UNITED STATES DEPARTMENT OF LABOR
FRANCES PERKINS, Secretary

BUREAU OF LABOR STATISTICS
ISADOR LUBIN, Commissioner

BULLETIN OF THE UNITED STATES BUREAU OF LABOR STATISTICS · · · · **No. 604**

WAGES AND HOURS OF LABOR SERIES

HISTORY OF
WAGES IN THE UNITED STATES
FROM COLONIAL TIMES
TO 1928

Revision of Bulletin No. 499
with
Supplement, 1929–1933 (Page 523)

UNITED STATES

GOVERNMENT PRINTING OFFICE

WASHINGTON : 1934

Republished by Gale Research Company, Book Tower, Detroit, 1966

ACKNOWLEDGMENT

Part 1 of this report was prepared by Estelle M. Stewart, of the United States Department of Labor. Part 2 was prepared under the direction of J. C. Bowen, of the Bureau of Labor Statistics, United States Department of Labor.

II

CONTENTS

APPENDIXES

Letter of Transmittal

UNITED STATES DEPARTMENT OF LABOR,
BUREAU OF LABOR STATISTICS,
Washington, May 11, 1934.

MADAM SECRETARY: I have the honor to transmit herewith a revised edition of Bulletin No. 499 of the Bureau of Labor Statistics entitled "History of Wages in the United States from Colonial Times to 1928." The revision consists principally of a supplement bringing the material down to the year 1933. The original bulletin, issued in 1929, had a very wide circulation and the edition has been exhausted. The continuing demand for the material contained in this bulletin makes it desirable to issue a new edition, incorporating the available wage data for the later years. A complete revision was impracticable because of the printing cost, but it was felt that a reprint of the original with a supplement for the later years would meet the demand in a reasonably satisfactory manner.

Respectfully submitted.

ISADOR LUBIN, *Commissioner.*

HON. FRANCES PERKINS,
    Secretary of Labor.

BULLETIN OF THE

U. S. BUREAU OF LABOR STATISTICS

| No. 604 | WASHINGTON | OCTOBER, 1929 |

HISTORY OF WAGES IN THE UNITED STATES FROM COLONIAL TIMES TO 1928

INTRODUCTION

This report attempts to present a picture of American wages from early colonial days to the present time. The picture is drawn necessarily in rather broad strokes. In general, the policy has been to select representative occupations in representative industries, and present for such occupations as continuous a record as possible of wages and hours of labor.

The main reason for the preparation of the present report was the desire to preserve in permanent form the principal contents of the bureau's early wage studies as well as the still earlier records of colonial America. The printed reports containing these early data are for the most part long out of print and the unpublished documents are inaccessible to many persons who desire to use them.

The present report incorporates, of course, only a small proportion of the bureau's published wage studies, but it does contain a sufficient volume of material to meet the needs of most readers. Moreover, by bringing together and coordinating the various studies and documents it makes reference very much easier than has been the case in the past, when the tracing of wage movements in particular occupations or industries over a period of years required the thumbing of many volumes.

The character of the source material makes necessary the dividing of the report into two distinct parts, Part 1 dealing with the period prior to 1840 and Part 2 covering the period from 1840 to 1928. For the period prior to 1840 the source material is scattered, lacking in consecutiveness, and seldom available in modern statistical form. Part 1 of the report, therefore, is largely in text form, and the basic information is derived from a multitude of sources.

Part 2, beginning with the year 1840, is entirely statistical in presentation, and the source material is derived entirely from the reports of the former United States Department of Labor and its successor, the Bureau of Labor Statistics of the present United States Department of Labor.

1

PART 1

FROM COLONIAL TIMES TO 1840

3

PART 1.—FROM COLONIAL TIMES TO 1840

Wages in and of themselves have been consistently overlooked by most writers of American history. Economic histories, to be sure, deal with wages, occasionally quite completely for a given era, locality, or trade, but even in them wages are incidental to the main theme. So far there has been no publication, at least within the bureau's knowledge, which deals specifically with the subject of early American wages.

In its effort to supply that lack the bureau drew first upon secondary sources, to bring together authoritative data scattered through many volumes of histories and economic studies. William B. Weeden's "Economic and Social History of New England, 1620–1789," and Philip A. Bruce's "Economic History of Virginia in the Seventeenth Century," furnished the general framework. As the work progressed and publication after publication was reviewed only to find that all of them covered practically the same ground, it was decided to go beyond secondary sources to original material to fill the gaps in the story.

Except for State archives and State historical societies, the most fruitful source has been the material now being collected by the Baker Library of the Harvard Graduate School of Business Administration. This material contains records, ledgers, account books, and correspondence of some of the earliest American industries, going back in one case, that of the Saugus (Lynn) Iron Works, to 1643. Pay rolls of the Slater textile mills for more than 50 years are in the Baker collection, as well as many other records of great value and interest. All of this material was generously placed at the disposal of the bureau.

The record so far as it has been preserved is scattered at best, and the most persistent research still leaves wide gaps which it seems impossible to fill. The first half of the eighteenth century, in particular, proved barren ground, but apparently that has been the experience of all students of early America, whatever special field they have tried to cover. Yet when it is considered that wages and working conditions did not change materially nor rapidly before the industrial era, probably the material gathered by the bureau constitutes an essentially complete picture of early American wages.

More than wage figures alone, however, is needed to tell the whole story. Methods of payment in the earliest periods are as important as the pay itself, and both must be interpreted in the light of customs, systems of labor, and working conditions peculiar to colonization. Hence the indenture and redemption systems, which were an important factor in influencing workmen to emigrate to the colonies, are dealt with in the study, although no wages, in the sense of regular money payments, were involved under those peculiar labor systems.

5

It has also been necessary to go, somewhat sketchily, into the question of the various currencies in which wages were paid, since currency values varied with time and place. No attempt has been made, however, to do more than convert these values into the present American equivalent. No comparison with the present-day purchasing value of that American equivalent is undertaken. Where contemporary evidence has been obtained which is suggestive of living costs and what the wages paid meant in terms of standards of living, it is used, but beyond that the report has not ventured.

Wage data and conditions of labor so far as the bureau has been able to secure them are given fully in Part 1 of this report for the following trades and industries: Building trades, shipbuilding, cabinetmaking, iron, glass, textiles, boots and shoes, clothing, printing, seamen, and agriculture. A few other trades are treated as fully as the scattered data permit. School-teachers have been included in the study.

Chapter 1.—EARLY WORKING CONDITIONS AND WAGE LEGISLATION

"High American wages" date from the beginning of the country, to judge from evidence contained in the earliest colonial records in which reference to wages is found. Letters and reports from agents of the British companies engaged in colonial settlement and from the early colonial governors, express consternation amounting to distress over the "exhorbitant demands" of craftsmen and laborers. A colonial treasurer of the Virginia Colony declared, about 1625, that the wages paid there were "intolerable" and "much in excess of the sum paid to the same class of persons in England."[1] In 1633 Governor Winthrop, of the Massachusetts Bay Colony, noted that the "excessive rates" charged by workmen "grew to a general complaint" which called for legislative action,[2] and a colonial governor in North Carolina complained that "the Price of Labour is very high."

From the workman's side of the story comes similar testimony treated from a different viewpoint. Gabriel Thomas, who wrote a history of "the Province and Countrey of Pensilvania" in 1698 for the purpose of inducing the poverty-stricken workers of England to emigrate, asserts that "the encouragements are very greate and inviting, for Poor People (both Men and Women) of all kinds can here get three times the wages for their Labour they can in England or Wales;"[3] and William Penn says in a letter that "all provisions are reasonable but Labour dear, which makes it a good Poor Man's country."[4] Another promoter, with a zeal suggestive of present-day publicity methods, wrote glowingly of the "happy circumstances" in which laborers in New Jersey were placed in 1641.[5]

Viewed from this distance, neither the wages nor the working conditions, so far as history records them, appear either "extravagant" or "inviting," but it is undoubtedly true that wages began in the colonies at a higher rate than was being paid in Europe at the same time. If, however, as Bruce concludes from contemporaneous writings, the "only thing dear" in the colonies "was labor,"[6] that condition arose chiefly from the scarcity of workers, especially skilled craftsmen.

SCARCITY OF LABOR

Throughout the colonial period this scarcity was a vital problem that influenced customs and legislation and resulted in the establishment of the elaborate system of securing workers by contract or "indenture" which became a definite labor policy in Pennsylvania and in the southern colonies and was widely practiced in all of them.

The record suggests that lack of sufficient craftsmen was a serious condition for more than a century. Governor Winthrop, of the

---

[1] Bruce, Philip A.: Economic History of Virginia in the Seventeenth Century, Vol. II, p. 48.
[2] Hart, Albert Bushnell, ed.: American History Told by Contemporaries (Governor Winthrop's Journal quoted), Vol. I, p. 374.
[3] Thomas, Gabriel: An Historical and Geographical Account of the Province and Countrey of Pensilvania, published 1698.
[4] Oldmixon, John: British Empire in America, Vol. I, p. 316.
[5] Evelin, Robert: Directions for Adventurers, in Force's Tracts, Vol. II.
[6] Bruce, Vol. I, p. 584.

Massachusetts Bay Colony, declared in 1630 that the "scarcity of workers caused them to raise their wages to an excessive rate;" [7] a century and a quarter later Governor Dobbs, of North Carolina, reported that "artificers and labourers being scarce in comparison to the number of Planters, when they are employed they won't work half, scarce a third part of work in a Day of what they do in Europe, and their wages are from two shillings to 3, 4, and 5 shillings per Diem this currency." [8]   During the intervening years the same story is told—New Amsterdam in 1658 had "no sawyers" and only "one articled smith.   Free smiths are extraordinarily scarce," and because of the price they were in consequence able to command "it is not advisable to get much work done by them." [9]   In Maine, in 1675, "handicraftsmen are but few, the Tumelor, or Cooper, Smiths and Carpenters are best welcomed amongst them;" [10] while "artificers" were "so scarce" in South Carolina in 1731 "that all sorts of work is very Dear; Taylors, Shoemakers, Smiths, &c would be particularly acceptable." [11]

CONTROL OF WORKERS

Both of these conditions, the scarcity of labor and the resulting high wages, were met differently by the northern and the southern colonies. Out of them grew the indenture system and, eventually in the South, slavery.   The indenture system will be taken up in a later chapter.

The New England colonies undertook to meet them by regulation and legislation.   If local laws limiting property holding and citizenship to "freemen" and "commoners" operated to exclude needed tradesmen from a town, the laws were either suspended in given cases or the town found some way to get around them in order to secure the desired services.   Both Boston and Charlestown in 1640 waived certain of the citizenship requirements to obtain carpenters.   As early as 1635 Lynn voted to admit a landless blacksmith, and later granted him 20 acres of land, thus keeping both the blacksmith and the letter of the law requiring that residents be landholders.

These concessions as a rule had strings to them.   When 20 citizens of Haverhill, Mass., raised a subscription among themselves to purchase a house and land in order that a blacksmith could come into the settlement, they required that the smith agree to remain for seven years, and did not permit him to work for any person other than the 20 subscribers.   The town of Windsor, Conn., presented a currier with a house and land and "something for a shop," but it was to belong to him and his heirs only on condition that "he lives and dies with us and affords us the use of his trade."   Otherwise the property was to revert to the town. [12]   In 1656 William How was granted "twelve acres of meadow land and twelve acres of upland" in what afterwards became the great textile center of Lowell, Mass., "provided he set up his trade of weaving and perform the town's work." [13]

Once established in the colony, workmen were under the rigid regulation and control of a governmental system which, to quote

[7] Hart, Vol. I, p. 374.
[8] North Carolina Records; Letter from Governor Dobbs to Lords of Trade, January 4, 1755, Vol. V, p. 315.
[9] O'Callaghan's Documents Relative to the Colonial History of the State of New York. (Letter from Director of Colony to the Commissioners), Vol. II, p. 52.
[10] Hart, Vol. I, p. 433.   An Account of Two Voyages to New England, by John Josselyn.
[11] Carroll, B. E., ed.: Historical Collections of South Carolina, Vol. II, p. 130.
[12] Weeden, William B.: Economic and Social History of New England, 1620–1789, Vol. I, p. 81.
[13] Bagnall, William R.: Textile Industries of the United States, p. 8.

Weeden, believed that it "could legislate prosperity and well-being for everyone, rich or poor." [14] Impressment of labor was one tenet of that system, and "either the public need or the demands of private business could enforce it." [15] As a rule it was only in harvest time that craftsmen were impressed into private service, but carpenters were sometimes drafted to build houses for individuals. Work on the public roads one day in the month was required of every workman in Salem, and he was subject to a fine of 3 shillings if he did not comply.[16] When the selectmen of Dedham, Mass., decided to build a meeting house, the committee in charge was authorized to "order men to worke upon the same." [17]

WAGE LEGISLATION

It was in legislation dealing with wages, however, that the authorities in the New England colonies made their most persistent efforts to control workers. Plymouth Colony and Massachusetts Bay Colony passed similar laws in 1630 fixing a maximum rate of pay. In Massachusetts Bay Colony:

It was ordered that Carpenters, Joyners, Brickelayers, Sawers and Thatchers shal not take above 2s. [48.6 cents] a day, and 16d. [32 cents] a day if they have meate and drinke, nor any man shall give more, under paine of 10s. [$2.43] to taker and giver; and that sawers shal not take above 4s. 6d. [$1.00] ye hundred for boards, att six score to the hundred, if they have their wood felled and squared for them, and not above 5s. 6d. [$1.33] if they fell and square their wood themselves.

It was ordered that labourers shal not take above 12d. [24.3 cents] a day for their worke, and not above 6d. [12 cents] and meat and drink, under paine of 10s. [$2.43].[18]

Although this law was not successful and operated less than six months, the court tried again in 1633, with lower rates and evidently greater determination, to dictate wages. The second ruling kept the same rate of 2s. a day for "master" workmen—building tradesmen, mowers, and wheelwrights—but the rate with "dyett" became 14d. (28 cents) a day instead of 16d. "Master taylors" were allowed 12d. (24.3 cents) and "inferior taylors" 8d. (16 cents) per day "with dyett." Instead of fixing the rate for laborers, or "inferior" workmen, as did the 1630 act, that of 1633 left its determination to the town constable and "two indifferent freemen," probably for each and every given case.

Apparently it was not a simple matter to employ craftsmen at that rate. There were few settlers in the Bay Colony who did not have some land, cultivation of which undoubtedly paid better than day work at an arbitrarily fixed rate. Employers were soon overbidding the rate, and in a few cases were "presented" before the court and fined for violating the law. After a year of this, the clause fixing a penalty for paying more than the legal rate was repealed. The penalty for taking more was assessed against several workmen after it was no longer illegal to pay more, but this ill-balanced arrangement resulted in the following year, 1635, in the repeal of the wage-fixing statute in its entirety.

---

[14] Weeden, Vol. I, p. 99.
[15] Idem, Vol. I, p. 82.
[16] Felt, Joseph B.: Annals of Salem, Vol. I, p. 285.
[17] Massachusetts Historical Society: Dedham Town Records.
[18] Massachusetts Bay Colony Records, Vol. I, p. 109.

Naturally wages went up. The highest rate for which workmen had been haled into court and fined was, according to the court records, 2s. 6d. (61 cents) per day. With legal restraints removed skilled workers commanded 3s. (73 cents) a day, perhaps more in specific instances. Colonial authorities recognized that their legislative policy had failed, but, as Weeden expresses it, the idea "that labor could fix its own reward worried them exceedingly." [19] Not unlike their successors of a much later day, when "divers complaints concerning oppression in wages, * * * to the great dishonor of God, the scandall of the gosple and the griefe of divers of God's people" began to follow upon the repeal of wage legislation, the court appointed a commission of 29 men, including Endicott, Winthrop, Bradstreet, and Mather, "to bring into the next Generall Court their thoughts for the remediing of the same." [20]

This communion of the best minds of Massachusetts Bay seems to have produced nothing more concrete than the adoption of a policy of "local option" by which each town was advised and requested to control its own wage rate, and the promulgation of the following declaration by the General Court:

The Court, having taken into consideration the scarsity of money and the great abatement in the prices of corne, cattle and other commodities of the countrey, whereby it is impossible that men shall bee able to give such wages to servants and other labourers and workmen as formerly, so as many think better to lay aside their busines and impliments (which would tende to the ruin of the Churches and the Commonwealth) than to spend the small remainder of their estates for the maintenance of others in such a way as will not afford them some equall recompence—it is therefore hearby declared that it is thought equall that all servants, labourers and workmen shall bee content to abate their wages according to the fall of the commodities wherein their labour is bestowed, and that they shall bee satisfied with payment in such things as are raised by their labour or other commodities which the countrey affoards, and that they are to be content to partake now in the present scarsity as well as they have had their advantage by the plenty of former times, and this Court shall account it great oppression in any that shall transgress the intention of this Order, and will have them proceeded with accordingly.[21]

While the General Court of the Bay Colony thus changed its policy from one of dictating a limit to what a workman might have for his work to one of thinking about what should content him, the court of Plymouth Colony retained its old legal rate of 2s. (48.6 cents), with no greater success at enforcement, and the towns of the Bay Colony undertook to carry out what the colonial authorities had passed on to them to handle. The wage rates fixed by the towns were lower than those in the colonial statutes, but that was because of the general depression and hard times following the crop failure of 1640. Carpenters in Hingham were reduced from 2s. to 1s. 10d. (44.5 cents), and wheelwrights from 2s. 3d. (54.6 cents) to 2s. a day; while mowers kept the old rate of 2s. and common labor rose to 1s. 6d. (36 cents).[22] As late as 1651 Thomas Trusler, of Salem, was presented before the Essex County Court for "taking excessive wages from John Alderman, viz., 10s. 6d. ($1.75)[23] for a day's work of 6 oxen and one man," [24] but no fine is recorded.

[19] Weeden, Vol. I, p. 179.
[20] Massachusetts Bay Colony Records, Vol. I, p. 223.
[21] Idem, Vol. I, p. 326.
[22] Weeden, Vol. I, p. 173.
[23] Colonial currency; shilling worth 16.7 cents in American equivalent.
[24] Essex County Court Records.

Twenty years after the New England colonies had given up the futile effort to control a commodity so urgently in demand as labor, Virginia attempted both impressment and wage fixing in its program of town building, and succeeded only in driving mechanics out of the colony.[25]

CRAFTSMEN AS PLANTERS

The many, constantly repeated efforts to control and regulate labor by legislative action were made inoperative by the continued scarcity of workers, especially in the skilled crafts, and by "the abundance of land and the common desire to plant settlers upon it."[26]

The tendency of craftsmen to become farmers was frowned upon in New England, since it was "more to the public welfare and the Glory of God to hold them to their trade," and specifically legislated against in Virginia. Agents of the Virginia Company were instructed to establish tradesmen in towns, in order "to remove them from temptation to plant on their own account."[27]

Nevertheless, the evidence, though slight, is that among the comparatively few skilled workers who emigrated to the colonies, a considerable number did as a matter of fact take up land and become farmers and tobacco planters. Weeden speaks of the opportunity afforded workers in New England to become landholders as "the countervailing privilege which lightened and ameliorated the severity toward laborers and those working for hire," and quotes Johnson's "Wonder-Working Providence" as declaring, in 1650, that "there are many hundreds of laboring men who had not enough to bring them over, yet now are worth scores, and some hundreds of pounds," through cultivating the land available to them.[26]

"While it would be erroneous to say that as a general class the free mechanics of Virginia in the seventeenth century enjoyed even a moderate degree of prosperity from the mere pursuit of their trades," Bruce believes that "there are nevertheless many evidences that numerous individuals belonging to this class were men in possession of considerable wealth, derived, there is reason to think, as much from cultivation of tobacco on their own account as from the accumulation of the proceeds of their mechanical work in the service of their neighbors."[28] He gives several instances on which he bases his conclusions:

The trade of blacksmith was perhaps the least remunerative of all the callings of that general character, since, the roads being level and free from stones, it was the habit of the planters to allow their horses to go unshod. * * * The county records of the period show that persons in this calling were able to acquire small estates.

* * * The trade of cooper was far more profitable, the field offered for the exercise of skill being a wider one. * * * There were few more important articles connected with the economy of the plantation than the hogsheads in which the tobacco, when cured, was stored for shipment. It was the business of the cooper to manufacture these receptacles, an occupation in which a handsome remuneration was assured owing to the abundance of work; it is not surprising, therefore, to discover that this class of tradesmen were in possession of considerable tracts of real estate and owned many kinds of personalty. Numerous patents to public lands were obtained by them. In 1657 alone, two were issued, aggregating seven hundred and fifty acres.[29]

[25] See p. 50.
[26] Weeden, Vol. I, p. 84.
[27] Bruce, Vol. II, p. 411.

[28] Bruce, Vol. II, p. 418.
[29] Idem, Vol. II, pp. 418–421.

Carpenters often "secured public lands, either in fee simple or by lease for a long term of years." [29]   Many tanners had large property holdings, and colonial records show substantial areas possessed by shoemakers.[30]

CRAFT LINES INDEFINITE

Craft distinctions as we know them were not made in the colonial and provincial eras, either in the performance of work or in the payment of wages.   The mechanic was apt to be a jack-of-all-trades, even though he might also be master of his own, for his skill could be used to advantage outside his own craft.   The building trades were frequently combined in one person; a blacksmith and wheelwright might be a silversmith at the same time, and the shoemaker was, very likely, a tanner as well.   "If any one could or would carry on ten trades, no one would have a right to prevent him," [31] since the guild system of the Old World had not been transplanted to the New.

It will be noticed that the rates fixed by the early colonial laws make slight distinction in the trades in the matter of wages, and that the difference between pay for skilled work and for unskilled work is not great.   In fact, in two instances of record, it is specifically stated that all work should be paid for at the same rate.   The men who worked upon the construction of the meeting house in Dedham, Mass., in 1637, were to be assigned tasks to which they were "severally apted," and the same wages were to be paid "in all cases." [32]   In the reconstruction of a fort on Point Comfort, Va., the General Court ordered that mechanics and laborers should "all receive the same wages." [33]

This condition held true until the beginning of the eighteenth century.   Even then the differences between the crafts were not marked until trade organizations began to spring up toward the close of the century.   By 1800 wage rates appear for numerous crafts, with fairly well-defined jurisdictional lines, but the rates themselves do not vary materially as between these different crafts, and the distinction between skilled and unskilled labor is not so strongly reflected in their pay as it became later, with the development of a pronounced craft consciousness.

An interesting analysis of the conditions which produced this slight difference in their wages is given by a pioneer textile manufacturer:

On a comparison of the prices of labor in this country with those of Great Britain, we perceive that although the wage of common labor is much higher here, yet that of the artificer is not.   Here the demand for labor is chiefly agricultural and the wages seem to be regulated by it.   There the mechanic arts afford so much employment that the demand for every species of skill and ingenuity is constant and high.   Hence it happens that we can satisfy our artists with wages very little above the common labor of the country, while those who come from Europe will not work without a much greater price.[34]

---

[29] Idem, Vol. II, pp. 418–421.
[30] Idem, Vol. II, pp. 478–479.
[31] Mittelberger, Gottlieb: Journey to Pennsylvania, 1750–1754, p. 56.
[32] Dedham Town Records (see p. 47).
[33] Bruce, Vol. II, p. 417.
[34] Manuscript letter of George Cabot, Sept. 6, 1791, in Hamilton Papers, Library of Congress.

Chapter 2.—MONEY AND MONEY EQUIVALENT

Although wages are fixed in terms of money in the early colonial statutes, money was not at first, in any of the colonies, the medium in which the workers were principally paid. A system of barter existed throughout the first century of settlement and the very scarce currency was little used in the payment of wages.

THE TOBACCO WAGES OF VIRGINIA

In Virginia wages were quoted not in coin but in pounds of tobacco. Tobacco was in fact money, the standard of value "in which all the supplies, both domestic and imported, were purchased; in which the tax imposed by public levy was settled; in which the tithables of the minister, the fees of the attorney and physician, the debts due the merchant, the remuneration of the free mechanic, the wages of the servant, the charges of the midwife and the grave digger were paid."[1]

Tobacco warehouse receipts, or "tobacco notes," took the place of metal currency and served all the purposes of a more usual monetary system in general business transactions, at least in the export trade. However, "the inconveniences of such a system were felt * * * in the working of internal affairs, in the transaction of local business, for instance, in the sale of the commodity of labor and professional knowledge and the like."[2] Another writer explains that "when we recall the constant fluctuation in the price of tobacco we can imagine what a clumsy and inefficient currency tobacco must have been. A tobacco note issued one year might lose half its value by a fall in the price of tobacco in the following year."[3]

Tobacco prices, on which wages were based, are shown in the following table, compiled by Jacobstein from Government figures and colonial statutes:[4]

Year	Per pound	Year	Per pound
1619	3s.	1665	1d.
1628	3d.	1690	2d.
1631	6d.	1722	¾d.
1640	12d.	1753	2d.
1645	1½d.	1763	2d.

The shilling in the first quotation was the British shilling, then worth 24.3 cents in the American equivalent. As will be pointed out later, the value of the colonial shilling began to diverge from that of the sterling shilling about 1640. Hence in addition to the materially lower value of tobacco per pound after 1640, the price is based on a currency of a lower standard, and the quotation of 1d. as for instance in 1665, probably represents less than 1.5 cents in American money. On that basis, the rate of 20 pounds of tobacco a day, fixed by court order in 1666 to be paid on a certain construction job,[5] converts into a trifle less than 30 cents a day in the American equivalent.

---

[1] Bruce, Philip A.: Economic History of Virginia in the 17th Century, Vol. II, p. 495.
[2] Bruce, Vol. II, p. 497.
[3] Jacobstein, Meyer: The Tobacco Industry in the United States. Columbia University Studies in History, Economics, and Public Law, Vol. XXVI, No. 3, p. 25.
[4] Idem, Vol. XXVI, No. 3, p. 23.
[5] See p. 50.

THE "COUNTRY PAY" OF NEW ENGLAND

The most widely used mediums of exchange in the New England colonies were beaver skins and "country pay," which means, substantially, agricultural products, corn chiefly. Beaver was "second in value only to the precious metals," and furnished "an equivalent for cash,"[6] since, like the tobacco of the southern colonies, it found a constant and fairly stable market in Europe. Its use was largely confined to foreign business and must have been rare indeed in the payment of wages, because it appears in only one instance in the wage material obtained from the early records. Weeden quotes from an account book dated Piscataqua, N. H., April 1, 1633: "I paid the Smith for work 2 lbs of Beaver and 2 shillings in Beaver at 2 several times. To the taylor for mending blanketts, beaver ½ lb." Beaver was worth at the time from 14s. to 20s. a pound.[7]

The standard medium in which workmen were paid was "corn," a generic term which included "several species of grain and even peas, which, together with livestock, lawfully received at the colonial treasury for public taxes, was often designated by the phrase 'country pay.'"[8] In 1631 the Massachusetts General Court ordered "that corne shall passe for payment of all debts at the usual rate it is solde for, unless money or beaver be expressly named."[9] For years the selling price of corn was alternately fixed and freed by the court, and the rate at which it would be received for taxes was established annually.

Corn sold in 1631, the year in which it was made a legal tender, at 10s. ($2.43) to 11s. ($2.67) a bushel; the next year the price had fallen to 4s. 6d. ($1.00), recovering slightly, in 1633, to 6s. ($1.46) per bushel. Its selling price fluctuated between 4s. 6d. and 6s. until 1641, and its currency value as set by the court varied accordingly. That year, following the poor crops of 1640, the court did not undertake to maintain a selling price, declaring instead that:

For servants and workmen's wages it is ordered that they may be paid in corne. For the price, if the parties can not agree, the corne is to be valued by 2 indifferent freemen, to be choesen the one by the master, the other by the servant or workman (who are to have respect to the valewe of the worke or service); and if they cannot agree then a third man is to be chosen by the magistrate.[10]

After 1642 the price of corn in colonial money, though rising occasionally as high as 6s. ($1) kept at a fairly steady level of 3s. (50 cents) a bushel until the close of the century, when the period of inflated paper money set in.

Depreciation in the value of articles other than corn in which workmen were paid materially lessened the amount actually received for work. To illustrate, Boston's first lawyer undertook a case for a carpenter of Cambridge who received as part of his pay for the construction of a house "one cowe and one steere calfe" valued, by the employer, at £25 ($121.50). According to the plaintiff, that price "was then overvalued £5 [$24.30] at least." The carpenter had to pay his workmen £9 ($43.75) in money for their work on the job. Later, when he tried to market his cattle, the price had fallen so that "now they are not worth above £12 [$58.32]." In addition to the

---

[6] Weeden, William B.: Economic and Social History of New England, 1620–1789, Vol. I, p. 39.
[7] Idem, Vol. I, p. 132.
[8] Felt, Joseph B.: Massachusetts Currency, p. 13.
[9] Massachusetts Bay Colony Records Vol. I, p. 192.
[10] Idem, Vol. I, p. 340.

loss of £13 ($63.18) in the value of the stock, the plaintiff had been at an expense of "£2 10s. [$12.15] for the keeping of them since, which amounts to £15 10s. [$75.33]," the amount entered in the petition for relief.[11]

Toward the close of the seventeenth century the expanding trade with the West Indies brought in an increasing supply of silver, and from the opening of the eighteenth century to the Revolution, while "country pay" was still a factor in the payment of wages, it does not appear in the record to so great an extent as in the colonial period. It was again resorted to during the Revolution, when money was practically worthless.

The custom of granting discounts from country-pay prices for cash payment in the purchase of goods was adopted after money became more plentiful, and the allowance ran from one-fourth to one-third of the barter price. On the other hand, workers who demanded money instead of, or in addition to, country pay had to accept from one-fourth to one-third less than the wages paid in barter. A building contract dated 1694 specifies that the contract price of £15 10s. ($51.67) is "to be payed in Rye at four shillings [66.7 cents] per bushel & Indian corne at three shillings [50 cents] a bushel;" should any part of the £15 10s. be paid in money, however, the builder "shall abate one-fourth part thereof."[12]

"FOUND"

Still another difficulty in the way of computing colonial wages arises from the almost universal practice of providing workers with board at the place where they were engaged. That custom was, of course, always followed in the case of farm laborers and domestic servants, as it still is, and wages for these classes can safely be regarded as in addition to maintenance.

In the earliest days that was also true of tailors, shoemakers, and to some extent of building tradesmen, but it is not always possible to determine which wage rates do and which do not include board. Frequently the record says specifically so much per day "and found" or "with dyett," and it is assumed that substantially higher rates for the same or comparable occupations in the same period must be straight wages. Often, too, the wage rate will be followed by the expression "the labourer finding himself," and by a comparison of rates in the two methods of payment it is possible to estimate when maintenance is a part of the pay in cases where the item itself does not cover that point.

Another early practice which became the subject of frequent legislation and constant agitation is suggested in the following statute of 1645:

Whereas it is found by too common and sad experience in all parts of the colony that the forcing of labourers and other workmen to take wine in pay for wages is a great nursery or preparative to drunkenness * * * it is therefore ordered and ordained by this Court that no labourer or workman whatsoever shall after ye publication and promulgation hereof be inforced or pressed to take wine in pay for his labour.[13]

---

[11] Lechford, Thomas: Manuscript Notebook, 1638–1641 (published by the American Antiquarian Society, 1885), p. 410.
[12] See p. 48.
[13] Massachusetts Bay Colony Records, Vol. II, p. 101.

Later, in 1672, another angle to this same problem developed. Instead of "being pressed to take wine in pay for his labour," workmen were accused of "demanding an allouance of licquors or wines every day, over and above their wages, without which it is found, by too sad experience, many refuse to worke." It was "therefore ordered by the Court and by the authority thereof, and be it hereby enacted, that if any person or persons after publication hereof shall give wine or strong licquors to any workmen or boys that work with them, except in case of necessity, shall pay twenty shillings [$3.33] for every such offence."[14]

A hundred years afterward Jefferson wrote of the crew of building tradesmen whom he employed on some remodeling work on his home: "I observe that their food and liquor has cost exactly 2s. [33.3 cents] on the day's labor."

COLONIAL CURRENCY

The earliest settlers in both the Virginia and the Massachusetts colonies used English money, of course, and while sterling lasted it had the same value in the colonies as in the mother country. Very early in the history of the colonies, however, this condition changed, and while the British form of pounds, shillings, and pence was retained until after the establishment of the Republic, it was not in fact the British monetary system. After 1640 colonial money was based on the Spanish dollar instead of on the pound sterling.

At the same time the value of the monetary unit, the colonial shilling, was exceedingly erratic, seldom, as an early statistician observed, "being the same in two different Provinces at a time, and often changing values in the same place." [15]

The Virginia shilling remained practically stable throughout the history of the colony. In 1645 the Assembly declared that the Spanish "piece of 8", which in time became the American dollar, should pass current and be valued as the equivalent of six shillings of Virginia money. This established the Virginia shilling at 16.7 cents in the American equivalent. For perhaps two decades following that order, through political manipulation the value fluctuated between 5s. and 6s. to the dollar, but by 1680 the standard was again firmly established at 6s., and discussion of the money of this colony can be dismissed with the statement that a Virginia shilling means 16.7 cents wherever quoted.

Pennsylvania also escaped most of the fluctuation and inflation of its currency that beset other colonies, but a shilling had two different values, each of which can be regarded as stable during the periods specified. The colonial shilling ran five to the Spanish dollar, making 20 cents in the American equivalent. The standard changed early in the provincial era to 7s. 6d. to the dollar, "at which, from 1742, it finally rested." [16]

The same situation was essentially true in New Jersey, Delaware, and Maryland. The shilling in these four colonies can therefore be quoted at 20 cents up to the close of the first quarter of the eighteenth century, and 13.3 cents thereafter.

The New York money unit during the first half century of settlement was the Dutch florin, which is 40 cents in the American equiva-

---

[14] Idem, Vol. IV, No. 2, p. 510.
[15] Wright, John: The American Negotiator (3d edition. London, 1767), p. 1.
[16] Phillips, Henry, jr.: Pennsylvania Paper Money, p. 13.

lent. With the disintegration of Dutch power in the colony, about 1665, New York adopted the shilling unit, but its value there was considerably less than in the other old settlements. The New York shilling, when introduced, was worth 12.5 cents, 8 shillings to the dollar, and maintained a fair degree of stability up to the Revolution.

The shilling of North Carolina had the same nominal value as that of New York, but suffered depreciation repeatedly and probably fell as low as did that of South Carolina, although by 1764 it had recovered, and afterward kept its position at 12.5 cents. Starting with a value in the American equivalent of 21.4 cents, 4s. 8d. to the dollar, South Carolina money was at first the highest in the American colonies. In 1710 a South Carolina shilling was quoted by the provincial governor [17] at slightly more than two-thirds the value of the sterling shilling, which gives it a value approximately that of the Virginia shilling. The Province issued paper money in 1712 to meet its proportion of expense in one of the Queen Anne wars, after which her currency fell headlong. . Wright computed 32 South Carolina shillings to the Spanish dollar in 1760.[18] This makes a paper shilling of the period worth a trifle more than 3 cents, and it fell ultimately to less than 3 cents.[19]

New England currency, however, has the most confused history. Information concerning it deals chiefly with Massachusetts, but in the main conditions in the Bay Colony were duplicated throughout the entire northern settlement.

Inflation at the close of the seventeenth century followed a standard New England shilling stabilized for 60 years at 16.7 cents. That was the value established after the sterling shilling had disappeared, maintained by the pine-tree shilling of the Hull mint, beginning in 1653, and fixed by statute in 1679.[20] The adoption of paper money at the close of the century did not result in immediate depreciation. With repeated emissions after 1712 to meet the cost of the military expeditions into Canada, however, the New England paper shilling fell steadily, dropping from 8s. to the Spanish dollar in 1713, to 45 in 1749.[20]

To avert ruin Massachusetts secured a substantial shipment of sterling money from England and set about to redeem her paper currency and to place her finances on a sounder footing. In 1750 "lawful money" was established and "old tenor" was gradually redeemed. Lawful money continued the old relation of 6 to 1 between the shilling and the Spanish dollar.

Conversion to the American equivalent of wages paid in old tenor from 1716 to 1750 is made on the basis of the relation between the paper shilling and the Spanish dollar, as follows:[21]

In 1716, 9¼ shillings to the Spanish dollar; in 1717, 12; in 1722, 14; in 1728, 18; in 1730, 20; in 1737, 26; in 1739, 27; in 1741, 28.

A conversion table printed in Boston in 1750 "to bring Old Tenor into Lawful Money" gives the relative value of old tenor as two-fifteenths the value of lawful money; in other words 15 shillings in

[17] Carroll, B. E., ed.: South Carolina Historical Collections, Vol. II, p. 122. History of South Carolina (attributed to Governor Glen).
[18] Wright's American Negotiator.
[19] Clark, Victor S.: History of Manufactures in the United States, 1607-1860, p. 584.
[20] Felt's Massachusetts Currency.
[21] Potter, Elisha R.: Emissions of Paper Money Made by the Colony of Rhode Island.

old tenor were worth 2 shillings in the new currency.[22] Felt puts the ratio of old tenor to lawful money as high as 10 to 1 in 1751. In Rhode Island in 1769 it took £8 in old tenor to pay a debt of 6 shillings, which was about the rate applied by that colony in redeeming her old tenor currency in 1770.[23]

Efforts at stabilization, fairly successful for several years, were defeated by the Revolution, when values were again completely upset by the depreciation and practical worthlessness of continental paper money. Then wage rates appear in pounds per day instead of shillings, and all wages and prices mount to fanciful heights which, for conversion purposes, make them quite literally "not worth a continental." This can be strikingly illustrated by the following items taken from the ordinary daily accounts of the Pennsylvania Hospital in 1780, which are expressed in continental currency: Mutton, $7 a pound; potatoes, $18 a peck; coffee, $12 a pound; sugar, $6 a pound; butter, $8 a pound; bread, $4 a loaf; eggs, $9 a dozen; three days' whitewashing at $55 a day; 2½ days' washing at $20 a day; servant girl, $50 a month.

Provincial and town governments undertook both price and wage fixing throughout the course of the war, trying to keep pace with the fictitious values of their worthless paper currencies. The earnestness, as well as the futility of this effort is suggested in the following declaration with which, on November 3, 1779, the New Hampshire Convention of Delegates followed up its November proclamation fixing prices and wages:[24]

Money is justly called the Sinews of War, and if the stipulated Prices are not complied with it is natural to conclude that Money will depreciate faster than it has ever done, and should that be unhappily our case, soon, very soon, it will not be in our Power to support our Army or even ourselves. * * * We must earnestly entreat every Merchant, Trader and Farmer and every other Rank of People to consider that if they vie with each other in obtaining High Prices and which will distress the other most, until the Money will not purchase any Article, what satisfaction will it be for the Merchant to recollect he received an hundred or an hundred and twenty dollars for a Yard of Cloth, the Farmer a thousand or 1200 dollars for a Yoke of Oxen, or any other Person to receive for what he has to sell or for his Labour at that Rate and so in Proportion for everything they sell, when all they receive may not purchase either Food or Raiment.

AMERICAN MONEY

The American monetary system adopted by the Republic at the close of the Revolution established itself slowly. Pounds, shillings, and pence remained the money terminology in most of the old communities for more than a generation after the adoption of the Constitution, although they were of course definitely convertible into dollars and cents. The personal accounts of Thomas Jefferson, even while he was President (1801–1809), are kept in pounds, shillings, and pence. In the pay rolls of the Slater mills in Rhode Island time and piece rates are given in shillings and total earnings in dollars and cents up to 1845, and probably longer. Massachusetts and New York, and the new Territories to the west, seem to have dropped the old form almost at once, but other parts of New England and the South did not.

---

[22] Massachusetts Bureau of Statistics of Labor: History of Wages and Prices in Massachusetts, 1752–1883 by Carroll D. Wright, p. 42.
[23] Potter, Elisha R.: Emissions of Paper Money Made by the Colony of Rhode Island.
[24] New Hampshire Broadsides, Library of Congress.

Moreover, the old complication remained. In Virginia, Rhode Island, and Connecticut a shilling meant 16.7 cents; in Pennsylvania, Maryland, Delaware, and New Jersey, 13.3 cents; and in New York and the Carolinas, 12.5 cents. Thus a hypothetical wage rate of 6s. a day in Virginia, 7s. 6d. a day in Philadelphia, and 8s. in New York City in 1800 would not mean that wages were one-third higher in New York than in Richmond. The actual money payment in all cases would have been an American dollar.

PRICES OF COMMODITIES USED AS BARTER

Truck payment entered so largely into the calculation of wages during the colonial and provincial eras that some conception of prices is necessary to interpret wages. It has been pointed out in an earlier wage study that, "as is well known, statistics of prices for any period are much easier to obtain than statistics of wages for the same period," [25] but unfortunately they are not easy to translate into terms of cost of living. Without attempting to do more than suggest the purchasing power of money wages, and the market value of the commodities given to workers in exchange for their labor, some price statistics are presented.

Tables 1 and 2 are a combination of various data, figures for the years 1633 to 1720 having been taken from the appendix to Weeden's "Economic and Social History of New England," which presents statutory prices for the most part; and figures from 1720 from Felt's "Annals of Salem." Felt's sources were contemporary account books, "prices current" broadsides, and grocery bills.

Table 1 gives the New England prices of wheat and corn per bushel, at 10-year periods, from 1630 to 1750. So little fluctuation was found in the price of these products from year to year that a single entry for each decade was considered sufficient.

TABLE **1.**—*Prices of wheat and corn in New England colonies, at 10-year periods, 1630 to 1750, with American equivalents*

Year	Value of shilling in American equivalent	Price of wheat, per bushel		Price of corn, per bushel	
		Shillings and pence	American equivalent	Shillings and pence	American equivalent
	Cents	*s. d.*		*s. d.*	
1630	24.3			10 0 11 0	$2.43 2.67
1640	24.3	7 0	$1.70	4 0	.97
1650	16.7	5 0	.84	3 0	.50
1660	16.7	4 0 5 0	.67 .84	3 0	.50
1670	16.7	5 0	.84	3 0	.50
1680	16.7	5 0	.84	3 0 2 0	.50 .33
1690	16.7	4 6	.75	3 0	.50
1700	16.7	5 0	.84	3 0	.50
1710	16.7	7 0	1.17	2 6	.42
1720	7.5	8 0 9 0	.60 .68	4 0	.30
1730	5.0	10 6	.60	6 6	.33
1740	3.6	21 0	.76	10 6	.38
1750	2.0	55 0	1.10	27 0	.54

[25] Wright's History of Wages and Prices, Massachusetts, 1752–1860, p. 41.

Table 2 shows no regularity in intervals of time.   The figures showing prices of butter, beef, and pork were used for all years for which they could be obtained.

TABLE 2.—*Prices of butter, beef, and pork in the New England Colonies, for specified years, 1633 to 1749, with American equivalents*

Year	Value of shilling in American equivalent	Price per pound					
		Butter		Beef		Pork	
		Shillings and pence	American equivalent	Shillings and pence	American equivalent	Shillings and pence	American equivalent
	Cents	*s. d.*		*s. d.*		*s. d.*	
1633	24.3	6	$0.12				
1637	24.3	7	.14				
1653	16.7			3	$0.04	4	$0.06
1655	16.7			{ 2	.03	3	.04
				3	.04	4	.06
1667	16.7	6	.08			3	.04
1670	16.7	6	.08			3	.04
1678	16.7	5	.07			2	.03
1685	16.7	9	.13	1½	.02	2½	.035
1687	16.7	4	.06	2	.03	3	.04
1690	16.7	4	.06				
1692	16.7			2	.03		
1695	16.7	4	.06				
1699	16.7			2	.03	3	.04
1704	16.7			1¼	.018	2	.03
1711	16.7	7	.10				
1712	16.7	10	.14	3½	.05	4½	.06
1719	8.3	11	.08				
1727	7.1	1 0	.07				
1733	5.0	1 6	.08	7	.03	8	.03
1740	3.6			10	.03		
1741	3.6			1 2	.04	1 2	.04
1747	2.5	5 0	.13	1 8	.04	2 6	.06
1748	2.5	7 0	.18	2 0	.05	2 9	.07
1749	2.0	8 0	.16	2 9	.055	4 0	.08

Table 3 was found in "Economica, a Statistical Manual for the United States of America," by Samuel Blodget, the imprint of which says that it was "printed for the Author in the City of Washington, 1806."   This table is reproduced exactly as printed.   The author's own comment on it is interesting.   In a footnote to the table he says:

The table shewing the variation of money is * * * not only one of the most important but cost more time and attention to bring it to its present state than either, if not all, in this book, the general table alone excepted; and yet it can not be made as complete as it ought to be to answer all the desirable purposes of a common measure for all estimates of *real* instead of merely *nominal* expenditures; the variations in prices have often been so sudden that an average for any three months must sometimes appear doubtful to those who have not full time for inquiry.   It is made up from prices current, and merchants' books and accounts of sales in every State in the Union.

This statistical presentation of a century and a quarter ago follows:

TABLE 3.—*Prices current in the principal cities, etc., of the United States, showing the variation of money, etc., for 20 years, from authentic documents*

Places	Averaged in the following years for first 6 mos.	Lands, improved near towns, per A	Rent, ditto, per c.	Labour, per day	Wheat, per bushel	Rye, per bushel	Corn, per bushel	Beef, per barrel	Pork, per cwt.	Butter, per lb.	Cheese, per lb.	Potatoes, per bu.	Tallow, per lb.	Lard, per lb.	Cod-fish, cwt.	Rice, cwt.	Flour, barrel	Tobacco, cwt.	Herring, barrel	Hams, per lb.
	Years	Dols.		Cts.	Cts.	Cts.	Cts.	Dols.	Dols.	Cts.	Cts.	Cts.	Cts.	Cts.	Dols.	Dols.	Dols.	Dols.	Dols.	Cts.
Boston		30	4	50	80	65	40	6	4	10	6½	11	6	6	2½	3	4½	3¼	2½	7½
New York		50	4	55	75	60	40	7	4	11	7	12	8	8	3½	3	4	3¼	2½	8
Philadelphia	1785	50	4	60	75	60	40	7	4	11	7	12	9	9	3½	3	4	3¼	2½	8
Baltimore		30	3½	50	75	65	35	7	4	11	7	14	9	9	3½	3	4	3	2½	8
Charleston		30	5	50	80	65	40	7	4¼	12	7	15	10	10	3½	2½	4½	3¼	2½	9
U. S. averaged	1785	2½	3½	50	60	45	35	5½	4	9	6	10½	7	7	3½	3	4	3	2½	7
Boston		50	4	50	85	60	50	8	5	12	8	14	10	11	3½	3½	5½	4¼	3	9
New York		60	5	50	80	60	45	8	5	12	8	15	11	12	3½	3½	5	4¼	3½	9½
Philadelphia	1790	55	5	50	80	60	45	8½	5	12	8	15	11	11	3½	3½	5	4¼	3½	9½
Baltimore		50	5	60	75	60	40	8½	5¼	13	9	16	11	12	3½	3½	5	4	3	10
Charleston		60	5	60	85	65	50	8½	5½	14	9	17	12	13	3½	3	5½	4	3½	10
U. S. averaged	1790	2½	4	50	75	50	45	8	4½	10	8	15	9	9	4	3½	4½	4	3½	9½
Boston		100	4½	95	130	75	60	8½	5½	13	11	18	11	11½	4	4	7	5¾	3	11
New York		120	5	100	120	75	60	9	5½	13½	11	19	12½	13	4½	4	6½	5½	3½	11½
Philadelphia	1795	120	5	100	120	75	60	9	5½	13	11	19	12½	13	4½	4	6½	5½	3½	11½
Baltimore		100	5	100	120	75	60	9	5½	14	12	20	12½	13	4½	4	6½	5¼	3½	11½
Charleston		100	6	105	135	75	60	9½	6	15	13	25	14	14	4½	3½	7	5¼	4	11½
U. S. averaged	1795	5½	4¼	95	120	75	55	9	5	12	10	19	11	11	4½	3½	6	5¼	4	10
Boston		150	4½	90	210	110	95	10	6	15	12	20	13	13½	4	4½	10½	6	4	12
New York		250	5	100	210	110	95	11	6½	15½	14	22	14	14	4½	4½	10¼	6	4	12½
Philadelphia	1800	250	5	100	210	110	95	11	6	15½	14	25	14	13½	4½	4½	10¼	6	4	12½
Baltimore		200	6	110	200	110	90	12	6½	16	14	30	14	14	4½	4½	10¼	5¾	4	12½
Charleston		200	6	110	210	110	95	12½	6½	16½	15	50	15	15	4½	4½	11	5¾	4	12½
U. S. averaged	1800	6	4½	90	200	100	85	10	6½	14	11	22	13	13	4½	4½	10	5¾	4½	11
Boston		250	5	75	205	106	95	12	7½	19	15	30	13½	13½	4½	5½	11½	7	4	13
New York		300	6	80	200	106	95	12½	7½	21	16	35	13½	13½	4½	5½	11¼	7¼	4½	13½
Philadelphia	1805	250	6	80	200	106	95	13	7½	21½	16	40	13½	13½	4½	5½	11¼	7	4½	13½
Baltimore		250	5	80	200	106	95	13	7½	22	18	60	14½	14½	5	5½	11	6½	4½	13½
Charleston		250	6	100	210	106	100	14	8	24	20	100	15	15	5	5	11¼	6½	5	14
U. S. averaged	1805	6¼	4½	75	180	100	90	12	7½	20	15	30	13	13	4¾	5¼	10	6½	4	12

Flour prices are thus reviewed in Clark's "History of Manufactures in the United States, 1607–1860" (p. 139):

The price of flour was subject to great variation, both at different seasons and from year to year. In local markets a hundredweight of flour usually sold for about the same as 3 bushels of wheat. In an age when every farmer took his own grain to the mill, and had it ground for toll in kind, there was little chance for speculation to affect prices in the local market. The scanty evidence at hand indicates that during the seventeenth century prices were at times very high. In 1629 wheat flour is rated at $3 a bushel, and in 1697 at between $11 and $12 a barrel. There had been an intervening period of moderate prices, but thereafter for some years quotations maintained a high level. In 1721, again, very low prices, possibly under $1 per 100 pounds, are quoted in New England. After this date we have a fairly continuous record of flour values in the middle colonies. From 1721 until 1748 quotations ranged between $1 and $1.50 a hundredweight, with an average probably not far from midway between those two figures. The latter year prices rose to $2.80 a hundredweight, and, with the exception of a few short seasons, they remained above $2 from that time until the Revolution. In other words, during the first part of the century flour cost in port towns under $3 a barrel, and from the middle of the century until the war with England, following the abrupt rise in 1748, it usually cost above $4 a barrel.

CONTEMPORARY DATA ON PRICES

Some contemporary material bearing on the general subject of prices and cost of living was found, chiefly with reference to board and lodging. Data of this character appear more frequently after the Revolution, and by 1800–1820 are not uncommon in the many books of travel of that period.

An early pronouncement of the relation between wages and prices is found in an order of the Massachusetts Bay Colony General Court of 1634, issued after the 1633 statute fixing wages. Referring to its wage enactment, by which "the wages of workmen were reduced to a certainety in regard of the great extorcion used by dyvers persons of little conscience," the court decides that:

Nowe, least the honest and conscionable workemen be wronged or discouraged by excessive prizes of those commodyties which are necessary for their life and comfort, wee have thought it very just and equall to sett order also therein; wee doe therefore hereby order, that after publique notice hereof noe persons shall sell to any of the inhabitants within this jurisdiction any provision, cloathinge, tooles or other commodities above the rate of four pence in a shilling more than the same cost or might be bought for ready money in England, on paine of forfeiting the valewe of the things solde, except cheese, which, in regard of the much hazard in bringing, and wyne and oyle, vinegar and strong waters, which in regard of leakeing may be solde att such rates (provided the same be moderate) as the buyer and seller can agree. And for lynnen and other commodyties which, in regard of their close stowage and small hazard, may be afforded att a cheape rate, wee doe advise all men to be a rule to themselves in keeping a good conscience, assuring them that if any man shall exccede the bounds of moderacion we shall punish them severely.[26]

A few years later the court, "aware that the board at public houses, if extravagant, not only required a corresponding price from the traveller, but also put him in the hazard of contracting a taste for similar fare at his own house, and thus promoted a costly mode of living, ever unfavorable to the pecuniary concerns of a community,"[27] tried another way of helping the consumer. It declared that:

Whereas complaint hath bene also made that diverse pore people, who would willingly content themselves with meane dyet are forced to take such dyet as is

[26] Massachusetts Bay Colony Records, Vol. I, p. 110.
[27] Felt's Massachusetts Currency, p. 22.

tendered them at 12d. [24.3 cents] the meale or more; it is now ordered that every keeper of such Inn or comon vicualling house shall sell and allow unto every of their guests such victuals as they shall call for, and not force them to take more or other than they desire, bee it never so meane and small in quantity, and shall affoard the same and all other dyet at reasonable prizes upon paine of such fine as the Court shall inflict according to the measure and quantity of the offence.[28]

This law was enacted in 1637. In 1639 Virginia fixed the price of a meal at an "ordinary" at 12d. "Five years later, the charge for a meal at an inn was not allowed to exceed 10 pounds of tobacco (15.4 cents). Only wholesome diet was to be furnished and that in sufficient quantity." [29]

Writing about Maine in 1675 an early chronicler says:

Massachusetts merchants furnish them with all things they stand in need of, keeping here and there fair Magazines stored with English goods, but they set excessive prices upon them. If they do not gain cent per cent they cry out that they are losers, hence English shoes are sold for 8 & 9s. [$1.33–$1.50] a pair; worsted stockings of 3/6 [95 cents] for 7/8 [$1.28] a pair; . . . serges of 2 or 3s. [48.6–73 cents] a yard for 6s. and 7s. [$1 and $1.17] a yard, and so all sorts of commodities, both for planters and fishermen.[30]

Bread prices were generally fixed by order of the colonial court or by town ordinances. These regulations controlled both the weight and the price of a loaf of bread, basing price on the current price of wheat flour. In the earliest days bread sold at a penny a loaf, and governmental control dealt only with the weight that must be given for a penny. Thus a New Haven, Conn., ordinance of 1640 stipulates that with wheat at 6s. 6d. ($1.58) a bushel, white bread must weigh 6 ounces per loaf; "wheat bread" 9½ ounces, and the "household loaf" 12¼ ounces. Each loaf sold at an English penny, which is about 2 cents. The Massachusetts General Court in 1696 fixed a sliding scale of loaf weights proportionate to the price of flour, ranging from 8¾ ounces when flour sold at 16 shillings ($2.67) per hundredweight, to 4⅜ ounces when flour cost 32s. ($5.33), the loaf of bread to sell in all cases at one penny.

Speaking of the women of Pennsylvania who in 1698 earned "their own Livelihood by their own Industry," Thomas found their charges very high, "for I can buy in London a cheesecake for Two pence, bigger than theirs for that price, when at the same time their milk is as cheap as we can buy it in London and their Flour cheaper by one-half."

A Salem, Mass., ordinance of April, 1726, declares that:

Wheat for this month is 11s. [61 cents] [31] a bushel. The price and weight of bread required to be 2d. [1 cent] for a loaf of 8 oz. 4 drs.; 4d. [4 cents] for a loaf 16 oz. 12 drs.; 6d. [6 cents] for a wheaten loaf of 2 lbs. 5 oz.; 6d. for a household loaf of 3 lbs. 2 oz.[32]

Board in Virginia in the middle of the seventeenth century was £5 sterling ($24.30) a year, on which "any one can live in a manner which in England would entail an outlay of thirty pound sterling [$145.80]." [33] A century later board in the Shenandoah Valley region

---

[28] Massachusetts Bay Colony Records, Vol. I, p. 214.
[29] Bruce, Vol. II, p. 203.
[30] Hart, Albert Bushnell, ed.: American History Told by Contemporaries, Vol. I, p. 433. An account of Two Voyages to New England, by John Josselyn. Conversion of these prices has been made on the assumption that Josselyn was comparing the cost of the articles in colonial money with the cost of the same article in England in terms of English money. Hence the sterling shilling has been used to convert the values he quotes, while the colonial shilling is used to convert actual prices charged.
[31] Depreciated currency, 18 shillings to the dollar. See p. 17.
[32] Quoted in Felt's Annals of Salem, Vol. II, p. 153.
[33] Bullock's Virginia, p. 37.

of Virginia was £15 [$50] a year in the account book of a local blacksmith.[34]

At about the same period board in Boston was 12s. ($2) a week,[34] practically twice the rate in rural Virginia. A generation later the same rate is given for board in New York outside New York City. In the city it was $7 a week.[35] The rate charged for board in Philadelphia in 1748 is reported by one of the numerous European travelers of the period: "I and my companion had a room, candles, beds, attendance, and three meals a day, if we chose to have so many, for 20s. ($2.67) per week in Pennsylvania currency. But wood, washing, and wine, if required, were to be paid for besides." [36] Speaking of the same period, another visitor says:

Provisions are cheap in Pennsylvania, but everything that is manufactured and brought into the country is three or four times as dear as in Germany. Even in the humblest and poorest houses in this country there is no meal without meat, and no one eats the bread without butter or cheese, although the bread is as good as with us. It is very annoying, however, that nothing but salt meat is eaten in summer and rarely fresh meat in winter. On account of the extensive stock raising, meat is very cheap.[37]

At the close of the century, 1790, Tench Coxe, then Assistant Secretary of the Treasury, in one of his papers on economic and industrial conditions in the young Republic, declares that—

Though the wages of the industrious poor are very good, yet the necessaries of life are cheaper than in Europe, and the articles used are more comfortable and pleasing. It may be safely affirmed that an american cent, being equal to the hundredth part of a mexican dollar, will buy as good butchers meat in the capitals of the several states as a penny sterling will buy in Amsterdam, Paris, or London. Fish, in all our cities and towns near the sea, are excellent, abundant, and cheaper far than butchers meat; and poultry is so low that a turkey of fourteen or fifteen pounds weight may be bought for three shillings and nine pence to four shillings and six pence sterling [90 cents to $1.09].[38]

Material on the cost of living for the years immediately following the War of 1812 is abundant in a 3-volume work entitled "A Statistical, Political and Historical Account of the United States," by D. B. Warden, published in Edinburgh in 1819. How accurate Warden's figures are has not been definitely determined. He was a Government official in Washington at one time and later United States consul at Paris, where his book was written. He seems not to have gained any standing as a historian, but McMaster quotes his figures occasionally, and they are consistent with other data of the same period. They are presented here as interesting rather than as authoritative. The period covered is in all cases the three years from 1815 to 1818.

Board in New York was $2 a week in the country and villages and $4 or $5 in towns, depending on their size and importance. The average rent of houses of the sort used by mechanics in the towns was $80 a year.

In Pennsylvania—

The price of living in a farmer's house, boarding, lodging and washing, $2 a week. It is well ascertained that a family may be comfortably supported, each, per day, for 20 cents, and even for 16 cents in some counties. On the western side of the mountains a resident has assured me that a family may be supported

---

[34] Manuscript accounts.
[35] McMaster, John Bach: History of the People of the United States, Vol. I, p. 242.
[36] Kalm, Peter: Journeys into North America, Vol. I, p. 24.
[37] Mittelberger, Gottlieb: Journey to Pennsylvania, 1750-1754, pp. 64-5.
[38] Coxe, Tench: View of America, pp. 95-6.

at the rate of 10 cents each. A gentleman who lived many years in Carlisle in reply to my inquiry on the subject observed that before the year 1812 the average expense for a family for living was $1 a week. [39]

Another writer, who traveled from Virginia to Illinois in 1817 looking for a homestead, and who made daily notes of his observations and experiences, found, in McConnellsburg, Pa., a blacksmith who "earns $20 a month and board, and he lives in a cabin of one room for which, with a garden, he pays $20 a year." [40]

Both men agree that "in general," as Warden reports it, cost of living in the Middle West Territories "is one-third cheaper than in the eastern States." In Kentucky "provisions are cheap and in great abundance. Board is $2 a week. The rent of a house containing five good rooms is from $100 to $200 a year; a house for mechanics from $20 to $50."

Curiously enough, Warden seems to find living higher in the South than in the East. "Beef, mutton and pork were 12 cents per pound" in Richmond in 1815, but were "in remote parts of the interior, about half that price." Board of workmen in Richmond was $3.50 to $5.50; in towns of lesser importance, $2 to $2.50 per week. "The rent of a house at Richmond, not of the handsomest class, was $1,400 a year; of a store, about one-third less."

New Orleans led in high cost of board, according to Warden, who says that "board is about $1 a day; in some of the best houses, twice that sum." As early as 1808 "the common price of French boarding houses was $45 a month without supper or wine; American boarding houses, $32."

Retail prices in Washington, D. C., in 1818, were: "Beef, 4½d. to 6d. [$0.06–$0.08] per pound; pork the same; potatoes, 3s. 4d. [$0.56] a bushel; bread, 2d. [$0.03] a pound; milk, 5½d. [$0.08] a quart; tea, 4/6 to 13s. 6d. [$0.75 to $2.25] per pound; coffee, 12½d. to 16d. [$0.14 to $0.22] per pound." Fuel wood was $4 a cord; shoes were $2.50 a pair. Bricks cost $5.75 to $6.50 per thousand, and "a house consisting of three stories, 26 feet in front and 40 feet deep, completely finished, costs from $4,000 to $6,000. A house of two stories of the same length and breadth is valued at from $3,000 to $4,000."

The following "estimated expense of clothing a family of 6" for a year is not for any specified locality, and unfortunately gives no hint as to either quantity or quality of clothing purchasable on that budget. It reads:

Man and wife, at $25.40 each _____ $50. 80
One child above 16 _____ 25. 40
Three children under 16, at $23.95 each _____ 71. 85

148. 05

Clothing prices are obtainable to some extent for all periods, but are not applicable in relation to wages, because practically always these prices are quoted on a class of goods which workingmen did not buy.

Living standards maintained on the basis of these cost of living data differed as radically from present-day conditions as did the prices themselves. Comment on the marked differences between living

[39] Warden, D. B.: A Statistical, Political, and Historical Account of the United States, Vol. II, p. 85.
[40] Birkbeck, Morris: Notes on a Journey in America from the Coast of Virginia to the Territory of Illinois, 1817.

conditions of wage earners at the beginning of the nineteenth century and those of wage earners of 1885 is made by Carroll D. Wright in his History of Wages and Prices in Massachusetts, 1752–1860 (pp. 10–11):

Laborers at the beginning of the century had few of the comforts and conveniences now common in the poorest families. China, glassware, and carpets, to say nothing of the numberless contrivances now in use for facilitating household labor, were then practically out of reach. Dwellings were warmed by open fires of wood, while churches were not warmed at all. The iron cook stove for economically and efficiently aiding in the culinary operations of the family had not yet appeared. Anthracite coal, though for fifteen years in use on blacksmiths' forges in the coal region, was unavailable for household purposes, and in 1806 the first freightage of a few hundred bushels was brought down to Philadelphia and there used experimentally, with indifferent success.

The artisan's food was simple, often coarse, and in fact confined to the bare necessities of life. The wide range of products which now enrich the workingman's table, brought to him from all the markets of the world by the modern system of rapid transportation, were many of them unknown, or if known were expensive luxuries only obtainable by the favored few.

McMaster, speaking of the food and clothing of the early American workingman, says:

Among the fruits and vegetables of which no one had then even heard, are cantaloupes, many varieties of peaches and pears, tomatoes and rhubarb, sweet corn, the cauliflower, the egg plant, head lettuce, and okra.

If the food of an artisan would now be thought coarse, his clothes would be thought abominable. A pair of yellow buckskin or leathern breeches, a checked shirt, a red flannel jacket, a rusty felt hat cocked up at the corners, shoes of neat's skin set off with huge buckles of brass, and a leathern apron, comprised his scanty wardrobe.[41]

---

[41] History of the People of the United States, Vol. I. p. 97.

Chapter 3.—THE INDENTURE SYSTEM OF LABOR

It is undoubtedly because free labor, hired on a wage basis, was in more general use in New England than in the other colonies that the existing wage data for the colonial period are so largely confined to New England. Conversely, probably the chief reason wage statistics covering the other settlements are so rarely found is that a labor system very different from employment for actual wages prevailed.

This system was that of "indentured" labor, generally referred to as white servitude, which grew out of the demand for land and for laborers in the colonies on one hand, and of the overpopulation and extreme poverty of Europe on the other.

"INDENTURED SERVANTS" AND "REDEMPTIONERS"

White servitude took two different forms—labor under a specific contract called an indenture and under a less definite agreement embodied in legislation or what came to be known as "the custom of the country."

An indentured servant was one who came to the New World under a contract either with a planter who imported him into the colony, or with the shipowner or merchant who transported him for the purpose of disposing of his services upon arrival. British law required that all British subjects emigrating as servants should, before sailing, execute indentures stipulating the number of years of service entered into, and whether the labor to be performed was a definite trade or any kind of work required by the other party to the contract. The master, in consideration of his right to the servant's labor, agreed to provide food, clothing, and lodging for the stated period of time, and generally to allow additional compensation in the nature of provisions, clothing, and equipment upon the expiration of the term. This allowance came to be known as "freedom dues" and sometimes, particularly in the beginning, included land. These indentures were similar in form; in fact a printed form came into use as the system developed. They were officially recorded at the port of embarkation, and had the full force of law in both England and the colonies.

Redemptioners were as a rule Europeans who, desiring to emigrate but having no means to pay for their own passage, permitted the shippers to dispose of their services, in exchange for transportation, under conditions controlled by colonial legislation or by "the custom of the country."

The distinction is largely one of procedure, because "when a redemptioner had been sold, he had the legal status of an indentured servant." [1]

IMPORTANCE OF SYSTEM

Basically the entire system of white servitude which developed in the American colonies "was only a modified form of the system of apprenticeship which had been in vogue in England for several

---

[1] Herrick, Cheesman A.: White Servitude in Pennsylvania, p. 4, footnote.

centuries preceding. The wide use of this system of labor during the fifteenth and sixteenth centuries accounts in a great measure for the readiness with which persons in later years entered into a contract of servitude in order to reach the New World." [2] The system is generally regarded as being economically necessary in its time, and "indentured servants have been long regarded as the chief support of the American industrial system in the seventeenth century," [3] because—

No system of free labor could have been maintained in the colonies until a comparatively late date. In the first place, the poor of Europe would not have been able to come to America had they been obliged to pay for their passage in advance. On the other hand, the planters could not afford to pay the wages of free laborers. Even with the large supply of servants and convicts, free labor was high and unprofitable. Laborers would not hire, except for very high wages, when they could easily obtain new lands and become planters themselves.[4]

Accordingly, "the economic importance of the servant in developing the resources of the colonies, especially the middle colonies, can hardly be overestimated." [5]

DEVELOPMENT OF SYSTEM

Social, political, and economic conditions in Great Britain during the seventeenth century produced unemployment and widespread poverty which created the supply of available workers out of which the indenture system evolved. Two conditions in the colonies produced the market for this supply. One was the desire for land—a desire which could be met by the importation of servants under the "headright" system, which allowed each settler a certain number of acres for each person brought into the colony; the other was the acute need for labor to clear and develop the land after it had been acquired. That the latter condition was the more compelling motive is evidenced by the fact that the importation of servants was in nowise diminished by the later abolition of the headright system.

Inevitably, then, the transportation and sale of servants from Europe to the colonies became an established business in the Old World, and a form of servitude which could be bought and controlled was adopted as the labor policy of the New World.

Actually most of the first colonists to settle Virginia were servants of the exploiting company, and were bound to its service for a definite period of time. Under the program of colonization carried out by the Virginia company—

The position of an early planter was theoretically that of a member of the Company who was to receive in lieu of his services for a term of years his maintenance during that time, or his transportation and maintenance at the Company's charge. For the adventure of his person, as well as for every subscription of £12 10s., [$60.75] he received a bill of adventure which entitled him to the proportion that would fall to a single share in the division of land and profits. As a member he stood on an equal footing with all other members and stockholders. Practically, however, he was, at least during the first twelve years of the Company's government, little better than a servant, manipulated in the interest of the Company, held in servitude beyond a stipulated term, and defrauded of his just share in the proceeds of the undertaking.[6]

[2] McCormac, Eugene Irving: White Servitude in Maryland; Johns Hopkins University Studies in Historical and Political Science, Series XXII, Nos. 3–4, p. 7.
[3] Herrick, p. 10.
[4] McCormac, pp. 33–34.
[5] Idem, p. 32.
[6] Ballagh, James Curtis: White Servitude in the Colony of Virginia; Johns Hopkins University Studies in Historical and Political Science, Series XIII, Nos. 6–7, 1895, p. 13.

The policy thus introduced at the outset was adopted by these same colonists when they were at last freed from their servile connection with the company and became planters on their own account, and "there gradually grew up after the year 1616 and the establishment of separate plantations, the practice on the part of societies of planters, and later of private persons, of transporting servants to settle and work their lands very much on the same conditions of service as those made with the company. This developed, as property began to be acquired by the planters generally, into the common mode of transporting servants on contract by indenture for a limited term of service, varying in individual cases according to the terms of the contract."[7]

Importation of servants was largely an individual matter at first. The planters who were in need of workers requested their representatives in England to send men out as needed, and the expenses of the voyage were met by the employer. Gradually the procuring of workers for the colonies grew into a business, and with the development of a steady market and greater shipping facilities, merchants and shippers began the transportation of servants, without previous solicitation on the part of the planters, solely as a commercial enterprise. That it was a profitable undertaking is suggested by the fact that "a servant might be transported at a cost of from £6 to £8 [$29.16 to $38.88], and sold for £40 or £60 [$194.40 to $291.16]."[8]

While in large part the business thus created was a legitimate form of assisted immigration, it led to evils both in procuring and in transporting which discredited the entire traffic. Systematic kidnaping of children and adults was resorted to and carried on openly and flagrantly in English seaports. The alarming proportions assumed by this outrage finally compelled legislative action which influenced the indenture system as a whole without, however, materially affecting the kidnaping evil itself. The law requiring that indentures be executed and recorded before sailing was a direct result of the practice of kidnaping. This law probably checked the operations of the organized kidnapers to some extent, but a few years later merchants in the colonial trade appealed to Parliament for measures to protect their legitimate business of supplying the colonies with laborers. Parliament granted the request with an act making the stealing and transporting of children and adults a crime punishable by death "without benefit of clergy."

"Not even this extreme penalty," Bruce states, "could put a stop to the mischief. Ten years after this act became a law, it was said that 10,000 persons were annually spirited away from the kingdom by the arts of the kidnapers."[9]

The operations, half a century later, of the agents, or "newlanders," on the Continent, especially in the German Palatinate, were comparable in their methods of persuasion to the "spirits," or professional kidnapers, of England during the seventeenth century. These newlanders were employed by the shipping companies to secure redemptioners for the colonies, specifically for the Pennsylvania trade. While perhaps physical force was not used by them, as it was by the English kidnapers, some of the worst abuses which attached to the

---

[7] Ballagh, p. 26.
[8] Idem, p. 41.
[9] Bruce, Philip A.: Economic History of Virginia in the Seventeenth Century, Vol. I, p. 618.

colonial labor system are attributable to the exploitations practiced by these promoters. Both the "spirits" and the "newlanders" were the prototypes of the emigrant runner who became an unpleasantly familiar figure in the induced immigration of a much later period in American history.

Exploitation of emigrating servants during the long waits for ships, and on shipboard, and appalling conditions resulting from over-crowding, insufficient food, and lack of sanitary provisions and pre-cautions during the voyage, constituted additional evils which both the home and the colonial governments tried in vain to control. That evil, far from being checked, grew in proportion to the continued increase in the importation of bound servants into the country, and as a feature of assisted immigration, long outlived the indenture system.

CHARACTER OF INDENTURED SERVANTS

The first laborers sent into the early settlements as indentured servants came chiefly from the great class of unemployed and unem-ployable unskilled workers and landless agricultural laborers—the unassimilable surplus population of Great Britain. Undoubtedly thoughout the history of the indenture system in all the colonies that remained true of a preponderance of the servant class from the British Isles and the Continent, in spite of the stigma of criminality which later attached to the class. Their poverty, as Bruce points out, was no obstacle to their emigration to a land in urgent need of their services, particularly since that poverty was the result of social and economic conditions of which they were merely victims, and which "could not destroy the great qualities inherent in the stock from which they sprung." [10]

Transportation to the colonies was a legitimate means of diverting an unwieldy overflow of population in order to mitigate the burdens of the English poor law, and to that end it was principally employed. Probably the comment made upon the character of those sent out in one of the first shipments of indentured servants could have been aptly applied to every shipment—"They are like those who are left behind, even of all sorts, better and worse."

The "worse" element increased, however, with the later practice of sentencing criminals to transportation to the colonies as long-term servants. Among the first convicts sent over in any numbers "politi-cal prisoners, or offenders against the government rather than against the law, constituted the larger class." [11] The political disturbances of the seventeenth century sent many into exile as indentured servants to the American colonists. Cromwell sent over 1,600 royalist soldiers, and the practice continued with each change in political domination until some time after the Restoration. The servants who were in this category, "far from always belonging to a low station in their native country, frequently represented the most useful and respectable elements in the kingdom." [12]

But the practice extended to the criminal class, and regardless of constant protest and resistance on the part of the colonies, trans-portation of "King's passengers," as they were euphemistically

[10] Bruce, Vol. I, p. 582.
[11] Herrick, p. 116.
[12] Bruce, Vol. I, p. 608.

called, increased rapidly throughout the eighteenth century, and was stopped only by the American Revolution.

The first recorded instance of the indenture of a criminal is in Virginia in 1618, "when a man convicted of manslaughter and sentenced to be hanged was reprieved, 'because he was a carpenter and the plantation needed carpenters.' " [13] English penal law, in the middle of the seventeenth century, prescribed the death penalty for more than 300 different crimes, among which "arson of cornstacks" and "killing of cattle" were included. Bruce suggests that transportation was seized upon as "a compromise on the part of the English judges" with the "pitiless rigidity of the criminal code then in force." [14]

Early in the eighteenth century an act was passed providing "that in cases of minor offenses, grand or petit larceny, and other misdemeanors for which benefit of clergy was allowed and upon which whipping and burning in the hand were visited, criminals might be sent to the American colonies for seven years. Similar offenders who were in the workhouses were included. Where persons had been convicted or stood attainted of any offense for which death might be inflicted under the law, or where they were convicted of any crime for which benefit of clergy was denied them, judges might commute the sentences to transportation for 14 years in the plantations." [15] Return to England before the expiration of the term to which they were sentenced carried a mandatory infliction of the death penalty, and completion of the term amounted to pardon.

The colonists opposed the introduction of convicts by every means within their power, but their efforts were not successful. Pennsylvania and Virginia controlled the matter to a considerable extent, but the other settlements were unable to do so. Maryland especially became "the dumping-ground for English jails, and received more convicts than any other plantation on the continent. A contemporary, in 1767, estimates the number imported into Maryland for the preceding thirty years at 600 per annum." [16]

The attitude of the American settlers toward the practice is shown in the many regulative and restrictive laws passed by the provincial legislatures, and by the bitter attacks upon it in the early newspapers. Franklin fought it vigorously in his paper and in England. Feeling grew more intense as the policy persisted in spite of growing opposition, and Herrick makes the point that "the sending of convicts rather than trade regulation led to early estrangement." [17]

Various estimates have been made of the entire number sent as servants into the colonies. "Between 1717 and 1775 the number sent from Old Bailey alone is thought to be 10,000, and the whole number from various places in Great Britain and Ireland at least 50,000." [18]

Most of these "King's passengers," McCormac holds, "were ordinary criminals. Among them were men and women of all ages and descriptions. They represented all crimes—if some of the offenses may be so classed—from stealing a loaf of bread to sustain life, to highway robbery. The worst criminals were seldom transported." [19]

[13] Ballagh, p. 36.
[14] Bruce, Vol. I, p. 603.
[15] Herrick, p. 119.
[16] McCormac, p. 98.
[17] Herrick, p 131.
[18] McCormac, p. 93, citing Butler, British Convicts Shipped to America—American Historical Review, Vol. II, p. 25; and Lang, Transportation and Colonization, pp. 37–38.
[19] Idem, p. 95.

An inconsiderable element of the indentured servant class came from the colonies themselves. These servants as a rule were either persons who had been sentenced to servitude by the colonial courts for misdemeanors, or who had voluntarily sold themselves to escape imprisonment for debt.

METHODS OF SALE AND DISTRIBUTION

After the emigrating servant, whether indentured or kidnaped, a free-willer or a convict, had survived the hardships and perils of the voyage, he became merely merchandise when the ship reached its American port. "When a large proportion of servants on board of a ship arriving in Virginia were consigned under indenture to planters named in the bills of lading, the vessel either proceeded directly to the landings of these planters, or to some general port where it could be conveniently reached by them." If, on the other hand, the cargo of servants was the property of the shipmaster, to be sold in port by him to the highest bidder, as was usually the case, "it seems to have been the habit of the planters residing in the neighborhood to go on board and make purchases of servants. The most prominent citizens did not disdain to buy in person in this manner." [20]

After the colonial press appeared, notices of the arrival of ships having servants to be disposed of were frequent. These advertisements gave the number, age, and sex of the human cargo, and frequently listed various trades and callings as being available in the person of those transported. The public was invited to inspect the outfit on board ship, where sales would be conducted by the captain.

Redemptioners were supposed to be allowed a certain number of days after arrival in port to obtain money with which to pay the captain for their passage, but "in practice they were usually sold without indenture as soon as the ship arrived." [21] One of the charges against the shippers was that no time was allowed the newcomer to make his own arrangements upon landing, but instead he was summarily disposed of in payment of his debt to the ship, sometimes with no real comprehension of the meaning of the transaction. The manner in which the sale of the German redemptioners who poured into Pennsylvania in the second quarter of the eighteenth century was carried on is given minutely by a contemporary who was presumably familiar with the custom. "The sale of human beings in the market on board the ship," he says, "is carried on thus:"

Every day Englishmen, Dutchmen, and High-German people come from the city of Philadelphia and other places, in part from a great distance, say 20, 30, or 40 hours away, and go on board the newly arrived ship that has brought and offers for sale passengers from Europe, and select among them the healthy persons such as they deem suitable for their business, and bargain with them how long they will serve for their passage money, which most of them are still in debt for. When they have come to an agreement, it happens that adult persons bind themselves in writing to serve 3, 4, 5, or 6 years for the amount due by them, according to their age and strength. But very young people, from 10 to 15 years, must serve till they are 21 years old.

Many parents must sell and trade away their children like so many head of cattle; for if their children take the debt upon themselves, the parents can leave

---

[20] Bruce, Vol. I, p. 633.
[21] McCormac, p. 43.

the ship free and unrestrained; but as the parents often do not know where and to what people their children are going, it often happens that such parents and children, after leaving the ship, do not see each other again for many years, perhaps no more in all their lives.

When people arrive who can not make themselves free, but have children under 5 years, the parents can not free themselves by them, for such children must be given to somebody without compensation to be brought up, and they must serve for their bringing up until they are 21 years old. Children from 5 to 10 years, who pay half price for their passage, viz, 30 florins [$12], must likewise serve for it until they are 21 years of age; they cannot, therefore, redeem their parents by taking the debt of the latter upon themselves. But children above 10 years can take part of their parents' debt upon themselves.

A woman must stand for her husband if he arrives sick, and in like manner a man for his sick wife, and take the debt upon herself or himself, and thus serve five to six years not alone for his or her own debt, but also for that of the sick husband or wife. But if both are sick, such persons are sent from the ship to the sick-house (hospital), but not until it appears probable that they will find no purchasers. As soon as they are well again they must serve for their passage, or pay if they have the means.

It often happens that whole families, husband, wife, and children, are separated by being sold to different purchasers, especially when they have not paid any part of their passage money.

When a husband or wife has died at sea, when the ship has made more than half of her trip, the survivor must pay or serve not only for himself or herself, but also for the deceased.

When both parents have died over half-way at sea, their children, especially when they are young and have nothing to pawn or to pay, must stand for their own and their parents' passage, and serve till they are 21 years old.[22]

Prices varied according to age, skill, length of service, and other considerations, but "the average price for adults seems to have been about £15 to £20 [$72.90 to $97.20]," while "convicts were regularly sold by the contractors at £8 to £20 [$38.88 to $97.20] each."[23] The price for which redemptioners were sold in Pennsylvania "was gradually advanced during the eighteenth century" and as the price increased "charges of passage were increased,"[24] so that whatever might be the market value of a man's services, the shippers put in a claim for his transportation of substantially that amount.

Opposition to the policy of transportation of criminals, and prejudice against convicts as servants, made their sale difficult. Colonies passed laws requiring ship captains having convicts for sale to declare them such, stating the nature of the offense and the length of the sentence. Virginia and Pennsylvania fixed duties upon transported convicts. The mother country could abrogate these legislative restrictions in its determination to foist its outcasts upon the colonies, but it had no such advantage when it came to the actual sale to the planters of a commodity which they did not want. Devious means had to be resorted to for disguising the true status of the convicts. One story is told of a vessel which landed at Annapolis, Md., carrying "sixty-six indentures signed by the Mayor of Dublin, and twenty-two wigs," the purpose of the wigs being "to set off as decent servants" a shipment of convicts.[25]

As settlement moved back from the seaboard a new business grew up analogous to that of servant shipping. Dealers would buy up servants in blocks at the port of entry and take them inland for sale in the new settlements. The trade practices of these dealers seem to

[22] Mittleberger, Gottlieb: Journey to Pennsylvania, 1750–1754, pp. 26–28.
[23] McCormac, p. 42.
[24] Herrick, p. 202.
[25] Annals of Philadelphia, quoted by Herrick, p. 118.

have earned for them their suggestive name of "soul drivers" and were in fact not unlike the better-known tactics of their contemporaries, the slave traders. The back country was depended upon largely to furnish the market for the criminal class which the more experienced buyers in the old settlements refused.

LEGAL STATUS OF SERVANTS

A servant became the property of his employer, or master, as soon as the sale of his services was effected. He could at any time during his servitude be resold for the remainder of his term, without his own consent. In Pennsylvania, however, the law did not permit his removal from the colony after resale without his consent.

The legal character of the institution of white servitude was definitely fixed in all the colonies and was practically identical in all in which it was the predominating labor system. An indenture executed in England covering the term and kind of service, the obligations of both master and servants, and the remuneration to be paid, was regarded as a legal contract enforceable by the colonial courts. As the practice of sending "free-willers" into the country without contract grew, the abuses inherent therein were very soon checked by legislation, particularly with respect to the length of service and the "freedom dues," that is, the amount payable at the expiration of the term. Maryland fixed the term of service for servants sold without indenture at four years for males 18 years of age and over and females 12 years of age and over. Males under 18 were to serve until they were 24; females under 12 were bound for seven years.[26] In Pennsylvania servitude was for five years for persons 17 years of age and over, and until the age of 22 for those under 17,[27] and Virginia, after frequent changes, settled upon a term of five years for persons 19 years of age and over, and one extending through the twenty-fourth year for those under 19.[28] Longer terms could not be enforced except as punishment, and then only as penalties inflicted by law or court order.

To protect the servant against manipulation in the matter of age, the laws required that masters present their servants in court within three months to record their ages, if known; if ages were not known, they were to be "adjudged" by the court and recorded. In the southern colonies a master's failure to comply with this regulation shortened the servant's term one year. Later a fine was imposed as an additional penalty.

Whether the servant was bound by an indenture specific in its terms, or merely by the custom of the country, "he had a legal as well as moral right to expect that provision would be made for his comfortable existence,"[29] and, according to a contemporary, "the laws of Virginia take great care for the good usage of servants as to necessities, Diet and Clothes."[30] Virginia law also provided that a sick or disabled servant "could claim support and medical attention at his master's charge during servitude without any reciprocal right on the part of the master therefor. The master was prevented by the liability of his goods and chattels to seizure from avoiding this obliga-

---

[26] McCormac, p. 44.
[27] Herrick, p. 291, citing laws.
[28] Bruce, Vol. II, p. 5, citing Hening's Statutes, Vol. II, p. 240.
[29] Idem, Vol. II, p. 5.
[30] Oldmixon, John: British Empire in America (1735), Vol. I, p. 426.

tion by freeing his servant and throwing him upon the parish."[31] Moreover, if the servant had become sick or disabled "in consequence of the meagreness of the provision made for his comfort, or as the result of punishment to which he might have been subjected, he was to be taken away from his master, * * * turned over to the church wardens of the parish, and until the expiration of his term supported at the expense of his original employer,"[32] if his condition did not permit resale.

Legally servants could always bring charges against their masters for mistreatment, violation of contract, and the like, but they were themselves subject to punishment if they failed to prove their case. "While there were laws granting to servants the right to bring their masters to justice for any cruel or unjust treatment," Geiser finds "few occasions on which this right was exercised,"[33] and Herrick agrees that "servants did not find it easy to get their rights."[34]   On the other hand, Bruce maintains that so far as legal safeguards went the servant was afforded "absolute security in the enjoyment of every comfort that he could reasonably claim," and "if in any case he suffered, it was to be attributed to his own supineness and not to any deficiency in the law prescribing the remedy,"[35] and still another student of the system asserts that "the courts carefully guarded his contract and effected speedy redress of his grievances."[36]   However, both of the writers just quoted were referring specifically to the early history of the system in Virginia, before it had become the complicated labor problem which it was in Pennsylvania in the time about which the two previously quoted authorities are writing.   Every history of the system which has been consulted gives instances of judicial decisions favorable to the servants, particularly in the important item of freedom dues.

EXTENDED TERMS AS PUNISHMENT

Nevertheless the laws themselves afforded almost unlimited opportunities for injustice and exploitation by providing for additional time in servitude as a penalty for countless infractions and misdemeanors.   In its practical application, extension of time as a legal theory worked two ways.   It was granted to the employer as compensation for damages in his claim against a servant who broke laws dealing solely with the master and servant relationship, and it was also granted even in criminal cases where the employer paid in money a fine assessed against a servant for violation of general laws having no connection with his status as servant.

Numerous laws were designed merely to protect the master in his right to his servant's time and labor.   Chief among these were those prohibiting trading with a servant without his master's consent; prohibiting marriage of servants, even to free persons, without such consent; and the laws relating to runaway servants.   Offenses against all of these laws were punished by extension of the period of servitude, the amount of added time being in some instances fixed by

---

[31] Ballagh, p. 64.
[32] Bruce, Vol. II, p. 12-13.
[33] Geiser, Karl Frederick: Redemptioners and Indentured Servants in the Colony and Commonwealth of Pennsylvania, p. 103.
[34] Herrick, p. 278.
[35] Bruce, Vol. II, p. 11.
[36] Ballagh, p. 44.

statute, in others determined by the court. Marriage between servants without the consent of their masters was penalized by an additional year of service. If a servant married a free person the latter must either pay a prohibitive fine to the employer, or serve him for one year. If a woman servant gave birth to an illegitimate child her time of service might be extended from one to two years, and in some colonies the children were placed at the disposal of the parish until they were 31 years of age. In Maryland "masters were compelled by law to maintain bastard children of their women servants. If the father could be found, he was held responsible for the support of the child; if not, the mother must repay the master by servitude or otherwise." [37] The Virginia law did not permit extended time in case the master was the father of the servant's child. Instead, the mother became the property of the parish for two years following the expiration of her term of service.

The problem of the runaway servant grew increasingly worse as the system developed, and resulted in stringent laws which restricted the liberties even of freemen, particularly those whose servitude had recently ended. Some colonies required passes of every person found outside his own immediate neighborhood, and if such pass or similar evidence of good faith were not produced on demand, the traveler was considered a runaway servant and treated accordingly. Often in such cases the person taken prisoner was really a runaway. If after due notice he was not claimed, he could be sold again into servitude to pay the costs of his apprehension and maintenance.

Extensions of service ranging from double the amount of lost time to 10 days for each day's absence were imposed after a servant was recovered. At first the county bore the cost of pursuit and capture. Later that was assessed against the servant, which, in actual practice, meant that the master paid the money cost and then recovered it from the servant in the form of extended servitude in addition to that already laid against him for lost time. In this way a servant's time could be so extended as practically to double the legal limit of an indenture.

The following bill against a runaway servant, dated Philadelphia, July 17, 1769,[38] illustrates the manner in which the money cost of capture was assessed against the runaway and in turn translated into a time value which was added to the period of servitude. The bill reads:

	£	s.	d.	
To Messrs. Fearis and LeTeliene for one day which they spent looking for you		10	10	($1.43)
To their ferriage twice, 1/4, & expences 1/1 (17.3 and 14.3¢)		2	5	($0.32)
To advertising in Gazette, Journal and Chronicle		15		($2.00)
To ditto in the York papers		5		($0.666)
To 100 handbills at York		7	6	($1.00)
To John LeTeliene for 10 days which he lost in search of you at York, at 3/4 per day (44 cents)	1	13	4	($4.44)
To ditto for cash which you took away from him		17		($2.27)
To ditto for his gold brooch which he lost when he was looking for you		17		($2.27)
To cash expended by LeTeliene in going to New York, while he was there and on his way back		3		($8.00)
To horse hire for ditto, 10 days at 5/ (66.6 cents)		2	10	($6.67)

37 McCormac, p. 70.
38 In Logan Papers, Vol. X, Historical Society of Pennsylvania.

	£	s.	d.

To Reward, Charges and Prison fees at Carlisle, as per Rob't
Semple's account_____ 7   6   ($19.49)
To cash paid waggoner for bringing you home_____ 2   5   ($6.00)
To time lost from the 16 July, the day you ran away, till the
21st of August, following, the day you were brought back,
is 1 monthe & 6 days.

Under the last item entered in the bill is a series of calculations, unintelligible now without some key by which to interpret them, but which seemed to work out in an orderly fashion to the closing notation on the bill: "To serve beyond his indented time, fifteen months."

WORKING CONDITIONS AND SOCIAL STATUS

To give an accurate idea of the actual condition of the indentured servant class is, as Geiser emphasizes, "no easy task, because there are almost as many different opinions as there are contemporary accounts." [39] Moreover, these contemporary accounts develop not only different opinions but distinctly contradictory evidence. One of the earliest records is subject to considerable discount because it was admittedly written by a pamphleteer for the purpose of attracting servants to Maryland. On the other hand, he is writing of a day before the system had assumed the formidable character it later developed. As Alsop sees it, the life of the indentured servants is a pleasant, easy one:

Five days and a half in the summer weeks is the allotted time that they work in; for two months when the sun predominates in the highest pitch of his heat they claim an ancient and customary privilege, to repose themselves three hours a day within the house, and this is undeniably granted to them that work in the field. [40]

A Virginia contemporary gives a similar account:

The labour servants are put to is not so hard nor of such continuance as Husbandmen nor Handicraft are kept at in England. I said little or nothing is done in the winter time. None ever work before sunrise nor after sunset. In the summer they rest, sleep or exercise themselves five houres in the heat of the day. Saturday afternoon is always their own, the olde Holidays are observed, and the Sabbath spent in good exercise. [41]

Half a century later an early historian declares that so far as conditions in Virginia are concerned "all the labour of the country, which consists chiefly in Tilling, Manuring the Ground, sawing and planting tobacco, is so easy that as hard work as 'tis represented to be, the Day Labourers in England are much the greater slaves, if hard Work and hard Living are signs of Slavery." [42] With the passage of another half century the picture grows less attractive, as evidenced by the available contemporary record. Servants in Maryland "are strained to the utmost to perform their allotted labors; and from a prepossession in many cases too justly founded, they are supposed to be receiving the just reward which is due to repeated offenses. There are doubtless many exceptions to this observation, yet, generally speaking, they groan beneath a worse than Egyptian bondage." [43] Mittelberger, who in 1750 was as frankly

[39] Geiser, p. 102.
[40] Alsop, George: Character of the Province of Maryland, p. 57.
[41] Hammond, John: Leah and Rachel (in Force's Tracts, Vol. III).
[42] Oldmixon, Vol. I, p. 426.
[43] Eddis, William: Letters from America (1775), p. 70.

writing to discourage servant immigration as Alsop in 1650 was to promote it, finds that—

Work and labor in this new and wild land are very hard and manifold, and many a one who came here in his old age must work very hard to his end for his bread. I will not speak of young people. Work mostly consists in cutting wood, felling oak-trees, rooting out, or as they say, clearing large tracts of forests. Such forests, being cleared, are then laid out for fields and meadows. From the best hewn wood, fences are made around the new fields; for there all meadows, orchards and fruit-fields are surrounded and fenced with planks made of thickly-split wood, laid one above the other, as in zigzag lines, and within such enclosures horses, cattle and sheep are permitted to graze. Our Europeans, who are purchased, must work hard, for new fields are constantly laid out, and so they learn that stumps of oak-trees are in America certainly as hard as in Germany. However hard he may be compelled to work in the fatherland, he will surely find it quite as hard, if not harder, in the new country.[44]

For an unbiassed estimate of the actual situation, "the middle ground" between the extreme viewpoints taken by those who saw the system in operation "seems to be nearer the truth," McCormac thinks, and—

It is quite probable that in the early years the servant differed little socially from the master whom he served. Both were ignorant and lived the happy-go-lucky life of the frontiersman. Many masters were themselves only freed servants. As society advanced the position of the servant did not advance with it, but rather deteriorated. The large importation of convicts and fugitives from justice and the mingling of servants with slaves tended to degrade the whole servant class.[45]

FREEDOM DUES

In relation to a wage study, the crux of the indenture system lies of course in the actual remuneration, over and above maintenance for the indenture period, which a servant could claim. Fortunately, unlike the elements of treatment and social status, the matter of freedom dues is quite definitely fixed, at least in terms of its day and time, however inconvertible those terms may be. Whether embodied definitely in an indenture executed in Europe years before they fell due, or in the laws of the colony prevailing at the time, colonial courts saw to it that freedom dues were granted the servant as a right. Laws and judicial decisions might lean strongly in the direction of the master class in all other particulars, but all the evidence indicates that the servant held the whip hand in the collection of his promised remuneration when his term of servitude was ended.

The "headright," which gave planters a tract of land, usually 50 acres but varying at different times and in different colonies, for each servant brought over, gave rise to the belief that the land thus obtained reverted to the servant when he became a freedman. That was true in only one colony, and there only for a period of little more than 20 years. The Maryland General Assembly in 1640 enumerated as one item of the legal freedom dues "fifty acres of land, five whereof at least to be plantable."[46] This was considered "a great burden by the planters, as it cancelled in great measure the profits derived from the labor of the servants," and was repealed in 1663, after which "the freed servant could no longer require land from his former master unless it was expressly stipulated in the indenture."[47] Hammond, in his tract, "Leah and Rachel, or the Two Fruitfull Sisters, Virginia and Mary-land," warns against the prevailing "old

---

44 Mittelberger, pp. 29–31.   46 Maryland State Archives, Vol. I, p. 97.
45 McCormac, p. 72.   47 McCormac, pp. 23–24.

delusion" that land is granted a servant "according to the Custome of the Countrey," for, he says, "their is no land accustomary due to the servant, but to the Master, and therefore that servant is unwise that will not dash out that custom in his covenant and make that due of Land absolutely his own."

Servants sometimes acquired land as part of their freedom dues, but except under the Maryland provision quoted, its acquisition was a legal right only when named in the indenture. Land was available to freedmen in the proprietary colonies by application to the governor, but that was uncleared land which had not been taken up.

Certain other provisions for the freedmen were uniformly made either by contract or by law, although details varied with time and place. The Pennsylvania law of 1700 is typical. It provided that—

Every servant that shall faithfully serve four years or more shall, at the expiration of their servitude, have a discharge, and shall be duly clothed with two complete suits of apparel, whereof one shall be new, and shall also be furnished with one axe, one grubbing hoe and one weeding hoe, at the charge of the master or mistress.[48]

Ten to fifteen bushels of Indian corn and a smaller amount of wheat were frequently included, and the regulations of New Jersey substituted horses for the hoes. A Maryland law of 1715 specifies what constituted a complete suit of apparel: "1 new Hat; 1 good suit (coat and breeches) either Kersey or broadcloth; 1 new shirt of white linen, 1 pair of French Fall shoes and stockings" for the men, and "Waste Coat and Pettycoat of new half-thick or Penistone; a new shift of white linen (Two Suits); Shoes and stockings; a blue apron and Two caps of white linen" for the women.[49]

Freedom dues seem to have been wholly a matter of agreement between master and servant in New England. In the Bay Colony these agreements were recorded in and enforced by the General Court. Boston's first lawyer executed an indenture calling for "double apparrell and five pounds [$24.30] in money"[50] at the end of seven years. In another instance he prosecuted a case for a servant whose indenture entitled him to "wages of foure pounds [$19.44] by the yeare and a pigg to be payd at every yeare's end and in the end of the terme [six years] to have a Convenient lott for his services. He [the master] promised also the said Servant three suits of apparell and six shirts."[51] A money consideration ranging from £3 to £10 ($14.58 to $48.60) appears in practically all of the indentures which Lechford drew up, for apprentices as well as for servants, and in those recorded in the proceedings of the Massachusetts Bay Colony General Court.

In the later history of the system, the value of the articles called for in the freedom dues was often given in cash. The last law passed in North Carolina dealing with freedom dues provided for "£3 [$7.50] proclamation money and one suit of clothes."[52]

---

[48] Pennsylvania Statutes at Large, II, 54–56, cited in Herrick, p. 293.
[49] Geiser, p. 72, footnote, citing A Complete Collection of the Laws of Maryland, 1692–1725, Annapolis, 1727.
[50] Lechford's Manuscript Note Book, p. 76.
[51] Idem, p. 251.
[52] Bassett, John Spencer: Slavery and Servitude in the Colony of North Carolina, Johns Hopkins University Studies in Historical and Political Science, 14th Series, 1896, Nos. IV–V, p. 84.

APPRENTICES AND CHILDREN

The apprenticing of children to trades followed in practically all particulars the indenture system, but there were two marked differences—the length of service and the fact that an apprentice could not be assigned, or transferred to a master other than the original contracting party, except in case of the death of the master. Studies of the old colonial labor system make almost no distinction between actual apprenticeship and the indenturing of children, so that it is difficult now to draw the line. The record is clearer in New England than in other colonies, probably because bound servitude was less general among workers other than apprentices, and more trades were practiced.

As a general rule an apprenticeship lasted for seven years, unless the child was very young when bound. In that case the term expired when the boy became 21. Apprentice contracts drawn up by Lechford generally called for "double apparel" and a money payment at the end of the term, although there is considerable variation. Two contracts binding boys to carpenters specify a 7-year term; in one case the boy is to have "an ewe kidd at the end of foure yeares if he doe his duty, and £5 [$24.30] at the end of the terme, meate, drinke & Clothes & Double Apparell when he goes forth"; [53] the other gives no terms for the apprentice period, but calls for one additional year's work as a journeyman, with "wages for that year £8 [$38.88]." [54] Suggestive of some of the curious provisions in apprentice contracts is one from Windsor, Conn., which obligates the master to teach the boy "to write and read English and cast accounts, and be at the cost and use his best endeavors to get his scurf head cured. Also to learn him the trade of a cooper, and at the end of his term to let him go free and give him double apparel, a musket, sword and bandoliers, and 20s [$4.86]." [55]

An apprenticeship indenture recorded in Roxbury, Mass., about 1678, under which the master was to teach the "art, trade, mistery and science" of shoemaking, is typical of the general terms of these contracts, traces of which are still found in apprentice indentures:

The said Josaph shall truly and faithfully serve, his Counsels lawful and honest obay, his secretts his shall keep, hurt to his master he shall not doe nor consent to be done, at unlawful games he shall not play, nor from his masters buisness absent himselfe by night or day, his masters goods he shall not wast nor imbezzell, nor them lend without his masters Consent. Taverns and Ale Howses he shall not frequent except about his masters buisness there to be done but as a true and faithful servant ought to behave himselfe in word and deed during the said terme, * * * and at the end of six years to give their said apprentice doubell apparell, one suit for the Lord's day and one suit for the working days meet and comely for one of his degree and calling.[56]

The contract between a Virginia planter and a boy whom he imported as an apprentice in 1659 is even more specific:

This indenture made the 6th Day of June in the year of our Lord Christ 1659, witnesseth, that Bartholomew Clarke ye son of John Clarke of the city of Canterbury, Sadler, of his own liking and with ye consent of Francis Plumber of ye City of Canterbury, Brewer, hath put himself apprentice unto Edward Rowzie

[53] Lechford, Thomas: Manuscript Notebook, 1638–1641 (published by American Antiquarian Society, 1885, p. 151).
[54] Idem, p. 153.
[55] Weeden, William B.: Economic and Social History of New England, 1620–1789, Vol. I, p. 84, quoting Stiles, Windsor, p. 146.
[56] Idem, Vol. I, p. 274, citing Drake's Roxbury, p. 64.

of Virginia, planter, as an apprentice with him to dwell from ye day of ye date mentioned above unto ye full term of four years from thence next ensuing fully to be complete and ended, all which said term the said Bartholomew Clarke well and faithfully the said Edward Rowzie as his master shall serve, his secrets keep, his commands just and lawful he shall observe, and fornication he shall not commit, nor contract matrimony with any woman during the said term, he shall not do hurt unto his master nor consent to ye doing of any, but to his power shall hinder and prevent ye doing of any; at cards, dice or any unlawful games he shall not play; he shall not waste the goods of his said master nor lend them to anybody without his master's consent; he shall not absent himself from his said master's service day or night, but as a true and faithful servant shall demean himself, and the said Edward Rowzie in ye mystery, art, and occupation of a planter which now * * * the best manner he can the said Bartholomew shall teach or cause to be taught, and also during said term shall find and allow his apprentice competent meat, drink, apparel, washing, lodging and all other things fitting for his degree and in the end thereof, fifty acres of land to be laid out for him, and all other things which according to the custom of the country is or ought to be done.[57]

Suggestive also of a later day is the complaint that journeymen took their own sons on as apprentices and did not carry them through the full term. Boston undertook to control that condition by a rule that no one could set up as an independent journeyman or mechanic unless he was 21 years of age and had served seven years under a master workman.

The custom developed during the eighteenth century of giving both apprentices and indentured children six weeks' schooling throughout the year. Pennsylvania law made that compulsory in 1810.

The indenture system was widely used as a means of emptying European orphan asylums and almshouses. The vice director of a Dutch colony on the Delaware River wrote thus to his commissioners in Holland in 1658:

The children sent over from the almshouse have safely arrived and were in sufficient request so that all are bound out with one and the other; the eldest for 2 years, the others, and the major portion, for 3 years, and the youngest for 4 years, earning 40, 60, and 80 guilders [$16, $24, and $32] during the above period, and at the end of the term will be fitted out in the same manner as they are at present. Please continue to send others from time to time but if possible none ought to come less than 15 years of age, and somewhat strong.[58]

The Virginia Company dispatched 100 poor and orphaned children to the colony in 1619, and the following year, at the instance of the company, the city of London sent an additional hundred. Virginia planters preferred children as servants, not only because they were "more easily controlled, but their terms continued for a greater length of time than those of persons who had reached maturity, and in consequence their masters were not called upon to supply their places so often nor so soon." [59]

The custom of indenturing pauper and orphan children, together with the practice of promiscuous kidnaping of children for transportation as servants, resulted in the presence in the colonies of a very considerable number of young people. "So great was the demand for these youthful laborers that in one year alone, 1627, fourteen or fifteen hundred children who had been gathered up in different parts of England were sent to Virginia." [60]

[57] Bruce, Vol. II, pp. 1–2, footnote, citing Records of Rappahanock County, 1664–1673, p. 21.
[58] Documents Relative to Colonial History of New York, Vol. II, pp. 51–52.
[59] Bruce, Vol. I, p. 595.
[60] Idem, p. 612.

New England children were subject to being bound out to servitude by court action if in the opinion of the authorities parents were too poor or unfit to care for them in the manner which the authorities considered proper and necessary. Apparently this practice went on to an extent that would seem quite appalling now.

It would be interesting to know to what extent throughout our history, from the time that 100 children landed in Virginia in 1619, to the time nearly 200 hundred years later, when Slater opened his cotton mill with nine small children, the work of a very young country was really carried on by its very young inhabitants.

FREEDMEN

Information regarding the indentured servant after he was freed is almost wholly lacking, either because students of the system stop at the dividing line, or because, as one of them says, the freed servant almost immediately "was merged into the great body of freemen, and all traces of his former occupations were soon obliterated."[61] Out of the little historical material which has survived, Ballagh finds that "enough remains to give decisive proof of a very rapid evolution of servants when free, and to show that they did not continue as a class at all." [62]

In the southern colonies the evidence seems strong that to a large extent freedmen became either tenants or overseers on the great tobacco plantations. "An overseer was usually allowed one-seventh of the calves, foals, grain, and tobacco, and one-half of the pigs raised on the plantation. If he were thrifty he was soon able to stock a plantation of his own. Many thus became men of wealth and good standing." [63]

Two very early records indicate that the freedman was not always an asset to the community. Governor Winthrop, of the Massachusetts Bay Colony, had an indentured servant who, when he was out of his time, "took great wages above others, in ready money only. In a year or a little more, he had scraped together about £25 [$121.50], and then returned with his prey to England." [64] One of "the Reasons and Causes Why and How New Netherlands is So Decayed," in the opinion of Junker Van der Cook "and Ten others," is that "it seems as if from the first the Company sought to stock this land with their own employees, which was a great mistake, for when their time was out they returned home, taking nothing with them except a little in their pockets and a bad name for the country." [65] Josselyn, who found in his journeys to New England much to lament about, decries the fact that "Servants, which are for the most part English, when they are out of their time will not work under half a crown [61 cents] a day, and for less I do not see how they can, by reason of the dearness of clothing. If they hire them by the year they pay them 14 or 15 pound, yea, 20 pound [$68.04–$72.90–$97.20] at the year's end in corn, cattle and fish."

Herrick quotes the pastor of a Lutheran church in Philadelphia as reporting in 1746 "that while the congregation over which he presided

61 Geiser, p. 109.
62 Ballagh, p. 81.
63 Bassett, p. 85.
64 Winthrop's Journal, quoted in Weeden, Vol. I, p. 179.
65 Hart, Albert Bushnell, ed.: American History Told by Contemporaries, Vol. I, p. 532.

was one of the largest it was also one of the poorest; its membership was of those who were temporary residents paying off the debt of their passage, and when this was paid they moved inland, to secure property for themselves." [66] Another evidence of the success of servants as citizens is contained in a letter which an Irish immigrant wrote from his new home in New York to his old home in Ireland, in 1737, in which he speaks with great enthusiasm of the opportunities in the New World, and declares that "there are Servants here out of Ireland and have served their time here who are now Justices of the Piece."[67]

Bruce finds "many evidences that it was common for servants upon the close of their terms to earn a subsistence in the character of hired laborers," [68] and Geiser says it was not uncommon in Pennsylvania for a newly liberated servant to enter into a second indenture.[69]

For the best of the servant class "the redemptioner's school of experience was severe, but it fitted him for the exacting demands of claiming a wilderness, and if health were not broken, those who completed indentures were well prepared to carve out a fortune in the New World." [70] For the worst, "the convict class disappeared by destroying itself," [71] since the criminals "frequently meet here with the end they deserved at Home"[72] and, according to Benjamin Franklin, were "commonly advanced to the gallows."

DECLINE OF SYSTEM

The bulk of the indentured servant traffic flowed into Virginia, Maryland, and Pennsylvania, and the system was economically more vital to those colonies than to the others. The economic value of the indenture system became markedly different as between the tobacco-growing South and industrial Pennsylvania, however. This is shown in the developments of the first half of the eighteenth century, during which the system declined in the plantation colonies almost as rapidly as it grew in Pennsylvania, and in the fact that it lasted in the latter colony nearly a century after it had become outgrown in Maryland and Virginia.

In the South white servitude went down "before the black man's superior endurance, docility, and labor capacity," [73] and from the planter's viewpoint more important still, the black man's inability to escape from a servitude which, far from being limited to a few years of his own life, outlived him and descended to his children.

"One of the most serious drawbacks to the employment of indentured laborers," Bruce points out, "was the inevitable frequency of change attending this form of service. A planter might introduce a hundred willing laborers, who might prove invaluable to him during the time covered by their covenants, but in a few years, when experience had made them efficient, and their bodies had become thoroughly enured to the change of climate, they recovered their freedom." [74] Their places then had to be filled again, involving a repeated outlay

---

[66] Herrick, p. 181.
[67] Letter from James Murray, in Memorial History of New York City, Vol. II, p. 203.
[68] Bruce, Vol. II, p. 47.
[69] Geiser, p. 75.
[70] Herrick, p. 270.
[71] Idem, p. 140.
[72] Jones, Hugh: Present State of Virginia (1724)—Extract in Documentary History of American Industrial Society, Vol. 1, p. 339.
[73] Bassett, p. 77.
[74] Bruce, Vol. II, p. 58.

of money to secure new hands, in addition to that expended in freedom dues for those whom they succeeded.

Indentured labor on the vast tobacco plantations became too expensive, as hired free labor had always been. Even with the great difference in the initial expenditure, the negro slave was cheaper than the white servant, and inevitably supplanted him. The same conditions of economic demand and a ready market which had produced traffic in white servants operated to develop the slave trade sufficiently to accommodate that market, and there was the added advantage that the natural increase in negro population in the colonies created a native supply.

The Carolinas and Georgia reacted immediately to the experience of the older colonies and adopted slavery from the start. White servitude never got a real foothold in these newer plantation colonies, and by the middle of the eighteenth century the system was practically at an end throughout the South.

Conditions resulting from a single-crop agricultural industry thus destroyed white servitude and established negro slavery in the tobacco growing colonies. Industrial conditions in Pennsylvania produced exactly the opposite result, because "the diversified production and industry which prevailed in Pennsylvania required a higher order of labor than that of slaves."[75] Hence "the introduction of white servants under indenture went hand in hand with the industrial progress of the country."[76] Pennsylvania began manufacturing from her immense store of raw material almost at once, and "after 1730 was regarded as one of the leading industrial and commercial settlements of America. It was in part to satisfy the labor demand of an industrial community with diversified production that the indentured labor system assumed such proportions."[77]

Indentured servants in the southern colonies were predominantly agricultural laborers. Except for the large influx of German farmers this seems not to have been true in Pennsylvania. Herrick gives a detailed analysis of advertisements of servants for sale and finds that "almost invariably" the dealer "made the claim that they were either all mechanics and tradesmen, or that tradesmen were included among those to be sold." He adds, however, that since "the trade to which a servant made claim was important in securing for him a ready sale," it is quite likely that dealers and servants were not above misrepresenting the degree of skill available.[78] Analyzing advertisements for runaway servants also to determine the extent of craftsmanship among them, Herrick found that the trade previously followed by the runaway "was given in approximately one-half of the advertisements, and as given shows a large proportion of skilled laborers."[79]

A contemporary account is that of the president of the Provincial Council who, in 1756, reported that "every kind of business here, as well among the Tradesmen and Mechanics as the Planters and Farmers, is chiefly carried on and supported by the labor of indentured servants."[80]

As a labor policy white servitude continued in Pennsylvania for a quarter of a century after the establishment of the Republic. It

---

75 Herrick, p. 23.   78 Idem, p. 73.
76 Idem, p. 60.   79 Idem, p. 75.
77 Idem, p. 57.   80 Quoted in Geiser, p. 25.

took on renewed vigor after the Revolution, and indentured servants figure largely in the heavy immigration at the close of the eighteenth century. The last officially recorded registry [81] of a redemptioner in Pennsylvania is dated December 1, 1831.

The system was never legally abolished. It died gradually as the economic conditions which had created it changed. As population increased, indentured immigrants were no longer necessary to an adequate labor supply, and with the introduction of machinery and the factory system employers found it cheaper to hire free labor by the day, or as needed, than to maintain servants by the year. One law, however, did affect the system materially. When imprisonment for debt was outlawed, carrying with it the master's power to compel the servant to discharge his debt, "the institution of indentured service received its legal death blow and necessarily died out without any special enactment." [82]

---

[81] Herrick, Cheesman A.: White Slavery in Pennsylvania. Reproduction of original register, fronting p. 266.
[82] Geiser, p. 42.

Chapter 4.—BUILDING TRADES

SEVENTEENTH CENTURY

Building, in the earliest days of colonial settlement, was not important, and skilled building mechanics were few, especially in the southern colonies. There were two bricklayers, four carpenters, and one mason among the first settlers at Jamestown in 1607, but later, in 1609 and 1610, the Virginia Company of London advertised for building tradesmen to emigrate to the colony, apparently without results.[1]

Bricks were made in Virginia at the very beginning of the colony, but, according to Bruce, they seem "to have entered only to a limited extent into the construction of the dwellings,"[2] being confined almost wholly to chimneys. The rough structures of plank or log which housed the first Virginia settlers were probably erected without the aid of skilled builders. At any rate, no mention is made of definite wages paid building tradesmen prior to 1624, when the price of bricklaying was fixed at 40 pounds of tobacco ($2.43) per thousand bricks.

Scarcity of artisans of all trades persisted throughout the early history of Virginia. The company repeatedly issued broadsides advertising for mechanics and offered special inducements, such as grants of town properties for home building; and planters frequently wrote home to their agents directing that carpenters, bricklayers, and masons be dispatched to the colony under terms considerably more advantageous to the worker than those customarily offered for plantation labor. Later, after the Colonial Assembly was established, a law was enacted (1661–62) which exempted "handicraftsmen" from taxation. Although short-lived, this legislation suggests the lengths to which the colony found it necessary to go in its effort to secure an adequate supply of skilled craftsmen.

"The most favorable legislation, however," Bruce says, "was unable to create a large and prosperous class of mechanics in Virginia,"[3] or at least to insure their remaining in the trades to which they had been trained. The tendency was always to abandon the trades and follow the general drift of labor to the plantations. In 1633 an effort was made to force mechanics to follow their trades by enacting a law forbidding them to perform agricultural labor of any kind.[4]

Neither legislative policy influenced conditions materially. The indenture system, which seems to have been almost exclusively followed in the southern colonies, was not a satisfactory method of maintaining a supply of mechanics. If a craftsman had completed his apprenticeship before emigrating his term of indenture was generally brief—four years at the most—and upon its expiration his place had to be filled by another craftsman, often with the attendant ex-

---

[1] Bruce, Philip A.: Economic History of Virginia in the Seventeenth Century. Vol. II, p. 400.
[2] Idem, Vol. II, p. 134.
[3] Idem, Vol. II, p. 413.
[4] Hening's Statutes of Virginia, Vol. I, p. 208.

pense increased by special inducements to tradesmen. Frequently indentured mechanics became planters themselves when their terms were out. All these many difficulties in the way of keeping a sufficient number of mechanics in the colony resulted in the adoption by the planters of a practice of training their negro slaves, whose terms of service did not expire, in the crafts necessary for the self-contained community which a tobacco plantation became. Accordingly, the building industry as such can hardly be said to have existed in the South of the colonial period, and information about it is rare.

While not leaving so specific a record to show it, the northern colonies undoubtedly suffered with the southern in the matter of scarcity of building tradesmen. On the other hand, there are quite early stories which suggest how the building problem was handled. The southern colonists settled on widely scattered plantations and had slight need for towns—in fact, opposed them. In the North, particularly in New England, the town was the important factor in colonial development.

The records of the town of Dedham, Mass., show that in 1637, within a few years of its founding, a committee was "choesen to contrive the Fabricke of a meetinghouse to be in length 30 foote & 20 foote in breadth & between the upper & nether sill in ye studds 12 foote, the same to be girte, and to order men to worke upon the same in all workes as they are severally apted accordingly. As also to proportion the same worke and wages in all cases." [5]

What the wages were, on the basis of a daily rate, the record does not show. It says only that the following terms were adopted:

There shall be allowed such as do fell Pynes of 2 foote over at ye carfe [6] six pence [12 cents] and for Oake of the same thickness eight pence [16 cents]: and for grater and smaler after ye same Rate. If any tree split by the default of ye feller he shal loose ye felling.

Crosse cutting every 2 foote over to be allowed six pence & so every scantling after that Rate.

To allow for saweing Pyne bords 5s. [$1.22] & for splitting 6s. [$1.46] per 100 And for ye breaking Carfe of 2 foote deepe 3d. [6 cents] per foote Running Measure.

Carpenters to have for makeing pitholes 12s. [$2.91] per pair.

Daily wages in Massachusetts probably were at the time 3 shillings (73 cents) a day. An agreement dated 1629 between the Massachusetts Bay Company and Richard Claydon, carpenter, specifies that the emigrant's debt to the company should be discharged by crediting him with 3s. a day for his work for the company. In 1630 the Colonial Court ordered that "carpenters, joyners, bricklayers, sawers, and thatchers shall not take above 2s. [48.6 cents] a day." [7] If "they have meate and drinke" the 2s. rate was cut to 16d. [32 cents].

Nevertheless, the rate apparently remained around 3s. a day, for three years later Governor Winthrop says that because carpenters and masons were receiving 3s. a day, on account of the scarcity of workmen, "it grew a general complaint which the Court, taking knowledge of, as also of some further evils which were springing out of the excessive rates of wages, they made an order that carpenters masons, etc., should take but 2s. a day." [8]

---

[5] Dedham Town Records, published by the Massachusetts Historical Society.
[6] The point of cutting.
[7] Massachusetts Bay Colony Records, Vol. I, pp. 74–75.
[8] Governor Winthrop's Journal.

The pay of bricklayers in New York in the year in which Dedham built its meeting house, 1637, was 80 cents a day.

Occasional items of record in the ensuing 10 years indicate, in most instances, somewhat lower rates. Mechanics engaged in the construction of Fort Charles and Fort James, on the Virginia coast, in 1643, were paid the equivalent of 1s. 2d. (19.5 cents) a day in tobacco, the rate being 7 pounds per day, a pound of which at this time "did not exceed two pence" [9] in value. Bricklayers in Plymouth Colony were still working at the legal rate of 2s. a day, which the Plymouth Colony Court had undertaken to maintain even after the Massachusetts Bay Colony had abandoned the effort to control wages by legislation. The New Amsterdam rate remained about the same, that is, 2 florins, or 80 cents a day, for skilled men, and 40 to 50 cents for day laborers.[10]

Dedham, Mass., built a schoolhouse in 1648, "the lengthe 18 foot being 14 foot beside the chimney, the wideness 15 foot, the studd 9 foote betwixt the joynts, one floor of joyce: 2 convenient windows in the lower roome and one in the chamber, the plancher layed, the stayers made, the sides boarded feather-edged and rabbited, the doors made and hanged." The total cost of construction was £17 6s. 10d. ($57.80), of which the builder received £11 3d. ($36.70) "for his worke about ye schoole house." Laborers working under him were paid 1s. 8d. (28 cents) a day.[11]

Nearly 50 years later Dedham needed a new schoolhouse to replace this early one. The selectmen met on March 8, 1694, "to go threw with the agreement with John Baker conserning the schoole house," and they agreed—

that the said John Baker shall goe on and build the schoole house, finding all timber, boards claubords shingles naills glasse bricke stone & clay & borde the outside and claubord the inside & make it close warm and desent suitable to such a schoole house & to make one door and two windows containing twelve foots of glass also a good stone chimney nine foots between gams and to carry it out of the house with good bricke and to find whatever else is necessary & to finish said house to the turning of the Key by the First of June 1695   Excepting the upar floor & clauboring the inside which flor and clauborING is also to be finished by the twenty-fifth day of October next after the date hereof   For and in consideration of this abovewritten we the Selectmen of Dedham doe agree in behalf of the towne that the abovesaid John Baker shall receive of the Town of Dedham twenty shillings [$3.33] in money att the time when said Schoole house is raised and fifteen pounds ten shillings [$51.67] at the twenty-fifth day of February next to be payed in corn in Rye at four shillings [66.7 cents] per bushell & Indian corn at three shillings [50 cents] per bushel & so much as shall be payed of the fifteen pounds ten shillings in mony the said John Baker shall abate one-fourth part thereof   He is also to receive the old schoole house with what belongs thereto & the stone and clay of the town's lying by it.[12]

TOWN BUILDING IN VIRGINIA

While towns multiplied in number and grew in size throughout the northern colonies, Virginia remained townless. Repeated efforts on the part of the British Government to promote or compel the erection of towns failed, because the land-holding system upon which the colony was founded made community living economically impossible. After the Restoration a very determined attempt was made by the

⁹ Bruce, Vol. II, p. 416.
¹⁰ Bishop, J. Leander: History of American Manufactures, 1608–1860.
¹¹ Dedham Town Records.
¹² Idem.

home government to establish towns, and when Berkeley returned to the governorship in 1662 he carried with him instructions to erect a town on each river. Bruce remarks that—

It is a significant commentary on the effect of the numerous laws which had been passed with a view to enlarging Jamestown that Berkeley was specially directed to begin at this place a new attempt at town-building in Virginia. Such was the recommendation which was necessary after all the carefully considered undertakings of fifty years.[13]

The General Assembly embodied the order of the British Government in the "Cohabitation act" of 1662, which, as analyzed by Bruce—

constitutes one of the most interesting acts of legislation in colonial history, and might be regarded as a remarkable triumph of legislative hope over practical experience were it not for the statement of the preamble that the assembly had undertaken to encourage the building of towns because they looked upon it as their duty to conform to the wishes of their sovereign in England.

Under the terms of this statute, it was provided that Jamestown should consist of thirty-two houses, a number which indicated that the General Assembly was disposed to be moderate and prudent in its requirements. Each house was to be forty feet from end to end, twenty feet in width in the interior, and eighteen feet in height. Each was to be constructed of brick. The walls were to be two bricks in thickness as far as the water table, and one and a half the remaining distance. The roof was to be covered with slate or tile, and was to be fifteen feet in pitch.

Although the colony had prospered in a fair measure for a period of fifty years without having a large settlement at Jamestown, nevertheless it had now been determined in earnest to establish one there. To accomplish this, each of the seventeen counties into which Virginia was divided at this time was ordered to build a house at Jamestown at its own expense. The authority was conferred on all to impress into service the mechanics needed for the work, such as bricklayers, carpenters, sawyers and other tradesmen. The strictest regulations were laid down to prevent every kind of exaction. The bricks were to be manufactured in the most careful manner and were in size to represent statute measure; the price was not to exceed one hundred and fifty pounds of tobacco ($2.10) for every thousand. In addition to receiving his food without charge the ordinary laborer engaged in erecting a house was to be paid at the rate of two thousand pounds of tobacco ($28) a year. The brickmakers and bricklayers were to be remunerated according to the number of bricks moulded and laid, while the wages of each carpenter were not to exceed thirty pounds of tobacco (42 cents) a day. Each sawyer was to receive half a pound of tobacco for every foot of plank and timber for joices which he fashioned into shape. The keepers of the taverns at Jamestown were required to supply the ordinary laborer with food at the rate of one thousand pounds of tobacco ($14) a year, and the most skilled workmen at the rate of fifteen hundred ($21). An important provision of the law was that after its passage no wooden house was to be erected in Jamestown, and all such houses then standing should not be repaired with the same material, but should be replaced by structures of brick.

This brief synopsis of the law of 1662 shows how elaborate were the provisions of that measure for the enlargement more especially of Jamestown. As far as legislation, independently of favorable local conditions, could create a town where none existed, it might be supposed that the law would have been successful in accomplishing its object, so far, at least, as the capital was concerned. It provided in detail for the erection of a number of houses at a cost which was distributed among the people of the seventeen counties. The mechanics to be employed in the work were to be provided for properly, and to be fully remunerated for their labor.

To answer the question of "what was the practical result of all these carefully considered provisions?" Bruce draws upon contemporary evidence and finds that "three years after their adoption Secretary Ludwell, writing to Secretary Bennett in England, stated that enough of the proposed town had been built to accommodate the officers employed in the civil administration of Virginia, but this,

---

[13] Bruce, Vol. II, p. 538.

it may be inferred, * * * amounted only to the construction of four or five houses. He declared that the erection of this scanty number of buildings had entailed the loss of hundreds of people, apprehension of impressment having driven many mechanics from the colony."[14]

The wages provided for in the cohabitation act seem to be higher than the prevailing rate, for later, in 1666, the Colonial Court ordered that in the reconstruction of the fort on Point Comfort workmen should receive 20 pounds of tobacco for a day's work, an order which applied equally to skilled mechanics and common laborers.[15] Tobacco is valued at this time at 1d. a pound,[16] which makes a day's pay in tobacco about equivalent to 1s. 8d. (28 cents) in currency.

WAGES AT CLOSE OF CENTURY

A few scattered records complete the available data for the seventeenth century. Under date of September 26, 1673, Hendrick Van Borsum of New Amsterdam contracted "to serve the Honorable Governor as Carpenter for the period of the current year commencing to-morrow; for which service he shall receive a salary of fl. 30 a month [equal to $12.—ED.] without board. * * * but whenever he shall be sent to work without the city he shall be provided with victuals."[17] Salem, Mass., built a town hall in 1677 and paid the carpenter £20 ($66.67), "one-third in money and two-thirds in provisions" for his work.[18]

A building contract entered into in Henrico County, Va., in 1679, called for the erection of a house 40 feet long and 20 feet wide, clapboarded and roofed, with a chimney at either end, "the upper and lower floors to be divided respectively into two rooms by a wooden partition." The house was to be finished in seven months, and the owner agreed to pay the builder "twelve hundred pounds of tobacco in cask." Tobacco was probably worth about 2d. a pound, and 1,200 pounds converted into American money would amount to $33.60. A few years later a carpenter in a neighboring county agreed to build a house of similar dimensions for £9 sterling, or $43.74.[19]

The usual rate of pay for building craftsmen in New Jersey in 1680–1685 was 2s. (40 cents) a day; in Amboy, "where building was active," mechanics received 2s. 6d. (50 cents)[20] a day. "The houses building at Amboy in 1683 are described as usually 30 feet long, 16 feet wide, 10 feet between joints, with double chimney of timber and clay 'as the manner of this country is to build,' and cost about £50 [$200] each."[21]

Thomas recorded that in Pennsylvania in 1698 "Carpenters, both House and Ship, Bricklayers, Masons, either of these Trades-Men will get between Five and Six Shillings [$1 and $1.20][20] every day constantly. Brickmakers have twenty shillings [$4] a thousand for their Bricks at the Kiln," and "Plasterers have commonly eighteen pence [30 cents] a yard for Plastering."

[14] Idem, Vol. II, pp. 540–545.
[15] General Court Orders, March 29, 1666—Robinson transcript, pp. 112–113.
[16] Jacobstein—See p. 13.
[17] New York Colonial Documents, Vol. II, p. 617.
[18] Felt's Annals of Salem, Vol. I, p. 390.
[19] Bruce, Vol. II, pp. 151–152.
[20] Colonial shilling of Pennsylvania and New Jersey, worth 20 cents. See p. 16.
[21] Bishop, p. 109, footnote.

EIGHTEENTH CENTURY

A gradual differentiation in building trades and in the rates paid different crafts becomes evident from the beginning of the eighteenth century. As wealth accumulated in the mercantile centers and on the plantations building began to develop along more pretentious, or at least more substantial, lines. The generic "carpenter" who did practically all the building in the colonial period, is joined by the brick and stone mason, the ornamental-iron worker, the painter and paper-hanger, the plasterer, the cabinetmaker and the wood carver. By the middle of the century such homes as Mount Vernon and Monticello, in Virginia, and the Harrison Gray Otis mansion, in Boston, were being erected, calling for the highest degree of skilled craftsmanship in various lines. Some figures showing the remuneration of these crafts have come down to us, often not as actual wages, as we understand the term, but rather in accounts of work done on a piece or job basis. Unfortunately there is little data which would enable us to translate the job basis to a time basis and thus get a clearer idea of what the sums received meant in terms of a day's work.

Rates of pay of carpenters, bricklayers, and building laborers are given by the day in the accounts of public building in Massachusetts during the first quarter of the century, beginning at 3s. 6d. and 3s. 8d. (58.4 and 61 cents) for carpenters and 4s. (66.7 cents) for bricklayers in 1701.[22] In 1712 carpenters on the Boston town hall were getting 5s. (83.3 cents) a day, "all cash," [23] and bricklayers 6s. ($1) a day. Common labor was usually paid 2s. 6d. (42 cents) a day.

In New York during this period "handicraftsmen such as Carpenters, Joyners, Masons and Bricklayers may earn at least five shillings New York money [62.5 cents] every day they will work," and common laborers "may earn two shillings and three pence [28 cents] New York money".[24] Rates in South Carolina in 1710 were: Bricklayers, 6s. ($1), carpenters and joiners, 3s. to 5s. (50 to 83.3 cents); "a labourer hath from one shilling and three pence to 2s. [21 to 33.3 cents] a day, with Lodging and Diett."[25]

For the years between 1710 and 1730 there is very little data, such figures as are found showing slight change from the earlier record. Money inflation had begun by 1730 and rates began to rise, particularly in New England. Virginia money, however, maintained a fairly even standard, and the higher rate of 3s. (50 cents) a day for carpenters in 1731[26] undoubtedly represents an actual increase in wages. A "skilful carpenter" in South Carolina in the same year "is not ashamed to demand his 30s. per day besides his Diet, and the Common wages of a Workman is 20s. a day provided he speaks English. * * * But this is Carolina money," [27] which at that time was worth about three cents a shilling in American money.[28]

---

[22] Massachusetts State Archives.
[23] Douglass, William: Discourse Concerning the Currencies of the British Plantations in America (1739). In Economic Studies of the American Economic Association, Vol. II, 1897, p. 322.
[24] O'Callaghan's Documents Relative to the Colonial History of the State of New York, Vol. V, p. 106.
[25] From "History of South Carolina" attributed to Gov. Glen of the Province, in South Carolina Historical Collections, Vol. II, p. 261.
[26] Manuscript account book, Library of Congress.
[27] South Carolina Historical Collections, Vol. II, p. 122.
[28] See p. 17.

The following is "an account of work done" by a carpenter in York County, Va., in 1733:[29]

	£	s.	d.	
To 30 squares of shingling at 4/5 (73.7 cents)	6	15	00	($22. 50)
To a sash frame and sashes		14	00	($2. 33)
To 1 days' work myself and Thomas at 3/ (50 cents), 7 days' work Daniel at 2/6 (42 cents) and 7 days Matt at 1/8 (28 cents)	1	14	00	($5. 67)
To putting in 71 diamond panes of glass at 2d. (2.8 cents)		11	10	($1. 97)
To putting in 5 sash panes of glass at 3d. (4.2 cents)		1	3	($0. 21)
To painting 80 yards outside house at 10 d.(14 cents)	3	6	8	($11. 11)

An Irish immigrant to New York wrote to his family in Ireland, in a letter dated November 7, 1737, that masons and carpenters in New York City "get 6 shillings [75 cents] a day." [30]

The rate on public works in Massachusetts from 1735 to 1740 [31] was 12s. (45.6 cents) a day for "master workmen" in all trades, 7s. 9d. (30 cents) for "hands," and 7s. to 7s. 6d. (27 to 29 cents) for laborers. Twelve shillings, however, were "equal to only 3 shillings 4 pence of Former Times"; and "even this is further reduced by obliging him to take one half in Shop Goods at 25 per cent or more Advance over the Money Price; this Iniquity still grows by reducing the Goods part to the least vendable, the Shopkeeper refusing to let them have Provisions, West India Goods or Goods of Great Britain that are in demand." [32]

Stonemasons were paid 15s. (57 cents) per perch, and 3s. 6d. (13.3 cents) was paid for a square yard of "finish plaistering." John Simpson billed the provincial "Committee on Repair of ye Powder House" for labor at the rate of 14s. (53 cents) per day each for himself and two of his assistants, and 12s. (45.6 cents) per day for the rest of his crew. The bill suffered a substantial disallowance at the hands of the House of Representatives before payment, however, because of "overcharge on daye's work." [33]

Interior painting of the Province House was charged for in 1737 at the rate of 3s. (11.4 cents) a "yard" (square yard) for "bright red," 2s. (7.6 cents) for "lead colour," and 12d. (3.8 cents) for priming. By 1741 prices on the same work had advanced to 1s. 6d. (5.4 cents) for priming, 10s. (36 cents) for "vermillion," 5s. (18 cents) for "light blue," 3s. 6d. (12.6 cents) for "pearl colour," and 8s. (29 cents) for green. The House reduced the rate on the green room 2s. a yard before approving the bill.[33] The price for painting in Virginia at this time was 10d. (14 cents) for outside work and 12d. (16.7 cents) for inside, "painting over three times." A day's work was worth 3s. (50 cents).

Masons repairing one of the fortifications in Boston harbor in 1740 received 10s. (36 cents) a day "and found," board being rated at 20s. (72 cents) a week. Masons' "attendants" received 5s. (18 cents) a day and board.[33]

Carpenters' rates in Salem, Mass., in 1743 were 13s. 6d. a day[34] and in Virginia 3s.[35] but in this instance the southerner apparently had the advantage, since transposed to the American equivalent,

[29] Manuscript account book, Jones Family Papers, Library of Congress.
[30] In Memorial History of New York City (Edited by James Grant Wilson, 1892), Vol. 2, p. 203.
[31] Depreciated currency—shilling worth about 3.8 cents. See p. 17.
[32] Douglass's Discourse on Currencies, p. 322.
[33] Massachusetts State Archives.
[34] Felt, Joseph B.: Annals of Salem, p. 200.
[35] Manuscript Account Book.

13s. 6d. in inflated Massachusetts paper currency was worth less than 40 cents, while in stable Virginia money three shillings amounted to half a dollar. Philadelphia carpenters at this time were earning 4s. 6d. (59 cents) a day.

Rates continued to soar in Massachusetts until 1750, when "lawful money" was established. After that, workmen on public construction were paid at the following rates and subsistence, which remained fairly constant up to the Revolution: [36]

	Per day
Bricklayers	6s. ($1. 00)
Bricklayers' helpers	4s. 8d. ($0. 78)
Laborers	4s. ($0. 667)
Carpenters	4s. ($0. 667)
Laborers	2s. ($0. 333)

Building-trades' rates in Pennsylvania from 1750 to 1775 were: Bricklayers, 5s. 6d. and 6s. (72.6 and 80 cents); bricklayers' helpers, 3s. 6d. to 5s. (46 to 66.7 cents); carpenters, 5s. to 6s. (66.7 to 80 cents); painters, 6s. (80 cents); and unskilled labor, 2s. 6d. to 3s. (32.6 to 40 cents) a day. These are the usual rates given in various manuscript accounts.[37] Lower rates also appear, especially in the Norris and Stiegel account books, in which, in the decade between 1756 and 1766, masons' rates are given as 3s. 6d. and 4s. (46 and 53 cents a day, 4s. being the summer rate. An agreement with a carpenter, dated 1758, has the memorandum: "Hitherto, William says, he charged 5s. (66.7 cents) a day, but now offers to work at 4s. (53 cents) a day and find himself." [38] A plasterer received only 2s. 6d. (32.6 cents), the rate for common labor, while shingle roofing paid 3s. (40 cents) a day.

A contract for shingle making, in Pennsylvania in 1763, calls for 8,000 shingles at 25s. ($3.33) and one-half gallon liquor per thousand, "but if any are found to be bad, to be deducted out of his wages, or if the above number should not come to hand." [39]

In North Carolina at the same time "artificers" received "from 3 to 4 shillings a day [37.5 to 50 cents], common labour 2s. [25 cents]." [40]

An advertisement in the Boston Gazette of November 6, 1760, calls for "a person who understands cutting slate to cover houses who will agree for one month or as many days as he will work this Fall and pay him 40s. O T (old tenor) or 4s. sterling (97 cents) per day, he finding himself; and if he wants to Board he may agree very reasonable with the Tenants who live nigh the works."

After the Revolution, from 1785 to the close of the century, the rates paid skilled building tradesmen in Philadelphia were 7s. 6d. ($1) for carpenters; 6s. and 6s. 5d. (80 and 85 cents) for painters, and 6s. (80 cents) for plasterers. Five shillings (66.7 cents) a day was paid for whitewashing.

PAINTING

Baker Library in Cambridge contains a file of account books of the firm of Rea & Johnston, painters, of Boston, dating from 1765 to the early 1800's. They were sign painters, ship painters, house painters, interior decorators, and portrait painters. Apparently they were high-grade craftsmen, and such names as Oliver Wendell, Asa Fuller,

---

[36] Massachusetts State Archives.
[37] In Historical Society of Pennsylvania, Philadelphia, manuscript collection.
[38] Charles Norris's Account Book, Historical Society of Pennsylvania.
[39] Mary Ann Furnace, Manuscript account books, Historical Society of Pennsylvania.
[40] North Carolina Records, Vol. V, p. 644. North Carolina shillings, 12.5 cents. See p. 17.

the Lowells, and Harrison Gray Otis appear in their accounts year after year.   Typical entries for various years follow:

	£	s.	d.	
1765—To 2 days' work papering a room_____		12		($2. 00)
1767—To 130 yards painting at 7s. O T per yard_____	45	11	00	($20. 24)
1772—To painting portico at Parish House, 26 yards, at 10d. (14 cents)_____	1	1	8	($3. 61)
To painting back chamber green, 8 yards, at 1s. 6d. (25 cents) _____		12		($2. 00)
1781—To painting front room, 85 yards, at 2s. (33.3 cents) a yard_____	8	10	0	($28. 33)
1783—To painting entry, staircase and upper chambers, 127 yards, at 1s. 1d. (18 cents) _____	7	8	2	($24. 69)

1791—To painting your house, outside, from the Garrett to the Ground, Fences &c Included, viz:

Measure

South Front___ 233 yards.
West End_____ 106 do.
Northwest_____ 156 do.
North End___ 86 do.

	£	s.	d.	
581 yards, at 1s. (16.7 cents)_	31	9	5	($104. 90)

East Side in ye
Tan Y a r d,
measure_____ 191 yards.
Garrett, Roof,
L o o k o u t,
G a n g b o a r d,
Eaves, Fences,
P u m p, a n d
Top of Cistern _____ 575 yards.

	£	s.	d.	
766 do. at 10d. (14 cents)_	31	18	4	($106. 38)
Four Luthern Windows, at 3s. (50 cents)_____		12		($2. 00)
40 window frames, at 2s. (33.3 cents)_____	4			($13. 33)
952 sash lights, at 2 cents each_____	5	14	2	($19. 03)
Grand Total_____	73	13	11	($245. 65)

In 1793 inside painting, which had been 7 to 10d. (9.8 to 14 cents) for about 15 years, is raised to 1s. (16.7 cents) per square yard.   The last entry in the 1793 account book reads:

Harrison Gray Otis, Dr.
To painting sundry parts of your house inside, viz:
Front Room_____ 84 yards.
Chamber_____ 81 do.
Dining parlour_____ 95 do.
Entry & stairway_____ 178 do.

438 yards, at 1s__ £21. 18. 0 ($73. 00)

The next year the rate went still higher, to 1s. 2d. (19.5 cents), and the price charged for painting Venetian blinds was raised from 10s. to 15s. ($1.67 to $2.50) a pair.   In 1797 American money appeared in the accounts.   Inside painting was 20 cents a yard, and a school was charged $1.25 for "one day's work of one of our painters."

GOVERNMENT BUILDING

The close of the century found public construction actively under way in various places.   The Federal Government began in 1793 the erection of the United States Capitol and other buildings, and the laying out and development of the District of Columbia, and two years later Massachusetts began to build its new statehouse. The Virginia scale for skilled building-trades men was, in 1796–97, 6s. a day ($1); for helpers, 4s. (66.7 cents); and for laborers, 2s. 6d. (42 cents),[41] and probably those rates prevailed on the Government work in the District of Columbia. "Hodcarriers and mortar mixers, diggers and choppers, who from 1793 to 1800 labored on the public buildings and cut the streets and avenues of Washington received $70 a year, or, if they wished, $60 for all the work they could do from March 1 to December 20. (They were of course found, but not clothed.) The hours of labor were invariably from sunrise to sunset." [42]

Data dealing with the cost of constructing the Massachusetts State Capitol appear in voluminous detail in the account books of the period in the State archives. The administrative end of the work was apparently intrusted to a committee, composed largely of members of the two houses of the State legislature. Charles Bulfinch, the architect who designed the building, was also a member of the committee. Whereas to-day an undertaking of that nature is turned over to a building contractor who handles the administrative work as well as the materials and labor, it was much more complicated than that in Massachusetts in 1795. Each material dealer billed the committee for the amount of material delivered, no matter how small, and a dozen different carters presented bills for delivery, often in form and writing so illiterate as to make their deciphering difficult.

Carters charged 6s. ($1) a load. The price of bricks seems to have been fixed at $9 a thousand, and bricks were sold to the committee at that price by a variety of dealers. The masonry was apparently contracted for by a firm of mason contractors, whose accounts were presented on a printed billhead, in a businesslike manner more like present-day bookkeeping than the countless little statements on torn scraps of paper which represent other classes of participants in the undertaking. The mason contractors charged the State $5 a thousand for laying brick and $1.33 a perch for setting stone, but paid their bricklayers and stone masons $1.50 per day.

A dollar and a half a day was the standard rate for most of the skilled trades. Common or "general labor," received 6s. to 8s. ($1 to $1.33) a day. The "master mechanics" and foremen received $2. The cabinetmakers who built the mahogany bookcases, the tables, the Speaker's chair, etc., were also paid $2.

Piece prices are given for lathing and plastering at 25 cents per square yard; those for ornamental stucco work run from 1s. (16.7 cents) a foot for straight molding to 3s. 6d. (58 cents) for the most elaborate design; the price charged by the woodcarver for the Corinthian capitals was $70 each for the 23-inch columns, and $50 for the 3¼-inch columns, while the pine cone on the top of the dome was $25. The columns range from $3 to $10 each for turning, depending upon the diameter.

The bill for painting reads thus:

	£	s.	d.	
To painting State House three times over, 10,822 square yards, at 1/6 (25 cents)	811	13	00	($2,705. 50)
To painting the Dome over the fourth time, 9½ days' work, at 9s. ($1.50)	4	5	6	($14. 25)

41 Thomas Jefferson's manuscript account books, Massachusetts Historical Society.
42 McMaster, John B., History of the People of United States, Vol. II, pp. 617–18.

NINETEENTH CENTURY

Wages rose steadily with the opening of the new century, after Federal and State Governments had begun really to function, and the new Republic to find itself. "It is impossible," McMaster states, "to read the many memorials which for twenty years (1790–1810) had been coming to Congress, without noticing the general complaint of the high price of wages. To us, when we consider the long hours of labor and the cost of living, these wages seem extremely low." John Jay calls the wage demands of mechanics and laborers at this period "very extravagant."

The carpenters of Boston in 1800 "chose a large and respectable committee out of their number" to formulate a new scale of piece rates to take the place of the 1774 "book of prices" which, "not considering that they were calculated upon a scale which bears no proportion to the price of other labor now, and which is by no means an equivalent compensation for the service, in reference to the raised price of the necessaries of life," was still in general use. This 1800 price list and "rules of work" will be found in full in Appendix B.

From about 1810 sources of information become numerous, and data from these various sources are on the whole consistent. They show enough uniformity to justify the conclusion that by that time wage standards had become fairly fixed for the respective crafts, and suggest about the same differences between geographic localities and trades that we find to-day.

McMaster reports that rates for all classes of work differed "in each of the three great belts along which population streamed westward." They were highest in the New England and New York area, as far west as Ohio, and lowest in the South, with the territory west of Ohio holding the middle ground. In each of these belts, wages were lower on the seaboard than inland.

Although Monticello, Thomas Jefferson's home in Virginia, was built in 1770–1772, most of the entries in his account books dealing with building costs and rates paid building-trades men cover a later period, 1800–1815. He gives not only rates, but a compilation of "observations," to use his own term, and data concerning both time and money costs in building which are worth reproducing substantially as he wrote them. Most of these entries, when dated at all, run from 1810 to 1815.[43]

JEFFERSON'S NOTES ON BUILDING

BRICK.—A demicord of earth (4-foot cube) makes 1,000 bricks. A man will turn up 4 such cubes, or even 5, a day. The price for turning up is 1s. [13.3 cents] (Maryland) the cube, or 1,000 bricks, the laborer finding himself.

A man moulds 2,000 bricks a day. His attendance is a man to temper, one to wheel the mortar to him, and a boy to bear off (Philadelphia).

At Georgetown in 1792 a brickmaker for 2½ dollars the thousand made the bricks, turning up the clay and finding himself everything except wood to burn and planks to cover them.

The brick work is about one-third of the whole cost, the carpenter's material and iron-mongery one-third, the carpenter's work one-third.

1814.—Chisolm and two apprentices (one of them a new beginner) lay 1,600 bricks a day.

STONE.—Paving or other stone cut at 8d. [11.2 cents] the superficial foot, the block being found, and provisions.

---

[43] Thomas Jefferson's Manuscript Account books, Massachusetts Historical Society.

The price for laying stone is 2s. 6d. [42 cents] per perch in an 18-inch wall. In Augusta it is 2s. [33.3 cents]. Such stone work is cheaper than brick in the proportion of £1,056.4 to £581.5 [$3,520.6⁷ to $1,937.50]. Everything calculated accurately by a workman at Georgetown, ...s brick work coming to $9.60 per thousand and his stone work $2 per perch, including the cost and carriage of everything, even of the rough stone. A man lays generally 3 perch a day, and even 5 in a very thick wall.

WOOD.—The sawmills over the mountains saw for 20s. [$3.33] the thousand, or one-half for the other.

Two mawlers and 3 rivers will rive 750 pine slabs a day, of 14 feet long, and double that number 6 feet long. Every slab clears about 4 inches, that is to say, 30 slabs properly clapped clear 10 feet.

Another estimate is that 3 men will get only 450 slabs a day if 6 feet long and 5 inches broad.

To rive and draw 500 shingles is a common day's work.⁴⁴ A man may joint 3,000 a day.

Four men got out and out 600 chestnut pales a day, 7 feet long, for the garden.

PAINT.—Venetian blinds. The Upholsterer's part costs 2 dollars and the painting (by a coach painter) a French crown [about $1].

FRESCO PAINTING.—Schneider charges a dollar a yard he finding paints, or 8s. [$1.33] a day, paint &c found him. He can do half a yard an hour.

CARPENTRY.—June, 1812: Johnny Heming and Lewis made a set of Venetian blinds, with fixed slats, i e 2 pair 3 feet 3 inche⁻ square, in 6 days, splitting out the slats from common plank with a handsaw. S⌄y a window a week.

March 21, 1814: Johnny Heming began the body of a landau January 12 and finished it this day, being 9 weeks and 5 days. He had not more help from Lewis than made up for his own interruptions. The smith work employed the 2 smiths perhaps one-third of the same time.

A panelled door is done in 5 days, all the stuff being previously planed up.

A Boston painter's bill in 1814 reads as follows:

To 2 days' work	$3. 75
To hanging 7½ rolls of paper	3. 50
To hanging 10½ rolls of paper, at 50 cents a roll	5. 25
To whiting ceiling	1. 00
To pinkwashing the sides	2. 00
To whiting and pinking 3 upper chambers at 4s. [66.7 cents] each	2. 00

Masons' wages had advanced in Massachusetts from $1.50 a day in 1795–1800, when the statehouse was under construction, to $2 in 1815, when Boston was building an almshouse and paying that rate for the brickwork, with bricks at $1 per 100, an advance of $1 per thousand over the price paid by the State for the capitol. Plastering at the almshouse was 50 cents a square yard, and slate roofers received $2 a day.⁴⁵

This rate is higher, however, than the prevailing rate at the time. Official statistics of the Massachusetts Bureau of Statistics of Labor show an average rate of $1.21 for masons over the entire State.⁴⁶

Across the State line, in Rhode Island, a manufacturing concern was building a road and a bridge connecting two factories. Foremen on this job received $1.75 a day, masons and carpenters, $1.50, and laborers, 6s. ($1). Carting was $2.50 for man and team.⁴⁷

A contemporary historian gives presumably authentic daily rates for carpenters and bricklayers in several States for the period 1815–1817, as follows: ⁴⁸

Bricklayers.—$1.50 in New York and South Carolina; $2 in Pennsylvania; $1 in Ohio; and $3 per M. in District of Columbia.

Carpenters.—$1.50 per day in Maine and New York and $1 in Ohio.

---

⁴⁴ Shingle makers in Ohio in 1815 were paid $1.50 per day.
⁴⁵ Manuscript account book, Baker Library.
⁴⁶ Massachusetts Bureau of Statistics of Labor. History of Wages and Prices, 1752–1883.
⁴⁷ Manuscript Account book, Moses Brown, John Carter Brown Library, Providence.
⁴⁸ Warden, D. B.: A Statistical, Political, and Historical Account of the United States (published in Edinburgh in 1819).

Another contemporary writer quotes a general average for the whole country in the following decade as $1.45 for carpenters and $1.62 for masons.[49]

In 1832 carpenters in Boston were offered $2 a day to break a strike for a 10-hour day.[50] In New York in 1836 they were getting $1.75, and in that year the Philadelphia carpenters struck for $1.50 per day from March 20 to November 20 and $1.25 for the remainder of the year. The rate at the time of the strike was $1.25 from April 1 to November 1, and $1.12½ for the winter.

Table 4 is compiled from Wright's Wages and Prices, 1752–1883, and shows rates paid certain of the building trades in the State of Massachusetts, from 1800 to 1838, giving high, medium, and low rates, per day.

TABLE 4.—*Daily wage rates (high, medium, and low) for specified building trades in Massachusetts, 1800 to 1838*

Year	Carpenters			Masons			Painters			Laborers		
	High	Medium	Low	High	Medium	Low	High	Medium	Low	High	Medium	Low
1800	6s.		5s. 2d.							4s. 2d.		2s.
1801	5s. 10½d.		4s. 6d.							5s. 8d.		3s. 10d.
1802								3s. 9d.		6s.	5s.	4s. 6d.
1803	5s.	$1.08			$1.66						$0.42	
1804	5s. 9d.	1.16	4s. 1d.					$1.33		5s. 3d.	.89	4s.
1805	$1.75	1.46	$1.17							$1.02	.84	$0.25
1806		1.46								1.27	1.00	.86
1807		1.50						1.50		6s.	4s. 6d.	3s. 6d.
1808	1.75	1.00	.67							$1.00	$0.85	$0.50
1809	1.33		1.06	$1.75		$1.33				1.67	1.23	.99
1810	1.11		1.00	1.33		1.00				1.10	.84	.51
1811	1.24	1.00	.75		1.50						1.00	
1812		1.40			3.25			1.50		1.25	1.07	.67
1813	1.43	1.26	1.00	1.74		1.50		1.50		1.33	1.00	.57
1814		1.04								1.35	1.00	.78
1815	[a]1.00		.75		[b]1.21				[c]1.13		.99	.50
1816		1.00								1.74	1.07	.79
1817	1.42		1.00							1.00		
1818												
1819		1.14								1.00		.75
1820		1.00								1.15	.80	.50
1821										1.00	.68	.50
1822		.89								1.00	.75	.64
1823		1.00								.80		.67
1824		.83								1.00		.73
1825	[a]1.33		1.00	[d]1.50	1.25	1.00	$1.25		$1.00	.99	.71	.50
1826										1.00	.79	.46
1827										1.13	1.00	.72
1828					1.26					1.00	.69	.50
1829											.76	
1830											.74	
1833										1.00		.88
1834											1.00	
1835	[e]1.25		1.12	[f]1.50		1.25	1.25		1.00	.83		.63
1837	[g]2.00		1.33									
1838	[g]2.00		1.33									

[a] With board, $0.625; with board in summer, high—$1.25; summer, low—$0.625).
[b] In winter, $0.88; with board, summer and winter, $0.628.
[c] Winter, high—$1.25; winter, low—$1. Summer, with board, high—$0.84; summer, with board, low—$0.50; winter, with board, high—$0.75; winter, with board, low—$0.50.
[d] Summer, board, high—$0.84; summer, board, low—$0.66; winter, board, high—$0.75; winter, board, low—$0.50.
[e] Summer, board, high—$0.90; summer, board, low—$0.60; winter, high—$1.12; winter, low—$1; winter, board, high—$0.84; winter, board, low—$0.50.
[f] Summer, board, high—$0.84; summer, board, low—$0.66; winter—$1 per day; winter, board, high—$0.75; winter, board, low—$0.50.
[g] Cotton-mill carpenters.

[49] Allen, Zachariah: Science of Mechanics (1829).
[50] Documentary History of American Industrial Society, Vol. VI, p. 86.

SHIPBUILDING

"As soon as colonial labor settled into organized work"[51] it began the first American industry, shipbuilding. The need of the colonies themselves for vessels and the abundance of readily accessible materials made its development natural.

Unlike most of the trades of the colonial period, that of shipbuilding was followed by skilled and specialized workers. "With timely wisdom," Weeden says, "the sagacious fathers had brought shipwrights from England who were complete masters of the art of building ships in their day. The descendants of these men, aided by the hardy seamen bred in the fisheries, could launch the best and cheapest vessel to be had in the latter half of the seventeenth century."[52]

The Virginia Company sent 25 skilled ship carpenters to Jamestown, who were "to be employed only in the trade in which they had been educated,"[53] and "Penn brought a shipbuilder on his first voyage."[54]

The development of the industry has been related frequently in maritime and economic histories, but for the specific purposes of the present study the available information is extremely meager. Old records show construction costs per ton over long periods, but details bearing on labor costs and wage rates are wholly lacking. The reason seems to be that given by Weeden, with particular reference to New England—that "this work of shipbuilding * * * was carried on substantially without money"[55] and the men engaged in it "saw little money * * * for their labor. West India sugar and rum, home produce, a few dry goods—in fact all their immediate and necessary consumption—was dealt out to them in return for their labor."[56]

One early record relates to New Jersey in 1641, but it is the work of one of the pamphleteers of the period and is very probably overstated. According to his report "ten men a day will build a tun of shipping as in England * * * which is 6s. [$1.20] a day's work, having the Timber without money."[57]

The rate of pay for ship carpenters in Massachusetts in the last quarter of the seventeenth century seems to have been 3s. and 3s. 6d. (50 and 58 cents) a day, the latter rate being for skilled work. The following account, dated 1680, is probably for repair work, except perhaps in the case of the last entry:[58]

	£	s.	d.	
To work on the Penelope, 10½ days	1	16	9	($6. 13)
Making half a mast for the Penelope		12	6	($2. 08)
6 daye's work on the Ketch George when Bayly was master	1	01	0	($3. 50)
6 daye's work on the Ketch George when Peter Miller was master	1	02	9	($3. 79)
Work done on the Ketch Swallow, 49½ dayes	8	13	3	($28. 87)

The daily rate is 3s. 6d. (58 cents) in all cases except "when Peter Miller was master," when it is 3s. 8d. (61 cents). No explanation is offered for the increase—perhaps Captain Miller was difficult to work for.

---

51 Weeden, William B.: Economic and Social History of New England, 1620–1789, Vol. I, p. 167.
52 Idem, Vol. I, p. 255.
53 Bruce, Vol. II, p. 429.
54 Herrick, Cheesman A.: White Servitude in Pennsylvania, p. 65.
55 Weeden, Vol. I, p. 167.
56 Idem, Vol. I, p. 366.
57 Evelin, Robert: Directions for Adventurers—Force's Tracts, Vol. II. (New Jersey, 20-cent shilling.)
58 Manuscript account book, Essex Institute.

A blacksmith billed a Salem shipbuilder in 1690 for £1 5s. ($4.17) for making an anchor weighing 50 pounds,[59] but unfortunately no time is entered in the statement. Gabriel Thomas quoted the rate of pay of ship carpenters in Pennsylvania in 1698 as "between five and six shillings" ($1 and $1.20) [60] a day.

A very early employer's liability case which was decided in favor of the plaintiff grew out of an accident in a Salem shipyard in 1641, in which a rigger was killed. The employer "was required by the Court of Assistants to pay £10 sterling [$48.60] to the wife and children of the deceased because they thought that sufficient care was not taken to have his tackle strong enough." [61]

Virginia produced some seagoing vessels, but large ships were not imperative because foreign shippers were always eager to furnish all that were needed to move the tobacco crops. On the other hand, small sloops and shallops which could navigate Virginia rivers to the wharves of the planters were in constant demand, and were built in the colony. Bruce quotes a statement of 1672, presenting in itemized form the cost of building a sloop:

> The total amount was 4,467 pounds of tobacco, which at the rate of two pence a pound represented an expense, perhaps, of about $925. In the construction of this sloop the various parts were supplied by different persons. It seems to have required four months to complete it, for the charges for the food furnished the carpenter run over that length of time; a cask of cider was also consumed by him during the same period.[62]

After more than a century of extensive shipbuilding on the New England seaboard the industry moved inland after more timber. While Weeden accounts for the decline of the industry in the old centers after 1750 by the exhaustion of the great trees,[63] another writer holds that "in Boston shipbuilding was a declining industry on account of the exorbitant wages, carpenters demanding 67 cents a day." [64] This exorbitant rate, however, represents an increase of only 6d. to 1s. (8.4 to 16.7 cents) over the rate of a century before. In Pennsylvania throughout the last quarter of the eighteenth century the rate for skilled workers was 9s. ($1.20) a day.[65]

Stephen Girard, of Philadelphia, apparently paid more than the prevailing rate to all his employees, whatever their occupation. Pay rolls for an overhauling and repair job on his ship Voltaire at Philadelphia in 1807 show the following daily rates: Carpenters and calkers, $2; sawyers, $1.25; painters, $1.25; laborers, $1.10 and $1.[66] These rates are considerably higher than those paid in Massachusetts at a later period, after the general rise in wages following the War of 1812. Shipyard wages in 1815, as given in the Massachusetts State report, are $1.13 a day for boat builders, or 50 cents a day with board, and $1.25 for riggers. In 1825–26 the average rate was $1.25, and $2 a day for calkers.[67]

A custom of long standing in the shipbuilding industry required employers to furnish workers with "drink or grog at various intervals in the day. The ceremony of laying the keel, and of commencing

[59] Manuscript account book, Essex Institute.
[60] Pennsylvania colonial shilling, 20 cents.
[61] Felt, Joseph B.: Annals of Salem, Vol. I, p. 178.
[62] Bruce, Vol. II, p. 436 (citing Records of York County, Va., Vol. 1671-1694, p. 25).
[63] Weeden, Vol. II, p. 765.
[64] Clark, Victor S.: History of Manufactures in the United States, 1607-1860, p. 208.
[65] Wharton & Humphreys Shipyard Accounts, 1773-1795, Historical Society of Pennsylvania.
[66] In Girard College Library, Philadelphia.
[67] Massachusetts Bureau of Statistics of Labor (16th annual report), History of Wages and Prices, p. 175.

each part of the work, as also the christening or naming of a vessel, was always accompanied with the use of ardent spirits."[68] In 1817 Thacher Magoun, a shipbuilder of Medford, Mass., "determined to abolish the grog privilege."

The hours of labor at that time were from sunrise to sunset, and all employers were obliged by custom to furnish liquor free at least twice a day. These two periods for drink were really periods of rest, and were called luncheon times, and Mr. Magoun's no-rum movement meant no luncheon time, and was practically an increase in the working time, the employer thus saving the cost of time as well as the cost of rum. The hours of this luncheon privilege were eleven o'clock in the forenoon and four o'clock in the afternoon. Many of the workmen who were temperance men were indignant at the action of their employer, as they felt that the luncheon times were as oases in the desert of unremitting toil.[68]

There was a brief, unsuccessful strike, "but finally all gave in and a ship was built without the use of liquor in any form."[68]

Ship workers "seem to have been the first to bring the question of the hours of labor to a direct issue."[69] The journeyman shipwrights and calkers of Boston organized in 1832 and "resolved that from and after March 20 until the first of September we will not labor more than ten hours a day unless paid extra for each and every hour."[70] The master builders promptly locked them out and advertised in the Boston papers for shipwrights who were "not pledged to any combination respecting hours," and offered $2 a day.[71] The Boston journeymen were defeated, but "while the merchants of Boston were saying that it was impossible to conduct their business on the ten-hour system, the system was adopted in New York and Philadelphia after a struggle, and it was working satisfactorily. Public sentiment grew stronger in favor of the ship workers" and the movement started in New York and Philadelphia "spread along the coast and culminated in the proclamation of President Van Buren fixing the hours of labor for persons employed in the navy yards"[72] at 10 a day.

Conditions in shipyards at the time were thus described:

Everywhere, from the Government shipyards down to the ten-ton sloop set up in the woods miles from any place, the rule holds good. Hurrah! Hurry and hiring men to-day; to-morrow, or day after, or next week, the place is as quiet as a grave yard; the crisis is passed, the hurry is over, the craft launched and gone, and so all the craftsmen—scattered in as many directions, perhaps, as there are men, in search of some other three-weeks' job.

In some four or five of our larger cities ship work is something more continuous and reliable; but even here they are by no means exempt from depressions and sudden fluctuations; and whenever the "slack time" comes if the ship carpenter, caulker, joiner, etc., is not absolutely discharged, his wages are reduced until he finds himself wondering "what he will do with it," his remuneration, at the highest figure, being no greater than that of some half a dozen other classes of mechanics whose employment is constant and always under shelter, so that whatever time they may lose is voluntary.[73]

CABINETMAKING

The cabinetmaker, as distinct from the carpenter and joiner, makes his appearance in the latter part of the eighteenth century. The earliest daily rate which the bureau was able to find is the $2

[68] McNeill, George E., ed.: The Labor Movement (1887), p. 333.
[69] Idem, p. 337.
[70] Idem, p. 339.
[71] Documentary History American Industrial Society, Vol. VI, pp. 85–86.
[72] McNeill, George E.: The Labor Movement, pp. 340–341.
[73] Idem, p. 341.

paid to the cabinetmakers who built the furniture in the Massachusetts State House in 1797.[74] This was undoubtedly much higher than the prevailing rate, as were most of the wages paid on that job, and was for expert work. Fifty years later the rate established by the Journeyman Cabinet Makers Beneficial Society of the District of Columbia was only "$1.50 for every ten hours' work when employed by the day." [75]

The usual method of payment in cabinetmaking, however, was by the job or piece. While specifications for each job are detailed, no suggestion is given as to the time involved in execution. A list of "Prices of Cabinet and Chair Work" was carefully recorded by Benjamin Lehman, a Philadelphia manufacturer, in 1786, with the notation: "The first column is of Mahogany, the second of Walnut, the third the Journeyman's Wages.[76] Various items selected from this list, with the amount paid to the journeyman for the work specified, follow:

	£	s.	d.	
High chest of drawers on a frame, head and corners and plain feet	3	10	0	($9. 33)
Ditto, claw feet, leaves on knees and shell drawers	5	0	0	($13. 33)
Low chest of drawers	1	12	6	($4. 33)
	1	17	6	($5. 00)
Chairs _____10s. ($1.33) to—		17		($2. 26)
Easy chairs		18		($2. 40)
Chair frames for stuffing		6		($0. 80)
Sofas, plain	1	0	0	($2. 67)
Ditto, with a fret on the feet and Rails and Carved Mouldings	2	10	0	($6. 67)
Dining Tables, 3' 6"	1	0	0	($2. 67)
4'	1	2	6	($3. 00)
4' 6"	1	5	0	($3. 33)
5' 6" with 6 legs	1	15	0	($4. 67)
Card tables		17	6	($2. 33)
Card tables with round corners	1	2	6	($3. 00)
Bedsteads, low posts with claw feet		10		($1. 31)
Bedsteads, high posts, fluted pillars and carved capital	1	10		($4. 00)
Ditto with plain turned pillars and bases		15		($2. 00)

Cabinetmakers in New York City were sufficiently well organized in 1802 to establish a "Book of Prices" which was agreed to by the employers in September of that year. This price list was maintained until 1817, when it was revised and again accepted by the employers. The next revision was begun in 1832, but was not signed by the employers and put into effect until two years later, a strike for enforcement having taken place in the meantime. The rates in the 1817 price list are considerably higher in most instances than those of 1834. Whether the 1817 prices held throughout the 15 years, or whether the revision of 1832 was an attempt to stabilize a falling scale is not known. The 1817 Book of Prices reflects the general advance in both wages and prices which followed the War of 1812, and it is altogether probable that it was not effectively enforced throughout the entire period in which it was presumably operative.

The bureau had access to a volume, privately owned, in which all three of these price lists—1802, 1817, and 1834—are combined. Items are listed in the minutest detail, with full specifications for the work and the manner in which it was to be performed. The articles listed change from household furniture which in 1802 is fairly simple,

[74] Massachusetts State Archives; see also p. 55.
[75] Constitution of 1842 in Library of Congress.
[76] In manuscript collection, Historical Society of Pennsylvania, Philadelphia.

through successive styles and periods to a seemingly endless number in 1834, specifications for which are intricate and detailed in the extreme. The simple styles of 1802 have largely disappeared from the list in 1817 and are wholly absent in 1834, and many of those introduced in 1817 have been replaced in the later revision. This makes comparison of prices difficult and uncertain. In tabulating this material, selection was made only of standard articles of furniture which seemed from the specifications to be reasonably comparable. The specifications as listed are taken from the 1802 book, elaborations on which in the later editions have been omitted.

The 1802 book states that "men working by the day are to be paid in proportion to their earnings by the piece, and find their own candles."

The preface to the 1817 list reads:

It appears from long experience that the late Book of Prices has been found deficient in many respects, owing to the late improvements and alterations in the work; therefore to better regulate the prices of cabinet work, the New York Society of Journeymen Cabinet Makers have determined to lay before their employers one which they trust will prevent, in some degree, those disputes which have frequently occurred by taking prices of work from improper places. They have endeavored to arrange them so that the present book will allow the work to average as much, and no more, than the late book, with the advance of 12½ per cent.

The following table shows the piece prices paid on selected articles for each of the three periods covered. In the original, prices are quoted in pounds, shillings, and pence for 1802 and 1817. Since that was not the money system of the time it has been converted for presentation here:

TABLE 5.—*Piece prices on selected articles of furniture, as given in union agreements in New York City, from 1802 to 1834*

Article	1802	1817	1834
Plain chest or bureau, 3 feet 6 inches long, 2 feet 7 inches high between the moldings, 4 drawers	$6.50	$8.25	$6.70
Each inch less in length, deduct	.08	.08	.08
Each inch more in length, add	.08	.08	.12
Each drawer	.68	.88	.68
Serpentine chest or bureau, 3 feet 8 inches long, 2 feet 10 inches high, 4 drawers	12.50	12.50	11.25
Secretary, 3 feet 10 inches long, 3 feet 1 inch high, 8 small drawers, 8 letter holes, 3 long drawers	15.00	--------	18.50
Straight front library bookcase, 5 feet long, 7 feet 6 inches high between plinth and cornice, 2 flat panel doors upper and 2 lower, 4 shelves in each side of upper part and 2 on each side of lower	20.00	{¹ 11.50 ²14.00}	¹ 10.00 ² 11.00
Low wardrobe, 4 feet 2 inches long, 3 feet 8 inches high between moldings, 2 flat panel doors, panels plowed in, with ovolo stuck on inner edge, 3 shelves inside, 2 short drawers in bottom	9.50	10.38	8.75
Wardrobe, 4 feet long, 6 feet 2 inches high between moldings, 2 flat panel doors, panels plowed in, an ovolo stuck in inner edge, four trays in upper part, 3 long drawers in lower	16.25	22.13	17.25
Inch more in length, add	.19	.30	.25
Inch more in height, add	.08	.15	.12
Inch less in length, deduct	.19	.30	.16
Inch less in height, deduct	.08	.15	.08
Half round dining table, 4 feet long, veneered rail, 3 plain legs, an astragal or five strings round the lower edge of the rail	2.50	3.13	3.75
Knee-hole library table, 4 feet long, 2 feet 6 inches wide, 9 drawers	14.50	--------	--------
Same, 5 feet 6 inches long, 2 feet 4 inches wide, 3 drawers in each pedestal and one in center, 6 plain tapered legs	--------	16.38	--------
Straight-front sideboard, 6 feet long, framing 21 inches deep, deep drawer at one end partitioned for bottles	20.00	15.00	14.00

¹ Lower.   ² Upper.

TABLE 5.—*Piece prices on selected articles of furniture, as given in union agreements in New York City, from 1802 to 1834*—Continued

Article	1802	1817	1834
Low post bedstead, four posts turned	$0.88	$1.13	$1.00
If made of hardwood, extra	.38	.63	.50
High post bedstead	2.00	2.00	2.00
If made of hardwood, extra	.50	.83	.75
Clock case, with arched head, scroll or cove pediment, the top of the body door serpentine, and quarter-round on ditto, frieze below top molding, etc	8.10	12.50	11.50
Cradle, plain, all solid	2.75	3.38	3.25
A square-back chair, with straight top and stay rail, four upright slats, straight seat, made for stuffing over the rails, plain tapered legs	1.50	2.13	(³)

³ Chair prices for 1834 period, various designs, range from $2.13 for Grecian chairs, to $5 for rocking chairs.
"All chairs for which a price can not be found in the list to be settled by a committee. Where a single Grecian chair is to be made, charge 25 cents extra; French chair, 50 cents extra. Shaping, gluing, veneering, all charged for in addition to price for body work."

Additional regulations in the 1817 agreement are: "All pine work to be done by the day, and the workman to be paid according to his earnings by the piece. When work, or any part of it, is made of cherry, ash, or plain maple, to be the same as mahogany. When glass plates are put in any piece of work, to pay 5 per cent on the value thereon, the workman to take the risk. It shall be optional with the employer to have them put in by the workman or not."

The latter provision was changed in 1834, when it was agreed that putting in glass plates was "to be paid for according to time, the employer to take the risk." Further, "all marble pillars, tops, etc., to be at the risk of the employers."

Prices which could not be fixed by the 1834 scale were "to be settled by a committee of employers and journeymen."

The time rate paid cabinetmakers in 1832, as given in the McLane report on statistics of manufactures, ranges from 75 cents to $1.25 a day, and averages a dollar a day in most of the States reporting. In Maine, however, 75 cents was the prevailing rate.

Chapter 5.—IRON INDUSTRY

A supply of iron was among the chief material advantages which England expected to derive from the American colonies, because of the abundance of good ore and of wood for charcoal, which was then used as coal. Iron manufacture was begun in Virginia very soon after its settlement, but the early efforts met with a series of disasters which discouraged further development throughout the seventeenth century.

The first iron works were established in 1620 at Falling Creek, about 60 miles above Jamestown, by a group of ironworkers from England. A promising beginning was followed immediately by the death of the superintendent and two of the master workmen. Later the Virginia Company sent over a new superintendent and 20 skilled men to put the enterprise back on its feet. These 20 men went at the expense of the company, were to be supported by it for the first year, and agreed to remain in its employ for seven years. Again the Falling Creek works were progressing toward success when the Indian massacre of 1622 put an end to the undertaking. All of the workmen were killed and the plant was destroyed.

The discovery of bog ore in Massachusetts led to the establishment of the first productive iron works in the colonies at Saugus (Lynn) about 1643. Governor Winthrop's son, John Winthrop, jr., was chiefly instrumental in organizing a company of "undertakers" in England which raised £1,000 ($4,860) for the enterprise. Winthrop returned to Massachusetts with skilled workmen and obtained concessions from the Colonial Government, provisional upon completing the works within three years and providing the colony with sufficient iron at £20 ($97.20) per ton. Later stock in the company was offered to the public and the General Court requested "all citizens * * * to take stock according to their ability." By 1648, Winthrop wrote, the furnace was producing "8 tuns per week, and their bar iron is as good as the Spanish." In capacity it "ranked with the larger establishments of this kind, either in America or abroad." [1]

The enterprise, which "embraced a blast furnace, or 'foundery,' and a refining forge," [2] was, according to an account written in 1677, "very much promoted and strenuously carried on for some time, but at length, instead of drawing out bars of iron for the country's use, there was hammered out nothing but contentions and lawsuits." [3] It became involved in many difficulties which resulted in the discontinuance of the plant about 1688, after it had passed through several hands.

Baker Library of the Harvard Graduate School of Business Administration has recently come into possession of a collection of manuscripts, chiefly letters, accounts, and inventories, of the Saugus

---

[1] Clark, Victor S.: History of Manufactures in the United States, 1607–1860, p. 170.
[2] Swank, James M.: Iron in All Ages, p. 83.
[3] Quoted by Swank, p. 83.

Iron Works. Some of these accounts are practically pay rolls. Those dealing particularly with the furnace and forge for the year 1652 are here reproduced as copied from the original manuscripts by the bureau representative:

To 26 weekes worke at Forge	£16–6s.	($54.33)
" 2 dayes worke at ye finnery chimneye	5s.	($0.83)
" 5 dayes worke and setting an anvill	15s.	($2.50)
" 14 dayes worke at Furnace	£1–15s.	($5.83)
" Hennry Leonard for 4 dayes worke	10s.	($1.67)
" James Leonard for 15 dayes worke about finnery chimneye and other worke about ye forge	£1–13s.	($5.50)
" ditto Leonard for dressing his bellows 3 times	£1–10s.	($5.00)
To accompte of Jno Vinton for 6½ dayes work	16/3	($2.71)
" accompte of Ralph Russel for 2½ dayes work	6/3	($1.04)
" accompte of Thomas Wiggins for 2 dayes worke	5s.	($0.83)
" 7 dayes work	17/6	($2.92)
To 4 dayes worke fashioning ye hammer beames	50s.	($8.33)
" ½ dayes work putting in ye furnace beames	5/3	($0.88)
" 30 dayes worke about ye workes at 2/6	£3–15s.	($12.50)
" acct Jno Turner, 49 weekes waiges	£29–8s.	($98.00)

These are wages paid the skilled workers. Reduced to a daily rate, the amount is 2s. 6d. (42 cents) in practically all instances. The cost of boarding these men, which is also entered in the accounts, runs from 5s. to 5s. 8d. (83.3 to 94.5 cents) per capita a week. The superintendent received £100 a year, probably sterling ($486), and his agreement with the company provided for "passadge for himself, his wife, 2 children, 3 servants; an howse to be built for him and ground to be allowed him for his horses and a few cowes."

Unskilled labor was done by Scotchmen taken prisoners by Cromwell and sent to the iron works under 10 years' indenture to the company. Nearly 40 of these indentured servants were employed in the plant. On one occasion the company in England protested the weekly charge of 5 shillings per head for boarding them, and insisted that this amount be cut to 3s. 6d. (58 cents), "you haveing ther plenty of fish, both fresh and salt, and pidgions and venison and corne and pease."

The woodsmen's accounts give a time rate in some cases and a piece rate in others. The time rate appears in such entries as: "To accompte of Samuel Harte for 9 months wages, £9 [$30]"; "to acct of Daniel Salmon for 20 weeks waiges at 9s. [$1.50] a week"; "to ditto for 27 weekes waiges at 12s. [$2.00] per weeke," and in occasional items of 1s. 6d. (25 cents) for a day's work felling trees. The piece rate is generally 2 s., 2 s. 4d., and 2s. 8d. (33.3, 39, and 44.5 cents) a cord for cutting and cording, depending on the length of the log. One entry is for 2s. 6d. (42 cents) "to a daye's work attendance on ye coarde woode, being afire."

The charge for loading "coale" is entered variously, ranging from 4s. 8d. to 5s. 8d. (78 to 94.5 cents) a "loade," but there is no way of determining what constituted a load. Colonel Spotswood, 70 years later, estimated the cost of coaling charcoal at his Virginia forge at 5s. (83.3 cents) per load of 160 bushels. Very likely a load meant the same thing at Saugus, as other rates are comparable in the two plants, particularly in cording wood, for which Spotswood paid 2s. (33.3 cents) a cord for wood "cut, mauled, cut to length (4 feet) and delivered at pits." [4]

---

[4] Pearse, John B.: A Concise History of the Iron Manufacture of the American Colonies, p. 12.

To obtain the raw material, bog ore, "men go out with boats and make use of instruments much like those with which oysters are taken, to get up the ore from the bottom of the pond."[5] The "bogg myne" accounts show that this work was paid for at the rate of 6s. ($1) a ton. "For a number of years," before the supply began to run out, "a man would take up and bring to shore two tons of it in a day."[5]

An account which may be credited to maintenance is "9 monthes carpenter work, £35 [$116.67]," which is about 3s. (50 cents) per day. Other items, which do not specify the occupation, are, "wages at 12s. 8d. [$2.11] per week"; "to 6 monthes waiges, £20 [$66.67]"; "to 26 weekes work at 12s. 8d. [$2.11]"; "to 4 weekes waiges, £2 [$6.67]."

Later records suggest that the employees of the company experienced difficulty in collecting their wages. Among the papers in the bankruptcy proceedings is a petition presented to the court by several of the workmen, whose names appear on the accounts, who "do most humbly petition this Honored Court to be pleased that before any judgment be entered your petitioners may be payed their just dues, or such order taken that they may be payd in some short time."

Weeden speaks of the Saugus Iron Works as "a school for instructing iron workers"[6] which influenced the industry materially, however limited the success of the enterprise itself. The Leonards, Henry and James, who appear in the accounts, were among the skilled men whom Winthrop secured in England. They left the Saugus works to start other plants throughout Massachusetts, the most successful of which was at Raynham, and founded a long line of New England iron masters. Ralph Russell also left Saugus to set up a forge of his own. Joseph Jenks, one of the early American inventors, was the machinist at the Saugus Iron Works. He made the molds for the first castings, and later obtained from the superintendent of the plant a concession to start a small forge for the manufacture of edged tools. He made the dies for the "pine tree shilling" coined by the Bay Colony, and in 1654, still working at his small forge in the Saugus plant, built the first fire engine made in America. His son left the Saugus plant in 1671 and started "the forge which founded Pawtucket," R. I.[7]

In the colonial period iron and steel manufacture, Clark says, "was entirely a workshop craft. A bloomery was simply a large blacksmith's forge, generally with a power-driven bellows, or a small furnace without a stack, in which rich ores could be deoxydized in an open charcoal fire so as to form a semimolten mass or bloom of wrought iron, which was refined by hammering upon an anvil. Almost any country smithy might become a bloomery upon occasion, and we have no record of how often small quantities of iron may have been made in this way."[8] Thomas, Pennsylvania's chronicler, records one instance (1698) which suggests how profitable the smith may have found these occasional incursions into iron manufacture: "A blacksmith, (my next Neighbor) who himself, with one

[5] From an old letter, quoted by Swank, p. 94.
[6] Vol. 1, p. 178.
[7] Pawtucket Times Historical Magazine, Oct. 8, 1921 (two hundred and fiftieth anniversary).
[8] Clark, p. 169.

negro man he had, got 50s. [$10] [9] in one Day, by working up a hundred pound weight of Iron, which at 6 pence [10 cents] per pound (and that is the Common Price) amounts to that Summ."

Iron manufacture developed rapidly in all the colonies during the first half of the eighteenth century. Several successful furnaces were operated in Maryland and Virginia, but because of the wide use of indentured labor wage data concerning them is obscure. "The Virginia works used slave labor, with English or German foremen," and "the Maryland furnaces, especially in later years, used either indentured English convicts or redemptioners whose labor was sold for a term of years." [10]

Colonel Alexander Spotswood, an English engineer, served as governor of the Virginia colony for 14 years and then became, in 1724, its most prominent ironmaster. He paid his superintendent £100 ($333) a year, and had in addition a pay roll of £500 ($1,665) a year for "the founder, miner, collier, stock taker, clerk, smith, carpenter, wheelright, and several carters." [11]

Colonial furnaces in the first half of the eighteenth century, during which many sprang up, operated successfully for a brief period and then died out, have been described as "baronial and patriarchal, resembling a feudal holding or a southern plantation. They were located where forests were within easy reach and generally had a farm adjacent; with the slaves, white servants and free laborers, one of these furnaces formed a little settlement." [12] Operating methods in use in 1759, in Pennsylvania and New Jersey specifically, are given thus by a contemporary:

> The workmen are partly English and partly Irish, with some few Germans, although the work is carried on after the English method. The pig iron is melted into geese and is cast from five to six feet long and a half foot broad, for convenience in forging. The pigs are first operated upon by the finers. Then the chiffery or hammermen take it back again into their hands and beat out the long bars.
> The finers are paid 30s. [$4] [13] a ton, the hammermen 23s. 9d. [$3.15] a ton; that is to say, both together £2.13.9 [$7.15] per ton. The laborers are generally composed partly of negroes (slaves) and partly of servants from Germany or Ireland bought for a term of years. [14]

The most ambitious undertakings of the latter half of the century were those of Hasenclever in New Jersey and Stiegel in Pennsylvania. Both of these enterprises, like that of the Saugus Iron Works a hundred years before, ended in bankruptcy within a few years. Hasenclever had enormous holdings and attempted operations on a scale which would be considerable even now. Business records and statements of costs of production which he left are reproduced in Pearse's History of Iron Manufacture in the American Colonies, thus: [15]

> He set out to build five blast furnaces and seven forges, with twelve hammers and twenty-five fires. He estimated the cost of building these works at about £40,000 [$100,000] [16], and the profits from them at £10,000 [$25,000] at least—the furnaces producing 3,500 tons pig iron yearly, at a profit of two pounds, eleven shillings four pence sterling [$12.47], and the forges one thousand two

[9] Pennsylvania colonial shilling equals 20 cents.
[10] Pearse, p. 16.
[11] Idem, p. 13.
[12] Herrick, Cheesman A.: White Servitude in Pennsylvania, p. 64.
[13] Pennsylvania Shilling of Provincial era—13.3 cents. See p. 16.
[14] Acrelius, Israel: History of New Sweden. In Pennsylvania Historical Society Memoirs, Vol. IX.
[15] Pearse, pp. 67-70.
[16] New York currency—shilling is 12.5 cents.

hundred and fifty tons bar iron yearly, at a profit of seven pounds thirteen shillings sterling [$37.18] per ton.

The actual costs of producing pig and bar iron are thus detailed:

Effective Account of the Expenses and Wages paid in the Province of New Jersey, in North America, to smelt five tons of Ore into three tons of Pig Iron, and to reduce three tons of Pig Iron into two tons of Bar Iron:

	£	s.	d.	
To 5 tons of ore, with all charges rendered, at the furnace, 15s. [$1.88] per ton_____	3	15	0	($9. 38)
9 loads of charcoal, of 96 bushels each, at 20s. [$2.50] per load_____	9	0	0	($22. 50)
Wages—1 founder, at 5s. [63 cents] per day, and 9 assistants, viz: 1 keeper, 2 fillers, 2 ore breakers, 2 coal stockers, 1 gutterman, 1 bankman, at 3s. [37.5 cents] per day_____	1	12	0	($4. 00)
Salaries and repair of buildings and roads per day_____	1	0	0	($2. 50)
	15	7	0	($38. 38)

Expenses to Reduce Three Tons of Pig Iron into Two Tons of Bar Iron:

	£	s.	d.	
To 3 tons of pig iron_____	15	7	0	($38. 38)
9 loads of coal, at 96 bushels per load, at 20s. [$2.50]__	9	0	0	($22. 50)
Forgemen's wages, at £4 5s. [$10.63] per ton_____	8	10	0	($21. 25)
Salaries and repair of buildings and roads, at £3 [$7.50] per ton_____	6	0	0	($15. 00)
Transport to New York and shipping, per ton, £1 10s. [$3.75]_____	3	0	0	($7. 50)
Two tons of bar iron on board ship at New York cost, in New York currency_____	41	17	0	($104. 63)

The expenses of making bar iron at Ringwood, out of the old material extracted from the cinder heaps, is stated as follows, for 4 tons, 1 hundredweight, 2 quarters:

	£	s.	d.	
To 3½ tons of cinder iron, at £1 10s. [$3.75], New York currency per ton_____	5	5	0	($13. 13)
5 tons old forge cinders, at £1 [$2.50] per ton_____	5	0	0	($12. 50)
21¾ loads of charcoal, at 96 bushels per load, at 20s. [$2.50].	21	15	0	($54. 38)
Forgeman's wages, at £5 14s. [$14.25] per ton—(one-third more than for common bar)_____	23	3	11	($57. 98)
	55	3	11	($137. 99)

Rates at the Stiegel furnaces in Pennsylvania in 1756–1760 were less than those paid at the Saugus Iron Works a hundred years before. The prevailing daily rates were 1s. 6d. and 2s. (19 cents and 26.6 cents), while monthly wages ranged from 30s. to 60s. ($4 to $8). The ore miners received more money, 2s. 10d. to 3s. 5d. (36.6 to 45 cents), but it is possible that they were not boarded, as were the men at the forge.[17] The Mary Ann Furnace,[17] a neighbor of Stiegel's Elizabeth Furnace, paid by the month almost entirely, although the accounts occasionally show entries by the day. The prevailing monthly wage for both the miners and the forgemen was 50s. ($6.67), the range being from 45s. ($6) to £3 ($8). A higher rate of 70s. ($9.33) which appears occasionally in the accounts was probably paid to foremen. The stoker received £4 ($10.68) a month, while "night work in the smith shop" was valued at £4.10 ($12). When a daily rate was paid it was 2s. 6d. (33 cents) in nearly all cases.

The rates for hauling differed with the material hauled. Ore paid 5s. (67 cents); limestone, 7s. 6d. ($1), and sand 6s. (80 cents) per load of 132½ bushels. A man with a team earned 12s. ($1.60) a day "on his own diet."

---

17 Manuscript account books in the Library of the Historical Society of Pennsylvania.

The items of expense as shown by the account books of still another contemporary "furnace" suggest that, with the exception of the bankman, the workers were indentured servants maintained entirely by the company. Clothing, shoes, medical attendance, and the like appear frequently in the account of expenditures. Wages to the bankman at 35s. ($4.67) a month are entered regularly, and a daily rate of 2s. (26.6 cents) appears occasionally.

An interesting story of the labor system and methods of wage payment practiced in a South Carolina iron works in 1785–1795 can be read into an advertisement in the Charleston City Gazette of May 12, 1795, which announces the works for sale at public auction.[18]

The plant holdings consisted of 15,000 acres of land "on which are about twenty-five improved farms," and a settlement containing four gristmills and two sawmills. The extent of available timber was great enough that "before there will be any occasion to go to an improper distance for coal, the woods will bear a second cutting." In addition to land, buildings, and plant equipment, "there are upwards of ninety negroes attached to the works, between 70 and 80 of whom are grown, the rest are children. Most of these negroes have been employed for a considerable time at the works and are very useful and valuable as forgemen, blacksmiths, founders, miners, and various other occupations."

Workmen were paid "either in bar iron or in castings, according to their respective branches." The value of a ton of bar iron at the time, as stated in the advertisement, was £37 10s. sterling ($182.25). This reduces to 9 cents a pound in American money. The price of castings as quoted in the advertisement is 3½d. sterling, or 7 cents, per pound. The following table has been made from the statement of wages paid at the works, as given in the advertisement. Conversion to a money equivalent has been made by using the rate per pound of castings and bar iron given above.

Monthly wages (in pounds of iron) paid at the works, with money equivalent

Occupation:	Castings (pounds)	Money equivalent
Founders and keepers	1, 250	$87. 50
Fellers	154	10. 78
	Bar iron	
Laborers	{ 100	9. 00
	{ 130	11. 70
Wheelwrights	250	22. 50
Carpenters	250	22. 50
Blacksmiths	175	15. 75
Master colliers	400	36. 00
Under colliers	250	22. 50

Those paid at piece rates were the finer, the hammerer, and the wood cutters. The finer was paid 200 pounds of bar iron ($18) per long ton of "anchonies" and the hammerer 150 pounds of bar iron ($13.50) per short ton of bar iron. The woodsmen received 6 pounds of iron (54 cents) for each 4 feet by 4 feet 4 inches by 8 feet cord.

In all cases the workmen "found themselves," and, in the case of the founder, whatever he paid his keeper came out of his own monthly wages. Board, according to the proprietors, "is generally 50 pounds

18 In Documentary History of American Industrial Society, Vol. II, pp. 306–312.

iron [$4.50] per month"; "wheat, 8 pounds iron [$0.72] per bushel; * * * 4 pounds of iron ($0.36) is given per bushel for corn," while meat was from 3 to 4 cents a pound.

The proprietors assured prospective bidders that "it is probable that hands of all professions may be procured to carry on the works, and that goods would answer them better than cash in payment." They are further of the opinion that "if a store of goods well laid in was established, the hands would be better satisfied to take goods for payment at 125 per cent advance than they now are with the present mode of payment" in bar iron or castings. That method had been followed, it was explained, because there was "no store now established to furnish a regular supply to the work people."

Massachusetts foundries paid $1.13 a day to skilled foundrymen and pattern makers in 1815, and 87½ cents to unskilled.[19] The scale at the Foxhall foundry at Georgetown, in the District of Columbia, where about 30 men were employed in 1818, was $2 a day for foremen, $1.50 for molders, and $0.66⅔ for laborers.[20] By 1825 the scale had advanced in Massachusetts to $1.25 and $1.50 for skilled men.[19] In the report of Louis McLane, Secretary of the Treasury, on Statistics of Manufactures in the United States in 1832, the average pay of workers in blast furnaces, rolling mills, and foundries, is a dollar a day in all States reporting. In Connecticut and New York the most highly skilled workers received $1.50, and one New Jersey mill reported $2. The rate in New Hampshire was as low as 67 and 75 cents, but most mills paid $1.

During the Revolution the demand for ironworkers in the manufacture of arms and cannon was great, and labor was so scarce that all men employed in iron works were exempt from military duty and prisoners of war were sent into the foundries to work.

BLACKSMITHS

The blacksmith, who was also the manufacturer of tools and household utensils, was a very important factor in colonial life. Numerous records show the concessions and efforts that were made to establish blacksmiths in the new settlements, and wherever mention is made of the scarcity of labor they are included among the needed craftsmen. Advertisements for blacksmith apprentices occur repeatedly in all the early newspapers, and as a rule boys apprenticed to that trade received money payment, sometimes as much as a pound a year, as an inducement. Since blacksmiths were independent craftsmen and proprietors of their own shops almost wholly, little material as to earnings or rates of pay is available. Blacksmiths were not specified in the wage-fixing statutes of the Massachusetts colonies, so it is safe to assume that few of them were employed as journeymen. In 1639 two of the craft in Massachusetts, "in behalfe of themselves and the rest of the blacksmiths within this Colony," petitioned the colonial court for "advice and help" in meeting an acute situation created by the rise in the price of coal from "30s. [$7.29] a chaldron (36 bushels) to £4 [$19.44] lacking but 2s. (i. e. £3 18s.) [$18.95] a chaldron." Moreover, "they are forced speedily

---

[19] Massachusetts Bureau of Statistics of Labor: History of Wages and Prices in Massachusetts, 1752-1883, p. 171.
[20] Warden, D. B.: A Statistical, Political, and Historical Account of the United States, Vol. III, p. 214, footnote.

to buy them at that great price or els they can not be gotten for money, but are bought up and sent away into other parts of this Continent." The petitioning blacksmiths feared that "unlesse some speedy remedy be found out to help and prevent these mischeifes their trade will be much hurt and the commonwealth deeply prejudiced." [21]

The blacksmiths and the commonwealth must have weathered the crisis some way without the necessary governmental aid to business, for the court took no action on the petition.

Journeyman blacksmiths were paid 1 florin (40 cents) a day in New Amsterdam in 1637. A hundred and fifty years later the rate in New York City was $1 a day, while the journeyman rate in Massachusetts toward the close of the eighteenth century was $0.66⅔. In a table of the "price of labour" in South Carolina in 1710, appearing in a brief history of the colony attributed to the governor of the period,[22] blacksmiths are the highest paid craftsmen in the list, at 7s. 6d. ($1.25) a day. In western Pennsylvania a hundred years later "a blacksmith earns $20 a month and board, and he lives in a cabin of one room for which, with a garden, he pays $20 a year." [23]

In 1774 Thomas Jefferson made an agreement "with Francis Bishop that he shall work at the smith trade with Barnaby, whom he is to teach. I am to build him a house and a shop at Shadwell and to find him 400 pounds of pork and corn for himself. Also I am to find him tools, but if I can not get them in time he is to use his own until I can. He and Barnaby are to get their own coal and wood (but I waggon in the coal) and we go halves in the profits of the business." The arrangement as to wood was apparently changed afterwards, as six weeks later, on the day "Bishop the blacksmith begins to work for me," an entry reads: "George Bradley goes to cutting wood for Bishop, for which I am to pay him, by the month, £8 [$26.67] and meat a year. He pays his own levies and taxes and clothes himself." [24]

At the close of the seventeenth century (1690) a Salem blacksmith charged 1s. (16.7 cents) for shoeing a horse and 1s. 6d. (25 cents) for "makeing a bolt." [25]   A bill for smith work done at Province House in Boston in 1742 reads: [26]

	£	s.	d.	
To 3 strong padlocks to stable	1	6	0	($0. 78)
To 2 hasps and 4 staples to ditto		7	0	($0. 21)
To a bar and 2 long staples to coach house		15	0	($0. 45)
To a strong pair H hinges and 8 screws and nails to a door under the Great Stairs		10	0	($0. 30)
To a new large lock and bolting on with screws on stable door	1	8		($0. 84)

Five years later, after the devastating fire which swept Boston in 1747,[27] a smith presents a bill for four days' work at the Province House, at 25 shillings [50 cents] a day, for "removing and taking care of ironwork preserved from the flames." [26]

[21] Lechford's Notebook, p. 184.
[22] In Carroll's South Carolina Historical Collections, Vol. 2, p. 261.
[23] Birkbeck, Morris: Notes on a Journey in America from the Coast of Virginia to the Territory of Illinois, p. 35.
[24] Jefferson's manuscript account books, Massachusetts Historical Society.
[25] Manuscript account book, Essex Institute.
[26] Massachusetts State Archives.
[27] Depreciated currency—shilling worth about 3 cents in 1712, and 2 cents in 1747.

These bills against the Province House are of course stated in "old tenor" currency, the depreciated paper of the period, which for the five years referred to ran 30s. to 50s. to the Spanish dollar.[28]

Shoeing a horse "all round" cost 3s. (40 cents) in Maryland in 1771, and 4s. (53 cents) during the war.[29] The Portsmouth, N. H., "Town Committee for Regulating Prices" fixed 5s. per pound as the price blacksmiths could charge "for weight work" and "for shoeing a horse all round not above £6 and for shifting a sett of shoes, 30s."[30] This proclamation was dated October 1, 1779, at which time, according to the State Committee's Scale of Depreciated Currency [30] it took £2,030 in continental paper to be worth £100 in coin. At that rate the staggering sum of £6 for shoeing a horse becomes about one-twentieth of that, or 6s. ($1), a figure somewhat more comparable to the Maryland price. Six pounds was also the price in Pennsylvania in the same year for "shoeing a horse with four new shoes." The pre-war price in that Province was 5s. (66.7 cents).[31]

NAILS

That nails should have been a really serious problem in any age seems almost fantastic now. Nevertheless the need for nails played an important part in colonial economics, and the value attached to their possession can be appreciated when one realizes that in early Virginia nails were a part of a planter's estate, listed in inventories and mentioned in wills. Throughout the first century of settlement, evidently, all the nails used by the colonists were imported, and so valuable were they that, Bruce relates—

Small landowners, in deserting their homes with a view to making a settlement elsewhere on more fertile soil, were in the habit of burning their cabins when abandoned, in order to secure the nails by which the planks were held together, and so general did this habit become that in 1644–45 it was provided by law, as a means of destroying the motive for setting the houses on fire, that each planter, when he gave up his dwelling, should be allowed, at public expense, as many nails as two impartial men should calculate to be in the frame of the deserted residence.[32]

After the manufacture of iron commenced in the colonies, slitting mills were established which cut bar iron into nail-rods, and the manufacture of nails became a widespread industry. It was a common practice for "country people to erect small forges in their chimney corners and in winter, and in evenings, when little other work can be done, great quantities of nails are made, even by children. These people take the rod iron of the merchant and return him the nails and in consequence of this easy mode of barter the manufacture is prodigiously great."[33] Advertisements of nails for sale in large or small quantities are pretty sure to be found in the early newspapers.

Factory production began to displace the home manufacture of hand wrought nails after 1790, with the introduction of a nail-cutting machine. Within a few years many machines for making nails were patented and put into operation, and "the occupation of making nails in the chimney corner met with a serious check."[34]

[28] See p. 17.
[29] Dixon manuscript account books, Library of Congress.
[30] New Hampshire Broadsides, Library of Congress.
[31] Norris Manuscript account books, Historical Society of Pennsylvania.
[32] Bruce, Philip A.: Economic History of Virginia in the 17th Century, Vol. II, p. 146–147.
[33] Quoted in Swank, p. 99.
[34] Swank, p. 99.

Thomas Jefferson ran a nail factory on his Monticello plantation, which must have been an enterprising business, to judge from the many entries in his account books of purchases of nail rods in large quantities. The work was done by slaves. It was Jefferson's practice to work negro boys between 16 and 19 years of age in the "nailery," under the supervision of an overseer. In 1803 he was paying the overseer £10 ($33.33) a year for his services as superintendent of the nailery, in addition to wages paid him for other duties about the plantation. Jefferson decided to change that method, however, and "from the commencement of the ensuing year he is to have 2 per cent on all the nails sold instead of the 10 pounds."[35]

In 1781 nail makers in one of the early factories in Massachusetts were paid 48 cents a day. By 1817 this rate had more than doubled and in the manufacture of tacks the workers were paid $1 a day. The piece rate in tack factories was 2.8 cents per thousand in 1822, by which time the day rate had increased to $1.25.[36] Daily earnings of pieceworkers in a Pennsylvania nail factory in 1832 were $1 to $1.50.[37]

Processes and earnings in a nail factory in Salem, Mass., in 1810, are given thus by a visitor to the works:

Two heading machines are contrived to support by two levers the nail against an immovable cap. * * * The rollers for the iron slitting mill are powerful. The cutting machines are of different sizes, with different motions. The larger machine is fed by tongs led by a pulley. The smaller is fed by hand and can give 1,400 strokes in a minute. The machine for heading is not used since the first experiment, as it is found heading is done better by hand than any machine as yet invented both as to time and goodness of execution. Board for the workmen can be had at 15s. [$2.50] a week, and the men who head have about an average of 5s. [83.3 cents] per hundredweight and can earn from 6s. to 9s. [$1 to $1.50] a day.[38]

---

[35] Jefferson's manuscript account books.
[36] Massachusetts Bureau of Statistics of Labor: History of Wages and Prices in Massachusetts, 1752–1883, p. 172.
[37] Statistics of Manufactures, Vol. II, p. 215.
[38] Diary of William Bentley, D. D. (published by Essex Institute), p. 498.

Chapter 6.—GLASS INDUSTRY

One of the first manufactures undertaken in the colonies was glass, but in spite of repeated efforts and the availability of excellent material, the industry attained no really successful footing for more than a century. A glasshouse was started in Virginia during the second year of settlement, manned by skilled workmen from Europe. The prime interest of the Virginia Company in promoting the manufacture of glass was "the necessity of providing a large quantity of beads for the use of the settlers in their trade with the Indian natives." [1] The first venture failed after Smith left the colony, and "nothing more was heard of glass manufacture in Virginia until 1621, in which year there was an effort to establish it on a permanent footing." [2]

This second effort consisted of transporting "four Italians skilled in glass-making" and erecting a factory, but the enterprise was a failure from the start.

Salem, Mass., granted land in 1639 to several men for the purpose of promoting the manufacture of glass. After the reorganization of the company a few years later the Salem glasshouse operated for 25 or 30 years, but "it is probable that nothing more was attempted than the manufacture of bottles and other coarse descriptions of glass."

The great increase in New England population and prosperity * * * and the improvements already taking place in the construction of the dwellings, would have rendered the domestic manufacture of window glass a special boon to the country. But its fabrication is altogether a more difficult and expensive matter than that of bottles and the coarser household wares. Hence we find that the first dwelling houses of the colonists, in all parts of the country, were very generally—with the exception of those of some of the wealthier emigrants—destitute of glass windows.[3]

New York, New Jersey, and Pennsylvania made early efforts at glassmaking, but "notwithstanding these attempts in different quarters to manufacture glass, and the existence of good material, from which the purest glass is now made, * * * no great progress was made before the Revolution." [4]

Two concerns, however, one in New Jersey and one in Pennsylvania, had achieved a fair degree of success and had passed out of existence before the close of the Revolution. Of these, the New Jersey plant was the older. It was established by Caspar Wistar, at Alloway, N. J., in 1739, and operated until 1780, manufacturing "bottles and coarse green window glass." [5]

Wistar made an agreement with four expert German glassmakers to pay their passage to America, "they to teach the art of glassmaking to him and his son Richard and to no one else; and he to provide land, fuel, servants, food, and material for a glass factory in the province of New Jersey; to advance money for all expenses, including

---

[1] Bruce, Philip A.: Economic History of Virginia in the Seventeenth Century, Vol. II, p. 440.
[2] Idem, p. 441.
[3] Bishop, J. Leander: History of American Manufactures, 1608-1860, Vol. I, p. 234.
[4] Idem, p. 236.
[5] Clark, Victor S.: History of Manufactures in the United States, 1607-1860, p. 209.

their support, and to give them one-third of the net profits of the enterprise."[6]

While nothing was found bearing directly on the working force of Wistar's plant, Bishop says it "employed quite a number of German workmen,"[7] and it is very likely that most of the operatives were indentured servants. That they were housed at the works is evident from the inventory published in the advertisement which offered the plant for sale. This inventory, printed in the Pennsylvania Journal of October 11, 1780, reads:[8]

Two furnaces with the necessary ovens for casting glass, drying wood, etc. Nearby are two flattening ovens in separate houses, a store house, a pot house, a house with tables for cutting glass, stamping mill, rolling mill for preparing glass for working pots. Dwellings for workmen. Mansion house, 6 rooms to a floor. Bake house and wash house. Store house.

Scarcity of skilled labor in the second generation seems to have been chiefly responsible for the failure of the Wistar works after 40 years of a fairly substantial business. In fact, the difficulty in getting and keeping trained workmen accounts in large part for the invariable failures of the many early attempts at glassmaking in the colonies. Governor Moore of New York wrote to the Lords of Trade and Plantations in 1767 that "the Master of a Glass House which was set up here a few years ago, now a bankrupt, assured me that his ruin was owing to no other cause than being deserted by the Servants he had imported at great expense."[9]

The first attempts at flint-glass manufacture to achieve any stability were those made by Henry William Stiegel, in Pennsylvania, beginning in 1763. Stiegel was an iron master, but branched out first into the manufacture of ordinary window glass and bottles, and later, at his last factory at Manheim, into the ambitious efforts in decorated and colored art glass which, though ending in speedy bankruptcy, produced nevertheless the first American flint glass of any artistic value or interest. In his study of "Stiegel Glass," Frederick William Hunter estimates flint glass to have been 30 per cent of the output of the Manheim factory.[10] To students of early glass, Hunter believes—

It is of course perfectly evident that Stiegel had expert help trained in the Bristol technique; also that he had German workmen whose knowledge of the use of vitrifiable enamels was a professional one. And not only were the blowers and decorators employed in the last glass house thus specially trained, but the pot men and foremen who mixed and made the delicately colored glasses of the later period of the factory were evidently experts. The conclusion is therefore warranted that Stiegel brought men over from Europe especially for the manning of his last factory. But the direct evidence of this that I have been able to find is so slight that the fact of his having, on June 5, 1772, taken on three indentured servants—Archibald Jackson for 4 years at £15 [$40]; Patrick Flanigan for 5 years at £15; and John Williams for 7 years at £15—is about the extent of it.[11]

Discussing processes in the Stiegel works, Hunter says:

It is likely, from the wording of his advertisements, that both the "crown" method (by which an opened bubble of glass was spun into a flat circular disc from which window panes were cut) and the "sheet" method (in which an oblong cylinder of glass was first fashioned and then cut longitudinally by a diamond and allowed to open and flatten out under the influence of heat), were practiced

[6] Hunter, Frederick William: Stiegel Glass, p. 159.
[7] Bishop, Vol. I, p. 236.
[8] Quoted by Hunter.
[9] O'Callaghan's Documentary History of New York, Vol. I, p. 733.
[10] Hunter, p. 225.
[11] Idem, p. 72.

at the works. On the other hand, the common run of bottles were usually, at this time, blown in crude clay moulds that were open at the top and about as deep as the body of the bottle. The body of the bottle being thus formed, the punty rod was attached to the bottom (driving it in a bit in the operation), and the neck of the bottle drawn out by means of the blowpipe.[12]

Fortunately the account books of the Manheim works have been preserved and are in the manuscript collection of the Historical Society of Pennsylvania, and while the bookkeeping is extremely crude, at times even erratic, it is possible to arrive at Stiegel's wage scale from the scattered entries.

From 1763 to 1770 most of the glassmakers were paid by the piece, the scales of prices for which, per dozen, were as follows:

Window glass:	s.	d.	Cents	Tableware—Continued.	s.	d.	Cents
8 x 10	6	0	80	Salts	2	0	26. 6
7 x 9	5	0	66. 7	Cream jugs (each)	0	2	2
6 x 8	4	0	53	Bottles:			
5 x 7	2	6	32. 6	Gallon	3	0	40
4 x 6	1	6	19	Quart	1	6	19
Tableware:				Pint	1	1	14
Small glasses	3	0	40	Gill	1	0	13. 3
Plates	4	0	53				

Some workers were time workers even in this early period. Daily rates, where quoted, are 2s. 8d. and 3s. (34.6 and 40 cents), while monthly wages ranged from £1 10s. ($4) for boys to £3 and £3 10s. ($8 and $9.33) for shearers.

Piecework seems to have been abolished at the beginning of 1771, and all of the regular staff put on a monthly basis under monthly or yearly agreements. Monthly wages remained about the same—the skilled men getting from £3 to £3 10s., while wages of unskilled workers and boys ranged between £1 ($2.67) and £2 15s. ($7.33).

The agreements state specifically that the employee is "to work at anything he is put to, Teazing alone excepted." In that occupation a definite agreement was made—for example, "this day agreed with George Kloppert for to teaze in the glasshouse for the time of one year from this date at £3 10s. per month." An agreement covering tender boys reads:

Agreement made this day with John Nowman for his Two Boys to work in the Glasshouse at tending the Glassmakers or any other work they shall be ordered to do by H. W. Stiegel or any of his Deputies for and during this present Blast, for which the said Nowman is to receive the sum of Two pounds Ten shillings [$6.67] per month. The said Nowman is to find them their accomodations.

Another agreement, probably covering unskilled labor of a general nature, states that "Martin Betz is to work in the glasshouse or anywhere else where he is ordered at any Business that he shall be ordered to do, during the time of 12 Months, for which he is to receive £31 [$82.67] or the value thereof, finding his own accommodations during the whole Time." A postscript adds that "he is also to have 10 pounds of Nails in Bargain." A teamster agreed "to drive ox team for one year at £33 [$88.20] and in Bargain one pair of Shoes."

Later, in 1773–1775, after Stiegel had begun to specialize in art glass, he paid considerably higher wages for the skilled work. Expert

---

[12] Hunter, p. 187.

workmen, largely imported from England, Germany, and Italy, were paid salaries ranging from £5 1s. 9d. to £5 11s. 4d. ($13.56 to $14.84) a month. One of his specialists, however, he did not import. Hunter reproduces in facsimile [13] a "Memorandum of Agreement made this Fourth Day of June, 1773, between Henry William Stiegel, owner of the American Flint Glass Manufactory of the one Side, and Lazarus Isaacs, Glass Cutter of Philadelphia, of the other Side." Isaacs was to be employed as "cutter and flowerer at £5 10s. ($14.67) per month." Stiegel was to furnish him "a house to live in and also a piece of land for a garden. As to firewood, he is to be supplied like the other workmen at five shillings [66.7 cents] per cord hawled to his Door. For the Rest of the Materials belonging to his Work said H. W. Stiegel is to find them, except his own Tools and Utensils belonging to his work." A penalty clause involving "£1,000 lawful money of Pennsylvania" [$2,670] was attached for violation of the agreement by either party.

After Stiegel's financial collapse, which he tried unsuccessfully to check by means of a lottery, the works were abandoned and no effort was ever made to revive the industry.

The manuscript accounts of the Boston Glass Works in 1794 show that "the aggregate week's wages of a foreman, 8 assistants and a boy, were $58.50. Probably the glassmakers, who were imported workmen, received about $1 a day.[14] Twenty-five years later, average daily wages in the industry in Massachusetts, according to State report, were $2.04 for gaffers, $1.63 for cutters, $1.05 for journeymen in unspecified occupations, and 54 cents for boys. By 1840 these rates had increased to $2.87 for gaffers, $2.22 for cutters, and $1.50 for unclassified journeymen. Boys' wages remained the same.[15]

The McLane report, covering about the same period, gives a general average for all skilled occupations of $1.30 a day, and 50 cents a day for boys, in the Massachusetts factories.[16]

In the glass industry in Pennsylvania boys earned $1.50 to $3.50 a week, while of the flint glassworks reporting, one stated that "wages vary from $5 to $20 per week for men."[17] Another gave $14 a week as the highest amount earned. In window-glass manufacture, one concern paid its blowers 85 cents per 100 feet, and its cutters $18 a box, while time workers received $18 a month. Boys were paid $4 a month. Another reported only annual earnings—"10 men at an average of $450 per annum; 5 at $200; 2 at $150; 1 at $125; and 10 boys at $50 per annum. Eight hours a day, nine months in the year."[18]

The oldest existing union scale in glass bottle blowing, dated June 22, 1846, is reproduced in the appendix. Union officials pointed out that piece rates for identical and comparable articles in the current union scale do not differ materially from these early rates, the difference in earning power lying, of course, in the vastly greater production by machine processes.

---

[13] Hunter, p. 73.
[14] Clark, p. 394.
[15] Massachusetts State Bureau of Statistics of Labor, History of Wages and Prices in Massachusetts 1752-1860, p. 166.
[16] Statistics of Manufactures, 1832, Vol. I, p. 525.
[17] Idem, Vol. II, p. 523.
[18] Idem, Vol. II, p. 532.

Chapter 7.—TEXTILE INDUSTRIES

HOUSEHOLD MANUFACTURE

During the first 75 years of colonial settlement textile manufacture was so wholly a household industry that, in New England and the middle colonies at least, nearly every home was a textile factory. The southern colonies, at a decided trade advantage in being able to exchange their tobacco for imported fabrics, were not under the necessity for home production which impelled their northern neighbors.

Because each household was practically self-sufficient, the question of rates of pay for cloth manufacture does not enter until the close of the seventeenth century, with the appearance of the itinerant and the custom weavers. Skilled workers were needed to finish the home product, and from the first they established "fulling mills" which dressed and finished the coarse home-made fabrics. But they have left no record of what their services were worth. The first fulling mill was established in Rowley, Mass., about 1643, by 20 skilled textile workers from Yorkshire, England, who brought their equipment with them. "This appears to have been the first place at which woolen cloth was made in New England." [1] Fulling mills sprang up rapidly throughout the colonies, and are the beginnings of mill production of cloth; but, according to Bishop, even after their introduction, "much of the woolen cloth of household manufacture was worn in its unfulled and unfinished state." [1]

Despite the mother country's policy of prohibiting the manufacture of textiles in the colonies, colonial authorities at various times throughout the first century offered bounties from public funds on cloth manufacture and on the necessary raw material. Furthermore, Massachusetts Bay Colony undertook to make home spinning obligatory by an order that—

All hands not necessarily employed on other occasions, as women, boys and girls, shall and are hereby enjoined to spin according to their skill and ability, and that the selectmen in every town do consider the condition and capacity of every family, and accordingly assess them as one or more spinners. And because several families are necessarily employed the greater part of their time in other business, yet, if opportunities were attended, some time might be spared, at least by some of them, for this work; the said selectmen shall therefore assess such families at half or a quarter of a spinner, according to their capacities. Secondly, and that every one thus assessed for a whole spinner, do after the present year, 1656, spin for 30 weeks eavery yeare 3 pounds per week of linnen, cotton or woollen, and so proportionally for half or quarter spinners, under the penalty of 12d. for every pound short. [2]

Later the spinning school was evolved, out of which, perhaps, grew the conception of employing child labor in textile manufacture. The Virginia colony passed a law in 1646 calling for the establishment of two flax houses, under the direction of a master and mistress appointed by the assembly, to which each county was required to send two

---

[1] Bishop, J. Leander: History of American Manufactures, 1608–1860, Vol. I, p. 304.
[2] Massachusetts Bay Colony Records, Vol. III, p. 396.

children, "male or female, of the age of eight or seven at least, whose parents were too poor to educate them, to be instructed in the art of carding, knitting, and spinning. In order that ample provision might be made for the health and comfort of the pupils, each county was required to supply the two children whom it sent with six barrels of Indian corn, a sow, two laying hens, linen and woolen apparel, shoes, hose, a bed, rug, blanket, two coverlets, a wooden bowl or tray, and two pewter spoons."[3] This school appears to have existed only on paper, and in 1663 the General Assembly passed another law directing each county to provide for "educating and instructing poor children in the knowledge of spinning, weaving, and other useful occupations."[4] Early in the eighteenth century two concurrent movements were started in Boston to establish spinning schools for children. One was a public enterprise, the funds for which were raised by popular subscription and later by a luxury tax. A large brick building was erected, and the school "was spiritedly conducted for a few years, but was soon abandoned."[5] The other spinning school was the philanthropic undertaking of a Boston merchant, to provide employment for the children of the poor. Textile manufacture as a means of poor relief was also tried in New York City when, in 1734, it built an almshouse and installed four spinning wheels, flax, and knitting equipment "for the relief and setting on work of poor needy persons" and inmates.

"These movements," Weeden says, "helped to make spinners at home, but went no further."[6] How extensive home manufacture was can be gathered from reports of colonial governors to the British Board of Trade. It was to the interests of the governors to minimize the degree of commercial manufacture, since it was specifically prohibited by the home government, but they could not cover up the fact that home manufacture made the rank and file of colonists independent of imports, even if their statements as to manufacture for sale were strictly true. A New York governor reported that in 1708 the inhabitants of the Province "already make very good serges, linsey-woolseys, and in some places they begin to make coarse cloth and without doubt in a short time they will so far improve in that as not to want the assistance of England to clothe themselves."[7] In Virginia at the same time Governor Spotswood found that—

The people being disappointed of the necessary supply of Cloathing for their familys in return for their tobacco found themselves under the necessity of attempting to Cloath themselves with their own manufacture. This is now become so universal that even in one of the best countys for tobacco I'm credibly informed that there has been made this last year above 40,000 yards of divers sorts of woolen, cotton and linnen Cloath.[8]

"Country people and planters" in Massachusetts at about the same time, according to a colonial official's statement, had "entered so far into making their own woolens that not one in forty but wears his own carding, spinning, etc."[9]

---

[3] Bruce, Philip A.: Economic History of Virginia in the 17th Century, Vol. II, p. 455.
[4] Hening's Virginia Statutes, Vol. II, p. 266.
[5] Bishop, Vol. I, p. 333.
[6] Weeden, William B.: Economic and Social History of New England, 1620–1789, Vol. I, p. 305.
[7] In O'Callaghan's Documents, Vol. V, p. 59.
[8] Gov. Spotswood's Report to British Council of Trade, Mar. 20, 1710, in Virginia Historical Society Collections, Vol. I, pp. 72–73.
[9] Clark, Victor S.: History of Manufactures in the United States, 1607–1860, p. 199.

Ten years before the Revolution Governor Moore, of New York, reported that—

The custom of making these coarse cloths prevails in private families throughout the whole province, and almost in very house a sufficient quantity is manufactured for the use of that family, without the least design of sending any of it to market. This I had the opportunity of seeing in the late tour that I made, and had the same accounts given me by all the persons of whom I made inquiry; for every house swarms with children, who are set to work as soon as they are able to spin and card, and as every family is furnished with a loom, the itinerant weavers who travel about the country put the finishing hand to the work.[10]

The implements used in this widespread household industry were the spinning wheel, "an antique form of the common hand loom, and, after its invention about the year 1670, * * * the weaver's loom in its present form; hand cards and combs for preparing the material, and a primitive form of shuttle. Stock cards, the drop box, the flying shuttle, and the whole series of later improvements in carding, spinning, and weaving, were not then invented. Nearly all the processes of manufacture were manual operations, and the appliances few and imperfect. Even the dressing of woolen cloth, with a tolerably good supply of fulling mills, was imperfectly and laboriously performed." [11]

The material produced was chiefly linsey-woolsey, made with linen warp and a coarse woolen filling, kersey, and serge, both of which consisted of wool in various forms combined with tow or linen, and fabrics made of linen and hemp. "The dress of apprentices and laborers almost invariably comprised shirts of home-manufactured 'ozenbrig' made of hemp or flax, and varying in price from one to one shilling and sixpence per yard; and vests and breeches of the same or of coarse tow cloth. Coats, or doublets, and breeches of leather, or enduring buckskin, and coats also of kersey, drugget, duroy, frieze, etc.; felt hats, coarse leather shoes with brass buckles and often wooden heels, and coarse yarn or worsted stockings, were the outer habiliments of that class and were principally of home manufacture." [12]

Weaving seems to have been the first process to break away from concentration within the household. Weaving on the home loom by itinerant weavers, and by men who used their own looms, working up their neighbors' homespun yarns for them on a contract basis, developed toward the end of the seventeenth century and was practiced by individuals who, presumably, had skill and speed superior to the general run of household workers. Itinerant weavers, according to Thomas, speaking of Pennsylvania in 1698, "have twelve pence (1s.) [20 cents] the yard for Weaving of that which is little more than half a yard in breadth." A Connecticut itinerant weaver in 1713 charged 1s. 3d. (21 cents) per yard for plain cloth and checked shirting, and 1s. (16.7 cents) a yard for drugget.

Contract or custom weaving must have developed specialized weave shops because of the skill of individual operatives, but the record, Weeden says, is "mostly but not all lost." An inventory filed at New Haven, Conn., in 1684, included five looms, one of them a silk loom, and because the man whose estate was inventoried was not wealthy Weeden infers that "his business consisted in weaving custom work on these five looms. He must have employed hired

---

[10] Reports to Board of Trade, quoted by Clark, p. 209.
[11] Bishop, Vol. I, pp. 332–333.
[12] Idem, Vol. I, p. 331.

laborers or his six children in the work. The fact of the silk loom evinces especial skill in the art."[13]

Later, in 1696, a record appears of "an humble dyer, comber, weaver, and fuller" of Boston who, Weeden thinks, was probably "the first organizer" of the textile industry in America.

He dyed wool, using two furnaces, and he combed it, either colored or white. Doubtless the spinning was done in the homesteads of eastern Massachusetts by the dames, or the daughters of the dames, who had been taught in the spinning classes. The wool might be their own, or "put out" by Cornish for the spinning. Evidently he traded his manufacture for that of others; he combed and wove, but he did not card or spin. Dyeing in two furnaces, combing with two combs, weaving with four looms, a detached and independent fulling mill, would make a considerable business.[14]

The record does not show, however, the value of his labor in carrying on his business. The inventory gives only the price per yard of the product, and it is not until 75 years later that figures are available showing the labor charge in a similar enterprise. An advertisement in the Virginia Gazette (Williamsburg) of January 13, 1774, reads:[15]

This is to inform the Publick and those Gentlemen in particular who were so kind to assist me in may Plan for executing my Fulling Mill that it is now complete and at Work. All persons that are disposed to encourage this laudable Undertaking I shall be obliged to for their Favours. I advise the Publick that I have two Looms at Work that weave five Quarter Yard wide Cloth, as it is much to the Manufacturers Advantage to have their Cloth wove of that Width. My Price for weaving is 1s. a yard; Fulling, Dying, Dressing, &c. 1s. more for common cloth, but dearer for Live Colours.

The advertisement states further that "it is to be observed for I Work for ready Money only."

An advertisement in the Boston News Letter of March 8, 1770, proposed the establishment of a woolen mill with the following estimated annual pay roll: 1 comber at £40 ($133.33); 4 weavers at £40 each; 15 spinners at £15 ($50); 3 winders of worsted and yarn at £12 ($40); 2 boys at £15 ($50); and a manager at £100 ($333).

These rates of course apply to mill production, rudimentary though it was. 'Rates paid to home spinners and weavers by the "manufactories," which were little more than distributing centers, the yarn merchants or the custom weavers, are here presented as compiled from various sources by Mr. Clark in his History of Manufactures, 1609–1860:

From the close of the seventeenth century until the introduction of automatic machinery for spinning and weaving the cost of textile operations in America remained constant. About the year 1700 yarns of cotton, flax or wool were spun for 8 cents a run, the equivalent of 4 cents a skein in later measurements; and the cost of spinning the coarse cotton or woolen yarns then used was about 20 cents a pound. During the Revolution the rates paid textile labor in New England remained the same as in the earlier period. Linen warps, cotton filling, and tow yarn were spun for 8 cents a run. In Virginia the price for spinning wool varied from 11 to 25 cents a pound, and for cotton from 33 to 67 cents. After the Revolution the spinners working at the Hartford woolen manufactory received 8 cents a run or about 20 cents a pound for spinning wool. In the South most of the spinning was done in families or by slave girls, and very few entries for this labor occur in southern account books, though weaving items are common. In 1782 the cost of spinning in Virginia varied from 17 cents a pound for coarse tow yarns used in making osnaburgs to 33 cents a pound for cotton warp used in mixed cotton and woolen goods.

---

[13] Weeden, Vol. I, p. 305.
[14] Idem, Vol. I, pp. 389–390.
[15] In Documentary History of American Industrial Society, Vol. II, p. 326.

These data, fragmentary as they are, indicate clearly that the price of household textile labor had remained stationary for over a century, and that the labor-cost of spinning normally ranged from 20 to 30 cents per pound of yarn, according to the fineness of the product and the material employed.

At the opening of the eighteenth century the usual price for making coarse fabrics of cotton and linen, kerseys, and worsteds, in Massachusetts, varied from 6 to 8 cents a yard. From that time until the Revolution cottons, woolens, and towcloth, plain and striped, were woven for 4.5 and 5 cents a yard. The Virginia price for weaving country cloth of cotton and linen was somewhat higher, or from 5.5 to 6.5 cents a yard. Jeans were woven for 21 cents, tickings for 25 cents, fine linen for 28 cents, and coarse osnaburgs for about 10 cents. In New Jersey during the Revolution the price of weaving linen cloth was about 7 and 8 cents a yard, "coating" 13 cents, and double-width linen 16 cents. Stripes from dyed weft, necessitating the use of three or four shuttles, were woven for 16 cents a yard, and sheetings for about the same price.

The New Jersey rate for weaving woolen cloth and worsted in 1787 and 1788 was 13.33 cents a yard, or 1 Pennsylvania shilling. The Hartford Woolen Manufactory a year later paid 12 to 14 cents a yard for weaving coarse cassimeres and coatings. At the close of the Revolution the price of weaving coarse cotton, and cotton and woolen cloths, in Virginia, was 5.67 cents, while fine woolen cloths were woven for three times that amount, or a shilling a yard. Shirtings that sold for 55 cents a yard were woven for 8.33 cents.[16]

Dyeing of yarn and cloth for the home weavers was carried on at first in 1-man shops quite independently of the textile mills. Newspaper advertisements give an idea of this business. John Hickey, "living at the South End of Boston next house to the Sign of the White Horse," advertised in the Boston Gazette of September 1, 1760, that he "has furnished himself with all sorts of utensils fit to carry on the Business of Silk or Cloth Dyeing. * * * and prints Linnens with True Blues and Whites." He worked for cash only, and charged 1 shilling (16.7 cents) per pound for dyeing linen or cotton blue "and all other goods in proportion, and engages his work as well as if sent to London."

A Nashville, Tenn., dyer in 1804 advertised: "Blue, Red, Green, Black and Yellow Dying—I will color cotton and linen thread a deep blue at four shillings sixpence [56 cents] per pound, and a light blue at two shillings sixpence [31 cents] per pound; and the other colors mentioned I will dye upon woolens at two shillings [25 cents] per pound."[17]

The many spinning mills which grew up after the Revolution greatly increased the amount of home weaving for the market, and as late as 1810 "only 2 per cent of the cloth made in America was produced in factories."[18] The way in which these sporadic establishments kept down labor costs is suggested by the very frank advertisement of a Connecticut plant appearing in the Connecticut Courant of May 4, 1795, which announced that a new mill had been opened which "proposes to receive as apprentices to the cotton and woolen manufactory any number of boys and girls from the age of 10 to 14. They will be instructed in the various branches of the factory, well clothed and well fed, and taught to read, write and cipher, and parents may be assured that the most particular attention will be paid to the morals as well as the education of the children." Timothy Dwight visited a Connecticut mill during his travels and reported that "the principal part of the labour in attending the machinery in the cotton and woolen manufactories is done by women and children; the former hired at from 50 cents to one dollar a week; the latter are apprentices who are regularly instructed in reading, writing and arithmetic. The wages of the men are from 5 to 21 dollars a month." [19]   According to an old letter, another Connecticut mill was at one time working 73 children from a New York almshouse as indentured apprentices.[20] Moses Brown, Slater's partner, expressed the opinion that the general practice of employing children had resulted in "nearly a total saving of labor to the country."[21]

Samuel Slater was the working superintendent of both the first two mills started by him and his several partners with Arkwright spinning machinery and "received in each case $1.50 per day for his services, making his wages $3.00 a day."[22]

These early spinning mills gave out the yarn to be woven by home weavers on hand looms.   There are abundant data on weaving rates per yard for hand weaving in the period between the rise of the spinning mill, after about 1790, and the introduction of power looms about 1817.   These rates show a very wide range, but unfortunately do not often specify the kind of cloth woven.   The Batchelder mill at New Ipswich, Mass., "often had more than 100 weavers, some of whom came 6 or 8 miles to receive the yarn and to return the woven cloth, the price paid for weaving being 3 to 7 cents a yard."[23]   The product in this case was sheeting and shirtings.   "A fair adult hand-loom weaver," according to Carroll D. Wright, could "weave from 42 to 48 yards of common shirting per week."[24]   Applying the rate paid at the New Ipswich mill, home weavers on this grade of goods might earn from $1.50 to $3 a week.   In the same year, 1807, a Rhode Island mill was paying from 8 to 17 cents a yard for dress plaids, probably ginghams.

A Maryland company, with mills at Baltimore and Ellicott City; was in 1812–1815 the largest spinning concern in the country, operating 8,000 spindles. Their weavers were paid 12 cents a yard for weaving a cotton fabric running 40 picks to the inch, 3 yards to the pound, and earned about 50 cents a day. The Virginia rate was 10 cents a yard.

The mill at Pittsfield, Mass., manufacturing high-grade broadcloth, paid its weavers 40 to 60 cents a yard in 1805. These weavers worked at the mill, however, on special looms.

A weaver's ticket used by the Slater mill in Pawtucket, R. I., is here reproduced. On the back, written in ink, is the date—July 4, 1817. These tickets, given out at the mill with the yarn, are the instructions to the weavers for producing the particular kind of fabric or pattern desired.

[19] Travels in New England and New York, quoted in Bagnall's Textile Industries in the United States, p. 354.
[20] Quoted in Bagnall, p. 357.
[21] Letter in Hamilton papers, Library of Congress, cited by Clark, p. 398.
[22] Lewton, Frederick L.: Samuel Slater and the Oldest Cotton Machinery in America, in Annual Report of Smithsonian Institution, 1926, p. 506.
[23] Bagnall, William: Textile Industries in the United States, p. 477.
[24] In "The Factory System of the United States," in Census of 1880, Vol. II, p. 585.

Pattern, No. *56*.
To be warped *31*. Beer in a *42*.
Slaie   Yards   Spools
Skeins on a Spool will warp the piece.
Weight *22* lb. *1* oz.   No.
  112 Skeins.   *D. Blue.*   Warp. *12*.
   28 do.   *White.*   do.
      do.   do.
      do.   do.
      do.   do.
      do.   do.
  112 Skeins.   *D. Blue.*   Filling.
   28 do.   *White.*   do.
      do.   do.
      do.   do.
To be striped in the Warp.
  8 Threads, *D. Blue.*
  2   *White.*

To be Filled.
  8 Threads, *D. Blue.*
  2   *White.*

PRICE of Weaving *6* Cents pr. Yard,
if well wove and trimmed.
   Weavers must return the Yarn left
of a piece, with the Cloth.—Cloth must
be trimmed, wove as thick at the ends
as in the middle, and returned free from
stains and dirt; and if it is made too
sleazy, or damaged in any way, a deduction will be made from the weaving.—
Return this with the Cloth.

WORKING AND LIVING CONDITIONS UNDER FACTORY SYSTEM

Power looms and improved spinning machinery had changed textile manufacture definitely from a domestic to a factory industry by
1820. Some home weaving was still done as late as 1850, but it was
insignificant. The weaving labor cost in a yard of sheeting, which
had been 12 cents on hand looms, became one-tenth of that on power
looms, a degree of competition which naturally hand weaving could
not survive. Ledgers of a Providence yarn factory [25] give the rates
paid home weavers over a series of years immediately following the
general adoption of power looms. Ginghams which were woven in
1818 for 8 cents a yard were worth only 3 cents to the weaver in
1824. The rate on stripes and checks which had been 6 cents in
1818 had fallen to 2⅞ cents in 1824.

Even under factory production the work was still carried on largely
by women and children. Their employment was looked upon then as
an unqualified good which made possible the development of manufacture without taking men from agriculture, while at the same time
it made women and children, to quote Alexander Hamilton, "more
useful than they otherwise would be," [26] and enabled them to escape
the evils of idleness and destitution. Agriculture was itself a gainer

[25] In Baker Library.
[26] Hamilton, Alexander: Report on Manufactures, 1791, p. 29.

by the new opportunities for women, according to Hamilton, because "the husbandman himself experiences a new source of profit and support from the increased industry of his wife and daughters." [26]

The employment of women and children was, moreover, a distinct advantage to the manufacturer in several ways, one of which is perhaps suggested in an observation made by one of their number, the man who first applied power to the weaving of woolen cloth. In his diary he says that after many experiments it had proved its practicability—

We commenced building power looms to take the place of hand looms with all possible dispatch. The saving in operating 60 looms by water instead of the old way, by hand, amounted to about $40 per day. Besides this saving, we got rid of 60 weavers, the most of them men who in those bygone days were intemperate and exceedingly troublesome, and substituted for them 30 girls, who were easily managed and did more and better work.[27]

The mill town soon followed the establishment of the factory system in cloth manufacture, but it assumed two different forms. These two systems, as they first developed in the two most important centers, are analyzed by a pioneer manufacturer:

Mr. Slater had proceeded upon the English plan of employing families in the mill, often including children at an age when it would have been more proper for them to be at school. The consequence was the bringing together, in a factory village, a collection of families dependent entirely upon their labor, and often of parents who were disposed to live upon the labor of their children rather than upon their own, and exposed to suffering, as the operatives have been in England, whenever there was any interruption in the business. It was also the custom, instead of making payments in money, to establish what was called a Factory Store, from which the families were furnished with provisions and other articles in payment for their labor, which resulted in a sort of dependence upon their employers.

At Waltham, they at once commenced the practice of the payment of wages in money, every week or fortnight, and also provided boarding-houses to accomodate all in their employ. This precluded the employment of children; as about half the usual wages of females would be required for the payment of board, the Company could not afford to pay board and wages to those who were not capable of doing full work. The result was that only those of mature age could find employment; and such usually having a home to which they could return in case of any interruption in the business, they were not subject to be left dependent or exposed to suffering.[28]

Pay rolls of one of the Slater spinning mills in Pawtucket have three headings—amount earned, charges, and net amount paid. The charges column is subdivided into two parts, one headed "cow," the other, "rent." The charge for pasturing the cow was usually 57 cents for each pay-roll period of two weeks. Rent runs from 96 cents to $1.08 for the same period. Unlike the mills using the boarding-house system, turnover in the Slater mills seems not to have been a serious matter. The same families appear on the pay rolls year after year, and generally the same members of the family as well. Changes seem to be occasioned chiefly by the marriage of the older girls, after which a new name appears at the end of the list of members of the family employed. The very nominal sum earned by the newcomer justifies the assumption, even without data on ages, that as one of the family's wage earners took up a new place in another family, her small brother or sister was drafted into service to help fill the gap. The domestic economy of the Howland family, over a period of three years, as shown by the pay rolls, is typical:

---

[26] Hamilton, Alexander: Report on Manufactures, 1791, p. 29.
[27] Manuscript Diary of Joshua Aubin, Amesbury, Mass., in Baker Library. (Citation probably refers to year 1821.)
[28] Batchelder, Samuel: Early Progress of Cotton Manufacture in the United States (1863). pp. 74-75.

TABLE **6.**—*Earnings of typical mill family employed in spinning room, with amounts owed the company, for specified pay-roll periods, 1828–1830*

[Occupations not specified]

Name of operative	Two weeks ending Nov. 28, 1828						Two weeks ending Aug. 1, 1829						Two weeks ending July 31, 1830					
	Days worked	Amount earned	Charges Cow	Rent	Net amount paid	Average net earnings per day[1]	Days worked	Amount earned	Charges Cow	Rent	Net amount paid	Average net earnings per day[1]	Days worked	Amount earned	Charges Cow	Rent	Net amount paid	Average net earnings per day[1]
Howland, Willard	12	$10.00			$10.00	$0.83	12	$10.00			$10.00	$0.83	11.0	$7.67			$7.67	$0.66
Howland, Malvin	12	5.50			5.50	.46	12	6.00			6.00	.50	11.6	5.75			5.75	.50
Howland, Munyan	12	1.33			1.33	.11	12	1.50			1.50	.13	11.3	1.40			1.40	.12
Howland, John	12	1.17			1.17	.09	12	1.33			1.33	.11	11.3	1.25			1.25	.11
Howland, Polly	12	4.00			4.00	.33	12	4.00			4.00	.33	---					
Howland, Hannah	12	2.00			2.00	.17	12	2.83			2.83	.24	11.3	2.72			2.72	.24
Howland, Lorinda							12	1.00			1.00	.08	---					
Total		24.00	$0.57	$0.96	22.47	1.87		26.66	$0.57	$0.96	25.13	2.09		18.79	$0.57	$1.06	17.16	1.43

[1] Inserted by bureau—not in original pay rolls.

While there was a company store in connection with the Slater mills at Pawtucket, truck payment does not seem to have been the practice, at least to an extent which would affect the pay rolls, and the only charges against the operatives are those of pasturage and rent, as shown in the table. In most New England mill towns, however, with the exception of Lowell, truck payment was the general method. The Fall River mill started out, in 1817, by paying only in goods—money was not used. The system was changed, according to a story, after the following incident:

Accounts so invariably showed a balance in favor of the mill owners that the employees began to be much dissatisfied. Hannah Borden's position was a peculiarly independent one, not merely because she was the daughter of a stockholder, but because she was the best weaver in the city and the company could not afford to lose her. She felt that it was unfair that the operatives should not be allowed to see their accounts, and felt so certain that her own were not correct that she went to the agent and threatened to leave unless he would let her see the books. He ordered them sent up, and she found articles like suspenders and rum charged against her. She finally demanded money wages as the only condition on which she would remain in the mill, and the granting of her demand led the other hands to insist on the same treatment, and money wages for every one became the rule.[29]

The Lowell mills were established later than those already mentioned and adopted the company boarding-house method of providing living quarters for their hands. In the earliest years the Lowell mills were unique in the class of operatives they attracted. These pioneer "mill girls" were, to quote a writer who was one of them in her early girlhood, "blooming and energetic New England women. They were naturally intelligent, had mother wit." [30] An impressive number of them became leaders in various fields after they left the mills; some of them became famous and all of them, as a class, were the subjects of much economic, social, and literary discussion both here and in England for 20 years. They carried on, from 1840 to 1847, the "Lowell Offering, a Repository of Original Articles written by Factory Girls," which was "not only the first work written by factory girls, but also the first magazine or journal written exclusively by women in all the world." [31]

The lives of the operatives were under a rigorous corporation paternalism which controlled working conditions and—

not only regulated the dwelling places and food of their operatives but dictated the time of going to bed and the rules of social intercourse. For the most part the operatives in the early days seem to have made few objections to the system, but occasionally a considerable measure of opposition is found. In one of the early factory tracts, issued by the Female Labor Reform Association of Lowell, complaint is made of the wearisome extent of corporation control. At the close of the day's work, the operative was said to be watched to see that her footsteps did not "drag beyond the corporation limits" and whether she wished it or not she was subjected to the manifold inconveniences of a large crowded boarding house where, too, it was said that the price paid for her accommodation was so utterly insignificant that it would not insure to her the common comforts of life.[32]

Board at the company boarding houses was $1.25 per capita for women and $1.75 for men a week, 25 cents of which, prior to 1836, was paid by the corporation. In 1836 the Merrimack plant, the largest of the Lowell mills, announced a cut in wages and the discontinuance of its contribution toward the maintenance of its em-

[29] Abbott, Edith: Women in Industry, p. 272.   [31] Abbott, p. 114.
[30] Robinson, Harriet H.: Loom and Spindle, p. 62.   [32] Idem, pp. 114-115.

ployees, and brought about its first strike.   Mrs. Robinson, who as a child took part in this "turn-out," says:

It is hardly necessary to say that so far as results were concerned this strike did no good. The dissatisfaction of the operatives subsided, or burned itself out, and though the authorities did not accede to their demands, the majority returned to their work and the corporation went on cutting down the wages.[33]

Nevertheless, these continued wage reductions had a decided effect upon the labor force in the Lowell mills. With each succeeding cut the "best of the girls left and went to their homes or to the other employments that were fast opening to women, until there were very few of the old guard left; and thus the status of the factory population of New England gradually became what we know it to be to-day."[34]

Out of her own experience in the Merrimack mills, Mrs. Robinson wrote thus of living and working conditions:

Except in rare instances, the rights of the early mill girls were secure. They were subject to no extortion, if they did extra work they were always paid in full, and their own account of labor done by the piece was always accepted. They kept the figures and were paid accordingly.

Their life in the factory was made pleasant to them. In those days there was no need of advocating the doctrine of the proper relation between employer and employed. Help was too valuable to be ill-treated.

Their surroundings were pure, and the whole atmosphere of their boarding houses was as refined as that of their homes.

The health of the girls was good. The regularity and simplicity of their lives and the plain and substantial food provided for them kept them free from illness.[35]

Another writer, of the later era of factory sanitation and legal control of working conditions for women, wonders a little if this picture is not after all a long backward view which reflects an idealized rather than an actual condition, and in which "long hours, unsanitary mills, crowded boarding houses, compulsorily supported corporation churches * * * are forgotten."[36] Miss Abbott notes an official complaint made by a physician in the Lowell Hospital, "not only of the lack of ventilation, but of the 'manifest disregard of cleanliness' and of the overcrowding in some of the corporation boarding houses."[37]

From an article in the census of 1880; making a comparison between the "modern" and improved factory of 1880 and the first large textile mills, we get some impression of the physical make-up of the old plants:

The first mills built were very considerable structures for their time, but they were low-studded, badly lighted, and were heated by stoves; and in these mills the operatives were compelled to work under arduous conditions (owing to the imperfection of the machinery) thirteen to fourteen hours a day. These narrow structures were in some places built seven stories in height. In the earlier mills the apparatus for the removal of dust from the factory was very imperfect.[38]

The Philadelphia Album, in its issue of March 8, 1834, described "the shop in which all the machinery employed in the mills is manufactured." This "machine shop, belonging to the Locks and Canal Company"

[33] Robinson, pp. 85–86.
[34] Idem, p. 86.
[35] Idem, p. 71 et seq.
[36] Abbott, p. 133.
[37] Idem, pp. 128–129.
[38] Atkinson, Edward: Special Report on Cotton Manufacture. Census of 1880, Vol. II, pp. 953–954.

is probably the largest shop in the country, being built of brick, four stories high, two hundred and twenty feet in length and forty-five in width. About 200 machinists, some of them the most skilful and ingenious workmen in the United States or in the world, are constantly employed. About 600 tons of cast and wrought iron, two-thirds of which at least are of American production, are annually converted into machinery, besides a large quantity of imported steel.

Working hours in the textile mills "extended from five o'clock in the morning until seven in the evening, with one-half hour for breakfast and for dinner. Even the doffers were forced to be on duty nearly fourteen hours a day, and this was the greatest hardship in the lives of these children. For it was not until 1842 that the hours of labor for children under twelve years of age were limited to ten per day; but the 'ten-hour law' itself was not passed until long after some of the little doffers were old enough to appear before the legislative committee on the subject and plead—by their presence—for a reduction of the hours of labor." [39]

Even with a 13-hour day, some overtime was worked, and "the young woman who is able is generally willing to engage in it, as she draws the pay, to the extent of the extra work, of two girls, while she incurs the expense of the board of but one." [40]

The working-day at Lowell seems to have been shortened to 12 hours about 1845.[41] Baker Library has a collection of time-schedule placards of the Lowell mills ranging from 1853 to 1875. A specimen schedule is given in the appendix.

On the other hand, the 12-hour day seems to have existed in the Slater and other Rhode Island mills as early as 1825. No definite evidence of this has been obtained—the statement is made by inference drawn from the fact that the pay rolls of the Rhode Island mills to which the bureau had access used 12 as the denominator in noting fractions of a working-day, as 3/12, 7/12, etc. The hours of labor in the Lonsdale mills in Rhode Island were 12 per day for all occupations, from 1830 to 1860.[42]

Saturday was often, perhaps generally, shorter by at least two hours, than the other working-days. The work week in the Rhode Island mills was probably 70 hours.

WAGES

Early data on wages in textile mills are scattered and frequently confusing. As a rule the few available pay rolls cover only weekly or monthly earnings and afford slight means of determining rates or any other basis by which earnings were calculated. Rates by occupations can not be had, because no distinction is made of occupations within a department, and the rates on a known occupation, such as frame spinning, may vary widely, probably according to the age of the operative. Thus earnings in the spinning room range all the way from those of doffers who may be 7 or 8 years old, to the skilled men, but only the overseers, and occasionally the second hands, are given an occupational designation.

From secondary sources the bureau has pay-roll data on the Waltham (Mass.) mill for the year 1821, and on the Merrimack

³⁹Robinson, p. 31.
⁴⁰ Miles, Henry A.: Lowell as It Was and As It Is (Lowell, 1845), p. 108.
⁴¹ Census of 1880, Vol. XX, p. 350.
⁴² Idem, p. 366.

mills (Lowell, Mass.) for 1824 and 1840. The data dealing with the Waltham mill were taken from original pay rolls by Edith Abbott, and appear in her book, Women in Industry. Information covering the Lowell plants is from the tabulated census material found in Volume XX of the census of 1880.

Data dealing with the Slater mills in Rhode Island were taken from the file of original pay-roll books in Baker Library by the bureau representative, and cover the years 1828 to 1843.

In only four departments—carding, spinning, weaving, and dressing—are figures available which are in any way adequate or comparable. The particular Slater mill from which the most definite data were secured is the "Steam Cotton Manufactory" established in Providence in 1827. Either the mill used only mule spinners, or else the pay rolls for the frame spinning department have been lost, as the only entries covering spinning were for mule spinning. Mule spinning was in its very earliest experimental stage at that time, and it is possible that Slater was merely experimenting at Providence, and getting most of the yarn for his Providence weave room from his Pawtucket yarn mills. Rates paid frame spinners at Pawtucket are shown in Table 6. The average daily earnings there were much lower than in the spinning departments of the other mills, probably because child labor was employed in the Slater mills to a much greater extent than was the case in Massachusetts. Hence, in the following table the spinning department in the Slater mill has been omitted as not being comparable with that of the other mills. Mule spinning will be considered separately.

Table 7 shows the average daily rates of operatives below the supervisory grades, for the four departments in each of the three plants discussed. As already stated, occupations within the department can not be specified, since no distinction is made of them in the pay rolls themselves.

TABLE 7.—*Average daily rates of pay of cotton mill operatives in certain New England mills, 1821 to 1828*

Department	Waltham, Mass., mill, 1821	Lowell, Mass., mill, 1824	Slater mill, Rhode Island, 1828
Carding	$0.39	$0.375	$0.31
Spinning	.43	.56	(¹)
Weaving	.45	.67	.50
Dressing	.50	.375	.375

¹ Mule spinners, rates not comparable.

We do not know the length of the working-day in the Waltham mill. Very likely it was the same as that at Lowell, 5 a. m. to 7 p. m., with two half-hour recesses for meals—that is, a 13-hour day. The 12-hour day obtained in the Providence plant.

The higher rate for weaving paid by the Lowell concern did not continue. Mention has been made of wage reductions, beginning in 1836. The 1840 rate quoted in the census tables is 50 cents a day. The high rate in the earlier years was admittedly paid as an effective inducement to attract a high grade of workers.

Average full-time weekly earnings at the rates given would be $2.34, $2.25, and $1.86 for carders; $2.60 and $3.36 for spinners; $2.70, $4.02, and $3 for weavers; $3 and $2.25 for dressers.

Actual earnings in the Lowell mills are not available. The Waltham pay rolls give weekly earnings, the Slater pay rolls, monthly. The range from lowest to highest in Waltham is: Carding, $1.50 to $6; spinning, $2.50 to $7.50; weaving, $1.75 to $6.60; dressing, $2.23 to $7.

The lowest monthly earnings in the weave room at the Slater mills for the month of November, 1828, is $1.25, the highest is $9, while the average monthly earnings of the 20 weavers employed, all women, is $7.58. During the month of October of the following year, 1829, three women earned more than $14 on two looms, and in the same month of 1830, working on three looms, 10 of the women weavers earned between $14 and $15.

It is only by inference that wages paid to overseers can be taken from the Waltham pay rolls. One man in the carding department and two in the weave room at $12 a week each were undoubtedly supervisors, as that is analogous to the rate of $2 per day for carding and weaving overseers in the Merrimack mills. In the Slater mills those two occupations were paid only $1.50 per day. Spinning-room overseers in both the Massachusetts plants received $1.75 a day, or $10.50 a week. These rates are all higher than those of dressing-room overseers, which were $1.76 at Waltham, $1.50 at Lowell, and $1.13 at Providence. Second hands in the card room got $1.25 a day in Lowell and $1 in Providence. The rate for loom fixers in the Slater pay rolls, the only one giving that occupation, is $1.25 a day, the same as the overseer's rate. The sizing maker in the dressing department received $1 a day. The superintendent of the Steam Cotton Manufactory was on a fixed salary of $50 a month.

Rates in the Slater mills, the only establishment for which data extending over a period of years are available, show practically no change in the 15 years studied except in the single occupation of mule spinning. The census report, after giving average weekly wages in two representative Massachusetts mills in 1828, says: "These rates did not vary much for several years," and follows that statement with average weekly earnings in the same plants in 1836, showing slightly lower wages in some cases and higher in others. For example, the average weekly earnings of women weavers was $2.61 in 1828 and $2.05 in 1836; of dressers, $2.82 in 1828 and $3.11 in 1836.[43]

Rates and earnings of the mule spinners employed at Slater's Steam Cotton Manufactory afford an interesting contrast to the low wages in the other departments. Mule spinners are always men, and it is quite likely that in the experimental undertaking at Providence the operatives were skilled men who had learned the work in England, where mule spinning was introduced several years before its advent here.

In the first year of operation of the Providence plant only five mule spinners were employed. They received $1.33 a day, and were the highest paid men in the plant except the carding and weaving overseers. The next year, 1829, piece rates were introduced. The overseer kept the $1.33 time rate, while the spinners were paid at the rate of 16 cents per 100 skeins of warp, and 13 cents per 100 skeins of filling. Actual monthly earnings in the month of October, 1829, range from $36.18 to $44.10, and average $39.54 for the seven men employed. By 1830 the rate had dropped 1 cent per 100 on filling, but earnings were even higher, ranging from $40.19 to $43.30 and averaging $41.48, with the same number engaged.

The rate in September, 1834, had increased to $1.50 a day for the overseer, while the piece rates paid the spinners had dropped to 14 cents per 100 skeins of warp and 10½ cents for filling. Twelve spinners were employed, whose actual monthly earnings ranged from $27.65 to $44.97. Ten years later the piece rate had dropped to 8½ and 6½ cents per 100 skeins, and the highest amount earned in May, 1844, was $35.70.

An earlier figure than any here quoted is taken from the May, 1817, pay roll of the Boston Manufacturing Co., which enters a mule spinner's earnings for one day at $2.50.[44]

A strike for shorter hours closed 10 textile mills in Paterson, N. J., in 1835. Testimony and affidavits [45] taken during the course of the strike showed that 600 of the strikers were children under 16 years of age, whose weekly earnings ranged from 50 cents to $1.75 and averaged $1.12½. The workday, the excessive length of which had brought about the strike, was from sunrise to sunset from March 1 to October 1, and from daylight to 8 p. m. from October 1 to March 1. One-half hour was allowed for breakfast during the period between March 15 and October 1. For the remainder of the year operatives ate their breakfast at home "by candle light" before reporting at the mill. The dinner period was 45 minutes throughout the year.

Actual weekly earnings of 10 young persons, whose occupations, however, were not given, were thus reported in affidavits: One boy, aged 19, and one girl, 18, at $2.75; four girls, ages 13 to 20, and one boy, aged 15, at $2; 1 girl, 13, at $1.50; 1 boy, 12, at $1.25; and a 10-year old girl at 44 cents.

SOUTHERN MILLS

While there were small textile mills in the South in the first half of the nineteenth century, information about them is very slight and wage data are almost wholly lacking for the period under discussion. Average weekly wages in 1831, covering all operatives and classified by sex instead of by occupational divisions, is all that it has been possible to secure, and that only from secondary sources. "Average weekly wages of males in Maryland amounted to $3.87 and of females, $1.91; male operatives in Virginia received $2.73 and females $1.58." [46]

Textile manufacture in the South was carried on almost wholly by slave and child labor. An early English student of economic conditions in the American slave States wrote of his visit and observations in a cotton mill in Athens, Ga., in 1839:

There is no difficulty * * * on account of color, the white girls working in the same room and at the same loom with the black girls, and boys of each color,

[44] Clark, p. 388.
[45] National Trades Union (New York), Aug. 15, 1835, quoted from the Paterson Courier, in Documentary History of American Industrial Society, Vol. V, pp. 63–66.
[46] Montgomery, James: Practical Details of Cotton Manufacture in the United States (Glasgow, 1840), p. 161.

as well as men and women, working together without repugnance or objection. The negroes here are found to be quite as easily taught to perform all the required duties of spinners and weavers as the whites, and are just as tractable when taught; but their labour is dearer than that of the whites, for whilst the free boys and girls employed receive about $7.00 per month, out of which they find themselves, the slaves are paid the same wages (which is handed over to their owners) and the mill-owner has to feed them in addition; so that the free labour is cheaper to him than the slave; and the hope expressed by the proprietor to me was that the progressive increase of the white population by immigration would enable him to employ wholly their free labour, which to him would be more advantageous.[47]

---

[47] From Slave States in America, cited in Documentary History of American Industrial Society, Vol. II, p. 357.

Chapter 8.—MARITIME INDUSTRIES

MERCHANT MARINE

A large part of the time of the Courts of Assistants of the Massachusetts Bay Colony was given to adjudicating disputes involving seamen's wages, and, while we can not know that the seamen actually collected the amounts due them, certainly the court almost uniformly declared in their favor. The importance to the general welfare of the colony of the merchant marine made it advisable to protect the interests of the seamen, at least so far as their wages were concerned. Living and working conditions on board ship were probably regarded as the individual concern of the shippers and their employees, but the court was apparently always ready to intercede in the matter of money payment due maritime workers.

Another indication that, legally at least, seamen's wages were safeguarded is found in the case of a privateer which was seized by order of the governor of New York in 1699. Writing to the Lords of Trade in London about the incident, the colonial governor, the Earl of Bellamont, says:

> The ship *Hester* that I ordered to be seized and brought from Perth Amboy was condemned and sold by Inch of Candle at New Yorke, but neither the King nor I as Governor had a shilling by that seizure; for the Master swore the seamen's wages amounted to more than the price the ship sold for, and Mr. Graham, the Atturny, asured me that it was law that in cases of that kind the seamen were to be paid their wages, and that the ship was a pledge for their wages.[1]

It is not often possible to determine accurately the rates paid seamen, as the court cases as a rule covered lump-sum payments for an entire voyage the duration of which is not stated. Occasionally, however, a monthly rate is specified. These rates vary somewhat on different ships, but from a considerable number of cases in the court records during the last quarter of the seventeenth century the scale can be fairly definitely stated. Ordinary seamen received from 27 to 35 shillings ($4.50 to $5.83), and able seamen from 32 to 40 shillings ($5.33 to $6.67), a month. Two different records put the rate for boatswains at 45 shillings ($7.50) per month. in one case "till ye ship arrived at Barbadoes," and 48s. ($8) from the time of leaving Barbadoes to the end of the voyage. The court in 1676 ordered the master of the ship *Nevis* to pay its pilot £5 ($16.67) and its carpenter 54s. ($9) a month for a voyage of five months. Five and six pounds ($16.67 and $20) a month were the usual rates for captains.

A Massachusetts law of 1680 decreed that masters and mariners in port should receive half pay.[2]

Rates paid on merchant vessels sailing from Virginia ports were practically the same as those paid by the New England ship owners, averaging, for seamen, about 30 shillings ($5) a month in 1668.

1 O'Callaghan's Documents Relative to History of Colony, of New York, Vol. IV, p. 591.
2 Massachusetts Archives, lxi, p. 214.

The pay per month on a ship sailing from Norfolk in 1695 was: Seamen, £2 4s. ($7.33); chief mate, £4 ($13.33); a ship physician and a ship carpenter, £3 10s. ($11.67) each.[3] The North Carolina fleet seems to have combined the functions of navy and merchant marine. The Shaftsbury papers[4] give detailed pay rolls of several ships in the fleet, of which the following, for the ship *Caroline* in the year 1669, is representative:

	£	s.	Per month
Henry Brayne, master	5		($24. 30)
John Comings, mate	3		($14. 58)
Richard Dyas, gunner		35	($8. 50)
Richard Cole, carpenter	3	5	($15. 80)
Peter Salter, trumpeter		35	($8. 50)
Arthur Roper, boatswain's mate		30	($7. 29)
Carpenter's mate		30	($7. 29)
11 seamen, each		30	($7. 29)

Available data for the eighteenth century show a gradual but not marked rise from these early rates. In 1707 the scale was £6 ($20) per month for master, £3 10s. ($11.67) for first mate,⁻ £2 15s. ($9.16) for second mate, and £1 15s. ($5.83) each for gunner, carpenter, and boatswain.[5] "In 1713 and 1714 seamen ranged from £2 2s. to £2 15s. [$7 to $9.16] per month, generally £2 10s. [$8.33]; mates got £3 5s. [$10.83]; captains, £4 10s. [$15]. In a picked crew of a Massachusetts sloop in 1730 to 1734 three men obtained £3 [$10] per month each; the mate, £4 [$13.33]; the captain, £6 [$20]. These seamen paid sixpence [8.4 cents] per month from their small wages to the collectors of different ports for the use of Greenwich Hospital."[6]

A slave ship owned by Peter Faneuil sailed from Sierra Leone on April 10 and arrived at Newport on August 1, 1743. Its pay roll,[7] in which sterling is specified, reads:

TABLE 8.—*Pay roll of slave ship, 1743*

Men's names	Qualities	When shipt	Wages sterling	When discharged	Wages due	American equivalent
			£ s.		£ s. d.	
Charles Winkham	Master	Apr. 10	6 00 ($29. 16)	Aug. 18	25 12 0	$124. 41
John Battey	Mate	do	3 10 (17. 01)	do. 17	14 16 4	72. 00
Oliver Arnold	2d mate	do	3 10 (17. 01)	do. —	12 14 0	61. 70
Alex McKinsey	Boatswain	do	3 00 (14. 58)	do. 16	12 12 0	61. 22
Silvester Sweet	Sailor	do	2 10 (12. 15)	do. 18	10 13 4	51. 83
Oliver Somes	do	do	2 10 (12. 15)	do. 16	10 10 0	51. 03
Wm. Umerey	do	May 1	2 00 (9. 72)	do. 16	7 1 4	34. 34
Wm. Wyat	do	do	2 10 (12. 15)	do. 18	8 18 4	43. 33

Perhaps the crews of ships engaged in the highly profitable slave trade shared some of the gains as well as the hazards of the business, as these' wages, in sterling, are considerably higher than others quoted for the same period.

The sloop *Hummingbird*, of Massachusetts, in the service of the Province, made an official voyage from Boston to Annapolis, Md., and return, in 1744. The master received £20 sterling ($97.20) for

---

[3] Bruce, Philip A.: Economic History of Virginia in the 17th Century, Vol. II, pp. 347-348.
[4] In Collections of South Carolina Historical Society, Vol. III, p. 141.
[5] Weeden, William B.: Economic and Social History of New England, 1620-1789, Vol. II, p. 889.
[6] Idem, Vol. II, p. 577.
[7] Original manuscript in Rhode Island State Archives, cited by Weeden, Vol. II, p. 469.

the voyage; the mate, who also served as pilot, was paid £25 sterling ($121.50) for the voyage. Monthly rates, also sterling, paid to the crew were: £1 10s. 6d. ($7.40) to the gunner; £1 7s. ($6.56) to the boatswain; and £1 4s. ($5.83) to each of the 16 seamen.[8]

A shipping contract[9] executed at New London, Conn., in 1767, reads:

That in consideration of the monthly or other wages, against each respective seaman and mariner's name hereunder set, They severally shall and will perform the above mentioned voyage and the said Master doth hereby hire the said Seamen and Mariners for the said voyage at such monthly wages to be paid pursuant to the Laws of Great Britain.

	Wages per month £ s.	
Master	4 16	($23. 30)
Seaman	2 00	($9. 72)
Seaman	1 15	($8. 50)
Seaman	1 10	($7. 29)
Mariner	1 15	($8. 50)
Mariner	1 10	($7. 29)
Mariner	1 5	($6. 08)

While sterling is not specified in this case, it is fair to conclude, by comparison with wages paid by the *Hummingbird*, that sterling was meant.

In January, 1776, the brig *Nancy*, sailing from Wickford, R. I., "and by God's grace bound for the Salt Islands," carried the following crew and pay roll:[10]

TABLE 9.—*Brig Nancy, Benjamin Baker, master, 1776*

Men's names	Quality	Wages per month	Advance wages	Wages on ye voige	Whole wages	American equivalent
		£ s.	£ s.	Month	£ s. d.	
Benjamin Baker	Captain	10 10 ($35.00)	10 10	2 27	30 9 0	$101.50
John Bissel	Mate	6 18 ($23.00)	6 18	2 27	20 0 6	66.75
Ezekil Mitchel	Saler	3 6 ($11.00)	3 6	2 22	9 0 4	30.05
John (x) Jones	Saler	3 6 ($11.00)	3 6	2 17		
Gid Jenkins	Raw hand	2 11 ($8.50)	2 11	2 25	7 4 6	24.08
Wm. Homes	Cook	2 2 ($7.00)	2 2	2 26	6 4 3	20.71
Simon (x) Laven	Saler	3 0 ($10.00)	3 0	2 23	8 6 0	27.67
Dom Smith	Saler	3 0 ($10.00)	3 0	2 23	8 6 0	27.67
Daniel Jones	Saler	3 6 ($11.00)	3 6	2 17	8 11 7	28.59

In this case, Rhode Island money was undoubtedly the currency in which these wages were paid.

"If we could look into the living of these hardy mariners in their dingy cabins"—there, Weeden thinks, "would be history indeed."

Plainly, there was a democratic simplicity instituted which contrasted somewhat with the modified aristocratic movement characteristic of New England. Forecastle and cabin, if separated in fact, were closely related in principle. Not only did fishing crews join interest in the catch, but ordinary seamen had small privileges for their own freight, which they ventured in the voyage and turned in trade. This diffusion of interest among the common seamen affected sensibly the working of a vessel. There was a common feeling engendered between owner and sailor, which fostered the proper energy of the voyage.[11]

Reported rates after the establishment of the Republic show some discrepancies. A broadside, posted in Baltimore in 1790, advertising for men for the mercantile marine, offered $30 a month to the mate,

---

[8] Massachusetts State Archives.
[9] Connecticut Broadsides, Library of Congress.
[10] In Rhode Island State Archives, cited in Weeden, Vol. II, p. 911.
[11] Weeden, Vol. II, p. 576.

$20 to able seamen, $18 to the cook, and $12 to the cabin steward.[12]
Between 1796 and 1820 Stephen Girard's ships sailing out of Philadelphia paid even higher wages to their crews.   The captain's salary
was $50 a month in all cases recorded, and that of first mate ran from
$30 to $38; of second mate, $25 to $34.   Seamen's rates were usually
either $22 or $32 a month, and cooks $20.   A large proportion of the
wages credited to the accounts of the crews appear in the Girard
receipt books as having been paid out in Philadelphia to the wives
and mothers of the sailors, throughout the duration of their voyages.

Girard's scale seems considerably higher than the average pay in
the merchant marine.   This was perhaps due to the fact that he
operated a fleet of privateers which, like the slave ships, may have
had to offer special inducements because of the greater risk.   Two
agreements are of record concerning men on the brig *Sally*, captured
by the British in 1800 and taken to Halifax.   The cook gave a receipt
for $20 on account and agreed to wait for the remainder due him
"until said Mr. Girard has recovered said brig and cargo under the
appeal which he has entered at Halifax."   The mate agreed that "if
said Stephen Girard recovers from the British his vessel and cargo,
he will pay me the remainder of my wages, after deducting the
proportion of charges.   Otherwise I will have no further demand
against him."   The mate's claim was settled two years later by the
payment of $107.

Speaking of conditions affecting the merchant marine in 1790 to
1795, McMaster says that "common sailors could scarcely be had
at $24 a month." [13]   Yet the "sailors' strike" of 1803 was the result of
an attempt of seamen shipping out of New York City to obtain an
increase in wages from $10 a month to $14,[14] and Warden reported
that from 1800 to 1815 monthly wages of seamen "varied from
$10 to $17." [15]

According to McMaster, river boatmen on the Mississippi and the
Ohio received a dollar a day,[16] while Warden quotes $25 a month.[17]
McMaster also sees in "the rush of men into the merchant marine" [16]
between 1800 and 1810 one of the chief causes for the abrupt rise in
wages paid unskilled labor during that decade.

Seamen's wages as quoted by Warden must have remained fairly
constant for the next 20 years, as a second sailors' strike, which
occurred in Boston in 1837, was an attempt to force an advance in
wages from $14 to $16 a month.   The strike failed because "plenty
of men could be obtained at the lower rate." [18]

The only rate for longshoremen that has been found pertains to
Massachusetts in 1756, and is given in "old tenor" currency, which
converts into 50 cents a day for white laborers and 45 cents for
negroes.[19]

Salaries of keepers of the lighthouses along the Massachusetts coast
ranged from $150 a year for Plymouth Light to $350 a year for that
on Thatcher's Island, in the period immediately following the War
of 1812.[20]

---

[12] Maryland Broadsides, Library of Congress.
[13] History of the People of the United States, Vol. I, p. 242.
[14] Third Annual Report, U. S. Commissioner of Labor (1887), p. 1031.
[15] Warden, D. B.: A Statistical, Political, and Historical Account of the United States, Vol. III, p. 274, footnote.
[16] Vol. III, p. 510.
[17] Vol. II, p. 340.
[18] Eleventh Annual Report, Massachusetts Bureau of Statistics of Labor (1880), p. 5.
[19] Massachusetts State Archives.
[20] Warden, Vol. I, p. 344.

FISHING

It is to be regretted that an industry which played so conspicuous a part in the economic life of New England, and engaged the services of so many people as did fishing, should have left behind it so slight an industrial history. The dependence of the early colonists on fishing and the later economic importance of the fish trade are always given prominence by both contemporary writers and historians in treating of colonial America, but reference to the earnings of the men engaged in the industry are so rare as to be practically nonexistent. This can probably be accounted for by the system of payment used even by large-scale operators like Faneuil—that of giving the fishermen a percentage of the value of the catch after each voyage, a system which, of course, made earnings a very uncertain factor.

An unknown, but undoubtedly considerable, proportion of the colonists earned their living fishing for the shippers, and "the business of the fisheries enters into all the doings of the time. Whenever we turn over the stray papers of a seventeenth century merchant we find evidences, great and small, of his constant intercourse with fish and fishermen."[21]

This early fishing system, like all the industries of the time, stimulated in the highest degree the personal powers of the participants. Great changes have been wrought gradually in the position of the individual fisherman, the laborer, and in capital, his environment, the tools and appliances of his work. At this period the capitalists, fitting out the expedition with boat, provisions, seines, etc., took one half the value of the catch, and the other part went to the crew. In the eighteenth century the capitalist's moiety was reduced to one-fifth—a proportion which gave great opportunity to the individual fisherman, and which lasted until near our own time.[22]

The value of the individual fisherman's share of the catch on one voyage might be as high as £8 or £9 ($26.67 or $30), according to Josselyn's report in 1675. A Massachusetts fisherman brought suit in the Essex County quarterly court in 1663 for payment of wages under a contract calling for "a year's employment fishing," for which the stipulated remuneration of £29 4s. ($97.33) was "to be paid mostly by bills of exchange on England."[23]

By the middle of the eighteenth century "New England employed 45,880 tons of shipping and 6,002 men"[24] in its fishing industry, but the extent of the industry in terms of earnings of the men engaged in it evidently can not now be determined.

WHALING

The whaling industry reached its peak somewhat later than the period dealt with in this study, but it was not unimportant even in the earliest years of the development of the maritime industries. Before the Revolution it had assumed considerable importance, and "New England easily led all the world"[25] in the trade. In 1774 it employed approximately 4,700 men. The Revolution and the War of 1812 checked its normal development, and it was not until about 1825 that the industry regained a substantial footing.

---

[21] Weeden, Vol. I, p. 247.
[22] Idem, Vol. I, pp. 245–246.
[23] Essex County Quarterly Court Records, Vol. III, p. 106. (Published by Essex Institute.)
[24] Weeden, Vol. II, p. 750.
[25] Idem, Vol. I, p. 443.

A recent book [26] goes exhaustively into the subject of whaling and presents, largely from original sources, "a study of life and labor" in the industry. Mr. Hohman's work will be liberally drawn upon in a brief treatment of an American industry which, although completely extinct now, played nevertheless a prominent part in the industrial history of early America.

Hohman fixes 1830 to 1860 as "the golden era" of the industry, an era which brought not only an enormous financial and industrial expansion but marked changes within the industry itself as well, particularly in relation to "the human material entering into the crews."

So gradual was this change that it is impossible to assign it to any given year. Yet so unmistakable was it, too, that the industry was divided into two roughly defined but clearly recognizable periods. For want of a more precise boundary line these two may be separated by the half decade 1825–1830. Before that time the crews were provincial and homogeneous; after 1830 they were cosmopolitan and heterogeneous. The early foremast hands were made up largely of Yankees from the New England seaboard, with an admixture of Gay Head Indians and a small representative of negroes; while during the second period individuals from every race and from a score of nationalities rubbed shoulders in the crowded forecastles and steerages. Coincident with this shift from provincialism to cosmopolitanism went a marked deterioration in skill, experience, efficiency and morale, as well as a striking increase in the total number of men engaged in the fishery.[27]

By 1833 the American whaling fleet was employing 10,000 seamen, whose most striking attribute was their youth.

Old men were virtually unknown at sea; and even middle-aged men were rare except among masters and mates. Voyage after voyage whaling vessels sailed with crews whose average ages were little in excess of twenty years. It was exceptional to find a man of thirty in the forecastle, while countless hands were still in their teens.

A logical corollary of such extreme youth was found in lack of experience. The percentage of green hands carried by many whalers was truly astounding. In one vessel which left New Bedford in 1832 only four of the fourteen men in the forecastle had ever been to·sea before.

But inexperience was by no means the worst characteristic exhibited in the forecastles. All too often the foremast hands came from the dregs of shore life. This heavy dilution of the labor supply with inexperienced and degenerate elements brought about a notable decrease in both efficiency and morality. Closer supervision and a more relentless driving were practiced in an effort to secure the adequate performance of necessary tasks.[28]

As the industry grew and the demand for whalemen increased, a system of labor recruiting developed which resorted to all manner of "suave deceit and shameless misrepresentation" to secure workers. Through this "funnel-like system" extending, by means of various shipping agencies, from the seaboard to the Great Lakes, "men from all parts of the country flowed into the forecastles, with the whaling ports at the receptive end." [29]

Prospective whalemen, herded into droves and dispatched to the whaling ports, passed from the hands of the shipping agent into those of the outfitter. "This individual may be characterized briefly as the entrepreneur of the labor supply phase of the industry. Usually, too, he was the organizer, guiding spirit, and main beneficiary of the

[26] Hohman, Elmo Paul: The American Whaleman (Longman, Green & Co.), 1928.
[27] Idem, p. 48.
[28] Idem, pp. 57–59.
[29] Idem, p. 90.

system of commercialized exploitation which fed upon the whale-man's earnings." [30]

The extent of the outfit sold to the recruit "varied with the igno-rance, need, or gullibility of the purchaser and with the shrewdness, rapacity, or dishonesty, of the seller." In most cases, however—

The outfits were exceedingly scanty (in view of the length of the voyage for which they were intended), shamelessly inferior in quality, and extortionate in price. At times the prices were only twenty to thirty per cent above the going rates charged for similar goods in ordinary stores; but in countless instances the discrepancy rose to one hundred per cent and more. In general, the coarsest and cheapest materials were provided for amounts which would have been more than sufficient, elsewhere, to purchase goods of excellent quality and workmanship.[31]

In actual money, these bills against the whalemen ran between $60 and $100. "The one figure most often mentioned by contemporary writers was $75; and an analysis of hundreds of accounts showed that a majority of the men were charged with amounts ranging from $70 to $90." [32]

This amount was paid by the employer to the merchant who sold the outfit, then charged against the whaleman, at interest which ran for the entire length of the voyage.

Whalers made longer and longer voyages as the industry grew, until toward the end "four and four and a half years became increas-ingly common." [33] In the earlier period, "a report made to the Secretary of the Navy in 1828 showed that during the years 1815 to 1824 inclusive, the average length of 178 cruises had been twenty-nine months." [34]

Living conditions on board the whalers, which were the homes of the men in the industry for these long terms, differed probably only in degree from those in the merchant marine or the fishing trade. The manufacturing element in whaling, however—that is, reducing the whale to the marketable products of oil, bone, and spermaceti, all of which was done on shipboard—aggravated what was very likely the most wretched conditions existing in maritime work.

Living quarters on a whaler are described thus:

Conditions in the cabin were usually adequate, if not wholly commendable. The captain occupied a large stateroom on the starboard side, with a bed so swung that the rocking of the vessel was counteracted. The mates had smaller staterooms, with ordinary bunks, just forward of the captain's quarters.

Still farther forward, and completely separated from the officers' staterooms, was the steerage, an irregular compartment ordinarily containing eight plainly constructed bunks. It was small, poorly ventilated and lighted, and allowed no privacy; but with care and favoring conditions it might be made passably comfortable.

In the forecastle, however, conditions were universally inadequate and often squalid and filthy. The average forecastle was a very low compartment, juts under the main deck in the extreme forward part of the vessel, which followed the curve of the bows back some sixteen to twenty-five feet and enclosed the lower portion of the foremast, thus diminishing still further the small deck space. The bunks, crudely constructed of rough planking, were ranged along the sides of the compartment in a double tier. The only ventilation and light came from the hole cut in the deck above for the purpose of giving access to the ladder which was the sole means of entrance and egress. This hole was thus entrance, exit, ventilator and skylight. In cold or stormy weather, when it has to be kept closed, there was no ventilation or daylight whatever. Such quarters commonly housed from twelve to twenty men (a number at once tragic and ridiculous).[35]

The method of payment in the whaling industry, like that in fishing, was the "lay" system—that is, each worker received a

[30] Hohman, p. 97.   [32] Idem, p. 98.   [34] Idem, p. 84.
[31] Idem, pp. 99–100.   [33] Idem, p. 85.   [35] Idem, pp. 125–126.

fractional part, called the "lay," of the total net proceeds of the voyage. "Captains, mates, boatsteerers, and coopers received 'short lays' ranging from $\frac{1}{8}$ to $\frac{1}{100}$ of the net proceeds; able and ordinary seamen, stewards, cooks, and blacksmiths were entitled to shares which varied from $\frac{1}{100}$ to $\frac{1}{160}$; green hands and boys had to be content with 'long lays' which fluctuated from $\frac{1}{160}$ to $\frac{1}{200}$; and instances of fractions as small as $\frac{1}{250}$, and even $\frac{1}{350}$, were not unknown." [36]

Only occasionally are these "lays" expressed in money. The account of one whaler for a voyage of practically two years, 1805 to 1807, gives earnings in money, as follows: Captain, $2,052.13; first mate, $1,381.41; second mate, $1,008.06; two boat steerers, $777.05 each; cooper, $621,64; boy, $310.82; seamen, including negroes and temporary hands, from $108.36 to $497.31 each.

The amount of the lay dropped steadily during the first half of the nineteenth century. Converting manuscript accounts of voyages of two vessels into averages, Hohman deduces the following data:

Average length of voyage and average earnings of 39 foremast hands carried by the bark *Minerva* during three consecutive voyages, 1836–1841: Average length of voyage, 614 days; average lay per voyage, $94.51; average earnings per month, $4.62; average earnings per day, 15.4 cents.

Average length of voyage and average earnings of 70 foremast hands carried by the bark *Marcella* during four consecutive voyages, 1845–1856: Average length of voyage, 935 days; average lay per voyage, $97.60; average earnings per month, $3.12; average earnings per day, 10.4 cents.[37]

Against earnings, however, was set the whaleman's indebtedness, first for his outfit, and later for all indebtedness incurred on shipboard, such as purchases from the ship's store, advanced wages, and the like, all of which bore extortionate interest for the entire length of the voyage. Hence "it was not uncommon for a seaman to find himself actually in debt to the agents of the vessel on which he had worked for a period of two to four years." [38] Frequently this situation was met by inducing, if not requiring, the debtor seaman to ship on the next voyage in order to work off his obligation.

Normally, "the strength of the lay was sufficient to prevail against its crowding adversaries" [39] on the debit side of the account, and there was, beside, even for those whose lays did not cover their debts, the incalculable item of maintenance for indefinite periods. "Even after allowing for the execrable fare that was commonly furnished, 'free board' for a period of two to four years was an important matter to the men in the forecastle," but "just how important it was, in accurate terms of dollars and cents, no one seems to have taken the trouble to ascertain." [40]

Hohman estimates that "in round terms, the average whaleman was receiving about 20 cents a day plus food and bunk space, at a time when the average unskilled shore worker was being paid about 90 cents a day without room and board." But—

Since wages paid in addition to board and room were from 33 per cent to 50 per cent lower than ordinary money wages, these same shore laborers would have received from forty-five cents to sixty cents per day if they had been living with their employers. That is, when average earnings were reckoned on a comparable basis, the lowest grade of landlubber could sell his untrained strength for an amount two or three times as great as that obtained by the occupant of a whaling forecastle.[41]

---

[36] Hohman, p. 217.
[37] Idem, pp. 236–237.
[38] Idem, p. 219.
[39] Idem, p. 265.
[40] Idem, p. 268.
[41] Idem, p. 240.

Chapter 9.—BOOTS AND SHOES

Throughout the period covered in this study, that is, up to 1840, boot and shoe making was wholly a handicraft. The history of the industry follows closely that of textiles from household manufacture through the stages of the itinerant journeyman and the small shop to power-driven machinery in the factory. One marked difference is that while by 1840 machine production of textiles was well underway, shoemaking machines had not yet been invented. Shoemaking "could be performed adequately * * * by any frontier farmer in his colonial kitchen"[1] but gradually the itinerant cobbler found his way into that colonial kitchen.

This cobbler was either a journeyman, "whipping the cat" after his apprenticeship to some master in a larger town was completed, or a self-taught farmer of their own community who could make more at this trade than at farming. His standard was apt to be higher, his experience wider, his number of lasts greater, and his knowledge of leather deeper than that of any other farmer in the village.[2]

Nothing accurate can be given as representing the earnings of the itinerant shoemaker of the colonial period, because his pay was chiefly in board and truck.

In the larger settlements journeyman shoemakers, working in their own home shops, developed a custom trade which in the language of the day was known as "bespoke work." Early wage rates undoubtedly always apply to this "bespoke work" and represent the amount of money paid by the customer to the journeyman for the labor on a pair of shoes, the material for which the customer himself supplied.

What was probably the first guild venture in America was made by the shoemakers of Boston in 1648, when they petitioned the General Court for authority to organize to protect the trade from "the damag which the country sustaynes by occasion of bad ware made by some of that trade."[3] A charter was granted under which shoemakers were given "libertie and powre" to assemble, elect officers, and "to make orders for the well governinge of theire company, in the mannginge of theire trade and all the affayres thereunto pertaining," such rules to be submitted to the county court for approval. "And for the better executing such orders" the elected officers "or any three of them shall have power to heare and determine all offenses against any of their said orders." Upon complaint to the county court "of any person or persons who shall use the art or trade of shoomaker or any part thereof, not being approved of by the officers of ye said shoomakers to be a sufficient workman, the said court shall have power to send for such persons and suppress them." The charter made the definite prohibition, however, "that no unlawful combination be made at any time by the said company of shoomakers for inhancinge the prices of shooes, bootes or wages." It also dictated that "no shoomaker shall refuse to make shooes for any inhabitant at reasonable rates of theire own leather for the use of themselves

---

[1] Hazard, Blanche Evans: The Organization of the Boot and Shoe Industry in Massachusetts before 1875, p. 4.
[2] Idem, p. 6.
[3] Massachusetts Bay Colony Records, Vol. III, pp. 132–133.

and families." Any craftsman who "shall find himselfe greived" by the actions or decisions of the "company" had recourse to the county court.

The working utensils of the craft were as simple as its organization. The colonial cobbler—

had a flat face hammer and an awl and pincers and knives, which he brought from England with him, a lapstone that was picked up on the seashore, some hand-forged nails, some linen thread spun perhaps by housewives of New England, some wax from the bee-hives of colonial farmers, and leather imported from Europe or made by some early tanner. His product was crude, for he had only crude tools and materials with which to work.[4]

While there is a record of a "shoe factory in which nine men were employed"[5] in Virginia as early as 1652, the shift of the industry from the household into the shop was neither marked nor important before the middle of the eighteenth century. John Adam Dagyr, a master craftsman who emigrated from Wales to Lynn, Mass., in 1750, is credited with being "the first organizer of the industry in this country"[6] and his skill gave to the business "a lift and impetus   *   *   *   equal to the moving power of a new invention."[7] Although even at that time "New England shoemakers led in the industry,"[8] Lynn, which was already a shoe center, had only three shops in which journeymen were employed.[9]

From the available records it appears, curiously, that in custom or "bespoke work" the charge for making a pair of shoes shows practically no change throughout the history of the handicraft. The first rate found is that given by Gabriel Thomas in his history of Pennsylvania and applies to Philadelphia in 1698. He says: "As to Journeymen Shoemakers, they have Two Shillings per Pair for both men and women's Shoes." Both the census of 1860, in its history of the boot and shoe industry,[10] and Bishop's History of American Manufactures [11] give the same rate, 2s. per pair, as the wages received by journeyman shoemakers in Philadelphia in 1698, and while the source is not given in either work, they are quite certainly quoting Thomas.

Two shillings in Pennyslvania currency of the period is 40 cents in the American equivalent.[12] Entries in the ledger of a Massachusetts shoemaker in 1806 [13] show such items as "to making 15 pairs boys' shoes, $6.25"; "to making 18 pairs men's shoes, $7.50," etc., which in each case makes an average labor cost of 42 cents per pair. The diary of a shoemaker of Lynn, Mass., apparently doing "bespoke work" exclusively, shows that in 1822 he was getting 40 and 45 cents per pair for his work.[14]

Unfortunately there are no data to show whether or not these prices are for comparable products. In the later development of the industry, rates varied decidedly on different kinds of work, as, for example, between women's shoes and men's work shoes, between pumps and high boots, and so on.

---

[4] Gannon, Fred A.: Shoemaking, Old and New, p. 9.
[5] Tryon, Rolla M.: Household Manufactures in the United States, 1640–1860, p. 4 (citing J. C. Wise's Eastern Shore of Virginia in the Seventeenth Century, p. 302).
[6] Allen, Frederick J.: The Shoe Industry, p. 6.
[7] Weeden, William B.: Economic and Social History of New England, 1620–1789, Vol. II, p. 682.
[8] Allen, p. 13.
[9] Weeden, p. 682.
[10] Census of Manufactures, 1860, p. lxi.
[11] Vol. I, p. 444.
[12] See p. 16.
[13] Hazard, p. 46.
[14] The Ways of a Worker of a Century Ago, as Shown by the Diary of Joseph Lye, Shoemaker (Published by Fred A. Gannon, Salem, Mass.)

The only definite information regarding productivity applies to the later era, 1817–1822, and comes from the diary just referred to. Lye's usual daily production seems to have been two pairs of shoes, although he sometimes made three pairs, and on one day he records making "two pairs of village walking boots at 45 cents, two pairs military at 40 cents."[15] At that rate, the usual daily earnings of a good shoemaker, working for himself on "bespoke work" in his own shop, would be 80 to 90 cents. Two of Lye's entries read: "This week's work comes to $5.87 exclusive of other work;" "this week's work amounts to $5.40;" items which in both cases refer only to his earnings at the shoemaking trade.

Developments beginning shortly after 1750 materially changed the nature of the industry from one carried on in 1-man shops for a custom trade to large-scale production for the open market. In the initial transition—

> Though apprentices and journeymen were employed, the less skilled and more irregular labor of the women and girls of the family was also utilized. The shoemaker turned over to the entrepreneur the completed shoe, often the combined labor of every member of his family besides his apprentices and journeymen, but with all the processes done in his shop under his direction.[16]

Ultimately came diversification and lessened skill, as the work was put out from a central shop to home workers who were not necessarily journeyman shoemakers.

> Domestic workers came from miles around to the central shop to "take out" work; women got boot legs to side up and cord; men got boots to last and bottom for their own work, and straps to stick, tops and counters to sew on for their children's work. All the members of a family, oftentimes of a whole community, would be found working on boots.[17]

The greatly increased output which was necessary during the Revolution to supply shoes to the Army resulted in the establishment of shoe factories, and introduced "a distinction between capital and labor in the industry" and a division of labor within the factory.

> It was known that workmen were usually expert in particular operations, for instance, in cutting and fitting the uppers, or in preparing soles, or in sewing the sole to the upper. This fact produced a division of labor. Shoemaking in factories during this period, until the introduction of machinery, was marked also by the custom of having what were called "teams" of workers. A team consisted of a number of workers, each performing a particular process, the whole team producing an entire shoe. On the other hand, a team might consist of a group of men all experts on a single process. Such a team was usually known as a "gang." A gang of bottomers, for instance, often went from factory to factory, or from employer to employer, having a contract with each to bottom all the shoes in process of making. The team or gang system gradually passed largely out of use after the introduction of shoe machinery.
>
> The typical shoemaker had long been his own master. He worked in his little shop at home as he pleased, doing perhaps farm work or engaging in some other occupation a part of the year. He objected to serving any other master than himself, and believed that obedience to a foreman was a surrender of his personal rights and liberties. He was reluctant to submit to factory hours, from seven in the morning until six at night, and to exacting factory regulations. He opposed in like manner the introduction of labor-saving machinery. The general industrial growth of communities was, however, an irresistible though a slowly coming tide. Progressive methods of employment and the introduction of machinery gradually broke down all opposition.[18]

---

[15] The Ways of a Worker of a Century Ago, p. 13.
[16] Hazard, p. 25.
[17] Idem, p. 52.
[18] Allen, pp. 17–21.

The average daily earnings of shoemakers in factories in Massa chusetts was 73 cents during the decade 1791–1800, and $1.06 from 1821 to 1830, according to the Massachusetts Bureau of Statistics of Labor.[19] Wages at Lynn, which in 1830 "ranged from $5 to $7 a week," were paid in scrip.

The Union Store, a noted store of 1830, was established and carried on by a group of Lynn manufacturers. It was stocked with goods of all kinds, indeed, with everything that a man might need in daily life. Shoe manufacturers who were interested in this store gave their employes orders on the store in payment of wages. Each order read: "Please deliver to the bearer goods to the amount of _____." The man who insisted on cash payment of his wages usually had a great deal of difficulty in finding employment. The order went into circulation, for shoemakers used them to pay for goods that they bought at stores other than the Union Store, and to pay the doctor, the druggist, and others. The orders were accepted as worth 60 or 70 per cent of their face value when in general circulation, but were worth their full value in exchange for goods at the Union Store.

Fortunately, necessities of life were cheap. So a shoemaker who brought in his week's work and got an order on the store in payment for his wages, was usually able to exchange that order for enough goods to keep himself and his family alive for the week.[20]

That system was not confined to Lynn. The entrepreneur in the shoe business in this period often had his own grocery business, and "by having the grocery store where his goods, bought at wholesale, could be paid out at retail prices to his domestic workers, he got rid of paying wages in cash."[21]

From the rise of the factory to the introduction of machinery after 1850, the work of stitching the uppers, called "binding," was done almost wholly by women as a home occupation.

Since the women did the work in their own homes, much of it was done at times when they were not engaged in household duties. The factories of Lynn gave out a great deal of work to the women of the neighboring towns and villages, as well as to those within the city. In the fishing villages of the coast, where shoemaking was a winter occupation for fishermen, their wives and daughters found employment at shoebinding through a great part of the year.[22]

Shoe binding was done as well by women who depended upon it for their livelihood, and "by working all day they were able to earn 50 or 75 cents."[23] In 1803 the piecework price for shoe binding ranged from 22 to 50 cents per dozen pairs.[24]

The report of the Secretary of the Treasury on Statistics of Manufactures in 1832 shows the prevailing wage rates in the shoe factories after factory production was well organized, but before the introduction of any machinery except the pegging machine. These data also show the difference in rates paid for different types of work.

The lowest wage rate reported in Massachusetts was paid at Essex, Ipswich, Topsfield, and Wenham, where the product was almost entirely rough work shoes for men and boys, which found their chief market in the South. The average rate was 46 cents a day for men and 14 cents for women. Daily earnings on this grade of work were as low as 33 cents. At Danvers, where a comparable grade of goods was produced, men averaged 66 cents, boys 30 cents, and women 25 cents per day. Marblehead specialized in children's shoes and men's

---

[19] History of Wages and Prices in Massachusetts, 1752–1883, p. 280.
[20] Gannon, pp. 15–16.
[21] Hazard, pp. 51–52.
[22] Abbott, Edith: Women in Industry, p. 155.
[23] Gannon, p. 22.
[24] Massachusetts Bureau of Statistics of Labor: History of Wages and Prices, p. 175.

slippers, the average daily rate on which was 52 cents for men, 28 cents for boys, and 13 cents for women. The report adds that "many citizens of this town go to sea or fishing in the summer and make shoes in the winter." [25]

In factories making men's shoes for general market the usual rate was 70 cents a day, although at Randolph the average was 83 cents for men, which is a higher rate than that paid at Lynn on high-grade women's shoes. The average daily rate in the Lynn factories was 72 cents for men, 45 cents for boys, and 22 cents for women. This rate is considerably lower than that reported by Braintree and Weymouth, which also manufactured women's shoes. In these towns the average rate is given as $1 a day. While many workers in the Lynn factories received that much, daily rates of 50 and 67 cents were not uncommon.

Wages were higher in Boston than elsewhere, averaging $1.10 per day for men, and 50 cents for women and boys. Referring to the shoe trade in Boston the report says:

> The boot and shoe manufacture in this city is so intimately connected with the same branches in the neighboring counties that it is not easy to separate it. Many of the principal establishments in Boston have shops in the country to which they furnish the stock and from which they receive the manufactured article. Most of the shoe stores, as they are termed, have one or more persons employed in making and repairing shoes in the city, while at the same time they have the greater part of their saleable stock from the country. Many of the persons who are taken into the above estimate are merely cobblers, keeping a small shop and employing one person, while many others employ from 12 to 20 constantly.[26]

In western Massachusetts both men's and women's shoes were made and the average daily rate was 88 cents, which was considerably higher than the average in Essex County, where the trade was concentrated. Women and boys were apparently not employed in the industry in the western part of the State; at any rate they are not shown in the reports. In Worcester, where the trade was "custom work entirely" [27] men earned 84 cents a day, a figure which still reflected the 40-cent rate on bespoke work, on the assumed production of two pairs daily.

The average daily rates in other States were: 67 cents for men, 50 cents for boys, and 30 cents for women, in New Hampshire; 78 cents for men in Maine; and "$18 a month in towns and from $8 to $10 in the country" [28] in Pennsylvania. The McLane report does not cover the boot and shoe industry in New York, although it was extensive at that time.

In 1835 "Philadelphia shoemakers publicly complained that the Eastern States, meaning Massachusetts, did not do shoemaking as well as they and charged less. This was probably true in all its order and sale work aside from its regular private custom work. New England was then specializing in brogans and cheap shoes for women. The Philadelphia shoe industry always made the highest grade shoes with skilled German workers." [29]

The working-day in 1832 in shoe factories reported in the McLane report was uniformly 12 hours.

---

[25] McLane, Louis: Statistics of Manufactures in the United States, 1832 (Report of U. S. Treasury), Vol. I, p. 238.
[26] McLane Report, Vol. I, p. 468.
[27] Idem, Vol. I, p. 569.
[28] Idem, Vol. II, p. 598.
[29] Hazard, p. 144, footnote.

SOUTHERN MANUFACTURE

Authorities on the boot and shoe industry agree that the manufacture of shoes in the southern colonies was negligible. Planters and the well-to-do in general imported foreign-made goods for their personal wear, while, on the other hand, the servants and slaves on the plantations afforded the best market for the inferior work shoes produced in certain sections of Massachusetts and Connecticut. In the earlier period, however, before New England began exporting shoes, there was undoubtedly a considerable home manufacture in Virginia.

The list of artificers for whom the London Company advertised in 1609 did not include tanners, curriers and shoemakers, from which it would be inferred that the corporation expected to furnish the settlers with shoes from England in addition to every other form of clothing. In the broadside issued by the company in 1611, tanners and shoemakers were among those to whom inducements to emigrate were offered; and these inducements proved effective, for it is known that there were shoemakers and tanners in the colony in 1616 who followed their trades as well as cultivated the ground.[30]

Captain Mathews was a prominent planter who made a point of demonstrating his theory that a well-managed plantation could produce successfully every commodity necessary to its maintenance. In 1648, "in addition to having spinners and weavers among his servants and slaves, he owned a tannery and employed eight shoemakers, a number so great that they must have been engaged in part in making shoes for sale." [31]   Reference has already been made to another Virginia colonist who employed nine men in his "shoe factory." [32]   Bruce also mentions this same planter, and adds that "there were few planters of easy fortune who did not have tradesmen of this character in their employment," [33] since "leading planters were in the habit of importing shoemakers from England for the same reasons that moved them to bring in representatives of other trades." [34]

Here again, in trying to determine wages paid these workers, we encounter the indenture system, and while Bruce asserts that "there are many indications in the records of the latter half of the seventeenth century that both tanners and shoemakers constituted a class of importance in the colony, including those who were free as well as those who were serving under articles of indenture," [35] there is no reference to earnings in the trade, and quite probably the work was chiefly that of indentured servants without wages.

Plantation accounts of a later period develop a new angle—the practice followed by planters who had shoemakers of hiring them out to neighbors who needed their services. Whether these craftsmen were indentured servants or negro slaves is not known, but in this connection it is immaterial, since in either case the amount paid for their work would have gone not to them but to their masters.

Letters in the "Jones Family Papers" [36] suggest that the shoemakers on the Jones estate were much in demand by neighboring planters. Bills against these planters in the Jones account books give a fair idea of the labor cost in the shoes made from their own stock, probably for their servants and slaves. In 1747 Thomas Jones billed one

[30] Bruce, Philip A.: Economic History of Virginia in the Seventeenth Century, Vol. II, pp. 474-475.
[31] Idem, Vol. II, pp. 475-476.
[32] See p. 101.
[33] Bruce, Vol. II, p. 476.
[34] Idem, Vol. II, p. 477.
[35] Idem, p. 476.
[36] Manuscript Collection, Library of Congress.

customer for: "Making 14 pairs of plains, 14s. [$2.67];" and "4 pairs of shoes, 5s. [83.3 cents]." The following year the account reads: "To making 8 pairs of men's and women's pumps, 12s. [$2]; 1 pair men's falls, 1/3 [21 cents]; 18 pairs of plains, 18s. [$3]." In 1749 another of Jones's neighbors was billed: "To two days' work of two shoemakers, 8s. [$1.33]"; and later in the same year, "to one day's work of one shoemaker, 1s. [16.7 cents]."

BOOTS

Boots, according to one history of the industry, "were little worn before the War for Independence."[37] Philadelphia seems to have been the center of the early manufacture of boots and the home of the early trade organizations of both workers and employers, as well as the scene of the prosecution of the first trial of trade-unionists for "combination and conspiracy to raise their wages."

The first organization of journeymen cordwainers was in Philadelphia in 1792, and during its life the scale for making ordinary boots rose from $1.40 in 1792 to $2.75 in 1796, for shop and bespoke work. The journeymen agreed to do order work for $2.50 "in order to encourage the exportation trade."

This was taken advantage of at the time of the cholera epidemic in 1798 when the journeymen were paid only $2.25. After the journeymen returned to the city they organized their second strike, in 1798, for an increase. This was immediately granted by the employers, but in the following year, 1799, the employers effected an organization and ordered a return to the former wage. This caused an obstinate strike and lockout of nine or ten weeks, ending in a compromise. Again in 1804 there was another brief strike, at which the journeymen won and the employers agreed to pay $2.75. But after Christmas, when work became slack, the price of order work was reduced to $2.50. This led to the obstinate strike of 1805 in which the journeymen demanded a flat increase all round to $3 on both wholesale and retail work.[38]

The testimony in the trial of the Philadelphia cordwainers in 1806 [39] which grew out of this strike contains considerable information dealing with wages and working conditions in the bootmaking trade in the first decade of the nineteenth century.

The scale current in 1805 and the proposed increase which the employers, through a general agreement, refused to grant were:[40]

	Prices in 1805	Prices proposed
Fancy tops	$4. 25	$5. 00
Back straps	3. 75	4. 00
Long boots	2. 75	3. 00
Cossacks	2. 75	3. 00
Bootees	2. 50	3. 00

Evidence was introduced to show that the new prices asked by the Philadelphia cordwainers were the rates then prevailing in New York and Baltimore.[41] In this connection the statement was made that "considering how much dearer house rent, firing, and marketing is at those places, the journeymen in Philadelphia have the advantage even at the present rates."[42]

[37] Census of Manufactures, 1860, p. lxix.
[38] Commons, John R.: Introduction to Trial of the Philadelphia Cordwainers, 1806, In Documentary History of American Industrial Society, Vol. III, p. 37.
[39] Documentary History of American Industrial Society, Vol. III.
[40] Idem, p. 106.
[41] Idem, p. 112.
[42] Idem, p. 103.

Replying to a question about journeymen's weekly earnings, one employer said:

I have had them earn but six and seven dollars, but some have earned eleven and a quarter and twelve dollars a week; a good workman may earn eleven and a quarter a week, for a good workman can make three pairs of back strap boots a week, which at $3.75 a pair is eleven dollars and a quarter.[40]

A journeyman called upon as witness was asked: "How many hours a day must a man work to earn $11.25 per week?" He replied, "I could not earn ten dollars at the present rates if I was to work all the twenty-four hours of the day." [43] Another journeyman testified:

A man can not make a pair of back straps under three days, setting steadily, late and early. I can not make twelve dollars a week, and I much doubt if any man can on full-dress, fancy-top, back strap boots.[44]

A third said:

I work very hard, and later hours than other men. At most I earn but ten dollars a week; I don't remember I ever earned eleven and a quarter. In common I could not earn more than seven or eight; on an average I can not make more than nine dollars.[45]

When fancy-top boots came into fashion in the summer of 1805, the employers granted an advance of 50 cents above the prevailing rate on backstrap boots for the new model. According to one witness who worked on fancy-top boots at the price originally fixed— "I could only make eight dollars and a half a week, and I worked from five in the morning until twelve or one at night. I can not make more than two pair a week." [46]

The strike was lost and the defendants in the conspiracy trial were found "guilty of a combination to raise their wages" and fined "eight dollars each, with costs of suit." [47] In the list of prices adopted by the employers at the close of the strike order work was not mentioned, and because of the failure of the strike "workmen were compelled to accept the employers' list."

Consequently in 1806, as compared with 1789, the price for boots (i. e. ordinary long boots and cossacks) paid to the journeymen on retail and custom work had advanced from $1.40 to $2.75, while the price on wholesale work of the same quality, after futile efforts of the journeymen to equalize it, was left open to individual bargains.[48]

The New York piece-price scale in effect in 1805 [49] was:

Back strap boots, fair tops	$4. 00
Back strapping the top	. 75
Ornament straps closed outside	. 25
Back strap bootees	3. 50
Wax legs closed outside, plain counters, fair tops	3. 25
Cordovan boots, fair-tops	3. 00
Cordovan bootees	2. 50
Suwarrow boots, closed outside	3. 00
Suwarrow, inside closed, bespoke	2. 75
Suwarrow, inside, inferior work	2. 50
Binding boots	. 25
Stabbing boots	. 25
Footing old boots	2. 00
Foxing new boots	. 50
Foxing and countering old boots	2. 00
Foxing without counters	1. 75
Shoes, best work	1. 12
Shoes, inferior work	1. 00

[40] Documentary History of American Industrial Society, Vol. III, p. 106.
[43] Idem, p. 118.   [45] Idem, p. 123.   [47] Idem, p. 236.
[44] Idem, pp. 121-122.   [46] Idem, p. 124.   [48] Commons, op. cit., p. 38.
[49] Documentary History of American Industrial Society, Vol. III, pp. 368-369.

Pumps, French edges_____ $1. 12
Pumps, shouldered edges_____ 1. 00
Golo shoes_____ 1. 50
Stitching rans_____ . 75
Cork soles_____ . 50

The organized journeymen cordwainers of Pittsburgh were defendants in 1815 in a conspiracy trial similar, in the indictment and developments, to that of the Philadelphia bootmakers nine years before. The wage scale and earnings, however, can not be so definitely established from the testimony in the Pittsburgh trial [50] as in the Philadelphia case. The price on cossacks, which had been $2.75, was raised to $3.25; bootees went from $2.25 to $2.75; fine shoes were to pay $1.25 and men's pumps, $1.12½.

The organized journeymen struck to enforce this new scale and the organized employers countered with the proposal to adopt the Philadelphia scale. The only indication of the outcome of the strike is the trial itself, which suggests that the men lost, and the fact that the defendants were found guilty and fined $1 each and costs.

One journeyman, testifying for the prosecution, said that an industrious man could support his family under the current scale, as living was cheaper than it had been. "A common week's work upon cossacks is nine dollars—I have earned twelve. Wages paid every Saturday evening." [51]

Apparently it was customary for the journeyman to live with their employers. In 1812 the members of the union "took an oath not to give more than two dollars a week for boarding and finding to any employer. We thought it duly proportioned to the wages given by them." [52] The employers, in their counterproposal at the time of the strike, three years later, "agreed to board them at $2.50 a week and find them with room, fires, candles, etc." [53]

An employer who "generally had from fourteen to twenty-two hands" and who paid $3 instead of $2.75 for work on cossacks, gave as his objection to the scale the fact that "they made no difference between good and bad workmen, or between customer and order work." [54]

In an "Address to the Journeymen Cordwainers of the City and County of Philadelphia", issued in 1835 by the 200 members of the "United Beneficial Society of Journeyman Cordwainers" it was declared that "the wages of $2.75 formerly paid for boots have fallen to $1.12½; that their earnings of $9 to $10 a week have fallen to $4 to $6; that, in order to earn such wages they must work in many instances fourteen hours a day" while other skilled tradesmen "are earning $8 to $12 a week" and often "only working ten hours a day." [55]

Boot and shoe workers were outstanding among the crafts which early formed trade organizations. These were sufficiently effective and active that "of the 17 trials for conspiracy prior to 1842, the shoemakers occasioned nine." [56]

[50] Documentary Histosy of American Industrial Society, Vol. IV, pp. 15–87.
[51] Idem, p. 32.
[52] Idem, p. 34.
[53] Idem, p. 46.
[54] Idem, p. 49.
[55] Commons, in Documentary History of American Industrial Society, Vol. III, p. 40.
[56] Idem, p. 19.

Chapter 10.—CLOTHING TRADES

TAILORING

Tailors were specifically included in the second act of Massachusetts Bay Colony General Court, 1633, fixing maximum wages for workers. In that statute "master taylors" were allowed 1s. (24.3 cents) a day with "dyett," while "inferior taylors" were to be content with 8d. (16 cents) and board.

Ten years later one of the Connecticut settlements which perhaps had identical or similar legal restraint upon the earnings of tailors, nevertheless made it possible for them to earn the prescribed amount by legislating work for them:

A public order of the colony of New Haven, in 1643, soon after its settlement, required the tailors to see that every family was provided with "a coat of cotton woole well and substantially made." In the following year the functions of the craft were again called into exercise for the public safety in a curious order requiring, under penalty, that so soon as canvas and cotton could be obtained from abroad, "every family within the plantation shall accordingly provide and after continue furnished with a coate well made and soe quilted with cotton woole as may be fit for service and a comfortable defence against Indian arrowes, and the taylors about town shall consider and advise how to make them and take care that they be done without unnecessary delay." [1]

While journeymen tailors of this period were, like the weavers and the shoemakers, largely itinerant workers, the tailoring shop had appeared in the larger settlements, to judge by a partnership agreement drawn up in Boston in 1639. By the terms of this 7-year agreement the—

Co-partners in the trade of Taylery shal be and continue together daylie in one shoppe and be at equall costs and charges in providing and paying for shoproome and all necessary utensills and things requisite to their saide trade and shall each of them have one Apprentice servant in their joynt shoppe from time to time during the said terme of seaven yeares. All the profitts, commodities and advantages which shal be gotten by them in theire said trade, and by the industry and worke of them the said partyes to these presents, and of theire Apprentice servants shal be equally Due and be divided and parted from time to time unto and betweene the saide partyes to these presents. In case of sickness or other necessary occasion of absence of them the saide parties to these presents from their saide joynt shopp during the said terme, if the saide absence shall be by the space of a Day or more, that then the one of the said parties shall allow unto the other 16d. [22.3 cents] for every Dayes absence of each other.[2]

Another agreement of record seems to be a modified indenture into which Luke Mathews, a tailor of Hereford, entered with Thomas Landon, of Virginia:

Mathews bound himself to serve Landon for a period of two years, his term to begin when he reached the Colony; the remuneration was to be six pence [8.4 cents] a day when working for members of Landon's family, but when for other persons he was to be entitled to one-half the proceeds of his labor, whatever it might be.[3]

Six tailors were sent to the Virginia colony in 1608 as indentured servants and many freemen "who followed this calling secured a livelihood by working by the day or by the task." [4] Earnings of

---

[1] Census of Manufactures, 1860, p. lxiii.
[2] Lechford, Thomas: Manuscript Notebook, 1638-1641 (published by American Antiquarian Society, 1885), pp. 91-92.
[3] Bruce, Philip A.: Economic History of Virginia in the 17th Century, Vol. II, p. 471.
[4] Idem, p. 472.

tailors of this period are always quoted in pounds of tobacco, conversion of which into American money, using the scant data on tobacco prices which we have,[5] produces rather inconsistent results.

In 1678, Philip Thomas of Henrico brought in a statement of indebtedness against Captain Crews of that county which showed that he had for forty-two and a half days been employed in the service of the latter under an agreement promising him twenty pounds of tobacco (1/8) [28 cents] each day. William Murray was in 1697 sued by John Nelson, a tailor, for the amount which had been agreed upon as his reward for services extending over six weeks. This was one thousand pounds of tobacco £8 6s. 8d., or about 4/4 per day [$27.77 or 72.3 cents a day].[6]

Bruce relates "a curious instance which throws light upon the social standing" of craftsmen in the Virginia colony:

James Bullock, a tailor, entered into a wager with Mr. Mathew Slader that in a race to take place between their horses he would prove the winner. The court, instead of allowing him the amount agreed upon in the bet, which he seems to have won, fined him one hundred pounds of tobacco, on the ground that it was illegal for laborers to participate in horse-racing, this being a sport reserved exclusively for gentlemen. Tailors, nevertheless, were considered sufficiently respectable to act as the attorneys of leading planters in special transactions.[7]

"There are numerous indications," Bruce adds, "that tailors enjoyed a large measure of prosperity."

Two accounts of wage rates in Pennsylvania, one referring to 1698,[8] the other to 1710,[9] give 12s. ($2.40) a week and board as the usual earnings of journeyman tailors. In New York in 1737 "a tailor gets 20s. [$2.50] for making a suit of clothes"[10] and in Virginia in 1757 a tailor's bill for "making a coat, waistcoat and 2 pair breeches" was £1 6s. ($4.33).[11]

A woman dressmaker in Salem, Mass., in 1768 charged 12s. old tenor (about 25 cents) for day work, and from £1 to £1 2s. 6d. (45 to 50 cents) for making a gown.[12]

A piece, or "job" system of payment in place of daily rates came into use toward the close of the eighteenth century, and "during the first half of the nineteenth century there seems to have been little uniformity in methods of payment, although it is probable that the piece system predominated."[13]

Journeyman tailors of Baltimore had a trade organization as early as 1795 which "forced wages up to seven shillings sixpence [$1] per job." Later, in 1805, "the pay per job was fixed at 8/9 [$1.16] and a system of 'extras' was introduced by which what had once been four jobs was at last made to count as eight."[14]

The wages of tailors, "finding themselves and working 14 and 15 hours a day, were from $7 to $9 a week"[15] in Ohio in 1819, according to a traveler, who, however, probably "made the estimate after talking with journeymen about their piece scales."[16] Another traveler

---

[5] See p. 13.
[6] Bruce, Vol. II, p. 472.
[7] Idem, p. 473.
[8] Thomas, Gabriel: An Historical and Geographical Account of the Province and Countrey of Pensilvania (1698).
[9] Captain Robert Boyles' Voayages and Adventures, in Hart's History Told by Contemporaries, Vol. II, p. 75.
[10] Letter in Memorial History of New York City, Vol. II, p. 203.
[11] Jones Family Papers, Manuscript, Library of Congress.
[12] Manuscript Account Book, Lee-Cabot Papers, Massachusetts Historical Society.
[13] Stowell, Charles Jacob: Studies in Trade-Unionism in the Custom Tailoring Trade, p. 18.
[14] McMaster, John Bach: History of the People of the United States, Vol. III, p. 511.
[15] Hulme's Journal, in Thwaite's Early Western Travels, Vol. X, p. 75.
[16] Stowell, p. 18.

reported that journeymen tailors were making $2 a day in Pittsburgh in 1817,[17] while in Kentucky at the same time "a tailor will charge from $5 to $10 for making a coat." [18]

Average weekly earnings of tailors in Massachusetts in 1815 was $6, or $3 with board. Ten years later the rate with board was the same, while the rate without board had advanced to $7 and $8. In 1828 daily rates were $1.25 and $1.50.[19]

The involved system of piece prices prevailing is shown in the "Trial of Twenty-four Journeymen Tailors Charged with a Conspiracy" in Philadelphia in 1827. The case rose out of an order which was not specifically covered by the bill of prices. The six men working on the garment, a "lady's riding habit of thin pongee,"[20] fixed $7.06 as the price for making, which, according to the employers, was $1 more than the bill of prices on thin material called for. They paid the men their price and then discharged them, after which most of their employees struck because, as one witness expressed it, they "saw no reason for discharging men for demanding the usual wages." [21] The defendants were acquitted of the charge of conspiracy to raise wages, but were found guilty on the third count in the indictment, that of trying to force the reinstatement of the discharged workers. The attorney for the defense gave notice of appeal, and if the case was followed further the record apparently has not been found.

The bill of prices introduced as evidence was:

Ladies' Habits, Coats and Pelisses [22]

Habits without skirts, plain	$4. 50
Habits with skirts, plain	6. 00
If loops or strings to tie up at bottom, extra	. 25
Vent at sleeve hand, without buttons, extra	. 12½
Wadding in breast, extra	. 25
Hussar skirts rantered to body, extra	. 12½
Each fly in breast, extra	. 25
Habits, hussar fashion, without skirts	6. 00
Habits, hussar fashion, with skirts	7. 50
Wadded sleeve heads, extra	. 18¾

The testimony contains no reference to the time involved, or to weekly earnings on piecework. One witness declared that "if regular prices are not paid we can't support ourselves."[23] Wages for week work were given as $12 in the testimony.[23]

An "Emigrants' Directory" of 1820, "advised tailors who might come to this country that in New York their trade had been 'much injured by the employment of women and boys who work from twenty-five to fifty per cent cheaper than the men.' A man that can cut, it was specified, 'will be occasionally very well paid, the women not being very clever in this branch of the business makes men more necessary. Trousers are all made by women.'" [24]

---

[17] Birkbeck, Morris: Notes on a Journey in America from the Coast of Virginia to the Territory of Illinois (1817).

[18] Warden, D. B.: A Statistical, Political and Historical Account of the United States, Vol. II, p. 340.

[19] Massachusetts Bureau of Statistics of Labor: History of Wages and Prices in Massachusetts, 1752–1883, p. 165.

[20] Trial, p. 16.

[21] Idem, p. 49.

[22] Idem, p. 129.

[23] Idem, p. 48.

[24] Abbott, Edith: Women in Industry, p. 218, quoting "View of the United States of America, A Complete Emigrant's Directory" (London, 1820), p. 371.

The McLane report of 1832 covers 100 tailoring shops in Boston, employing 300 men at $2 a day, and 100 boys and 1,300 women at 50 cents a day.[25]

READY-MADE CLOTHING

"The first ready-made clothing of which we have record was 'shirts for the Indians,' which were made by at least one woman in Northfield, Mass., about 1725 for 8d. [11.2 cents] each, and 'men's Breeches' which were made for 1s. 6d. [25 cents] a pair." [26] While "we are accustomed to associate the ready-made industry with the introduction of machinery * * * the industry was known long before." The custom trade was the first to begin supplying the demand for ready-made clothes, a demand which came "with the development of a middle class who demanded better clothing than a workingman's suit, but were still unable to pay for the expensive custom suit." [27]

By 1835 "the manufacture of ready-made clothing had become a thriving business" but "it was practically confined to men's and boys' clothing of the cheaper grades and to shirts, and the quantities manufactured were necessarily small, the work being all done by hand. It is probable, though there are practically no statistics on the subject, that during this period women retained all their former work, the lighter forms of sewing, and at the same time slowly encroached upon the domain of the man tailor." [28]

In its treatment of wages, hours, and working conditions of women in the clothing trades in the early years of the industry,[29] the report of the United States Department of Commerce and Labor on Woman and Child Wage Earners in the United States [30] draws upon the labor papers of the period, and the investigations of Mathew Carey, for most of its data. It prefaces its summary with the declaration that "the history of this period, like that of the better-known period of the machine, is a tale of long hours, low wages, and exploitation." [31]

It was declared that in Philadelphia in 1829 it required "great expertness, unceasing industry from sunrise till 10 or 11 o'clock at night, constant employment (which few of them have) without any interruption whatever from sickness or attention to their families, to earn a dollar and a half a week," and that much of the workers' time had to be given to "travelling 8, 10, 12, or 14 squares for work and as many to take it back when finished." [32]

Conditions in New York a year later were, according to the New York Sentinel, the first labor daily, as bad as those in Philadelphia, and "no means had been discovered or adopted to mitigate the distress."

Many women in New York, said the Sentinel, were employed "in making duck pantaloons for a readymade clothes store for 4 cents a pair, and cotton shirts for 7 cents apiece. These women stated," said the Sentinel, "that with the most unremitting industry they could sew no more than three pair of pantaloons, or one shirt, in a day, and that they were obliged to labor for this paltry pittance

[25] McLane, Louis: Statistics of Manufactures in the United States, 1832, Vol. I, p. 465.
[26] Sumner, Helen L.: History of Women in Industry in the United States. In Vol. IX of the U. S. Department of Commerce and Labor Report on Conditions of Women and Child Wage Earners in the United States, p. 120.
[27] Stowell, p. 20.
[28] Sumner, p. 123.
[29] In Vol. IX, pp. 115–174.
[30] Senate Document No. 645, 61st Congress, 2d session.
[31] Sumner, p. 123.
[32] Sumner, p. 123, quoting Free Trade Advocate, Philadelphia, Mar. 14, 1829.

or be entirely without employment." The storekeeper, for whom they wrought, could procure the services of emigrants wretchedly poor, or get his work done at the almshouse, and would give no higher wages. In consequence, the price of such work was reduced to nearly a similar rate throughout the city.[33]

In Boston, the report continues, "conditions were as bad as in Philadelphia and New York—

The Rev. Joseph Tuckerman recorded in 1830 that he had recently been told "by a very respectable keeper of a slop shop that he has for some time past had 50 applications a day from females for work with which he could not supply them; and the work sought by them is coarse shirts to be made at 10, 8, or even 6¼ cents each, or laborers' frocks, or duck pantaloons, at the same prices." The average weekly wages for such work, when a woman was fully employed, he gave as but a dollar or a dollar and a quarter—less, apparently, than in Philadelphia. Rents, moreover, he stated to be higher in Boston than in Philadelphia, the common price of a room being a dollar a week. [34]

Pittsburgh tailors in 1830 were paying for "making a pair of pantaloons, which took about 15 hours, 25 cents, and for making a shirt, 'that takes a woman a whole day if she attends to any other work in her family,' 12½ cents." [35] These rates are practically identical with those of 8d. (11.2 cents) for shirts and 1s. 6d. (25 cents) for "men's breeches" paid a century before, as previously noted.

Mathew Carey estimated yearly receipts and expenditures of the woman worker in the clothing trade as follows: [36]

Forty-four weeks, at $1.25 _____ $55. 00
Lodgings, 50 cents per week _____ $26. 00
Fuel, 25 cents per week, but say only 12½ _____ 6. 50
                                                            ———— 32. 50

Remains for victuals and clothes _____ 22. 50

Later, in 1833, Carey "made still another calculation of the receipts and expenditures of the seamstress. Laying aside all consideration of unemployment, sickness, or lack of skill and rapidity, and taking as a basis the highest wages paid, he made, for a woman without children, the following calculation per annum:" [37]

Nine shirts per week, $1.12½ _____ $58. 50
Rent, at 50 cents _____ $26. 00
Shoes and clothes, suppose _____ 10. 00
Fuel per week, say 15 cents _____ 7. 80
Soap, candles, etc., 8 cents _____ 4. 16
Remain for food and drink 20 cents per week, or about 2¾ cents
  per day _____ 10. 54
                                                            ———— 58. 50

Expert seamstresses could not make more than eight or nine shirts or duck pantaloons a week, which at the highest price paid, 12½ cents, would amount to only $1.12½.[38]

During the decade 1825–1835 women employed in the clothing trades in the three largest centers, New York, Philadelphia, and Baltimore, instituted a number of movements toward organization. Most of these were benevolent societies chiefly, but one organized in Baltimore in 1833 seems to have been not only economic but militant. It organized for the purpose of striking for increased wages, and "resolved that, more effectively to accomplish our purpose, we enter into a positive agreement to take out no work from the shops until proper rates be established." The women "strenuously advised and

---

[33] Sumner, p. 124.
[34] Idem, p. 125.
[35] Idem, p. 127.
[36] Idem., p. 127.
[37] Idem, pp. 128–129.
[38] Idem, pp. 127–128.

requested" all other women in the trade to cooperate "in the present attempt to establish such a bill of wages as shall remunerate us for our labor."

At a later meeting a bill of prices was drawn up and a strike to enforce it was called for October 1. "On the following day the journeymen tailors of Baltimore issued a call for a special meeting for the purpose of assisting the women in their stand for higher wages. The women's organization was called the Female Union Society of Tailoresses and Seamstresses. The result of the strike and the further work of the Female Union Society are unknown." [39]

---

[39] Andrews, John B.: History of Women in Trade Unions. Vol. X of Report on Conditions of Woman and Child Wage Earners in the United States, pp. 38–39.

Chapter 11.—PRINTING AND PUBLISHING

Harvard College owned and controlled the first printing press in the American Colonies, and the first printers were in the employ of the colonial government. Governmental control went so far that in 1664 the Massachusetts Bay Colony General Court ordered that "for the Preventing of Irregularyties and Abuse to the authority of this Country by the Printing Presse * * * their shall no Printing Press be allowed in any Town within this Jurisdiction but in Cambridge, nor shall any person or persons presume to print any copie but by the allowance first had and obtayned under the hand of such as this court shall from time to time Impower."[1] Shortly afterward, this law was amended "to permit the use of a press at Boston, and a person was authorized to conduct it, subject, however, to the licensers who were appointed for the purpose of inspecting it."[2] Even with some liberalization from time to time, it was not until well along in the eighteenth century that printers became craftsmen independent of the control of colonial authorities.

Stephen Daye, the first printer, was "granted three hundred acres of land where it may be convenient, without prejudice to any town." The grant was made to him as printer for the Colony, in 1641, but he did not take up the land, and in 1655, six years after he had left the position, he appealed to the court for "Recompence of his Care and Charge in furtheringe the work of Printing." The court confirmed the original grant of land, but two years later Daye was still complaining to the General Court that "he hath suffered much damage by Erecting the Printing Presse at Cambridge for which he never had yett any Considerable Sattisfaction."[3]

His successor, Samuel Green, was ordered by the General Court, in 1654, to print the laws of the Colony "to the number of five, six, or seven hundred as the Court shall order, all which coppies the Treasurer shall take and pay for in wheate for the number of five hundred after the rate of one penny [1.4 cents] a sheete, or eight shillings [$1.33] a hundred for five hundred sheets."[4]

Green printed the Indian Bible on the Cambridge presses, the second of which had been shipped from England for the purpose by the Society for Propagating the Gospel among the Indians. In the account [5] presented to the society by its colonial agent for that piece of work were the following labor charges. Other items in the original, not quoted here, cover stock and repairs to the presses.

	£	s.	d.	
To printing the Title Sheete to the New Testament	1	0	0	($3.33)
To printing 1500 Cattechisms	15	0	0	($50.00)
To printing 21 sheets of the Old Testament, att 3 lb. 10s. [$11.67] per sheete, Mr. Johnson being absent	73	10	0	($245.00)
To printing 25 sheetes with his healp, att 50s. [$8.33] per sheete	62	10	0	($208.33)
To binding 200 Testaments att 6d. [8.4 cents] a peece	5	0	0	($16.67)

[1] Thomas, Isaiah: History of Printing in America (1st ed. Mass. 1810), Vol. I, p. 247. Massachusetts Bay Colony Records quoted.
[2] Idem, Vol. I, p. 207.
[3] Idem, Vol. I, p. 230.
[4] Idem, Vol. I, p. 236–237.
[5] Idem, Vol. I, p. 243.

118

Johnson, mentioned in Green's account, was sent from England by the society under a 3-year contract, to assist in the work of printing the Indian Bible. The printers estimated that with two men working together they could "print a sheete every weeke" and computed the whole job "to amount to a hundred and fifty sheetes." Johnson proved unreliable, however, and "absented himselfe from the worke more than halfe a yeare att one time," which is given by the agent of the society as accounting for the fact that Green had worked alone on 21 sheets of the Bible and had in consequence raised his price from £2 10s. to £3 10s. [$8.33 to $11.67].[6]

There is apparently no available record of the wages of journeyman printers from the time, after the opening of the eighteenth century, when they began to work independently, in the publication of tracts, books, and newspapers, until the close of the century. Perhaps that is explained in Thomas's statement that "it seems to have been the custom with master printers in Boston at that time, when their business was on a very small scale, instead of hiring those who had served a regular apprenticeship to the trade as journeymen, to admit them as temporary partners in work and to draw a proportion of the profit."[7] Thomas relates that he himself "accepted an offer for board for his services" on one job,[8] and Benjamin Franklin, while he frequently refers to the low wages he received as a journeyman, fails to state what those wages were.

Thomas mentions salaries paid to two printers who were employed as official printers to provincial governments before the Revolution. One of these was retained by both Virginia and Maryland, each of which paid him "a salary of two hundred pounds per annum in country produce." Later, in 1740, Maryland terminated that arrangement and appointed another man "printer for the colony" at an annual salary of £500 ($1,335)[9] currency. "For this sum he printed the laws as they were made from session to session, proclamations, &c., he being paid the cost of paper used in the work."[10] When he died in 1767 his widow succeeded him as official printer.

Apparently it was quite the custom for wives of printers to take over the business of a printing establishment upon the death of their husbands. Thomas makes frequent reference, in his biographies of early printers, to the succession of the widow to the business. In most cases she was an employer only, but Anne Franklin, widow of James and sister-in-law of Benjamin, "printed for the colony" of Rhode Island, in 1745, assisted by her two daughters, who "were correct and quick compositors at case,"[11] having been instructed by their father.

Before the Revolution "printing was confined to the capitals of the colonies, but the war occasioned the dispersion of the presses," largely to insure their safety, and "after the establishment of our independence presses multiplied very fast not only in seaports but in all the principal inland towns and villages."[12]

Following this rapid development of printing and the increase in the number of newspapers, a number which Thomas found "almost

---

[6] Idem, Vol. I, p. 266 (quoting letter from colonial agent to society in London).
[7] Idem, Vol. I, p. 301.
[8] Idem, Vol. I, p. 370.
[9] Maryland currency—pound worth $2.67.
[10] Thomas, Vol. II, pp. 128–129.
[11] Idem, Vol. I, p. 420.
[12] Idem, Vol. I, p. 210.

incredible" in 1810,[13] sporadic organizations of journeymen sprang up to establish and stabilize rates of wages. A study of these organizations was published by the Bureau of Labor of the United States Department of Commerce and Labor in its Bulletin No. 61, November, 1905.[14] Except where otherwise noted, data on printers' wages from 1786 are taken from this report of the bureau, and apply only to what were, substantially, union scales. Rates at which the "tramp printer" and partially skilled men worked have not been found to an extent which would justify their inclusion.

In 1786, 26 journeyman printers of Philadelphia, "probably comprising a majority of the competent men in the city at that time," met and unanimously resolved to resist an attempted wage reduction, and agreed not "to engage to work for any printing establishment in this city or county under the sum of $6.00 per week," and to support "such of our brethren as shall be thrown out of employment by refusing to work for less than $6 per week."

The rate in New York was substantially lower than that in Philadelphia at the time, evidently 87½ cents a day, and not until 1795 did the journeymen of New York succeed in raising their rate to $1. Four years later the Franklin Typographical Society of Journeyman Printers of New York was formed. It drew up a complete wage scale and struck to enforce it. This scale called for 25 cents for 1,000 ems, not less than $7 a week in book and job work, and $8 a week on newspapers.

The Philadelphia Typographical Society was organized in 1802 and drew up a bill of prices, which is believed to be the oldest printers' scale which has been preserved. In presenting the scale to the master printers for acceptance the society asserted that "we have confined ourselves to what a majority of employers in this city gives" and that its chief purpose was "to have one uniform price established." The scale was:

Composition:
Per week, not less than _____ $8. 00
Every 1,000 m's, from brevier to English, inclusive_____ . 25
Common rule or figure work_____ . 50
Press work:
Per week, not less than_____ $8. 00
All paper below medium, per token (240 sheets)_____ . 30
All paper above medium, per token_____ . 37½
Broadsides, per token_____ . 75
Cards, per pack_____ . 12½
All small jobs_____ . 30

A year later the price of composition on newspapers was increased to 30 cents per 1,000 ems, and a charge was placed on each alteration from copy after proofs had been corrected.

While the Philadelphia society was growing stronger numerically and economically, the craft in New York was losing ground. By 1804 the scale previously adopted had been so demoralized that compositors were taking 5 cents per 1,000 ems less, and pressmen were working for 25 cents per token instead of 37½ cents. Boys were displacing journeymen in typesetting, at $4 and $4.50 a week. The New York society drafted a new scale in 1809 in which it attempted little more than to restore the 1800 scale. In some shops strikes were

[13] Idem, Vol. II, p. 183.
[14] Stewart, Ethelbert: Documentary History of the Early Organizations of Printers, pp. 857–1033.

called to enforce the standard. It was adopted, but apparently represented no advance over conditions in 1800. Six publishers then made an agreement to raise their subscription price from $8 to $10 a year, because, at the 25 cents per 1,000 ems rate, compositors were earning as high as $8 a week, and "such great wages, combined with the cost of paper and type," and of clerk hire, which "had risen from $350 to $400 and even $500 a year," [15] were ruining their business.

New York made its next advance in 1815, when it secured substantial increases. Piece prices in typesetting ranged from 27 to 50 cents per 1,000 ems, and "all workmen employed by the week shall receive not less than $9 in book offices and on evening papers, and on morning papers not less than $10." The scale for pressmen ranged from 33 cents to 39 cents per token, depending on the size of type and weight of paper, "a token of paper, if on bookwork, to consist of no more than 10½ quires, and if on a daily paper, of no more than 10." Three cents extra was to be paid "on forms containing wood engravings." Pressmen working by the week received $10 a week on morning papers and $9 on evening papers. When teaching apprentices they were to be given 5 cents additional per token for the first three months, and 3 cents per token for the next three months.

The society went beyond its immediate jurisdiction and undertook "to induce" other organizations, those of Philadelphia, Albany, New York, and Washington, D. C., especially, "to raise their prices to at least the same standard as ours."

The scale in Washington at the time was:

Compositors

During the recess of Congress, in book or newspaper offices, to receive not less than $9 per week. During the session, in· offices engaged on congressional work, or in newspaper offices, to receive not less than $10 per week, and $2 for each and every Sunday.

By the piece: For every 1,000 ems, from brevier to pica, 28 cents; for smaller letter than brevier, 33⅓ cents; on newspapers, not less than 30 cents per 1,000 ems; above pica, to be charged as pica.

Alterations: Compositors to receive, for alterations from copy, at the rate of 25 cents per hour.

Pressmen

During the recess of Congress, shall receive not less than $9 per week; by the piece, in newspaper offices, not less than 27½ cents per token for royal or superroyal; nor less than 45 cents per token for imperial.

During the session, in offices engaged on congressional work, or in newspaper offices, not to receive less than $10 per week, and $2 for each and every Sunday.

Paper: Medium, and below medium, when the form consists of brevier or larger letter, 33⅓ cents per token; below brevier, not less than 35 cents per token; royal and upward, on brevier or larger letter, not less than 37½ cents per token; all under brevier, not less than 50 cents per token.

Jobs not less than 35 cents per token.

Cards, for one pack and not exceeding two packs, 35 cents; when exceeding two packs, to be paid at the rate of 15 cents per pack.

Broadsides shall be paid for double, according to the size of the paper.

For taking down or putting up a press, $3.

For working down a new press, $6.

When an alteration in a form takes place, each pressman shall be paid 16¼ cents an hour.

No pressman shall teach an apprentice presswork without the benefit of his work for 13 weeks, or half his wages for 6 months; nor shall he teach an apprentice who is more than 18 years old, and who is bound for less than three years.

The same scale was in force in Baltimore, and placed both cities well ahead of most of the northern cities. Weekly earnings in Boston

---

[15] McMaster, John Bach: History of the People of the United States, Vol. I, pp. 617–618.

were less than $7 a week in 1815, and did not reach $9 until 1825, in which year that is recorded as the highest rate paid both pressmen and compositors, with $7.50 as the medium and $6 as the low rate per week.[16]

There is a lapse of nearly 20 years in the wage data given in the bureau bulletin. During that time the early organizations were either collapsing entirely or changing their functions to those of benevolent societies wholly. About 1830 a new wave of organization set in, this time along definite trade-union lines, and wage rates were again brought up for revision. Perhaps this gap in the story is more apparent than real, however, because in Washington, for example, the 1815 wage scale was actually in continuous application for more than 20 years. Baltimore, on the other hand, had not maintained its scale, and the prices asked by the union founded in 1831 were appreciably lower than those paid in 1815. Whether or not the scale represented an increase over the prevailing rate is not recorded. The 1831 scale was 25 cents per 1,000 ems on the usual run of work, and $8 a week for compositors employed by the week. Piece rates per token for pressmen were 30 to 37½ cents on ordinary work. Pressmen employed by the week were to receive $8 in book and job offices and on evening papers, $9 on morning papers. Overtime appears for the first time, at the rate of 20 cents an hour after 10 hours for time workers, 4 cents extra per token and 5 cents additional per 1,000 ems for pieceworkers.

This lowered scale suggests deteriorated trade conditions which the record for the 20 years definitely shows. Women were appearing in printing offices, boys without training were taking the places of journeymen, and apprenticeship was almost demoralized. Mechanical changes, such as stereotyping, were affecting earnings materially.

When the printers of New York founded a trade-union, they prefaced their constitution, adopted in 1833, with "Introductory Remarks" which give an idea of the disturbed state of the trade. The printing industry, it said, prospered for several years following the stabilization which grew out of the 1815 uniform scale, and—

Some printers from a distance, having heard that business was good, and being determined to obtain it at all hazards, located themselves among us; and to secure a sufficient quantity of work commenced operations on terms that could not be afforded, if they wished to obtain a fair remuneration for their labor, or act honestly by the workman. The consequence was that while a few grew rich at the expense of the journeymen, old established printers [employers] who had before paid honorable prices, were obliged to reduce their charges for work or lose much of their business; and as their receipts were diminished, the wages of the journeymen were reduced by degrees until, instead of a uniform scale of prices, every man was compelled to work for what he could obtain.

Another cause of depression was the practice, which then prevailed, and has continued more or less to the present time, of employing runaway or dismissed apprentices for a small compensation. These were called two-thirds men, and have always proved a great pest to the profession. Added to this, roller boys, having gained admission to the interior of a printing office, have in a short time fought their way from the rear to the front of the press, to the discharge of the regular pressman.

The trade also, as far as pressmen are concerned, had suffered extremely by the applications of machinery to that branch of the business; and while a few individuals were growing rich, as they asserted, for the benefit of the public at large, many who had spent from five to seven years of the flower of their lives in acquiring a knowledge of their profession were left without employment.

[16] Massachusetts Bureau of Statistics of Labor: History of Wages and Prices in Massachusetts, 1752–1883, p. 174.

Matters continued in this condition for a number of years. Meantime the business of stereotyping had increased to a great extent; and the numerous improvements in the art   *   *   *   rendered it every year more and more difficult for compositors to support themselves and their families. To the disgrace of some employers, every advantage was taken of the necessities of the workmen, and impositions were continually practiced upon them.

The scale adopted by this New York organization in 1833 differed little from that of Baltimore, except in the rate for time workers which was set at $12 a week for compositors on morning papers, and $9 for those on evening papers and in book and job offices; and $9 a week for pressmen. Two years later, the printers of Philadelphia, where prices had fallen much below the scale of 20 years before, attempted to establish weekly rates at $9 for evening papers and in book and job offices, and $10 for morning papers. Ten hours remained the working day everywhere, and the overtime rate was still 20 cents an hour.

No material increase above these rates was obtained in the old cities up to 1840 except in Washington, where the printers secured some advances in the scale of 1837. Time workers received $11 a week during sessions of Congress and $10 during recesses, while the piece rate went to 31 cents per 1,000 ems and 37 cents per token. Sunday work was to receive $2, with 25 cents additional for each hour in excess of eight. On other days the overtime rate was still 20 cents an hour after 10 hours.

The Washington union had had a stormy time for several years on the apprentice question with Duff Green, printer to the Senate, who not only fought long-term apprenticeship and made a point of employing "two-thirders" and runaway apprentices as journeymen, but proposed to establish a school where printing would be taught in one year to 200 boys annually. The 1837 scale contained the unequivocal declaration, acceded to by the employers, that—

After the 1st day of January, 1839, the Columbia Typographical Society will not permit members of said society to work in any office where boys may be taken on as apprentices to the printing business to serve for a less period than five years.

During the late 30's the printers in some of the southern cities organized and established rates considerably higher than any of those current in the east. In Nashville, Tenn., the time rate was $11 a week for compositors and $12 for pressmen; the piece rate, 35 cents per 1,000 ems and 40 cents per token on ordinary work.

The New Orleans rate, fixed in its 1839 scale, was 62½ cents per 1,000 ems, increased from 50 cents; 75 cents per token for printing newspapers and $1 per token on bookwork. Weekly rates, which had been $15, were raised to $19 for compositors and pressmen on evening papers and in book and job offices. Pressmen on morning papers got $22 a week, while compositors were to work by the piece only. Foremen's wages were $25 a week on morning papers and $22.50 on evening papers. Overtime paid 40 cents an hour.

In Tallahassee, Fla., $18 a week was paid, but the organization there issued a warning to the trade not to be tempted by that apparently high wage, because "they will have to pay here, for board, from $6 to $10 a week; clothing and other expenses double, and often treble to that of the northern prices, and all other things in proportion."

The various union scales referred to will be found in full in Appendix E.

Chapter 12.—AGRICULTURAL LABOR

Agricultural labor during the first century of colonial settlement was probably not free labor to any appreciable extent, even in New England. The indentured servants discussed in chapter 3 were farm hands chiefly, hence any extensive treatment of the working conditions and pay of agricultural laborers in the seventeenth century would be largely repetition of what has already been given in that chapter in reference to the working conditions of the indentured servants.

There are, however, some data on the wages of free laborers who engaged in farm work. Early in the history of the Virginia settlement hired laborers commanded wages of 1 pound of tobacco (3 shillings) (73 cents)[1] a day and their food. By the close of the seventeenth century this rate had fallen to 1s. (16.7 cents)[2] by the day, and £6 sterling ($29.16) by the year.[3]

In Massachusetts, in the first few years of settlement, labor at a maximum wage fixed by law was compulsory during planting and harvesting seasons. "Artificers and mechanics, compelled by the constable, must leave their crafts unless they had harvesting of their own, and betake themselves to the fields of their neighbors 'needing ym.'" [4] The first legal rate, fixed in 1630, was from 6d. to 1s. (12 to 24.3 cents) per day and board. The act of 1633 raised the rate to 8d. (16 cents) with board, 1s. 6d. (36 cents) without board, for field laborers, and 2s. (48.6 cents) a day for mowers, who were classed with the skilled craftsmen. After the repeal of the wage-fixing laws, mowers increased their rates to 2s. 6d. (60 cents) per day; farm laborers, to 2s. (48.6 cents) per day from February 10 to November 10, and 1s. 6d. (36 cents) per day for the winter months.

This rate held for only two years, and in 1641, following the crop failure and depression of 1640, mowers had dropped back to 2s., and field hands to 1s. 8d. (40 cents) from March to September, 1s. 4d. (32 cents) from September to March. By 1644 wages were higher, but had not quite reached the level of 1639. Data for that year fix the price of a day's work for a man and 4 oxen at 4s. 6d. ($1.09); for a man and 6 oxen at 7s. ($1.70); and for a man and 8 oxen at 8s. ($1.94).[4] A Salem man was "presented" to the county court in 1651 for demanding "excessive wages," which in this case were 10s. 6d. ($1.75) for a day's work of one man and six oxen.[5]

The scarcity of labor produced, besides conscription in the interest of the farmers, the system of communal herding on the village common.

Cowherd, swineherd, goatherd, and shepherd, each and all served in various towns, caring for the animals of the villagers. By embodying in one communal herd the cattle of many owners, the best care was obtained with the least effort. Labor was scarce on the widening estates of the proprietors and in the growing towns. In some cases, as at Cambridge, the cows were brought into the village twice in twenty-four hours to be milked, and were pastured out day and night. The Cambridge arrangement is typical of the customs prevailing in 1635, as well as at later periods. Richard Rice was to keep 100 cows for three months, receiving

1 English sterling shilling—24.3 cents. See p. 13.
2 Colonial shilling.
3 Bruce, Philip A.: Economic History of Virginia in the 17th century, Vol. II, pp. 48, 50.
4 Weeden, William B.: Economic and Social History of New England, 1620–1789, Vol. II, pp. 877–880.
5 Essex County (Mass.) Quarterly Court Records, Vol. II. Colonial shilling—16.7 cents.

ten pounds [$48.60] in pay. The town gives him two men to help him the first fourteen days, and one man the next seven days. Then that the morals of Richard, the "cowkeep," might not deteriorate in this enforced daily duty, he was to be allowed two Sabbaths out of three for worship, the town providing for the herd on those days. He was to pay three pence fine for any night when he failed to bring in all his charge. He could not keep any other cattle without consent of the townsmen.

Always at half an hour after sunrise and again before sunset, the herdsman went through the village street gathering or dispersing his herd. He signalled by winding his horn, and the owners waited at their home gates to attend the patient kine as they went out and in.[6]

The herdsman of Salem was paid 15s. ($3.64) a week, "one-half in English corn, the other half in Indian." [7]

Another angle of the scarcity and urgency of farm labor is the protest against using their time in military training which one farmer voiced to the General Court "in behalfe of himself and all other husbandmen of the Country," declaring that—

> Whereas husbandry and tillage much concerne the good of this Commonwealth and your petiçoners have undertaken the managing and tillage of divers ffarmes in the Country & sowing of English corne their servants are oftentimes drawne from their worke to trayne in seed time, hay tyme & harvest to the great discouragement & dammage of your petiçoners and your petiçoner the said Zacheus Gould for himselfe saith that for one days trayning this yeare he was much damnnfyed in his hay. And fforasmuch as fishermen upon just grounds are exempted from trayning because their trade is also for the Common wealth, Your petiçoners humbly pray that this Court will be pleased to take the premises into their grave Consideration and thereupon to give order for the incouragement of your petiçoners who are husbandmen imployed about English graine that they & their servants may be exempted from ordinary traynings in seed tyme hay tyme and harvest.[8]

Because the colonists were always "hard driven in obtaining the necessary servants," Indians "were forced into servitude for one reason and another." This servitude was enforced not by definite indenture, such as covered and, in a measure, protected white laborers, but by methods which, as Weeden observes, "would not satisfy modern criticism." [9]

Colonial farming implements were primitive in the extreme, even in comparison with those in use in the mother country at the same time. The exorbitant price of imported iron and the roughness of the newly cleored lands made the use of plows impracticable, and they were not widely used in Virginia until the end of the century. With the crude plow then used in Virginia, composed of wood, "with the exception of the tips and shares, which were pieces of iron fastened to the parts most inclined to wear from their more direct contact with the soil," [10] it required "a month to turn over 12 acres, although by exercising great industry a man and boy might accomplish this work in 12 days. Two ablebodied laborers were sufficient to sow 60 acres in wheat in the course of one season, and to reap the grain when it was in a condition to be harvested." [11]

At the iron works at Saugus, Mass.,[12] Joseph Jenks was inventing and manufacturing edged tools for household and farm use during the middle of the century. He "thickened the back of his scythe; at

6 Weeden, Vol. I, pp. 64–65.
7 Salem Town Records.
8 Lechford, Thomas: Manuscript Notebook, 1638–1641 (published by American Antiquarian Society, 1885), p. 322.
9 Weeden, Vol. I, p. 103.
10 Bruce, Vol. I, p. 200.
11 Idem, Vol. I, p. 329 (citing Williams's Virginia Richly Valued, p. 13, in Force's Tracts, Vol. III).
12 See p. 67

the same time he lightened and lengthened the blade, increasing its cutting force and thus giving the mower greater advantage in the crucial struggle of the harvest time." [13]

The foundation of New England agriculture was grass; "cut and dried into hay it became the main stay of industry, the maintenance of animal life through the hard winters," and "the leader of a mowing field was honored among men, a rustic hero in the uncertain season when hay must be secured or perish." [14] The rustic hero benefited financially by the demands for his labor, for mowing was always paid at a higher rate than other farm work. In a later period a manuscript account book shows 6s. ($1) a day for mowing, while the same man earned only 4s. 6d. (75 cents) a day when employed in weeding.

Practices which probably added more than did the higher wage rate to the cost of hay to the consumer are suggested in an advertisement appearing in the Boston Weekly Newsletter of April 15, 1742, signed by the official weighmaster of the Port of Boston. It reads:

This is to notify the Town of Boston that they have been imposed upon and wronged by the carters and sloopmen in taking the Hay that comes by Water by only guessing at the Weight. To make it easier to the Buyer and to prevent such unjust Dealings, I do hereby notify the Town that from this Day forward I will weigh the Hay that comes by Water for three pence a Hundred.

While the southern colonies tended more and more to large-scale cultivation of tobacco and became strictly agricultural communities producing a single crop, New England was subordinating agriculture to commerce so completely that farming left "few distinctive marks on the economic development of the time," and was confined almost wholly to the "wants of each homestead." [15] Tobacco growing required immense plantations and many hands in its cultivation. Labor was secured through the indenture system and through slavery, and on most plantations the only free labor, paid on a wage basis, was that of the overseers. New England farming, on the other hand, was done chiefly by the family, with occasional help hired by the day at the old 2s. rate, which held almost without change until the Revolution.

The day rate in Pennsylvania for extra hands was about the same as that paid in New England. According to Watson's Annals of Philadelphia [16] "at and after the period of the Revolution, when wheat was 5s. (66.7 cents) a bushel, the price of labour in the harvest time was 2s. 6d. (32.6 cents) for men, and for boys, 1s. 3d. (16 cents)." The writer, in passing, makes a rather familiar comment of the older generation on the new by adding: "I have seen wealthy men in Chester County who had in their boyhood worked many days at reaping for 1s. 3d., and afterwards, in manhood, for 2s. 6d. The sons of such men won't now labour at all."

The change which took place within the years just preceding the Revolution was one of method of employment and payment rather than a change in rates. The institution of the "hired hand" who lived with the family and was paid by the month was introduced about 1775, and by the close of the century was in general use. The prevailing monthly wage was $7.

An interesting debate which indirectly concerns wages of farm hands took place in the House of Representatives on January 6,

---

[13] Weeden, Vol. I, p. 184.
[14] Idem, Vol. I, p. 184.

[15] Idem, p. 330.
[16] Vol. II, p. 263.

1794.[17] A bill was under discussion "for augmenting the pay of soldiers from $3 to $4 a month," an amendment to which "proposed an addition of a fifth dollar." The increase was opposed by some members for two distinct reasons. One was the effect upon the morale of the soldiers themselves; the other was the danger that the new rate would attract farm laborers who were less well off under existing conditions than they would be in the army if the bill were adopted. Mr. Wadsworth of New York declared that "in the States north of Pennsylvania the wages of a common laborer were not superior on the whole to those of the common soldier." According to the congressional reporter Mr. Smith, presumably of Vermont, "said that as to the rate of labor, good men were hired to work in Vermont for £18 a year, which is equal to $4 a month, and out of that they find their own clothes. He thought it a very dangerous plan to raise the wages of soldiers at this time, when every article was above its natural price, because when they returned to their old level it would be impossible to reduce wages." Speaking in support of the bill, "Mr. Boudinot said that he would be very sorry to recommend the augmentation if he thought it would induce farmers to quit their professions for a military life," but "he had no apprehensions of that kind. America would be in a very bad situation indeed if additional pay of $12 a year could bribe a farmer to enlist. He would look strange at any of his neighbors who should tell him that they had embraced such an offer."

Fifteen years later the monthly pay of farm hands, as reported by McMaster, was $7 in winter and $10 in summer in Maine and eastern Massachusetts; $9 in western Massachusetts and $10 in Connecticut, apparently all year; $13 and $14 without board in New York, and $8 "and found" in Pennsylvania for a 26-day month.[18]

After the War of 1812 these rates rose to $12 and $15 a month, even $18 in the new Territories. Farm laborers in Maine, in 1815, according to Warden, "have from $9 to $12 per month with food and half a pint of rum a day; and $20 without provisions."[19] By 1816 the rate per day, when used, was $1 in Massachusetts, as shown in a manuscript account book.[20] This rate is listed as "high" for 1820–21, in the official Massachusetts report[21] and "medium" in 1823. One dollar was again the high rate in 1825, and continued so for more than 20 years.

In the South, as has been stated, only the overseers received actual wages. Frequently, perhaps usually in the earlier periods, these men became overseers upon the expiration of their terms as indentured servants. "In the seventeenth, as in the eighteenth and nineteenth centuries, the position of an overseer furnished many opportunities to the incumbent for the improvement of his condition by the accumulation of property."[22] An overseer "was usually allowed one-seventh of the calves, foals, grain and tobacco, and one-half of the pigs raised on the plantation. If he were thrifty he was soon able to stock a plantation of his own."[23] When paid in money the rate varied from £15 to £40 ($50 to $133.33) a year in 1710.[24] One of

[17] Annals of Congress, 3d Congress, 1st session, House of Representatives, p. 159–163.
[18] McMaster, John Bach: History of the People of the United States, Vol. III, pp. 511–514.
[19] Warden, D. B.: A Statistical, Political, and Historical Account of the United States, Vol. I, p. 369.
[20] In Baker Library.
[21] Massachusetts Bureau of Statistics of Labor: History of Wages and Prices, pp. 161–162.
[22] Bruce, Vol. II, p. 47.
[23] Bassett, John Spencer: Slavery and Servitude in the Colony of North Carolina, p. 85.
[24] Governor Glenn's History of South Carolina, in South Carolina Historical Collections, Vol. II, p. 261.

Washington's account books shows that he "paid John Allison in full for his year's service as overseer, £37.6.8" ($124.45) in cash on December 31, 1797.[25]

Jefferson paid the overseer on his Bedford plantation, in charge of 16 hands, $200 a year in 1811.[26] An overseer on a rice plantation in Georgia was getting $250 a year in 1830.

Jefferson as a rule employed his overseers on a share basis, at any rate on his home estate of Monticello. His notes contain the following contract, which he considered a model agreement for plantation supervisors:

Articles for Contracts with Overseers [26]

The employer to have his share of grain at a fixed price at the end of the year if he chuses it.

Not to share till seed grain is taken out, and then of what is sold or eaten by measure only.

Allow one-half a share for every horse, and the same for a plough-boy, a share for every 8 hands as far as 16, but never more than 2 shares.

Provisions—400 lbs. of pork if single, 500 lbs. if married.

To be turned off at any time of year if his employer disapproves of his conduct, on paying a proportion of what shall be made according to the time he has staid.

To pay for carrying his share of the crops to market.

To pay the carriage of all refused to ditto.

To pay his own taxes and levies.

To pay his share of liquor and hiring at harvest.

To exchange clear profits with his employer at the end of the year if the employer chuses.

Not allowed to keep a horse or a goose or to keep a woman for waiting on him out of the crops.

---

[25] Manuscript account book—John Carter Brown Library.
[26] Thomas Jefferson's manuscript note books, in Massachusetts Historical Society Library.

Chapter 13.—SCHOOL-TEACHERS

Wide as was the application of the indenture system of labor to the economic life of early America, it is a matter of curious interest, from the modern viewpoint, to find that it was no less generally applied to the first educational efforts of the groping young colonies. Indeed, as one student of the system sees it, "perhaps in nothing was the influence of the servant more marked in his effect on society than in that powerful agency for good or evil,"[1] the school.

An early custom in the South, afterward adopted in the middle colonies, was for a family or a group of families to purchase imported servants who were represented as being qualified to teach. One servant advertised himself for sale as a schoolmaster in Pennsylvania, stating that his indenture might be taken by a group of families for a period not to exceed seven years.

Incoming servants were frequently mentioned as knowing Latin, and sometimes French and other languages, also as writing a good hand and being able to teach reading and accounts. Mention of these and the occasional notices of school masters who had run away, broken jail, and forged passes, show that servant school masters were common.[2]

The diary of an English bookkeeper[3] who, "being reduced to the last shilling I hade, was obliged to go to Virginia for four years as a schoolmaster for Bedd, Board, washing and five pounds [$24.30][4] during the whole time," gives a fair idea of the way the system worked. He arrived at Fredericksburg, Va., in April, 1774, and after two weeks spent in search of a master he was bought by Colonel Daingerfield, a planter living "about seven miles below the Toun of Fredericksburgh," on the Rappahannock. He was given "a neat little house at the upper end of an Avenue of planting at 500 yds from the Main House, where I was to keep the school and Lodge myself in it."

The next day, April 27—

About 8 A M the colonel delivered his three Sons to my Charge to teach them to read, write and figure. his oldest son Edwin 10 years of age, intred into two syllables in the spelling book, Bathourest his second son six years of age in the Alphabete and William his third son 4 years of age does not know the letters. * * * My School Houres is from 6 to 8 in the morning; in the forenoon from 9 to 12, and from 3 to 6 in the afternoon.

The diary continues:

Munday, June 20th. This morning entred to school Philip and Dorethea Edge's Children of Mr Benjamin Edge Planter.

Tuesday, 21st. This day Mr Smuel Edge Planter came to me and begged me to take a son of his to school who was both deaf and dum, and I consented to try what I could do with him.

When he was not busy teaching he acted as bookkeeper and purchasing agent for his master, and when in town in the latter capacity he occasionally picked up such additional jobs as writing "a love letter from Mr Anderson to one Peggie Dewar at the Howse

---

[1] Geiser, Karl Frederick: Redemptioners and Indentured Servants in the Colony and Commonwealth of Pennsylvania, p. 107.

[2] Herrick, Cheesman A.: White Servitude in Pennsylvania, p. 271.

[3] Diary of John Harrower, 1773-1776, American Historical Review, Vol. VI, pp. 72-106; Extracts in Documentary History of American Industrial Society, Vol. I, pp. 366-369.

[4] English money.

of Mr John Mitchel at the Wilderness." An entry dated April 23, 1776, two years after he entered service, reads:

At noon rode to Town, got the Newspapers and settled with Mr. Porter for teaching his two sons 12 months when he verry genteely allowed me £6 [$20][5] for them, besides a present of two silk vests and two pair of Nankeen Breeches last summer and a Gallon of rum at Christenmass, both he and Mrs Porter being extreamly well satisfied with what I hade don to them.

Harrower's difficulties in finding a purchaser, while the boat builder, two coopers, and a barber who sailed with him sold readily, substantiates the statement of a contemporary that "schoolmasters did not find so ready a sale or bring such good prices as others." [6]

In spite of the fact that in the southern and middle colonies "it was largely the redemptioners and indentured servants that instructed the youths of the time," the schoolmaster of that class was not "a model of excellence."

In fact he was not supposed to be, and his character was usually in keeping with his reputation. Too often their moral standard was low, their habits dissolute and their methods and discipline extremely crude. That sobriety was at a premium among this class may be inferred from the following advertisement: "Wanted, a sober person that is capable of teaching a school; such a person coming well recommended may find encouragement in said employ." There is no evidence that convicts were thus employed in Pennsylvania, but the servant formed no small proportion of the teaching force of the colony. Scarcely a vessel arrived in which there were not schoolmasters regularly advertised for sale. In none of the middle colonies at this time did the teacher occupy an exalted position. He was regarded as an unproductive laborer. Agricultural laborers or artisans was what the colony wanted and needed most, and they were nearly always sold at a higher price than the schoolmasters.[7]

Maryland, also—

depended largely upon servant schoolmasters for the instruction of its youth. "At least two-thirds of the little education we receive," says Boucher, "are derived from instructors who are either indented servants or transported felons." This was not a random statement, but was made after an investigation of the subject. Concerning the character of these servant schoolmasters, there is little said by other contemporaries.[8]

In New York and New England the seed of the public school was planted early in the course of settlement. During the period of Dutch control in New York "religion and education received early and constant attention," and teaching was largely in the hands of the clergy.

In 1650 William Vestens was sent from Amsterdam as schoolmaster and consoler of the sick. A common school was maintained at the time with a succession of teachers. In 1652 Domine Samuel Drisius, who could preach in Dutch, French, and English, was sent * * * at a salary of fourteen hundred and fifty guilders [$580],[9] and Domine Gideon Schaats, at a salary of eight hundred guilders [$320], came out to Rensselaerwyck as preacher and schoolmaster. In 1658 a petition was submitted to the Amsterdam chamber for a master for a Latin school (at Jamaica, Long Island), and the next year * * * a professor came out in that capacity, but he gave way in 1661 to Domine Aegidius Luyck, whose reputation drew pupils from families as far away as Virginia and the Carolinas.[10]

The school system which the Dutch had founded and fostered very nearly collapsed under English rule in the colony, the representatives of which were "occupied with other things."

---

[5] Virginia money.
[6] Herrick, p. 271, quoting Jonathan Boucher, "a Maryland rector who was tutor to Washington's stepson."
[7] Geiser, p. 107-108.
[8] McCormac, Eugene Irving: White Servitude in Maryland, p. 76.
[9] Guilder is 40 cents in the American equivalent.
[10] Roberts, Ellis H.: New York (Scudder's American Commonwealths), pp. 77, 87.

Schools there were, but so poorly supported that our historian Smith testifies that after he was born, "such was the negligence of the day, that an instructor could not find bread from the voluntary contributions of the inhabitants." It was high time to care for the youth of the province, for its population had become, in 1731, 50,289. Yet an act passed in 1732 "to encourage a public school in the city of New York" went no further. * * * This school was free to all pupils.[11]

The professional opportunities afforded by the Latin schools of New York City were promising enough in 1737 to prompt one resident to write to his pastor in Ireland that "if your sons would come here they would get more in one year teaching a Latin school than you yourself will get for three years' preaching."[12]

An early act of the legislature after New York became a State was to appropriate $50,000, "of which the interest was to be applied in the ratio of the population, with like sums raised by local tax, in the payment of wages of teachers in the common schools."[13]

Massachusetts, to the end "that learning may not be buried in ye grave of our fathers in ye church and commonwealth," established schools by law in 1647, ordering each town of 50 householders "to appoint one within their towne to teach all such children as shall resort to him to write and reade, whose wages shall be paid either by ye parents or masters of such children, or by ye inhabitants in general, by way of supply." Towns of 100 householders were ordered "to set up a grammar school, ye master thereof being able to instruct youth so farr as they may be fited for ye university."[14]

Several towns had schools before this law was enacted. Boston started one in 1635, and in 1644 the inhabitants of Dedham "did resolve and consent * * * to rayse the summe of £20 [$66.67] per annum toward maintaining a schoolmaster to keep a free school in our town."[15] Dedham thereupon founded the first real public school, free to pupils and supported wholly out of tax funds.

There was no uniformity in the salaries paid schoolmasters by the different towns. At the same time that Dedham was paying £20, Essex was paying only £14 ($46.67) and Watertown £30 ($100). "The Watertown salary continued about the same for some seventy years; in 1715 or 1720 it was raised to £36 [$120]."[16]

Woburn also paid at the rate of £30 ($100) a year for a number of years after its school began to function; but the town seems to have had a struggle to establish one. The first effort was made in 1685, when a teacher was employed at £5 ($16.67) per annum to teach all the children who applied. None applied, and the schoolmaster received only £1 10s. ($5) of the fixed salary. Fifteen years later a school was run for four months and the teacher was paid £9 ($30) for his services. After that the salary varied from £30 "and horse kept," in 1709, to £21 15s. ($72.50) and board in 1714. Wages in old tenor during the second quarter of the century went as high as £100 a year in 1745 to 1748, but after 1760 the rate settled to £40 ($133.33) lawful money for an 11-month term.[17]

Dedham raised the salary of its school master in 1695 to £25 ($83.33) per year, "whereof eight pounds is to be in money, the other

11 Roberts, p. 262.
12 Letter in Memorial History of New York City, Vol. II, p. 203.
13 Robert's New York, Vol. II, p. 457.
14 Massachusetts Bay Colony Records, Vol. II, p. 6.
15 Slafter, Carlos: Citing Dedham Town Records (Schools and Teachers of Dedham, Mass., 1644–1904, p. 7).
16 Weeden, William B.: Economic and Social History of New England, 1620–1789, Vol. I, p. 222.
17 Sewall, Samuel: History of Woburn, Mass., Appendix No. xiii, pp. 586–587.

£17 [$56.67] in corne, Rye at 4s. [66.7 cents] per bushell and Indian corne at 3s. [50 cents] per bushell." [18] The next year "the town began to pay the salary of the school master entirely in money." [19] Thereafter the scale was £28 [$93.33] in 1705 and £200 [$88.67] in 1751. The last entry is in old tenor, and represented about £25 in lawful money, so that in actual money the salary was about the same for the entire half century.

Many other towns paid the schoolmaster a small sum out of the town treasury, and whatever else he made came through tuition fees paid by the pupils. This was true of both Cambridge and Northampton, among others. Each of these towns paid only £10 [$33.33] out of the public funds toward the teacher's salary. Northampton pupils paid, in addition, "ffowre pence [5.6 cents] per weeke for such as are in the Primer and other English books and sixpense [8.4 cents] per week to learn the Accidence (Latin grammar) wrighting and Casting Accounts." [20]

In 1687 the town changed its method of paying the master. He was still to collect tuition fees, but whatever he lacked of getting forty pounds [$133.33] was to be made up by the town. There was always much delinquency in paying on the part of those who sent children to school, and when the teacher was thus relieved from any absolute necessity for following up his debtors, it can easily be imagined that the amount collected dwindled. The result was that the town voted shortly afterward to allow "the Scholars to go free." [21]

While the towns were inclined to be lax in the matter of school maintenance, the colonial authorities were persistent in enforcing the school law, and many town records show instances in which the town is "presented" for violations, frequently caused by inability to secure a teacher. Framingham, for example, voted in 1716 "to have a moving school in the four quarters of the town. Mr. Goddard consented to teach four weeks in each place for £15 [$50] and all taught at his house were to pay 6d. [8.4 cents] per head per week." The plan was not successful, apparently, for the records two years later show that "a committee having reported their inability, after the utmost diligence, to obtain a schoolmaster, and the town again having been presented, another committee was appointed to obtain one, 'and that forthwith.' It was voted that the gentlemen of the committee go first to Captain Edward Goddard and see upon what terms he would serve the town; if he would serve the town as cheap as, or something cheaper than another, then the committee was to make a bargain with him for the year." [22]

In the New Haven and Connecticut colonies schools were established almost at once, parents paying a stated sum for each child. At Guilford this fee was 4s. [66.7 cents] per quarter for each pupil. The New Haven colonial court ordered in 1657 that each town not already maintaining a school should open one and pay one-third the cost of operation, the rest to be carried on a per capita basis by the families using it.

Plymouth Colony "farmed its fisheries of bass and mackerel on the Cape coast and gave the proceeds to the support of the public schools. In 1684–1693 the rental was £30 [$100] per annum." [23]

[18] Records of Selectmen, Dedham, Mass., 1695.
[19] Slafter, p. 34.
[20] Johnson, Clifton: Old Time Schools and School Books, p. 5 (Northampton Town Records quoted).
[21] Idem, p. 5.
[22] Barry, William: History of Framingham, Mass., p. 75.
[23] Weeden, Vol. 1, p. 247.

The salary of President Rogers, of Harvard, as fixed by the court in 1682 was £100 ($333) in money and £50 ($166.67) in commodities; while each of his two assistants received £50 in money.

The routine of the early schools is suggested in the Dorchester school rules of 1645, which provided that—

for seven months in the warmer part of the year the master should every day begin to teach at seven o'clock in the morning and dismiss the scholars at five in the afternoon, while in the colder and darker months of the remainder of the year he was to begin at eight and close at four. There was to be a midday intermission from eleven to one except on Monday, when the master "shall call his scholars together between twelve and one of the clock to examine them what they have learned, at which time also he shall take notice of any misdemeanor or outrage that any of his scholars shall have committed on the sabbath, to the end that at some convenient time due admonition and correction may be administered." [24]

The women who taught the "dame schools" received salaries that were modest in the extreme, generally amounting to 10 shillings ($1.67) a year in the earliest period. To be sure, these schools were usually held in the women's homes, and were casual affairs so far as instruction was concerned. Later, when the dame school was taking care of the smallest children and leaving the schoolmaster freer to carry on the "grammar school," the relative importance attached to the two classes of teachers is suggested by the action of the overseers of the town of Manchester, Mass., who in 1736—

Voted that "the £50 [$166.67] voted for the support of a free school in Manchester the one half of sd £50 to be expended to supporte four school dames to keep a free school" in various parts of the town, "the other half of sd £50 to be expended to supporte a school master to keep a free schoole in the schoole house in Manchester in fall and winter season." [25]

Twenty years later the pay of the keeper of a dame school was even less, as £12 lawful money ($40) was assessed "to be distributed to Three School Mistresses in Three different parts of ye town." [25]

Before the Revolutionary period the dame school had been absorbed into the town school, and women teachers were taking over the town schools for the summer months, to leave the men free for farm work. In 1773 Lydia Warner kept school in Northfield, Mass., for 18 weeks at 5 shillings (83 cents) a week. [26]

From the close of the eighteenth century until well into the nineteenth—

The usual sum paid to a master was ten or twelve dollars a month, though a wealthy district might, in exceptional cases, give twenty dollars to retain a man of culture and experience. Women earned from four to ten dollars. Even after the middle of the nineteenth century the standard pay for a woman teacher in many districts was one dollar a week. Thus a "qualified woman teacher" in a Connecticut town in 1798 received a weekly stipend of sixty-seven cents, and some masters of that period were paid no more. Besides the money remuneration, the districts boarded the teachers. Otherwise the salary would have loomed much larger, and the town appropriation would have quickly melted away. The teacher "boarded round" among the homes of the pupils, spending at each house a length of time proportioned to the number of school children in the family. The custom was common until after 1850. [27]

[24] Johnson, p. 11.
[25] Lamson, D. F.: History of the Town of Manchester, Mass., pp. 206–208.
[26] Temple, Josiah H., and Sheldon, George: History of Northfield, Mass., p. 316.
[27] Johnson, p. 126.

Chapter 14.—OTHER OCCUPATIONS

Scattered data for a few other trades and occupations, unskilled chiefly, were found among the many sources drawn upon for material, but they are too fragmentary to be worked into a continuous story. They are therefore presented in a sketchy fashion which makes no claim to completeness.

DOMESTIC SERVANTS

Household servants, like agricultural laborers, were almost without exception indentured, but there are instances in which the need of housekeepers was so compelling that money considerations in addition to the usual terms of indenture were offered.

Domestic servants shipped from Holland into Pennsylvania in 1663, for example, were under indenture to serve "for a term of years to defray the expense of bringing them over," but they also received "yearly wages of 60, 70 and 80 guilders [$24.00, $28.00 and $32.00]." [1]

A Virginia planter sent to England in 1680 for "a trained housekeeper, offering to pay her passage money, to allow her three pounds sterling ($14.58) by the year, and to furnish her food without charge. He considered that this would be highly acceptable, as the remuneration, he said, would be equal to that which was received by the same class of domestics in the mother country." [2] The same terms were made "betweene Elisabeth Evans of Bridgend, in the County of Glamorgan, and John Wheelewright, minister," of Exeter, N. H., in a contract executed by Lechford, in 1639. [3]

A much better bargain was made in Virginia in 1697 by a woman already in the colony who "was to receive remuneration for her work during a period of two months and a half, at the rate of five pounds, sixteen shillings and six pence [$19.42] [4] a month," a rate which, it is added, was "probably not considered extraordinary." [2] In Pennsylvania at the time "maidservants' wages is commonly betwixt six and ten pounds [$24 and $40] per annum, with very good accomodations." [5]

"The women who were exported from England to the Colony" (Virginia), Bruce says, "had unusual opportunities for advancing their welfare in life. If they enjoyed an honorable reputation, they found no difficulty in marrying into a higher station than they had been accustomed to; Bullock mentioned the fact that no maid whom he had brought over failed to find a husband in the course of three months after she had entered his service." [6] Another contemporaneous account asserts that the "dearness" of women's work in Pennsylvania at the beginning of the eighteenth century "proceeds from the smallness of the number and the scarcity of workers, for even the

[1] Herrick, Cheesman A.: White Servitude in Pennsylvania, p. 27. Guilder is 40 cents in the American equivalent.
[2] Bruce, Philip A.: Economic History of Virginia in the 17th century, Vol. II, p. 49.
[3] Lechford, Thomas: Manuscript Notebook, 1638-1641., p. 107.
[4] Virginia currency.
[5] Thomas, Gabriel: An Historical and Geographical Account of the Province and Country of Pensilvania (1698). Pennsylvania currency, pound worth $4.
[6] Bruce, Vol. II, p. 51.

meanest single women marry well, and being above Want are above Work." [7]

An account book kept in Salem, Mass., in 1695 [8] notes three days' work by a laundress at 1s. (16.7 cents) a day, while "the old steward's book of Harvard College shows that the wages of a laundress between 1687–1719 were ten shillings [$1.67] a quarter." [9]

Peter Kalm reported wages of household servants in Philadelphia in 1748 as £8 to £10 ($21.33 to $26.67) for women and £16 to £20 ($42.67 to $53.33) for men a year, which, he added, was much more than was paid in the rural districts of Pennsylvania.[10] A contemporary gives £1 5s. ($3.13) as the monthly wages of domestics in Georgia in 1735.[11]

At the close of the century domestic servants were getting $7 a month in Virginia [12] and $8 at New York.[13]

The Pennsylvania Hospital of Philadelphia is the oldest existing hospital in the country. The wages paid its household servants— cooks, housemaids, and laundresses—can be traced for consecutive years beginning with 1752, from the old account books still kept at the institution.

In 1752 cooks were paid £10 to £15 ($26.68 to $40) a year; housemaids, £10, and the matron, £30 ($80). After the Revolution, 1785 to 1800, the weekly rate is 5s (66.7 cents) for the cook, 7s. 6d. ($1) for the baker, and 3s. 9d. (49 cents) each for housemaids. Laundresses earned 2s. 6d. (32.6 cents) a day. From 1801 to 1810 the baker and the housemaids were getting $10 a month; the cook, $1 a week; laundresses, 50 cents, and a cleaning woman 60 cents a day. These rates later show very little change except in the case of the baker and the cook, who in 1820 were receiving $16 a month and $2 a week, respectively.

The laundresses, at $3 a week, were paid more than the nurses, whose wages rose in 1817 to $2 a week, after a yearly wage of £14 to £18 ($37.34 to $48) extending back 50 years. Probably, however, the laundresses were not maintained at the hospital as the nurses were. Laundry work was reduced to $2 a week in 1822.

One of Stephen Girard's housemaids, who had been indentured to him, agreed in 1801 to remain with him after the expiration of her servitude at $1.25 a week. Charges for house cleaning in his accounts[14] show a rate of 5s. (66.7 cents) a day.

Sweeping chimneys cost the hospital 6d. (6 cents) per chimney in 1752, but the rate rose steadily to 1s. 6d. (19 cents) apiece in 1800, at which time Girard was paying 25 cents a chimney.

Thomas Jefferson's account books contain many items covering the wages of the household staff of his large establishment at Monticello. In 1801 he engaged a French steward at $40 a month "for himself and his wife as femme de charge." A typical pay roll for the period of

---

[7] Hart, Albert B., ed.: American History Told by Contemporaries, Vol. II, p. 75. Captain Robert Boyle's Adventures.
[8] In Essex Institute, Salem.
[9] Abbott, Edith: Women in Industry, p. 264, citing manuscript records in library of Harvard University.
[10] Travels in North American, vol. 1, p. 387.
[11] Oldmixon, John: British Empire in America, Vol. I, p. 541.
[12] Thomas Jefferson's manuscript accounts.
[13] McMaster, John Bach: History of the People of the United States, Vol. I, p. 242.
[14] In Girard College Library.

this steward's incumbency, at which time Jefferson himself was living in the White House, reads:

M. Rapin, 47 days	$62. 67
M. Julien, May 4 to June 4	25. 00
Joseph Daugherty, May 4 to June 4	16. 00
Chris Silverman, May 4 to June 4	14. 00
Edward Maher, May 4 to June 4	14. 00
Maria Murphy, May 4 to June 4	9. 00
Garcon de cuisine, April 26 to May 26	8. 00
The cook woman, March 20 to May 20	30. 00
John (baker), May 4 to June 4	10. 00

These are all white servants. A later pay roll in the account concludes with the statement that "this makes the regular establishment of servants $135 per month, besides liveries and besides Rapin's forty dollars—175 D."

Warden gives $15 to $20 a month as the wages of a first-class cook in Washington a few years later, and $2 to $4 a month for "maid servants." [15] Domestics in Massachusetts at about that time were paid at the rate of 50 cents a week.[16]

The report of the United States Department of Commerce and Labor on the History of Women in Industry [17] gives the following data, compiled from various sources, on wages of domestic servants during the second quarter of the nineteenth century:[18]

In 1829 a writer in the Mechanics' Free Press stated that for a period of at least thirty years the wages of female domestics had remained practically stationary, but that they had profited somewhat by the fall in prices which had occurred during that period. In New England, however, the opening of the cotton factories, especially those at Lowell, had caused a decided increase in the wages of women domestics. Wages in New England, which had averaged about 70 cents a week in 1808 and 50 cents in 1815, ranged from $1.25 to $1.50 in 1849. In New York the usual wages, which appear to have been between $4 and $5 a month in 1826, were said to have been about $6 a month in 1835. In Pottsville, Pa., the wages of servant girls in 1830 were $1 a week, and women who could clean house and wash clothes could readily obtain 50 cents a day. A writer in the Delaware Advertiser in 1830 stated that a servant in his family received 75 cents a week, or $39 a year, which, he said, was almost the lowest wages ever paid for housework.

While on the whole "the conditions of labor of domestic servants have changed but little," as Miss Sumner remarks, nevertheless in the early history of the country, when many of the industries were carried on in the home, "a large part of the time of domestic servants was spent in manufacturing occupations of one kind or another," an aspect of that field of work which changed conditions have completely eliminated.

COMMON LABOR

The expressions "common labour" and "labouring men" appear frequently in the old records, but it is not at all certain that common labor then meant what it does now, or that the "labouring men" referred to were unskilled workers and not craftsmen. In some cases a difference in the rates quoted for workers so designated, compared with those for specified trades, justify the assumption that they apply to unskilled, or common labor. For example, Gabriel Thomas is

   [15] Warden, D. B.: A Statistical, Political, and Historical Account of the United States, Vol. III, p. 195.
   [16] Massachusetts Bureau of Statistics of Labor: History of Wages and Prices, in Massachusetts, 1752–1883. p. 82.
   [17] Sumner, Helen L.: Vol. IX of Report on Conditions of Woman and Child Wage Earners.
   [18] Idem, Ch. IV, pp. 179–180.

specific in his references to skilled workers, listing the separate crafts and quoting the wages paid them. Then he adds that "labouring men have commonly 14 and 15 pound ($56 and $60)[19] a year and their Meate, Drink, Washing and Lodgeing." Governor Glenn, also, in his History of South Carolina (1710), distinguishes between designated craftsmen whose daily wages range from 4s. to 7s. 6d. ($0.67 to $1.25) and "labourers" who have "from 1s. 3d. to 2s. [21 to 33.3 cents][20] a day." Undoubtedly in both cases the workers were of the class now grouped as common labor.

Laborers as distinguished from both agricultural laborers and craftsmen in the History of Wages and Prices in Massachusetts were paid 33 cents (2s.) a day, with slight variation, from 1752 to the Revolution. In four years of that period, 1758 to 1761, the average rate fell to 25 cents, and in 1762 to 17.8 cents. The highest rate given in the decade following the outbreak of the war was 79 cents in 1779; the lowest, 22 cents in 1777.[21]

A story of danger, labor difficulties, privation, and tragedy for the rough, unskilled labor that forced a path into a wilderness runs through the prosaic clerical entries in the account against "the Province of Pennsylvania for charges on opening a Ro*d from the Back Settlements of said Province towards the Ohio for the King's Service, in Pursuance of an Application from the late General Braddock."[22]

The road led out from Carlisle, Pa., toward the west, across the mountains. Work was begun on May 5, 1755. The trail blazers went first, and were paid 2s. 6d. (32.6 cents) and 3s. (40 cents) a day. They were followed by the surveyors, probably the only skilled men on the job, who were paid 6s. (80 cents) a day.

Road gangs were organized wherever they could be gathered together and sent to the camps. Working time was "calculated from the day each man arrived at the Road. No allowance made for coming to the Road before Entry, and no time allowed for returning home, both which the labourers seem to insist upon." Enemy Indians attacked the camps and the labor force was seriously disrupted not only by killings at the hands of the Indians, but by the loss of the men who "deserted the service at the time our People was scalped by the Indians."

The laborers were paid 2s. 6d. (32.6 cents) a day. The scale for the gang foremen, or "overseers," as they were called, was 3s. 6d. (46 cents), which was considered too low. The commission in charge of the project wrote that "the overseers think if more is not allowed they will not have justice done."

Teamsters received 2s. 6d. a day, the same as the laborers, unless they drove their own horses, in which case they were allowed 2s. (26.6 cents) a day for each horse. A wagon, team, and driver earned 12s. ($1.60) a day. Horses were rented from the neighboring farmers as they went along, at 2s. a day, and frequently fell victim to the arrows and thefts of the Indians. After the project was aban-

---

[19] Pennsylvania colonial currency—shilling worth 20 cents.
[20] In South Carolina Historical Collections, Vol. II, p. 261.
[21] History of Wages and Prices in Massachusetts, p. 167.
[22] In Norris Papers, manuscript collection of Historical Society of Pennsylvania.

doned, following Braddock's defeat and death, one of the commissioners petitioned the provincial assembly thus:

The most of these persons who has lost their horses are very poor people and some of them were heads of families, that were killed and have left their Widows and Children behind them, very poor, and no horses to work on their Plantations, and they and all others as before mentioned were in the Government service doing what they could toward the work of the Roads, although it has to our great disadvantage turned out to little account at present, as General Braddock did not succeed, notwithstanding these poor people who suffered on the Roads even at the expence of their Lives. And I hope the Honorable House will consider the Widow and the Fatherless, altho' they live in this unhappy county of Cumberland, whose Inhabitants are exposed to many Dangers, and as it was I that Employed these Poor People they give me a great deal of uneasiness in coming daily looking for Redress for their Labour and Losses, which I hope, Gentlemen, you'll consider.

Some degree of protection from enemy Indians was necessary to keep the camps from complete demoralization, so the commissioners, in the absence of a militia, employed a guard of "70 men and 70 horses Ten Days Guarding the Cattle and Provisions, Burying the Dead and Endeavoring to preserve some of the Provisions that was lost. As we Labour under many Disadvantages of the kind by reason we have no Militia therefore must do all Business by Money, and these persons whom we promised to pay demanded 4s. [53.3 cents] per Diem," a sum which the commissioner "leaves to the Consideration of the House."

Speaking of conditions in the country as a whole in 1784 McMaster says that the wage of the unskilled common laborer was 25 cents a day. "Sometimes when laborers were few he was paid more, and became the envy of his fellows if at the end of the week he took home to his family 15s. Yet all authorities agree that in 1784 the hire of workmen was twice as great as in 1774." [23]   Later—

Between 1800 and 1810 the spread of population, the increase in the number of farms, the rush of men into the merchant marine, raised the pay of the unskilled laborer very perceptibly. From the estimates of the cost of internal improvements, from the pay rolls of turnpike companies, from town records, from private diaries, from newspaper advertisements, it appears that during this period men who could drive piles, or build roads, or dig ditches, or pave streets, or tend a machine in any of the factories, or were engaged in transportation, were paid from one dollar to a dollar and a third per day. One advertisement for 30 men to work on the road from Genessee River to Buffalo offers $12 a month, food, lodging, and whisky every day.[24]

Warden's figures for common labor in 1815 are $1 a day in Maine [25] and New York; [26] 60 to 70 cents by the day and $140 by the year "with food," in Pennsylvania; [27] and 50 cents a day with food or 75 cents without food, in Ohio.[28]

An unidentified southern newspaper printed the following advertisement on May 24, 1833: [29]

Five Hundred Laborers Wanted: We will employ the above number of laborers to work on the Muscle Shoals Canal, etc., at the rates of Fifteen Dollars per month for twenty-six working days, or we will employ Negroes by the year or for a less time as may suit the convenience of the planters. We will also be

[23] McMaster, Vol. I, p. 96.
[24] Idem, Vol. III, p. 510.
[25] Warden, Vol. I, p. 367.
[26] Idem, Vol. I, p. 539.
[27] Idem, Vol. II, p. 85.
[28] Idem, Vol. II, p. 262.
[29] Quoted in E. S. Abdy's Journal of a Residence in the United States (London, 1835), Vol. II, p 109, in Documentary History of American Industrial Society, Vol. II, p. 348.

responsible to slave-holders who hire their Negroes to us for any injury or damage that may hereafter happen in the progress of blasting rocks or of caving in of banks.

Going outside the chronological limits of this study to cite the pay rolls of the Rutland and Burlington Railroad [30] which was under construction in 1849, unskilled workers in the construction gangs were paid $1 a day, which is 50 cents less than the rate for skilled tradesmen. Common laborers in the road gangs, which cleared the right of way for the construction men, received 85 cents a day.

BARBERS

The practice of barbers in the early days apparently was to charge for their services by the month or quarter, instead of by the job. Judging from the few items found by the bureau these charges are confusingly dissimilar, except perhaps in the case of Boston barbers, who seem to have had a trade organization. This is inferred from a news item in the New England Courant of November 31–December 7, 1724, which announced that—

On Tuesday, the first of this Instant, in the Evening, Thirty-two Principal Barbers of this place assembled at the Golden Ball, with a Trumpeter attending them, to debate some important Articles relating to their Occupations; where it was proposed that they should raise their Shaving from 8s. to 10s. [48 to 60 cents][31] per Quarter, and that they should advance 5s. [30 cents] on the Price of making Common Wiggs and 10s. [60 cents] on their Tye ones. It was also proposed that no one of this Faculty should shave or dress wiggs on Sunday mornings for the Future, on Penalty of forfeiting Ten pounds [$12] for every such Offence; From whence it may be fairly concluded that in the past such a Practice has been too common among them.

Two bills against Mr. Jones of Virginia in the manuscript collection of Jones Family Papers are:

To one year's shaving, July, 1724 to 1725_____   15s. ($2.50)
To one and one-half years' shaving, from July, 1725, to December, 1726_____   £1 2s. 6d. ($3.75)

Sixty years later Thomas Jefferson's monthly bill at the barbers was 20 shillings ($3.33). Another entry in Jefferson's account book for the same year, 1784, reads: "Bob begins work with a barber at 15s. ($2.50) a month." Bob must have been an assistant of some sort, as that rate seems too low for a journeyman and too high for an apprentice, but the notebook sheds no further light.

An agreement made in Philadelphia in 1807 between a hatter and a barber calls for "three shaves a week, at $2 a quarter, to be paid for in hats." [32]

[30] Baker Library.
[31] Depreciated currency—shilling worth about 6 cents.
[32] Manuscript Account Book, Historical Society of Pennsylvania

LIST OF PUBLISHED SOURCES

Abbott, Edith—Women in Industry.
Acrelius, Israel—History of New Sweden (in Pennsylvania Historical Society Memoirs, Vol. IX).
Allen, Frederick J.—The Shoe Industry.
Allen, Zachariah—Science of Mechanics (1829).
Alsop, George—Character of the Province of Maryland (1650).
Andrews, John B.—History of Women in Trade Unions (Vol. X of Report on Conditions of Woman and Child Wage Earners in United States).
Annals of Congress—Third Congress, 1st session.
Atkinson, Edward—Special Report on Cotton Manufacture (in Census of 1880, Vol. II).
Bagnall, William—Textile Industries in the United States (1860).
Ballagh, James Curtis—White Servitude in the Colony of Virginia (in Johns Hopkins University Studies in Historical and Political Science, Series XIII),
Barry, William—History of Framingham, Mass.
Bassett, John Spencer—Slavery and Servitude in the Colony of North Carolina (in Johns Hopkins University Studies in Historical and Political Science. Series XIV).
Batchelder, Samuel—Early Progress of Cotton Manufacture in the United States.
Bently, William D. D.—Diary of (Published by Essex Institute, Salem, Mass.).
Birkbeck, Morris—Notes on a Journey in America from the Coast of Virginia to the Territory of Illinois (1817).
Bishop, J. Leander—History of American Manufacturers, 1608–1860. 2 vols.
Blodgett, Samuel—Economica, a Statistical Manual for the United States of America (privately published in Washington, D. C., 1806).
Bruce, Philip A.—Economic History of Virginia in the Seventeenth Century. 2 vols.
Bullock, William—Virginia (London, 1649).
Clark, Victor S.—History of Manufactures in the United States, 1607–1860.
Commons, John R.—Introduction to Trial of Journeyman Cordwainers, 1806 (in Vol. III, Documentary History of American Industrial Society).
Coxe, Tench—View of America (1794).
Dedham (Mass.) Town Records—Published by Massachusetts Historical Society.
Documentary History of American Industrial Society. 10 vols. John R. Commons, editor.
Douglass, William—Discourse Concerning the Currencies of the British Plantations in America (1739). (In Economic Studies of American Economic Association, Vol. II, 1897.)
Eddis, William—Letters from America (1775).
Essex County (Mass.) Court Records—Published by Essex Institute.
Evelin, Robert—Directions for Adventurers (in Force's Tracts, Vol. II).
Felt, Joseph B.:
    Annals of Salem. 2 vols.
    Massachusetts Currency.
Force, Peter—Tracts and Other Papers Relating to the Origin, Settlement and Progress of the Colonies in North America. 4 vols.
Gannon, Fred A.—Shoe Making, Old and New.
Geiser, Karl Frederick—Redemptioners and Indentured Servants in the Colony and Commonwealth of Pennsylvania.
Hamilton, Alexander—Report on Manufactures, 1791.
Hammond, John—Leah and Rachel, or the Two Fruitfull Sisters, Virginia and Mary-land (in Force's Tracts, Vol. III).
Harrower, John—Diary of (in American Historical Review, Vol. VI).
Hart, Albert Bushnell—Editor, American History Told by Contemporaries.
Hazard, Blanche Evans—The Organization of the Boot and Shoe Industry in Massachusetts Before 1875.
Hening, William Waller—Virginia Statutes at Large.
Herrick, Cheesman A.—White Servitude in Pennsylvania.

Hohman, Elmo Paul—The American Whaleman.
Hunter, Frederick William—Stiegel Glass.
Jacobstein, Meyer—The Tobacco Industry in the United States (in Columbia University Studies in History, Economics and Political Law, Vol. XXVI).
Johnson, Clifton—Old Time Schools and School Books.
Josselyn, John—An Account of Two Voyages to New England (in Vol. I of Hart's American History Told by Contemporaries).
Kalm, Peter—Journeys into North America. 2 vols.
Lamson, D. F.—History of the Town of Manchester (Mass.).
Lechford, Thomas—Manuscript Notebook, 1638–1641 (published by American Antiquarian Society, 1885).
Lewton, Frederick L.—Samuel Slater and the Oldest Cotton Machinery in America (in Annual Report of Smithsonian Institution, 1926).
Lye, Joseph—The Ways of a Worker of a Century Ago, as Shown by the Diary of Joseph Lye, Shoemaker (published by Fred A. Gannon, Salem).
McCormac, Eugene Irving—White Servitude in Maryland (in Johns Hopkins University Studies in Historical and Political Science, Series XXII).
McLane, Louis—Statistics of Manufacturers in the United States, 1832 (Report of U. S. Treasury).
McMaster, John Bach—History of the People of the United States. 8 vols.
McNeill, George—The Labor Movement.
Massachusetts:
    Records of the Governor and Company of the Massachusetts Bay in New England (Including Records of the General Court and Courts of Assistants), 1628–1686. 5 vols.
    Bureau of Statistics of Labor, 11th Annual Report (1880).
Miles, Henry A.—Lowell as it Was and as It is (1845).
Mittelberger, Gottlieb—Journey to Pennsylvania, 1750–1754.
Montgomery, James—Practical Details of Cotton Manufacture in the United States (Glasgow, 1840).
New York—Documents Relative to the Colonial History of the State of New York (edited by E. B. O'Callaghan).
New York City—Memorial History (edited by James Grant Wilson).
North Carolina Records. 15 vols.
Oldmixon, John—British Empire in America (1735), 3 vols.
Pearse, John B.—A Concise History of the Iron Manufacture of the American Colonies.
Phillips, Henry, Jr.—Pennsylvania Paper Money.
Potter, Elisha R.—Emissions of Paper Money Made by the Colony of Rhode Island.
Roberts, Ellis H.—New York (American Commonwealths, Horace E. Scudder, editor).
Robinson, Harriet H.—Loom and Spindle.
Salem (Mass.) Town Records.
Sewall, Samuel—History of Woburn, Mass.
Slafter, Carlos—Schools and Teachers of Dedham, Mass., 1644–1904.
South Carolina Historical Collections—B. E. Carroll, editor.
Stewart, Ethelbert—Documentary History of the Early Organizations of Printers (Bulletin of U. S. Bureau of Labor, November, 1905).
Stowell, Charles Jacob—Studies in Trade Unionism in the Custom Tailoring Trade.
Sumner, Helen L.—History of Women in Industry in the United States (Vol. IX of the Report on Conditions of Woman and Child Wage Earners in the United States).
Swank, James M.—Iron in all Ages.
Temple, Josiah H., and Sheldon, George—History of Northfield (Mass.).
Thwaites, Reuben Gold—Editor, Early Western Travels. 32 vols.
Thomas, Gabriel—An Historical and Geographical Account of the Province and Countrey of Pensilvania (1698).
Thomas, Isaiah—History of Printing in America (1810).
Trial of Twenty-Four Journeyman Tailors Charged with a Conspiracy (Transcript of Testimony, Philadelphia, 1827).
Tryon, Rolla Melton—Household Manufactures in the United States, 1640–1860.

United States:
  Department of Labor, Third Annual Report, 1887.
  Department of Commerce and Labor, Report on Conditions of Woman and Child Wage Earners in the United States.   10 vols.   (Senate Document No. 645, 61st Congress, 2nd Session).
  Census of Manufactures, 1860.
  Census of Manufactures, 1880.
Virginia Historical Society Collections.
Warden, D. B.—A Statistical, Political and Historical Account of the United States.   3 vols. (1819).
Weeden, William B.—Economic and Social History of New England, 1620–1789 2 vols.
Winthrop, Governor John—Journal (In Hart's Contemporaries, Vol. I)
Wright, Carroll D.:
  Factory System in the United States (in Vol. II, Census of 1880)
  History of Wages and Prices, 1752–1883.   From 16th Annual Report of the Massachusetts Bureau of Statistics of Labor, 1885.
Wright, John—The American Negotiator (3rd edition, London, 1767)

PART 2

FROM 1840 TO 1928

PART 2.—FROM 1840 TO 1928

INTRODUCTION

The work of the Bureau of Labor Statistics has always covered a wide field. In the early years of the bureau it was the policy to make a thorough study of at least one important subject each year, but no attempt was made to specialize in particular lines of work and to collect and publish data on each of those lines each year. As a consequence, the list of publications of the bureau in the early years shows very disconnected subject titles.

To illustrate this point the first of the annual reports of the bureau published in 1886, related to industry depressions; the second report related to convict labor; the third report related to strikes and lockouts; the fourth report to working women in large cities; the fifth report related to railroad labor. In 1889 the bureau also published a special report relating to marriage and divorce. This policy required the personnel of the bureau to be general practitioners, competent to handle fairly well almost any subject that might come up for investigation, but it did not permit of a development of specialists in particular lines of work. This condition has been remedied, but only in part. The personnel of the bureau has always been small and there has not been an opportunity for the specialization which is now so desirable.

The subject of wages was covered quite fully in some of the early publications of the bureau and scarcely at all in other publications. The fifth annual report was devoted largely to the wages of railroad employees and the chapters on wages formed a very important part of the sixth annual report which bears the title "Cost of Production." Wages constituted quite a large part of the eleventh annual report relating to work and wages of men, women, and children, and also of the thirteenth annual report, relating to hand and machine labor. The first really large wage study, however, was published as part of the so-called "Aldrich" report. This report, although published as a Senate document, was mainly prepared by the then Department of Labor, now the Bureau of Labor Statistics. It contained a quantity of information on wages, running back as far as 1840, and coming down to 1891.

The nineteenth annual report published in 1904 was devoted entirely to wages and hours of labor. It contained figures by occupations for many of the major industries of the United States. As the Aldrich report ended with 1891, it was decided that this report should include wage data as far back as 1890. This gave a continuity of partially comparable information on wages and hours of labor from 1840 to 1903. The report was compiled on rather different lines than the Aldrich report and was more systematically planned. It was possible to get for this report substantially such figures as were wanted while in compiling the Aldrich report, because of the long period

145

covered, it was more often a case of getting such figures as could be obtained than in getting the figures that were wanted. The nineteenth annual report, therefore, is much better balanced in its material than the Aldrich report.

The wage study made in the nineteenth annual report was continued in an abridged form each year down to and including 1907. The figures for each year were published in the bulletins of the bureau. After 1907 the annual collection of wage data was dropped for a few years while the bureau was devoting its limited resources and personnel to other lines of work. The major work of the bureau for a period of two or three years was a report on condition of women and child wage earners in the United States. This report when finally published consisted of 19 volumes and was a monumental piece of work. It included quite a fund of information concerning wages in some few industries, but the wage figures applied only to the time of the study.

In 1912 the bureau began to devote much more of its time to the study of wages. Several industries were covered at this time and the wage data were collected back to the year 1907. At this time also the bureau began the collection of union-wage figures as such, and on this subject a study and report has been made each year down to the present time.

It was the intention of the bureau when the wage surveys were resumed in 1912 that several of the major industries should be studied each year and a considerable number of industries were thus covered for two or three years. Then the bureau, because of the pressure of other lines of work, changed its policy and decided to cover several of the major industries on alternate years, covering some of them one year and others the next, without an attempt being made to fill in data for the missing year. This is the policy of the bureau to-day, although it has never been able strictly to adhere to the "alternate year" plan and for some industries there are gaps of three or four years in the figures. It would be highly desirable to cover all of the important industries each year so that there might be available at all times wage information not more than one year out of date, but because of the limitation of funds and the necessity of carrying other lines of work the bureau is unable to do more on the subject of wages than it is doing at the present time.

This explanation will show why this report can not give directly connected figures for industries and occupations through the period from 1840 to the present time. It is also to be noted that the report does not contain by any means all of the wage data available, but from the publications of the bureau enough wage data have been collected and are presented to show what the rates of wages in general have been over the entire period covered and also to furnish a very good idea as to the trend of wages throughout the period.

All the wage data presented in Part 2 are from studies made by the Bureau of Labor Statistics, except the data for farm laborers in Tables D–2 and D–3 (pp. 227 and 228) which are taken from reports of the United States Department of Agriculture.

A.—BAKERY TRADES

BAKERS

The sources from which wage data were secured are the fifteenth and the nineteenth annual reports of the Commissioner of Labor Statistics and bulletins of the Bureau of Labor Statistics Nos. 59, 65, 71, 77, 131, 143, 171, 194, 214, 245, 259, 274, 286, 302, 325, 354, 388, 404, 431, 457, and 482.

In some of these reports the data are present,·¹ by cities, in others by States or geographic divisions; whenever such data were not available for any of these, the information is shown for the United States. In some instances there are overlapping periods. These represent information from different sources and are considered valuable for that reason. The details are shown here in the same manner as published in the above-noted reports.

An inspection of these tables will show that in the early years from 1880 to 1900 bakers were grouped into one class as presented in Table A–1, and again from 1905 to 1907 in Table A–4. In Table A–2, which presents data for the years 1890 to 1904, and Table A–5, which covers the period from 1907 to 1928, inclusive, bakers are presented as first hands and second hands, mixers, benchmen, ovenmen, etc. The occupation terms first hand, second hand, etc., do not represent identical work in all of the different cities where these terms are used. A particular kind of work in one city may be considered as first-hand work and in another city the same work may be classed as second-hand. These reports have followed the terminology used in each city.

The wage data reported for the early periods and extending to 1907 were copied by agents of the Bureau of Labor Statistics direct from pay rolls or other records of representative establishments in the various localities. Both hours and earnings as shown here represent averages computed from these reports.

For the period from 1907 to 1928 the wage data reported here represents minimum rates of wages paid to union workers through agreements with their employers or group of employers. The hours represent the maximum which may be worked beyond which extra for overtime is usually paid. For further explanation of the source of these details see "Building trades," page 153.

TABLE A-1.—*Bakers, 1880-1900, by year and State*

Year and State	Sex	Hours per week	Rate per day (dollars)
1880:			
Georgia	M.	60- 66- 63	1.67-2.00-1.88
New Jersey	M.	80- 80- 80	1 1.50-1.50-1.50
Pennsylvania	M.	60- 60- 60	2.33-3.33-2.81
1881:			
Connecticut	M.	72- 90- 84	1.16-1.46-1.24
Illinois	M.	74-100- 87	1.75-1.75-1.75
New Jersey	M.	72-102- 89	1.50-1.70-1.68
New York	M.	74-112-100	1.20-2.25-1.65
Do	M.	112-112-112	1 1.65-1.65-1.65
1882:			
Illinois	M.	74-102- 99	2.00-2.50-2.04
Missouri	M.	60- 72- 67	1.67-4.17-2.28
New Jersey	M.	(2)	1.33-1.67-1.55
Do	M.	(2)	1 1.67-1.67-1.67
Ohio	(2)	60- 60- 60	1.68-1.68-1.68
1883:			
Massachusetts	M.	(2)	1.33-3.83-2.12
Michigan	M.	(2)	.50-4.00-1.76
New Jersey	M.		1.33-3.00-1.69
Ohio	M.	72- 72- 72	1.67-1.67-1.67
West Virginia	M.	60- 60- 60	1.33-1.33-1.33
1884:			
California	M.	60- 72- 64	1 1.92-3.00-2.62
Illinois	M.	78- 78- 78	1.25-1.50-1.42
Iowa	M.	72- 72- 72	2.00-2.25-2.08
Michigan	M.	(2)	1.25-2.88-1.76
New Jersey	M.	48- 84- 62	1.33-2.83-1.80
New York	M.	120-120-120	2.17-2.17-2.17
Ohio	M.	60- 60- 60	1.83-1.83-1.83
Pennsylvania	M.	59- 60- 60	1.25-3.00-1.85
1885:			
Iowa	M.	60- 60- 60	2.33-2.33-2.33
New Jersey	M.	60- 78- 63	1.17-3.00-1.79
New York	M.	60- 86- 82	.60-2.50-2.22
1886:			
California	M.	60- 60- 60	2.30-2.30-2.30
Do	(2)	48- 84- 64	1.34-2.50-1.73
Do	(2)	60- 90- 69	1 1.34-2.50-2.03
Connecticut	M.	60- 60- 60	1.88-2.25-2.00
Georgia	M.	60- 66- 61	1.25-1.75-1.49
Illinois	M.	54- 86- 73	1.50-2.50-2.02
Iowa	M.	60- 77- 72	1.00-2.25-1.65
Kentucky	M.	69- 69- 69	1.21-1.21-1.21
Louisiana	M.	105-105-105	1 1.25-1.25-1.25
Massachusetts	M.	62- 62- 62	2.32-2.32-2.32
Michigan	(2)	48- 60- 54	1.75-1.75-1.75
Minnesota	M.	80- 80- 80	1.75-1.75-1.75
Missouri	M.	54- 60- 55	1.00-1.58-1.16
Do	M.	(2)	1 1.00-1.23-1.10
New Jersey	M.	78- 78- 78	2.00-2.00-2.00
New York	M.	60-120- 79	.80-2.67-1.92
Do	F.	60- 60- 60	1.67-2.00-1.91
Ohio	M.	87- 87- 87	1.66-1.66-1.66
Pennsylvania	M.	84- 84- 84	1.50-1.50-1.50
Wisconsin	M.	80- 80- 80	1.50-1.50-1.50
1887:			
Connecticut	M.	(2)	.81-2.09-1.93
Kansas	M.	(2)	1.00-1.00-1.00
New York	M.	74- 74- 74	1 2.83-2.83-2.83
Ohio	M.	60- 78 (2)	1.00-2.50-1.71
Do	F.	60- 78 (2)	.60-1.00- .85
Wisconsin	M.	(2)	1.00-1.00-1.00
1888:			
Colorado	M.	60- 60- 60	5.00-5.00-5.00
Iowa	M.	72- 72- 72	2.00-2.00-2.00
Kansas	M.	(2)	2.14-2.50-2.27
New Jersey	(2)	72- 81- 74	2.00-3.00-2.67
New York	M.	55- 81- 67	1.50-5.00-2.17
Do	M.	73- 73- 73	1 1.00-1.50-1.25
Rhode Island	(2)	(2)	2.50-2.50-2.50
1890:			
Minnesota	M.	(2)	1.00-2.00-1.64
New York	M.	(2)	.67-3.33-1.39
Ohio	(2)	60- 72- 61	1.20-2.50-1.69
1891:			
Michigan	F.	(2)	.50-1.00- .67
New York	M.	(2)	.58-5.00-1.57
Ohio	M.	48- 72- 61	1.00-3.00-1.77
1892:			
California	M.	(2)	.77-3.33-1.81
Illinois	M.	48- 60- 57	1.00-1.67-1.13
Do	F.	63- 63- 63	3 .96- .96- .96
Iowa	M.	48- 72- 62	1.16-3.00-1.88
Missouri	M.	(2)	1.33-2.08-1.69
1893:			
Illinois	M.	59- 96- 67	.83-4.17-2.07
Do	F.	36- 56- 49	.50-2.00-1.06
Maryland	M.	30- 96- 68	.67-5.00-2.06
Do	F.	72- 72- 72	4.17-4.17-4.17
Missouri	M.	84- 84- 84	1.17-3.00-1.55
Montana	M.	57- 77- 61	2.00-4.17-3.58
Do	M.	48- 48- 48	3 .96-2.50-1.73
New York	M.	48-117- 73	.67-4.17-1.67
Do	M.	56-102- 69	1 .58-1.33- .99
Do	F.	70- 84- 75	.54-2.00-1.40
Ohio	M.	54- 72- 62	1.00-2.50-1.73
Do	M.	60- 60- 60	1 1.40-1.50-1.44
Do	F.	60- 60- 60	.50-1.00- .54
Pennsylvania	M.	42-108- 71	.42-3.33-1.90
Do	M.	60- 84- 73	1 .67-1.92-1.01
1894:			
District of Columbia	M.	60- 60- 60	2.00-3.00-2.50
Iowa	M.	60- 84- 66	1.17-3.75-2.05
Do	M.	60- 60- 60	1 2.17-2.17-2.17
New Hampshire	M.	60- 72- 63	2.17-3.50-2.88
Ohio	M.	54- 72- 62	1.14-4.17-1.76
Do	F.	48- 66- 58	.50- .66- .59
1895:			
Georgia	M.	59- 59- 59	1.25-2.33-1.46
Illinois	M.	60- 60- 60	2.00-2.00-2.00
Iowa	M.	60- 60- 60	2.33-2.33-2.33
Massachusetts	M.	60- 60- 60	2.10-2.25-2.14
Missouri	M.	(2)	.67-2.29-1.85
New York	M.	60- 60- 60	2.00-3.33-2.39
North Carolina	M.	60- 60- 60	1.50-1.50-1.50
Ohio	M.	54- 72- 60	.66-3.33-1.90
Do	F.	54- 60- 55	.58- .75- .71
Rhode Island	M.	66- 66- 66	.67-3.00-1.83
1896:			
Colorado	(2)	66- 66- 66	2.00-2.00-2.00
Florida	M.	(2)	2.00-2.00-2.00
Georgia	M.	60- 66- 62	1.00-2.00-1.84
Illinois	M.	60- 72- 61	.67-3.00-2.01
Iowa	M.	72- 72- 72	1.67-1.67-1.67
Kansas	M.	60- 60- 60	1.17-1.17-1.17
Missouri	M.	48- 72- 62	1.40-2.25-1.91
Do	F.	54- 60- 59	.92-1.20- .98
Nebraska	M.	60-108- 63	.50-4.25-1.85
New York	M.	60- 60- 60	.83-3.00-1.72
Ohio	M.	60- 68- 62	.87-2.35-1.71
Do	F.	63- 63- 63	.54- .54- .54
Pennsylvania	M.	54- 57- 55	1.50-3.33-2.16
West Virginia	M.	60- 60- 60	1.83-1.83-1.83
1897:			
Illinois	M.	60- 60- 60	2.00-2.17-2.09
Kansas	M.	70- 75- 75	.86-1.71-1.46
Michigan	M.	(2)	2.04-2.04-2.04
Nebraska	M.	(2)	2.00-2.00-2.00
Do	(2)	(2)	1.00-1.00-1.00
Virginia	M.	54- 96- 63	.69-3.00- .92
Do	F.	48- 72- 60	.50-1.50- .86
1898:			
Michigan	M.	(2)	1.25-1.50-1.41
Nebraska	M.	48- 96- 62	1.00-2.50-1.83
1899:			
Georgia	M.	60- 60- 60	.60-2.00-1.06
Massachusetts	M.	66- 70- 68	1.17-4.17-2.17
1900:			
Georgia	M.	60- 60- 60	.60-2.00-1.06
Massachusetts	M.	66- 70- 68	1.17-4.17-2.15

1 And board.   2 Not reported.   3 And board and lodging.

TABLE A-2.—*Bakers, first hands, males, 1890–1904, by geographic division and year*

Year	North Atlantic		South Atlantic		North Central		South Central	
	Hours per week	Rate per hour	Hours per week	Rate per hour	Hours per week	Rate per hour	Hours per week	Rate per hour
1890	64.6	$0.259	67.6	$0.198	65.8	$0.230	71.4	$0.224
1891	64.7	.261	67.6	.198	65.8	.230	71.4	.224
1892	64.6	.259	67.6	.198	65.9	.231	71.4	.224
1893	64.3	.258	67.6	.198	65.9	.226	71.4	.224
1894	65.1	.255	67.6	198	64.4	.226	71.4	.224
1895	65.1	.256	67.6	197	64.3	.228	71.4	.225
1896	65.1	.257	67.6	.201	64.2	.231	71.4	.225
1897	65.1	.258	67.6	.203	64.1	.232	71.4	.225
1898	65.4	.257	67.6	.210	62.7	.239	71.4	.226
1899	65.2	.258	67.6	.208	61.2	.253	70.7	.232
1900	63.4	.268	67.6	.217	60.9	.258	69.5	.240
1901	63.6	.271	65.2	.234	60.8	.261	68.5	.247
1902	63.6	.275	65.2	.234	60.4	.274	68.5	.247
1903	63.4	.279	63.4	.240	59.6	.280	67.4	.232
1904	61.3	.272	60.9	.262	59.2	.283	65.3	.250

TABLE A-3.—*Bakers, second hands, males, 1890–1904, by geographic division and year*

Year	North Atlantic		South Atlantic		North Central		South Central	
	Hours per week	Rate per hour	Hours per week	Rate per hour	Hours per week	Rate per hour	Hours per week	Rate per hour
1890	68.2	$0.181	63.2	$0.154	64.0	$0.192	74.3	$0.158
1891	68.1	.184	63.2	.154	64.0	.193	74.3	.158
1892	68.1	.185	63.5	.153	64.7	.192	74.3	.158
1893	67.8	.185	63.2	.156	64.7	.191	74.3	.158
1894	67.3	.187	62.8	.157	64.5	.190	74.3	.158
1895	67.9	.187	63.6	.154	63.7	.192	74.3	.158
1896	67.8	.188	63.7	.158	63.7	.194	74.3	.158
1897	68.1	.186	63.7	.158	63.1	.197	74.3	.158
1898	67.7	.188	66.1	.158	62.2	.201	74.3	.158
1899	68.2	189	63.5	.163	60.4	.209	74.3	.158
1900	66.5	.194	63.8	.164	59.8	.216	73.7	.166
1901	67.4	.198	62.2	.179	59.6	.217	73.3	.169
1902	67.4	.204	62.2	.179	58.5	.233	72.9	.172
1903	66.6	.210	61.5	.175	59.2	.229	68.3	.181
1904	60.4	.226	61.0	.204	58.4	.239	66.6	.197

TABLE A-4.—*Bakers, males, 1905–1907, by geographic division and year*

Year	North Atlantic		South Atlantic		North Central		South Central	
	Hours per week	Rate per hour	Hours per week	Rate per hour	Hours per week	Rate per hour	Hours per week	Rate per hour
1905	61.8	$0.242	59.8	$0.239	58.0	$0.248	65.4	$0.220
1906	61.2	.251	60.0	.240	57.5	.257	67.5	.210
1907	61.3	.251	59.4	.245	57.6	.258	66.4	.218

TABLE A-5.—*Bakers, first hands, hand, day work, males, 1907–1928, by city and year*

Year	Cincinnati, Ohio [1]		Dallas, Tex. [2]		Denver, Colo. [3]		Fall River, Mass.	
	Hours per week	Rate per hour	Hours per week	Rate per hour	Hours per week	Rate per hour	Hours per week	Rate per hour
1907	54.0	$0.278	78.0	$0.205			60.0	$0.283
1908	54.0	.278	72.0	.250			60.0	.283
1909	54.0	.278	72.0	.278			60.0	.283
1910	54.0	.278	66.0	.333	57.0	$0.316	60.0	.300
1911	54.0	.278	60.0	.367	57.0	.333	54.0	.333
1912	54.0	.278	60.0	.367	54.0	.370	54.0	.333
1913	54.0	.296	60.0	.367	54.0	.370		
1914	54.0	.296	57.0	.386	54.0	*.370	60.0	.300
1915	54.0	.315	54.0	.407	54.0	.370		
1916	54.0	.315	51.0	.431	54.0	.370		
1917	54.0	.333	51.0	.431	54.0	.389		
1918	54.0	.370	51.0	.529	54.0	.426		
1919	54.0	.444	51.0	.627	51.0	.539		
1920	48.0	.750	51.0	.824	51.0	.608		
1921	48.0	.750	51.0	.824	51.0	.627		
1922	48.0	.750	51.0	.741	48.0	.615		
1923	48.0	.771	51.0	.765	48.0	.667		
1924	48.0	.771	51.0	.765	48.0	.708		
1925	48.0	.771	51.0	.765	48.0	.792		
1926	48.0	.771	51.0	.765	48.0	.792		
1927	48.0	.771	51.0	.765	48.0	.792		
1928	48.0	.771	51.0	.765	48.0	.792		

Year	Indianapolis, Ind. [4]		Kansas City, Mo. [5]		Louisville, Ky. [1]		New York, N. Y.	
1907	60.0	$0.267	54.0	$0.296	57.0	$0.263	74.0	$0.216
1908	60.0	.267	54.0	.296	57.0	.263	74.0	.243
1909	60.0	.267	54.0	.333	57.0	.281	74.0	.243
1910	60.0	.267	54.0	.333	57.0	.281	62.0	.323
1911	60.0	.265	54.0	.352	57.0	.281	62.0	.323
1912	60.0	.265	54.0	.352	57.0	.281	56.0	.357
1913	60.0	.267	54.0	.389	57.0	.281	54.0	.333
1914	60.0	.267	54.0	.407	57.0	.281	54.0	.370
1915	57.0	.316	54.0	.407	57.0	.281	54.0	.370
1916	57.0	.316	54.0	.407	57.0	.281	60.0	.300
1917	57.0	.368	54.0	.444	57.0	.316	54.0	.370
1918	54.0	.463	54.0	.481			51.0	.412
1919	54.0	.556	54.0	.556			51.0	.510
1920	54.0	.648	48.0	.813	48.0	.583	48.0	.854
1921	54.0	.694	48.0	.813	48.0	.583	48.0	.979
1922	54.0	.694	48.0	.813	48.0	.583	48.0	.979
1923	54.0	.694	48.0	.813	48.0	.583	48.0	.979
1924	54.0	.694	48.0	.875	48.0	.625	48.0	.979
1925	54.0	.694	48.0	.875	48.0	.625	48.0	.979
1926	54.0	.694	48.0	.875	48.0	.625	48.0	.979
1927	54.0	.694	48.0	.896	48.0	.625	48.0	.979
1928	54.0	.694	48.0	.896	48.0	.625	48.0	.979

Year	Omaha, Nebr.		San Francisco, Calif. [7]		Seattle, Wash. [8]		Washington, D. C. [9]	
1907	60.0	$0.267	60.0	$0.367	60.0	$0.400	54.0	$0.306
1908	60.0	.267	54.0	.463	60.0	.400	54.0	.320
1909	54.0	.296	54.0	.463	60.0	.417	54.0	.320
1910	54.0	.296	54.0	.463	54.0	.463	54.0	.320
1911	54.0	.296	54.0	.463	48.0	.521	54.0	.333
1912	54.0	.296	54.0	.463	48.0	.521	54.0	.333
1913	54.0	.296	54.0	.463	48.0	.458	54.0	.361
1914	54.0	.296	54.0	.463	48.0	.458	54.0	.361
1915	54.0	.296	54.0	.463	48.0	.458	54.0	.361
1916			54.0	.463	48.0	.458	54.0	.361
1917			54.0	.463	48.0	.500	54.0	[10].361
1918			54.0	.556	48.0	.688	48.0	.563
1919			51.0	.725	48.0	.813	48.0	.640
1920			48.0	.875	48.0	.938	48.0	.900
1921			48.0	.958	48.0	.938	48.0	.900
1922			48.0	.896	48.0	.875	48.0	.900
1923			48.0	.958	48.0	.938	48.0	1.000
1924			48.0	.958	48.0	1.000	48.0	1.000
1925			48.0	.958	48.0	1.000	48.0	1.000
1926			48.0	.958	48.0	1.000	48.0	1.000
1927			48.0	.958	48.0	1.000	48.0	1.000
1928			48.0	.958	48.0	1.000	48.0	1.000

[1] Oven men.
[2] Foremen, 1916–1928, inclusive.
[3] Oven men, 1910–1924, inclusive.
[4] Oven men, 1907–1912, inclusive; foremen, 1913–1928, inclusive.
[5] Oven men, 1913–1928, inclusive.
[6] Scale became 51 cents on May 25, 1918.
[7] Oven men, 1914–1928, inclusive.
[8] Benchmen in charge of ovens, 1913–1917, inclusive; oven men, 1918–1928, inclusive.
[9] Not classified, 1907–1922, inclusive; journeymen, 1923–1928, inclusive.
[10] Scale became 40 cents per hour on June 2, 1917.

TABLE **A-6.**—*Bakers, first hands, machine, day work, males, 1907–1928, by city and year*

Year	Kansas City, Mo.[1]		Washington, D. C.[2]		Cincinnati, Ohio[3]		New York, N. Y.[4]		San Francisco, Calif.[3]		Denver, Colo.[5]	
	Hours per week	Rate per hour	Hours per week	Rate per hour	Hours per week	Rate per hour	Hours per week	Rate per hour	Hours per week	Rate per hour	Hours per week	Rate per hour
1907	54.0	$0.333	48.0	$0.344								
1908	54.0	.333	48.0	.360								
1909	54.0	.333	48.0	.360								
1910	54.0	.333	48.0	.360								
1911	48.0	.417	48.0	.375								
1912	48.0	.438	48.0	.375								
1913	48.0	.438	48.0	.406	48.0	$0.375	54.0	$0.370	48.0	$0.521		
1914	54.0	.458	48.0	.406	48.0	.375	54.0	.370	48.0	.521		
1915	54.0	.458	48.0	.406	48.0	.375	54.0	.370	48.0	.521		
1916	48.0	.458	48.0	.406	48.0	.396	51.0	.392	48.0	.521		
1917	48.0	.500	48.0	⁶.406	48.0	.396	51.0	.431	48.0	.521		
1918	48.0	.542	48.0	.563	48.0	.438	51.0	⁷.431	48.0	.625		
1919	48.0	.625			48.0	.521	51.0	.529	48.0	.771		
1920	48.0	.813			48.0	.750	48.0	.875	48.0	.875		
1921											48.0	$0.667
1922											48.0	.615
1923							48.0	1.021			48.0	.667
1924							48.0	1.021			48.0	.708
1925							48.0	1.083			48.0	.708
1926							48.0	1.083			48.0	.708
1927											48.0	.708
1928	⁸48.0	⁸.833									48.0	.708

¹ Oven men, 1907–1920, inclusive.	⁵ Oven men, 1921–1928, inclusive.
² Not classified, 1907–1918, inclusive.	⁶ Scale became 45 cents on June 2, 1917.
³ Oven men, 1913–1920, inclusive.	⁷ Scale became 52.9 cents on May 25, 1918.
⁴ Oven men, 1913–1924, inclusive.	⁸ Benchmen and machine hands.

TABLE **A-7.**—*Bakers, first hands, machine, night work, males, 1907–1912, by city and year*

Year	Cincinnati, Ohio[1]		Indianapolis, Ind.[1]	
	Hours per week	Rate per hour	Hours per week	Rate per hour
1907	54.0	$0.315	60.0	$0.300
1908	54.0	.315	60.0	.300
1909	54.0	.315	60.0	.300
1910	54.0	.315	60.0	.300
1911	54.0	.315	60.0	.300
1912	54.0	.315	60.0	.300

¹ Oven men, 1907–1912, inclusive.

TABLE A-8.—*Bakers, second hands, hand, day work, males, 1907-1928, by city and year*

Year	Cincinnati, Ohio [1]		Dallas, Texas [1]		Denver, Colo. [1]		Fall River, Mass. [2]	
	Hours per week	Rate per hour	Hours per week	Rate per hour	Hours per week	Rate per hour	Hours per week	Rate per hour
1907	54.0	$0.241	78.0	$0.180			60.0	$0.233
1908	54.0	.241	72.0	.222			60.0	.233
1909	54.0	.241	72.0	.250			60.0	.233
1910	54.0	.241	66.0	.303	57.0	$0.263	60.0	.250
1911	54.0	.241	60.0	.333	57.0	.298	54.0	.278
1912	54.0	.241	60.0	.333	54.0	.333	54.0	.278
1913	54.0	.259	60.0	.333	54.0	.333		
1914	54.0	.259	57.0	.351	54.0	.333	60.0	.250
1915	54.0	.278	54.0	.370	54.0	.333		
1916	54.0	.278	51.0	.392	54.0	.333		
1917	54.0	.296	51.0	.392	54.0	.352		
1918	54.0	.333	51.0	.471	54.0	.389		
1919	54.0	.407	51.0	.569	51.0	.490		
1920	48.0	.688	51.0	.765	51.0	.559	48.0	.667
1921	48.0	.688	51.0	.765	51.0	.588		
1922	48.0	.688	51.0	.688	48.0	.573		
1923	48.0	.708	51.0	.716	48.0	.625		
1924	48.0	.708	51.0	.716	48.0	.667		
1925	48.0	.708			48.0	.667		
1926	48.0	.708	51.0	.716	48.0	.667		
1927	48.0	.708	51.0	.716	48.0	.667		
1928	48.0	.708	51.0	.716	48.0	.667		

Year	Indianapolis, Ind. [3]		Kansas City, Mo. [4]		Louisville, Ky. [5]		New York, N. Y.	
1907	60.0	$0.233	54.0	$0.278	57.0	$0.228	74.0	$0.189
1908	60.0	.233	54.0	.278	57.0	.228	74.0	.189
1909	60.0	.233	54.0	.296	57.0	.246	74.0	.216
1910	60.0	.233	54.0	.296	57.0	.246	62.0	.258
1911	60.0	.233	54.0	.333	57.0	.246	62.0	.258
1912	60.0	.267	54.0	.352	57.0	.246	56.0	.286
1913	60.0	.267	54.0	.352	57.0	.246	54.0	.296
1914	60.0	.250	54.0	.370	57.0	.246	54.0	.315
1915	57.0	.263	54.0	.370	57.0	.246	54.0	.315
1916	57.0	.298	54.0	.370	57.0	.246	60.0	.267
1917	57.0	.333	54.0	.407	57.0	.272	54.0	.333
1918	54.0	.389	54.0	.444			51.0	[6] .353
1919	54.0	.481	54.0	.519			51.0	.451
1920	54.0	.574	48.0	.750	48.0	.500	48.0	.792
1921	54.0	.556	48.0	.750	48.0	.500	48.0	.917
1922	54.0	.556	48.0	.750	48.0	.500	48.0	.917
1923	54.0	.556	48.0	.750	48.0	.542	48.0	.917
1924	54.0	.556	48.0	.813	48.0	.583	48.0	.917
1925	54.0	.556	48.0	.813	48.0	.583	48.0	.917
1926	54.0	.556	48.0	.813	48.0	.583	48.0	.917
1927	54.0	.556	48.0	.833	48.0	.583	48.0	.917
1928	54.0	.556	48.0	.833	48.0	.583	48.0	.917

Year	Omaha, Nebr.		San Francisco, Calif. [5]		Seattle, Wash. [5]	
1907	60.0	$0.250	60.0	$0.300	60.0	$0.333
1908	60.0	.250	54.0	.389	60.0	.333
1909	54.0	.278	54.0	.389	60.0	.333
1910	54.0	.278	54.0	.389	54.0	.370
1911	54.0	.278	54.0	.389	48.0	.417
1912	54.0	.278	54.0	.389	48.0	.417
1913	54.0	.278	54.0	.389	48.0	.417
1914	54.0	.278	54.0	.389	48.0	.417
1915	54.0	.278	54.0	.389	48.0	.417
1916			54.0	.389	48.0	.417
1917			54.0	.389	48.0	.458
1918			54.0	.500	48.0	.625
1919			51.0	.667	48.0	.750
1920	51.0	.725	48.0	.813	48.0	.875
1921			48.0	.896	48.0	.875
1922			48.0	.833	48.0	.813
1923			48.0	.896	48.0	.875
1924			48.0	.896	48.0	.938
1925			48.0	.896	48.0	.938
1926			48.0	.896	48.0	.938
1927			48.0	.896	48.0	.938
1928			48.0	.896	48.0	.938

[1] Benchmen, 1913-1928, inclusive.
[2] Benchmen, 1920.
[3] Benchmen, 1914-15, inclusive; second hands and benchmen, 1916-17, inclusive; benchmen, mixers, and oven men, 1921-1928, inclusive.
[4] Benchmen.
[5] Benchmen, 1913-1928, inclusive.
[6] Scale became 45.1 cents on May 24, 1918.

B.—BUILDING TRADES

The sources from which these wage data were taken are the fifteenth and the nineteenth annual reports of the Commissioner of Labor Statistics and bulletins of the Bureau of Labor Statistics Nos. 59, 65, 71, 77, 131, 143, 171, 194, 214, 245, 259, 274, 286, 302, 325, 354, 362, 388, 404, 422, 431, 457, 471, and 482.

The wage data reported for the early periods and extending to 1907 were obtained by agents of the Bureau of Labor Statistics direct from pay rolls or other records of representative establishments in the various localities. The hours shown here are basic or regular full-time working hours of the various establishments reduced to an average for each particular occupation. The earnings are averages obtained by dividing the actual earnings of all employees working in each specified occupation during a representative pay period by their actual hours worked during this same representative pay period.

For the period from 1907 to 1928 the rates represent the minimum union scales of wages which have been agreed to or accepted by the union men and the employers. The hours represent the maximum which may be worked beyond which extra payment for overtime is usually made. In many instances workmen are actually paid more than the scale, and in other instances they work fewer hours than the scale designates.

A large part of this union wage data were obtained by agents of the Bureau of Labor Statistics through personal visits to business agents and secretaries of the respective trade unions in the various cities. Through the cooperation of the State labor bureau officials in Massachusetts, Ohio, and Pennsylvania, certain details from their reports were furnished to this bureau. Whenever available the wage scales, written agreements, and trade-union records were consulted.

The various wage agreements as reported represent wages for different units of time, some per hour, others per day or month. For the purpose of comparison, all of these varying rates have been converted into a common unit of a rate per hour.

Electricians were designated as inside wiremen in the overlapping period from 1890 to 1900 and from 1900 to 1928, Tables B–6 and B–7.

The data for laborers here presented cover those engaged in work on or about building construction for the period of 1890 to 1928. For other laborers see Tables D–1, D–2, D–3 (pp. 225, 227, and 228), G–1 (p. 253), I–16, I–17, I–18 (pp. 295 and 296), O–11, and O–12 (p. 464).

TABLE **B-1.**—*Bricklayers, 1840–1900, by year and State*

Year and State	Sex	Hours per week	Rate per day (dollars)	Year and State	Sex	Hours per week	Rate per day (dollars)
1840:				1866:			
New York	M.	60–60–60	1.75–1.75–1.75	Massachusetts	M.	60–60–60	2.25–3.75–2.95
1841:				New York	M.	60–60–60	3.00–4.00–3.58
New York	M.	60–60–60	1.50–2.50–1.79	Ohio	M.	60–60–60	4.00–4.00–4.00
1842:				Pennsylvania	M.	54–54–54	3.00–3.00–3.00
New York	M.	60–60–60	1.50–2.50–2.00	1867:			
1843:				Massachusetts	M.	60–60–60	2.25–4.00–3.17
New York	M.	60–60–60	2.50–2.50–2.50	New York	M.	60–60–60	3.50–5.00–4.67
1844:				Ohio	M.	60–60–60	5.00–5.00–5.00
New York	M.	60–60–60	2.50–2.50–2.50	Pennsylvania	M.	54–54–54	3.50–3.50–3.50
1845:				1868:			
New York	M.	60–60–60	2.50–2.50–2.50	Massachusetts	M.	60–60–60	3.00–4.00–3.76
1846:				New York	M.	60–60–60	4.00–4.50–4.35
New York	M.	60–60–60	1.75–2.00–1.79	Ohio	M.	60–60–60	5.00–5.00–5.00
1847:				Pennsylvania	M.	54–54–54	3.50–3.50–3.50
Massachusetts	M.	60–60–60	1.33–1.33–1.33	1869:			
New York	M.	60–60–60	1.75–2.00–1.88	Massachusetts	M.	60–60–60	2.25–4.00–3.44
1848:				New York	M.	60–60–60	4.00–5.00–4.88
Massachusetts	M.	60–60–60	1.33–1.67–1.39	Ohio	M.	60–60–60	5.00–5.00–5.00
New York	M.	60–60–60	1.75–2.00–1.88	Pennsylvania	M.	54–54–54	3.50–3.50–3.50
1849:				1870:			
New York	M.	60–60–60	1.75–2.00–1.88	California	M.	48–48–48	5.00–5.00–5.00
1850:				Illinois	M.	60–60–60	3.00–3.50–3.38
New York	M.	60–60–60	2.00–2.00–2.00	Louisiana	M.	60–60–60	2.25–3.00–2.50
1851:				Maryland	M.	59–59–59	4.00–4.50–4.15
New York	M.	C0–60–60	1.75–2.00–1.88	Massachusetts	M.	60–60–60	3.00–5.00–3.97
1852:				Minnesota	M.	60–60–60	3.50–3.50–3.50
New York	M.	60–60–60	1.75–2.00–1.93	Missouri	M.	60–60–60	3.00–3.00–3.00
1853:				New York	M.	60–60–60	3.00–5.00–3.89
New York	M.	60–60–60	1.75–2.00–1.96	Ohio	M.	60–60–60	4.50–5.00–4.63
1854:				Pennsylvania	M.	54–60–57	3.00–5.00–4.01
New York	M.	60–60–60	1.75–2.00–1.94	Virginia	M.	60–60–60	3.50–3.50–3.50
1855:				1871:			
New York	M.	60–60–60	1.75–2.25–2.00	California	M.	48–48–48	5.00–5.00–5.00
1856:				Illinois	M.	60–60–60	5.00–5.00–5.00
New York	M.	60–60–60	1.75–2.25–2.00	Louisiana	M.	60–60–60	2.25–3.00–2.50
Ohio	M.	60–60–60	2.00–2.00–2.00	Maryland	M.	59–59–59	4.00–4.50–4.29
1857:				Massachusetts	M.	60–60–60	2.50–5.00–4.07
New York	M.	60–60–60	1.75–2.50–2.08	Minnesota	M.	60–60–60	3.50–3.50–3.50
Ohio	M.	60–60–60	2.00–2.00–2.00	Missouri	M.	60–60–60	3.00–3.00–3.00
1858:				New York	M.	60–60–60	3.00–4.00–3.85
New York	M.	60–60–60	1.50–2.50–1.86	Ohio	M.	60–60–60	5.00–5.00–5.00
Ohio	M.	60–60–60	2.00–2.00–2.00	Pennsylvania	M.	54–60–55	3.00–4.00–3.89
1859:				Virginia	M.	60–60–60	3.50–3.50–3.50
Massachusetts	M.	60–60–60	1.25–2.25–1.74	1872:			
New York	M.	60–60–60	1.50–2.50–1.80	California	M.	48–48–48	5.00–5.00–5.00
Ohio	M.	60–60–60	2.25–2.25–2.25	Illinois	M.	60–60–60	5.00–5.00–5.00
1860:				Louisiana	M.	60–60–60	2.25–3.00–2.58
Massachusetts	M.	60–60–60	1.25–2.00–1.53	Maryland	M.	59–59–59	4.00–4.50–4.19
New York	M.	60–60–60	2.00–2.75–2.05	Massachusetts	M.	60–60–60	2.25–4.75–3.86
Ohio	M.	60–60–60	1.67–2.25–1.98	Minnesota	M.	60–60–60	3.50–3.50–3.50
Pennsylvania	M.	54–54–54	2.00–2.00–2.00	Missouri	M.	60–60–60	3.00–3.00–3.00
1861:				New York	M.	48–60–59	3.00–4.00–3.84
Massachusetts	⁷I.	60–60–60	1.50–2.25–1.81	Ohio	M.	60–60–60	3.33–5.00–4.69
New York	M.	60–60–60	2.00–2.50–2.03	Pennsylvania	M.	54–60–56	3.00–5.00–4.02
Ohio	M.	60–60–60	2.25–2.25–2.25	Virginia	M.	60–60–60	3.50–3.50–3.50
Pennsylvania	M.	54–54–54	2.00–2.00–2.00	1873:			
1862:				California	M.	48–48–48	5.00–5.00–5.00
Massachusetts	M.	60–60–60	1.25–2.00–1.79	Illinois	M.	60–60–60	3.50–3.50–3.50
New York	M.	60–60–60	2.00–2.50–2.11	Louisiana	M.	60–60–60	2.25–3.00–2.50
Ohio	M.	60–60–60	2.50–2.50–2.50	Maryland	M.	59–59–59	3.00–4.50–3.72
Pennsylvania	M.	54–54–54	2.25–2.25–2.25	Massachusetts	M.	60–60–60	2.25–4.75–3.88
1863:				Minnesota	M.	60–60–60	3.50–3.50–3.50
Massachusetts	M.	60–60–60	1.40–2.50–2.05	Missouri	M.	60–60–60	2.75–2.75–2.75
New York	M.	60–60–60	1.50–2.50–2.25	New York	M.	48–60–59	3.00–5.00–3.83
Ohio	M.	60–60–60	2.75–2.75–2.75	Ohio	M.	60–60–60	5.00–5.00–5.00
1864:				Pennsylvania	M.	54 60 57	3.25–5.00–3.94
Massachusetts	M.	60–60–60	1.75–3.00–2.31	Virginia	M.	60–60–60	3.50–3.50–3.50
New York	M.	60–60–60	1.75–3.00–2.77	1874:			
Ohio	M.	60–60–60	3.00–3.00–3.00	California	M.	48–48–48	5.00–5.00–5.00
Pennsylvania	M.	54–54–54	2.50–2.50–2.50	Illinois	M.	60–60–60	2.50–2.50–2.50
1865:				Louisiana	M.	60–60–60	2.25–2.75–2.42
Massachusetts	M.	60–60–60	2.00–3.00–2.59	Maryland	M.	59–59–59	3.00–3.50–3.20
New York	M.	60–60–60	2.25–3.00–2.81	Massachusetts	M.	60–60–60	3.00–4.00–3.50
Ohio	M.	60–60–60	4.00–4.00–4.00	Minnesota	M.	60–60–60	3.50–3.50–3.50
Pennsylvania	M.	54–54–54	3.00–3.00–3.00	Missouri	M.	60–60–60	2.75–2.75–2.75

TABLE **B-1.**—*Bricklayers, 1840–1900, by year and State*—Continued

Year and State	Sex	Hours per week	Rate per day (dollars)	Year and State	Sex	Hours per week	Rate per day (dollars)
1874—Continued.				**1880—Continued.**			
New York	M.	48-60-59	3.00-4.50-3.42	New York	M.	48-60-59	2.75-3.50-3.12
Ohio	M.	60-60-60	5.00-5.00-5.00	Ohio	M.	60-60-60	3.50-3.75-3.50
Pennsylvania	M.	54-60-57	2.00-4.00-3.07	Pennsylvania	M.	54-60-57	1.75-3.50-2.32
Virginia	M.	60-60-60	3.00-3.00-3.00	Virginia	M.	60-60-60	2.50-2.50-2.50
1875:				**1881:**			
California	M.	48-60-59	5.00-5.00-5.00	California	M.	48-60-57	4.00-4.00-4.00
Illinois	M.	60-60-60	2.50-2.50-2.50	Illinois	M.	60-60-60	3.50-3.50-3.50
Louisiana	M.	60-60-60	2.25-3.00-2.50	Louisiana	M.	60-60-60	2.75-3.00-2.88
Maryland	M.	59-59-59	3.50-4.00-3.71	Maryland	M.	48-48-48	3.50-4.00-3.67
Massachusetts	M.	60-60-60	3.00-4.50-3.48	Massachusetts	M.	60-60-60	2.50-3.50-2.83
Minnesota	M.	60-60-60	3.50-3.50-3.50	Minnesota	M.	59-60-60	4.00-5.00-4.55
Missouri	M.	60-60-60	2.75-2.75-2.75	Missouri	M.	60-60-60	4.00-4.10-4.04
New York	M.	48-60-59	3.00-4.00-3.35	New Jersey	M.	60-60-80	2.67-4.00-3.28
Ohio	M.	60-60-60	4.50-4.50-4.50	New York	M.	48-60-59	2.75-4.50-3.52
Pennsylvania	M.	54-60-57	3.00-4.00-3.33	Ohio	M.	59-60-60	2.50-4.00-3.54
Virginia	M.	60-60-60	2.75-2.75-2.75	Pennsylvania	M.	54-60-57	2.00-3.50-2.94
1876:				Virginia	M.	60-60-60	2.50-2.50-2.50
California	M.	48-60-57	4.00-5.00-4.22	**1882:**			
Illinois	M.	60-60-60	3.00-3.00-3.00	California	M.	48-60-57	4.00-5.50-5.15
Louisiana	M.	60-60-60	2.25-3.00-2.58	Connecticut	M.	60-60-60	3.50-3.50-3.50
Maryland	M.	59-59-59	3.50-4.00-3.69	Delaware	M.	50-50-50	3.00-3.25-3.13
Massachusetts	M.	60-60-60	2.88-4.00-3.45	Illinois	M.	60-60-60	2.68-3.50-3.42
Minnesota	M.	60-60-60	3.50-3.50-3.50	Iowa	M.	60-60-60	2.50-4.50-3.93
Missouri	M.	60-60-60	2.75-2.75-2.75	Louisiana	M.	60-60-60	2.25-3.00-2.50
New York	M.	48-60-58	2.50-4.00-3.11	Maryland	M.	48-48-48	4.00-4.00-4.00
Ohio	M.	60-60-60	4.50-4.50-4.50	Massachusetts	M.	60-60-60	2.25-5.00-3.18
Pennsylvania	M.	54-60-57	1.29-4.00-2.92	Minnesota	M.	59-60-60	3.25-5.00-4.14
Virginia	M.	60-60-60	2.50-2.50-2.50	Missouri	M.	60-60-60	4.00-4.75-4.29
1877:				New Jersey	M.	(1)	2.75-2.75-2.75
California	M.	48-60-58	4.00-5.00-4.14	New York	M.	48-60-59	3.50-4.00-3.89
Illinois	M.	60-60-60	3.00-3.00-3.00	Ohio	M.	60-60-60	3.50-4.00-3.66
Louisiana	M.	60-60-60	2.25-3.00-2.56	Do	(1)	59-60-59	3.50-4.00-3.75
Maryland	M.	53-53-53	3.50-4.00-3.72	Pennsylvania	M.	54-60-57	2.00-4.50-3.07
Massachusetts	M.	60-60-60	2.50-4.00-2.96	Virginia	M.	60-60-60	3.00-3.00-3.00
Minnesota	M.	60-60-60	3.50-3.50-3.50	**1883:**			
Missouri	M.	60-60-60	2.75-2.75-2.75	California	M.	48-54-53	4.00-5.50-5.25
New York	M.	48-60-58	2.50-4.00-2.85	Illinois	M.	59-60-59	3.50-4.00-3.75
Ohio	M.	60-60-60	4.00-4.00-4.00	Indiana	M.	60-60-60	3.50-3.67-3.54
Pennsylvania	M.	54-60-57	1.80-3.60-2.84	Iowa	M.	59-60-60	4.00-4.50-4.17
Virginia	M.	60-60-60	2.50-2.50-2.50	Louisiana	M.	60-60-60	2.25-3.00-2.50
1878:				Maryland	M.	48-48-48	4.00-4.00-4.00
California	M.	48-60-54	4.00-4.00-4.00	Massachusetts	M.	60-60-60	2.25-4.00-3.25
Illinois	M.	60-60-60	3.00-3.00-3.00	Michigan	M.	(1)	1.25-6.00-3.17
Louisiana	M.	60-60-60	2.25-3.00-2.56	Minnesota	M.	60-60-60	5.00-5.00-5.00
Maryland	M.	53-53-53	3.50-4.00-3.71	Missouri	M.	60-60-60	4.50-4.50-4.50
Massachusetts	M.	60-60-60	2.50-3.50-2.90	New Jersey	M.	60-60-60	2.00-3.00-2.67
Minnesota	M.	60-60-60	3.50-3.50-3.50	New York	M.	48-60-58	3.50-4.00-4.00
Missouri	M.	60-60-60	3.00-3.00-3.00	Ohio	M.	59-100-61	2.50-5.00-3.82
New York	M.	48-60-58	2.50-4.00-2.81	Pennsylvania	M.	54-60-57	2.54-4.50-3.36
Ohio	M.	60-60-60	2.00-4.00-2.41	Texas	M.	60-60-60	4.50-5.00-4.75
Pennsylvania	M.	54-72-57	1.25-3.50-2.44	**1884:**			
Virginia	M.	60-60-60	2.50-2.50-2.50	California	M.	48-60-54	3.00-5.50-4.22
1879:				Illinois	M.	60-60-60	3.50-5.00-3.53
California	M.	48-60-55	4.00-4.00-4.00	Iowa	M.	60-72-60	2.00-10.00-3.66
Illinois	M.	60-60-60	3.50-3.50-3.50	Louisiana	M.	60-60-60	2.25-3.50-3.42
Louisiana	M.	60-60-60	2.00-2.50-2.25	Maryland	M.	48-48-48	4.00-4.50-4.25
Maryland	M.	53-53-53	3.50-4.00-3.70	Massachusetts	M.	60-60-60	2.25-4.00-3.20
Massachusetts	M.	60-60-60	2.40-3.25-2.71	Michigan	M.	(1)	1.75-4.00-2.93
Minnesota	M.	60-60-60	3.50-3.50-3.50	Minnesota	M.	59-60-60	3.60-5.00-4.16
Missouri	M.	60-60-60	1.50-3.00-2.67	Missouri	M.	60-60-60	4.00-5.00-4.47
New Jersey	(1)	60-60-60	1.50-1.50-1.50	New Jersey	M.	59-60-59	2.33-4.00-3.05
New York	M.	48-60-58	2.50-3.50-3.13	New York	M.	53-60-57	3.50-4.00-4.00
Ohio	M.	60-60-60	2.00-4.00-3.33	Ohio	M.	60-60-60	3.48-4.50-3.67
Pennsylvania	M.	54-60-56	1.67-3.25-2.39	Pennsylvania	M.	54-60-56	2.50-4.00-3.35
Virginia	M.	60-60-60	2.50-2.50-2.50	Texas	M.	60-60-60	3.50-3.50-3.50
1880:				Virginia	M.	60-60-60	3.50-3.50-3.50
California	M.	48-60-56	4.00-4.00-4.00	**1885:**			
Illinois	M.	60-60-60	3.50-3.50-3.50	California	M.	48-54-52	5.00-5.50-5.36
Louisiana	M.	60-60-60	2.25-3.00-2.56	Illinois	M.	48-60-48	2.80-4.00-3.99
Maryland	M.	53-53-53	3.50-4.00-3.70	Kansas	M.	60-60-60	3.50-4.00-3.93
Massachusetts	M.	60-60-60	2.50-3.25-2.68	Kentucky	M.	60-60-60	3.50-3.50-3.50
Minnesota	M.	60-60-60	3.50-3.50-3.50	Louisiana	M.	60-60-60	2.00-3.00-2.50
Missouri	M.	60-60-60	3.50-3.50-3.50	Maryland	M.	48-48-48	4.00-4.50-4.04
New Jersey	(1)	58-60-59	2.00-2.50-2.25				

1 Not reported.

TABLE **B-1.**—*Bricklayers, 1840–1900, by year and State*—Continued

| Year and State | Sex | Lowest, highest, and average— | | Year and State | Sex | Lowest, highest, and average— | |
		Hours per week	Rate per day (dollars)			Hours per week	Rate per day (dollars)
1885—Continued.				**1889—Continued.**			
Massachusetts____	M.	60–60–60	2. 75–4. 50–3. 37	Massachusetts____	M.	54–60–56	2. 25–3. 87–3. 46
Minnesota_____	M.	60–60–60	5. 00–5. 00–5. 00	Minnesota_____	M.	60–60–60	5. 00–5. 00–5. 00
Missouri_____	M.	60–60–60	4. 50–4. 50–4. 50	Missouri_____	M.	48–48–48	2. 25 4. 40–4. 27
New Jersey_____	M.	60–60–60	3. 00–3. 25–3. 00	New York_____	M.	48–60–51	3. 50–4. 05–4. 03
New York_____	M.	54–60–54	3. 50–4. 00–3. 82	North Carolina___	M.	60–72–62	2. 00–2. 50–2. 30
Ohio_____	M.	60–72–61	1. 50–4. 50–3. 78	Ohio_____	M.	60–60–60	3. 25–5. 00–4. 71
Oregon_____	M.	59–59–59	6. 00–6. 00–6. 00	Pennsylvania_____	M.	54–60–54	2. 50–5. 50–3. 78
Pennsylvania_____	M.	54–72–60	2. 70–4. 50–3. 38	Tennessee_____	M.	66–66–66	4. 00–4. 00–4. 00
Virginia_____	M.	60–60–60	3. 00–3. 50–3. 46	Virginia_____	M.	60–60–60	3. 50–3. 50–3. 50
1886:				West Virginia_____	M.	60–60–60	2. 50–4. 00–3. 50
California_____	M.	48–60–59	2. 30–5. 50–3. 19	Wisconsin_____	M.	(1)	1. 84–4. 32–3. 22
Do_____	M.	48–48–48	3. 50–3. 50–3. 50	**1890:**			
Dist. of Columbia.	M.	53–58–54	4. 50–4. 50–4. 50	California_____	M.	48–54–53	5. 00–6. 00–5. 83
Illinois_____	M.	48–60–52	2. 00–4. 00–3. 76	Illinois_____	M.	48–48–48	4. 00–4. 00–4 00
Indiana_____	M.	54–60–57	4. 00–4. 05–4. 03	Kansas_____	M.	(1)	2. 50–5 00–4. 05
Iowa_____	M.	48–78–59	1. 00–6. 00–3. 12	Louisiana_____	M.	60–60–60	2. 00–3. 50–2. 75
Kansas_____	M.	60–60–60	3. 50–4. 50–4. 00	Maryland_____	M.	48–48–48	3. 50–4. 00–3. 75
Louisiana_____	M.	60–60–60	2. 25–3. 00–2. 56	Massachusetts____	M.	54–60–55	2. 50–4. 05–3. 55
Maryland_____	M.	48–48 48	3. 50–4. 00–3. 88	Minnesota_____	M.	60–60–60	2. 25–4. 75–3. 93
Massachusetts____	M.	58–60–59	2. 50–4. 00–3. 50	Missouri_____	M.	48–48–48	2. 50–6. 00–4. 43
Minnesota_____	M.	54–66–57	3. 60–5. 00–4. 23	New York_____	M.	48–60–48	2. 00–4. 50–3. 98
Missouri_____	M.	48–48–48	3. 60–3. 60–3. 60	Ohio_____	M.	54–60–58	3. 25–4. 95–3. 83
New York_____	M.	48–60–51	3. 00–4. 05–3. 59	Pennsylvania_____	M.	54–54–54	3. 60–4. 50–3. 86
Ohio_____	M.	60–60–60	1. 69–4. 50–3. 54	Virginia_____	M.	60–60–60	4. 00–4. 00–4. 00
Pennsylvania_____	M.	54–54–54	3. 00–4. 50–3. 72	**1891:**			
South Carolina____	M.	59–60–60	2. 75–5. 00–3. 88	California_____	M.	48–54–53	5. 00–6. 00–5. 81
Virginia_____	M.	58–60–59	3. 50–4. 50–4. 17	Illinois_____	M.	48–48–48	4. 00–4. 00–4. 00
Wisconsin_____	M.	59–59–59	2. 50–2. 50–2. 50	Louisiana_____	M.	54–54–54	4. 05–4. 05–4. 05
1887:				Maryland_____	M.	48–48–48	3. 50–4. 00–3. 72
California_____	M.	48–54 53	5. 00–5. 50–5. 39	Massachusetts____	M.	54–60–56	2. 25–3. 78–3. 51
Illinois_____	M.	48–48–48	4. 00–4. 00–4. 00	Minnesota_____	M.	60–60–60*	4. 50–4. 50–4. 50
Kansas_____	M.	60–60–60	4. 00–5. 00–4. 33	Missouri_____	M.	48–48–48	2. 66–4. 40–4. 12
Louisiana_____	M.	60–60–60	2. 25–2. 50–2. 38	New York_____	M.	48–60–48	2. 00–4. 00–3. 98
Maryland_____	M.	48–48–48	1. 90–5. 50–3. 66	Ohio_____	M.	54–60–59	3. 25–4. 95–3. 84
Massachusetts____	M.	54–60–58	1. 75–4. 00–2. 94	Pennsylvania_____	M.	54–54–54	3. 60–4. 05–3. 99
Michigan_____	M.	60–60–60	2. 00–4. 00–3. 15	Virginia_____	M.	60–60–60	4. 00–4. 00–4. 00
Do_____	M.	(1)	3 .30– .30– .30	Wisconsin_____	M.	(1)	2 .20– .70– .37
Minnesota_____	M.	60–60–60	5. 00–5. 00–5. 00	**1892:**			
Missouri_____	M.	48–48–48	2. 50–4. 00–3. 40	California_____	M.	48–54–53	3. 00–6. 00–5. 02
New Jersey_____	M.	(1)	2. 40–2. 40–2. 40	Illinois_____	M.	48–48–48	4. 00–4. 00–4. 00
New York_____	M.	53–60–54	3. 00–4. 05–3. 93	Iowa_____	M.	54–60–55	3. 50–4. 50–3. 97
North Carolina___	M.	60–66–61	1. 50–3. 00–2. 19	Louisiana_____	M.	54–54–54	4. 05–4. 05–4. 05
Ohio_____	M.	54–60–59	1. 50–5. 00–3. 22	Maryland_____	M.	48–48–48	3. 50–4. 00–3. 77
Pennsylvania_____	M.	54–60–54	2. 00–4. 50–3. 61	Massachusetts____	M.	54–54–54	3. 00–4. 05–3. 68
Virginia_____	M.	60–60–60	3. 00–4. 00–3. 47	Michigan_____	M.	54–60–55	1. 00–9. 44–3. 43
Wisconsin_____	M.	(1)	1. 50–4. 50–2. 81	Minnesota_____	M.	60–60–60	4. 50–4. 50–4. 50
1888:				Missouri_____	M.	48–54–54	2. 82–4. 50–4. 41
California_____	M.	48–54–53	5. 00–5. 50–5. 42	New York_____	M.	48–60–48	3. 50–4. 00–4. 00
Georgia_____	M.	(1)	2. 00–2. 00–2. 00	Ohio_____	M.	54–60–57	2. 00–4. 95–3. 93
Illinois_____	M.	48–48–48	4. 00–4. 00–4. 00	Do_____	(1)	48–72–54	1.25–10.00–4.01
Iowa_____	M.	48–60–57	2. 17–4. 00–3. 17	Pennsylvania_____	M.	54–54–54	3. 60–4. 05–3. 87
Kansas_____	M.	48–48–48	4. 00–5. 33–4. 84	Virginia_____	M.	54 54–54	3. 60–3. 60–3. 60
Lousiana_____	M.	60–60–60	2. 25–2. 50–2. 42	**1893:**			
Maine_____	M.	60–60–60	3. 00–3. 50–3. 25	California_____	M.	48–48–48	5. 00–5. 00–5. 00
Maryland_____	M.	48–48 48	4. 00–4. 00–4. 00	Illinois_____	M.	48–48–48	1. 67–4. 00–3. 94
Massachusetts____	M.	54–60–56	2. 50–4. 50–3. 30	Louisiana_____	M.	54–54–54	4. 05–4. 05–4. 05
Michigan_____	M.	60–60–60	1. 50–3. 26–2. 17	Maryland_____	M.	45–60–50	. 50–5. 00–3. 40
Minnesota_____	M.	60–60–60	5. 00–5. 00–5. 00	Massachusetts____	M.	54–54–54	3. 15–4. 05–3. 75
Missouri_____	M.	48–48–48	4. 40–4. 40–4. 40	Minnesota_____	M.	60–60–60	4. 50–4. 50–4. 50
New Jersey_____	(1)	54–54–54	2. 50–4. 05–3. 50	Missouri_____	M.	48–48–48	4. 40–4. 40–4. 40
New York_____	M.	53–60–55	3. 00–5. 00–3. 78	Montana_____	M.	48–54–48	5. 00–6. 00–5. 82
North Carolina___	M.	60–72–64	1. 00–3. 00–1. 86	New York_____	M.	47–60–49	1. 50–4. 50–3. 83
Ohio_____	M.	60–60–60	1. 75–4. 50–3. 23	Ohio_____	M.	54–60–59	2. 00–4. 50–3. 53
Pennsylvania_____	M.	54–54–54	3. 15–4. 50–3. 84	Pennsylvania_____	M.	48–60–54	1. 33–5. 00–3. 65
South Carolina____	M.	(1)	1. 00–1. 75–1. 38	Virginia_____	M.	54–54–54	3. 60–3. 60–3. 60
Tennessee_____	M.	(1)	4. 00–5. 00–4. 08	Wisconsin_____	M.	(1)	2 .20– .42½–.33
Virginia_____	M.	60–60–60	3. 00–3. 50–3. 29	**1894:**			
1889:				California_____	M.	48–48–48	5. 00–5. 00–5. 00
California_____	M.	48–54–53	5. 00–6. 00–5. 77	Illinois_____	M.	48–48–48	4. 00–4. 00–4. 00
Illinois_____	M.	48–60–49	3. 00–4. 00–3. 94	Iowa_____	M.	48–66–57	2. 50–4. 67–3. 71
Indiana_____	M.	60–60–60	3. 50–3. 50–3. 50	Louisiana_____	M.	54–54–54	4. 05–4. 05–4. 05
Kansas_____	M.	(1)	3. 25–3. 25–3. 25	Maryland_____	M.	48–48–48	3. 50–4. 00–3. 70
Louisiana_____	M.	60–60–60	2. 25–3. 00–2. 58	Massachusetts____	M.	48–54–52	3. 36–4. 05–3. 65
Maryland_____	M.	48–48–48	4. 00–4. 00–4. 00	Minnesota_____	M.	60–60–60	4. 50–4. 50–4. 50

Table B-1.—Bricklayers, 1840-1900, by year and State—Continued

Year and State	Sex	Hours per week	Rate per day (dollars)	Year and State	Sex	Hours per week	Rate per day (dollars)
1894—Continued.				**1897—Continued.**			
Missouri	M.	48-48-48	4.40-4.40-4.40	Montana	(1)	(1)	2.73-2.73-2.73
New York	M.	48-48-48	4.00-4.00-4.00	Nebraska	(1)	48-54-48	2.25-4.00-3.93
North Carolina	(1)	60-72-64	1.25-3.00-2.13	New York	M.	48-48-48	4.00-4.00-4.00
Ohio	M.	48-60-59	1.63-4.50-2.59	Ohio	M.	48-48-48	3.20-3.20-3.20
Pennsylvania	M.	54-54-54	3.00-4.25-3.26	Do	(1)	54-60-60	1.50-8.10-3.02
Virginia	M.	54-54-54	3.60-3.60-3.60	Pennsylvania	M.	54-54-54	2.70-4.05-3.54
1895:				Virginia	M.	54-54-54	2.50-2.50-2.50
California	M.	48-48-48	5.00-5.00-5.00	**1898:**			
Illinois	M.	48-48-48	4.00-4.00-4.00	California	M.	48-48-48	5.00-5.00-5.00
Louisiana	M.	54-54-54	4.05-4.05-4.05	Illinois	M.	48-48-48	4.00-4.00-4.00
Maryland	M.	48-48-48	3.00-3.00-3.00	Kansas	M.	48-48-48	3.20-4.50-4.07
Massachusetts	M.	48-48-48	2.40-3.60-3.34	Louisiana	M.	54-54-54	3.15-3.60-3.38
Minnesota	M.	60-60-60	4.50-4.50-4.50	Maryland	M.	53-53-53	3.00-3.00-3.00
Missouri	M.	48-48-48	2.70-5.50-4.51	Massachusetts	M.	48-48-48	3.20-4.40-3.41
New York	M.	48-48-48	4.00-4.00-4.00	Michigan	M.	(1)	2.37-3.60-3.41
North Carolina	M.	60-66-61	1.50-3.00-2.27	Minnesota	M.	54-54-54	4.50-4.50-4.50
Ohio	M.	48-72-60	1.50-5.00-3.07	Missouri	M.	48-48-48	3.20-3.20-3.20
Pennsylvania	M.	54-54-54	3.00-4.05-3.56	Nebraska	(1)	42-60-56	.75-5.00-2.93
Virginia	M.	54-54-54	3.60-3.60-3.60	New York	M.	48-48-48	4.00-4.00-4.00
1896:				Ohio	M.	48-48-48	3.00-4.00-3.42
Alabama	M.	(1)	3.00-3.00-3.00	Pennsylvania	M.	44-54-48	1.90-3.83-2.89
California	M.	48-48-48	5.00-5.00-5.00	Virginia	M.	54-54-54	2.25-2.25-2.25
Colorado	M.	48-48-48	4.00-4.00-4.00	Do	(1)	54-54-54	4.00-4.00-4.00
Georgia	M.	(1)	.75-3.00-1.86	**1899:**			
Illinois	M.	48-48-48	2.00-4.00-3.98	Alabama	M.	50-60-50	4.05-4.40-4.05
Louisiana	M.	54-54-54	3.15-3.60-3.38	California	M.	48-48-48	4.00-5.00-4.75
Maryland	M.	48-54-53	2.99-3.50-3.02	Georgia	M.	60-60-60	1.75-2.25-2.11
Massachusetts	M.	48-84-50	2.40-7.70-3.87	Illinois	M.	48-48-48	4.50-4.50-4.50
Minnesota	M.	60-60-60	4.50-4.50-4.50	Massachusetts	M.	48-48-48	3.60-3.60-3.60
Missouri	M.	48-48-48	4.40-4.40-4.40	Montana	M.	48-48-48	6.00-6.00-6.00
New York	M.	48-60-48	1.04-4.00-3.97	New Jersey	M.	53-53-53	3.09-3.09-30.9
North Carolina	M.	60-72-62	1.00-2.50-1.88	New York	M.	44-54-47	3.20-4.03-3.50
Ohio	M.	48-60-56	1.85-3.75-3.41	North Carolina	M.	48-84-61	1.25-3.00-2.17
Pennsylvania	M.	50-60-52	2.50-5.49-4.30	Ohio	M.	60-60-60	1.82-4.68-3.47
Rhode Island	M.	60-60-60	2.00-2.00-2.00	Pennsylvania	M.	48-48-48	2.15-4.60-3.56
South Carolina	M.	66-66-66	2.25-2.25-2.25	**1900:**			
Tennessee	M.	(1)	2.00-3.33-2.79	Alabama	M.	54-54-54	4.05-4.40-4.05
Virginia	M.	54-54-54	3.15-3.15-3.15	California	M.	48-48-48	4.00-5.00-4.74
1897:				Georgia	M.	60-60-60	2.00-3.00-2.38
California	M.	48-48-48	5.00-5.00-5.00	Illinois	M.	48-48-48	4.50-4.50-4.50
Illinois	M.	48-48-48	4.00-4.00-4.00	Massachusetts	M.	48-48-48	3.60-3.60-3.60
Louisiana	M.	54-54-54	3.15-3.60-3.40	Montana	M.	48-48-48	6.00-6.00-6.00
Maryland	M.	53-53-53	3.00-3.00-3.00	New Jersey	M.	53-53-53	3.53-3.53-3.53
Massachusetts	M.	48-48-48	2.40-4.00-3.45	New York	M.	44-54-47	3.20-4.03-3.53
Michigan	(1)	(1)	² .45-.45-.45	North Carolina	M.	60-60-60	1.75-3.00-2.29
Minnesota	M.	60-60-60	4.50-4.50-4.50	Ohio	M.	60-60-60	2.75-4.25-3.63
Missouri	M.	48-48-48	4.40-4.40-4.40	Pennsylvania	M.	48-48-48	4.00-4.00-4.00

¹ Not reported.   ² Per hour.

Table B-2.—Bricklayers, males, 1890-1928, by city and year

Year	Atlanta, Ga. Hours per week	Atlanta, Ga. Rate per hour	Birmingham, Ala. Hours per week	Birmingham, Ala. Rate per hour	Boston, Mass. Hours per week	Boston, Mass. Rate per hour	Chicago, Ill. Hours per week	Chicago, Ill. Rate per hour
1890	60.0	$0.230	59.9	$0.496	53.8	$0.398	48.0	$0.500
1891	60.0	.230	59.8	.493	53.8	.427	48.0	.500
1892	60.0	.225	59.7	.445	50.9	.431	48.0	.500
1893	60.0	.225	59.3	.393	49.4	.441	48.0	.500
1894	60.0	.225	59.7	.303	48.8	.450	48.0	.500
1895	60.0	.236	58.6	.314	48.1	.448	48.0	.500
1896	60.0	.257	59.1	.272	48.0	.449	46.5	.500
1897	60.0	.257	58.2	.327	48.0	.457	48.0	.500
1898	60.0	.267	58.4	.327	48.0	.466	46.2	.500
1899	60.0	.267	57.8	.339	48.0	.475	46.3	.500
1900	60.0	.292	59.3	.314	48.0	.480	46.3	.500
1901	60.0	.292	58.7	.367	48.0	.505	46.2	.500
1902	60.0	.313	48.0	.539	48.0	.503	46.2	.550
1903	57.7	.380	48.0	.500	48.0	.525	44.0	.600

TABLE B-2.—*Bricklayers, males, 1890-1928, by city and year*—Continued

Year	Atlanta, Ga.		Birmingham, Ala.		Boston, Mass.		Chicago, Ill.	
	Hours per week	Rate per hour	Hours per week	Rate per hour	Hours per week	Rate per hour	Hours per week	Rate per hour
1904	57.4	$0.404	48.0	$0.491	48.0	$0.537	45.1	$0.600
1905	55.3	.445	48.0	.497	48.0	.550	45.5	.630
1906	56.0	.462	49.7	.604	47.7	.589	45.2	.627
1907	53.0	.400	----	----	44.0	.600	48.0	.625
1908	53.0	.450	----	----	44.0	.600	48.0	.625
1909	53.0	.450	----	----	44.0	.600	48.0	.675
1910	53.0	.450	----	----	44.0	.600	44.0	.675
1911	53.0	.450	----	----	44.0	.600	44.0	.675
1912	53.0	.450	----	----	44.0	.600	44.0	.725
1913	53.0	.450	----	----	44.0	.650	44.0	.750
1914	50.0	.450	----	----	44.0	.650	44.0	.750
1915	50.0	.450	----	----	44.0	.650	44.0	.750
1916	50.0	.500	----	----	44.0	.650	44.0	.750
1917	50.0	.600	----	----	44.0	.700	44.0	.750
1918	50.0	.600	----	----	44.0	.800	44.0	750
1919	44.0	.700	----	----	44.0	.800	44.0	.875
1920	44.0	1.125	----	----	44.0	1.000	44.0	1.250
1921	44.0	1.000	----	----	44.0	1.000	44.0	1.250
1922	44.0	1.000	----	----	44.0	1.000	44.0	1.100
1923	44.0	1.125	----	----	44.0	1.250	44.0	1.100
1924	44.0	1.250	----	----	44.0	1.250	44.0	1.250
1925	44.0	1.250	----	----	44.0	1.250	44.0	1.500
1926	44.0	1.400	----	----	44.0	1.400	44.0	1.500
1927	44.0	1.400	44.0	1.500	44.0	1.400	44.0	1.625
1928	44.0	1.400	44.0	1.500	44.0	1.400	44.0	1.625

Year	Cincinnati, Ohio		Denver, Colo.		Detroit, Mich.		New Orleans, La.	
1890	49.1	$0.495	48.0	$0.625	54.0	$0.389	54.0	$0.397
1891	48.5	.504	48.0	.625	54.0	.389	54.0	.388
1892	48.6	.505	48.0	.625	54.0	.389	54.0	.388
1893	48.4	.500	48.0	.625	54.0	.346	54.0	.396
1894	48.0	.563	48.0	.375	54.0	.308	54.0	.395
1895	48.0	.563	48.0	.375	54.0	.391	54.0	.409
1896	48.0	.550	48.0	.375	48.0	.400	54.0	.409
1897	48.0	.453	48.0	.469	48.0	.391	54.0	.378
1898	48.0	.456	48.0	.625	48.0	.375	54.0	.356
1899	48.0	.473	48.0	.625	48.0	.400	54.0	.450
1900	48.0	.500	48.0	.625	48.0	.450	51.2	.474
1901	48.0	.518	48.0	.625	48.0	.450	48.0	.500
1902	48.0	.563	44.0	.638	48.0	.514	48.0	.500
1903	48.0	.563	44.0	.665	48.0	.530	48.0	.625
1904	45.0	.600	44.0	.641	48.0	.500	48.0	.625
1905	45.0	.617	44.0	.639	48.0	.550	48.0	.625
1906	45.0	.621	44.0	.703	48.0	.572	48.0	.629
1907	45.0	.600	44.0	.750	48.0	.575	48.0	.625
1908	45.0	.600	44.0	.750	48.0	.600	48.0	.625
1909	45.0	.600	44.0	.750	48.0	.600	44.0	.625
1910	45.0	.625	44.0	.750	[1]48.0	.625	44.0	.625
1911	45.0	.625	44.0	.750	[1]48.0	.625	44.0	.625
1912	45.0	.650	44.0	.750	[1]48.0	.625	44.0	.625
1913	45.0	.650	44.0	.750	[3]48.0	.650	44.0	.625
1914	45.0	.650	44.0	.750	[3]44.0	.650	44.0	.625
1915	45.0	.700	44.0	.750	[3]44.0	.650	44.0	.625
1916	45.0	.700	44.0	.875	[4]44.0	.700	44.0	.625
1917	45.0	.750	44.0	.875	[4]44.0	.750	44.0	.625
1918	45.0	.900	44.0	1.000	[4]44.0	.800	44.0	.625
1919	45.0	.900	44.0	1.000	[4]44.0	.900	44.0	.750
1920	45.0	1.250	44.0	1.250	44.0	1.250	44.0	1.000
1921	45.0	1.250	44.0	1.250	44.0	1.000	44.0	1.000
1922	45.0	1.250	44.0	1.250	44.0	1.000	44.0	1.000
1923	45.0	1.250	44.0	1.375	44.0	1.350	44.0	1.000
1924	45.0	1.500	44.0	1.500	44.0	1.500	44.0	1.250
1925	44.0	1.500	44.0	1.500	44.0	1.500	44.0	1.250
1926	44.0	1.625	44.0	1.500	44.0	1.500	44.0	1.250
1927	44.0	1.625	44.0	1.500	44.0	1.575	44.0	1.250
1928	44.0	1.625	44.0	1.500	44.0	1.575	44.0	1.500

[1] 44 hours, June 15 to Sept. 15.
[2] 44 hours, October to April, both inclusive.
[3] 48 hours, November to April, both inclusive.
[4] 48 hours, December to February, both inclusive.

TABLE **B-2.**—*Bricklayers, males, 1890–1928, by city and year*—Continued

Year	New York, N. Y.[5]		Philadelphia, Pa.		St. Louis, Mo.		San Francisco, Calif.	
	Hours per week	Rate per hour	Hours per week	Rate per hour	Hours per week	Rate per hour	Hours per week	Rate per hour
1890	49. 6	$0. 471	50. 4	$0. 447	53. 5	$0. 481	49. 7	$0. 637
1891	49. 3	. 473	50. 1	. 450	53. 7	. 478	49. 6	. 636
1892	48. 0	. 500	50. 2	. 449	54. 1	. 463	48. 0	. 625
1893	47. 7	. 500	50. 1	. 449	52. 6	. 450	48. 0	. 625
1894	47. 9	. 500	50. 1	. 450	48. 0	. 493	48. 0	. 625
1895	47. 5	. 500	50. 2	. 449	48. 0	. 491	48. 0	. 625
1896	47. 9	. 500	50. 2	. 449	48. 0	. 502	48. 0	. 625
1897	48. 0	. 500	50. 2	. 448	48. 0	. 504	48. 0	. 625
1898	47. 6	. 500	45. 8	. 403	48. 0	. 457	48. 0	. 625
1899	44. 8	. 550	44. 0	. 463	46. 6	. 533	48. 0	. 625
1900	44. 4	. 562	44. 0	. 494	45. 9	. 550	48. 0	. 625
1901	44. 0	. 590	44. 0	. 496	45. 8	. 550	48. 0	. 625
1902	44. 0	. 648	44. 0	. 550	44. 0	. 582	48. 0	. 640
1903	44. 0	. 637	44. 0	. 600	44. 0	. 642	45. 6	. 759
1904	44. 0	. 650	44. 0	. 600	44. 0	. 658	44. 0	. 750
1905	44. 0	. 700	44. 0	. 600	44. 0	. 708	44. 0	. 750
1906	44. 0	. 700	44. 0	. 625	44. 0	. 737	44. 0	. 889
1907	44. 0	. 700	44. 0	. 625	44. 0	. 650	44. 0	. 875
1908	44. 0	. 700	44. 0	. 625	44. 0	. 650	44. 0	. 875
1909	44. 0	. 700	44. 0	. 625	44. 0	. 650	44. 0	. 875
1910	44. 0	. 700	44. 0	. 625	44. 0	. 700	44. 0	. 875
1911	44. 0	. 700	44. 0	. 625	44. 0	. 700	44. 0	. 875
1912	44. 0	. 700	44. 0	. 625	44. 0	. 700	44. 0	. 875
1913	44. 0	. 700	44. 0	. 625	44. 0	. 700	44. 0	. 875
1914	44. 0	. 750	44. 0	. 650	44. 0	. 750	44. 0	. 875
1915	44. 0	. 750	44. 0	. 650	44. 0	. 750	44. 0	. 875
1916	44. 0	. 750	44. 0	. 650	44. 0	. 750	44. 0	. 875
1917	44. 0	. 750	44. 0	. 700	44. 0	. 750	44. 0	. 875
1918	44. 0	. 813	44. 0	. 800	44. 0	. 850	44. 0	1. 000
1919	44. 0	. 875	44. 0	. 800	44. 0	1. 000	44. 0	1. 125
1920	44. 0	1. 250	44. 0	1. 300	44. 0	1. 250	44. 0	1. 250
1921	44. 0	1. 250	44. 0	1. 300	44. 0	1. 250	44. 0	1. 250
1922	44. 0	1. 250	44. 0	1. 250	44. 0	1. 250	44. 0	1. 250
1923	44. 0	1. 500	44. 0	1. 375	44. 0	1. 500	44. 0	1. 375
1924	44. 0	1. 500	[6] 44. 0	1. 500	44. 0	1. 750	44. 0	1. 375
1925	44. 0	1. 500	[6] 44. 0	1. 500	44. 0	1. 750	44. 0	1. 375
1926	44. 0	1. 750	[6] 44. 0	1. 625	44. 0	1. 750	44. 0	1. 375
1927	44. 0	1. 750	40. 0	1. 625	44. 0	1. 750	44. 0	1. 375
1928	44. 0	1. 750	40. 0	1. 625	44. 0	1. 750	44. 0	1. 375

[5] Greater New York, 1903-1907.
[6] Full holiday on Saturday, June to September, inclusive.

TABLE **B-3.**—*Carpenters and joiners, 1840–1900, by year and State*

Year and State	Sex	Lowest, highest, and average—		Year and State	Sex	Lowest, highest, and average—	
		Hours per week	Rate per day (dollars)			Hours per week	Rate per day (dollars)
1840:				1844:			
Connecticut	M.	60-60-60	1. 25-1. 62-1. 46	Connecticut	M.	60-60-60	1. 37-1. 62-1. 50
Massachusetts	M.	60-84-65	1. 17-1. 67-1. 25	Massachusetts	M.	60-84-68	. 91-1. 50-1. 27
New York	M.	60-60-60	1. 13-1. 50-1. 29	New York	M.	60-60-60	1. 25-1. 75-1. 50
Pennsylvania	M.	60-60-60	1. 00-1. 25-1. 20	Pennsylvania	M.	60-60-60	1. 25-1. 25-1. 25
1841:				1845:			
Connecticut	M.	60-60-60	1. 25-1. 62-1. 46	Connecticut	M.	60-60-60	1. 25-1. 62-1. 44
Massachusetts	M.	60-84-65	1. 17-1. 67-1. 28	Massachusetts	M.	60-84-69	1. 00-1. 58-1. 22
New York	M.	60-60-60	1. 25-1. 75-1. 50	New York	M.	60-72-61	1. 00-1. 75-1. 55
Pennsylvania	M.	60-60-60	1. 25-1. 25-1. 25	Pennsylvania	M.	60-60-60	1. 25-1. 25-1. 25
1842:				1846:			
Connecticut	M.	60-60-60	1. 37-1. 50-1. 43	Connecticut	M.	60-60-60	1. 37-1. 62-1. 50
Massachusetts	M.	60-84-71	. 88-1. 67-1. 28	Massachusetts	M.	60-84-65	1. 00-1. 67-1. 29
New York	M.	60-60-60	1. 25-1. 75-1. 50	New York	M.	60-60-60	1. 00-2. 00-1. 76
Pennsylvania	M.	60-60-60	1. 25-1. 25-1. 25	Pennsylvania	M.	60-60-60	1. 25-1. 25-1. 25
1843:				1847:			
Connecticut	M.	60-60-60	1. 37-1. 62-1. 50	Connecticut	M.	60-60-60	1. 37-1. 62-1. 50
Massachusetts	M.	60-84-63	. 91-1. 75-1. 29	Massachusetts	M.	60-84-69	. 60-1. 50-1. 28
New York	M.	60-60-60	1. 00-1. 50-1. 33	New York	M.	60-60-60	1. 00-2. 00-1. 72
Pennsylvania	M.	60-60-60	1. 25-1. 25-1. 25	Pennsylvania	M.	60-60-60	1. 25-1. 50-1. 47

Table **B-3.**—*Carpenters and joiners, 1840-1900, by year and State*—Continued

Year and State	Sex	Lowest, highest, and average—		Year and State	Sex	Lowest, highest, and average—	
		Hours per week	Rate per day (dollars)			Hours per week	Rate per day (dollars)
1848:				**1860:**			
Connecticut	M.	60–60–60	1.25–1.62–1.44	Connecticut	M.	60–72–61	1.25–1.75–1.65
Massachusetts	M.	60–84–65	.60–1.63–1.32	Maryland	M.	60–60–60	1.38–1.38–1.38
New Jersey	M.	(¹)	²1.25–1.25–1.25	Massachusetts	M.	60–78–63	1.00–3.00–1.35
New York	M.	60–60–60	1.00–2.50–1.71	New York	M.	60–72–60	1.00–2.50–1.90
Pennsylvania	M.	60–60–60	1.25–1.50–1.48	Ohio	M.	60–60–60	1.00–1.67–1.39
1849:				Pennsylvania	M.	60–60–60	1.75–1.75–1.75
Connecticut	M.	60–60–60	1.25–1.62–1.44	**1861:**			
Massachusetts	M.	75–84–80	.75–1.58–1.31	Connecticut	M.	60–60–60	1.25–1.75–1.50
New York	M.	60–72–62	1.35–2.00–1.74	Massachusetts	M.	60–78–63	1.00–1.83–1.40
Pennsylvania	M.	60–60–60	1.25–1.50–1.43	New York	M.	60–72–60	1.25–2.50–1.91
1850:				Ohio	M.	60–60–60	1.50–1.63–1.57
Connecticut	M.	60–60–60	1.37–1.75–1.58	Pennsylvania	M.	60–60–60	1.75–2.00–1.89
Massachusetts	M.	60–84–66	.60–2.00–1.33	**1862:**			
New York	M.	60–60–60	1.00–2.00–1.71	Connecticut	M.	60–60–60	1.25–1.75–1.48
Pennsylvania	M.	60–60–60	1.25–1.50–1.44	Massachusetts	M.	60–72–62	1.00–3.00–1.36
1851:				New York	M.	60–72–60	1.25–2.50–1.89
Connecticut	M.	60–60–60	1.37–1.75–1.60	Ohio	M.	60–60–60	1.50–1.63–1.57
Massachusetts	M.	60–84–68	.75–2.00–1.30	Pennsylvania	M.	60–60–60	1.75–2.50–2.21
New York	M.	60–60–60	1.00–2.00–1.74	**1863:**			
Pennsylvania	M.	60–60–60	1.25–1.50–1.44	Connecticut	M.	60–72–60	1.50–2.50–1.86
1852:				Maryland	M.	60–60–60	1.50–1.75–1.69
Connecticut	M.	60–60–60	1.37–1.75–1.60	Massachusetts	M.	60–72–62	1.00–3.00–1.40
Massachusetts	M.	60–78–63	.75–1.50–1.30	New York	M.	60–60–60	1.34–2.50–1.97
New York	M.	60–60–60	1.00–2.00–1.80	Ohio	M.	60–60–60	1.75–1.75–1.75
Pennsylvania	M.	60–60–60	1.25–1.50–1.45	Pennsylvania	M.	60–60–60	1.25–3.00–2.44
1853:				**1864:**			
Connecticut	M.	60–60–60	1.50–1.75–1.67	Connecticut	M.	60–72–60	1.63–3.00–2.05
Massachusetts	M.	60–78–67	1.00–1.73–1.30	Maryland	M.	60–60–60	1.50–2.25–2.07
New York	M.	60–60–60	1.00–2.00–1.88	Massachusetts	M.	60–72–63	1.10–2.50–1.65
Pennsylvania	M.	60–60–60	1.25–1.50–1.48	New Jersey	M.	60–60–60	2.00–2.00–2.00
1854:				New York	M.	60–60–60	1.34–3.00–2.70
Connecticut	M.	60–60–60	1.75–2.00–1.88	Ohio	M.	60–60–60	2.25–2.25–2.25
Maryland	M.	60–60–60	1.38–1.38–1.38	Pennsylvania	M.	60–60–60	2.25–3.00–2.52
Massachusetts	M.	60–78–64	1.00–1.83–1.38	**1865:**			
New York	M.	60–60–60	1.00–2.25–1.89	Connecticut	M.	60–60–60	1.62–3.00–2.25
Pennsylvania	M.	60–60–60	1.50–1.50–1.50	Maryland	M.	60–60–60	1.67–2.50–2.33
1855:				Massachusetts	M.	60–72–61	1.42–3.00–2.14
Connecticut	M.	60–60–60	1.25–1.75–1.50	New Jersey	M.	60–60–60	2.00–2.00–2.00
Maryland	M.	60–60–60	1.38–1.38–1.38	New York	M.	60–72–60	1.67–3.25–2.90
Massachusetts	M.	60–72–62	1.00–2.50–1.42	Ohio	M.	60–60–60	2.50–2.50–2.50
New Jersey	M.	60–72–68	1.50–1.50–1.50	Pennsylvania	M.	60–60–60	2–25–2.50–2.39
New York	M.	60–72–60	2.25–1.25–1.85	**1866:**			
Pennsylvania	M.	60–60–60	1.50–1.50–1.50	Connecticut	M.	60–66–61	2.25–3.00–2.63
1856:				Maryland	M.	60–60–60	1.67–2.75–2.52
Connecticut	M.	60–60–60	1.37–1.50–1.46	Massachusetts	M.	60–72–62	1.33–4.00–2.03
Maryland	M.	60–60–60	1.38–1.38–1.38	New Jersey	M.	60–60–60	2.30–2.30–2.30
Massachusetts	M.	60–72–64	1.08–1.75–1.40	New York	M.	60–72–60	1.75–3.50–3.19
New York	M.	60–72–60	1.13–2.25–1.76	Ohio	M.	60–60–60	3.00–3.00–3.00
Ohio	M.	60–60–60	1.50–1.50–1.50	Pennsylvania	M.	60–60–60	2.50–2.75–2.57
Pennsylvania	M.	60–60–60	1.50–1.50–1.50	**1867:**			
1857:				Connecticut	M.	60–60–60	2.75–3.25–3.03
Connecticut	M.	60–60–60	1.50–2.00–1.69	Georgia	M.	66–66–66	1.25–1.75–1.50
Maryland	M.	60–60–60	1.38–1.38–1.38	Maryland	M.	60–60–60	1.67–3.00–2.67
Massachusetts	M.	60–72–62	1.00–2.50–1.37	Massachusetts	M.	60–72–62	1.50–4.00–2.42
New York	M.	60–72–60	1.25–2.25–1.79	New Jersey	M.	60–60–60	2.50–2.50–2.50
Ohio	M.	60–60–60	1.50–1.50–1.50	New York	M.	60–72–60	1.67–3.75–3.27
Pennsylvania	M.	60–60–60	1.50–1.50–1.50	Ohio	M.	60–60–60	2.50–2.50–2.50
1858:				Pennsylvania	M.	60–60–60	2.50–2.75–2.59
Connecticut	M.	60–72–62	1.25–2.00–1.50	**1868:**			
Maryland	M.	60–60–60	1.38–1.38–1.38	Connecticut	M.	60–60–60	2.25–3.25–3.05
Massachusetts	M.	60–78–64	1.00–2.75–1.34	Maryland	M.	60–60–60	1.67–3.25–2.84
New York	M.	60–72–60	1.25–2.50–1.85	Massachusetts	M.	60–66–62	1.25–4.00–2.23
Ohio	M.	60–60–60	1.50–1.50–1.50	New Jersey	M.	60–60–60	2.50–2.50–2.50
Pennsylvania	M.	60–60–60	1.50–1.50–1.50	New York	M.	60–72–60	1.50–4.00–3.58
1859:				Ohio	M.	60–60–60	2.50–2.50–2.50
Connecticut	M.	60–72–61	1.50–1.75–1.67	Pennsylvania	M.	60–60–60	2.50–2.75–2.60
Illinois	M.	60–60–60	2.00–2.00–2.00	**1869:**			
Maryland	M.	60–60–60	1.38–1.38–1.38	Connecticut	M.	60–60–60	2.00–4.00–2.98
Massachusetts	M.	60–78–63	1.00–1.75–1.38	Maryland	M.	60–60–60	1.67–3.25–2.73
New Jersey	M.	60–60–60	1.50–1.50–1.50	Massachusetts	M.	60–66–62	1.25–3.00–2.22
New York	M.	60–72–60	1.13–3.50–1.90	New Jersey	M.	60–60–60	2.50–2.50–2.50
Ohio	M.	60–60–60	1.50–1.50–1.50	New York	M.	59–72–60	1.75–4.00–3.63
Pennsylvania	M.	60–60–60	1.50–1.75–1.58	Ohio	M.	60–60–60	2.25–2.25–2.25
				Pennsylvania	M.	60–60–60	2.00–2.75–2.57

¹ Not reported.   ² And board.

TABLE **B-3.**—*Carpenters and joiners, 1840–1900, by year and State*—Continued

| Year and State | Sex | Lowest, highest, and average— | | Year and State | Sex | Lowest, highest, and average— | |
		Hours per week	Rate per day (dollars)			Hours per week	Rate per day (dollars)
1870:				**1875:**			
California	M.	60–60–60	3. 50–4. 00–3. 83	California	M.	60–60–60	3. 50–3. 50–3. 50
Connecticut	M.	60–60–60	1. 75–4. 00–2. 77	Connecticut	M.	60–60–60	2. 00–3. 50–2. 68
Illinois	M.	60–60–60	2. 50–3. 00–2. 58	Illinois	M.	60–60–60	2. 00–2. 70–2. 21
Louisiana	M.	54–54–54	2. 50–3. 50–2. 88	Louisiana	M.	54–54–54	2. 50–3. 25–2. 81
Maryland	M.	60–60–60	1. 67–3. 00–2. 58	Maryland	M.	60–60–60	1. 67–2. 75–2. 12
Massachusetts	M.	60–66–62	1. 16–3. 50–2. 34	Massachusetts	M.	60–60–60	1. 50–3. 00–2. 15
Minnesota	M.	60–60–60	1. 75–2. 00–1. 94	Minnesota	M.	60–60–60	1. 75–2. 00–1. 85
Missouri	M.	60–60–60	3. 50–3. 50–3. 50	Missouri	M.	60–60–60	3. 50–3. 50–3. 50
New Jersey	M.	60–60–60	2. 50–2. 50–2. 50	New Hampshire	M.	72–72–72	2. 25–2. 25–2. 25
New York	M.	59–72–60	2. 00–3. 75–3. 50	New Jersey	M.	60–60–60	2. 67–2. 67–2. 67
Ohio	M.	60–60–60	1. 80–3. 25–2. 45	New York	M.	54–72–57	1. 55–3. 75–3. 10
Pennsylvania	M.	60–60–60	2. 00–3. 50–2. 67	Ohio	M.	60–60–60	1. 67–3. 00–2. 46
Virginia	M.	60–60–60	2. 00–2. 75–2. 27	Pennsylvania	M.	60–72–61	1. 63–3. 67–2. 05
1871:				Rhode Island	M.	60–60–60	2. 25–2. 25–2. 25
California	M.	60–60–60	3. 50–4. 00–3. 77	Virginia	M.	60–60–60	2. 00–2. 75–2. 46
Connecticut	M.	60–66–60	1. 75–3. 50–2. 79	**1876:**			
Illinois	M.	60–60–60	2. 30–3. 00–2. 89	California	M.	54–60–56	3. 50–3. 50–3. 50
Louisiana	M.	54–54–54	2. 50–3. 50–2. 89	Connecticut	M.	60–66–60	1. 75–3. 50–2. 51
Maryland	M.	60–60–60	1. 67–3. 00–2. 58	Illinois	M.	60–60–60	2. 00–2. 40–2. 15
Massachusetts	M.	53–66–61	1. 33–3. 50–2. 45	Louisiana	M.	54–54–54	2. 50–3. 25–2. 68
Minnesota	M.	60–60–60	1. 75–2. 00–1. 94	Maryland	M.	60–60–60	1. 67–3. 00–2. 05
Missouri	M.	60–60–60	3. 50–3. 50–3. 50	Massachusetts	M.	60–60–60	1. 40–2. 75–2. 08
New Jersey	M.	60–60–60	2. 50–2. 50–2. 50	Minnesota	M.	60–60–60	1. 75–2. 00–1. 86
New York	M.	59–72–60	2. 00–3. 75–3. 39	Missouri	M.	60–60–60	3. 50–3. 50–3. 50
Ohio	M.	60–60–60	1. 80–3. 50–2. 50	New Hampshire	M.	72–72–72	2. 25–2. 25–2. 25
Pennsylvania	M.	60–60–60	2. 00–3. 50–2. 70	New Jersey	M.	60–60–60	2. 67–2. 67–2. 67
Rhode Island	M.	60–60–60	2. 00–2. 00–2. 00	New York	M.	54–72–57	1. 75–3. 75–2. 92
Virginia	M.	60–60–60	2. 00–2. 75–2. 23	North Carolina	M.	60–60–60	1. 50–1. 50–1. 50
1872:				Ohio	M.	60–60–60	1. 86–2. 75–2. 45
California	M.	60–60–60	3. 50–4. 00–3. 76	Pennsylvania	M.	48–66–57	1. 10–3. 67–2. 02
Connecticut	M.	60–66–61	2. 00–3. 50–2. 73	Rhode Island	M.	60–60–60	2. 50–2. 50–2. 50
Illinois	M.	60–60–60	2. 40–3. 15–2. 82	Virginia	M.	60–60–60	2. 00–2. 75–2. 52
Louisiana	M.	54–54–54	2. 50–3. 00–2. 86	**1877:**			
Maryland	M.	60–60–60	1. 67–3. 00–2. 56	California	M.	54–60–55	3. 50–3. 50–3. 50
Massachusetts	M.	60–66–61	1. 50–4. 50–2. 51	Connecticut	M.	60–60–60	1. 75–2. 75–2. 20
Minnesota	M.	60–60–60	1. 75–2. 00–1. 85	Georgia	M.	66–66–66	2. 25–2. 25–2. 25
Missouri	M.	60–60–60	3. 50–3. 50–3. 50	Illinois	M.	60–60–60	2. 20–2. 50–2. 24
New Hampshire	M.	72–72–72	2. 25–2. 25–2. 25	Louisiana	M.	54–54–54	2. 50–3. 25–2. 68
New Jersey	M.	60–60–60	2. 50–2. 50–2. 50	Maryland	M.	60–60–60	1. 50–3. 00–2. 06
New York	M.	54–72–57	1. 75–3. 75–3. 25	Massachusetts	M.	60–60–60	1. 39–2. 50–1. 81
Ohio	M.	60–60–60	1. 83–3. 50–2. 52	Minnesota	M.	60–60–60	1. 75–2. 00–1. 86
Pennsylvania	M.	60–60–60	2. 00–3. 50–2. 69	Missouri	M.	60–60–60	3. 50–3. 50–3. 50
South Carolina	M.	72–72–72	1. 75–1. 75–1. 75	New Hampshire	M.	72–72–72	2. 25–2. 25–2. 25
Virginia	M.	60–60–60	2. 25–2. 75–2. 43	New Jersey	M.	53–60–55	1. 00–2. 67–1. 80
1873:				New York	M.	54–72–57	1. 50–3. 50–2. 85
California	M.	60–60–60	3. 50–4. 00–3. 71	Ohio	M.	60–84–65	1. 17–4. 00–2. 04
Connecticut	M.	60–66–60	2. 50–4. 50–3. 04	Pennsylvania	M.	48–72–58	1. 15–3. 50–2. 04
Illinois	M.	60–60–60	2. 50–3. 15–2. 56	Do	M.	(1)	³ . 22– . 22– . 22
Louisiana	M.	54–54–54	2. 50–3. 50–2. 87	Rhode Island	M.	60–60–60	1. 25–2. 00–1. 63
Maryland	M.	60–60–60	1. 67–3. 00–2. 05	Virginia	M.	60–60–60	1. 50–2. 25–1. 87
Massachusetts	M.	60–60–60	1. 25–3. 25–2. 40	**1878:**			
Minnesota	M.	60–60–60	1. 75–2. 00–1. 84	California	M.	54–60–56	3. 50–3. 50–3. 50
Missouri	M.	60–60–60	3. 50–3. 50–3. 50	Connecticut	M.	60–72–66	2. 00–3. 00–2. 53
New Hampshire	M.	72–72–72	2. 25–2. 25–2. 25	Georgia	M.	66–66–66	1. 75–2. 42–2. 08
New Jersey	M.	60–60–60	2. 50–3. 00–2. 90	Illinois	M.	60–60–60	2. 00–2. 40–2. 14
New York	M.	54–72–57	1. 75–4. 00–3. 28	Louisiana	M.	54–54–54	2. 50–3. 25–2. 69
Ohio	M.	60–60–60	1. 90–3. 25–2. 67	Maryland	M.	60–60–60	1. 25–2. 50–1. 93
Pennsylvania	M.	60–60–60	2. 00–4. 00–2. 31	Massachusetts	M.	60–60–60	1. 39–2. 75–1. 82
Virginia	M.	60–60–60	2. 00–2. 75–2. 49	Minnesota	M.	60–60–60	2. 00–2. 25–2. 10
1874:				Missouri	M.	48–48–48	2. 80–2. 80–2. 80
California	M.	60–60–60	3. 50–4. 00–3. 63	New Hampshire	M.	72–72–72	2. 25–2. 25–2. 25
Connecticut	M.	60–66–60	2. 50–4. 50–2. 89	New Jersey	M.	60–60–60	1. 75–2. 67–1. 93
Illinois	M.	60–60–60	2. 00–2. 50–2. 21	New York	M.	54–72–56	1. 50–3. 50–2. 93
Louisiana	M.	54–54–54	2. 50–3. 25–2. 80	Ohio	M.	48–60–60	1. 10–2. 75–1. 91
Maryland	M.	60–60–60	1. 67–2. 75–2. 16	Pennsylvania	M.	48–72–59	. 80–3. 00–1. 87
Massachusetts	M.	60–66–61	1. 25–4. 50–2. 33	Virginia	M.	60–60–60	1. 25–2. 00–1. 58
Minnesota	M.	60–60–60	1. 75–2. 00–1. 86	**1879:**			
Missouri	M.	60–60–60	3. 50–3. 50–3. 50	California	M.	54–60–56	3. 50–3. 50–3. 50
New Hampshire	M.	72–72–72	2. 25–2. 25–2. 25	Connecticut	M.	60–66–61	1. 75–2. 75–2. 04
New Jersey	M.	60–60–60	2. 67–2. 67–2. 67	Illinois	M.	60–60–60	2. 00–2. 40–2. 24
New York	M.	54–72–57	1. 75–4. 00–3. 30	Louisiana	M.	54–54–54	2. 50–3. 00–2. 69
Ohio	M.	60–60–60	1. 90–3. 50–2. 50	Maryland	M.	60–60–60	1. 25–2. 50–1. 91
Pennsylvania	M.	60–60–60	1. 08–3. 67–2. 15	Massachusetts	M.	60–60–60	1. 00–2. 75–1. 91
Virginia	M.	60–60–60	2. 00–2. 75–2. 41	Minnesota	M.	60–60–60	2. 00–2. 25–2. 10

¹ Not reported.　　　　³ Per hour.

TABLE **B-3.**—*Carpenters and joiners, 1840-1900, by year and State*—Continued

| Year and State | Sex | Lowest, highest, and average— | | Year and State | Sex | Lowest, highest, and average— | |
		Hours per week	Rate per day (dollars)			Hours per week	Rate per day (dollars)
1879—Continued.				**1883—Continued.**			
Missouri	M.	48-60-51	1. 17-2. 80-2. 19	Maryland	M.	60-60-60	1. 67-2. 75-2. 34
New Hampshire	M.	72-72-72	2. 00-2. 00-2. 00	Massachusetts	M.	60-60-60	1. 15-3. 50-2. 35
New Jersey	M.	50-60-58	. 70-3. 00-1. 66	Michigan	M.	(¹)	. 50-4. 00-2. 00
New York	M.	54-72-56	1. 50-3. 50-2. 90	Minnesota	M.	60-60-60	2. 25-2. 50-2. 34
Ohio	M.	60-60-60	1. 50-3. 75-2. 00	Missouri	M.	48-48-48	2. 80-2. 80-2. 80
Pennsylvania	M.	54-78-60	. 60-3. 00-1. 68	New Hampshire	M.	72-72-72	2. 00-2. 00-2. 00
Do	M.	(¹)	² 2. 25-2. 25-2. 25	New Jersey	M.	51-72-60	1. 35-3. 00-2. 20
Do	M.	(¹)	⁴ . 77- . 77- . 77	New York	M.	54-72-59	1. 25-3. 50-3. 22
Virginia	M.	60-60-60	1. 25-1. 75-1. 50	North Carolina	M.	(¹)	1. 00-1. 00-1. 00
1880:				Ohio	M.	59-60-60	1. 50-3. 25-2. 40
California	M.	54-60-57	3. 50-3. 50-3. 50	Pennsylvania	M.	60-60-60	1. 67-4. 00-2. 68
Connecticut	M.	60-66-61	2. 00-2. 75-2. 15	Rhode Island	M.	60-60-60	1. 25-3. 00-2. 11
Georgia	M.	66-69-68	1. 50-2. 00-1. 76	South Carolina	M.	70-72-71	1. 25-1. 25-1. 25
Illinois	M.	43-60-56	1. 56-2. 50-2. 03	Tennessee	M.	66-66-66	1. 33-2. 00-1. 67
Louisiana	M.	54-54-54	2. 00-3. 00-2. 67	Virginia	M.	60-60-60	1. 50-2. 50-1. 95
Maryland	M.	60-60-60	1. 75-2. 50-2. 12	**1884:**			
Massachusetts	M.	60-60-60	1. 25-2. 75-1. 90	California	M.	54-60-60	2. 00-3. 50-2. 75
Minnesota	M.	60-60-60	2. 00-2. 25-2. 11	Connecticut	M.	60-66-60	2. 17-3. 75-2. 53
Missouri	M.	48-48-48	2. 80-2. 80-2. 80	Georgia	M.	66-70-68	1. 25-2. 50-1. 95
New Hampshire	M.	72-72-72	2. 00-2. 00-2. 00	Illinois	M.	59-60-60	2. 00-3. 00-2. 74
New Jersey	M.	54-84-60	1. 00-3. 00-1. 54	Indiana	M.	(¹)	1. 75-2. 25-2. 00
New York	M.	54-72-57	1. 50-4. 00-2. 96	Iowa	M.	57-72-61	1. 00-4. 00-2. 40
North Carolina	M.	60-60-60	1. 50-1. 50-1. 50	Louisiana	M.	54-66-60	2. 00-2. 75-2. 26
Ohio	M.	60-60-60	1. 25-2. 75-1. 99	Maryland	M.	60-60-60	2. 00-2. 75-2. 42
Pennsylvania	M.	50-66-60	. 90-3. 00-2. 28	Massachusetts	M.	60-60-60	1. 35-3. 00-2. 08
Rhode Island	M.	60-60-60	1. 25-2. 25-1. 77	Michigan	M.	(¹)	. 46-5. 75-1. 84
Virginia	M.	60-60-60	1. 13-1. 75-1. 42	Minnesota	M.	60-60-60	2. 25-2. 50-2. 34
1881:				Missouri	M.	48-60-51	1. 67-3. 00-2. 76
California	M.	54-60-56	3. 00-3. 50-3. 45	New Hampshire	M.	72-72-72	2. 00-2. 00-2. 00
Connecticut	M.	60-60-60	1. 75-2. 75-2. 33	New Jersey	M.	42-60-59	1. 20-3. 00-2. 28
Georgia	M.	66-66-66	1. 50-1. 50-1. 50	New York	M.	54-72-57	1. 66-3. 50-3. 02
Illinois	M.	60-60-60	2. 00-2. 50-2. 37	Ohio	M.	54-60-60	1. 50-3. 25-2. 30
Louisiana	M.	54-54-54	2. 25-3. 00-2. 48	Pennsylvania	M.	60-60-60	1. 50-4. 00-1. 97
Maryland	M.	60-60-60	1. 50-2. 50-2. 17	Rhode Island	M.	60-60-60	1. 25-3. 00-2. 24
Massachusetts	M.	60-60-60	1. 35-2. 75-2. 12	South Carolina	M.	69-69-69	1. 25-2. 00-1. 63
Michigan	M.	60-60-60	1. 75-1. 75-1. 75	Tennessee	M.	66-66-66	2. 00-2. 00-2. 00
Minnesota	M.	60-60-60	2. 25-2. 50-2. 35	Virginia	M.	55-60-59	1. 50-2. 50. 2. 01
Missouri	M.	48-60-60	2. 25-2. 80-2. 40	Wisconsin	M.	(¹)	2. 33-2. 33-2. 33
New Hampshire	M.	65-72-65	. 75-2. 50-1. 80	**1885:**			
New Jersey	M.	60-60-60	1. 75-2. 50-2. 11	California	M.	54-60-57	2. 25-3. 50-3. 12
New York	M.	54-72-58	1. 50-3. 50-2. 87	Connecticut	M.	60-69-61	1. 50-3. 75-2. 32
Ohio	M.	59-72-60	1. 00-3. 47-2. 10	Delaware	M.	60-60-60	1. 50-2. 25-1. 81
Pennsylvania	M.	60-72-60	1. 70-3. 17-2. 21	Dist. of Columbia	M.	60-60-60	3. 00-3. 00-3. 00
Rhode Island	M.	60-60-60	1. 25-2. 25-1. 81	Georgia	M.	69-69-69	. 90-1. 25-1. 17
South Carolina	M.	72-72-72	1. 25-1. 27-1. 26	Illinois	M.	60-72-60	1. 50-4. 00-2. 28
Virginia	M.	60-60-60	1. 25-2. 25-1. 75	Ind' n	M.	57-57-57	2. 25-2. 25-2. 25
1882:				Iow	M.	48-60-57	1. 36-3. 00-2. 13
California	M.	54-60-57	3. 00-3. 50-3. 42	Kansas	M.	60-60-60	1. 65-1. 65-1. 65
Connecticut	M.	60-66-61	2. 17-2. 75-2. 49	Kentucky	M.	54-54-54	2. 25-2. 75-2. 51
Georgia	M.	72-72-72	1. 50-1. 50-1. 50	Maine	M.	44-66-65	1. 25-3. 00-1. 92
Illinois	M.	60-60-60	1. 15-2. 50-2. 04	Maryland	M.	54-72-61	1. 50-2. 75-2. 31
Louisiana	M.	54-54-54	2. 25-2. 75-2. 50	Massachusetts	M.	60-60-60	1. 25-3. 00-1. 97
Maine	M.	66-66-66	1. 50-1. 50-1. 50	Michigan	M.	66-66-66	1. 30-3. 07-2. 01
Maryland	M.	60-60-60	1. 67-2. 75-2. 34	Minnesota	M.	60-60-60	2. 25-2. 50-2. 34
Massachusetts	M.	59-60-60	1. 35-3. 00-2. 08	Missouri	M.	48-60-50	1. 50-3. 00-2. 11
Minnesota	M.	60-60-60	2. 25-2. 50-2. 35	New Hampshire	M.	59-72-63	1. 05-2. 83-1. 97
Missouri	M.	48-60-54	1. 67-3. 25-2. 75	New Jersey	M.	42-66-59	1. 25-3. 33-2. 37
New Hampshire	M.	66-72-67	1. 75-2. 10-1. 98	New York	M.	54-72-58	1. 00-3. 50-2. 99
New Jersey	M.	60-72-63	2. 00-2. 50-2. 14	North Carolina	M.	60-69-61	. 75-2. 25-1. 50
New York	M.	54-72-58	1. 50-3. 50-3. 08	Ohio	M.	60-72-61	1. 30-3. 25-2. 08
North Carolina	M.	60-60-60	1. 25-1. 25-1. 25	Pennsylvania	M.	48-72-60	1. 75-4. 00-1. 86
Ohio	M.	60-60-60	1. 60-3. 17-2. 35	Rhode Island	M.	60-60-60	1. 25-3. 00-2. 14
Do	(¹)	54-75-60	1. 25-3. 00-1. 91	Tennessee	M.	60-60-60	1. 58-1. 58-1. 58
Pennsylvania	M.	45-66-60	1. 25-4. 00-2. 63	Vermont	M.	66-66-66	1. 92-2. 00-1. 93
Rhode Island	M.	60-60-60	1. 25-2. 50-2. 00	Virginia	M.	48-72-60	1. 35-2. 50-1. 93
South Carolina	M.	61-69-66	1. 25-2. 00-1. 53	West Virginia	M.	60-60-60	1. 50-2. 00-1. 87
Virginia	M.	60-60-60	1. 25-2. 25-1. 77	Wisconsin	M.	60-60-60	1. 85-2. 67-2. 10
1883:				**1886:**			
Alabama	M.	(¹)	1. 00-1. 50-1. 25	California	M.	48-60-60	2. 00-5. 00-3. 05
California	M.	54-60-56	3. 00-3. 50-3. 30	Do	M.	60-60-60	² 2. 49-2. 49-2. 49
Connecticut	M.	60-66-63	2. 17-3. 50-2. 57	Connecticut	M.	54-60-58	1. 25-3. 38-2. 46
Georgia	M.	66-66-66	2. 00-2. 75-2. 21	Dist. of Columbia	M.	53-58-55	3. 00-3. 00-3. 00
Illinois	M.	60-60-60	2. 00-2. 50-2. 33	Illinois	M.	48-60-55	1. 50-3. 00-2. 18
Louisiana	M.	54-54-54	2. 25-2. 75-2. 54				

¹ Not reported.   ² And board.   ⁴ And rent.

TABLE **B-3.**—*Carpenters and joiners, 1840–1900, by year and State*—Continued

Year and State	Sex	Hours per week	Rate per day (dollars)
1886—Continued.			
Iowa	M.	54-69-60	1.00-5.00-2.26
Kansas	M.	48-60-60	1.50-3.00-2.28
Louisiana	M.	54-54-54	2.25-2.75-2.51
Maryland	M.	54-60-57	2.00-2.75-2.50
Massachusetts	M.	54-66-60	1.35-3.00-2.16
Michigan	M.	60-60-60	1.67-1.67-1.67
Minnesota	M.	60-60-60	2.00-2.50-2.14
Missouri	M.	48-60-53	2.60-2.80-2.72
New Hampshire	M.	60-72-61	1.50-2.00-1.71
New Jersey	M.	54-66-57	1.50-3.25-2.59
New York	M.	48-72-55	1.67-4.16-2.84
North Carolina	M.	60-60-60	1.50-1.50-1.50
Ohio	M.	48-60-58	1.06-3.80-2.40
Pennsylvania	M.	54-60-57	1.75-3.60-2.45
Rhode Island	M.	60-60-60	1.25-3.00-2.21
Vermont	M.	66-66-66	2.50-2.50-2.50
Virginia	M.	60-60-60	1.50-2.50-1.78
1887:			
California	M.	54-60-56	3.00-3.50-3.24
Connecticut	M.	54-60-55	.92-3.38-2.24
Delaware	M.	[1]	[1].12½-.22½-.20
Florida	M.	[1]	1.25-3.00-2.05
Illinois	M.	60-60-60	2.20-2.75-2.48
Do	[1]	[1]	2.08-2.08-2.08
Kansas	M.	48-60-57	1.50-3.00-2.36
Louisiana	M.	54-54-54	2.25-2.75-2.51
Maine	M.	60-60-60	1.50-2.50-1.74
Maryland	M.	54-60-54	1.20-3.00-1.90
Do	M.	[1]	[1].20-.25-.23
Massachusetts	M.	54-60-60	1.00-3.50-2.06
Michigan	M.	60-60-60	1.25-3.50-1.95
Do	M.	[1]	[1].15-.21½-.18½
Minnesota	M.	60-60-60	2.25-2.50-2.34
Missouri	M.	48-72-56	1.25-3.26-2.31
Do	[1]	[1]	1.87-2.64-2.56
Nebraska	[1]	54-60-58	1.50-4.79-2.34
New Hampshire	M.	60-60-60	1.50-2.75-2.18
New Jersey	M.	60-60-60	1.30-3.00-1.89
New York	M.	53-72-56	1.25-3.50-2.34
North Carolina	M.	60-72-64	1.00-2.75-1.47
Ohio	M.	54-72-59	1.00-3.25-2.07
Oregon	M.	[1]	2.00-4.00-2.99
Pennsylvania	M.	54-60-56	1.00-3.60-2.12
Do	M.	[1]	[1].15-.25-.19
Rhode Island	M.	60-60-60	1.50-3.00-2.24
Virginia	M.	54-54-54	1.00-2.50-1.76
West Virginia	M.	[1]	1.15-2.25-1.65
Wisconsin	M.	[1]	1.25-3.50-2.01
Do	M.	[1]	[2]1.35-1.35-1.35
1888:			
California	M.	54-60-56	3.00-3.50-3.25
Colorado	M.	60-60-60	1.92-5.50-2.55
Connecticut	M.	54-60-54	2.00-3.38-2.56
Delaware	M.	[1]	2.00-2.25-2.13
Georgia	M.	66-66-66	1.50-2.25-1.73
Illinois	M.	60-60-60	2.00-2.75-2.47
Indiana	M.	54-60-59	1.46-2.88-2.08
Iowa	M.	54-62-59	1.80-2.68-2.23
Kansas	M.	57-60-58	1.75-2.86-2.41
Louisiana	M.	54-54-54	2.25-2.75-2.51
Maine	M.	60-60-60	1.75-2.00-1.90
Maryland	M	54-60-54	2.00-2.75-2.43
Massachusetts	M.	54-60-59	1.35-3.00-2.06
Michigan	M.	60-66-60	1.00-4.22-2.09
Minnesota	M.	60-60-60	2.25-2.50-2.34
Missouri	M.	48-48-48	2.40-2.40-2.40
Do	[1]	[1]	1.92-2.68-2.37
New Hampshire	M.	60-60-60	1.50-2.00-1.75
New Jersey	M.	48-60-57	1.67-3.00-2.24
New York	M.	45-72-57	1.00-4.16-2.68
Do	M.	[1]	[3].30-.30-.30
Do	M.	[1]	[4]1.50-1.50-1.50
North Carolina	M.	57-72-65	.75-2.50-1.46
Ohio	M.	54-60-60	1.10-3.25-2.11
Pennsylvania	M.	54-60-55	1.00-3.60-2.66
Rhode Island	M.	60-60-60	1.00-3.25-2.26

Year and State	Sex	Hours per week	Rate per day (dollars)
1888—Continued.			
South Carolina	M.	66-66-66	0.75-1.75-1.13
Tennessee	M.	[1]	1.50-1.50-1.50
Virginia	M.	54-72 [1]	1.00-2.25-1.76
West Virginia	M.	60-63-62	2.40-2.40-2.40
1889:			
Alabama	M.	48-84-62	1.00-5.00-1.90
California	M.	54-60-56	3.00-3.60-3.32
Colorado	[1]	[1]	3.00-3.00-3.00
Connecticut	M.	54-60-56	1.84-3.25-2.53
Georgia	M.	66-72-70	1.25-2.00-1.81
Illinois	M.	48-70-54	1.48-2.88-2.28
Indiana	M.	48-60-58	1.25-2.75-1.84
Do	[1]	[1]	1.50-2.50-2.00
Iowa	M.	48-60-58	1.50-2.75-2.21
Kansas	[1]	[1]	2.50-2.50-2.50
Do	M.	54-60-60	1.50-3.33-2.29
Louisiana	M.	54-54-54	2.25-2.75-2.48
Maine	M.	60-60-60	1.25-3.00-1.93
Maryland	M.	54-60-55	1.17-2.75-2.33
Massachusetts	M.	54-60-59	1.23-3.25-2.14
Michigan	M.	60-65-60	1.00-3.45-2.01
Minnesota	M.	60-60-60	2.25-2.50-2.33
Missouri	M.	48-72-49	1.50-3.00-2.36
Do	[1]	[1]	1.12-2.67-2.00
New Hampshire	M.	60-60-60	1.50-3.00-1.81
New Jersey	M.	60-60-60	1.25-2.67-2.05
New York	M.	48-72-51	1.25-4.00-3.14
North Carolina	M.	60-72-62	1.00-2.00-1.42
Ohio	M.	54-84-60	1.40-3.25-2.16
Do	[1]	[1]	2.50-2.50-2.50
Pennsylvania	M.	54-84-57	1.15-3.60-2.44
Do	[1]	[1]	2.50-3.50-2.82
Rhode Island	M.	60-60-60	1.50-3.34-2.23
South Carolina	M.	69-69-69	1.00-1.00-1.00
Tennessee	M.	60-84-67	1.00-3.00-1.72
Virginia	M.	54-72-64	1.50-2.25-2.01
West Virginia	M.	00-63-60	1.80-3.00-2.42
Do	[1]	[1]	2.50-2.50-2.50
Wisconsin	M.	60-60-60	.79-4.97-1.92
1890:			
Alabama	M.	60-60-60	1.00-3.00-2.20
California	M.	54-60-56	3.00-3.50-3.22
Connecticut	M.	54-60-54	2.25-3.25-2.64
Illinois	M.	48-60-54	2.10-2.40-2.30
Indiana	M.	54-60-60	1.40-2.75-1.98
Iowa	M.	[1]	1.13-2.50-2.07
Kansas	M.	[1]	1.75-3.25-2.39
Kentucky	M.	[1]	2.00-2.00-2.00
Louisiana	M.	54-54-54	2.25-2.75-2.50
Maine	M.	60-60-60	1.50-2.00-1.75
Maryland	M.	54-60-54	1.25-2.75-2.41
Massachusetts	M.	54-60-59	1.35-3.25-2.11
Michigan	M.	60-60-60	1.33-3.00-1.91
Minnesota	M.	60-60-60	1.00-2.75-2.15
Mississippi	M.	[1]	1.13-1.40-1.27
Missouri	M.	48-48-48	2.30-2.80-2.79
Nebraska	M.	[1]	1.50-3.00-2.13
New Hampshire	M.	60-60-60	1.72-2.25-1.81
New Jersey	M.	54-60-59	1.35-3.00-1.83
New York	M.	48-72-49	.38-5.25-2.46
North Carolina	M.	60-60-60	1.00-1.42-1.23
Ohio	M.	54-60-57	1.25-3.00-2.02
Do	[1]	48-69-58	.92-3.41-2.07
Pennsylvania	M.	54-70-56	1.65-3.60-2.77
Rhode Island	M.	60-60-60	1.50-3.00-2.34
Tennessee	M.	[1]	1.25-2.00-1.63
Virginia	M.	54-66-56	1.88-2.50-2.14
Wisconsin	M.	60-60-60	2.50-2.50-2.50
1891:			
California	M.	54-60-56	3.00-3.50-3.25
Connecticut	M.	54-60-55	2.25-3.25-2.69
Florida	M.	60-60-60	1.54-2.00-1.85
Illinois	M.	48-60-53	2.10-2.80-2.58
Indiana	M.	48-60-58	1.47-2.66-1.87
Louisiana	M.	54-54-54	2.00-2.75-2.35
Maine	M.	54-00-59	1.38-3.00-1.97

[1] Not reported. [2] And board. [3] Per hour. [4] And rent.

TABLE **B–3.**—*Carpenters and joiners, 1840–1900, by year and State*—Continued

Year and State	Sex	Hours per week	Rate per day (dollars)	Year and State	Sex	Hours per week	Rate per day (dollars)
1891—Continued.				**1894—Continued.**			
Maine	M.	(¹)	³0.20–0.20–0.20	Iowa	M.	42–72–59	1.10–3.75–2.19
Maryland	M.	54–60–54	2.00–2.75–2.42	Kansas	M.	58–58–58	1.92–2.00–1.93
Massachusetts	M.	54–60–59	1.35–3.25–2.09	Louisiana	M.	54–54–54	2.00–2.75–2.34
Minnesota	M.	60–60–60	2.00–2.25–2.20	Maine	M.	54–66–60	1.25–2.50–1.99
Missouri	M.	48–48–48	.81–3.25–2.17	Maryland	M.	54–54–54	2.25–2.50–2.43
New Hampshire	M.	60–60–60	2.00–2.00–2.00	Massachusetts	M.	54–60–56	1.16–4.06–2.24
New Jersey	M.	60–60–60	3.00–3.00–3.00	Minnesota	M.	60–60–60	2.00–2.25–2.11
New York	M.	48–72–49	.38–5.25–2.46	Missouri	M.	48–48–48	3.20–3.20–3.20
North Carolina	M.	60–75–63	.65–1.75–1.34	Montana	M.	(¹)	2.41–3.35–2.73
Do	(¹)	(¹)	.70–2.12–1.57	New Hampshire	M.	60–60–60	1.50–2.50–1.89
Ohio	M.	54–72–58	1.25–3.00–2.17	New York	(¹)	(¹)	2.50–2.50–2.50
Pennsylvania	M.	60–60–54	1.67–3.60–2.76	Do	M.	48–60–48	1.25–3.75–3.33
Rhode Island	M.	60–60–60	1.50–3.00–2.39	North Carolina	M.	60–66 60	.50–2.75–1.51
South Carolina	M.	60–60–60	1.42–1.75–1.54	Ohio	M.	54–72–58	1.08–5.00–2.01
Virginia	M.	54–54–54	2.00–2.50–2.22	Pennsylvania	M.	54–60–57	1.60–3.60–2.51
Wisconsin	M.	(¹)	2.00–2.00–2.00	Rhode Island	M.	60–60–60	1.50–2.50–1.94
Do	M.	(¹)	³.12½–.30–.23	Virginia	M.	54–54–54	2.00–2.50–2.20
1892:				West Virginia	M.	48–60–55	1.15–2.88–1.58
California	M.	48–60–50	.75–4.00–3.29	**1895:**			
Connecticut	M.	45–60–56	2.03–4.81–2.63	Alabama	M.	66–66–66	1.50–1.50–1.50
Delaware	M.	60–60–60	1.50–3.00–2.05	Connecticut	M.	60–72–62	1.80–2.89–2.27
Florida	M.	60–66–63	1.75–3.00–2.01	Delaware	M.	60–60–60	1.50–2.84–1.91
Illinois	M.	48–60–53	2.20–2.80–2.59	Georgia	M.	66–66–66	1.25–2.25–1.68
Indiana	M.	54–72–60	1.16–2.58–2.01	Illinois	M.	48–60–50	2.20–3.00–2.70
Iowa	M.	54–60–59	1.00–3.00–2.22	Indiana	M.	48–60–59	1.23–2.00–1.85
Louisiana	M.	54–54–54	2.00–2.75–2.33	Iowa	(¹)	(¹)	1.52–2.50–1.96
Maine	M.	60–60–60	1.82–2.75–2.06	Kansas	M.	60–60–60	.86–2.88–2.13
Maryland	M.	¹48–60–51	1.50–3.00–2.14	Kentucky	M.	60–60–60	2.50–2.50–2.50
Massachusetts	M.	54–60–59	1.35–4.00–2.06	Louisiana	M.	54–63–55	2.00–2.75–2.33
Do	(¹)	60–60–60	2.25–2.25–2.25	Maine	M.	60–60–60	1.25–2.75–2.12
Michigan	M.	24–72–57	.50–11.22–2.05	Maryland	M.	54–54–54	2.25–2.50–2.40
Minnesota	M.	60–60–60	2.00–2.25–2.20	Massachusetts	M.	41–60–57	1.16–4.06–2.22
Missouri	M.	48–48–48	2.25–3.20–2.81	Michigan	M.	(¹)	1.52–2.25–1.89
New Jersey	M.	60–60–60	2.50–3.00–2.75	Minnesota	M.	60–60–60	2.00–2.25–2.10
New York	M.	48–60–50	1.50–3.75–3.14	Missouri	M.	48–60–48	1.50–3.00–2.67
North Carolina	M.	60–60–60	1.50–1.50–1.50	Montana	M.	(¹)	2.06–3.50–2.72
Do	(¹)	(¹)	1.00–2.02–1.62	New Hampshire	M.	59–60–60	1.10–2.42–1.80
Ohio	M.	54–60–56	1.58–3.00–2.21	New Jersey	M.	53–60–59	2.00–2.75–2.35
Do	(¹)	53–72–55	1.25–2.50–2.17	New York	M.	48–60–48	1.50–3.75–3.33
Pennsylvania	M.	54–60–55	1.76–3.60–2.72	North Carolina	M.	60–72–61	.75–2.75–1.61
Rhode Island	M.	42–60–59	.77–3.50–2.36	Ohio	M.	48–72–57	1.00–3.50–1.97
South Carolina	M.	60–60–60	1.50–1.75–1.69	Pennsylvania	M.	54–60–56	1.60–3.60–2.37
Virginia	M.	54–54–54	2.00–2.50–2.16	Rhode Island	M.	57–66–60	1.50–3.00–2.31
1893:				South Carolina	M.	61–66–64	1.20–2.50–1.59
California	M.	54–60–56	3.00–3.50–3.23	Tennessee	M.	66–66–66	1.10–2.00–1.44
Connecticut	M.	60–60–60	2.20–4.81–2.53	Virginia	M.	54–55–54	2.00–2.50–2.30
Delaware	M.	60–60–60	1.50–2.84–2.07	Wisconsin	(¹)	48–84–60	.95–2.70–1.77
Illinois	M.	40–66–50	.33–7.83–2.89	**1896:**			
Indiana	M.	48–60–59	1.61–2.47–2.01	Alabama	M.	(¹)	1.33–2.50–1.85
Kansas	M.	(¹)	2.22–2.22–2.22	California	M.	54–60–55	2.75–3.50–3.12
Louisiana	M.	54–54–54	2.00–2.75–2.30	Colorado	M.	48–60–55	2.00–5.20–2.86
Maryland	M.	46–60–55	.67–3.00–2.26	Connecticut	M.	60–60–60	1.50–2.94–2.04
Massachusetts	M.	54–60–56	1.34–4.06–2.23	Dist. of Columbia	M.	(¹)	1.00–2.50–1.75
Michigan	M.	42–78–59	1.20–3.64–1.93	Florida	M.	(¹)	1.50–2.17–1.93
Minnesota	M.	60–60–60	2.00–2.25–2.11	Georgia	M.	60–66–66	.25–3.00–1.56
Missouri	M.	48–60–55	1.46–3.20–2.57	Illinois	M.	48–60–55	1.50–3.00–2.47
Montana	M.	45–60–51	2.50–5.00–4.19	Indiana	M.	48–65–59	1.11–2.61–1.99
New Hampshire	M.	48–66–59	1.25–4.00–2.23	Iowa	(¹)	(¹)	1.52–2.46–2.00
New Jersey	M.	60–60–60	2.00–2.90–2.90	Kansas	M.	48–60–57	1.50–2.25–2.09
New York	M.	36–72–49	.67–3.75–3.08	Louisiana	M.	54–54–54	2.00–2.75–2.32
North Carolina	M.	(¹)	1.00–1.93–1.58	Maryland	M.	48–60–54	1.50–2.81–2.37
Ohio	M.	45–60–58	1.05–3.15–2.03	Massachusetts	M.	53–84–56	2.00–3.30–2.48
Pennsylvania	M.	60–60–60	.67–3.00–2.52	Michigan	M.	55–60–56	1.67–2.50–2.22
Rhode Island	M.	60–60–60	.92–3.00–2.47	Minnesota	M.	60–60–60	2.00–2.25–2.10
Virginia	M.	54–54–54	2.00–2.50–2.18	Mississippi	M.	(¹)	.42–1.25–.78
Wisconsin	M.	(¹)	³.10–.35–.21	Missouri	M.	48–48–48	2.80–2.80–2.80
1894:				Do	(¹)	(¹)	1.70–2.57–2.24
California	M.	54–60–56	2.75–3.50–3.17	Montana	M.	(¹)	2.26–3.49–2.71
Connecticut	M.	60–60–60	1.80–2.89–2.26	Nebraska	M.	48–60–52	1.50–3.40–2.56
Delaware	M.	60–60–60	1.50–2.84–1.97	New Hampshire	M.	60–60–60	1.60–1.95–1.74
Georgia	M.	60–60–60	2.00–2.00–2.00	New York	M.	48–70–50	1.20–4.95–3.13
Illinois	M.	48–60–49	2.20–3.00–2.95	North Carolina	M.	60–72–62	.45–2.50–1.66
Indiana	M.	48–60–56	1.35–2.62–1.95	Ohio	M.	48–60–57	1.30–3.15–1.92

¹ Not reported. ³ Per hour.

Table **B-3.**—*Carpenters and joiners, 1840–1900, by year and State*—Continued

Year and State	Sex	Lowest, highest, and average—		Year and State	Sex	Lowest, highest, and average—	
		Hours per week	Rate per day (dollars)			Hours per week	Rate per day (dollars)
1896—Continued.				1898—Continued.			
Pennsylvania	M.	47–72–56	1. 50–4. 05–2. 70	Minnesota	M.	60–60–60	2. 00–2. 25–2. 18
Rhode Island	M.	60–60–60	2. 00–2. 25–2. 16	Missouri	M.	48–48–48	2. 80–2. 80–2. 80
South Carolina	M.	66–66–66	. 50–1. 50–1. 17	Do	(1)	48–60–59	1. 60–2. 62–2. 24
Tennessee	M.	(1)	. 83–3. 00–1. 67	Nebraska	(1)	48–60–56	1. 00–4. 50–2. 27
Vermont	M.	64–66–65	2. 00–2. 25–2. 13	Do	(1)	(1)	3. 17½–. 25–. 22½
Virginia	M.	54–54–54	1. 75–2. 50–2. 03	New Jersey	M.	60–60–60	1. 71–2. 50–2. 05
Wisconsin	M.	60–60–60	2. 00 -2. 25–2. 02	New York	M.	48–60–49	1. 35–3. 50–2. 61
1897:				North Carolina	(1)	(1)	1. 00–2. 23–1. 59
California	M.	54–60–56	2. 75–3. 50–3. 08	Ohio	M.	54–60–57	1. 33–3. 15–1. 86
Connecticut	M.	54–60–58	2. 25–2. 50–2. 33	Pennsylvania	M.	54–60–56	1. 60–4. 05–2. 49
Illinois	M.	48–60–51	2. 20–2. 80–2. 67	Virginia	M.	54–54–54	2. 00–2. 50–2. 18
Iowa	(1)	(1)	1. 63–2. 42–1. 98	1899:			
Kansas	M.	42–84–61	1. 50–2. 70–2. 00	Alabama	M.	60–60–60	1. 50–3. 25–2. 00
Do	M.	(1)	3. 16–. 20–. 18	California	M.	48–48–48	2. 50–3. 50–3. 06
Louisiana	M.	54–54–54	2. 00–2. 75–2. 33	Georgia	M.	59–60–60	1. 25–2. 75–1. 83
Maryland	M.	54–54–54	2. 25–2. 50–2. 43	Illinois	M.	48–48–48	3. 40–3. 40–3. 40
Do	(1)	54–60–59	1. 60–2. 44–2. 00	Massachusetts	M.	48–48–48	2. 40–2. 64–2. 42
Massachusetts	M.	54–54–54	2. 25–3. 00–2. 54	Michigan	(1)	(1)	1. 97–1. 97–1. 97
Michigan	M.	(1)	1. 72–2. 25–1. 89	Montana	M.	53–53–53	4. 42–4. 42–4. 42
Minnesota	M.	60–60–60	2. 00–2. 25–2. 18	New Jersey	M.	53–53–53	1. 96–2. 50–1. 97
Missouri	M.	48–48–48	2. 80–2. 80–2. 80	New York	M.	44–54–51	1. 80–3. 50–2. 14
Montana	(1)	(1)	2. 24–3. 59–2. 67	North Carolina	M.	48–72–60	. 75–3. 00–1. 40
Nebraska	M.	48–60–51	1. 00–3. 00–2. 30	Do	(1)	(1)	1. 00–2. 24–1. 57
New York	M.	48–60–49	1. 31–4. 05–2. 63	Ohio	M.	48–54–51	1. 65–2. 70–2. 20
North Carolina	(1)	(1)	1. 24–2. 23–1. 62	Pennsylvania	M.	54–54–54	1. 65–3. 00–2. 69
Ohio	M.	54–60–57	1. 45–3. 15–1. 94	Tennessee	M.	(1)	1. 35–2. 04–1. 59
Do	(1)	60–72–62	1. 00–2. 50–1. 73	Virginia	(1)	(1)	1. 00–2. 41–1. 62
Pennsylvania	M.	54–72–49	1. 12–4. 05–2. 46	1900:			
Virginia	M.	54–66–59	1. 12–2. 50–1. 62	Alabama	M.	54–60–54	1. 50–3. 25–2. 48
1898				California	M.	48–48–48	3. 00–3. 50–3. 08
California	M.	54–60–55	2. 75–3. 50–3. 05	Georgia	M.	59–60–60	1. 50–2. 75–1. 96
Illinois	M.	48–60–56	2. 20–2. 80–2. 44	Illinois	M.	48–48–48	3. 40–3. 40–3. 40
Indiana	(1)	48–60–58	1. 35–2. 31–1. 93	Massachusetts	M.	48–48–48	2. 40–2. 64–2. 42
Iowa	(1)	(1)	1. 69–2. 36–2. 02	Montana	M.	53–53–53	4. 42–4. 42–4. 42
Kansas	M.	33–60–52	1. 24–2. 75–2. 34	New Jersey	M.	53–53–53	2. 04–3. 00–2. 24
Louisiana	M.	54–54–54	2. 00–2. 75–2. 35	New York	M.	44–54–51	1. 80–4. 00–2. 25
Maryland	M.	54–54–54	2. 25–2. 50–2. 42	North Carolina	M.	60–60–60	. 80–2. 40–1. 39
Massachusetts	M.	54–54–54	2. 50–3. 00–2. 54	Ohio	M.	48–54–51	1. 80–2. 70–2. 22
Michigan	M.	(1)	1. 50–2. 00–1. 73	Pennsylvania	M.	48–48–48	2. 80–2. 80–2. 80

1 Not reported.   2 Per hour.

Table **B-4.**—*Carpenters, males, 1890–1928, by city and year*

Year	Atlanta, Ga.		Birmingham, Ala.		Boston, Mass.		Chicago, Ill.	
	Hours per week	Rate per hour	Hours per week	Rate per hour	Hours per week	Rate per hour	Hours per week	Rate per hour
1890	60. 0	$0. 189	59. 5	$0. 284	54. 0	$0. 300	48. 0	$0. 350
1891	60. 0	. 185	59. 6	. 288	54. 0	. 301	48. 0	. 350
1892	60. 0	. 183	59. 5	. 270	54. 0	. 303	48. 0	. 350
1893	60. 0	. 182	58. 3	. 263	54. 0	. 304	48. 0	. 350
1894	60. 0	. 188	59. 2	. 248	54. 0	. 305	48. 0	. 350
1895	60. 0	. 204	57. 3	. 217	54. 0	. 303	48. 0	. 350
1896	60. 0	. 206	58. 0	. 206	54. 0	. 303	48. 0	. 350
1897	60. 9	. 206	58. 8	. 229	54. 0	. 303	48. 0	. 350
1898	60. 0	. 216	58. 4	. 248	54. 0	. 305	48. 0	. 375
1899	60. 0	. 217	57. 4	. 240	54. 0	. 305	44. 0	. 425
1900	60. 0	. 235	56. 0	. 263	49. 4	. 305	44. 0	. 450
1901	60. 0	. 229	54. 2	. 291	48. 9	. 338	44. 0	. 450
1902	60. 0	. 234	49. 3	. 316	48. 9	. 337	44. 0	. 450
1903	60. 0	. 239	49. 2	. 327	48. 5	. 349	44. 0	. 500
1904	59. 8	. 243	50. 0	. 321	48. 1	. 374	44. 0	. 500
1905	59. 8	. 243	49. 2	. 369	48. 2	. 384	44. 0	. 500
1906	59. 4	. 274	48. 0	. 374	48. 1	. 405	44. 0	. 550
1907	54. 0	. 300	48. 0	. 400	48. 0	. 438	44. 0	. 563
1908	54. 0	. 300	48. 0	. 400	48. 0	. 438	44. 0	. 563
1909	54. 0	. 300	48. 0	. 400	48. 0	. 478	44. 0	. 563
1910	54. 0	. 300	48. 0	. 400	44. 0	. 500	44. 0	. 600
1911	54. 0	. 350	48. 0	. 450	44. 0	. 500	44. 0	. 600

TABLE **B-4.**—*Carpenters, males, 1890-1928, by city and year*—Continued

Year	Atlanta, Ga.		Birmingham, Ala.		Boston, Mass.		Chicago, Ill.	
	Hours per week	Rate per hour	Hours per week	Rate per hour	Hours per week	Rate per hour	Hours per week	Rate per hour
1912	54.0	$0.350	48.0	$0.450	44.0	$0.500	44.0	$0.650
1913	50.0	.400	48.0	.525	44.0	.500	44.0	.650
1914	50.0	.400	48.0	.450	44.0	.550	44.0	.650
1915	50.0	.400	48.0	.450	44.0	.550	44.0	.650
1916	50.0	.400	48.0	.450	44.0	.570	44.0	.700
1917	50.0	.500	48.0	.450	44.0	.600	44.0	.700
1918	50.0	.500	48.0	.550	40.0	.650	44.0	.700
1919	44.0	.600	44.0	.650	40.0	.750	44.0	.800
1920	44.0	.800	44.0	.750	40.0	1.000	44.0	1.250
1921	44.0	.700	44.0	.750	40.0	1.000	44.0	1.250
1922	44.0	.700	44.0	.750	40.0	1.000	44.0	1.100
1923	44.0	.700	44.0	.750	44.0	1.050	44.0	1.250
1924	44.0	.800	44.0	.875	44.0	1.100	44.0	1.250
1925	44.0	.800	44.0	.875	44.0	1.100	44.0	1.250
1926	44.0	.800	44.0	.950	44.0	1.250	44.0	1.375
1927	44.0	.800	44.0	1.000	44.0	1.250	44.0	1.500
1928	44.0	.800	44.0	1.000	44.0	1.250	44.0	1.500

Year	Cincinnati, Ohio		Denver, Colo.		Detroit, Mich.		New Orleans, La.	
1890	54.0	$0.275	48.0	$0.344	54.0	$0.229	54.0	$0.279
1891	54.0	.292	48.0	.344	54.0	.211	54.0	.269
1892	54.0	.318	48.0	.344	54.0	.221	54.0	.269
1893	54.0	.310	48.0	.263	54.0	.223	54.0	.262
1894	54.0	.326	48.0	.250	54.0	.193	54.0	.265
1895	54.0	.283	48.0	.265	54.0	.196	54.0	.264
1896	54.0	.283	48.0	.261	54.0	.204	54.0	.264
1897	54.0	.274	48.0	.250	54.0	.210	54.0	.261
1898	54.0	.258	48.0	.313	54.0	.207	54.0	.264
1899	51.2	.270	48.0	.375	54.0	.220	54.0	.259
1900	48.0	.296	48.0	.375	54.0	.239	51.6	.280
1901	48.0	.323	48.0	.406	48.0	.257	48.8	.298
1902	48.0	.356	46.2	.450	48.0	.296	49.7	.298
1903	48.0	.370	45.8	.450	48.0	.319	48.0	.353
1904	48.0	.379	44.0	.450	48.0	.342	48.0	.356
1905	48.0	.404	44.0	.450	48.0	.342	49.4	.358
1906	48.0	.402	44.0	.500	48.0	.349	49.3	.360
1907	44.5	.450	44.0	.500	48.0	.350	48.0	.450
1908	44.5	.450	44.0	.550	48.0	.375	48.0	.450
1909	44.5	.450	44.0	.600	48.0	.375	48.0	.450
1910	44.5	.500	44.0	.600	48.0	.400	48.0	.400
1911	44.5	.500	44.0	.600	48.0	.450	48.0	.400
1912	44.5	.500	44.0	.600	48.0	.500	48.0	.400
1913	44.5	.500	44.0	.600	48.0	.500	48.0	.400
1914	44.5	.500	44.0	.600	48.0	.500	48.0	.400
1915	44.5	.550	44.0	.600	48.0	.500	48.0	.400
1916	44.5	.600	44.0	.600	44.0	.500	48.0	.400
1917	44.5	.625	44.0	.700	44.0	.600	48.0	.400
1918	44.5	.650	44.0	.750	44.0	.600	48.0	.500
1919	44.5	.700	44.0	.875	44.0	.800	48.0	.600
1920	44.5	1.000	44.0	1.125	44.0	1.000	48.0	.750
1921	44.5	1.000	44.0	1.125	44.0	.850	44.0	1.000
1922	44.5	.950	44.0	1.000	44.0	.850	44.0	1.000
1923	44.5	1.050	44.0	1.125	44.0	1.150	44.0	.900
1924	44.5	1.150	44.0	1.125	44.0	1.150	44.0	.900
1925	44.5	1.250	44.0	1.125	44.0	1.150	44.0	.900
1926	44.5	1.313	44.0	1.125	44.0	1.150	44.0	.900
1927	44.5	1.350	40.0	1.250	44.0	1.150	44.0	.900
1928	44.5	1.375	40.0	1.250	44.0	1.150	44.0	.900

Year	New York, N. Y.[1]		Philadelphia, Pa.		St. Louis, Mo.		San Francisco, Calif.	
1890	48.2	$0.431	55.0	$0.295	48.0	$0.305	56.2	$0.369
1891	48.1	.435	55.3	.298	48.0	.306	56.4	.369
1892	48.1	.436	54.9	.299	48.0	.324	56.2	.373
1893	48.2	.433	55.2	.298	48.0	.357	56.4	.352
1894	48.0	.435	54.7	.300	48.0	.360	55.8	.334
1895	48.1	.433	54.7	.298	48.0	.350	55.5	.331
1896	48.0	.436	55.0	.298	48.0	.350	52.6	.367
1897	48.0	.437	55.1	.296	48.0	.350	52.4	.370
1898	48.0	.438	54.0	.314	48.0	.350	53.0	.368

[1] Greater New York, 1903-1907; Manhattan, 1907-1927.

TABLE **B-4.**—*Carpenters, males, 1890–1928, by city and year*—Continued

Year	New York, N. Y.		Philadelphia, Pa.		St. Louis, Mo.		San Francisco, Calif.	
	Hours per week	Rate per hour	Hours per week	Rate per hour	Hours per week	Rate per hour	Hours per week	Rate per hour
1899	47.0	$0.451	54.0	$0.311	48.0	$0.325	52.9	$0.379
1900	44.1	.495	48.0	.343	46.7	.383	52.6	.394
1901	44.1	.497	47.8	.347	44.0	.410	52.4	.396
1902	44.1	.514	46.2	.392	44.0	.424	48.7	.427
1903	44.0	.536	46.3	.400	44.0	.532	45.1	.497
1904	44.0	.530	46.4	.400	44.0	.523	44.0	.500
1905	44.0	.537	46.1	.400	44.0	.550	44.0	.504
1906	44.0	.575	44.9	.450	44.0	.550	44.0	.608
1907	44.0	.607	44.1	.462	44.0	.596	44.0	.625
1907	44.0	.625	44.0	.450	44.0	.550	44.0	.625
1908	44.0	.625	44.0	.450	44.0	.550	44.0	.625
1909	44.0	.625	44.0	.450	44.0	.600	44.0	.625
1910	44.0	.625	44.0	.500	44.0	.600	44.0	.625
9911	44.0	.625	44.0	.500	44.0	.625	44.0	.625
1912	44.0	.625	44.0	.500	44.0	.625	44.0	.625
1913	44.0	.625	44.0	.500	44.0	.625	44.0	.625
1914	44.0	.625	44.0	.550	44.0	.625	44.0	.625
1915	44.0	.625	44.0	.550	44.0	.625	44.0	.625
1916	44.0	.625	44.0	.550	44.0	.625	44.0	.625
1917	44.0	.688	44.0	.600	44.0	.650	44.0	.688
1918	44.0	.688	44.0	.700	44.0	.700	44.0	.750
1919	44.0	.750	44.0	.800	44.0	.825	44.0	.875
1920	44.0	1.125	44.0	1.125	44.0	1.000	44.0	1.063
1921	44.0	1.125	44.0	1.125	44.0	1.250	44.0	1.125
1922	44.0	1.125	44.0	.900	44.0	1.100	44.0	1.044
1923	44.0	1.125	44.0	1.125	44.0	1.250	44.0	1.044
1924	44.0	1.313	44.0	1.125	44.0	1.500	44.0	1.044
1925	44.0	1.313	44.0	1.125	44.0	1.500	44.0	1.044
1926	44.0	1.500	44.0	1.250	44.0	1.500	44.0	1.125
1927	44.0	1.500	44.0	1.250	44.0	1.500	44.0	1.125
1928	44.0	1.500	44.0	1.250	40.0	1.500	44.0	1.125

TABLE **B-5.**—*Electricians (inside wiremen), 1880–1900, by year and State*

Year and State	Sex	Lowest, highest, and average—		Year and State	Sex	Lowest, highest, and average—	
		Hours per week	Rate per day (dollars)			Hours per week	Rate per day (dollars)
1880:				**1893:**			
New Jersey	(¹)	56–56–56	2.00–2.00–2.00	Illinois	M.	60–60–60	3.00–3.00–3.00
1883:				Montana	M.	49–70–60	3.50–5.75–4.11
Massachusetts	M.	(¹)	1.17–3.25–2.15	New Hampshire	M.	53–60–58	2.00–5.00–2.88
1884:				Ohio	M.	54–54–54	3.00–3.00–3.00
Michigan	M.	(¹)	2.25–3.00–2.63	Pennsylvania	M.	60–70–65	3.00–3.83–3.42
1885:				**1894:**			
Ohio	M.	60–60–60	1.89–1.89–1.89	Iowa	M.	60–72–62	1.92–2.71–2.31
Pennsylvania	M.	60–60–60	2.00–2.00–2.00	New Hampshire	M.	57–60–59	1.75–2.50–2.00
1887:				New York	(¹)	(¹)	3.00–3.00–3.00
Maryland	M.	(¹)	1.25–2.88–2.08	Ohio	M.	60–72–62	1.50–3.00–1.88
Massachusetts	M.	(¹)	2.00–4.11–2.53	Pennsylvania	M.	60–60–60	2.70–2.70–2.70
New York	M.	(¹)	3.19–3.64–3.42	**1895:**			
Ohio	M.	60–60–60	1.50–2.90–2.33	Georgia	M.	66–66–66	1.50–2.25–1.88
Wisconsin	M.	(¹)	2.47–2.47–2.47	Maine	M.	60–60–60	1.75–2.75–2.08
1888:				Massachusetts	M.	60–60–60	2.25–2.50–2.38
New York	M.	54–72–58	1.50–8.33–3.78	Michigan	M.	(¹)	.75–3.30–1.88
1889:				Missouri	M.	(¹)	2.50–2.50–2.50
Indiana	M.	60–60–60	1.25–1.25–1.25	New Hampshire	M.	59–60–60	1.18–2.50–1.42
Pennsylvania	(¹)	(¹)	2.30–2.30–2.30	New York	M.	48–48–48	3.00–3.00–3.00
1890:				Ohio	M.	60–60–60	1.66–2.50–1.98
Michigan	M.	60–60–60	.67–2.50–1.51	Pennsylvania	M.	60–60–60	2.70–2.70–2.70
New York	M.	(¹)	1.52–2.92–2.34	Vermont	M.	60–60–60	1.50–1.50–1.50
1891:				**1896:**			
Maine	M.	72–72–72	2.00–2.00–2.00	Connecticut	M.	60–60–60	3.00–3.00–3.00
Missouri	M.	(¹)	2.95–2.95–2.95	Georgia	M.	66–66–66	1.50–1.50–1.50
New York	M.	(¹)	1.67–5.83–2.54	Illinois	M.	54–54–54	2.50–2.50–2.50
1892:				Maryland	M.	54–54–54	4.00–4.00–4.00
Pennsylvania	M.	60–60–60	3.50–3.50.3.50	Massachusetts	M.	60–60–60	4.17–4.17–4.15

¹ Not reported.

TABLE **B-5.**—*Electricians (inside wiremen), 1880-1900, by year and State*—Con.

Year and State	Sex	Lowest, highest, and average—		Year and State	Sex	Lowest, highest, and average—	
		Hours per week	Rate per day (dollars)			Hours per week	Rate per day (dollars)
1896—Continued.				1898—Continued.			
Nebraska	M.	60-60-60	2. 00-2. 75-2. 17	Michigan	M.	(¹)	1. 50-2. 75-2. 62
New York	M.	(¹)	. 83-3. 50-1. 94	Missouri	M.	60-72-61	2. 00-5. 00-2. 50
Ohio	M.	60-60-60	1. 60-2. 25-1. 98	Nebraska	M.	60-60-60	1. 00-5. 00-2. 61
Pennsylvania	M.	60-60-60	1. 60-2. 50-2. 41	Pennsylvania	M.	(¹)	2. 10-2. 10-2. 10
South Carolina	M.	(¹)	1. 17-1. 17-1. 17	Washington	(¹)	(¹)	1-62. 3. 33-2. 33
Wisconsin	M.	60-72-66	1. 50-2. 25-1. 88	1899:			
1897:				Michigan	M.	60-60-60	2. 08-3. 12-2. 37
Nebraska	M.	(¹)	2. 00-2. 00-2. 00	New York	M.	(¹)	2. 50-2. 50-2. 50
Ohio	(¹)	(¹)	2. 25-2. 25-2. 25	North Carolina	M.	(¹)	2. 25-2. 25-2. 25
Pennsylvania	M.	60-60-60	2. 75-2. 75-2. 75	Pennsylvania	M.	(¹)	2. 40-2. 50-2. 45
Virginia	M.	60-60-60	1. 80-1. 80-1. 80	Virginia	(¹)	(¹)	1. 50-3. 65-2. 18
1898:				1900:			
Iowa	(¹)	(¹)	1. 75-1. 75-1. 75	New York	M.	(¹)	2. 50-2. 50-2. 50
Kansas	M.	60-60-60	2. 07-2. 88-2. 48				

¹ Not reported.

TABLE **B-6.**—*Inside wiremen, males, 1890-1907, by geographic division and year*

Year	North Atlantic		South Atlantic		North Central		South Central	
	Hours per week	Rate per hour	Hours per week	Rate per hour	Hours per week	Rate per hour	Hours per week	Rate per hour
1890	56. 0	$0. 266	59. 2	$0. 226	53. 3	$0. 266	59. 3	$0. 229
1891	56. 0	. 266	58. 8	. 218	53. 2	. 267	59. 3	. 231
1892	55. 6	. 274	58. 7	. 217	49. 4	. 276	59. 3	. 230
1893	55. 3	. 292	58. 8	. 217	52. 4	. 310	59. 3	. 228
1894	55. 0	. 289	58. 4	. 213	53. 0	. 301	59. 3	. 229
1895	53. 7	. 302	58. 3	. 218	53. 9	. 316	59. 3	. 247
1896	53. 0	. 300	57. 8	. 229	52. 0	. 345	59. 3	. 247
1897	51. 2	. 328	58. 1	. 228	51. 6	. 345	59. 4	. 248
1898	50. 7	. 338	58. 2	. 242	52. 0	. 367	54. 7	. 279
1899	51. 1	. 344	58. 6	. 242	51. 8	. 365	54. 7	. 279
1900	48. 7	. 396	57. 9	. 275	51. 0	. 359	52. 5	. 291
1901	48. 9	. 380	56. 6	. 278	50. 7	. 373	52. 1	. 296
1902	48. 7	. 402	56. 6	. 292	49. 6	. 397	52. 1	. 306
1903	46. 1	. 434	53. 8	. 309	47. 8	. 430	50. 2	. 321
1904	46. 8	. 416	51. 8	. 314	48. 5	. 387	52. 3	. 337
1905	46. 5	. 412	51. 3	. 340	47. 6	. 427	52. 7	. 307
1906	46. 6	. 423	50. 8	. 363	48. 4	. 394	52. 9	. 314
1907	46. 5	. 425	50. 5	. 379	48. 0	. 419	51. 4	. 344

TABLE **B-7.**—*Inside wiremen, males, 1907-1928, by city and year*

Year	Atlanta, Ga.		Birmingham, Ala.		Boston, Mass.		Chicago, Ill.	
	Hours per week	Rate per hour	Hours per week	Rate per hour	Hours per week	Rate per hour	Hours per week	Rate per hour
1907			48. 0	$0. 438	48. 0	$0. 450	44. 0	$0. 625
1908			48. 0	. 438	48. 0	. 450	44. 0	. 625
1909			48. 0	. 438	48. 0	. 450	44. 0	. 688
1910			48. 0	. 500	¹ 44. 0	. 500	44. 0	. 688
1911	54. 0	$0. 333	48. 0	. 500	¹ 44. 0	. 500	44. 0	. 750
1912	54. 0	. 389	44. 0	. 563	44. 0	. 550	44. 0	. 750
1913	54. 0	. 444	44. 0	. 625	44. 0	. 550	44. 0	. 750
1914			44. 0	. 625	44. 0	. 550	44. 0	. 750
1915			44. 0	. 500	44. 0	² . 600	44. 0	. 750
1916			44. 0	. 500	44. 0	. 625	44. 0	. 750
1917	54. 0	. 389	44. 0	. 500	44. 0	. 650	44. 0	. 750
1918	48. 0	. 550	44. 0	³ . 625	44. 0	. 700	44. 0	. 813
1919	44. 0	. 750	44. 0	. 800	44. 0	. 775	44. 0	. 875
1920	44. 0	. 900	44. 0	1. 000	44. 0	1. 000	44. 0	1. 250

¹ 48 hours October to April.   ² 62.5 cents effective July 1.   ³ 75 cents on June 21.

TABLE **B-7.**—*Inside wiremen, males, 1907-1928, by city and year*—Continued

Year	Atlanta, Ga. Hours per week	Atlanta, Ga. Rate per hour	Birmingham, Ala. Hours per week	Birmingham, Ala. Rate per hour	Boston, Mass. Hours per week	Boston, Mass. Rate per hour	Chicago, Ill. Hours per week	Chicago, Ill. Rate per hour
1921	44.0	$0.900	44.0	$1.000	44.0	[4]$1.000	44.0	[3]$1.250
1922	44.0	.900	44.0	.850	44.0	[4]1.000	44.0	1.100
1923	44.0	.900	44.0	1.000	44.0	1.050	44.0	1.100
1924	44.0	.900	44.0	1.125	44.0	1.100	44.0	1.250
1925	44.0	.900	44.0	1.125	44.0	1.100	44.0	1.500
1926	44.0	.900	44.0	1.125	44.0	1.200	44.0	1.500
1927	44.0	.900	44.0	1.250	44.0	1.250	44.0	1.563
1928	44.0	1.000	44.0	1.250	44.0	1.250	44.0	1.625

Year	Cincinnati, Ohio Hours per week	Cincinnati, Ohio Rate per hour	Denver, Colo. Hours per week	Denver, Colo. Rate per hour	Detroit, Mich. Hours per week	Detroit, Mich. Rate per hour	New Orleans, La., Hours per week	New Orleans, La., Rate per hour
1907	48.0	$0.406	44.0	$0.531	48.0	$0.400	48.0	$0.450
1908	48.0	.406	44.0	.531	48.0	.400	48.0	.450
1909	48.0	.406	44.0	.531	48.0	.400	48.0	.450
1910	48.0	.406	44.0	.563	48.0	.438	48.0	.450
1911	44.5	.450	44.0	.563	48.0	.438	48.0	.450
1912	44.5	.450	44.0	.563	48.0	.469	48.0	.450
1913	44.5	.500	44.0	.563	48.0	.469	48.0	.450
1914	44.0	.500	44.0	.563	[5]48.0	.500	48.0	.500
1915	44.5	.531	44.0	.563	[5]48.0	[6].531	48.0	.500
1916	44.5	.563	44.0	.600	48.0	.594	48.0	.500
1917	44.5	.625	44.0	.625	44.0	.669	48.0	[7].563
1918	44.5	.688	44.0	.825	44.0	.750	48.0	.700
1919	44.5	[8].719	44.0	.825	44.0	.938	44.0	.900
1920	44.5	1.000	44.0	1.000	44.0	1.250	44.0	1.000
1921	44.5	1.000	44.0	1.000	44.0	1.000	44.0	1.000
1922	44.5	.950	44.0	1.000	44.0	1.000	44.0	.900
1923	44.5	1.050	44.0	1.125	44.0	1.125	44.0	1.050
1924	44.5	1.150	44.0	1.125	44.0	1.250	44.0	1.100
1925	44.5	1.250	44.0	1.250	44.0	1.300	44.0	1.100
1926	44.5	1.313	44.0	1.375	44.0	1.400	44.0	1.200
1927	44.5	1.350	44.0	1.375	44.0	1.500	44.0	1.250
1928	44.5	1.375	44.0	1.375	44.0	1.500	44.0	1.250

Year	New York, N. Y. Hours per week	New York, N. Y. Rate per hour	Philadelphia, Pa. Hours per week	Philadelphia, Pa. Rate per hour	St. Louis, Mo. Hours per week	St. Louis, Mo. Rate per hour	San Francisco, Calif. Hours per week	San Francisco, Calif. Rate per hour
1907	44.0	$0.500	[5]48.0	$0.450	44.0	$0.650	44.0	$0.625
1908	44.0	.563	[5]48.0	.450	44.0	.650	44.0	.625
1909	44.0	.563	[5]48.0	.450	44.0	.650	44.0	.625
1910	44.0	.563	[5]48.0	.450	44.0	.650	44.0	.625
1911	44.0	.563	[5]48.0	.450	44.0	.650	44.0	.625
1912	44.0	.563	[5]48.0	.450	44.0	.650	44.0	.625
1913	44.0	.563	44.0	.450	44.0	.650	44.0	.625
1914	44.0	.600	44.0	.450	44.0	.700	44.0	.625
1915	44.0	.600	44.0	.500	44.0	.750	44.0	.625
1916	44.0	.600	44.0	.563	44.0	.750	44.0	.625
1917	44.0	.650	44.0	[10].650	44.0	.750	44.0	.750
1918	44.0	[9].650	44.0	.750	44.0	[11].750	44.0	.750
1919	44.0	.750	44.0	[12]1.000	44.0	.875	44.0	.875
1920	44.0	1.125	44.0	1.125	44.0	1.000	44.0	1.125
1921	44.0	[13]{1.125 / 1.000}	44.0	1.125	44.0	1.250		
1922	44.0	[13]{1.125 / 1.000}	44.0	.900	44.0	1.250	44.0	1.000
1923	44.0	[13]{1.125 / 1.000}	44.0	1.000	44.0	1.250	44.0	1.000
1924	44.0	[13]{1.313 / 1.000}	44.0	1.125	44.0	1.500	44.0	1.000
1925	44.0	1.313	[14]44.0	1.125	44.0	1.500	44.0	1.000
1926	44.0	1.500	[14]44.0	1.250	44.0	1.500	44.0	1.063
1927	44.0	1.500	[14]44.0	1.250	44.0	1.500	44.0	1.125
1928	44.0	1.500	44.0	1.250	44.0	1.500	44.0	1.125

[3] 75 cents on June 21.
[4] Old scale; strike pending.
[5] 44 hours June to September.
[6] Effective Nov. 1.
[7] 70 cents on June 1.
[8] Nominal only; all received more.
[9] 75 cents on June 15.
[10] 75 cents on June 1.
[11] 86.3 cents on July 15.
[12] 25 per cent received $1.25.
[13] 2 unions.
[14] 40 hours June to August.

TABLE **B-8.**—*Engineers, stationary, 1840–1900, by year and State*

Year and State	Sex	Hours per week	Rate per day (dollars)	Year and State	Sex	Hours per week	Rate per day (dollars)
1840:				**1855:**			
Massachusetts	M.	84-84-84	2.00-2.00-2.00	Connecticut	M.	60-60-60	1.25-1.67-1.47
1841:				Florida	M.	60-60-60	3.00-3.00-3.00
Massachusetts	M.	84-84-84	2.00-2.00-2.00	Maryland	M.	60-60-60	1.50-1.50-1.50
New York	M.	84-84-84	1.50-1.50-1.50	Massachusetts	M.	72-72-72	2.50-2.50-2.50
1842:				New Hampshire	M.	60-60-60	1.00-1.00-1.00
Connecticut	M.	60-60-60	1.75-1.75-1.75	New York	M.	60-84-64	1.00-2.50-1.54
Massachusetts	M.	84-84-84	2.00-2.00-2.00	Pennsylvania	M.	72-72-72	1.50-1.56-1.53
New York	M.	84-84-84	1.75-1.75-1.75	**1856:**			
Pennsylvania	M.	(¹)	1.00-1.00-1.00	Connecticut	M.	60-60-60	1.25-2.00-1.64
1843:				Maryland	M.	60-60-60	1.50-1.50-1.50
Massachusetts	M.	84-84-84	2.00-2.00-2.00	Massachusetts	M.	72-72-72	2.50-2.50-2.50
New York	M.	84-84-84	1.75-1.75-1.75	New Hampshire	M.	60-60-60	1.17-1.17-1.17
Pennsylvania	M.	(¹)	1.00-1.00-1.00	New York	M.	60-84-67	1.13-2.30-1.60
1844:				Pennsylvania	M.	72-72-72	1.50-1.80-1.65
Connecticut	M.	60-60-60	1.34-1.34-1.34	**1857:**			
Massachusetts	M.	84-84-84	2.00-2.00-2.00	Connecticut	M.	60-60-60	1.25-2.00-1.64
New York	M.	60-84-72	1.00-1.75-1.38	Maryland	M.	60-60-60	1.50-1.50-1.50
Pennsylvania	M.	(¹)	1.00-1.00-1.00	Massachusetts	M.	72-72-72	2.75-2.75-2.75
1845:				New Hampshire	M.	60-60-60	1.17-1.17-1.17
Connecticut	M.	60-60-60	1.50-1.50-1.50	New York	M.	60-84-66	1.13-2.30-1.53
Massachusetts	M.	84-84-84	2.25-2.25-2.25	Pennsylvania	M.	72-72-72	1.50-1.80-1.65
New York	M.	60-84-72	1.00-1.75-1.38	**1858:**			
Pennsylvania	M.	(¹)	1.42-1.42-1.42	Connecticut	M.	60-60-60	1.38-1.67-1.51
1846:				Maryland	M.	60-60-60	1.50-1.50-1.50
Connecticut	M.	60-60-60	1.50-1.50-1.50	Massachusetts	M.	72-72-72	2.75-2.75-2.75
Massachusetts	M.	84-84-84	2.25-2.25-2.25	New Hampshire	M.	60-60-60	1.17-1.17-1.17
New York	M.	60-84-72	.75-1.75-1.25	New York	M.	60-84-76	1.00-2.30-1.56
Pennsylvania	M.	(¹)	1.42-1.42-1.42	Pennsylvania	M.	72-72-72	1.50-2.04-1.77
1847:				**1859:**			
Connecticut	M.	60-60-60	1.50-1.50-1.50	Connecticut	M.	60-60-60	1.17-1.67-1.40
Massachusetts	M.	84-84-84	2.25-2.25-2.25	Maryland	M.	60-60-60	1.50-1.50-1.50
New York	M.	60-84-68	.83-2.00-1.24	Massachusetts	M.	72-72-72	2.75-2.75-2.75
¹ Not reported.				New Hampshire	M.	60-60-60	1.08-1.08-1.08
1848:				New York	M.	60-84-72	1.00-2.30-1.64
Connecticut	M.	60-60-60	1.50-1.50-1.50	Pennsylvania	M.	72-72-72	1.50-2.04-1.77
Massachusetts	M.	84-84-84	2.25-2.25-2.25	**1860:**			
New York	M.	60-84-68	1.00-2.00-1.33	Connecticut	M.	60-60-60	1.17-1.50-1.34
1849:				Maryland	M.	60-60-60	1.50-1.50-1.50
Connecticut	M.	60-60-60	1.50-1.50-1.50	Massachusetts	M.	60-72-68	2.50-3.00-2.67
Massachusetts	M.	84-84-84	2.25-2.25-2.25	New Hampshire	M.	60-60-60	1.17-1.17-1.17
New York	M.	60-84-66	1.00-2.00-1.56	New York	M.	60-84-68	1.00-2.50-1.63
Pennsylvania	M.	(¹)	1.00-1.00-1.00	Pennsylvania	M.	60-72-66	1.50-2.40-1.80
1850:				**1861:**			
Connecticut	M.	60-60-60	1.17-1.50-1.34	Connecticut	M.	60-60-60	1.17-1.50-1.34
Massachusetts	M.	84-84-84	2.25-2.25-2.25	Massachusetts	M.	66-66-66	3.00-3.00-3.00
New York	M.	60-84-63	.75-2.00-1.36	New York	M.	60-84-68	1.00-2.50-1.82
Pennsylvania	M.	72-72-72	1.00-1.56-1.30	Pennsylvania	M.	60-72-66	1.50-2.40-1.80
1851:				**1862:**			
Connecticut	M.	50-60-60	1.50-1.50-1.50	Connecticut	M.	60-60-60	1.25-2.00-1.69
Massachusetts	M.	84-84-84	2.25-2.25-2.25	Massachusetts	M.	66-66-62	2.25-3.00-2.50
New York	M.	60-84-66	.75-2.00-1.38	New Hampshire	M.	60-60-60	1.17-1.17-1.17
Pennsylvania	M.	72-72-72	1.34-1.56-1.45	New York	M.	60-84-70	1.00-2.00-1.77
1852:				Pennsylvania	M.	60-72-66	1.50-2.40-1.86
Connecticut	M.	60-60-60	1.50-1.50-1.50	**1863:**			
Massachusetts	M.	72-72-72	2.25-2.25-2.25	Connecticut	M.	60-60-60	1.50-1.67-1.54
New Hampshire	M.	60-60-60	1.00-1.00-1.00	Maryland	M.	60-60-60	1.34-1.67-1.51
New York	M.	60-84-68	1.00-2.00-1.58	Massachusetts	M.	66-66-66	3.00-3.00-3.00
Pennsylvania	M.	72-72-72	1.34-1.56-1.45	New Hampshire	M.	60-60-60	1.17-1.17-1.17
1853:				New York	M.	60-84-67	1.00-2.75-1.69
Connecticut	M.	60-60-60	1.17-1.50-1.34	Pennsylvania	M.	60-72-64	1.50-2.40-1.86
Massachusetts	M.	72-72-72	2.50-2.50-2.50	**1864:**			
New Hampshire	M.	60-60-60	1.00-1.00-1.00	Connecticut	M.	60-60-60	1.67-2.50-1.92
New York	M.	60-84-68	1.25-2.00-1.67	Maryland	M.	60-60-60	1.67-2.17-1.92
Pennsylvania	M.	72-72-72	1.34-1.56-1.44	Massachusetts	M.	54-66-62	2.50-3.00-2.67
1854:				New Hampshire	M.	60-60-60	1.25-1.25-1.25
Connecticut	M.	60-60-60	1.06-1.50-1.30	New Jersey	M.	60-60-60	2.00-2.00-2.00
Maryland	M.	60-60-60	1.50-1.50-1.50	New York	M.	60-84-73	1.17-2.93-2.04
Massachusetts	M.	72-72-72	2.50-2.50-2.50	Ohio	M.	70-70-70	2.25-2.25-2.25
New Hampshire	M.	60-60-60	1.00-1.00-1.00	Pennsylvania	M.	60-72-64	1.67-2.64-2.10
New York	M.	60-84-66	1.00-2.00-1.53				
Pennsylvania	M.	72-72-72	1.34-1.56-1.45				

¹ Not reported.

TABLE B-8.—*Engineers, stationary, 1840–1900, by year and State*—Continued

Year and State	Sex	Hours per week	Rate per day (dollars)
1865:			
Connecticut	M.	60–60–60	2.00–2.50–2.25
Maryland	M.	60–60–60	2.17–2.17–2.17
Massachusetts	M.	66–66–66	2.75–3.10–2.93
New Hampshire	M.	60–60–60	1.50–1.50–1.50
New Jersey	M.	60–60–60	2.00–2.17–2.09
New York	M.	60–84–70	1.34–3.32–2.34
Ohio	M.	70–70–70	3.00–3.00–3.00
Pennsylvania	M.	60–72–64	1.67–3.00–2.14
Rhode Island	M.	78–78–78	1.50–1.50–1.50
1866:			
Connecticut	M.	60–60–60	1.75–2.50–2.08
Maryland	M.	60–60–60	2.17–2.17–2.17
Massachusetts	M.	66–66–66	2.75–3.00–2.88
New Hampshire	M.	60–60–60	1.75–1.75–1.75
New Jersey	M.	60–60–60	2.00–2.50–2.33
New York	M.	60–84–70	1.34–3.32–2.43
Ohio	M.	70–70–70	3.00–3.00–3.00
Pennsylvania	M.	60–72–63	1.75–3.00–2.40
Rhode Island	M.	78–78–78	1.75–1.75–1.75
1867:			
Connecticut	M.	60–60–60	2.00–2.50–2.25
Maryland	M.	60–60–60	2.17–2.17–2.17
Massachusetts	M.	66–66–66	3.00–3.00–3.00
New Hampshire	M.	60–60–60	1.75–1.75–1.75
New Jersey	M.	60–60–60	2.50–2.50–2.50
New York	M.	60–84–70	1.34–3.50–2.63
Ohio	M.	70–70–70	3.00–3.00–3.00
Pennsylvania	M.	60–72–63	1.75–3.00–2.42
Rhode Island	M.	78–78–78	1.75–1.75–1.75
1868:			
Connecticut	M.	60–60–60	2.25–2.50–2.42
Maryland	M.	60–60–60	2.17–2.17–2.17
Massachusetts	M.	60–66–64	2.50–3.00–2.83
New Hampshire	M.	60–60–60	1.75–1.75–1.75
New Jersey	M.	60–60–60	2.50–2.50–2.50
New York	M.	60–84–70	1.34–3.50–2.66
Ohio	M.	70–70–70	3.00–3.00–3.00
Pennsylvania	M.	60–72–63	1.75–3.00–2.44
Rhode Island	M.	72–72–72	2.00–2.00–2.00
1869:			
Connecticut	M.	60–60–60	2.50–2.50–2.50
Maryland	M.	60–60–60	2.17–2.17–2.17
Massachusetts	M.	66–66–66	2.50–3.00–2.83
New Hampshire	M.	60–60–60	1.50–2.50–1.85
New Jersey	M.	60–60–60	2.50–2.50–2.50
New York	M.	59–84–69	1.34–3.50–2.66
Ohio	M.	70–70–70	3.00–3.00–3.00
Pennsylvania	M.	60–72–64	2.00–3.00–2.50
Rhode Island	M.	72–72–72	2.25–2.25–2.25
1870:			
Connecticut	M.	60–60–60	2.75–2.75–2.75
Maryland	M.	60–60–60	2.17–2.17–2.17
Massachusetts	M.	66–66–66	2.50–3.00–2.75
New Hampshire	M.	60–60–60	2.00–2.00–2.90
New Jersey	M.	60–60–60	2.50–3.00–2.67
New York	M.	59–84–66	1.34–4.17–2.97
Ohio	M.	70–70–70	3.00–3.00–3.00
Pennsylvania	M.	60–72–64	2.00–3.00–2.50
Rhode Island	M.	72–72–72	2.50–2.50–2.50
1871:			
Connecticut	M.	60–60–60	2.67–3.00–2.84
Maryland	M.	60–60–60	2.17–2.17–2.17
Massachusetts	M.	48–66–60	1.33–3.00–2.49
New Hampshire	M.	60–60–60	2.00–2.00–2.00
New Jersey	M.	60–60–60	2.50–2.50–2.50
New York	M.	59–84–70	1.34–3.84–2.86
Pennsylvania	M.	60–72–64	2.00–2.64–2.35
Rhode Island	M.	72–72–72	2.50–2.50–2.50
1872:			
Connecticut	M.	60–60–60	2.67–4.00–3.25
Maryland	M.	60–60–60	2.17–2.17–2.17
Massachusetts	M.	66–66–66	2.75–3.00–2.92
1872—Continued.			
New Hampshire	M.	60–72–66	1.63–2.00–1.82
New Jersey	M.	60–60–60	2.50–2.50–2.50
New York	M.	59–84–65	1.67–4.15–2.62
Ohio	M.	(¹)	1.80–2.67–2.23
Pennsylvania	(¹)	60–60–60	4.00–4.00–4.00
Rhode Island	M.	72–72–72	2.75–2.75–2.75
1873:			
Connecticut	M.	60–60–60	2.67–3.34–3.00
Maryland	M.	60–60–60	2.17–2.17–2.17
Massachusetts	M.	66–66–66	2.75–3.00–2.92
New Hampshire	M.	60–72–66	1.75–2.00–1.88
New Jersey	M.	60–60–60	2.50–2.50–2.50
New York	M.	60–84–64	2.00–4.15–2.70
Pennsylvania	M.	60–72–64	1.50–3.83–2.52
Rhode Island	M.	72–72–72	2.75–2.75–2.75
1874:			
Alabama	M.	72–72–72	2.00–2.00–2.00
Connecticut	M.	60–60–60	2.67–3.34–3.00
Delaware	M.	60–60–60	2.00–2.00–2.00
Illinois	M.	59–59–59	2.50–2.50–2.50
Maryland	M.	60–60–60	2.17–2.17–2.17
Massachusetts	M.	60–66–63	2.50–3.08–2.73
New Hampshire	M.	60–72–66	1.80–2.00–1.90
New Jersey	M.	60–60–60	2.50–2.50–2.50
New York	M.	60–84–67	2.00–4.15–2.94
Oregon	M.	60–60–60	4.17–4.17–4.17
Pennsylvania	M.	60–72–62	1.10–3.00–1.88
Rhode Island	M.	72–72–72	2.75–2.75–2.75
1875:			
Connecticut	M.	60–60–60	2.50–3.00–2.67
Maryland	M.	60–60–60	2.17–2.17–2.17
Massachusetts	M.	60–60–60	3.00–3.00–3.00
New Hampshire	M.	60–72–66	1.80–2.00–1.90
New Jersey	M.	60–60–60	2.50–2.50–2.50
New York	M.	60–84–71	2.00–4.60–3.21
Pennsylvania	M.	60–72–65	1.35–2.67–2.38
Rhode Island	M.	72–72–72	2.75–2.75–2.75
1876:			
Connecticut	M.	60–60–60	3.00–3.00–3.00
Maryland	M.	60–60–60	2.17–2.17–2.17
Massachusetts	M.	60–60–60	3.00–3.00–3.00
New Hampshire	M.	60–72–66	1.35–2.00–1.65
New Jersey	M.	60–60–60	2.50–2.50–2.50
New York	M.	59–84–70	2.00–4.60–3.09
Pennsylvania	M.	60–72–62	.75–5.00–2.00
Do	M.	(¹)	².18–.18–.18
Rhode Island	M.	72–72–72	2.75–2.75–2.75
South Carolina	M.	66–66–66	2.00–2.00–2.00
1877:			
Connecticut	M.	60–60–60	2.75–2.75–2.75
Maryland	M.	60–60–60	2.17–2.17–2.17
Massachusetts	M.	60–60–60	3.00–3.25–3.08
New Hampshire	M.	72–72–72	1.50–1.50–1.50
New Jersey	M.	60–60–60	2.00–2.00–2.00
New York	M.	59–84–70	2.00–4.60–3.10
Ohio	M.	60–84–79	1.00–5.00–1.97
Pennsylvania	M.	48–72–65	1.35–2.91–2.14
Rhode Island	M.	72–72–72	2.75–2.75–2.75
1878:			
Connecticut	M.	60–72–68	2.50–3.33–2.86
Georgia	M.	66–66–66	3.00–3.00–3.00
Maryland	M.	60–60–60	2.17–2.17–2.17
Massachusetts	M.	60–60–60	3.00–3.25–3.08
New Hampshire	M.	72–72–72	1.50–1.50–1.50
New Jersey	M.	60–60–60	2.00–2.00–2.00
New York	M.	59–84–70	1.84–4.60–3.04
North Carolina	M.	(¹)	1.33–1.33–1.33
Ohio	M.	59–59–59	1.25–3.07–1.87
Pennsylvania	M.	54–72–67	.80–3.50–1.68
Rhode Island	M.	72–72–72	2.75–2.75–2.75

¹ Not reported.   ² Per hour.

TABLE **B-8.**—*Engineers, stationary, 1840–1900, by year and State*—Continued

Year and State	Sex	Hours per week	Rate per day (dollars)	Year and State	Sex	Hours per week	Rate per day (dollars)
1879:				**1884:**			
Connecticut	M.	60-60-60	2.00-2.50-2.25	Connecticut	M.	60-60-60	2.00-2.75-2.38
Maryland	M.	60-60-60	2.17-2.17-2.17	Florida	M.	(1)	2.00-2.00-2.00
Massachusetts	M.	60-60-60	2.29-3.50-2.90	Georgia	M.	66-66-66	1.33-2.75-2.06
Missouri	M.	70-70-70	1.32-1.32-1.32	Indiana	M.	(1)	2.25-2.25-2.25
New Hampshire	M.	60-72-66	1.15-1.60-1.38	Kentucky	M.	54-66-62	2.00-3.33-2.78
New Jersey	M.	60-60-60	2.00-2.00-2.00	Louisiana	M.	63-66-65	3.00-3.50-3.25
New York	M.	59-84-72	.84-4.60-2.55	Maryland	M.	60-60-60	2.00-2.00-2.00
Pennsylvania	M.	54-72-60	.50-3.50-1.73	Massachusetts	M.	60-60-60	2.08-4.00-3.04
Do	M.	(1)	³.77-.77-.77	Michigan	M.	(1)	.85-5.50-2.54
Rhode Island	M.	72-72-72	3.00-3.00-3.00	Missouri	M.	70-70-70	2.50-2.74-2.74
1880:				New Hampshire	M.	60-72-66	1.15-1.65-1.40
Connecticut	M.	60-60-60	2.00-2.50-2.25	New Jersey	M.	54-84-67	1.33-3.67-1.93
Georgia	M.	(1)	2.50-2.50-2.50	New York	M.	59-84-64	1.67-4.60-2.28
Illinois	M.	60-61-60	1.24-2.95-1.94	Ohio	M.	54-59-57	1.00-2.75-1.96
Kentucky	M.	60-60-60	1.50-1.50-1.50	Pennsylvania	M.	54-72-61	1.00-3.33-1.75
Maryland	M.	60-60-60	2.17-2.17-2.17	Rhode Island	M.	60-72-66	2.50-3.00-2.75
Massachusetts	M.	60-60-60	2.00-3.50-2.58	Tennessee	M.	59-66-63	1.33-2.50-1.92
Missouri	M.	(1)	2.00-2.00-2.00	Virginia	M.	55-59-57	1.67-3.33-2.50
New Hampshire	M.	60-72-67	1.15-1.65-1.40	West Virginia	M.	60-60-60	2.50-3.00-2.67
New Jersey	M.	60-60-60	2.00-2.00-2.00	Wisconsin	M.	60-60-60	2.00-2.00-2.00
New York	M.	59-84-65	1.00-4.60-2.48	**1885:**			
Ohio	M.	(1)	2.50-2.50-2.50	Alabama	M.	66-72-71	1.08-3.50-2.08
Pennsylvania	M.	53-72-61	1.75-2.59-2.25	Arkansas	M.	60-60-60	3.00-3.00-3.00
Rhode Island	M.	72-72-72	3.25-3.25-3.25	California	M.	60-72-62	1.40-6.00-4.10
South Carolina	M.	(1)	.83-.83-.83	Connecticut	M.	60-66-61	1.25-3.00-2.20
1881:				Delaware	M.	60-72-69	1.50-2.00-1.82
Connecticut	M.	60-60-60	2.00-2.50-2.25	Georgia	M.	59-69-63	1.33-2.50-1.78
Georgia	M.	66-66-66	2.50-2.50-2.50	Illinois	M.	55-72-68	1.50-4.50-2.57
Kentucky	M.	(1)	1.67-1.67-1.67	Indiana	M.	60-72-62	1.50-3.33-2.13
Maryland	M.	60-60-60	2.17-2.17-2.17	Iowa	M.	60-63-63	1.67-3.00-1.73
Massachusetts	M.	60-60-60	1.92-3.50-2.57	Kentucky	M.	60-66-62	1.50-3.00-2.02
Michigan	M.	60-60-60	2.50-2.50-2.50	Louisiana	M.	55-60-58	2.00-3.00-2.50
New Hampshire	M.	60-72-66	1.15-1.65-1.40	Maine	M.	60-72-69	1.40-2.50-1.92
New Jersey	M.	60-60-60	2.00-2.00-2.00	Maryland	M.	54-72-67	1.45-3.00-1.95
New York	M.	59-84-65	1.34-4.60-2.29	Massachusetts	M.	50-72-61	1.17-4.00-2.34
North Carolina	M.	(1)	.75-.75-.75	Michigan	M.	60-66-65	.85-4.75-2.52
Ohio	M.	55-72-63	1.20-3.68-2.11	Missouri	M.	48-72-58	1.35-5.33-2.27
Pennsylvania	M.	60-72-63	1.75-2.64-2.22	New Hampshire	M.	60-72-64	1.20-3.00-1.72
Rhode Island	M.	66-72-69	3.25-3.25-3.25	New Jersey	M.	42-84-65	1.33-2.50-1.96
1882:				New York	M.	49-84-64	1.25-5.83-2.32
Connecticut	M.	60-66-62	1.50-3.00-2.32	North Carolina	M.	60-69-62	1.00-2.83-2.43
Georgia	M.	72-72-72	1.50-2.00-1.75	Ohio	M.	54-72-66	1.00-3.84-1.85
Kentucky	M.	66-66-63	1.75-2.00-1.88	Oregon	M.	72-72-72	2.25-2.25-2.25
Maine	M.	66-66-66	1.25-1.75-1.50	Pennsylvania	M.	48-72-53	1.08-5.75-1.76
Maryland	M.	60-60-60	2.00-2.00-2.00	Rhode Island	M.	48-72-60	2.50-3.25-2.88
Massachusetts	M.	60-60-60	2.29-3.72-3.01	South Carolina	M.	(1)	1.00-1.00-1.00
Missouri	M.	59-59-59	3.00-3.00-3.00	Tennessee	M.	60-72-69	1.25-2.10-1.68
New Hampshire	M.	60-72-66	1.15-1.65-1.40	Vermont	M.	60-66-61	1.90-4.33-2.53
New Jersey	M.	60-72-67	1.50-3.00-2.11	Virginia	M.	60-72-65	1.13-3.33-1.82
New York	M.	59-84-62	1.34-4.60-2.29	West Virginia	M.	60-66-61	1.25-2.50-1.81
North Carolina	M.	72-72-72	1.50-1.50-1.50	Wisconsin	M.	59-72-62	1.50-5.00-2.45
Ohio	M.	60-60-60	2.00-2.00-2.00	**1886:**			
Do	(1)	54-112-64	.83-4.17-1.99	Connecticut	M.	60-60-60	2.00-2.75-2.38
Pennsylvania	M.	60-72-62	1.75-2.64-2.26	Delaware	M.	72-72-72	2.08-2.08-2.08
Rhode Island	M.	60-72-66	2.25-3.25-2.75	Illinois	M.	48-72-57	2.00-3.33-2.75
South Carolina	M.	61-69-65	.90-2.00-1.63	Indiana	M.	60-60-60	1.92-2.00-1.96
Virginia	M.	60-60-60	1.50-1.50-1.50	Iowa	M.	60-60-60	1.50-2.00-1.86
West Virginia	M.	59-59-59	1.50-2.00-1.75	Kentucky	M.	60-60-60	1.50-1.50-1.50
1883:				Maryland	M.	48-60-57	1.67-2.50-2.05
Alabama	M.	(1)	3.50-3.50-3.50	Massachusetts	M.	60-60-60	2.00-4.25-2.92
Connecticut	M.	60-60-60	2.00-2.75-2.33	Michigan	M.	48-60-59	1.25-4.17-2.21
Georgia	M.	66-69-68	.83-2.75-1.86	Minnesota	M.	60-60-60	2.00-2.00-2.00
Kentucky	M.	(1)	2.00-2.00-2.00	New Hampshire	M.	60-72-66	1.20-1.70-1.45
Maryland	M.	60-60-60	2.00-2.00-2.00	New Jersey	M.	55-72-65	1.33-2.50-1.94
Massachusetts	M.	60-60-60	1.25-5.00-2.50	New York	M.	54-84-61	1.33-4.60-2.34
Mississippi	M.	(1)	2.92-2.92-2.92	Pennsylvania	M.	48-72-60	1.42-4.17-2.43
New Hampshire	M.	60-72-66	1.15-1.65-1.40	Rhode Island	M.	60-60-60	2.00-3.58-2.71
New Jersey	M.	48-75-58	1.33-3.00-2.03	**1887:**			
New York	M.	59-84-64	1.17-4.60-2.24	Connecticut	M.	60-60-60	1.50-4.59-2.52
North Carolina	M.	60-60-60	1.00-1.00-1.00	Delaware	M.	(1)	³.13-.13-.13
Ohio	M.	60-60-60	1.60-3.00-2.31	Florida	M.	(1)	1.00-1.53-1.37
Pennsylvania	M.	60-72-62	1.75-2.64-2.18	Maryland	M.	60-60-60	.77-3.75-1.65
Rhode Island	M.	72-72-72	2.50-2.50-2.50	Massachusetts	M.	60-60-60	1.50-4.25-2.35
Tennessee	M.	66-66-66	3.00-3.00-3.00	Michigan	M.	60-60-60	1.25-2.30-1.81

¹ Not reported.   ² Per hour.   ³ And rent.

TABLE **B-8.**—*Engineers, stationary, 1840–1900, by year and State*—Continued

Year and State	Sex	Hours per week	Rate per day (dollars)	Year and State	Sex	Hours per week	Rate per day (dollars)
1887—Continued.				**1890—Continued.**			
Michigan	M.	(¹)	²0. 20–0. 20–0. 20	Indiana	M.	60–60–60	1. 50–2. 50–2. 41
Missouri	M.	74–74–74	1. 65–2. 68–1. 92	Kentucky	M.	(¹)	3. 00–3. 00–3. 00
New Hampshire	M.	60–60–60	1. 25–1. 70–1. 48	Louisiana	M.	(¹)	4. 00–4. 00–4. 00
New Jersey	M.	60–60–60	. 50–3. 64–1. 94	Maryland	M.	48–84–63	1. 25–2. 67–1. 93
New York	M.	60–84–64	. 38–4. 60–2. 12	Massachusetts	M.	60–60–60	1. 65–4. 25–2. 56
Ohio	M.	54–72–60	1. 25–2. 75–1. 94	Michigan	M.	60–60–60	. 50–3. 75–1. 87
Oregon	M.	(¹)	. 58–2. 88–2. 34	Mississippi	M.	(¹)	3. 19–3. 19–3. 19
Pennsylvania	M.	(¹)	³. 13– . 25–. 17½	Missouri	M.	(¹)	1. 97–1. 97–1. 97
Do	M.	60–72–62	1. 05–3. 25–2. 10	New Hampshire	M.	60–60–60	1. 25–2. 00–1. 63
Rhode Island	M.	60–60–60	1. 50–2. 50–1. 95	New Jersey	M.	60–84–68	1. 20–3. 50–1. 84
Virginia	M.	(¹)	1. 34–1. 34–1. 34	New York	M.	54–84–63	. 67–7. 33–2. 26
Wisconsin	M.	(¹)	1. 50–3. 07–2. 08	Do	M.	(¹)	³1. 13–1. 13–1. 13
1888:				North Carolina	M.	(¹)	1. 00–2. 50–1. 72
California	M.	61–61–61	3. 75–5. 00–4. 38	Ohio	M.	60–84–74	1. 00–2. 20–1. 77
Colorado	M.	(¹)	1. 73–2. 09–1. 92	Do	(¹)	42–84–61	1. 17–5. 00–2. 13
Connecticut	M.	60–60–60	2. 00–3. 25–2. 63	Pennsylvania	M.	54–84–65	1. 00–3. 24–2. 13
Delaware	M.	(¹)	1. 83–1. 83–1. 83	Rhode Island	M.	60–60–60	2. 38–2. 75–2. 57
Illinois	M.	60–84–67	1. 63–3. 25–2. 35	Tennessee	M.	(¹)	3. 00–3. 07–3. 04
Indiana	M.	(¹)	2. 13–2. 13–2. 13	Wisconsin	M.	55–84–77	2. 35–3. 25–2. 69
Kansas	M.	60–72–67	1. 25–4. 17–2. 08	**1891:**			
Maryland	M.	60–60–60	2. 00–2. 00–2. 00	Connecticut	M.	60–60–60	2. 25–3. 00–2. 67
Massachusetts	M.	60–60–60	1. 65–4. 25–2. 65	Florida	M.	60–60–60	1. 92–4. 79–2. 80
Michigan	M.	48–78–61	. 80–3. 83–2. 15	Illinois	(¹)	72–84–78	2. 68–3. 00–2. 84
New Hampshire	M.	60–60–60	1. 25–1. 75–1. 50	Kansas	M.	60–60–60	1. 60–2. 50–2. 11
New Jersey	M.	60–60–60	1. 50–3. 50–2. 30	Maine	M.	60–72–66	1. 67–2. 50–2. 01
New York	M.	48–84–63	1. 00–5. 00–2. 45	Maryland	M.	60–60–60	2. 00–2. 00–2. 00
Do	M.	(¹)	⁴2. 00–2. 00–2. 00	Massachusetts	M.	60–60–60	1. 65–4. 25–2. 52
Do	M.	58–58–58	⁵1. 83–1. 83–1. 83	Michigan	M.	60–60–60	3. 00–3. 00–3. 00
Do	M.	60–60–60	⁶1. 83–1. 83–1. 83	Minnesota	M.	60–60–60	2. 00–3. 00–2. 50
Do	M.	(¹)	⁶2. 00–2. 00–2. 00	Missouri	M.	(¹)	1. 50–4. 09–2. 25
North Carolina	M.	(¹)	3. 00–3. 00–3. 00	New Hampshire	M.	60–60–60	1. 25–1. 75–1. 50
Ohio	M.	54–84–65	1. 75–3. 07–2. 59	New Jersey	M.	60–60–60	2. 00–2. 08–2. 04
Pennsylvania	M.	60–84–77	1. 05–5. 00–2. 36	New York	M.	(¹)	³1. 13–1. 13–1. 13
Rhode Island	M.	60–60–60	1. 67–3. 33–2. 44	Do	M.	54–84–63	. 67–7. 33–2. 26
South Carolina	M.	66–66–66	1. 50–1. 50–1. 50	Ohio	M.	48–84–62	. 75–5. 00–2. 10
Tennessee	M.	(¹)	1. 40–2. 00–1. 79	Pennsylvania	M.	60–72–62	2. 00–3. 24–2. 54
Virginia	M.	60–84–78	1. 00–2. 30–1. 64	Rhode Island	M.	60–60–60	2. 75–2. 75–2. 75
West Virginia	M.	60–72–67	1. 50–2. 66–2. 10	South Carolina	M.	60–60–60	1. 50–3. 20–2. 15
1889:				Wisconsin	M.	60–60–60	3. 00–3. 00–3. 00
Alabama	M.	48–84–67	1. 10–3. 48–2. 13	Do	M.	(¹)	⁴3. 51–3. 51–3. 51
California	M.	(¹)	3. 00–4. 84–3. 92	**1892:**			
Colorado	(¹)	(¹)	2. 50–2. 50–2. 50	California	M.	54–66–59	1. 34–5. 50–3. 22
Connecticut	M.	60–60–60	1. 84–3. 25–2. 47	Connecticut	M.	60–60–60	2. 00–3. 00–2. 42
Delaware	M.	60–60–60	2. 25–2. 25–2. 25	Florida	M.	54–66–61	1. 00–4. 00–1. 93
Georgia	M.	66–84–78	1. 50–5. 00–2. 22	Indiana	M.	48–72–61	1. 25–3. 00–1. 84
Illinois	M.	60–72–65	1. 50–4. 41–2. 24	Iowa	M.	60–72–68	1. 45–1. 92–1. 67
Indiana	M.	60–72–63	1. 53–3. 00–2. 03	Kansas	M.	60–60–60	2. 11–2. 11–2. 11
Do	(¹)	(¹)	3. 50–3. 50–3. 50	Maine	M.	60–60–60	2. 30–2. 30–2. 30
Kansas	(¹)	(¹)	1. 50–1. 50–1. 50	Maryland	M.	54–72–61	1. 75–4. 80–2. 53
Do	M.	54–90–65	1. 00–3. 50–2. 04	Massachusetts	M.	60–60–60	2. 00–2. 00–2. 00
Maine	M.	60–60–60	2. 00–2. 50–2. 25	Michigan	M.	60–60–60	3. 00–3. 00–3. 00
Maryland	M.	60–72–62	1. 38–2. 50–2. 15	Minnesota	M.	60–60–60	2. 00–3. 00–2. 50
Massachusetts	M.	60–84–61	1. 65–4. 25–2. 61	New Hampshire	M.	60–60–60	1. 25–1. 25–1. 25
Michigan	M.	60–84–61	. 67–3. 83–1. 97	New Jersey	M.	60–60–60	2. 25–2. 25–2. 25
Minnesota	M.	60–60–60	2. 05–2. 31–2. 16	New York	M.	60–77–63	2. 00–4. 60–2. 72
Mississippi	M.	(¹)	1. 25–1. 25–1. 25	Ohio	M.	84–84–84	2. 00–2. 50–2. 39
Missouri	M.	72–72–72	1. 00–3. 00–1. 75	Do	(¹)	48–72–65	. 90–3. 83–2. 04
Do	(¹)	(¹)	1. 04–3. 00–1. 77	Do	(¹)	(¹)	⁷. 20– . 20– . 20
New Hampshire	M.	60–60–60	1. 25–3. 00–2. 33	Pennsylvania	M.	60–60–60	2. 00–2. 67–2. 41
New Jersey	M.	60–72–66	1. 53–2. 83–2. 02	Rhode Island	M.	53–60–57	1. 75–3. 00–2. 14
New York	M.	59–84–65	1. 30–4. 60–2. 00	South Carolina	M.	60–60–60	1. 60–3. 45–2. 74
Do	M.	(¹)	3. 25–3. 25–3. 25	Wisconsin	M.	60–60–60	3. 00–3. 00–3. 00
North Carolina	M.	(¹)	1. 50–1. 50–1. 50	**1893:**			
Ohio	M.	(¹)	1. 35–4. 00–2. 12	Illinois	M.	60–84–72	1. 67–3. 00–2. 34
Pennsylvania	M.	45–84–67	1. 20–4. 00–2. 16	Maryland	M.	72–72–72	1. 67–1. 67–1. 67
Rhode Island	M.	60–60–60	2. 50–2. 91–2. 72	Massachusetts	M.	60–63–61	1. 75–3. 30–2. 31
Tennessee	M.	60–60–60	1. 00–4. 79–2. 12	Michigan	M.	57–81–64	1. 50–3. 00–1. 94
Virginia	M.	60–84–74	1. 25–2. 75–2. 05	Minnesota	M.	60–60–60	2. 00–3. 00–2. 50
West Virginia	M.	49–84–66	1. 05–3. 15–2. 24	Montana	(¹)	60–60–60	3. 00–3. 69–3. 52
Wisconsin	M.	60–60–60	1. 50–2. 50–1. 90	Do	(¹)	(¹)	⁷2. 27–2. 27–2. 27
1890:				New Jersey	M.	84–84–84	1. 60–1. 60–1. 60
Alabama	M.	60–84–70	1. 50–3. 67–2. 41	New York	M.	60–66–63	2. 20–2. 31–2. 26
California	M.	(¹)	2. 50–2. 50–2. 50	North Carolina	M.	(¹)	. 50– . 50– . 50
Connecticut	M.	60–60–60	2. 00–3. 33–2. 73	Ohio	M.	48–78–62	. 83–5. 00–2. 13
Illinois	M.	60–84–68	1. 75–2. 50–2. 12				

¹ Not reported.
² Per hour.
³ And rent.
⁴ And board.

⁵ And rent and fuel.
⁶ And a percentage.
⁷ And board and lodging.

TABLE **B-8.**—*Engineers, stationary, 1840–1900, by year and State*—Continued

Year and State	Sex	Lowest, highest, and average—		Year and State	Sex	Lowest, highest, and average—	
		Hours per week	Rate per day (dollars)			Hours per week	Rate per day (dollars)
1893—Continued.				**1896—Continued.**			
Pennsylvania	M.	60-60-60	2.00-2.67-2.35	Iowa	M.	48-60-59	1.50-2.67-2.11
Rhode Island	M.	(1)	3.00-3.00-3.00	Kentucky	M.	54-63-60	1.50-3.33-2.11
Wisconsin	M.	60-60-60	2.08-3.00-2.54	Maine	M.	53-53-53	2.00-2.00-2.00
1894:				Maryland	M.	48-70-60	1.33-3.50-2.19
Connecticut	M.	60-60-60	2.75-2.75-2.75	Massachusetts	M.	48-84-63	1.75-4.00-2.61
Dist. of Columbia	M.	54-60-58	2.35-2.67-2.51	Michigan	M.	54-72-60	1.22-4.17-2.05
Georgia	M.	60-72-62	.75-2.75-1.85	Minnesota	M.	60-60-60	2.10-2.10-2.10
Indiana	M.	48-72-60	.88-3.25-2.08	Do	M.	54-60-59	[4]2.25-3.83-2.96
Maine	M.	54-60-59	1.50-2.50-1.94	Missouri	M.	48-72-60	.75-4.50-2.32
Maryland	M.	60-72-68	2.00-2.50-2.08	Montana	M.	(1)	2.59-2.59-2.59
Massachusetts	M.	54-72-60	1.50-3.30-2.38	Nebraska	M.	48-72-62	.77-5.00-2.08
Michigan	M.	60-60-60	2.70-2.70-2.70	New Hampshire	M.	60-60-60	2.50-2.75-2.63
Minnesota	M.	60-60-60	2.00-2.56-2.35	New Jersey	M.	56-60-60	2.00-4.00-3.13
Montana	M.	(1)	3.37-3.50-3.43	New York	M.	48-84-63	1.25-5.00-2.62
New Hampshire	M.	53-53-53	1.75-2.75-2.33	North Carolina	M.	54-69-67	.70-1.50-1.04
New York	M.	60-72-60	1.00-3.33-2.00	Ohio	M.	48-72-61	1.00-4.50-2.12
North Carolina	M.	60-72-63	.75-3.00-1.20	Pennsylvania	M.	47-72-59	1.28-4.17-2.31
Ohio	M.	23-84-61	.50-5.00-2.04	Rhode Island	M.	60-60-60	1.92-4.00-3.09
Pennsylvania	M.	60-60-60	2.00-2.67-2.24	South Carolina	M.	66-66-66	.90-3.50-1.97
Rhode Island	M.	(1)	2.70-2.70-2.70	Vermont	M.	60-64-62	2.00-2.50-2.25
West Virginia	M.	60-72-66	1.25-2.75-2.00	West Virginia	M.	55-60-59	1.25-3.13-2.23
Wisconsin	M.	60-60-60	3.00-3.00-3.00	Wisconsin	M.	48-72-61	1.50-5.83-2.48
1895:				**1897:**			
Alabama	M.	60-66-64	2.25-3.50-3.08	Connecticut	M.	58-60-60	2.50-4.00-3.46
Connecticut	M.	59-72-61	1.50-3.25-2.51	Georgia	M.	66-66-66	4.16-4.16-4.16
Florida	M.	63-63-63	1.00-1.00-1.00	Illinois	M.	60-60-60	2.67-3.50-3.00
Georgia	M.	51-66-64	1.00-3.00-1.94	Kansas	M.	28-98-74	.82-2.49-1.43
Illinois	M.	54-60-57	2.67-3.83-2.79	Maine	M.	54-60-59	2.00-2.50-2.25
Iowa	M.	54-60-57	2.00-2.00-2.00	Massachusetts	M.	60-63-60	2.03-3.50-2.68
Louisiana	M.	55-63-59	2.00-4.00-3.19	Michigan	M.	60-60-60	1.97-2.25-1.97
Maine	M.	54-60-60	1.50-3.00-2.01	Montana	(1)	(1)	2.41-2.76-2.61
Maryland	M.	54-90-62	1.50-3.00-2.12	Nebraska	M.	48-72-61	1.00-4.00-1.79
Massachusetts	M.	48-72-59	1.50-4.17-2.52	New York	M.	54-72-70	1.50-6.00-3.00
Michigan	M.	60-60-60	2.70-2.70-2.70	North Carolina	M.	66-75-69	.65-.90-.73
Minnesota	M.	60-60-60	2.00-2.56-2.35	Ohio	M.	54-72-66	.75-4.00-2.03
Mississippi	M.	60-60-60	2.92-2.92-2.92	Pennsylvania	M.	48-60-56	1.35-3.00-2.20
Missouri	M.	59-60-60	1.51-4.85-2.89	Vermont	M.	72-72-72	2.50-2.50-2.50
Montana	M.	(1)	1.53-2.25-1.86	Virginia	M.	48-72-63	.62-3.33-1.59
New Hampshire	M.	60-66-61	1.25-3.00-1.77	**1898:**			
New Jersey	M.	48-60-58	1.67-8.00-2.50	Iowa	(1)	(1)	2.50-2.50-2.50
New York	M.	48-66-59	1.25-5.00-2.52	Missouri	(1)	72-72-72	2.47-3.00-2.60
North Carolina	M.	54-72-64	.30-2.60-1.08	Nebraska	(1)	60-66-61	1.00-4.60-1.85
Ohio	M.	45-84-63	.75-4.80-2.09	New Jersey	M.	60-72-66	1.50-3.00-1.83
Pennsylvania	M.	42-60-59	1.25-3.50-2.54	New York	M.	60-60-60	1.50-7.50-3.17
Rhode Island	M.	55-66-59	1.67-4.17-2.64	Ohio	M.	(1)	1.25-2.80-1.92
South Carolina	M.	54-66-64	.83-2.08-1.39	Pennsylvania	M.	(1)	1.50-3.75-2.06
Tennessee	M.	59-67-65	1.00-3.33-2.13	Washington	(1)	(1)	1.73-3.00-2.35
Vermont	M.	60-72-66	1.25-2.50-1.88	**1899:**			
Virginia	M.	54-72-63	1.15-3.67-2.17	Massachusetts	M.	48-48-48	3.00-3.00-3.00
West Virginia	M.	59-60-60	2.00-2.33-2.17	Michigan	M.	(1)	1.83-2.25-2.01
Wisconsin	M.	60-60-60	2.00-3.00-2.33	New York	M.	53-59-56	2.50-3.00-2.63
Do	(1)	48-90-65	1.50-5.00-2.39	North Carolina	M.	59-90-66	1.00-3.00-1.50
1896:				Ohio	M.	(1)	1.38-3.45-2.16
Alabama	M.	63-63-63	1.10-1.10-1.10	Pennsylvania	M.	84-84-84	1.60-3.25-2.24
California	M.	48-60-59	1.25-3.00-2.19	Tennessee	M.	(1)	1.50-2.00-1.90
Colorado	M.	48-72-54	1.53-3.50-2.98	Virginia	(1)	(1)	1.50-3.00-2.20
Connecticut	M.	60-60-60	2.00-4.00-2.80	**1900:** [8]			
Delaware	M.	72-72-72	2.25-2.25-2.25	Alabama	M.	63-63-63	1.25-1.25-1.50
Florida	M.	60-60-60	1.00-2.50-1.67	Massachusetts	M.	48-48-48	3.00-3.00-3.20
Georgia	M.	60-72-63	.75-3.50-1.68	New York	M.	53-59-56	2.50-3.00-2.03
Illinois	M.	51-60-58	2.00-5.00-2.66	North Carolina	M.	59-69-65	1.00-3.00-1.61
Indiana	M.	60-65-62	1.75-2.50-2.16	Ohio	(1)	(1)	2.50-2.50-2.65

[1] Not reported.   [4] And board.   [8] No available wage data after 1900.

TABLE **B-9.**—*Firemen, stationary, 1840–1900, by year and State*

| Year and State | Sex | Lowest, highest, and average— | | Year and State | Sex | Lowest, highest, and average— | |
		Hours per week	Rate per day (dollars)			Hours per week	Rate per day (dollars)
1840:				**1868:**			
Massachusetts	M.	84-84-84	1.25-1.25-1.25	Connecticut	M.	66-66-66	1.50-1.50-1.50
New York	M.	72-72-72	.75-.75-.75	Massachusetts	M.	66-66-66	1.45-2.00-1.64
1841:				New York	M.	66-66-66	1.75-1.75-1.75
Massachusetts	M.	84-84-84	1.25-1.25-1.25	**1869:**			
1842:				Connecticut	M.	66-66-66	1.25-1.50-1.38
Massachusetts	M.	84-84-84	1.25-1.25-1.25	Massachusetts	M.	66-66-66	1.45-2.00-1.67
1843:				New Hampshire	M.	(¹)	1.75-1.75-1.75
Massachusetts	M.	84-84-84	1.25-1.30-1.28	New York	M.	66-66-66	1.75-1.75-1.75
1844:				**1870:**			
Massachusetts	M.	84-84-84	1.25-1.30-1.28	Connecticut	M.	66-66-66	1.50-1.50-1.50
1845:				Massachusetts	M.	66-66-66	1.40-2.00-1.73
Massachusetts	M.	84-84-84	1.25-1.30-1.28	New Jersey	M.	60-60-60	2.00-2.00-2.00
1846:				New York	M.	66-66-62	1.75-2.50 2.25
Massachusetts	M.	84-84-84	1.30-1.35-1.33	**1871:**			
1847:				Connecticut	M.	66-66-66	1.50-1.60-1.55
Massachusetts	M.	84-84-84	1.35-1.35-1.35	Massachusetts	M.	59-70-63	1.45-2.00-1.86
1848:				New York	M.	66-66-66	1.75-1.75-1.75
Massachusetts	M.	84-84-84	1.25-1.35-1.30	**1872:**			
1849:				Connecticut	M.	60-66-64	1.60-2.00-1.74
Massachusetts	M.	84-84-84	1.25-1.35-1.32	Massachusetts	M.	66-66-66	1.45-2.00-1.61
1850:				New York	M.	66-66-66	1.75-1.75-1.75
Massachusetts	M.	84-84-84	1.35-1.35-1.35	South Carolina	M.	72-72-72	1.25-1.25-1.25
1851:				**1873:**			
Massachusetts	M.	84-84-84	1.35-1.35-1.35	Connecticut	M.	66-66-66	1.75-1.75-1.75
1852:				Massachusetts	M.	66-66-66	1.50-1.75-1.67
Massachusetts	M.	72-72-72	1.35-1.40-1.38	New York	M.	60-66-62	1.38-1.75-1.50
1853:				**1874:**			
Massachusetts	M.	72-72-72	1.40-1.50-1.45	Alabama	M.	72-72-72	1.50-1.50-1.50
New York	M.	72-72-72	.84-.84-.84	Connecticut	M.	66-66-66	1.75-2.00-1.88
1854:				Massachusetts	M.	66-66-66	1.67-1.75-1.72
Massachusetts	M.	72-72-72	1.42-1.45-1.44	New York	M.	66-66-66	1.50-1.50-1.50
New York	M.	72-72-72	.84-.84-.84	Pennsylvania	M.	(¹)	1.40-1.90-1.66
1855:				**1875:**			
Massachusetts	M.	72-72-72	1.45-1.50-1.48	Connecticut	M.	66-66-66	1.75-1.75-1.75
New York	M.	60-72-62	1.00-1.00-1.00	Massachusetts	M.	60-60-60	1.50-1.75-1.60
1856:				New York	M.	66-66-66	1.63-1.63-1.63
Massachusetts	M.	72-72-72	1.00-1.50-1.32	Pennsylvania	M.	(¹)	1.50-2.25-1.88
New York	M.	72-72-72	1.00-1.00-1.00	**1876:**			
1857:				Connecticut	M.	66-66-66	1.75-1.80-1.78
Massachusetts	M.	72-72-72	1.00-1.50-1.32	Massachusetts	M.	60-60-60	1.35-1.75-1.57
New York	M.	72-72-72	1.00-1.00-1.00	New Hampshire	M.	66-66-66	1.35-1.50-1.40
1858:				New York	M.	66-66-66	1.42-1.42-1.42
Massachusetts	M.	72-72-72	1.17-1.50-1.36	Pennsylvania	M.	(¹)	.85-2.90-1.62
New York	M.	72-72-72	.75-.75-.75	South Carolina	M.	66-66-66	1.00-1.00-1.00
1859:				**1877:**			
Massachusetts	M.	72-72-72	1.17-1.50-1.41	Connecticut	M.	66-66-66	1.80-1.80-1.80
New York	M.	72-72-72	.75-.75-.75	Georgia	M.	66-66-66	1.50-1.50-1.50
1860:				Massachusetts	M.	60-60-60	1.20-1.75-1.51
Massachusetts	M.	60-72-70	1.00-1.50-1.33	New York	M.	66-66-66	1.27-1.27-1.27
New York	M.	72-72-72	.75-.75-.75	Ohio	M.	84-84-84	1.00-1.92-1.40
1861:				Pennsylvania	M.	60-72-64	1.38-2.21-1.81
Massachusetts	M.	66-66-66	1.25-1.50-1.38	**1878:**			
New York	M	72-72-72	.75-.75-.75	Connecticut	M.	66-72-71	1.80-2.25-2.14
1862:				Georgia	M.	66-66-66	1.00-1.00-1.00
Massachusetts	M.	66-66-66	1.25-1.50-1.41	Massachusetts	M.	60-60-60	1.20-1.75-1.49
New York	M.	72-72-72	.75-.75-.75	New York	M.	66-66-66	1.27-1.27-1.27
1863:				Ohio	M.	(¹)	2.30-2.30-2.30
Massachusetts	M.	66-66-66	1.25-1.67-1.48	Pennsylvania	M.	54-84-68	.45-2.00-1.25
1864:				Virginia	M.	72-72-72	1.00-1.00-1.00
Connecticut	M.	72-72-72	1.25-1.25-1.25	**1879:**			
Massachusetts	M.	66-66-66	1.35-1.50-1.46	Connecticut	M.	66-66-66	1.80-1.80-1.80
1865:				Massachusetts	M.	60-60-60	1.20-1.60-1.36
Massachusetts	M.	66-66-66	1.40-1.75 1.51	Missouri	M.	60-60-60	1.19-1.19-1.19
New York	M.	60-72-62	1.50-2.00-1.58	New York	M.	66-66-66	1.27-1.27-1.27
1866:				Pennsylvania	M.	(¹)	.44-2.50-1.39
Connecticut	M.	66-66-66	1.50-1.50-1.50	Do	M.	(¹)	².75-.75-.75
Massachusetts	M.	66-66-66	1.50-1.83-1.58	**1880:**			
New York	M.	72-72-72	2.00-2.00-2.00	Massachusetts	M.	60-60-60	1.10-1.60-1.37
1867:				New Hampshire	M.	69-69-69	1.27-2.50-2.09
Connecticut	M.	66-66-66	1.75-1.75-1.75	New York	M.	59-66-61	1.25-1.67-1.47
Massachusetts	M.	66-66-66	1.50-2.00-1.67	Pennsylvania	M.	60-60-60	1.25-1.67-1.47
New York	M.	72-72-72	2.00-2.00-2.00	Rhode Island	M.	72-72-72	1.25-1.45-1.35
				Virginia	M.	68-68-68	1.25-1.25-1.25

¹ Not reported.　　² And board.

TABLE **B-9.**—*Firemen, stationary, 1840–1900, by year and State*—Continued

Year and State	Sex	Lowest, highest, and average— Hours per week	Lowest, highest, and average— Rate per day (dollars)
1881:			
Connecticut	M.	66–66–66	1.25–1.80–1.58
Georgia	M.	66–66–66	1.00–1.00–1.00
Massachusetts	M.	60–60–60	1.25–1.60–1.42
New Hampshire	M.	65–65–65	1.25–2.00–1.45
New Jersey	M.	72–72–72	1.68–1.68–1.68
New York	M.	66–66–66	1.40–1.40–1.40
North Carolina	M.	(1)	.60–.60–.60
Ohio	M.	60–72–69	1.25–2.00–1.55
Rhode Island	M.	72–72–72	1.25–1.45–1.32
1882:			
Connecticut	M.	66–66–66	1.25–1.75–1.46
Georgia	M.	70–70–70	.75–.75–.75
Maine	M.	(1)	1.50–1.50–1.50
Massachusetts	M.	60–60–60	1.20–1.60–1.39
Missouri	M.	59–59–59	1.75–1.75–1.75
New Hampshire	M.	66–66–66	1.50–1.50–1.50
New Jersey	M.	48–72–55	1.50–2.50–2.15
New York	M.	66–66–66	1.25–1.25–1.25
North Carolina	M.	72–72–72	1.00–1.00–1.00
Ohio	M.	57–72–65	.50–2.50–1.46
Rhode Island	M.	72–72–72	1.25–1.45–1.35
South Carolina	M.	61–69–65	1.00–1.25–1.08
Virginia	M.	(1)	1.25–1.50–1.38
West Virginia	M.	59–59–59	1.40–1.40–1.40
1883:			
Alabama	M.	(1)	1.17–1.17–1.17
Connecticut	M.	60–66–64	1.25–2.00–1.70
Georgia	M.	69–69–69	.75–1.60–1.26
Kentucky	M.	(1)	1.00–1.00–1.00
Massachusetts	M.	60–60–60	1.00–2.08–1.50
Michigan	M.	(1)	1.25–2.58–1.85
Mississippi	M.	(1)	1.33–1.33–1.33
New Jersey	M.	54–72–64	1.25–3.33–1.74
New York	M.	66–66–66	1.25–1.25–1.25
Pennsylvania	M.	(1)	1.50–1.50–1.50
Rhode Island	M.	72–72–72	1.25–1.60–1.43
Tennessee	M.	65–66–66	1.00–1.17–1.09
1884:			
Connecticut	M.	60–66–64	1.25–1.75–1.50
Georgia	M.	66–70–67	1.00–1.25–1.07
Indiana	M.	(1)	.90–2.00–1.48
Iowa	M.	63–63–63	1.37–1.37–1.37
Kentucky	M.	66–66–66	1.75–2.00–1.88
Louisiana	M.	63–66–64	1.67–2.25–1.89
Massachusetts	M.	60–60–60	1.20–1.60–1.48
Michigan	M.	(1)	1.00–4.50–1.76
New Jersey	M.	60–70–61	1.33–2.04–1.70
New York	M.	66–66–66	1.25–1.25–1.25
Ohio	M.	54–54–54	3.00–3.33–3.17
Pennsylvania	M.	(1)	1.48–1.48–1.48
Rhode Island	M.	72–72–68	1.37–1.60–1.49
South Carolina	M.	69–69–69	.83–.83–.83
West Virginia	M.	60–60–60	1.50–1.67–1.59
1885:			
Alabama	M.	66–84–82	.75–1.50–1.21
Arkansas	M.	60–60–60	1.75–1.75–1.75
California	M.	60–72–62	1.00–2.50–1.52
Connecticut	M.	60–69–64	1.25–2.10–1.76
Delaware	M.	60–60–60	1.16–1.25–1.21
Georgia	M.	69–69–69	.65–.85–.75
Illinois	M.	60–72–69	1.50–2.33–1.86
Indiana	M.	60–66–61	1.20–1.63–1.49
Kentucky	M.	60–66–62	1.50–1.65–1.54
Louisiana	M.	55–55–55	2.00–2.00–2.00
Maine	M.	60–72–67	1.15–2.50–1.86
Maryland	M.	60–84–75	1.25–2.14–1.86
Massachusetts	M.	59–60–60	1.00–2.25–1.54
Michigan	M.	60–66–65	1.15–2.75–1.64
Minnesota	M.	(1)	1.75–1.75–1.75
Missouri	M.	60–72–69	1.50–2.85–2.11
New Hampshire	M.	60–66–61	1.35–1.80–1.56
New Jersey	M.	55–72–62	.75–1.83–1.31
New York	M.	60–72–66	1.10–3.00–1.54
North Carolina	M.	60–69–62	.75–1.00–.90
Ohio	M.	58–84–68	1.00–2.33–1.31
1885—Continued.			
Pennsylvania	M.	60–84–63	1.45–1.92–1.64
Rhode Island	M.	72–72–72	1.25–1.60–1.43
Tennessee	M.	66–67–67	1.00–1.00–1.00
Vermont	M.	66–66–66	1.40–1.50–1.43
Virginia	M.	60–84–71	1.00–1.50–1.22
West Virginia	M.	60–60–60	1.25–1.25–1.25
Wisconsin	M.	60–72–63	1.67–2.00–1.77
1886:			
Alabama	M.	60–60–60	.60–.60–.60
Connecticut	M.	66–66–66	1.62–1.62–1.62
Delaware	M.	72–72–72	1.67–1.67–1.67
Illinois	M.	54–60–56	1.50–2.33–1.98
Kansas	M.	(1)	2.17–2.17–2.17
Massachusetts	M.	60–60–60	1.25–1.60–1.48
Michigan	M.	60–60–60	1.00–1.50–1.39
New Hampshire	M.	60–60–60	1.25–1.33–1.26
New Jersey	M.	60–72–63	.83–1.67–1.44
New York	M.	54–66–57	1.00–2.00–1.63
Pennsylvania	M.	57–64–60	1.25–2.25–1.66
Rhode Island	M.	60–60–60	1.25–1.75–1.47
1887:			
Connecticut	M.	60–60–60	1.50–2.50–1.77
Maryland	M.	(1)	1.10–2.50–1.53
Massachusetts	M.	60–60–60	1.00–2.00–1.53
Michigan	M.	60–60–60	.77–1.75–1.33
Missouri	M.	(1)	1.75–1.75–1.75
Nebraska	(1)	54–60–55	1.35–2.37–1.84
New Jersey	M.	(1)	1.15–2.11–1.93
New York	M.	58–60–59	1.04–3.50–2.42
Ohio	M.	54–60–57	1.25–3.00–1.57
Oregon	M.	(1)	2.49–2.49–2.49
Pennsylvania	M.	(1)	[3].12–.20–.14
Rhode Island	M.	72–72–72	1.40–2.10–1.53
Wisconsin	M.	60–60–60	1.25–1.50–1.36
1888:			
California	M.	61–61–61	2.31–2.50–2.41
Connecticut	M.	60–60–60	1.50–1.75–1.59
Delaware	M.	(1)	1.17–1.17–1.17
Georgia	M.	66–66–66	1.25–1.50–1.38
Illinois	M.	60–60–60	.80–2.29–1.64
Indiana	M.	(1)	1.63–1.63–1.63
Kansas	M.	(1)	1.75–1.75–1.75
Massachusetts	M.	60–60–60	1.00–2.00–1.43
Michigan	M.	36–78–58	.58–2.15–1.97
Missouri	M.	(1)	1.50–1.50–1.50
New Jersey	M.	(1)	1.50–4.50–2.67
New York	M.	(1)	[3].12½–.12½–.12½
Do.	M.	48–72–65	.67–3.33–1.89
North Carolina	M.	(1)	1.25–1.25–1.25
Ohio	M.	54–72–63	1.73–2.00–1.85
Rhode Island	M.	60–60–60	1.25–1.67–1.48
South Carolina	M.	66–66–66	.75–1.25–.95
Tennessee	M.	(1)	1.00–1.50–1.23
Virginia	M.	72–72–72	1.00–1.56–1.30
West Virginia	M.	66–66–66	1.86–1.86–1.86
1889:			
Alabama	M.	48–90–64	1.10–1.80–1.42
California	M.	(1)	1.75–2.50–2.13
Connecticut	M.	60–60–60	1.00–2.00–1.53
Georgia	M.	66–84–75	1.00–1.50–1.19
Illinois	M.	60–72–68	.55–2.35–1.63
Indiana	M.	60–72–62	1.50–2.00–1.70
Kansas	M.	54–72–61	1.25–1.83–1.50
Maine	M.	60–70–63	1.27–1.75–1.55
Maryland	M.	60–60–60	1.00–1.65–1.42
Massachusetts	M.	60–60–60	1.25–2.00–1.67
Michigan	M.	56–70–61	.83–2.25–1.67
Minnesota	M.	60–60–60	1.75–1.95–1.89
Mississippi	M.	(1)	1.25–1.25–1.25
Missouri	M.	(1)	1.50–2.17–1.73
Do.	(1)		1.19–1.64–1.37
New Hampshire	M.	60–72–70	1.50–2.17–1.62
New Jersey	M.	60–60–60	1.50–1.50–1.50
New York	M.	60–72–66	1.25–2.10–1.74

[1] Not reported.   [3] Per hour.

TABLE B-9.—*Firemen, stationary, 1840-1900, by year and State*—Continued

Year and State	Sex	Hours per week	Rate per day (dollars)
1889—Continued.			
North Carolina___	M.	(1)	1.00-1.00-1.00
Ohio___	M.	50-84-67	1.13-2.25-1.56
Pennsylvania___	M.	55-84-63	1.25-2.50-1.69
Rhode Island___	M.	60-60-60	1.25-1.60-1.42
South Carolina___	M.	69-69-69	.75-.75-.75
Tennessee___	M.	60-72-66	1.00-2.00-1.33
Virginia___	M.	60-84-72	1.00-1.75-1.64
West Virginia___	M.	60-70-66	1.25-2.25-1.83
Wisconsin___	M.	60-60-60	1.50-2.00-1.78
1890:			
Alabama___	M.	60-60-60	.50-1.50-1.03
Connecticut___	M.	60-87-78	1.50-2.00-1.81
Kentucky___	M.	(1)	1.00-1.25-1.13
Louisiana___	M.	(1)	2.00-2.00-2.00
Maine___	M.	70-70-70	1.25-1.50-1.33
Massachusetts___	M.	60-60-60	1.00-2.00-1.48
Michigan___	M.	60-60-60	.67-2.05-1.54
Mississippi___	M.	(1)	1.00-1.50-1.25
New Hampshire__	M.	60-60-60	1.50-1.50-1.50
New Jersey___	M.	60-60-60	1.00-1.75-1.47
New York___	M.	45-63-55	1.00-5.00-1.83
Do___	M.	(1)	[4]1.13-1.13-1.13
North Carolina___	M.	(1)	.50-1.25-.99
Ohio___	(1)		.75-3.00-1.64
Pennsylvania___	M.	60-60-60	1.58-1.83-1.70
Rhode Island___	M.	60-60-60	1.25-1.63-1.46
Tennessee___	M.	69-69-69	.75-1.50-1.14
Wisconsin___	M.	84-84-84	1.50-1.50-1.50
1891:			
Connecticut___	M.	60-60-60	1.50-1.50-1.50
Florida___	M.	60-60-60	1.50-1.50-1.50
Kansas___	M.	60-60-60	2.00-2.00-2.00
Maine___	M.	60-72-69	1.50-2.00-1.74
Massachusetts___	M.	60-60-60	1.25-2.25-1.63
Michigan___	M.	60-60-60	1.88-1.88-1.88
Minnesota___	M.	60-60-60	1.75-2.00-1.88
Missouri___	M.	(1)	1.24-2.84-2.28
New York___	M.	60-60-60	.50-5.00-1.82
Do___	(1)	(1)	[4]1.13-1.13-1.13
North Carolina___	M.	71-71-71	.50-.50-.50
Ohio___	M.	36-84-63	1.00-3.00-1.74
Pennsylvania___	M.	60-60-60	2.00-2.00-2.00
Rhode Island___	M.	60-60-60	1.25-1.50-1.38
South Carolina___	M.	60-60-60	.84-1.25-1.10
Wisconsin___	M.	60-60-60	1.65-2.00-1.83
1892:			
California___	M.	54-60-56	2.49-2.67-2.63
Connecticut___	M.	60-60-60	1.50-1.50-1.50
Florida___	M.	60-66-61	1.00-1.54-1.33
Indiana___	M.	60-60-60	1.12-1.25-1.19
Maine___	M.	60-60-60	1.43-2.00-1.66
Massachusetts___	M.	58-72-62	1.45-2.25-1.79
Michigan___	M.	60-60-60	1.75-1.75-1.75
Minnesota___	M.	60-60-60	1.75-2.00-1.88
New Hampshire__	M.	60-60-60	1.25-1.25-1.25
New York___	M.	54-72-64	1.58-2.00-1.73
Ohio___	M.	48-84-69	.50-3.50-1.72
Rhode Island___	M.	60-60-60	1.50-1.50-1.50
South Carolina___	M.	60-60-60	1.00-1.50-1.30
Wisconsin___	M.	60-60-60	2.50-2.50-2.50
1893:			
Connecticut___	M.	60-60-60	2.25-2.25-2.25
Maryland___	M.	72-72-72	1.67-1.67-1.67
Massachusetts___	M.	60-72-69	1.80-1.98-1.89
Michigan___	M.	60-72-66	1.25-1.75-1.50
Minnesota___	M.	60-60-60	1.75-2.00-1.88
Missouri___	M.	54-72-68	.67-4.17-1.85
New Hampshire__	M.	60-60-60	1.25-1.25-1.25
New Jersey___	M.	84-84-84	1.40-1.40-1.40
New York___	M.	60-60-60	1.67-2.00-1.84
Ohio___	M.	36-81-62	.75-2.50-1.59
Pennsylvania___	M.	60-60-60	1.73-2.49-2.11
Rhode Island___	M.	(1)	1.50-1.50-1.50
Wisconsin___	M.	60-60-60	1.50-2.50-1.89
1894:			
Connecticut___	M.	60-60-60	1.90-1.90-1.90
Georgia___	M.	60-60-60	1.00-1.00-1.00
Indiana___	M.	72-72-72	1.33-1.33-1.33
Maine___	M.	60-66-62	1.19-2.00-1.50
Massachusetts___	M.	60-84-74	1.65-2.00-1.84
Michigan___	M.	60-60-60	1.75-1.75-1.75
Minnesota___	M.	60-60-60	1.50-1.75-1.56
Montana___	M.	(1)	2.43-2.43-2.43
New Hampshire_	M.	53-60-57	1.25-2.00-1.63
New York___	M.	54-60-60	1.00-2.00-1.53
North Carolina___	M.	60-84-63	.52-1.25-.96
Ohio___	M.	54-72-64	1.48-3.22-1.88
Rhode Island___	M.	(1)	1.35-1.35-1.35
Do___	(1)		1.40-1.67-1.51
South Carolina___	M.	66-66-66	1.00-1.00-1.00
West Virginia___	M.	60-72-69	1.10-1.25-1.19
Wisconsin___	M.	60-60-60	2.00-2.00-2.00
1895:			
Alabama___	M.	60-66-62	1.00-1.75-1.32
Connecticut___	M.	45-72-63	1.25-2.00-1.73
Florida___	M.	60-63-62	1.00-1.00-1.00
Georgia___	M.	66-66-66	.75-1.60-1.05
Illinois___	M.	54-54-54	2.30-2.30-2.30
Kansas___	M.	48-48-48	1.00-1.00-1.00
Louisiana___	M.	55-63-61	1.72-2.25-1.95
Maine___	M.	60-60-60	1.13-2.50-1.92
Maryland___	M.	54-72-62	1.08-2.33-1.65
Massachusetts___	M.	54-72-60	1.25-3.00-1.78
Michigan___	M.	54-72-60	1.15-1.63-1.41
Minnesota___	M.	60-60-60	1.50-1.60-1.53
Mississippi___	M.	60-60-60	1.50-1.50-1.50
Missouri___	M.	59-60-60	1.25-2.56-1.71
Montana___	M.	(1)	2.17-2.17-2.17
New Hampshire_	M.	59-66-60	1.13-2.25-1.56
New Jersey___	M.	53-60-59	1.17-3.00-1.94
New York___	M.	48-60-60	1.00-3.50-1.88
North Carolina___	M.	60-72-65	.60-1.25-.89
Ohio___	M.	36-84-65	.67-2.81-1.63
Pennsylvania___	M.	54-60-59	1.50-2.50-1.76
Rhode Island___	M.	55-66-60	1.50-2.00-1.66
South Carolina___	M.	60-66-64	1.00-1.50-1.07
Tennessee___	M.	59-67-65	.50-1.25-1.05
Virginia___	M.	60-72-68	1.08-1.75-1.37
Wisconsin___	M.	60-60-60	2.00-2.00-2.00
Do___	(1)	60-78-65	1.25-2.50-1.68
1896:			
Alabama___	M.	63-63-63	1.10-1.10-1.10
California___	M.	60-60-60	1.50-2.00-1.75
Colorado___	M.	60-72-62	1.50-2.63-2.04
Connecticut___	M.	60-60-60	1.25-2.45-1.91
Delaware___	M.	72-72-72	1.79-1.79-1.79
Florida___	M.	(1)	1-25-1.25-1.25
Georgia___	M.	54-66-64	.40-1.35-1.00
Illinois___	M.	54-60-57	1.50-2.33-1.91
Indiana___	M.	60-65-64	1.00-1.60-1.45
Iowa___	M.	(1)	1.92-1.92-1.92
Kentucky___	M.	60-63-61	1.00-1.75-1.30
Maryland___	M.	60-77-67	1.00-2.01-1.84
Massachusetts___	M.	54-70-68	1.25-2.28-2.08
Michigan___	M.	54-72-61	.66-2.00-1.32
Minnesota___	M.	60-60-60	[2]1.15-1.15-1.15
Do___	M.	60-60-60	1.20-2.00-1.67
Montana___	M.	(1)	2.91-2.98-2.94
Nebraska___	M.	48-60-55	1.66-2.50-2.02
New Hampshire_	M.	60-77-67	1.17-1.75-1.35
New Jersey___	M.	56-60-59	1.50-2.33-1.97
New York___	M.	48-84-65	1.00-2.50-1.96
North Carolina___	M.	66-69-69	.60-1.00-.85
Ohio___	M.	36-72-64	.99-3.50-1.69
Pennsylvania___	M.	54-84-60	1.17-2.25-1.69
Rhode Island___	M.	60-60-60	1.50-2.00-1.75
South Carolina___	M.	66-66-66	.75-1.50-1.09
Tennessee___	M.	(1)	1.00-1.00-1.00
Vermont___	M.	66-66-66	1.75-1.75-1.75

¹ Not reported.   ² And board.   ⁴ And rent.

TABLE B-9.—*Firemen, stationary, 1840–1900, by year and State*—Continued

Year and State	Sex	Hours per week	Rate per day (dollars)	Year and State	Sex	Hours per week	Rate per day (dollars)
1896—Continued.				1898—Continued.			
West Virginia	M.	55–59–57	1.67–2.63–1.99	Missouri	[1]	48–72–63	1.75–1.90–1.80
Wisconsin	M.	48–72–63	1.67–2.00–1.75	Nebraska	[1]	60–96–83	.40–3.00–1.80
1897:				New York	M.	[1]	1.00–3.00–1.84
Connecticut	M.	60–60–60	1.75–2.00–1.90	Ohio	M.	[1]	1.35–1.75–1.58
Georgia	M.	66–66–66	1.50–1.50–1.50	Pennsylvania	M.	[1]	1.40–2.00–1.65
Illinois	M.	60–60–60	2.00–2.50–2.25	Washington	[1]	[1]	1.50–2.25–1.81
Kansas	M.	56–84–71	.86–2.14–1.48	1899:			
Maine	M.	60–66–65	1.50–1.50–1.50	Michigan	M.	[1]	1.67–1.96–1.89
Massachusetts	M.	60–60–60	1.40–2.25–1.97	New York	M.	59–59–59	1.67–1.67–1.67
Michigan	M.	60–60–60	1.40–1.53–1.53	North Carolina	M.	66–66–66	.60–.60–.60
Nebraska	M.	60–60–60	2.25–2.50–2.38	Ohio	M.	[1]	1.48–1.72–1.65
New York	M.	54–72–70	1.25–3.00–2.46	Pennsylvania	M.	84–84–84	1.50–1.00–1.82
Ohio	[1]	48–72–66	.80–2.00–1.53	Tennessee	M.	[1]	1.10–1.74–1.39
Pennsylvania	M.	48–60–65	1.35–2.32–1.56	Virginia	[1]	[1]	1.15–1.75–1.34
Virginia	M.	48–72–63	.50–1.75–1.14	1900: [5]			
1898:				New York	M.	59–59–59	1.67–1.67–1.67
Iowa	[1]	[1]	1.75–1.75–1.75	Ohio	[1]	[1]	1.65–1.65–1.65
Kansas	M.	48–78–63	1.40–1.75–1.58	Pennsylvania	M.	84–84–84	2.00–2.00–2.00

[1] Not reported.   [5] No available wage data later than 1900.

TABLE B-10.—*Hod carriers, 1840–1900, by year and State*

Year and State	Sex	Hours per week	Rate per day (dollars)	Year and State	Sex	Hours per week	Rate per day (dollars)
1840:				1855:			
New York	M.	60–60–60	0.75–1.13–0.85	Connecticut	M.	48–60–56	0.80–1.00–0.93
1841:				Massachusetts	M.	78–78–78	1.00–1.00–1.00
New York	M.	60–60–60	.75–1.13–.94	New York	M.	60–60–60	.75–1.50–1.00
1842:				1856:			
New York	M.	60–60–60	.75–1.13–.84	Connecticut	M.	48–60–55	.80–1.00–.92
1843:				Massachusetts	M.	78–78–78	.87–1.12–.97
New York	M.	60–60–60	1.13–1.13–1.13	New York	M.	60–60–60	.75–1.50–1.03
1844:				1857:			
New York	M.	60–60–60	1.13–1.25–1.23	Connecticut	M.	48–60–53	1.00–1.25–1.13
1845:				Massachusetts	M.	78–78–78	.87–.87–.87
New York	M.	60–60–60	.75–1.25–.84	New York	M.	60–60–60	.75–1.50–1.04
1846:				1858:			
New York	M.	60–60–60	.75–1.25–1.00	Connecticut	M.	60–60–60	1.00–1.00–1.00
1847:				Massachusetts	M.	78–78–78	1.00–1.17–1.07
New York	M.	60–60–60	.81–1.25–1.03	New York	M.	60–60–60	.75–1.50–1.10
1848:				1859:			
New York	M.	60–60–60	.88–1.25–1.07	Connecticut	M.	48–60–53	.80–1.33–1.04
1849:				Massachusetts	M.	60–78–63	.87–1.25–1.11
Massachusetts	M.	[1]	.75–.84–.80	New York	M.	60–60–60	.75–1.50–1.03
New York	M.	60–60–60	.88–1.25–1.07	1860:			
1850:				Connecticut	M.	48–60–56	.80–1.16–1.04
Massachusetts	M.	60–60–60	.75–1.00–.86	Massachusetts	M.	60–78–65	1.00–1.17–1.04
New York	M.	60–60–60	.88–1.25–.94	New York	M.	60–60–60	.81–1.50–1.18
1851:				Ohio	M.	[1]	1.00–1.00–1.00
New York	M.	60–60–60	.88–1.13–1.00	Pennsylvania	M.	54–54–54	1.12–1.12–1.12
1852:				1861:			
Connecticut	M.	[1]	1.00–1.00–1.00	Connecticut	M.	60–60–60	1.00–1.00–1.00
Massachusetts	M.	[1]	.87–.87–.87	Massachusetts	M.	60–78–61	.90–1.25–1.08
New York	M.	60–60–60	.88–1.38–1.13	New York	M.	60–60–60	.81–1.75–1.20
1853:				Pennsylvania	M.	54–54–54	1.25–1.25–1.25
Connecticut	M.	48–48–48	.80–1.00–.91	1862:			
Massachusetts	M.	78–78–78	.87–1.00–.94	Connecticut	M.	60–60–60	1.00–1.00–1.00
New York	M.	60–60–60	.75–1.50–1.06	Massachusetts	M.	60–78–63	1.00–1.25–1.18
1854:				New York	M.	60–60–60	.81–1.75–1.15
Connecticut	M.	60–60–60	.80–1.20–1.08	Pennsylvania	M.	54–54–54	1.25–1.25–1.25
Massachusetts	M.	78–78–78	.87–1.00–.94	1863:			
New York	M.	60–60–60	.88–1.50–1.00	Connecticut	M.	48–60–53	1.50–1.62–1.55
				Massachusetts	M.	60–78–63	1.00–1.25–1.19
				New York	M.	60–60–60	.96–1.75–1.31

[1] Not reported.

TABLE **B-10.**—*Hod carriers, 1840-1900, by year and State*—Continued

Year and State	Sex	Hours per week	Rate per day (dollars)	Year and State	Sex	Hours per week	Rate per day (dollars)
1864:				**1873—Continued.**			
Connecticut	M.	60-60-60	1.50-1.67-1.60	Maryland	M.	59-59-59	2.50-3.00-2.63
Massachusetts	M.	60-78-63	1.00-1.50-1.43	Massachusetts	M.	60-60-60	1.50-2.50-2.03
New York	M.	60-60-60	1.06-2.25-1.68	Minnesota	M.	60-60-60	1.50-1.50-1.50
Pennsylvania	M.	54-54-54	1.50-1.50-1.50	Missouri	M.	60-60-60	1.25-1.50-1.32
1865:				New York	M.	48-60-59	1.50-2.50-2.37
Connecticut	M.	60-60-60	1.67-1.67-1.67	Ohio	M.	60-60-60	3.00-3.00-3.00
Massachusetts	M.	60-60-60	1.50-1.75-1.55	Pennsylvania	M.	54-60-57	2.25-2.50-2.47
New York	M.	60-60-60	1.38-2.25-1.71	Virginia	M.	60-60-60	1.25-1.25-1.25
Pennsylvania	M.	54-54-54	2.00-2.00-2.00	**1874:**			
1866:				California	M.	48-54-52	3.00-3.00-3.00
Connecticut	M.	60-60-60	1.67-1.67-1.67	Connecticut	M.	48-60-52	1.50-2.00-1.72
Massachusetts	M.	60-60-60	1.50-2.00-1.74	Illinois	M.	60-60-60	1.00-1.00-1.00
New York	M.	60-60-60	1.44-2.50-2.16	Louisiana	M.	60-60-60	1.50-1.50-1.50
Pennsylvania	M.	54-54-54	2.00-2.00-2.00	Maryland	M.	59-59-59	1.25-1.50-1.38
1867:				Massachusetts	M.	60-60-60	1.75-2.50-1.95
Connecticut	M.	48-60-59	1.33-1.75-1.70	Minnesota	M.	60-60-60	1.50-1.50-1.50
Massachusetts	M.	60-60-60	1.50-2.00-1.59	Missouri	M.	60-60-60	1.25-1.50-1.32
New York	M.	60-60-60	1.44-2.75-2.21	New York	M.	48-60-58	1.44-2.50-2.01
Pennsylvania	M.	54-54-54	2.25-2.25-2.25	Ohio	M.	60-60-60	3.00-3.00-3.00
1868:				Pennsylvania	M.	54-60-57	2.25-2.50-2.26
Connecticut	M.	48-60-57	1.20-2.00-1.80	Virginia	M.	60-60-60	1.13-1.13-1.13
Massachusetts	M.	60-60-60	2.00-2.00-2.00	**1875:**			
New York	M.	60-60-60	1.44-2.50-2.09	California	M.	48-60-58	3.00-3.00-3.00
Pennsylvania	M.	54-54-54	2.25-2.25-2.25	Connecticut	M.	48-60-54	1.20-2.00-1.58
1869:				Illinois	M.	60-60-60	1.00-1.25-1.06
Connecticut	M.	48-60-55	1.75-2.00-1.90	Louisiana	M.	60-60-60	1.50-1.50-1.50
Massachusetts	M.	60-60-60	1.50-2.25-1.93	Maryland	M.	59-59-59	1.25-1.75-1.45
New York	M.	60-60-60	1.44-2.75-2.43	Massachusetts	M.	60-60-60	1.62-2.50-1.91
Pennsylvania	M.	54-54-54	2.00-2.00-2.00	Minnesota	M.	60-60-60	1.50-1.50-1.50
1870:				Missouri	M.	60-60-60	1.25-1.50-1.32
California	M.	48-54-52	3.00-3.00-3.00	New York	M.	48-60-59	1.25-2.25-1.98
Connecticut	M.	48-60-58	1.40-2.00-1.90	Ohio	M.	60-60-60	2.75-2.75-2.75
Illinois	M.	60-60-60	1.50-1.50-1.50	Pennsylvania	M.	54-60-57	2.00-2.50-2.04
Louisiana	M.	60-60-60	1.50-1.50-1.50	Virginia	M.	60-60-60	1.00-1.00-1.00
Maryland	M.	59-59-59	2.50-2.75-2.63	**1876:**			
Massachusetts	M.	60-60-60	1.75-2.50-2.12	California	M.	48-60-57	2.50-3.00-2.63
Minnesota	M.	60-60-60	1.50-1.50-1.50	Connecticut	M.	48-60-56	1.20-2.00-1.48
Missouri	M.	60-60-60	1.50-1.75-1.58	Illinois	M.	60-60-60	1.00-1.25-1.05
New York	M.	60-60-60	1.44-2.75-2.39	Louisiana	M.	60-60-60	1.50-1.50-1.50
Ohio	M.	60-60-60	2.75-2.75-2.75	Maryland	M.	59-59-59	1.50-1.75-1.57
Pennsylvania	M.	54-60-57	2.00-2.50-2.12	Massachusetts	M.	60-60-60	1.62-2.50-1.84
Virginia	M.	60-60-60	1.25-1.25-1.25	Minnesota	M.	60-60-60	1.50-1.50-1.50
1871:				Missouri	M.	60-60-60	1.25-1.50-1.33
California	M.	48-54-52	3.00-3.00-3.00	New York	M.	48-60-58	1.25-2.25-1.92
Connecticut	M.	48-60-57	1.60-2.00-1.93	Ohio	M.	60-60-60	2.75-2.75-2.75
Illinois	M.	60-60-60	1.50-1.50-1.50	Pennsylvania	M.	54-60-58	1.75-2.25-1.80
Louisiana	M.	60-60-60	1.50-1.50-1.50	Virginia	M.	60-60-60	1.00-1.00-1.00
Maryland	M.	59-59-59	2.50-3.00-2.70	**1877:**			
Massachusetts	M.	60-60-60	1.17-2.50-2.09	California	M.	48-60-57	2.50-3.00-2.63
Minnesota	M.	60-60-60	1.50-1.50-1.50	Connecticut	M.	48-60-58	1.00-2.00-1.42
Missouri	M.	60-60-60	1.50-1.75-1.58	Illinois	M.	60-60-60	1.00-1.00-1.00
New York	M.	48-60-59	1.44-2.50-2.37	Louisiana	M.	60-60-60	1.50-1.50-1.50
Ohio	M.	60-60-60	3.00-3.00-3.00	Maryland	M.	53-53-53	1.50-2.00-1.67
Pennsylvania	M.	54-60-55	2.25-2.50-2.27	Massachusetts	M.	60-60-60	1.50-2.00-1.79
Virginia	M.	60-60-60	1.25-1.25-1.25	Minnesota	M.	60-60-60	1.50-1.50-1.50
1872:				Missouri	M.	60-60-60	1.25-1.50-1.34
California	M.	48-54-52	3.00-3.00-3.00	New York	M.	48-60-58	1.00-2.25-1.77
Connecticut	M.	48-60-56	1.60-2.00-1.84	Ohio	M.	60-60-60	2.50-2.50-2.50
Illinois	M.	60-60-60	1.50-1.50-1.50	Pennsylvania	M.	54-60-58	1.50-2.25-1.65
Louisiana	M.	60-60-60	1.50-1.50-1.50	Virginia	M.	60-60-60	1.00-1.00-1.00
Maryland	M.	59-59-59	2.50-3.00-2.67	**1878:**			
Massachusetts	M.	60-60-60	1.75-2.50-1.98	California	M.	48-60-53	2.25-2.50-2.35
Minnesota	M.	60-60-60	1.50-1.50-1.50	Connecticut	M.	48-60-54	1.25-1.75-1.48
Missouri	M.	60-60-60	1.50-1.75-1.58	Illinois	M.	60-60-60	1.50-1.50-1.50
New York	M.	48-60-59	1.44-2.50-2.37	Louisiana	M.	60-60-60	1.50-1.50-1.50
Ohio	M.	60-60-60	2.00-3.00-2.80	Maryland	M.	53-53-53	1.50-2.00-1.76
Pennsylvania	M.	54-60-56	2.25-2.50-2.48	Massachusetts	M.	60-60-60	1.50-2.00-1.83
Virginia	M.	60-60-60	1.25-1.25-1.25	Minnesota	M.	60-60-60	1.75-1.75-1.75
1873:				Missouri	M.	60-60-60	1.50-1.75-1.60
California	M.	48-54-52	3.00-3.00-3.00	New York	M.	48-60-58	1.00-2.25-1.73
Connecticut	M.	48-60-58	1.50-2.00-1.92	Ohio	M.	60-60-60	2.50-2.50-2.50
Illinois	M.	60-60-60	1.50-1.50-1.50	Pennsylvania	M.	54-60-56	.85-2.25-1.44
Louisiana	M.	60-60-60	1.50-1.50-1.50	Virginia	M.	60-60-60	1.00-1.00-1.00

Table **B-10.**—*Hod carriers, 1840–1900, by year and State*—Continued

Year and State	Sex	Lowest, highest, and average— Hours per week	Rate per day (dollars)
1879:			
California	M.	48–60–55	2.50–3.00–2.70
Connecticut	M.	60–60–60	1.25–1.75–1.28
Illinois	M.	60–60–60	1.50–1.50–1.50
Louisiana	M.	60–60–60	1.50–1.50–1.50
Maryland	M.	53–53–53	1.50–2.00–1.74
Massachusetts	M.	60–60–60	1.62–2.00–1.82
Minnesota	M.	60–60–60	1.75–1.75–1.75
Missouri	M.	60–60–60	1.50–1.75–1.61
New York	M.	48–60–58	1.00–2.25–1.83
Ohio	M.	60–60–60	1.25–2.25–2.00
Pennsylvania	M.	54–60–56	1.25–2.00–1.47
Virginia	M.	60–60–60	1.00–1.00–1.00
1880:			
California	M.	48–60–56	2.50–2.50–2.50
Connecticut	M.	48–60–58	1.10–1.75–1.49
Illinois	M.	60–60–60	1.50–1.50–1.50
Louisiana	M.	60–60–60	1.50–1.50–1.50
Maryland	M.	53–53–53	1.50–2.00–1.73
Massachusetts	M.	60–60–60	1.75–2.25–1.82
Minnesota	M.	60–60–60	1.75–2.00–1.92
Missouri	M.	60–60–60	1.75–2.00–1.83
New York	M.	48–60–58	1.13–2.25–1.99
Ohio	M.	60–60–60	2.25–2.25–2.25
Pennsylvania	M.	54–60–57	1.50–2.00–1.62
Virginia	M.	60–60–60	1.00–1.00–1.00
1881:			
California	M.	48–60–56	2.50–2.50–2.50
Connecticut	M.	48–60–55	1.50–2.00–1.79
Dist. of Columbia	M.	60–60–60	1.87–1.87–1.87
Illinois	M.	60–60–60	1.50–1.50–1.50
Louisiana	M.	60–60–60	1.50–1.50–1.50
Maryland	M.	48–48–48	1.50–2.00–1.73
Massachusetts	M.	60–60–60	1.50–2.00–1.62
Minnesota	M.	60–60–60	1.75–2.00–1.90
Missouri	M.	60–60–60	1.75–3.00–1.84
New York	M.	48–60–58	1.00–2.50–2.21
Ohio	M.	60–60–60	2.50–2.50–2.50
Pennsylvania	M.	54–60–59	1.50–2.00–1.78
Virginia	M.	60–60–60	1.00–1.00–1.00
1882:			
California	M.	48–60–57	3.00–3.00–3.00
Connecticut	M.	48–60–54	1.60–2.25–1.96
Delaware	M.	50–50–50	2.00–2.00–2.00
Illinois	M.	60–60–60	1.50–1.75–1.65
Louisiana	M.	60–60–60	1.50–1.50–1.50
Maryland	M.	48–48–48	1.50–1.75–1.61
Massachusetts	M.	60–60–60	1.50–2.25–1.71
Minnesota	M.	60–60–60	2.00–2.00–2.00
Missouri	M.	60–60–60	1.85–3.00–1.97
New Jersey	M.	(1)	2.00–2.00–2.00
New York	M.	48–60–58	1.00–2.50–2.35
Ohio	M.	60–60–60	2.50–2.50–2.50
Pennsylvania	M.	54–60–57	1.75–2.00–1.84
Virginia	M.	60–60–60	1.13–1.13–1.13
1883:			
California	M.	48–57–55	3.00–3.00–3.00
Connecticut	M.	60–60–60	1.67–2.00–1.99
Illinois	M.	60–60–60	1.50–1.50–1.50
Louisiana	M.	60–60–60	1.50–1.50–1.50
Maryland	M.	48–48–48	1.50–2.00–1.75
Massachusetts	M.	60–60–60	1.35–2.25–1.94
Minnesota	M.	60–60–60	2.00–2.00–2.00
Missouri	M.	60–60–60	1.75–3.00–2.12
New Jersey	M.	60–60–60	2.00–2.75–2.36
New York	M.	48–60–58	1.38–2.75–2.37
Ohio	M.	60–60–60	2.75–2.75–2.75
Pennsylvania	M.	54–60–57	1.75–2.50–2.04
Virginia	M.	60–60–60	1.25–1.25–1.25
1884:			
California	M.	48–60–59	2.00–3.00–2.29
Connecticut	M.	48–60–55	1.60–2.25–1.96
Dist. of Columbia	M.	58–58–58	2.00–2.00–2.00
Illinois	M.	60–60–60	1.75–1.75–1.75
Louisiana	M.	60–60–60	1.50–1.50–1.50
Maryland	M.	48–48–48	1.50–2.00–1.75
1884—Continued.			
Massachusetts	M.	60–60–60	1.50–2.00–1.72
Michigan	M.	(1)	1.50–1.75–1.67
Minnesota	M.	60–60–60	2.00–2.00–2.00
Missouri	M.	60–60–60	2.75–3.00–2.83
New Jersey	M.	59–60–59	1.67–2.50–1.85
New York	M.	54–60–57	1.25–2.50–2.33
Ohio	M.	60–60–60	2.75–2.75–2.75
Pennsylvania	M.	54–60–56	1.75–2.25–2.01
Virginia	M.	60–60–60	1.25–1.25–1.25
1885:			
California	M.	48–57–54	3.00–3.00–3.00
Connecticut	M.	48–60–51	1.60–2.25–1.94
Illinois	M.	48–48–48	1.75–1.75–1.75
Indiana	M.	60–60–60	1.25–1.25–1.25
Kansas	M.	60–60–60	1.50–1.50–1.50
Kentucky	M.	60–60–60	1.50–1.50–1.50
Louisiana	M.	60–60–60	1.50–1.50–1.50
Maryland	M.	48–48–48	2.00–2.50–2.23
Massachusetts	M.	60–60–60	1.15–2.25–1.66
Minnesota	M.	60–60–60	2.00–2.00–2.00
Missouri	M.	60–60–60	2.75–3.00–2.85
New Jersey	M.	54–60–57	1.10–2.50–2.34
Ohio	M.	60–72–63	1.25–2.75–2.32
Pennsylvania	M.	54–60–58	1.65–2.25–2.08
Virginia	M.	60–60–60	1.25–1.25–1.25
1886:			
California	M.	48–60–59	1.04–3.00–1.66
Do	M.	48–48–48	[2] 2.50–2.50–2.50
Connecticut	M.	48–54–52	1.60–2.00–1.88
Dist. of Columbia	M.	53–53–53	2.00–2.00–2.00
Illinois	M.	48–60–56	1.50–2.00–1.61
Kansas	M.	60–60–60	2.00–2.00–2.00
Kentucky	M.	60–60–60	2.00–2.00–2.00
Louisiana	M.	60–60–60	1.50–1.50–1.50
Maryland	M.	48–48–48	2.00–2.25–2.13
Massachusetts	M.	58–60–60	1.25–2.00–1.69
Minnesota	M.	60–60–60	2.00–2.00–2.00
Missouri	M.	48–48–48	2.20–2.40–2.26
New Jersey	M.	60–60–60	2.00–2.00–2.00
New York	M.	53–60–54	1.35–2.50–2.38
Ohio	M.	60–60–60	2.75–2.75–2.75
Pennsylvania	M.	54–54–54	2.00–2.50–2.21
Virginia	M.	58–60–60	1.25–1.75–1.47
1886:			
California	M.	48–57–55	3.00–3.00–3.00
Connecticut	M.	48–54–52	1.75–2.00–1.91
Delaware	M.	(1)	[3] .14–.14–.14
Illinois	M.	48–48–48	1.75–1.75–1.75
Kansas	M.	60–60–60	1.40 2.00–1.64
Louisiana	M.	60–60–60	1.50–1.50–1.50
1887:			
Maine	M.	(1)	1.25–1.25–1.25
Maryland	M.	48–48–48	1.00–2.50–1.83
Massachusetts	M.	54–60–59	1.20–2.07–1.67
Michigan	M.	(1)	1.50–1.60–1.56
Minnesota	M.	60–60–60	2.00–2.00–2.00
Missouri	M.	48–48–48	1.25–2.60–2.18
New Jersey	M.	(1)	1.40–1.70–1.60
New York	M.	(1)	[3] .10–.20–.15
Do	M.	53–60–54	1.25–2.52–2.13
Ohio	M.	54–60–58	1.10–2.50–1.95
Pennsylvania	M.	(1)	[3] .10–.17½–.13
Do	M.	54–60–60	1.20–3.50–1.57
Rhode Island	M.	(1)	1.25–1.25–1.24
Virginia	M.	60–60–60	1.25–1.25–1.22
Wisconsin	M.	(1)	1.50–1.75–1.55
1888:			
California	M.	48–57–54	3.00–3.00–3.00
Connecticut	M.	48–54–53	1.78–2.00–1.83
Illinois	M.	48–48–48	1.75–1.75–1.75
Louisiana	M.	60–60–60	1.50–1.50–1.50
Maryland	M.	48–48–48	2.25–2.50–2.39
Massachusetts	M.	54–60–58	1.50–2.07–1.73
Minnesota	M.	60–60–60	2.00–2.00–2.00

¹ Not reported.   ² And board.   ³ Per hour.

TABLE **B-10.**—*Hod carriers, 1840-1900, by year and State*—Continued

Year and State	Sex	Hours per week	Rate per day (dollars)	Year and State	Sex	Hours per week	Rate per day (dollars)
1888—Continued.				**1893—Continued.**			
Missouri	M.	48-48-48	2.80-3.00-2.90	Massachusetts	M.	54-54-54	2.07-2.25-2.22
New Jersey	(1)	51-60-54	1.60-2.50-2.21	Michigan	M.	60-60-60	1.25-1.25-1.25
New York	M.	53-60-56	1.13-2.75-1.83	Minnesota	M.	60-60-60	1.75-1.75-1.75
Ohio	M.	60-60-60	2.50-2.50-2.50	Missouri	M.	48-48-48	2.80-3.00-2.88
Pennsylvania	M.	54-54-54	2.00-2.50-2.23	Montana	M.	48-48-48	3.75-4.00-3.83
Virginia	M.	60-60-60	1.25-1.25-1.25	New York	M.	48-60-49	1.25-2.50-2.33
1889:				Ohio	M.	54-60-58	2.00-2.81-2.27
Alabama	M.	60-66-65	1.00-1.20-1.03	Pennsylvania	M.	53-60-54	1.50-2.67-2.28
California	M.	48-57-54	3.00-3.00-3.00	Rhode Island	M.	(1)	2.24-2.25-2.25
Connecticut	M.	48-54-51	1.75-2.00-1.89	Virginia	M.	54-54-54	1.25-1.25-1.25
Illinois	M.	48-60-50	1.25-1.75-1.70	Wisconsin	M.	(1)	³.12½-.22½-.15½
Kansas	M.	60-60-60	1.40-1.75-1.53	**1894**			
Louisiana	M.	60-60-60	1.50-1.50-1.50	California	M.	48-54-52	3.00-3.00-3.00
Maryland	M.	48-48-48	2.25-2.50-2.38	Illinois	M.	48-48-48	1.75-1.75-1.75
Massachusetts	M.	54-60-58	1.50-2.07-1.69	Louisiana	M.	54-54-54	1.35-1.35-1.35
Minnesota	M.	60-60-60	2.00-2.00-2.00	Maine	M.	60-60-60	1.50-1.75-1.58
Missouri	M.	48-48-48	2.80-3.00-2.86	Maryland	M.	48-48-48	2.00-2.50-2.20
New Hampshire	M.	(1)	1.25-1.25-1.25	Massachusetts	M.	48-54-52	2.00-2.25-2.19
New York	M.	48-60-51	1.25-2.52-2.40	Minnesota	M.	60-60-60	1.75-1.75-1.75
Ohio	M.	60-60-60	1.13-2.50-1.99	Missouri	M.	48-48-48	2.80-3.00-2.84
Pennsylvania	M.	54-60-55	1.25-2.50-2.07	New York	M.	48-48-48	2.40-2.40-2.40
Virginia	M.	60-60-60	1.25-1.25-1.25	Ohio	M.	48-60-56	1.25-2.50-1.67
West Virginia	M.	(1)	1.71-1.71-1.71	Pennsylvania	M.	54-54-54	2.00-2.50-2.22
Wisconsin	M.	(1)	1.43-2.18-1.68	Rhode Island	M.	60-60-60	1.50-1.50-1.50
1890:				Virginia	M.	54-54-54	1.25-1.25-1.25
California	M.	48-57-55	3.00-3.00-3.00	**1895:**			
Connecticut	M.	48-54-51	1.78-2.00-1.91	California	M.	48-54-52	3.00-3.00-3.00
Illinois	M.	48-48-48	1.50-1.75-1.75	Illinois	M.	48-48-48	1.50-1.50-1.50
Louisiana	M.	60-60-60	1.50-1.50-1.50	Louisiana	M.	54-54-54	1.35-1.35-1.35
Maryland	M.	48-48-48	2.25-2.50-2.37	Maine	M.	60-60-60	1.50-2.50-1.63
Massachusetts	M.	54-60-57	1.50-2.07-1.80	Maryland	M.	48-48-48	1.75-2.00-1.94
Minnesota	M.	60-60-60	1.25-2.00-1.85	Massachusetts	M.	48-48-48	1.84-2.00-2.00
Missouri	M.	48-48-48	2.80-3.00-2.86	Minnesota	M.	60-60-60	1.75-1.75-1.75
Nebraska	M.	(1)	1.80-2.25-1.99	Missouri	M.	48-48-48	1.33-2.60-2.39
New York	M.	48-60-50	1.25-2.52-2.39	New York	M.	48-48-48	2.40-2.40-2.40
Ohio	M.	54-54-54	2.52-2.52-2.52	Ohio	M.	48-60-54	1.25-2.50-1.94
Pennsylvania	M.	54-54-54	2.25-2.50-2.35	Pennsylvania	M.	54-54-54	2.00-2.50-2.19
Virginia	M.	60-60-60	1.35-1.35-1.35	Virginia	M.	54-54-54	1.25-1.25-1.25
1891:				**1896:**			
California	M.	48-57-55	3.00-3.00-3.00	California	M.	48-54-52	3.00-3.00-3.00
Connecticut	M.	48-54-53	1.78-2.12-2.03	Connecticut	M.	60-60-60	1.50-1.50-1.50
Illinois	M.	48-48-48	1.75-1.75-1.75	District of Columbia	M.	(1)	1.50-1.67-1.59
Louisiana	M.	54-54-54	1.35-1.35-1.35	Illinois	M.	48-60-49	.90-2.33-1.48
Maine	M.	60-60-60	1.50-2.00-1.64	Maryland	M.	48-54-53	1.75-2.50-2.09
Maryland	M.	48-48-48	2.25-2.50-2.36	Massachusetts	M.	47-77-49	1.84-3.41-2.15
Massachusetts	M.	54-60-58	1.50-2.07-1.77	Minnesota	M.	60-60-60	1.75-1.75-1.75
Minnesota	M.	60-60-60	1.75-2.00-1.85	Missouri	M.	48-48-48	2.60-2.80-2.70
Missouri	M.	48-48-48	2.80-3.00-2.90	New York	M.	44-60-48	1.50-2.50-2.35
New York	M.	48-60-48	1.25-2.50-2.30	Ohio	M.	48-60-56	1.25-2.00-1.50
Ohio	M.	54-54-54	2.48-2.48-2.48	Pennsylvania	M.	45-60-50	1.56-2.71-2.34
Pennsylvania	M.	54-54-54	2.00-2.50-2.26	Tennessee	M.	(1)	.83-.83-.83
Virginia	M.	60-60-60	1.35-1.35-1.35	Virginia	M.	54-54-54	1.13-1.13-1.13
Wisconsin	M.	(1)	.12½-.27½-.18½	**1897:**			
1892:				California	M.	48-54-52	3.00-3.00-3.00
California	M.	48-57-53	3.00-3.50-3.17	Illinois	M.	48-48-48	2.00-2.00-2.00
Connecticut	M.	54-54-54	2.13-2.13-2.13	Louisiana	M.	54-54-54	1.35-1.35-1.35
Illinois	M.	48-48-48	1.75-1.75-1.75	Maryland	M.	53-53-53	1.75-2.00-1.91
Iowa	M.	60-60-60	1.50-1.50-1.50	Massachusetts	M.	48-48-48	1.84-2.00-2.00
Louisiana	M.	54-54-54	1.35-1.35-1.35	Minnesota	M.	60-60-60	1.75-1.75-1.75
Maryland	M.	48-48-48	2.25-2.50-2.38	Missouri	M.	48-48-48	2.60-2.80-2.68
Massachusetts	M.	54-54-54	2.07-2.25-2.24	New York	M.	48-48-48	2.40-2.40-2.40
Michigan	M.	54-60-56	1.25-2.00-1.58	Ohio	M.	48-48-48	2.00-2.00-2.00
Minnesota	M.	60-60-60	1.75-2.00-1.88	Pennsylvania	M.	54-54-54	2.00-2.25-2.12
Missouri	M.	48-48-48	2.80-3.00-2.91	Virginia	M.	54-54-54	1.00-1.00-1.00
New York	M.	48-60-50	1.50-2.50-2.34	**1898:**			
Ohio	M.	54-54-54	2.48-2.48-2.48	California	M.	48-54-52	3.00-3.00-3.00
Do	(1)	53-60-55	.75-2.50-2.05	Illinois	M.	48-48-48	2.00-2.00-2.00
Pennsylvania	M.	54-54-54	2.00-2.50-2.23	Louisiana	M.	54-54-54	1.35-1.35-1.35
Rhode Island	M.	54-60-59	1.50-2.50-1.85	Maryland	M.	53-53-53	1.75-2.00-1.89
Virginia	M.	54-54-54	1.25-1.25-1.25	Massachusetts	M.	48-48-48	1.60-2.00-1.97
1893:				Minnesota	M.	54-54-54	1.75-1.75-1.75
California	M.	48-54-53	3.00-3.00-3.00	Missouri	M.	48-48-48	2.60-2.80-2.70
Illinois	M.	48-60-48	1.50-2.50-1.76	Nebraska	(1)	48-72-62	1.00-1.75-1.40
Louisiana	M.	54-54-54	1.35-1.35-1.35	New York	M.	48-48-48	2.40-2.40-2.40
Maryland	M.	48-60-49	1.50-2.50-2.13				

¹ Not reported.   ³ Per hour.

TABLE **B–10.**—*Hod carriers, 1840–1900, by year and State*—Continued

| Year and State | Sex | Lowest, highest, and average— | | Year and State | Sex | Lowest, highest, and average— | |
		Hours per week	Rate per day (dollars)			Hours per week	Rate per day (dollars)
1898—Continued.				1898—Continued.			
Ohio	M.	48–48–48	1. 25–2. 00–1. 50	Ohio	M.	60–60–60	1. 20–1. 66–1. 44
Pennsylvania	M.	44–54–51	1. 35–2. 00–1. 88	Pennsylvania	M.	48–48–48	1. 50–2. 50–2. 39
Virginia	M.	54–54–54	1. 00–1. 00–1. 00	1900:			
1899:				California	M.	54–54–54	1. 75–3. 00–2. 54
California	M.	54–54–54	1. 75–3. 00–2. 44	Massachusetts	M.	48–48–48	2. 00–2. 50–2. 10
Massachusetts	M.	48–48–48	2. 00–2. 50–2. 10	Montana	M.	48–48–48	˙4. 00–4. 50–4. 33
Montana	M.	48–48–48	4. 00–4. 50–4. 28	New York	M.	44–54–49	1. 20–2. 42–1. 71
New York	M.	44–54–49	1. 20–2. 42–1. 69	Ohio	M.	60–60–60	1. 40–˙. 70–1. 43
Do	(¹)	(¹)	3. 00–3. 00–3. 00	Pennsylvania	M.	48–48–48	2. 40–2. 50–2. 42

¹ Not reported.

TABLE **B–11.**—*Hod carriers, males, 1890–1928, by city and year*

[Where two rates are shown for one year, the first rate is for brick and the second for mortar]

| Year | Atlanta, Ga. | | Birmingham, Ala. | | Boston, Mass. | | Chicago, Ill. | |
	Hours per week	Rate per hour	Hours per week	Rate per hour	Hours per week	Rate per hour	Hours per week	Rate per hour
1890					53. 5	$0. 257	48. 0	$0. 219
1891					53. 6	. 256	48. 0	. 219
1892					53. 4	. 259	48. 0	. 219
1893					52. 4	. 260	48. 0	. 219
1894					51. 8	. 261	48. 0	. 219
1895					50. 7	. 260	48. 0	. 213
1896					50. 4	. 260	48. 0	. 214
1897					50. 7	. 261	48. 0	. 250
1898					51. 0	. 261	48. 0	. 250
1899					47. 7	. 281	48. 0	. 250
1900					47. 7	. 288	48. 0	. 250
1901					47. 7	. 287	48. 0	. 250
1902					47. 7	. 291	46. 1	. 264
1903					47. 8	. 291	44. 0	. 312
1904	59. 1	$0. 103			47. 0	. 304	44. 0	. 319
1905	56. 1	. 123			46. 9	. 309	45. 6	. 315
1906	54. 8	. 150			46. 9	. 321	45. 7	. 357
1907					44. 0	. 300	48. 0	. 350
1908					44. 0	. 300	48. 0	. 350
1909					44. 0	. 300	48. 0	. 350
1910					44. 0	. 350	44. 0	. 425
1911					44. 0	. 350	44. 0	. 450
1912	54. 0	. 281	44. 0	. 300	44. 0	. 350	44. 0	. 450
1913	54. 0	. 281	44. 0	. 300	44. 0	. 350	44. 0	. 480
1914			44. 0	. 300	44. 0	. 350	44. 0	. 400
1915			44. 0	. 300	44. 0	. 350	44. 0	. 500
1916			44. 0	. 250	44. 0	. 350	44. 0	. 425
1917			44. 0	. 250	44. 0	. 400	44. 0	. 450
1918					44. 0	. 425	44. 0	. 500
1919					{ 44. 0 / 44. 0	. 425 / . 501 }	44. 0	. 575
1920					44. 0	. 700	44. 0	1. 000
1921					44. 0	. 700	44. 0	1. 000
1922					44. 0	. 700	44. 0	. 725
1923					44. 0	. 700	44. 0	. 725
1924					44. 0	. 700	44. 0	. 725
1925			47. 0	. 500	44. 0	. 700	44. 0	. 825
1926					44. 0	. 790	44. 0	. 875
1927					44. 0	. 790	44. 0	. 900
1928					44. 0	. 790	44. 0	. 900

TABLE **B-11.**—*Hod carriers, males, 1890-1928, by city and year*—Continued

Year	Cincinnati, Ohio		Denver, Colo.		Detroit, Mich.		New Orleans, La.	
	Hours per week	Rate per hour	Hours per week	Rate per hour	Hours per week	Rate per hour	Hours per week	Rate per hour
1890	49.7	$0.285	48.0	$0.303	53.1	$0.170	54.0	$0.212
1891	48.8	.297	48.0	.313	53.5	.168	54.0	.212
1892	48.9	.296	48.0	.315	53.5	.168	54.0	.212
1893	48.6	.301	48.0	.301	53.0	.170	54.0	.212
1894	48.0	.313	48.0	.286	53.1	.156	54.0	.212
1895	48.0	.313	48.0	.286	53.4	.169	54.0	.212
1896	48.0	.300	48.0	.290	48.0	.171	54.0	.212
1897	48.0	.250	48.0	.299	48.0	.168	54.0	.212
1898	48.0	.250	48.0	.301	48.0	.169	54.0	.212
1899	48.0	.264	48.0	.312	48.0	.185	54.0	.212
1900	48.0	.299	48.0	.314	48.0	.200	54.0	.212
1901	48.0	.299	53.9	.295	48.0	.214	54.0	.212
1902	48.0	.350	52.0	.305	48.0	.234	48.0	.238
1903	48.0	.350	52.7	.306	48.0	.232	48.0	.210
1904	44.9	.356	44.0	.350	48.0	.244	53.0	.179
1905	45.0	.355	44.0	.349	48.0	.241	52.9	.187
1906	44.9	.367	44.0	.372	48.0	.244	48.0	.275
1907	45.0	.375	44.0	.344 / .375	----	----	----	----
1908	45.0	.375	44.0	.375 / .406	----	----	----	----
1909	45.0	.375	44.0	.375 / .406	----	----	----	----
1910	45.0	.375	44.0	.375 / .406	----	----	----	----
1911	45.0	.375	44.0	.375 / .406	----	----	----	----
1912	45.0	.425	44.0	.375 / .406	48.0	.350	----	----
1913	45.0	.425	44.0	.375 / .406	48.0	.350	----	----
1914	45.0	.425	44.0	.375 / .406	44.0	.350	----	----
1915	45.0	.425	44.0	.375 / .406	44.0	.350	----	----
1916	45.0	.425	44.0	.375 / .406	44.0	.350 / .400	----	----
1917	45.0	.425	44.0	.438 / .469	44.0	.400 / .438	----	----
1918	45.0	.500	44.0	.531 / .563	44.0	.500	----	----
1919	45.0	.575	44.0	.625 / .656	44.0	.650	----	----
1920	45.0	.850	44.0	.750 / .781	44.0	1.000	45.0	.500
1921	45.0	.850	44.0	.750 / .781	44.0	.750	45.0	.650
1922	45.0	.725	44.0	.750 / .781	44.0	.750	45.0	.650
1923	45.0	.825	44.0	.750 / .781	49.5	.750	45.0	.650
1924	45.0	.900	44.0	.813 / .844	49.5	.750	45.0	.750
1925	45.0	.925	44.0	.813 / .844	44.0	.750	45.0	.750
1926	45.0	.950	44.0	.813 / .844	44.0	.750	----	----
1927	45.0	.975	44.0	.813 / .844	44.0	.750	----	----
1928	45.0	.975	44.0	.813 / .844	44.0	.750	----	----

TABLE **B-11.**—*Hod carriers, males, 1890-1928, by city and year*—Continued

Year	New York, N. Y.[1]		Philadelphia, Pa.		St. Louis, Mo.		San Francisco, Calif.	
	Hours per week	Rate per hour	Hours per week	Rate per hour	Hours per week	Rate per hour	Hours per week	Rate per hour
1890	48.4	$0.283	51.4	$0.278	49.4	$0.320	52.7	$0.357
1891	47.6	.282	50.7	.271	49.2	.319	52.9	.352
1892	46.8	.294	50.7	.275	49.5	.313	49.3	.384
1893	46.8	.299	50.6	.276	49.1	.297	49.7	.375
1894	47.0	.303	50.3	.282	48.0	.296	49.1	.382
1895	46.8	.299	50.6	.274	48.0	.283	49.5	.377
1896	47.2	.298	50.7	.274	48.0	.333	49.8	.374
1897	47.5	.295	50.9	.268	48.0	.325	49.9	.374
1898	46.7	.304	48.1	.262	48.0	.319	49.8	.376
1899	45.2	.326	46.8	.271	46.4	.338	49.5	.372
1900	44.8	.332	46.4	.283	44.8	.346	49.6	.380
1901	44.0	.329	46.9	.279	44.7	.355	49.5	.379
1902	44.0	.361	45.7	.309	44.0	.381	48.9	.376
1903	44.0	.360	44.2	.348	44.0	.399	46.1	.432
1904	44.0	.359	44.0	.313	44.0	.406	44.0	.438
1905	44.0	.361	46.0	.306	44.3	.439	44.0	.445
1906	44.0	.379	46.9	.308	44.4	.440	44.0	.527
1907	44.0	.381	46.8	.314	44.3	.453	44.0	.519
1908	44.0	.375	44.0	.350	44.0	{ .375 .400 }	44.0	.500
1909	44.0	.375	44.0	.350	44.0	{ .375 .400 }	44.0	.500
1910	44.0	.375	44.0	.350	44.0	{ .375 .400 }	44.0	.500
1911	44.0	.375	44.0	.350	44.0	{ .425 .450 }	44.0	.500
1912	44.0	.375	44.0	.350	44.0	{ .425 .450 }	44.0	.500
1913	44.0	.375	44.0	.350	44.0	{ .425 .450 }	44.0	.500
1914	44.0	.375	44.0	.350	44.0	{ .475 .500 }	44.0	.500
1915	44.0	.375	44.0	.350	44.0	{ .475 .500 }	44.0	.500
1916	44.0	.375	44.0	.400	44.0	{ .475 .500 }	44.0	.500
1917	44.0	.425	44.0	.450	44.0	{ .475 .500 }	44.0	.500
1918	44.0	.470	44.0	.600	44.0	.550	44.0	.625
1919	44.0	.575	44.0	.700	44.0	.650	44.0	.750
1920	44.0	.875	44.0	1.000	44.0	.700	44.0	.938
1921	44.0	.875	44.0	.850	44.0	.850	44.0	1.000
1922			44.0	.850	44.0	.850	46.3	.713
1923			44.0	1.000	44.0	1.000	46.3	.772
1924	44.0	.700	44.0	1.000	44.0	1.150	46.3	.772
1925	44.0	1.000	44.0	1.000	44.0	1.150	44.0	.875
1926	44.0	1.125	44.0	1.000	44.0	1.150	44.0	.875
1927	44.0	1.125	44.0	1.000	44.0	1.150	44.0	.875
1928	44.0	1.125	44.0	{ .850 1.000 }	44.0	1.150	44.0	.875

[1] Greater New York, 1903-1907.

TABLE **B-12.**—*Laborers, males, 1890-1928, by city and year*

[For other laborers see Tables D-1, D-2, D-3, G-1, I-16, I-17, I-18, O-11, and O-12]

Year	Atlanta, Ga.		Birmingham, Ala.		Boston, Mass.[1]		Chicago, Ill.[2]	
	Hours per week	Rate per hour	Hours per week	Rate per hour	Hours per week	Rate per hour	Hours per week	Rate per hour
1890			60. 0	$0. 101	59. 8	$0. 173	60. 0	$0. 167
1891			60. 0	. 101	59. 8	. 173	60. 0	. 167
1892			59. 1	. 123	59. 7	. 173	60. 0	. 172
1893			58. 9	. 144	59. 8	. 173	60. 0	. 170
1894			59. 7	. 101	59. 8	. 173	60. 0	. 170
1895			58. 4	. 086	59. 7	. 173	60. 0	. 170
1896			59. 1	. 081	59. 7	. 173	60. 0	. 171
1897			58. 6	. 084	59. 6	. 175	60. 0	. 172
1898			58. 0	. 086	59. 8	. 175	60. 0	. 172
1899			58. 8	. 083	59. 5	. 175	60. 0	. 170
1900			58. 8	. 084	59. 4	. 177	60. 0	. 169
1901			56. 9	. 107	59. 5	. 176	60. 0	. 192
1902			56. 8	. 125	54. 6	. 192	60. 0	. 192
1903	58. 1	$0. 107	58. 1	. 125	57. 4	. 172	46. 2	. 284
1904	59. 3	. 103	58. 5	. 125	56. 3	. 166	46. 4	. 292
1905	58. 4	. 119	56. 8	. 132	54. 5	. 178	47. 7	. 276
1906	59. 0	. 127	57. 7	. 147	53. 4	. 189	50. 9	. 294
1907					48. 0	. 250	48. 0	. 350
1908					48. 0	. 300	48. 0	. 350
1909					48. 0	. 300	48. 0	. 350
1910					48. 0	. 300	44. 0	. 375
1911					48. 0	. 300	44. 0	. 375
1912					44. 0	. 300	44. 0	. 375
1913	54. 0	. 200			48. 0	. 350	44. 0	. 400
1914	54. 0	. 200			48. 0	. 350	44. 0	. 400
1915					48. 0	. 350	44. 0	. 400
1916					48. 0	. 350	44. 0	. 425
1917					48. 0	. 375	44. 0	. 450
1918					48. 0	. 400	44. 0	. 500
1919					44. 0	. 400	44. 0	. 575
1920					44. 0	. 675	44. 0	1. 000
1921					44. 0	. 675	44. 0	1. 000
1922					44. 0	. 675	44. 0	. 725
1923					48. 0	. 675	44. 0	. 725
1924					48. 0	. 650	44. 0	. 725
1925					48. 0	. 650	44. 0	. 825
1926					48. 0	. 740	44. 0	. 875
1927					48. 0	. 740	44. 0	. 900
1928					48. 0	. 740	44. 0	. 900

[1] English excavators, 1907-1911; excavators, 1912-13.
[2] Excavators, 1912-1916; building workers, 1917-18.

TABLE B-12.—*Laborers, males, 1890-1928, by city and year*—Continued

Year	Cincinnati, Ohio		Denver, Colo.		Detroit, Mich.		New Orleans, La.	
	Hours per week	Rate per hour	Hours per week	Rate per hour	Hours per week	Rate per hour	Hours per week	Rate per hour
1890							54.0	$0.153
1891							54.0	.156
1892							54.0	.156
1893							54.0	.153
1894							54.0	.153
1895							54.0	.153
1896							54.0	.153
1897							54.0	.154
1898							54.0	.155
1899							54.0	.142
1900							51.0	.177
1901							48.2	.194
1902							48.2	.198
1903	54.6	$0.174			56.0	$0.186	48.0	.201
1904	54.9	.186	51.8	$0.217	57.0	.180	50.4	.206
1905	56.2	.190	51.5	.237	58.0	.179	49.3	.209
1906	52.9	.202	51.3	.243	55.6	.179	48.8	.214
1907	52.1	.204	53.0	.264	55.7	.195	49.2	.216
1912	60.0	.200						
1913	60.0	.200						
1914	50.0	.250						
1915	50.0	.250			54.0	.300		
1916	50.0	.250	44.0	.375	54.0	.300		
1917	50.0	.300	44.0	.438	54.0	.400		
1918	50.0	.350	48.0	.500				
1919	50.0	.400	48.0	.500	44.0	.650		
1920	50.0	.450	44.0	.500	44.0	.750		
1921	50.0	.500	44.0	.625	44.0	.600	45.0	.4..
1922	50.0	.400			44.0	.500	45.0	.500
1923	50.0	.450			49.5	.600	45.0	.500
1924	50.0	.525			49.5	.600	45.0	...00
1925	50.0	.550	44.0	.813	44.0	.600		
1926	50.0	.580	44.0	.813	44.0	.600		
1927	50.0	.600			44.0	.600		
1928	50.0	.600			44.0	.600		

Year	New York, N. Y.[3]		Philadelphia, Pa.		St. Louis, Mo.[4]		San Francisco, Calif.[5]	
	Hours per week	Rate per hour	Hours per week	Rate per hour	Hours per week	Rate per hour	Hours per week	Rate per hour
1890			58.5	$0.156	60.0	$0.169		
1891			58.2	.157	60.0	.169		
1892			58.4	.157	60.0	.163		
1893			57.3	.159	60.0	.159		
1894			56.8	.161	60.0	.142		
1895			57.7	.158	60.0	.156		
1896			57.7	.159	60.0	.138		
1897			57.9	.158	60.0	.155		
1898			57.8	.158	60.0	.142		
1899			57.1	.159	60.0	.139		
1900			56.5	.160	60.0	.140		
1901			56.6	.167	60.0	.181		
1902			56.1	.163	60.0	.187		
1903	58.8	$0.157	57.3	.156	60.0	.206		
1904	53.7	.188	57.6	.156				
1905	51.5	.202	56.1	.164				
1906	50.4	.210	58.1	.179				
1907	44.0	.219			44.0	.250	54.0	$0.278
1908	44.0	.219			44.0	.250	54.0	.278
1909	44.0	.219			44.0	.250	54.0	.278
1910	44.0	.219			44.0	.250	54.0	.278
1911	44.0	.219			44.0	.250	54.0	.278
1912	48.0	.225			44.0	.250	54.0	.278
1913	48.0	.225			44.0	.250	54.0	.278
1914	48.0	.225			44.0	.250	48.0	.313
1915	48.0	.250			44.0	.250	48.0	.313
1916	48.0	.250			44.0	.250	48.0	.313
1917	48.0	.300	44.0	.350	44.0	.300	48.0	.375
1918	48.0	.405	44.0	.625	44.0	.400	48.0	.438
1919	48.0	.405	44.0	.625	44.0	.450	48.0	.625
1920	48.0	.750	44.0	.750	44.0	.675	48.0	.750
1921	44.0	.875	44.0	1.000	44.0	.675	48.0	.813
1922	44.0	.875			44.0	.575	44.0	.625
1923	44.0	1.000	44.0	.850	44.0	.675	44.0	.625
1924	44.0	1.000	44.0	.850	44.0	.750	44.0	.625
1925	44.0	1.000	44.0	.850	44.0	.750	44.0	.625
1926	44.0	1.050			44.0	.750	48.0	.625
1927	44.0	1.150	44.0	1.125	44.0	.750	48.0	.688
1928	44.0	1.150	44.0	.600	44.0	.750	48.0	.688

³ Excavators, 1907-1920, inclusive.   ⁴ Building work, 1916.   ⁵ Building ork, 1914-1916, inclusive.

TABLE **B-13.**—*Marble cutters, 1840-1899, by year and State*

Year and State	Sex	Hours per week	Rate per day (dollars)	Year and State	Sex	Hours per week	Rate per day (dollars)
1840:				**1871:**			
New York	M.	60–60–60	1. 50–1. 50–1. 50	Maryland	M.	60–60–60	3. 50–3. 50–3. 50
1841:				Massachusetts	M.	59–59–59	2. 50–2. 50–2. 50
New York	M.	60–60–60	1. 50–1. 75–1. 63	New York	M.	60–60–60	2. 00–4. 00–3. 22
1842:				**1872:**			
New York	M.	60–60–60	1. 50–1. 50–1. 50	Maryland	M.	60–60–60	3. 50–3. 50–3. 50
1843:				New York	M.	60–60–60	2. 00–4. 00–3. 27
New York	M.	60–60–60	1. 50–1. 50–1. 50	**1873:**			
1844:				Maryland	M.	60–60–60	3. 00–3. 50–3. 45
New York	M.	60–60–60	1. 25–1. 50–1. 44	New York	M.	60–60–60	2. 25–4. 00–3. 25
1845:				**1874:**			
New York	M.	60–60–60	1. 50–1. 75–1. 56	Maryland	M.	60–60–60	3. 00–3. 50–3. 44
1846:				New York	M.	60–60–60	2. 25–3. 75–3. 11
New York	M.	60–60–60	1. 67–1. 75–1. 73	**1875:**			
1847:				Maryland	M.	60–60–60	3. 00–3. 50–3. 43
New York	M.	60–60–60	1. 75–1. 75–1. 75	New York	M.	60–60–60	2. 25–3. 75–3. 10
1848:				**1876:**			
New York	M.	60–60–60	1. 50–1. 75–1. 63	Maryland	M.	60–60–60	2. 75–3. 50–3. 30
1851:				New York	M.	60–60–60	2. 25–3. 75–2. 93
New York	M.	60–60–60	2. 13–2. 13–2. 13	**1877:**			
1852:				Maryland	M.	60–60–60	2. 75–3. 50–2. 85
New York	M.	60–60–60	2. 25–2. 25–2. 25	New York	M.	60–60–60	2. 25–3. 00–2. 77
1853:				Ohio	M.	(1)	2. 00–2. 00–2. 00
New York	M.	60–60–60	2. 00–2. 25–2. 13	**1878:**			
1854:				Maryland	M.	60–60–60	2. 50–2. 75–2. 72
Maryland	M.	60–60–60	2. 00–2. 00–2. 00	New York	M.	60–60–60	2. 00–3. 00–2. 47
New York	M.	60–60–60	2. 00–3. 00–2. 50	**1879:**			
1855:				Maryland	M.	60–60–60	2. 50–2. 75–2. 72
Maryland	M.	60–60–60	2. 00–2. 00–2. 00	Missouri	M.	59–60–60	1. 83–2. 17–2. 00
New York	M.	60–60–60	1. 75–2. 50–2. 19	New York	M.	60–60–60	2. 25–2. 75–2. 38
1856:				**1880:**			
Maryland	M.	54–60–58	2. 00–2. 25–2. 11	Maryland	M.	60–60–60	2. 50–2. 50–2. 50
New York	M.	60–60–60	2. 00–2. 50–2. 28	New York	M.	60–60–60	2. 13–2. 50–2. 40
1857:				**1881:**			
Maryland	M.	54–60–58	2. 00–2. 25–2. 17	Maryland	M.	60–60–60	2. 50–2. 50–2. 50
New York	M.	60–60–60	1. 63–2. 50–2. 21	New York	M.	60–60–60	2. 00–3. 00–2. 57
1858:				**1882:**			
Maryland	M.	54–60–58	2. 00–2. 25–2. 16	Maryland	M.	60–60–60	2. 50–2. 75–2. 65
New York	M.	60–60–60	1. 88–2. 00–1. 99	Massachusetts	M.	60–60–60	2. 90–3. 40–3. 15
1859:				Missouri	M.	60–60–60	1. 67–3. 00–2. 29
Maryland	M.	54–60–58	2. 00–2. 25–2. 15	New York	M.	60–60–60	2. 00–3. 00–2. 05
New York	M.	60–60–60	1. 67–2. 25–2. 04	**1883:**			
1860:				Maryland	M.	60–60–60	2. 50–2. 75–2. 66
Maryland	M.	54–60–58	2. 00–2. 25–2. 16	Massachusetts	M.	(1)	2. 00–2. 75–2. 30
New York	M.	60–60–60	1. 34–2. 38–2. 04	New York	M.	60–60–60	2. 25–3. 00–2. 69
1861:				**1884:**			
Maryland	M.	60–60–60	2. 00–2. 50–2. 07	California	M.	60–60–60	2. 50–3. 00–2. 88
New York	M.	60–60–60	1. 34–2. 13–1. 62	Iowa	M.	60–60–60	2. 50–2. 50–2. 50
1862:				Maryland	M.	60–60–60	2. 50–2. 75–2. 69
New York	M.	60–60–60	1. 25–1. 88–1. 58	Michigan	M.	(1)	2. 25–2. 50–2. 38
1863:				Missouri	M.	60–60–60	1. 67–3. 00–2. 38
Maryland	M.	60–60–60	2. 25–2. 25–2. 25	New York	M.	60–60–60	2. 50–3. 50–2. 85
New York	M.	60–60–60	1. 67–2. 25–1. 95	**1885:**			
1864:				Maryland	M.	60–60–60	2. 50–2. 75–2. 71
Maryland	M.	60–60–60	2. 25–3. 00–2. 78	New York	M.	60–60–60	2. 50–3. 50–2. 82
New York	M.	60–60–60	1. 75–3. 00–2. 52	**1886:**			
1865:				California	M.	60–60–60	2. 50–4. 00–2. 68
Maryland	M.	60–60–60	3. 25–3. 25–3. 25	Do.	M.	72–72–72	[2]3. 00–3. 00–3. 00
New York	M.	60–60–60	2. 00–3. 50–2. 91	Illinois	M.	48–60–52	1. 60–3. 00–2. 07
1866:				Iowa	M.		. 90–2. 50–1. 70
Maryland	M.	60–60–60	3. 25–3. 25–3. 25	Kansas	M.	60–60–60	2. 00–2. 00–2. 00
New York	M.	60–60–60	2. 00–3. 75–2. 94	Maryland	M.	60–60–60	2. 25–2. 75–2. 63
1867:				New York	M.	60–60–60	2. 50–3. 50–2. 94
Maryland	M.	60–60–60	3. 25–3. 50–3. 41	Vermont	M.	60–60–60	2. 60–2. 60–2. 60
New York	M.	60–60–60	2. 25–4. 00–3. 39	**1887:**			
1868:				Kansas	M.	60–60–60	2. 00–2. 00–2. 00
Maryland	M.	60–60–60	3. 50–3. 50–3. 50	Maryland	M.	60–60–60	2. 50–2. 75–2. 71
New York	M.	60–60–60	2. 00–4. 00–3. 46	New York	M.	60–60–60	2. 75–3. 00–2. 98
1869:				Ohio	M.	54–60–60	1. 50–3. 00–2. 58
Maryland	M.	60–60–60	3. 50–3. 50–3. 50	Wisconsin	M.	(1)	2. 00–3. 00–2. 50
New York	M.	60–60–60	2. 25–4. 50–3. 69	**1888:**			
1870:				Maryland	M.	60–60–60	2. 75–3. 00–2. 89
Maryland	M.	60–60–60	3. 50–3. 50–3. 50	New York	M.	48–60–54	1. 67–3. 94–3. 01
New York	M.	60–60–60	2. 25–4. 50–3. 19				

1 Not reported.   2 And board.

TABLE **B-13.**—*Marble cutters, 1840–1899, by year and State*—Continued

| Year and State | Sex | Lowest, highest, and average— | | Year and State | Sex | Lowest, highest, and average— | |
		Hours per week	Rate per day (dollars)			Hours per week	Rate per day (dollars)
1889:				1894:			
Maryland	M.	54-54-54	2.75-3.00-2.88	Iowa	M.	60-60-60	1.67-2.50-2.08
New York	M.	54-54-54	2.50-3.50-2.89	New York	M.	54-54-54	2.50-3.50-2.77
1890:				North Carolina	(¹)	60-60-60	2.50-2.50-2.50
Maryland	M.	54-54-54	2.75-3.00-2.86	1895:			
Minnesota	M.	(¹)	1.50-2.75-2.19	New York	M.	54-54-54	2.50-3.50-2.80
New York	M.	54-54-54	2.00-3.90-3.21	North Carolina	M.	60-60-60	3.00-3.00-3.00
Ohio	(¹)	60-60-60	1.66-1.75-1.72	Vermont	M.	60-60-60	2.50-3.50-3.00
1891:				Wisconsin	(¹)	60-60-60	1.25-2.50-1.75
Maryland	M.	54-54-54	2.75-3.00-2.88	1896:			
New York	M.	48-54-50	2.00-3.90-3.27	Kansas	M.	60-60-60	1.50-2.50-2.00
Ohio	M.	54-60-58	2.00-2.75-2.45	New York	M.	54-54-54	2.50-3.50-2.83
1892:				Ohio	M.	52-54-53	1.81-2.50-2.19
California	M.	54-57-55	1.83-3.50-2.67	Vermont	M.	60-60-60	2.00-2.15-2.08
Maryland	M.	54-54-54	2.50-3.00-2.83	1897:			
Massachusetts	M.	60-60-60	4.00-5.00-4.33	Kansas	M.	54-60-57	1.35-2.25-1.80
Michigan	M.	(¹)	1.28-2.34-1.81	New York	M.	48-54-48	2.50-4.50-3.94
New York	M.	48-54-49	2.75-3.50-3.38	Virginia	M.	54-60-59	1.50-2.75-1.93
1893:				1898:			
Illinois	M.	48-60-56	2.50-4.00-3.42	New York	M.	48-54-48	2.50-4.50-4.22
Missouri	M.	54-54-54	1.86-1.86-1.86	1899:			
Montana	M.	54-54-54	4.00-4.00-4.00	North Carolina	M.	54-54-54	2.00-2.00-2.00
New York	M.	48-59-53	1.33-3.50-2.51				
Ohio	M.	54-60-59	2.00-3.00-2.20				
Pennsylvania	M.	59-60-60	1.17-2.33-1.75				

¹ Not reported.

TABLE **B-14.**—*Marble cutters, males, 1890–1907, by geographic division and year*

| Year | North Atlantic | | South Atlantic | | North Central | | South Central | |
	Hours per week	Rate per hour	Hours per week	Rate per hour	Hours per week	Rate per hour	Hours per week	Rate per hour
1890	52.7	$0.380	56.6	$0.287	57.5	$0.249	56.8	$0.282
1891	50.4	.415	56.3	.281	57.1	.250	56.7	.290
1892	50.9	.392	56.3	.277	53.0	.327	56.8	.291
1893	50.9	.392	56.4	.280	52.9	.327	56.8	.288
1894	50.6	.388	56.6	.278	57.6	.248	57.0	.288
1895	50.5	.386	56.9	.278	57.2	.240	57.4	.284
1896	50.6	.415	56.3	.288	56.4	.246	57.1	.284
1897	50.2	.422	56.6	.284	56.4	.246	56.8	.281
1898	49.9	.425	56.8	.282	56.7	.242	56.8	.284
1899	47.1	.447	56.9	.267	57.1	.235	56.3	.288
1900	46.8	.447	56.5	.277	57.3	.255	56.2	.289
1901	46.7	.486	56.3	.275	56.1	.271	56.2	.292
1902	46.4	.531	55.6	.283	56.3	.283	56.3	.290
1903	46.6	.536	53.8	.318	53.2	.302	55.9	.296
1904	47.0	.477	52.1	.333	54.0	.304	56.6	.298
1905	46.9	.491	52.5	.351	53.9	.302	57.0	.306
1906	46.8	.490	52.1	.373	54.7	.320	55.6	.305
1907 [1]	46.5	.496	51.4	.374	55.1	.321	53.9	.358

[1] No available wage data after 1907.

TABLE B-15.—*Masons, 1840-1900, by year and State*

Year and State	Sex	Lowest, highest, and average—	
		Hours per week	Rate per day (dollars)
1840:			
Massachusetts	M.	60–60–60	1.75–1.75–1.75
New York	M.	60–60–60	1.50–1.50–1.50
1841:			
Massachusetts	M.	60–60–60	1.75–2.00–1.88
New York	M.	60–60–60	1.50–1.50–1.50
1842:			
Massachusetts	M.	60–60–60	1.88–1.88–1.88
1843:			
Massachusetts	M.	60–60–60	1.54–2.00–1.84
1844:			
Massachusetts	M.	60–60–60	1.54–2.00–1.76
New York	M.	60–60–60	1.50–1.50–1.50
1845:			
Massachusetts	M.	60–60–60	1.54–1.88–1.79
New York	M.	60–60–60	1.50–1.50–1.50
1846:			
Massachusetts	M.	60–60–60	1.54–1.88–1.84
New York	M.	60–60–60	1.50–1.75–1.55
1847:			
Massachusetts	M.	60–60–60	1.75–2.00–1.82
New York	M.	60–60–60	1.50–1.75–1.63
1848:			
Massachusetts	M.	60–60–60	2.00–2.00–2.00
New York	M.	60–60–60	1.50–1.50–1.50
1849:			
Massachusetts	M.	60–00–60	1.25–2.00–1.63
New York	M.	60–60–60	1.50–1.50–1.50
1850:			
Massachusetts	M.	60–60–60	1.25–2.00–1.51
New York	M.	60–60–60	1.50–1.75–1.60
1851:			
Massachusetts	M.	60–60–60	1.50–2.00–1.63
New York	M.	60–60–60	1.50–1.63–1.60
1852:			
Connecticut	M.	(1)	1.50–2.00–1.80
Massachusetts	M.	60–60–60	1.50–2.00–1.83
New York	M.	60–60–60	1.50–1.75–1.63
1853:			
Connecticut	M.	54–60–59	1.40–2.00–1.68
Massachusetts	M.	60–78–63	1.75–2.00–1.94
New York	M.	60–60–60	1.75–2.50–1.95
1854:			
Connecticut	M.	48–60–54	1.75–2.25–2.04
Massachusetts	M.	78–78–78	1.75–2.00–1.93
New York	M.	60–60–60	1.50–2.50–2.00
1855:			
Connecticut	M.	48–60–57	1.50–2.00–1.76
Massachusetts	M.	72–78–76	1.00–2.00–1.79
New York	M.	60–60–60	1.75–2.50–2.03
1856:			
Connecticut	M.	48–60–59	1.40–2.00–1.89
Massachusetts	M.	60–78–75	1.00–2.00–1.80
New York	M.	60–60–60	1.50–2.50–1.62
Pennsylvania	M.	72–72–72	.77–.77–.77
1857:			
Connecticut	M.	60–60–60	1.75–2.25–2.00
Massachusetts	M.	60–78–71	1.00–2.00–1.75
New York	M.	60–60–60	1.75–2.50–2.04
1858:			
Connecticut	M.	48–60–59	1.75–2.25–2.03
Massachusetts	M.	60–78–74	.83–2.25–1.90
New York	M.	60–60–60	1.75–2.50–2.13
1859:			
Connecticut	M.	48–60–58	1.40–2.50–2.03
Massachusetts	M.	60–78–67	1.00–2.25–1.88
New York	M.	60–60–60	1.50–2.50–1.90
1860:			
Connecticut	M.	48–60–56	1.60–2.25–1.94
Massachusetts	M.	60–78–67	1.00–2.25–1.84
New York	M.	60–60–60	2.50–2.50–2.50
1861:			
Connecticut	M.	48–60–50	1.75–2.00–1.78
Massachusetts	M.	60–78–64	.83–2.25–1.77
New York	M.	60–60–60	2.50–2.50–2.50
1862:			
Connecticut	M.	60–60–60	1.75–2.25–2.00
Massachusetts	M.	60–78–65	1.08–2.25–1.80
New York	M.	60–60–60	1.84–2.50–2.05
1863:			
Connecticut	M.	48–60–54	2.25–3.25–2.72
Massachusetts	M.	60–78–65	1.08–2.50–2.03
New York	M.	60–60–60	1.50–2.50–1.98
1864:			
Connecticut	M.	60–60–60	2.00–2.50–2.48
Massachusetts	M.	60–78–65	1.33–2.52–2.17
New York	M.	60–60–60	2.00–2.67–2.35
1865:			
Connecticut	M.	60–60–60	2.50–3.00–2.82
Massachusetts	M.	60–66–61	2.00–3.00–2.73
New York	M.	60–60–60	2.00–2.67–2.40
1866:			
Connecticut	M.	60–60–60	3.00–3.00–3.00
Massachusetts	M.	60–66–60	1.75–4.00–2.91
New York	M.	60–60–60	2.00–3.50–2.73
1867:			
Connecticut	M.	60–60–60	3.00–3.50–3.42
Massachusetts	M.	60–66–61	2.50–4.00–3.29
New York	M.	60–60–60	2.00–3.50–2.72
1868:			
Connecticut	M.	48–60–56	3.25–4.00–3.76
Massachusetts	M.	60–66–61	2.50–4.50–3.52
New York	M.	60–60–60	2.00–3.50–2.72
1869:			
Connecticut	M.	48–60–55	3.20–4.00–3.68
Massachusetts	M.	60–66–60	2.75–4.50–3.64
New York	M.	60–60–60	2.00–3.50–2.72
1870:			
California	M.	48–54–52	5.00–5.00–5.00
Connecticut	M.	48–60–59	3.20–4.00–3.93
Illinois	M.	60–60–60	3.00–3.50–3.33
Maryland	M.	59–60–60	4.00–4.50–4.20
Massachusetts	M.	60–66–61	2.50–4.50–3.65
Minnesota	M.	60–60–60	2.25–2.25–2.25
Missouri	M.	60–60–60	2.25–2.25–2.25
New York	M.	60–60–60	2.25–4.67–3.41
Ohio	M.	60–60–60	3.00–3.00–3.00
Pennsylvania	M.	54–60–58	2.50–3.25–3.01
Virginia	M.	60–60–60	3.50–3.50–3.50
1871:			
California	M.	48–54–52	5.00–5.00–5.00
Connecticut	M.	48–60–58	2.50–4.00–3.71
Illinois	M.	60–60–60	5.00–5.00–5.00
Maryland	M.	59–60–60	4.00–4.50–4.20
Massachusetts	M.	60–66–60	2.50–4.25–3.54
Minnesota	M.	60–60–60	2.25–2.25–2.25
Missouri	M.	60–60–60	2.25–2.25–2.25
New York	M.	60–60–60	2.25–4.67–3.42
Ohio	M.	60–60–60	3.00–3.00–3.00
Pennsylvania	M.	54–60–58	2.25–3.50–2.97
Virginia	M.	60–60–60	4.50–4.50–4.50
1872:			
California	M.	48–54–53	5.00–5.00–5.00
Connecticut	M.	48–60–56	2.50–4.00–3.71
Illinois	M.	60–60–60	5.00–5.00–5.00
Maryland	M.	59–60–60	4.00–4.50–4.23
Massachusetts	M.	60–66–60	2.87–4.50–3.13
Minnesota	M.	60–60–60	2.25–2.25–2.25
Missouri	M.	60–60–60	2.25–2.25–2.25
New York	M.	60–60–60	2.25–4.67–3.38
Ohio	M.	60–60–60	3.00–4.00–3.15
Pennsylvania	M.	54–60–59	2.25–3.75–3.35
Virginia	M.	60–60–60	4.50–4.50–4.50
1873:			
California	M.	48–54–52	5.00–5.00–5.00
Connecticut	M.	48–60–59	3.00–4.00–3.90
Illinois	M.	60–60–60	3.50–3.50–3.50
Maryland	M.	59–60–60	4.00–4.50–4.25
Massachusetts	M.	60–66–62	2.50–4.00–3.29
Minnesota	M.	60–60–60	2.25–2.25–2.25

¹ Not reported.

TABLE **B-15.**—*Masons, 1840–1900, by year and State*—Continued

Year and State	Sex	Lowest, highest, and average—		Year and State	Sex	Lowest, highest, and average—	
		Hours per week	Rate per day (dollars)			Hours per week	Rate per day (dollars)
1873—Continued.				**1879—Continued.**			
Missouri	M.	60–60–60	2. 25–2. 25–2. 25	Ohio	M.	60–60–60	2. 00–2. 50–2. 06
New York	M.	60–60–60	2. 38–4. 67–3. 36	Pennsylvania	M.	54–60–60	1. 17–2. 50–2. 19
Ohio	M.	60–60–60	3. 50–3. 50–3. 50	Virginia	M.	60–60–60	3. 50–3. 50–3. 50
Pennsylvania	M.	54–60–59	3. 00–3. 50–3. 33	**1880:**			
Virginia	M.	60–60–60	4. 50–4. 50–4. 50	California	M.	48–54–53	4. 00–5. 00–4. 89
1874:				Connecticut	M.	48–60–58	2. 00–4. 00–2. 59
California	M.	48–54–53	5. 00–5. 00–5. 00	Illinois	M.	60–60–60	2. 20–3. 50–2. 98
Connecticut	M.	48–60–53	3. 00–4. 00–3. 53	Maryland	M.	53–54–54	3. 00–4. 50–3. 78
Illinois	M.	60–60–60	2. 50–2. 50–2. 50	Massachusetts	M.	60–60–60	2. 00–3. 50–2. 52
Maryland	M.	59–60–60	2. 25–4. 50–3. 29	Minnesota	M.	60–60–60	2. 75–3. 00–2. 89
Massachusetts	M.	60–66–61	2. 08–4. 50–3. 27	Missouri	M.	48–48–48	4. 00–4. 00–4. 00
Minnesota	M.	60–60–60	2. 25–2. 25–2. 25	New Jersey	(¹)	54–60–59	1. 25–2. 50–1. 72
Missouri	M.	60–60–60	2. 25–2. 25–2. 25	New York	M.	60–60–60	2. 38–2. 75–2. 58
New York	M.	60–60–60	2. 50–3. 00–2. 95	Ohio	M.	60–60–60	2. 00–2. 25–2. 25
Ohio	M.	60–60–60	3. 25–3. 25–3. 25	Pennsylvania	M.	54–60–59	1. 50–2. 50–2. 14
Pennsylvania	M.	54–60–59	1. 75–3. 50–2. 42	Virginia	M.	60–60–60	3. 50–3. 50–3. 50
Virginia	M.	60–60–60	3. 50–3. 50–3. 50	**1881:**			
1875:				California	M.	48–54–54	4. 00–5. 00–4. 95
California	M.	48–54–54	5. 00–5. 00–5. 00	Colorado	M.	60–60–60	3. 50–3. 50–3. 50
Connecticut	M.	48–60–54	2. 40–4. 00–2. 98	Connecticut	M.	48–60–56	1. 80–4. 00–2. 77
Illinois	M.	60–60–60	2. 50–2. 50–2. 50	Illinois	M.	60–60–60	3. 50–3. 50–3. 50
Maryland	M.	59–60–60	2. 25–4. 50–3. 29	Maryland	M.	48–54–51	3. 00–4. 50–3. 68
Massachusetts	M.	60–60–60	2. 00–4. 25–3. 02	Massachusetts	M.	60–60–60	2. 00–3. 50–2. 70
Minnesota	M.	60–60–60	2. 25–2. 25–2. 25	Minnesota	M.	60–60–60	3. 50–3. 50–3. 50
Missouri	M.	60–60–60	2. 25–2. 25–2. 25	Missouri	M.	48–48–48	4. 00–4. 00–4. 00
New York	M.	60–60–60	2. 50–4. 00–3. 01	New Jersey	M.	60–60–60	2. 50–2. 50–2. 50
Ohio	M.	60–60–60	3. 00–3. 00–3. 00	New York	M.	60–60–60	2. 38–3. 00–2. 92
Pennsylvania	M.	54–60–59	2. 25–3. 50–2. 88	Ohio	M.	60–60–60	2. 50–3. 00–2. 95
Virginia	M.	60–60–60	3. 50–3. 50–3. 50	Pennsylvania	M.	54–66–59	2. 00–3. 00–2. 85
1876:				Virginia	M.	60–60–60	3. 50–3. 50–3. 50
California	M.	48–54–54	5. 00–5. 00–5. 00	**1882:**			
Connecticut	M.	48–60–56	2. 40–4. 00–2. 70	California	M.	48–54–54	4. 00–5. 00–4. 94
Illinois	M.	60–60–60	3. 00–3. 00–3. 00	Colorado	M.	60–60–60	4. 00–4. 00–4. 00
Maryland	M.	54–59–57	3. 00–4. 50–3. 64	Connecticut	M.	48–60–59	2. 25–4. 00–3. 35
Massachusetts	M.	60–60–60	1. 75–4. 00–3. 00	Illinois	M.	60–60–60	3. 50–3. 50–3. 50
Minnesota	M.	60–60–60	2. 25–2. 25–2. 25	Maryland	M.	48–54–50	3. 00–4. 50–3. 62
Missouri	M.	48–48–48	4. 00–4. 00–4. 00	Massachusetts	M.	60–60–60	2. 00–4. 00–2. 80
New York	M.	60–60–60	2. 50–2. 75–2. 52	Minnesota	M.	60–60–60	3. 50–3. 50–3. 50
Ohio	M.	60–60–60	2. 75–3. 00–2. 89	Missouri	M.	48–60–49	2. 50–4. 00–3. 95
Pennsylvania	M.	54–60–60	2. 25–3. 50–2. 47	New Jersey	M.	(¹)	2. 75–3. 00–2. 86
Virginia	M.	60–60–60	3. 50–3. 50–3. 50	New York	M.	60–60–60	2. 38–4. 00–3. 22
1877:				Ohio	M.	60–60–60	2. 75–3. 00–2. 98
California	M.	48–54–53	5. 00–5. 00–5. 00	Do	(¹)	60–60–60	2. 00–2. 63–2. 32
Connecticut	M.	48–60–59	2. 25–4. 00–2. 56	Pennsylvania	M.	54–60–58	1. 30–3. 25–2. 77
Illinois	M.	60–60–60	3. 00–3. 00–3. 00	Virginia	M.	60–60–60	3. 50–3. 50–3. 50
Maryland	M.	53–54–53	3. 00–4. 50–3. 67	**1883:**			
Massachusetts	M.	60–60–60	1. 70–3. 50–2. 68	California	M.	48–54–53	4. 00–5. 00–4. 91
Minnesota	M.	60–60–60	2. 25–2. 25–2. 25	Connecticut	M.	48–60–49	2. 50–4. 00–3. 46
Missouri	M.	48–48–48	4. 00–4. 00–4. 00	Illinois	M.	60–60–60	3. 50–3. 50–3. 50
New York	M.	60–60–60	2. 00–2. 75–2. 12	Maryland	M.	48–54–50	3. 00–4. 50–3. 61
Ohio	M.	60–60–60	2. 00–2. 25–2. 06	Massachusetts	M.	60–60–60	1. 25–5. 00–2. 68
Pennsylvania	M.	48–60–59	2. 00–3. 50–2. 36	Michigan	M.	(¹)	1. 00–3. 75–2. 74
Virginia	M.	60–60–60	3. 50–3. 50–3. 50	Minnesota	M.	60–60–60	3. 50–3. 50–3. 50
1878:				Missouri	M.	48–48–48	4. 00–4. 00–4. 00
California	M.	48–54–53	4. 00–5. 00–4. 88	New Jersey	M.	60–60–60	2. 50–2. 88–2. 60
Connecticut	M.	60–60–60	1. 75–4. 00–2. 50	New York	M.	60–60–60	2. 50–4. 00–3. 31
Illinois	M.	60–60–60	3. 00–3. 00–3. 00	Ohio	M.	59–70–60	2. 00–4. 17–3. 14
Maryland	M.	53–54–53	3. 00–4. 50–3. 57	Pennsylvania	M.	54–60–59	2. 00–3. 30–3. 11
Massachusetts	M.	60–60–60	1. 88–3. 25–2. 52	Virginia	M.	60–60–60	3. 50–3. 50–3. 50
Minnesota	M.	60–60–60	2. 75–3. 00–2. 89	**1884:**			
Missouri	M.	48–48–48	4. 00–4. 00–4. 00	California	M.	48–60–55	2. 50–5. 00–4. 16
New York	M.	60–60–60	2. 00–2. 75–2. 11	Connecticut	M.	48–60–57	3. 00–4. 00–3. 55
Ohio	M.	60–60–60	2. 00–2. 25–2. 11	Illinois	M.	60–60–60	3. 50–3. 50–3. 50
Pennsylvania	M.	54–72–59	1. 25–2. 75–1. 98	Iowa	M.	60–60–60	1. 50–4. 50–2. 48
Virginia	M.	60–60–60	3. 50–3. 50–3. 50	Maryland	M.	48–54–50	3. 00–4. 50–3. 57
1879:				Massachusetts	M.	60–60–60	2. 00–4. 00–3. 22
California	M.	48–54–53	4. 00–5. 00–4. 83	Michigan	M.	(¹)	1. 00–4. 00–2. 56
Connecticut	M.	48–60–59	1. 75–4. 00–2. 24	Minnesota	M.	60–60–60	3. 50–3. 50–3. 50
Illinois	M.	60–60–60	3. 50–3. 50–3. 50	Missouri	M.	48–48–48	4. 00–4. 00–4. 00
Maryland	M.	53–54–53	3. 50–4. 50–3. 57	New Jersey	M.	60–72–60	1. 50–3. 51–2. 87
Massachusetts	M.	60–60–60	1. 73–3. 50–2. 59	New York	M.	60–60–60	2. 38–3. 90–3. 26
Minnesota	M.	60–60–60	2. 75–3. 00–2. 89	Ohio	M.	59–60–60	2. 50–3. 25–3. 00
Missouri	M.	48–48–48	4. 00–4. 00–4. 00	Pennsylvania	M.	54–54–54	2. 00–4. 00–2. 41
New Jersey	M.	59–60–60	1. 00–1. 75–1. 50	Virginia	M.	60–60–60	3. 50–3. 50–3. 50
New York	M.	60–60–60	2. 00–2. 50–2. 47				

¹ Not reported.

TABLE **B-15.**—*Masons, 1840–1900, by year and State*—Continued

Year and State	Sex	Lowest, highest, and average—		Year and State	Sex	Lowest, highest, and average—	
		Hours per week	Rate per day (dollars)			Hours per week	Rate per day (dollars)
1885:				**1888—Continued.**			
California	M.	48–54–54	4. 00–5. 00–4. 92	Missouri	M.	48–48–48	4. 00–4. 00–4. 00
Connecticut	M.	48–60–53	2. 75–4. 00–3. 30	New Jersey	M.	51–60–56	1. 49–3. 50–2. 86
Georgia	M.	69–69–69	2. 25–2. 25–2. 25	New York	M.	(¹)	². 33½–.45–.39½
Illinois	M.	48–60–49	4. 00–5. 00–4. 05	Do	M.	48–60–55	1. 37–4. 05–3. 37
Indiana	M.	60–60–60	1. 75–2. 50–2. 00	North Carolina	M.	60–78–66	1. 00–2. 50–1. 42
Kansas	M.	60–60–60	1. 25–3. 00–2. 70	Ohio	M.	54–54–54	1. 25–3. 50–2. 68
Maine	M.	66–66–66	1. 13–2. 75–1. 88	Pennsylvania	M.	54–54–54	2. 00–3. 30–2. 97
Maryland	M.	48–54–50	3. 00–4. 50–3. 57	Rhode Island	M.	(¹)	2. 00–5. 00–2. 97
Massachusetts	M.	60–60–60	1. 50–4. 00–3. 11	South Carolina	M.	66–66–66	1. 00–2. 25–1. 25
Michigan	M.	(¹)	1. 50–3. 75–2. 40	Tennessee	M.	60–60–60	3. 45–3. 45–3. 45
Minnesota	M.	60–60–60	3. 50–3. 50–3. 50	Virginia	M.	54–54–54	3. 00–3. 00–3. 00
Missouri	M.	48–48–48	4. 00–4. 00–4. 00	**1889:**			
Nebraska	M.	60–60–60	3. 50–3. 50–3. 50	Alabama	M.	60–66–61	1. 50–5. 00–2. 73
New Jersey	M.	51–60–60	1. 50–3. 50–2. 68	California	M.	48–54–53	4. 00–5. 00–4. 85
New York	M.	54–66–56	1. 87–3. 50–3. 05	Connecticut	M.	48–54–50	2. 25–4. 00–3. 30
Ohio	M.	60–60–60	1. 52–4. 00–3. 14	Illinois	M.	48–72–53	1. 53–6. 13–3. 44
Pennsylvania	M.	48–60–54	2. 00–3. 50–2. 50	Indiana	M.	66–66–66	2. 25–3. 00–2. 75
Vermont	M.	66–66–66	2. 25–2. 25–2. 25	Kansas	M.	60–60–60	1. 75–3. 12–2. 69
Virginia	M.	48–54–51	3. 00–3. 50–3. 28	Maine	M.	60–60–60	1. 25–2. 25–1. 83
West Virginia	M.	60–60–60	3. 50–3. 50–3. 50	Maryland	M.	48–54–51	3. 00–4. 50–3. 75
1886:				Massachusetts	M.	60–60–60	1. 75–5. 50–3. 20
California	M.	48–54–54	4. 00–5. 00–4. 94	Michigan	M.	(¹)	3. 00–4. 00–3. 50
Connecticut	M.	54–54–54	2. 75–4. 00–3. 50	Minnesota	M.	60–60–60	3. 50–3. 50–3. 50
Illinois	M.	48–60–55	1. 75–4. 00–3. 30	Missouri	M.	(¹)	1. 92–2. 00–1. 96
Iowa	M.	60–60–60	1. 00–4. 00–2. 78	Do	M.	48–48–48	1. 50–4. 00–3. 91
Kansas	M.	48–60–60	1. 50–3. 50–2. 80	New Hampshire	M.	(¹)	1. 50–3. 00–1. 97
Maryland	M.	48–54–51	3. 50–4. 50–3. 86	New York	M.	54–60–57	1. 50–4. 00–3. 32
Massachusetts	M.	60–60–60	1. 80–4. 00–3. 04	North Carolina	M.	60–60–60	1. 00–1. 50–1. 25
Minnesota	M.	53–60–59	2. 25–2. 25–2. 36	Ohio	M.	54–66–59	1. 34–6. 37–2. 84
Missouri	M.	48–48–48	4. 00–4. 00–4. 00	Pennsylvania	M.	54–60–57	1. 35–4. 17–3. 00
New Hampshire	M.	60–60–60	1. 13–2. 25–1. 63	Tennessee	M.	60–72–64	2. 00–3. 75–2. 58
New Jersey	M.	60–60–60	2. 50–3. 00–2. 98	Virginia	M.	54–72–64	1. 75–3. 50–2. 79
New York	M.	53–60–54	2. 50–4. 00–2. 75	West Virginia	M.	60–60–60	2. 50–4. 17–3. 44
Ohio	M.	54–54–54	2. 70–2. 93–2. 87	Wisconsin	M.	(¹)	2. 26–5. 00–3. 49
Pennsylvania	M.	53–60–57	2. 00–3. 30–3. 13	**1890:**			
Virginia	M.	54–54–54	3. 50–3. 50–3. 50	California	M.	48–54–53	4. 00–5. 00–4. 80
1887:				Connecticut	M.	48–54–50	2. 50–4. 00–3. 39
California	M.	48–54–53	4. 00–5. 00–4. 89	Illinois	M.	48–48–48	2. 18–4. 00–3. 88
Connecticut	M.	48–54–51	1. 50–4. 00–2. 81	Indiana	M.	60–60–60	2. 00–2. 00–2. 00
Delaware	M.	(¹)	². 15–.35½–.29½	Kansas	M.	(¹)	2. 00–3. 75–3. 08
Florida	M.	(¹)	3. 00–3. 00–3. 00	Maryland	M.	48–54–51	3. 60–4. 50–3. 98
Illinois	M.	48–48–48	4. 00–4. 00–4. 00	Massachusetts	M.	60–60–60	1. 94–5. 50–3. 29
Kansas	M.	60–60–60	1. 50–3. 50–2. 89	Minnesota	M.	60–60–60	1. 75–3. 50–2. 81
Maine	M.	60–60–60	2. 25–3. 00–2. 54	Missouri	M.	48–48–48	4. 00–4. 00–4. 00
Maryland	M.	(¹)	². 32½–.32½–.32½	Nebraska	M.	(¹)	1. 50–3. 00–2. 50
Do	M.	48–54–51	1. 50–4. 50–2. 73	New York	M.	48–60–50	1. 25–5. 00–3. 39
Massachusetts	M.	60–60–60	1. 25–5. 50–2. 39	North Carolina	M.	(¹)	1. 25–2. 87–1. 84
Michigan	M.	(¹)	2. 50–4. 00–3. 23	Ohio	M.	54–54–54	3. 60–4. 50–3. 74
Minnesota	M.	60–60–60	3. 50–3. 50–3. 50	Pennsylvania	M.	54–54–54	2. 00–4. 00–3. 40
Missouri	M.	48–48–48	1. 50–4. 00–3. 52	Virginia	M.	54–54–54	3. 00–3. 00–3. 00
Nebraska	M.	60–60–60	2. 50–4. 00–3. 52	**1891:**			
New Jersey	M.	(¹)	2. 50–3. 10–2. 80	California	M.	48–54–53	4. 00–5. 00–4. 86
New York	M.	(¹)	². 13–.35–.24	Connecticut	M.	48–54–53	2. 50–4. 05–3. 71
Do	M.	48–60–56	1. 50–4. 00–3. 35	Illinois	M.	48–48–48	4. 00–4. 00–4. 00
North Carolina	M.	72–72–72	1. 00–1. 00–1. 00	Kansas	M.	60–60–60	2. 63–2. 63–2. 63
Ohio	M.	54–72–57	1. 25–3. 50–2. 82	Maine	M.	60–60–60	3. 00–3. 25–2. 68
Pennsylvania	M.	(¹)	². 10–.30–.18½	Maryland	M.	48–54–51	3. 60–4. 50–3. 98
Do	M.	54–60–56	1. 40–3. 50–2. 66	Massachusetts	M.	60–60–60	1. 94–5. 50–3. 11
Rhode Island	M.	(¹)	2. 50–3. 00–2. 75	Minnesota	M.	48–48–48	3. 50–3. 50–3. 50
Virginia	M.	54–54–54	3. 00–3. 00–3. 00	Missouri	M.	48–48–48	4. 00–4. 00–4. 00
West Virginia	M.	(¹)	1. 50–2. 50–1. 81	New York	M.	48–60–49	1. 13–5. 00–3. 18
Wisconsin	M.	(¹)	2. 00–4. 00–2. 73	North Carolina	M.	(¹)	1. 65–1. 65–1. 65
1888:				Ohio	M.	54–54–54	3. 24–3. 60–3. 55
California	M.	48–54–53	4. 00–5. 00–4. 83	Pennsylvania	M.	54–54–54	2. 00–3. 60–3. 39
Colorado	M.	60–60–60	4. 00–4. 50–4. 75	Virginia	M.	54–54–54	3. 00–3. 00–3. 00
Connecticut	M.	48–54–53	2. 50–4. 00–3. 55	Wisconsin	M.	(¹)	². 20–.45–.30
Georgia	M.	66–66–66	2. 50–2. 75–2. 56	**1892:**			
Illinois	M.	48–48–48	4. 00–4. 00–4. 00	California	M.	48–54–53	3. 00–4. 50–4. 00
Iowa	M.	54–60–58	2. 50–3. 30–2. 94	Connecticut	M.	54–54–54	1. 50–4. 05–3. 77
Kansas	M.	(¹)	2. 00–3. 58–3. 24	Illinois	M.	48–48–48	4. 00–4. 00–4. 00
Maryland	M.	48–54–51	3. 50–4. 50–3. 96	Iowa	M.	54–60–60	2. 00–4. 00–3. 25
Massachusetts	M.	60–60–60	1. 94–5. 50–3. 49	Kansas	M.	60–60–60	2. 38–2. 38–2. 38
Michigan	M.	48–60–59	1. 00–2. 99–2. 45	Maine	M.	60–60–60	2. 00–2. 00–2. 00
Minnesota	M.	60–60–60	3. 50–3. 50–3. 50	Maryland	M.	48–54–51	3. 40–4. 50–3. 95

¹ Not reported.   ² Per hour.

Table B-15.—*Masons, 1840-1900, by year and State*—Continued

Year and State	Sex	Lowest, highest, and average—		Year and State	Sex	Lowest, highest, and average—	
		Hours per week	Rate per day (dollars)			Hours per week	Rate per day (dollars)
1892—Continued.				1896:			
Massachusetts	M.	58–60–59	1.88–4.00–3.18	California	M.	48–54–53	4.00–4.50–4.38
Michigan	M.	36–60–57	1.50–5.00–3.25	Connecticut	M.	60–60–60	3.00–3.62–3.31
Minnesota	M.	60–60–60	2.25–2.50–2.41	Georgia	M.	(¹)	.67–2.50–1.54
Missouri	M.	48–48–48	4.00–4.00–4.00	Illinois	M.	48–48–48	3.00–4.00–3.91
New York	M.	48–60–49	2.50–4.00–3.90	Kansas	M.	60–60–60	2.50–2.50–2.50
Ohio	M.	48–60–55	1.15–4.00–3.41	Maryland	M.	53–60–56	2.99–3.51–3.19
Pennsylvania	M.	54–54–54	2.00–3.60–3.47	Massachusetts	M.	48–60–50	2.00–4.20–3.37
Rhode Island	M.	54–60–59	1.00–5.00–3.08	Michigan	(¹)	60–60–60	3.00–3.00–3.00
Virginia	M.	54–54–54	3.00–3.00–3.00	Minnesota	M.	60–60–60	2.25–2.50–2.39
1893:				Missouri	M.	48–48–48	3.60–3.60–3.60
California	M.	48–54–53	4.00–4.50–4.40	Nebraska	M.	48–48–48	3.00–3.00–3.00
Connecticut	M.	54–60–56	1.50–4.05–3.72	New Hampshire	M.	60–60–60	2.25–3.00–2.92
Illinois	M.	48–48–48	2.25–5.00–3.94	New York	M.	48–60–49	2.50–4.00–3.92
Kansas	M.	(¹)	3.50–3.50–3.50	North Carolina	M.	60–66–63	1.00–1.50–1.25
Maryland	M.	48–60–52	2.00–4.50–3.72	Ohio	M.	48–60–56	2.50–3.26–3.09
Massachusetts	M.	58–58–58	1.88–4.00–2.96	Pennsylvania	M.	50–60–53	2.58–3.75–3.22
Michigan	M.	60–60–60	1.75–1.75–1.75	Rhode Island	M.	60–60–60	3.00–3.00–3.00
Minnesota	M.	60–60–60	2.25–2.50–2.36	Tennessee	M.	(¹)	1.00–2.50–1.58
Missouri	M.	48–60–48	2.03–4.00–2.08	Virginia	M.	54–54–54	3.00–3.00–3.00
Montana	M.	42–54–51	4.50–6.00–5.17	1897:			
New Hampshire	M.	54–60–59	1.50–3.75–2.98	California	M.	48–54–53	4.00–4.50–4.40
New York	M.	47–60–51	2.00–4.00–3.07	Connecticut	M.	54–54–54	2.00–3.60–2.70
Ohio	M.	54–60–58	2.50–3.60–3.15	Illinois	M.	48–48–48	4.00–4.00–4.00
Pennsylvania	M.	48–60–56	1.00–4.00–2.94	Kansas	M.	48–60–56	2.00–3.20–2.39
Rhode Island	M.	60–60–60	2.00–3.50–3.23	Do	M.	(¹)	².17½–.17½–.17½
Virginia	M.	54–54–54	3.00–3.00–3.00	Maryland	M.	53–54–54	3.00–3.50–3.13
Wisconsin	M.	(¹)	².20–.40–.30	Michigan	M.	(¹)	2.71–2.71–2.71
1894:				Minnesota	M.	60–60–60	2.25–2.50–2.39
California	M.	48–54–53	4.00–4.50–4.42	Missouri	M.	48–48–48	3.60–3.60–3.60
Connecticut	M.	54–54–54	1.75–4.05–3.73	Nebraska	(¹)	48–48–48	4.00–4.00–4.00
Illinois	M.	48–48–48	4.00–4.00–4.00	New York	M.	48–53–48	3.00–4.05–3.38
Iowa	M.	48–60–59	1.67–3.67–2.90	Ohio	M.	48–48–48	2.56–2.56–2.56
Kansas	M.	58–58–58	2.22–3.50–2.24	Pennsylvania	M.	54–54–54	1.64–3.15–2.83
Maine	M.	54–60–60	1.75–3.00–2.48	Virginia	M.	54–54–54	3.00–3.00–3.00
Maryland	M.	48–54–51	4.00–4.50–4.11	1898:			
Massachusetts	M.	58–58–58	1.30–3.62–2.07	California	M.	48–54–53	4.00–4.50–4.41
Minnesota	M.	60–60–60	2.25–2.50–2.36	Illinois	M.	48–48–48	4.00–4.00–4.00
Missouri	M.	48–48–48	4.00–4.00–4.00	Kansas	M.	54–54–54	2.25–3.00–2.65
New York	M.	48–48–48	2.50–4.00–3.95	Maryland	M.	53–54–54	3.00–3.50–3.13
Ohio	M.	48–60–56	2.50–3.30–3.04	Michigan	M.	(¹)	2.00–2.72–2.37
Pennsylvania	M.	54–54–54	2.00–3.15–2.81	Minnesota	M.	54–54–54	2.25–2.50–2.39
Rhode Island	M.	60–60–60	1.75–2.75–2.17	Missouri	M.	48–48–48	2.80–2.80–2.80
Virginia	M.	54–54–54	3.00–3.00–3.00	Nebraska	(¹)	48–60–56	1.00–3.37–2.33
1895:				Do	(¹)	(¹)	².17½–.17½–.17½
California	M.	48–54–53	4.00–4.50–4.44	New York	M.	48–54–48	3.20–4.05–3.67
Connecticut	M.	54–54–54	1.75–4.05–3.74	Ohio	M.	48–48–48	2.40–2.50–2.41
Illinois	M.	48–48–48	4.00–4.00–4.00	Pennsylvania	M.	54–54–54	2.00–3.15–2.87
Kansas	M.	60–60–60	1.50–2.00–1.75	Virginia	M.	54–54–54	3.00–3.00–3.00
Maine	M.	60–60–60	1.50–3.00–2.09	1899:			
Maryland	M.	48–54–52	3.00–3.50–3.13	California	M.	48–48–48	3.00–3.00–3.00
Massachusetts	M.	58–58–58	1.30–3.75–2.64	Georgia	M.	60–60–60	2.00–2.25–2.13
Minnesota	M.	60–60–60	2.25–2.50–2.36	Massachusetts	M.	48–48–48	3.60–3.60–3.60
Missouri	M.	48–48–48	3.60–3.60–3.60	New York	M.	44–60–48	2.93–3.60–3.06
Nebraska	(¹)	60–60–60	1.00–2.00–1.50	Ohio	M.	(¹)	2.75–2.75–2.75
New Hampshire	M.	60–60–60	1.35–3.25–1.83	Pennsylvania	M.	54–54–54	2.50–3.00–3.00
New York	M.	48–48–48	2.50–4.00–3.94	1900:			
North Carolina	M.	60–60–60	1.00–1.50–1.33	California	M.	48–48–48	3.50–3.50–3.50
Ohio	M.	48–60–55	2.50–4.00–3.57	Georgia	M.	60–60–60	2.00–2.25–2.13
Pennsylvania	M.	54–54–54	2.00–3.42–3.03	Massachusetts	M.	48–48–48	3.60–3.60–3.60
Rhode Island	M.	60–60–60	2.00–2.50–2.25	New York	M.	44–60–48	2.93–3.60–3.04
Virginia	M.	54–54–54	3.00–3.00–3.00	Pennsylvania	M.	48–48–48	3.00–3.00–3.00
Wisconsin	(¹)	48–60–55	1.50–3.60–2.72				

¹ Not reported.   ² Per hour.

TABLE **B-16.**—*Stone masons, males, 1890–1907, by geographic division and year*

Year	North Atlantic		South Atlantic		North Central		South Central	
	Hours per week	Rate per hour	Hours per week	Rate per hour	Hours per week	Rate per hour	Hours per week	Rate per hour
1890	56. 2	$0. 323	54. 3	$0. 368	52. 6	$0. 420	56. 3	$0. 350
1891	56. 4	.318	54. 4	.364	52. 6	.421	56. 3	.350
1892	56. 3	.315	54. 7	.359	52. 3	.421	56. 3	.360
1893	56. 0	.316	54. 7	.362	51. 7	.417	55. 8	.363
1894	55. 9	.313	55. 1	.343	51. 6	.382	55. 6	.369
1895	55. 7	.312	56. 0	.314	51. 2	.398	55. 2	.348
1896	55. 6	.315	54. 6	.382	51. 2	.404	54. 6	.346
1897	55. 1	.319	53. 9	.354	50. 1	.414	54. 6	.342
1898	53. 3	.333	53. 9	.333	50. 6	.395	54. 5	.344
1899	54. 4	.329	53. 9	.339	50. 1	.426	54. 4	.363
1900	53. 0	.340	53. 6	.352	50. 0	.424	54. 4	.369
1901	52. 9	.354	53. 7	.376	48. 5	.457	51. 8	.371
1902	51. 5	.381	51. 3	.445	48. 0	.485	50. 4	.421
1903	49. 8	.423	51. 0	.467	48. 6	.499	50. 8	.448
1904	48. 6	.443	51. 5	.461	47. 7	.532	52. 4	.408
1905	47. 6	.465	51. 8	.456	48. 0	.510	51. 1	.421
1906	47. 5	.477	52. 0	.467	48. 1	.526	49. 5	.463
1907	47. 3	.493	51. 2	.458	47. 6	.546	49. 5	.474

TABLE **B-17.**—*Stone masons, males, 1907–1928, by city and year*

Year	Atlanta, Ga.		Birmingham, Ala.		Boston, Mass.		Chicago, Ill.	
	Hours per week	Rate per hour	Hours per week	Rate per hour	Hours per week	Rate per hour	Hours per week	Rate per hour
1907	53. 0	$0. 408			44. 0	[1] $0. 600	48. 0	$0. 628
1908	53. 0	.459			44. 0	[1] . 600	48. 0	.628
1909	53. 0	.459			44. 0	.600	48. 0	.675
1910	53. 0	.459			44. 0	.600	44. 0	.675
1911	53. 0	.459			44. 0	.600	44. 0	.675
1912	53. 0	.450			44. 0	.600	44. 0	.725
1913	53. 0	.450	[2] 44. 0	$0. 700	44. 0	.650	44. 0	.750
1914	{ 3 50. 0 53. 0 }	.450	44. 0	.700	44. 0	.650	44. 0	.750
1915	50. 0	.450	44. 0	.700	44. 0	.650	44. 0	.750
1916	4 50. 0	.500	44. 0	.700	44. 0	.650	44. 0	.750
1917	50. 0	.600	44. 0	.700	44. 0	.700	44. 0	.750
1918	50. 0	5 . 600	44. 0	.875	44. 0	.800	44. 0	6 . 750
1919	44. 0	7 . 700	44. 0	.875	44. 0	.800	44. 0	.875
1920	44. 0	7 1. 125	44. 0	1. 000	44. 0	1. 000	44. 0	1. 250
1921	44. 0	1. 000	44. 0	1. 000	44. 0	8 1. 000	44. 0	8 1. 250
1922	44. 0	1. 000	44. 0	1. 000	44. 0	1. 000	44. 0	1. 100
1923	44. 0	1. 125	44. 0	1. 125	44. 0	1. 250	44. 0	1. 100
1924	44. 0	{ 3 1. 250 1. 125 }	44. 0	1. 250	44. 0	1. 250	44. 0	1. 500
1925	44. 0	{ 3 1. 250 1. 125 }	44. 0	1. 375	44. 0	1. 250	44. 0	1. 500
1926	44. 0	1. 400	44. 0	1. 500	44. 0	1. 400	44. 0	1. 500
1927	44. 0	1. 400	44. 0	1. 500	44. 0	1. 400	44. 0	1. 625
1928	44. 0	1. 400	44. 0	1. 500	44. 0	1. 400	44. 0	1. 625

[1] Rough foundation, 55 cents.
[2] 48 hours October to December.
[3] Two unions.
[4] 53 hours October to April.

[5] 70 cents on June 1.
[6] 81.3 cents on August 1.
[7] Nominal rate; all received more.
[8] Old scale; strike pending.

TABLE **B-17.**—*Stone masons, males, 1907–1928, by city and year*—Continued

Year	Cincinnati, Ohio		Denver, Colo.		Detroit, Mich.		New Orleans, La.	
	Hours per week	Rate per hour	Hours per week	Rate per hour	Hours per week	Rate per hour	Hours per week	Rate per hour
1907	45.0	$0.540	44.0	$0.625	48.0	$0.550	48.0	$0.625
1908	45.0	.540	44.0	.625	48.0	.550	48.0	.625
1909	45.0	.540	44.0	.625	48.0	.550	44.0	.625
1910	45.0	.540	44.0	.625	48.0	.550	44.0	.625
1911	45.0	.540	44.0	.625	48.0	.550	44.0	.625
1912	45.0	.540	44.0	.625	48.0	.550	44.0	.625
1913	45.0	.600	44.0	.625	48.0	.600	44.0	.625
1914	45.0	.600	44.0	.625	[9] 44.0	.650	44.0	.625
1915	45.0	.600	44.0	.625	[9] 44.0	.650	44.0	.625
1916	45.0	.600	44.0	.625	[10] 44.0	.700	44.0	.625
1917	45.0	.650	44.0	.750	[10] 44.0	.750	44.0	.625
1918	45.0	.700	44.0	.875	[10] 44.0	.800	44.0	.625
1919	45.0	.700	44.0	.875	[10] 44.0	.900	44.0	.750
1920	45.0	.900	44.0	1.125	44.0	1.250	44.0	1.000
1921	45.0	1.000	44.0	1.125	44.0	1.000	44.0	1.250
1922	45.0	1.000	44.0	1.250	44.0	1.000	44.0	1.000
1923	45.0	1.125	44.0	1.375	44.0	1.350	44.0	1.000
1924	45.0	1.125	44.0	1.500	44.0	1.500	44.0	1.250
1925	45.0	1.250	44.0	1.500	44.0	1.500	44.0	1.250
1926	45.0	1.250	44.0	1.500	44.0	1.500	44.0	1.250
1927	44.0	1.500	44.0	1.500	44.0	1.575	44.0	1.250
1928	44.0	1.500	44.0	1.500	44.0	1.575	44.0	1.500

Year	New York, N. Y.[11]		Philadelphia, Pa.		St. Louis, Mo.		San Francisco, Calif.	
1907	44.0	$0.525	44.0	$0.500	44.0	$0.600		
1908	44.0	.550	44.0	.500	44.0	.600		
1909	44.0	.550	44.0	.500	44.0	.600		
1910	44.0	.550	44.0	.500	44.0	.600		
1911	44.0	.575	44.0	.500	44.0	.600		
1912	44.0	.575	44.0	.500	44.0	.600	44.0	$0.875
1913	44.0	.600	44.0	.500	44.0	.600	44.0	.875
1914	44.0	.600	44.0	.550	44.0	.700		
1915	44.0	.600	44.0	.550	44.0	.700		
1916	44.0	.625	44.0	.550	44.0	.700		
1917	44.0	{ .625 to .750 }	44.0	.600	44.0	.700		
1918	44.0	.750	44.0	.700	44.0	.700		
1919	44.0	[12] .800	44.0	[13] .800	44.0	.850	44.0	1.000
1920	44.0	1.250	44.0	1.300	44.0	1.000	44.0	1.125
1921	44.0	1.250	44.0	1.300	44.0	1.000	44.0	[8] 1.125
1922	44.0	1.250	44.0	1.000	44.0	1.250	44.0	1.250
1923	44.0	1.500	44.0	1.250	44.0	1.500	44.0	1.375
1924	44.0	1.500	44.0	1.300	44.0	1.500	44.0	1.375
1925	44.0	1.500	44.0	1.300	44.0	1.500		
1926	44.0	1.750	[14] 44.0	1.500	44.0	1.500		
1927	44.0	1.750	44.0	1.500	44.0	1.500	44.0	1.375
1928	44.0	1.750	44.0	1.500	44.0	1.500	44.0	1.375

[8] Old scale; strike pending.
[9] 48 hours November to April, inclusive.
[10] 48 hours December to February, inclusive.
[11] Manhattan and Bronx, 1912 to 1920.

[12] Rate for foundation work.
[13] 50 per cent received more.
[14] 40 hours July and August.

TABLE **B-18.**—*Painters, 1840–1900, by year and State*

Year and State	Sex	Hours per week	Rate per day (dollars)
1840:			
Connecticut	M.	66-66-66	1.50-1.50-1.50
Maryland	M.	60-60-60	1.25-1.25-1.25
Massachusetts	M.	60-60-60	1.42-1.67-1.50
New York	M.	60-60-60	1.25-1.50-1.49
1841:			
Maryland	M.	60-60-60	1.25-1.25-1.25
Massachusetts	M.	60-60-60	1.33-1.67-1.50
New York	M.	60-60-60	1.25-1.50-1.49
1842:			
Connecticut	M.	66-66-66	1.50-1.50-1.50
Maryland	M.	60-60-60	1.25-1.38-1.33
Massachusetts	M.	60-60-60	1.42-1.67-1.55
New York	M.	60-60-60	1.25-1.50-1.49
1843:			
Maryland	M.	60-60-60	1.25-1.38-1.35
Massachusetts	M.	60-60-60	1.33-1.67-1.44
New York	M.	60-60-60	1.25-1.50-1.49
1844:			
Maryland	M.	60-60-60	1.25-1.50-1.40
Massachusetts	M.	60-60-60	1.42-1.67-1.48
New York	M.	60-60-60	1.25-1.50-1.49
1845:			
Maryland	M.	60-60-60	1.38-1.50-1.43
Massachusetts	M.	60-60-60	1.33-1.42-1.34
New York	M.	60-60-60	1.25-1.50-1.49
1846:			
Maryland	M.	60-60-60	1.38-1.50-1.43
Massachusetts	M.	60-60-60	.96-1.42-1.23
New York	M.	60-60-60	1.25-1.50-1.49
1847:			
Maryland	M.	60-60-60	1.50-1.50-1.50
Massachusetts	M.	60-60-60	1.67-1.67-1.67
New York	M.	60-60-60	1.25-1.50-1.49
1848:			
Maryland	M.	60-60-60	1.50-1.50-1.50
Massachusetts	M.	60-75-64	1.00-1.50-1.37
New York	M.	60-60-60	1.25-1.50-1.49
1849:			
Maryland	M.	60-60-60	1.50-1.50-1.50
Massachusetts	M.	60-75-65	1.42-1.67-1.49
New York	M.	60-60-60	1.25-1.50-1.49
Pennsylvania	M.	60-60-60	1.50-2.50-1.75
1850:			
Maryland	M.	60-60-60	1.50-1.50-1.50
Massachusetts	M.	60-75-70	1.42-1.50-1.47
New York	M.	60-60-60	1.25-1.75-1.72
Pennsylvania	M.	60-60-60	1.25-1.50-1.47
1851:			
Maryland	M.	60-60-60	1.50-1.50-1.50
Massachusetts	M.	60-75-64	1.42-1.50-1.44
New York	M.	60-60-60	1.25-1.75-1.73
Pennsylvania	M.	60-60-60	1.12-1.50-1.37
1852:			
Maryland	M.	60-60-60	1.50-1.50-1.50
Massachusetts	M.	60-75-62	.96-1.50-1.17
New York	M.	60-60-60	1.00-1.75-1.61
Pennsylvania	M.	60-60-60	1.25-2.50-1.55
1853:			
Massachusetts	M.	60-75-64	1.42-1.67-1.48
New York	M.	60-60-60	1.25-1.75-1.73
Pennsylvania	M	60-60-60	1.25-3.00-1.75
Do	F.	54-54-54	.59-.84-.70
1854:			
Massachusetts	M.	60-66-62	1.12-1.75-1.40
New York	M.	60-60-60	1.25-2.00-1.97
Pennsylvania	F.	54-54-54	.59-.84-.69
1855:			
Massachusetts	M.	60-72-64	1.00-1.75-1.48
New York	M.	60-60-60	1.25-2.00-1.96
Pennsylvania	F.	54-54-54	.67-.84-.73
1856:			
Maryland	M.	60-60-60	1.75-1.75-1.75
Massachusetts	M.	60-72-61	.96-1.75-1.34
New York	M.	60-60-60	1.25-2.00-1.93
Pennsylvania	F.	54-60-58	.67-.94-.73
1857:			
Maryland	M.	60-60-60	1.75-1.75-1.75
Massachusetts	M.	60-78-63	1.00-1.75-1.42
New York	M.	60-60-60	1.25-2.00-1.95
Pennsylvania	F.	54-54-54	.67-.84-.77
Virginia	M.	72-72-72	1.00-1.00-1.00
1858:			
Maryland	M.	60-60-60	1.75-1.75-1.75
Massachusetts	M.	60-78-67	.87-1.75-1.28
New York	M.	60-60-60	1.25-1.75-1.73
Pennsylvania	F.	54-54-54	.67-.84-.75
1859:			
Maryland	M.	60-60-60	1.50-1.75-1.64
Massachusetts	M.	60-78-70	.75-1.75-1.20
New York	M.	60-60-60	1.25-2.00-1.96
Pennsylvania	F.	54-54-54	.67-.84-.75
1860:			
Maryland	M.	60-60-60	1.50-1.75-1.67
Massachusetts	M.	60-78-69	.75-1.75-1.23
New York	M.	60-60-60	1.25-2.00-1.97
Ohio	M.	(1)	1.25-2.00-1.63
Pennsylvania	M.	60-60-60	1.50-1.50-1.50
Do	F.	54-54-54	.67-.84-.75
1861:			
Maryland	M.	60-60-60	1.50-1.67-1.59
Massachusetts	M.	60-78-73	1.00-2.00-1.23
New York	M.	60-60-60	1.25-2.00-1.93
Pennsylvania	F.	54-54-54	.67-.84-.72
1862:			
Maryland	M.	60-60-60	1.17-1.50-1.45
Massachusetts	M.	60-78-68	.83-1.75-1.29
New York	M.	60-60-60	1.75-2.00-1.98
Pennsylvania	F.	54-54-54	.67-.84-.78
1863:			
Maryland	M.	60-60-60	1.50-1.75-1.57
Massachusetts	M.	60-78-66	1.00-1.83-1.35
New York	M.	60-60-60	1.75-2.50-2.21
Pennsylvania	F.	54-54-54	.67-.84-.78
1864:			
Delaware	M.	60-60-60	1.67-2.42-2.06
Maryland	M.	60-60-60	1.50-2.50-2.40
Massachusetts	M.	60-78-66	.75-2.50-1.57
New York	M.	60-60-60	1.75-3.00-2.93
Pennsylvania	F.	54-54-54	.75-.84-.81
1865:			
Delaware	M.	60-60-60	1.25-2.50-1.89
Maryland	M.	60-72-63	2.50-2.50-2.50
Massachusetts	M.	60-72-60	1.16-2.50-1.88
New York	M.	60-72-60	1.38-3.60-2.82
Pennsylvania	M.	60-60-60	1.84-1.84-1.84
Do	F.	54-54-54	.84-.84-.84
1866:			
Maryland	M.	60-72-62	2.50-3.00-2.54
Massachusetts	M.	60-60-60	1.25-3.00-2.08
New York	M.	60-60-60	1.75-3.50-3.35
Pennsylvania	M.	60-60-60	2.00-2.00-2.00
Do	F.	54-54-54	.75-1.00-.86
1867:			
Delaware	M.	60-60-60	2.00-3.33-2.55
Maryland	M.	60-60-60	2.50-3.00-2.96
Massachusetts	M.	60-72-61	1.42-3.50-2.11
New York	M.	60-60-60	1.75-4.00-3.86
Pennsylvania	M.	60-60-60	2.17-2.17-2.17
Do	F.	54-60-55	.75-1.00-.87
1868:			
Delaware	M.	60-60-60	2.25-3.33-2.54
Maryland	M.	60-60-60	2.50-3.00-2.96
Massachusetts	M.	60-66-62	1.00-4.00-3.43
New York	M.	60-60-60	1.75-4.00-3.43
Pennsylvania	M.	60-60-60	2.17-2.17-2.17
Do	F.	54-54-54	.75-1.17-.89
1869:			
Delaware	M.	60-60-60	2.00-3.50-2.46
Maryland	M.	60-60-60	2.50-3.00-2.94
Massachusetts	M.	60-66-62	1.25-4.50-2.22
New York	M.	60-60-60	1.75-4.50-4.29

¹ Not reported.

TABLE **B-18.**—*Painters, 1840-1900, by year and State*—Continued

Year and State	Sex	Hours per week	Rate per day (dollars)	Year and State	Sex	Hours per week	Rate per day (dollars)
1869—Continued.				**1875—Continued.**			
Pennsylvania	M.	60-60-60	2.17-2.17-2.17	Illinois	M.	60-60-60	1.50-2.65-2.17
Do	F.	54-54-54	.84-1.17-.96	Louisiana	M.	60-60-60	2.00-2.00-2.00
1870:				Maryland	M.	60-60-60	2.00-2.50-2.50
California	M.	60-60-60	3.50-4.00-3.72	Massachusetts	M.	60-60-60	1.50-3.00-2.22
Delaware	M.	60-60-60	2.00-3.50-2.47	Minnesota	M.	60-60-60	2.50-3.00-2.67
Illinois	M.	60-60-60	1.75-3.25-2.17	Missouri	M.	60-60-60	2.50-2.50-2.50
Louisiana	M.	60-60-60	2.50-2.50-2.50	New York	M.	60-72-60	1.75-4.00-3.08
Maryland	M.	60-60-60	2.50-3.00-2.53	Ohio	M.	59-59-59	2.50-2.50-2.50
Massachusetts	M.	60-66-61	1.25-4.50-2.37	Pennsylvania	M.	60-60-60	.50-4.20-2.23
Minnesota	M.	60-60-60	2.50-3.00-2.77	Do	F.	54-54-54	.75-1.50-1.15
Missouri	M.	60-60-60	2.50-2.50-2.50	Virginia	M.	60-60-60	1.75-1.75-1.75
New York	M.	60-60-60	1.75-3.50-3.15	**1876:**			
Ohio	M.	59-59-59	2.50-2.50-2.50	California	M.	54-54-54	3.00-3.50-3.26
Pennsylvania	M.	60-60-60	2.00-4.50-2.69	Delaware	M.	60-60-60	1.50-2.33-1.87
Do	F.	54-54-54	.75-1.17-.97	Illinois	M.	60-60-60	1.50-2.50-2.00
Virginia	M.	60-60-60	2.00-2.00-2.00	Louisiana	M.	60-60-60	2.00-2.00-2.00
1871:				Maryland	M.	60-60-60	2.00-2.50-2.47
California	M.	60-60-60	3.50-4.00-3.66	Massachusetts	M.	54-60-59	1.02-4.00-2.05
Delaware	M.	60-60-60	2.00-3.00-2.43	Minnesota	M.	60-60-60	2.50-3.00-2.60
Illinois	M.	60-60-60	2.00-3.50-2.22	Missouri	M.	60-60-60	2.50-2.50-2.50
Louisiana	M.	60-60-60	2.50-2.50-2.50	New York	M.	60-60-60	1.75-4.00-3.02
Maryland	M.	60-60-60	2.50-3.00-2.52	Ohio	M.	59-59-59	2.50-2.50-2.50
Massachusetts	M.	66-66-61	.75-4.25-2.35	Pennsylvania	M.	48-60-59	.56-4.00-2.02
Minnesota	M.	60-60-60	2.50-3.00-2.77	Do	F.	54-54-54	.75-1.34-1.03
Missouri	M.	60-60-60	2.50-2.50-2.50	Virginia	M.	60-60-60	1.75-1.75-1.75
New York	M.	60-60-60	1.75-3.50-3.16	**1877:**			
Ohio	M.	59-59-59	2.50-2.50-2.50	California	M.	54-54-54	3.00-3.50-3.10
Pennsylvania	M.	60-60-60	2.00-4.50-2.72	Delaware	M.	60-60-60	1.67-2.00-1.77
Do	F.	54-54-54	.75-1.17-.97	Illinois	M.	60-60-60	1.50-2.50-2.02
Virginia	M.	60-60-60	2.00-2.00-2.00	Louisiana	M.	60-60-60	2.25-2.25-2.25
1872:				Maryland	M.	60-60-60	2.00-2.50-2.48
California	M.	60-60-60	3.50-4.00-3.70	Massachusetts	M.	54-60-59	1.45-3.00-2.09
Delaware	M.	60-60-60	2.17-3.00-2.56	Minnesota	M.	60-60-60	2.50-3.00-2.60
Illinois	M.	60-60-60	2.50-3.25-2.67	Missouri	M.	60-60-60	2.50-2.50-2.50
Louisiana	M.	60-60-60	3.00-3.00-3.00	New Jersey	M.	60-60-60	2.00-2.10-2.09
Maryland	M.	60-60-60	2.50-2.50-2.50	New York	M.	60-60-60	1.55-4.00-2.59
Massachusetts	M.	66-66-61	1.00-4.50-2.47	Ohio	M.	59-60-59	1.50-2.50-1.86
Minnesota	M.	60-60-60	2.50-3.00-2.67	Pennsylvania	M.	48-60-58	.90-4.00-2.33
Missouri	M.	60-60-60	2.50-2.50-2.50	Do	M.	(¹)	².20-.20-.20
New York	M.	60-60-60	1.50-3.75-3.12	Do	F.	54-54-54	1.00-1.34-1.17
Ohio	M.	59-59-59	1.85-3.00-2.61	Virginia	M.	60-60-60	1.75-1.75-1.75
Pennsylvania	M.	60-60-60	2.00-4.50-2.78	**1878:**			
Do	F.	54-54-54	.75-1.50-1.08	California	M.	54-54-54	3.00-3.50-3.19
Virginia	M.	60-60-60	2.00-2.00-2.00	Connecticut	M.	72-72-72	2.25-2.25-2.25
1873:				Delaware	M.	60-60-60	1.50-1.67-1.58
California	M.	60-60-60	3.50-4.00-3.69	Illinois	M.	60-60-60	1.75-2.50-2.05
Delaware	M.	60-60-60	2.00-3.00-2.55	Louisiana	M.	60-60-60	2.25-2.25-2.25
Illinois	M.	60-60-60	1.75-3.00-2.26	Maryland	M.	60-60-60	1.75-2.50-2.48
Louisiana	M.	60-60-60	3.00-3.00-3.00	Massachusetts	M.	54-60-59	1.25-3.00-1.99
Maryland	M.	60-60-60	2.50-2.50-2.50	Minnesota	M.	60-60-60	2.50-3.00-2.65
Massachusetts	M.	66-66-61	1.50-4.50-2.72	Missouri	M.	60-60-60	2.50-2.50-2.50
Minnesota	M.	60-60-60	2.50-3.00-2.67	New York	M.	60-60-60	1.50-4.00-2.61
Missouri	M.	60-60-60	2.50-2.50-2.50	Ohio	M.	59-60-59	1.67-4.00-1.80
New York	M.	60-60-60	1.75-4.00-3.13	Pennsylvania	M.	48-60-58	1.00-4.00-2.17
Ohio	M.	59-59-59	2.50-2.50-2.50	Do	M.	54-60-57	.85-1.34-1.01
Pennsylvania	M.	60-60-60	1.50-4.50-2.65	Virginia	M.	60-60-60	1.75-1.75-1.75
Do	F.	54-54-54	.75-1.50-1.14	**1879:**			
Virginia	M.	60-60-60	1.75-1.75-1.75	California	M.	54-54-54	3.00-3.50-3.11
1874:				Delaware	M.	60-60-60	1.67-1.83-1.71
California	M.	60-60-60	3.00-3.50-3.25	Illinois	M.	60-60-60	1.75-2.50-2.13
Delaware	M.	60-60-60	1.67-2.92-2.41	Louisiana	M.	60-60-60	2.00-2.00-2.00
Illinois	M.	60-60-60	1.75-2.65-2.07	Maryland	M.	60-60-60	2.00-2.50-2.48
Louisiana	M.	60-60-60	2.00-2.00-2.00	Massachusetts	M.	54-60-59	.75-2.75-1.88
Maryland	M.	60-60-60	2.50-2.50-2.50	Minnesota	M.	60-60-60	2.50-3.00-2.65
Massachusetts	M.	66-66-61	1.60-4.50-2.45	Missouri	M.	59-60-60	1.25-3.33-2.18
Minnesota	M.	60-60-60	2.50-3.00-2.67	New Jersey	M.	(¹)	.62-2.00-1.65
Missouri	M.	60-60-60	2.50-2.50-2.50	New York	M.	60-72-60	1.75-3.25-2.84
New York	M.	60-60-60	1.75-4.00-3.02	Ohio	M.	59-59-59	.75-2.50-1.91
Ohio	M.	59-59-59	2.50-2.50-2.50	Pennsylvania	M.	54-72-60	1.10-4.00-1.95
Pennsylvania	M.	60-60-60	1.25-4.50-2.37	Do	F.	54-54-54	1.00-1.34-1.17
Do	F.	54-54-54	.75-1.50-1.10	Virginia	M.	60-60-60	1.75-1.75-1.75
Virginia	M.	60-60-60	1.75-1.75-1.75	**1880:**			
1875:				California	M.	54-54-54	3.00-3.50-3.10
California	M.	60-60-60	3.00-3.50-3.17	Illinois	M.	49-60-57	1.74-2.50-2.02
Delaware	M.	60-60-60	1.50-2.50-1.89	Louisiana	M.	60-60-60	2.00-2.00-2.00

---

¹ Not reported.   ² Per hour.

TABLE B-18.—*Painters, 1840-1900, by year and State*—Continued

Year and State	Sex	Hours per week	Rate per day (dollars)
1880—Continued.			
Maryland	M.	60-60-60	1.75-2.50-2.47
Massachusetts	M.	54-60-59	.75-2.50-1.95
Minnesota	M.	60-60-60	2.75-2.75-2.75
Missouri	M.	60-60-60	2.50-2.50-2.50
New Jersey	(1)	55-60-60	1.00-2.50-1.62
New York	M.	60-72-60	1.75-3.00-2.94
Ohio	M.	59-59-59	1.50-2.00-1.52
Pennsylvania	M.	60-60-60	1.50-3.33-2.36
Do	M.	54-54-54	1.00-1.34-1.17
Virginia	M.	60-60-60	2.00-2.00-2.00
1881:			
California	M.	54-54-54	3.00-3.00-3.00
Delaware	M.	60-60-60	1.66-2.50-1.92
Dist. of Columbia	M.	58-58-58	2.00-2.25-2.13
Illinois	M.	60-60-60	1.75-3.00-2.30
Louisiana	M.	60-60-60	2.00-2.00-2.00
Maryland	M.	60-60-60	1.75-2.50-2.47
Massachusetts	M.	54-60-59	1.00-3.00-2.04
Minnesota	M.	60-60-60	2.75-2.75-2.75
Missouri	M.	60-60-60	2.50-2.50-2.50
New Hampshire	M.	65-65-65	1.35-2.25-1.63
New Jersey	M.	54-60-59	1.37-2.50-1.91
New York	M.	58-72-58	1.75-3.50-2.76
Ohio	M.	54-60-59	1.20-3.00-1.61
Pennsylvania	M.	60-60-60	1.70-3.33-2.50
Do	F.	54-54-54	1.00-1.34-1.17
Virginia	M.	60-60-60	2.00-2.00-2.00
Wisconsin	M.	59-59-59	1.85-1.85-1.85
1882:			
California	M.	54-54-54	3.00-3.00-3.00
Delaware	M.	60-60-60	1.67-2.67-2.09
Illinois	M.	60-60-60	2.00-3.00-2.55
Louisiana	M.	60-60-60	2.00-2.00-2.00
Maryland	M.	60-60-60	1.75-2.50-2.47
Massachusetts	M.	54-60-57	1.10-3.00-2.11
Minnesota	M.	60-60-60	2.75-2.75-2.75
Missouri	M.	60-60-60	1.25-3.33-2.71
New Jersey	M.	60-60-60	1.50-3.00-2.70
New York	M.	58-72-58	1.92-3.50-2.86
Ohio	M.	59-59-59	2.25-2.50-2.38
Do	(1)	57-72-60	1.00-3.50-1.71
Pennsylvania	M.	60-60-60	1.67-3.67-2.49
Do	F.	54-54-54	1.00-1.34-1.17
Virginia	M.	60-60-60	2.00-2.00-2.00
1883:			
California	M.	54-54-54	3.00-3.50-3.17
Delaware	M.	60-60-60	1.83-2.67-2.13
Dist. of Columbia	M.	58-58-58	2.50-3.00-2.75
Georgia	M.	(1)	1.75-1.75-1.75
Illinois	M.	60-60-60	2.00-3.00-2.62
Louisiana	M.	60-60-60	2.00-2.00-2.00
Maryland	M.	60-60-60	1.75-2.50-2.49
Massachusetts	M.	54-60-57	1.00-3.00-2.11
Do	(1)	(1)	.83-1.15-.97
Michigan	M.	(1)	.40-5.00-1.97
Minnesota	M.	60-60-60	2.75-2.75-2.75
Missouri	M.	60-60-60	2.50-2.50-2.50
New Jersey	M.	60-60-60	1.33-3.00-2.50
New York	M.	58-72-58	1.93-3.50-3.25
Ohio	M.	48-60-59	1.50-3.00-2.20
Pennsylvania	M.	60-60-60	2.00-3.33-2.65
Do	F.	54-54-54	.92-1.17-1.05
Texas	M.	60-60-60	2.50-2.50-2.50
Virginia	M.	60-60-60	2.00-2.00-2.00
1884:			
California	M.	54-60-54	2.00-5.00-3.12
Delaware	M.	60-60-60	2.00-3.00-2.21
Illinois	M.	54-60-60	2.30-3.00-2.48
Indiana	M.	(1)	1.50-1.50-1.50
Iowa	M.	54-72-60	1.50-4.00-2.40
Louisiana	M.	60-60-60	2.25-2.25-2.25
Maryland	M.	60-60-60	1.75-2.50-2.49
Massachusetts	M.	54-60-58	1.15-3.50-2.12
Michigan	M.	(1)	.50-4.25-1.88
Minnesota	M.	60-60-60	2.75-2.75-2.75
Missouri	M.	48-60-51	2.17-4.00-2.45
New Jersey	M.	54-60-60	.83-3.00-2.29
New York	M.	58-72-58	1.92-3.50-3.26
1884—Continued.			
Ohio	M.	48-60-58	1.30-2.50-1.89
Pennsylvania	M.	60-63-60	1.67-3.67-2.14
Do	F.	54-54-54	.92-1.17-1.04
Virginia	M.	60-60-60	2.50-2.50-2.50
1885:			
California	M.	54-60-54	2.25-3.00-2.98
Connecticut	M.	60-60-60	1.50-3.50-2.10
Delaware	M.	60-60-60	1.50-2.50-1.76
Georgia	M.	69-69-69	1.00-1.00-1.00
Illinois	M.	60-60-60	1.00-4.00-2.17
Indiana	M.	60-60-60	.65-2.25-1.68
Iowa	M.	57-57-57	2.00-2.00-2.00
Kansas	M.	48-60-56	1.92-3.00-2.32
Louisiana	M.	60-60-60	2.25-2.25-2.25
Maine	M.	54-66-61	1.33-2.03-1.70
Maryland	M.	54-60-60	1.75-2.50-2.49
Massachusetts	M.	54-60-58	1.04-3.50-2.13
Michigan	M.	(1)	1.00-3.08-1.94
Minnesota	M.	60-60-60	2.75-2.75-2.75
Missouri	M.	48-60-51	1.92-2.75-2.40
New Hampshire	M.	66-66-66	1.25-1.25-1.25
New Jersey	M.	54-60-59	1.00-4.67-2.40
Do	F.	60-60-60	.58-.58-.58
New York	M.	56-72-69	1.12-3.50-2.96
Do	F.	59-59-59	.67-1.00-.87
North Carolina	M.	60-60-60	1.50-2.50-1.75
Ohio	M.	59-60-60	1.25-3.85-1.73
Pennsylvania	M.	60-60-60	1.88-3.67-2.03
Do	F.	54-54-54	.92-1.17-1.04
Rhode Island	M.	48-48-48	1.31-1.75-1.53
Vermont	M.	60-66-60	1.50-2.00-1.61
Virginia	M.	60-60-60	1.80-2.50-2.30
Wisconsin	M.	48-48-48	1.00-1.00-1.00
1886:			
California	M.	54-60-59	1.92-5.00-2.57
Do	M.	48-48-48	2.88-3.00-2.99
Connecticut	M.	60-60-60	2.00-2.25-2.14
Delaware	M.	60-60-60	1.50-2.50-1.79
Dist. of Columbia	M.	53-58-55	3.00-3.00-3.00
Illinois	M.	48-60-53	1.50-3.50-2.54
Iowa	M.	(1)	.50-5.00-2.13
Kansas	M.	54-72-60	1.00-2.90-2.12
Louisiana	M.	60-60-60	2.25-2.25-2.25
Maryland	F.	60-60-60	.67-.67-.67
Do	M.	54-60-57	1.75-2.50-2.49
Massachusetts	M.	54-60-59	1.25-3.50-2.40
Michigan	M.	60-60-60	2.15-2.15-2.15
Minnesota	M.	60-60-60	.75-2.75-2.67
Missouri	M.	48-60-50	2.40-2.50-2.42
New Hampshire	M.	60-60-60	1.60-1.60-1.60
New Jersey	M.	54-60-59	2.50-3.00-2.74
Do	F.	59-59-59	1.08-1.08-1.08
New York	M.	48-72-54	1.90-3.50-3.18
Ohio	M.	59-59-59	1.21-3.34-2.14
Pennsylvania	F.	44-54-50	.92-1.17-1.11
Do	M.	54-60-55	1.26-3.67-2.65
Rhode Island	M.	60-60-60	2.00-2.00-2.00
Virginia	M.	60-60-60	2.50-2.50-2.50
1887:			
California	M.	54-54-54	3.00-3.00-3.00
Connecticut	M.	(1)	.84-3.00-2.20
Do	F.	(1)	.91-.91-.91
Delaware	M.	(1)	[2] 17½-.22½-.20
Do	M.	60-60-60	1.75-3.00-2.01
Florida	M.	(1)	1.00-4.00-1.99
Illinois	F.	47-60-57	.58-1.68-.94
Do	M.	48-60-54	2.20-2.80-2.39
Do	(1)	(1)	1.77-1.77-1.77
Kansas	M.	60-60-60	2.00-3.75-2.41
Louisiana	M.	60-60-60	2.25-2.25-2.25
Maine	M.	60-60-60	1.50-2.25-1.88
Maryland	M.	54-60-54	.80-2.50-2.04
Massachusetts	F.	48-60-57	.92-1.17-1.02
Do	M.	54-60-58	1.00-3.35-1.98
Michigan	M.	(1)	1.75-2.50-1.96
Do	M.	(1)	[2] 15-.21-.17½
Minnesota	M.	60-60-60	2.75-2.75-2.75

¹ Not reported.   ² Per hour.

TABLE **B–18.**—*Painters, 1840–1900, by year and State*—Continued

Year and State	Sex	Hours per week	Rate per day (dollars)	Year and State	Sex	Hours per week	Rate per day (dollars)
1887—Continued.				**1890—Continued.**			
Missouri	M.	48-72-52	1.73-3.00-2.39	Louisiana	M.	60-60-60	2.25-2.25-2.25
Do	([1])		2.30-2.95-2.73	Maryland	M.	54-60-54	2.00-2.50-2.50
Nebraska	([1])	54-60-59	1.00-3.50-2.26	Massachusetts	M.	54-60-58	1.25-3.25-2.16
New Hampshire	M.	([1])	2.50-2.50-2.50	Michigan	M.	60-60-60	.33-3.33-1.50
New Jersey	M.	([1])	2.25-2.25-2.25	Minnesota	M.	60-60-60	1.00-2.75-2.28
New York	F.	52-60-57	[2].35-1.17-.74	Missouri	M.	48-48-48	2.40-2.50-2.43
Do	M.	48-72-54	1.25-3.50-2.93	Nebraska	M.	([1])	2.50-2.50-2.50
Do	M.	([1])	[2].12-.25-.18	New Hampshire	M.	60-60-60	1.70-2.00-1.80
North Carolina	M.	60-72-63	1.00-2.00-1.48	New York	M.	48-72-55	.50-5.00-2.16
Ohio	F.	57-60-60	.42-1.00-.82	Do	F.	([1])	.88-1.17-1.06
Do	M.	48-60-59	.50-3.50-1.94	Ohio	M.	59-59-59	2.50-2.50-2.50
Oregon	M.	([1])	1.50-3.60-2.83	Do	([1])	42-60-57	.65-5.00-1.71
Pennsylvania	M.	54-60-55	.60-3.67-2.17	Pennsylvania	M.	53-60-55	2.00-4.16-2.70
Do	M.	([1])	[2].15-.20-.18½	Do	F.	54-54-54	1.25-1.25-1.25
Do	F.	54-54-54	.92-1.17-1.08	Virginia	M.	60-60-60	1.75-1.75-1.75
Rhode Island	M.	([1])	1.70-2.50-2.20	Wisconsin	M.	([1])	.89-4.47-1.93
Virginia	M.	60-60-60	1.75-2.00-1.95	**1891:**			
West Virginia	M.	([1])	1.25-2.00-1.75	California	M.	48-48-48	2.50-3.50-2.93
Wisconsin	M.	([1])	.71-3.00-1.66	Delaware	M.	60-60-60	1.75-3.00-2.17
1888:				Illinois	M.	48-60-51	2.20-2.80-2.41
California	M.	54-54-54	3.00-3.00-3.00	Indiana	M.	48-60-57	1.10-2.38-1.81
Colorado	M.	48-60-56	2.03-3.25-2.19	Louisiana	M.	60-60-60	2.25-2.25-2.25
Delaware	M.	60-60-60	1.75-3.00-2.01	Maine	M.	60-60-60	1.17-2.75-1.98
Georgia	M.	66-66-66	1.25-2.48-1.40	Maryland	M.	54-60-54	2.00-2.50-2.50
Illinois	M.	48-60-53	2.20-3.00-2.48	Massachusetts	M.	54-60-58	1.25-3.25-2.21
Indiana	M.	60-72-60	1.15-2.57-2.04	Michigan	F.	([1])	.50-.77-.59
Iowa	M.	51-60-59	1.50-3.00-2.17	Minnesota	M.	60-60-60	2.75-2.75-2.75
Kansas	M.	([1])	1.75-2.75-2.29	Missouri	M.	48-48-48	1.09-3.00-2.17
Louisiana	M.	60-60-60	2.25-2.25-2.25	New York	M.	48-72-51	.50-5.00-2.09
Maine	M.	60-60-60	2.00-2.50-2.25	Do	F.	([1])	1.00-1.17-1.06
Maryland	M.	54-60-54	1.75-2.50-2.49	Ohio	M.	42-72-58	.75-2.75-1.81
Massachusetts	M.	54-60-57	1.00-3.25-2.22	Pennsylvania	M.	54-60-55	2.00-4.16-2.73
Michigan	M.	60-60-60	1.99-2.49-2.09	Do	F.	54-54-54	1.25-1.25-1.25
Minnesota	M.	60-60-60	2.75-2.75-2.75	Virginia	M.	60-60-60	1.75-1.75-1.75
Missouri	M.	48-60-51	2.40-2.50-2.43	Wisconsin	M.	([1])	[2].12½-.45-.23½
Do	([1])	([1])	1.80-2.33-2.01	**1892:**			
New Jersey	M.	54-60-55	1.54-2.75-1.65	California	M.	48-60-50	1.50-4.00-3.00
Do	F.	([1])	1.00-1.00-1.00	Delaware	M.	60-60-60	1.33-3.00-2.00
New York	M.	46-72-57	.75-4.17-2.59	Illinois	M.	48-60-50	2.20-2.80-2.56
Do	M.	([1])	[2].16½-.17½-.17½	Do	F.	58-60-59	.83-1.77-1.26
North Carolina	M.	60-72-62	.83-2.25-1.39	Indiana	M.	54-60-60	1.10-2.79-1.84
Ohio	M.	59-60-59	1.28-2.74-1.94	Iowa	M.	60-60-60	.50-2.50-2.21
Pennsylvania	M.	53-60-55	1.90-3.67-2.69	Louisiana	M.	54-54-54	2.70-2.70-2.70
Do	F.	54-54-54	.92-1.17-1.05	Maine	M.	60-60-60	1.83-1.90-1.88
Rhode Island	M.	([1])	1.16-3.00-2.27	Maryland	M.	54-60-56	1.50-2.50-2.21
South Carolina	M.	66-66-66	1.00-1.00-1.00	Massachusetts	M.	54-60-57	1.25-3.25-2.23
Virginia	M.	60-60-60	1.00-2.00-1.93	Michigan	M.	42-60-58	.50-7.00-2.05
1889:				Minnesota	M.	60-60-60	2.50-2.75-2.63
California	M.	54-54-54	3.00-3.00-3.00	Missouri	M.	48-60-52	1.17-3.00-2.62
Connecticut	M.	([1])	2.00-2.00-2.00	New York	M.	48-60-51	1.75-3.50-3.43
Delaware	M.	60-60-60	1.83-3.00-2.08	Ohio	M.	53-53-53	2.61-2.61-2.61
Illinois	M.	48-60-54	2.10-2.93-2.40	Do	([1])	53-60-56	.50-3.00-1.94
Indiana	M.	48-60-59	1.25-2.22-1.67	Pennsylvania	M.	53-60-55	1.40-4.16-2.61
Iowa	M.	48-60-57	1.50-2.40-1.95	Rhode Island	M.	54-60-57	1.25-4.00-2.38
Kansas	M.	60-60-60	1.20-3.00-2.28	Virginia	M.	60-60-60	2.00-2.00-2.00
Louisiana	M.	60-60-60	2.25-2.25-2.25	**1893:**			
Maine	M.	([1])	1.50-2.00-1.75	California	M.	48-48-48	2.50-3.50-2.89
Maryland	M.	54-60-54	1.35-2.50-2.47	Delaware	M.	60-60-60	1.33-3.00-1.95
Massachusetts	M.	54-60-58	1.00-3.25-2.05	Illinois	M.	48-72-50	.47-4.33-2.67
Michigan	M.	60-60-60	.67-3.00-1.13	Indiana	M.	48-60-58	1.65-2.31-1.95
Minnesota	M.	60-60-60	2.75-2.75-2.75	Louisiana	M.	54-54-54	2.70-2.70-2.70
Missouri	M.	48-60-51	2.40-2.50-2.43	Maryland	M.	44-72-55	.67-3.33-2.33
New Hampshire	M.	60-60-60	1.25-2.20-1.80	Massachusetts	M.	54-60-55	1.25-3.00-2.35
New York	M.	54-72-55	1.50-3.50-3.40	Michigan	M.	54-60-59	.75-3.83-1.89
North Carolina	M.	60-72-63	1.00-2.00-1.75	Minnesota	M.	60-60-60	2.50-2.50-2.50
Ohio	M.	59-59-59	2.50-2.50-2.50	Missouri	M.	48-60-57	1.75-2.75-2.31
Pennsylvania	M.	53-60-55	.75-4.16-2.68	Montana	M.	48-54-50	2.50-5.00-3.74
Do	F.	54-54-54	.95-1.25-1.09	New Hampshire	M.	48-66-59	1.25-4.00-2.13
Virginia	M.	60-60-60	2.00-2.00-2.00	New York	M.	48-60-50	.67-4.17-2.93
1890:				Do	F.	48-60-50	.50-1.08-.75
California	M.	54-54-54	2.50-3.50-2.89	Ohio	M.	30-60-56	1.00-5.00-1.75
Delaware	M.	60-60-60	1.75-3.00-2.17	Do	F.	54-54-54	.75-1.20-1.16
Illinois	M.	48-60-52	2.00-2.60-2.32	Pennsylvania	M.	48-60-56	.50-4.16-2.49
Indiana	M.	54-60-60	1.10-2.50-1.92	Rhode Island	M.	60-60-60	1.66-3.50-2.48
Kansas	M.	([1])	1.70-2.75-2.22	Virginia	M.	60-60-60	2.00-2.00-2.00
				Wisconsin	M.	([1])	[2].10-.50-.23

[1] Not reported.   [2] Per hour.

TABLE B-18.—*Painters, 1840-1900, by year and State*—Continued

Year and State	Sex	Hours per week	Rate per day (dollars)	Year and State	Sex	Hours per week	Rate per day (dollars)
1894:				**1896—Continued.**			
California	M.	48-48-48	2.50-3.50-2.89	Ohio	F.	54-60-60	0.75-0.90-0.81
Delaware	M.	60-60-60	1.33-3.00-1.86	Pennsylvania	M.	48-60-55	1.10-3.30-2.73
Illinois	M.	48-60-49	2.30-3.00-2.61	Rhode Island	M.	60-60-60	1.33-1.83-1.54
Indiana	M.	48-60-56	1.20-2.75-1.84	South Carolina	M.	66-66-66	1.05-1.05-1.05
Iowa	M.	45-84-59	.75-3.50-2.03	Tennessee	M.	(1)	1.00-1.33-1.15
Kansas	M.	54-54-54	2.32-2.32-2.32	Vermont	M.	60-60-60	1.25-1.25-1.25
Louisiana	M.	54-54-54	2.70-2.70-2.70	Virginia	M.	60-60-60	1.75-1.75-1.75
Maine	M.	60-60-60	1.50-3.00-2.11	**1897:**			
Maryland	M.	54-54-54	2.50-2.50-2.50	California	M.	48-48-48	2.50-3.50-2.72
Massachusetts	M.	54-58-55	1.25-4.50-2.60	Connecticut	M.	48-55-52	2.00-2.06-2.03
Do.	(1)	(1)	2.00-2.00-2.00	Illinois	M.	48-60-49	2.35-3.00-2.77
Minnesota	M.	60-60-60	2.50-2.50-2.50	Kansas	M.	48-60-57	1.30-2.30-1.98
Missouri	M.	48-48-48	2.50-2.50-2.50	Louisiana	M.	54-54-54	2.00-2.00-2.00
New Hampshire	M.	60-60-60	1.50-1.50-1.50	Maryland	M.	54-54-54	2.50-2.50-2.50
New York	M.	48-60-54	1.25-3.50-2.61	Do.	(1)	54-54-54	1.90-2.00-1.95
Do.	(1)	(1)	2.50-2.50-2.50	Massachusetts	M.	54-54-54	2.25-3.38-2.63
North Carolina	M.	60-60-60	1.00-1.25-1.22	Michigan	M.	(1)	1.62-1.62-1.62
Do.	(1)	60-60-60	1.35-2.50-1.90	Do.	(1)	48-54-50	.99-2.44-1.86
Ohio	M.	24-60-54	.60-3.00-1.68	Minnesota	M.	60-60-60	2.50-2.50-2.50
Pennsylvania	M.	53-60-55	1.12-4.16-2.61	Missouri	M.	48-48-48	2.50-2.50-2.50
Rhode Island	(1)	(1)	1.04-1.50-1.27	Montana	(1)	(1)	1.72-3.45-2.46
Virginia	M.	60-60-60	2.00-2.00-2.00	Nebraska	M.	48-60-49	1.35-2.70-2.44
West Virginia	M.	54-54-54	1.80-1.80-1.80	New York	M.	48-60-49	1.25-3.50-2.45
1895:				Ohio	M.	53-53-53	2.61-2.61-2.61
California	M.	48-48-48	2.50-3.50-2.83	Pennsylvania	M.	53-60-54	1.80-3.00-2.61
Connecticut	M.	60-60-60	2.00-2.00-2.00	Virginia	M.	54-60-59	.65-2.00-1.51
Delaware	M.	60-60-60	1.33-2.75-1.62	**1898:**			
Illinois	M.	48-60-49	2.35-3.00-2.63	California	M.	48-48-48	2.50-3.50-2.76
Indiana	M.	54-60-60	1.49-3.30-1.85	Illinois	M.	48-60-49	2.35-3.00-2.74
Kansas	(1)	48-48-48	1.53-1.53-1.53	Indiana	(1)	42-72-58	1.14-2.37-1.87
Louisiana	M.	54-54-54	2.25-2.25-2.25	Kansas	M.	48-54-52	1.35-2.03-1.75
Maine	M.	60-60-60	1.25-2.25-1.89	Louisiana	M.	54-54-54	2.00-2.00-2.00
Maryland	M.	54-54-54	2.50-2.50-2.50	Maryland	M.	54-54-54	2.50-2.50-2.50
Massachusetts	M.	41-60-55	1.00-3.00-2.15	Massachusetts	M.	54-54-54	2.25-3.92-2.86
Michigan	M.	(1)	1.50-2.00-1.74	Michigan	M.	(1)	1.32-1.87-1.56
Minnesota	M.	60-60-60	2.50-2.50-2.50	Minnesota	M.	60-60-60	2.50-2.50-2.50
Missouri	M.	48-48-48	2.00-2.50-2.49	Missouri	M.	48-48-48	2.50-2.50-2.50
Montana	M.	(1)	4.29-4.29-4.29	Do.	(1)	48-60-56	1.91-2.50-2.29
New Hampshire	M.	60-60-60	1.00-1.00-1.60	Nebraska	(1)	48-60-56	1.00-4.00-2.14
New York	M.	48-60-56	.88-3.50-2.32	Do.	(1)	(1)	².25-.25-.25
North Carolina	M.	60-72-63	1.00-1.75-1.29	New York	M.	48-60-50	1.00-4.00-2.47
Ohio	M.	36-72-55	.50-3.00-1.68	Ohio	M.	53-53-53	2.61-2.61-2.61
Do.	F.	60-60-60	.60-.90-.73	Pennsylvania	M.	48-60-58	1.70-3.00-2.50
Pennsylvania	M.	53-60-55	.90-4.16-2.58	Virginia	M.	60-60-60	1.75-1.75-1.75
Rhode Island	M.	55-55-55	3.33-3.33-3.33	Do.	(1)	54-54-54	2.50-2.50-2.50
Virginia	M.	60-60-60	1.75-1.75-1.75	**1899:**			
Wisconsin	(1)	48-84-59	.64-4.00-1.74	Alabama	M.	54-60-54	1.50-3.00-2.22
1896:				California	M.	48-48-48	3.00-3.00-3.00
California	M.	48-48-48	2.50-3.50-2.83	Georgia	M.	60-60-60	1.75-2.00-1.84
Colorado	M.	48-48-48	2.50-2.50-2.50	Illinois	M.	48-60-49	2.40-3.00-2.96
Connecticut	M.	60-60-60	1.25-1.75-1.40	Massachusetts	M.	48-53-48	2.25-3.00-2.56
Dist. of Columbia	M.	(1)	2.50-2.50-2.50	Michigan	(1)	(1)	1.50-1.50-1.50
Georgia	M.	66-66-66	.50-1.75-1.27	Montana	M.	48-48-48	4.05-4.05-4.05
Illinois	M.	48-60-49	.32-3.00-2.52	New Jersey	M.	54-54-54	2.50-2.50-2.30
Indiana	M.	48-65-58	1.40-2.35-1.88	New York	M.	47-54-52	2.25-3.50-2.57
Kansas	M.	48-72-57	1.50-2.50-2.13	North Carolina	M.	54-72-62	1.00-2.65-1.52
Louisiana	M.	54-54-54	2.25-2.25-2.25	Ohio	M.	48-48-48	2.00-2.00-2.00
Maryland	M.	53-60-55	1.51-2.50-2.28	Pennsylvania	M.	48-48-48	2.80-2.80-2.80
Massachusetts	M.	48-60-51	1.50-2.81-2.40	Virginia	(1)	(1)	2.15-2.50-2.40
Michigan	M.	60-60-60	.40-3.25-1.51	**1900:**			
Minnesota	M.	60-60-60	2.50-2.50-2.50	Alabama	M.	54-60-54	1.50-3.00-2.25
Mississippi	M.	(1)	2.50-2.50-2.50	California	M.	48-48-48	3.00-3.00-3.00
Missouri	M.	48-60-57	1.08-2.50-1.94	Georgia	M.	60-60-60	1.75-2.00-1.84
Montana	M.	(1)	3.64-3.64-3.64	Illinois	M.	48-48-48	3.00-3.20-3.15
Nebraska	M.	48-48-48	2.00-3.16-2.87	Massachusetts	M.	48-53-48	2.25-3.00-2.56
Do.	(1)	60-60-60	.75-3.00-1.44	Montana	M.	48-48-48	4.05-4.05-4.05
New Hampshire	M.	60-60-60	1.55-1.60-1.59	New Jersey	M.	53-53-53	2.50-2.50-2.50
New Jersey	M.	60-60-60	1.50-1.50-1.50	New York	M.	47-54-53	2.25-3.50-2.39
New York	M.	48-60-51	.50-4.00-2.08	North Carolina	M.	60-60-60	1.25-1.50-1.38
Do.	F.	59-59-59	.50-1.00-.75	Ohio	M.	48-48-48	2.00-2.25-2.14
North Carolina	M.	60-72-62	1.50-2.50-1.88	Pennsylvania	M.	48-48-48	2.80-2.80-2.80
Ohio	M.	46-60-54	.75-3.00-1.64				

1 Not reported.   2 Per hour.

TABLE B-19.—*Painters, males, 1890-1928, by city and year*

Year	Atlanta, Ga.		Birmingham, Ala.		Boston, Mass.		Chicago, Ill.	
	Hours per week	Rate per hour	Hours per week	Rate per hour	Hours per week	Rate per hour	Hours per week	Rate per hour
1890	60.0	$0.163	60.0	$0.250	54.0	$0.283	48.0	$0.305
1891	60.0	.173	60.0	.250	54.0	.285	48.0	.309
1892	60.0	.187	60.0	.250	54.0	.287	48.0	.324
1893	60.0	.186	60.0	.227	54.0	.290	48.0	.347
1894	60.0	.189	60.0	.205	54.0	.297	48.0	.327
1895	60.0	.189	60.0	.200	54.0	.289	48.0	.337
1896	60.0	.192	60.0	.200	52.8	.294	48.0	.337
1897	60.0	.193	60.0	.200	52.4	.302	48.0	.351
1898	60.0	.189	60.0	.221	51.7	.317	48.0	.351
1899	60.0	.189	56.0	.233	48.4	.314	48.0	.383
1900	60.0	.212	56.2	.250	48.4	.317	48.0	.379
1901	60.0	.211	54.0	258	48.0	.321	45.6	.400
1902	60.0	.238	48.0	.301	48.0	.321	45.4	.400
1903	55.8	.228	48.0	.400	48.0	.240	44.0	.400
1904	54.5	.242	48.0	.353	48.0	.350	44.0	.450
1905	54.8	.249	48.0	.356	48.0	.352	44.0	.450
1906	54.6	.275	48.0	.356	48.0	.375	44.0	.481
1907	1 53.0	.278	48.0	.350	48.0	.395	44.0	.500
1908	1 53.0	.278	48.0	.350	44.0	.410	44.0	.500
1909	1 53.0	.278	48.0	.375	44.0	.410	44.0	.550
1910	1 53.0	.307	48.0	.400	44.0	.455	44.0	.600
1911	1 53.0	.307	48.0	.400	44.0	.455	44.0	.600
1912	1 53.0	.333	48.0	.450	44.0	.500	44.0	.600
1913	1 53.0	.333	48.0	.450	44.0	.500	44.0	.650
1914	1 53.0	.333	48.0	.450	44.0	.550	44.0	.700
1915	1 53.0	.333	48.0	.450	44.0	.550	44.0	.700
1916	1 53.0	.333	48.0	.450	40.0	.605	44.0	.700
1917	1 53.0	.361	44.0	.500	40.0	.625	44.0	.725
1918	48.0	.500	44.0	.625	40.0	.750	44.0	.750
1919	44.0	.600	44.0	.750	40.0	.825	44.0	.875
1920	44.0	.600	44.0	.875	40.0	1.000	44.0	1.250
1921	44.0	.850	44.0	.875	40.0	1.000	44.0	1.250
1922	44.0	.750	44.0	.750	40.0	1.000	44.0	1.100
1923	44.0	.750	44.0	.875	40.0	1.050	44.0	1.250
1924	44.0	.750	44.0	.875	40.0	1.100	44.0	1.250
1925	44.0	.750	44.0	1.000	40.0	1.100	44.0	1.500
1926	44.0	.800	44.0	1.000	40.0	1.250	44.0	1.500
1927	44.0	.850	44.0	1.125	40.0	1.250	44.0	1.500
1928	44.0	.850	44.0	1.000	40.0	1.250	40.0	1.625

Year	Cincinnati, Ohio		Denver, Colo.		Detroit, Mich.		New Orleans, La.	
1890	58.8	$0.275	54.0	$0.285	54.0	$0.227	52.8	$0.236
1891	56.4	.283	54.0	.287	54.0	.232	52.9	.235
1892	54.4	.290	54.0	.292	54.0	.231	52.0	.251
1893	52.1	.300	54.0	.282	54.0	.235	51.8	.250
1894	54.7	.284	54.0	.265	54.0	.233	51.9	.253
1895	54.6	.286	54.0	.265	54.0	.216	51.7	.239
1896	54.6	.286	54.0	.278	54.0	.222	51.9	.252
1897	54.7	.264	48.0	.324	54.0	.220	52.1	.253
1898	53.9	.280	48.0	.331	54.0	.226	52.2	.261
1899	51.1	.278	48.0	.338	54.0	.231	52.4	.264
1900	48.6	.306	48.0	.361	54.0	.237	48.0	.285
1901	48.0	.331	48.0	.375	48.0	.264	48.0	.290
1902	48.0	.346	44.0	.437	48.0	.283	48.0	.286
1903	48.0	.350	44.0	.437	48.0	.296	48.0	.285
1904	48.0	.375	44.0	.437	48.0	.327	48.0	.313
1905	48.0	.375	44.0	.437	48.0	.332	48.0	.313
1906	48.0	.375	44.0	.451	48.0	.342	48.0	.360
1907	48.0	.400	44.0	.500	48.0	.350	48.0	.375
1908	48.0	.400	44.0	.500	48.0	.350	48.0	.375
1909	48.0	.425	44.0	.500	48.0	.375	48.0	.400
1910	44.0	.432	44.0	.500	48.0	.375	48.0	.400
1911	44.0	.450	44.0	.500	48.0	.400	48.0	.400
1912	44.0	.450	44.0	.500	48.0	.400	48.0	.400
1913	44.0	.450	44.0	.500	48.0	.450	48.0	.400
1914	44.0	.500	44.0	.500	48.0	.450	48.0	.400
1915	44.0	.500	44.0	.500	48.0	.450	48.0	.400
1916	44.0	.550	44.0	.550	44.0	.500	48.0	.400
1917	44.0	.550	44.0	.625	44.0	.600	48.0	.400
1918	44.0	.600	44.0	.688	44.0	.700	48.0	.500
1919	44.0	.625	44.0	.850	44.0	.800	44.0	.650
1920	44.0	.875	44.0	1.000	44.0	1.000	44.0	.750
1921	44.0	1.000	44.0	1.125	44.0	1.000	44.0	.900

1 Work 53 hours; paid for 54.

TABLE **B-19.**—*Painters, males, 1890-1928, by city and year*—Continued

Year	Cincinnati, Ohio Hours per week	Rate per hour	Denver, Colo. Hours per week	Rate per hour	Detroit, Mich. Hours per week	Rate per hour	New Orleans, La. Hours per week	Rate per hour
1922	44.0	$0.875	44.0	$1.000	44.0	$0.900	44.0	$0.800
1923	44.0	.975	44.0	1.000	44.0	1.00?	44.0	.800
1924	44.0	1.075	44.0	1.125	44.0	1.125	44.0	.850
1925	44.0	1.175	44.0	1.125	44.0	1.125	44.0	.850
1926	44.0	1.250	44.0	1.250	44.0	1.250	44.0	.850
1927	40.0	1.313	40.0	1.250	44.0	1.250	44.0	.900
1928	40.0	1.313	40.0	1.250	44.0	1.250	44.0	.900

Year	New York, N. Y.[1] Hours per week	Rate per hour	Philadelphia, Pa. Hours per week	Rate per hour	St. Louis, Mo. Hours per week	Rate per hour	San Francisco, Calif. Hours per week	Rate per hour
1890	51.0	$0.396	54.0	$0.293	48.0	$0.305	51.6	$0.334
1891	50.7	.394	54.0	.289	48.0	.305	50.9	.336
1892	48.0	.420	54.0	.286	48.0	.313	51.0	.337
1893	48.0	.420	54.0	.287	48.0	.313	48.7	.363
1894	48.1	.420	54.0	.286	48.0	.313	48.8	.332
1895	47.9	.417	54.0	.288	48.0	.313	48.4	.341
1896	47.8	.414	54.0	.285	48.0	.313	48.6	.346
1897	47.9	.414	54.0	.283	48.0	.313	48.8	.352
1898	47.8	.417	54.0	.286	48.0	.323	48.0	.375
1899	47.8	.417	48.0	.350	44.6	.375	48.0	.375
1900	47.6	.417	48.0	.350	44.6	.375	48.0	.424
1901	44.4	.466	48.0	.350	44.0	.427	48.0	.438
1902	44.1	.479	48.0	.375	44.0	.449	48.0	.438
1903	44.1	.455	48.0	.375	44.0	.450	47.8	.438
1904	44.1	.459	48.0	.375	44.0	.457	47.8	.438
1905	44.1	.470	48.0	.375	44.0	.501	44.0	.564
1906	44.0	.500	44.0	.400	44.0	.500	48.0	.500
1907	44.0	.500	44.0	.400	44.0	.500	48.0	.500
1908	44.0	.500	44.0	.400	44.0	.500	48.0	.500
1909	44.0	.500	44.0	.425	44.0	.525	44.0	.563
1910	44.0	.500	44.0	.425	44.0	.550	44.0	.563
1911	44.0	.500	44.0	.425	44.0	.550	44.0	.563
1912	44.0	.500	44.0	.425	44.0	.575	44.0	.563
1913	44.0	.500	44.0	.425	44.0	.600	44.0	.594
1914	44.0	.500	44.0	.425	44.0	.625	44.0	.625
1915	44.0	.625	44.0	.425	44.0	.625	44.0	.625
1916	44.0	.625	44.0	.450	44.0	.625	44.0	.625
1917	44.0	.625	44.0	.600	44.0	.750	44.0	.750
1918	44.0	.750	44.0	.750	44.0	.750	44.0	.875
1919	40.0	1.125	40.0	1.000	44.0	1.000	44.0	1.063
1920	40.0	1.125	40.0	1.000	44.0	1.250	44.0	1.063
1921	40.0	1.125	44.0	1.000	44.0	1.000	44.0	1.000
1922	40.0	1.125	44.0	1.000	44.0	1.125	44.0	1.044
1923	40.0	1.313	44.0	1.000	44.0	1.300	44.0	1.044
1924	40.0	1.313	44.0	1.000	44.0	1.300	44.0	1.044
1925	40.0	1.500	44.0	[3] 1.000	44.0	1.350	44.0	1.044
1926	40.0	{ 1.500 1.750 }	44.0	1.050	44.0	1.438	44.0	1.125
1927	40.0	1.500	44.0	1.050	44.0	1.438	44.0	1.125
1928								

[1] Greater New York, 1903-1906; includes Manhattan, Bronx, Kings, and Richmond, 1907-1928.
[3] Old scale; strike pending.

TABLE **B-20**.—*Plasterers, 1840–1900, by year and State*

Year and State	Sex	Hours per week	Rate per day (dollars)	Year and State	Sex	Hours per week	Rate per day (dollars)
1840:				**1869:**			
Pennsylvania	M.	60-60-60	1.50-1.50-1.50	New York	M.	60-60-60	5.00-5.00-5.00
1841:				Pennsylvania	M.	60-60-60	3.00-4.00-3.67
Pennsylvania	M.	60-60-60	1.50-1.50-1.50	**1870:**			
1842:				New York	M.	60-60-60	3.75-5.00-3.91
Pennsylvania	M.	60-60-60	1.50-1.50-1.50	Pennsylvania	M.	60-60-60	2.50-3.00-2.86
1843:				**1871:**			
Pennsylvania	M.	60-60-60	1.50-1.50-1.50	New York	M.	60-60-60	3.75-4.00-3.77
1844:				Pennsylvania	M.	60-60-60	2.50-3.00-2.88
Pennsylvania	M.	60-60-60	1.50-1.50-1.50	**1872:**			
1845:				Massachusetts	M.	60-60-60	3.75-3.75-3.75
Pennsylvania	M.	60-60-60	1.50-1.50-1.50	New York	M.	48-60-59	3.75-4.00-3.77
1846:				Ohio	M.	(¹)	3.50-3.50-3.50
Pennsylvania	M.	60-60-60	1.50-1.50-1.50	Pennsylvania	M.	60-60-60	2.50-3.00-2.86
1847:				**1873:**			
Pennsylvania	M.	60-60-60	1.50-1.75-1.63	New York	M.	48-60-59	3.75-4.00-3.77
1848:				Pennsylvania	M.	60-60-60	2.50-3.00-2.92
Pennsylvania	M.	60-60-60	1.50-1.75-1.61	**1874:**			
1849:				New York	M.	48-60-59	3.25-3.50-3.27
Pennsylvania	M.	60-60-60	1.50-1.75-1.64	Pennsylvania	M.	60-60-60	2.50-3.00-2.86
1850:				**1875:**			
Pennsylvania	M.	60-60-60	1.50-1.75-1.63	New York	M.	48-60-59	3.00-3.25-3.24
1851:				Pennsylvania	M.	60-60-60	2.50-3.00-2.88
New York	M.	60-60-60	1.75-1.75-1.75	**1876:**			
Pennsylvania	M.	60-60-60	1.50-1.75-1.63	New York	M.	48-60-59	2.50-2.75-2.76
852:				Pennsylvania	M.	60-60-60	1.75-2.50-2.31
New York	M.	60-60-60	1.75-175.-1.75	**1877::**			
Pennsylvania	M.	60-60-60	1.50-1.75-1.65	New York	M.	48-60-59	2.25-2.50-2.26
1853:				Ohio	M.	60-60-60	2.00-2.00-2.00
New York	M.	60-60-60	1.75-1.75-1.75	Pennsylvania	M.	60-60-60	1.75-2.00-1.94
Pennsylvania	M.	60-60-60	1.50-1.75-1.60	**1878:**			
1854:				New York	M.	48-60-59	2.25-2.50-2.27
New York	M.	60-60-60	1.75-1.75-1.75	Ohio	M.	60-60-60	2.00-2.50-2.03
Pennsylvania	M.	60-60-60	1.50-1.75-1.63	Pennsylvania	M.	60-60-60	1.75-2.00-1.94
1855:				**1879:**			
New York	M.	60-60-60	1.75-1.75-1.75	Missouri	M.	(¹)	2.00-3.00-2.75
Pennsylvania	M.	60-60-60	1.50-1.75-1.66	New Jersey	(¹)	60-60-60	1.00-1.00-1.00
1856:				New York	M.	48-60-59	2.50-2.75-2.74
New York	M.	60-60-60	1.75-1.75-1.75	Pennsylvania	M.	54-72-60	.83-1.83-1.58
Pennsylvania	M.	60-60-60	1.50-1.75-1.64	**1880:**			
1857:				New York	M.	48-60-60	2.75-3.00-2.75
New York	M.	60-60-60	1.75-1.75-1.75	North Carolina	M.	72-72-72	2.50-2.50-2.50
Pennsylvania	M.	60-60-60	1.50-1.75-1.66	Ohio	M.	(¹)	2.50-2.50-2.50
1858:				Pennsylvania	M.	60-60-60	1.50-2.00-1.81
New York	M.	60-60-60	1.50-1.50-1.50	**1881:**			
Pennsylvania	M.	60-60-60	1.50-1.75-1.67	Dist. of Columbia	M.	58-58-58	1.75-2.50-2.13
1859:				Massachusetts	M.	60-60-60	2.25-2.75-2.50
New York	M.	60-60-60	1.50-1.50-1.50	New York	M.	48-60-60	2.86-4.50-3.16
Pennsylvania	M.	60-60-60	1.50-1.75-1.68	Ohio	M.	60-60-60	2.00-3.00-2.55
1860:				Pennsylvania	M.	60-60-60	1.50-3.00-1.97
New York	M.	60-60-60	2.00-2.00-2.00	**1882:**			
Pennsylvania	M.	60-60-60	1.50-1.75-1.69	Dist. of Columbia	M.	58-58-58	3.00-3.50-3.25
1861:				Illinois	M.	60-60-60	3.00-3.00-3.00
New York	M.	60-60-60	2.00-2.00-2.00	Missouri	M.	60-60-60	3.00-3.50-3.41
Pennsylvania	M.	60-60-60	1.50-1.75-1.66	New York	(¹)	48-60-60	3.32-4.00-3.41
1862:				Ohio	M.	60-60-60	3.00-3.50-3.25
New York	M.	60-60-60	2.25-2.25-2.25	Pennsylvania	M.	60-60-60	1.75-3.50-2.39
Pennsylvania	M.	60-60-60	1.50-1.75-1.67	**1883:**			
1863:				Iowa	M.	60-60-60	3.00-3.50-3.17
New York	M.	60-60-60	2.50-2.50-2.50	Massachusetts	M.	(¹)	2.00-3.50-3.05
Pennsylvania	M.	60-60-60	1.75-2.00-1.92	Michigan	M.	(¹)	1.25-4.00-2.68
1864:				Minnesota	M.	59-60-60	4.50-4.50-4.50
New York	M.	60-60-60	3.00-3.00-3.00	Missouri	M.	59-59-59	4.00-4.50-4.25
Pennsylvania	M.	60-60-60	1.75-2.00-1.93	New Jersey	M.	60-60-60	1.67-2.50-2.00
1865:				New York	M.	48-60-60	2.50-4.00-3.12
New York	M.	60-60-60	3.00-3.00-3.00	Ohio	M.	60-60-60	2.50-3.33-2.99
Pennsylvania	M.	60-60-60	1.75-2.50-2.29	Pennsylvania	M.	59-60-59	2.50-3.00-2.98
1966:				**1884:**			
New York	M.	60-60-60	4.00-4.00-4.00	California	M.	60-60-60	3.00-4.00-3.42
Pennsylvania	M.	60-60-60	2.00-3.00-2.60	Illinois	M.	59-59-59	4.00-4.50-4.41
1867:				Iowa	M.	60-72-60	1.50-8.00-3.00
New York	M.	60-60-60	5.00-5.00-5.00	Louisiana	M.	60-60-60	3.00-3.00-3.00
Pennsylvania	M.	60-60-60	3.00-4.00-3.70	Michigan	M.	54-54-54	1.50-3.50-3.16
1868:				Missouri	M.	60-60-60	4.00-4.00-4.00
New York	M.	60-60-60	4.50-4.50-4.50	New Jersey	M.	60-60-60	2.33-3.00-2.64
Pennsylvania	M.	60-60-60	3.00-4.00-3.67	New York	M.	54-60-55	2.94-4.00-3.44

¹ Not reported.

TABLE B-20.—*Plasterers, 1840-1900, by year and State*—Continued

Year and State	Sex	Hours per week	Rate per day (dollars)	Year and State	Sex	Hours per week	Rate per day (dollars)
1884—Continued.				**1892—Continued.**			
Ohio	M.	60-60-60	3.02-3.02-3.02	New York	M.	48-48-48	4.00-4.00-4.00
Pennsylvania	M.	54-60-59	2.00-3.50-3.25	Ohio	[1]	53-60-56	1.25-3.60-3.13
1885:				Pennsylvania	M.	48-48-48	3.20-3.20-3.20
Kansas	M.	60-60-60	2.00-3.50-2.92	Rhode Island	M.	54-60-55	2.50-3.50-3.39
New Jersey	M.	60-60-60	2.25-3.00-2.50	**1893:**			
New York	M.	54-60-57	3.45-4.00-3.52	Illinois	M.	48-84-57	1.25-4.17-2.56
Pennsylvania	M.	54-54-54	3.50-3.50-3.50	Maryland	M.	48-60-55	.83-3.00-1.79
1886:				Michigan	M.	60-60-60	1.46-1.46-1.46
California	M.	60-60-60	2.50-5.00-2.97	Missouri	M.	48-48-48	4.00-4.00-4.00
Do	M.	48-48-48	[2] 2.88-2.88-2.88	New Hampshire	M.	60-60-60	2.25-3.00-2.63
Dist. of Columbia	M.	48-53-51	3.00-3.50-3.25	New York	M.	60-60-60	.83-4.00-3.85
Illinois	M.	60-60-60	1.67-4.00-2.67	Ohio	M.	60-60-60	2.50-2.50-2.50
Iowa	M.	45-60-60	1.00-6.50-2.81	Pennsylvania	M.	54-60-57	1.33-3.00-2.17
Kansas	M.	60-60-60	1.00-4.00-2.80	Wisconsin	M.	[1]	[3] .20-.40-.30
New York	M.	53-58-55	1.00-4.00-3.66	**1894:**			
Ohio	M.	[1]	3.10-3.10-3.10	Iowa	M.	48-60-57	1.75-4.00-2.88
Pennsylvania	M.	48-59-52	2.66-3.50-2.85	New Hampshire	M.	60-60-60	1.75-1.75-1.75
Texas	M.	47-60-54	3.00-3.50-3.25	New York	M.	48-48-48	4.00-4.00-4.00
1887:				North Carolina	[1]	60-60-60	2.00-2.50-2.25
Florida	M.	[1]	2.50-2.50-2.50	Ohio	M.	[1]	1.17-4.00-3.12
Kansas	M.	[1]	2.25-5.00-3.17	**1895:**			
Maryland	M.	[1]	1.75-2.00-1.92	New York	M.	48-48-48	4.00-4.00-4.00
Massachusetts	M.	[1]	3-50.3.50-3.50	North Carolina	M.	60-63-61	1.50-2.35-1.75
Missouri	M.	[1]	2.50-2.50-2.50	**1896:**			
New York	M.	53-54-54	3.78-4.00-3.79	Colorado	M.	48-48-48	3.00-3.00-3.00
Ohio	M.	54-60-58	1.50-3.50-2.59	Georgia	M.	[1]	.42-.83-.63
Pennsylvania	M.	54-54-54	2.00-3.50-3.00	Illinois	M.	48-48-48	1.50-1.50 1.50
Wisconsin	M.	[1]	3.00-3.00-3.00	Kansas	M.	60-60-60	2.00-2.50-2.25
1888:				Massachusetts	M.	47-48-47	3.37-4.00-3.46
Colorado	M.	54-60-57	4.00-5.00-4.50	New York	M.	44-48-45	4.00-4.00-4.00
Iowa	M.	51-60-59	2.00-3.67-2.93	North Carolina	M.	60-60-60	1.50-3.00-2.33
Kansas	M.	[1]	3.00-3.50-3.25	Pennsylvania	M.	48-54-49	2.75-3.51-3.19
Michigan	M.	60-60-60	1.92-1.92-1.92	**1897:**			
New Jersey	[1]	54-54-54	4.00-4.00-4.00	Kansas	M.	60-70-65	1.20-2.50-1.73
New York	M.	53-60-55	3.00-4.00-3.53	Nebraska	[1]	48-48-48	2.00-4.00-3.90
North Carolina	M.	60-72-62	1.00-2.50-1.83	New York	M.	48-54-49	2.75-4.00-3.25
Ohio	M.	[1]	1.50-3.12-2.59	**1898:**			
Pennsylvania	M.	54-54-54	3.50-3.50-3.50	New York	M.	48-54-48	3.00-4.00-3.57
1889:				**1899:**			
Kansas	M.	[1]	2.70-2.70-2.70	Alabama	M.	54-54-54	2.00-2.50-2.25
New York	M.	54-54-54	3.78-4.00-3.78	California	M.	48-48-48	3.00-4.00-3.60
Pennsylvania	M.	54-54-54	3.50-3.50-3.50	Georgia	M.	60-60-60	1.50-2.50-2.85
Wisconsin	M.	[1]	1.27-3.68-2.52	Illinois	M.	48-48-48	3.50-4.00-3.88
1890:				Massachusetts	M.	48-48-48	3.44-3.60-3.57
Kansas	M.	[1]	2.25-3.00-2.78	Montana	M.	48-48-48	6.00-6.00-6.00
Minnesota	M.	[1]	1.75-4.00-3.36	New York	M.	44-54-48	3.00-4.50-3.47
Nebraska	M.	[1]	4.00-4.00-4.00	North Carolina	M.	60-60-60	1.75-2.50-2.15
New York	M.	48-54-48	2.00-4.50-3.94	Pennsylvania	M.	48-48-48	3.20-3.20-3.20
Pennsylvania	M.	54-54-54	3.50-3.50-3.50	**1900:**			
1891:				Alabama	M.	48-48-48	4.00-4.00-4.00
Missouri	M.	[1]	2.50-2.50-2.50	California	M.	48-48-48	3.00-4.50-4.11
New York	M.	48-48-48	2.00-4.00-3.90	Georgia	M.	60-60-60	1.50-2.50-1.85
Pennsylvania	M.	48-48-48	3.20-3.20-3.20	Illinois	M.	48-48-48	4.00-4.00-4.00
Wisconsin	M.	[1]	[3] .15-.45-.33	Massachusetts	M.	48-48-48	3.44-3.60-3.58
1892:				Montana	M.	48-48-48	7.00-7.00-7.00
California	M.	48-48-48	5.00-5.00-5.00	New York	M.	44-54-48	2.88-4.50-3.60
Michigan	M.	54-60-55	1.00-4.05-2.95	North Carolina	M.	60-60-60	1.75-2.50-2.14
Missouri	M.	48-48-48	4.00-4.00-4.00	Pennsylvania	M.	48-48-48	3.20-3.20-3.20

[1] Not reported. [2] And board. [3] Per hour.

TABLE **B-21.**—*Plasterers, males, 1890-1928, by city and year*

Year	Atlanta, Ga.		Birmingham, Ala.		Boston, Mass.		Chicago, Ill.	
	Hours per week	Rate per hour	Hours per week	Rate per hour	Hours per week	Rate per hour	Hours per week	Rate per hour
1890			59. 0	$0. 441	53. 1	$0. 398	48. 0	$0. 442
1891			59. 2	. 411	53. 1	. 398	48. 0	. 442
1892			59. 5	. 382	52. 5	. 403	48. 0	. 500
1893			58. 9	. 368	52. 5	. 403	48. 0	. 500
1894			59. 3	. 256	52. 6	. 403	48. 0	. 438
1895			58. 2	. 249	52. 4	. 404	48. 0	. 438
1896			58. 5	. 266	52. 5	. 404	48. 0	. 495
1897			59. 0	. 261	52. 5	. 404	48. 0	. 500
1898			57. 0	. 298	49. 4	. 403	48. 0	. 500
1899			57. 1	. 330	44. 4	. 453	48. 0	. 500
1900			57. 4	. 331	44. 4	. 454	44. 0	. 500
1901			56. 3	. 408	44. 4	. 454	44. 0	. 500
1902			48. 6	. 473	44. 3	. 455	44. 0	. 500
1903	54. 0	$0. 317	48. 0	. 521	44. 6	. 456	44. 0	. 563
1904	54. 0	. 350	48. 0	. 464	44. 0	. 500	44. 0	. 563
1905	54. 0	. 400	48. 0	. 479	44. 0	. 502	44. 0	. 585
1906	54. 0	. 440	46. 2	. 538	44. 0	. 551	44. 0	. 688
1907	53. 0	. 450	44. 0	. 563	44. 0	. 600	44. 0	. 688
1908	53. 0	. 450	44. 0	. 563	44. 0	. 600	44. 0	. 688
1909	53. 0	. 450	44. 0	. 563	44. 0	. 650	44. 0	. 688
1910	53. 0	. 450	44. 0	. 563	44. 0	. 650	44. 0	. 688
1911	¹ 53. 0	. 400	44. 0	. 625	44. 0	. 650	44. 0	. 688
1912	¹ 53. 0	. 444	44. 0	. 625	44. 0	. 650	44. 0	. 750
1913	¹ 53. 0	. 444	44. 0	. 625	44. 0	. 650	44. 0	. 750
1914	¹ 53. 0	. 444	44. 0	. 625	44. 0	. 650	44. 0	. 750
1915	¹ 53. 0	. 444	44. 0	. 625	44. 0	. 650	44. 0	. 750
1916	¹ 53. 0	. 444	44. 0	. 625	40. 0	. 700	44. 0	. 750
1917	¹ 53. 0	. 444	44. 0	. 625	40. 0	. 700	44. 0	. 750
1918	44. 0	. 688	44. 0	. 625	40. 0	. 700	44. 0	. 813
1919	44. 0	. 750	44. 0	. 750	40. 0	. 800	44. 0	. 875
1920	44. 0	. 750	44. 0	. 750	40. 0	1. 000	44. 0	1. 250
1921	44. 0	. 750	44. 0	1. 000	40. 0	1. 250	44. 0	1. 250
1922	44. 0	1. 000	44. 0	1. 000	40. 0	1. 125	44. 0	1. 100
1923	44. 0	1. 000	44. 0	1. 000	40. 0	1. 125	44. 0	1. 500
1924	44. 0	1. 125	44. 0	1. 250	40. 0	1. 250	44. 0	1. 500
1925	44. 0	1. 125	44. 0	1. 250	40. 0	1. 250	44. 0	1. 500
1926	44. 0	1. 250	44. 0	1. 250	40. 0	1. 500	44. 0	1. 500
1927	44. 0	1. 250	44. 0	1. 250	40. 0	1. 500	44. 0	1. 625
1928	41. 0	1. 250	44. 0	1. 250	40. 0	1. 500	44. 0	1. 625

Year	Cincinnati, Ohio		Denver, Colo.		Detroit, Mich.		New Orleans, La.	
1890	54. 0	$0. 366	48. 0	$0. 500			54. 0	$0. 244
1891	54. 0	. 364	48. 0	. 500			54. 0	. 248
1892	54. 0	. 400	48. 0	. 500			54. 0	. 246
1893	50. 7	. 400	48. 0	. 432			54. 0	. 246
1894	51. 3	. 400	48. 0	. 281			54. 0	. 248
1895	51. 2	. 423	48. 0	. 359			54. 0	. 246
1896	48. 0	. 450	48. 0	. 375			54. 0	. 248
1897	48. 0	. 413	48. 0	. 455			54. 0	. 248
1898	48. 0	. 375	48. 0	. 500			54. 0	. 248
1899	48. 0	. 400	48. 0	. 500			54. 0	. 248
1900	48. 0	. 422	48. 0	. 500			54. 0	. 250
1901	48. 0	. 500	48. 0	. 500			51. 0	. 250
1902	48. 0	. 500	44. 0	. 553			48. 0	. 281
1903	45. 6	. 563	44. 0	. 638	48. 0	$0. 500	48. 0	. 375
1904	44. 5	. 625	44. 0	. 625	48. 0	. 500	48. 0	. 400
1905	44. 5	. 625	44. 0	. 625	46. 5	. 509	48. 0	. 450
1906	44. 5	. 625	44. 0	. 666	45. 6	. 555	48. 0	. 479
1907	44. 5	. 625	44. 0	. 688	44. 0	. 531	48. 0	. 500
1908	44. 5	. 625	44. 0	. 688	44. 0	. 563	48. 0	. 500
1909	44. 5	. 625	44. 0	. 688	44. 0	. 563	48. 0	. 500
1910	44. 5	. 625	44. 0	. 688	44. 0	. 600	48. 0	. 500
1911	44. 5	. 625	44. 0	. 688	44. 0	. 600	48. 0	. 500
1912	ʹ.5	. 625	44. 0	. 688	44. 0	. 625	48. 0	. 625
1913	44. 5	. 688	44. 0	. 750	44. 0	. 688	48. 0	. 625
1914	44. 5	. 750	44. 0	. 750	44. 0	. 688	48. 0	. 625
1915	44. 5	. 750	44. 0	. 750	44. 0	. 688	48. 0	. 500
1916	44. 5	. 750	44. 0	. 750	44. 0	. 688	48. 0	. 500
1917	44. 5	. 750	44. 0	. 875	44. 0	. 750	45. 0	. 625
1918	44. 5	. 750	44. 0	. 875	44. 0	. 750	45. 0	. 625
1919	44. 5	. 875	44. 0	. 875	44. 0	. 875	45. 0	. 750
1920	44. 5	1. 000	44. 0	1. 250	44. 0	1. 250	45. 0	1. 000

¹ Work 53 hours; paid for 54.

TABLE **B-21.**—*Plasterers, males, 1890–1928, by city and year*—Continued

Year	Cincinnati, Ohio		Denver, Colo.		Detroit, Mich.		New Orleans, La.	
	Hours per week	Rate per hour	Hours per week	Rate per hour	Hours per week	Rate per hour	Hours per week	Rate per hour
1921	44.5	$1.125	44.0	$1.250	44.0	$1.250	45.0	$1.000
1922	44.5	1.125	44.0	1.250	44.0	1.125	45.0	1.000
1923	44.5	1.250	44.0	1.250	44.0	1.500	45.0	1.000
1924	44.5	1.500	44.0	1.500	44.0	1.563	45.0	1.250
1925	44.5	1.500	44.0	1.500	44.0	1.563	44.0	1.250
1926	44.5	1.500	44.0	1.500	44.0	1.563	45.0	1.250
1927	44.5	1.500	44.0	1.500	44.0	1.625	44.0	1.250
1928	44.5	1.500	44.0	1.500	44.0	1.625	45.0	1.250

Year	New York, N. Y.[2]		Philadelphia, Pa.		St. Louis, Mo.		San Francisco, Calif.	
1890	48.0	$0.500	53.2	$0.390	48.0	$0.500	48.0	$0.652
1891	44.0	.500	51.5	.394	48.0	.500	48.0	.625
1892	44.0	.500	51.0	.394	48.0	.532	48.0	.625
1893	44.0	.500	48.0	.442	48.0	.488	48.0	.625
1894	44.0	.500	48.0	.400	48.0	.488	48.0	.625
1895	44.0	.500	48.0	.400	48.0	.492	48.0	.500
1896	44.0	.500	48.0	.400	48.0	.413	48.0	.375
1897	44.0	.500	48.0	.400	48.0	.443	48.0	.313
1898	44.0	.500	48.0	.400	48.0	.450	48.0	.375
1899	44.0	.563	48.0	.400	46.3	.500	48.0	.500
1900	44.0	.563	48.0	.400	44.0	.563	48.0	.417
1901	44.0	.563	46.0	.450	44.0	.563	44.0	.625
1902	44.0	.625	45.8	.450	44.0	.625	44.0	.693
1903	44.0	.682	44.0	.500	44.0	.750	44.0	.727
1904	44.0	.680	44.0	.500	44.0	.750	44.0	.750
1905	44.0	.688	44.0	.563	44.0	.750	44.0	.750
1906	44.0	.688	44.0	.563	44.0	.750	44.0	.875
1907	44.0	.688	44.0	.594	44.0	.750	44.0	.875
1908	44.0	.688	44.0	.594	44.0	.750	44.0	.875
1909	44.0	.688	44.0	.594	44.0	.750	44.0	.875
1910	44.0	.688	44.0	.625	44.0	.750	44.0	.875
1911	44.0	.688	44.0	.625	44.0	.750	44.0	.875
1912	44.0	.688	44.0	.625	44.0	.750	44.0	.875
1913	44.0	.688	44.0	.625	44.0	.750	44.0	.875
1914	44.0	.688	44.0	.625	44.0	.750	44.0	.875
1915	44.0	.688	40.0	.625	44.0	.750	44.0	.875
1916	44.0	.750	40.0	.625	44.0	.750	40.0	.875
1917	44.0	.750	40.0	.700	44.0	.750	40.0	.875
1918	44.0	.750	40.0	.750	44.0	.875	40.0	1.000
1919	44.0	.900	40.0	.800	44.0	1.000	40.0	1.125
1920	44.0	1.250	40.0	1.250	44.0	1.250	40.0	1.250
1921	44.0	1.250	40.0	1.250	44.0	1.375	40.0	1.375
1922	44.0	1.250	40.0	1.250	44.0	1.375	44.0	1.275
1923	44.0	1.250	40.0	1.250	44.0	1.500	44.0	1.275
1924	44.0	1.500	40.0	1.500	44.0	1.750	44.0	1.275
1925	44.0	1.500	40.0	1.500	44.0	1.750	44.0	1.500
1926	40.0	1.750	40.0	1.750	44.0	1.750	44.0	1.500
1927	40.0	1.750	40.0	1.750	44.0	1.750	44.0	1.500
1928	40.0	1.750	40.0	1.750	40.0	1.750	44.0	1.500

[2] Greater New York, 1903–1907.

TABLE B–22.—*Plumbers, 1850–1900, by year and State*

Year and State	Sex	Lowest, highest, and average—		Year and State	Sex	Lowest, highest, and average—	
		Hours per week	Rate per day (dollars)			Hours per week	Rate per day (dollars)
1850:				**1871—Continued.**			
Massachusetts____	M.	60–60–60	2. 00–2. 00–2. 00	Louisiana_____	M.	60–60–60	2. 50–3. 00–2. 70
New Jersey_____	M.	60–60–60	1. 50–1. 50–1. 50	Maryland_____	M.	60–60–60	2. 50–3. 25–2. 91
1851:				Massachusetts____	M.	59–60–60	3. 00–5. 00–3. 45
New Jersey_____	M.	60–60–60	1. 50–1. 50–1. 50	Minnesota_____	M.	60–60–60	3. 50–4. 00–3. 63
New York_____	M.	60–60–60	1. 75–2. 00–1. 90	Missouri_____	M.	60–60–60	3. 50–3. 50–3. 50
1852:				New Jersey_____	M.	60–60–60	2. 50–3. 75–3. 25
New Jersey_____	M.	60–60–60	1. 50–1. 50–1. 50	New York_____	M.	54–60–57	2. 50–4. 00–3. 36
New York_____	M.	60–60–60	1. 75–2. 00–1. 90	Ohio_____	M.	60–60–60	3. 50–3. 75–3. 58
1853:				Pennsylvania_____	M.	60–60–60	2. 50–3. 75–3. 02
New Jersey_____	M.	60–60–60	1. 50–1. 50–1. 50	Virginia_____	M.	60–60–60	3. 00–3. 50–3. 10
New York_____	M.	60–60–60	2. 00–2. 25–2. 17	**1872:**			
1854:				California_____	M.	60–60–60	3. 00–4. 00–3. 70
New Jersey_____	M.	60–60–60	1. 50–1. 75–1. 58	Illinois_____	M.	54–54–54	3. 15–3. 15–3. 15
New York_____	M.	60–60–60	2. 00–2. 25–2. 17	Louisiana_____	M.	60–60–60	2. 50–3. 00–2. 75
1855:				Maryland_____	M.	60–60–60	2. 50–3. 25–2. 89
New Jersey_____	M.	60–60–60	1. 50–2. 00–1. 75	Massachusetts____	M.	59–60–60	3. 00–4. 50–3. 42
New York_____	M.	60–60–60	2. 00–2. 25–2. 17	Minnesota_____	M.	60–60–60	3. 50–4. 00–3. 60
1856:				Missouri_____	M.	60–60–60	3. 50–3. 50–3. 50
New Jersey_____	M.	60–60–60	1. 75–1. 75–1. 75	New Jersey_____	M.	60–60–60	2. 50–3. 75–3. 31
New York_____	M.	60–60–60	2. 00–2. 25–2. 17	New York_____	M.	54–60–57	2. 50–4. 00–3. 22
1857:				Ohio_____	M.	60–60–60	1. 67–2. 50–2. 29
Connecticut_____	M.	60–60–60	1. 62–1. 62–1. 62	Pennsylvania_____	M.	60–60–60	2. 50–4. 17–2. 92
New Jersey_____	M.	60–60–60	1. 50–1. 75–1. 63	Virginia_____	M.	60–60–60	3. 00–3. 50–3. 10
New York_____	M.	60–60–60	2. 00–2. 25–2. 15	**1873:**			
1858:				California_____	M.	60–60–60	3. 00–4. 00–3. 66
New Jersey_____	M.	60–60–60	1. 50–1. 88–1. 69	Illinois_____	M.	54–54–54	3. 15–3. 15–3. 15
New York_____	M.	60–60–60	2. 00–2. 25–2. 17	Louisiana_____	M.	60–60–60	2. 50–3. 00–2. 70
1859:				Maryland_____	M.	60–60–60	2. 50–3. 25–2. 89
New Jersey_____	M.	60–60–60	2. 00–2. 00–2. 00	Massachusetts____	M.	59–60–60	3. 00–4. 00–3. 50
New York_____	M.	60–60–60	1. 75–2. 00–1. 90	Minnesota_____	M.	60–60–60	3. 50–4. 00–3. 58
1860:				Missouri_____	M.	60–60–60	3. 50–3. 50–3. 50
New Jersey_____	M.	60–60–60	2. 00–2. 00–2. 00	New Jersey_____	M.	60–60–60	2. 50–3. 75–3. 25
New York_____	M.	60–60–60	1. 75–2. 00–1. 88	New York_____	M.	54–60–57	2. 50–4. 00–3. 18
1861:				Ohio_____	M.	60–60–60	2. 50–3. 00–2. 56
New Jersey_____	M.	60–60–60	2. 00–2. 00–2. 00	Pennsylvania_____	M.	60–60–60	2. 50–4. 17–2. 89
New York_____	M.	60–60–60	1. 75–2. 00–1. 88	Virginia_____	M.	60–60–60	3. 00–3. 50–3. 13
1862:				**1874:**			
New Jersey_____	M.	60–60–60	1. 38–2. 00–1. 69	California_____	M.	60–60–60	3. 00–4. 00–3. 61
New York_____	M.	60–60–60	1. 75–2. 00–1. 93	Illinois_____	M.	54–54–54	3. 15–3. 15–3. 15
1863:				Louisiana_____	M.	60–60–60	2. 50–3. 00–2. 75
New Jersey_____	M.	60–60–60	2. 00–2. 00–2. 00	Maryland_____	M.	60–60–60	2. 25–3. 00–2. 74
New York_____	M.	60–60–60	2. 50–2. 50–2. 50	Massachusetts____	M.	59–60–60	3. 00–4. 00–3. 36
1864:				Minnesota_____	M.	60–60–60	3. 50–4. 00–3. 56
New Jersey_____	M.	60–60–60	2. 50–2. 50–2. 50	Missouri_____	M.	60–60–60	3. 50–3. 50–3. 50
New York_____	M.	60–60–60	3. 50–3. 50–3. 50	New Jersey_____	M.	60–60–60	2. 83–3. 50–3. 28
1865:				New York_____	M.	54–60–57	2. 50–4. 00–3. 11
New Jersey_____	M.	60–60–60	3. 00–3. 00–3. 00	Ohio_____	M.	60–60–60	3. 00–3. 33–3. 11
New York_____	M.	60–60–60	3. 50–3. 50–3. 50	Pennsylvania_____	M.	60–60–60	2. 50–4. 17–2. 77
1866:				Virginia_____	M.	60–60–60	3. 00–3. 50–3. 13
New Jersey_____	M.	60–60–60	1. 75–3. 33–2. 77	**1875:**			
New York_____	M.	60–60–60	3. 50–3. 50–3. 50	California_____	M.	60–60–60	3. 00–4. 00–3. 62
1867:				Illinois_____	M.	54–54–54	3. 15–3. 15–3. 15
New Jersey_____	M.	60–60–60	2. 00–3. 33–2. 90	Louisiana_____	M.	60–60–60	2. 50–3. 00–2. 72
New York_____	M.	60–60–60	3. 75–4. 00–3. 85	Maryland_____	M.	60–60–60	2. 25–3. 00–2. 74
1868:				Massachusetts____	M.	59–60–60	3. 00–4. 00–3. 30
New Jersey_____	M.	60–60–60	2. 50–3. 75–3. 19	Minnesota_____	M.	60–60–60	3. 50–4. 00–3. 56
New York_____	M.	60–60–60	3. 75–4. 00–3. 85	Missouri_____	M.	60–60–60	3. 50–3. 50–3. 50
1869:				New Jersey_____	M.	60–60–60	2. 83–3. 50–3. 26
New Jersey_____	M.	60–60–60	2. 50–3. 75–3. 25	New York_____	M.	54–60–57	2. 50–4. 00–3. 16
New York_____	M.	60–60–60	3. 75–4. 00–3. 85	Ohio_____	M.	60–60–60	2. 00–3. 67–3. 24
1870:				Pennsylvania_____	M.	60–60–60	2. 50–4. 17–3. 09
California_____	M.	60–80–60	3. 00–4. 00–3. 66	Virginia_____	M.	60–60–60	3. 00–3. 50–3. 17
Illinois_____	M.	54–54–54	3. 15–3. 15–3. 15	**1876:**			
Louisiana_____	M.	60–60–60	2. 50–3. 00–2. 75	California_____	M.	60–60–60	3. 00–4. 00–3. 60
Maryland_____	M.	60–60–60	2. 50–3. 25–2. 87	Illinois_____	M.	54–54–54	3–15–3. 15–3. 15
Massachusetts____	M.	59–60–60	3. 00–5. 50–3. 50	Louisiana_____	M.	60–60–60	2. 50–3. 00–2. 64
Minnesota_____	M.	60–60–60	3. 50–4. 00–3. 63	Maryland_____	M.	60–60–60	2. 25–3. 00–2. 74
Missouri_____	M.	60–60–60	3. 50–3. 50–3. 50	Massachusetts____	M.	59–60–60	3. 00–4. 00–3. 30
New Jersey_____	M.	60–60–60	2. 50–3. 75–3. 25	Minnesota_____	M.	60–60–60	3. 50–3. 50–3. 50
New York_____	M.	54–60–57	2. 75–4. 00–3. 37	Missouri_____	M.	60–60–60	3. 50–3. 50–3. 50
Ohio_____	M.	60–60–60	3. 75–3. 75–3. 75	New Jersey_____	M.	60–60–60	2. 83–3. 50–3. 17
Pennsylvania_____	M.	60–60–60	2. 50–3. 75–2. 96	New York_____	M.	54–60–57	2. 50–3. 50–3. 13
Virginia_____	M.	60–60–60	3. 00–3. 50–3. 10	Ohio_____	M.	60–60–60	2. 00–3. 33–2. 90
1871:				Pennsylvania_____	M.	60–60–60	2. 25–4. 17–2. 93
California_____	M.	60–60–60	3. 00–4. 00–3. 62	Virginia_____	M.	60–60–60	3. 00–3. 50–3. 17
Illinois_____	M.	54–54–54	3. 15–3. 15–3. 15				

TABLE B-22.—*Plumbers, 1850-1900, by year and State*—Continued

Year and State	Sex	Hours per week	Rate per day (dollars)	Year and State	Sex	Hours per week	Rate per day (dollars)
1877:				**1882—Continued.**			
California	M.	60–60–60	3.00–4.00–3.60	New York	M.	54–60–54	3.50–3.50–3.50
Illinois	M.	54–54–54	3.15–3.15–3.15	Ohio	M.	60–60–60	2.00–3.50–3.10
Louisiana	M.	60–60–60	2.50–3.00–2.72	Pennsylvania	M.	59–60–60	2.00–3.00–2.67
Maryland	M.	60–60–60	2.25–3.00–2.74	Virginia	M.	60–60–60	2.50–3.00–2.60
Massachusetts	M.	59–60–60	3.00–3.50–3.22	**1883:**			
Minnesota	M.	60–60–60	3.50–3.50–3.50	California	M.	54–54–54	3.00–4.00–3.53
Missouri	M.	60–60–60	3.50–3.50–3.50	Illinois	M.	48–48–48	3.50–3.50–3.50
New Jersey	M.	60–60–60	2.83–3.00–2.92	Louisiana	M.	60–60–60	2.50–3.00–2.64
New York	M.	54–60–57	2.50–3.50–3.16	Maryland	M.	60–60–60	2.25–3.00–2.71
Ohio	M.	60–60–60	3.00–3.00–3.00	Massachusetts	M.	59–60–60	1.75–3.50–3.04
Pennsylvania	M.	60–60–60	2.50–3.33–2.58	Michigan	M.	(1)	.60–3.00–2.27
Virginia	M.	60–60–60	3.00–3.50–3.13	Minnesota	M.	60–60–60	3.50–3.50–3.50
1878:				Missouri	M.	60–60–60	3.50–3.50–3.50
California	M.	80–60–60	3.00–4.00–3.55	New Jersey	M.	60–60–60	2.00–3.00–2.50
Illinois	M.	54–54–54	3.15–3.15–3.15	New York	M.	54–60–58	3.50–3.50–3.50
Louisiana	M.	60–60–60	2.50–3.00–2.63	Ohio	M.	60–60–60	2.50–3.25–2.86
Maryland	M.	60–60–60	2.25–3.00–2.74	Pennsylvania	M.	60–60–60	1.75–3.16–2.89
Massachusetts	M.	59–60–60	2.00–3.00–2.45	Virginia	M.	60–60–60	2.00–2.50–2.13
Minnesota	M.	60–60–60	3.50–3.50–3.50	**1884:**			
Missouri	M.	60–60–60	3.50–3.50–3.50	California	M.	54–60–57	3.00–4.00–3.26
New Jersey	M.	80–60–60	2.50–2.75–2.63	Illinois	M.	48–48–48	3.00–3.50–3.49
New York	M.	54–60–54	2.50–3.50–3.13	Iowa	M.	60–60–60	3.00–3.00–2.67
Ohio	M.	60–60–60	2.00–3.33–2.89	Louisiana	M.	60–60–60	2.50–3.00–2.75
Pennsylvania	M.	60–60–60	1.75–2.75–2.35	Maryland	M.	60–60–60	2.25–3.00–2.70
Virginia	M.	60–60–60	3.00–3.50–3.13	Massachusetts	M.	59–60–60	2.75–3.50–3.12
1879:				Michigan	M.	(1)	1.00–3.00–2.27
California	M.	60–60–60	3.00–4.00–3.62	Minnesota	M.	60–60–60	3.50–3.50–3.50
Illinois	M.	54–54–54	3.15–3.15–3.15	Missouri	M.	60–60–60	3.00–4.50–3.53
Louisiana	M.	60–60–60	2.50–3.00–2.70	New Jersey	M.	60–60–60	2.08–3.00–2.44
Maryland	M.	60–60–60	2.25–3.00–2.76	New York	M.	54–60–60	2.50–3.50–3.50
Massachusetts	M.	59–60–60	2.00–2.50–2.23	Ohio	M.	60–60–60	2.00–3.79–2.83
Minnesota	M.	60–60–60	3.50–3.50–3.50	Pennsylvania	M.	60–60–60	2.00–3.00–2.72
Missouri	M.	60–60–60	3.50–3.50–3.50	Virginia	M.	60–60–60	2.00–2.50–2.10
New Jersey	M.	60–60–60	1.00–2.75–1.94	**1885:**			
New York	M.	54–60–54	2.50–3.50–3.12	California	M.	54–54–54	3.00–4.00–3.56
Ohio	M.	60–60–60	2.17–3.33–2.83	Dist. of Columbia	M.	60–60–60	3.50–3.50–3.50
Pennsylvania	M.	60–60–60	2.00–3.00–2.55	Illinois	M.	48–48–48	3.50–3.50–3.50
Virginia	M.	60–60–60	3.00–3.50–3.13	Louisiana	M.	60–60–60	2.50–3.00–2.70
1880:				Maryland	M.	60–60–60	2.25–3.00–2.70
California	M.	60–60–60	3.00–4.00–3.63	Massachusetts	M.	59–60–60	2.50–3.50–3.21
Illinois	M.	48–48–48	3.00–3.15–3.08	Minnesota	M.	48–60–54	3.50–3.50–3.50
Louisiana	M.	60–60–60	2.50–3.00–2.75	Missouri	M.	60–60–60	3.00–3.50–3.53
Maryland	M.	60–60–60	2.25–3.00–2.70	New Jersey	M.	54–60–57	2.17–3.50–2.69
Massachusetts	M.	59–60–60	2.00–3.00–2.66	New York	M.	45–60–56	2.75–3.50–3.17
Minnesota	M.	60–60–60	3.50–3.50–3.50	Ohio	M.	60–60–60	1.92–2.92–2.68
Missouri	M.	60–60–60	3.50–3.50–3.50	Pennsylvania	M.	60–60–60	2.50–3.50–2.86
New Jersey	M.	60–60–60	2.38–2.50–2.44	Virginia	M.	60–60–60	2.00–2.50–2.13
Do	(1)	67–67–67	3.11–3.11–3.11	**1886:**			
New York	M.	54–60–54	3.00–3.50–3.37	California	M.	54–60–58	2.50–4.00–3.05
Ohio	M.	60–60–60	2.00–3.33–2.74	Dist. of Columbia	M.	53–54–54	3.50–3.50–3.50
Pennsylvania	M.	60–60–60	2.00–3.00–2.42	Illinois	M.	48–60–50	2.00–6.00–3.36
Virginia	M.	60–60–60	2.00–3.00–2.42	Iowa	M.	60–60–60	2.00–4.00–2.63
1881:				Kansas	M.	60–60–60	3.00–3.00–3.00
California	M.	60–60–60	3.00–4.00–3.43	Louisiana	M.	60–60–60	2.50–3.00–2.72
Illinois	M.	48–48–48	3.50–3.50–3.50	Maryland	M.	60–60–60	2.25–3.00–2.73
Louisiana	M.	60–60–60	2.50–3.00–2.67	Massachusetts	M.	54–59–54	2.50–4.00–3.24
Maryland	M.	60–60–60	2.25–3.00–2.70	Minnesota	M.	48–60–57	2.25–3.50–2.33
Massachusetts	M.	59–60–60	2.00–3.33–2.72	Missouri	M.	48–60–59	3.00–3.50–3.04
Minnesota	M.	60–60–60	3.50–3.50–3.50	New Jersey	M.	53–60–56	2.25–3.50–2.74
Missouri	M.	60–60–60	3.50–3.50–3.50	New York	M.	48–60–54	1.67–4.00–3.28
New Jersey	M.	60–60–60	2.50–2.50–2.50	Ohio	M.	60–60–60	2.50–3.50–3.10
New York	M.	54–60–54	3.00–3.50–3.43	Pennsylvania	M.	60–60–60	2.00–3.50–2.81
Ohio	M.	60–60–60	2.67–4.17–3.11	Virginia	M.	60–60–60	2.00–2.50–2.13
Pennsylvania	M.	60–60–60	1.75–2.75–2.34	**1887:**			
Virginia	M.	60–60–60	2.50–3.00–2.63	California	M.	54–54–54	3.00–4.00–3.50
1882:				Connecticut	M.	(1)	1.50–4.00–2.57
California	M.	60–60–60	3.00–4.00–3.50	Illinois	M.	48–48–48	3.50–3.60–3.57
Illinois	M.	48–60–51	3.00–3.50–3.39	Kansas	M.	54–60–58	2.35–3.50–2.73
Louisiana	M.	60–60–60	2.50–3.00–2.60	Louisiana	M.	60–60–60	2.50–3.00–2.67
Maryland	M.	60–60–60	2.25–3.00–2.70	Maryland	M.	54–54–54	1.70–3.00–2.53
Massachusetts	M.	59–60–60	2.50–3.00–2.78	Massachusetts	M.	54–59–54	2.00–4.00–3.12
Minnesota	M.	60–60–60	3.50–3.50–3.50	Michigan	M.	(1)	2.35–2.61–2.48
Missouri	M.	60–60–60	3.50–3.50–3.25	Minnesota	M.	48–60–54	3.50–3.50–3.50
New Jersey	M.	60–60–60	2.50–2.50–2.50	Missouri	M.	48–48–48	3.50–3.50–3.50

1 Not reported.

TABLE **B-22**.—*Plumbers, 1850-1900, by year and State*—Continued

Year and State	Sex	Hours per week	Rate per day (dollars)	Year and State	Sex	Hours per week	Rate per day (dollars)
1887—Continued.				**1892—Continued.**			
New Jersey	M.	60-60-60	2.50-3.00-2.75	Minnesota	M.	48-48-48	3.50-3.50-3.50
New York	M.	48-54-52	2.10-3.75-3.52	Missouri	M.	48-48-48	3.50-3.50-3.50
Do	M.	(1)	[2].20-.30-.23	New Jersey	M.	60-60-60	3.00-3.00-3.00
Ohio	M.	54-60-59	1.25-3.83-2.76	New York	M.	48-48-48	3.50-3.75-3.58
Oregon	M.	(1)	4.79-4.79-4.79	Ohio	M.	54-54-54	3.50-3.50-3.50
Pennsylvania	M.	60-72-61	2.00-3.50-2.94	Do	(1)	53-60-55	1.00-5.50-3.26
Virginia	M.	60-60-60	2.00-2.50-2.13	Pennsylvania	M.	54-60-57	2.50-3.50-3.06
Wisconsin	M.	(1)	2.42-2.42-2.42	Rhode Island	M.	49-60-55	1.00-3.50-2.69
1888:				Virginia	M.	60-60-60	2.00-2.50-2.20
California	M.	54-54-54	3.00-4.00-3.50	**1893:**			
Illinois	M.	48-48-48	3.50-3.60-3.58	California	M.	48-48-48	3.00-4.00-3.55
Louisiana	M.	60-60-60	2.50-3.00-2.58	Illinois	M.	48-60-49	1.50-4.50-3.53
Maryland	M.	54-54-54	2.00-3.00-2.64	Louisiana	M.	54-54-54	2.50-3.00-2.60
Massachusetts	M.	54-59-55	2.83-4.00-3.18	Maryland	M.	54-72-56	.67-4.17-2.56
Michigan	M.	60-60-60	2.30-3.26-2.78	Massachusetts	M.	54-54-54	3.00-3.50-3.30
Minnesota	M.	48-60-54	3.50-3.50-3.50	Michigan	M.	57-60-59	1.35-2.00-1.68
Missouri	M.	48-48-48.	3.50-3.50-3.50	Minnesota	M.	48-48-48	3.50-3.50-3.50
New Jersey	M.	60-60-60	2.50-3.00-2.75	Missouri	M.	48-48-48	3.50-3.50-3.50
Do	(1)		2.50-3.50-3.00	Montana	M.	42-60-50	3.00-5.00-4.38
New York	M.	48-60-54	1.00-4.00-3.37	New Hampshire	M.	59-60-60	1.75-3.50-2.54
Do	M.	(1)	[2].22½-.22½-.22½	New York	M.	48-60-49	1.17-3.75-3.53
Ohio	M.	54-54-54	1.50-3.83-2.77	Ohio	M.	48-60-56	1.50-3.67-2.49
Pennsylvania	M.	54-60-59	2.50-4.00-3.15	Pennsylvania	M.	48-66-55	1.00-3.83-2.81
Virginia	M.	60-60-60	2.00-2.50-2.10	Rhode Island	M.	(1)	3.00-3.50-3.42
1889:				Virginia	M.	48-48-48	2.00-2.50-2.25
California	M.	54-54-54	3.00-4.00-3.45	Wisconsin	M.	(1)	[2].15-.45-.30
Illinois	M.	48-48-48	3.50-3.60-3.57	**1894:**			
Louisiana	M.	60-60-60	2.50-3.00-2.67	California	M.	48-48-48	3.00-4.00-3.57
Maryland	M.	54-54-54	2.00-3.00-2.65	Illinois	M.	48-48-48	3.75-3.75-3.75
Massachusetts	M.	54-59-54	2.83-4.00-3.24	Iowa	M.	48-60-55	1.00-3.50-2.64
Michigan	M.	60-60-60	1.10-2.50-1.80	Louisiana	M.	54-54 54	2.50-3.00-2.70
Minnesota	M.	48-60-54	3.50-3.50-3.50	Maryland	M.	54-54-54	2.50-3.00-2.82
Missouri	M.	48-48-48	3.50-3.50-3.50	Massachusetts	M.	54-54-54	3.00-3.50-3.13
New Jersey	M.	60-60-60	2.50-3.00-2.75	Minnesota	M.	48-48-48	3.50-3.50-3.50
New York	M.	48-54-48	3.50-3.75-3.59	Missouri	M.	48-48-48	3.50-3.50-3.50
Ohio	M.	54-54-54	2.00-3.50-3.13	New York	M.	48-60-48	1.50-3.75-3.72
Pennsylvania	M.	54-60-59	2.50-3.50-3.13	North Carolina	(1)	60-60-60	2.88-2.88-2.88
Virginia	M.	60-60-60	2.00-2.50-2.20	Ohio	M.	54-60-58	1.67-3.50-2.50
Wisconsin	M.	(1)	1.66-3.48-2.35	Pennsylvania	M.	54-54-54	2.50-3.50-3.06
1890:				Virginia	M.	48-48-48	2.00-2.50-2.25
California	M.	48-54-53	3.00-4.00-3.55	**1895:**			
Illinois	M.	48-48-48	3.75-3.75-3.75	California	M.	48-48-48	3.00-4.00-3.59
Kansas	M.	(1)	2.50-3.50-3.04	Illinois	M.	48-48-48	3.75-3.75-3.75
Louisiana	M.	60-60-60	2.50-3.00-2.64	Louisiana	M.	54-54-54	2.50-3.00-2.58
Maryland	M.	54-54-54	2.50-3.00-2.79	Maryland	M.	54-54-54	2.50-3.00-2.75
Massachusetts	M.	54-54-54	2.50-4.00-3.19	Massachusetts	M.	48-54-49	2.50-3.00-3.28
Michigan	M.	60-60-60	1.33-2.67-2.00	Minnesota	M.	48-48-48	3.50-3.50-3.50
Minnesota	M.	48-60-54	1.50-4.00-3.12	Missouri	M.	48-48-48	3.50-3.50-3.50
Missouri	M.	48-48-48	3.50-3.50-3.50	New York	M.	48-48-48	3.50-3.75-3.74
New Jersey	M.	60-60-60	2.50-3.00-2.75	North Carolina	M.	60-60-60	2.50-2.50-2.50
New York	M.	48-54-48	1.50-3.75-2.94	Ohio	M.	54-60-55	2.00-3.50-2.75
Ohio	M.	54-54-54	1.80-3.33-2.90	Pennsylvania	M.	50-54-53	2.70-3.50-3.07
Pennsylvania	M.	54-60-59	2.50-3.50-3.00	Virginia	M.	48-48-48	2.00-2.50-2.25
Virginia	M.	60-60-60	2.00-2.50-2.20	**1896:**			
1891:				Alabama	M.	(1)	1.25-1.25-1.25
California	M.	48-48-48	3.00-4.00-3.56	California	M.	48-48-48	3.00-4.00-3.59
Illinois	M.	48-48-48	3.75-3.75-3.75	Colorado	M.	48-48-48	4.00-4.00-4.00
Louisiana	M.	60-60-60	2.50-3.00-2.67	Florida	M.	(1)	1.25-1.25-1.25
Maryland	M.	54-54-54	2.50-3.00-2.79	Illinois	M.	48-54-48	2.00-3.75-3.71
Massachusetts	M.	54-54-54	2.50-4.00-3.25	Kansas	M.	60-60-60	2.00-2.00-2.00
Minnesota	M.	48-48-48	3.50-3.50-3.50	Louisiana	M.	54-54-54	2.50-3.00-2.67
Missouri	M.	48-48-48	3.50-3.50-3.50	Maryland	M.	54-54-54	2.50-3.00-2.53
New Jersey	M.	60-60-60	2.50-2.50-2.50	Massachusetts	M.	48-56-48	2.50-4.50-3.77
New York	M.	48-48-48	.55-3.75-2.87	Minnesota	M.	48-48-48	3.50-3.50-3.50
Ohio	M.	54-60-58	1.50-3.50-2.50	Missouri	M.	48-48-48	3.50-3.50-3.50
Pennsylvania	M.	54-60-59	2.50-3.50-3.06	New York	M.	48-60-49	1.00-3.85-3.49
Virginia	M.	60-60-60	2.00-2.50-2.20	North Carolina	M.	54-54-54	2.50-2.50-2.50
Wisconsin	M.	(1)	[2].17½-.40-.30½	Ohio	M.	48-60-55	1.50-3.50-2.32
1892:				Pennsylvania	M.	48-60-53	2.08-3.51-3.05
California	M.	48-54-49	1.50-4.00-3.65	Virginia	M.	48-48-48	2.00-2.50-2.25
Illinois	M.	48-48-48	3.75-3.75-3.75	**1897:**			
Louisiana	M.	54-54-54	2.50-3.00-2.72	California	M.	48-48-48	3.00-4.00-3.54
Maryland	M.	54-54-54	2.50-3.00-2.82	Illinois	M.	48-48-48	3.75-3.75-3.75
Massachusetts	M.	54-54-54	2.50-4.00-3.17	Kansas	M.	(1)	[2].30-.30-.30
Michigan	M.	54-60-59	.42-5.00-2.44	Louisiana	M.	54-54-54	2.50-3.00-2.72

[1] Not reported.   [2] Per hour.

TABLE **B-22.**—*Plumbers, 1850-1900, by year and State*—Continued

Year and State	Sex	Lowest, highest, and average—		Year and State	Sex	Lowest, highest, and average—	
		Hours per week	Rate per day (dollars)			Hours per week	Rate per day (dollars)
1897—Continued.				1898—Continued.			
Maryland	M.	54–54–54	2. 50–3. 00–2. 79	Pennsylvania	M.	50–54–52	1. 67–3. 50–2. 92
Massachusetts	M.	48–54–49	2. 50–3. 50–3. 31	Virginia	M.	48–48–48	2. 00–2. 50–2. 25
Michigan	M.	(1)	1. 98–1. 98–1. 98	1899:			
Minnesota	M.	48–48–48	3. 50–3. 50–3. 50	California	M.	48–48–48	4. 00–4. 00–4. 00
Missouri	M.	48–48–48	3. 50–3. 50–3. 50	Illinois	M.	44–44–44	3. 67–3. 90–3. 69
Nebraska	(1)	48–60–52	3. 00–4. 00–3. 35	Massachusetts	M.	48–48–48	3. 75–3. 75–3. 75
New York	M.	48–48–48	3. 25–3. 75–3. 73	Montana	M.	48–48–48	5. 60–5. 60–5. 60
Ohio	M.	53–53–53	1. 67–3. 50–2. 79	New Jersey	M.	54–54–54	3. 00–3. 00–3. 00
Pennsylvania	M.	50–54–53	1. 67–3. 50–2. 95	New York	M.	48–54–50	2. 50–3. 50–3. 19
Virginia	M.	48–48–48	2. 00–2. 50–2. 25	North Carolina	M.	54–60–57	2. 50–2. 70–2. 60
1898:				Ohio	M.	48–48–48	2. 25–3. 50–2. 69
California	M.	48–48–48	3. 00–4. 00–3. 61	Pennsylvania	M.	54–54–54	3. 00–3. 50–3. 31
Illinois	M.	48–48–48	3. 75–3. 75–3. 75	1900:			
Louisiana	M.	54–54–54	2. 50–3. 00–2. 64	California	M.	48–48–48	4. 00–4. 00–4. 00
Maryland	M.	54–54–54	2. 50–3. 00–2. 79	Illinois	M.	44–44–44	3. 67–3. 90–3. 68
Massachusetts	M.	48–48–48	2. 50–3. 50–3. 27	Massachusetts	M.	48–48–48	3. 75–3. 75–3. 75
Michigan	M.	(1)	2. 00–2. 50–2. 17	Montana	M.	48–48–48	5. 60–5. 60–5. 60
Minnesota	M.	48–48–48	3. 50–3. 50–3. 50	New Jersey	M.	48–48–48	3. 00–3. 00–3. 00
Missouri	M.	48–48–48	3. 50–3. 50–3. 50	New York	M.	48–54–50	2. 50–3. 50–3. 19
Nebraska	(1)	54–60–56	. 75–6. 00–2. 51	Ohio	M.	48–48–48	2. 25–3. 50–2. 71
New York	M.	48–48–48	3. 50–3. 75–3. 74	Pennsylvania	M.	54–54–54	3. 00–3. 50–3. 31
Ohio	M.	53–53–53	1. 83–3. 50–2. 93				

1 Not reported.

TABLE **B-23.**—*Plumbers, males, 1890-1928, by city and year*

Year	Atlanta, Ga.[1]		Birmingham, Ala.[2]		Boston, Mass.		Chicago, Ill.[1]	
	Hours per week	Rate per hour	Hours per week	Rate per hour	Hours per week	Rate per hour	Hours per week	Rate per hour
1890					51. 5	$0. 426	48. 0	$0. 469
1891					51. 4	. 425	48. 0	. 469
1892					50. 4	. 430	48. 0	. 469
1893					50. 4	. 432	48. 0	. 469
1894					50. 2	. 428	48. 0	. 469
1895					49. 0	. 440	48. 0	. 469
1896					49. 1	. 438	48. 0	. 469
1897					49. 1	. 439	48. 0	. 469
1898					49. 3	. 433	48. 0	. 469
1899					48. 0	. 446	46. 9	. 500
1900					48. 0	. 448	46. 7	. 500
1901					48. 0	. 447	46. 9	. 500
1902					48. 0	. 450	46. 7	. 500
1903	54. 7	$0. 378	47. 8	$0. 502	48. 0	. 453	44. 0	. 563
1904	53. 1	. 397	47. 8	. 503	48. 0	. 456	44. 0	. 563
1905	53. 1	. 392	48. 0	. 563	48. 0	. 456	44. 0	. 563
1906	53. 0	. 425	47. 0	. 575	48. 0	. 476	44. 0	. 563
1907	3 53. 0	. 400	47. 0	. 575	48. 0	. 500	44. 0	. 625
1908	3 53. 0	. 400	47. 0	. 638	48. 0	. 500	44. 0	. 650
1909	3 53. 0	. 400	44. 0	. 638	48. 0	. 550	44. 0	. 650
1910	3 53. 0	. 400	44. 0	. 688	48. 0	. 550	44. 0	. 688
1911	53. 0	. 450	44. 0	. 688	44. 0	. 550	44. 0	. 688
1912	53. 0	. 450	44. 0	. 688	44. 0	. 600	44. 0	. 750
1913	53. 0	. 450	44. 0	. 688	44. 0	. 600	44. 0	. 750
1914	53. 0	. 450	44. 0	. 750	44. 0	. 650	44. 0	. 750
1915	53. 0	. 450	44. 0	. 750	44. 0	. 650	44. 0	. 750
1916	53. 0	. 450	44. 0	. 750	44. 0	. 650	44. 0	. 750
1917	53. 0	. 450	44. 0	. 750	44. 0	. 688	44. 0	. 750
1918	49. 5	. 500	44. 0	. 875	44. 0	. 750	44. 0	. 750
1919	49. 5	. 600	44. 0	1. 125	44. 0	. 800	44. 0	. 844
1920	44. 0	1. 000	44. 0	1. 500	44. 0	1. 000	44. 0	1. 250
1921	44. 0	1. 000	44. 0	1. 500	44. 0	1. 000	44. 0	1. 250
1922	44. 0	1. 000	44. 0	1. 250	44. 0	1. 000	44. 0	1. 100
1923	44. 0	1. 000	44. 0	1. 500	44. 0	1. 050	44. 0	1. 100
1924	44. 0	1. 000	44. 0	1. 500	44. 0	1. 100	44. 0	1. 250
1925	44. 0	1. 000	44. 0	1. 500	44. 0	1. 100	44. 0	1. 250
1926	44. 0	1. 250	44. 0	1. 500	44. 0	1. 250	44. 0	1. 500
1927	44. 0	1. 250	44. 0	1. 500	44. 0	1. 250	44. 0	1. 500
1928	44. 0	1. 250	44. 0	1. 500	44. 0	1. 375	44. 0	1. 625

1 Includes gas fitters, 1907–1928.
2 Includes gas fitters, 1912–1928.
3 Work 53 hours; paid for 54.

TABLE **B-23.**—*Plumbers, males, 1890–1928, by city and year*—Continued

Year	Cincinnati, Ohio [1]		Denver, Colo.[1]		Detroit, Mich.		New Orleans, La.[1]	
	Hours per week	Rate per hour	Hours per week	Rate per hour	Hours per week	Rate per hour	Hours per week	Rate per hour
1890	54.7	$0.388	48.0	$0.500	54.0	$0.302	52.8	$0.325
1891	54.7	.388	48.0	.500	54.0	.289	53.1	.322
1892	55.4	.383	48.0	.500	54.0	.296	53.3	.322
1893	54.7	.388	48.0	.500	54.0	.303	52.2	.325
1894	54.9	.387	48.0	.500	54.0	.303	52.3	.321
1895	55.0	.386	48.0	.500	54.0	.299	52.3	.321
1896	51.9	.406	48.0	.500	54.0	.299	52.5	.322
1897	51.9	.406	48.0	.500	54.0	.296	52.5	.323
1898	51.9	.406	48.0	.500	54.0	.289	52.5	.339
1899	51.6	.408	48.0	.500	54.0	.279	52.7	.340
1900	51.4	.410	48.0	.500	48.0	.327	52.8	.334
1901	48.8	.431	48.0	.500	48.0	.355	48.0	.388
1902	48.0	.438	44.0	.531	48.0	.370	48.0	.404
1903	48.0	.460	44.0	.531	48.0	.367	48.0	.431
1904	48.0	.500	44.0	.531	48.0	.424	48.0	.490
1905	48.0	.500	44.0	.545	48.0	.454	48.0	.500
1906	48.0	.500	44.0	.625	48.0	.401	48.0	.494
1907	44.5	.500	48.0	.563	48.0	.469	48.0	.500
1908	44.5	.500	44.0	.625	48.0	.469	48.0	.500
1909	44.5	.500	44.0	.625	48.0	.469	48.0	.563
1910	44.5	.563	44.0	.625	48.0	.500	48.0	.563
1911	44.5	.563	44.0	.625	48.0	.500	48.0	.563
1912	44.5	.563	44.0	.625	48.0	.500	48.0	.563
1913	44.5	.618	44.0	.625	48.0	.563	48.0	.563
1914	44.5	.618	44.0	.625	48.0	.563	48.0	.563
1915	44.5	.618	44.0	.625	48.0	.600	48.0	.563
1916	44.5	.618	44.0	.625	44.0	.625	48.0	.563
1917	44.0	.656	44.0	.750	44.0	.688	48.0	.563
1918	44.0	.656	44.0	.875	44.0	.750	48.0	.688
1919	44.0	.750	44.0	.875	44.0	.900	48.0	.800
1920	44.0	1.000	44.0	1.000	44.0	1.250	48.0	.900
1921	44.0	1.000	44.0	1.063	44.0	1.000	44.0	1.000
1922	44.0	1.000	44.0	1.063	44.0	1.000	44.0	.900
1923	44.0	1.125	44.0	1.188	44.0	1.250	44.0	.900
1924	44.0	1.250	44.0	1.188	44.0	1.300	44.0	1.050
1925	44.0	1.250	44.0	1.250	44.0	1.300	44.0	1.125
1926	44.0	1.350	44.0	1.375	44.0	1.400	44.0	1.250
1927	44.0	1.375	44.0	1.375	44.0	1.500	44.0	1.250
1928	44.0	1.375	44.0	1.375	44.0	1.500	44.0	1.250

Year	New York, N. Y.[4]		Philadelphia, Pa.[1]		St. Louis, Mo.		San Francisco, Calif.	
1890	48.5	$0.439	55.2	$0.340	48.0	$0.409	48.0	$0.455
1891	48.6	.438	55.6	.336	48.0	.438	48.0	.455
1892	48.6	.439	55.0	.339	48.0	.438	48.0	.473
1893	48.7	.454	54.1	.343	48.0	.438	48.0	.470
1894	48.5	.458	53.5	.352	48.0	.438	48.0	.467
1895	48.5	.459	53.5	.345	48.0	.438	48.0	.469
1896	48.7	.454	53.4	.347	48.0	.438	48.0	.470
1897	48.7	.455	53.6	.348	48.0	.438	48.0	.466
1898	48.7	.456	53.7	.346	48.0	.438	48.0	.474
1899	48.8	.457	53.0	.345	46.8	.457	18.0	.488
1900	48.2	.461	52.7	.354	44.0	.500	48.0	.488
1901	48.2	.488	51.1	.369	44.0	.500	48.0	.492
1902	44.4	.526	48.3	.385	44.0	.500	48.0	.521
1903	44.4	.525	47.2	.405	44.0	.625	47.9	.564
1904	44.1	.560	47.8	.438	44.0	.625	47.5	.632
1905	44.0	.593	47.7	.438	44.0	.625	47.5	.632
1906	44.0	.595	47.7	.438	44.0	.625	44.0	.800
1907	44.0	.625	44.0	.438	44.0	.625		
1908	44.0	.625	44.0	.438	44.0	.663		
1909	44.0	.625	44.0	.438	44.0	.663		
1910	44.0	.625	44.0	.438	44.0	.663		
1911	44.0	.688	44.0	.500	44.0	.663	44.0	.750
1912	44.0	.688	44.0	.500	44.0	.663	44.0	.750
1913	44.0	.688	44.0	.500	44.0	.663	44.0	.750
1914	44.0	.688	44.0	.500	44.0	.750	44.0	.750
1915	44.0	.688	44.0	.500	44.0	.750	44.0	.750
1916	44.0	.688	44.0	.500	44.0	.750	44.0	.750
1917	44.0	.688	44.0	.563	44.0	.750	44.0	.813
1918	44.0	.750	44.0	.625	44.0	.813	44.0	.875
1919	44.0	.750	44.0	.800	44.0	1.000	44.0	1.000
1920	44.0	1.125	44.0	.900	44.0	1.250	44.0	1.250
1921	44.0	1.125	44.0	1.150	44.0	1.250	44.0	1.250
1922	44.0	1.125	44.0	.900	44.0	1.250	44.0	1.250
1923	44.0	1.250	44.0	1.150	44.0	1.250	44.0	1.250
1924	44.0	1.375	44.0	1.150	44.0	1.500	44.0	1.125
1925	44.0	1.375	44.0	1.150	44.0	1.500	44.0	1.125
1926	44.0	1.500	44.0	1.150	44.0	1.500		
1927	44.0	1.500	44.0	1.150	44.0	1.500	44.0	1.250
1928	44.0	1.500	44.0	1.150	44.0	1.500	44.0	1.250

[1] Includes gas fitters, 1907–1928.
[4] Greater New York, 1903–1906; Manhattan and Bronx (includes gas fitters), 1907–1928.

TABLE **B-24.**—*Stonecutters, 1850–1900, by year and State*

| Year and State | Sex | Lowest, highest, and average— | | Year and State | Sex | Lowest, highest, and average— | |
		Hours per week	Rate per day (dollars)			Hours per week	Rate per day (dollars)
1850:				**1872:**			
New York	M.	60-60-60	2.00-2.00-2.00	California	M.	48-60-56	4.00-5.00-4.07
1851:				Illinois	M.	48-48-48	5.00-5.00-5.00
New York	M.	60-60-60	2.00-2.00-2.00	Louisiana	M.	60-60-60	4.50-4.50-4.50
1852:				Maryland	M.	59-59-59	4.00-4.00-4.00
New York	M.	60-60-60	2.00-2.00-2.00	Massachusetts	M.	54-60-59	3.25-4.50-4.02
1853:				Minnesota	M.	60-60-60	3.00-3.00-3.00
New York	M.	60-60-60	2.00-2.00-2.00	Missouri	M.	54-60-56	2.00-4.00-2.46
1854:				New York	M.	60-60-60	4.00-4.00-4.00
New York	M.	60-60-60	2.00-2.00-2.00	Ohio	M.	60-60-60	3.50-5.00-4.45
1855:				Pennsylvania	M.	59-60-59	3.50-4.50-3.85
New York	M.	60-60-60	2.00-2.00-2.00	Virginia	M.	60-60-60	3.50-3.50-3.50
1856:				**1873:**			
New York	M.	60-60-60	2.00-2.00-2.00	California	M.	48-60-55	4.00-5.00-4.07
1857:				Illinois	M.	48-48-48	3.00-3.00-3.00
New York	M.	60-60-60	2.00-2.00-2.00	Louisiana	M.	60-60-60	4.50-4.50-4.50
1858:				Maryland	M.	59-59-59	4.00-4.00-4.00
New York	M.	60-60-60	2.00-2.00-2.00	Massachusetts	M.	54-60-57	3.25-5.00-4.50
1859:				Minnesota	M.	60-60-60	3.00-3.00-3.00
Massachusetts	M.	60-60-60	1.10-1.57-1.25	Missouri	M.	54-60-56	2.00-3.50-2.50
New York	M.	60-60-60	2.00-2.00-2.00	New York	M.	60-60-60	4.00-4.00-4.00
1860:				Ohio	M.	60-60-60	4.50-4.50-4.50
Massachusetts	M.	60-60-60	1.12-2.00-1.37	Pennsylvania	M.	59-60-59	3.50-4.50-3.82
New York	M.	60-60-60	2.00-2.00-2.00	Virginia	M.	48-60-54	3.50-4.50-3.97
Ohio	M.	(¹)	1.67-1.67-1.67	**1874:**			
Pennsylvania	M.	60-60-60	1.75-1.75-1.75	California	M.	48-60-54	4.00-5.00-4.04
1861:				Illinois	M.	48-48-48	2.50-2.50-2.50
Massachusetts	M.	60-60-60	1.12-2.00-1.43	Louisiana	M.	60-60-60	4.50-4.50-4.50
New York	M.	60-60-60	2.00-2.00-2.00	Maryland	M.	59-59-59	4.00-4.00-4.00
Pennsylvania	M.	60-60-60	1.75-1.75-1.75	Massachusetts	M.	54-60-58	3.00-5.00-3.97
1862:				Minnesota	M.	60-60-60	3.00-3.00-3.00
New York	M.	60-60-60	2.00-2.00-2.00	Missouri	M.	54-60-57	2.00-3.50-2.46
Pennsylvania	M.	60-60-60	1.75-1.75-1.75	New York	M.	60-60-60	4.00-4.00-4.00
1863:				Ohio	M.	60-60-60	4.00-4.00-4.00
New York	M.	60-60-60	2.25-2.25-2.25	Pennsylvania	M.	59-60-59	3.25-4.50-3.73
Pennsylvania	M.	60-60-60	2.00-2.00-2.00	Virginia	M.	60-60-60	3.00-3.00-3.00
1864:				**1875:**			
New York	M.	60-60-60	2.75-2.75-2.75	California	M.	48-54-52	4.00-5.00-4.04
Pennsylvania	M.	60-60-60	2.50-2.75-2.69	Illinois	M.	48-48-48	2.25-2.25-2.25
1865:				Louisiana	M.	60-60-60	4.00-4.00-4.00
New York	M.	60-60-60	3.50-3.50-3.50	Maryland	M.	59-59-59	4.00-4.00-4.00
Pennsylvania	M.	60-60-60	3.00-3.25-3.05	Massachusetts	M.	54-60-58	2.50-4.00-3.10
1866:				Minnesota	M.	60-60-60	3.00-3.00-3.00
New York	M.	60-60-60	3.75-3.75-3.75	Missouri	M.	54-60-57	2.00-3.00-2.40
Pennsylvania	M.	60-60-60	3.25-3.25-3.25	New York	M.	60-60-60	3.50-3.50-3.50
1867:				Ohio	M.	60-60-60	4.00-4.00-4.00
Pennsylvania	M.	60-60-60	3.25-3.25-3.25	Pennsylvania	M.	59-60-59	3.00-4.50-3.65
1868:				Virginia	M.	60-60-60	3.00-3.00-3.00
Pennsylvania	M.	60-60-60	3.75-3.75-3.75	**1876:**			
1869:				California	M.	48-54-52	3.50-5.00-3.77
New York	M.	60-60-60	4.25-4.25-4.25	Illinois	M.	48-48-48	2.50-4.00-2.54
Pennsylvania	M.	60-60-60	2.50-2.50-2.50	Louisiana	M.	60-60-60	3.75-3.75-3.75
1870:				Maryland	M.	59-59-59	3.00-3.00-3.00
California	M.	48-60-55	4.00-5.00-4.14	Massachusetts	M.	54-60-59	2.25-3.50-2.75
Illinois	M.	48-48-48	3.50-3.50-3.50	Minnesota	M.	60-60-60	3.00-3.00-3.00
Louisiana	M.	60-60-60	4.50-4.50-4.50	Missouri	M.	48-60-54	2.25-4.00-2.88
Maryland	M.	59-59-59	4.00-4.00-4.00	New York	M.	60-60-60	3.00-3.00-3.00
Massachusetts	M.	54-60-59	3.50-4.50-4.09	Ohio	M.	60-60-60	3.00-3.50-3.25
Minnesota	M.	60-60-60	3.00-3.00-3.00	Pennsylvania	M.	59-60-59	2.50-4.50-3.24
Missouri	M.	54-60-56	2.00-4.00-2.50	Virginia	M.	60-60-60	3.00-3.00-3.00
New York	M.	60-60-60	4.25-4.25-4.25	**1877:**			
Ohio	M.	60-60-60	3.50-3.50-3.50	California	M.	48-54-52	3.50-5.00-3.79
Pennsylvania	M.	48-60-57	3.00-4.00-3.58	Illinois	M.	48-48-48	2.50-2.50-2.50
Virginia	M.	60-60-60	3.50-3.50-3.50	Louisiana	M.	60-60-60	2.50-2.50-2.50
1871:				Maryland	M.	59-59-59	3.00-3.00-3.00
California	M.	48-60-55	4.00-5.00-4.11	Massachusetts	M.	54-60-57	2.25-3.00-2.62
Illinois	M.	48-48-48	3.50-3.50-3.50	Minnesota	M.	60-60-60	3.00-3.50-3.23
Louisiana	M.	60-60-60	4.50-4.50-4.50	Missouri	M.	48-60-54	2.25-4.00-2.68
Maryland	M.	59-59-59	4.00-4.00-4.00	New Jersey	M.	60-60-60	2.00-2.00-2.00
Massachusetts	M.	54-60-59	3.50-4.50-3.87	New York	M.	60-60-60	3.00-3.00-3.00
Minnesota	M.	60-60-60	3.00-3.00-3.00	Ohio	M.	60-60-60	2.00-2.50-2.30
Missouri	M.	54-60-56	2.00-4.00-2.62	Pennsylvania	M.	59-60-59	2.00-3.75-2.79
New York	M.	60-60-60	4.00-4.00-4.00	Virginia	M.	60-60-60	3.00-3.00-3.00
Ohio	M.	60-60-60	3.50-3.50-3.50	**1878:**			
Pennsylvania	M.	59-60-59	3.00-4.00-3.52	California	M.	48-54-53	3.50-4.00-3.67
Virginia	M.	60-60-60	3.50-3.50-3.50	Illinois	M.	48-48-48	2.50-2.50-2.50

¹ Not reported.

TABLE **B–24.**—*Stonecutters, 1850–1900, by year and State*—Continued

Year and State	Sex	Lowest, highest, and average—		Year and State	Sex	Lowest, highest, and average—	
		Hours per week	Rate per day (dollars)			Hours per week	Rate per day (dollars)
1878—Continued.				**1883—Continued.**			
Louisiana	M.	60–60–60	2.50–2.50–2.50	New York	M.	53–60–60	2.75–3.75–2.92
Maryland	M.	59–59–59	3.00–3.00–3.00	Ohio	M.	59–60–60	2.50–3.50–2.86
Massachusetts	M.	54–60–56	2.25–3.00–2.83	Pennsylvania	M.	54–60–60	3.25–3.75–3.30
Minnesota	M.	60 60–60	3.50–3.50–3.50	Virginia	M.	60–60–60	3.00–3.00–3.00
Missouri	M.	48–60–54	2.25–4.00–2.63	**1884:**			
New York	M.	60–60–60	3.00–3.00–3.00	California	M.	48–60–54	3.50–4.00–3.61
Ohio	M.	60–60–60	1.50–2.50–2.20	Dist. of Columbia	M.	48–48–48	3.00–3.60–3.44
Pennsylvania	M.	59–60–59	2.00–3.25–2.56	Illinois	M.	48–57–48	3.00–4.00–3.09
Virginia	M.	60–60–60	3.00–3.00–3.00	Iowa	M.	60–60–60	3.00–3.00–3.00
1879:				Louisiana	M.	60–60–60	2.50–2.50–2.50
California	M.	48–54–53	3.50–4.00–3.70	Maine	M.	58–58–58	3.00–3.00–3.00
Illinois	M.	48–48–48	2.50–2.50–2.50	Maryland	M.	59–59–59	3.00–3.00–3.00
Louisiana	M.	60–60–60	2.50–2.50–2.50	Massachusetts	M.	54–59–55	2.70–4.00–3.59
Maryland	M.	59–59–59	3.00–3.00 –3.00	Michigan	M.	(¹)	1.50–3.50–2.63
Massachusetts	M.	54–60–57	2.25–3.00–2.68	Minnesota	M.	60–60–60	3.50–3.50–3.50
Minnesota	M.	60–60–60	3.50–3.50–3.50	Missouri	M.	48–60–56	2.25–4.00–3.02
Missouri	M.	48–60–54	1.67–4.00–2.29	New Jersey	M.	60–60–60	2.75–3.50–2.88
New York	M.	60–60–60	3.00–3.00–3.00	New York	M.	60–60–60	3.75–3.75–3.75
Ohio	M.	60–60–60	2.00–3.00–2.30	Ohio	M.	54–60–55	3.50–3.50–3.50
Pennsylvania	M.	59–60–59	1.00–2.50–2.11	Pennsylvania	M.	54–60–59	3.25–3.75–3.31
Virginia	M.	60–60–60	3.00–3.00–3.00	Texas	M.	59–60–60	4.00–5.00–4.93
1880:				Virginia	M.	60–60–60	3.00–3.00–3.00
California	M.	48–54–53	3.50–4.00–3.66	**1885:**			
Illinois	M.	48–48–48	3.00–3.00–3.00	California	M.	48–54–53	3.50–4.00–3.62
Louisiana	M.	60–60–60	2.50–2.50–2.50	Illinois	M.	48–48–48	3.00–3.00–3.00
Maryland	M.	59–59–59	3.00–3.00–3.00	Kansas	M.	60–60–60	3.00–3.50–3.25
Massachusetts	M.	54–60–58	2.00–3.00–2.58	Louisiana	M.	60–60–60	2.50–2.50–2.50
Minnesota	M.	60–60–60	3.50–3.50–3.50	Maryland	M.	53–60–55	3.00–3.25–3.10
Missouri	M.	48–60–54	2.25–4.00–2.79	Massachusetts	M.	54–59–58	2.46–4.00–3.04
New Jersey	(¹)	48–48–48	3.50–3.50–3.50	Minnesota	M.	48–60–54	3.50–5.00–3.78
New York	M.	60–60–60	3.00–3.00–3.00	Missouri	M.	48–60–55	2.25–4.00–2.81
Ohio	M.	60–60–60	1.25–3.00–2.90	New Jersey	M.	53–60–54	1.67–3.42–3.14
Pennsylvania	M.	59–60–59	1.25–3.00–2.49	New York	M.	48–54–49	3.75–4.50–4.33
Virginia	M.	60–60–60	3.00–3.00–3.00	Ohio	M.	57–60–59	3.15–3.50–3.47
1881:				Pennsylvaia	M.	53–60–56	3.25–3.75–3.42
California	M.	48–54–53	3.50–4.00–3.68	Virginia	M.	54–54–54	3.00–3.00–3.00
Illinois	M.	48–60–58	3.00–3.50–3.33	**1886:**			
Louisiana	M.	60–60–60	2.75–2.75–2.75	California	M.	48–60–59	2.00–4.00–2.66
Maryland	M.	59–59–59	3.00–3.00–3.00	Do.	M.	60–60–60	²1.92–1.92–1.92
Massachusetts	M.	54–59–57	2.46–4.00–3.12	Connecticut	M.	54–54–54	3.25–3.25–3.25
Michigan	M.	60–60–60	2.10–2.60–2.35	Dist. of Columbia	M.	53–53–53	3.50–3.60–3.55
Minnesota	M.	60–60–60	3.50–3.50–3.50	Georgia	M.	54–54–54	4.00–4.00–4.00
Missouri	M.	48–60–54	2.25–4.00–2.80	Illinois	M.	48–60–56	1.50–3.50–3.22
New York	M.	60–60–60	3.00–3.00–3.00	Iowa	M.	66–66–66	1.28–4.00–2.10
Ohio	M.	60–60–60	1.55–3.25–2.75	Kansas	M.	60–60–60	3.00–3.50–3.04
Pennsylvania	M.	54–60–58	2.75–3.25–2.95	Louisiana	M.	60–60–60	2.50–2.50–2.50
Virginia	M.	60–60–60	3.00–3.00–3.00	Maryland	M.	53–53–53	3.25–3.25–3.25
1882:				Massachusetts	M.	54–59–58	2.46–4.00–2.99
California	M.	48–54–53	3.50–4.00–3.65	Minnesota	M.	48–60–54	2.50–3.50–3.18
Dist. of Columbia	M.	52–58–55	3.00–3.00–3.00	Missouri	M.	48–54–51	2.25–4.00–2.88
Illinois	M.	48–48–48	3.00–3.00–3.00	New Jersey	M.	50–50–50	3.50–3.50–3.50
Indiana	M.	60–60–60	3.00–3.50–3.11	New York	M.	48–60–58	2.80–3.75–3.36
Louisiana	M.	60–60–60	3.00–3.00–3.00	Ohio	M.	48–60–54	3.25–3.60–3.33
Maryland	M.	59–59–59	3.00–3.00–3.00	Pennsylvania	M.	53–54–54	3.00–3.60–3.21
Massachusetts	M.	54–59–56	2.21–3.00–2.77	South Dakota	M.	(¹)	4.00–4.00–4.00
Michigan	M.	60–60–60	2.99–3.99–3.57	Vermont	M.	60–60–60	2.50–2.50–2.50
Minnesota	M.	60–60–60	3.50–3.50–3.50	Virginia	M.	54–54–54	3.00–3.00–3.00
Missouri	M.	48–60–57	2.25–4.00–3.21	**1887:**			
New Jersey	M.	53–53–53	2.50–3.75–2.73	California	M.	48–54–53	3.50–4.00–3.63
New York	M.	53–60–60	2.90–3.75–3.16	Delaware	M.	(¹)	³.20–.27¼–.26½
Ohio	M.	60–60–60	2.06–3.50–2.46	Illinois	M.	48–48–48	3.50–3.50–3.50
Pennsylvania	M.	59–60–60	3.00–3.75–3.07	Kansas	M.	48–60–49	3.50–4.25–3.60
Virginia	M.	60–60–60	3.00–3.00–3.00	Louisiana	M.	60–60–60	2.50–2.50–2.50
1883:				Maine	M.	60–60–60	2.00–2.75–2.54
California	M.	48–54–53	3.50–4.00–3.65	Maryland	M.	53–53–53	1.35–3.25–2.91
Illinois	M.	48–48–48	3.00–3.00–3.00	Massachusetts	M.	54–59–57	1.35–4.00–2.95
Indiana	M.	60–60–60	3.00–3.00–3.00	Minnesota	M.	60–60–60	3.50–3.50–3.50
Louisiana	M.	60–60–60	2.50–3.00–2.75	Missouri	M.	48–51–51	2.25–4.00–3.00
Maryland	M.	54–59–55	3.00–3.25–3.11	New York	M.	54–54–54	2.50–3.75–3.05
Massachusetts	M.	54–59–58	2.50–3.50–2.99	Ohio	M.	53–60–57	1.25–4.69–3.46
Michigan	M.	(¹)	1.25–5.00–2.74	Pennsylvania	M.	53–54–53	2.00–3.65–2.90
Minnesota	M.	60–60–60	3.50–3.50–3.50	Virginia	M.	54–54–54	3.00–3.00–3.00
Missouri	M.	48–60–54	2.25–4.00–3.07	West Virginia	M.	(¹)	2.75–3.00–2.90
New Jersey	M.	51–54–53	3.42–3.50–3.48	Wisconsin	M.	(¹)	2.50–3.50–3.00

¹ Not reported.   ² And board.   ³ Per hour.

TABLE **B-24.**—*Stonecutters, 1850-1900, by year and State*—Continued

Year and State	Sex	Hours per week	Rate per day (dollars)
1888:			
California	M.	48-54-53	3.50-4.00-3.68
Colorado	M.	60-60-60	3.00-4.17-3.59
Illinois	M.	48-48-48	3.50-3.50-3.50
Kansas	M.	(1)	3.33-3.60-3.53
Louisiana	M.	60-60-60	2.50-2.50-2.50
Maine	M.	57-60-60	2.00-3.00-2.61
Maryland	M.	53-53-53	3.60-3.60-3.60
Massachusetts	M.	54-59-58	2.70-4.00-3.04
Michigan	M.	60-60-60	1.99-3.99-3.63
Minnesota	M.	60-60-60	3.50-3.50-3.50
Missouri	M.	48-54-51	2.25-4.00-3.13
New Jersey	(1)	51-60-55	3.00-4.50-3.43
New York	M.	48-60-53	1.63-4.50-3.83
North Carolina	M.	60-72-65	1.50-3.00-2.20
Ohio	M.	53-53-53	4.05-4.05-4.05
Pennsylvania	M.	53-54-53	3.25-3.75-3.33
Rhode Island	M.	(1)	1.16-4.00-2.50
Virginia	M.	54-54-54	3.00-3.00-3.00
1889:			
California	M.	48-54-53	3.50-4.00-3.69
Illinois	M.	48-48-48	3.50-3.50-3.50
Kansas	M.	(1)	3.25-3.60-3.50
Louisiana	M.	60-60-60	2.50-2.50-2.50
Maryland	M.	53-53-53	3.60-3.60-3.60
Massachusetts	M.	54-59-58	2.70-4.00-3.12
Minnesota	M.	60-60-60	3.50-3.50-3.50
Missouri	M.	48-54-51	2.25-4.00-3.13
New York	M.	54-54-54	3.75-3.75-3.75
Ohio	M.	53-53-53	4.05-4.05-4.05
Pennsylvania	M.	53-54-53	3.25-4.00-3.45
Virginia	M.	54-54-54	3.00-3.00-3.00
Wisconsin	M.	(1)	1.84-4.05-2.98
1890:			
California	M.	48-54-53	3.50-4.00-3.67
Illinois	M.	48-48-48	4.00-4.00-4.00
Kansas	M.	(1)	2.60-5.00-3.43
Louisiana	M.	60-60-60	2.50-2.50-2.50
Maryland	M.	53-53-53	3.60-3.60-3.60
Massachusetts	M.	48-59-57	2.70-4.00-3.28
Minnesota	M.	60-60-60	2.25-4.00-3.73
Missouri	M.	48-54-50	2.25-4.00-3.36
New York	M.	54-54-54	2.00-4.00-2.99
Ohio	M.	53-53-53	4.05-4.05-4.05
Do	(1)	54-60-59	1.50-3.60-2.21
Pennsylvania	M.	53-54-53	3.25-4.00-3.33
Virginia	M.	54-54-54	3.00-3.00-3.00
1891:			
California	M.	48-54-51	3.50-4.00-3.72
Illinois	M.	48-48-48	4.00-4.00-4.00
Louisiana	M.	54-54-54	2.50-2.50-2.50
Maryland	M.	48-53-51	3.44-3.64-3.56
Massachusetts	M.	48-54-52	2.79-4.00-3.32
Minnesota	M.	60-60-60	3.50-3.50-3.50
Missouri	M.	48-54-50	2.25-4.00-3.42
New York	M.	54-54-54	2.00-4.00-3.00
Ohio	M.	53-60-58	3.00-4.05-3.39
Pennsylvania	M.	53-54-53	3.50-4.14-3.63
Virginia	M.	54-54-54	3.00-3.00-3.00
Wisconsin	M.	(1)	³ .22- .60- .37
1892:			
California	M.	48-54-51	3.00-5.00-3.78
Illinois	M.	48-48-48	4.50-4.50-4.50
Indiana	M.	60-60-60	1.95-3.50-2.13
Louisiana	M.	54-54-54	2.50-2.50-2.50
Maryland	M.	48-48-48	3.44-3.44-3.44
Massachusetts	M.	48-60-54	2.16-3.52-2.93
Michigan	M.	(1)	.50-5.00-3.39
Minnesota	M.	60-60-60	3.25-3.50-3.38
Missouri	M.	48-60-55	2.25-4.00-3.51
Ohio	M.	53-53-53	4.05-4.05-4.05
Do	(1)	48-60-55	1.25-5.00-3.52
Pennsylvania	M.	53-54-53	3.50-4.14-3.57
Rhode Island	M.	48-60-54	1.53-4.00-2.72
Vermont	M.	60-60-60	2.15-2.15-2.15
Virginia	M.	54-54-54	3.00-3.00-3.00
1893:			
California	M.	48-54-53	3.50-4.00-3.61
Illinois	M.	44-60-49	1.50-4.50-3.79
Louisiana	M.	54-54-54	2.50-2.50-2.50
Maryland	M.	48-60-49	1.00-3.44-3.37
Massachusetts	M.	48-54-53	2.16-3.15-2.76
Minnesota	M.	60-60-60	3.25-3.50-3.40
Missouri	M.	48-60-48	2.25-4.00-2.40
Montana	M.	42-54-52	5.00-5.00-5.00
New Hampshire	M.	53-60-54	1.50-3.90-2.73
New York	M.	48-72-56	1.50-4.00-2.70
Ohio	M.	53-54-53	3.60-4.05-4.02
Pennsylvania	M.	53-60-54	.50-4.14-3.54
Rhode Island	M.	(1)	2.75-2.80-2.76
Virginia	M.	54-54-54	3.00-3.00-3.00
Wisconsin	M.	(1)	³ .15- .50- .33½
1894:			
California	M.	48-54-52	3.50-4.00-3.66
Dist. of Columbia	M.	48-48-48	3.60-3.60-3.60
Illinois	M.	48-48-48	4.00-4.00-4.00
Iowa	M.	60-60-60	2.50-4.00-3.25
Louisiana	M.	54-54-54	2.50-3.00-2.63
Maryland	M.	48-48-48	3.44-3.44-3.44
Massachusetts	(1)	(1)	3.00-3.00-3.00
Do	M.	48-54-52	2.25-3.00-2.81
Minnesota	M.	60-60-60	3.25-3.50-3.40
Missouri	M.	48-54-50	2.25-3.60-3.14
New Hampshire	M.	53-54-53	2.00-3.00-2.93
New York	(1)	(1)	3.00-3.00-3.00
North Carolina	(1)	48-48-48	3.00-4.00-3.33
Ohio	M.	48-48-48	1.67-3.60-3.21
Pennsylvania	M.	53-54-53	3.50-4.00-3.55
Virginia	M.	54-54-54	3.00-3.00-3.00
1895:			
California	M.	48-54-52	3.50-4.00-3.63
Connecticut	M.	60-60-60	3.00-3.00-3.00
Illinois	M.	48-48-48	4.00-4.00-4.00
Louisiana	M.	54-54-54	3.00-3.00-3.00
Maryland	M.	48-48-48	3.44-3.44-3.44
Massachusetts	M.	48-60-54	1.80-3.00-2.60
Minnesota	M.	60-60-60	3.25-3.50-3.40
Missouri	M.	48-54-49	2.25-3.60-3.30
North Carolina	M.	60-60-60	3.00-3.50-3.10
Ohio	M.	48-60-52	2.50-3.60-3.35
Pennsylvania	M.	53-54-53	3.50-4.00-3.57
Virginia	M.	54-54-54	3.00-3.00-3.00
Wisconsin	(1)	54-54-54	1.50-3.50-2.50
1896:			
California	M.	48-54-52	3.50-4.00-3.68
Illinois	M.	44-54-48	1.00-4.63-3.75
Kansas	M.	48-48-48	2.50-2.50-2.50
Louisiana	M.	54-54-54	2.50-2.50-2.50
Maryland	M.	48-60-50	3.24-3.51-3.38
Massachusetts	M.	48-60-54	2.00-4.40-2.70
Minnesota	M.	60-60-60	3.25-3.50-3.40
Missouri	M.	48-60-51	1.75-3.60-2.94
Nebraska	M.	60-60-60	2.00-3.00-2.50
New York	M.	48-48-48	3.50-3.50-3.50
Ohio	M.	48-56-54	3.11-3.60-3.25
Pennsylvania	M.	50-54-51	2.70-4.00-3.40
Virginia	M.	54-54-54	3.00-3.00-3.00
1897:			
California	M.	48-54-52	3.00-4.00-3.61
Illinois	M.	48-48-48	4.00-4.00-4.00
Kansas	M.	48-60-57	1.25-3.00-2.25
Do	M.	(1)	³ .25- .25- .25
Louisiana	M.	54-54-54	2.50-3.00-2.75
Maryland	M.	48-48-48	3.44-3.44-3.44
Massachusetts	M.	48-54-52	2.70-3.20-2.83
Michigan	M.	(1)	2.80-2.80-2.80
Minnesota	M.	60-60-60	3.25-3.50-3.40
Missouri	M.	48-54-51	2.25-3.80-3.06
Nebraska	(1)	48-48-48	3.20-3.20-3.20
New York	M.	48-60-49	1.09-4.50-3.41
Ohio	M.	48-48-48	3.60-3.60-3.60
Pennsylvania	M.	54-54-54	2.70-4.05-3.23
Virginia	M.	54-60-55	1.50-3.00-2.86

¹ Not reported. ³ Per hour.

TABLE **B-24.**—*Stonecutters, 1850-1900, by year and State*—Continued

| Year and State | Sex | Lowest, highest, and average— | | Year and State | Sex | Lowest, highest, and average— | |
		Hours per week	Rate per day (dollars)			Hours per week	Rate per day (dollars)
1898:				**1899:**			
California	M.	48–54–53	3. 00–4. 00–3. 52	Alabama	M.	54–54–54	3. 15–3. 15–3. 15
Illinois	M.	48–48–48	4. 50–4. 50–4. 50	California	M.	48–48–48	2. 75–2. 75–2. 75
Louisiana	M.	54–54–54	2. 50–3. 00–2. 75	Montana	M.	48–48–48	5. 33–5. 33–5. 33
Maryland	M.	48–48–48	3. 44–3. 44–3. 44	New York	M.	44–48–47	3. 00–4, 50–3. 51
Massachusetts	M.	48–54–51	2. 70–3. 20–2. 95	Pennsylvania	(¹)	50–50–50	3. 50–3. 50 3. 50
Michigan	M.	(¹)	1. 50–2. 50–1. 95	**1900:**			
Minnesota	M.	60–60–60	3. 25–3. 50–3. 40	Alabama	M.	54–54–54	3. 60–3. 60–3. 60
Missouri	M.	48–54–52	2. 25–3. 20–2. 57	California	M.	48–48–48	3. 60–3. 60–3. 60
Nebraska	(¹)	54–60–56	. 75–4. 00–2. 66	Georgia	M.	60–60–60	3. 00–3. 60–3. 30
New York	M.	44–60–47	2. 00–4. 53–3. 45	Montana	M.	48–48–48	6. 00–6. 00–6. 00
Ohio	M.	48–48–48	3. 00–3. 00–3. 00	New York	M.	44 48–46	3. 00–4. 50–3. 62
Pennsylvania	M.	54–54–54	3. 06–4. 05–3. 25	Pennsylvania	(¹)	50 50–50	3. 50–3. 50–3. 50
Virginia	M.	54–54–54	2. 50–3. 00–2. 67				

¹ Not reported.

TABLE **B-25.**—*Stonecutters, soft stone, males, 1890-1906, by geographic division and year*

| Year | North Atlantic | | South Atlantic | | North Central | | South Central | |
	Hours per week	Rate per hour	Hours per week	Rate per hour	Hours per week	Rate per hour	Hours per week	Rate per hour
1890	51. 1	$0. 418	53. 6	$0. 403	50. 2	$0. 418	55. 0	$0. 360
1891	48. 9	. 440	51. 2	. 415	50. 2	. 425	55. 3	. 348
1892	48. 7	. 440	48. 3	. 425	49. 9	. 434	55. 2	. 361
1893	48. 3	. 440	48. 3	. 425	51. 0	. 413	55. 3	. 358
1894	48. 3	. 432	48. 4	. 423	50. 2	. 408	55. 4	. 341
1895	47. 9	. 423	48. 4	. 424	50. 3	. 401	55. 6	. 329
1896	47. 4	. 439	48. 4	. 424	50. 8	. 392	54. 8	. 329
1897	47. 0	. 442	48. 4	. 423	49. 0	. 417	54. 4	. 318
1898	46. 5	. 451	48. 4	. 427	48. 5	. 432	54. 5	. 315
1899	46. 6	. 457	48. 7	. 425	48. 8	. 416	54. 5	. 319
1900	46. 5	. 466	48. 6	. 426	49. 4	. 408	54. 4	. 324
1901	45. 8	. 475	48. 7	. 425	48. 5	. 419	53. 9	. 360
1902	45. 8	. 503	48. 0	. 431	48. 6	. 450	53. 0	. 344
1903	45. 1	. 558	48. 0	. 456	47. 0	. 486	47. 3	. 465
1904	45. 2	. 541	48. 2	. 449	47. 2	. 495	46. 1	. 472
1905	45. 5	. 523	48. 3	. 474	46. 8	. 498	46. 2	. 489
1906	45. 2	. 522	48. 2	. 484	46. 3	. 514	46. 3	. 495

TABLE **B–26.**—*Stonecutters, soft stone, males, 1907–1928, by city and year*

Year	Atlanta, Ga. Hours per week	Rate per hour	Birmingham, Ala. Hours per week	Rate per hour	Boston, Mass.[1] Hours per week	Rate per hour	Chicago, Ill. Hours per week	Rate per hour
1907	48.0	$0.500	44.0	$0.450	48.0	$0.500		
1908	48.0	.500	44.0	.450	48.0	.500		
1909	48.0	.500	44.0	.450	48.0	.500		
1910	48.0	.500	44.0	.500	48.0	.500		
1911	48.0	.500	44.0	.500	48.0	.500	44.0	$0.625
1912	48.0	.500	44.0	.500	44.0	.500	44.0	.625
1913	48.0	.500	44.0	.500	44.0	.563	44.0	.625
1914	48.0	.500	44.0	.500	44.0	.563	44.0	.625
1915	48.0	.500	44.0	.500	44.0	.563	44.0	.625
1916	44.0	.500	44.0	.500	44.0	.563	44.0	.700
1917	44.0	.500	44.0	.500	44.0	.625	44.0	.700
1918	44.0	.625	44.0	.625	44.0	.700	44.0	.700
1919	44.0	.750	44.0	.625	44.0	.700	44.0	.813
1920	44.0	1.000	44.0	.900	44.0	1.000	44.0	1.250
1921	44.0	1.000			44.0	1.000	44.0	1.250
1922	44.0	.900			44.0	1.000	44.0	1.025
1923	44.0	1.000			44.0	1.125	44.0	1.025
1924	44.0	1.000			44.0	1.100	44.0	1.250
1925	44.0	1.125	44.0	1.000	44.0	1.100	44.0	1.375
1926			44.0	1.000	44.0	1.250	44.0	1.500
1927			44.0	1.000	44.0	1.250	44.0	1.500
1928					44.0	1.250	44.0	1.500

Year	Cincinnati, Ohio Hours per week	Rate per hour	Denver, Colo. Hours per week	Rate per hour	Detroit, Mich.[2] Hours per week	Rate per hour	New Orleans, La. Hours per week	Rate per hour
1907	44.5	$0.563	44.0	$0.625	44.0	$0.500		
1908	44.5	.563	44.0	.625	44.0	.500		
1909	44.5	.563	44.0	.625	44.0	.500		
1910	44.5	.563	44.0	.625	44.0	.563		
1911	44.5	.563	44.0	.625	44.0	.563		
1912	44.5	.563	44.0	.625	44.0	.563		
1913	44.5	.563	44.0	.625	44.0	.625		
1914	44.0	.563	44.0	.625	44.0	.625		
1915	44.5	.600	44.0	.625	44.0	.625		
1916	44.5	.625	44.0	.625	44.0	.650		
1917	44.0	.650	44.0	.625	44.0	.700		
1918	44.0	.700	44.0	.750	44.0	.800		
1919	44.0	.775	44.0	.875	44.0	1.000		
1920	44.0	1.150	44.0	1.000	44.0	1.250	44.0	$1.000
1921	44.0	1.250	44.0	1.125	44.0	1.125	44.0	1.250
1922	44.0	1.250	44.0	1.000	44.0	1.125	44.0	1.250
1923	44.0	1.250	44.0	1.125	44.0	1.250	44.0	1.250
1924	44.0	1.250	44.0	1.125	50.0	1.220	44.0	1.250
1925	44.0	1.250	44.0	1.250	44.0	1.375	44.0	1.250
1926	44.0	1.325	44.0	1.250	44.0	1.375	44.0	1.250
1927	44.0	1.500	44.0	1.250	44.0	1.375	44.0	1.250
1928	44.0	1.500	44.0	1.250	44.0	1.375	44.0	1.250

Year	New York, N. Y.[3] Hours per week	Rate per hour	Philadelphia, Pa.[4] Hours per week	Rate per hour	St. Louis, Mo.[5] Hours per week	Rate per hour	San Francisco, Calif. Hours per week	Rate per hour
1907	44.0	$0.625	44.0	$0.500	44.0	$0.563	44.0	$0.625
1908	44.0	.625	44.0	.500	44.0	.563	44.0	.625
1909	44.0	.625	44.0	.500	44.0	.563	44.0	.625
1910	44.0	.625	44.0	.500	44.0	.563	44.0	.625
1911	44.0	.625	44.0	.500	44.0	.563	44.0	.625
1912	44.0	.625	44.0	.500	44.0	.563	44.0	.625
1913	44.0	.684	44.0	.500	44.0	.563	44.0	.700
1914	44.0	.688	44.0	.530	44.0	.625	44.0	.700
1915	44.0	.688	44.0	.563	44.0	.625	44.0	.700
1916	44.0	.688	44.0	.563	44.0	.625	44.0	.700
1917	44.0	.688	44.0	.650	44.0	.625	44.0	.700
1918	44.0	.688	44.0	.650	44.0	.700	44.0	.700
1919	44.0	.844	44.0	.825	44.0	.850	44.0	1.000
1920	44.0	1.125	44.0	1.100	44.0	1.000	44.0	1.000
1921	44.0	1.125	44.0	1.200	44.0	1.000	44.0	1.125
1922	44.0	1.125	44.0	1.000	44.0	1.000	44.0	1.000
1923	44.0	1.250	44.0	1.125	44.0	1.125		
1924	44.0	1.313	44.0	1.250	44.0	1.250		
1925	44.0	1.375	44.0	1.250	44.0	1.250	44.0	1.125
1926	44.0	1.500			44.0	1.250	44.0	1.125
1927	44.0	1.500	44.0	1.313	44.0	1.250	44.0	1.125
1928	44.0	1.500	44.0	1.313	44.0	1.250	44.0	1.125

[1] Inside men only, 1912–1920 and 1923–1928, inclusive.
[2] Not classified, 1909–1914 and 1922–1924; outside men only, 1915–1921 and 1925–1928.
[3] First class only.
[4] Inside men only, 1914–1916 and 1919–1921.
[5] Inside men only, 1921–1922.

TABLE **B-27**.—*Granite cutters, males, 1890–1906, by geographic division and year*

Year	North Atlantic		South Atlantic		North Central		Western	
	Hours per week	Rate per hour	Hours per week	Rate per hour	Hours per week	Rate per hour	Hours per week	Rate per hour
1890	54.5	$0.330	50.1	$0.366	54.6	$0.340	48.9	$0.487
1891	54.2	.337	51.6	.367	52.9	.352	49.0	.486
1892	53.9	.339	51.0	.379	53.1	.351	49.6	.480
1893	53.9	.344	50.4	.376	53.3	.341	51.1	.457
1894	52.9	.346	53.2	.340	53.2	.344	51.0	.455
1895	53.4	.341	50.6	.386	52.7	.342	50.6	.455
1896	53.4	.337	50.6	.386	52.6	.348	51.4	.447
1897	53.4	.333	52.1	.364	52.9	.341	51.0	.454
1898	53.5	.325	53.1	.350	52.2	.352	50.0	.474
1899	52.0	.328	50.4	.396	52.3	.362	50.3	.471
1900	50.1	.356	52.4	.363	52.1	.354	48.3	.496
1901	49.6	.363	53.4	.353	51.1	.367	48.1	.500
1902	49.5	.370	50.0	.376	51.1	.381	47.9	.503
1903	48.5	.389	50.1	.361	52.1	.355	47.1	.503
1904	47.9	.383	48.2	.396	53.4	.338	47.6	.552
1905	47.5	.411	48.4	.397	52.7	.344	47.3	.549
1906	47.6	.413	48.3	.394	52.8	.372	47.6	.556

TABLE **B-28**.—*Granite cutters, inside, males, 1907–1928, by city and year*

Year	Atlanta, Ga.[1]		Boston, Mass.[2]		Chicago, Ill.[3]		Cincinnati, Ohio[4]	
	Hours per week	Rate per hour	Hours per week	Rate per hour	Hours per week	Rate per hour	Hours per week	Rate per hour
1907	48.0	$0.375			48.0	$0.375		
1908	48.0	.375			48.0	.406		
1909	48.0	.375			48.0	.406		
1910	48.0	.400			48.0	.406		
1911	48.0	.400	44.0	$0.444	48.0	.406		
1912	45.0	.413	44.0	.444	48.0	.563		
1913	45.0	.413	44.0	.456	44.0	.625		
1914	45.0	.413	44.0	.456	44.0	.500	45.0	$0.500
1915	45.0	.413	44.0	.456	44.0	.500	44.0	.500
1916	44.0	.500	44.0	.500	44.0	.531	44.0	.500
1917	44.0	.500	44.0	.500	44.0	.563	44.0	.500
1918	44.0	.600	44.0	.600	44.0	.663	44.0	.625
1919	44.0	.700	44.0	.750	44.0	.763	44.0	.750
1920	44.0	.750	44.0	1.000	44.0	.863	44.0	1.000
1921	44.0	1.000	44.0	1.000	44.0	1.125	44.0	1.000
1922	44.0	1.000	44.0	1.000	44.0	1.125	40.0	1.000
1923	44.0	1.000	44.0	1.000	44.0	1.125	44.0	1.000
1924			44.0	1.000	44.0	1.125	44.0	1.125
1925			44.0	1.000	44.0	1.500	44.0	1.125
1926			44.0	1.100	[4]44.0	1.250	44.0	1.125
1927			44.0	1.125	[4]44.0	1.375	44.0	1.125
1928			44.0	1.125	[4]44.0	1.500	44.0	1.125

Year	Denver, Colo.[5]		Detroit, Mich.		New Orleans, La.[6]		New York, N. Y.[7]	
	Hours per week	Rate per hour	Hours per week	Rate per hour	Hours per week	Rate per hour	Hours per week	Rate per hour
1907	44.0	$0.500	48.0	$0.375	54.0	$0.333	44.0	$0.438
1908	44.0	.500	48.0	.375	48.0	.333	44.0	.438
1909	44.0	.570	48.0	.375	48.0	.400	44.0	.438
1910	44.0	.570	44.0	.406	48.0	.400	44.0	.438
1911	44.0	.570	44.0	.406	48.0	.400	44.0	.438
1912	44.0	.571	44.5	.438	48.0	.400	44.0	.500
1913	44.0	.570	44.5	.450	45.0	.450	44.0	.500
1914	44.0	.570	44.5	.450	45.0	.450	44.0	.500
1915	44.0	.570	44.5	.450	45.0	.450	44.0	.500
1916	44.0	.570	44.0	.500	44.0	.500	44.0	.500
1917	44.0	.570	44.0	.513	44.0	.500	44.0	.500
1918	44.0	.688	44.0	.625	44.0	.500	44.0	.688
1919	44.0	.850	44.0	.750	44.0	.750	44.0	.790
1920	44.0	1.000	44.0	1.000	44.0	.800	44.0	1.000
1921	44.0	1.063	44.0	1.000	44.0	1.000	44.0	1.125
1922	44.0	1.063	44.0	1.000	44.0	1.000	44.0	1.125
1923	44.0	1.063	44.0	1.000	44.0	1.000	44.0	1.125
1924	44.0	1.063	44.0	1.000	44.0	1.000	44.0	1.125
1925	44.0	1.063	44.0	1.000	44.0	1.000	44.0	1.125
1926	44.0	1.125	44.0	1.000	44.0	1.000	44.0	1.375
1927	44.0	1.125	44.0	1.125	44.0	1.125	44.0	1.375
1928	44.0	1.125	44.0	1.125	44.0	1.125	44.0	1.375

[1] Not classified, 1915–1923, inclusive.
[2] Not classified, 1919–1928, inclusive.
[3] Includes machine men, 1914–1921; not classified, 1922–1924; building work, 1925–1928.
[4] 40 hours per week, November to March, inclusive.
[5] Not classified, but includes outside men, 1907–1912.
[6] Not classified, 1907–1911, inclusive.
[7] Not classified, 1919–1928.

TABLE **B-28.**—*Granite cutters, inside, males, 1907–1928, by city and year*—Contd.

Year	Philadelphia, Pa.⁸		St. Louis, Mo.		San Francisco, Calif.⁹	
	Hours per week	Rate per hour	Hours per week	Rate per hour	Hours per week	Rate per hour
1907	44.0	$0.478	44.0	$0.500	48.0	$0.563
1908	44.0	.478	44.0	.500	48.0	.563
1909	44.0	.478	44.0	.500	48.0	.625
1910	44.0	.478	44.0	.500	48.0	.625
1911	44.0	.500	44.0	.500	44.0	.625
1912	44.0	.500	44.0	.500	44.0	.625
1913	44.0	.500	44.0	.500	44.0	.625
1914	44.0	.563	44.0	.500	44.0	.625
1915	44.0	.563	44.0	.500	44.0	.625
1916	44.0	.563	44.0	.500	44.0	.663
1917	44.0	.563	44.0	.500	44.0	.675
1918	44.0	.700	44.0	.600	44.0	.700
1919	44.0	.800	44.0	.750	44.0	.875
1920	44.0	1.000	44.0	1.000	44.0	1.000
1921	44.0	1.000	44.0	1.000	44.0	1.125
1922	44.0	1.000	44.0	1.000	44.0	1.125
1923	44.0	1.125	44.0	1.000	44.0	1.125
1924	44.0	1.125	44.0	1.125	44.0	1.125
1925	44.0	1.125	44.0	1.125	44.0	1.125
1926	44.0	1.188	44.0	1.250	44.0	1.188
1927	44.0	1.125	44.0	1.250	44.0	1.188
1928	44.0	1.250	44.0	1.250	44.0	1.188

⁸ Not classified, but includes outside men, 1907–1913; includes outside men and machine men, 1916–1928.
⁹ Not classified, 1925–1927, inclusive.

TABLE **B-29.**—*Tile layers, 1886–1899, by year and State*

Year and State	Sex	Lowest, highest, and average—		Year and State	Sex	Lowest, highest, and average—	
		Hours per week	Rate per day (dollars)			Hours per week	Rate per day (dollars)
1886:				1893:			
Illinois	M.	54–60–60	1.75–3.50–3.36	Illinois	M.	48–48–48	4.00–4.00–4.00
1888:				1894:			
New York	M.	53–59–54	3.00–4.00–3.88	Ohio	M.	60–60–60	2.50–2.50–2.50
1890:				1895:			
Minnesota	M.	(¹)	2.50–2.75–2.54	Ohio	M.	54–54–54	4.50–4.50–4.50
1892:				1896:			
California	M.	48–48–48	3.00–5.50–4.17	Ohio	M.	54–54–54	2.50–2.50–2.50
Michigan	M.	(¹)	2.65–2.65–2.65	1899:			
				New York	(¹)	44–44–44	4.50–4.50–4.50

¹ Not reported.

TABLE **B–30.**—*Tile layers, males, 1912–1928, by city and year*

Year	Atlanta, Ga.		Birmingham, Ala.		Boston, Mass.		Chicago, Ill.	
	Hours per week	Rate per hour	Hours per week	Rate per hour	Hours per week	Rate per hour	Hours per week	Rate per hour
1912					44.0	$0.625	44.0	$0.750
1913					44.0	.688	44.0	.750
1914					44.0	.688	44.0	.750
1915					44.0	.688	44.0	.750
1916					44.0	.688	44.0	.750
1917					40.0	.750	44.0	.750
1918					40.0	.750	44.0	.750
1919					40.0	.800	44.0	.875
1920	44.0	$1.125			40.0	1.000	44.0	1.250
1921	44.0	1.000			40.0	1.000	44.0	1.250
1922	44.0	1.000			40.0	1.000	44.0	1.025
1923	44.0	1.125	44.0	$1.250	44.0	1.125	44.0	1.154
1924	44.0	1.250	44.0	1.250	44.0	1.250	44.0	1.300
1925	44.0	{ 1.125 / 1.250 }	44.0	1.375	44.0	1.250	44.0	1.300
1926	44.0	1.400	44.0	1.500	44.0	1.250	44.0	1.300
1927	44.0	1.400	44.0	1.500	44.0	1.400	44.0	1.625
1928	44.0	1.400	44.0	1.500	44.0	1.400	44.0	1.625

Year	Cincinnati, Ohio		Denver, Colo.		Detroit, Mich.		New Orleans, La.	
	Hours per week	Rate per hour	Hours per week	Rate per hour	Hours per week	Rate per hour	Hours per week	Rate per hour
1912	45.5	$0.625	44.0	$0.625				
1913	44.0	.625	44.0	.625	48.0	$0.500		
1914	44.0	.625	44.0	.625	48.0	.500		
1915	44.0	.688	44.0	.625	48.0	.600		
1916	44.0	.688	44.0	.625	44.0	.600		
1917	44.0	.688	44.0	.700	44.0	.688		
1918	44.0	.688	44.0	.700	44.0	.688		
1919	44.0	.719	44.0	.875	44.0	.719		
1920	44.0	1.000	44.0	1.000	44.0	1.000	44.0	$1.000
1921	44.0	1.000	44.0	1.000	44.0	1.000	44.0	1.000
1922	44.0	1.000	44.0	1.000	44.0	1.000	44.0	1.000
1923	44.0	1.125	44.0	1.125	44.0	1.125	44.0	1.125
1924	44.0	1.250	44.0	1.125	44.0	1.125	44.0	1.125
1925	44.0	1.250	44.0	1.250	44.0	1.375	44.0	1.125
1926	44.0	1.313	44.0	1.250	44.0	1.500	44.0	1.250
1927	44.0	1.500	44.0	1.250	44.0	1.500	44.0	1.250
1928	44.0	1.500	44.0	1.375	44.0	1.500	44.0	1.250

Year	New York, N. Y.		Philadelphia, Pa.		St. Louis, Mo.		San Francisco, Calif.	
	Hours per week	Rate per hour	Hours per week	Rate per hour	Hours per week	Rate per hour	Hours per week	Rate per hour
1912	44.0	$0.625	44.0	$0.625	44.0	$0.625	44.0	$0.750
1913	44.0	.688	44.0	.625	44.0	.625	44.0	.750
1914	44.0	.688	44.0	.625	44.0	.688	44.0	.750
1915	44.0	.688	44.0	.625	44.0	.688	44.0	.750
1916	44.0	.688	44.0	.650	44.0	.688	44.0	.750
1917	44.0	.750	44.0	.675	44.0	.688	44.0	.750
1918	44.0	.750	44.0	.700	44.0	.750	44.0	.813
1919	44.0	.813	44.0	.800	44.0	.850	44.0	1.000
1920	44.0	1.125	44.0	1.000	44.0	1.000	44.0	1.125
1921	44.0	1.125	44.0	1.000	44.0	1.000	44.0	1.125
1922	44.0	1.125	44.0	1.000	44.0	1.000	44.0	1.000
1923	44.0	1.125	44.0	1.250	44.0	1.250	44.0	1.125
1924	44.0	1.313	44.0	1.500	44.0	1.500	44.0	1.250
1925	44.0	1.313	44.0	1.500	44.0	1.500	44.0	1.250
1926	44.0	1.500	44.0	1.500	44.0	1.500	44.0	1.250
1927	44.0	1.500	44.0	1.500	44.0	1.500	44.0	1.250
1928	44.0	1.500	44.0	1.500	44.0	1.500	44.0	1.250

C.—CLOTHING INDUSTRY

The sources from which this wage data were secured are the fifteenth and the nineteenth annual reports of the Commissioner of Labor Statistics and bulletins of the Bureau of Labor Statistics Nos. 59, 65, 71, 77, 135, 161, 187, 265, 329, 387, 435, and 503. The wage data shown here for dressmakers is very incomplete, no information of this character being available for any period after the year 1898.

The details for sewing-machine operators in men's clothing are shown by States from 1865 to 1900, Table C-2; by geographic divisions from 1890 to 1907, Tables C-3 and C-4; and by cities, Tables C-5 and C-6, for the various specified periods from 1911 to 1928, inclusive, whenever reports on men's clothing were published.

The wage data presented here includes employees working on all grades from a cheap suit up to a garment of very high class.

In the early history of the clothing industry it required years of experience to become an all-round expert workman. The present-day employee is a specialist who performs a particular operation or a limited number of operations. By this constant repetition of the same operation an inexperienced employee soon acquires both skill and speed. When an employee has learned a particular occupation he seldom ever changes to another.

There are two distinct types of clothing manufacturers—one who buys, cuts, and manufactures the materials into finished garments and sells the product; the other is a contractor who cuts and manufactures the garments for a specified piece price per garment. These contractors usually provide their own help, machinery, and workrooms.

TABLE C-1.—*Dressmakers, 1851-1898, by year and State*

Year and State	Sex	Lowest, highest, and average—		Year and State	Sex	Lowest, highest, and average—	
		Hours per week	Rate per day (dollars)			Hours per week	Rate per day (dollars)
1851:				**1879:**			
New York	F.	(¹)	1. 33–1. 33–1. 33	Illinois	F.	(¹)	0. 33–1. 00–0. 67
1871:				Indiana	F.	(¹)	1. 00–1. 00–1. 00
Massachusetts	F.	60–60–60	1. 00–2. 00–1. 35	Massachusetts	F.	(¹)	. 83– . 83– . 83
New York	F.	(¹)	. 33– . 33– . 33	New Jersey	F.	(¹)	1. 00–1. 00–1. 00
1872:				New York	F.	(¹)	. 33– . 83– . 58
New York	F.	(¹)	² 2. 00–2. 00–2. 00	Pennsylvania	F.	(¹)	. 67–1. 25– . 96
1873:				**1880:**			
Pennsylvania	F.	(¹)	. 83– . 83– . 83	Illinois	F.	(¹)	1. 00–1. 00–1. 00
1874:				New York	F.	(¹)	. 67– . 67– . 67
Illinois	F.	(¹)	1. 00–1. 00–1. 00	Pennsylvania	F.	(¹)	1. 50–1. 50–1. 50
Pennsylvania	F.	(¹)	1. 17–1. 17–1. 17	Rhode Island	F.	(¹)	1. 00–1. 00–1. 00
1875:				**1881:**			
Ohio	F.	(¹)	. 83– . 83– . 83	Illinois	F.	(¹)	. 50– . 83– . 67
1876:				Massachusetts	F.	(¹)	1. 00–1. 00–1. 00
Illinois	F.	(¹)	1. 00–1. 08–1. 04	**1882:**			
New York	F.	(¹)	. 25– . 25– . 25	Illinois	F.	57–57–57	. 67– . 90– . 82
Pennsylvania	F.	(¹)	. 67–1. 17– . 92	Missouri	F.	(¹)	. 42– . 42– . 42
Texas	F.	(¹)	1. 33–1. 33–1. 33	Do	(¹)	60–60–60	1. 50–1. 50–1. 50
1877:				New Jersey	F.	(¹)	. 67–1. 00– . 99
Illinois	F.	(¹)	. 25– . 25– . 25	New York	F.	(¹)	. 50– . 83– . 67
New Jersey	F.	(¹)	1. 50–1. 50–1. 50	Pennsylvania	F.	(¹)	1. 00–1. 00–1. 00
				Do	F.	(¹)	². 75– . 75– . 75

¹ Not reported. ² And board.

219

TABLE **C-1.**—*Dressmakers, 1851–1898, by year and State*—Continued

| Year and State | Sex | Lowest, highest, and average— | | Year and State | Sex | Lowest, highest, and average— | |
		Hours per week	Rate per day (dollars)			Hours per week	Rate per day (dollars)
1883:				**1887—Continued.**			
California	F.	(1)	1.00-1.00-1.00	Ohio	F.	53-72-60	0.38-4.00-0.77
Illinois	F.	(1)	.50-1.00-.78	Pennsylvania	F.	50-53-52	.83-1.00-.89
Do	F.	(1)	³1.00-1.00-1.00	**1888:**			
Indiana	F.	(1)	.92-.92-.92	California	F.	54-60-54	.42-2.00-.95
Kentucky	F.	55-57-56	.54-1.00-.77	Colorado	F.	54-90-58	.33-2.67-1.21
Michigan	F.	(1)	.35-2.00-.87	Georgia	F.	54-66-59	.83-2.00-.91
Missouri	F.	(1)	.42-.42-.42	Indiana	F.	54-63-57	.29-1.33-.84
New Jersey	F.	90-96-93	.67-.92-.81	Iowa	F.	81-81-81	.38-1.50-.98
New York	F.	(1)	.50-3.33-1.44	Maine	F.	60-96-69	1.00-1.25-1.06
Pennsylvania	F.	(1)	.83-.83-.83	New Jersey	F.	60-60-60	1.25-1.25-1.25
Wisconsin	F.	(1)	.50-.50-.50	New York	F.	(1)	1.17-1.67-1.63
1884:				South Carolina	F.	36-48-39	.50-1.67-.84
California	F.	60-60-60	1.00-2.50-1.31	**1889:**			
Georgia	F.	60-60-60	.50-.50-.50	Kansas	F.	(1)	.92-.92-.92
Illinois	F.	(1)	.67-1.17-.94	Rhode Island	F.	42-72-55	.50-2.00-1.07
Massachusetts	F.	(1)	1.17-1.17-1.17	**1890:**			
Michigan	F.	(1)	.17-3.00-.91	New York	F.	(1)	².83-1.67-1.34
Minnesota	F.	(1)	.33-.33-.33	**1891:**			
Missouri	F.	(1)	.58-.58-.58	Michigan	F.	(1)	².18-1.39-.66
New Jersey	F.	60-72-68	.33-1.33-.88	New York	F.	(1)	².83-2.00-1.47
New York	F.	(1)	.58-1.67-1.00	North Carolina	F.	60-60-60	.75-.75-.75
Pennsylvania	F.	56-56-56	.25-1.25-.91	**1892:**			
1885:				California	F.	54-72-56	.50-2.75-1.22
California	F.	(1)	.50-.83-.67	Illinois	F.	48-54-50	.58-6.67-1.97
Georgia	F.	(1)	1.00-1.25-1.10	Iowa	F.	54-84-62	.50-1.75-.78
Illinois	F.	(1)	1.17-1.17-1.17	Maine	F.	60-60-60	.33-2.50-.87
Do	F.	(1)	.83-.83-.83	Do	F.	60-60-60	².42-.42-.42
Indiana	F.	(1)	.58-.58-.58	Do	F.	60-60-60	².42-.42-.42
Massachusetts	F.	(1)	.50-1.33-.92	**1893:**			
Missouri	F.	(1)	.75-.75-.75	Illinois	F.	36-90-58	.33-3.33-1.21
New Jersey	F.	60-72-60	.67-2.83-.99	Do	F.	70-70-70	².83-.83-.83
New York	F.	54-72-55	.50-7.50-1.48	Maryland	M.	60-72-66	1.00-1.00-1.00
Ohio	F.	(1)	.33-.83-.58	Do	F.	46-84-62	.17-2.00-.87
Pennsylvania	F.	(1)	.67-1.33-.96	Montana	F.	42-51-48	.17-5.75-1.06
Wisconsin	F.	(1)	.50-.50-.50	New Jersey	F.	58-58-58	.42-2.50-1.07
1886:				New York	M.	68-68-68	1.67-1.67-1.67
California	F.	(1)	.67-.75-.71	Do	F.	36-72-57	.38-2.50-1.16
Illinois	F.	54-54-54	.58-4.17-1.50	Pennsylvania	M.	50-60-57	.50-4.17-2.13
Indiana	F.	(1)	.83-1.00-.92	Do	F.	36-72-59	.33-2.00-1.04
Iowa	F.	66-66-66	1.07-1.07-1.07	**1894:**			
Maryland	F.	54-65-59	.25-2.00-.81	Indiana	F.	55-58-57	.25-2.00-.98
Minnesota	F.	(1)	.42-.42-.42	Iowa	F.	60-72-62	.50-1.67-1.18
Do	F.	(1)	1.00-1.00-1.00	Kansas	F.	61-61-61	1.18-1.18-1.18
Missouri	F.	42-72-57	.22-2.50-.93	New York	F.	(1)	1.50-1.50-1.50
New Jersey	F.	51-57-54	.18-1.00-.72	Ohio	F.	(1)	.58-1.33-.96
Do	F.	72-72-72	1.25-1.25-1.25	Pennsylvania	F.	48-84-58	.67-1.50-1.06
New York	F.	51-66-57	.67-2.50-1.42	**1895:**			
Ohio	F.	(1)	.25-1.00-.61	Louisiana	M.	60-60-60	5.83-5.83-5.83
Pennsylvania	F.	53-56-55	.50-1.25-.91	Do	F.	60-60-60	.33-4.17-1.30
Rhode Island	F.	54-58-55	.67-1.67-1.01	Maine	F.	57-57-57	.38-1.50-1.02
Wisconsin	F.	(1)	.67-1.00-.84	New York	F.	54-54-54	.67-2.67-1.45
1887:				Ohio	F.	60-60-60	.53-1.34-.72
California	F.	54-60-56	.42-2.00-1.02	**1896:**			
Illinois	F.	50-72-54	.33-3.00-1.27	Colorado	F.	54-54-54	1.35-2.00-1.68
Indiana	F.	(1)	.50-.67-.59	Florida	F.	(1)	1.33-1.33-1.33
Kentucky	F.	54-65-58	.08½-2.00-.94	Georgia	F.	54-57-56	.83-1.67-1.10
Louisiana	F.	54-60-59	.25-1.42-.86	Illinois	F.	54-54-54	.83-1.67-1.34
Massachusetts	F.	53-57-54	.52-1.67-1.15	Massachusetts	F.	(1)	1.17-1.17-1.17
Minnesota	F.	(1)	.42-.42-.42	Pennsylvania	F.	56-59-58	.67-1.50-.94
Montana	F.	57-57-57	2.00-2.00-2.00	**1898:**			
New York	F.	51-66-58	.17-3.00-.94	Michigan	F.	(1)	.74-1.50-.93
Do	F.	54-54-54	².83-.83-.83	Nebraska	F.	(1) 60-60-60	.75-2.00-1.17

¹ Not reported.   ² And board.   ³ And dinner.

TABLE C-2.—*Sewing-machine operators, 1865–1900, by year and State*

Year and State	Sex	Lowest, highest, and average— Hours per week	Lowest, highest, and average— Rate per day (dollars)
1865:			
New York	F.	51-51-51	1.17-1.75-1.40
1870:			
New York	F.	52-54-52	.75-1.50-1.04
1871:			
Massachusetts	F.	48-60-60	.75-2.33-1.31
1872:			
Massachusetts	F.	60-60-60	1.00-2.50-1.28
1873:			
Connecticut	F.	60-60-60	.58-1.33-1.04
1874:			
Connecticut	F.	(1)	.75-1.00-.76
1875:			
New York	F.	54-72-70	1.09-1.42-1.30
1877:			
Maine	F.	66-66-66	.88-.90-.89
1880:			
Georgia	F.	(1)	.75-.75-.75
Maryland	F.	60-60-60	.75-1.21-.92
Massachusetts	F.	60-60-60	.67-.92-.79
New York	M.	60-60-60	2.88-3.20-3.04
Do	F.	54-60-55	.85-2.61-1.24
Pennsylvania	M.	60-60-60	1.50-2.00-1.75
Do	F.	57-57-57	.83-1.00-.92
South Carolina	F.	60-60-60	.58-1.00-.81
1881:			
Connecticut	F.	60-60-60	1.41-1.41-1.41
Missouri	F.	54-54-54	.73-1.41-1.15
New Hampshire	F.	65-65-65	1.10-1.10-1.10
Pennsylvania	F.	(1)	1.17-1.17-1.17
1882:			
Missouri	F.	59-59-59	.64-1.53-1.13
New Hampshire	M.	66-66-66	.70-1.15-.99
Do	F.	66-66-66	.75-1.50-.98
New Jersey	F.	(1)	1.25-1.50-1.42
North Carolina	M.	(1)	.42-.42-.42
Do	F.	72-72-72	.50-.50-.50
Pennsylvania	F.	52-59-55	.67-1.00-.82
South Carolina	M.	69-69-69	1.00-1.00-1.00
Virginia	F.	54-54-54	1.00-1.33-1.16
1883:			
Massachusetts	F.	(1)	.83-3.33-1.68
New Jersey	M.	60-60-60	1.50-2.00-1.83
Do	F.	60-72-60	.67-1.33-1.01
North Carolina	F.	60-60-60	.50-.83-.68
1884:			
Georgia	F.	(1)	.75-.75-.75
Missouri	F.	60-60-60	.66-1.08-.86
New Jersey	M.	60-60-60	1.00-1.00-1.00
Do	F.	59-60-60	.50-2.50-.97
Pennsylvania	F.	48-60-54	.83-1.17-1.01
Rhode Island	F.	60-60-60	1.00-1.17-1.09
South Carolina	M.	69-69-69	.75-.75-.75
Virginia	F.	55-55-55	.67-.83-.75
1885:			
Alabama	F.	(1)	.83-.93-.88
California	F.	63-63-63	1.00-1.00-1.00
Connecticut	M.	60-60-60	.85-1.00-.93
Do	F.	60-69-61	.60-1.17-.91
Illinois	M.	54-54-54	2.00-4.17-2.68
Do	F.	54-60-55	.83-2.36-1.19
Iowa	F.	53-63-61	.35-1.45-.72
Louisiana	F.		.63-1.35-1.00
Maine	M.	66-66-66	1.19-1.19-1.19
Do	F.		.80-1.00-.95
Maryland	M.	54-60-58	1.25-3.33-2.15
Do	F.	54-60-59	.33-2.08-.78
Massachusetts	F.	60-60-60	.33-1.83-1.09
Michigan	F.	60-60-60	.31-1.15-.73
Minnesota	F.	(1)	.60-1.50-.89
New Jersey	F.	40-59-50	.58-1.67-1.06
New York	M.	54-54-54	1.21-3.20-1.86
Do	F.	51-72-57	.33-2.23-1.10
Ohio	F.	60-60-60	1.15-1.15-1.15
Pennsylvania	F.	60-60-60	.41-.41-.41
Wisconsin	F.	60-60-60	.53-1.05-.82

Year and State	Sex	Lowest, highest, and average— Hours per week	Lowest, highest, and average— Rate per day (dollars)
1886:			
California	F.	54-54-54	1.25-1.25-1.25
Connecticut	F.	60-60-60	.85-1.00-.93
Illinois	M.	57-57-57	1.67-2.33-2.00
Do	F.	57-57-57	1.00-1.67-1.19
Iowa	F.	60-60-60	.41-1.83-1.01
Maryland	F.	42-61-58	.17-2.04-.85
Massachusetts	F.	59-60-60	.62-.89-.89
Michigan	F.	54-60-58	.43-1.44-.91
Missouri	F.	47-57-55	.25-2.00-.80
Montana	F.	(1)	.67-.67-.67
New Jersey	F.	38-62-57	.33-1.67-1.00
New York	M.	(1)	1.50-2.33-1.88
Do	F.	45-64-58	.50-1.49-1.00
Pennsylvania	(1)	60-60-60	1.25-1.25-1.25
Do	M.	56-60-59	.21-2.50-.99
Do	F.	36-60-58	.20-2.43-1.08
Rhode Island	F.	48-61-58	.50-1.42-.89
1887:			
California	F.	55-63-61	.50-1.63-1.11
Connecticut	F.	(1)	1.42-1.42-1.42
Illinois	F.	48-62-55	.50-1.67-1.07
Iowa	F.	54-56-55	1.00-1.08-1.06
Kentucky	F.	48-63-58	.25-1.33-.76
Louisiana	F.	57-60-59	.42-1.17-.75
Maryland	F.	54-54-54	.50-.50-.50
Massachusetts	F.	42-60-54	.46-2.33-1.09
Minnesota	F.	54-60-57	.50-2.17-1.30
Montana	F.	60-60-60	.58-.58-.58
New York	F.	43-72-54	.25-3.00-1.15
Ohio	F.	52-61-59	.18-1.67-.77
Pennsylvania	F.	46-60-55	.15-2.00-.96
Wisconsin	F.	42-60-54	.83-.83-.83
1888:			
California	F.	57-63-59	.50-1.17-1.00
Georgia	F.	55-55-55	.42-.60-.49
Indiana	F.	55-57-56	.29-.73-.54
Maine	F.	60-60-60	1.42-1.42-1.42
New Jersey	F.	59-78-62	.40-1.50-.98
New York	M.	53-60-55	.50-2.67-1.27
Do	F.	53-60-59	.83-1.67-1.23
Do	(1)	48-59-57	.83-2.00-1.39
South Carolina	F.	60-60-60	.50-.83-.70
Do	M.	66-66-66	.75-.75-.75
Do	(1)	66-66-66	.70-.70-.70
Virginia	F.	50-61-56	.31-.75-.53
1889:			
Maine	F.	60-60-60	1.25-1.25-1.25
Massachusetts	F.	60-60-60	.90-.95-.93
New Hampshire	M.	(1)	.80-.80-.80
Do	F.	(1)	1.35-1.35-1.35
Rhode Island	F.	57-60-59	.50-.70-.60
1890:			
New York	M.	(1)	.17-4.17-1.26
Do	F.	(1)	.42-2.50-1.01
Tennessee	F.	(1)	.65-.65-.65
1891:			
Michigan	F.	(1)	.65-1.08-.84
New York	M.	(1)	.17-4.17-1.01
Do	F.	(1)	.42-2.50-1.01
Ohio	F.	51-51-51	1.00-1.00-1.00
1892:			
California	F.	54-57-55	.58-1.50-1.06
Illinois	F.	47-60-54	.31-2.23-.99
Maine	F.	60-60-60	.50-1.50-.86
1893:			
Missouri	M.	84-84-84	2.83-3.33-3.13
New Jersey	F.	49-59-58	.42-1.83-.90
New York	M.	60-70-65	1.67-1.67-1.67
Do	F.	58-72-63	.50-1.50-.82
Ohio	M.	54-60-54	1.50-3.50-1.85
Do	F.	48-60-56	.75-1.42-1.16
1894:			
Massachusetts	F.	54-60-59	1.17-1.25-1.23
New York	F.	60-60-60	.67-1.25-.89
Ohio	M.	48-60-54	1.50-2.00-1.77
Do	F.	42-60-52	.60-1.50-.96

¹ Not reported.

TABLE **C-2.**—*Sewing-machine operators, 1865-1900, by year and State*—Continued

Year and State	Sex	Lowest, highest, and average—		Year and State	Sex	Lowest, highest, and average—	
		Hours per week	Rate per day (dollars)			Hours per week	Rate per day (dollars)
1895:				1896—Continued.			
Connecticut	F.	59–60–59	0. 62–1. 51–1. 09	Minnesota	F.	60–60–60	1. 26–1. 80–1. 61
Georgia	M.	66–66–66	. 75– . 75– . 75	Missouri	F.	54–60–55	. 70–1. 50– . 90
Do	F.	66–66–66	. 75– . 75– . 75	Do	M.	48–66–59	. 67–3. 35–1. 70
Illinois	M.	'54–54–54	1. 33–4. 08–2. 45	Nebraska	F.	57–60–58	. 40–1. 65– . 90
Do	F.	. 75–1. 50–1. 04	New Jersey	M.	60–60–60	1. 66–1. 66–1. 66
Iowa	F.	54–54–54	. 20–1. 43– . 74	Do	F.	56–56–56	1. 00–1. 25–1. 11
Louisiana	F.	60–60–60	. 50–1. 50– . 95	New York	M.	57–60–60	. 83–2. 67–1. 84
Maryland	M.	54–57–56	1. 17–3. 33–2. 06	Do	F.	54–60–56	. 54–1. 67– . 98
Do	F.	48–60–56	. 46–2. 13–1. 06	North Carolina	M.	69–69–69	. 40– . 40– . 40
Massachusetts	M.	58–60–60	1. 00–1. 34–1. 24	Do	F.	68–68–68	. 60– . 60– . 60
Do	F.	54–60–58	. 38–3. 00–1. 11	Ohio	M.	54–58–58	1. 25–3. 00–1. 86
Missouri	F.	54–60–57	. 66–1. 62–1. 05	Do	F.	36–60–54	. 50–1. 40– . 89
New Hampshire	M.	60–60–60	1. 15–1. 25–1. 18	Pennsylvania	M.	54–60–55	. 42–2. 50–1. 76
Do	F.	60–60–60	. 80–1. 26–1. 03	Do	F.	48–60–57	. 32–2. 23– . 98
New Jersey	M.	55–55–55	. 93–2. 00–1. 62	Rhode Island	M.	60–60–60	1. 00–1. 00–1. 00
Do	F.	48–60–55	. 33–2. 50–1. 01	Do	F.	60–60–60	1. 00–1. 57–1. 45
New York	M.	51–60–53	. 67–3. 83–2. 46	South Carolina	M.	66–66–66	. 75–1. 00– . 88
Do	F.	49–60–55	. 23–2. 85–1. 22	1897:			
North Carolina	F.	60–60–60	. 50–1. 00– . 68	Massachusetts	F.	51–63–52	1. 25–1. 50–1. 38
Do	M.	66–70–68	. 75– . 90– . 83	Nebraska	F.	(¹)	1. 00–1. 00–1. 00
Ohio	M.	54–60–57	1. 60–3. 50–1. 84	New Jersey	M.	(¹)	1. 68–1. 88–1. 87
Do	F.	45–60–56	. 73–1. 25– . 97	Do	F.	(¹)	. 81–1. 25–1. 06
Pennsylvania	F.	60–60–60	1. 67–1. 67–1. 67	New York	F.	54–£4–54	1. 00–1. 50–1. 33
Rhode Island	F.	60–60–60	1. 00–1. 17–1. 09	Do	M.	(¹)	1. 50–1. 50–1. 50
South Carolina	F.	60–66–61	. 58–1. 00– . 80	Virginia	F.	48–60–59	. 60–1. 00– . 73
Virginia	F.	54–55–55	. 67–1. 25– . 77	1898:			
1896:				New Jersey	M.	60–60–60	. 67–2. 50–1. 46
Alabama	F.	63–63–63	. 70– . 70– . 70	Do	F.	60–60–60	. 58–1. 50– . 90
Connecticut	F.	60–60–60	. 80–2. 00–1. 10	New York	M.	60–60–60	1. 00–3. 00–1. 73
Georgia	M.	66–66–66	1. 00–1. 00–1. 00	1899:			
Do	F.	63–63–63	. 75–1. 00– . 85	Georgia	F.	60–60–60	. 40–1. 12– . 73
Illinois	M.	57–57–57	1. 67–2. 00–1. 75	North Carolina	F.	60–63–61	. 40–1. 52– . 79
Do	F.	48–60–53	. 83–2. 31–1. 39	1900:			
Iowa	F.	48–60–51	. 23–2. 42– . 91	Georgia	F.	60–66–62	. 40–1. 12– . 65
Maryland	F.	54–60–59	. 42–2. 25– . 88	North Carolina	F.	60–63–61	. 40–1. 52– . 80
Michigan	F.	54–60–58	. 35–1. 69– . 92				

¹ Not reported.

TABLE **C-3.**—*Sewing-machine operators, males, men's clothing, 1890-1907, by geographic division and year*

Year	North Atlantic		South Atlantic		North Central		South Central	
	Hours per week	Rate per hour	Hours per week	Rate per hour	Hours per week	Rate per hour	Hours per week	Rate per hour
1890	59	$0. 263						
1891	59	. 263						
1892	59	. 270						
1893	59	. 270						
1894	59	. 261						
1895	59	. 261						
1896	59	. 263						
1897	59	. 261						
1898	59	. 261						
1899	59	. 275						
1900	54	. 274						
1901	54	. 299						
1902	54	. 299						
1903	54. 3	. 226	60. 0	$0. 227	55. 3	$0. 304	58. 3	$0. 217
1904	55. 2	. 203	58. 8	. 257	54. 7	. 280	56. 4	. 172
1905	55. 0	. 208	58. 6	. 233	54. 1	. 289	54. 1	. 178
1906	54. 9	. 219	58. 7	. 258	54. 0	. 310	57. 5	. 279
1907	55. 1	. 224	55. 9	. 235	54. 0	. 316	56. 8	. 281

TABLE C-4.—*Sewing-machine operators, females, men's clothing, 1890–1907, by geographic division and year*

Year	South Atlantic		North Central		South Central		North Atlantic	
	Hours per week	Rate per hour	Hours per week	Rate per hour	Hours per week	Rate per hour	Hours per week	Rate per hour
1890	60.0	$0.085	58.1	$0.072	55.0	$0.100		
1891	60.0	.081	57.8	.076	55.0	.100		
1892	60.0	.080	57.9	.078	55.0	.100		
1893	60.0	.081	58.5	.074	55.0	.100		
1894	60.0	.085	58.0	.075	55.1	.091		
1895	60.0	.085	58.0	.076	55.1	.091		
1896	60.0	.085	57.9	.079	55.1	.091		
1897	60.0	.085	57.7	.076	55.0	.098		
1898	60.0	.087	57.5	.081	55.0	.109		
1899	60.0	.088	57.7	.080	55.0	.109		
1900	60.0	.089	57.8	.076	55.0	.109		
1901	60.0	.090	57.7	.078	55.0	.109		
1902	60.0	.090	57.4	.082	55.0	.109		
1903	57.0	.107	55.2	.112	57.2	.109	54.0	$0.126
1904	55.9	.112	55.1	.147	54.9	.103	54.1	.126
1905	55.8	.116	55.8	.161	53.9	.113	54.0	.132
1906	56.3	.137	54.1	.194	54.6	.130	53.8	.133
1907	56.6	.141	54.1	.189	55.0	.132	53.7	.138

TABLE C-5.—*Operators, coat, males, men's clothing, 1911–1928, by city and year*

Year	Baltimore, Md.		Boston, Mass.		Chicago, Ill.		Cincinnati, Ohio	
	Hours per week	Rate per hour	Hours per week	Rate per hour	Hours per week	Rate per hour	Hours per week	Rate per hour
1911	59.5	$0.190			54.0	$0.317		
1912	59.2	.200	53.2	$0.307	54.0	.313	53.8	$0.208
1913	53.9	.224	50.0	.403	52.0	.344	50.9	.292
1914	53.8	.265	50.0	.399	52.0	.344	51.4	.292
1919	48.0	.614	45.8	.611	48.0	.565	49.9	.493
1922	44.0	.863	44.1	.803	44.0	1.043	42.5	.811
1924	44.0	.945	44.0	1.000	44.0	1.092	41.2	1.011
1926	44.0	.887	44.0	1.037	44.0	1.181	41.4	.914
1928	44.0	.786	42.5	.973	44.0	1.192	41.5	1.265

Year	Cleveland, Ohio [1]		New York, N. Y.[1]		Philadelphia, Pa.[1]		Rochester, N. Y.[1]	
1911			56.1	$0.270	54.4	$0.257	54.7	$0.305
1912			56.5	.272	54.4	.251	54.6	.286
1913			51.8	.335	53.9	.266	52.0	.337
1914			51.3	.331	54.0	.266	50.0	.354
1919	49.8	$0.505	46.8	.639	48.0	.609	48.0	.562
1922			44.3	1.002	44.0	.787	44.0	.872
1924			44.2	1.050	44.0	.901	44.0	1.028
1926			44.3	1.035	44.0	.952	44.0	1.102
1928	44.0	.892	44.3	1.018	44.0	.919	43.8	.975

[1] Includes operators on coats, vests, and pants, 1919.

TABLE C-6.—*Operators, coat, females, men's clothing, 1911-1928, by city and year*

Year	Baltimore, Md.[1]		Boston, Mass.[1]		Chicago, Ill.[1]		Cincinnati, Ohio[1]	
	Hours per week	Rate per hour	Hours per week	Rate per hour	Hours per week	Rate per hour	Hours per week	Rate per hour
1911	57.6	$0.129			54.0	$0.224	53.7	$0.164
1912	56.2	.132	54.0	$0.157	54.0	.209	53.3	.161
1913	53.3	.153	50.0	.164	52.0	.222	50.4	.184
1914	52.2	.168	50.0	.179	52.0	.248	50.6	.186
1919	48.0	.375	46.0	.313	48.0	.400	49.0	.255
1922	44.0	.492	44.2	.419	44.0	.755	42.4	.550
1924	44.0	.410	44.0	.581	44.0	.905	39.1	.610
1926	44.4	.461	44.0	.570	44.0	.941	40.0	.632
1928	44.0	.424	42.7	.489	44.0	1.019	38.1	.718

Year	Cleveland, Ohio[1]		New York, N. Y.[1]		Philadelphia, Pa.[1]		Rochester, N. Y.[1]	
1911			54.8	$0.152	54.0	$0.145	54.4	$0.191
1912			56.0	.138	54.1	.150	54.6	.190
1913			52.5	.170	54.0	.173	52.0	.204
1914			52.2	.170	54.0	.172	50.0	.222
1919	48.1	$0.381	46.8	.394	48.0	.347	48.0	.374
1922			45.3	.604	44.0	.466	44.0	.538
1924			45.4	.648	44.0	.476	44.0	.680
1926	46.3	.614	45.2	.644	44.0	.588	44.0	.682
1928	44.0	.607	45.1	.642	44.0	.529	42.2	.645

[1] Includes operators on coats, vests, and pants, 1919.

D.—FARMING

FARM LABORERS

The sources from which wage data were secured are the Fifteenth Annual Report of the Commissioner of Labor Statistics and the reports of the United States Department of Agriculture. For other laborers see Tables B–12 (p. 185), G–1 (p. 253), I–16, I–17, I–18 (pp. 295 and 296), O–11, and O–12 (p. 464).

TABLE D–1.—*Farm laborers, 1841–1899, by year and State*

Year and State	Sex	Hours per week	Rate per day (dollars)	Year and State	Sex	Hours per week	Rate per day (dollars)
1841:				**1860:**			
Texas	M.	66–66–66	0.50–0.50–0.50	Illinois	M.	60–66–61	1.00–1.00–1.00
1843:				New Jersey	M.	[1]	.42–.42–.42
Florida	M.	66–66–66	.75–.75–.75	New York	M.	66–66–66	.88–.88–.88
1844:				**1861:**			
Kentucky	M.	60–60–60	.30–.30–.30	New Jersey	M.	[1]	.46–.46–.46
1845:				New York	M.	66–66–66	.88–.88–.88
New Jersey	M.	[1]	[2] .25–.40–.31	**1862:**			
1846:				New Jersey	M.	[1]	.23–.27–.25
New Jersey	M.	[2]	.40–.40–.40	New York	M.	66–66–66	1.00–1.00–1.00
Do	M.	[2]	[3] .23–.35–.29	**1863:**			
1847:				New Jersey	M.	[1]	.31–.31–.31
New Jersey	M.	[1]	.27–.40–.33	Do	M.	[1]	[3] .50–.50–.50
1848:				New York	M.	66–66–66	1.13–1.13–1.13
New Jersey	M.	[2]	.23–.50–.37	**1864:**			
Wisconsin	M.	60–60–60	[2] .63–.63–.63	New Jersey	M.	[1]	.31–.58–.42
1849:				Do	M.	[1]	[3] .67–1.00–.84
New Jersey	M.	[1]	.32–.50–.41	New York	M.	66–66–66	1.50–1.50–1.50
1850:				**1865:**			
Illinois	M.	60–60–60	.40–1.00–.58	New Jersey	M.	[1]	[2] .77–.77–.77
Kentucky	M.	60–60–60	.50–1.00–.96	New York	M.	66–66–66	1.50–1.50–1.50
New Jersey	M.	[1]	.33–.50–.42	**1866:**			
Rhode Island	M.	60–60–60	.75–.75–.75	Iowa	M.	60–60–60	1.00–1.00–1.00
1851:				New York	M.	66–66–66	1.50–1.50–1.50
New Jersey	M.	[2]	.29–.50–.37	South Carolina	M.	60–60–60	.77–.77–.77
1852:				**1867:**			
New Jersey	M.	[2]	.27–.50–.38	New York	M.	66–66–66	1.50–1.50–1.50
1853:				**1868:**			
Florida	M.	60–60–60	.31–.31–.31	Illinois	M.	60–60–60	1.00–1.00–1.00
New Jersey	M.	[1]	.38–.50–.44	New York	M.	66–66–66	1.50–1.50–1.50
Wisconsin	M.	60–60–60	[2] .75–.75–.75	**1869:**			
1854:				Alabama	M.	60–60–60	.75–.75–.75
New Jersey	M.	[1]	.35–.38–.37	Missouri	M.	60–60–60	1.50–1.50–1.50
New York	M.	66–66–66	1.00–1.00–1.00	New York	M.	66–66–66	1.75–1.75–1.75
1855:				**1870:**			
Illinois	M.	60–60–60	.40–1.00–.64	Florida	M.	60–60–60	.40–.50–.47
Louisiana	M.	66–66–66	1.00–1.00–1.00	Illinois	M.	60–60–60	1 00–1.50–1.46
New Jersey	M.	[1]	.23–.35–.29	Louisiana	M.	66–66–66	1.00–1.00–1.00
Do	M.	[1]	[2] .63–.63–.63	Missouri	M.	60–60–60	1.00–1.00–1.00
New York	M.	66–66–66	.88–.88–.88	New York	M.	66–66–66	1.50–1.50–1.50
1856:				**1871:**			
New Jersey	M.	[1]	.43–.63–.51	New York	M.	66–66–66	1.50–1.50–1.50
New York	M.	66–66–66	.88–.88–.88	**1872:**			
Wisconsin	M.	60–60–60	[2] .63–.63–.63	Illinois	M.	60–60–60	.65–1.25–1.05
1857:				New York	M.	66–66–66	1.50–1.50–1.50
New Jersey	M.	[1]	.38–.54–.48	**1873:**			
New York	M.	66–66–66	.88–.88–.88	New York	M.	66–66–66	1.50–1.50–1.50
1858:				**1874:**			
Illinois	M.	60–60–60	1.00–1.00–1.00	New York	M.	66–66–66	1.25–1.25–1.25
New Jersey	M.	[1]	.38–.50–.44	**1875:**			
New York	M.	66–66–66	.88–.88–.88	New York	M.	66–66–66	1.25–1.25–1.25
1859:				**1876:**			
New Jersey	M.	[1]	.42–.42–.42	New York	M.	63–63–63	1.25–1.25–1.25
Do	M.	[1]	[2] .38–.38–.38	Pennsylvania	M.	[1]	.60–1.00–.85
New York	M.	66–66–66	.88–.88–.88				

[1] Not reported. [2] And board. [3] And house.

225

TABLE **D–1.**—*Farm laborers, 1841–1899, by year and State*—Continued

Year and State	Sex	Lowest, highest, and average—		Year and State	Sex	Lowest, highest, and average—	
		Hours per week	Rate per day (dollars)			Hours per week	Rate per day (dollars)
1877:				**1892:**			
New York	M.	63–66–63	1.00–1.00–1.00	Iowa	(¹)	60–90–71	0.38–1.25–0.85
1878:				North Carolina	M.	72–72–72	.50–.50–.50
New York	M.	63–63–63	.88–.88–.88	**1893:**			
1879:				Florida	M.	60–60–60	.75–.75–.75
New Jersey	(¹)	70–70–70	.60–.75–.68	Illinois	M.	60–72–61	1.00–1.50–1.45
New York	M.	63–63–63	.88–.88–.88	Maryland	M.	60–72–69	.50–1.67–.80
1880:				Missouri	M.	60–60–60	1.00–2.00–1.19
New Jersey	(¹)	40–90–61	.39–1.50–1.05	Montana	M.	54–54–54	1.92–1.92–1.92
New York	M.	63–63–63	1.25–1.25–1.25	Do	M.	54–66–58	⁴1.15–1.34–1.21
North Carolina	M.	60–60–60	.75–.75–.75	Do	M.	60–78–62	².77–1.53–1.31
1881:				New York	M.	60–84–66	1.00–1.25–1.17
Louisiana	M.	60–60–60	.75–.75–.75	Do	M.	72–72–72	².33–.33–.33
New York	M.	63–63–63	1.25–1.25–1.25	North Carolina	M.	60–72–71	.50–1.00–.67
1882:				Pennsylvania	M.	72–72–72	1.38–1.38–1.38
New York	M.	63–63–63	1.50–1.50–1.50	Wisconsin	M.	(¹)	1.25–1.25–1.25
1883:				**1894:**			
New York	M.	63–63–63	1.25–1.25–1.25	Georgia	M.	60–60–60	.50–.50–.50
1884:				Illinois	M.	60–66–60	1.00–2.50–1.32
California	M.	60–72–68	².96–1.15–1.08	Iowa	M.	60–96–78	.75–1.00–.82
Michigan	M.	(¹)	1.00–2.00–1.61	Do	M.	72–84–78	².77–.77–.77
New York	M.	63–63–63	1.25–1.25–1.25	Michigan	M.	(¹)	.19–2.00–.73
1885:				Do	M.	(¹)	⁵1.00–1.00–1.00
Florida	M.	60–60–60	.50–.60–.55	Do	M.	(¹)	⁶.58–1.15–.87
Kansas	M.	60–60–60	1.00–1.00–1.00	Montana	M.	60–78–62	².77–1.53–1.20
New Jersey	M.	60–60–60	1.00–1.00–1.00	New York	M.	60–60–60	.50–1.50–1.25
Do	M.	72–72–72	².69–.69–.69	North Carolina	M.	60–72–69	.20–1.00–.56
New York	M.	63–63–63	1.38–1.38–1.38	Do	F.	72–72–72	.40–.40–.40
1886:				**1895:**			
Alabama	M.	60–60–60	.60–.60–.60	Florida	M.	60–60–60	.25–.65–.48
Connecticut	M.	(¹)	1.00–1.00–1.00	Illinois	M.	60–66–60	.75–1.25–1.10
Florida	M.	60–60–60	.35–.75–.62	Do	F.	60–60–60	.75–1.00–.92
Illinois	M.	60–96–75	.46–1.25–.70	Iowa	M.	60–60–60	1.00–1.50–1.08
Kansas	M.	(¹)	1.00–2.00–1.39	Kentucky	M.	48–66–58	.50–2.00–.84
Louisiana	M.	70–70–70	1.00–1.00–1.00	Louisiana	M.	66–66–66	.65–.65–.65
Do	F.	70–70–70	.75–.75–.75	Missouri	M.	60–60–60	.85–.85–.85
New York	M.	63–63–63	1.38–1.38–1.38	Montana	M.	(¹)	⁴.61–1.51–1.03
1887:				Nebraska	M.	60–60–60	1.25–1.25–1.25
Connecticut	M.	(¹)	.75–2.00–1.27	North Carolina	M.	60–60–60	.50–1.00–.63
Do	M.	(¹)	².13–1.50–.75	North Dakota	M.	(¹)	.41–1.58–.91
Kansas	M.	60–78–72	.75–1.70–1.15	South Carolina	M.	60–60–60	.58–.58–.58
New York	M.	63–63–63	1.38–1.38–1.38	Texas	M.	60–60–60	.50–1.00–.55
Wisconsin	M.	(¹)	1.00–1.00–1.00	Wisconsin	M.	(¹)	.58–1.34–.86
1888:				Do	M.	60–60–60	².27–1.50–.75
Colorado	M.	72–72–72	.75–2.25–1.50	**1896:**			
Iowa	M.	(¹)	².50–1.67–.90	California	M.	60–60–60	1.50–2.50–1.90
New York	M.	59–63–63	1.30–1.67–1.40	Georgia	M.	(¹)	.29–.83–.56
Ohio	M.	(¹)	².42–1.27–.73	Missouri	(¹)	(¹)	.38–.77–.58
1889:				New York	M.	(¹)	.46–1.73–.74
Minnesota	(¹)	(¹)	.91–1.52–1.15	Tennessee	M.	(¹)	.58–.58–.58
New York	M.	63–63–63	1.50–1.50–1.50	Do	F.	(¹)	.75–.75–.75
North Carolina	M.	66–66–66	.40–.40–.40	**1897:**			
1890:				Kansas	M.	54–112–75	.88–1.15–.77
Maine	M.	(¹)	.17–2.08–1.00	**1898:**			
Nebraska	M.	(¹)	1.50–1.50–1.50	Nebraska	(¹)	60–72–67	.20–3.00–.88
New York	M.	63–63–63	1.15–1.50–1.49	Pennsylvania	M.	(¹)	1.15–1.15–1.15
North Carolina	M.	78–78–78	.40–.50–.45	**1899:**			
North Dakota	M.	(¹)	².50–1.61–1.10	Pennsylvania	M.	(¹)	1.34–1.34–1.34
1891:							
New York	M.	63–63–63	1.15–1.50–1.37				
North Dakota	(¹)	(¹)	².58–1.50–1.11				
Wisconsin	M.	(¹)	1.25–1.25–1.25				

¹ Not reported.
³ And board.
⁴ And board and lodging.

⁵ And fuel.
⁶ And perquisites.

TABLE **D-2.**—*Farm laborers, males, 1866–1927, by year and index number*

Year	Average farm wage [1]				Index numbers of farm wages— 1910–1914 =100 [2]
	Per month—		Per day—		
	With board	Without board	With board	Without board	
1866 [3]	$10. 09	$15. 50	$0. 64	$0. 90	55
1869	9. 97	15. 50	. 63	. 87	54
1874 or 1875	11. 16	17. 10	. 68	. 94	59
1877 or 1879 [4]	10. 86	16. 79	. 61	. 84	56
1879 or 1880	11. 70	17. 53	. 64	. 89	59
1880 or 1881	12. 32	18. 52	. 67	. 92	62
1881 or 1882	12. 88	19. 11	. 70	. 97	65
1884 or 1885	13. 08	19. 22	. 71	. 96	65
1887 or 1888	13. 29	19. 67	. 72	. 98	66
1889 or 1890	13. 29	19. 45	. 72	. 97	66
1891 or 1892	13. 48	20. 02	. 73	. 98	67
1893	13. 85	19. 97	. 72	. 92	67
1894	12. 70	18. 57	. 65	. 84	61
1895	12. 75	18. 74	. 65	. 85	62
1898	13. 29	19. 16	. 71	. 94	65
1899	13. 90	19. 97	. 75	. 99	68
1902	15. 51	22. 12	. 83	1. 09	76
1906	18. 73	26. 19	1. 03	1. 32	92
1909	20. 48	28. 09	1. 04	1. 31	96
1910	19. 58	28. 04	1. 07	1. 40	97
1911	19. 85	28. 33	1. 07	1. 40	97
1912	20. 46	29. 14	1. 12	1. 44	101
1913	21. 27	30. 21	1. 15	1. 48	104
1914	20. 90	29. 72	1. 11	1. 43	101
1915	21. 08	29. 97	1. 12	1. 45	102
1916	23. 04	32. 58	1. 24	1. 60	112
1917	28. 64	40. 19	1. 56	2. 00	140
1918	35. 12	49. 13	2. 05	2. 61	176
1919	40. 14	56. 77	2. 44	3. 10	206
1920	47. 24	65. 05	2. 84	3. 56	239
1921	30. 25	43. 58	1. 66	2. 17	150
1922	29. 31	42. 09	1. 64	2. 14	146
1923	33. 09	46. 74	1. 91	2. 45	166
1924	33. 34	47. 22	1. 88	2. 44	166
1925	33. 88	47. 80	1. 89	2. 46	168
1926	34. 86	48. 86	1. 91	2. 49	171
1927	34. 58	48. 63	1. 90	2. 46	170

[1] Yearly averages are from reports by crop reporters, giving average wages for the year in their localities and published by United States Department of Agriculture.
[2] In constructing the farm wage index numbers the rates of wages per day with and without board and wages per month with and without board were used.
[3] Years 1866 to 1878 paid in gold.
[4] 1877 or 1878, 1878 or 1879 (combined).

TABLE **D-3.**—*Farm laborers, males, 1910–1928, by geographic division and State*

Per month with board

Geographic division and State	1910	1917	1922	1923	1925	1926	1927	1928
NORTH ATLANTIC								
Maine	$23.50	$36.00	$38.00	$41.00	$43.00	$45.00	$45.00	$47.00
New Hampshire	23.50	35.00	38.60	46.50	46.00	50.00	49.00	49.00
Vermont	25.00	35.00	35.00	40.60	46.00	36.00	47.00	48.00
Massachusetts	22.75	38.00	41.00	50.00	50.00	52.00	52.00	49.00
Rhode Island	21.00	31.00	40.00	50.00	50.00	51.00	52.00	54.00
Connecticut	21.00	35.00	40.00	52.00	51.00	54.00	54.00	53.00
New York	23.50	35.00	39.70	45.50	48.00	50.50	49.75	49.75
New Jersey	19.50	32.00	40.00	44.50	46.00	54.00	47.00	47.00
Pennsylvania	18.75	30.00	33.00	38.00	39.50	41.75	41.00	39.75
Average	21.65	33.26	37.14	43.42	45.29	47.75	47.01	46.58
NORTH CENTRAL								
Ohio	21.00	31.00	32.60	36.80	38.00	39.00	39.25	38.75
Indiana	20.50	29.00	30.20	35.40	35.00	37.00	37.00	37.00
Illinois	24.50	33.00	33.90	40.20	42.00	42.00	42.50	43.25
Michigan	23.00	34.00	33.60	40.00	41.00	43.50	42.50	43.00
Wisconsin	26.00	36.00	37.00	45.00	46.50	48.50	49.00	48.75
Minnesota	26.00	39.00	35.00	37.00	45.00	46.75	47.25	47.00
Iowa	28.00	41.00	36.80	43.30	45.50	46.25	46.75	47.75
Missouri	21.50	29.00	28.70	31.00	32.00	34.00	33.00	33.00
North Dakota	29.00	41.00	38.70	40.30	49.50	49.50	53.25	54.25
South Dakota	27.00	42.00	36.40	43.20	46.50	43.75	48.25	48.25
Nebraska	26.50	39.00	34.50	40.00	40.00	40.00	43.00	43.00
Kansas	24.00	33.00	32.50	35.90	36.00	37.00	37.75	39.25
Average	(¹)	(¹)	(¹)	(¹)	40.80	41.91	42.47	42.73
SOUTH ATLANTIC								
Delaware	16.00	29.00	27.10	32.80	32.00	35.00	33.00	32.00
Maryland	13.50	24.00	28.50	32.00	34.50	35.75	36.75	36.00
Virginia	14.00	22.00	24.80	28.00	30.00	30.00	31.00	30.00
West Virginia	19.40	31.00	33.20	35.50	36.50	34.75	34.00	33.25
North Carolina	13.60	25.00	24.00	28.00	29.00	30.00	27.50	27.75
South Carolina	12.00	18.00	16.20	20.00	21.25	21.00	20.50	21.00
Georgia	13.00	19.00	15.60	17.30	20.50	21.50	20.25	19.50
Florida	15.00	22.00	23.40	26.00	26.00	28.00	24.25	24.00
Average	13.77	22.44	22.12	24.93	26.20	26.76	25.77	25.43
SOUTH CENTRAL								
Kentucky	16.00	24.00	25.90	28.10	27.25	28.50	27.50	27.25
Tennessee	14.00	21.00	22.30	24.60	25.50	24.75	25.75	24.50
Alabama	13.00	16.00	17.60	19.90	26.00	22.50	22.00	21.00
Mississippi	13.30	17.00	18.20	20.00	22.00	23.75	23.50	21.75
Arkansas	16.25	23.00	21.35	23.00	25.00	30.00	25.50	26.00
Louisiana	13.50	19.00	22.40	21.00	23.00	24.00	23.50	25.75
Oklahoma	19.10	28.00	26.00	27.40	29.50	31.50	30.25	31.25
Texas	18.00	25.00	24.20	28.30	29.00	30.00	26.50	31.25
Average	15.28	21.88	22.33	24.13	26.32	27.14	25.57	26.57
WESTERN								
Montana	38.00	46.00	42.20	48.00	56.50	52.50	60.25	60.50
Idaho	35.00	51.00	46.00	53.00	54.50	56.00	58.25	55.50
Wyoming	35.00	45.00	39.50	44.50	47.00	49.00	51.75	53.00
Colorado	29.50	41.00	35.00	40.00	40.00	41.30	43.00	40.50
New Mexico	24.50	32.00	31.00	32.50	33.00	34.00	35.25	36.25
Arizona	30.00	48.00	40.00	54.00	44.50	45.00	50.50	52.00
Utah	35.00	50.00	47.00	54.00	56.50	54.50	59.75	53.50
Nevada	37.00	50.00	48.00	58.00	55.50	59.25	63.25	62.00
Washington	33.00	47.00	45.00	54.30	52.00	51.00	53.75	52.75
Oregon	32.00	44.00	43.50	52.50	45.00	51.00	53.25	49.00
California	33.00	43.00	55.00	56.00	60.00	63.00	65.00	62.00
Average	32.69	44.25	45.57	51.25	52.02	53.61	56.39	54.21
United States	19.21	28.87	29.17	33.18	34.91	36.00	35.68	35.75

¹ Not reported.

TABLE D–3.—*Farm laborers, males, 1910–1928, by geographic division and State—* Continued

Per month without board

Geographic division and State	1910	1917	1922	1923	1925	1926	1927	1928
NORTH ATLANTIC								
Maine	$34.50	$53.00	$53.50	$61.00	$63.00	$64.00	$66.00	$65.00
New Hampshire	35.50	51.00	60.00	69.00	71.00	76.00	71.00	74.00
Vermont	35.50	50.00	52.00	60.30	66.00	65.00	69.00	72.00
Massachusetts	37.20	58.00	68.00	80.00	78.00	79.00	83.00	80.00
Rhode Island	34.00	48.00	65.00	80.00	72.00	78.00	82.00	80.00
Connecticut	36.00	52.00	67.00	75.00	76.00	80.00	82.00	81.00
New York	35.00	48.00	56.50	64.00	69.00	70.25	69.50	70.75
New Jersey	31.50	46.00	62.00	67.00	72.00	77.00	72.00	70.00
Pennsylvania	29.00	45.00	50.90	55.50	58.50	60.00	61.50	59.75
Average	33.19	48.06	55.82	63.31	66.88	68.67	69.03	68.71
NORTH CENTRAL								
Ohio	29.00	43.00	46.50	50.40	53.00	55.00	54.50	53.75
Indiana	28.40	41.00	42.70	48.60	48.00	50.00	50.00	49.00
Illinois	32.90	44.00	45.00	52.50	55.00	55.00	55.00	55.00
Michigan	33.00	47.00	47.30	55.00	58.00	61.00	59.25	60.00
Wisconsin	37.25	52.00	54.00	63.00	64.00	66.00	67.25	65.25
Minnesota	38.00	54.00	50.00	55.50	61.00	62.00	63.75	63.75
Iowa	39.00	53.00	49.70	56.60	57.00	56.75	55.00	58.50
Missouri	29.50	39.00	39.50	42.50	43.00	44.00	45.00	44.00
North Dakota	42.00	60.00	55.50	58.80	68.50	69.50	72.00	75.75
South Dakota	39.00	61.00	53.00	61.70	61.50	60.00	66.50	66.00
Nebraska	38.00	53.00	48.50	54.00	54.50	53.50	55.75	58.00
Kansas	34.00	46.00	46.70	50.60	50.00	51.00	52.25	54.25
Average	(1)	(1)	(1)	(1)	55.10	56.12	56.67	56.96
SOUTH ATLANTIC								
Delaware	24.75	43.00	40.00	51.00	48.00	48.00	50.00	46.00
Maryland	21.50	37.00	42.00	48.00	50.75	51.00	52.25	51.25
Virginia	19.50	32.00	35.50	40.00	42.00	43.00	43.00	42.00
West Virginia	29.00	45.00	47.90	50.50	52.25	49.50	48.75	48.00
North Carolina	19.50	30.00	33.00	39.00	40.00	41.00	38.00	39.25
South Carolina	16.50	25.00	23.20	27.50	30.00	29.50	29.25	28.00
Georgia	18.00	26.00	23.00	24.50	28.75	29.50	28.75	27.25
Florida	25.00	33.00	35.50	40.00	38.00	42.50	36.75	·37.00
Average	19.75	30.80	31.72	35.55	36.84	37.58	36.44	35.78
SOUTH CENTRAL								
Kentucky	23.10	33.00	36.30	38.60	38.25	39.75	38.25	38.00
Tennessee	20.00	29.00	30.75	35.25	35.25	33.00	33.50	33.25
Alabama	18.50	24.00	25.80	28.20	34.00	31.50	27.00	30.00
Mississippi	19.50	24.00	25.90	29.40	32.00	33.70	32.00	31.25
Arkansas	24.00	32.00	31.60	33.90	35.00	37.50	36.00	35.75
Louisiana	20.25	30.00	32.60	33.00	34.75	36.00	33.00	35.25
Oklahoma	28.10	40.00	37.00	38.30	42.00	45.00	47.25	43.25
Texas	24.50	35.00	35.40	39.70	42.00	44.00	43.25	42.50
Average	21.90	31.07	32.09	34.55	37.25	38.15	36.85	36.74
WESTERN								
Montana	50.00	70.00	63.00	65.50	76.25	75.00	77.50	83.25
Idaho	49.50	70.00	66.00	72.70	76.00	77.00	79.50	77.75
Wyoming	49.00	68.00	60.00	62.50	69.00	70.00	73.25	77.00
Colorado	44.50	60.00	54.00	58.30	59.00	63.80	65.00	60.50
New Mexico	34.35	48.00	46.00	48.00	49.00	50.00	49.75	49.25
Arizona	40.00	68.00	58.00	66.00	73.50	65.00	69.00	72.00
Utah	47.50	68.00	64.00	73.70	76.50	75.00	80.75	74.00
Nevada	54.00	72.00	65.00	86.00	71.75	81.50	89.00	80.00
Washington	50.00	66.00	65.00	77.00	76.00	75.00	77.75	78.00
Oregon	44.50	61.00	63.00	70.00	65.00	76.00	72.00	69.75
California	47.00	63.00	79.00	82.00	87.00	90.00	90.00	90.00
Average	46.48	63.59	66.03	72.79	75.19	77.31	78.33	77.68
United States	27.50	40.43	41.79	46.91	48.99	50.10	49.77	49.60

1 Not reported.

TABLE D-3.—*Farm laborers, males, 1910-1928, by geographic division and State—*
Continued

Per day with board

Geographic division and State	1910	1917	1922	1923	1925	1926	1927	1928
NORTH ATLANTIC								
Maine	$1.23	$2.02	$2.08	$2.50	$2.50	$2.60	$2.75	$2.60
New Hampshire	1.18	1.92	2.11	2.70	2.60	2.50	2.70	2.55
Vermont	1.21	1.98	1.96	2.55	2.50	2.60	2.55	2.60
Massachusetts	1.22	2.00	2.31	2.95	2.90	2.75	2.90	2.90
Rhode Island	1.12	1.90	2.37	2.65	2.80	2.80	2.70	3.00
Connecticut	1.07	1.85	2.05	2.80	2.70	2.85	2.90	2.80
New York	1.28	1.94	2.46	3.00	2.05	3.10	3.05	3.00
New Jersey	1.11	1.95	2.25	2.55	2.65	2.90	2.90	2.85
Pennsylvania	1.04	1.80	2.10	2.48	2.60	2.60	2.60	2.55
Average	1.17	1.91	2.24	2.73	2.78	2.82	2.83	2.78
NORTH CENTRAL								
Ohio	1.20	1.88	2.00	2.18	2.55	2.55	2.50	2.45
Indiana	1.14	1.65	1.80	2.25	2.20	2.55	2.25	2.20
Illinois	1.31	1.85	1.95	2.40	2.35	2.35	2.25	2.30
Michigan	1.22	1.97	2.10	2.58	2.65	2.75	2.70	2.75
Wisconsin	1.35	2.00	2.20	2.45	2.50	2.45	2.55	2.50
Minnesota	1.48	2.17	2.20	2.55	2.85	2.80	2.75	2.80
Iowa	1.57	2.23	2.11	2.52	2.50	2.50	2.55	2.55
Missouri	1.02	1.44	1.46	1.62	1.75	1.70	1.65	1.70
North Dakota	1.60	2.45	2.50	2.50	3.80	3.35	4.20	4.15
South Dakota	1.54	2.52	2.25	2.65	2.85	2.45	2.95	3.00
Nebraska	1.57	2.31	2.15	2.42	2.35	2.25	2.55	2.45
Kansas	1.42	2.00	2.19	2.32	2.20	2.20	2.40	2.50
Average	(¹)	(¹)	(¹)	(¹)	2.45	2.41	2.47	2.48
SOUTH ATLANTIC								
Delaware	.98	1.75	1.60	2.25	2.75	2.50	2.50	2.30
Maryland	.88	1.52	1.54	1.95	2.35	2.25	2.20	2.30
Virginia	.78	1.25	1.31	1.61	1.60	1.65	1.65	1.65
West Virginia	.94	1.55	1.55	1.90	1.95	1.80	1.75	1.75
North Carolina	.73	1.18	1.35	1.55	1.50	1.50	1.40	1.50
South Carolina	.70	.93	.85	1.12	1.05	1.05	1.00	1.00
Georgia	.73	1.00	.88	1.00	1.10	1.10	1.05	1.05
Florida	.96	1.14	1.15	1.44	1.35	1.50	1.20	1.25
Average	.77	1.17	1.18	1.41	1.42	1.42	1.35	1.38
SOUTH CENTRAL								
Kentucky	.85	1.20	1.23	1.51	1.45	1.60	1.35	1.40
Tennessee	.77	1.02	1.07	1.28	1.20	1.20	1.15	1.20
Alabama	.85	1.00	1.00	1.20	1.20	1.25	1.20	1.15
Mississippi	.83	.95	1.10	1.29	1.25	1.25	1.20	1.15
Arkansas	.90	1.20	1.15	1.30	1.25	1.25	1.30	1.20
Louisiana	.77	1.11	1.26	1.45	1.40	1.35	1.25	1.25
Oklahoma	1.11	1.65	1.52	1.60	1.80	1.85	1.75	1.80
Texas	1.04	1.28	1.30	1.45	1.55	1.70	1.55	1.60
Average	.89	1.18	1.20	1.38	1.40	1.46	1.36	1.37
WESTERN								
Montana	1.77	2.44	2.40	2.70	3.25	3.20	3.65	3.70
Idaho	1.70	2.48	2.22	2.85	2.85	2.85	3.05	3.00
Wyoming	1.73	2.15	1.95	2.50	2.55	2.50	2.65	2.65
Colorado	1.47	2.15	1.90	2.20	2.20	2.40	2.40	2.35
New Mexico	1.12	1.55	1.30	1.58	1.60	1.70	1.75	1.85
Arizona	1.34	2.22	1.75	2.10	1.95	1.75	2.05	2.20
Utah	1.55	2.42	2.16	2.47	2.65	2.40	2.70	2.40
Nevada	1.39	2.25	2.40	2.45	2.40	2.55	2.85	2.65
Washington	1.72	2.40	2.38	2.95	2.80	2.90	3.05	2.85
Oregon	1.51	2.15	2.25	2.80	2.40	2.50	2.70	2.75
California	1.44	2.04	2.53	2.80	2.55	2.55	2.65	2.70
Average	1.51	1.87	2.23	2.64	2.49	2.51	2.67	2.66
United States	1.06	1.56	1.65	1.93	1.95	1.97	1.96	1.96

¹ Not reported.

TABLE D-3.—*Farm laborers, males, 1910–1928, by geographic division and State—*
Continued

Per day without board

Geographic division and State	1910	1917	1922	1923	1925	1926	1927	1928
NORTH ATLANTIC								
Maine	$1.60	$2.56	$2.70	$3.10	$3.30	$3.25	$3.30	$3.30
New Hampshire	1.65	2.50	2.84	3.60	3.30	3.30	3.45	3.65
Vermont	1.60	2.45	2.53	3.20	3.20	3.20	3.35	3.40
Massachusetts	1.66	2.55	3.18	3.90	3.65	3.80	3.75	3.75
Rhode Island	1.56	2.45	3.20	3.65	3.65	3.60	3.70	3.80
Connecticut	1.55	2.50	2.95	3.75	3.70	3.80	3.85	3.75
New York	1.66	2.47	3.15	3.70	3.80	3.90	3.80	3.80
New Jersey	1.46	2.40	3.00	3.55	3.65	3.75	3.80	3.85
Pennsylvania	1.49	2.35	2.70	3.15	3.40	3.35	3.40	3.30
Average	1.58	2.43	2.91	3.48	3.58	3.62	3.62	3.58
NORTH CENTRAL								
Ohio	1.57	2.37	2.60	2.92	3.25	3.25	3.25	3.10
Indiana	1.45	2.10	2.32	2.83	2.85	2.85	2.90	2.75
Illinois	1.63	2.32	2.48	2.96	3.05	3.05	2.95	2.95
Michigan	1.66	2.50	2.70	3.23	3.35	3.50	3.35	3.40
Wisconsin	1.78	2.52	2.90	3.15	3.25	3.15	3.10	3.10
Minnesota	1.90	2.77	2.95	3.29	3.50	3.40	3.50	3.55
Iowa	1.98	2.76	2.67	3.12	3.15	3.10	3.15	3.20
Missouri	1.32	1.82	1.90	2.10	2.30	2.20	2.20	2.20
North Dakota	2.20	3.30	3.40	3.50	4.50	4.20	4.90	5.05
South Dakota	2.00	3.15	3.10	3.45	3.75	3.25	3.70	3.80
Nebraska	1.96	2.95	2.85	3.00	3.15	3.00	3.30	3.30
Kansas	1.84	2.50	2.75	2.90	2.90	2.90	3.10	3.20
Average	(1)	(1)	(1)	(1)	3.14	3.08	3.14	3.14
SOUTH ATLANTIC								
Delaware	1.22	2.16	2.07	2.75	3.30	3.10	3.15	3.05
Maryland	1.18	2.00	2.11	2.50	3.10	2.95	2.90	2.90
Virginia	1.01	1.65	1.76	2.08	2.10	2.15	2.15	2.15
West Virginia	1.27	2.06	2.10	2.50	2.55	2.50	2.40	2.45
North Carolina	.97	1.50	1.75	1.95	2.00	1.90	1.75	1.90
South Carolina	.90	1.16	1.08	1.42	1.35	1.40	1.35	1.25
Georgia	.95	1.31	1.12	1.30	1.35	1.45	1.40	1.35
Florida	1.32	1.55	1.60	2.00	1.85	2.00	1.70	1.70
Average	1.01	1.52	1.55	1.82	1.84	1.86	1.78	1.78
SOUTH CENTRAL								
Kentucky	1.12	1.59	1.63	1.97	1.95	2.05	1.75	1.80
Tennessee	1.02	1.35	1.40	1.64	1.50	1.60	1.55	1.50
Alabama	1.05	1.26	1.30	1.50	1.55	1.60	1.45	1.50
Mississippi	1.10	1.27	1.45	1.68	1.70	1.65	1.60	1.55
Arkansas	1.20	1.58	1.52	1.66	1.75	1.70	1.70	1.60
Louisiana	1.02	1.39	1.60	1.75	1.65	1.80	1.60	1.55
Oklahoma	1.47	2.10	1.96	2.00	2.35	2.50	2.20	2.25
Texas	1.32	1.65	1.66	1.88	2.05	2.20	2.00	2.00
Average	1.15	1.53	1.56	1.76	1.83	1.91	1.75	1.74
WESTERN								
Montana	2.36	3.30	3.20	3.55	3.85	3.85	4.40	4.35
Idaho	2.27	3.20	3.00	3.45	3.70	3.65	3.75	3.75
Wyoming	2.29	3.17	2.75	3.40	3.40	3.40	3.55	3.55
Colorado	2.00	2.79	2.60	2.90	3.00	3.20	3.20	3.15
New Mexico	1.58	1.97	1.80	2.10	2.15	2.20	2.15	2.30
Arizona	2.04	2.83	2.50	2.70	2.65	2.50	2.75	2.70
Utah	2.00	3.00	2.81	3.05	2.90	3.10	3.30	3.15
Nevada	1.96	3.00	3.40	3.58	3.15	2.95	3.50	3.50
Washington	2.26	3.10	3.15	3.75	3.75	3.60	3.70	3.70
Oregon	2.07	2.80	2.95	3.48	3.10	3.25	3.45	3.25
California	2.02	2.67	3.40	3.70	3.60	3.65	3.60	3.65
Average	2.06	2.82	3.00	3.42	3.33	3.37	3.45	3.44
United States	1.38	2.02	2.15	2.47	2.53	2.55	2.51	2.51

¹ Not reported.

E.—GLASS AND CLAY PRODUCTS

The sources from which these wage data were taken are the fifteenth and the nineteenth annual reports of the Commissioner of Labor Statistics and bulletins of the Bureau of Labor Statistics Nos. 59, 65, 71, 77, 265, and 412.

The available reports on wages and hours of labor in the glass and the pottery industries are very few in number.

A large per cent of the workers in the pottery industry are on piecework. They are paid at rates per dozen pieces of ware, per "kiln day," per 100 cubic feet, or other piece units. A "kiln day" is a specified number of cubic feet of kiln space. The space varies with the product which is being produced.

In establishments where no record of time actually worked by pieceworkers was regularly kept, a special day by day record of actual time worked by each employee was kept for a representative pay period, at the request of the Bureau of Labor Statistics. These actual hours worked at piece rates thus obtained enabled the bureau to arrive at the earnings per hour for employees in each occupation. These were computed by dividing the combined earnings of all employees in each occupation which were received during the selected pay period by the combined hours worked by all employees in each specified occupation.

The same method has been used in arriving at hours and earnings in other industries where pieceworkers are found.

In the early history of glass blowing the work was almost entirely a handicraft. No machinery and only a very few tools were used. The experienced blower usually had one or more unskilled assistants, generally boys, who did his carrying and cleaned blowpipes, etc. In later years molds were introduced to aid in shaping the articles, and a few more years later mechanical devices were introduced which pressed the simpler articles in molds without the need of blowing, and finally, in 1895, machines appeared on the market which actually did the blowing of glass. These machines dispensed with the blower as such, but still required the services of a skilled glass gatherer to feed the machine and a skilled glass worker to operate the pressing and blowing levers. In the year 1898 there appeared an entirely automatic bottle-blowing machine. Machinists were required on this new device, but no glass workers of the old type.

These improved methods affected all classes of labor, both skilled and unskilled. Their numbers, their duties, and the conditions under which they worked underwent many changes.

Improved methods, however, did not supersede entirely the old hand methods. Machines were limited to certain classes of wares, therefore the old systems of working and the old devices of the past were continued in active use, and not infrequently, side by side in the same factory.

232

TABLE E-1.—Glass blowers, bottles, 1841-1898, by year and State

Year and State	Sex	Hours per week	Rate per day (dollars)	Year and State	Sex	Hours per week	Rate per day (dollars)
		Lowest, highest, and average—				*Lowest, highest, and average—*	
1841:				1877:			
New Jersey	M.	(¹)	1.60-4.00-2.49	New Jersey	M.	(¹)	3.38-3.90-3.68
1842:				1878:			
New Jersey	M.	(¹)	1.60-4.00-2.49	New Jersey	M.	(¹)	3.38-3.90-3.68
1843:				1879:			
New Jersey	M.	(¹)	1.60-4.00-2.49	New Jersey	M.	(¹)	3.38-3.90-3.68
1844:					Pennsylvania	M.	(¹)	3.00-4.00-3.45
New Jersey	M.	(¹)	2.10-4.76-3.09	1880:			
1845:				New Jersey	M.	(¹)	3.50-3.90-3.70
New Jersey	M.	(¹)	2.35-4.76-3.22	Pennsylvania	M.	54-54-54	5.00-5.00-5.00
1846:				1881:			
New Jersey	M.	(¹)	2.35-4.76-3.22	New Jersey	M.	(¹)	4.87-5.47-5.15
1847:				Ohio	M.	43-50-45	3.58-4.17 3.96
New Jersey	M.	(¹)	2.60-4.75-3.39	Pennsylvania	M.	58-58-58	4.00-5.00-4.50
1848:				1882:			
New Jersey	M.	(¹)	2.60-4.75-3.39	New Jersey	M.	(¹)	4.87-5.47-5.15
1849:				Pennsylvania	M.	54-54-54	4.00-4.50-4.13
New Jersey	M.	(¹)	2.45-4.00-3.01	1883:			
1850:				Kentucky	M.	52-52-52	5.00-5.00-5.00
New Jersey	M.	(¹)	2.45-4.00-3.01	New Jersey	M.	48-60-51	2.68-6.33-4.23
1851:				Pennsylvania	M.	54-54-54	4.00-4.00-4.00
New Jersey	M.	(¹)	2.45-4.00-3.01	1884:			
1852:				Illinois	M.	60-60-60	4.00-4.00-4.00
New Jersey	M.	(¹)	2.50-3.75-2.99	Kentucky	M.	52-52-52	5.00-5.00-5.00
1853:				New Jersey	M.	36-60-51	1.73-6.00-4.08
New Jersey	M.	(¹)	2.50-3.75-2.99	Ohio	M.	48-54-53	3.28-3.88-3.74
1854:				Pennsylvania	M.	54-58-58	4.00-5.00-4.83
New Jersey	M.	(¹)	2.50-3.75-2.99	1885:			
1855:				California	M.	60-60-60	4.33-4.33-4.33
New Jersey	M.	(¹)	2.25-3.60-2.77	Illinois	M.	60-60-60	4.00-4.00-4.00
1856:				Kentucky	M.	52-60-56	4.00-5.00-4.46
New Jersey	M.	(¹)	2.25-3.60-2.77	Massachusetts	M.	59-59-59	2.89-2.89-2.89
1857:				New Jersey	M.	36-60-52	1.67-15.00-4.14
New Jersey	M.	(¹)	2.25-3.60-2.77	Ohio	M.	54-54-54	3.84-4.50-4.13
1858:				Pennsylvania	M.	48-60-58	3.98-5.00-4.37
New Jersey	M.	(¹)	2.25-3.60-2.77	West Virginia	M.	60-60-60	4.90-4.90-4.90
1859:				1886:			
New Jersey	M.	(¹)	2.25-3.08-2.59	Illinois	M.	51-51-51	4.50-4.50-4.50
1860:				New Jersey	M.	48-60-54	1.33-11.53-4.22
New Jersey	M.	(¹)	2.25-3.08-2.59	New York	M.	54-60-55	2.00-4.75-3.76
1861:				Pennsylvania	M.	54-60-58	4.10-4.50-4.21
New Jersey	M.	(¹)	2.10-2.90-2.44	1887:			
1862:				New Jersey	M.	(¹)	4.61-5.25-4.84
New Jersey	M.	(¹)	2.25-3.85-2.95	Ohio	M.	60-60-60	3.20-5.00-4.21
1863:				1888:			
New Jersey	M.	(¹)	2.25-3.85-2.95	New Jersey	M.	45-54-52	2.65-8.00-4.95
1864:				New York	M.	50-54-52	5.00-5.50-5.27
New Jersey	M.	(¹)	2.25-3.85-2.95	1889:			
1865:				Indiana	M.	54-54-54	4.50-5.33-4.56
New Jersey	M.	(¹)	3.36-4.76-3.95	New Jersey	M.	54-54-54	4.00-5.47-4.05
1866:				New York	M.	(¹)	2.01-6.84-4.78
New Jersey	M.	(¹)	3.36-4.76-3.95	1890:			
1867:				California	M.	(¹)	(²)
New Jersey	M.	(¹)	4.90-5.40-5.14	Illinois	M.	54-54-54	2.59-6.50-5.34
1868:				Indiana	M.	54-54-54	3.55-9.70-4.65
New Jersey	M.	(¹)	4.87-5.60-5.19	Maryland	M.	52-52-52	3.68-4.85-4.35
1869:				Missouri	M.	54-54-54	3.13-6.00-5.37
New Jersey	M.	(¹)	4.87-5.60-5.19	New Jersey	M.	48-54-51	1.13-5.74-3.80
1870:				New York	M.	44-55-46	3.29-7.73-4.44
New Jersey	M.	(¹)	4.87-5.60-5.19	Ohio	M.	54-54-54	1.67-6.15-4.27
1871:				Pennsylvania	M.	51-54-53	1.87-9.21-4.40
New Jersey	M.	(¹)	4.87-5.60-5.17	1891:			
1872:				Illinois	(¹)	53-53-53	3.83-4.07-3.96
New Jersey	M.	(¹)	4.87-5.60-5.19	New Jersey	M.	(¹)	4.87-5.47-5.15
1873:				New York	M.	(¹)	3.92-5.00-4.85
New Jersey	M.	(¹)	4.87-5.60-5.19	1892:			
1874:				Indiana	M.	54-54-54	5.90-5.90-5.90
New Jersey	M.	(¹)	4.60-5.40-4.96	New Jersey	M.	(¹)	4.87-5.47-5.15
1875:				1893:			
New Jersey	M.	(¹)	4.34-5.00-4.64	New Jersey	F.	55-55-55	.75-.75-.75
1876:				1898:			
New Jersey	M.	(¹)	4.07-4.75-4.36	New Jersey	M.	54-60-54	2.50-10.00-3.97
Pennsylvania	M.	(¹)	3.50-3.50-3.50				

¹ Not reported.   ² $10.00-$10.00-$10.00.

TABLE E-2.—*Blowers .(green glass), males, 1890–1907, by geographic division and year*

Year	North Atlantic		North Central		South Atlantic	
	Hours per week	Rate per hour	Hours per week	Rate per hour	Hours per week	Rate per hour
1890	52.7	$0.511				
1891	51.7	.499				
1892	52.1	.538				
1893	52.8	.503				
1894	51.8	.507				
1895	51.6	.495				
1896	51.7	.502				
1897	51.8	.486				
1898	52.7	.478				
1899	50.8	.538				
1900	51.0	.593				
1901	51.0	.633				
1902	51.0	.597				
1903	51.0	.605				
1904	51.1	.710				
1905	50.9	.672	49.0	$0.788		
1906	47.9	.762	49.6	.785	50.0	$0.799
1907	47.8	.796	49.5	.770	50.0	.891

TABLE E-3.—*Blowers (flint glass), males, 1890–1907, by geographic division and year*

Year	North Atlantic		North Central		South Atlantic	
	Hours per week	Rate per hour	Hours per week	Rate per hour	Hours per week	Rate per hour
1890	50.6	$0.555	49.5	$0.452		
1891	50.5	.559	49.5	.452		
1892	50.5	.534	49.5	.469		
1893	50.7	.543	49.5	.472		
1894	50.5	.581	49.5	.482		
1895	50.6	.541	49.5	.496		
1896	50.6	.562	49.5	.494		
1897	50.6	.572	49.5	.492		
1898	50.6	.532	49.5	.476		
1899	50.6	.562	49.5	.505		
1900	50.8	.567	49.5	.498		
1901	50.5	.600	49.5	.496		
1902	50.5	.588	49.5	.526		
1903	50.7	.561	49.5	.515		
1904	49.6	.605	50.5	.618		
1905	49.8	.604	49.0	.656		
1906	49.6	.641	50.0	.672	55.4	$0.574
1907	49.7	.657	49.9	.681	55.5	.570

TABLE E-4.—*Blowers (bottles, tableware, window and lighting ware), males, 1919, by State and year*

Year	Indiana		New Jersey		New York		Ohio	
	Hours per week	Rate per hour	Hours per week	Rate per hour	Hours per week	Rate per hour	Hours per week	Rate per hour
1919	(1)	$1.011	(1)	$0.856	(1)	$0.809	(1)	$0.905

Year	Pennsylvania		Virginia		West Virginia			
1919	(1)	$1.055	(1)	$0.852	(1)	$0.980		

1 Not reported.

TABLE E–5.—*Potters, 1840–1895, by year and State*

Year and State	Sex	Lowest, highest, and average—		Year and State	Sex	Lowest, highest, and average—	
		Hours per week	Rate per day (dollars)			Hours per week	Rate per day (dollars)
1840:				**1886—Continued.**			
Ohio	M.	60–60–60	0. 80–1. 20–1. 00	Illinois	M.	54–60–57	1. 35–2. 50–1. 89
1865:				Ohio	M.	(¹)	1. 15–2. 42–1. 87
Massachusetts	M.	60–60–60	2. 50–2. 50–2. 50	**1887:**			
1872:				Ohio	M.	48–63–55	. 66–3. 50–2. 31
Ohio	M.	(¹)	1. 50–2. 50–2. 08	Wisconsin	M.	(¹)	1. 25–1. 25–1. 25
1877:				**1888:**			
New Jersey	M.	64–64–64	2. 25–2. 25–2. 25	Michigan	M.	60–60–60	1. 75–1. 75–1. 75
Ohio	M.	(¹)	2. 00–2. 50–2. 46	New Jersey	M.	60–60–60	1. 60–3. 50–1. 92
1879:				New York	M.	60–60–60	1. 25–3. 00–2. 68
Ohio	M.	(¹)	1. 75–2. 50–2. 20	**1890:**			
1880:				Minnesota	M.	(¹)	1. 25–2. 75–1. 64
Massachusetts	M.	60–60–60	3. 00–3. 00–3. 00	New York	M.	(¹)	3. 00–3. 00–3. 00
New Jersey	(¹)	58–65–61	1. 00–2. 00–1. 56	**1891:**			
1881:				New York	M.	(¹)	. 42–3. 00–2. 41
New Jersey	M.	60–60–60	2. 00–2. 00–2. 00	**1892:**			
Ohio	M.	56–60–60	2. 00–2. 00–2. 00	Ohio	M.	45–60–57	. 50–4. 00–2. 14
1882:				**1893:**			
Ohio	(¹)	48–60–57	2. 00–3. 00–2. 50	Illinois	M.	60–60–60	2. 00–2. 00–2. 00
1883:				Maryland	M.	55–72–60	. 42–3. 33–1. 60
New Jersey	(¹)	60–60–60	2. 50–2. 50–2. 50	Do	F.	60–60–60	. 25–1. 67– . 76
Ohio	M.	48–66–58	1. 50–3. 00–2. 28	Massachusetts	M.	60–60–60	2. 80–5. 70–3. 83
1884:				New York	M.	59–59–59	2. 17–2. 17–2. 17
Iowa	M.	60–60–60	1. 00–2. 00–1. 50	Ohio	M.	60–60–60	4. 00–4. 00–4. 00
Michigan	M.	(¹)	1. 50–1. 50–1. 50	**1894:**			
New Jersey	M.	60–60–60	2. 71–2. 71–2. 71	Massachusetts	M.	60–60–60	2. 50–3. 60–3. 05
1886:				Ohio	M.	54–60–54	2. 00–2. 61–2. 54
California	M.	60–60–60	1. 00–4. 00–2. 00	West Virginia	M.	60–60–60	1. 80–1. 80–1. 80
Do	M.	60–60–60	³1. 50–1. 50–1. 50	**1895:**			
				Massachusetts	M.	60–60–60	2. 50–3. 36–2. 79

¹ Not reported.   ² And board.

TABLE E–6.—*Jiggers, males, 1919, by State and year*

Year	New York		New Jersey		West Virginia		Ohio	
	Hours per week	Rate per hour	Hours per week	Rate per hour	Hours per week	Rate per hour	Hours per week	Rate per hour
1919	(¹)	$0. 830	(¹)	$0. 772	(¹)	$0. 812	(¹)	$0. 721

¹ Not reported.

TABLE E–7.—*Jiggers, males, 1925, by group and year*

[Group 1 includes 5 East Liverpool, Ohio, and 6 near-by West Virginia potteries; Group 2 includes 11 small potteries in East Liverpool, Ohio; Group 3 includes 15 potteries outside of East Liverpool, Ohio, 2 in Pennsylvania, and 1 in West Virginia; Group 4 includes 3 potteries in Trenton, N. J.; and Group 5 covers 1 pottery each in Maryland, Tennessee, and Virginia]

Year	Group 1		Group 2		Group 3		Group 4		Group 5	
	Hours per week	Rate per hour	Hours per week	Rate per hour	Hours per week	Rate per hour	Hours per week	Rate per hour	Hours per week	Rate per hour
1925	(¹)	$0. 955	(¹)	$0. 836	(¹)	$0. 909	(¹)	$0. 892	(¹)	$0. 794

¹ Not reported.

TABLE E-8.—*Kiln placers, males, 1919, by State and year*

Year	New York		New Jersey		West Virginia		Ohio	
	Hours per week	Rate per hour	Hours per week	Rate per hour	Hours per week	Rate per hour	Hours per week	Rate per hour
1919	(1)	$0.809	(1)	$0.844	(1)	$0.870	(1)	$0.800

1 Not reported.

TABLE E-9.—*Kiln placers, males, 1925, by group and year*

[For explanation of groups see Table E-7.]

Year	Group 1		Group 2		Group 3		Group 4		Group 5	
	Hours per week	Rate per hour	Hours per week	Rate per hour	Hours per week	Rate per hour	Hours per week	Rate per hour	Hours per week	Rate per hour
1925	(1)	$1.076	(1)	$0.978	(1)	$1.012	(1)	$1.127	(1)	$1.154

1 Not reported.

TABLE E-10.—*Turners, clay and pottery products, 1872–1896, by year and State*

Year and State	Sex	Lowest, highest, and average—		Year and State	Sex	Lowest, highest, and average—	
		Hours per week	Rate per day (dollars)			Hours per week	Rate per day (dollars)
1872:				1888:			
Ohio	M.	(1)	3.33–3.33–3.33	New York	M.	53–54–54	1.67–2.50–2.12
1877:				1890:			
Ohio	M.	(1)	2.50–2.50–2.50	New York	M.	(1)	2.00–3.45–3.21
1879:				Ohio	(1)	42–60–53	1.00–3.00–2.26
Ohio	M.	(1)	2.50–2.50–2.50	1891:			
1879:				New York	M.	(1)	2.00–3.45–2.68
Pennsylvania	(1)	54–60–57	1.00–1.50–1.25	Ohio	M.	48–60–57	2.00–3.40–2.44
1882:				1892:			
Ohio	(1)	48–60–52	1.50–3.00–2.56	Ohio	(1)	44–60–53	.75–5.00–2.55
1884:				1893:			
New Jersey	M.	60–60–60	2.08–2.08–2.08	Ohio	M.	48–60–58	2.00–3.00–2.50
Ohio	M.	30–54–48	1.00–2.78–2.25	1894:			
1886:				Ohio	M.	54–60–55	1.37–3.00–2.31
New Jersey	M.	60–60–60	3.00–3.00–3.00	Do	F.	60–60–60	.75–.75–.75
1887:				1896:			
Ohio	F.	54–54–56	1.00–1.33–1.11	Ohio	M.	54–54–54	2.63–2.79–2.71
Do	M.	48–60–54	1.50–3.00–2.42				

1 Not reported.

TABLE E-11.—*Turners, males, 1919, by State and year*

Year	New York		New Jersey		West Virginia		Ohio	
	Hours per week	Rate per hour	Hours per week	Rate per hour	Hours per week	Rate per hour	Hours per week	Rate per hour
1919	(1)	$0.860	(1)	$0.636	(1)	$0.845	(1)	$0.807

1 Not reported.

TABLE E-12.—*Turners, males, 1925, by group and year*

Year	Group 1		Group 2		Group 3		Group 4		Group 5	
	Hours per week	Rate per hour	Hours per week	Rate per hour	Hours per week	Rate per hour	Hours per week	Rate per hour	Hours per week	Rate per hour
1925	(¹)	$0.928	(¹)	$0.922	(¹)	$0.982	(¹)	$0.602	(¹)	$1.169

¹ Not reported.

F.—IRON AND STEEL INDUSTRY

The sources from which wage data were secured are the fifteenth and the nineteenth annual reports of the Commissioner of Labor Statistics and bulletins of the Bureau of Labor Statistics Nos. 59, 65, 71, 77, 151, 168, 218, 265, 305, 353, 381, and 442.

In the early years, 1840 to 1900, Table F–16, certain employees were reported as fillers. These reports may have included those who did both top and bottom filling.

In later years and in the overlapping period from 1890 to 1926 details are shown for top fillers, Tables F–17 and F–18. Bottom fillers were reported from 1897 to 1915, and for two districts in a few later years, Table F–19. Wages and hours are also shown for skip operators from 1907 to 1926, see Table F–20. These employees have largely supplanted the work performed by top fillers. Mechanical filling instead of hand filling of stacks is merely a short term covering a whole series of improvements in the method of charging the furnace. It does away with bottom fillers and their helpers, top fillers and their helpers, and substitutes larrymen and their helpers and skip operators. In some plants this change alone cut the time in man-hours of labor per ton of output by one-half.

The pig-casting machine displaces a considerable number of sand cutters, iron carriers, and miscellaneous yard labor. The pig machine brings about a savings of labor in the iron yard because of the fact that the pigs are elevated in the process of cooling and permits them to drop into gondolas and open cars from which they are unloaded by locomotive cranes.

The ore bridge and car dumper have also exerted an influence on labor time. One or two men with a car dumper can handle all the ore that a one or two furnace plant can use whereby if it had to be shoveled out by hand the labor cost would be prohibitive. An ore bridge with a crew of two operators and two oilers removes the ore from the stock pile and keeps the bins supplied and eliminates the use of several locomotive cranes and reduces the amount of railroad transportation in the plant, thus cutting the labor force.

Charging machines in open hearth furnaces have eliminated many men, as furnaces were originally charged by hand the materials being laid on a peel and pushed into the furnace, but with modern large furnaces both on account of the time required and the arduousness of the labor this is done by a charging machine.

The 3-high roll mill which took the place of the old 2-high makes it possible to greatly increase the output of mills' rolling plates and shapes of large size, as it takes too long and too many men to drag and shove the piece back over the top of the roll after the first pass, but about 1857 the idea of a 3-high mill was conceived, which has three rolls set one above the other in which the center roll rotates in the opposite direction of the upper and lower rolls. In mills of this

238

type the rolls can be operated at great speed and the material carried through in some types of mills almost at the rate of better than a half mile a minute. The only disadvantage of a 3-high mill is the power necessary to raise large weights up to the pass over the middle roll. The continuous rolling mills which are now coming into use in rolling sheet product is revolutionizing the old hand method of rolling sheets. This is the newest invention in the iron and steel industry. About 20 men in the electrical, mechanical, and operating crews in charge of an entire mill for an 8-hour shift will produce a tonnage equal to that of 360 men on the hot-mill crews of 40 hand mills in an 8-hour shift.

Mechanical puddling machines are now taking the place of hand puddling with a great saving in labor time, but this operation is so new that no available data can be given, the bureau having made no study of this process.

TABLE **F-1.**—*Catchers, bar mills, 1840–1899, by year and State*

| Year and State | Sex | Lowest, highest, and average— | | Year and State | Sex | Lowest, highest, and average— | |
		Hours per week	Rate per day (dollars)			Hours per week	Rate per day (dollars)
1840:				1866:			
New York	M.	60–60–60	1. 00–1. 25–1. 13	New York	M.	60–60–60	1. 00–4. 25–1. 95
1842:				1867:			
New York	M.	60–60–60	. 75–1. 25–1. 00	New York	M.	60–60–60	1. 00–4. 25–2. 03
1843:				1868:			
New York	M.	60–60–60	. 75– . 75– . 75	New York	M.	60–60–60	1. 38–1. 75–1. 60
1844:				1869:			
New York	M.	60–60–60	. 88– . 88– . 88	New York	M.	60–60–60	1. 06–1. 75–1. 41
1845:				1870:			
New York	M.	60–60–60	1. 25–1. 25–1. 25	New York	M.	60–60–60	1. 00–1. 75–1. 52
1847:				1871:			
New York	M.	60–60–60	. 56– . 56– . 56	New York	M.	60–60–60	1. 13–1. 75–1. 48
1849:				1872:			
New York	M.	60–60–60	. 44–1. 00– . 54	New York	M.	60–60–60	1. 00–2. 13–1. 55
1850:				1873:			
New York	M.	60–60–60	· . 44–1. 00– . 73	New York	M.	60–60–60	. 63–2. 13–1. 57
1851:				1874:			
New York	M.	60–60–60	. 44–1. 00– . 61	New York	M.	60–60–60	1. 25–1. 88–1. 51
1852:					Pennsylvania	M.	(¹)	1. 25–3. 67–2. 31
New York	M.	60–60–60	. 50– . 63– . 57	1875:			
1853:				New York	M.	60–60–60	1. 13–1. 75–1. 42
New York	M.	60–60–60	. 38– . 63– . 50	Pennsylvania	M.	(¹)	1. 68–2. 82–2. 28
1854:				1876:			
New York	M.	60–60–60	. 44–1. 00– . 63	New York	M.	60–60–60	1. 04–1. 40–1. 20
1855:				Pennsylvania	M.	(¹)	. 64–6. 00–1. 88
New York	M.	60–60–60	. 44– . 81– . 60	1877:			
1856:				New York	M.	60–60–60	1. 13–1. 40–1. 24
New York	M.	60–60–60	. 63–1. 13– . 95	Ohio	M.	(¹)	1. 33–4. 17–2. 60
1857:				1878:			
New York	M.	60–60–60	. 44–1. 13– . 82	New York	M.	60–60–60	1. 00–1. 25–1. 10
1858:				Pennsylvania	M.	48–72–58	. 98–2. 75–1. 75
New York	M.	60–60–60	. 50– . 88– . 77	1879:			
1859:				New York	M.	60–60–60	. 50–1. 25– . 97
New York	M.	60–60–60	. 50–1. 00– . 83	Pennsylvania	M.	60–60–60	. 60–4. 00–2. 10
1860:				1880:			
New York	M.	60–60–60	. 56–1. 06– . 85	New Jersey	(¹)	55–55–55	1. 50–1. 50–1. 50
1861:				New York	M.	60–60–60	1. 20–1. 70–1. 55
New York	M.	60–60–60	. 56–1. 25– . 90	Pennsylvania	M.	66–66–66	1. 44–1. 44–1. 44
1862:				1881:			
New York	M.	60–60–60	. 56–1. 06– . 87	New York	M.	60–60–60	1. 00–1. 95–1. 59
1863:				1882:			
New York	M.	60–60–60	. 63–1. 38–1. 06	New York	M.	60–60–60	. 65–1. 68–1. 35
1864:				1883:			
New York	M.	60–60–60	. 75–2. 00–1. 39	New Jersey	M.	72–72–72	1. 17–2. 00–1. 54
1865:				New York	M.	60–60–60	1. 00–1. 68–1. 47
New York	M.	60–60–60	1. 13–2. 00–1. 59				

TABLE **F-1.**—*Catchers, bar mills, 1840–1899, by year and State*—Continued

Year and State	Sex	Lowest, highest, and average—		Year and State	Sex	Lowest, highest, and average—	
		Hours per week	Rate per day (dollars)			Hours per week	Rate per day (dollars)
1884:				**1889—Continued.**			
New Jersey	M.	54–72–59	1. 62–2. 53–1. 84	Virginia	M.	55–55–55	1. 00–2. 25–1. 86
New York	M.	60–60–60	. 90–1. 50–1. 40	West Virginia	M.	(¹)	2. 50–2. 50–2. 50
1885:				**1890:**			
Delaware	M.	60–60–60	1. 77–1. 77–1. 77	Alabama	M.	55–60–56	2. 25–5. 00–3. 11
Illinois	M.	60–60–60	2. 00–6. 30 3. 83	Wisconsin	M.	55–55–55	3. 60–3. 60–3. 60
Indiana	M.	60–60–60	3. 75–3. 75–3. 75	**1891:**			
Kentucky	M.	60–60–60	2. 75–4. 00–3. 25	New York	M.	(¹)	1. 50–2. 08–1. 88
New Jersey	M.	54–72–63	. 83–1. 33–1. 17	**1892:**			
New York	M.	60–72–64	1. 50–2. 60–1. 97	Missouri	M.	48–48–48	2. 10–2. 75–2. 45
Ohio	M.	60–72–64	1. 25–4. 84–2. 54	New York	M.	(¹)	1. 35–1. 35–1. 35
Pennsylvania	M.	60–72–68	2. 07–4. 00–2. 69	Ohio	M.	(¹)	48–63–54	1. 00–8. 00–2. 74
Virginia	M.	48–60–52	1. 38–2. 25–1. 69	**1893:**			
West Virginia	M.	60–60–60	2. 50–2. 50–2. 50	New York	M.	(¹)	1. 35–1. 35–1. 35
1886:				**1894:**			
New Jersey	M.	60–60–60	1. 00–1. 47–1. 27	New York	M.	(¹)	1. 35–1. 35–1. 35
New York	M.	60–60–60	1. 50–1. 50–1. 50	**1895:**			
1887:				Ohio	M.	48–72–55	1. 00–7. 70–2. 67
New York	M.	60–60–60	1. 30–1. 30–1. 30	Wisconsin	(¹)	66–66–66	4. 00–4. 00–4. 00
Ohio	M.	54–60–57	1. 50–4. 00–2. 40	**1896:**			
Pennsylvania	M.	(¹)	2. 31–9. 47–3. 63	Connecticut	M.	60–60–60	2. 25–2. 25–2. 25
Wisconsin	M.	(¹)	4. 00–4. 00–4. 00	New York	M.	60–60–60	1. 75–1. 75–1. 75
1888:				Pennsylvania	M.	60–72–69	. 98–2. 25–1. 94
New Jersey	M.	(¹)	1. 40–3. 43–2. 44	**1897:**			
1889:				New York	M.	60–60–60	1. 65–1. 65–1. 65
Alabama	M.	(¹)	1. 15–2. 17–1. 83	Ohio	(¹)	48–72–53	. 70–8. 00–2. 51
Delaware	M.	60–60–60	1. 40–1. 66–1. 60	Pennsylvania	M.	(¹)	1. 58–2. 87–2. 10
Illinois	M.	60–72–70	1. 31–7. 76–2. 83	**1898:**			
Indiana	M.	66–72–68	1. 20–4. 41–2. 16	Ohio	M.	(¹)	1. 04–7. 00–2. 90
Maryland	M.	(¹)	1. 87–1. 87–1. 87	Pennsylvania	M.	(¹)	1. 17–5. 00–3. 11
New York	M.	60–60–60	1. 34–2. 54–1. 81	**1899:**			
Ohio	M.	44–66–55	1. 35–7. 00–2. 68	Ohio	M.	(¹)	1. 25–8. 40–3. 39
Pennsylvania	M.	50–66–59	1. 25–5. 32–2. 10	Pennsylvania	M.	(¹)	1. 70–7. 09–3. 42
Tennessee	M.	(¹)	1. 50–2. 50–1. 74				

¹ Not reported.

TABLE **F-2.**—*Catchers, males, bar mills, 1890–1907, by geographic division ana year*

Year	North Atlantic		South Atlantic		North Central		South Central	
	Hours per week	Rate per hour	Hours per week	Rate per hour	Hours per week	Rate per hour	Hours per week	Rate per hour
1890	65. 6	$0. 324	60. 0	$0. 232	72. 0	$0. 594	60. 0	$0. 132
1891	65. 7	. 287	60. 0	. 232	72. 0	. 600	60. 0	. 153
1892	65. 7	. 283	60. 0	. 219	72. 0	. 535	60. 0	. 147
1893	65. 9	. 301	60. 0	. 204	72. 0	. 484	60. 0	. 108
1894	65. 6	. 262	60. 0	. 217	72. 0	. 475	60. 0	. 095
1895	64. 8	. 282	60. 0	. 212	72. 0	. 510	60. 0	. 093
1896	64. 8	. 293	60. 0	. 225	72. 0	. 497	60. 0	. 135
1897	64. 8	. 299	60. 0	. 180	57. 6	. 502	60. 0	. 143
1898	64. 8	. 284	60. 0	. 176	57. 6	. 536	60. 0	. 126
1899	64. 8	. 335	60. 0	. 180	56. 4	. 541	60. 0	. 157
1900	64. 8	. 350	60. 0	. 225	60. 0	. 504	60. 0	. 146
1901	64. 8	. 336	60. 0	. 233	59. 5	. 475	60. 0	. 132
1902	65. 9	. 358	60. 0	. 248	60. 3	. 626	60. 0	. 162
1903	66. 2	. 418	60. 0	. 242	63. 8	. 688	72. 0	. 141
1904	61. 4	. 295	60. 0	. 228	64. 4	. 517	72. 0	. 266
1905	65. 6	. 298	60. 0	. 253	66. 7	. 488	72. 0	. 253
1906	64. 0	. 334	60. 9	. 253	67. 4	. 549	72. 0	. 265
1907	63. 9	. 348	60. 9	. 273	67. 4	. 532	72. 0	. 306

TABLE F–3.—*Catchers, males, bar mills, 1907–1926, by geographic division and year*

Year	Eastern		Pittsburgh		Great Lakes and Middle West		Southern	
	Hours per week	Rate per hour	Hours per week	Rate per hour	Hours per week	Rate per hour	Hours per week	Rate per hour
1907	61.6	$0.314	65.9	$0.478	55.4	$0.440		
1908	59.1	.301	66.2	.375	55.4	.456		
1909	59.1	.297	66.0	.428	55.4	.423		
1910	58.9	.326	62.2	.452	55.4	.465		
1911	58.5	.309	62.0	.417	55.4	.455		
1912	57.8	.332	61.3	.419	55.5	.568		
1913	56.5	.389	61.8	.438	56.0	.522	54.7	$0.429
1914	57.2	.398	62.2	.400	57.0	.484	54.8	.433
1915	57.2	.400	61.5	.426	58.3	.471	55.4	.402
1919	(1)	.797	(1)	.922	(1)	1.047	(1)	.741
1920	56.7	.840	62.8	.983	50.2	1.290	63.6	.858
1922	56.9	.606	57.6	.752	54.1	.805	64.3	.650
1924	55.2	.717	52.6	.822	56.2	.955	58.1	.714
1926	55.2	.711	51.9	.908	52.7	.962	56.7	.615

1 Not reported.

TABLE F–4.—*Rollers, bar mills, 1840–1899, by year and State*

Year and State	Sex	Lowest, highest, and average—		Year and State	Sex	Lowest, highest, and average—	
		Hours per week	Rate per day (dollars)			Hours per week	Rate per day (dollars)
1840:				1858:			
Pennsylvania___	M.	(1)	2.88- 2.88- 2.88	Pennsylvania___	M.	(1)	3.00- 3.00- 3.00
1841:				1859:			
Pennsylvania___	M.	(1)	2.88- 2.88- 2.88	Pennsylvania___	M.	(1)	3.00- 3.00- 3.00
1842:				1860:			
New York_____	M.	60-60-60	2.75- 2.75- 2.75	Pennsylvania___	M.	(1)	3.20- 3.20- 3.20
Pennsylvania___	M.	(1)	2.88- 2.88- 2.88	1861:			
1843:				Pennsylvania___	M.	(1)	3.20- 3.20- 3.20
New York_____	M.	60-60-60	2.00- 2.00- 2.00	1862:			
Pennsylvania___	M.	(1)	2.88- 2.88- 2.88	Pennsylvania___	M.	(1)	4.00- 4.00- 4.00
1844:				1863:			
New York_____	M.	60-60-60	2.00- 2.00- 2.00	Pennsylvania___	M.	(1)	4.40- 4.40- 4.40
Pennsylvania___	M.	(1)	2.88- 2.88- 2.88	1864:			
1845:				New York_____	M.	60-60-60	4.00- 4.00- 4.00
New York_____	M.	60-60-60	2.00- 2.00- 2.00	Pennsylvania___	M.	(1)	5.60- 5.60- 5.60
Pennsylvania___	M.	(1)	2.88- 2.88- 2.88	1865:			
1846:				New York_____	M.	60-60-60	4.00- 4.25- 4.14
New York_____	M.	60-60-60	2.00- 2.00- 2.00	Pennsylvania___	M.	(1)	4.40- 4.40- 4.40
Pennsylvania___	M.	(1)	2.88- 2.88- 2.88	1866:			
1847:				New York_____	M.	60-60-60	4.00- 5.00- 4.15
Pennsylvania___	M.	(1)	2.88- 2.88- 2.88	Pennsylvania___	M.	(1)	5.28- 5.28- 5.28
1848:				1867:			
New York_____	M.	60-60-60	2.00- 2.00- 2.00	New York_____	M.	60-60-60	4.00- 5.00- 4.23
Pennsylvania___	M.	(1)	2.88- 2.88- 2.88	Pennsylvania___	M.	(1)	4.95- 4.95- 4.95
1849:				68:			
New York_____	M.	60-60-60	2.00- 2.00- 2.00	New York_____	M.	60-60-60	4.00- 4.00- 4.00
Pennsylvania___	M.	(1)	2.88- 2.88- 2.88	18 Pennsylvania___	M.	(1)	5.67- 5.67- 5.67
1850:				1869:			
Pennsylvania___	M.	(1)	2.52- 2.52- 2.52	New York_____	M.	60-60-60	4.00- 4.00- 4.00
1851:				Pennsylvania___	M.	(1)	4.50- 4.50- 4.50
Pennsylvania___	M.	(1)	2.52- 2.52- 2.52	1870:			
1852:				Pennsylvania___	M.	(1)	4.50- 4.50- 4.50
Pennsylvania___	M.	(1)	2.52- 2.52- 2.52	1871:			
1853:				Massachusetts__	M.	60-60-60	2.25- 2.68- 2.35
New York_____	M.	60-60-60	2.00- 2.00- 2.00	New York_____	M.	60-60-60	4.50- 4.50- 4.50
Pennsylvania___	M.	(1)	3.20- 3.20- 3.20	Pennsylvania___	M.	(1)	4.50- 4.50- 4.50
1854:				1872:			
New York_____	M.	60-60-60	2.00- 2.00- 2.00	New York_____	M.	60-60-60	4.50- 4.50- 4.50
Pennsylvania___	M.	(1)	3.20- 3.20- 3.20	Ohio_____	M.	(1)	5.00-10.83- 7.11
1855:				Pennsylvania___	(1)	60-60-60	7.29- 7.29- 7.29
New York_____	M.	60-60-60	2.00- 2.00- 2.00	Do_____	M.	(1)	5.76- 5.76- 5.76
Pennsylvania___	M.	(1)	3.20- 3.20- 3.20	1873:			
1856:				New York_____	M.	60-60-60	4.50- 4.50- 4.50
Pennsylvania___	M.	(1)	3.48- 3.48- 3.48	Pennsylvania___	M.	(1)	4.50- 4.50- 4.50
1857:				1874:			
Pennsylvania___	M.	(1)	3.48- 3.48- 3.48	Pennsylvania___	M.	(1)	1.50- 7.33- 2.86

1 Not reported.

TABLE F-4.—*Rollers, bar mills, 1840–1899, by year and State*—Continued

Year and State	Sex	Lowest, highest, and average—		Year and State	Sex	Lowest, highest, and average—	
		Hours per week	Rate per day (dollars)			Hours per week	Rate per day (dollars)
1875:				**1888:**			
Pennsylvania___	M.	(¹)	1. 92– 4. 92– 3. 47	New Jersey_____	M.	(¹)	1. 67– 7. 67– 3. 78
1876:				Pennsylvania___	M.	(¹)	3. 71– 3. 71– 3. 71
Pennsylvania___	M.	(¹)	1. 40– 8. 80– 3. 53	Tennessee_____	M.	(¹)	5. 00– 6. 00– 5. 67
1877:				West Virginia___	M.	66–66–66	4. 47– 4. 47– 4. 47
Ohio_____	M.	65–72–68	1. 67– 8. 33– 5. 33	**1889:**			
Pennsylvania___	M.	(¹)	3. 60– 3. 60– 3. 60	Alabama_____	M.	60–60–60	5. 00–10. 00– 7. 04
1878:				Delaware_____	M.	60–60–60	1. 64– 2. 80– 2. 38
Ohio_____	M.	(¹)	2. 50– 8. 00– 4. 02	Illinois_____	M.	60–72–72	2. 50– 7. 00– 6. 05
Pennsylvania___	M.	48–72–61	1. 50– 7. 00– 4. 39	Indiana_____	M.	66–66–66	3. 13– 4. 86– 4. 00
1879:				Maryland_____	M.	60–60–60	1. 50– 2. 80– 2. 37
Ohio_____	M.	(¹)	2. 58–10. 00– 5. 14	New York_____	M.	60–60–60	2. 25– 7. 50– 5. 22
Pennsylvania___	M.	57–72–61	1. 20– 7. 00– 2. 81	Ohio_____	M.	44–70–56	4. 00–25. 83– 7. 20
1880:				Pennsylvania___	M.	50–66–60	1. 63–19. 23– 5. 13
Ohio_____	M.	(¹)	4. 17–10. 00– 6. 18	Tennessee_____	M.	(¹)	1. 50–10. 40– 4. 10
Pennsylvania___	M.	48–72–66	2. 85– 8. 00– 5. 07	Virginia_____	M.	55–55–55	12. 90–12. 90–12. 90
1881:				West Virginia___	M.	66–66–66	5. 29– 7. 67– 6. 01
New York_____	M.	60–60–60	4. 00– 5. 00– 4. 50	**1890:**			
Ohio_____	M.	42–60–57	4. 00–15. 00– 5. 88	Alabama_____	M.	55–60–56	4. 17– 5. 50– 4. 68
Pennsylvania___	M.	48–72–60	3. 00–10. 00– 6. 02	New York_____	M.	60–60–60	2. 50– 4. 50– 2. 68
1882:				Pennsylvania___	M.	(¹)	3. 96– 3. 96– 3. 96
New York_____	M.	60–60–60	5. 00– 5. 00– 5. 00	Wisconsin_____	M.	55–55–55	4. 25– 4. 25– 4. 25
Ohio_____	M.	53–66–60	4. 17– 6. 67– 5. 61	**1891:**			
Pennsylvania___	M.	42–72–56	3. 50– 7. 00– 4. 78	New York_____	M.	(¹)	1. 00– 5. 00– 2. 13
1883:				Pennsylvania___	M.	(¹)	3. 96– 3. 96– 3. 96
Michigan_____	M.	(¹)	3. 00– 4. 00– 3. 29	**1892:**			
New Jersey_____	M.	66–72–72	3. 00– 7. 00– 4. 31	Indiana_____	M.	48–60–56	3. 05– 5. 50– 4. 13
New York_____	M.	60–60–60	5. 00– 6. 50– 5. 75	Missouri_____	M.	48–48–48	7. 00–10. 50– 9. 36
Ohio_____	M.	54–72–61	3. 17– 6. 00– 4. 56	New York_____	M.	(¹)	6. 75– 6. 75– 6. 75
Pennsylvania___	M.	(¹)	3. 60– 3. 60– 3. 60	Ohio_____	(¹)	48–63–55	3. 50–30. 00– 9. 96
1884:				Pennsylvania___	M.	(¹)	3. 96– 3. 96– 3. 96
Illinois_____	M.	66–66–66	4. 00–10. 00– 8. 00	**1893:**			
New Jersey_____	M.	48–72–69	3. 17– 3. 65– 3. 24	New York_____	M.	(¹)	6. 75– 6. 75– 6. 75
Ohio_____	M.	(¹)	3. 25–12. 50– 6. 95	**1894:**			
Pennsylvania___	M.	(¹)	3. 15– 3. 15– 3. 15	Indiana_____	M.	48–51–50	6. 00– 9. 00– 7. 50
1885:				New York_____	M.	(¹)	6. 75– 6. 75– 6. 75
Delaware_____	M.	60–60–60	1. 50– 2. 75– 2. 29	West Virginia___	M.	54–54–54	1. 25– 1. 25– 1. 25
Illinois_____	M.	60–60–60	5. 30–11. 65– 7. 72	**1895:**			
Indiana_____	M.	60–60–60	4. 50–10. 00– 7. 17	New York_____	M.	60–60–60	1. 25– 6. 75– 4. 92
Kentucky_____	M.	60–60–60	3. 50– 9. 25– 7. 44	Ohio_____	M.	48–72–55	2. 00–13. 50– 7. 27
New Jersey_____	M.	54–72–65	. 83– 2. 00– 1. 32	Pennsylvania___	M.	60–60–60	1. 25– 1. 25– 1. 25
New York_____	M.	48–60–59	4. 40– 6. 00– 4. 94	**1896:**			
Ohio_____	M.	60–72–63	1. 54–12. 00– 6. 92	Illinois_____	M.	60–60–60	1. 75– 1. 75– 1. 75
Pennsylvania___	M.	48–60–55	3. 15–10. 00– 5. 53	Pennsylvania___	M.	60–72–69	2. 17– 5. 00– 4. 06
Virginia_____	M.	48–60–54	2. 30– 4. 50– 3. 64	**1897:**			
West Virginia___	M.	60–60–60	5. 00– 7. 00– 6. 00	Ohio_____	(¹)	48–72–54	. 80–25. 00– 8. 33
Wisconsin_____	M.	60–60–60	3. 66– 3. 66– 3. 66	Pennsylvania___	M.	(¹)	4. 37– 6. 32– 5. 37
1886:				**1898:**			
New Jersey_____	M.	60–60–60	1. 00– 1. 83– 1. 31	Ohio_____	M.	(¹)	3. 56–20. 84– 7. 43
New York_____	M.	60–60–60	4. 50– 4. 50– 4. 50	Pennsylvania___	M.	(¹)	. 90– 8. 50– 3. 86
Ohio_____	M.	(¹)	3. 02– 6. 01– 4. 20	**1899:**			
Pennsylvania__	M.	(¹)	3. 38– 3. 38– 3. 38	Ohio_____	M.	(¹)	4. 75–25. 00–10. 69
1887:				Pennsylvania___	M.	(¹)	. 95–15. 47– 2. 99
New York_____	M.	60–60–60	4. 50– 4. 50– 4. 50				
Ohio_____	M.	42–72–60	3. 00–33. 82– 6. 53				
Pennsylvania___	M.	(¹)	3. 00–21. 86– 7. 95				
Wisconsin_____	M.	(¹)	3. 00–10. 00– 9. 15				

TABLE **F–5.**—*Rollers, males, bar mills, 1890–1907, by geographic division and year*

Year	North Atlantic		South Atlantic		North Central		South Central	
	Hours per week	Rate per hour	Hours per week	Rate per hour	Hours per week	Rate per hour	Hours per week	Rate per hour
1890	64.4	$0.563	60.0	$0.720	72.0	$1.022	60.0	$0.519
1891	64.8	.554	60.0	.697	72.0	1.032	60.0	.589
1892	65.1	.531	60.0	.707	72.0	.900	60.0	.552
1893	64.6	.554	60.0	.627	72.0	.894	60.0	.378
1894	64.8	.528	60.0	.631	72.0	.793	60.0	.328
1895	64.4	.546	60.0	.568	72.0	.880	60.0	.325
1896	64.4	.539	60.0	.624	72.0	.933	60.0	.540
1897	64.4	.585	60.0	.562	57.6	1.050	60.0	.542
1898	64.4	.553	60.0	.536	57.6	1.084	60.0	.476
1899	64.4	.581	60.0	.540	57.6	1.429	60.0	.600
1900	64.4	.625	60.0	.655	64.0	1.127	60.0	.600
1901	64.4	.645	60.0	.663	64.0	1.192	60.0	.585
1902	64.8	.657	60.0	.653	64.0	1.441	60.0	.681
1903	64.8	.737	60.0	.654	64.0	1.423	60.0	.594
1904	62.2	.698	60.0	.560	70.3	1.063	72.0	.629
1905	63.6	.719	60.0	.668	71.7	.966	72.0	.806
1906	63.8	.704	61.3	.700	70.3	1.085	72.0	.940
1907	63.7	.773	61.3	.774	70.3	1.040	72.0	1.006

TABLE **F–6.**—*Rollers, males, bar mills, 1907–1926, by geographic division and year*

Year	Eastern		Pittsburgh		Great Lakes and Middle West		Southern	
	Hours per week	Rate per hour	Hours per week	Rate per hour	Hours per week	Rate per hour	Hours per week	Rate per hour
1907	60.7	$0.777	66.9	$1.097	65.6	$0.999		
1908	59.8	.776	67.3	.929	66.7	.853		
1909	59.8	.830	66.9	1.014	66.7	.799		
1910	58.6	.748	62.9	1.048	66.8	.785		
1911	58.4	.741	62.2	.937	65.8	.854		
1912	58.6	.772	61.3	.933	66.2	.803		
1913	57.4	.811	61.7	1.074	60.3	1.019	55.1	$1.006
1914	58.0	.823	61.7	.926	59.7	1.050	55.2	.945
1915	57.9	.836	60.9	.987	60.4	1.014	55.2	.876
1919	(¹)	1.375	(¹)	1.748	(¹)	2.077	(¹)	1.745
1920	56.6	1.566	61.0	1.912	57.7	2.433	62.7	1.941
1922	58.5	1.063	56.7	1.470	58.9	1.676	63.1	1.408
1924	56.5	1.347	51.4	1.681	54.1	1.673	57.9	1.474
1926	55.9	1.379	51.0	1.756	52.9	1.832	57.2	1.589

¹ Not reported.

TABLE **F-7.**—*Roughers, bar mills, 1843–1899, by year and State*

Year and State	Sex	Lowest, highest, and average— Hours per week	Lowest, highest, and average— Rate per day (dollars)
1843:			
New York	M.	60–60–60	1.38–1.50–1.40
1844:			
New York	M.	60–60–60	1.13–1.38–1.26
1845:			
New York	M.	60–60–60	1.50–1.50–1.50
1846:			
New York	M.	60–60–60	1.50–1.50–1.50
1847:			
New York	M.	60–60–60	1.50–1.50–1.50
1848:			
New York	M.	60–60–60	1.63–1.63–1.63
1849:			
New York	M.	60–60–60	1.63–1.63–1.63
1850:			
New York	M.	60–60–60	1.63–1.63–1.63
1851:			
New York	M.	60–60–60	1.63–1.63–1.63
1852:			
New York	M.	60–60–60	1.63–1.63–1.63
1853:			
New York	M.	60–60–60	1.50–1.63–1.56
1854:			
New York	M.	60–60–60	1.50–1.75–1.64
1855:			
New York	M.	60–60–60	1.38–1.75–1.61
1856:			
New York	M.	60–60–60	1.38–1.88–1.62
1857:			
New York	M.	60–60–60	1.50–1.88–1.65
1858:			
New York	M.	60–60–60	1.25–1.50–1.43
1859:			
New York	M.	60–60–60	1.25–1.63–1.45
1860:			
New York	M.	60–60–60	1.25–1.63–1.51
Ohio	M.	[1]	5.00–5.00–5.00
1861:			
New York	M.	60–60–60	1.25–1.63–1.52
1862:			
New York	M.	60–60–60	1.13–1.88–1.58
1863:			
New York	M.	60–60–60	1.50–2.50–1.91
1864:			
New York	M.	60–60–60	1.75–3.50–2.53
865:			
New York	M.	60–60–60	1.94–1.94–1.94
1866:			
New York	M.	60–60–60	1.25–3.50–2.89
1867:			
New York	M.	60–60–60	1.25–3.50–2.78
1868:			
New York	M.	60–60–60	3.00–3.38–3.19
1869:			
New York	M.	60–60–60	1.38–2.50–1.94
1870:			
New York	M.	60–60–60	1.38–3.75–2.21
1871:			
New York	M.	60–60–60	1.63–3.25–2.29
1872:			
New York	M.	60–60–60	1.85–2.75–2.24
Ohio	M.	[1]	7.50–7-50–7.50
1873:			
New York	M.	60–60–60	2.00–3.25–2.42
1874:			
New York	M.	60–60–60	1.88–1.88–1.88
Pennsylvania	M.	[1]	2.33–3.25–2.56
1875:			
New York	M.	60–60–60	2.20–2.20–2.20
Pennsylvania	M.	[1]	3.24–3.24–3.24
1876:			
New York	M.	60–60–60	1.75–2.20–1.90
Pennsylvania	M.	[1]	1.74–2.00–1.78
1877:			
New York	M.	60–60–60	1.75–1.75–1.75
1878:			
New York	M.	60–60–60	1.60–1.75–1.68
1879:			
Missouri	M.	60–60–60	1.75–1.75–1.75

Year and State	Sex	Lowest, highest, and average— Hours per week	Lowest, highest, and average— Rate per day (dollars)
1879—Continued.			
New York	M.	60–60–60	0.95–2.00–1.42
Ohio	M.	[1]	5.00–5.00–5.00
Pennsylvania	M.	54–72–62	1.30–4.59–2.83
1880:			
New York	M.	60–60–60	1.80–2.10–1.95
Pennsylvania	M.	66–66–66	2.70–3.50–2.97
1881:			
New York	M.	60–60–60	2.10–3.00–2.51
Ohio	M.	48–48–48	5.00–5.00–5.00
Pennsylvania	M.	66–66–66	2.70–3.00–2.85
1882:			
New York	M.	60–60–60	2.10–3.75–2.77
1883:			
Michigan	M.	[1]	1.00–3.00–2.44
New Jersey	M.	72–72–72	1.33–3.50–2.32
New York	M.	60–60–60	2.10–3.63–2.56
1884:			
New Jersey	M.	60–60–60	2.17–2.17–2.17
New York	M.	60–60–60	2.00–3.60–2.32
1885:			
Illinois	M.	60–60–60	3.50–3.50–3.50
Indiana	M.	60–60–60	3.75–3.75–3.75
Kentucky	M.	60–60–60	1.75–3.00–2.48
New York	M.	60–72–67	1.50–3.15–2.58
Ohio	M.	60–72–65	1.62–4.00–3.04
Pennsylvania	M.	48–60–52	2.50–4.00–3.56
Virginia	M.	48–60–53	1.60–2.50–1.96
1886:			
New Jersey	M.	60–60–60	1.67–2.92–2.25
New York	M.	60–60–60	1.50–2.50–1.82
Ohio	---	60–60–60	2.03–3.35–2.86
1887:			
Ohio	M.	54–72–60	2.25–5.00–2.95
Pennsylvania	M.	[1]	2.00–4.67–3.37
Rhode Island	M.	60–60–60	3.50–3.50–3.50
Wisconsin	M.	[1]	4.50–4.50–4.50
1888:			
New Jersey	M.	[1]	2.75–4.47–3.47
New York	M.	60–72–69	1.25–2.93–2.21
1889:			
Alabama	M.	54–54–54	1.04–2.67–1.68
Illinois	M.	72–72–72	2.18–5.04–3.58
Indiana	M.	66–72–69	1.75–3.69–2.47
Missouri	M.	[1]	1.65–1.98–1.82
New York	M.	60–60–60	1.25–3.05–2.49
Ohio	M.	44–72–56	2.00–4.81–3.12
Pennsylvania	M.	55–66–59	1.61–4.93–3.08
Tennessee	M.	[1]	2.00–2.50–2.11
Virginia	M.	55–55–55	4.00–4.00–4.00
West Virginia	M.	[1]	2.50–2.50–2.50
1890:			
Alabama	M.	55–60–56	2.75–3.67–3.17
1891:			
New York	M.	[1]	2.00–2.00–2.00
1892:			
Missouri	M.	48–48–48	1.67–2.75–2.64
New York	M.	[1]	1.80–2.93–2.55
Ohio	[1]	48–63–56	1.75–7.85–3.28
1893:			
New York	M.	[1]	180–2.93–2.55
1894:			
Indiana	M.	60–60–60	4.50–4.50–4.50
New York	M.	[1]	1.80–2.93–2.55
Ohio	M.	60–60–60	2.70–2.70–2.70
1895:			
New York	M.	[1]	1.80–2.93–2.65
Ohio	M.	48–72–57	1.40–5.75–2.93
1896:			
Pennsylvania	M.	60–72–70	2.50–3.00–2.93
1897:			
Ohio	[1]	48–72–55	.85–4.85–2.85
1898:			
Ohio	M.	[1]	1.75–4.75–3.41
Pennsylvania	M.	[1]	1.17–4.00–2.94
1899:			
Ohio	M.	[1]	2.34–6.00–4.10
Pennsylvania	M.	[1]	2.52–4.77–3.73

[1] Not reported.

TABLE **F–8.**—*Roughers, males, 1890–1907, by geographic division and year*

Year	North Atlantic		South Atlantic		North Central		South Central	
	Hours per week	Rate per hour	Hours per week	Rate per hour	Hours per week	Rate per hour	Hours per week	Rate per hour
1890	63.6	$0.309	60.0	$0.361	72.0	$0.475	60.0	$0.220
1891	63.7	.302	60.0	.335	72.0	.546	60.0	.245
1892	63.8	.313	60.0	.329	72.0	.454	60.0	.236
1893	64.1	.321	60.0	.315	72.0	.406	60.0	.193
1894	63.8	.294	60.0	.315	72.0	.418	60.0	.150
1895	63.7	.281	60.0	.302	72.0	.430	60.0	.140
1896	63.9	.288	60.0	.301	72.0	.412	60.0	.196
1897	63.8	.302	60.0	.279	56.0	.430	60.0	.217
1898	63.7	.283	60.0	.257	55.4	.390	60.0	.189
1899	63.7	.337	60.0	.273	55.4	.467	60.0	.256
1900	63.4	.342	60.0	.326	59.9	.516	60.0	.219
1901	63.7	.345	60.0	.317	60.1	.567	60.0	.216
1902	63.9	.367	60.0	.336	60.0	.646	60.0	.281
1903	63.2	.421	60.0	.308	63.7	.612	72.0	.207
1904	62.4	.329	60.0	.330	60.7	.519	72.0	.323
1905	65.7	.359	60.0	.355	61.5	.504	72.0	.347
1906	65.4	.385	61.1	.341	61.0	.518	72.0	.332
1907	65.3	.404	61.1	.379	61.4	.576	72.0	.352

TABLE **F–9.**—*Roughers, males, bar mills, 1907–1926, by geographic division and year*

Year	Eastern		Pittsburgh		Great Lakes and Middle West		Southern	
	Hours per week	Rate per hour	Hours per week	Rate per hour	Hours per week	Rate per hour	Hours per week	Rate per hour
1907	60.4	$0.316	66.4	$0.424	56.7	$0.487	----------	----------
1908	59.4	.301	67.0	.341	58.6	.365	----------	----------
1909	59.4	.337	66.7	.370	58.5	.379	----------	----------
1910	58.3	.356	62.7	.412	60.2	.422	----------	----------
1911	58.3	.358	61.9	.375	59.8	.393	----------	----------
1912	57.5	.384	61.1	.372	59.8	.435	----------	----------
1913	56.8	.410	62.5	.450	55.9	.516	55.9	$0.434
1914	57.6	.412	62.5	.413	56.7	.483	56.2	.427
1915	57.7	.409	61.8	.444	57.9	.468	56.2	.406
1919	(¹)	.846	(¹)	.947	(¹)	1.045	(¹)	.768
1920	56.9	.927	60.4	1.008	49.9	1,301	64.3	.852
1922	58.0	.628	56.1	.722	53.8	.830	61.8	.605
1924	55.7	.773	52.3	.824	55.2	.953	58.8	.669
1926	55.3	.783	52.8	.865	52.5	1.002	55.7	.639

¹ Not reported.

TABLE **F–10.**—*Puddlers, puddling mills, 1840–1899, by year and State*

Year and State	Sex	Lowest, highest, and average—		Year and State	Sex	Lowest, highest, and average—	
		Hours per week	Rate per day (dollars)			Hours per week	Rate per day (dollars)
1840: Pennsylvania	M.	(¹)	2.30–3.69–3.00	1845: Pennsylvania	M.	(¹)	2.30–3.69–3.00
1841: Pennsylvania	M.	(¹)	2.30–3.45–2.88	1846: Pennsylvania	M.	(¹)	2.30–3.69–3.00
1842: Pennsylvania	M.	(¹)	2.30–3.13–2.72	1847: Pennsylvania	M.	(¹)	2.30–3.69–3.00
1843: Pennsylvania	M.	(¹)	2.30–3.13–2.72	1848: Pennsylvania	M.	(¹)	2.30–3.69–3.00
1844: Pennsylvania	M.	(¹)	2.30–3.13–2.72	1849: Pennsylvania	M.	(¹)	2.30 3.69 3.00

¹ Not reported.

TABLE F–10.—*Puddlers, puddling mills, 1840–1899, by year and State*—Con.

Year and State	Sex	Hours per week	Rate per day (dollars)
1850:			
Pennsylvania	M.	(1)	2.01-3.00-2.51
1851:			
Pennsylvania	M.	(1)	2.01-3.00-2.51
1852:			
Pennsylvania	M.	(1)	1.73-3.00-2.37
1853:			
Pennsylvania	M.	(1)	2.59-3.00-2.80
1854:			
Pennsylvania	M.	(1)	2.59-3.00-2.80
1855:			
Pennsylvania	M.	(1)	2.59-2.67-2.63
1856:			
Pennsylvania	M.	(1)	2.67-2.88-2.78
1857:			
Pennsylvania	M.	(1)	2.67-2.88-2.78
1858:			
Pennsylvania	M.	(1)	2.01-2.33-2.17
1859:			
Pennsylvania	M.	(1)	2.01-2.67-2.34
1860:			
Pennsylvania	M.	(1)	2.01-2.67-2.34
1861:			
Pennsylvania	M.	(1)	2.01-2.67-2.34
1862:			
Pennsylvania	M.	(1)	2.30-3.00-2.65
1863:			
Pennsylvania	M.	(1)	3.79-4.00-3.90
1864:			
Pennsylvania	M.	(1)	5.17-5.33-5.25
1865:			
Pennsylvania	M.	(1)	3.83-4.14-3.99
1866:			
Pennsylvania	M.	(1)	4.83-5.37-5.10
1867:			
Pennsylvania	M.	(1)	4.14-5.37-4.76
1868:			
Pennsylvania	M.	(1)	4.36-4.83-4.60
1869:			
Pennsylvania	M.	(1)	4.14-4.81-4.48
1870:			
Pennsylvania	M.	(1)	4.14-4.50-4.32
1871:			
Massachusetts	M.	(1)	2.68-2.68-2.68
Pennsylvania	M.	(1)	4.14-4.66-4.40
1872:			
Ohio	M.	(1)	2.67-5.83-4.47
Pennsylvania	(1)	60-60-60	5.72-5.72-5.72
Do	M.	(1)	5.35-5.60-5.48
1873:			
Pennsylvania	M.	(1)	4.29-4.84-4.57
1874:			
Pennsylvania	M.	(1)	2.50-4.40-3.04
1875:			
Pennsylvania	M.	(1)	2.75-3.75-3.42
1876:			
Pennsylvania	M.	(1)	2.00-3.60-2.96
1877:			
Ohio	M.	55-62-59	2.33-5.00-4.11
Pennsylvania	M.	(1)	2.50-3.15-2.83
1878:			
Ohio	M.	60-65-63	2.50-4.50-3.06
Pennsylvania	M.	42-72-58	2.00-5.00-3.04
1879:			
Ohio	M.	(1)	3.00-4.70-3.41
Pennsylvania	M.	54-72-63	1.67-4.75-3.39
1880:			
New Jersey	(1)	55-58-57	2.50-3.40-2.95
Ohio	M.	(1)	2.50-6.00-3.75
Pennsylvania	M.	60-66-63	2.50-4.50-3.35
1881:			
Ohio	M.	40-72-56	3.00-6.13-3.91
Pennsylvania	M.	54-78-61	2.44-5.05-3.32
Tennessee	M.	75-75-75	6.00-6.25-6.13
1882:			
Missouri	M.	60-60-60	4.57-4.66-4.62
Ohio	M.	60-72-65	3.86-6.50-5.50
1882—Continued.			
Ohio	(1)	44-70-61	2.67-4.00-3.69
Pennsylvania	M.	55-66-59	2.80-4.83-3.06
1883:			
Illinois	M.	60-66-63	1.75-2.00-1.88
Indiana	M.	60-60-60	4.00-4.00-4.00
Michigan	M.	(1)	1.50-5.50-3.24
New Jersey	M.	72-72-72	3.35-5.00-4.09
Ohio	M.	53-66-57	3.25-4.00-3.33
Pennsylvania	M.	55-72-58	2.60-3.46-2.78
1884:			
Illinois	M.	(1)	4.33-4.33-4.33
New Jersey	M.	54-72-66	1.75-3.50-2.40
Ohio	M.	42-66-56	2.50-4.58-3.55
Pennsylvania	M.	60-60-60	2.50-3.46-2.55
1885:			
Delaware	M.	60-60-60	2.50-2.50-2.50
Illinois	M.	60-60-60	4.00-4.00-4.00
Indiana	M.	60-60-60	4.00-4.00-4.00
Kentucky	M.	60-60-60	2.00-3.75-3.08
New Jersey	M.	72-72-72	1.67-1.92-1.79
New York	M.	60-60-60	2.36-3.15-2.82
Ohio	M.	42-72-58	3.00-4.17-3.64
Pennsylvania	M.	55-60-60	2.30-3.62-3.22
Virginia	M.	48-60-58	2.35-2.40-2.36
West Virginia	M.	60-60-60	2.75-2.75-2.75
1886:			
Illinois	M.	54-54-54	6.00-6.00-6.00
Missouri	M.	48-48-48	2.75-2.75-2.75
New Jersey	M.	60-60-60	1.75-2.50-1.99
Pennsylvania	M.	60-72-61	2.40-3.34-2.76
Virginia	M.	60-60-60	2.50-2.50-2.50
Wisconsin	M.	66-66-66	4.00-4.00-4.00
1887:			
Ohio	M.	48-72-59	2.00-5.50-3.88
Pennsylvania	M.	60-60-60	2.91-4.00-3.50
Wisconsin	M.	(1)	4.25-4.25-4.25
1888:			
New Jersey	M.	60-72-66	2.27-3.00-2.81
New York	M.	54-54-54	2.66-2.66-2.66
Ohio	M.	(1)	2.00-5.50-3.75
Pennsylvania	M.	(1)	2.73-3.67-3.20
Tennessee	M.	(1)	3.00-3.00-3.00
1889:			
Alabama	M.	48-48-48	3.60-3.60-3.60
Delaware	M.	60-66-64	2.44-2.44-2.44
Illinois	M.	60-72-70	3.21-4.75-3.73
Indiana	M.	66-72-68	3.67-4.00-3.77
Maryland	M.	60-60-60	2.57-2.57-2.57
New York	M.	60-60-60	2.70-6.09-3.92
Ohio	M.	44-66-56	3.88-7.30-4.57
Pennsylvania	M.	50-66-59	2.16-5.68-3.19
Virginia	M.	55-55-55	1.01-2.41-1.78
West Virginia	M.	(1)	2.76-3.84-3.09
1890:			
Alabama	M.	55-55-55	3.67-3.67-3.67
Pennsylvania	M.	(1)	2.91-3.67-3.29
Wisconsin	M.	55-55-55	4.50-4.50-4.50
1891:			
New York	M.	(1)	3.50-3.50-3.50
Pennsylvania	M.	(1)	2.91-3.67-3.29
1892:			
Indiana	M.	48-60-57	2.90-3.13-3.02
Pennsylvania	M.	(1)	2.55-3.67-3.11
1893:			
Ohio	M.	60-60-60	3.70-4.00-3.83
1894:			
Indiana	M.	48-72-60	3.25-4.00-3.63
1895:			
Wisconsin	(1)	66-72-69	3.00-3.03-3.02
1896:			
Pennsylvania	M.	72-72-72	4.50-4.50-4.50
1898:			
Ohio	M.	(1)	1.92-5.18-3.30
Pennsylvania	M.	(1)	2.51-5.50-2.92
1899:			
Ohio	M.	(1)	2.30-5.75-4.26
Pennsylvania	M.	(1)	2.75-6.00-3.50

[1] Not reported.

TABLE **F–11.**—*Puddlers, males, puddling mills, muck bar, 1890–1903, by geographic division and year*

Year	North Atlantic		South Atlantic		North Central		South Central	
	Hours per week	Rate per hour	Hours per week	Rate per hour	Hours per week	Rate per hour	Hours per week	Rate per hour
1890	57.8	$0.386	57.0	$0.344	54.0	$0.521	60.0	$0.263
1891	57.8	.378	56.5	.346	54.0	.528	60.0	.249
1892	56.7	.379	57.0	.343	54.0	.523	60.0	.242
1893	57.7	.417	56.2	.323	54.0	.475	60.0	.260
1894	59.9	.351	56.5	.280	54.0	.357	60.0	.208
1895	59.6	.357	55.4	.295	54.0	.378	60.0	.229
1896	55.4	.358	55.7	.312	54.0	.400	60.0	.219
1897	58.2	.365	55.5	.288	54.0	.356	60.0	.233
1898	59.3	.366	55.5	.292	54.0	.327	60.0	.210
1899	58.6	.350	54.4	.378	54.0	.453	60.0	.226
1900	58.6	.327	56.4	.318	69.7	.414	60.0	.245
1901	57.8	.340	55.5	.304	69.7	.361	54.8	.344
1902	57.9	.357	55.7	.329	69.7	.378	54.8	.387
1903	57.9	.374	56.6	.347	69.7	.425	56.2	.308

TABLE **F–12.**—*Puddlers, males, puddling mills, 1914–1926, by geographic division and year*

Year	Eastern		Pittsburgh		Great Lakes and Middle West		Southern		United States	
	Hours per week	Rate per hour	Hours per week	Rate per hour	Hours per week	Rate per hour	Hours per week	Rate per hour	Hours per week	Rate per hour
1914	55.2	$0.406	51.4	$0.514	54.5	$0.515	57.7	$0.316		
1915	52.3	.367	51.7	.527	54.5	.488	57.9	.283		
1919	(1)	1.146	(1)	1.444	(1)	1.217	(1)	1.018		
1920	48.2	1.282	51.8	1.588			58.0	1.228		
1922	49.9	.651	46.8	.795			43.4	.888		
1924	53.0	.904	47.9	1.230			53.1	.889		
1926									53.5	$0.767

[1] Not reported.

TABLE **F–13.**—*Furnace keepers, pig-iron blast furnaces, 1840–1900, by year and State*

Year and State	Sex	Lowest, highest, and average—		Year and State	Sex	Lowest, highest, and average—	
		Hours per week	Rate per day (dollars)			Hours per week	Rate per day (dollars)
1840:				1849:			
Pennsylvania	M.	(1)	1.00–1.00–1.00	Pennsylvania	M.	(1)	1.40–1.40–1.40
1841:				1850:			
Pennsylvania	M.	(1)	1.00–1.00–1.00	Pennsylvania	M.	(1)	1.65–1.65–1.65
1842:				1851:			
Pennsylvania	M.	(1)	1.00–1.00–1.00	Pennsylvania	M.	(1)	1.69–1.69–1.69
1843:				1852:			
Pennsylvania	M.	(1)	1.00–1.00–1.00	Pennsylvania	M.	(1)	1.53–1.53–1.53
1844:				1853:			
Pennsylvania	M.	(1)	1.21–1.21–1.21	Pennsylvania	M.	(1)	1.63–1.63–1.63
1845:				1854:			
Pennsylvania	M.	(1)	1.41–1.41–1.41	Pennsylvania	M.	(1)	1.63–1.63–1.63
1846:				1855:			
Pennsylvania	M.	(1)	1.42–1.42–1.42	Pennsylvania	M.	(1)	1.92–1.92–1.92
1847:				1856:			
Pennsylvania	M.	(1)	1.70–1.70–1.70	Pennsylvania	M.	72–72–72	.72–1.94–1.13
1848:				1857:			
Pennsylvania	M.	(1)	1.67–1.67–1.67	Pennsylvania	M.	(1)	1.94–1.94–1.94

[1] Not reported.

TABLE **F-13.**—*Furnace keepers, pig-iron blast furnaces, 1840–1900, by year and State*—Continued

Year and State	Sex	Lowest, highest, and average—		Year and State	Sex	Lowest, highest, and average—	
		Hours per week	Rate per day (dollars)			Hours per week	Rate per day (dollars)
1858:				**1885:**			
Pennsylvania	M.	(¹)	1. 70–1. 70–1. 70	Indiana	M.	70–70–70	1. 85–1. 85–1. 85
1859:				Maryland	M.	84–84–84	1. 50–1. 50–1. 50
Pennsylvania	M.	(¹)	1. 67–1. 67–1. 67	New York	M.	84–84–84	1. 67–1. 85–1. 79
1860:				Ohio	M.	72–84–84	1. 35–2. 00–1. 64
Pennsylvania	M.	(¹)	1. 85–1. 85–1. 85	Pennsylvania	M.	84–84–84	1. 80–2. 25–2. 02
1861:				Tennessee	M.	84–84–84	1. 80–1. 80–1. 80
Pennsylvania	M.	(¹)	1. 90–1. 90–1. 90	Virginia	M.	84–84–84	1. 50–2. 30–1. 93
1862:				**1886:**			
Pennsylvania	M.	(¹)	1. 68–1. 68–1. 68	Pennsylvania	M.	(¹)	2. 05–2. 05–2. 05
1863:				**1887:**			
Pennsylvania	M.	(¹)	1. 90–1. 90–1. 90	Ohio	M.	70–84–74	1. 40–2. 25–1. 91
1864:				Pennsylvania	M.	84–84–84	2. 10–2. 25–2. 18
Pennsylvania	M.	(¹)	2. 70–2. 70–2. 70	Wisconsin	M.	(¹)	3. 10–3. 10–3. 10
1865:				**1888:**			
Pennsylvania	M.	(¹)	2. 49–2. 49–2. 49	Illinois	M.	84–84–84	3. 25–3. 25–3. 25
1866:				Michigan	M.	84–84–84	1. 80–2. 00–1. 90
Pennsylvania	M.	(¹)	2. 41–2. 41–2. 41	New York	M.	70–84–75	1. 88–2. 15–1. 98
1867:				Ohio	M.	84–84–84	2. 40–2. 40–2. 40
Pennsylvania	M.	(¹)	2. 53–2. 53–2. 53	Pennsylvania	M.	84–84–84	1. 85–2. 25–2. 04
1868:				Tennessee	M.	(¹)	1. 85–1. 85–1. 85
Pennsylvania	M.	(¹)	2. 53–2. 53–2. 53	Virginia	M.	84–84–84	1. 40–2. 00–1. 67
1869:				West Virginia	M.	84–84–84	2. 40–2. 40–2. 40
Pennsylvania	M.	(¹)	2. 77–2. 77–2. 77	**1889:**			
1870:				Alabama	M.	84–84–84	1. 25–2. 00–1. 89
Pennsylvania	M.	(¹)	2. 77–2. 77–2. 77	Georgia	M.	84–84–84	1. 65–1. 65–1. 65
1871:				Illinois	M.	84–84–84	3. 10–3. 25–3. 21
Pennsylvania	M.	(¹)	2. 78–2. 78–2. 78	Indiana	M.	84–84–84	1. 70–1. 70–1. 70
1872:				Maryland	M.	72–72–72	1. 58–1. 58–1. 58
Pennsylvania	M.	(¹)	3. 15–3. 15–3. 15	Michigan	M.	84–84–84	2. 00–2. 00–2. 00
1873:				Missouri	M.	84–84–84	1. 70–1. 70–1. 70
Pennsylvania	M.	(¹)	2. 58–3. 27–2. 81	New York	M.	84–84–84	1. 85–2. 15–1. 98
1874:				Ohio	M.	84–84–84	1. 80–2. 50–2. 07
Pennsylvania	M.	(¹)	1. 25–4. 00–1. 94	Pennsylvania	M.	56–84–83	1. 08–3. 00–1. 91
1875:				Tennessee	M.	77–84–82	1. 75–2. 00–1. 89
Pennsylvania	M.	(¹)	1. 60–1. 94–1. 71	Virginia	M.	84–84–84	1. 50–2. 00–1. 83
1876:				West Virginia	M.	84–84–84	1. 65–2. 40–2. 01
Pennsylvania	M.	(¹)	. 85–2. 37–1. 67	**1890:**			
1877:				Alabama	M.	84–84–84	2. 00–2. 00–2. 00
Ohio	M.	60–84–77	. 86–1. 90–1. 32	New York	M.	(¹)	2. 00–2. 00–2. 00
Pennsylvania	M.	(¹)	1. 56–1. 56–1. 56	Ohio	M.	72–84–76	1. 00–2. 30–1. 43
1878:				Pennsylvania	M.	84–84–84	1. 90–2. 25–2. 02
Ohio	M.	(¹)	. 86–1. 75–1. 37	Wisconsin	M.	84–84–84	3. 00–3. 00–3. 00
Pennsylvania	M.	67–84–82	. 79–2. 25–1. 36	**1891:**			
1879:				New York	M.	(¹)	1. 75–2. 20–1. 93
Ohio	M.	(¹)	. 86–2. 80–1. 51	Pennsylvania	M.	(¹)	2. 00–2. 00–2. 00
Pennsylvania	M.	84–84–84	. 79–2. 50–1. 59	**1892:**			
Do	M.	(¹)	². 66– . 66– . 66	Ohio	M.	58–84–72	1. 00–3. 00–1. 69
1880:				Pennsylvania	M.	(¹)	2. 25–2. 25–2. 25
Ohio	M.	60–84–78	1. 07–2. 50–1. 63	**1893:**			
Pennsylvania	M.	84–84–84	1. 30–1. 78–1. 62	New Jersey	M.	84–84–84	1. 75–1. 75–1. 75
1881:				**1895:**			
Ohio	M.	70–84–77	1. 00–2. 65–1. 65	Ohio	M.	84–84–84	. 75–2. 25–1. 70
Pennsylvania	M.	84–84–84	1. 78–1. 90–1. 84	**1896:**			
1882:				Pennsylvania	M.	84–84–84	1. 68–1. 69–1. 69
Pennsylvania	M.	84–84–84	1. 90–2. 00–1. 95	**1897:**			
1883:				Ohio	(¹)	84–84–84	. 75–2. 20–1. 50
Pennsylvania	M	(¹)	2. 25–2. 25–2. 25	Pennsylvania	M.	(¹)	2. 00–2. 10–2. 06
1884:				**1898:**			
Michigan	M.	(¹)	1. 85–1. 85–1. 85	Pennsylvania	M.	(¹)	2. 10–2. 20–2. 17
New Jersey	M.	70–84–80	1. 59–2. 53–1. 82	**1899:**			
Ohio	M.	(¹)	1. 00–2. 25–1. 64	Alabama	M.	84–84–84	1. 75–1. 85–1. 82
Pennsylvania	M.	(¹)	2. 25–2. 25–2. 25	Pennsylvania	M.	(¹)	2. 40–2. 50–2. 47
				1900:			
				Alabama	M.	84–84–84	1. 80–1. 85–1. 83

¹ Not reported.　　　　　　　　² And rent.

TABLE F-14.—*Keepers, males, blast furnaces, 1890–1907, by geographic division and year*

Year	North Atlantic		South Atlantic		North Central		South Central	
	Hours per week	Rate per hour	Hours per week	Rate per hour	Hours per week	Rate per hour	Hours per week	Rate per hour
1890	84.0	$0.182	84.0	$0.180	84.0	$0.220	84.0	$0.159
1891	84.0	.178	84.0	.180	84.0	.238	84.0	.156
1892	84.0	.175	84.0	.180	84.0	.247	84.0	.150
1893	84.0	.165	84.0	.176	84.0	.246	84.0	.147
1894	84.0	.163	84.0	.208	84.0	.173	84.0	.133
1895	84.0	.155	84.0	.208	84.0	.215	84.0	.130
1896	84.0	.159	84.0	.179	84.0	.215	84.0	.134
1897	84.0	.155	84.0	.153	84.0	.183	84.0	.130
1898	84.0	.155	84.0	.160	84.0	.187	84.0	.130
1899	84.0	.168	84.0	.170	84.0	.208	84.0	.132
1900	84.0	.180	84.0	.174	84.0	.209	84.0	.141
1901	84.0	.178	84.0	.177	84.0	.215	84.0	.141
1902	84.0	.191	84.0	.175	84.0	.219	84.0	.144
1903	84.0	.192	84.0	.183	84.0	.221	84.0	.148
1904	84.0	.190	84.0	.170	84.0	.201	84.0	.155
1905	84.0	.201	84.0	.184	84.0	.210	84.0	.158
1906	84.0	.202	84.0	.184	84.0	.213	84.0	.166
1907	84.0	.214	84.0	.187	84.0	.223	84.0	.166

TABLE F-15.—*Keepers, males, blast furnaces, 1907–1926, by geographic division and year*

Year	Eastern		Pittsburgh		Great Lakes and Middle West		Southern	
	Hours per week	Rate per hour	Hours per week	Rate per hour	Hours per week	Rate per hour	Hours per week	Rate per hour
1907	84.0	$0.173	84.0	$0.231	84.0	$0.235	84.0	$0.170
1908	84.0	.161	84.0	.230	84.0	.224	84.0	.161
1909	84.0	.150	84.0	.219	84.0	.225	84.0	.150
1910	84.0	.177	84.0	.236	84.0	.229	84.0	.171
1911	81.6	.174	84.0	.236	80.3	.231	84.0	.169
1912	81.6	.179	78.5	.248	79.1	.231	82.1	.170
1913	82.2	.196	84.0	.259	79.1	.247	82.7	.181
1914	81.8	.199	78.9	.259	77.1	.245	84.0	.177
1915	82.5	.195	78.8	.258	76.3	.246	84.0	.172
1919	(1)	.487	(1)	.605	(1)	.572	(1)	.389
1920	84.0	.526	77.3	.684	66.3	.662	78.3	.462
1922	83.5	.404	75.6	.457	71.7	.446	76.0	.318
1924	62.7	.530	54.7	.647	55.3	.619	62.4	.405
1926	63.0	.519	55.5	.632	55.4	.622	62.5	.412

1 Not reported.

Table F-16.—*Fillers, pig iron, blast furnaces, 1840–1900, by year and State*

| Year and State | Sex | Lowest, highest, and average— | | Year and State | Sex | Lowest, highest, and average— | |
		Hours per week	Rate per day (dollars)			Hours per week	Rate per day (dollars)
1840:				**1878:**			
Pennsylvania	M.	(¹)	0.65–0.65–0.65	Ohio	M.	(¹)	0.86–1.50–1.18
1841:				Pennsylvania	M.	67–84–83	.60–2.00–1.14
Pennsylvania	M.	(¹)	.65–.65–.65	**1879:**			
1842:				Ohio	M.	(¹)	.77–1.70–1.37
Pennsylvania	M.	(¹)	.65–.65–.65	Pennsylvania	M.	(¹)	.72–2.00–1.38
1843:				Do	M.	(¹)	².66–.66–.66
Pennsylvania	M.	(¹)	.65–.65–.65	**1880:**			
1844:				Ohio	M.	60–84–81	0.86–1.82–1.46
Pennsylvania	M.	(¹)	.85–.85–.85	Pennsylvania	M.	(¹)	1.56–1.56–1.56
1845:				**1881:**			
Pennsylvania	M.	(¹)	1.01–1.01–1.01	Ohio	M.	70–84–78	.86–1.75–1.49
1846:				Pennsylvania	M.	(¹)	1.56–1.56–1.56
Pennsylvania	M.	(¹)	.99–.99–.99	**1882:**			
1847:				New Jersey	M.	84–84–84	1.65–1.75–1.69
Pennsylvania	M.	(¹)	1.13–1.13–1.13	Pennsylvania	M.	84–84–84	1.71–1.75–1.74
1848:				**1883:**			
Pennsylvania	M.	(¹)	1.12–1.12–1.12	New Jersey	M.	(¹)	1.29–1.72–1.49
1849:				Pennsylvania	M.	(¹)	1.88–1.88–1.88
Pennsylvania	M.	(¹)	1.02–1.02–1.02	**1884:**			
1850:				New Jersey	M.	70–84–81	1.35–1.58–1.48
Pennsylvania	M.	(¹)	1.07–1.07–1.07	Ohio	M.	48–84–59	.81–1.70–1.45
1851:				Pennsylvania	M.	(¹)	1.88–1.88–1.88
Pennsylvania	M.	(¹)	1.09–1.09–1.09	**1885:**			
1852:				Indiana	M.	70–70–70	1.35–1.35–1.35
Pennsylvania	M.	(¹)	1.05–1.05–1.05	Maryland	M.	84–84–84	1.25–1.50–1.35
1853:				Ohio	M.	48–84–64	.73–1.46–1.30
Pennsylvania	M.	(¹)	1.16–1.16–1.16	Pennsylvania	M.	84–84–84	1.65–1.71–1.65
1854:				Virginia	M.	84–84–84	1.10–1.10–1.10
Pennsylvania	M.	(¹)	1.16–1.16–1.16	**1886:**			
1855:				Pennsylvania	M.	(¹)	1.71–1.71–1.71
Pennsylvania	M.	(¹)	1.32–1.32–1.32	**1887:**			
1856:				Ohio	M.	70–70–70	1.40–1.40–1.40
Pennsylvania	M.	(¹)	1.36–1.36–1.36	Pennsylvania	M.	(¹)	1.88–1.88–1.88
1857:				**1888:**			
Pennsylvania	M.	(¹)	1.36–1.36–1.36	New York	M.	77–77–77	1.50–1.50–1.50
1858:				Ohio	M.	84–84–84	1.65–1.65–1.65
Pennsylvania	M.	(¹)	1.30–1.30–1.30	Pennsylvania	M.	84–84–84	1.50–1.75–1.61
1859:				Tennessee	M.	(¹)	1.00–1.20–1.18
Pennsylvania	M.	(¹)	1.25–1.25–1.25	Virginia	M.	84–84–84	1.00–1.30–1.20
1860:				West Virginia	M.	84–84–84	1.65–1.65–1.65
Pennsylvania	M.	(¹)	1.37–1.37–1.37	**1889:**			
1861:				Alabama	M.	70–84–84	1.10–1.70–1.23
Pennsylvania	M.	(¹)	1.44–1.44–1.44	Georgia	M.	84–84–84	1.10–1.25–1.18
1862:				Illinois	M.	70–70–70	2.10–2.10–2.10
Pennsylvania	M.	(¹)	1.25–1.25–1.25	Maryland	M.	72–72–72	1.35–1.35–1.35
1863:				Missouri	M.	84–84–84	1.50–1.50–1.50
Pennsylvania	M.	(¹)	1.38–1.38–1.38	New York	M.	70–84–74	1.29–1.70–1.43
1864:				Ohio	M.	56–84–80	1.35–2.00–1.58
Pennsylvania	M.	(¹)	2.10–2.10–2.10	Pennsylvania	M.	56–84–80	1.08–1.88–1.48
1865:				Tennessee	M.	84–84–84	1.20–1.30–1.23
Pennsylvania	M.	(¹)	1.93–1.93–1.93	West Virginia	M.	70–84–76	1.40–1.65–1.64
1866:				**1890:**			
Pennsylvania	M.	(¹)	1.95–1.95–1.95	Alabama	M.	84–84–84	1.10–1.10–1.10
1867:				New York	M.	(¹)	1.75–1.75–1.75
Pennsylvania	M.	(¹)	2.05–2.05–2.05	Ohio	M.	72–84–83	1.00–1.70–1.58
1868:				Pennsylvania	M.	84–84–84	1.65–1.88–1.67
Pennsylvania	M.	(¹)	2.05–2.05–2.05	Wisconsin	M.	84–84–84	1.92–1.92–1.92
1869:				**1891:**			
Pennsylvania	M.	(¹)	2.25–2.25–2.25	New York	M.	(¹)	1.50–1.75–1.55
1870:				Pennsylvania	M.	(¹)	1.70–1.70–1.70
Pennsylvania	M.	(¹)	2.25–2.25–2.25	**1892:**			
1871:				Pennsylvania	M.	(¹)	1.88–1.88–1.88
Pennsylvania	M.	(¹)	2.25–2.25–2.25	**1896:**			
1872:				Pennsylvania	M.	70–84–74	1.10–1.38–1.22
Pennsylvania	M.	(¹)	2.56–2.56–2.56	**1897:**			
1873:				Pennsylvania	M.	(¹)	1.50–1.50–1.50
Pennsylvania	M.	(¹)	2.40–2.66–2.43	**1898:**			
1874:				Pennsylvania	M.	(¹)	1.65–1.65–1.65
Pennsylvania	M.	(¹)	1.10–1.79–1.49	**1899:**			
1875:				Alabama	M.	84–84–84	1.15–1.20–1.19
Pennsylvania	M.	(¹)	1.35–1.70–1.40	Pennsylvania	M.	(¹)	1.90–1.90–1.90
1876:				**1900:**			
Pennsylvania	M.	(¹)	.79–1.87–1.37	Alabama	M.	84–84–84	1.20–1.25–1.21
1877:							
Ohio	M.	60–84–80	.77–1.60–1.22				
Pennsylvania	M.	(¹)	1.37–1.37–1.37				

¹ Not reported.　　　　² And rent.

TABLE F-17.—*Top fillers, males, blast furnaces, 1890–1907, by geographic division and year*

Year	North Atlantic		South Atlantic		North Central		South Central	
	Hours per week	Rate per hour	Hours per week	Rate per hour	Hours per week	Rate per hour	Hours per week	Rate per hour
1890	84.0	$0.133	84.0	$0.149	84.0	$0.173	84.0	$0.133
1891	84.0	.143	84.0	.143	84.0	.178	84.0	.127
1892	84.0	.132	84.0	.155	84.0	.181	84.0	.127
1893	84.0	.128	84.0	.145	84.0	.180	84.0	.124
1894	84.0	.125	84.0	.204	84.0	.139	84.0	.112
1895	84.0	.124	84.0	.204	84.0	.144	84.0	.110
1896	84.0	.127	84.0	.151	84.0	.157	84.0	.118
1897	84.0	.123	84.0	.134	84.0	.154	84.0	.109
1898	84.0	.120	84.0	.142	84.0	.156	84.0	.105
1899	84.0	.135	84.0	.145	84.0	.174	84.0	.115
1900	84.0	.145	84.0	.145	84.0	.176	84.0	.123
1901	84.0	.140	84.0	.160	84.0	.178	84.0	.124
1902	84.0	.148	84.0	.154	84.0	.182	84.0	.129
1903	84.0	.148	84.0	.145	71.5	.232	84.0	.131
1904	84.0	.144	84.0	.135	72.0	.212	84.0	.142
1905	82.0	.164	84.0	.135	81.3	.190	84.0	.146
1906	82.0	.164	84.0	.133	79.5	.200	84.0	.158
1907	82.0	.176	84.0	.154	79.5	.210	84.0	.159

TABLE F-18.—*Top fillers, males, blast furnaces, 1907–1926, by geographic division and year*

Year	Eastern		Pittsburgh		Great Lakes and Middle West		Southern	
	Hours per week	Rate per hour	Hours per week	Rate per hour	Hours per week	Rate per hour	Hours per week	Rate per hour
1907	84.0	$0.155	84.0	$0.217	84.0	$0.212	84.0	$0.152
1908	84.0	.136	84.0	.206	84.0	.193	84.0	.154
1909	84.0	.136	84.0	.206	84.0	.203	84.0	.138
1910	84.0	.158	84.0	.217	74.7	.240	84.0	.150
1911	84.0	.153	84.0	.217	75.6	.227	84.0	.147
1912	84.0	.154	84.0	.217	78.4	.218	79.1	.147
1913	84.0	.189	84.0	.227	78.4	.238	80.8	.164
1914	84.0	.200	84.0	.238	70.5	.251	84.0	.162
1915	84.0	.200	84.0	.238	70.5	.251	84.0	.161
1919					(¹)	.644	(¹)	.336
1920					62.7	.859	78.9	.388
1922					60.0	.549	76.1	.288
1924					55.2	.766	57.7	.424
1926					53.0	.643	54.0	.474

¹ Not reported.

TABLE **F–19.**—*Bottom fillers, males, blast furnaces, 1907–1926, by geographic division and year*

Year	Eastern		Pittsburgh		Great Lakes and Middle West		Southern	
	Hours per week	Rate per hour	Hours per week	Rate per hour	Hours per week	Rate per hour	Hours per week	Rate per hour
1907	84.0	$0.141	84.0	$0.182	84.0	$0.186	84.0	$0.142
1908	84.0	.127	84.0	.173	84.0	.167	84.0	.143
1909	84.0	.128	84.0	.172	84.0	.177	84.0	.114
1910	84.0	.143	84.0	.186	84.0	.182	84.0	.133
1911	84.0	.136	84.0	.186	84.0	.175	84.0	.133
1912	84.0	.142	84.0	.186	84.0	.178	77.6	.131
1913	84.0	.164	84.0	.208	84.0	.196	78.2	.144
1914	84.0	.171	84.0	.210	80.9	.192	84.0	.139
1915	84.0	.172	84.0	.210	79.4	.190	84.0	.137
1919					(1)	.487	(1)	.340
1920					61.7	.691	78.7	.423
1922					70.2	.417	75.2	.266
1924					55.3	.594	53.6	.414
1926					53.0	.584	53.6	.412

1 Not reported.

TABLE **F–20.**—*Skip operators, males, blast furnaces, 1907–1926, by geographic division and year*

Year	Eastern		Pittsburgh		Great Lakes and Middle West		Southern	
	Hours per week	Rate per hour	Hours per week	Rate per hour	Hours per week	Rate per hour	Hours per week	Rate per hour
1907			84.0	$0.192	84.0	$0.219	84.0	$0.152
1908			84.0	.191	84.0	.204	84.0	.140
1909			84.0	.184	84.0	.202	84.0	.155
1910	84.0	$0.167	84.0	.207	84.0	.204	84.0	.161
1911	78.0	.173	84.0	.205	84.0	.208	84.0	.160
1912	78.0	.186	77.4	.217	81.2	.214	84.0	.161
1913	79.2	.196	84.0	.227	81.1	.225	84.0	.170
1914	80.0	.194	78.4	.230	78.2	.224	84.0	.169
1915	81.6	.196	78.7	.231	76.8	.224	84.0	.169
1919	(1)	.468	(1)	.565	(1)	.558	(1)	.379
1920	84.0	.511	77.2	.620	63.2	.663	78.5	.456
1922	83.5	.387	76.0	.419	71.5	.423	76.0	.328
1924	62.7	.513	54.9	.580	55.1	.589	65.6	.392
1926	63.6	.506	55.8	.583	55.4	.605	68.3	.356

1 Not reported.

G.—LABORERS

The source from which these wage data were taken is the Fifteenth Annual Report of the Commissioner of Labor Statistics. This report covers the period from 1840 to 1900. No information is available as to the nature of the work on which these employees were engaged. Wage data for other laborers are also reported in the building, the metal, and the woodworking trades groups, Tables B–12, I–16, I–17, I–18, O–11, and O–12, and as "farm laborers" Tables D–1, D–2, and D–3

TABLE G–1.—*Laborers, 1840–1900, by year and State*

Year and State	Sex	Lowest, highest, and average—		Year and State	Sex	Lowest, highest, and average—	
		Hours per week	Rate per day (dollars)			Hours per week	Rate per day (dollars)
1840:				**1850:**			
Massachusetts....	M.	78–84–81	0.75–1.00–0.91	Connecticut........	M.	60–60–60	0.96–.96–0.96
New York........	M.	60–60–60	.75–1.25– .95	Massachusetts....	M.	60–84–67	.75–1.33– .90
Ohio.............	M.	60–60–60	.30– .60– .56	New Hampshire..	M.	60–60–60	.80–1.00– .90
Pennsylvania.....	M.	(¹)	1.00–1.00–1.00	New Jersey........	M.	60–60–60	.75– .75– .75
1841:				New York........	M.	60–60–60	.63–1.25– .92
Massachusetts....	M.	78–84–80	.87–1.00– .96	Ohio.............	M.	60–60–60	.88– .88– .88
New York........	M.	60–60–60	.69–1.25– .99	Pennsylvania.....	M.	60–60–60	.80–1.00– .95
1842:				**1851:**			
Massachusetts....	M.	78–84–83	.75–1.00– .86	Connecticut........	M.	60–60–60	.96– .96– .96
New York........	M.	60–72–61	.50–1.25– .89	Maryland.........	M.	60–60–60	1.00–1.00–1.00
Pennsylvania.....	M.	(¹)	1.00–1.00–1.00	Massachusetts....	M.	60–84–63	.60–1.25– .89
1843:				New Hampshire..	M.	60–60–60	.80–1.00– .91
Massachusetts....	M.	78–84–81	.87–1.00– .94	New Jersey........	M.	60–60–60	.75– .88– .82
New York........	M.	60–72–61	.56–1.25– .86	New York........	M.	60–60–60	.68–1.25– .89
Pennsylvania.....	M.	(¹)	1.00–1.00–1.00	Ohio.............	M.	60–60–60	.88– .88– .88
1844:				Pennsylvania.....	M.	60–60–60	1.00–1.00–1.00
Massachusetts....	M.	78–84–81	.87–1.00– .94	**1852:**			
New York........	M.	60–72–61	.59–1.25– .90	Connecticut........	M.	60–60–60	.84–1.00– .95
Pennsylvania.....	M.	(¹)	1.00–1.00–1.00	Massachusetts....	M.	60–72–63	.60–1.25– .87
1845:				New Hampshire..	M.	60–60–60	.80–1.25– .99
Massachusetts....	M.	72–84–80	.65–1.00– .80	New Jersey........	M.	60–60–60	.88– .88– .88
New York........	M.	60–60–60	.63–1.25– .84	New York........	M.	60–60–60	.63–1.25– .94
Ohio.............	M.	60–60–60	.70– .70– .70	Ohio.............	M.	60–60–60	.88–1.00– .92
Pennsylvania.....	M.	(¹)	1.00–1.45–1.03	Pennsylvania.....	M.	60–60–60	1.00–1.50–1.03
1846:				**1853:**			
Massachusetts....	M.	72–84–81	.65–1.00– .85	Connecticut........	M.	60–60–60	.83–1.00– .92
New Hampshire..	M.	66–66–66	.67–1.00– .83	Massachusetts....	M.	60–72–64	.55–1.25– .87
New York........	M.	60–60–60	.63–1.25– .83	New Hampshire..	M.	60–60–60	.80–1.00– .89
Pennsylvania.....	M.	(¹)	1.00–1.00–1.00	New Jersey........	M.	60–60–60	.88–1.00– .98
1847:				New York........	M.	60–72–60	.63–1.50–1.15
Massachusetts....	M.	72–84–79	.70–1.17– .88	Ohio.............	M.	60–60–60	1.00–1.00–1.00
New Hampshire..	M.	66–66–66	.67–1.00– .80	Pennsylvania.....	M.	60–60–60	1.00–1.61–1.03
New York........	M.	60–60–60	.46–1.25– .86	**1854:**			
Pennsylvania.....	M.	(¹)	1.00–1.00–1.00	Connecticut........	M.	60–60–60	.83–1.25–1.04
1848:				Maryland.........	M.	60–60–60	1.00–1.00–1.00
Connecticut........	M.	60–60–60	.96– .96– .96	Massachusetts....	M.	60–72–63	.62–1.25– .88
Massachusetts....	M.	72–84–78	.70–1.17– .87	New Hampshire..	M.	60–60–60	.83–1.00– .95
New Hampshire..	M.	60–60–60	.80–1.00– .90	New Jersey........	M.	60–60–60	1.00–1.00–1.00
New York........	M.	60–60–60	.63–1.25– .86	New York........	M.	60–72–60	.50–1.25– .97
Pennsylvania.....	M.	(¹)	1.00–1.00–1.00	Ohio.............	M.	60–60–60	1.00–2.00–1.53
1849:				Pennsylvania.....	M.	60–60–60	1.00–1.61–1.03
Connecticut........	M.	60–60–60	.96– .96– .96	**1855:**			
Massachusetts....	M.	60–84–66	.60–1.00– .84	Connecticut........	M.	60–60–60	.83–1.25–1.06
New Hampshire..	M.	60–60–60	.80–1.17– .97	Maryland.........	M.	60–60–60	1.00–1.00–1.00
New York........	M.	60–60–60	.63–1.25– .93	Massachusetts....	M.	60–72–63	.63–1.25– .89
Ohio.............	M.	60–60–60	.88– .88– .88	New Hampshire..	M.	60–60–60	.83–1.00– .94
Pennsylvania.....	M.	60–60–60	.80–1.00– .94	New York........	M.	60–72–60	.63–1.44– .95
				Ohio.............	M.	60–60–60	1.00–1.00–1.00
				Pennsylvania.....	M.	60–60–60	1.00–1.67–1.05

¹ Not reported.

TABLE **G–1.**—*Laborers, 1840–1900, by year and State*—Continued

Year and State	Sex	Hours per week	Rate per day (dollars)	Year and State	Sex	Hours per week	Rate per day (dollars)
1856:				**1862:**			
Connecticut	M.	60–60–60	.83–1.25–1.04	Maryland	M.	60–60–60	0.83– .83–0.83
Maryland	M.	60–60–60	1.00–1.13–1.03	Massachusetts	M.	60–72–62	.62–1.50– .99
Massachusetts	M.	60–72–61	.63–1.25– .90	Michigan	M.	(1)	.90– .90– .90
New Hampshire	M.	60–60–60	1.00–1.33–1.11	New Hampshire	M.	60–60–60	1.00–1.33–1.11
New Jersey	M.	60–60–60	1.00–1.00–1.00	Do	M.	72–72–72	².46– .46– .46
New York	M.	60–72–61	.63–1.13– .98	New Jersey	M.	60–60–60	1.00–1.00–1.00
Ohio	M.	60–60–60	1.00–1.00–1.00	New York	M.	60–60–60	1.00–1.00–1.00
Pennsylvania	M.	60–60–60	1.00–1.67–1.09	Ohio	M.	60–72–61	1.00–1.00–1.00
Rhode Island	M.	84–84–84	.71– .71– .71	Pennsylvania	M.	60–60–60	.83–1.67–1.09
1857:				Rhode Island	M.	78–78–78	.96– .96– .96
Connecticut	M.	60–60–60	.72–1.34–1.03	**1863:**			
Maryland	M.	60–60–60	1.00–1.13–1.03	Maryland	M.	60–60–60	1.00–1.75–1.38
Massachusetts	M.	60–72–61	.65–1.25– .94	Massachusetts	M.	60–72–62	.50–1.75–1.11
Michigan	M.	(1)	.75– .75– .75	Michigan	M.	(1)	1.75–1.75–1.75
New Hampshire	M.	60–60–60	.83–1.25–1.13	New Hampshire	M.	60–60–60	1.00–1.42–1.08
New Jersey	M.	60–60–60	1.00–1.25–1.06	Do	M.	72–72–72	².62– .62– .62
New York	M.	60–72–62	.63–1.50– .97	New Jersey	M.	60–60–60	1.13–1.50–1.26
Ohio	M.	60–60–60	1.00–1.00–1.00	New York	M.	60–72–61	.25–1.75–1.16
Pennsylvania	M.	60–60–60	.90–1.67–1.05	Ohio	M.	60–60–60	1.15–1.15–1.15
Rhode Island	M.	84–84–84	.71– .71– .71	Pennsylvania	M.	60–60–60	.83–1.65–1.19
Virginia	M.	72–72–72	.50– .75– .63	Rhode Island	M.	78–78–78	.96– .96– .96
1858:				**1864:**			
Connecticut	M.	60–60–60	.72–1.34–1.10	Maryland	M.	60–60–60	1.25–1.67–1.42
Maryland	M.	60–60–60	1.00–1.13–1.04	Massachusetts	M.	60–72–63	.70–1.75–1.29
Massachusetts	M.	60–72–63	.50–1.00– .93	New Hampshire	M.	60–60–60	1.00–1.67–1.34
Michigan	M.	(1)	.75– .75– .75	Do	M.	72–72–72	².69– .69– .69
New Hampshire	M.	60–60–60	.92–1.25–1.06	New Jersey	M.	60–60–60	1.13–1.66–1.45
Do	M.	72–72–72	².39– .39– .39	New York	M.	60–72–61	.88–1.75–1.30
New Jersey	M.	60–60–60	1.00–1.00–1.00	Ohio	M.	60–60–60	1.50–1.50–1.50
New York	M.	60–72–62	.63–1.25– .97	Pennsylvania	M.	60–60–60	1.00–1.75–1.29
Ohio	M.	60–60–60	1.00–1.00–1.00	Rhode Island	M.	78–78–78	.92– .92– .92
Pennsylvania	M.	60–60–60	1.00–1.67–1.07	**1865:**			
Rhode Island	M.	84–84–84	.79– .79– .79	Connecticut	M.	60–60–60	1.25–1.25–1.25
1859:				Maryland	M.	60–72–62	.50–1.67–1.47
Maryland	M.	60–60–60	1.00–1.13–1.04	Massachusetts	M.	60–72–64	.75–1.83–1.53
Massachusetts	M.	60–72–63	.50–1.25– .95	Michigan	M.	(1)	2.00–2.00–2.00
Michigan	M.	(1)	.75– .75– .75	New Hampshire	M.	60–60–60	.92– .92– .92
New Hampshire	M.	60–60–60	.92–1.17–1.05	Do	M.	72–72–72	².69– .69– .69
Do	M.	72–72–72	².39– .39– .39	New Jersey	M.	60–60–60	1.33–2.00–1.70
New Jersey	M.	60–60–60	1.00–1.25–1.16	New York	M.	60–72–61	.96–2.25–1.60
New York	M.	60–72–61	.63–1.50–1.02	North Carolina	M.	60–60–60	.75– .75– .75
Ohio	M.	60–60–60	1.00–1.00–1.00	Ohio	M.	60–60–60	1.75–1.75–1.75
Pennsylvania	M.	60–60–60	1.00–1.67–1.04	Pennsylvania	M.	60–60–60	1.00–2.00–1.56
Rhode Island	M.	84–84–84	.96– .96– .96	Rhode Island	M.	78–78–78	1.00–1.00–1.00
1860:				**1866:**			
Illinois	M.	60–60–60	1.00–1.00–1.00	Maryland	M.	60–60–60	1.60–2.00–1.65
Maryland	M.	60–72–64	.92–1.25–1.05	Massachusetts	M.	60–72–62	.65–2.00–1.58
Massachusetts	M.	60–72–66	.62–1.50–1.01	Michigan	M.	(1)	2.00–2.00–2.00
Michigan	M.	(1)	1.25–1.25–1.25	New Hampshire	M.	60–60–60	1.25–1.50–1.42
New Hampshire	M.	60–60–60	1.00–1.25–1.13	Do	M.	72–72–72	².69– .69– .69
Do	M.	72–72–72	².39– .39– .39	New Jersey	M.	60–60–60	1.24–1.83–1.57
New Jersey	M.	60–60–60	1.13–1.25–1.18	New York	M.	60–72–62	.96–2.25–1.61
New York	M.	60–72–61	.44–2.00– .99	Ohio	M.	60–60–60	1.90–1.90–1.90
Ohio	M.	60–60–60	1.00–1.00–1.00	Pennsylvania	M.	60–60–60	1.50–2.00–1.60
Pennsylvania	M.	60–60–60	.92–2.25–1.37	Rhode Island	M.	78–78–78	1.00–1.00–1.00
Rhode Island	M.	78–78–78	.96– .96– .96	**1867:**			
1861:				Georgia	M.	66–66–66	.50– .75– .67
Maryland	M.	60–60–60	.75–1.13– .86	Maryland	M.	60–60–60	1.50–2.00–1.63
Massachusetts	M.	60–72–62	.62–1.50– .98	Massachusetts	M.	60–72–62	.62–2.00–1.54
Michigan	M.	(1)	1.00–1.00–1.00	Michigan	M.	(1)	2.00–2.00–2.00
New Hampshire	M.	60–60–60	1.00–1.00–1.00	New Hampshire	M.	60–60–60	1.42–1.50–1.48
Do	M.	72–72–72	².39– .39– .39	Do	M.	72–72–72	².69– .69– .69
New Jersey	M.	60–60–60	1.00–1.00–1.00	New Jersey	M.	60–60–60	1.75–1.83–1.78
New York	M.	60–72–61	.69–1.38–1.00	New York	M.	60–72–62	.68–2.25–1.51
Ohio	M.	60–60–60	1.00–1.00–1.00	Ohio	M.	60–60–60	1.90–1.90–1.90
Pennsylvania	M.	60–60–60	.83–1.67–1.08	Pennsylvania	M.	60–60–60	1.50–1.75–1.58
Rhode Island	M.	78–78–78	.96– .96– .96	Rhode Island	M.	78–78–78	1.00–1.00–1.00

¹ Not reported.   ² And board.

TABLE G–1.—*Laborers, 1840–1900, by year and State*—Continued

Year and State	Sex	Hours per week	Rate per day (dollars)
1868:			
Connecticut	M.	60–60–60	1.50–1.75–1.63
Delaware	M.	60–60–60	1.42–1.67–1.47
Maine	M.	66–66–66	1.00–1.25–1.13
Maryland	M.	60–60–60	1.50–2.00–1.63
Massachusetts	M.	60–72–62	1.00–2.00–1.58
Michigan	M.	(1)	1.80–1.80–1.80
New Hampshire	M.	60–60–60	1.33–1.33–1.33
Do	M.	72–72–72	2 .69–.69–.69
New Jersey	M.	60–60–60	1.50–1.83–1.73
New York	M.	60–72–62	.68–2.35–1.56
Ohio	M.	60–60–60	1.75–1.75–1.75
Pennsylvania	M.	60–62–60	1.00–2.00–1.53
Rhode Island	M.	72–72–72	1.00–1.00–1.00
1869:			
Connecticut	M.	60–60–60	1.50–1.75–1.63
Delaware	M.	60–60–60	1.17–1.50–1.37
Maryland	M.	60–60–60	1.50–2.00–1.62
Massachusetts	M.	60–72–62	1.00–2.00–1.57
Michigan	M.	(1)	1.80–1.80–1.80
New Hampshire	M.	60–60–60	1.33–1.75–1.48
Do	M.	72–72–72	2 .69–.69–.69
New Jersey	M.	60–60–60	1.50–1.88–1.76
New York	M.	60–72–61	.88–2.50–1.66
Ohio	M.	60–60–60	1.75–1.75–1.75
Pennsylvania	M.	60–60–60	.83–2.00–1.53
Rhode Island	M.	72–72–72	1.00–1.00–1.00
1870:			
California	M.	60–60–60	2.00–2.00–2.00
Delaware	M.	60–60–60	1.33–1.50–1.37
Illinois	M.	60–60–60	1.75–2.00–1.90
Louisiana	M.	60–60–60	1.50–1.50–1.50
Maryland	M.	60–60–60	1.25–2.00–1.41
Massachusetts	M.	60–72–62	1.00–2.00–1.58
Michigan	M.	(1)	1.75–1.75–1.75
Minnesota	M.	60–60–60	1.25–1.25–1.25
Missouri	M.	54–54–54	1.50–1.50–1.50
New Hampshire	M.	60–60–60	1.33–1.58–1.48
Do	M.	72–72–72	2 .69–.69–.69
New Jersey	M.	60–60–60	1.00–2.50–2.05
New York	M.	60–72–62	.75–2.50–1.66
North Carolina	M.	60–60–60	.75–.75–.75
Ohio	M.	60–60–60	1.50–2.00–1.59
Pennsylvania	M.	54–64–59	1.00–1.83–1.50
Rhode Island	M.	72–72–72	1.33–1.33–1.33
1871:			
California	M.	60–60–60	2.00–2.00–2.00
Delaware	M.	60–60–60	1.33–1.67–1.44
Illinois	M.	60–60–60	1.75–2.00–1.90
Louisiana	M.	60–60–60	1.50–1.50–1.50
Maryland	M.	60–60–60	1.25–2.00–1.41
Massachusetts	M.	48–72–61	.90–2.08–1.68
Michigan	M.	(1)	1.75–1.75–1.75
Minnesota	M.	60–60–60	1.25–1.25–1.25
Missouri	M.	54–54–54	1.50–1.50–1.50
New Hampshire	M.	60–60–60	1.33–1.58–1.48
Do	M.	72–72–72	2 .69–.69–.69
New Jersey	M.	60–60–60	1.17–2.00–1.73
New York	M.	60–72–61	.75–2.50–1.72
Ohio	M.	60–60–60	1.50–2.00–1.75
Pennsylvania	M.	54–60–55	1.00–1.83–1.46
Rhode Island	M.	72–72–72	.83–.83–.83
1872:			
California	M.	60–60–60	2.00–2.00–2.00
Connecticut	M.	60–60–60	1.75–2.00–1.92
Delaware	M.	60–60–60	1.33–1.67–1.50
Illinois	M.	60–60–60	1.75–2.00–1.91
Louisiana	M.	60–60–60	1.50–1.50–1.50
Maryland	M.	60–60–60	1.25–2.00–1.41
Massachusetts	M.	60–72–61	1.00–2.00–1.55
Michigan	M.	(1)	1.75–1.75–1.75
Do	M.	60–60–60	2 1.00–1.00–1.00
Minnesota	M.	60–60–60	1.25–1.25–1.25
Missouri	M.	54–60–54	1.50–1.50–1.50
New Hampshire	M.	60–60–60	1.15–2.00–1.36
Do	M.	72–72–72	2 .69–.69–.69
1872—Continued			
New Jersey	M.	60–60–60	1.83–2.00–1.96
New York	M.	60–72–61	.63–2.50–1.70
Ohio	M.	60–60–60	1.50–2.83–1.79
Pennsylvania	M.	54–60–57	1.17–2.00–1.43
Rhode Island	M.	72–72–72	.83–.83–.83
South Carolina	M.	72–72–72	.75–.75–.75
1873:			
California	M.	60–60–60	2.00–2.00–2.00
Connecticut	M.	60–60–60	1.00–2.00–1.67
Delaware	M.	60–60–60	1.33–1.58–1.49
Illinois	M.	60–60–60	1.75–2.00–1.90
Louisiana	M.	60–60–60	1.50–1.50–1.50
Maryland	M.	60–60–60	1.25–2.00–1.40
Massachusetts	M.	60–72–62	1.00–2.00–1.55
Michigan	M.	(1)	2.00–2.00–2.00
Minnesota	M.	60–60–60	1.25–1.25–1.25
Missouri	M.	54–60–55	1.50–1.50–1.50
New Hampshire	M.	60–60–60	1.00–1.58–1.39
Do	M.	72–72–72	2 .69–.69–.69
New Jersey	M.	60–60–60	1.67–2.00–1.77
New York	M.	60–72–61	.88–3.50–1.73
Ohio	M.	60–60–60	1.50–2.75–1.69
Pennsylvania	M.	60–60–60	1.25–2.00–1.52
Rhode Island	M.	72–72–72	.83–.83–.83
1874:			
Alabama	M.	72–72–72	1.00–1.00–1.00
California	M.	60–60–60	2.00–2.00–2.00
Connecticut	M.	60–60–60	2.00–2.00–2.00
Delaware	M.	60–60–60	1.17–1.83–1.42
Illinois	M.	60–60–60	1.00–2.22–1.51
Indiana	M.	(1)	1.47–1.73–1.72
Iowa	M.	(1)	1.53–1.53–1.53
Louisiana	M.	60–60–60	1.50–1.50–1.50
Maryland	M.	60–60–60	1.25–2.00–1.32
Massachusetts	M.	60–72–62	1.00–2.00–1.49
Michigan	M.	(1)	1.35–1.35–1.35
Minnesota	M.	60–60–60	1.25–1.25–1.25
Missouri	M.	54–60–55	1.50–1.50–1.50
New Hampshire	M.	60–60–60	1.15–1.58–1.46
Do	M.	72–72–72	2 .69–.69–.69
New Jersey	M.	60–60–60	1.50–2.00–1.88
New York	M.	60–72–61	.75–3.00–1.72
Ohio	M.	60–60–60	1.16–2.00–1.59
Pennsylvania	M.	54–60–56	.75–2.05–1.38
Do	M.	(1) 54–60–59	1.40–1.50–1.49
Rhode Island	M.	72–72–72	.83–.83–.83
Virginia	M.	60–60–60	1.00–1.00–1.00
1875:			
California	M.	60–60–60	1.50–2.00–1.81
Connecticut	M.	60–60–60	1.50–2.00–1.75
Delaware	M.	60–60–60	1.00–1.50–1.31
Illinois	M.	60–60–60	1.50–1.75–1.75
Louisiana	M.	60–60–60	1.75–1.75–1.75
Maine	M.	72–72–72	1.50–1.75–1.67
Maryland	M.	60–60–60	1.25–2.00–1.30
Massachusetts	M.	60–72–61	1.25–2.00–1.44
Michigan	M.	(1)	1.35–1.35–1.35
Minnesota	M.	60–60–60	1.25–1.25–1.25
Missouri	M.	54–60–56	1.50–1.50–1.50
New Hampshire	M.	60–60–60	1.33–1.50–1.44
Do	M.	72–72–72	2 .69–.69–.69
New Jersey	M.	60–60–60	.75–2.00–1.67
New York	M.	60–72–61	.63–2.75–1.53
Ohio	M.	60–60–60	1.33–1.83–1.56
Pennsylvania	M.	54–72–61	1.00–2.14–1.59
Rhode Island	M.	72–72–72	.92–.92–.92
Virginia	M.	60–60–60	1.00–1.00–1.00
1876:			
California	M.	60–60–60	1.00–2.00–1.86
Connecticut	M.	60–60–60	1.20–1.84–1.52
Delaware	M.	60–60–60	1.17–1.50–1.32
Illinois	M.	60–60–60	1.50–1.60–1.60
Louisiana	M.	60–60–60	1.75–1.75–1.75
Maryland	M.	60–60–60	1.15–2.00–1.28
Massachusetts	M.	60–72–61	.90–1.83–1.38

1 Not reported.   2 And board.

TABLE **G-1.**—*Laborers, 1840–1900, by year and State*—Continued

Lowest, highest, and average—

Year and State	Sex	Hours per week	Rate per day (dollars)	Year and State	Sex	Hours per week	Rate per day (dollars)
1876—Continued				**1880:**			
Michigan	M.	(1)	1.35–1.35–1.35	Alabama	(1)	(1)	1.20–1.47–1.29
Minnesota	M.	60–60–60	1.25–1.25–1.25	California	M.	60–60–60	2.00–2.00–2.00
Missouri	M.	54–60–57	1.50–1.50–1.50	Connecticut	M.	60–60–60	1.50–1.50–1.50
New Hampshire	M.	60–66–65	1.35–1.50–1.41	Georgia	M.	60–69–67	.67–2.00–.93
Do	M.	72–70–72	[2].69–.69–.69	Illinois	M.	44–70–59	.96–1.60–1.20
New Jersey	M.	60–60–60	1.50–2.00–1.81	Kentucky	M.	60–60–60	1.00–1.00–1.00
New York	M.	60–72–61	.56–2.75–1.49	Do	(1)	(1)	1.03–1.03–1.03
Ohio	M.	60–60–60	1.50–1.83–1.55	Louisiana	M.	60–60–60	1.50–1.50–1.50
Pennsylvania	M.	48–60–59	.65–4.00–1.50	Maine	(1)	66–66–66	1.00–1.00–1.00
Do	M.	(1)	[2].14–.14–.14	Maryland	M.	60–60–60	1.12–1.67–1.27
Rhode Island	M.	72–72–72	.92–.92–.92	Massachusetts	M.	60–72–61	.75–1.75–1.20
South Carolina	M.	66–66–66	.50–.83–.66	Michigan	M.	(1)	.55–1.55–1.55
Virginia	M.	60–60–60	.83–.83–.83	Do	(1)	(1)	1.60–1.73–1.67
1877:				Minnesota	M.	60–60–60	1.50–1.50–1.50
California	M.	60–60–60	2.00–2.00–2.00	Do	(1)	(1)	1.90–1.96–1.93
Connecticut	M.	60–60–60	1.50–1.50–1.50	Missouri	M.	54–60–58	1.50–1.50–1.50
Delaware	M.	60–60–60	1.17–1.50–1.34	Do	(1)	(1)	1.20–1.36–1.23
Illinois	M.	60–60–60	1.50–1.50–1.50	New Hampshire	M.	60–60–60	1.00–1.25–1.19
Louisiana	M.	60–60–60	1.50–1.50–1.50	Do	M.	72–72–72	[2].69–.69–.69
Maine	M.	66–66–66	.75–1.25–.97	Do	(1)	66–66–66	1.00–1.10–1.05
Maryland	M.	60–60–60	1.00–1.83–1.27	New Jersey	M.	60–60–60	1.33–1.75–1.53
Massachusetts	M.	60–72–61	.85–1.90–1.33	Do	(1)	54–84–61	.90–1.90–1.21
Michigan	M.	(1)	1.35–1.35–1.35	Do	(1)	(1)	1.21–1.24–1.23
Minnesota	M.	60–60–60	1.25–1.25–1.25	New York	M.	52–72–61	.63–2.00–1.30
Missouri	M.	54–60–57	1.50–1.50–1.50	Do	(1)	(1)	1.20–1.37–1.26
New Hampshire	M.	72–72–72	[2].69–.69–.69	Ohio	M.	60–84–75	1.00–2.00–1.27
New Jersey	M.	60–67–64	1.00–2.00–1.27	Do	(1)	(1)	1.03–1.25–1.05
New York	M.	60–72–61	.65–2.50–1.30	Pennsylvania	M.	50–72–59	.75–2.00–1.29
Ohio	M.	60–84–76	.80–2.13–1.21	Do	(1)	(1)	1.10–1.12–1.10
Pennsylvania	M.	42–72–58	.80–2.25–1.51	Rhode Island	M.	72–72–72	1.10–1.10–1.10
Do	M.	(1)	[3].11–.11–.11	Do	(1)	66–72–68	1.00–1.25–1.09
Rhode Island	M.	72–72–72	.92–.92–.92	Tennessee	(1)	(1)	1.00–1.05–1.05
Virginia	M.	60–60–60	1.00–1.00–1.00	Texas	(1)	(1)	.53–.53–.53
1878:				Virginia	M.	60–60–60	1.00–1.25–1.01
California	M.	60–60–60	2.00–2.00–2.00	West Virginia	M.	60–60–60	1.50–1.50–1.50
Connecticut	M.	60–72–71	1.00–1.75–1.47	Wisconsin	(1)	(1)	1.68–1.81–1.74
Delaware	M.	60–60–60	1.17–1.50–1.50	**1881:**			
Illinois	M.	60–60–60	1.38–1.50–1.50	California	M.	60–60–60	2.00–2.00–2.00
Louisiana	M.	60–60–60	1.50–1.50–1.50	Connecticut	M.	60–60–60	1.50–1.50–1.50
Maryland	M.	60–60–60	1.00–1.83–1.27	Delaware	M.	60–60–60	1.00–1.54–1.28
Massachusetts	M.	60–72–61	1.00–1.90–1.30	Georgia	M.	66–66–66	.90–1.17–1.08
Michigan	M.	(1)	1.35–1.35–1.35	Illinois	M.	54–60–56	1.15–1.60–1.32
Minnesota	M.	60–60–60	1.25–1.50–1.35	Indiana	M.	60–60–60	1.00–1.35–1.25
Missouri	M.	54–60–58	1.50–1.50–1.50	Kentucky	M.	60–60–60	1.10–1.10–1.10
New Hampshire	M.	60–60–60	1.25–1.25–1.25	Louisiana	M.	60–60–60	1.50–1.50–1.50
Do	M.	72–72–72	[2].69–.69–.69	Maryland	M.	60–60–60	1.16–1.67–1.28
New Jersey	M.	60–60–60	1.08–2.00–1.17	Massachusetts	M.	60–72–60	.65–2.00–1.05
New York	M.	60–72–61	.65–2.25–1.25	Michigan	M.	60–60–60	1.25–1.50–1.27
Ohio	M.	54–72–60	.83–1.67–1.18	Minnesota	M.	60–66–64	1.50–1.50–1.50
Pennsylvania	M.	45–72–60	.70–2.50–1.30	Missouri	M.	54–60–58	1.15–1.50–1.38
Do	M.	(1)	[2].12–.12–.12	New Hampshire	M.	60–60–60	1.00–1.30–1.20
Rhode Island	M.	72–72–72	.92–.92–.92	Do	M.	72–72–72	[2].75–.75–.75
Virginia	M.	60–60–60	.83–.83–.83	New Jersey	M.	60–72–61	1.00–1.75–1.24
1879:				New York	M.	54–72–61	.50–2.25–1.48
California	M.	60–60–60	2.00–2.00–2.00	Ohio	M.	48–84–61	.75–2.25–1.34
Connecticut	M.	60–60–60	1.25–1.25–1.25	Pennsylvania	M.	54–80–60	1.00–1.83–1.24
Delaware	M.	60–60–60	1.00–1.50–1.32	Rhode Island	M.	66–72–71	1.06–1.10–1.09
Illinois	M.	60–60–60	1.38–1.50–1.49	Virginia	M.	60–69–65	1.00–1.00–1.00
Louisiana	M.	60–60–60	1.50–1.50–1.50	Wisconsin	M.	65–71–68	1.25–2.50 1.67–1.53
Maryland	M.	60–60–60	1.00–1.67–1.36	**1882:**			
Massachusetts	M.	60–72–61	1.00–1.75–1.25	California	M.	60–60–60	2.00–2.00–2.00
Michigan	M.	(1)	1.35–1.35–1.35	Connecticut	M.	60–66–60	1.25–1.50–1.28
Minnesota	M.	60–60–60	1.25–1.50–1.35	Delaware	M.	60–60–60	1.00–1.50–1.26
Missouri	M.	45–72–59	.75–1.73–1.30	Georgia	M.	70–70–71	.50–1.25–.94
New Hampshire	M.	60–60–60	1.00–1.25–1.19	Illinois	M.	60–60–60	.77–2.30–1.19
Do	M.	72–72–72	[2].69–.69–.69	Louisiana	M.	60–60–60	1.50–1.50–1.50
New Jersey	M.	60–60–60	1.33–2.00–1.52	Maryland	M.	60–60–60	1.20–1.67–1.29
Do	(1)	46–78–60	.75–2.00–1.12	Massachusetts	M.	60–72–60	.90–2.00–1.26
New York	M.	60–72–61	.45–2.25–1.25	Michigan	M.	60–60–60	1.40–1.75–1.62
Ohio	M.	60–60–60	.88–1.80–1.26	Minnesota	M.	60–60–60	1.40–1.75–1.62
Pennsylvania	M.	42–84–58	.50–2.59–1.27	Missouri	M.	39–72–58	1.00–2.25–1.46
Do	M.	(1)	[2].75–.75–.75	Nebraska	M.	60–60–60	1.25–1.25–1.25
Do	M.	(1)	[4].77–.77–.77	New Hampshire	M.	60–66–65	.50–1.30–.90
Rhode Island	M.	72–72–72	.92–.92–.92	Do	M.	72–72–72	[5].75–.75–.75
Virginia	M.	60–60–60	1.00–1.00–1.00	New Jersey	M.	60–72–64	1.00–2.00–1.17

[1] Not reported.   [2] And board.   [3] Per hour.

TABLE **G-1.**—*Laborers, 1840-1900, by year and State*—Continued

Left half

Year and State	Sex	Lowest, highest, and average—	
		Hours per week	Rate per day (dollars)
1882—Continued.			
New York	M.	57-72-59	.75-2.25-1.57
North Carolina	M.	(1)	.75-.75-.75
Ohio	M	60-60-60	1.17-1.25-1.35
Do	(1)	54-92-60	.75-2.00-1.37
Pennsylvania	M.	54-66-59	1.00-1.75-1.34
Rhode Island	M.	60-72-61	1.10-1.83-1.54
South Carolina	M.	61-69-66	.60-1.25-.81
Virginia	M.	60-60-60	1.00-1.25-1.01
West Virginia	M.	59-59-59	1.25-1.25-1.25
Wisconsin	M.	57-57-57	1.75-1.75-1.75
1883:			
Alabama	M.	(1)	.67-.67-.67
California	M.	60-60-60	1.00-2.00-1.01
Colorado	M.	60-60-60	2.00-2.00-2.00
Connecticut	M.	60-60-60	1.50-1.50-1.50
Delaware	M.	60-60-60	1.00-1.50-1.27
Georgia	M.	66-69-69	.50-1.25-.82
Illinois	M.	60-60-60	1.50-1.68-1.50
Louisiana	M.	60-63-60	.83-1.50-1.47
Maryland	M.	60-60-60	1.20-1.67-1.28
Massachusetts	M.	60-72-60	.90-2.00-1.30
Michigan	M.	(1)	.75-3.00-1.44
Minnesota	M.	60-60-60	1.50-1.50-1.50
Mississippi	M.	(1)	1.00-1.00-1.00
Missouri	M.	54-60-58	1.50-1.75-1.66
New Hampshire	M.	60-60-60	1.00-1.30-1.20
Do	M.	72-72-72	[2] .75-.75-.75
New Jersey	M.	48-75-61	.91-2.00-1.20
New York	M.	60-72-61	.75-2.50-1.51
Ohio	M.	45-84-61	1.20-2.17-1.36
Pennsylvania	M.	54-60-59	1.20-1.75-1.46
Rhode Island	M.	72-72-72	1.10-1.10-1.10
South Carolina	M.	66-66-66	.65-1.35-1.28
Tennessee	M.	66-66-66	.80-1.00-.93
Virginia	M.	60-60-60	1.00-1.00-1.00
West Virginia	M.	60-60-60	1.00-1.00-1.00
1884:			
Alabama	M.	84-84-84	1.00-1.00-1.00
California	M.	60-84-61	2.00-2.49-2.31
Colorado	M.	72-72-72	2.50-2.50-2.50
Delaware	M.	60-72-70	1.00-2.50-1.29
Georgia	M.	66-70-68	.75-1.00-.78
Illinois	M.	60-60-60	1.10-2.00-1.50
Indiana	M.	(1)	1.00-1.25-1.19
Iowa	M.	60-84-63	.67-2.00-1.28
Louisiana	M.	60-66-60	1.00-1.50-1.48
Maryland	M.	60-60-60	1.20-1.67-1.28
Massachusetts	M.	60-72-60	.75-2.00-1.30
Do	M.	60-60-60	[2] 1.50-1.50-1.50
Michigan	M.	(1)	.46-2.75-1.42
Minnesota	M.	60-60-60	1.50-1.50-1.50
Missouri	M.	54-60-58	1.25-1.75-1.49
New Hampshire	M.	60-60-60	1.00-1.30-1.20
Do	M.	72-72-72	[2] .75-.75-.75
New Jersey	M.	54-72-61	.83-2.00-1.26
New York	M.	53-72-56	.63-2.50-1.20
Ohio	M.	54-72-60	.67-2.25-1.20
Pennsylvania	M.	54-60-59	.67-2.00-1.27
Rhode Island	M.	72-72-72	1.10-1.10-1.10
South Carolina	M.	69-69-69	.58-.75-.73
Virginia	M.	60-60-60	.67-1.25-1.01
Washington	M.	60-60-60	.80-1.00-.90
West Virginia	M.	59-60-59	.83-1.50-1.16
1885:			
Alabama	M.	72-72-72	.80-1.50-1.12
Arkansas	M.	60-60-60	1.50-1.50-1.50
California	M.	60-72-61	.75-3.50-1.74
Connecticut	M.	59-66-59	.67-1.38-1.30
Delaware	M.	60-72-61	.42-1.65-1.21
Georgia	M.	69-69-69	.32-.85-.51
Illinois	M.	54-72-60	.50-2.00-1.44
Indiana	M.	60-72-60	.80-2.12-1.33
Iowa	M.	60-70-70	1.35-1.50-1.36
Kansas	M.	48-108-60	.75-2.00-1.37
Kentucky	M.	54-66-60	.75-2.00-1.28

Right half

Year and State	Sex	Lowest, highest, and average—	
		Hours per week	Rate per day (dollars)
1885—Continued.			
Louisiana	M.	60-60-60	1.50-1.50-1.50
Maine	M.	54-72-66	.90-2.17-1.32
Maryland	M.	60-72-67	.95-2.00-1.18
Massachusetts	M.	50-72-61	.67-2.00-1.22
Michigan	M.	60-66-66	.58-3.00-1.35
Minnesota	M.	60-72-64	1.25-1.62-1.39
Missouri	M.	48-72-55	1.00-2.00-1.39
New Hampshire	M.	59-66-61	.71-2.17-1.24
Do	M.	72-72-72	[2] .75-.75-.75
New Jersey	M.	42-72-60	.63-2.50-1.27
Do	M.	60-60-60	[2] .96-.96-.96
New York	M.	53-72-57	.60-2.50-1.63
North Carolina	M.	60-69-62	.67-1.00-.83
Ohio	M.	54-72-61	.50-2.08-1.12
Oregon	M.	72-72-72	1.75-1.75-1.75
Pennsylvania	M.	48-72-58	.75-2.60-1.27
Rhode Island	M.	48-72-58	.83-2.00-1.32
South Carolina	M.	66-66-66	.85-1.25-.88
Tennessee	M.	60-72-66	.90-1.50-1.01
Texas	M.	60-60-60	1.50-1.50-1.50
Vermont	M.	60-66-60	1.10-1.12-1.10
Virginia	M.	48-72-57	.75-1.30-.94
West Virginia	M.	54-66-60	1.00-1.42-1.20
Wisconsin	M.	60-69-65	1.00-1.67-1.39
1886:			
California	M.	60-60-60	1.75-2.00-1.87
Connecticut	M.	60-60-60	.75-2.00-1.63
Delaware	M.	60-72-64	1.00-1.42-1.25
Dist. of Columbia	M.	58-58-58	2.00-2.00-2.00
Illinois	M.	48-78-56	.83-2.00-1.58
Indiana	M.	60-60-60	1.20-1.20-1.20
Iowa	M.	60-78-61	.50-4.00-1.30
Kansas	M.	30-78-60	.75-2.00-1.36
Maryland	M.	48-60-60	1.00-2.00-1.09
Massachusetts	M.	60-72-61	.75-1.84-1.28
Michigan	M.	54-60-53	1.00-2.00-1.26
Minnesota	M.	60-60-60	1.13-1.50-1.28
Missouri	M.	54-60-58	1.50-1.50-1.50
New Hampshire	M.	60-60-60	1.20-1.40-1.31
Do	M.	72-72-72	[2] .75-.75-.75
New Jersey	M.	57-72-58	.55-2.00-1.17
New York	M.	42-72-60	.75-2.50-1.75
North Dakota	M.	60-60-60	1.75-1.75-1.75
Ohio	M.	60-60-60	.65-2.25-1.29
Pennsylvania	M.	54-60-59	.83-1.80-1.31
Rhode Island	M.	72-72-72	1.25-1.25-1.25
Tennessee	M.	60-60-60	1.25-1.25-1.25
Vermont	M.	60-60-60	1.00-1.00-1.00
Virginia	M.	66-66-66	1.10-1.10-1.10
West Virginia	M.	48-72-60	.94-1.50-1.23
1887:			
California	M.	60-63-60	1.75-2.00-1.92
Connecticut	M.	60-60-60	.72-2.00-1.48
Delaware	M.	60-60-60	1.00-1.67-1.30
Florida	M.	(1)	[3] .10-.20-.12
Do	M.	(1)	.27-2.00-1.03
Do	M.	(1)	[3] .14-.14
Illinois	M.	60-60-60	1.50-1.50-1.50
Do	(1)	(1)	1.64-1.64-1.64
Kansas	M.	54-72-60	.75-2.25-1.63
Do	M.	(1)	[2] .75-.75-.75
Kentucky	F.	60-60-60	1.00-1.00-1.00
Louisiana	M.	60-60-60	1.75-1.75-1.75
Maine	M.	60-72-60	.75-2.00-1.23
Maryland	M.	60-60-60	.38-2.30-1.17
Do	M.	(1)	[3] .13-.18-.15
Do	M.	60-72-61	[3] .16½-.20-.17
Michigan	M.	60-60-60	1.00-1.33-1.33
Do	M.	(1)	[3] .10-.17-.13
Minnesota	M.	60-60-60	1.50-1.50-1.50
Missouri	M.	54-72-58	1.00-2.57-1.40
Do	(1)	(1)	1.13-1.62-1.53
Nebraska	M.	54-60-58	1.00-2.50-1.63

[1] Not reported.   [2] And board.   [3] Per hour.

Table G-1.—*Laborers, 1840–1900, by year and State*—Continued

Year and State	Sex	Lowest, highest, and average— Hours per week	Rate per day (dollars)
1887—Continued.			
New Hampshire	M.	60-60-60	1.25-1.40-1.30
Do	M.	60-60-60	[2].75-.75-.75
New Jersey	M.	60-60-60	1.20-2.00-1.39
New York	M.	53-72-60	.58-2.50-1.39
Do	M.	(1)	[3].10-.18½-.14
North Carolina	M.	60-78-62	.50-1.75-.80
Ohio	M.	42-72-60	.50-2.50-1.37
Oregon	M.	(1)	1.53-2.49-2.03
Pennsylvania	M.	48-72-59	.31-3.54-1.29
Do	M.	(1)	[3].07½-.20-.12
Rhode Island	M.	48-60-54	1.10-2.50-1.43
Do	M.	(1)	[3].15-.25-.16½
Virginia	M.	60-60-60	.46-2.00-1.06
West Virginia	M.	(1)	.54-1.53-1.15
Wisconsin	M.	(1)	1.00-2.00-1.41
1888:			
California	M.	60-60-60	2.00-2.00-2.00
Colorado	M.	48-60-58	1.15-2.00-1.88
Connecticut	M.	60-60-60	1.25-1.25-1.25
Delaware	M.	60-60-60	1.00-1.67-1.29
Georgia	M.	66-66-66	.50-1.75-.89
Illinois	M.	60-84-61	1.40-3.00-1.55
Indiana	M.	(1)	1.25-1.25-1.25
Iowa	M.	54-63-60	1.00-1.75-1.28
Do	M.	(1)	[3]1.25-1.25-1.25
Kansas	M.	54-72-61	.75-2.00-1.48
Louisiana	M.	60-60-60	1.75-1.75-1.75
Maine	M.	60-72-63	1.00-2.00-1.49
Maryland	M.	60-60-60	1.20-1.67-1.28
Massachusetts	M.	60-72-61	.75-1.84-1.24
Michigan	M.	36-90-60	.77-2.38-1.51
Minnesota	M.	60-60-60	1.50-1.50-1.50
Missouri	M.	54-60-58	1.50-1.50-1.50
Do	(1)	(1)	1.15-1.60-1.34
New Hampshire	M.	60-60-60	1.25-1.50-1.33
Do	M.	60-60-60	[2].75-.75-.75
New Jersey	M.	48-84-60	1.00-2.00-1.38
New York	M.	48-93-60	.66-3.00-1.52
Do	M.	(1)	[3].14-.25-.21
Do	M.	(1)	[2].96-.96-.96
Do	M.	60-60-60	[2].75-.75-.75
Do	M.	66-66-66	[4]1.25-1.25-1.25
North Carolina	M.	60-72-66	.31-1.00-.61
Ohio	M.	60-60-60	.91-2.00-1.32
Pennsylvania	M.	54-84-61	1.00-2.45-1.39
Rhode Island	M.	60-60-60	1.00-2.00-1.20
South Carolina	M.	66-66-66	.50-1.00-.59
Tennessee	M.	60-60-60	.40-1.85-1.03
Virginia	M.	60-72-64	.50-1.90-1.01
West Virginia	M.	60-66-63	1.40-1.80-1.42
1889:			
Alabama	M.	48-84-63	.75-2.50-1.23
Do	(1)	(1)	.83-1.47-1.26
Alaska	(1)	(1)	2.00-2.82-2.61
Arizona	(1)	(1)	1.49-3.20-2.42
Arkansas	(1)	(1)	1.22-2.06-1.65
California	M.	60-60-60	1.75-2.00-1.95
Do	(1)	(1)	1.16-3.70-2.06
Colorado	(1)	(1)	1.63-3.75-2.66
Connecticut	M.	60-60-60	1.25-1.50-1.29
Do	(1)	(1)	1.48-1.74-1.57
Delaware	M.	60-60-60	1.00-1.67-1.16
Do	(1)	(1)	1.50-1.50-1.50
Georgia	M.	66-84-69	.50-2.00-1.02
Do	(1)	(1)	.80-1.05-.99
Idaho	(1)	(1)	1.77-3.50-3.05
Illinois	M.	60-72-63	.52-3.00-1.46
Do	(1)	(1)	1.00-2.00-1.68
Indiana	M.	60-60-61	1.00-2.05-1.29
Do	(1)	(1)	.96-1.91-1.45
Indian Territory	(1)	(1)	1.90-2.41-2.27
Iowa	(1)	(1)	1.19-2.13-1.67
Do	M.	48-60-58	1.16-1.46-1.30
Kansas	(1)	(1)	.75-1.95-1.58
Do	M.	48-72-60	.50-2.25-1.54
1889—Continued.			
Kentucky	(1)	(1)	1.01-1.84-1.31
Louisiana	M.	60-60-60	1.75-1.75-1.75
Maine	(1)	(1)	1.62-1.75-1.67
Maine	M.	60-60-60	.75-2.00-1.40
Maryland	M.	60-72-60	.89-1.87-1.31
Do	(1)	(1)	1.05-1.86-1.57
Massachusetts	M.	60-72-61	.75-1.90-1.22
Do	(1)	(1)	1.25-1.80-1.56
Michigan	M.	57-84-60	.33-2.13-1.66
Do	(1)	(1)	1.25-2.10-1.65
Minnesota	M.	60-60-60	1.50-1.85-1.76
Do	(1)	(1)	1.48-1.96-1.84
Missouri	M.	54-72-65	.75-2.00-1.24
Do	(1)	(1)	1.12-1.91-1.54
Do	(1)	(1)	.60-2.21-1.41
Montana	(1)	(1)	1.50-3.58-3.17
Nebraska	(1)	(1)	1.54-1.54-1.54
Nevada	(1)	(1)	2.00-3.88-3.15
New Hampshire	M.	60-60-60	1.05-1.50-1.17
Do	(1)	(1)	1.50-1.68-1.65
Do	M.	60-60-60	[2].75-.75-.75
New Jersey	M.	60-60-60	1.25-2.00-1.32
Do	(1)	(1)	1.21-1.45-1.33
New Mexico	(1)	(1)	1.00-3.00-2.30
New York	M.	54-84-61	.40-2.50-1.36
Do	(1)	(1)	1.20-1.75-1.37
North Carolina	M.	60-72-67	.40-1.25-.73
Do	(1)	(1)	.75-1.00-.86
North Dakota	(1)	(1)	1.50-1.88-1.72
Ohio	M.	48-84-62	.95-3.50-1.40
Do	(1)	(1)	1.00-2.00-1.43
Oregon	(1)	(1)	1.00-3.50-2.28
Pennsylvania	M.	42-84-61	.75-3.50-1.41
Do	(1)	(1)	1.00-2.03 1.51
Rhode Island	(1)	(1)	1.36-1.54-1.53
Do	(1)	(1)	1.10-1.10-1.10
South Carolina	M.	69-69-69	.50-.82-.65
Do	(1)	(1)	.78-1.20-.98
South Dakota	(1)	(1)	1.50-3.00-2.67
Tennessee	M.	60-84-78	.60-1.85-1.07
Do	(1)	(1)	.60-1.65-1.14
Texas	(1)	(1)	.53-2.50-1.32
Utah	(1)	(1)	1.75-3.31-2.86
Vermont	(1)	(1)	1.03-1.45-1.33
Virginia	M.	54-77-68	.75-1.50-1.05
Do	(1)	(1)	.75-1.70-1.18
Washington	(1)	(1)	2.06-3.34-2.53
West Virginia	M.	54-84-62	.75-3.22-1.43
Do	(1)	(1)	.93-2.00-1.41
Wisconsin	M.	60-60-60	1.00-2.10-1.62
Do	(1)	(1)	1.37-1.81-1.65
Wyoming	(1)	(1)	2.00-4.00-2.38
1890:			
Alabama	M.	55-72-63	.31-2.00-1.20
California	M.	60-60-60	1.75-2.00-1.84
Connecticut	M.	60-60-60	.92-1.75-1.38
Delaware	M.	60-60-60	1.00-1.67-1.29
Illinois	M.	60-60-60	1.00-2.00-1.51
Indiana	M.	60-60-60	.75-1.63-1.26
Kansas	M.	(1)	1.10-1.75-1.43
Louisiana	M.	60-60-60	.50-1.50-1.44
Maine	M.	60-60-60	1.25-1.25-1.25
Maryland	M.	48-60-60	1.10-1.67-1.27
Massachusetts	M.	60-72-61	.90-1.84-1.30
Michigan	M.	60-60-60	.33-2.50-1.33
Minnesota	M.	60-60-60	1.00-2.10-1.45
Mississippi	M.	(1)	.90-1.00-.99
Missouri	M.	54-60-57	.75-2.00-1.50
Nebraska	M.	(1)	1.20-2.03-1.62
New Hampshire	M.	60-60-60	1.00-1.50-1.25
Do	M.	60-60-60	[2].75-.75-.75
New Jersey	M.	48-70-59	.67-2.00-1.27
New York	M.	54-72-60	.60-2.50-1.57
Do	M.	(1)	[3].14-.14-.14
North Carolina	M.	60-72-66	.50-1.00-.75

1 Not reported.   2 And board.   3 Per hour.   4 And rent.   5 And board and washing.

TABLE G–1.—*Laborers, 1840–1900, by year and State*—Continued

Year and State	Sex	Hours per week	Rate per day (dollars)
1890—Continued.			
Ohio	M.	54-72.60	.82-2.00-1.36
Do	(1)	48-72-60	.75-2.00-1.37
Pennsylvania	M.	54-60-57	.75-2.00-1.42
Rhode Island	M.	60-60-60	.75-1.43-1.02
Tennessee	M.	69-69-69	.30-1.00- .59
Virginia	M.	60-60-60	1.00-1.00-1.00
Wisconsin	M.	60-84-63	1.40-2.15-1.55
1891:			
California	M.	60-60-60	1.75-2.00-1.84
Connecticut	M.	60-60-60	1.50-1.50-1.50
Delaware	M.	60-60-60	1.00-1.67-1.29
Illinois	M.	60-60-60	1.50-1.75-1.63
Do	M.	60-60-60	1.50-1.75-1.51
Kansas	M.	36-72-63	1.50-2.05-1.67
Louisiana	M.	60-60-60	1.50-1.50-1.50
Maine	M.	60-84-61	.87-2.00-1.44
Do	M.	(1)	[2].20- .20- .20
Maryland	M.	60-60-60	1.20-1.67-1.29
Massachusetts	M.	60-72-61	.90-1.84-1.32
Michigan	M.	60-60-60	1.25-1.55-1.28
Minnesota	M.	60-60-60	1.50-1.75-1.65
Do	M.	(1)	[2].84-1.15- .91
Missouri	M.	54-60-58	1.02-2.07-1.38
New Hampshire	M.	60-60-60	.75-1.50-1.08
New Jersey	M.	60-60-60	1.00-1.75-1.46
New York	M.	54-72-61	.60-2.75-1.44
Do	M.	(1)	[2].14- .14- .14
North Carolina	M.	60-72-64	.38-1.50- .85
Ohio	M.	42-72-59	.60-2.00-1.40
Pennsylvania	M.	54-60-57	1.00-2.00-1.41
Rhode Island	M.	60-60-60	1.10-1.10-1.10
South Carolina	M.	60-60-60	1.00-1.00-1.00
Virginia	M.	60-60-60	1.00-1.00-1.00
Wisconsin	M.	60-60-60	1.00-1.71-1.40
Do	M.	(1)	[2].10- .20- .15
1892:			
California	M.	48-66-60	1.00-2.25-1.90
Do	M.	60-60-60	[2]1.15-1.25-1.15
Connecticut	M.	54-60-55	.83-2.13-2.02
Delaware	M.	60-60-60	1.00-2.00-1.30
Florida	M.	60-60-60	1.00-1.25-1.09
Illinois	M.	59-60-60	1.50-1.75-1.51
Indiana	M.	48-66-59	.72-1.77-1.29
Iowa	M.	54-96-61	.76-1.80-1.34
Kansas	M.	60-60-60	1.60-1.75-1.62
Louisiana	M.	60-60-60	1.50-1.50-1.50
Maine	M.	60-60-60	1.41-1.84-1.52
Maryland	M.	60-60-60	1.20-1.67-1.28
Massachusetts	M.	58-72-61	.80-2.00-1.45
Michigan	M.	54-60-60	.75-2.00-1.32
Minnesota	M.	60-60-60	1.50-1.75-1.72
Do	M.	(1)	[2].84-1.15- .91
Missouri	M.	54-60-58	1.50-1.50-1.50
New Hampshire	M.	60-60-60	1.25-1.25-1.25
New Jersey	M.	60-60-60	1.67-1.75-1.72
New York	M.	54-66-60	1.00-2.50-1.72
Ohio	M.	36-84-59	.75-3.00-1.45
Pennsylvania	M.	54-60-58	1.00-2.00-1.41
Rhode Island	M.	53-60-59	1.25-1.75-1.55
South Carolina	M.	60-60-60	1.00-1.00-1.00
Vermont	M.	60-60-60	1.25-1.25-1.25
Virginia	M.	60-60-60	1.00-1.00-1.00
Wisconsin	M.	60-60-60	1.50-1.60-1.55
1893:			
California	M.	60-60-60	1.50-2.00-1.73
Connecticut	M.	54-54-54	2.13-2.13-2.13
Delaware	M.	60-60-60	.83-2.00-1.31
Illinois	M.	40-84-60	.33-2.75-1.57
Do	M.	65-72-69	[2].67-1.17- .92
Kansas	M.	(1)	1.50-1.50-1.50
Louisiana	M.	60-60-60	1.50-1.50-1.50
Maine	M.	(1)	1.62-1.62-1.62
Maryland	M.	42-95-61	.25-3.00-1.25
Massachusetts	M.	58-60-59	.87-2.00-1.51
Michigan	M.	48-72-60	.96-2.00-1.30

Year and State	Sex	Hours per week	Rate per day (dollars)
1893—Continued.			
Minnesota	M.	60-60-60	1.50-1.70-1.61
Do	M.	(1)	[2].61-1.15- .78
Missouri	M.	54-72-61	.69-2.00-1.59
Montana	M.	54-66-55	1.50-2.50-1.78
Do	M.	54-54-54	[6]1.53-1.53-1.53
New Hampshire	M.	55-60-59	1.00-2.00-1.36
New Jersey	M.	60-84-73	1.20-1.55-1.39
New York	M.	42-84-59	.67-3.00-1.49
North Carolina	M.	60-60-60	.75- .75- .75
Ohio	M.	36-72-59	.50-2.75-1.41
Pennsylvania	M.	48-84-59	.25-3.00-1.38
Virginia	M.	(1)	2.00-2.00-2.00
Do	M.	60-60-60	1.00-1.00-1.00
Do	M.	60-60-60	.75-1.76-1.47
Do	M.	(1)	[2].12½-.20-.14½
Do	M.	(1)	[2].50- .84- .81
1894:			
California	M.	60-60-60	1.50-2.00-1.75
Connecticut	M.	54-54-54	2.13-2.13-2.13
Delaware	M.	60-60-60	.83-2.00-1.27
Georgia	M.	60-60-60	.60- .80- .73
Illinois	M.	60-60-60	1.50-1.50-1.50
Indiana	M.	48-64-56	1.25-1.57-1.41
Iowa	M.	48-84-62	.67-2.25-1.43
Kansas	M.	62-62-62	1.05-1.43-1.08
Louisiana	M.	60-60-60	1.25-1.25-1.25
Maine	M.	57-66-60	1.00-2.00-1.47
Maryland	M.	60-72-62	1.00-1.50-1.27
Massachusetts	M.	54-72-62	.75-2.00-1.54
Michigan	M.	60-60-60	1.13-1.38-1.25
Minnesota	M.	60-60-60	1.25-1.75-1.50
Do	M.	(1)	[2].61-1.00- .70
Missouri	M.	54-60-58	1.50-1.50-1.50
Montana	M.	(1)	1.46-2.42-2.15
Do	M.	(1)	[6]1.22-1.22-1.22
New Hampshire	M.	54-69-60	1.17-2.00-1.53
New York	M.	54-60-60	.60-2.00-1.51
North Carolina	M.	60-72-62	.40-1.50- .79
Do	(1)	60-72-68	.40-1.50- .82
Ohio	M.	30-72-59	.50-3.33-1.36
Pennsylvania	M.	54-60-56	1.10-1.83-1.44
Rhode Island	(1)	(1)	.75-1.75-1.17
Virginia	M.	(1)	1.00-1.00-1.00
West Virginia	M.	48-60-59	.80-1.83-1.35
Wisconsin	M.	60-60-60	1.25-1.25-1.25
1895:			
Alabama	M.	60-66-64	.50- .90- .69
California	M.	60-60-60	1.50-2.00-1.76
Connecticut	M.	54-72-60	.75-2.13-1.67
Delaware	M.	60-60-60	.83-1.83-1.23
Florida	M.	60-63-62	.60-1.00- .80
Georgia	M.	51-66-63	.70-1.50-1.04
Illinois	M.	60-60-60	1.50-1.50-1.50
Kansas	M.	42-72-60	.75-2.30-1.54
Kentucky	M.	60-60-60	1.00-1.33-1.08
Louisiana	M.	60-63-61	.75-2.00-1.22
Maine	M.	60-60-60	.92-2.77-1.61
Maryland	M.	60-90-64	1.00-2.00-1.28
Massachusetts	M.	41-72-60	.67-2.17-1.47
Michigan	M.	60-60-60	.50-2.00-1.26
Minnesota	M.	60-60-60	1.37-1.75-1.39
Do	M.	(1)	[2].58- .77- .62
Mississippi	M.	60-60-60	.90- .90- .90
Missouri	M.	54-60-58	1.00-2.10-1.45
Montana	M.	(1)	1.10-2.17-1.32
New Hampshire	M.	59-60-60	.60-2.75-1.43
New Jersey	M.	48-60-58	.75-2.00-1.34
New York	M.	48-72-60	.58-2.50-1.49
North Carolina	M.	60-72-63	.50-1.50- .75
Ohio	M.	36-72-60	.40-4.00-1.36
Pennsylvania	M.	54-60-57	.53-2.00-1.36
Rhode Island	M.	55-60-59	.92-2.00-1.50
South Carolina	M.	54-66-66	.50-1.33- .72
Tennessee	M.	60-66-65	.80-1.30- .99
Virginia	M.	48-72-59	.67-1.25-1.04

[1] Not reported.　　[2] And board.　　[3] Per hour.　　[6] And board and lodging.

TABLE G-1.—*Laborers, 1840-1900, by year and State*—Continued

Year and State	Sex	Lowest, highest, and average—	
		Hours per week	Rate per day (dollars)
1895—Continued.			
West Virginia	M.	59-59-59	1.25-1.25-1.25
Wisconsin	M.	60-60-60	1.25-1.25-1.25
Do	[1]	42-96-60	.40-2.33-1.22
1896:			
Alabama	M.	[1]	.75-.90-.83
California	M.	60-60-60	1.00-2.00-1.29
Colorado	M.	54-60-60	.75-1.75-1.47
Connecticut	M.	60-60-60	1.00-1.75-1.24
Delaware	M.	54-72-64	.50-1.33-.89
Dist. of Columbia	M.	[1]	.83-.83-.83
Florida	M.	[1]	1.00-2.00-1.31
Georgia	M.	54-72-65	.50-1.58-.88
Illinois	M.	42-77-59	.83-2.25-1.32
Indiana	M.	60-65-62	1.10-2.00-1.21
Iowa	M.	48-58-51	.58-1.67-1.42
Kansas	M.	48-78-59	.58-2.30-1.28
Kentucky	M.	60-60-60	.45-1.00-.71
Louisiana	M.	60-60-60	1.25-1.25-1.25
Maryland	M.	48-70-60	1.00-2.00-1.27
Massachusetts	M.	54-84-60	1.00-2.25-1.61
Michigan	M.	54-60-59	1.00-2.00-1.35
Do	[1]	60-60-60	.67-2.00-1.19
Minnesota	M.	60-60-60	1.25-1.75-1.41
Do	M.	60-60-60	[2].50-.77-.52
Mississippi	M.	[1]	.50-.50-.50
Missouri	M.	48-72-60	.50-2.75-1.39
Montana	M.	[1]	1.14-2.51-1.52
Nebraska	M.	48-72-59	.75-3.50-1.72
New Hampshire	M.	54-60-59	1.20-2.00-1.45
New Jersey	M.	60-60-60	2.00-2.00-2.00
New York	M.	36-84-61	.38-3.00-1.50
North Carolina	M.	69-72-70	.75-.75-.75
Ohio	M.	45-72-59	.46-2.70-1.36
Do	F.	48-60-57	.40-1.33-.80
Pennsylvania	M.	47-72-60	.55-2.01-1.35
Rhode Island	M.	60-60-60	1.00-2.00-1.35
South Carolina	M.	66-66-66	.50-.75-.72
Tennessee	M.	[1]	.23-1.50-1.00
Vermont	M.	60-66-62	1.00-1.25-1.19
Virginia	M.	60-60-60	1.00-1.00-1.00
West Virginia	M.	48-60-58	.83-1.50-1.15
Wisconsin	M.	48-60-58	.75-2.50-1.25
1897:			
California	M.	60-60-60	1.50-1.75-1.58
Connecticut	M.	30-60-57	.75-1.75-1.44
Illinois	M.	60-60-60	1.00-1.67-1.50
Kansas	M.	30-84-63	.58-2.00-1.15
Louisiana	M.	60-60-60	1.25-1.25-1.25
Maine	M.	60-60-60	1.50-2.25-1.84

Year and State	Sex	Lowest, highest, and average—	
		Hours per week	Rate per day (dollars)
1897—Continued.			
Maryland	M.	54-60-58	1.25-1.50-1.27
Massachusetts	M.	60-60-60	.95-1.75-1.48
Michigan	M.	60-60-60	.75-1.35-1.25
Minnesota	M.	60-60-60	1.50-1.50-1.50
Missouri	M.	54-60-58	1.50-1.50-1.50
Montana	[1]	[1]	1.71-2.49-2.03
Nebraska	M.	48-60-55	1.00-3.00-1.58
New Hampshire	M.	53-53-53	1.75-1.75-1.75
New York	M.	48-70-54	.75-2.75-1.87
North Carolina	M.	66-66-66	.60-.60-.60
Ohio	M.	42-72-61	.40-5.00-1.38
Pennsylvania	M.	48-60-54	.60-2.20-1.43
Virginia	M.	48-72-61	.50-1.50-.95
1898:			
California	M.	60-60-60	1.50-1.75-1.59
Illinois	M.	60-60-60	1.25-1.75-1.50
Do	[1]	[1]	1.25-1.50-1.48
Iowa	[1]	[1]	1.40-1.50-1.42
Kansas	M.	42-72-53	.58-1.50-1.41
Louisiana	M.	60-60-60	1.25-1.25-1.25
Maine	M.	60-60-60	1.25-1.25-1.25
Maryland	M.	48-60-55	1.25-1.67-1.44
Massachusetts	M.	60-60-60	1.25-1.50-1.38
Michigan	M.	[1]	1.10-1.32-1.23
Minnesota	M.	60-60-60	1.50-1.50-1.50
Missouri	M.	54-60-58	1.50-1.50-1.50
Nebraska	[1]	60-60-60	1.50-1.50-1.50
Do	[1]	48-84-59	[3].30-4.00-1.74
New Jersey	M.	54-60-57	.75-1.67-1.29
New York	M.	48-60-55	.50-2.75-2.09
Ohio	M.	53-54-54	.50-2.50-1.36
Pennsylvania	M.	54-54-54	1.05-2.63-1.41
Virginia	M.	60-60-60	1.00-1.00-1.00
Washington	[1]	[1]	1.42-1.76-1.54
1899:			
Alabama	M.	84-84-84	1.05-2.00-1.60
Michigan	M.	64-64-64	1.27-1.63-1.33
New York	M.	44-44-44	1.50-2.46-1.51
North Carolina	M.	60-60-60	.65-.75-.71
Ohio	M.	[1]	1.21-2.25-1.46
Pennsylvania	[1]	[1]	1.10-3.43-1.52
Virginia	[1]	[1]	.75-1.10-.99
1900:			
Alabama	M.	84-84-84	1.10-2.00-1.64
New York	M.	44-44-44	1.50-2.46-1.51
North Carolina	M.	60-60-60	.65-.75-.71
Ohio	[1]	[1]	1.50-1.50-1.50

[1] Not reported.   [2] And board.   [3] Per hour.

H.—LEATHER AND ITS PRODUCTS

BOOTS AND SHOES

The sources from which this information was taken are the fifteenth and the nineteenth annual reports of the Commissioner of Labor Statistics and bulletins of the Bureau of Labor Statistics Nos. 59, 65, 71, 77, 134, 154, 178, 232, 260, 278, 324, 374, 450, and 498.

In nearly all of these reports the data are presented by States and by sex. For the period from 1907 to 1910 details were not available by States. They are here shown for the United States only. See Table H–4. In some instances there are overlapping periods. These reports are from different sources and are considered valuable. The details are presented here in the same manner as published in the above-noted reports.

The shoemaker as shown in this report represents a worker who made the entire shoe. Beginning by taking measurements of the customer's feet, cutting and matching the various parts of upper and sole, and then stitching these parts together by hand to form a complete shoe.

This 1-man method was followed by the shop which employed three or four workmen; then came the small factory in which most of the work was still done by hand. In these small factories the discovery was made that some workers were much more proficient than others in certain operations, therefore the work on the shoe was divided among the workmen, each doing a particular part, some cutting and stitching the upper, others preparing the sole, fastening it to the upper, etc. By this constant attention to a particular part of the shoe the worker was able to accomplish much more in a given length of time, do the work better and with less effort than when making the entire shoe. This division of the work into selected parts continued to increase and in a much larger degree after the introduction of machinery.

There is shown in Table H–6 the hours and rates for a group of employees reported as stitchers, upper. These workers stitch together the various parts of lining and upper and are here classed in a general group. The sewing machine used for stitching together these parts was first introduced in 1852 and marked the beginning of factory development. The figures cover the years 1859 to 1900. Tables H–7, H–8, H–9, H–10, H–11, H–12, and H–13 present wages and hours of vampers who represent a specific group. The figures relate to the years 1879 to 1928.

Wages and hours of work are shown in Tables H–20, H–21, H–22, and H–23 for McKay stitchers for various periods from 1875 to 1928, inclusive. This machine is used to fasten the sole and upper parts of the shoe together. It was introduced in the year 1858 and is said to be the first bottom sewing machine ever used in the manufacture of shoes. A very large per cent of all shoes are still manufactured by the McKay process.

Details are also shown for cutters, upper, hand, and lasters, machine.

261

TABLE **H–1.**—*Shoemakers, 1855–1899, by year and State*

Year and State	Sex	Hours per week	Rate per day (dollars)	Year and State	Sex	Hours per week	Rate per day (dollars)
1855;				**1887—Continued.**			
Massachusetts....	M.	72–72–72	1.50–2.40–1.95	Rhode Island.....	F.	48–48–48	1.00–1.00–1.00
1858:				Wisconsin........	M.	(1)	1.00–2.00–1.41
Massachusetts....	M.	60–60–60	2.50–2.50–2.50	Do.............	M.	(1)	[3].75–.75–.75
1859:				**1888:**			
Massachusetts....	M.	60–60–60	3.00–3.00–3.00	Colorado.........	M.	72–72–72	2.00–2.00–2.00
1860:				Iowa.............	M.	59–72–62	1.00–1.70–1.48
Ohio.............	M.	(1)	1.50–1.50–1.50	Kansas...........	......	(1)	1.50–1.50–1.50
1863:				Maine...........	M.	60–60–60	1.33–2.00–1.69
Massachusetts....	M.	60–60–60	2.50–2.50–2.50	Do.............	F.	60–60–60	.75–1.17–.97
1864:				New York........	M.	51–57–56	1.33–2.50–2.28
Massachusetts....	M.	60–60–60	2.50–2.50–2.50	North Carolina...	M.	60–72–64	1.00–1.66–1.34
1865:				**1889:**			
Massachusetts....	M.	60–60–60	2.50–2.50–2.50	Kansas...........	M.	(1)	2.12–2.12–2.12
1866:				North Carolina...	M.	48–48–48	1.00–1.00–1.00
Kansas..........	M.	(1)	1.50–1.50–1.50	**1890:**			
Massachusetts....	M.	60–60–60	3.00–3.00–3.00	Kansas...........	M.	(1)	1.70–2.00–1.88
1867:				Minnesota.......	M.	(1)	1.00–4.15–2.18
Massachusetts....	M.	60–60–60	2.50–3.00–2.75	New York........	M.	(1)	1.00–2.00–1.60
1868:				**1891:**			
Massachusetts....	M.	60–60–60	2.00–3.00–2.50	Michigan.........	F.	(1)	1.03–1.03–1.03
1872:				New York........	M.	(1)	1.00–2.33–1.79
Massachusetts....	M.	54–63–60	1.75–3.25–2.48	North Carolina...	M.	(1)	.50–.50–.50
Ohio.............	M.	(1)	2.50–4.17–3.27	Ohio............	M.	48–60–59	1.26–2.50–1.77
1873:				**1892:**			
Massachusetts....	M.	(1)	2.00–2.00–2.00	California........	M.	60–63–62	2.33–2.75–2.54
1875:				Missouri........	M.	60–60–60	2.50–2.50–2.50
Massachusetts....	M.	60–60–60	2.50–2.50–2.50	**1893:**			
1877:				Illinois.........	M.	60–80–63	1.00–2.33–1.62
New Jersey......	M.	60–60–60	1.16–2.50–1.51	Maryland........	M.	30–84–64	.50–3.33–1.32
Ohio.............	M.	54–60–59	1.50–3.00–2.14	Montana.........	M.	54–66–57	1.92–4.17–3.08
1878:				Do.............	M.	54–54–54	[3].67–.67–.67
Ohio.............	M.	60–65–63	1.25–2.00–1.63	New York........	M.	24–96–62	.33–4.17–1.41
1879:				Do.............	M.	84–84–84	[2].50–.50–.50
Missouri........	M.	60–75–66	1.17–2.50–1.71	Ohio............	M.	54–60–60	.75–3.00–1.63
New Jersey......	(1)	25–60–58	.75–3.00–1.30	Do.............	M.	54–60–60	.60–1.00–.99
Ohio.............	M.	(1)	1.33–2.33–1.86	Pennsylvania.....	M.	33–84–60	.25–3.33–1.49
Pennsylvania.....	M.	54–78–63	1.00–1.50–1.31	Do.............	F.	60–60–60	1.17–1.17–1.17
1880:				**1894:**			
New Jersey......	(1)	46–88–60	.82–3.75–1.59	Dist. of Columbia.	M.	60–60–60	3.00–3.00–3.00
Ohio.............	M.	(1)	1.75–1.75–1.75	Georgia.........	M.	60–60–60	1.50–1.50–1.50
1881:				Iowa,...........	M.	36–84–60	.58–4.17–1.69
Ohio.............	M.	48–72–60	1.00–2.67–1.78	Massachusetts....	M.	60–60–60	2.00–3.50–2.83
Pennsylvania.....	M.	60–60–60	2.00–2.00–2.00	New York........	M.	60–60–60	2.00–2.50–2.25
1882:				North Carolina...	M.	60–60–60	1.25–1.75–1.50
Illinois.........	M.	72–72–72	2.00–2.00–2.00	Do.............	(1)	60–60–60	1.00–2.00–1.67
Missouri........	M.	60–90–78	1.50–2.00–1.90	Ohio............	M.	42–60–58	1.25–3.00–1.69
New Jersey......	M.	(1)	1.67–1.67–1.67	Do.............	F.	60–60–60	1.00–1.00–1.00
Ohio.............	(1)	57–60–58	2.00–2.50–2.11	**1895:**			
Pennsylvania.....	M.	72–72–72	.85–1.75–1.30	Massachusetts....	M.	60–60–60	2.50–3.00–2.70
1883:				New York........	M.	60–60–60	1.50–2.50–2.00
Michigan........	M.	(1)	.50–4.00–1.67	North Carolina...	M.	60–60–60	[2].75–2.00–1.27
New Jersey......	M.	60–60–60	1.33–2.50–1.67	Ohio............	M.	54–60–59	1.18–1.75–1.60
Ohio.............	M.	59–60–60	1.67–2.50–2.21	Do.............	F.	54–54–54	1.00–1.00–1.00
1884:				Wisconsin........	(1)	36–60–58	.90–3.00–1.65
California........	M.	60–60–60	2.50–3.00–2.66	**1896:**			
Iowa............	M.	48–72–63	.96–3.50–1.74	Alabama.........	M.	(1)	.92–1.17–1.05
Michigan........	M.	(1)	.65–2.50–1.57	Georgia.........	M.	(1)	.42–.83–.63
Missouri........	M.	60–60–60	1.00–2.50–1.45	Illinois.........	M.	30–90–61	.32–2.50–1.13
New Jersey......	M.	60–72–68	1.67–2.00–1.95	Kansas..........	M.	48–48–48	1.60–1.60–1.60
Ohio.............	M.	64–64–64	1.83–1.83–1.83	Massachusetts....	M.	(1)	1.67–1.67–1.67
1885:				New York........	M.	(1)	.63–3.00–1.41
Kansas..........	M.	60–96–74	1.00–2.00–1.77	North Carolina...	M.	60–66–62	.65–1.50–1.13
New Jersey......	M.	60–60–60	1.67–2.50–2.00	Ohio............	M.	54–60–59	10.2–1.72–1.52
1886:				Do.............	F.	54–60–57	.75–1.00–.89
California........	M.	48–72–60	1.25–3.00–2.23	South Carolina...	M.	(1)	.67–.67–.67
Do.............	M.	60–72–62	[2]1.50–2.25–1.65	Tennessee	M.	(1)	.83–1.17–1.00
Illinois.........	M.	60–84–60	1.25–2.42–2.29	**1897:**			
Iowa............	M.	48–90–60	.75–4.00–1.64	Kansas..........	M.	58–60–59	1.45–2.00–1.66
Kansas..........	M.	60–90–66	1.25–2.50–1.67	Do.............	M.	(1)	[4].10–.10–.10
Ohio.............	M.	(1)	.53–2.03–1.48	Michigan........	M.	(1)	1.81–1.81–1.81
Rhode Island.....	F.	48–48–48	1.33–1.33–1.33	New York........	M.	57–60–59	.67–5.00–1.94
1887:				Do.............	F.	60–60–60	.75–.75–.75
Connecticut.....	M.	(1)	1.58–1.77–1.67	**1898:**			
Kansas..........	M.	90–90–90	1.50–2.50–1.91	Michigan........	M.	(1)	1.24–2.00–1.32
Maine...........	M.	60–72–61	.72–3.00–1.52	Nebraska........	(1)	48–48–48	.87–.87–.87
North Carolina...	M.	60–72–62	.80–2.00–1.36	New York........	M.	60–60–60	.60–3.00–1.87
Ohio.............	M.	60–60–60	1.25–2.25–1.77	Do.............	F.	60–60–60	.40–2.00–.89
Do.............	F.	60–60–60	1.25–1.25–1.25				

¹ Not reported.   ² And board.   ³ And board and lodging.   ⁴ Per hour.

TABLE **H-2.**—*Cutters, upper, 1883–1900, by year and State*

| Year and State | Sex | Lowest, highest, and average— | | Year and State | Sex | Lowest, highest, and average— | |
		Hours per week	Rate per day (dollars)			Hours per week	Rate per day (dollars)
1899:				**1894—Continued.**			
North Carolina___	M.	60–60–60	2. 00–2. 00–2. 00	Ohio_____	M.	48–60–59	1. 00–3. 00–2. 01
1883:				Do_____	F.	60–60–60	. 75–2. 00– . 96
Massachusetts____	M.	(¹)	1. 67–1. 83–1. 75	**1895:**			
Do_____	(¹)	(¹)	1. 17–1. 17–1. 17	Maine_____	M.	60–60–60	0. 83–2. 25–1. 32
1885:				Massachusetts____	M.	57–60–60	2. 00–3. 83–2. 61
Maine_____	M.	60–60–60	. 56–2. 29–1. 46	Missouri_____	M.	(¹)	. 41–4. 17–1. 72
1886:				Ohio_____	M.	42–60–59	1. 30–3. 00–2. 19
Missouri_____	F.	59–59–59	. 83– . 83– . 83	Do_____	F.	60–60–60	1. 15–2. 00–1. 29
Pennsylvania_____	M.	(¹)	1. 17–2. 00–1. 67	**1896:**			
1888:				Missouri_____	M.	54–60–59	1. 25–2. 50–2. 05
New York_____	M.	55–60–59	. 83–1. 08–1. 06	Do_____	F.	60–60–60	. 46–1. 85– . 91
1890:				Ohio_____	M.	57–60–58	1. 50–2. 13–1. 92
New York_____	M.	(¹)	. 50–3. 50–1. 89	Do_____	F.	60–60–60	1. 22–2. 00–1. 27
1891:				Pennsylvania_____	M.	60–60–60	1. 25–2. 00–1. 67
Michigan_____	F.	(¹)	. 89– . 89– . 89	**1897:**			
New York_____	M.	(¹)	. 50–3. 50–1. 85	Virginia_____	M.	60–60–60	1. 50–1. 50–1. 50
1893:				**1898:**			
Illinois_____	M.	59–59–59	3. 00–3. 00–3. 00	New York_____	M.	60–60–60	2. 00–2. 67–2. 50
1894:				**1899:**			
Maine_____	M.	60–60–60	1. 50–2. 25–1. 89	Massachusetts____	M.	58–58–58	1. 75–3. 00–2. 16
New Hampshire__	M.	60–60–60	1. 25–1. 25–1. 25	**1900:**			
New York_____	M.	60–60–60	1. 25–2. 25–1. 84	Massachusetts____	M.	58–58–58	1. 75–3. 00–2. 40
Do_____	F.	60–60–60	1. 00–1. 00–1. 00				

¹ Not reported.

TABLE **H-3.**—*Cutters, upper, males, 1890–1907, by State and year*

| Year | Massachusetts | | New Hampshire | | New York | | Ohio | |
	Hours per week	Rate per hour	Hours per week	Rate per hour	Hours per week	Rate per hour	Hours per week	Rate per hour
1890_____	59. 2	$0. 250	59. 8	$0. 235	57. 0	$0. 315	60. 0	$0. 233
1891_____	59. 4	. 250	59. 6	. 229	57. 0	. 302	60. 0	. 236
1892_____	59. 2	. 255	59. 4	. 225	59. 0	. 267	60. 0	. 269
1893_____	59. 2	. 262	59. 4	. 226	59. 0	. 268	60. 0	. 250
1894_____	58. 9	. 257	59. 4	. 224	57. 6	. 303	60. 0	. 210
1895_____	59. 0	. 258	59. 3	. 227	56. 4	. 296	60. 0	. 241
1896_____	59. 1	. 253	59. 3	. 226	57. 2	. 282	60. 0	. 236
1897_____	59. 0	. 255	59. 3	. 232	57. 4	. 280	60. 0	. 235
1898_____	59. 0	. 254	59. 3	. 231	57. 8	. 282	60. 0	. 243
1899_____	58. 8	. 260	59. 4	. 226	56. 9	. 282	60. 0	. 248
1900_____	58. 9	. 260	59. 3	. 226	55. 9	. 281	60. 0	. 263
1901_____	58. 9	. 256	59. 3	. 225	56. 2	. 291	60. 0	. 268
1902_____	57. 3	. 268	59. 3	. 228	53. 9	. 304	60. 0	. 274
1903_____	56. 0	. 282	59. 3	. 227	55. 3	. 308	60. 0	. 273
1904_____	55. 5	. 285	59. 3	. 233	55. 8	. 306	60. 0	. 304
1905_____	55. 0	. 292	59. 3	. 246	55. 6	. 314	56. 1	. 329
1906_____	54. 8	. 291	59. 4	. 246	55. 6	. 321	56. 3	. 341
1907_____	54. 7	. 314	59. 2	. 251	55. 0	. 334	56. 3	. 365

TABLE **H-4.**—*Cutters, vamp and whole shoe, hand, males, 1907–1912, United States*

| Year | United States | |
	Hours per week	Rate per hour
1907_____	54. 9	$0. 325
1908_____	54. 8	. 332
1909_____	54. 7	. 340
1910_____	56. 0	. 319
1911_____	56. 2	. 313
1912_____	55. 0	. 322

TABLE **H-5.**—*Cutters, vamp and whole shoe, hand, males, 1910–1928, by State and year*

Year	Massachusetts		New Hampshire		New York		Ohio	
	Hours per week	Rate per hour	Hours per week	Rate per hour	Hours per week	Rate per hour	Hours per week	Rate per hour
1910	54.3	$0.341	57.4	$0.218	56.1	$0.359	59.9	$0.292
1911	54.4	.334	57.4	.226	55.5	.340	59.9	.294
1912	53.1	.337	58.0	.242	54.6	.347	56.4	.322
1913	53.0	.362			53.7	.371	55.6	.372
1914	53.1	.373			52.1	.368	53.9	.412
1916	53.0	.395	55.0	.298	51.9	.420	53.6	.373
1918	51.2	.499	50.5	.393	51.6	.525	54.6	.496
1920	47.2	.936	49.0	.896	48.1	.833	47.8	.803
1922	46.7	.915	48.6	.689	47.5	.757	50.0	.766
1924	47.6	.920	48.0	.750	47.5	.896	49.9	.783
1926	48.2	.857	49.8	.676	47.4	.948	49.9	.975
1928	48.0	.895	49.1	.699	46.9	.974	49.9	.866

TABLE **H-6.**—*Stitchers, upper, 1859–1900, by year and State*

Year and State	Sex	Lowest, highest, and average—		Year and State	Sex	Lowest, highest, and average—	
		Hours per week	Rate per day (dollars)			Hours per week	Rate per day (dollars)
1859:				1885—Continued.			
Massachusetts	M.	60–60–60	2.00–2.00–2.00	New York	M.	60–60–60	.83–2.00–1.34
1869:				Do	F.	53–60–60	.83–1.35–1.30
Massachusetts	(¹)	57–57–57	1.85–1.85–1.85	Ohio	F.	59–60–60	.73–1.77–1.22
1873:				Pennsylvania	M.	60–60–60	1.50–2.65–1.78
Illinois	F.	(¹)	2.33–2.33–2.33	Do	F.	60–60–60	.50–1.32–1.07
1875:				Wisconsin	F.	60–60–60	1.00–1.00–1.00
Massachusetts	M.	(¹)	1.25–1.90–1.83	1886:			
Do	F.	(¹)	1.12–1.50–1.27	Illinois	F.	57–57–57	1.25–1.25–1.25
1877:				Maryland	F.	50–60–57	.50–2.00–1.04
Ohio	F.	(¹)	1.50–1.50–1.50	Massachusetts	F.	59–59–59	1.11–1.50–1.17
1879:				Missouri	F.	55–61–59	.50–1.67–1.08
Pennsylvania	F.	57–57–57	.30–2.00–1.12	New Hampshire	M.	59–59–59	1.50–1.50–1.50
Do	(¹)	60–60–60	.54–.80–.64	Do	F.	59–59–59	1.65–1.65–1.65
1880:				New Jersey	F.	48–60–60	.50–1.33–1.03
Ohio	F.	(¹)	.89–1.02–.92	New York	F.	56–60–58	.33–2.39–.95
1881:				Pennsylvania	F.	51–56–53	.41–1.17–.81
Massachusetts	F.	60–60–60	.23–1.84–.92	1887:			
New Jersey	M.	(¹)	1.67–1.67–1.67	California	F.	54–60–57	.50–2.00–1.56
Do	F.	(¹)	1.08–1.08–1.08	Connecticut	F.	(¹)	.67–1.14–1.08
1882:				Illinois	F.	53–60–59	.58–1.70–1.16
Missouri	(¹)	60–60–60	.67–1.33–1.00	Kentucky	F.	47–60–54	.28–1.25–.82
New Jersey	F.	60–60–60	1.10–1.33–1.20	Louisiana	F.	59–60–60	.38–1.33–.71
New York	F.	60–60–60	.67–.83–.73	Maryland	F.	59–59–59	.25–.25–.25
Ohio	(¹)	57–60–60	1.00–3.00–1.18	Massachusetts	F.	51–59–58	.67–1.75–1.15
Massachusetts	M.	(¹)	1.67–4.17–2.67	Minnesota	F.	59–60–60	.50–2.00–1.09
Do	F.	(¹)	1.17–2.00–1.50	New York	F.	45–60–57	.38–1.83–1.00
Missouri	F.	60–60–60	1.00–1.00–1.00	Ohio	F.	48–60–60	.50–1.67–.97
New Jersey	F.	60–60–60	.75–1.67–1.07	Pennsylvania	F.	52–57–54	.83–1.68–1.19
1884:				Wisconsin	(¹)	(¹)	.93–1.05–.97
Massachusetts	F.	59–59–59	1.80+2.00–1.91	1888:			
New Jersey	F.	60–60–60	.67–2.00–1.18	California	F.	54–59–57	.50–2.00–1.39
1885:				Indiana	F.	53–56–54	.83–1.00–.94
California	M.	60–60–60	1.37–1.37–1.37	Maine	F.	60–60–60	1.25–1.33–1.29
Do	F.	60–60–60	1.50–1.50–1.50	New Jersey	F.	60–60–60	1.00–1.25–1.12
Connecticut	F.	60–60–60	1.00–1.17–1.10	New York	M.	48–61–56	.88–2.00–1.41
Illinois	F.	60–60–60	1.50–1.50–1.50	Do	F.	44–61–59	.55–1.67–1.30
Kentucky	F.	60–60–60	1.00–1.00–1.00	Virginia	F.	52–52–52	.83–1.00–.94
Maine	M.	60–60–60	.50–2.50–1.24	1890:			
Do	F.	60–60–60	.43–2.36–1.06	New York	M.	(¹)	.33–4.25–1.23
Maryland	F.	60–60–60	.83–1.16–.93	Do	F.	(¹)	.22–1.50–1.02
Massachusetts	M.	48–60–60	1.00–3.33–1.83	1891:			
Do	F.	54–60–60	.35–2.79–1.38	Maine	F.	60–60–60	.64–1.33–.97
Do	(¹)	60–60–60	1.30–1.30–1.30	Do	(¹)	(¹)	1.07–1.58–1.17
Missouri	F.	59–59–59	.67–1.00–.80	Michigan	F.	(¹)	.67–1.18–1.10
New Jersey	F.	48–60–58	.67–2.00–1.06	New York	M.	(¹)	.33–4.25–1.18
Do	M.	54–54–54	2.33–4.17–3.25	Do	F.	(¹)	.22–1.58–1.01
				Ohio	F.	48–60–59	.49–1.25–.98

¹ Not reported.

TABLE **H–6.**—*Stitchers, upper, 1859–1900, by year and State*—Continued

Year and State	Sex	Hours per week	Rate per day (dollars)	Year and State	Sex	Hours per week	Rate per day (dollars)
1892:				1895—Continued.			
California	F.	47–60–58	.42–2.17–1.24	New Jersey	F.	54–60–56	.75–2.00–1.23
Illinois	F.	56–59–57	.42–2.16–1.17	New York	F.	50–60–54	.33–3.07–1.33
Maine	F.	(¹)	.50–1.50–.91	North Carolina	M.	60–60–60	1.50–1.50–1.50
1893:				Ohio	M.	42–42–42	.75–2.00–.79
Maryland	F.	60–60–60	.58–1.33–.99	Do	F.	48–60–60	.50–2.25–.95
New Jersey	F.	56–56–56	.58–1.33–1.00	1896:			
Ohio	M.	60–60–60	1.00–1.00–1.00	New York	F.	56–60–59	.28–2.84–1.15
Do	F.	42–60–59	.45–1.75–.97	Ohio	F.	55–60–59	.55–1.92–1.00
Pennsylvania	F.	58–60–59	.50–.67–:56	Do	M.	54–60–59	2.00–2.46–2.36
1894:				Pennsylvania	F.	59–59–59	.68–.83–.75
Indiana	(¹)	56–56–56	1.00–1.00–1.00	1898:			
New York	F.	60–60–60	.83–.83–.83	New Jersey	F.	60–60–60	1.58–2.00–1.80
Ohio	M.	60–60–60	1.00–2.50–1.56	New York	M.	60–60–60	.50–1.67–1.00
Do	F.	42–60–59	.50–2.00–.94	1899:			
1895:				Massachusetts	M.	58–58–58	1.75–3.00–2.24
Connecticut	F.	60–60–60	.83–1.33–1.03	Do	F.	58–58–58	.67–3.18–1.90
Maine	M.	60–60–60	1.00–3.33–2.14	1900:			
Do	F.	60–60–60	.50–2.42–1.24	Massachusetts	M.	58–58–58	1.75–3.00–2.28
Massachusetts	M.	55–60–57	1.23–3.03–2.11	Do	F.	58–58–58	.67–3.17–1.91
Do	F.	55–60–57	.83–2.78–1.52				
Missouri	F.	59–59–59	.33–3.50–.95				
Do	M.	(¹)	.50–3.00–1.42				

¹ Not reported.

TABLE **H–7.**—*Vampers, 1879–1900, by year and State*

Year and State	Sex	Hours per week	Rate per day (dollars)	Year and State	Sex	Hours per week	Rate per day (dollars)
1879:				1890:			
Pennsylvania	F.	57–57–57	0.70–2.24–1.49	New York	M.	(¹)	1.00–1.17–1.04
1884:				Do	F.	(¹)	1.25–1.25–1.25
New Jersey	F.	60–60–60	.92–1.33–1.23	1891:			
1885:				Maine	F.	60–60–60	.75–1.80–1.07
California	M.	60–60–60	2.25–2.58–2.36	Do	(¹)	(¹)	1.51–1.66–1.57
Connecticut	F.	60–60–60	1.17–1.17–1.17	Michigan	F.	(¹)	1.67–1.67–1.67
Massachusetts	M.	48–60–59	.75–2.25–1.98	New York	M.	(¹)	1.00–1.67–1.44
Do	F.	59–60–59	1.41–2.34–1.84	Do	F.	(¹)	1.17–1.17–1.17
New Jersey	F.	60–60–60	.50–1.33–.99	1892:			
New York	M.	60–60–60	1.67–1.75–1.73	California	F.	48–60–55	1.50–2.00–1.77
Do	F.	59–59–59	2.00–2.00–2.00	Do	(¹)	51–51–51	2.00–2.00–2.00
Ohio	F.	59–60–60	.75–1.62–1.14	Illinois	F.	56–58–57	1.05–2.11–1.58
Pennsylvania	M.	60–60–60	1.90–1.90–1.90	Maine	F.	(¹)	.67–2.50–1.29
1886:				1893:			
Maryland	F.	50–59–54	.75–1.58–1.21	New Jersey	F.	56–56–56	.58–1.67–1.08
Missouri	F.	58–61–59	1.17–1.50–1.30	1894:			
New Jersey	F.	48–60–58	.50–1.60–1.15	New York	F.	60–60–60	1.00–1.00–1.00
Pennsylvania	F.	50–50–50	1.00–2.13–1.61	1895:			
1887:				Connecticut	F.	60–60–60	1.33–1.33–1.33
Illinois	F.	53–60–57	1.17–2.17–1.58	Massachusetts	F.	59–59–59	1.15–2.47–1.73
Maine	M.	60–60–60	1.67–1.75–1.71	Do	F.	58–60–59	.85–2.50–2.01
Massachusetts	F.	51–59–54	1.17–1.50–1.39	New York	F.	59–60–60	1.50–2.00–1.75
Minnesota	F.	59–60–60	1.25–1.67–1.42	1896:			
New York	F.	52–60–56	.80–2.59–1.22	Ohio	F.	59–60–60	.79–1.62–1.21
Ohio	F.	56–60–59	.39–1.50–.94	Pennsylvania	F.	59–60–59	.67–1.85–1.23
Do	M.	60–60–60	1.50–1.50–1.50	1899:			
Pennsylvania	F.	57–57–57	1.67–1.67–1.67	Massachusetts	F.	58–58–58	2.07–3.07–2.53
1888:				1900:			
Indiana	F.	59–59–59	1.08–1.08–1.08	Massachusetts	F.	58–58–58	1.88–3.01–2.56
Maine	F.	60–60–60	1.35–2.00–1.71				
New York	M.	53–53–53	1.67–1.67–1.67				

¹ Not reported.

TABLE **H-8.**—*Vampers, males, 1890–1907, by geographic division and year*

Year	North Atlantic		North Central		South Central	
	Hours per week	Rate per hour	Hours per week	Rate per hour	Hours per week	Rate per hour
1890					54. 0	$0. 278
1891	58. 0	$0. 234			54. 0	. 278
1892	58. 0	. 225			54. 0	. 278
1893	56. 2	. 264	60. 0	$0. 113	54. 0	. 278
1894	56. 3	. 216	60. 0	. 160	54. 0	. 278
1895	56. 3	. 219	60. 0	. 187	54. 0	. 278
1896	56. 4	. 250	60. 0	. 223	54. 0	. 278
1897	56. 6	. 275	60. 0	. 279	54. 0	. 278
1898	56. 6	. 236	60. 0	. 342	54. 0	. 333
1899	56. 0	. 254	60. 0	. 303	54. 0	. 333
1900	56. 7	. 270	60. 0	. 251	54. 0	. 333
1901	56. 5	. 256	60. 0	. 311	54. 0	. 333
1902	56. 1	. 281	60. 0	. 291	54. 0	. 333
1903	54. 7	. 315	56. 5	. 252		
1904	54. 7	. 297	58. 1	. 331		
1905	55. 1	. 297	57. 0	. 280		
1906	55. 1	. 312	56. 5	. 295		
1907	55. 3	. 310	56. 2	. 315		

TABLE **H-9.**—*Vampers, males, 1907–1912, United States, by year*

Year	United States	
	Hours per week	Rate per hour
1907	54. 9	$0. 318
1908	55. 2	. 287
1909	54. 6	. 287
1910	55. 5	. 293
1911	55. 5	. 315
1912	54. 9	. 310

TABLE **H-10.**—*Vampers, males, 1910–1928, by State and year*

Year	Massachusetts		New Hampshire		New York	
	Hours per week	Rate per hour	Hours per week	Rate per hour	Hours per week	Rate per hour
1910	54. 1	$0. 315	56. 6	$0. 237	56. 2	$0. 302
1911	54. 2	. 339	56. 7	. 248	55. 6	. 324
1912	54. 0	. 322	57. 2	. 240	54. 6	. 333
1913	53. 9	. 346	55. 7	. 249	53. 6	. 346
1914	53. 9	. 332	55. 0	. 259	52. 7	. 327
1916	54. 2	. 349	55. 0	. 279	52. 7	. 401
1918	51. 3	. 455	50. 1	. 415	52. 4	. 553
1920	47. 7	. 695	48. 5	. 655	47. 6	. 858
1922	47. 4	. 674	48. 7	. 454	47. 3	. 625
1924	48. 1	. 720	48. 8	. 564	47. 1	. 774
1926	48. 0	. 709	49. 8	. 586	46. 5	. 903
1928	48. 0	. 736	50. 1	. 497	46. 8	. 743

TABLE **H–11.**—*Vampers, females, 1890–1907, by geographic division and year*

Year	North Atlantic		North Central	
	Hours per week	Rate per hour	Hours per week	Rate per hour
1890	56.9	$0.206	59.1	$0.150
1891	56.6	.195	59.2	.144
1892	56.8	.207	59.1	.146
1893	56.6	.211	59.2	.151
1894	56.6	.211	59.2	.147
1895	56.5	.215	59.4	.147
1896	56.3	.207	59.3	.159
1897	56.3	.204	59.2	.158
1898	56.6	.202	59.4	.153
1899	56.4	.198	59.4	.158
1900	56.5	.206	59.4	.163
1901	56.3	.211	59.3	.161
1902	55.5	.217	59.6	.163
1903	56.9	.227	57.4	.187
1904	56.2	.218	57.4	.202
1905	56.5	.226	57.6	.207
1906	56.1	.241	57.8	.212
1907	55.7	.247	57.6	.224

TABLE **H–12.**—*Vampers, females, 1907–1912, United States, by year*

Year	United States	
	Hours per week	Rate per hour
1907	55.7	$0.246
1908	55.9	.242
1909	55.5	.253
1910	56.9	.238
1911	56.5	.238
1912	55.1	.233

TABLE **H–13.**—*Vampers, females, 1910–1928, by States and year*

Year	Massachusetts		New Hampshire		New York		Ohio	
	Hours per week	Rate per hour	Hours per week	Rate per hour	Hours per week	Rate per hour	Hours per week	Rate per hour
1910	54.5	$0.268	57.1	$0.224	56.4	$0.245	59.8	$0.204
1911	54.8	.276	57.0	.212	55.6	.235	59.9	.203
1912	53.8	.246	57.1	.217	55.6	.251	54.0	.213
1913	53.7	.266	55.4	.226	53.7	.276	53.9	.220
1914	53.9	.260	55.0	.237	52.1	.266	53.8	.223
1916	53.7	.273	55.0	.248	52.0	.291	53.8	.211
1918	51.6	.338	50.1	.367	50.0	.344	50.0	.254
1920	47.2	.581	48.4	.584	47.9	.657	50.0	.438
1922	47.3	.560	48.4	.413	47.8	.545	50.0	.447
1924	47.6	.681	48.8	.556	48.3	.525	49.9	.448
1926	47.9	.635	49.2	.505	48.6	.525	49.9	.489
1928	48.0	.628	49.2	.502	48.4	.534	49.9	.428

TABLE **H–14.**—*Lasters, 1872–1900, by year and State*

Year and State	Sex	Lowest, highest, and average—		Year and State	Sex	Lowest, highest, and average—	
		Hours per week	Rate per day (dollars)			Hours per week	Rate per day (dollars)
1872:				**1886—Continued.**			
Massachusetts____	M.	(¹)	2. 10–2. 10–2. 10	New York_____	M.	58–60–59	1. 05–3. 56–2. 10
1875:				Pennsylvania_____	M.	(¹)	1. 53–2. 22–1. 88
Massachusetts____	M.	(¹)	1. 55–2. 09–2. 05	Wisconsin_____	M.	59–59–59	1. 75–1. 75–1. 75
Do_____	F.	(¹)	1. 25–1. 25–1. 25	**1887:**			
1877:				Massachusetts____	M.	59–60–59	1. 83–2. 33–2. 15
Ohio_____	M.	(¹)	2. 00–3. 00–2. 56	Ohio_____	M.	54–60–60	1. 16–3. 00–2. 27
1879:				Do_____	F.	60–60–60	. 55– . 55– . 55
New Jersey_____	M.	60–60–60	1. 00–1. 25–1. 13	Wisconsin_____	(¹)	(¹)	1. 75–1. 75–1. 75
Pennsylvania_____	M.	57–60–58	1. 08–3. 33–1. 85	**1888:**			
1880:				Maine_____	M.	60–60–60	2. 25–2. 25–2. 25
Ohio_____	M.	(¹)	1. 25–1. 41–1. 35	New Jersey_____	(¹)	48–60–58	1. 50–3. 00–2. 59
1881:				New York_____	M.	44–60–56	1. 00–3. 17–2. 41
New Jersey_____	M.	(¹)	2. 00–2. 00–2. 00	**1890:**			
Do_____	M.	59–59–59	1. 83–2. 00–1. 92	New York_____	M.	(¹)	. 67–2. 67–2. 01
1882:				**1891:**			
Maine_____	M.	60–60–60	2. 00–2. 00–2. 00	Maine_____	M.	60–60–60	1. 16–2. 75–1. 90
Massachusetts____	(¹)	59–59–59	3. 00–3. 25–3. 13	Do_____	(¹)	(¹)	1. 42–1. 79–1. 51
New Jersey_____	M.	60–60–60	1. 88–2. 00–1. 94	New York_____	M.	(¹)	. 67–3. 43–2. 01
New York_____	(¹)	60–60–60	2. 00–2. 25–2. 13	**1892:**			
Ohio_____	M.	60–60–60	2. 16–2. 38–2. 26	California_____	M.	54–60–60	1. 00–3. 50–1. 77
Do_____	(¹)	57–60–59	1. 80–2. 75–2. 18	**1893:**			
1883:				Maryland_____	M.	60–60–60	2. 00–2. 00–2. 00
Massachusetts____	M.	60–60–60	1. 67–3. 25–2. 31	New York_____	M.	50–65–58	1. 17–2. 00–1. 59
Missouri_____	M.	59–59–59	1. 65–2. 50–1. 99	Ohio_____	M.	42–60–59	1. 25–2. 50–1. 91
New Hampshire__	M.	59–59–59	2. 00–2. 50–2. 25	**1894:**			
New Jersey_____	M.	48–60–60	1. 44–3. 24–2. 09	Indiana_____	(¹)	60–60–60	2. 00–2. 00–2. 00
New York_____	(¹)	59–59–59	1. 25–1. 61–1. 43	Maine_____	M.	60–60–60	1. 75–2. 00–1. 88
1884:				New Hampshire__	M.	48–60–57	. 83–2. 33–1. 69
Maine_____	M.	59–59–59	2. 00–2. 38–2. 17	New York_____	M.	60–60–60	1. 67–1. 75–1. 69
Massachusetts____	M.	59–60–60	1. 75–3. 00–2. 24	Ohio_____	M.	42–60–59	. 75–3. 00–1. 91
New Jersey_____	M.	60–65–60	1. 50–3. 33–2. 27	**1895:**			
New York_____	(¹)	57–57–57	1. 50–1. 70–1. 60	Maine_____	M.	60–60–60	. 67–3. 00–2. 06
Pennsylvania_____	M.	60–60–60	1. 95–1. 95–1. 95	Massachusetts____	M.	54–60–58	. 83–3. 66–2. 12
1885:				Missouri_____	M.	59–59–59	1. 00–3. 33–2. 06
California_____	M.	60–60–60	1. 37–1. 75–1. 58	New Jersey_____	M.	54–60–57	1. 67–2. 17–2. 02
Illinois_____	M.	60–60–60	2. 25–2. 25–2. 25	New York_____	M.	59–59–59	1. 37–2. 00–1. 63
Kentucky_____	M.	60–60–60	2. 00–2. 00–2. 00	Ohio_____	M.	42–60–59	1. 00–3. 25–1. 76
Maine_____	M.	59–60–59	. 83–2. 83–1. 79	**1896:**			
Maryland_____	M.	60–60–60	1. 33–2. 00–1. 59	Missouri_____	M.	54–60–60	1. 08–2. 50–2. 00
Massachusetts____	M.	48–60–60	1. 50–3. 31–2. 63	New York_____	M.	59–60–59	1. 01–4. 61–2. 24
Missouri_____	M.	59–59–59	1. 31–2. 07–1. 64	Ohio_____	M.	56–60–58	1. 25–2. 87–1. 77
New Hampshire__	M.	59–59–59	1. 75–2. 00–1. 82	Pennsylvania_____	M.	59–60–59	. 77–2. 17–1. 50
New Jersey_____	F.	54–54–54	1. 33–1. 33–1. 33	**1897:**			
Do_____	M.	48–60–58	1. 00–3. 33–1. 91	New York_____	M.	60–60–60	1. 50–2. 00–1. 80
New York_____	M.	59–60–60	1. 42–2. 50–2. 22	Virginia_____	M.	60–60–60	1. 25–1. 25–1. 25
Ohio_____	M.	59–60–60	1. 40–2. 18–1. 79	Do_____	F.	54–54–54	. 75– . 75– . 75
Pennsylvania_____	M.	60–60–60	1. 73–2. 24–1. 92	**1898:**			
1886:				New York_____	M.	60–60–60	1. 33–3. 00–1. 86
Illinois_____	(¹)	59–59–59	3. 00–3. 00–3. 00	**1899:**			
Maine_____	(¹)	60–60–60	1. 87–2. 45–2. 16	Massachusetts____	M.	58–60–59	2. 53–3. 47–2. 63
Massachusetts____	M.	59–60–59	1. 66–3. 70–2. 34	**1900:**			
New Hampshire__	M.	59–60–60	1. 75–2. 12–1. 90	Massachusetts____	M.	58–60–58	1. 76–3. 48–2. 65
New Jersey_____	M.	60–65–60	. 92–3. 33–2. 06				

¹ Not reported.

TABLE **H–15**.—*Lasters, machine, males, 1890–1907, by State and year*

Year	Maine		Massachusetts		New Hampshire		Wisconsin	
	Hours per week	Rate per hour	Hours per week	Rate per hour	Hours per week	Rate per hour	Hours per week	Rate per hour
1890	58.0	$0.209	51.8	$0.307	54.8	$0.183	59.4	$0.237
1891	58.0	.227	51.7	.268	57.0	.195	59.4	.237
1892	58.0	.224	53.0	.298	56.9	.199	59.4	.237
1893	58.0	.219	54.1	.259	56.9	.185	59.4	.237
1894	58.0	.234	55.9	.278	56.9	.194	59.5	.234
1895	58.0	.245	55.9	.275	56.9	.191	59.5	.234
1896	58.0	.204	56.1	.279	56.9	.204	59.5	.247
1897	58.0	.208	55.1	.252	56.9	.190	59.5	.247
1898	58.0	.209	55.0	.266	54.1	.191	59.5	.253
1899	57.5	.206	55.7	.270	56.9	.186	59.5	.253
1900	57.4	.219	55.3	.277	55.3	.188	59.5	.255
1901	57.4	.232	55.1	.277	56.9	.196	59.5	.260
1902	57.5	.233	53.7	.299	56.9	.211	59.5	.268
1903	58.4	.238	55.2	.332	59.3	.215	59.5	.271
1904	58.9	.224	55.8	.332	59.3	.211	59.3	.291
1905	59.0	.243	55.8	.354	59.3	.248	59.4	.287
1906	59.0	.240	55.8	.350	59.3	.257	56.9	.290
1907	59.0	.242	54.9	.346	59.2	.253	56.4	.315

TABLE **H–16**.—*Bed-machine operators, males, 1907–1912, United States, by year*

Year	United States	
	Hours per week	Rate per hour
1907	54.7	$0.350
1908	54.8	.334
1909	54.8	.342
1910	56.4	.311
1911	56.1	.321
1912	55.5	.304

TABLE **H–17**.—*Bed-machine operators, males, 1910–1928, by State and year*

Year	Massachusetts		New Hampshire		New York		Ohio	
	Hours per week	Rate per hour	Hours per week	Rate per hour	Hours per week	Rate per hour	Hours per week	Rate per hour
1910	54.2	$0.343	56.9	$0.246	57.9	$0.329	59.8	$0.298
1911	54.3	.352	56.6	.247	56.5	.344	59.9	.298
1912	54.4	.304	57.2	.230	54.7	.346	57.9	.330
1913	54.2	.342	55.8	.252	53.8	.362	55.7	.360
1914	54.0	.332	55.0	.245	53.1	.319	56.7	.356
1916	54.2	.370	55.0	.298	53.3	.363	56.6	.386
1918	51.1	.541	50.2	.491	50.8	.484	56.3	.534
1920	47.8	.780	48.4	.790	47.6	.897	50.0	.959
1922	47.6	.669	48.4	.531	47.5	.706	50.0	.864
1924	47.9	.740	48.8	.661	47.9	.666	49.9	.713
1926	48.2	.737	49.2	.632	48.2	.715	50.0	.837
1928	48.1	.731	49.5	.655	48.2	.714	49.9	.749

TABLE **H-18.**—*Hand-method lasting machine operators, males, 1907-1912, United States, by year*

Year	United States	
	Hours per week	Rate per hour
1907	57. 1	$0. 311
1908	56. 6	. 307
1909	56. 7	. 309
1910	57. 4	. 306
1911	57. 0	. 316
1912	55. 8	. 324

TABLE **H-19.**—*Hand-method lasting machine operators, males, 1910-1928, by State and year*

Year	Massachusetts		New Hampshire		New York		Ohio	
	Hours per week	Rate per hour	Hours per week	Rate per hour	Hours per week	Rate per hour	Hours per week	Rate per hour
1910	55. 3	$0. 348	57. 1	$0. 252	55. 4	$0. 343	59. 9	$0. 324
1911	55. 0	. 368	57. 2	. 222	55. 6	. 323	59. 9	. 287
1912	53. 9	. 344	57. 0	. 291	55. 9	. 353	55. 6	. 337
1913	54. 1	. 377	55. 0	. 277	54. 2	. 378	54. 9	. 361
1914	54. 8	. 348	55. 0	. 276	53. 8	. 391	55. 7	. 384
1916	54. 4	. 384					55. 9	. 353
1918	52. 1	. 510					57. 0	. 460
1920	47. 1	1. 024	50. 9	. 684			50. 0	. 765
1922	46. 3	. 906	50. 9	. 587			50. 0	. 731
1924	48. 8	. 672			44. 0	. 801	50. 0	. 651
1926	48. 5	. 751					50. 0	. 575
1928	48. 2	. 995					50. 0	. 626

TABLE **H-20.**—*McKay stitchers, 1875-1900, by year and State*

Year and State	Sex	Lowest, highest, and average—		Year and State	Sex	Lowest, highest, and average—	
		Hours per week	Rate per day (dollars)			Hours per week	Rate per day (dollars)
1875:				1888:			
Massachusetts	M.	(1)	1. 25-2. 50-1. 88	New Jersey	(1)	60-60-60	4. 50-4. 50-4. 50
1877:				New York	M.	51-61-57	1. 00-3. 75-2. 75
Ohio	M.	(1)	2. 50-3. 00-2. 75	1890:			
1879:				New York	M.	(1)	1. 67-3. 33-2. 50
Pennsylvania	M.	60-60-60	1. 67-1. 75-1. 71	1891:			
1881:				Maine	M.	60-60-60	1. 64-3. 04-2. 82
Massachusetts	M.	60-60-60	2. 10-2. 10-2. 10	New York	M.	(1)	1. 67-3. 33-2. 48
1882:				1893:			
New Jersey	M.	60-60-60	. 83-2. 00-1. 70	Ohio	M.	54-54-54	2. 50-2. 50-2. 50
1883:				1894:			
New Jersey	M.	60-60-60	1. 67-2. 00-1. 80	Maine	M.	60-60-60	3. 00-3. 00-3. 00
1884:				New Hampshire	M.	45-45-45	1. 67-1. 67-1. 67
New Jersey	M.	60-60-60	1. 67-2. 50-1. 95	1895:			
1885:				Maine	M.	60-60-60	3. 00-3. 00-3. 00
California	M.	60-60-60	1. 50-2. 00-1. 75	Massachusetts	M.	55-59-58	1. 55-4. 21-2. 67
Massachusetts	M.	59-60-60	2. 50-2. 94-2. 72	Missouri	M.	(1)	3. 33-3. 50-3. 39
New Jersey	M.	60-60-60	. 83-2. 50-1. 78	New Jersey	M.	54-54-54	2. 00-2. 00-2. 00
New York	M.	60-60-60	2. 67-2. 79-2. 68	1896:			
Ohio	M.	60-60-60	2. 92-3. 36-3. 06	New York	M.	59-59-59	2. 00-4. 03-3. 02
Pennsylvania	M.	60-60-60	3. 25-3. 25-3. 25	Ohio	M.	59-60-60	2. 73-3. 12-2. 98
1886:				Pennsylvania	M.	59-59-59	2. 17-2. 67-2. 42
New Jersey	M.	60-60-60	. 83-2. 50-1. 98	1900:			
New York	M.	59-59-59	3. 05-3. 05-3. 05	Massachusetts	M.	58-58-58	3. 75-3. 75-3. 75
1887:							
Wisconsin	(1)	(1)	2. 45-2. 45-2. 45				

1 Not reported.

TABLE H-21. —*McKay stitchers, males, 1890-1907, by geographic division and year*

Year	North Atlantic		North Central	
	Hours per week	Rate per hour	Hours per week	Rate per hour
1890	57.3	$0.320	59.5	$0.237
1891	57.2	.310	59.5	.245
1892	56.6	.324	59.5	.242
1893	56.7	.344	59.5	.238
1894	56.3	.327	59.5	.243
1895	56.7	.338	59.5	.247
1896	56.3	.318	59.5	.245
1897	55.7	.324	59.5	.260
1898	55.3	.331	59.5	.252
1899	55.3	.317	59.5	.261
1900	54.0	.318	59.5	.253
1901	54.6	.314	59.6	.270
1902	53.6	.317	59.6	.280
1903	57.6	.319	58.1	.294
1904	56.7	.290	58.8	.317
1905	56.3	.289	58.7	.315
1906	56.4	.300	59.2	.316
1907	56.0	.294	59.2	.294

TABLE H-22.—*McKay sewers, males, 1907-1912, United States, by year*

Year	United States	
	Hours per week	Rate per hour
1907	55.2	$0.288
1908	55.3	.311
1909	55.7	.274
1910	57.1	.290
1911	56.5	.296
1912	56.3	.285

TABLE H-23.—*McKay sewers, males, 1910-1928, by State and year*

Year	Massachusetts		New Hampshire		New York		Ohio	
	Hours per week	Rate per hour	Hours per week	Rate per hour	Hours per week	Rate per hour	Hours per week	Rate per hour
1910	54.9	$0.327						
1911	55.0	.345						
1912	54.9	.307						
1913	54.8	.341						
1914	54.7	.372	55.0	$0.245	52.2	$0.349		
1916	54.2	.395	55.0	.268	50.9	.445	55.3	$0.337
1918	52.0	.461	51.8	.457	49.3	.531	56.7	.373
1920	46.9	.784	49.5	.668	48.0	1.057	50.0	.655
1922	47.2	.764	50.2	.535	48.0	.995	50.0	.697
1924	48.2	.769			48.0	.786	50.0	.664
1926	48.5	.857	50.9	.612	48.0	.910	49.9	.709
1928	46.8	1.058	51.6	.570	48.0	.783	50.0	.636

TANNERY

The sources from which this information was taken are the fifteenth and the nineteenth annual reports of the Commissioner of Labor Statistics and bulletins of the Bureau of Labor Statistics Nos. 56, 65, 71, and 77.

The reports showing details on wages and hours of labor in the tanning industry are very incomplete. No strictly comparable information of this character is available for any period after the year 1907. There is, however, a very complete study of tanneries to be found in Bulletin No. 265 of the bureau.

TABLE **H–24.**—*Tanners, 1860–1900, by year and State*

Year and State	Sex	Hours per week	Rate per day (dollars)
1860:			
Massachusetts....	M.	60–72–62	1.25–2.00–1.41
1866:			
Delaware........	M.	60–60–60	1.82–1.82–1.82
Massachusetts....	M.	60–60–60	1.67–2.00–1.92
1868:			
Delaware........	M.	60–60–60	1.67–2.00–1.95
1869:			
Delaware........	M.	60–60–60	1.83–2.00–1.99
1870:			
Delaware........	M.	60–60–60	1.67–1.67–1.67
Massachusetts....	M.	60–60–60	1.67–1.67–1.67
1871:			
Delaware........	M.	60–60–60	1.33–2.17–1.69
1872:			
Delaware........	M.	60–60–60	1.83–2.11–1.91
Ohio............	M.	(1)	2.50–2.50–2.50
1873:			
Delaware........	M.	60–60–60	1.83–2.55–1.96
1874:			
Delaware........	M.	60–60–60	1.33–2.00–1.80
1875:			
Delaware........	M.	60–60–60	1.33–2.17–1.83
1876:			
Delaware........	M.	60–60–60	1.58–2.00–1.86
1877:			
Delaware........	M.	60–60–60	1.58–1.83–1.73
Ohio............	M.	(1)	1.17–1.67–1.42
1878:			
Delaware........	M.	60–60–60	1.59–1.83–1.71
Pennsylvania....	M.	60–60–60	1.00–2.50–1.46
1879:			
Delaware........	M.	60–60–60	1.50–1.83–1.58
New Jersey......	(1)	59–59–59	1.25–1.25–1.25
Ohio............	M.	(1)	1.67–1.67–1.67
Pennsylvania....	M.	60–72–61	.58–3.00–1.38
1880:			
Delaware........	M.	60–60–60	1.42–2.00–1.75
Ohio............	M.	(1)	1.50–1.50–1.50
Pennsylvania....	M.	66–66–66	1.25–3.20–2.23
1881:			
Delaware........	M.	60–60–60	1.50–1.83–1.69
Michigan........	M.	60–60–60	1.45–1.45–1.45
New Jersey......	M.	60–60–60	1.67–1.67–1.67
Ohio............	M.	60–60–60	1.67–1.67–1.67
Pennsylvania....	M.	60–60–60	1.40–1.40–1.40
1882:			
Delaware........	M.	60–60–60	1.50–1.83–1.67
Illinois........	M.	60–60–60	1.70–1.70–1.70
Missouri........	M.	60–60–60	1.67–2.25–1.96
Pennsylvania....	M.	60–60–60	1.35–2.00–1.70
1883:			
Delaware........	M.	60–60–60	1.50–1.83–1.61
Michigan........	M.	(1)	.50–2.50–1.49
New Jersey......	M.	60–60–60	1.67–1.67–1.67
1884:			
California.......	M.	60–60–60	2.50–2.50–2.50
Do...........	M.	60–60–60	² 1.53–1.53–1.53
Delaware........	M.	60–60–60	1.50–1.83–1.63
Michigan........	M.	(1)	1.25–1.75–1.50
New Jersey......	M.	60–60–60	1.50–1.68–1.64
Ohio............	M.	65–65–65	1.83–1.83–1.83

Year and State	Sex	Hours per week	Rate per day (dollars)
1885:			
Delaware........	M.	60–60–60	.75–1.83–1.64
Massachusetts....	M.	60–60–60	1.53–1.53–1.53
Pennsylvania....	M.	60–60–60	1.50–2.15–1.81
Wisconsin.......	M.	60–60–60	1.68–1.68–1.68
1886:			
California.......	M.	60–60–60	1.53–3.00–1.98
Do...........	M.	60–60–60	² 1.15–1.75–1.72
Delaware........	M.	60–60–60	1.50–1.83–1.63
Illinois........	M.	54–60–57	2.00–2.00–2.00
Ohio............	M.	(1)	1.92–1.92–1.92
1887:			
Delaware........	M.	60–60–60	1.67–1.83–1.78
Ohio............	M.	60–60–60	1.50–6.66–1.99
Wisconsin.......	M.	(1)	2.00–2.50 2.33
1888:			
Delaware........	M.	60–60–60	1.50–1.83–1.67
New York........	M.	59–60–60	1.33–2.00–1.84
North Carolina...	M.	60–60–60	1.00–2.00–1.50
1889:			
Delaware........	M.	60–60–60	1.50–1.83–1.67
1890:			
Delaware........	M.	60–60–60	1.50–1.83–1.63
New York........	M.	(1)	1.00–2.50–1.65
1891:			
Delaware........	M.	60–60–60	1.53–1.83–1.50
New York........	M.	(1)	1.00–2.75–1.59
Ohio............	M.	60–60–60	1.25–1.85–1.67
1892:			
California.......	M.	60–68–61	2.00–3.33–2.47
Delaware........	M.	60–60–60	1.00–1.84–1.45
1893:			
Delaware........	M.	(1)	1.00–1.83–1.42
Illinois........	M.	54–60–57	1.33–1.33–1.33
Maryland........	M	60–72–64	.50–2.50–1.39
Missouri........	M.	60–60–60	2.00–2.00–2.00
New York........	M.	65–65–65	2.00–2.00–2.00
Ohio............	M.	54–60–57	1.35–2.06–1.64
Pennsylvania....	M.	60–60–60	1.00–1.33–1.11
1894:			
Delaware........	M.	(1)	1.00–1.17–1.09
Iowa............	M	48–72–59	1.00–1.60–1.25
New Hampshire...	M.	60–60–60	1.33–1.33–1.33
New York........	M.	60–60–60	1.35–1.50–1.48
North Carolina...	M.	60–60–60	.60–.75–.68
Do...........	(²)	60–60–60	1.50–1.50–1.50
Ohio............	M.	54–60–57	1.25–1.83–1.56
West Virginia....	M.	60–60–60|	1.35–1.35–1.35
1895:			
Delaware........	M.	(1)	1.17–1.33–1.22
North Carolina...	M.	60–60–60	.65–2.50–1.25
Ohio............	M.	60–60–60	.50–1.50–.84
Wisconsin.......	(²)	30–60–58	.88–3.84–1.70
1896:			
Massachusetts....	M.	60–60–60	1.00–2.00–1.50
Missouri........	M.	54–60–58	1.70–2.65–2.00
North Carolina...	M.	60–84–65	.50–1.50–.84
Ohio............	M.	58–60–60	1.29–1.66–1.56
1897:			
Virginia........	M.	60–72–60	.65–2.00–1.24
1899:			
Massachusetts....	M	59–59–59	1.67–1.67–1.67
1900:			
Massachusetts....	M.	59–59–59	1.67–1.67–1.67

¹ Not reported.   ² And board.

TABLE **H-25.**—*Tanners, males, 1890-1907, by geographic division and year*

Year	North Atlantic		South Atlantic		North Central		South Central		Western	
	Hours per week	Rate per hour	Hours per week	Rate per hour	Hours per week	Rate per hour	Hours per week	Rate per hour	Hours per week	Rate per hour
1890	59.3	$0.160	60.0	$0.112	56.9	$0.164	58.3	$0.128	60.0	$0.221
1891	59.3	.161	60.0	.110	56.7	.166	58.3	.128	60.0	.221
1892	59.2	.164	60.0	.111	56.9	.165	58.3	.128	60.0	.220
1893	59.3	.162	60.0	.111	57.1	.165	59.1	.115	60.0	.205
1894	59.3	.162	60.0	.104	57.3	.146	58.9	.119	60.0	.212
1895	59.2	.160	60.0	.104	57.7	.145	58.7	.121	60.0	.215
1896	59.2	.159	60.0	.111	58.0	.147	58.7	.120	60.0	.203
1897	59.3	.160	60.0	.111	58.7	.150	58.9	.118	60.0	.197
1898	59.3	.160	60.0	.111	59.6	.144	59.2	.114	60.0	.202
1899	59.3	.160	60.0	.111	58.5	.147	59.2	.113	60.0	.197
1900	59.3	.159	60.0	.116	58.4	.155	59.0	.115	60.0	.195
1901	59.3	.160	60.0	.117	58.4	.159	59.1	.114	60.0	.189
1902	59.3	.160	60.0	.121	58.4	.164	59.2	.114	60.0	.199
1903	58.9	.165	60.0	.120	58.2	.179	59.4	.119	60.0	.206
1904	58.8	.158	60.0	.121	58.8	.178	59.8	.110	57.5	.226
1905	59.1	.157	60.0	.124	59.1	.170	59.9	.110	57.8	.200
1906	59.0	.165	60.0	.133	59.6	.171	60.0	.126	54.7	.231
1907	59.0	.168	60.0	.136	59.5	.177	60.0	.127	54.6	.243

TABLE **H-26.**—*Tanners, males, 1904-1907, by State and year*

Year	California		Delaware		Illinois		Kentucky	
	Hours per week	Rate per hour	Hours per week	Rate per hour	Hours per week	Rate per hour	Hours per week	Rate per hour
1904	57.5	$0.226	60.0	$0.128	55.7	$0.180	59.7	$0.122
1905	57.8	.200	60.0	.135	57.9	.181	59.7	.123
1906	54.5	.228	60.0	.133	59.0	.180	60.0	.142
1907	54.4	.241	60.0	.136	59.0	.182	60.0	.152

Year	Massachusetts		Michigan		New Jersey		New York	
1904	59.0	$0.161			58.4	$0.159	58.8	$0.154
1905	59.0	.159			58.3	.161	59.9	.148
1906	59.0	.160	59.9	$0.179	57.9	.174	59.8	.161
1907	59.0	.161	59.9	.181	57.8	.176	59.8	.166

Year	Ohio		Pennsylvania		Virginia		Wisconsin	
1904	57.1	$0.170	59.0	$0.158	60.0	$0.122	60.0	$0.179
1905	56.7	.176	59.2	.158	60.0	.125	60.0	.166
1906	57.8	.174	59.2	.163	60.0	.130	59.9	.167
1907	57.8	.180	59.3	.168	60.0	.133	59.9	.174

I.—METAL TRADES (OTHER THAN IRON AND STEEL)

The sources from which these wage data were taken are the fifteenth · and the nineteenth annual reports of the Commissioner of Labor Statistics and bulletins of the Bureau of Labor Statistics Nos. 59, 65, 71, 77, 131, 143, 171, 194, 214, 245, 259, 274, 286, 302, 325, 354, 363, 388, 404, 422, 431, 457, 471, and 482.

The wage data reported for the early periods and extending to 1907 and from 1924 to 1928 were copied by agents of the Bureau of Labor Statistics direct from pay rolls or other records of representative establishments in the various localities. Both hours and earnings as shown here represent averages computed from these reports.

For the period from 1907 to 1924 the wage data reported here represents minimum rates of wages paid to union workers through agreements with their employers or group of employers. The hours represent the maximum which may be worked at single rate beyond which extra for overtime is usually paid. For further explanation of the source of these details see Building Trades, page 153.

The reports showing data for horseshoers are found only in the fifteenth and the nineteenth annual reports of the Commissioner of Labor Statistics and bulletins of the Bureau of Labor Statistics Nos. 59, 65, 71, and 77, and cover the period from 1870 to 1907. No other reports are available. In subsequent years the horse has been largely supplanted by the automobile. In many localities horseshoeing is done by blacksmiths. It is very probable that the data shown for blacksmiths in late years also include wages of those who did horseshoeing.

The data for laborers in this section (Table I–16) covers the period of 1890 to 1907; the data for foundry laborers (Table I–17) and those for machine shop laborers (Table I–18) cover the years 1923, 1925, and 1927. For other laborers see Tables B–12 (p. 185), D–1, D–2, D–3 (pp. 225, 227, and 228), G–1 (p. 253), O–11, and O–12 (p. 464).

The reports showing data for millwrights are only the fifteenth and the nineteenth annual reports of the Commissioner of Labor Statistics and bulletins of the Bureau of Labor Statistics Nos. 59, 65, 71, 77, 294, 373, 421, and 472. No reports were available for the period from 1907 to 1917.

274

TABLE I-1.—*Blacksmiths, 1840–1900, by year and State*

| Year and State | Sex | Lowest, highest, and average— | | Year and State | Sex | Lowest, highest, and average— | |
		Hours per week	Rate per day (dollars)			Hours per week	Rate per day (dollars)
1840:				**1855:**			
Maine	M.	60–60–60	2.00–2.00–2.00	Connecticut	M.	60–60–60	1.50–2.00–1.75
Massachusetts	M.	60–78–69	1.50–2.00–1.75	Maine	M.	60–60–60	2.00–2.00–2.00
New York	M.	60–60–60	1.25–1.75–1.45	Maryland	M.	60–60–60	1.50–1.67–1.53
Pennsylvania	M.	60–60–60	2.25–2.25–2.25	Massachusetts	M.	66–72–70	1.42–1.75–1.68
1841:				New Hampshire	M.	60–60–60	1.50–1.67–1.59
Massachusetts	M.	78–78–78	1.50–1.50–1.50	New Jersey	M.	60–60–60	1.50–1.50–1.50
New York	M.	60–60–60	1.25–1.75–1.45	New York	M.	60–72–61	1.06–2.50–1.73
1842:				Ohio	M.	60–60–60	1.50–1.50–1.50
Massachusetts	M.	78–78–78	1.50–1.50–1.50	Pennsylvania	M.	60–60–60	1.50–2.20–1.85
New York	M.	60–60–60	1.25–1.75–1.54	**1856:**			
1843:				Connecticut	M.	60–60–60	1.17–2.00–1.61
Massachusetts	M.	78–78–78	1.50–1.50–1.50	Maryland	M.	60–60–60	1.50–1.67–1.55
New York	M.	60–60–60	1.25–1.63–1.43	Massachusetts	M.	66–72–69	1.42–1.75–1.67
1844:				New Hampshire	M.	60–60–60	1.42–1.42–1.42
Massachusetts	M.	78–78–78	1.50–1.50–1.50	New York	M.	60–60–60	1.06–2.00–1.66
New York	M.	60–60–60	1.13–1.88–1.42	Ohio	M.	60–60–60	1.50–1.50–1.50
1845:				Pennsylvania	M.	60–72–62	.77–2.50–1.80
Massachusetts	M.	78–78–78	1.50–1.50–1.50	**1857:**			
New Hampshire	M.	66–66–66	1.17–1.17–1.17	Connecticut	M.	60–60–60	1.17–2.25–1.68
New York	M.	60–72–62	1.00–1.88–1.40	Maryland	M.	60–60–60	1.50–1.67–1.56
1846:				Massachusetts	M.	66–72–70	1.42–2.00–1.68
Massachusetts	M.	78–78–78	1.50–1.50–1.50	New Jersey	M.	60–60–60	1.88–1.88–1.88
New Hampshire	M.	66–66–66	1.17–1.33–1.25	New York	M.	60–60–60	1.13–2.13–1.70
New York	M.	60–60–60	1.13–1.88–1.50	Pennsylvania	M.	60–60–60	1.25–2.50–1.95
1847:				**1858:**			
Massachusetts	M.	78–78–78	1.50–1.50–1.50	Connecticut	M.	60–60–60	1.25–2.25–1.83
New York	M.	60–60–60	1.25–2.00–1.70	Florida	M.	60–60–60	1.50–1.50–1.50
1848:				Maryland	M.	60–60–60	1.50–1.67–1.59
Massachusetts	M.	78–78–78	1.50–1.50–1.50	Massachusetts	M.	66–72–70	1.50–2.00–1.73
New Hampshire	M.	60–60–60	1.25–1.25–1.25	New Hampshire	M.	60–60–60	1.50–1.50–1.50
New York	M.	60–60–60	1.13–2.00–1.57	New Jersey	M.	60–60–60	1.50–1.50–1.50
1849:				New York	M.	60–60–60	1.06–2.50–1.63
Massachusetts	M.	78–78–78	1.50–1.50–1.50	Ohio	M.	60–60–60	1.00–1.50–1.25
New Hampshire	M.	60–60–60	1.25–1.25–1.25	Pennsylvania	M.	60–72–62	1.50–2.20–1.84
New York	M.	60–60–60	1.13–2.00–1.68	**1859:**			
Ohio	M.	60–60–60	1.50–1.50–1.50	Connecticut	M.	60–60–60	1.25–2.50–1.92
Pennsylvania	M.	60–72–64	1.50–1.70–1.63	Florida	M.	60–60–60	1.50–1.50–1.50
1850:				Maryland	M.	60–60–60	1.50–1.67–1.59
Connecticut	M.	60–60–60	1.50–1.50–1.50	Massachusetts	M.	66–72–70	1.67–2.00–1.78
Massachusetts	M.	72–72–72	1.50–1.50–1.50	New Hampshire	M.	60–60–60	1.33–1.33–1.33
New Hampshire	M.	60–60–60	1.33–1.33–1.33	New Jersey	M.	60–60–60	2.00–2.00–2.00
New York	M.	60–72–60	1.13–2.00–1.58	New York	M.	60–60–60	1.06–3.00–1.65
Ohio	M.	60–60–60	1.50–1.50–1.50	Ohio	M.	60–60–60	1.50–1.50–1.50
Pennsylvania	M.	60–60–60	1.70–1.70–1.70	Pennsylvania	M.	60–60–60	2.20–2.34–2.25
1851:				**1860:**			
Massachusetts	M.	72–72–72	1.50–1.75–1.63	Connecticut	M.	60–60–60	1.75–2.25–2.00
New Hampshire	M.	60–60–60	1.33–1.33–1.33	Florida	M.	60–60–60	2.00–2.00–2.00
New York	M.	60–60–60	1.00–2.00–1.56	Maryland	M.	60–60–60	1.50–1.83–1.61
Ohio	M.	60–60–60	1.50–1.50–1.50	Massachusetts	M.	60–72–68	1.25–2.00–1.74
Pennsylvania	M.	60–60–60	1.70–1.70–1.70	New Hampshire	M.	60–60–60	1.50–1.50–1.50
1852:				New York	M.	60–60–60	1.13–3.00–1.78
Massachusetts	M.	72–72–72	1.50–1.75–1.63	Ohio	M.	60–60–60	1.50–1.67–1.57
New Hampshire	M.	60–60–60	1.42–1.42–1.42	Pennsylvania	M.	6C–60–60	1.67–2.34–2.01
New York	M.	60–60–60	1.25–2.00–1.63	**1861:**			
Ohio	M.	60–60–60	1.50–1.50–1.50	Maryland	M.	60–60–60	1.50–1.67–1.59
Pennsylvania	M.	60–60–60	1.70–1.70–1.70	Massachusetts	M.	66–66–66	1.50–2.00–1.79
1853:				New Hampshire	M.	60–60–60	1.42–1.42–1.42
Connecticut	M.	60–60–60	1.17–2.25–1.62	New York	M.	60–60–60	1.13–3.00–1.83
Massachusetts	M.	72–72–72	1.08–1.75–1.44	Ohio	M.	60–60–60	1.50–1.50–1.50
New Hampshire	M.	60–60–60	1.33–1.75–1.53	Pennsylvania	M.	60–60–60	1.75–2.34–2.00
New York	M.	60–60–60	1.13–2.00–1.65	**1862:**			
Ohio	M.	60–60–60	1.50–1.50–1.50	Connecticut	M.	60–60–60	1.13–2.50–1.85
Pennsylvania	M.	60–60–60	2.00–2.00–2.00	Maryland	M.	60–60–60	1.42–1.50–1.48
1854:				Massachusetts	M.	66–66–66	1.50–2.00–1.79
Connecticut	M.	60–60–60	1.17–2.50–1.82	New Hampshire	M.	60–60–60	1.50–1.58–1.54
Massachusetts	M.	72–72–72	1.08–1.75–1.44	New York	M.	60–60–60	1.13–3.00–1.98
New Hampshire	M.	60–60–60	1.50–1.50–1.50	Ohio	M.	60–60–60	1.50–1.75–1.63
New York	M.	60–60–60	1.13–2.50–1.69	Pennsylvania	M.	60–60–60	1.75–2.34–2.02
Ohio	M.	60–60–60	1.50–1.50–1.50				
Pennsylvania	M.	60–60–60	2.00–2.00–2.00				
South Carolina	M.	60–60–60	2.00–2.00–2.00				

TABLE I-1.—*Blacksmiths, 1840–1900, by year and State*—Continued

Year and State	Sex	Lowest, highest, and average—		Year and State	Sex	Lowest, highest, and average—	
		Hours per week	Rate per day (dollars)			Hours per week	Rate per day (dollars)
1863:				**1870--Continued.**			
Connecticut	M.	60–60–60	1. 20–2. 50–1. 92	Massachusetts	M.	59–66–61	1. 75–4. 50–3. 11
Maryland	M.	60–60–60	1. 75–2. 00–1. 83	Minnesota	M.	60–60–60	2. 75–3. 00–2. 85
Massachusetts	M.	66–66–66	1. 67–2. 00–1. 93	Missouri	M.	60–60–60	2. 50–2. 50–2. 50
New Hampshire	M.	60–60–60	1. 50–1. 67–1. 59	New Hampshire	M.	60–60–60	2. 00–2. 50–2. 33
New Jersey	M.	60–60–60	1. 66–1. 66–1. 66	New Jersey	M.	60–60–60	3. 00–3. 13–3. 04
New York	M.	60–60–60	1. 00–3. 00–1. 96	New York	M.	60–60–60	1. 50–4. 00–2. 82
Ohio	M.	60–60–60	1. 75–2. 00–1. 92	Ohio	M.	60–60–60	1. 80–3. 92–2. 52
Pennsylvania	M.	60–60–60	1. 50–2. 15–2. 04	Pennsylvania	M.	60–60–60	1. 55–3. 67–2. 40
South Carolina	M.	60–60–60	2. 50–2. 50–2. 50	Virginia	M.	60–60–60	2. 00–2. 50–2. 42
1864:				**1871:**			
Connecticut	M.	60–60–60	1. 60–3. 50–2. 43	California	M.	54–60–56	3. 00–6. 00–3. 53
Maryland	M.	60–60–60	2. 00–3. 50–2. 56	Connecticut	M.	60–60–60	2. 00–3. 75–2. 97
Massachusetts	M.	60–66–64	1. 75–2. 25–2. 00	Delaware	M.	60–60–60	2. 25–4. 00–2. 64
New Hampshire	M.	60–60–60	1. 50–1. 91–1. 71	Illinois	M.	60–60–60	2. 50–3. 75–2. 99
New Jersey	M.	60–60–60	2. 00–3. 00–2. 56	Louisiana	M.	60–60–60	4. 50–4. 50–4. 50
New York	M.	60–60–60	1. 13–4. 00–2. 13	Maryland	M.	58–60–59	2. 00–3. 00–2. 40
Ohio	M.	60–60–60	2. 25–2. 75–2. 58	Massachusetts	M.	59–66–61	2. 00–4. 50–2. 49
Pennsylvania	M.	60–60–60	2. 25–3. 00–2. 58	Minnesota	M.	60–60–60	2. 75–3. 00–2. 85
1865:				Missouri	M.	60–60–60	2. 60–2. 60–2. 60
Connecticut	M.	60–60–60	2. 00–3. 50–2. 67	New Hampshire	M.	60–60–60	2. 25–2. 25–2. 25
Maryland	M.	60–60–60	2. 25–4. 00–2. 64	New Jersey	M.	60–60–60	2. 63–3. 13–2. 94
Massachusetts	M.	60–66–65	2. 38–3. 00–2. 64	New York	M.	60–60–60	1. 60–4. 00–2. 89
New Hampshire	M.	60–60–60	2. 50–2. 50–2. 50	Ohio	M.	60–60–60	1. 90–3. 92–2. 52
New Jersey	M.	60–60–60	2. 16–3.·00–2. 53	Pennsylvania	M.	60–60–60	1. 75–3. 50–2. 53
New York	M.	60–60–60	1. 50–4. 00–2. 90	Virginia	M.	60–60–60	2. 00–2. 50–2. 42
Ohio	M.	60–60–60	2. 50–3. 00–2. 83	**1872:**			
Pennsylvania	M.	60–60–60	2. 50–3. 34–2. 80	California	M.	54–60–56	3. 06–6. 00–3. 60
1866:				Connecticut	M.	60–60–60	2. 00–3. 75–2. 95
Connecticut	M.	60–60–60	2. 00–3. 50–2. 71	Delaware	M.	60–60–60	2. 33–4. 00–2. 76
Maine	M.	60–60–60	3. 60–3. 60–3. 60	Illinois	M.	60–60–60	2. 70–3. 75–3. 15
Maryland	M.	60–60–60	2. 50–4. 00–2. 78	Louisiana	M.	60–60–60	4. 50–4. 50–4. 50
Massachusetts	M.	60–66–65	2. 38–3. 00–2. 71	Maryland	M.	58–60–59	2. 00–3. 00–2. 41
New Hampshire	M.	60–60–60	2. 17–2. 50–2. 39	Massachusetts	M.	59–66–61	2. 00–4. 00–3. 14
New Jersey	M.	60–60–60	2. 75–3. 25–2. 93	Minnesota	M.	60–60–60	2. 75–3. 00–2. 85
New York	M.	60–60–60	1. 50–4. 00–2. 90	Missouri	M.	50–60–54	2. 65–3. 50–2. 99
Ohio	M.	60–60–60	2. 75–3. 50–3. 25	New Hampshire	M.	60–60–60	2. 50–2. 50–2. 50
Pennsylvania	M.	60–60–60	2. 50–3. 67–2. 71	New Jersey	M.	60–60–60	2. 63–3. 25–2. 96
1867:				New York	M.	60–60–60	1. 63–4. 00–2·94
Connecticut	M.	60–60–60	2. 25–3. 50–2. 73	Ohio	M.	60–60–60	1. 75–5. 00–2. 61
Delaware	M.	60–60–60	2. 00–3. 00–2. 40	Pennsylvania	(¹)	60–60–60	3. 25–3. 25–3. 25
Georgia	M.	66–66–66	2. 33–2. 33–2. 33	Do	M.	60–60–60	1. 70–3. 50–2. 58
Maryland	M.	60–60–60	2. 50–2. 75–2. 61	Virginia	M.	60–60–60	2. 00–2. 50–2. 42
Massachusetts	M.	66–66–66	2. 50–3. 00–2. 90	**1873:**			
New Hampshire	M.	60–60–60	2. 17–2. 50–2. 39	California	M.	54–60–57	2. 84–6. 00–3. 66
New Jersey	M.	60–60–60	2. 00–3. 25–2. 72	Connecticut	M.	60–60–60	3. 00–3. 75–3. 42
New York	M.	66–60–60	1. 50–4. 00–2. 98	Delaware	M.	60–60–60	2. 00–2. 83–2. 58
Ohio	M.	60–60–60	2. 75–3. 50–3. 25	Illinois	M.	60–60–60	2. 90–3. 75–3. 11
Pennsylvania	M.	60–60–60	2. 50–3. 67–2. 75	Louisiana	M.	60–60–60	4. 50–4. 50–4. 50
1868:				Maryland	M.	58–60–59	1. 75–3. 00–2. 28
Connecticut	M.	60–60–60	2. 50–3. 50–2. 92	Massachusetts	M.	59–66–62	2. 00–4. 00–3. 02
Delaware	M.	60–60–60	2. 25–3. 00–2. 48	Minnesota	M.	60–60–60	2. 75–3. 00–2. 85
Maryland	M.	60–60–60	2. 50–2. 75–2. 60	Missouri	M.	50–60–54	2. 50–3. 50–2. 94
Massachusetts	M.	60–66–65	2. 50–3. 08–2. 90	New Hampshire	M.	60–60–60	2. 75–2. 75–2. 75
New Hampshire	M.	60–60–60	2. 25–2. 25–2. 25	New Jersey	M.	60–60–60	2. 63–3. 25–2. 90
New Jersey	M.	60–60–60	2. 00–3. 25–2. 78	New York	M.	60–60–60	1. 70–4. 00–3. 03
New York	M.	60–60–60	1. 50–4. 00–3. 03	North Carolina	M.	60–60–60	2. 00–2. 00–2. 00
Ohio	M.	60–60–60	2. 75–3. 50–3. 25	Ohio	M.	60–60–60	1. 90–3. 83–2. 58
Pennsylvania	M.	60–60–60	2. 50–3. 67–2. 83	Pennsylvania	M.	60–60–60	1. 90–4. 00–2. 52
1869:				Virginia	M.	48–60–58	2. 00–4. 00–2. 65
Connecticut	M.	60–60–60	2. 00–4. 00–3. 06	**1874:**			
Delaware	M.	60–72–61	2. 17–3. 33–2. 48	California	M.	54–60–57	2. 84–6. 00–3. 63
Maryland	M.	60–60–60	2. 50–2. 75–2. 58	Connecticut	M.	60–60–60	2. 75–3. 50–3. 19
Massachusetts	M.	60–66–65	2. 50–3. 08–2. 53	Delaware	M.	60–60–60	2. 00–2. 50–2. 43
New Hampshire	M.	60–60–60	1. 75–2. 50–2. 13	Illinois	M.	60–60–60	2. 00–3. 50–3. 07
New Jersey	M.	60–60–60	2. 75–2. 88–2. 82	Louisiana	M.	60–60–60	4. 00–4. 00–4. 00
New York	M.	60–60–60	1. 50–3. 90–2. 92	Maryland	M.	58–60–59	1. 67–2. 83–2. 14
Ohio	M.	60–60–60	2. 75–3. 50–3. 25	Massachusetts	M.	59–66–62	2. 00–4. 00–2. 97
Pennsylvania	M.	60–60–60	2. 60–3. 67–2. 88	Minnesota	M.	60–60–60	2. 75–3. 00–2. 88
1870:				Missouri	M.	50–60–54	2. 60–3. 50–2. 93
California	M.	54–60–57	3. 00–6. 00–3. 90	New Hampshire	M.	60–60–60	2. 75–2. 75–2. 75
Connecticut	M.	60–60–60	2. 00–3. 75–2. 94	New Jersey	M.	60–60–60	2. 75–3. 25–2. 96
Delaware	M.	60–60–60	2. 00–4. 00–2. 49	New York	M.	60–60–60	1. 65–4.·00–3. ¡7
Illinois	M.	60–60–60	2. 50–3. 75–3. 06	Ohio	M.	60–60–60	1. 90–3. 50–2. 56
Louisiana	M.	60–60–60	4. 50–4. 50–4. 50	Pennsylvania	M.	60–60–60	1. 25–3. 50–2. 16
Maryland	M.	58–60–59	2. 00–3. 00–2. 40	Virginia	M.	60–60–60	2. 17–2. 25–2. 24

TABLE I–1.—*Blacksmiths, 1840–1900, by year and State*—Continued

Year and State	Sex	Hours per week	Rate per day (dollars)
1875:			
California	M.	54–60–57	2. 84–6. 00–3. 59
Connecticut	M.	60–60–60	2. 00–3. 50–2. 97
Delaware	M.	60–60–60	1. 83–2. 50–2. 06
Illinois	M.	60–60–60	2. 75–3. 30–2. 90
Louisiana	M.	60–60–60	3. 00–3. 00–3. 00
Maine	M.	72–72–72	2. 25–2. 25–2. 25
Maryland	M.	58–60–59	1. 67–2. 83–2. 12
Massachusetts	M.	59–60–60	1. 92–3. 50–2. 28
Minnesota	M.	60–60–60	2. 75–3. 00–2. 88
Missouri	M.	50–60–53	2. 65–3. 50–3. 05
New Hampshire	M.	60–60–60	2. 75–2. 75–2. 75
New Jersey	M.	60–60–60	2. 75–3. 25–2. 93
New York	M.	60–60–60	1. 38–4. 00–2. 82
Ohio	M.	60–60–60	2. 48–3. 50–2. 80
Pennsylvania	M.	60–60–60	1. 42–3. 46–2. 02
Virginia	M.	60–60–60	2. 17–2. 25–2. 24
1876:			
California	M.	54–60–57	2. 84–6. 00–3. 61
Connecticut	M.	60–60–60	2. 00–3. 15–2. 65
Delaware	M.	60–60–60	1. 83–2. 50–2. 03
Illinois	M.	60–60–60	2. 65–3. 25–2. 84
Louisiana	M.	60–60–60	3. 00–3. 00–3. 00
Maryland	M.	58–60–59	1. 67–3. 00–2. 23
Massachusetts	M.	54–60–59	1. 50–3. 60–2. 68
Minnesota	M.	60–60–60	2. 75–3. 00–2. 86
Missouri	M.	50–60–53	2. 60–3. 50–3. 03
New Jersey	M.	60–60–60	2. 50–2. 88–2. 71
New York	M.	60–60–60	1. 50–4. 00–2. 95
Ohio	M.	60–60–60	2. 03–3. 50–2. 56
Pennsylvania	M.	48–60–57	1. 15–3. 50–2. 02
Do	M.	(1)	[2]. 06–. 22–. 21
South Carolina	M.	60–60–60	2. 25–2. 25–2. 25
Vermont	M.	66–66–66	2. 00–2. 00–2. 00
Virginia	M.	60–60–60	1. 83–2. 25–2. 15
1877:			
California	M.	54–60–57	2. 84–6. 00–3. 58
Connecticut	M.	60–60–60	2. 75–3. 25–2. 93
Delaware	M.	60–60–60	1. 75–2. 50–2. 07
Illinois	M.	60–60–60	2. 50–3. 15–2. 72
Louisiana	M.	60–60–60	3. 00–3. 00–3. 00
Maryland	M.	58–60–59	1. 67–3. 00–2. 23
Massachusetts	M.	54–60–59	1. 50–3. 50–2. 69
Minnesota	M.	60–60–60	2. 75–3. 00–2. 86
Missouri	M.	50–60–54	2. 60–3. 50–2. 93
New Jersey	M.	57–60–59	1. 00–3. 00–2. 10
New York	M.	60–60–60	1. 55–4. 50–2. 76
Ohio	M.	60–84–69	1. 17–3. 25–2. 16
Pennsylvania	M.	42–72–55	1. 50–3. 00–2. 12
Do	M.	(1)	[2]. 22–. 22–. 22
Virginia	M.	60–60–60	1. 75–2. 25–2. 00
1878:			
California	M.	54–60–56	2. 70–6. 00–3. 33
Connecticut	M.	60–72–62	2. 50–4. 50–3. 25
Delaware	M.	60–72–61	1. 25–2. 50–1. 69
Illinois	M.	60–60–60	2. 50–2. 90–2. 64
Louisiana	M.	60–60–60	3. 00–3. 00–3. 00
Maryland	M.	58–60–59	1. 67–3. 00–2. 23
Massachusetts	M.	54–66–59	1. 25–3. 20–2. 52
Minnesota	M.	60–60–60	2. 75–3. 00–2. 86
Missouri	M.	50–60–54	2. 65–3. 50–2. 99
New Jersey	M.	60–60–60	1. 75–2. 75–2. 35
New York	M.	60–60–60	1. 55–4. 50–2. 80
Ohio	M.	59–66–60	1. 50–3. 00–2. 07
Pennsylvania	M.	48–72–58	. 80–5. 00–1. 85
Virginia	M.	60–60–60	1. 75–2. 25–2. 13
1879:			
California	M.	54–60–57	2. 93–6. 00–3. 47
Connecticut	M.	60–60–60	2. 50–2. 75–2. 58
Delaware	M.	60–60–60	1. 25–2. 50–1. 93
Illinois	M.	60–60–60	2. 50–3. 15–2. 70
Louisiana	M.	60–60–60	3. 00–3. 00–3. 00
Maryland	M.	58–60–59	1. 67–3. 00–2. 23
Massachusetts	M.	54–60–59	1. 25–3. 20–2. 37
Minnesota	M.	60–60–60	2. 75–3. 00–2. 88
1879—Continued.			
Missouri	M.	48–60–54	0. 67–5. 00–2. 30
New Hampshire	M.	60–60–60	2. 00–2. 00–2. 00
New Jersey	M.	60–60–60	2. 25–2. 75–2. 49
Do	(1)	58–60–60	1. 50–2. 25–1. 90
New York	M.	60–60–60	1. 50–3. 50–2. 71
Ohio	M.	60–60–60	1. 50–3. 00–2. 25
Pennsylvania	M.	54–78–60	. 50–4. 00–1. 80
Do	M.	(1)	[3]. 77–. 77–. 77
Virginia	M.	60–60–60	1. 50–2. 25–1. 94
1880:			
California	M.	54–60–57	2. 93–6. 00–3. 59
Connecticut	M.	60–60–60	2. 50–3. 50–2. 92
Georgia	M.	66–66–66	1. 75–1. 75–1. 75
Illinois	M.	43–60–54	1. 72–2. 90–2. 25
Louisiana	M.	60–60–60	3. 00–3. 00–3. 00
Maryland	M.	58–60–59	1. 67–3. 00–2. 23
Massachusetts	M.	54–60–58	1. 50–3. 15–2. 57
Minnesota	M.	60–60–60	2. 50–2. 75–2. 59
Missouri	M.	50–60–54	2. 50–3. 00–2. 65
New Hampshire	M.	60–60–60	2. 00–2. 00–2. 00
New Jersey	M.	50–70–59	. 75–2. 75–1. 62
New York	M.	60–60–60	1. 50–3. 25–2. 50
Ohio	M.	60–60–60	2. 00–3. 00–2. 33
Pennsylvania	M.	60–72–60	1. 00–3. 34–2. 09
Virginia	M.	60–60–60	1. 50–2. 25–1. 76
1881:			
California	M.	54–60–57	2. 93–6. 00–3. 58
Connecticut	M.	60–60–60	2. 25–3. 00–2. 67
Delaware	M.	60–60–60	1. 34–2. 50–1. 97
Illinois	M.	60–60–60	2. 65–3. 15–2. 91
Louisiana	M.	60–60–60	3. 00–3. 00–3. 00
Maryland	M.	58–60–59	1. 67–3. 00–2. 22
Massachusetts	M.	54–60–58	1. 50–3. 50–2. 74
Minnesota	M.	60–60–60	2. 50–2. 75–2. 61
Missouri	M.	50–60–54	2. 50–2. 80–2. 61
New Hampshire	M.	60–65–65	1. 20–3. 15–1. 61
New Jersey	M.	60–60–60	. 96–3. 67–2. 39
New York	M.	60–60–60	1. 60–3. 50–2. 57
Ohio	M.	48–72–59	1. 00–4. 17–2. 05
Pennsylvania	M.	60–60–60	1. 50–3. 20–2. 17
Virginia	M.	60–60–60	1. 50–2. 25–1. 80
1882:			
California	M.	54–60–57	3. 00–6. 00–3. 54
Connecticut	M.	60–60–60	2. 00–3. 00–2. 65
Delaware	M.	72–72–72	1. 83–2. 75–2. 20
Georgia	M.	60–60–60	1. 25–1. 25–1. 25
Illinois	M.	60–60–60	2. 10–3. 15–2. 81
Louisiana	M.	60–60–60	3. 00–3. 00–3. 00
Maryland	M.	58–60–59	1. 83–3. 00–2. 38
Massachusetts	M.	54–60–58	1. 50–3. 25–2. 67
Minnesota	M.	60–60–60	2. 50–2. 75–2. 59
Missouri	M.	50–60–59	1. 50–4. 00–2. 55
New Hampshire	M.	60–60–60	2. 00–2. 00–2. 00
New Jersey	M.	60–72–65	1. 75–3. 00–2. 43
New York	M.	60–60–60	1. 50–3. 88–2. 61
North Carolina	M.	(1)	1. 25–1. 25–1. 25
Ohio	M.	60–60–60	1. 95–3. 25–2. 46
Do	(1)	54–75–60	. 60–4. 50–2. 24
Pennsylvania	M.	60–60–60	1. 80–4. 50–2. 37
South Carolina	M.	66–66–66	1. 25–1. 25–1. 25
Virginia	M.	60–60–60	1. 75–2. 25–2. 08
1883:			
California	M.	54–60–57	3. 15–6. 00–3. 54
Connecticut	M.	60–60–60	2. 00–3. 50–3. 00
Delaware	M.	60–60–60	1. 83–2. 75–2. 19
Georgia	M.	(1)	2. 25–2. 25–2. 25
Illinois	M.	60–60–60	2. 60–3. 00–2. 83
Indiana	M.	(1)	. 86–2. 76–1. 72
Louisiana	M.	60–60–60	3. 00–3. 00–3. 00
Maryland	M.	58–60–59	1. 83–3. 00–2. 28
Massachusetts	M.	54–60–59	1. 10–3. 50–2. 36
Michigan	M.	(1)	. 50–5. 00–2. 00
Minnesota	M.	60–60–60	2. 50–2. 75–2. 59
Missouri	M.	50–60–55	2. 50–2. 83–2. 64

[1] Not reported. [2] Per hour. [3] And rent free.

TABLE I–1.—*Blacksmiths, 1840–1900, by year and State*—Continued

Year and State	Sex	Hours per week	Rate per day (dollars)
1883—Continued.			
New Hampshire..	M.	60–60–60	2.00–2.00–2.00
New Jersey	M.	48–72–60	1.67–4.50–2.40
New York	M.	60–60–60	1.50–3.75–2.67
Ohio	M.	53–60–59	.83–4.17–2.32
Pennsylvania	M.	60–60–60	2.00–3.75–2.39
Tennessee	M.	66–66–66	1.50–1.50–1.50
Virginia	M.	60–60–60	1.67–2.25–2.00
1884:			
California	M.	54–60–59	1.50–6.00–2.63
Connecticut	M.	60–60–60	2.25–3.50–2.32
Delaware	M.	60–60–60	1.92–2.75–2.22
Georgia	M.	70–70–70	2.00–2.00–2.00
Illinois	M.	60–60–60	2.60–3.15–2.81
Iowa	M.	48–69–60	.64–6.00–2.46
Kansas	M.	60–60–60	2.11–2.11–2.11
Louisiana	M.	60–60–60	3.00–3.00–3.00
Maine	M.	58–58–58	2.75–2.75–2.75
Maryland	M.	58–60–59	1.83–3.00–2.31
Massachusetts	M.	54–60–59	1.75–3.25–2.53
Michigan	M.	(1)	.45–5.00–2.02
Minnesota	M.	60–60–60	2.40–2.50–2.44
Missouri	M.	50–81–60	1.25–3.08–2.40
New Hampshire..	M.	60–60–60	1.75–1.75–1.75
New Jersey	M.	54–72–60	1.00–4.00–2.43
New York	M.	60–60–60	1.50–3.60–2.56
Ohio	M.	59–60–59	1.80–3.17–2.26
Pennsylvania	M.	60–66–60	1.43–3.75–2.13
South Carolina	M.	69–69–69	1.50–1.50–1.50
Virginia	M.	60–60–60	1.67–2.25–2.12
West Virginia	M.	60–60–60	2.00–2.50–2.20
1885:			
California	M.	54–60–58	2.00–6.00–3.41
Connecticut	M.	60–60–60	2.00–3.50–2.78
Delaware	M.	60–60–60	1.50–2.30–2.13
Georgia	M.	69–69–69	1.50–1.70–1.60
Illinois	M.	60–60–60	1.50–4.00–2.50
Indiana	M.	60–60–60	1.50–2.75–2.17
Kansas	M.	54–60–59	1.50–3.81–2.60
Kentucky	M.	60–60–60	2.25–3.00–2.60
Louisiana	M.	60–60–60	3.00–3.00–3.00
Maine	M.	60–66–61	1.75–2.50–2.10
Maryland	M.	58–72–62	1.50–3.00–2.12
Massachusetts	M.	54–60–59	1.50–3.70–2–53
Michigan	M.	60–66–65	1.35–3.83–2.14
Minnesota	M.	60–60–60	2.40–2.50–2.44
Missouri	M.	48–60–55	1.75–3.08–2.50
New Hampshire..	M.	60–66–63	1.63–2.00–1.80
New Jersey	M.	42–62–60	1.50–3.60–2.64
New York	M.	59–72–62	1.35–3.25–2.34
North Carolina	M.	60–60–60	1.75–2.35–2.05
Ohio	M.	54–72–61	1.50–3.75–2.17
Pennsylvania	M.	60–72–62	1.35–3.75–2.14
Tennessee	M.	60–72–65	1.35–2.10–1.75
Vermont	M.	60–66–61	1.50–2.10–1.82
Virginia	M.	48–72–60	1.35–3.00–2.12
West Virginia	M.	60–66–60	2.00–2.50–2.12
Wisconsin	M.	60–60–60	3.30–3.30–3.30
1886:			
California	M.	48–60–60	4 1.73–6.00–2.68
Do	M.	60–60–60	2.30–2.50–2.44
Connecticut	M.	60–60–60	2.00–3.50–2.33
Delaware	M.	60–60–60	1.50–2.17–1.75
Illinois	M.	54–60–59	1.50–3.15–2.38
Indiana	M.	60–60–60	1.75–1.75–1.75
Iowa	M.	48–72–60	.50–7.00–2.02
Kansas	M.	60–70–61	1.66–4.00–2.23
Louisiana	M.	60–60–60	3.00–3.00–3.00
Maryland	M.	58–60–59	1.83–3.00–2.29
Massachusetts	M.	54–60–58	1.50–3.25–2.66
Minnesota	M.	60–60–60	2.40–2.50–2.44
Missouri	M.	50–60–54	2.50–2.80–2.61
New Hampshire..	M.	60–60–60	1.13–1.75–1.62
New Jersey	M.	60–60–60	1.73–3.33–2.57
New York	M.	60–60–60	1.50–3.25–2.64

Year and State	Sex	Hours per week	Rate per day (dollars)
1886—Continued.			
Ohio	M.	60–60–60	0.84–3.49–2.09
Pennsylvania	M.	60–60–60	1.90–3.75–2.41
Rhode Island	M.	60–60–60	2.67–2.67–2.67
Vermont	M.	60–60–60	2.25–2.25–2.25
Virginia	M.	60–60–60	2.00–2.25–2.09
1887:			
California	M.	54–60–57	3.00–6.00–3.56
Connecticut	M.	60–60–60	1.63–3.50–2.38
Delaware	M.	(1)	2.20–.25.22¼
Do	M.	60–60–60	1.83–2.33–2.06
Florida	M.	(1)	1.34–3.25–2.63
Illinois	M.	60–60–60	2.65–3.15–2.91
Kansas	M.	42–70–56	1.56–2.85–2.44
Louisiana	M.	60–60–60	3.00–3.00–3.00
Maine	M.	60–60–60	2.00–2.85–2.28
Maryland	M.	58–60–59	1.25–3.00–1.91
Massachusetts	M.	54–60–59	1.50–3.25–2.29
Michigan	M.	60–60–60	1.50–3.15–2.26
Do	M.	(1)	2.16–.30–.22
Minnesota	M.	60–60–60	2.40–2.50–2.44
Missouri	M.	50–72–60	1.60–3.67–2.62
Nebraska	(2)	54–60–57	1.75–3.85–2.63
New Hampshire..	M.	60–60–60	2.00–2.00–2.00
New Jersey	M.	60–60–60	1.00–3.00–2.08
New York	M.	60–60–60	1.45–3.50–2.22
North Carolina	M.	60–72–67	.75–2.50–1.25
Ohio	M.	48–72–59	.75–4.50–2.02
Oregon	M.	(1)	2.25–3.75–3.10
Pennsylvania	M.	(1)	2.22–.30–.24¼
Do	M.	60–60–60	1.25–3.75–2.26
Rhode Island	M.	48–60–54	1.75–2.75–2.21
Virginia	M.	60–60–60	1.15–2.75–2.10
West Virginia	M.	(1)	1.50–2.50–1.73
Wisconsin	M.	60–66–61	1.15–5.77–1.90
Do	M.	(1)	4 .96–.96–.96
1888:			
California	M.	54–60–57	3.00–6.00–368
Colorado	M.	60–60–60	2.50–3.45–3.03
Connecticut	M.	60–60–60	2.25–3.50–2.88
Delaware	M.	60–60–60	1.83–2.33–2.11
Georgia	M.	66–66–66	2.00–2.00–2.00
Illinois	M.	60–60–60	2.00–3.00–2.81
Indiana	M.	60–60–60	2.50–2.50–2.50
Iowa	M.	54–68–59	1.50–3.45–2.25
Kansas	M.	57–72–59	1.50–3.05–2.57
Louisiana	M.	60–60–60	3.00–3.00–3.00
Maine	M.	60–60–60	.96–2.75–1.76
Maryland	M.	58–60–59	1.83–3.00–2.21
Massachusetts	M.	54–60–58	1.50–3.50–2.78
Michigan	M.	60–72–60	1.15–3.26–2.18
Minnesota	M.	60–60–60	2.40–2.50–2.45
Missouri	M.	50–60–55	2.50–2.80–2.61
New Hampshire..	M.	60–60–60	2.00–2.00–2.00
New Jersey	M.	58–60–59	1.75–3.67–2.30
New York	M.	48–60–59	1.41–5.00–2.58
Do	M.	(1)	2.20–.33½–.29½
North Carolina	M.	48–72–59	.35–2.50–1.38
Ohio	M.	60–72–60	1.22–3.17–2.11
Pennsylvania	M.	60–65–60	1.75–3.75–2.33
Rhode Island	M.	60–60–60	1.10–2.75–2.02
South Carolina	M.	(1)	1.00–1.70–1.35
Tennessee	M.	60–60–60	2.00–2.25–2.13
Virginia	M.	60–72–62	1.40–2.25–2.00
West Virginia	M.	66–72–68	2.50–2.90–2.77
1889:			
Alabama	M.	48–84–63	1.25–3.00–2.19
California	M.	54–60–56	3.00–6.00–3.54
Connecticut	M.	60–60–60	2.00–3.50–2.94
Delaware	M.	60–60–60	1.67–2.50–2.06
Florida	M.	60–60–60	3.00–3.00–3.00
Georgia	M.	84–84–84	1.50–2.00–1.75
Illinois	M.	60–72–60	1.60–4.17–2.53
Indiana	M.	60–72–61	1.75–3.33–2.30
Iowa	M.	48–60–49	1.50–2.51–2.25

¹ Not reported. ² Per hour. ⁴ And board.

TABLE I–1.—*Blacksmiths, 1840–1900, by year and State*—Continued

Year and State	Sex	Hours per week	Rate per day (dollars)
1889—Continued.			
Kansas	M.	36-60-59	1.00-3.25-2.26
Louisiana	M.	60-60-60	3.00-3.00-3.00
Maine	M.	60-60-60	1.75-3.00-2.25
Maryland	M.	58-60-59	1.50-2.83-2.06
Massachusetts	M.	54-60-59	1.50-3.25-2.37
Michigan	M.	60-60-60	1.25-3.19-2.19
Minnesota	M.	60-60-60	2.25-2.75-2.60
Missouri	M.	50-72-58	1.60-3.00-2.27
Do	(1)	(1)	.85-3.35-2.32
New Hampshire	M.	(1)	2.00-2.40-2.13
New Jersey	M.	60-60-60	2.50-3.07-2.83
New York	M.	60-72-60	1.58-3.65-2.67
North Carolina	M.	60-66-61	.58-2.00-1.31
Ohio	M.	40-84-60	1.15-3.35-2.15
Pennsylvania	M.	48-84-60	1.20-4.00-2.24
Do	(1)	(1)	2.30-2.30-2.30
Tennessee	M.	60-84-68	1.50-3.00-1.37
Virginia	M.	60-72-65	1.50-2.75-1.97
West Virginia	M.	54-72-64	1.50-3.67-2.32
Wisconsin	M.	60-60-60	2.25-2.50-2.39
1890:			
Alabama	M.	60-60-60	1.00-3.65-2.20
California	M.	48-60-52	2.80-6.00-3.35
Connecticut	M.	60-60-60	2.25-3.50-3.08
Delaware	M.	60-60-60	2.00-2.33-2.17
Florida	M.	60-60-60	3.00-3.00-3.00
Illinois	M.	60-60-60	1.75-3.00-2.79
Indiana	M.	54-60-59	2.17-3.33-3.09
Kansas	M.	(1)	1.50-3.00-2.28
Louisiana	M.	60-60-60	3.00-3.00-3.00
Maryland	M.	48-60-59	1.67-3.33-2.22
Massachusetts	M.	54-60-58	1.50-3.25-2.58
Michigan	M.	60-60-60	.50-3.83-1.82
Minnesota	M.	60-60-60	2.00-3.00-2.42
Missouri	M.	50-60-55	1.25-2.80-2.42
Nebraska	M.	(1)	1.75-2.75-2.25
New Jersey	M.	60-72-62	1.33-3.03-2.18
New York	M.	59-60-60	1.00-4.50-2.27
North Carolina	M.	60-60-60	.80-2.00-1.40
Ohio	M.	54-75-60	1.25-3.00-2.29
Do	(1)	48-66-58	1.15-5.00-2.18
Pennsylvania	M.	54-70-60	1.34-4.00-2.38
Rhode Island	M.	(1)	1.50-1.50-1.50
Tennessee	M.	(1)	1.50-1.50-1.50
Virginia	M.	60-60-60	2.08-2.25-2.22
Wisconsin	M.	60-66-62	2.75-2.75-2.75
1891:			
California	M.	48-60-51	2.80-6.00-3.34
Connecticut	M.	60-60-60	2.50-3.50-3.06
Delaware	M.	60-72-61	2.00-2.50-2.19
Florida	M.	60-60-60	1.50-1.50-1.50
Illinois	(1)	53-60-57	2.50-4.00-3.25
Do	M.	60-60-60	2.40-3.00-2.83
Kansas	M.	60-60-60	1.75-2.00-1.94
Louisiana	M.	60-60-60	2.50-3.00-2.75
Maine	M.	60-60-60	1.25-3.00-2.05
Maryland	M.	58-60-59	1.33-2.83-2.02
Massachusetts	M.	54-60-58	1.50-3.25-2.56
Michigan	M.	60-60-60	1.50-1.50-1.50
Minnesota	M.	60-60-60	2.25-2.50-2.38
Do		(1)	[4]1.73-2.30-1.92
Missouri	M.	50-60-54	1.22-3.17-2.07
New Jersey	M.	60-60-60	2.50-3.00-2.75
New York	M.	60-60-60	.65-6.67-2.20
North Carolina	M.	60-60-60	1.50-1.50-1.50
Ohio	M.	42-72-58	1.25-5.00-2.06
Pennsylvania	M.	60-60-60	1.80-3.75-2.32
South Carolina	M.	60-60-60	1.25-1.75-1.45
Virginia	M.	60-60-60	1.75-2.25-2.10
Wisconsin	M.	60-60-60	2.25-2.65-2.50
1892:			
California	M.	48-60-54	2.00-6.00-3.06
Colorado	M.	60-60-60	3.23-3.23-3.23
1892—Continued.			
Connecticut	M.	45-60-59	1.85-3.50-2.63
Delaware	M.	60-60-60	1.75-2.50-2.15
Florida	M.	60-66-61	1.50-2.30-1.93
Illinois	M.	60-60-60	2.40-3.00-2.71
Indiana	M.	48-60-59	1.44-3.00-1.92
Iowa	M.	54-60-60	.87-2.75-2.47
Kansas	M.	60-60-60	2.63-2.85-2.78
Louisiana	M.	60-60-60	2.50-3.00-2.75
Maryland	M.	58-60-59	1.33-2.83-2.05
Massachusetts	M.	54-60-59	1.50-3.20-2.40
Michigan	M.	60-60-60	.75-3.00-1.58
Minnesota	M.	60-60-60	2.00-2.75-2.68
Do	M.	(1)	[4]1.73-2.30-1.92
Missouri	M.	60-60-54	2.50-2.80-2.63
New Jersey	M.	60-60-60	2.75-2.75-2.75
New Mexico	M.	60-60-60	3.22-3.22-3.22
New York	M.	48-60-60	1.75-4.00-2.69
Ohio	M.	60-60-60	1.75-2.90-2.31
Do	(1)	54-72-60	1.16-4.00-2.11
Pennsylvania	M.	54-60-59	1.00-3.75-2.37
Rhode Island	M.	53-60-54	2.48-3.00-2.57
South Carolina	M.	60-60-60	1.50-1.50-1.50
Vermont	M.	60-60-60	2.00-2.00-2.00
Virginia	M.	60-60-60	1.75-2.25-2.15
Wisconsin	M.	60-60-60	2.25-2.25-2.25
1893:			
California	M.	48-60-51	2.80-6.00-3.22
Connecticut	M.	45-60-59	1.85-3.40-2.53
Delaware	M.	60-60-60	1.75-2.50-2.15
Florida	M.	60-60-60	2.00-3.00-2.25
Illinois	M.	48-63-59	1.00-3.33-2.62
Louisiana	M.	60-60-60	2.50-3.00-2.75
Maryland	M.	48-72-60	.33-5.00-1.96
Massachusetts	M.	54-60-58	1.50-3.32-2.46
Michigan	M.	48-60-58	1.34-3.83-2.28
Minnesota	M.	60-60-60	2.00-2.50-2.45
Do	M.	(1)	[4]1.34-1.73-1.63
Missouri	M.	50-72-60	1.23-3.50-2.44
Montana	M.	42-57-53	2.50-4.50-3.33
Do	M.	75-75-75	[5]1.34-2.41-2.19
New Jersey	M.	60-60-60	2.11-2.11-2.11
New York	M.	48-78-60	1.00-4.00-2.44
Ohio	M.	42-60-56	.50-5.00-2.00
Pennsylvania	M.	54-84-60	1.00-3.33-2.35
Virginia	M.	60-60-60	2.17-2.33-2.27
Wisconsin	M.	60-60-60	2.25-2.50-2.38
1894:			
California	M.	48-60-51	2.80-6.00-3.19
Connecticut	M.	45-60-56	1.85-2.89-2.22
Delaware	M.	60-60-60	1.75-2.09-1.88
Florida	M.	60-60-60	1.00-2.00-1.67
Illinois	M.	60-60-60	2.40-3.00-2.72
Indiana	M.	49-60-54	1.50-3.25-2.26
Iowa	M.	45-78-57	.73-2.85-1.87
Louisiana	M.	60-60-60	2.50-3.00-2.75
Maine	M.	54-60-59	1.50-2.50-1.93
Maryland	M.	58-60-59	1.33-2.83-1.99
Massachusetts	M.	54-60-57	1.40-3.29-2.49
Minnesota	M.	60-60-60	2.00-2.50-2.38
Do	M.	(1)	[4]1.34-1.73-1.63
Missouri	M.	50-60-53	2.50-2.80-2.63
Montana	M.	(1)	2.63-3.60-3.25
New Hampshire	M.	40-60-55	[5]2.25-2.25-2.25
New York	M.	48-60-60	1.00-4.00-2.43
North Carolina	M.	60-60-60	1.00-2.00-1.71
Do	(1)	60-60-60	1.25-2.50-1.98
Ohio	M.	42-72-56	1.12-5.00-1.94
Pennsylvania	M.	54-60-59	1.00-3.75-2.32
Rhode Island	M.	(1)	1.45-2.00-1.73
Virginia	M.	60-60-60	2.17-2.25-2.23
West Virginia	M.	48-60-51	1.05-3.30-1.94
Wisconsin	M.	60-60-60	2.00-2.00-2.00

1 Not reported.   4 And board.   5 And board and lodging.

TABLE I-1.—*Blacksmiths, 1840–1900, by year and State*—Continued

Year and State	Sex	Lowest, highest, and average—		Year and State	Sex	Lowest, highest, and average—	
		Hours per week	Rate per day (dollars)			Hours per week	Rate per day (dollars)
1895:				**1897:**			
California	M.	48–60–51	2. 80–6. 00–3. 19	California	M.	48–60–52	2. 20–6. 00–3. 13
Connecticut	M.	60–60–60	1. 85–3. 25–2. 37	Connecticut	M.	60–60–60	2. 75–2. 75–2. 75
Delaware	M.	60–60–60	1. 75–2. 09–1. 92	Georgia	M.	66–66–66	1. 25–1. 25–1. 25
Florida	M.	60–60–60	1. 00–3. 00–2. 25	Illinois	M.	60–60–60	2. 50–3. 00–2. 81
Georgia	M.	48–66–62	1. 25–3. 00–1. 85	Kansas	M.	40–60–57	1. 00–3. 20–2. 10
Illinois	M.	54–60–59	2. 00–3. 50–2. 76	Do	(¹)	(¹)	². 25– . 28– . 27
Kansas	M.	60–60–60	2. 00–2. 00–2. 00	Louisiana	M.	60–60–60	2. 50–3. 00–2. 75
Louisiana	M.	60–60–60	2. 50–3. 00–2. 75	Maine	M.	54–60–58	2. 50–2. 50–2. 50
Maine	M.	54–60–58	2. 25–2. 50–2. 42	Maryland	M.	58–60–59	1. 33–3. 00–2. 06
Maryland	M.	58–60–59	1. 33–2. 83–1. 99	Massachusetts	M.	54–60–58	2. 00–2. 85–2. 51
Massachusetts	M.	54–60–57	1. 15–3. 00–2. 48	Michigan	M.	(¹)	1. 88–1. 88–1. 88
Michigan	M.	60–60–60	1. 50–3. 00–2. 00	Minnesota	M.	60–60–60	2. 50–2. 50–2. 50
Minnesota	M.	60–60–60	2. 00–2. 50–2. 38	Missouri	M.	50–60–53	2. 50–2. 80–2. 63
Do	M.	(¹)	1. 34–1. 73–1. 63	Montana	(¹)	(¹)	2. 25–3. 49–3. 07
Missouri	M.	50–60–55	1. 50–2. 80–2. 30	Nebraska	M.	60–60–60	1. 25–2. 50–1. 95
Montana	M.	(¹)	3. 60–3. 60–3.'60	New York	M.	60–60–60	1. 90–3. 75–3. 05
New Hampshire	M.	59–60–60	1. 20–2. 75–1. 66	Ohio	M.	48–72–60	1. 00–3. 50–2. 20
New Jersey	M.	54–60–59	2. 00–2. 40–2. 07	Pennsylvania	M.	50–60–59	1. 12–3. 50–2. 15
New York	M.	48–60–60	1. 25–4. 00–2. 22	Virginia	M.	54–60–60	. 95–3. 00–1. 77
North Carolina	M.	60–60–60	. 50–2. 00–1. 36	**1898:**			
Ohio	M.	36–72–57	. 98–4. 00–1. 93	California	M.	48–60–52	2. 20–6. 00–3. 11
Pennsylvania	M.	54–60–59	1. 00–3. 50–2. 26	Illinois	M.	60–60–60	2. 50–3. 00–2. 82
South Carolina	M.	60–60–60	2. 25–3. 00–2. 56	Iowa	(¹)	(¹)	1. 85–1. 85–1. 85
Tennessee	M.	66–67–67	1. 50–1. 50–1. 50	Kansas	M.	36–60–53	1. 80–3. 50–2. 60
Virginia	M.	60–60–60	2. 00–2. 25–2. 16	Louisiana	M.	60–60–60	2. 50–3. 00–2. 75
Wisconsin	M.	60–60–60	2. 00–2. 00–2. 00	Maryland	M.	58–60–59	1. 33–3. 00–2. 00
Wisconsin	(¹)	54–60–60	. 83–3. 50–1. 85	Massachusetts	M.	54–60–57	2. 00–2. 85–2. 62
1896:				Michigan	M.	(¹)	1. 00–2. 32–1. 92
Alabama	M.	(¹)	. 58– . 58– . 58	Missouri	M.	50–60–53	2. 50–2. 80–2. 59
California	M.	48–60–51	2. 20–6. 00–3. 15	Do	(¹)	60–60–60	2. 00–3. 00–2. 58
Colorado	M.	48–60–57	2. 00–3. 50–3. 27	Nebraska	(¹)	48–66–58	. 75–4. 00–2. 12
Connecticut	M.	60–60–60	1. 50–3. 00–2. 48	New Jersey	M.	60–60–60	1. 67–3. 33–2. 39
Georgia	M.	66–66–66	. 67–2. 50–1. 50	New York	M.	60–60–60	2. 10–3. 75–3. 14
Illinois	M.	55–60–60	1, 50–3. 00–2. 74	Ohio	M.	60–60–60	1. 50–3. 00–2. 12
Indiana	M.	65–65–65	1. 75–1. 75–1. 75	Pennsylvania	M.	54–60–59	1. 15–3. 50–2. 14
Kansas	M.	60–60–60	2. 00–2. 35–2. 25	Virginia	M.	60–60–60	2. 00–2. 25–2. 15
Louisiana	M.	60–60–60	2. 50–3. 00–2. 75	Do	(¹)	54–54–54	2. 35–2. 35–2. 35
Maine	M.	53–53–53	2. 75–2. 75–2. 75	Washington	(¹)	(¹)	1. 54–3. 13–2. 54
Maryland	M.	58–C0–60	1. 33–3. 00–2. 16	**1899:**			
Massachusetts	M.	54–60–57	2. 00–3. 00–2. 55	Alabama	M.	60–60–60	2. 00–3. 25–2. 57
Michigan	M.	48–78–60	. 45–3. 83–1. 72	Georgia	M.	60–60–60	2. 00–3. 50–2. 45
Minnesota	M.	60–60–60	2. 00–2. 50–2. 43	Massachusetts	M.	51–59–55	1. 00–4. 67–2. 32
Do	M.	(¹)	⁴1. 34–1. 53–1. 48	Michigan	M.	(¹)	1. 83–2. 02–1. 98
Mississippi	M.	(¹)	. 50–1. 00– . 75	New York	M.	54–60–59	1. 89–3. 00–2. 18
Missouri	M.	48–60–57	1. 17–6. 00–2. 01	North Carolina	M.	60–72–62	. 50–2. 50–1. 37
Montana	M.	(¹)	3. 46–3. 46–3. 46	Ohio	M.	60–80–60	1. 65–3. 50–2. 34
Nebraska	M.	48–60–52	1. 50–3. 85–2. 89	Pennsylvania	M.	(¹)	1. 75–4. 25–2. 54
New Hampshire	M.	60–60–60	1. 45–1. 90–1. 68	Tennessee	M.	(¹)	1. 25–2. 31–1. 81
New York	M.	48–60–57	1. 00–5. 21–2. 61	Virginia	M.	(¹)	1. 25–2. 25–1. 79
North Carolina	M.	60–72–63	. 75–2. 00–1. 55	**1900:**			
Ohio	M.	44–60–53	. 62–4. 00–1. 92	Alabama	M.	60–60–60	1. 20–3. 25–2. 37
Pennsylvania	M.	54–60–60	1. 00–3. 50–2. 57	Georgia	M.	60–60–60	2. 00–3. 50–2. 5C
Rhode Island	M.	60–60–60	1. 75–1. 75–1. 75	Massachusetts	M.	51–59–55	1. 75–4. 67–2. 41
South Carolina	M.	66–66–66	1. 25–1. 65–1. 45	New York	M.	54–60–58	1. 80–3. 00–2. 25
Tennessee	M.	(¹)	1. 17–1. 67–1. 38	North Carolina	M.	60–60–60	1. 50–1. 67–1. 59
Vermont	M.	48–60–60	1. 25–3. 00–2. 06	Ohio	M.	60–60–60	2. 00–4. 00–2. 33
Virginia	M.	60–60–60	2. 00–2. 25–2. 16				
West Virginia	M.	55–55–55	1. 50–2. 00–1. 73				
Wisconsin	M.	60–60–60	2. 00–2. 00–2. 00				

¹ Not reported.   ⁴ And board.

TABLE I–2.—*Blacksmiths, males, 1890–1906, by city and year*

Year	Atlanta, Ga.		Birmingham, Ala.		Boston, Mass.		Chicago, Ill.	
	Hours per hour	Rate per hour	Hours per week	Rate per hour	Hours per week	Rate per hour	Hours per week	Rate per hour
1890	59.5	$0.328			59.3	$0.284	59.8	$0.293
1891	59.5	.340			59.3	.284	59.8	.287
1892	59.5	.340			58.0	.290	58.6	.293
1893	59.7	.327			58.0	.289	53.6	.291
1894	59.7	.305			57.8	.285	57.7	.266
1895	59.7	.305			57.8	.286	58.3	.249
1896	59.7	.305			58.0	.283	58.3	.264
1897	59.\7	.305			57.8	.285	57.7	.263
1898	59.7	.317			57.8	.285	58.4	.264
1899	59.7	.317			55.9	.295	58.2	.287
1900	59.7	.327			55.9	.300	58.4	.295
1901	59.7	.327			55.9	.300	56.4	.296
1902	59.7	.327			55.5	.296	56.3	.318
1903	59.8	.330			54.7	.303	54.0	.326
1904	59.7	.340			55.1	.291	54.0	.334
1905	59.7	.318			55.1	.282	54.0	.342
1906	59.7	.344	59.5	$0.350	55.0	.272	51.9	.355

Year	Cincinnati, Ohio		Denver, Colo.		Detroit, Mich.		New Orleans, La.	
1890					60.0	$0.207	58.9	$0.331
1891					60.0	.202	58.8	.332
1892					60.0	.202	58.7	.333
1893					60.0	.200	58.8	.337
1894					60.0	.191	58.8	.339
1895					60.0	.194	58.8	.334
1896					60.0	.217	58.8	.329
1897					60.0	.201	58.8	.327
1898					60.0	.189	58.7	.333
1899					60.0	.196	58.7	.338
1900					60.0	.213	58.7	.341
1901					60.0	.215	54.0	.364
1902					60.0	.218	52.9	.372
1903	56.7	$0.283	(¹)	(¹)	59.6	.230	54.0	.352
1904	54.8	.288	53.8	$0.350	59.5	.230	54.0	.350
1905	54.8	.290	56.1	.329	59.3	.238	54.0	.358
1906	54.8	.309	55.5	.331	59.3	.247	54.0	.360

Year	New York, N. Y.		Philadelphia, Pa.		St. Louis, Mo		San Francisco, Calif.	
1890	59.0	$0.313	60.0	$0.283	60.0	$0.291	57.3	$0.346
1891	59.1	.314	60.0	.286	60.0	.291	55.5	.342
1892	59.1	.316	60.0	.310	60.0	.291	59.3	.355
1893	59.1	.320	60.0	.325	60.0	.291	55.7	.378
1894	59.1	.324	60.0	.306	60.0	.281	59.2	.334
1895	59.1	.323	60.0	.297	60.0	.281	59.2	.342
1896	59.1	.321	60.0	.306	60.0	.280	52.4	.346
1897	59.1	.310	60.0	.320	60.0	.280	59.1	.338
1898	59.1	.309	60.0	.280	57.0	.280	54.7	.333
1899	56.9	.325	58.0	.349	56.3	.280	59.1	.333
1900	55.5	.337	58.3	.304	56.3	.280	59.2	.332
1901	55.3	.335	58.3	.321	56.3	.280	59.2	.334
1902	52.6	.356	58.0	.339	56.2	.288	58.1	.336
1903	52.7	.364	56.7	.309	54.0	310	57.7	.344
1904	53.7	.389	56.1	.297	54.0	.310	54.0	.382
1905	53.7	.394	56.2	.324	54.0	.327	54.0	.404
1906	53.8	.400	56.4	.297	54.0	.344	54.0	.438

¹ Not reported.

TABLE **I-3.**—*Blacksmiths, males, railroad shops, 1907–1922, by city and year*

Year	Atlanta, Ga.		Birmingham, Ala.		Boston, Mass.		Chicago, Ill.	
	Hours per week	Rate per hour	Hours per week	Rate per hour	Hours per week	Rate per hour	Hours per week	Rate per hour
1907	54.0	$0.325	54.0	$0.340			1 49.0	$0.345
1908	54.0	.325	54.0	.340			1 49.0	.345
1909	54.0	.380	54.0	.340			1 49.0	.365
1910	54.0	.390	54.0	.375			1 49.0	.380
1911	54.0	.390	54.0	.390			1 49.0	.380
1912	54.0	.410	54.0	.390			1 49.0	.380
1913	54.0	.410	54.0	.410	2 53.0	$0.285	54.0	.400
1914	54.0	.410	54.0	.410	53.0	.305	54.0	.410
1915	54.0	.410	54.0	.410	53.0	.305	54.0	.410
1916	54.0	.420	54.0	.420	53.0	.305	54.0	.420
1917	54.0	.505	54.0	.505	3 53.0	.345	54.0	.420
1918	48.0	.680	48.0	.680	48.0	.680	48.0	.688
1919	48.0	.720	48.0	.720	48.0	.720	48.0	.720
1920	48.0	.850	4 48.0	.850	48.0	.850	5 48.0	.850
1921	4 48.0	.850	4 48.0	.850	4 48.0	.850	48.0	.850
1922	4 48.0	.770	4 48.0	.770	4 48.0	.770	48.0	.770

Year	Cincinnati, Ohio		Denver, Colo.		Detroit, Mich.		New Orleans, La.	
1907			54.0	$0.350				
1908			54.0	.385				
1909			54.0	.385				
1910			54.0	.415				
1911			48.0	.425				
1912	54.0	$0.325	48.0	.425			54.0	$0.395
1913	54.0	.335	48.0	.425			54.0	.395
1914	54.0	.335	48.0	.425			54.0	.415
1915	54.0	.335	48.0	.425			54.0	.415
1916	54.0	.350	48.0	.435			54.0	.410
1917	54.0	.375	48.0	.450			54.0	.420
1918	48.0	.680	48.0	.680	48.0	$0.680	48.0	.680
1919	48.0	.720	48.0	.720	48.0	.720	48.0	.720
1920	48.0	.850	48.0	.850	48.0	.850	48.0	.850
1921	48.0	.850	48.0	.850	48.0	.850	48.0	.850
1922	48.0	.770	48.0	.770	48.0	.770	48.0	.770

Year	New York, N. Y.		Philadelphia, Pa.		St. Louis, Mo.		San Francisco, Calif.	
1907					54.0	$0.320		
1908					54.0	.340		
1909					54.0	.340		
1910					54.0	.380		
1911					54.0	.380		
1912					54.0	.400	54.0	$0.400
1913					54.0	.400	54.0	.400
1914					54.0	.410	54.0	.400
1915					54.0	.410		
1916			54.0	$0.370	54.0	.410		
1917			54.0	.370	54.0	.435		
1918			48.0	.680	48.0	.680		
1919	5 45.0	$0.720	48.0	.720	48.0	.720		
1920	6 45.0	.850	48.0	.850	48.0	.850	6 48.0	850
1921	48.0	.850	48.0	.850	48.0	.850	48.0	850
1922	48.0	.770	48.0	.770	48.0	.770	48.0	770

1 54, September to April.
2 Paid for 54.
3 50, July and August; paid for 53.
4 General fire.
5 Paid for 49.
6 Paid for 46.

TABLE I–4.—*Blacksmiths, males, machine shops, 1923–1927, by State and year*

Year	California		Connecticut		Illinois		Indiana	
	Hours per week	Rate per hour	Hours per week	Rate per hour	Hours per week	Rate per hour	Hours per week	Rate per hour
1923	47.2	$1.061	50.6	$0.689	51.0	$0.713	54.5	$0.606
1925	46.8	.930	50.4	.743	50.2	.752	51.6	.706
1927	46.5	.852	50.7	.741	50.1	.764	51.8	.704

	Massachusetts		Michigan		Minnesota		New Jersey	
1923	48.2	$0.648	51.3	$0.653	51.0	$0.626	49.6	$0.726
1925	48.7	.693	51.4	.697	50.1	.602	49.6	.727
1927	49.4	.688	51.0	.689	50.1	.633	49.7	.748

	New York		Ohio		Pennsylvania		Wisconsin	
1923	47.3	$0.776	52.2	$0.610	51.7	$0.659	52.7	$0.619
1925	48.3	.727	50.8	.710	51.4	.718	49.5	.679
1927	49.1	.741	49.9	.700	50.9	.737	52.4	.757

TABLE I–5.—*Boiler makers, 1844–1900, by year and State*

Year and State	Sex	Lowest, highest, and average—		Year and State	Sex	Lowest, highest, and average—	
		Hours per week	Rate per day (dollars)			Hours per week	Rate per day (dollars)
1844:				**1860:**			
New York	M.	60–60–60	1.00–1.25–1.17	Connecticut	M.	60–60–60	1.63–2.00–1.77
1845:				Maryland	M.	60–60–60	1.50–2.50–1.79
New York	M.	60–60–60	1.00–1.38–1.13	New York	M.	60–60–60	1.13–1.25–1.21
1846:				**1861:**			
New York	M.	60–60–60	1.00–1.38–1.09	Connecticut	M.	60–60–60	1.75–1.88–1.79
1847:				Maryland	M.	60–60–60	1.50–1.50–1.50
New York	M.	60–60–60	1.00–1.50–1.16	New York	M.	60–60–60	1.50–1.75–1.60
1848:				**1862:**			
New York	M.	60–60–60	1.00–1.50–1.21	Connecticut	M.	60–60–60	1.25–2.50–1.68
1849:				Maryland	M.	60–60–60	1.67–2.25–1.96
New York	M.	60–60–60	1.25–1.50–1.33	New York	M.	60–60–60	1.25–1.75–1.55
1850:				**1863:**			
New York	M.	60–60–60	1.25–1.38–1.30	Connecticut	M.	60–60–60	1.40–2.75–1.92
1851:				Maryland	M.	60–60–60	1.83–2.00–1.92
New York	M.	60–60–60	1.13–1.50–1.28	New York	M.	60–60–60	1.00–2.13–1.51
1852:				**1864:**			
New York	M.	60–60–60	1.13–1.90–1.42	Connecticut	M.	60–60–60	1.40–3.50–2.24
1853:				Maryland	M.	60–60–60	2.00–3.00–2.22
Connecticut	M.	60–60–60	1.00–2.25–1.49	New York	M.	60–60–60	1.25–2.50–1.78
1854:				**1865:**			
Connecticut	M.	60–60–60	1.00–2.25–1.41	Connecticut	M.	60–60–60	2.00–4.00–2.66
New York	M.	60–60–60	1.13–1.63–1.45	Maryland	M.	60–60–60	2.50–3.50–2.87
1855:				New York	M.	60–60–60	1.38–2.75–2.32
Connecticut	M.	60–60–60	1.10–2.25–1.49	**1866:**			
Maryland	M.	60–60–60	1.50–2.50–1.79	Connecticut	M.	60–60–60	2.00–4.00–2.66
New York	M.	60–60–60	1.13–1.75–1.51	Maryland	M.	60–60–60	2.25–3.33–2.57
1856:				New York	M.	60–60–60	1.25–2.63–2.06
Connecticut	M.	60–60–60	1.20–2.37–1.59	**1867:**			
Maryland	M.	60–60–60	1.50–2.50–1.69	Connecticut	M.	60–60–60	2.00–5.00–2.73
New York	M.	60–60–60	1.25–1.88–1.54	Maryland	M.	60–60–60	2.50–3.33–2.94
1857:				New York	M.	60–60–60	1.38–3.00–2.17
Connecticut	M.	60–60–60	1.20–2.50–1.72	**1868:**			
Maryland	M.	60–60–60	1.50–2.50–1.83	Connecticut	M.	60–60–60	2.00–5.00–2.55
New York	M.	60–60–60	1.25–1.88–1.58	Maryland	M.	60–60–60	1.33–3.00–2.39
1858:				New York	M.	60–60–60	1.40–2.80–2.09
Connecticut	M.	60–60–60	1.25–2.37–1.67	**1869:**			
Maryland	M.	60–60–60	1.83–2.50–2.17	Connecticut	M.	60–60–60	2.00–5.00–2.66
New York	M.	60–60–60	1.37–1.37–1.37	Maryland	M.	60–60–60	2.25–3.33–2.40
1859:				New York	M.	60–60–60	1.40–3.00–2.07
Connecticut	M.	60–60–60	1.25–2.00–1.63				
Maryland	M.	60–60–60	1.25–2.50–1.67				

TABLE I-5.—*Boiler makers, 1844–1900, by year and State*—Continued

| Year and State | Sex | Lowest, highest, and average— | | Year and State | Sex | Lowest, highest, and average— | |
		Hours per week	Rate per day (dollars)			Hours per week	Rate per day (dollars)
1870:				**1876:**			
California	M.	54–60–56	3.00–4.00–3.38	California	M.	54–60–56	3.00–4.00–3.34
Connecticut	M.	60–60–60	1.88–3.50–2.54	Connecticut	M.	60–60–60	2.00–3.00–2.46
Illinois	M.	60–60–60	2.75–3.50–3.28	Illinois	M.	60–60–60	2.80–3.05–2.90
Louisiana	M.	60–60–60	3.50–4.00–3.63	Louisiana	M.	60–60–60	3.50–4.00–3.65
Maryland	M.	60–60–60	2.00–3.33–2.23	Maryland	M.	60–60–60	2.00–3.50–2.21
Massachusetts	M.	60–60–60	2.00–3.75–2.62	Massachusetts	M.	60–60–60	2.00–3.50–2.44
Minnesota	M.	60–60–60	3.50–3.50–3.50	Minnesota	M.	60–60–60	3.00–3.00–3.00
Missouri	M.	60–60–60	2.50–3.00–2.89	Missouri	M.	60–60–60	2.50–3.25–2.57
New York	M.	60–60–60	1.50–3.00–2.20	New York	M.	60–60–60	1.40–3.20–2.02
Ohio	M.	60–60–60	2.00–3.25–2.63	Ohio	M.	60–60–60	2.16–3.38–2.53
Pennsylvania	M.	60–60–60	1.80–3.00–2.21	Pennsylvania	M.	48–60–58	1.62–3.00–2.10
1871:				Do	M.	(1)	2.20–.20–.20
California	M.	54–60–55	2.88–4.00–3.19	Virginia	M.	60–60–60	2.00–2.00–2.00
Connecticut	M.	60–60–60	2.00–3.00–2.46	**1877:**			
Illinois	M.	60–60–60	2.70–3.75–3.35	California	M.	54–60–55	2.50–4.00–3.26
Louisiana	M.	60–60–60	3.50–4.00–3.64	Connecticut	M.	60–60–60	1.75–2.75–2.27
Maryland	M.	60–60–60	2.00–3.33–2.24	Illinois	M.	60–60–60	2.80–3.05–2.90
Massachusetts	M.	60–60–60	1.86–2.75–1.94	Louisiana	M.	60–60–60	3.50–4.00–3.63
Minnesota	M.	60–60–60	3.50–3.50–3.50	Maryland	M.	60–60–60	2.00–3.00–2.19
Missouri	M.	60–60–60	2.50–3.00–2.90	Massachusetts	M.	60–60–60	1.92–3.25–2.39
New York	M.	60–60–60	1.40–3.00–2.18	Minnesota	M.	60–60–60	3.00–3.00–3.00
Ohio	M.	60–60–60	2.00–3.25–2.54	Missouri	M.	60–60–60	2.50–3.25–2.62
Pennsylvania	M.	60–60–60	2.00–3.50–2.28	New York	M.	60–60–60	1.40–3.00–1.99
1872:				Ohio	M.	60–60–60	1.45–3.38–2.13
California	M.	54–60–55	2.88–4.00–3.19	Pennsylvania	M.	42–60–57	1.62–3.45–2.04
Connecticut	M.	60–60–60	1.75–4.50–2.52	Do	M.	(1)	2.16–.16–.16
Illinois	M.	60–60–60	3.00–3.75–3.38	Virginia	M.	60–60–60	2.00–2.00–2.00
Louisiana	M.	60–60–60	3.50–4.00–3.61	**1878:**			
Maryland	M.	60–60–60	2.00–3.33–2.25	California	M.	54–60–55	2.50–4.00–3.26
Massachusetts	M.	60–60–60	2.00–3.42–2.45	Connecticut	M.	60–60–60	1.75–3.00–2.44
Minnesota	M.	60–60–60	2.50–3.00–2.90	Illinois	M.	60–60–60	2.90–3.15–2.93
Missouri	M.	60–60–60	1.50–3.00–2.21	Louisiana	M.	60–60–60	3.50–4.00–3.64
New York	M.	60–60–60	2.00–3.25–2.53	Maryland	M.	60–60–60	2.00–3.00–2.19
Ohio	M.	60–60–60	2.00–3.80–2.36	Massachusetts	M.	60–60–60	1.92–3.25–2.31
Pennsylvania	M.	60–60–60		Minnesota	M.	60–60–60	3.00–3.00–3.00
1873:				Missouri	M.	60–60–60	2.50–3.25–2.59
California	M.	54–60–55	3.00–4.50–3.40	New York	M.	60–60–60	1.40–2.70–1.92
Connecticut	M.	60–60–60	1.75–4.50–2.59	Ohio	M.	60–60–60	1.75–3.38–2.01
Illinois	M.	60–60–60	2.75–3.75–3.35	Pennsylvania	M.	48–60–57	1.50–3.00–2.16
Louisiana	M.	60–60–60	3.50–4.00–3.63	Virginia	M.	60–60–60	1.50–1.67–1.59
Maryland	M.	60–60–60	2.00–3.33–2.25	**1879:**			
Massachusetts	M.	60–60–60	2.00–3.50–2.49	California	M.	54–60–57	2.50–3.75–3.18
Minnesota	M.	60–60–60	3.50–3.50–3.50	Connecticut	M.	60–60–60	1.50–2.50–1.96
Missouri	M.	60–60–60	2.50–3.07–2.89	Illinois	M.	60–60–60	2.80–3.05–2.90
New York	M.	60–60–60	1.60–3.00–2.24	Louisiana	M.	60–60–60	3.50–4.00–3.65
Ohio	M.	60–60–60	2.00–3.25–2.61	Maryland	M.	60–60–60	2.00–3.00–2.19
Pennsylvania	M.	60–60–60	2.00–3.80–2.37	Massachusetts	M.	60–60–60	1.92–3.25–2.33
1874:				Minnesota	M.	60–60–60	3.00–3.00–3.00
California	M.	54–60–55	2.88–4.50–3.39	Missouri	M.	60–60–60	2.27–5.00–2.53
Connecticut	M.	60–60–60	1.75–3.50–2.53	New York	M.	60–60–60	1.30–2.70–1.93
Delaware	M.	60–60–60	2.50–2.50–2.50	Ohio	M.	60–60–60	2.25–3.50–2.62
Illinois	M.	60–60–60	3.15–3.25–3.20	Pennsylvania	M.	57–60–58	1.25–2.67–1.81
Louisiana	M.	60–60–60	3.50–4.00–3.63	Virginia	M.	60–60–60	1.75–1.75–1.75
Maryland	M.	60–60–60	2.00–3.33–2.25	**1880:**			
Massachusetts	M.	66–60–60	2.00–3.75–2.57	California	M.	54–60–56	2.50–3.75–3.22
Minnesota	M.	60–60–60	3.50–3.50–3.50	Connecticut	M.	60–60–60	1.50–3.00–2.10
Missouri	M.	60–60–60	2.50–3.07–2.86	Illinois	M.	48–61–54	1.46–3.15–2.28
New York	M.	60–60–60	1.50–3.00–2.21	Louisiana	M.	60–60–60	3.50–3.50–3.50
Ohio	M.	60–60–60	2.00–3.38–2.64	Maryland	M.	60–60–60	2.00–3.50–2.20
Pennsylvania	M.	60–60–60	1.60–3.30–2.17	Massachusetts	M.	60–60–60	1.94–3.25–2.29
Virginia	M.	60–60–60	2.00–2.00–2.00	Minnesota	M.	60–60–60	3.00–3.00–3.00
1875:				Missouri	M.	60–60–60	2.27–4.00–2.49
California	M.	54–60–55	3.00–4.50–3.34	New Jersey	M.	60–65–63	2.00–2.25–2.13
Connecticut	M.	60–60–60	2.00–3.00–2.56	New York	M.	60–60–60	1.30–2.60–1.91
Illinois	M.	60–60–60	3.00–3.15–3.05	Ohio	M.	60–60–60	2.25–3.38–2.50
Louisiana	M.	60–60–60	3.50–4.00–3.62	Pennsylvania	M.	60–60–60	2.00–2.67–2.21
Maryland	M.	60–60–60	2.00–3.50–2.23	Virginia	M.	60–60–60	1.67–2.00–1.89
Massachusetts	M.	60–60–60	2.00–3.00–2.50	**1881:**			
Minnesota	M.	60–60–60	3.50–3.50–3.50	California	M.	54–60–57	2.50–3.75–3.18
Missouri	M.	60–60–60	2.50–3.07–2.85	Connecticut	M.	60–60–60	1.75–3.00–2.28
New York	M.	60–60–60	1.40–3.20–2.18	Illinois	M.	60–60–60	2.50–3.00–2.70
Pennsylvania	M.	60–60–60	1.60–3.00–1.82	Louisiana	M.	60–60–60	3.00–3.00–3.00
Ohio	M.	60–60–60	2.00–3.38–2.50	Maryland	M.	60–60–60	2.00–3.50–2.22
Virginia	M.	60–60–60	2.00–2.00–2.00	Massachusetts	M.	60–60–60	2.00–4.00–2.52

¹ Not reported.　　　　² Per hour.

TABLE **I–5.**—*Boiler makers, 1844–1900, by year and State*—Continued

Year and State	Sex	Hours per week	Rate per day (dollars)
1881—Continued.			
Minnesota	M.	60–60–60	3.00–3.00–3.00
Missouri	M.	60–60–60	2.27–4.00–2.49
New Jersey	M.	60–60–60	2.25–2.25–2.25
New York	M.	60–60–60	1.40–2.80–1.97
Ohio	M.	60–66–60	1.94–3.38–2.40
Pennsylvania	M.	60–60–60	1.83–3.00–2.35
Virginia	M.	60–60–60	2.25–2.50–2.38
1882:			
California	M.	54–60–57	2.50–3.75–3.21
Connecticut	M.	60–60–60	1.75–3.50–2.44
Illinois	M.	60–60–60	2.50–3.15–2.90
Louisiana	M.	60–60–60	3.00–3.00–3.00
Maryland	M.	60–60–60	2.00–3.50–2.30
Massachusetts	M.	60–60–60	2.00–5.00–2.61
Minnesota	M.	60–60–60	3.00–3.00–3.00
Missouri	M.	60–60–60	2.25–3.00–2.66
New York	M.	60–60–60	1.30–3.00–2.31
Ohio	M.	60–60–60	2.00–3.38–2.38
Do	M.	57–60–60	2.00–3.50–2.34
Pennsylvania	M.	60–60–60	2.00–3.00–2.29
Virginia	M.	60–60–60	2.25–2.92–2.59
1883:			
California	M.	54–60–57	2.50–4.00–3.16
Connecticut	M.	60–60–60	2.00–3.00–2.45
Illinois	M.	60–60–60	2.90–3.00–2.90
Louisiana	M.	60–60–60	3.00–3.00–3.00
Maryland	M.	60–60–60	2.00–3.50–2.42
Massachusetts	M.	60–60–60	1.67–5.00–2.34
Michigan	M.	(1)	.85–4.00–2.21
Minnesota	M.	60–60–60	3.00–3.00–3.00
Missouri	M.	60–60–60	2.50–3.00–2.64
New Jersey	M.	60–60–60	1.50–2.75–2.19
New York	M.	60–60–60	1.30–3.00–2.17
Ohio	M.	60–60–60	1.75–3.38–2.40
Pennsylvania	M.	60–60–60	2.00–3.00–2.29
Virginia	M.	60–60–60	2.00–2.00–2.00
1884:			
California	M.	54–60–57	2.75–4.00–3.32
Connecticut	M.	60–60–60	2.00–3.00–2.44
Illinois	M.	60–60–60	2.90–3.00–2.90
Iowa	M.	60–60–60	2.00–2.50–2.36
Louisiana	M.	60–60–60	3.00–3.00–3.00
Maryland	M.	60–60–60	2.00–3.50–2.47
Massachusetts	M.	60–60–60	2.00–5.00–2.52
Michigan	M.	(1)	1.00–7.67–2.33
Minnesota	M.	60–60–60	3.00–3.00–3.00
Missouri	M.	60–60–60	2.50–3.00–2.65
Nebraska	M.	60–60–60	2.45–2.45–2.45
New Jersey	M.	60–72–60	1.60–3.00–2.40
New York	M.	60–60–60	1.40–3.00–2.27
Ohio	M.	52–60 59	2.00–3.38–2.45
Pennsylvania	M.	60–60–60	2.00–3.50–2.33
Virginia	M.	60–60–60	1.67–1.67–1.67
1885:			
California	M.	54–60–58	2.75–4.25–3.31
Connecticut	M.	60–60–60	2.00–3.00–2.46
Illinois	M.	60–60–60	2.75–2.90–2.78
Indiana	M.	60–60–60	1.50–3.33–2.01
Louisiana	M.	60–60–60	2.50–3.00–2.63
Maryland	M.	60–60–60	2.00–3.50–2.47
Massachusetts	M.	60–60–60	2.00–5.00–2.55
Michigan	M.	(1)	1.25–3.45–2.29
Minnesota	M.	60–60–60	3.00–3.00–3.00
Missouri	M.	60–60–60	2.50–3.00–2.60
New Jersey	M.	60–60–60	1.25–3.00–2.54
New York	M.	60–60–60	1.25–2.70–2.24
Ohio	M.	60–72–60	1.75–3.00–2.09
Pennsylvania	M.	60–60–60	1.80–3.00–2.15
Vermont	M.	60–60–60	1.80–1.80–1.80
Virginia	M.	48–60–59	1.67–2.30–2.18
1886:			
California	M.	54–60–58	2.50–4.00–3.13
Connecticut	M.	60–60–60	2.00–3.00–2.48
Illinois	M.	59–60–60	1.90–3.00–2.39
Iowa	M.	48–60–55	1.25–3.50–2.55
Do	M.	(1)	[2] .25–.25–.25
1886—Continued.			
Kansas	M.	60–60–60	1.50–2.70–2.15
Louisiana	M.	60–60–60	2.50–3.00–2.63
Maryland	M.	60–60–60	2.00–3.50–2.47
Massachusetts	M.	60–60–60	2.00–5.00–2.46
Minnesota	M.	60–60–60	3.00–3.00–3.00
Missouri	M.	60–60–60	2.50–3.00–2.61
New York	M.	59–60–59	1.25–3.00–2.21
Ohio	M.	54–60–57	1.58–2.48–2.06
Pennsylvania	M.	60–60–60	2.00–3.00–2.34
Virginia	M.	60–60–60	1.67–2.10–1.81
1887:			
California	M.	54–60–57	3.00–4.00–3.40
Connecticut	M.	60–60–60	1.30–3.10–2.20
Delaware	M.	(1)	[2] .25–.27–.25½
Florida	M.	(1)	2.50–3.00–2.81
Illinois	M.	60–60–60	2.90–2.90–2.90
Kansas	M.	60–60–60	2.25–3.00–2.45
Louisiana	M.	60–60–60	2.50–3.00–2.64
Maine	M.	60–60–60	2.17–2.17–2.17
Maryland	M.	60–60–60	1.40–3.50–2.16
Massachusetts	M.	60–60–60	1.25–5.00–2.21
Michigan	M.	60–60–60	1.60–3.00–2.27
Do	M.	(1)	[2] .25–.30–.26½
Minnesota	M.	60–60–60	3.00–3.00–3.00
Missouri	M.	60–60–60	2.00–3.00–2.63
Nebraska	(1)	54–60–58	1.70–3.75–2.78
New Jersey	M.	(1)	1.70–2.75–2.23
New York	M.	60–60–60	1.35–3.83–2.25
North Carolina	M.	48–48–48	1.15–1.15–1.15
Ohio	M.	48–60–59	1.50–3.50–2.32
Oregon	M.	(1)	2.25–3.75–3.25
Pennsylvania	M.	(1)	[2] .22–.26–.24½
Do	M.	60–60–60	1.53–3.45–2.35
Rhode Island	M.	(1)	2.25–2.50–2.42
Virginia	M.	60–60–60	1.67–2.40–2.04
West Virginia	M.	(1)	1.50–1.50–1.50
Wisconsin	M.	(1)	1.50–3.25–2.59
1888:			
California	M.	54–60–57	3.00–4.00–3.41
Colorado	M.	60–60–60	3.25–3.25–3.25
Connecticut	M.	60–60–60	2.00–2.85–2.40
Illinois	M.	60–60–60	2.90–3.00–2.90
Iowa	M.	48–60–51	2.00–3.50–2.92
Kansas	M.	(1)	3.00–3.00–3.00
Louisiana	M.	60–60–60	2.50–3.00–2.60
Maryland	M.	60–60–60	2.00–3.50–2.46
Massachusetts	M.	60–60–60	2.00–5.00–2.42
Michigan	M.	60–72–64	1.73–3.83–2.49
Minnesota	M.	60–60–60	3.25–3.25–3.25
Missouri	M.	60–60–60	2.50–3.00–2.60
New Jersey	M.	60–60–60	1.92–3.00–2.22
New York	M.	53–60–58	1.40–4.50–2.20
Do	M.	(1)	[2] .27–.27–.27
North Carolina	M.	60–60–60	1.25–2.25–1.75
Ohio	M.	54–54–54	2.03–2.62–2.15
Pennsylvania	M.	60–60–60	2.00–3.00–2.36
Virginia	M.	60–60–60	1.50–1.67–1.59
1889:			
California	M.	54–60–58	3.24–4.00–3.46
Connecticut	M.	60–60–60	2.00–2.85–2.36
Illinois	M.	60–60–60	2.25–2.90–2.82
Kansas	M.	60–60–60	2.00–3.00–2.57
Louisiana	M.	60–60–60	2.50–3.00–2.64
Maryland	M.	60–60–60	2.00–3.50–2.46
Massachusetts	M.	60–60–60	2.00–5.00–2.48
Minnesota	M.	00–60–60	3.25–3.25–3.25
Missouri	M.	60–60–60	2.50–3.00–2.60
New York	M.	60–60–60	1.50–2.75–2.21
Ohio	M.	54–54–54	2.03–2.62–2.15
Pennsylvania	M.	60–60–60	1.80–3.00–2.31
Virginia	M.	60–60–60	1.33–2.00–1.67
1890:			
California	M.	48–60–56	2.80–4.00–3.32
Connecticut	M.	60–60–60	2.00–3.00–2.42
Illinois	M.	60–60–60	2.90–2.90–2.90

[1] Not reported.   [2] Per hour.

TABLE I-5.—*Boiler makers, 1844–1900, by year and State*—Continued

Year and State	Sex	Hours per week	Rate per day (dollars)
1890—Continued.			
Kansas	M.	(¹)	2.00-2.75-2.53
Louisiana	M.	60-60-60	2.50-3.00-2.63
Maryland	M.	60-60-60	2.00-3.50-2.47
Massachusetts	M.	60-60-60	2.00-5.00-2.56
Michigan	M.	60-60-60	.75-4.67-2.19
Minnesota	M.	60-60-60	1.25-3.25-2.66
Missouri	M.	60-60-60	2.50-3.00-2.60
Nebraska	M.	(¹)	2.50-2.85-2.68
New York	M.	60-60-60	1.25-4.00-2.35
Ohio	M.	54-54-54	2.03-2.62-2.16
Do	(¹)	(¹)	2.25-2.25-2.25
Pennsylvania	M.	60-60-60	1.80-3.00-2.32
Virginia	M.	60-60-60	2.17-2.17-2.17
1891:			
California	M.	48-60-56	2.80-4.00-3.24
Connecticut	M.	60-60-60	2.00-3.00-2.58
Illinois	M.	60-60-60	2.90-2.90-2.90
Louisiana	M.	60-60-60	2.50-3.00-2.64
Maryland	M.	60-60-60	2.00-3.50-2.47
Massachusetts	M.	60-60-60	2.00-5.00-2.47
Minnesota	M.	60-60-60	3.25-3.25-3.25
Missouri	M.	60-60-60	2.50-3.00-2.61
New York	M.	60-60-60	.50-6.39-2.09
Ohio	M.	54-60-60	1.25-2.75-2.17
Pennsylvania	M.	54-60-60	1.75-3.00-2.31
Virginia	M.	60-60-60	2.25-2.33-2.28
1892:			
California	M.	48-60-55	2.20-4.00-3.12
Colorado	M.	60-60-60	3.15-3.15-3.15
Connecticut	M.	60-60-60	2.00-3.00-2.71
Illinois	M.	60-60-60	2.25-3.25-2.64
Indiana	M.	54-60-60	1.91-2.92.2.39
Iowa	M.	60-60-60	1.75-2.80-2.65
Kansas	M.	60-60-60	2.60-2.83-2.76
Louisiana	M.	60-60-60	2.50-3.00-2.63
Maryland	M.	60-60-60	2.00-3.00-2.45
Massachusetts	M.	60-60-60	2.00-5.00-2.56
Michigan	M.	60-60-60	1.50-3.00-2.37
Minnesota	M.	60-60-60	3.25-3.25-3.25
Missouri	M.	60-60-60	2.50-3.00-2.61
New Mexico	M.	60-60-60	3.16-3.16-3.16
New York	M.	60-60-60	1.90-2.80-2.37
Ohio	M.	54-54-54	1.58-2.62-2.01
Pennsylvania	M.	54-60-60	1.75-3.00-2.29
Virginia	M.	60-60-60	2.25-2.33-2.29
1893:			
California	M.	48-60-53	2.20-4.00-2.94
Illinois	M.	54-60-59	2.17-3.25-2.79
Louisiana	M.	60-60-60	2.50-3.00-2.66
Maryland	M.	58-60-60	1.17-3.00-2.32
Massachusetts	M.	54-54-54	1.80-5.00-2.38
Michigan	M.	30-60-59	1.00-3.83-2.16
Minnesota	M.	60-60-60	3.00-3.00-3.00
Missouri	M.	60-60-60	2.49-3.00-2.53
Montana	M.	54-54-54	2.68-4.41-3.53
New York	M.	60-60-60	2.25-3.00-2.65
Ohio	M.	48-72-58	1.44-2.75-2.04
Pennsylvania	M.	54-60-60	1.75-3.00-2.29
Virginia	M.	60-60-60	1.67-2.25-1.96
1894:			
California	M.	48-60-51	2.20-3.50-2.74
Illinois	M.	60-60-60	2.90-3.00-2.91
Indiana	M.	50-60-56	1.87-3.00-2.43
Iowa	M.	48-66-54	1.50-3.00-2.32
Louisiana	M.	60-60-60	2.50-3.00-2.64
Maryland	M.	60-60-60	2.00-2.75-2.44
Massachusetts	M.	54-54-54	1.83-5.00-2.47
Minnesota	M.	60-60-60	3.00-3.00-3.00
Missouri	M.	60-60-60	2.50-3.00-2.58
Montana	M.	(¹)	2.93-4.14-3.23
New York	(¹)	(¹)	2.50-2.50-2.50
Do	M.	60-60-60	2.25-3.00-2.73
Ohio	M.	54-60-59	1.50-3.00-2.04
Pennsylvania	M.	54-60-60	1.75-2.75-2.23
Virginia	M.	60-60-60	1.67-2.25-1.96
West Virginia	M.	48-48-48	1.84-1.92-1.88
1895:			
California	M.	48-60-53	2.20-4.00-2.98
Illinois	M.	60-60-60	2.90-3.00-2.91
Kansas	M.	48-48-48	.69-1.50-1.06
Louisiana	M.	60-60-60	2.50-3.00-2.64
Maryland	M.	60-60-60	2.00-2.75-2.44
Massachusetts	M.	54-54-54	1.83-5.00-2.48
Minnesota	M.	60-60-60	3.00-3.00-3.00
Missouri	M.	60-80-60	2.50-3.00-2.57
Montana	M.	(¹)	3.60-3.60-3.60
Ohio	M.	48-60-60	1.25-3.00-1.87
Pennsylvania	M.	54-60-60	1.75-2.75-2.30
Virginia	M.	60-60-60	1.67-2.08-1.88
Wisconsin	(¹)	60-60-60	1.75-4.17-2.66
1896:			
California	M.	48-60-53	2.20-4.00-2.96
Illinois	M.	60-60-60	2.90-3.00-2.91
Kansas	M.	60-72-66	3.00-3.19-3.10
Louisiana	M.	60-60-60	2.50-3.00-2.64
Maryland	M.	60-60-60	2.00-2.75-2.31
Massachusetts	M.	54-56-54	1.83-5.00-2.37
Minnesota	M.	60-60-60	3.00-3.00-3.00
Missouri	M.	36-60-59	2.50-3.00-2.60
Montana	M.	(¹)	3.45-3.45-3.45
New York	M.	54-60-58	2.00-3.85-2.59
North Carolina	M.	60-60-60	2.50-2.50-2.50
Ohio	M.	48-60-58	1.44-2.70-1.94
Pennsylvania	M.	54-60-60	1.67-2.90-2.45
Virginia	M.	60-60-60	2.08-2.08-2.08
1897:			
California	M.	48-60-53	2.20-4.00-2.95
Illinois	M.	60-60-60	2.90-3.00-2.91
Kansas	(¹)	56-62-59	2.42-3.00-2.71
Louisiana	M.	60-60-60	2.50-3.00-2.63
Maryland	M.	60-60-60	2.00-2.75-2.44
Massachusetts	M.	54-54-54	1.83-5.00-2.48
Michigan	M.	36-60-51	1.28-2.93-2.11
Minnesota	M.	60-60-60	3.00-3.00-3.00
Missouri	M.	60-60-60	2.50-3.00-2.58
Montana	(¹)	(¹)	2.15-4.14-3.48
Nebraska	M.	48-48-48	2.50-2.50-2.50
New York	M.	54-60-54	1.50-5.60-2.45
Ohio	M.	54-54-54	1.53-2.70-1.97
Pennsylvania	M.	54-60-59	1.67-2.90-2.23
Virginia	M.	60-60-60	2.00-2.50-2.24
1898:			
California	M.	48-60-53	2.20-4.00-2.96
Illinois	M.	60-60-60	2.90-3.00-2.91
Kansas	M.	52-54-54	2.25-2.75-2.64
Louisiana	M.	60-60-60	2.50-3.00-2.60
Maryland	M.	60-60-60	2.00-2.75-2.44
Massachusetts	M.	54-54-54	1.83-5.00-2.48
Michigan	M.	(¹)	1.50-2.50-2.25
Minnesota	M.	60-60-60	3.00-3.00-3.00
Missouri	M.	60-60-60	2.50-3.00-2.59
Nebraska	(¹)	48-60-53	1.40-4.00-2.69
New Jersey	M.	60-60-60	1.75-3.00-2.20
New York	M.	54-60-56	1.75-3.50-2.21
Ohio	M.	54-54-54	1.58-2.70-2.05
Pennsylvania	M.	54-60-60	1.75-2.90-2.28
Virginia	M.	60-60-60	1.75-2.08-1.92
Washington	(¹)	(¹)	2.88-3.25-2.93
1899:			
Alabama	M.	60-60-60	2.75-3.00-2.88
Georgia	M.	59-59-59	1.60-2.50-2.14
Massachusetts	M.	54-54-54	2.50-3.50-2.70
New York	M.	54-54-54	1.80-2.70-2.48
North Carolina	M.	60-60-60	5.00-5.00-5.00
Ohio	M.	60-60-60	1.92-2.75-2.40
1900:			
Alabama	M.	60-60-60	2.75-3.00-2.88
Georgia	M.	59-59-59	1.60-2.75-2.23
Massachusetts	M.	54-54-54	2.50-3.50-2.70
New York	M.	54-54-54	1.98-2.70-2.52
Ohio	M.	60-60-60	2.00-3.00-2.48

¹ Not reported.   ² Per hour.

TABLE I–6.—*Boiler makers, males, foundries and machine shops,1890–1907, by city and year*

Year	Boston, Mass.		Chicago, Ill.		Denver, Colo.		New Orleans, La.	
	Hours per week	Rate per hour	Hours per week	Rate per hour	Hours per week	Rate per hour	Hours per week	Rate per hour
1890	59.8	$0.275	60.0	$0.272			57.3	$0.320
1891	59.8	.269	60.0	.271			57.7	.303
1892	58.4	.280	57.5	.272			57.1	.272
1893	56.8	.282	53.3	.282			59.4	.302
1894	56.9	.306	55.1	.281			58.0	.319
1895	56.8	.306	55.2	.279			57.1	.291
1896	54.1	.307	55.4	.279			56.4	.315
1897	54.2	.307	55.3	.271			57.7	.303
1898	54.1	.306	55.9	.273			57.3	.297
1899	54.2	.312	55.2	.269			55.9	.356
1900	54.2	.316	54.7	.272			55.2	.348
1901	54.2	.315	54.1	.282			54.0	.324
1902	54.2	.315	53.5	.290			52.3	.368
1903	54.0	.294	53.1	.332			54.0	.394
1904	54.0	.300	54.0	.348	54.0	$0.319	54.0	.393
1905	54.0	.302	54.0	.359	55.8	.306	54.0	.393
1906	54.0	.300	51.6	.365	57.0	.320	54.0	.393

Year	New York, N. Y.		Philadelphia, Pa.		San Francisco, Calif.	
	Hours per week	Rate per hour	Hours per week	Rate per week	Hours per week	Rate per hour
1890	59.0	$0.266			56.2	$0.348
1891	59.0	.272			55.9	.348
1892	59.0	.271			56.7	.344
1893	59.0	.271			59.2	.347
1894	59.0	.277			59.2	.326
1895	59.0	.268			59.2	.333
1896	59.0	.273			56.3	.321
1897	59.0	.268			59.2	.326
1898	59.0	.275			59.1	.323
1899	55.4	.295			59.1	.324
1900	53.0	.306			59.1	.321
1901	53.0	.308			59.1	.319
1902	51.4	.319			56.6	.318
1903	52.8	.331	55.6	$0.240	57.4	.345
1904	53.3	.339	56.2	.254	54.0	.393
1905	53.3	.342	56.2	.258	54.0	.389
1906	53.4	.346	56.0	.262	54.0	.427

TABLE I-7.—*Boiler makers, males, manufacturing shops, 1907–1924, by city and year*

Year	Atlanta, Ga.		Birmingham, Ala.		Boston, Mass.		Chicago, Ill.	
	Hours per week	Rate per hour	Hours per week	Rate per hour	Hours per week	Rate per hour	Hours per week	Rate per hour
1907	54.0	$0.300	60.0	$0.350	54.0	$0.306	[1] 49.5	$0.375
1908	54.0	.315	60.0	.350	54.0	.306	[1] 49.5	.375
1909	54.0	.320	60.0	.350	54.0	.306	[1] 49.5	.375
1910	54.0	.340	60.0	.375	54.0	.306	[1] 49.5	.400
1911	54.0	.380	60.0	.375	54.0	.306	[1] 49.5	.400
1912	54.0	.390	60.0	.375	54.0	.306	[1] 49.5	.400
1913	54.0	.400	60.0	.400	54.0	.306	54.0	.400
1914	54.0	.350	60.0	.400	54.0	.321	54.0	.400
1915	54.0	.350	60.0	.400	54.0	.321	54.0	.400
1916	54.0	.350	60.0	.425			54.0	.400
1917	50.0	.440	60.0	.475			54.0	.420
1918	50.0	.550	48.0	.675			54.0	.520
1919	50.0	.680	48.0	.800	48.0	.700	54.0	.600
1920	[2] 50.0	.720	48.0	.900	44.0	.800	54.0	.740
1921			48.0	[2] .750	44.0	.800	54.0	[2] .740
1922			48.0	.750			54.0	[2] .700
1923			48.0	.750			54.0	.700
1924							54.0	.700

Year	Cincinnati, Ohio		Denver, Colo.		Detroit, Mich.		New Orleans, La.	
1907	54.0	$0.335	54.0	$0.370	60.0	$0.300	54.0	$0.333
1908	54.0	.335	54.0	.370	60.0	.350	54.0	.333
1909	54.0	.350	54.0	.370	60.0	.350	54.0	.389
1910	54.0	.350	54.0	.370	60.0	.350	54.0	.389
1911	54.0	.350	54.0	.370	60.0	.350	54.0	.389
1912	54.0	.400	54.0	.410	60.0	.340	54.0	.389
1913	54.0	.400	54.0	.410	55.0	.400	54.0	.389
1914	49.5	.350	54.0	.410	55.0	.400	54.0	.389
1915	49.5	.350	54.0	.410	55.0	.400	54.0	.389
1916	49.5	.350	54.0	.400	55.0	.400	54.0	.389
1917	49.5	.380	51.0	[4] .425	55.0	.400	48.0	.438
1918	49.5	.400	48.0	.520	54.0	.625	48.0	.625
1919	49.5	.550	48.0	.680	54.0	.850	48.0	.800
1920	50.0	1.000	48.0	.720	44.0	1.000	48.0	.800
1921	50.0	.800	48.0	.640			44.0	.800
1922	49.5	.700					44.0	.750
1923	49.5	.700					44.0	.750
1924	49.5	.700					44.0	.750

Year	New York, N. Y.		Philadelphia, Pa.		St. Louis, Mo.		San Francisco, Calif.	
1907	54.0	$0.361			54.0	$0.350	[5] 54.0	$0.500
1908	54.0	.361			54.0	.350	[5] 54.0	.500
1909	54.0	.361			54.0	.380	[5] 52.5	.500
1910	54.0	.361			54.0	.380	[5] 49.5	.500
1911	54.0	.417			54.0	.400	[5] 48.0	.500
1912	54.0	.417	54.0	$0.333	54.0	.400	48.0	.500
1913	44.0	.625	49.0	.333	[6] 49.5	.400	48.0	.500
1914	54.0	.389	49.0	.333	[7] 49.5	.400	48.0	.500
1915	54.0	.389	49.0	.333	[6] 49.5	.400	48.0	.500
1916	48.0	.438	49.0	.333	[6] 49.5	.400	48.0	.531
1917	48.0	.494	48.0	.500	[6] 49.5	.400	48.0	.531
1918	48.0	.700	44.0	.700	48.0	.500	[5] 48.0	.725
1919	48.0	.800	44.0	.800	48.0	.700	44.0	.800
1920	[8] 48.0	.800	44.0	.900	48.0	.900	44.0	.900
1921	[9] 48.0	[9] .720	44.0	.900	48.0	.900	44.0	.900
1922	[8] 48.0	.640	44.0	.800	44.0	.800	44.0	.781
1923	[8] 48.0	.720	44.0	.800	44.0	.800	44.0	.844
1924	48.0	.720	44.0	.800	44.0	.900	44.0	.844

[1] 54, October to April.
[2] More than 50 per cent received more.
[3] More than 25 per cent received more.
[4] And bonus.
[5] Shopmen and outside men.
[6] 54, September to April, inclusive.
[7] 55, September to April, inclusive.
[8] 44, June to August, inclusive.
[9] And marine.

TABLE I-8.—*Core makers, 1850-1900, by year and State*

Year and State	Sex	Lowest, highest, and average—Hours per week	Rate per day (dollars)
1850:			
Massachusetts	F.	66-66-66	0.75-0.75-0.75
1854:			
Pennsylvania	M.	60-60-60	1.10-1.10-1.10
1855:			
Pennsylvania	M.	60-60-60	1.10-1.10-1.10
1856:			
Pennsylvania	M.	60-60-60	1.10-1.34-1.22
1857:			
Pennsylvania	M.	60-60-60	1.10-1.34-1.22
1858:			
Pennsylvania	M.	60-60-60	1.20-1.34-1.23
1859:			
New York	M.	60-60-60	1.25-1.25-1.25
Pennsylvania	M.	60-60-60	1.20-1.34-1.24
1860:			
New York	M.	60-60-60	1.25-1.25-1.25
Pennsylvania	M.	60-60-60	1.20-1.34-1.22
1861:			
New York	M.	60-60-60	1.25-1.25-1.25
Pennsylvania	M.	60-60-60	1.20-1.34-1.22
1862:			
New York	M.	60-60-60	1.25-1.25-1.25
Pennsylvania	M.	60-60-60	1.34-1.40-1.38
1863:			
New York	M.	60-60-60	1.25-1.25-1.25
Pennsylvania	M.	60-60-60	1.34-1.40-1.39
1864:			
New York	M.	60-60-60	1.25-1.25-1.25
Pennsylvania	M.	60-60-60	1.40-1.67-1.50
1865:			
New York	M.	60-60-60	1.50-1.50-1.50
Pennsylvania	M.	60-60-60	1.70-2.00-1.79
1866:			
New York	M.	60-60-60	1.50-1.50-1.50
Pennsylvania	M.	60-60-60	2.00-2.00-2.00
1867:			
New York	M.	60-60-60	1.50-1.50-1.50
Pennsylvania	M.	60-60-60	2.00-2.00-2.00
1868:			
New York	M.	60-60-60	1.67-1.67-1.67
Pennsylvania	M.	60-60-60	2.00-2.00-2.00
1869:			
New York	M.	60-60-60	1.67-1.67-1.67
Pennsylvania	M.	60-60-60	2.00-2.00-2.00
1870:			
New York	M.	60-60-60	1.67-1.67-1.67
Pennsylvania	M.	60-60-60	2.00-2.00-2.00
1871:			
New York	M.	60-60-60	1.67-1.67-1.67
Pennsylvania	M.	60-60-60	1.60-2.00-1.76
1872:			
New Hampshire	M.	72-72-72	.75-1.50-1.05
New York	M.	60-60-60	1.67-1.75-1.71
Pennsylvania	M.	60-60-60	1.40-1.80-1.56
1873:			
New Hampshire	M.	72-72-72	.75-1.50-1.08
New Jersey	M.	(1)	3.33-5.00-4.00
New York	M.	60-60-60	1.75-1.84-1.80
Pennsylvania	M.	60-60-60	1.50-1.80-1.63
1874:			
New Hampshire	M.	72-72-72	.75-1.50-1.21
New York	M.	60-60-60	1.75-1.84-1.80
Pennsylvania	M.	60-60-60	1.60-1.60-1.60
1875:			
New Hampshire	M.	60-60-60	.75-1.50-1.00
New York	M.	60-60-60	1.84-1.84-1.84
Pennsylvania	M.	60-60-60	1.40-1.40-1.40
1876:			
New Hampshire	M.	72-72-72	.75-.75-.75
Pennsylvania	M.	60-60-60	1.40-2.00-1.62
1877:			
New Hampshire	M.	72-72-72	.75-.75-.75
Ohio	M.	(1)	2.00-2.00-2.00
Pennsylvania	M.	60-60-60	1.30-1.70-1.48
1878:			
New Hampshire	M.	72-72-72	.75-2.00-1.25
New Jersey	M.	(1)	2.00-2.00-2.00
Pennsylvania	M.	54-60-59	1.30-1.70-1.48
1879:			
New York	M.	60-60-60	1.50-1.50-1.50
Pennsylvania	M.	60-60-60	1.30-1.70-1.51
1880:			
Illinois	M.	60-60-60	1.75-1.90-1.80
Do.	F.	60-60-60	.77-1.44-1.14
New York	M.	60-60-60	1.50-1.50-1.50
Pennsylvania	M.	60-60-60	1.40-1.60-1.44
1881:			
New Jersey	M.	60-60-60	2.25-2.50-2.42
New York	M.	60-60-60	1.50-1.50-1.50
Pennsylvania	M.	60-60-60	1.40-1.80-1.61
1882:			
New Jersey	M.	60-60-60	1.60-1.60-1.60
New York	M.	60-60-60	1.50-1.50-1.50
Ohio	(1)	60-60-60	1.00-1.00-1.00
Pennsylvania	M.	60-60-60	1.50-1.80-1.63
1883:			
Massachusetts	M.	(1)	1.75-3.00-2.27
Do.	(1)	(1)	.90-.90-.90
New Jersey	M.	(1)	1.50-3.00-2.34
New York	M.	60-60-60	1.50-1.50-1.50
Pennsylvania	M.	60-60-60	1.70-2.00-1.85
1884:			
Michigan	M.	(1)	.65-1.75-1.13
New Jersey	M.	54-60-60	1.67-2.67-2.59
New York	M.	60-60-60	1.50-1.50-1.50
Ohio	M.	(1)	.67-2.17-1.65
Pennsylvania	M.	60-60-60	1.70-2.00-1.83
1885:			
California	M.	60-60-60	2.50-3.75-3.00
Delaware	M.	60-60-60	1.50-1.95-1.80
Indiana	M.	60-60-60	1.40-1.70-1.50
Do.	F.	60-60-60	.65-.90-.68
New Jersey	M.	48-60-59	1.33-3.50-2.44
New York	M.	60-60-60	1.25-1.50-1.33
Ohio	M.	60-60-60	.75-2.17-1.50
Pennsylvania	M.	60-60-60	1.50-1.70-1.55
Tennessee	M.	60-60-60	1.35-1.35-1.35
1886:			
Connecticut	M.	60-60-60	1.00-1.00-1.00
New Jersey	M.	54-66-64	2.25-3.75-2.53
New York	M.	60-60-60	1.25-1.25-1.25
Ohio	M.	(1)	1.62-1.62-1.62
Pennsylvania	F.	56-56-56	1.17-1.17-1.17
Do.	M.	60-60-60	1.50-1.70-1.54
Texas	M.	60-60-60	2.00-2.00-2.00
1887:			
Connecticut	M.	(1)	.92-1.71-1.12
Illinois	F.	59-59-59	.49-1.33-.80
Maryland	M.	(1)	.60-1.70-1.04
New York	M.	(1)	1.40-1.50-1.43
Ohio	M.	54-60-60	1.00-2.25-1.58
Do.	F.	60-60-60	.60-.60-.60
Pennsylvania	M.	60-60-60	1.25-2.00-1.58
Wisconsin	M.	(1)	1.42-1.42-1.42
1888:			
New Hampshire	M.	60-60-60	1.25-1.50-1.38
New Jersey	F.	60-60-60	.50-.50-.50
Do.	(1)	60-60-60	1.10-2.00-1.70
New York	M.	51-60-58	.75-2.55-1.83
Do.	F.	55-55-55	1.50-1.50-1.50
Pennsylvania	M.	60-60-60	1.50-1.70-1.55
1889:			
New Hampshire	M.	60-60-60	1.50-1.50-1.50
New York	M.	60-60-60	1.50-1.50-1.50
Pennsylvania	M.	60-60-60	1.70-1.70-1.70
1890:			
Michigan	M.	60-60-60	.40-2.50-1.25
New Hampshire	M.	60-60-60	1.50-1.50-1.50
New York	M.	60-60-60	.67-3.38 1.65
Pennsylvania	M.	60-60-60	1.70-1.70-1.70

1 Not reported.

TABLE I-8.—*Core makers, 1850-1900, by year and State*—Continued

Year and State	Sex	Lowest, highest, and average—		Year and State	Sex	Lowest, highest, and average—	
		Hours per week	Rate per day (dollars)			Hours per week	Rate per day (dollars)
1891:				**1895:**			
Michigan	F.	(¹)	.39–.39–.39	Ohio	M.	48-60-59	.50-2.75-1.58
Missouri	M.	(¹)	.41-2.00-1.19	Do	F.	60-60-60	.60-1.25–.77
New Hampshire	M.	60-60-60	1.75-1.75-1.75	Pennsylvania	M.	60-60-60	1.50-1.60-1.52
New York	M.	60-60-60	.50-3.38-1.69	**1896:**			
Ohio	M.	42-60-59	.70-3.00-1.39	Illinois	M.	56-56-56	1.75-1.90-1.81
Pennsylvania	M.	60-60-60	1.70-1.70-1.70	Do	F.	56-56-56	.78-1.48-1.14
1892:				Michigan	(¹)	60-60-60	1.04-1.04-1.04
California	M.	56-56-56	2.50-3.00-2.67	Ohio	M.	49-62-59	.75-2.04-1.61
Indiana	M.	60-60-60	1.39-1.94-1.62	Do	F.	48-54-49	.60-1.25–.72
New York	M.	60-60-60	1.50-1.50-1.50	Pennsylvania	M.	60-60-60	1.75-1.75-1.75
Pennsylvania	M.	60-60-60	1.20-2.50-1.64	**1897:**			
1893:				Connecticut	F.	60-60-60	1.25-1.25-1.25
Montana	M.	54-54-54	3.50-4.00-3.75	Nebraska	M.	48-48-48	1.85-1.85-1.85
New York	M.	59-60-60	1.67-2.67-2.17	New York	M.	60-60-60	1.75-2.50-2.04
Ohio	M.	54-60-59	.75-2.75-1.37	Pennsylvania	M.	(¹)	1.87-2.37-2.04
Do	F.	54-60-58	.50-1.00–.70	Virginia	M.	60-60-60	1.25-2.00-1.93
Pennsylvania	M.	60-60-60	1.50-1.80-1.64	**1898:**			
Rhode Island	M.	(¹)	1.80-1.80-1.80	Nebraska	(¹)	54-54-54	.50-3.20-2.80
1894:				New York	M.	60-60-60	1.75-3.00-2.06
Indiana	M.	54-60-56	1.31-1.83-1.68	**1899:**			
Iowa	M.	60-66-62	.67-2.00-1.38	Massachusetts	M.	59-59-59	1.50-2.50-2.07
New York	M.	60-60-60	1.50-1.50-1.50	New York	M.	54-54-54	1.50-2.00-1.67
North Carolina	M.	60-60-60	1.25-1.25-1.25	Ohio	M.	60-60-60	2.00-2.25-2.10
Ohio	M.	48-60-59	.50-2.75-1.43	**1900:**			
Do	F.	54-60-58	.50-1.25–.73	Massachusetts	M.	59-59-59	1.50-3.00-2.56
Pennsylvania	M.	60-60-60	1.50-1.80-1.57	New York	M.	54-54-54	1.50-2.00-1.67
				Ohio	M.	60-60-60	2.25-2.50-2.29

¹ Not reported.

TABLE I-9.—*Core makers, males, 1890-1907, by geographic division and year*

Year	North Atlantic		North Central		South Central		Western		North Atlantic		North Central	
	Hours per week	Rate per hour	Hours per week	Rate per hour	Hours per week	Rate per hour	Hours per week	Rate per hour	Hours per week	Rate per hour	Hours per week	Rate per hour
1890	59.9	$0.209	59.8	$0.201	60.0	$0.143	60.0	$0.250	59.8	$0.076		
1891	59.9	.211	59.5	.187	60.0	.143	60.0	.264	59.7	.093		
1892	59.9	.212	59.5	.185	60.0	.144	60.0	.269	59.6	.100		
1893	59.9	.208	59.6	.174	60.0	.144	60.0	.278	59.5	.106		
1894	59.7	.201	59.5	.185	60.0	.144	59.0	.267	59.7	.096		
1895	59.9	.205	59.8	.170	60.0	.144	59.7	.253	59.7	.096		
1896	59.9	.207	59.5	.193	60.0	.144	58.9	.264	59.6	.098		
1897	59.7	.208	59.5	.191	54.9	.161	59.1	.263	59.7	.089		
1898	59.9	.209	59.5	.186	54.9	.161	59.5	.276	59.8	.088		
1899	59.9	.212	59.3	.192	54.9	.161	59.9	.278	59.7	.069		
1900	59.7	.215	59.1	.192	54.9	.164	59.8	.287	59.8	.081		
1901	59.0	.223	58.3	.202	54.9	.164	59.8	.286	59.8	.086		
1902	58.4	.220	57.6	.202	54.9	.164	59.6	.297	59.8	.079		
1903	57.5	.243	55.8	.222	55.1	.224	55.6	.316	59.0	.082	55.2	$0.110
1904	57.0	.253	55.3	.238	55.4	.252	53.9	.355	55.8	.111	54.4	.123
1905	57.0	.250	55.5	.244	55.2	.281	53.9	.368	55.7	.132	54.5	.119
1906	56.5	.271	55.2	.251	55.5	.287	53.5	.413	54.8	.131	54.9	.126
1907	55.6	.282	55.3	.260	56.0	.293	53.2	.424	54.7	.147	54.9	.150

TABLE I–10.—*Core makers, males, 1907–1924, by city and year*

Year	Atlanta, Ga.		Birmingham, Ala.		Boston, Mass.		Chicago, Ill.	
	Hours per week	Rate per hour	Hours per week	Rate per hour	Hours per week	Rate per hour	Hours per week	Rate per hour
1907	--------	--------	60.0	$0.300	54.0	$0.306	54.0	$0.3 1
1908	--------	--------	60.0	.300	54.0	.306	54.0	.3 1
1909	--------	--------	60.0	.300	54.0	.306	54.0	.361
1910	--------	--------	60.0	.300	54.0	.306	54.0	.389
1911	60.0	$0.300	60.0	.300	54.0	.333	54.0	.389
1912	60.0	.300	60.0	.300	54.0	.333	54.0	.389
1913	60.0	.300	54.0	.361	54.0	.389	54.0	.444
1914	60.0	.300	54.0	.361	54.0	.389	54.0	.444
1915	--------	--------	54.0	.361	54.0	.389	54.0	.444
1916	--------	--------	--------	--------	54.0	.444	48.0	.500
1917	--------	--------	--------	--------	54.0	.500	48.0	.563
1918	--------	--------	--------	--------	54.0	.583	48.0	.688
1919	--------	--------	--------	--------	54.0	.583	48.0	.800
1920	--------	--------	--------	--------	48.0	.900	48.0	1.050
1921	--------	--------	--------	--------	48.0	.900	48.0	.900
1922	--------	--------	--------	--------	48.0	.750	48.0	.750
1923 [1]	50.0	.700	--------	--------	48.0	.900	48.0	.875
1924 [1]	50.0	.700	--------	--------	48.0	.900	[2] 44.0	1.000

Year	Cincinnati, Ohio		Denver, Colo.		Detroit, Mich		New Orleans, La.	
1907	54.0	$0.306	54.0	$0.417	60.0	$0.250	54.0	$0.361
1908	54.0	.306	54.0	.389	60.0	.250	54.0	.361
1909	54.0	.306	54.0	.389	54.0	.278	54.0	.361
1910	54.0	.306	54.0	.389	54.0	.361	54.0	.361
1911	54.0	.361	54.0	.417	54.0	.361	54.0	.361
1912	54.0	.361	54.0	.417	54.0	.361	54.0	.361
1913	54.0	.361	54.0	.417	54.0	.389	54.0	.361
1914	54.0	.389	54.0	.417	54.0	.389	54.0	.361
1915	54.0	.389	54.0	.417	54.0	.389	54.0	[3] .361
1916	54.0	.444	54.0	.417	54.0	.444	54.0	.389
1917	54.0	.444	48.0	.500	54.0	.500	48.0	.500
1918	54.0	[4] .556	48.0	[5] .594	54.0	.611	48.0	[6] .625
1919	54.0	.583	[7] 48.0	.750	48.0	.800	48.0	.800
1920	48.0	.813	[7] 48.0	.800	48.0	1.000	48.0	.800
1921	48.0	.750	[7] 48.0	[8] 1.00	48.0	.900	48.0	.800
1922	48.0	.688	48.0	.781	48.0	.750	48.0	.750
1923 [1]	48.0	.750	[7] 48.0	.781	48.0	.850	48.0	.750
1924 [1]	48.0	.875	48.0	.800	48.0	.900	44.0	.800

Year	New York, N. Y.		Philadelphia, Pa.		St. Louis, Mo.		San Francisco, Calif	
1907	54.0	$0.333	54.0	$0.306	54.0	$0.339	54.0	$0.444
1908	54.0	.333	54.0	.306	54.0	.339	54.0	.444
1909	54.0	.333	54.0	.306	54.0	.339	52.5	.457
1910	54.0	.361	54.0	.306	54.0	.339	49.5	.485
1911	54.0	.389	54.0	.344	54.0	.372	48.0	.500
1912	54.0	.389	54.0	.344	54.0	.372	48.0	.500
1913	54.0	.389	54.0	.344	54.0	.389	48.0	.500
1914	54.0	.417	54.0	.389	54.0	.389	48.0	.500
1915	54.0	.417	54.0	.389	54.0	.389	48.0	.500
1916	54.0	.417	54.0	.444	54.0	.417	48.0	.500
1917	54.0	.472	54.0	.500	54.0	.500	48.0	.531
1918	54.0	.528	48.0	.688	54.0	.611	[9] 48.0	.725
1919	48.0	.750	48.0	[10] .688	48.0	.750	44.0	.800
1920	48.0	.880	48.0	1.000	48.0	.900	44.0	.880
1921	48.0	.880	48.0	.900	48.0	.850	44.0	1.000
1922	48.0	.781	48.0	.780	48.0	.750	44.0	.800
1923 [1]	48.0	.781	48.0	.850	48.0	.875	44.0	.875
1924 [1]	48.0	1.000	48.0	.969	48.0	.938	44.0	.938

[1] Includes iron molders.
[2] 48, November to April, inclusive.
[3] 38.9 cents on Sept. 1.
[4] 58.3 cents on May 16.
[5] 75 cents on June 1.
[6] 68.8 cents on July 15.
[7] Off every other Saturday, June to August, inclusive.
[8] Old scale; strike pending.
[9] 44, June to August inclusive.
[10] 75 per cent received more.

TABLE I-11.—*Core makers, males, 1925 and 1927, by State and year*

Year	California		Connecticut		Illinois		Indiana	
	Hours per week	Rate per hour	Hours per week	Rate per hour	Hours per week	Rate per hour	Hours per week	Rate per hour
1925	47.5	$0.838	49.6	$0.750	51.3	$0.796	49.0	$0.681
1927	45.6	.919	49.7	.774	49.7	.818	51.0	.664

	Iowa		Massachusetts		Michigan		New Jersey	
1925	52.6	$0.669	48.4	$0.720	50.5	$0.747	50.6	$0.820
1927	53.9	.719	49.1	.823	51.4	.714	50.7	.804

	New York		Ohio		Pennsylvania		Wisconsin	
1925	49.2	$0.753	52.0	$0.744	49.4	$0.757	51.1	$0.695
1927	48.6	.765	51.1	.793	50.4	.789	52.4	.732

TABLE I-12.—*Diesinkers, 1872–1900, by year and State*

Year and State	Sex	Lowest, highest, and average—		Year and State	Sex	Lowest, highest, and average—	
		Hours per week	Rate per day (dollars)			Hours per week	Rate per day (dollars)
1872:				1892:			
Connecticut	M.	60–60–60	4.50–4.50–4.50	California	M.	60–60–60	3.50–3.50–3.50
1880:				Illinois	M.	59–59–59	1.75–1.75–1.75
Massachusetts	M.	60–60–60	3.33–4.83–4.27	Massachusetts	M.	60–60–60	2.50–2.75–2.63
1881:				1893:			
Massachusetts	M.	60–60–60	5.00–5.00–5.00	Illinois	M.	59–59–59	1.75–1.75–1.75
1882:				Massachusetts	M.	60–60–60	2.75–2.75–2.75
Pennsylvania	M.	60–60–60	1.67–2.17–1.87	Ohio	M.	54–60–59	1.66–3.25–2.46
1884:				Pennsylvania	M.	60–60–60	2.50–2.50–2.50
Pennsylvania	M.	59–59–59	2.33–2.67–2.44	1894:			
1885:				Massachusetts	M.	60–60–60	3.00–3.00–3.00
Massachusetts	M.	60–60–60	4.50–4.50–4.50	Ohio	M.	48–60–59	1.75–3.50–2.42
New Hampshire	M.	60–60–60	4.33–4.66–4.40	1895:			
New Jersey	M.	(¹)	4–17–4.17–4.17	Massachusetts	M.	60–60–60	2.00–5.00–3.93
Do	M.	60–60–60	2.17–2.17–2.17	New Jersey	M.	60–60–60	3.50–3.50–3.50
1887:				Ohio	M.	60–60–60	2.10–3.50–2.66
Connecticut	M.	(¹)	2.95–4.21–3.48	Pennsylvania	M.	60–60–60	2.50–2.50–2.50
Ohio	M.	60–60–60	1.50–1.50–1.50	1896:			
1888:				Connecticut	M.	60–60–60	4.00–6.00–5.50
New Jersey	(¹)	58–58–58	2.75–2.75–2.75	Ohio	M.	60–60–60	2.25–3.50–2.86
New York	M.	57–59–58	1.00–6.00–3.42	Pennsylvania	M.	55–60–59	1.67–3.33–2.34
1889:				Rhode Island	M.	60–60–60	5.00–5.00–5.00
New Hampshire	M.	60–60–60	4.67–4.67–4.67	1897:			
1890:				Connecticut	M.	54–60–59	3.25–6.00–4.89
Illinois	M.	(¹)	2.00–2.00–2.00	1898:			
New York	M.	(¹)	1.13–5.00–2.18	New Jersey	M.	60–60–60	3.33–5.83–4.97
1891:				1899:			
Illinois	M.	(¹)	2.00–2.00–2.00	Pennsylvania	M.	54–54–54	3.33–3.33–3.33
New York	M.	(¹)	2.50–5.00–3.53	1900: ²			
				Pennsylvania	M.	54–54–54	3.33–3.33–3.33

¹ Not reported.
² Wage data for diesinkers in all periods after 1900 are combined with toolmakers, and are reported as tool and die makers.

TABLE I-13.—*Horseshoers, 1870–1900*

Year and State	Sex	Hours per week	Rate per day (dollars)	Year and State	Sex	Hours per week	Rate per day (dollars)
1870:				**1885:**			
California	M.	60–60–60	2.50–4.00–3.13	California	M.	60–60–60	3.00–3.50–3.33
Louisiana	M.	60–60–60	3.00–3.00–3.00	Illinois	M.	59–59–59	3.25–3.25–3.25
Missouri	M.	60–60–60	3.00–3.50–3.17	Louisiana	M.	60–60–60	3.00–3.00–3.00
1871:				Missouri	M.	60–60–60	2.25–3.00–2.58
California	M.	60–60–60	2.50–4.00–3.13	New Jersey	M.	60–60–60	2.00–3.00–2.58
Louisiana	M.	60–60–60	3.00–3.00–3.00	Ohio	M.	60–60–60	2.26–2.26–2.26
Massachusetts	M.	60–60–60	2.50–2.50–2.50	Pennsylvania	M.	60–60–60	2.00–2.66–2.33
Missouri	M.	60–60–60	3.00–3.50–3.17	**1886:**			
1872:				California	M.	60–60–60	3.00–3.50–3.33
California	M.	60–60–60	2.50–4.00–3.13	Louisiana	M.	60–60–60	3.00–3.00–3.00
Louisiana	M.	60–60–60	3.00–3.00–3.00	Missouri	M.	60–60–60	2.50–3.00–2.63
Missouri	M.	60–60–60	3.00–3.50–3.17	New Jersey	M.	58–60–59	2.25–2.87–2.56
1873:				New York	M.	60–60–60	2.37–3.12–2.75
California	M.	60–60–60	2.50–4.00–3.13	**1887:**			
Louisiana	M.	60–60–60	3.00–3.00–3.00	California	M.	60–60–60	3.00–3.50–3.33
Missouri	M.	60–60–60	3.00–3.50–3.17	Kansas	M.	60–60–60	2.50–2.50–2.50
1874:				Louisiana	M.	60–60–60	3.00–3.00–3.00
California	M.	60–60–60	2.50–4.00–3.13	Missouri	M.	60–72–60	2.25–3.00–2.61
Louisiana	M.	60–60–60	3.00–3.00–3.00	New York	M.	54–60–59	1.50–3.00–2.48
Missouri	M.	60–60–60	3.00–3.50–3.17	Wisconsin	M.	(1)	2.41–2.41–2.41
1875:				**1888:**			
California	M.	60–60–60	2.50–4.00–3.13	California	M.	60–60–60	3.00–3.50–3.33
Louisiana	M.	60–60–60	3.00–3.00–3.00	Louisiana	M.	60–60–60	3.00–3.00–3.00
Missouri	M.	60–60–60	3.00–3.50–3.14	Missouri	M.	60–60–60	2.50–2.00–2.63
1876:				New York	M.	42–60–48	1.50–3.50–2.70
California	M.	60–60–60	2.50–4.00–3.13	Ohio	M.	60–60–60	1.50–2.50–2.16
Louisiana	M.	60–60–60	3.00–3.00–3.00	**1889:**			
Missouri	M.	60–60–60	3.00–3.50–3.14	California	M.	60–60–60	3.00–3.50–3.33
1877:				Kansas	M.	(1)	2.00–2.00–2.00
California	M.	60–60–60	2.50–4.00–3.13	Louisiana	M.	60–60–60	3.00–3.00–3.00
Louisiana	M.	60–60–60	3.00–3.00–3.00	Missouri	M.	60–60–60	2.50–3.00–2.63
Missouri	M.	60–60–60	3.00–3.50–3.14	**1890:**			
1878:				California	M.	60–60–60	3.00–3.50–3.33
California	M.	60–60–60	3.00–3.50–3.33	Connecticut	M.	57–60–59	2.00–2.50–2.23
Louisiana	M.	60–60–60	3.00–3.00–3.00	Kansas	M.	(1)	2.50–3.00–2.71
Missouri	M.	60–60–60	3.00–3.50–3.14	Louisiana	M.	60–60–60	3.00–3.00–3.00
1879:				Minnesota	M.	(1)	1.25–2.90–2.09
California	M.	60–60–60	3.00–3.50–3.33	Missouri	M.	60–60–60	2.50–3.00–2.63
Louisiana	M.	60–60–60	3.00–3.00–3.00	New York	M.	(1)	2.00–2.28–2.14
Missouri	M.	60–60–60	2.50–3.00–2.65	**1891:**			
1880:				California	M.	60–60–60	3.00–3.50–3.33
California	M.	60–60–60	3.00–3.50–3.33	Louisiana	M.	60–60–60	3.00–3.00–3.00
Louisiana	M.	60–60–60	3.00–3.00–3.00	Missouri	M.	60–60–60	2.50–3.25–2.65
Missouri	M.	60–60–60	2.50–3.00–2.65	New York	M.	(1)	2.00–2.00–2.00
Ohio	M.	(1)	2.35–2.35–2.35	**1892:**			
1881:				California	M.	60–60–60	3.00–3.50–3.33
California	M.	60–60–60	3.00–3.50–3.33	Louisiana	M.	60–60–60	3.00–3.00–3.00
Illinois	M.	59–59–59	2.75–3.25–2.95	Missouri	M.	59–60–60	2.50–3.00–2.66
Louisiana	M.	60–60–60	3.00–3.00–3.00	Ohio	(1)	60–72–63	2.00–2.50–2.40
Missouri	M.	60–60–60	2.50–3.00–2.66	**1893:**			
Ohio	M.	60–60–60	2.50–2.50–2.50	California	M.	60–60–60	3.00–3.50–3.33
1882:				Illinois	M.	48–60–56	2.33–4.17–3.25
California	M.	60–60–60	3.00–3.50–3.33	Louisiana	M.	60–60–60	3.00–3.00–3.00
Illinois	M.	59–59 59	2.75–3.25–3.00	Maryland	M.	60–60–60	2.00–2.50–2.25
Louisiana	M.	60–60–60	3.00–3.00–3.00	Missouri	M.	60–60–60	2.50–3.00–2.64
Missouri	M.	60–60–60	1.67–3.33–2.60	Pennsylvania	M.	58–58–58	2.33–2.67–2.50
New Jersey	M.	(1)	2.25–2.50–2.28	Rhode Island	M.	(1)	2.50–3.00–2.75
New York	M.	69–76–70	2.00–3.25–2.78	**1894:**			
1883:				California	M.	60–60–60	3.00–3.50–3.33
California	M.	60–60–60	3.00–3.50–3.33	Iowa	M.	48–60–58	1.75–3.00–2.15
Illinois	M.	59–59–59	3.25–3.25–3.25	Louisiana	M.	60–60–60	3.00–3.00–3.00
Louisiana	M.	60–60–60	3.00–3.00–3.00	Missouri	M.	60–60–60	2.50–3.00–2.63
Michigan	M.	(1)	2.25–2.50–2.38	New Hampshire	M.	60–60 60	1.75–2.50–2.08
Missouri	M.	60–60–60	2.50–3.00–2.63	**1895:**			
New Jersey	M.	60–60–60	1.25–2.50–1.68	Georgia	M.	48–48–48	2.50–2.50–2.50
Ohio	M.	60–60–60	2.00–3.00–2.81	Louisiana	M.	60–60–60	3.00–3.00–3.00
1884:				Missouri	M.	60–60–60	2.50–3.00–2.63
California	M.	60–60–60	3.00–3.50–3.33	**1896:**			
Louisiana	M.	60–60–60	2.00–3.00–2.01	California	M.	60–60–60	3.00–3.50–3.33
Michigan	M.	(1)	2.00–3.00–2.38	Louisiana	M.	60–60–60	3.00–3.00–3.00
Missouri	M.	60–60–60	2.50–3.00–2.63	Massachusetts	M.	53–53–53	2.01–2.76–2.39
New Jersey	M.	60–60–60	1.00–3.00–2.45	Missouri	M.	53–53–53	2.00–3.00–2.25
New York	M.	58–75–63	2.50–3.00–2.74				

1 Not reported.

TABLE I-13.—*Horseshoers, 1870–1900*—Continued

Year and State	Sex	Lowest, highest, and average—		Year and State	Sex	Lowest, highest, and average—	
		Hours per week	Rate per day (dollars)			Hours per week	Rate per day (dollars)
1897:				1890—Continued.			
California	M.	60–60–60	3.00–3.50–3.33	Missouri	M.	53–53–53	2.00–2.50–2.12
Louisiana	M.	60–60–60	3.00–3.00–3.00	New York	M.	58–60–59	2.50–3.50–2.85
Missouri	M.	53–53–53	2.00–2.50–2.12	1899:			
New York	M.	58–60–59	2.00–3.50–2.74	Georgia	M.	60–60–60	2.00–3.00–2.33
1898:				1900:			
California	M.	60–60–60	3.00–3.50–3.33	Georgia	M.	60–60–60	2.00–3.00–2.33
Louisiana	M.	60–60–60	3.00–3.00–3.00				

¹ Not reported.

TABLE I-14.—*Horseshoers, fitters, males, 1890–1904, by geographic division and year*

Year	North Atlantic		South Atlantic		North Central		South Central	
	Hours per week	Rate per hour	Hours per week	Rate per hour	Hours per week	Rate per hour	Hours per week	Rate per hour
1890	57.6	$0.317	60.0	$0.212	59.6	$0.299	59.3	$0.315
1891	57.9	.314	60.0	.215	59.6	.299	59.3	.315
1892	57.8	.316	60.0	.215	59.6	.301	59.3	.315
1893	54.9	.332	60.0	.214	59.6	.301	56.7	.332
1894	54.9	.333	60.0	.223	59.6	.293	56.7	.332
1895	54.5	.335	60.0	.223	59.6	.295	56.7	.332
1896	54.5	.336	60.0	.225	59.6	.304	56.7	.332
1897	54.1	.339	60.0	.237	59.6	.306	56.7	.332
1898	54.1	.339	60.0	.238	59.6	.309	56.7	.332
1899	54.4	.333	60.0	.238	59.6	.309	56.0	.336
1900	54.4	.333	60.0	.240	58.8	.319	56.0	.336
1901	54.1	.335	60.0	.263	58.0	.328	56.3	.322
1902	54.2	.331	60.0	.257	57.4	.326	56.3	.322
1903	58.5	.333	60.0	.258	56.5	.345	55.3	.328
1904	53.9	.341	60.0	.258	56.7	.341	55.0	.366

TABLE I-15.—*Horseshoers, floor men, males, 1890–1907, by geographic division and year*

Year	North Atlantic		South Atlantic		North Central		South Central	
	Hours per week	Rate per hour	Hours per week	Rate per hour	Hours per week	Rate per hour	Hours per week	Rate per hour
1890	58.5	$0.259	59.4	$0.171	59.4	$0.250	59.6	$0.243
1891	58.6	.258	59.5	.170	59.3	.250	59.6	.243
1892	59.6	.260	59.5	.169	59.3	.250	59.6	.243
1893	57.1	.268	59.4	.169	59.2	.249	57.8	.251
1894	57.0	.281	59.4	.170	57.2	.260	57.8	.251
1895	56.9	.270	59.4	.171	57.0	.261	57.8	.251
1896	56.8	.270	59.4	.172	56.9	.263	58.0	.248
1897	56.5	.273	59.4	.172	56.8	.263	58.0	.248
1898	56.6	.274	59.4	.175	56.6	.265	57.3	.252
1899	56.6	.272	58.5	.182	56.7	.268	56.0	.257
1900	55.9	.279	58.1	.188	56.6	.269	56.0	.257
1901	55.6	.281	58.1	.188	55.6	.277	55.5	.260
1902	55.2	.288	57.5	.185	55.6	.278	55.5	.260
1903	54.4	.299	58.0	.218	55.6	.300	55.9	.268
1904	53.9	.304	56.2	.251	54.9	.313	55.8	.258
1905	53.9	.312	55.6	.265	54.6	.314	54.8	.263
1906	53.8	.313	55.2	.279	54.4	.321	54.4	.270
1907	53.5	.330	55.1	.288	54.3	.335	54.3	.290

TABLE I-16.—*Laborers, males, 1890-1907, by city and year*

[Other laborers are reported under the titles of "laborei." (kind of work not specified), "farm laborers" and in the "building" and the "woodworking" trades]

Year	Atlanta, Ga.		Birmingham, Ala.		Boston, Mass.		Chicago, Ill.	
	Hours per week	Rate per hour	Hours per week	Rate per hour	Hours per week	Rate per hour	Hours per week	Rate per hour
1890	59.7	$0.111			59.3	$0.163	59.3	$0.151
1891	59.8	.109			59.3	.164	59.2	.151
1892	59.7	.111			59.1	.164	59.0	.152
1893	59.8	.109			59.1	.165	57.9	.152
1894	59.7	.108			59.1	.164	58.5	.148
1895	59.7	.108			59. _	.173	58.7	.147
1896	59.7	.109			59.1	.173	58.7	.147
1897	59.8	.108			59.2	.169	58.4	.148
1898	59.8	.106			59.1	.175	58.7	.147
1899	59.8	.107			59.1	.172	58.7	.147
1900	59.8	.107			59.1	.170	58.8	.160
1901	59.8	.108			58.9	.172	56.0	.160
1902	59.8	.108			58.4	.175	55.5	.163
1903	59.8	.107			56.0	.185	54.2	.175
1904	59.8	.108	59.8	$0.100	56.0	.166	54.1	.181
1905	59.8	.114	59.8	.113	54.5	.174	54.2	.179
1906	59.8	.138	59.7	.131	54.6	.180	54.0	.194
1907	59.8	.135	59.6	.141	54.4	.184	54.0	.195

Year	Cincinnati, Ohio		Denver, Colo.		Detroit, Mich.		New Orleans, La.	
1890					60.0	$0.143	60.0	$0.162
1891					60.0	.141	60.0	.167
1892					60.0	.142	60.0	.167
1893					60.0	.142	60.0	.166
1894					60.0	.128	60.0	.164
1895					60.0	.142	60.0	.160
1896					60.0	.134	60.0	.169
1897					60.0	.141	60.0	.165
1898					60.0	.137	60.0	.163
1899					60.0	.142	60.0	.163
1900					60.0	.146	60.0	.164
1901					60.0	.149	54.0	.175
1902					60.0	.152	54.0	.185
1903	56.7	$0.158			59.4	.155	54.0	.173
1904	55.6	.152	53.4	$0.179	59.4	.159	54.0	.174
1905	56.4	.155	56.0	.182	59.5	.154	54.0	.173
1906	55.5	.161	55.2	.191	59.3	.159	54.0	.183
1907	55.5	.169	54.5	.210	59.4	.163	54.0	.194

Year	New York, N. Y.		Philadelphia, Pa.		St. Louis, Mo.		San Francisco, Calif.	
1890	58.9	$0.160			60.0	$0.168	59.0	$0.192
1891	59.0	.166			60.0	.169	59.0	.189
1892	58.9	.166			60.0	.170	59.0	.177
1893	58.9	.166			60.0	.169	59.0	.191
1894	58.8	.164			60.0	.170	59.0	.175
1895	58.9	.162			60.0	.168	59.0	.176
1896	58.9	.165			60.0	.166	56.3	.175
1897	58.9	.163			60.0	.166	59.0	.173
1898	58.9	.164			60.0	.164	59.0	.177
1899	58.8	.170			58.0	.164	59.0	.175
1900	57.6	.176			57.9	.163	59.0	.177
1901	57.0	.177			58.1	.164	59.0	.182
1902	53.8	.182			58.1	.165	56.1	.188
1903	54.1	.190	56.7	$0.142	54.0	.168	56.1	.202
1904	54.3	.192	56.8	.152	54.0	.181	54.0	.230
1905	54.0	.192	56.7	.152	54.0	.196	54.0	.230
1906	54.0	.196	57.0	.149	54.0	.193	54.0	.264
1907	54.0	.201	56.8	.153	54.0	.208	54.0	.281

TABLE **I-17.**—*Laborers, males, foundries, 1923, 1925, and 1927, by State and year*

Year	Alabama		California		Illinois		Louisiana	
	Hours per week	Rate per hour	Hours per week	Rate per hour	Hours per week	Rate per hour	Hours per week	Rate per hour
1923	53.4	$0.249	46.4	$0.473	52.5	$0.496	53.4	$0.274
1925	56.1	.274	48.7	.496	52.8	.543	52.4	.334
1927	54.0	.306	48.4	.557	50.5	.549	51.6	.353
	Maryland		Massachusetts		Michigan		Missouri	
1923	54.8	$0.353	49.5	$0.428	54.6	$0.400	54.4	$0.396
1925	55.8	.385	49.1	.502	51.0	.522	54.1	.413
1927	53.1	.381	50.7	.501	52.3	.529	51.8	.445
	New Hampshire		New York		Ohio		Pennsylvania	
1923	49.2	$0.476	52.6	$0.455	54.4	$0.404	57.4	$0.413
1925	48.8	.492	51.6	.500	54.5	.465	51.5	.476
1927	47.4	.466	52.0	.525	54.2	.475	51.3	.497

TABLE **I-18.**—*Laborers, males, machine shops, 1923, 1925, and 1927, by State and year*

Year	Alabama		California		Illinois		Louisiana	
	Hours per week	Rate per hour	Hours per week	Rate per hour	Hours per week	Rate per hour	Hours per week	Rate per hour
1923	53.8	$0.258	46.2	$0.534	50.5	$0.457	57.9	$0.253
1925	53.8	.285	46.2	.548	50.1	.505	48.3	.371
1927	54.5	.304	45.9	.535	49.9	.498	54.9	.329
	Maryland		Massachusetts		Michigan		Missouri	
1923	47.6	$0.392	49.2	$0.437	51.9	$0.405	52.6	$0.378
1925	49.9	.443	49.2	.484	51.5	.467	53.6	.372
1927	49.6	.430	49.7	.459	51.3	.490	52.2	.409
	New Hampshire		New York		Ohio		Pennsylvania	
1923	51.6	$0.463	47.8	$0.458	52.2	$0.413	52.7	$0.396
1925	50.7	.464	48.6	.449	51.2	.448	50.7	.449
1927	50.3	.469	48.6	.460	50.6	.453	51.6	.444

TABLE **I–19.**—*Lathe hands, machine shops, 1842–1896, by year and State*

Year and State	Sex	Lowest, highest, and average—		Year and State	Sex	Lowest, highest, and average—	
		Hours per week	Rate per day (dollars)			Hours per week	Rate per day (dollars)
1842:				1891:			
Connecticut	M.	66–66–66	1. 25–1. 50–1. 38	New York	M.	(¹)	. 75–3. 83–2. 14
1878:				1892:			
Pennsylvania	M.	(¹)	2. 00–2. 00–2. 00	Indiana	M.	60–60–60	2. 16–2. 23–2. 20
1879:				New York	M.	60–60–60	1. 50–1. 50–1. 50
Pennsylvania	M.	60–60–60	2. 50–2. 50–2. 50	Ohio	(¹)	55–55–55	3. 83–3. 83–3. 83
1882:				Pennsylvania	M.	60–60–60	1. 03–3. 28–2. 54
Ohio	(¹)	54–72–60	1. 30–2. 75–2. 12	1893:			
1883:				Michigan	M.	54–54–54	1. 50–1. 50–1. 50
New Jersey	(¹)	60–60–60	2. 25–3. 00–2. 63	New York	M.	60–60–60	1. 33–1. 33–1. 33
1884:				Do	M.	60–60–60	1. 50–1. 50–1. 50
New Jersey	M.	59–60–60	2. 00–2. 88–2. 63	Do	M.	60–60–60	1. 33–1. 50–1. 44
Ohio	M.	(¹)	1. 25–4. 00–2. 39	Ohio	M.	54–60–60	1. 00–2. 50–1. 79
1885:				1894:			
Massachusetts	F.	59–59–59	1. 00–1. 30–1. 15	Indiana	M.	48–60–54	. 68–2. 25–1. 47
New Jersey	M.	60–60–60	1. 83–3. 00–2. 62	New Hampshire	M.	55–60–58	1. 50–2. 25–1. 83
Ohio	M.	(¹)	1. 25–3. 33–2. 17	New York	M.	60–60–60	1. 50–1. 50–1. 50
1887:				Ohio	M.	54–60–60	1. 33–2. 75–1. 95
New York	M.	(¹)	1. 70–1. 80–1. 78	1895:			
Do	M.	(¹)	². 15– . 27– . 22	Connecticut	M.	59–59–59	2. 21–2. 21–2. 21
Ohio	M.	60–60–60	1. 00–2. 00–1. 65	Massachusetts	M.	59–59–59	1. 00–1. 90–1. 47
Pennsylvania	M.	(¹)	². 20– . 20– . 20	Do	F.	59–59–59	1. 00–1. 40–1. 23
1888:				Ohio	M.	54–72–59	1. 00–2. 25–1. 82
New Jersey	M.	66–66–66	2. 25–2. 50–2. 33	1896:			
New York	M.	57–60–59	1. 75–2. 50–2. 06	Connecticut	M.	60–60–60	1. 00–2. 25–1. 64
Ohio	M.	60–60–60	2. 50–2. 50–2. 50	Missouri	M.	48–60–58	1. 50–5. 25–2. 76
1889:				New York	M.	60–60–60	2. 00–2. 25–2. 05
New York	M.	60–60–60	1. 50–1. 75–1. 63	Ohio	M.	54–60–60	1. 00–2. 36–1. 81
1890:							
New York	M.	(¹)	. 83–2. 70–2. 32				

¹ Not reported.   ² Per hour.

TABLE **I–20.**—*Lathe hands and operators, turret, males, 1919–1927, by State and year*

Year	California		Connecticut		Illinois		Indiana	
	Hours per week	Rate per hour	Hours per week	Rate per hour	Hours per week	Rate per hour	Hours per week	Rate per hour
1919	(¹)	² $0. 677	(¹)	(¹)	(¹)	³ $0. 509	(¹)	³ $0. 657
1923	46. 5	. 875	50. 9	$0. 616	49. 6	. 694	53. 1	. 551
1925	46. 9	. 786	50. 9	. 646	49. 2	. 743	53. 4	. 605
1927	45. 8	. 809	51. 4	. 705	49. 3	. 720	51. 9	. 608

Year	Massachusetts		Michigan		Minnesota		New Jersey	
	Hours per week	Rate per hour	Hours per week	Rate per hour	Hours per week	Rate per hour	Hours per week	Rate per hour
1919	(¹)	³ $0. 511	(¹)	(¹)	(¹)	(¹)	(¹)	³ $0. 540
1923	51. 4	. 595	53. 1	$0. 542	49. 9	$0. 559	49. 6	. 625
1925	49. 0	. 651	52. 4	. 588	51. 0	. 656	49. 4	. 660
1927	49. 1	. 670	50. 6	. 674	49. 5	. 601	49. 5	. 713

Year	New York		Ohio		Pennsylvania		Wisconsin	
	Hours per week	Rate per hour	Hours per week	Rate per hour	Hours per week	Rate per hour	Hours per week	Rate per hour
1919	(¹)	³ $0. 666	(¹)	(¹)	(¹)	³ $0. 742	(¹)	³ $0. 547
1923	47. 1	. 688	49. 8	$0. 564	52. 0	. 580	52. 3	. 612
1925	48. 9	. 648	51. 0	. 623	49. 0	. 681	52. 3	. 651
1927	49. 2	. 681	50. 4	. 652	50. 1	. 672	53. 0	. 676

¹ Not reported.   ² 2-week or half-month pay period.   ³ 1-week pay period.

TABLE I–21.—*Lathe hands and operators, engine, males, 1919–1927, by State and year*

Year	California		Connecticut		Illinois		Indiana	
	Hours per week	Rate per hour	Hours per week	Rate per hour	Hours per week	Rate per hour	Hours per week	Rate per hour
1919	(¹)	² $0.698	(¹)	³ $0.542	(¹)	³ $0.530	(¹)	³ $0.575
1923	46.6	.851	50.4	.612	50.4	.642	52.8	.590
1925	46.6	.807	50.3	.644	50.2	.720	52.4	.628
1927	45.5	.848	51.1	.678	49.9	.767	49.7	.643

	Massachusetts		Michigan		New Jersey		New York	
1919	(¹)	³ $0.532	(¹)	³ $0.504	(¹)	³ $0.614	(¹)	³ $0.709
1923	50.6	.600	52.6	.556	49.4	.700	47.7	.687
1925	49.7	.607	52.5	.629	49.0	.716	48.5	.705
1927	49.2	.638	51.5	.643	49.5	.723	49.2	.724

	Ohio		Pennsylvania		Rhode Island		Wisconsin	
1919	----	----	(¹)	³ $0.713	(¹)	³ $0.482	(¹)	² $0.517
1923	51.8	$0.611	55.3	.640	50.0	.556	52.4	.596
1925	50.5	.636	51.0	.677	50.5	.602	51.8	.656
1927	50.7	.694	51.4	.687	50.4	.607	53.5	.695

¹ Not reported.   • ² 2-week or half-month pay period.   ³ 1-week pay period.

TABLE I–22.—*Machinists, 1840–1900, by year and State*

Year and State	Sex	Lowest, highest, and average—		Year and State	Sex	Lowest, highest, and average—	
		Hours per week	Rate per day (dollars)			Hours per week	Rate per day (dollars)
1840:				**1849:**			
Connecticut	M.	60–72–66	1.25–1.25–1.25	Massachusetts	M.	60–84–68	1.00–2.50–1.50
Massachusetts	M.	78–84–83	1.25–2.00–1.51	New Hampshire	M.	60–60–60	1.00–2.08–1.36
New York	M.	60–60–60	1.25–1.50–1.38	Ohio	M.	60–60–60	.63–2.25–1.38
1841:				Pennsylvania	M.	60–60–60	1.23–1.50–1.43
Massachusetts	M.	78–84–83	1.25–2.00–1.51	**1850:**			
1842:				Connecticut	M.	60–60–60	1.50–1.50–1.50
Connecticut	M.	66–66–66	2.25–2.25–2.25	Massachusetts	M.	60–84–68	1.00–2.50–1.52
Massachusetts	M.	78–84–84	1.25–2.00–1.48	New Hampshire	M.	60–60–60	1.00–2.50–1.41
New York	M.	60–60–60	1.50–1.50–1.50	New York	M.	60–60–60	.58–2.00–1.35
1843:				Ohio	M.	60–60–60	1.31–1.50–1.45
Massachusetts	M.	78–84–84	1.17–2.00–1.44	Pennsylvania	M.	60–60–60	1.20–1.50–1.30
New York	M.	60–C0–60	.75–2.00–1.22	**1851:**			
1844:				Connecticut	M.	60–66–62	1.50–1.50–1.50
Massachusetts	M.	78–84–83	1.00–2.00–1.34	Massachusetts	M.	60–84–68	1.00–2.50–1.52
New York	M.	60–60–60	.62–2.00–1.19	New Hampshire	M.	60–60–60	1.00–2.50–1.45
1845:				New York	M.	60–60–60	.67–2.25–1.37
Massachusetts	M.	72–84–81	1.16–2.00–1.41	Ohio	M.	60–60–60	1.38–1.50–1.47
New Hampshire	M.	66–66–66	1.00–2.00–1.25	Pennsylvania	M.	60–60–60	1.20–1.50–1.30
New York	M.	60–60–60	.75–2.00–1.27	**1852:**			
1846:				Massachusetts	M.	60–78–64	1.00–2.50–1.50
Massachusetts	M.	72–84–80	1.00–2.00–1.46	New Hampshire	M.	60–60–60	1.17–2.50–1.53
New Hampshire	M.	66–66–66	1.00–2.25–1.30	New York	M.	60–60–60	.63–2.75–1.47
New York	M.	60–60–C0	.75–2.00–1.32	Ohio	M.	60–60–60	1.38–1.50–1.48
1847:				Pennsylvania	M.	60–60–60	1.20–1.50–1.29
Massachusetts	M.	72–84–79	1.00–2.00–1.46	**1853:**			
New Hampshire	M.	66–66–66	1.00–2.08–1.35	Connecticut	M.	60–60–60	.92–3.83–1.55
New York	M.	60–60–60	.75–2.25–1.43	Massachusetts	M.	60–78–65	1.00–2.50–1.53
1848:				New Hampshire	M.	60–60–60	1.00–2.00–1.39
Massachusetts	M.	72–84–77	1.08–2.00–1.50	New York	M.	60–72–60	.75–2.50–1.54
New Hampshire	M.	60–60–60	1.00–2.08–1.34	Ohio	M.	60–60–60	1.50–1.54–1.51
New York	M.	60–60–60	.75–2.25–1.42	Pennsylvania	M.	60–60–60	1.20–1.67–1.41

TABLE I-22.—*Machinists, 1840-1900, by year and State*—Continued

Year and State	Sex	Hours per week	Rate per day (dollars)	Year and State	Sex	Hours per week	Rate per day (dollars)
1854:				**1862—Continued.**			
Connecticut	M.	60–60–60	.92–3.83–1.66	New York	M.	60–72–60	0.59–2.63–1.47
Masschusetts	M.	60–84–65	1.00–2.75–1.57	Ohio	M.	60–60–60	1.63–1.65–1.63
New Hampshire	M.	60–60–60	1.17–2.50–1.51	Pennsylvania	M.	60–60–60	1.33–2.00–1.79
New York	M.	60–72–60	.75–3.00–1.62	**1863:**			
Ohio	M.	60–60–60	1.65–1.75–1.73	Connecticut	M.	60–60–60	1.00–3.83–1.75
Pennsylvania	M.	60–60–60	1.20–1.67–1.45	Maryland	M.	60–60–60	1.67–2.50–1.98
1855:				Massachusetts	M.	60–72–62	1.00–3.52–2.04
Connecticut	M.	60–60–60	.90–3.83–1.61	New Hampshire	M.	60–60–60	1.33–2.00–1.68
Maryland	M.	60–60–60	1.50–1.83–1.64	New Jersey	M.	60–60–60	1.33–3.00–1.76
Massachusetts	M.	60–72–64	1.00–3.83–1.62	New York	M.	60–60–60	.63–2.75–1.57
New Hampshire	M.	60–60–60	1.00–1.75–1.41	Ohio	M.	60–60–60	1.75–1.75–1.75
New York	M.	60–72–60	75–2.50–1.71	Pennsylvania	M.	60–60–60	1.33–2.00–1.79
Ohio	M.	60–60–60	1.65–1.75–1.73	**1864:**			
Pennsylvania	M.	60–60–60	1.50–1.70–1.57	Connecticut	M.	60–60–60	.75–4.79–2.01
1856:				Maryland	M.	60–60–60	2.00–3.00–2.58
Connecticut	M.	60–60–60	.90–3.83–1.67	Massachusetts	M.	60–72–62	1.00–4.00–2.03
Maryland	M.	60–60–60	1.50–2.00–1.68	New Hampshire	M.	60–60–60	1.42–2.17–1.81
Massachusetts	M.	60–72–62	1.00–3.83–1.55	New Jersey	M.	60–60–60	1.50–3.00–2.14
New Hampshire	M.	60–60–60	1.17–2.00–1.46	New York	M.	60–60–60	.75–5.00–2.02
New Jersey	M.	60–60–60	1.25–3.00–1.67	Ohio	M.	60–60–60	2.25–2.25–2.25
New York	M.	60–72–60	.80–2.50–1.75	Pennsylvania	M.	60–60–60	1.33–2.20–2.06
Ohio	M.	60–60–60	1.65–1.75–1.73	**1865:**			
Pennsylvania	M.	60–60–60	1.50–1.70–1.56	Connecticut	M.	60–66–60	1.00–6.39–2.23
1857:				Maryland	M.	60–60–60	2.00–3.00–2.72
Connecticut	M.	60–60–60	.90–3.83–1.65	Massachusetts	M.	60–72–62	1.00–4.00–2.37
Maryland	M.	60–60–60	1.50–2.00–1.68	New Hampshire	M.	60–60–60	1.00–2.50–2.06
Massachusetts	M.	60–72–61	1.00–3.83–1.60	New Jersey	M.	60–60–60	1.50–4.17–2.41
New Hampshire	M.	60–60–60	1.17–2.00–1.46	New York	M.	60–72–60	.75–5.00–2.22
New Jersey	M.	60–66–60	1.25–3.00–1.71	Ohio	M.	60–60–60	2.50–2.50–2.50
New York	M.	60–72–60	.84–3.20–1.67	Pennsylvania	M.	60–60–60	1.83–2.84–2.48
Ohio	M.	60–60–60	1.65–1.75–1.74	**1866:**			
Pennsylvania	M.	60–60–60	1.50–1.70–1.57	Connecticut	M.	60–66–60	1.00–6.39–2.39
1858:				Maryland	M.	60–60–60	2.50–3.00–2.70
Connecticut	M.	60–60–60	1.00–3.84–1.63	Massachusetts	M.	60–72–62	1.00–5.00–2.56
Maryland	M.	60–60–60	1.50–2.00–1.70	New Hampshire	M.	60–60–60	1.00–2.50–2.02
Massachusetts	M.	60–84–63	1.00–3.00–1.61	New Jersey	M.	60–60–60	1.50–4.17–2.50
New Hampshire	M.	60–60–60	1.00–1.91–1.44	New York	M.	60–72–60	.67–4.00–2.37
New Jersey	M.	60–60–60	1.25–3.00–1.57	Ohio	M.	60–60–60	2.75–2.75–2.75
New York	M.	60–72–60	.75–2.50–1.50	Pennsylvania	M.	60–60–60	1.83–3.00–2.69
Ohio	M.	60–60–60	1.63–1.65–1.63	**1867:**			
Pennsylvania	M.	60–60–60	1.50–1.80–1.61	Connecticut	M.	60–66–60	1.00–6.39–2.46
1859:				Georgia	M.	66–66–66	2.50–3.33–2.78
Connecticut	M.	60–60–60	1.00–3.84–1.55	Maryland	M.	60–60–60	2.50–3.00–2.88
Maine	M.	(¹)	1.50–1.50–1.50	Massachusetts	M.	60–72–62	1.50–5.00–2.58
Maryland	M.	60–60–60	1.50–2.00–1.62	New Hampshire	M.	60–60–60	1.00–3.52–2.28
Massachusetts	M.	60–78–64	1.12–3.00–1.63	New Jersey	M.	60–60–60	1.67–4.17–2.64
New Hampshire	M.	60–60–60	1.00–1.67–1.38	New York	M.	60–72–60	1.00–5.75–2.45
New Jersey	M.	60–60–60	1.25–3.00–1.71	Ohio	M.	60–60–60	2.75–2.75–2.75
New York	M.	60–72–60	.75–2.00–1.33	Pennsylvania	M.	60–60–60	2.00–3.00–2.79
Ohio	M.	60–60–60	1.63–1.65–1.63	**1868:**			
Pennsylvania	M.	60–60–60	1.60–1.84–1.70	Connecticut	M.	60–66–60	1.50–6.39–2.50
1860:				Maryland	M.	60–60–60	2.50–3.00–2.76
Connecticut	M.	60–60–60	1.00–4.79–1.72	Massachusetts	M.	60–66–62	1.25–5.00–2.60
Maryland	M.	60–60–60	1.50–2.00–1.65	New Hampshire	M.	60–60–60	1.00–3.00–2.17
Massachusetts	M.	60–78–64	.70–3.33–1.65	New Jersey	M.	60–60–60	1.67–4.17–2.67
New Hampshire	M.	60–60–60	1.17–2.00–1.49	New York	M.	60–66–60	.50–4.00–2.47
New York	M.	60–60–60	.75–2.00–1.42	Ohio	M.	60–60–60	3.00–3.00–3.00
Ohio	M.	60–60–60	1.50–2.25–1.75	Pennsylvania	M.	60–60–60	2.50–3.00–2.80
Pennsylvania	M.	60–60–60	1.60–1.84–1.67	**1869:**			
1861:				Connecticut	M.	60–66–60	1.09–6.39–2.51
Connecticut	M.	60–60–60	1.00–4.79–1.58	Maryland	M.	60–60–60	2.25–3.00–2.66
Maryland	M.	60–60–60	1.42–2.00–1.57	Massachusetts	M.	60–66–62	1.00–5.00–2.62
Massachusetts	M.	60–78–62	.70–3.33–1.70	New Hampshire	M.	60–60–60	1.00–3.00–2.32
New Hampshire	M.	60–72–60	1.33–1.75–1.52	New Jersey	M.	60–60–60	1.67–4.17–2.72
New York	M.	60–72–60	.75–2.50–1.43	New York	M.	59–66–60	.42–4.00–2.28
Ohio	M.	60–60–60	1.63–1.65–1.63	Ohio	M.	60–60–60	3.00–3.00–3.00
Pennsylvania	M.	60–60–60	1.60–1.84–1.69	Pennsylvania	M.	60–60–60	2.50–3.00–2.79
1862:				**1870:**			
Connecticut	M.	60–60–60	1.00–4.79–1.58	California	M.	54–60–55	2.25–3.60–3.18
Maryland	M.	60–60–60	1.42–2.00–1.68	Connecticut	M.	60–66–60	1.09–6.39–2.66
Massachusetts	M.	60–72–62	.70–3.50–1.83	Illinois	M.	60–60–60	1.60–3.50–3.01
New Hampshire	M.	60–60–60	1.17–2.00–1.54	Louisiana	M.	60–60–60	1.50–4.00–3.07

¹ Not reported.

TABLE **I-22.**—*Machinists, 1840–1900, by year and State*—Continued

Year and State	Sex	Lowest, highest, and average—		Year and State	Sex	Lowest, highest, and average—	
		Hours per week	Rate per day (dollars)			Hours per week	Rate per day (dollars)
1870—Continued.				**1875:**			
Maryland	M.	60-60-60	1.25-3.00-2.28	California	M.	54-60-55	1.80-4.00-2.92
Massachusetts	M.	59-66-62	1.00-5.00-2.66	Connecticut	M.	60-66-61	1.50-5.75-2.65
Minnesota	M.	60-60-60	1.50-3.00-2.24	Delaware	M.	60-60-60	1.67-2.75-2.17
Missouri	M.	58-59-59	.42-2.75-1.85	Illinois	M.	60-60-60	1.50-3.25-2.58
New Hampshire	M.	60-60-60	1.75-3.00-2.39	Louisiana	M.	60-60-60	2.00-4.00-2.95
New Jersey	M.	60-60-60	1.67-4.17-2.72	Maryland	M.	60-60-60	1.25-2.75-2.25
New York	M.	52-66-60	.90-5.00-2.43	Massachusetts	M.	59-60-60	1.20-5.00-2.44
Ohio	M.	60-60-60	1.67-3.50-2.64	Minnesota	M.	60-60-60	1.50-3.00-2.21
Pennsylvania	M.	60-60-60	1.20-3.40-2.06	Missouri	M.	58-59-59	.42-2.75-2.03
Virginia	M.	60-60-60	1.00-2.50-1.69	New Hampshire	M.	60-60-60	1.00-3.00-2.35
1871:				New Jersey	M.	60-60-60	1.75-4.17-2.70
California	M.	54-60-55	2.03-3.60-3.05	New York	M.	60-66-60	1.00-6.00-2.48
Connecticut	M.	60-66-60	1.09-6.39-2.63	Ohio	M.	60-60-60	1.50-4.00-2.51
Delaware	M.	60-60-60	1.92-3.17-2.48	Pennsylvania	M.	60-60-60	1.20-3.75-1.91
Illinois	M.	60-60-60	1.75-3.50-2.91	Virginia	M.	60-60-60	.90-2.25-1.71
Louisiana	M.	60-60-60	2.00-4.00-3.20	**1876:**			
Maryland	M.	60-60-60	1.25-3.00-2.28	California	M.	54-60-55	1.80-4.50-2.90
Massachusetts	M.	53-66-61	1.35-5.50-2.52	Connecticut	M.	60-66-61	1.00-5.75-2.46
Minnesota	M.	60-60-60	1.50-3.00-2.24	Delaware	M.	60-60-60	1.67-2.50-1.88
Missouri	M.	58-59-59	.42-3.00-1.97	Illinois	M.	60-60-60	1.50-3.25-2.40
New Hampshire	M.	60-60-60	2.00-3.00-2.48	Louisiana	M.	60-60-60	1.60-3.50-2.32
New Jersey	M.	60-60-60	1.67-4.17-2.61	Maryland	M.	60-60-60	1.25-2.75-2.23
New York	M.	59-66-60	1.00-5.00-2.40	Massachusetts	M.	59-60-60	1.08-6.39-2.38
Ohio	M.	60-60-60	1.67-3.50-2.75	Minnesota	M.	60-60-60	1.50-3.00-2.20
Pennsylvania	M.	60-60-60	1.20-3.50-2.13	Missouri	M.	58-59-59	.50-2.75-2.03
Virginia	M.	60-60-60	1.00-2.50-1.69	New Hampshire	M.	60-60-60	1.00-3.00-2.12
1872:				New Jersey	M.	60-60-60	2.00-5.00-2.73
California	M.	54-60-55	2.03-3.75-3.06	New York	M.	59-66-60	.67-6.00-2.25
Connecticut	M.	60-66-60	1.00-6.39-2.60	Ohio	M.	60-60-60	1.67-4.00-2.30
Delaware	M.	60-60-60	2.25-3.17-2.66	Pennsylvania	M.	(1)	2.17-.20-.19
Illinois	M.	60-60-60	1.75-3.50-2.92	Do	M.	48-66-57	2.75-4.60-2.07
Louisiana	M.	60-60-60	2.00-4.00-3.10	South Carolina	M.	66-66-66	2.00-3.00-2.50
Maryland	M.	60-60-60	1.25-3.00-2.28	Virginia	M.	60-60-60	.90-2.25-1.51
Massachusetts	M.	60-60-60	1.25-5.50-2.62	**1877:**			
Minnesota	M.	59-78-60	1.50-3.00-2.24	California	M.	54-60-55	1.80-4.00-2.83
Missouri	M.	58-59-59	.42-2.75-1.81	Connecticut	M.	60-66-61	.90-5.18-2.22
New Hampshire	M.	60-60-60	1.00-3.00-2.24	Delaware	M.	60-60-60	1.50-2.33-1.81
New Jersey	M.	60-60-60	1.67-4.17-2.58	Georgia	M.	66-66-66	2.50-2.50-2.50
New York	M.	54-66-60	.67-6.00-2.52	Illinois	M.	60-60-60	1.50-3.25-2.31
Ohio	M.	60-60-60	1.67-4.00-2.75	Louisiana	M.	60-60-60	1.60-3.00-2.30
Pennsylvania	(1)	60-60-60	1.79-3.00-2.47	Maine	M.	66-66-66	2.25-2.25-2.25
Do	M.	60-60-60	1.35-3.50-2.08	Maryland	M.	60-60-60	1.25-2.50-2.21
South Carolina	M.	72-72-72	1.25-1.75-1.56	Massachusetts	M.	59-60-60	1.00-5.75-2.19
Virginia	M.	60-60-60	1.00-2.50-1.69	Minnesota	M.	60-60-60	1.50-3.00-2.20
1873:				Missouri	M.	58-59-59	.42-2.75-2.04
California	M.	54-60-56	1.80-4.00-3.08	New Jersey	M.	57-60-59	1.50-5.00-2.14
Connecticut	M.	60-66-60	1.00-5.75-2.76	New York	M.	59-66-60	.67-6.00-2.09
Delaware	M.	60-60-60	1.67-3.17-2.52	Ohio	M.	59-60-60	1.50-3.75-2.15
Illinois	M.	60-60-60	1.65-3.50-2.99	Pennsylvania	(1)		2.19-.19-.19
Louisiana	M.	60-60-60	2.00-4.00-3.08	Do	M.	42-72-55	1.00-3.50-2.07
Maryland	M.	60-60-60	1.25-3.00-2.29	Virginia	M.	60-60-60	.90-2.25-1.51
Massachusetts	M.	59-66-62	1.00-6.25-2.74	**1878:**			
Minnesota	M.	60-60-60	1.50-3.00-2.24	California	M.	54-60-55	1.62-3.75-2.80
Missouri	M.	58-59-59	.42-2.50-1.76	Connecticut	M.	60-72-62	1.09-4.60-2.22
New Hampshire	M.	60-60-60	1.50-3.00-2.43	Delaware	M.	60-60-60	1.17-2.33-1.72
New Jersey	M.	60-60-60	1.83-4.17-2.68	Illinois	M.	60-60-60	1.35-2.90-2.39
New York	M.	54-66-60	.67-6.00-2.49	Louisiana	M.	60-60-60	1.60-3.00-2.39
Ohio	M.	60-60-60	1.50-4.00-2.67	Maryland	M.	60-60-60	1.25-2.50-2.21
Pennsylvania	M.	60-60-60	1.20-4.15-2.21	Massachusetts	M.	59-60-60	1.00-5.75-2.14
Virginia	M.	60-60-60	1.00-2.50-1.69	Minnesota	M.	60-60-60	1.50-3.00-2.19
1874:				Missouri	M.	58-59-59	.58-3.00-2.19
California	M.	54-60-56	1.80-4.00-2.96	New Jersey	M.	60-60-60	1.75-5.00-2.49
Connecticut	M.	60-66-61	1.09-5.75-2.71	New York	M.	59-66-60	.67-6.00-2.08
Delaware	M.	60-60-60	1.42-2.75-2.39	Ohio	M.	48-60-60	1.25-3.33-1.87
Illinois	M.	60-60-60	1.70-3.25-2.76	Pennsylvania	M.	48-72-58	1.00-3.50-1.73
Louisiana	M.	60-60-60	2.00-4.00-3.15	Virginia	M.	60-60-60	.90-2.25-1.53
Maryland	M.	60-60-60	1.25-3.00-2.30	**1879:**			
Massachusetts	M.	59-66-61	1.25-5.50-2.66	California	M.	54-60-55	1.62-3.60-2.73
Minnesota	M.	60-60-60	1.50-3.00-2.21	Connecticut	M.	60-66-60	.90-4.14-2.02
Missouri	M.	58-59-59	.42-2.75-1.85	Delaware	M.	60-60-60	1.75-2.33-2.11
New Hampshire	M.	60-60-60	1.50-3.00-2.39	Illinois	M.	60-60-60	1.35-3.25-2.26
New Jersey	M.	60-60-60	2.00-4.17-2.73	Louisiana	M.	60-60-60	1.60-3.00-2.30
New York	M.	59-66-60	.92-6.00-2.43	Maryland	M.	60-60-60	1.25-2.50-2.20
Ohio	M.	60-60-60	1.50-4.00-2.61	Massachusetts	M.	59-60-60	.92-6.39-2.09
Pennsylvania	M.	60-60-60	1.00-4.15-2.22	Minnesota	M.	60-60-60	1.50-3.00-2.19
Virginia	M.	60-60-60	.90-2.25-1.62	Missouri	M.	48-70-59	.42-3.50-2.21

¹ Not reported.   ² Per hour.

TABLE I-22.—*Machinists, 1840–1900, by year and State*—Continued

Year and State	Sex	Lowest, highest, and average—		Year and State	Sex	Lowest, highest, and average—	
		Hours per week	Rate per day (dollars)			Hours per week	Rate per day (dollars)
1879—Continued.				**1883—Continued.**			
New Hampshire__	M.	60–60–60	1.38–3.33–2.29	Maryland_____	M.	60–60–60	1.25–3.00–2.28
New Jersey_____	M.	60–60–60	1.50–4.17–2.35	Massachusetts____	M.	59–60–60	.90–5.21–2.22
Do._____	(¹)	36–60–55	1.25–2.60–1.82	Michigan_____	M.	(¹)	.75–6.00–2.18
New York_____	M.	59–66–60	.42–5.43–1.99	Minnesota_____	M.	60–60–60	1.50–3.00–2.20
Ohio_____	M.	60–60–60	1.25–3.33–1.86	Mississippi_____	M.	(¹)	1.50–1.50–1.50
Pennsylvania____	M.	57–78–60	.75–4.00–1.90	Missouri_____	M.	58–59–59	.42–3.00–2.20
Virginia_____	M.	60–60–60	.90–2.25–1.60	New Hampshire__	M.	60–60–60	1.40–3.33–2.41
1880:				New Jersey_____	M.	60–75–60	1.50–5.00–2.26
California_____	M.	54–60–55	1.80–3.60–2.79	New York_____	M.	59–66–60	.92–5.43–2.25
Connecticut_____	M.	60–66–60	.95–4.14–1.97	North Carolina___	M.	(¹)	1.35–1.35–1.35
Georgia_____	M.	69–69–69	1.75–1.75–1.75	Ohio_____	M.	48–70–59	1.50–5.00–2.40
Illinois_____	M.	43–60–54	.91–3.25–1.95	Pennsylvania____	M.	60–60–60	1.00–4.00–2.11
Louisiana_____	M.	60–60–60	1.50–3.00–2.27	South Carolina___	M.	72–72–72	1.25–1.25–1.25
Maryland_____	M.	60–60–60	1.25–3.00–2.24	Tennessee_____	M.	66–66–66	1.50–2.50–1.88
Massachusetts___	M.	59–60–60	.92–6.39–2.16	Virginia_____	M.	60–60–60	.80–2.25–1.41
Minnesota_____	M.	60–60–60	1.50–3.00–2.19	**1884:**			
Missouri_____	M.	58–59–59	.42–3.00–2.17	California_____	M.	54–60–56	1.89–3.60–3.02
New Hampshire__	M.	60–60–60	1.40–3.33–2.31	Connecticut_____	M.	60–66–60	.95–4.79–2.13
New Jersey_____	M.	60–60–60	1.67–4.17–2.39	Delaware_____	M.	60–60–60	1.58–3.33–2.12
Do._____	(¹)	59–60–60	1.00–3.50–2.38	Georgia_____	M.	70–70–70	1.25–2.50–1.92
New York_____	M.	54–66–60	.50–5.43–1.98	Illinois_____	M.	57–60–60	1.60–3.25–2.43
Ohio_____	M.	60–60–60	1.42–3.33–1.92	Indiana_____	M.	(¹)	1.25–3.85–1.84
Pennsylvania____	M.	53–72–60	1.00–3.50–1.91	Iowa_____	M.	54–84–61	1.43–5.77–2.83
South Carolina___	M.	(¹)	4.17–4.17–4.17	Kentucky_____	M.	66–66–66	1.25–3.08–2.19
Virginia_____	M.	60–68–60	.90–2.25–1.67	Louisiana_____	M.	60–66–62	1.25–3.00–2.22
1881:				Maryland_____	M.	60–60–60	1.25–3.00–2.28
California_____	M.	54–60–57	1.80–3.60–2.92	Massachusetts____	M.	59–60–60	.90–4.79–2.28
Connecticut_____	M.	60–60–60	.95–4.79–2.08	Michigan_____	M.	(¹)	.65–4.00–2.18
Delaware_____	M.	60–60–60	1.42–3.00–1.84	Minnesota_____	M.	60–60–60	1.50–3.00–2.19
Georgia_____	M.	66–66–66	2.50–2.50–2.50	Missouri_____	M.	58–60–59	.42–3.00–2.24
Illinois_____	M.	60–60–60	1.65–2.90–2.45	New Hampshire__	M.	60–60–60	1.30–3.33–2.21
Indiana_____	M.	(¹)	1.75–2.75–2.21	New Jersey_____	M.	59–60–60	1.00–6.67–2.21
Louisiana_____	M.	60–60–60	1.00–3.00–2.22	New York_____	M.	59–60–60	.50–5.43–2.31
Maryland_____	M.	60–60–60	1.25–3.00–2.27	Ohio_____	M.	54–60–58	1.42–3.45–2.32
Massachusetts___	M.	59–60–60	.92–6.39–2.28	Pennsylvania____	M.	59–60–60	1.00–4.00–2.01
Michigan_____	M.	60–60–60	2.00–2.50–2.25	Rhode Island____	M.	58–60–59	2.50–2.75–2.63
Minnesota_____	M.	60–60–60	1.50–3.00–2.19	South Carolina___	M.	69–69–69	1.17–1.50–1.42
Missouri_____	M.	58–59–60	.42–5.00–2.23	Tennessee_____	M.	66–66–66	2.00–2.00–2.00
New Hampshire__	M.	60–65–62	1.40–3.33–2.57	Virginia_____	M.	55–60–59	.80–3.33–1.89
New Jersey_____	M.	60–60–60	1.33–4.17–2.34	West Virginia____	M.	60–60–60	2.00–2.00–2.00
New York_____	M.	59–66–60	.50–5.43–2.17	**1885:**			
Ohio_____	M.	48–72–59	1.35–4.58–2.11	Alabama_____	M.	(¹)	1.25–2.00–1.63
Pennsylvania____	M.	60–60–60	1.00–3.50–1.98	California_____	M.	54–63–58	.67–4.00–2.72
South Carolina___	M.	72–72–72	.83–.83–.83	Connecticut_____	M.	59–69–60	.95–4.79–2.12
Virginia_____	M.	60–60–60	.90–2.25–1.71	Delaware_____	M.	60–72–61	1.25–3.00–2.33
1882:				Georgia_____	M.	69–69–69	1.00–1.70–1.47
California_____	M.	54–60–57	1.89–3.60–2.98	Illinois_____	M.	60–66–60	1.50–4.00–2.41
Connecticut_____	M.	60–66–60	.95–4.79–2.19	Indiana_____	M.	60–66–60	.83–3.25–2 06
Delaware_____	M.	60–60–60	1.75–2.17–1.97	Iowa_____	M.	63–63–63	2.50–2.50–2.50
Georgia_____	M.	72–72–72	2.50–2.50–2.50	Kansas_____	M.	48–72–60	1.35–3.50–2.30
Illinois_____	M.	60–60–60	1.65–2.90–1.98	Kentucky_____	M.	60–60–60	1.00–3.50–1.91
Indiana_____	M.	(¹)	1.11–2.75–2.22	Louisiana_____	M.	60–60–60	1.50–3.00–2.38
Louisiana_____	M.	60–60–60	1.00–3.00–2.13	Maine_____	M.	60–72–64	1.25–3.00–1.98
Maryland_____	M.	60–60–60	1.25–3.00–2.27	Maryland_____	M.	54–72–61	1.25–3.33–2.24
Massachusetts___	M.	59–60–60	.80–5.75–2.30	Massachusetts____	M.	59–60–60	.82–4.50–2.20
Minnesota_____	M.	60–60–60	1.50–3.00–2.20	Michigan_____	M.	60–66–63	.58–4.79–2.06
Missouri_____	M.	58–60–59	.42–3.00–2.34	Minnesota_____	M.	60–72–62	1.50–3.00–2.22
New Hampshire__	M.	60–66–60	1.40–3.33–2.30	Missouri_____	M.	48–60–57	.42–3.00–2.00
New Jersey_____	M.	60–66–60	1.50–4.17–2.22	Do._____	(¹)	(¹)	2.42–2.42–2.42
New York_____	M.	59–66–60	.50–4.00–2.22	New Hampshire__	M.	59–66–61	1.25–3.50–2.02
North Carolina___	M.	60–72–63	.83–2.50–1.64	New Jersey_____	M.	42–66–60	.67–4.00–2.07
Ohio_____	(¹)	54–72–60	1.50–3.83–2.38	New York_____	M.	54–72–61	.50–5.00–2.07
Do._____	M.	60–60–60	1.42–3.45–2.17	North Carolina___	M.	60–69–61	1.67–3.50–2.01
Pennsylvania____	M.	59–66–60	1.00–4.00–2.03	Ohio_____	M.	60–72–60	.50–3.60–2.05
South Carolina___	M.	69–69–69	1.25–2.00–1.72	Pennsylvania____	M.	48–60–58	1.00–5.00–1.98
Virginia_____	M.	60–60–60	.80–2.42–1.73	Rhode Island____	M.	48–60–54	2.50–2.50–2.50
1883:				Tennessee_____	M.	60–60–60	1.00–2.80–2.59
Alabama_____	M.	(¹)	1.67–1.67–1.67	Vermont_____	M.	60–66–61	1.65–3.46–1.98
California_____	M.	54–60–56	1.89–3.60–3.01	Virginia_____	M.	48–72–58	.63–2.75–2.04
Connecticut_____	M.	60–66–60	.95–4.79–2.18	Wisconsin_____	M.	57–66–60	1.92–3.84–2.56
Delaware_____	M.	60–60–00	1.92–3.00–2.18	**1886:**			
Georgia_____	M.	66–66–66	1.50–2.50–2.07	California_____	M.	54–60–56	1.80–5.00–3.05
Illinois_____	M.	60–60–60	1.50–2.90–2.35	Connecticut_____	M.	60–66–60	1.09–4.79–2.15
Indiana_____	M.	(¹)	1.71–3.00–2.36	Delaware_____	M.	60–72–62	1.25–2.83–1.88
Louisiana_____	M.	60–60–60	1.50–3.00–2.13	Illinois_____	M.	54–60–60	1.33–3.50–2.34

¹ Not reported.

TABLE **I-22.**—*Machinists, 1840–1900, by year and State*—Continued

Year and State	Sex	Hours per week	Rate per day (dollars)
1886—Continued.			
Indiana	M.	(¹)	1.20-2.58-1.89
Iowa	M.	54-63-60	1.15-7.00-2.52
Kansas	M.	42-60-51	1.25-2.82-2.43
Louisiana	M.	60-60-60	1.75-3.00-2.71
Maryland	M.	60-60-60	1.25-2.75-2.25
Massachusetts	M.	59-60-60	1.00-5.00-2.16
Michigan	M.	60-60-60	1.50-2.75-2.45
Minnesota	M.	60-60-60	1.50-3.00-2.18
Missouri	M.	58-59-59	.42-3.00-2.05
New Hampshire	M.	60-60-60	1.40-3.25-2.25
New Jersey	M.	55-60-60	.50-4.00-2.10
New York	M.	44-66-58	.50-4.50-2.17
Ohio	M.	60-60-60	1.15-4.79-2.21
Pennsylvania	M.	57-60-60	.70-3.50-2.10
Rhode Island	M.	60-60-60	1.75-3.50-2.35
Virginia	M.	60-60-60	.80-2.17-1.54
1887:			
California	M.	54-60-56	1.80-3.60-3.03
Connecticut	M.	60-60-60	.61-6.41-2.30
Delaware	M.	(¹)	².14-.25-.20
Do	M.	60-60-60	1.42-3.33-2.10
Florida	M.	(¹)	1.00-3.50-2.34
Illinois	M.	60-60-60	1.50-3.25-2.38
Kansas	M.	50-60-58	2.00-3.84-2.49
Louisiana	M.	60-60-60	1.50-3.00-2.50
Maine	M.	60-60-60	1.00-3.00-2.13
Maryland	M.	(¹)	².22-.26-.23
Do	M.	60-60-60	.60-4.79-1.86
Massachusetts	M.	59-60-60	.75-5.00-2.19
Michigan	M.	60-60-60	1.50-3.13-2.23
Do	M.	(¹)	².23-.23-.23
Minnesota	M.	60-60-60	1.50-3.00-2.19
Missouri	(¹)	(¹)	1.60-3.50-3.02
Do	M.	58-59-59	.42-4.60-2.43
Nebraska	M.	54-60-57	1.25-3.75-2.47
New Hampshire	M.	60-60-60	1.45-3.20-2.25
New Jersey	M.	60-60-60	1.00-4.00-2.73
New York	M.	(¹)	².10-.28-.20
Do	M.	60-60-60	.75-5.17-2.29
North Carolina	M.	60-72-60	1.00-2.50-2.02
Ohio	M.	48-62-60	.75-4.00-2.17
Oregon	M.	(¹)	1.00-4.60-2.89
Pennsylvania	M.	60-60-60	².07½-.35-.22
Do	M.	60-60-60	.50-5.29-2.16
Rhode Island	M.	60-60-60	1.75-4.79-2.46
Virginia	M.	60-60-60	.80-2.75-1.91
West Virginia	M.	(¹)	1.50-2.50-1.80
Wisconsin	M.	(¹)	.50-5.00-2.08
1888:			
California	M.	54-60-56	1.80-3.60-3.03
Colorado	M.	60-66-62	1.65-4.50-2.77
Connecticut	M.	60-60-60	.84-4.79-2.19
Delaware	M.	60-60-60	1.42-3.33-2.13
Georgia	M.	66-66-66	1.50-3.50-1.97
Illinois	M.	60-60-60	1.50-3.00-2.40
Indiana	M.	54-60-59	1.73-2.99-2.32
Iowa	M.	54-60-58	1.73-3.87-2.25
Kansas	M.	57-60-58	1.74-2.88-2.49
Louisiana	M.	60-60-60	1.50-3.00-2.56
Maine	M.	60-60-60	2.00-2.00-2.00
Maryland	M.	60-60-60	1.25-3.00-2.28
Massachusetts	M.	59-60-60	1.00-5.00-2.24
Michigan	M.	60-72-60	.77-3.83-2.10
Minnesota	M.	60-60-60	1.50-3.00-2.19
Missouri	M.	58-59-59	.42-3.00-2.03
Do	(¹)	(¹)	1.88-2.58-2.09
New Hampshire	M.	60-60-60	1.33-3.08-2.07
New Jersey	M.	54-60-59	1.40-4.17-1.95
New York	M.	(¹)	².15-.28-.26
Do	M.	45-72-59	.50-5.75-2.22
North Carolina	M.	54-72-63	1.00-5.00-2.05
Ohio	M.	60-60-60	1.25-3.00-2.47
Pennsylvania	M.	60-60-60	1.10-4.00-2.15
Rhode Island	M.	60-60-60	1.50-3.00-2.20
South Carolina	M.	66-66-66	.75-3.50-1.98
Tennessee	M.	60-60-60	2.25-3.00-2.50
Virginia	M.	60-72-61	.80-3.26-1.85
West Virginia	M.	63-63-63	2.90-2.90-2.90
1889:			
Alabama	M.	48-84-68	1.00-4.79-2.66
California	M.	54-60-55	1.80-3.60-3.04
Connecticut	M.	60-60-60	.84-4.79-2.06
Delaware	M.	60-60-60	1.42-3.33-2.13
Georgia	M.	66-72-69	1.25-3.00-2.11
Illinois	M.	60-72-61	1.25-3.50-2.34
Indiana	M.	48-60-58	1.67-2.62-2.03
Iowa	M.	48-60-59	1.75-3.00-2.21
Kansas	M.	60-60-60	.75-3.25-2.18
Louisiana	M.	60-60-60	1.50-3.00-2.21
Maine	M.	60-60-60	1.25-3.42-2.01
Maryland	M.	60-60-60	.60-4.79-2.25
Massachusetts	M.	59-60-60	1.00-5.00-2.26
Michigan	M.	60-84-60	.78-3.50-1.83
Minnesota	M.	60-60-60	1.50-3.00-2.20
Missouri	M.	58-59-59	.42-3.50-2.10
New Hampshire	M.	60-60-60	1.00-4.81-2.02
New Jersey	M.	60-60-60	2.30-4.17-2.81
New York	M.	59-72-60	.75-5.17-2.28
North Carolina	M.	(¹)	1.50-1.50-1.50
Ohio	M.	54-84-61	1.33-4.00-2.06
Pennsylvania	M.	33-84-60	1.10-5.00-2.16
Rhode Island	M.	(¹)	1.00-2.25-1.75
South Carolina	M.	69-69-69	.75-1.90-1.33
Tennessee	M.	66-72-68	1.00-3.25-2.14
Virginia	M.	60-72-63	.80-3.00-1.84
West Virginia	M.	60-63-61	1.00-3.85-2.30
Wisconsin	M.	(¹)	3.45-3.45-3.45
1890:			
Alabama	M.	(¹)	1.10-4.00-2.25
California	M.	48-60-51	1.60-3.50-2.78
Connecticut	M.	60-60-60	.84-4.79-2.08
Delaware	M.	60-60-60	1.42-3.33-2.16
Illinois	M.	60-60-60	1.50-3.00-2.39
Indiana	M.	54-60-59	1.51-2.61-2.11
Iowa	M.	(¹)	.90-3.83-2.14
Kansas	M.	(¹)	1.75-3.25-2.51
Kentucky	M.	(¹)	.75-2.50-1.50
Louisiana	M.	60-60-60	1.50-4.00-2.56
Maine	M.	60-60-60	2.25-2.30-2.28
Maryland	M.	60-60-60	1.25-3.00-2.30
Massachusetts	M.	59-60-60	1.00-5.00-2.28
Michigan	M.	60-60-60	.40-4.17-1.89
Minnesota	M.	60-60-60	1.50-4.60-2.47
Mississippi	M.	(¹)	1.50-2.00-1.75
Missouri	M.	58-59-59	1.92-5.00-2.77
Nebraska	M.	(¹)	2.25-2.25-2.25
New Hampshire	M.	60-60-60	1.50-3.25-1.98
New Jersey	M.	60-60-60	1.69-4.17-2.68
New York	M.	59-60-60	.50-6.00-2.34
North Carolina	M.	60-72-66	.78-2.50-1.71
Ohio	M.	51-78-60	.70-3.58-2.25
Pennsylvania	M.	60-60-60	1.00-5.00-2.09
Rhode Island	M.	(¹)	2.00-2.75-2.38
Tennessee	M.	(¹)	2.00-2.00-2.00
Virginia	M.	60-60-60	.75-2.33-1.76
1891:			
California	M.	48-60-51	1.60-3.50-2.81
Connecticut	M.	60-60-60	.75-4.79-2.05
Delaware	M.	60-60-60	1.42-3.33-2.16
Illinois	M.	60-60-60	1.50-3.50-2.42
Indiana	M.	48-72-58	1.56-3.20-2.01
Louisiana	M.	60-60-60	1.50-3.00-2.21
Maine	M.	60-60-60	1.10-2.76-2.14
Maryland	M.	60-60-60	1.25-3.00-2.31
Massachusetts	M.	59-60-60	1.00-5.00-2.26
Minnesota	M.	60-60-60	1.75-3.25-2.48
Missouri	M.	58-59-59	.42-3.50-1.99
New Hampshire	M.	60-60-60	1.50-3.00-2.04
New Jersey	M.	60-60-60	2.00-4.17-2.85
New York	M.	59-60-60	.41-9.17-2.23
North Carolina	M.	60-72-67	1.00-4.00-2.14
Do	(¹)	(¹)	1.77-3.55-2.39
Ohio	M.	48-72-59	1.72-4.17-2.09
Pennsylvania	M.	54-60-59	1.00-5.50-2.13
South Carolina	M.	60-60-60	1.75-3.34-2.55
Virginia	M.	60-60-60	.75-2.34-1.77
Wisconsin	M.	(¹)	2.00-3.25-2.50

¹ Not reported.   ² Per hour.

Table **I-22.**—*Machinists, 1840–1900, by year and State*—Continued

Year and State	Sex	Lowest, highest, and average— Hours per week	Lowest, highest, and average— Rate per day (dollars)	Year and State	Sex	Lowest, highest, and average— Hours per week	Lowest, highest, and average— Rate per day (dollars)
1892:				**1895—Continued.**			
California	M.	48-63-54	1.30-4.00-2.87	Iowa	(1)	(1)	1.54-2.84-2.07
Colorado	M.	60-60-60	2.65-3.20-2.77	Kansas	M.	48-60-55	2.00-3.00-2.59
Connecticut	M.	60-60-60	1.50-4.79-2.26	Louisiana	M.	60-63-61	.50-4.00-2.12
Delaware	M.	60-60-60	1.17-3.75-1.97	Maine	M.	54-60-60	1.25-3.33-2.25
Florida	M.	60-66-61	1.50-3.84-2.45	Maryland	M.	54-60-60	1.25-3.00-2.25
Illinois	M.	59-60-60	1.50-3.50-2.54	Massachusetts	M.	55-60-60	1.00-5.83-2.21
Indiana	M.	42-72-57	1.38-2.90-2.08	Michigan	M.	(1)	.55-2.75-1.99
Iowa	M.	60-60-60	1.75-3.00-2.55	Minnesota	M.	60-60-60	1.50-3.00-2.21
Kansas	M.	60-60-60	2.68-2.77-2.73	Mississippi	M.	60-60-60	1.42-1.75-1.59
Louisiana	M.	60-60-60	1.50-3.00-2.11	Missouri	M.	58-60-59	.42-3.75-1.90
Maryland	M.	60-60-60	1.25-3.00-2.24	Montana	M.	53-53-53	2.80-5.00-3.10
Massachusetts	M.	58-60-60	.60-5.00-2.27	New Hampshire	M.	59-60-60	.85-3.50-1.92
Michigan	M.	60-60-60	.50-4.00-1.72	New Jersey	M.	53-60-58	1.70-3.50-2.68
Minnesota	M.	60-60-60	1.75-3.25-2.45	New York	M.	48-60-60	.75-5.83-2.59
Missouri	M.	59-59-59	.42-3.50-2.13	North Carolina	M.	60-72-66	.83-3.50-2.30
New Hampshire	M.	60-60-60	1.25-3.00-1.93	Ohio	M.	42-72-59	.50-4.00-2.05
New Jersey	M.	60-60-60	2.25-4.17-2.75	Pennsylvania	M.	42-60-59	1.00-5.00-2.08
New Mexico	M.	60-60-60	3.21-3.21-3.21	Rhode Island	M.	55-60-59	1.00-4.00-2.25
New York	M.	60-60-60	1.10-5.84-2.38	South Carolina	M.	54-66-65	.60-4.17-1.82
North Carolina	(1)	(1)	1.76-3.00-2.31	Tennessee	M.	66-67-66	.65-3.00-1.57
Ohio	(1)	58-60-59	2.50-3.00-2.75	Virginia	M.	55-60-59	.75-3.67-1.87
Do	M.	60-60-60	1.33-3.45-2.04	West Virginia	M.	60-60-60	.83-2.42-1.37
Pennsylvania	M.	54-60-59	1.00-6.00-2.17	Wisconsin	(1)	48-60-60	1.50-3.65-2.39
Virginia	M.	60-60-60	.75-2.33-1.83	**1896:**			
1893:				Alabama	M.	63-63-63	1.25-1.25-1.25
California	M.	48-60-50	1.60-3.50-2.75	California	M.	48-60-51	1.60-3.50-2.69
Connecticut	M.	60-60-60	2.40-2.50-2.49	Colorado	M.	48-66-53	1.50-4.00-2.87
Delaware	M.	60-60-60	1.17-3.42-1.72	Connecticut	M.	60-60-60	1.50-3.12-2.04
Illinois	M.	45-60-59	1.33-3.75-2.42	Delaware	M.	72-72-72	2.50-2.50-2.50
Indiana	M.	45-72-58	1.61-2.90-2.18	Georgia	M.	60-66-65	1.25-5.00-2.31
Kansas	M.	36-54-49	1.68-2.70-2.29	Illinois	M.	54-60-60	1.00-3.25-2.33
Louisiana	M.	60-60-60	1.50-3.00-2.21	Indiana	M.	48-65-56	1.10-3.00-2.22
Maryland	M.	60-60-60	1.25-3.00-2.25	Iowa	(1)	(1)	1.69-2.97-2.10
Massachusetts	M.	58-60-60	1.00-5.00-2.30	Kansas	M.	48-60-56	1.25-3.00-2.09
Michigan	M.	45-72-59	.60-3.83-2.14	Kentucky	M.	60-60-60	.83-2.93-1.71
Minnesota	M.	60-60-60	1.50-3.00-2.24	Louisiana	M.	60-60-60	1.50-3.00-2.29
Missouri	M.	54-63-60	.42-3.00-2.19	Maryland	M.	57-69-60	.67-7.00-2.07
Montana	M.	47-60-54	1.80-7.67-3.70	Massachusetts	M.	56-60-59	1.00-3.50-2.29
New Hampshire	M.	60-60-60	1.25-3.00-2.00	Michigan	M.	54-60-58	1.50-3.04-2.42
New York	M.	48-65-60	1.00-3.33-2.43	Minnesota	M.	60-60-60	1.50-3.33-2.18
North Carolina	M.	(1)	.62-3.19-2.27	Missouri	M.	45-60-58	.42-5.50-2.16
Ohio	M.	24-72-58	1.00-3.50-2.02	Montana	M.	(1)	2.45-3.53-2.95
Pennsylvania	M.	54-60-60	1.00-6.00-2.18	Nebraska	M.	48-60-48	1.75-3.50-3.09
Rhode Island	M.	(1)	1.50-3.30-2.24	New Hampshire	M.	60-60-60	2.50-3.00-2.75
Virginia	M.	60-60-60	.75-3.33-1.78	New Jersey	M.	56-56-56	3.00-6.00-4.00
Wisconsin	M.	(1)	2.25-3.25-2.75	New York	M.	48-70-57	.33-6.67-2.43
1894:				North Carolina	M.	60-72-63	1.00-3.50-2.30
California	M.	48-60-49	1.60-3.50-2.65	Ohio	M.	48-60-57	.50-3.66-2.00
Connecticut	M.	60-60-60	1.90-2.50-2.41	Pennsylvania	M.	51-60-60	.85-5.40-2.29
Delaware	M.	60-60-60	1.17-3.42-1.73	Rhode Island	M.	60-60-60	1.83-5.00-2.70
Georgia	M.	72-72-72	2.00-2.00-2.00	South Carolina	M.	66-66-66	1.00-2.00-1.51
Illinois	M.	60-60-60	1.50-2.90-2.27	Vermont	M.	60-66-60	.75-2.50-1.78
Indiana	M.	42-72-55	1.35-3.50-2.09	West Virginia	M.	55-55-55	1.50-2.50-2.02
Iowa	M.	48-60-56	1.00-3.50-2.02	Wisconsin	M.	60-60-60	1.00-3.00-2-22
Louisiana	M.	60-60-60	1.50-3.00-2.50	**1897:**			
Maine	M.	60-60-60	1.33-1.75-1.47	California	M.	48-60-51	2.00-3.50-2.72
Maryland	M.	60-60-60	1.25-3.00-2.27	Connecticut	M.	50-60-59	2.21-3.00-2.68
Massachusetts	M.	58-60-60	1.00-5.00-2.04	Georgia	M.	66-66-66	1.25-2.50-1.88
Minnesota	M.	60-60-60	1.50-3.00-2.22	Illinois	M.	60-60-60	1.50-3.00-2.36
Missouri	M.	58-59-59	.42-3.00-2.00	Iowa	(1)	(1)	1.59-2.95-2.07
Montana	M.	(1)	3.07-4.14-3.22	Kansas	M.	48-63-57	1.28-2.61-2.12
New Hampshire	M.	40-80-57	1.00-3.50-2.06	Do	M.	(1)	[2] .20-.20-.20
New York	M.	60-60-60	.88-3.50-2.49	Louisiana	M.	60-60-60	1.50-3.00-2.50
North Carolina	M.	60-72-62	1.68-3.50-2.48	Maryland	M.	60-60-60	1.25-2.50-2.11
Ohio	M.	42-72-58	.50-5.00-2.07	Do	(1)	54-60-59	1.33-2.50-2.08
Pennsylvania	M.	54-60-59	1.00-5.40-2.07	Massachusetts	M.	59-60-60	1.00-5.00-2.38
Rhode Island	M.	(1)	1.00-1.27-1.17	Michigan	M.	60-72-64	1.25-2.65-2.19
Virginia	M.	60-60-60	.75-2.25-1.75	Do	M.	(1)	[2] .25-.25-.25
West Virginia	M.	48-72-62	1.29-3.07-1.79	Minnesota	M.	60-60-60	1.50-3.00-2.20
1895:				Missouri	M.	58-59-59	.42-3.00-1.85
Alabama	M.	60-66-62	1.54-2.33-1.88	Montana	M.	(1)	2.12-3.62-2.65
California	M.	48-60-50	1.60-3.75-2.70	Nebraska	M.	48-60-57	1.00-3.00-1.88
Connecticut	M.	59-72-61	.67-3.50-2.22	New Hampshire	M.	60-60-60	2.00-2.00-2.00
Georgia	M.	60-66-66	1.00-4.17-2.18	New York	M.	48-60-58	.75-4.17-2.41
Illinois	M.	54-60-60	1.50-3.50-2.38	North Carolina	M.	75-75-75	2.00-2.00-2.00
Indiana	M.	48-60-59	1.50-2.70-2.10	Do	(1)	(1)	1.26-2.83-2.30

¹ Not reported. ² Per hour.

TABLE **I-22.**—*Machinists, 1840–1900, by year and State*—Continued

| Year and State | Sex | Lowest, highest, and average— | | Year and State | Sex | Lowest, highest, and average— | |
		Hours per week	Rate per day (dollars)			Hours per week	Rate per day (dollars)
1897—Continued.				1899:			
Ohio	M.	60–60–60	1.17–2.50–1.78	Alabama	M.	60–60–60	2.00–3.00–2.65
Do	(¹)	60–60–60	1.30–4.50–3.30	Connecticut	M.	(¹)	2.37–2.37–2.37
Pennsylvania	M.	48–60–59	.93–5.00–2.10	Georgia	M.	59–60–60	1.50–3.00–2.28
Virginia	M.	54–60–60	.75–3.50–2.05	Illinois	M.	60–60–60	1.65–3.30–2.85
1898:				Massachusetts	M.	54–54–54	1.35–3.15–2.34
California	M.	48–60–51	1.60–3.50–2.72	Michigan	(¹)	(¹)	1.83–1.83–1.83
Illinois	M.	60–60–60	1.50–3.00–2.33	New Jersey	(¹)	(¹)	2.22–2.22–2.22
Indiana	(¹)	48–60–56	1.61–2.68–2.12	New York	M.	60–60–60	1.00–3.00–2.16
Iowa	(¹)	(¹)	2.00–2.00–2.00	North Carolina	(¹)	(¹)	1.25–3.09–2.36
Do	(¹)	(¹)	1.72–2.85–2.16	Do	M.	60–72–61	1.00–4.00–2.43
Kansas	M.	42–60–51	.90–3.14–2.50	Pennsylvania	M.	54–54–54	1.25–4.00–2.27
Louisiana	M.	60–60–60	1.50–3.00–2.50	Tennessee	M.	(¹)	1.10–2.12–1.69
Maryland	M.	60–60–60	1.25–2.50–2.09	Virginia	(¹)	(¹)	1.42–2.83–2.29
Massachusetts	M.	59–60–60	1.00–5.00–2.33	1900.			
Michigan	M.	60–60–60	1.12–2.35–2.18	Alabama	M.	60–60–60	2.00–3.25–2.71
Minnesota	M.	60–60–60	1.50–3.00–2.20	Georgia	M.	59–60–60	1.75–3.25–2.28
Missouri	M.	58–59–59	.42–3.00–1.89	Illinois	M.	60–60–60	1.65–3.30–2.78
Do	(¹)	48–60–59	1.85–3.14–2.26	Massachusetts	M.	54–54–54	1.35–3.15–2.33
Nebraska	(¹)	48–72–50	1.00–3.50–2.73	New Jersey	(¹)	(¹)	2.28–2.28–2.28
New Jersey	M.	60–60–60	1.67–5.00–2.28	New York	M.	60–60–60	1.00–3.00–1.95
New York	M.	48–60–59	1.00–4.00–2.40	North Carolina	M.	60–60–60	1.25–2.75–2.40
North Carolina	(¹)	(¹)	1.25–2.83–2.28	Ohio	M.	60–60–60	1.25–3.25–2.07
Ohio	M.	60–60–60	1.17–4.60–2.02	Pennsylvania	M.	48–48–48	2.00–3.00–2.50
Pennsylvania	M.	54–60–59	.80–5.62–2.07				
Virginia	M.	60–60–60	.75–2.25–1.60				
Do	(¹)	60–60–60	2.38–2.38–2.38				
Washington	(¹)	(¹)	1.54–4.02–2.44				

¹ Not reported.

TABLE **I-23.**—*Machinists, males, 1890–1906, by city and year*

| Year | Atlanta, Ga. | | Birmingham, Ala. | | Boston, Mass. | | Chicago, Ill. | |
	Hours per week	Rate per hour	Hours per week	Rate per hour	Hours per week	Rate per hour	Hours per week	Rate per hour
1890	59.9	$0.261			59.4	$0.263	59.9	$0.271
1891	60.0	.265			59.4	.256	59.8	.277
1892	59.9	.267			58.1	.266	58.5	.278
1893	59.9	.271			57.4	.274	53.9	.276
1894	59.9	.250			57.0	.269	57.6	.245
1895	59.9	.247			57.2	.270	58.2	.249
1896	59.9	.256			57.4	.267	58.2	.252
1897	59.9	.241			57.3	.270	57.3	.253
1898	59.9	.241			57.2	.269	58.2	.251
1899	59.9	.248			56.6	.272	58.2	.257
1900	60.0	.253			56.5	.274	58.4	.263
1901	60.0	.259			55.9	.278	56.8	.271
1902	59.9	.257			54.3	.285	56.8	.302
1903	59.9	.287			54.2	.287	54.0	.297
1904	59.6	.292	59.8	$0.294	54.3	.286	54.0	.302
1905	59.7	.297	59.9	.297	54.0	.288	54.0	.327
1906	59.6	.302	59.8	.309	54.0	.299	52.2	.330

TABLE I-23.—*Machinists, males, 1890–1906, by city and year*—Continued

Year	Cincinnati, Ohio		Denver, Colo.		Detroit, Mich.		New Orleans, La.	
	Hours per week	Rate per hour	Hours per week	Rate per hour	Hours per week	Rate per hour	Hours per week	Rate per hour
1890	60.0	$0.232			60.0	$0.221	58.9	$0.298
1891	60.0	.233			60.0	.221	58.9	.302
1892	60.0	.232			60.0	.228	58.3	.313
1893	60.0	.219			60.0	.230	59.0	.298
1894	60.0	.197			60.0	.219	59.2	.300
1895	60.0	.200			60.0	.217	58.7	.296
1896	60.0	.206			60.0	.222	59.0	.297
1897	60.0	.211			60.0	.330	59.0	.298
1898	60.0	.212			60.0	.225	59.2	.293
1899	60.0	.222			60.0	.238	57.9	.299
1900	60.0	.228			60.0	.253	58.2	.309
1901	59.1	.247			60.0	.243	54.0	.325
1902	59.1	.249			60.0	.255	53.2	.344
1903	56.6	.229			59.3	.267	54.0	.345
1904	55.5	.246	53.8	$0.306	59.2	.277	54.0	.339
1905	55.4	.246	56.1	.320	59.1	.270	54.0	.345
1906	55.4	.258	56.3	.318	59.1	.276	54.0	.348

Year	New York, N. Y.		Philadelphia, Pa.		St. Louis, Mo.		San Francisco, Calif.	
1890	59.1	$0.242	60.0	$0.244	59.6	$0.260	59.1	$0.317
1891	59.1	.246	60.0	.243	59.6	.262	59.2	.315
1892	59.1	.242	60.0	.251	59.5	.260	59.2	.311
1893	59.1	.246	60.0	.246	59.5	.260	59.2	.316
1894	59.1	.232	60.0	.228	59.6	.257	59.1	.304
1895	59.1	.231	60.0	.226	59.6	.256	59.1	.297
1896	59.1	.234	59.8	.242	59.7	.265	57.0	.300
1897	59.1	.232	59.8	.235	59.8	.267	59.2	.301
1898	59.1	.239	59.8	.233	58.0	.269	59.2	.301
1899	58.8	.241	57.7	.246	57.0	.278	59.1	.303
1900	58.5	.245	57.0	.252	57.1	.284	59.2	.305
1901	58.2	.242	57.1	.257	56.6	.289	59.1	.311
1902	54.0	.268	56.7	.265	55.8	.303	58.1	.325
1903	53.8	.302	56.1	.300	54.0	.321	57.2	.331
1904	54.0	.302	55.9	.272	54.0	.301	54.0	.356
1905	56.5	.311	55.9	.277	54.0	.307	54.0	.366
1906	54.0	.321	56.0	.283	54.0	.303	54.0	.391

TABLE I-24.—*Machinists, all-round, males, 1907–1924, by city and year*

Year	Boston, Mass.		Chicago, Ill. [1]		Cincinnati, Ohio		Detroit, Mich.		New York, N. Y.		Philadelphia, Pa.	
	Hours per week	Rate per hour	Hours per week	Rate per hour	Hours per week	Rate per hour	Hours per week	Rate per hour	Hours per week	Rate per hour	Hours per week	Rate per hour
1907	54.0	$0.306			55.0	$0.300						
1908	54.0	.306			55.0	.300						
1909	54.0	.333			55.0	.300						
1910	54.0	.389			55.0	.300						
1911	54.0	.389	49.5	$0.390	55.0	.300	55.0	$0.333				
1912	50.0	.420	49.5	.390	55.0	.300	55.0	.333	51.0	$0.382	54.0	$0.333
1913	50.0	.420	54.0	.390	55.0	.300			51.0	.382	54.0	.333
1914	50.0	.420			52.5	.325						
1917			48.0	.550	48.0	.420	55.0	.420				
1918			48.0	.650	48.0	.420	55.0	.725				
1919			44.0	.800	48.0	.500	55.0	.850				
1920			44.0	1.000	48.0	.750	50.0	.900				
1921			44.0	.900	48.0	.750						
1922			44.0	[2] .830	48.0	.600						
1923			44.0	.930	48.0	.700						
1924			44.0	.950	48.0	.700						

[1] And specialists.   [2] More than 50 per cent received more.

TABLE **I–25.**—*Machinists, males, manufacturing and jobbing shops, 1907–1924, by city and year*

Year	Atlanta, Ga.		Birmingham, Ala.		Boston, Mass.		Chicago, Ill.	
	Hours per week	Rate per hour	Hours per week	Rate per hour	Hours per week	Rate per hour	Hours per week	Rate per hour
1907	60.0	$0.300	60.0	$0.275				
1908	60.0	.325	60.0	.275				
1909	60.0	.325	60.0	.300				
1910	60.0	.325	60.0	.300				
1911	60.0	.350	60.0	.325				
1912	60.0	.350	60.0	.325				
1913	60.0	.350	60.0	.350				
1914	54.0	.350	60.0	.350	54.0	$0.389	54.0	$0.417
1915	54.0	.400	60.0	.400	54.0	.389	54.0	.417
1916	54.0	.400	54.0	.450	54.0	.389	54.0	.450
1917	54.0	.400	54.0	.475	50.0	.500		
1918	54.0	1.550	54.0	.600	50.0	.550		
1919	54.0	.700	48.0	2.680	48.0	.650		
1920	54.0	.800	48.0	3.785	48.0	.750		
1921			48.0	2.750	48.0	.750		
1922			48.0	.750	48.0	.900		
1923			48.0	.750	44.0	.800		
1924			45.0	.750	44.0	.800		

Year	Cincinnati, Ohio		Denver, Colo.		Detroit, Mich.		New Orleans, La.	
1907			54.0	$0.375			54.0	$0.333
1908			54.0	.375			54.0	.333
1909			54.0	.375			54.0	.389
1910			54.0	.375			54.0	.389
1911			54.0	.375			54.0	.389
1912			54.0	.400	54.0	$0.333	54.0	.389
1913			54.0	.400	54.0	.350	54.0	.389
1914	54.0	$0.325	54.0	.400	54.0	.350	54.0	.389
1915	54.0	.325	54.0	.400	54.0	.350	54.0	.389
1916	48.0	.325	54.0	.400	54.0	.400	48.0	.438
1917	48.0	.420	51.0	.425	54.0	.450	48.0	.500
1918	48.0	.420	48.0	.520	54.0	.725	48.0	.688
1919	48.0	.550	48.0	.680	54.0	.850	48.0	.800
1920	48.0	.750	48.0	.720			48.0	.800
1921	48.0	.850	48.0	.850			44.0	.800
1922	48.0	.800	48.0	.720			44.0	.750
1923	48.0	.800						
1924	48.0	.800						

Year	New York, N. Y.		Philadelphia, Pa.[4]		St. Louis, Mo.		San Francisco, Calif.	
1907	54.0	$0.361	54.0	$0.333	54.0	$0.300		
1908	54.0	.361	54.0	.333	54.0	.330		
1909	54.0	.361	54.0	.333	54.0	.330		
1910	54.0	.361	54.0	.333	54.0	.330		
1911	54.0	.361	54.0	.333	54.0	.330		
1912	48.0	.406	54.0	.333	54.0	.330		
1913	48.0	.406	54.0	.333	54.0	.330		
1914	48.0	.406	54.0	.333	54.0	.370		
1915	48.0	.406	54.0	.350	54.0	.370		
1916	48.0	.469	54.0	.450	54.0	.370		
1917	48.0	.563	48.0	.480	54.0	.440		
1918	48.0	.730	48.0	.725	48.0	.600		
1919	48.0	.730	48.0	.800	48.0	2.700	44.0	$0.800
1920	48.0	.800	48.0	.800	48.0	2.850		
1921	48.0	.800	48.0	5.750	48.0	.900	44.0	.900
1922	48.0	.800	48.0	.750	48.0	5.700	44.0	.900
1923	48.0	.800	48.0	.750				
1924	48.0	.850	48.0	.750				

1 70 cents Aug. 1.
2 More than 50 per cent received more.
5 More than 25 per cent received more.
3 85 per cent received 82.5 to 90 cents.
4 Type of machinist not specified, 1907–1912.

TABLE I–26.—*Machinists, males, railroad shops, 1907–1922, by city and year*

Year	Atlanta, Ga.		Birmingham, Ala.		Boston, Mass.		Chicago, Ill.	
	Hours per week	Rate per hour	Hours per week	Rate per hour	Hours per week	Rate per hour	Hours per week	Rate per hour
1907	60.0	$0.300						
1908	54.0	.320						
1909	54.0	.320						
1910	54.0	.355						
1911	54.0	.380	54.0	$0.390				
1912	54.0	.380	54.0	.390	54.0	$0.285	49.5	$0.395
1913	54.0	.400	54.0	.390	¹ 53.0	.285	49.5	.395
1914	54.0	.410	54.0	.410	53.0	.305	50.0	.410
1915	54.0	.410	54.0	.410	53.0	.305	50.0	.410
1916	54.0	.420	54.0	.410	¹ 53.0	.305	54.0	.435
1917	54.0	.505	54.0	.435	53.0	.325	54.0	.435
1918	48.0	.680	48.0	.680	48.0	.680	48.0	.680
1919	48.0	.720	48.0	.720	48.0	.720	48.0	.720
1920	48.0	.850	48.0	.850	² 48.0	.850	² 48.0	.850
1921	48.0	.850	48.0	.850	48.0	.850	48.0	.850
1922	48.0	.770	48.0	.770	48.0	.770	48.0	.770

Year	Cincinnati, Ohio		Denver, Colo.		Detroit, Mich.		New Orleans, La.	
1907	54.0	$0.320	54.0	$0.400				
1908	54.0	.320	54.0	.400				
1909	54.0	.320	54.0	.400				
1910	54.0	.335	54.0	.400				
1911	54.0	.366	48.0	.410				
1912	54.0	.366	48.0	.410	60.0	$0.345	54.0	$0.400
1913	54.0	.386	48.0	.410	54.0	.355	54.0	.400
1914	54.0	.386	48.0	.410	54.0	.355	54.0	.410
1915	54.0	.386	48.0	.410	54.0	.355	54.0	.410
1916	54.0	.426	48.0	.420	54.0	.355	54.0	.410
1917	54.0	.426	48.0	.500	54.0	.355	54.0	.420
1918	48.0	.680	48.0	.680	48.0	.680	48.0	.680
1919	48.0	.720	48.0	.720	48.0	.720	48.0	.720
1920	48.0	.850	² 48.0	.850	48.0	.850	² 48.0	.850
1921	48.0	.850	48.0	.850	48.0	.850	48.0	.850
1922	48.0	.770	48.0	.770	48.0	.770	48.0	.770

Year	New York, N. Y		Philadelphia, Pa.		St. Louis, Mo.		San Francisco, Calif.	
1907					54.0	$0.360		
1908					54.0	.360		
1909					54.0	.360		
1910					54.0	.390		
1911					54.0	.390		
1912			55.0	$0.350	54.0	.390		
1913			55.0	.350	54.0	.415		
1914			54.0	.350	54.0	.415		
1915			54.0	.350	54.0	.415		
1916			54.0	.370	54.0	.415		
1917			54.0	.420	54.0	.465		
1918			48.0	.680	48.0	.680		
1919	48.0	$0.720	48.0	.720	48.0	.720		
1920	² 48.0	.850	48.0	.850	² 48.0	.850	² 48.0	.850
1921	48.0	.850	48.0	.850	48.0	.850	48.0	.850
1922	48.0	.770	48.0	.780	48.0	.770	48.0	.770

¹ Paid for 54.   ² Paid for 49.

TABLE I-27.—*Machinists, males, machine shops, 1923, 1925, and 1927, State and year*

Year	Alabama		California		Illinois		Louisiana	
	Hours per week	Rate per hour	Hours per week	Rate per hour	Hours per week	Rate per hour	Hours per week	Rate per hour
1923	54.9	$0.641	44.7	$0.793	50.4	$0.674	54.6	$0.804
1925	53.2	.673	45.3	.831	49.5	.775	47.9	.806
1927	52.3	.708	45.2	.844	48.5	.794	45.1	.866

	Maryland		Massachusetts		Michigan		Missouri	
1923	47.3	$0.637	48.8	$0.597	51.4	$0.659	50.3	$0.718
1925	47.8	.655	48.8	.654	50.4	.702	50.8	.727
1927	47.9	.686	47.5	.702	52.0	.736	48.6	.745

	New Hampshire		New York		Ohio		Pennsylvania	
1923	53.4	$0.631	48.4	$0.728	50.6	$0.669	51.1	$0.705
1925	53.5	.637	48.5	.710	52.1	.675	51.5	.711
1927	51.5	.679	49.6	.743	50.6	.678	50.7	.734

TABLE I-28.—*Millwrights, 1840–1900, by year and State*

Year and State	Sex	Lowest, highest, and average—Hours per week	Lowest, highest, and average—Rate per day (dollars)
1840: New York	M.	60-60-60	1.50-1.75-1.63
1841: New York	M.	60-60-60	1.50-1.50-1.50
1843: New York	M.	60-60-60	1.38-1.50-1.46
1844: New York	M.	60-60-60	1.38-1.50-1.44
1845: New York	M.	60-60-60	1.50-1.50-1.50
1846: New York	M.	60-60-60	1.50-1.50-1.50
1847: New York	M.	60-60-60	1.50-1.50-1.50
1848: New York	M.	60-60-60	1.25-1.63-1.50
1849: New York	M.	60-60-60	1.63-1.63-1.63
1851: New York	M.	60-60-60	1.63-1.63-1.63
Pennsylvania	M.	60-60-60	1.50-1.50-1.50
1852: Pennsylvania	M.	60-60-60	1.70-1.70-1.70
1853: New York	M.	60-60-60	1.38-1.38-1.38
Pennsylvania	M.	60-60-60	1.90-1.90-1.90
1854: New York	M.	60-60-60	1.50-1.50-1.50
Pennsylvania	M.	60-60-60	2.00-2.00-2.00
1855: New York	M.	60-60-60	1.25-1.50-1.38
Pennsylvania	M.	60-60-60	2.00-2.00-2.00
1856: Pennsylvania	M.	60-60-60	2.00-2.00-2.00
1857: Pennsylvania	M.	60-60-60	2.00-2.00-2.00
1858: Pennsylvania	M.	60-60-60	2.00-2.00-2.00
1859: Pennsylvania	M.	60-60-60	2.00-2.00-2.00
1860: Pennsylvania	M.	60-60-60	2.00-2.00-2.00
1861: Pennsylvania	M.	60-60-60	2.00-2.00-2.00
1862: Pennsylvania	M.	60-60-60	2.00-2.00-2.00
1863: Pennsylvania	M.	60-60-60	2.00-2.00-2.00
1864: Pennsylvania	M.	60-60-60	2.30-2.30-2.30
1865: Pennsylvania	M.	60-60-60	3.00-3.00-3.00
1866: Pennsylvania	M.	60-60-60	3.70-3.70-3.70
1867: Pennsylvania	M.	60-60-60	3.70-3.70-3.70
1868: New York	M.	60-60-60	2.00-2.25-2.19
Pennsylvania	M.	60-60-60	3.70-3.70-3.70
1869: New Hampshire	M.	(1)	2.50-2.75-2.63
Pennsylvania	M.	60-60-60	3.30-3.30-3.30
1870: Pennsylvania	M.	60-60-60	3.50-3.50-3.50
1871: Massachusetts	M.	59-59-59	2.00-2.00-2.00
Pennsylvania	M.	60-60-60	3.50-3.50-3.50
1872: Pennsylvania	M. (1)	60-60-60	4.00-4.00-4.00
Do.	M.	60-60-60	3.75-3.75-3.75
1873: Pennsylvania	M.	60-60-60	3.00-3.50-3.25
1874: Delaware	M.	60-60-60	2.33-2.33-2.33
Pennsylvania	M.	60-60-60	3.00-3.00-3.00
1875: New York	M.	60-60-60	2.00-2.25-2.08
Pennsylvania	M.	60-60-60	2.80-2.80-2.80
1876: New Hampshire	M.	66-66-66	2.70-2.70-2.70
New York	M.	60-60-60	2.00-2.25-2.13
Pennsylvania	M.	60-60-60	2.00-3.33-2.52

1 Not reported.

TABLE I-28.—*Millwrights, 1840–1900, by year and State*—Continued

Year and State	Sex	Hours per week	Rate per day (dollars)	Year and State	Sex	Hours per week	Rate per day (dollars)
1877:				1889—Continued.			
New York	M.	60–60–60	2.00–2.25–2.08	Pennsylvania	M.	60–60–60	2.00–5.50–3.10
Ohio	M.	(1)	2.25–3.21–2.41	Virginia	M.	60–60–60	3.00–3.00–3.00
Pennsylvania	M.	60–60–60	3.00–3.85–3.21	West Virginia	M.	(1)	2.00–2.25–2.13
1878:				1890:			
Connecticut	M.	72–72–72	3.00–3.00–3.30	Michigan	M.	60–60–60	2.00–5.00–2.67
New York	M.	60–60–60	2.00–2.25–2.10	New York	M.	60–60–60	1.50–3.19–2.42
Ohio	M.	(1)	2.13–2.13–2.13	Pennsylvania	M.	60–60–60	2.80–2.80–2.80
Pennsylvania	M.	54–66–60	2.00–3.20–2.49	1891:			
1879:				Missouri	M.	(1)	3.16–3.16–3.16
New Jersey	M.	60–60–60	2.50–2.50–2.50	New York	M.	60–60–60	1.25–3.50–2.33
New York	M.	60–60–60	2.00–2.00–2.00	Ohio	M.	54–72–60	2.00–3.25–2.49
Pennsylvania	M.	60–60–60	1.25–3.33–2.25	Pennsylvania	M.	60–60–60	2.80–2.80–2.80
1880:				Wisconsin	M.	60–60–60	2.25–3.25–2.75
New York	M.	60–60–60	2.00–2.50–2.25	1892:			
Pennsylvania	M.	60–60–60	2.50–2.50–2.50	Indiana	M.	60–60–60	2.50–2.50–2.50
1881:				Michigan	M.	60–60–60	1.75–4.00–2.65
New Jersey	M.	60–60–60	1.75–2.25–2.00	Minnesota	M.	60–60–60	2.50–2.50–2.50
New York	M.	60–60–60	2.00–2.50–2.25	Ohio	(1)	54–72–61	2.25–5.00–2.99
Ohio	M.	60–60–60	2.00–5.00–2.52	Pennsylvania	M.	60–60–60	2.00–3.60–2.73
Pennsylvania	M.	60–60–60	2.50–2.50–2.50	Wisconsin	M.	60–60–60	2.75–2.75–2.75
1882:				1893:			
New York	M.	60–60–60	2.00–2.50–2.25	Massachusetts	M.	(1)	2.85–2.85–2.85
Ohio	(1)	60–60–60	2.25–8.00–3.10	Minnesota	M.	60–60–60	2.50–2.50–2.50
Pennsylvania	M.	60–60–60	2.50–2.50–2.50	Missouri	M.	60–60–60	3.00–3.00–3.00
1883:				Ohio	M.	50–60–59	1.50–3.35–2.37
Michigan	M.	(1)	2.00–5.00–2.71	Pennsylvania	M.	60–60–60	2.00–3.55–2.81
New Jersey	M.	60–60–60	1.90–3.00–2.05	Wisconsin	M.	60–60–60	2.25–3.25–2.75
New York	M.	60–60–60	2.00–2.50–2.25	1894:			
Pennsylvania	M.	60–60–60	2.80–2.80–2.80	Indiana	M.	48–72–60	2.50–3.00–2.88
1884:				Iowa	M.	54–60–57	2.00–2.25–2.13
Iowa	M.	63–63–63	2.60–2.60–2.60	Massachusetts	M.	(1)	2.85–2.85–2.85
Michigan	M.	(1)	2.00–5.00–2.86	Michigan	M.	60–60–60	1.75–1.75–1.75
New Jersey	M.	60–60–60	2.67–2.67–2.67	Minnesota	M.	60–60–60	2.25–2.25–2.25
New York	M.	60–60–60	2.00–2.25–2.13	Ohio	M.	30–72–59	1.67–3.17–2.39
Ohio	M.	60–60–60	2.42–2.50–2.49	Pennsylvania	M.	60–60–60	2.20–2.80–2.45
Pennsylvania	M.	60–60–60	2.80–2.80–2.80	Wisconsin	M.	60–60–60	2.25–2.25–2.25
West Virginia	M.	60–60–60	2.25–2.25–2.25	1895:			
1885:				Massachusetts	M.	60–60–60	2.85–3.00–2.93
Delaware	M.	60–60–60	2.25–2.50–2.37	Michigan	M.	60–60–60	1.75–1.75–1.75
Illinois	M.	66–66–66	2.85–3.50–3.06	Minnesota	M.	60–60–60	2.25–2.56–2.41
Indiana	M.	60–72–61	2.10–3.00–2.29	New Hampshire	M.	60–66–63	2.00–3.00–2.50
Kentucky	M.	60–60–60	5.00–5.00–5.00	New York	M.	60–60–60	2.25–2.25–2.25
Massachusetts	M.	60–60–60	2.50–3.00–2.67	Ohio	M.	54–72–61	1.50–5.00–2.60
Michigan	M.	66–66–66	1.50–3.25–2.28	Pennsylvania	M.	60–60–60	1.60–2.80–2.32
Minnesota	M.	72–72–72	2.62–2.62–2.62	Wisconsin	M.	60–60–60	2.25–2.25–2.25
New Jersey	M.	60–60–60	2.00–3.33–2.71	Do	(1)	60–72–61	1.54–3.33–2.36
New York	M.	60–60–60	2.00–2.25–2.11	1896:			
Ohio	M.	60–72–65	1.60–3.60–2.32	Connecticut	M.	60–60–60	2.50–2.50–2.50
Pennsylvania	M.	60–60–60	2.50–4.00–3.18	Delaware	M.	72–72–72	2.25–2.50–2.38
Virginia	M.	48–60–52	2.25–2.25–2.25	Kansas	M.	60–60–60	2.33–2.33–2.33
Wisconsin	M.	72–72–72	2.00–2.00–2.00	Michigan	M.	60–60–60	1.75–1.75–1.75
1886:				Minnesota	M.	60–60–60	1.75–2.56–2.27
Delaware	M.	72–72–72	2.00–2.25–2.13	New York	M.	60–60–60	3.00–3.50–3.25
New York	M.	60–60–60	2.00–2.25–2.13	Ohio	M.	54–64–58	1.92–3.17–2.55
Ohio	M.	(1)	2.24–2.24–2.24	Pennsylvania	M.	54–60–54	2.50–2.67–2.67
Pennsylvania	M.	60–60–60	2.50–2.50–2.50	West Virginia	M.	60–60–60	2.25–2.25–2.25
1887:				Wisconsin	M.	60–72–68	2.00–2.25–2.08
Connecticut	M.	(1)	3.00–3.00–3.00	1897:			
New York	M.	60–60–60	2.00–2.25–2.08	Kansas	M.	70–77–72	1.85–2.75–2.37
North Carolina	M.	60–72–66	1.50–3.00–2.25	Michigan	M.	(1)	2.25–2.25–2.25
Ohio	M.	60–60–60	2.50–3.00–2.92	Ohio	(1)	60–72–61	1.50–5.00–2.43
Pennsylvania	M.	60–60–60	2.15–3.90–2.52	Pennsylvania	M.	(1)	1.86–2.47–2.06
1888:				Virginia	M.	60–72–61	1.50–2.00–1.57
Kansas	M.	60–72–61	2.00–3.55–2.68	1898:			
New Jersey	M.	(1)	2.50–2.50–2.50	Iowa	(1)	(1)	2.50–2.50–2.50
New York	M.	53–60–58	2.00–5.00–2.89	Kansas	M.	60–60–60	2.75–3.00–2.88
Pennsylvania	M.	60–60–60	2.80–2.80–2.80	Michigan	M.	(1)	1.90–2.66–2.20
1889:				Ohio	M.	(1)	1.44–2.70–1.97
Alabama	M.	60–60–60	4.45–4.45–4.45	Pennsylvania	M.	(1)	2.50–3.75–3.30
Delaware	M.	60–60–60	2.25–2.25–2.25	1899:			
Indiana	M.	60–60–60	2.75–2.75–2.75	New York	M.	60–60–60	2.00–3.80–2.27
Kansas	M.	54–72–66	1.75–3.00–2.50	North Carolina	M.	72–72–72	2.00–2.00–2.00
Michigan	M.	60–60–60	1.75–3.00–2.27	Ohio	M.	(1)	1.66–3.12–2.39
Missouri	M.	(1)	3.00–3.50–3.25	Pennsylvania	M.	(1)	1.75–4.97–3.09
New York	M.	60–60–60	2.00–2.45–2.21	1900:			
Ohio	M.	59–80–62	1.30–4.17–2.77	New York	M.	60–60–60	2.00–3.00–2.31

1 Not reported.

TABLE I-29.—*Millwrights, males, flour mills, 1890-1907, by geographic division and year*

Year	North Atlantic		North Central		South Central		Western	
	Hours per week	Rate per hour	Hours per week	Rate per hour	Hours per week	Rate per hour	Hours per week	Rate per hour
1890	60. 0	$0. 250	63. 5	$0. 256	60. 0	$0. 300	60. 0	$0. 350
1891	60. 0	. 250	63. 8	. 255	60. 0	. 300	60. 0	. 350
1892	60. 0	. 250	63. 5	. 257	60. 0	. 300	60. 0	. 350
1893	60. 0	. 250	62. 8	. 262	60. 0	. 250	60. 0	. 350
1894	60. 0	. 250	63. 4	. 257	60. 0	. 250	60. 0	. 300
1895	60. 0	. 263	63. 6	. 253	60. 0	. 250	60. 0	. 300
1896	60. 0	. 263	63. 3	. 253	60. 0	. 250	60. 0	. 300
1897	60. 0	. 263	64. 1	. 252	60. 0	. 300	60. 0	. 300
1898	60. 0	. 263	63. 2	. 259	60. 0	. 300	60. 0	. 300
1899	60. 0	. 263	63. 3	. 259	60. 0	. 300	60. 0	. 300
1900	60. 0	. 263	63. 5	. 263	60. 0	. 300	60. 0	. 350
1901	60. 0	. 288	63. 7	. 263	60. 0	. 350	60. 0	. 350
1902	60. 0	. 288	63. 7	. 267	60. 0	. 317	60. 0	. 350
1903	60. 0	. 308	61. 1	. 286	60. 0	. 300	50. 7	. 464
1904	57. 8	. 389	61. 1	. 299	59. 6	. 307	65. 0	. 298
1905	57. 9	. 394	60. 4	. 287	59. 7	. 293	64. 8	. 326
1906	57. 0	. 421	60. 3	. 291	59. 8	. 303	66. 0	. 334
1907	57. 0	. 434	59. 9	. 299	58. 2	. 334	66. 0	. 351

TABLE I-30.—*Millwrights, males, slaughtering and meat packing, 1917-1927, by districts*

Year	District 1, Chicago		District 2 [1]		District 3 [2]		District 4 [3]	
	Hours per week	Rate per hour	Hours per week	Rate per hour	Hours per week	Rate per hour	Hours per week	Rate per hour
1917	(4)	$0. 366	(4)	$0. 338	(4)	$0. 344	(4)	$0. 357
1921	47. 9	. 659	48. 0	. 609	33. 7	. 605	48. 0	. 615
1923	51. 3	. 673	49. 8	. 598	51. 2	. 610	48. 0	. 640
1925	49. 0	. 701	48. 8	. 604	50. 3	. 624	48. 0	. 631
1927	48. 5	. 675	47. 8	. 613	50. 0	. 644	48. 2	. 621

Year	District 5 [5]		District 6 [6]		District 7 [7]		District 8 [8]	
1917	(4)	$0. 339	(4)	$0. 413				
1921	54. 9	. 551	48. 0	. 632				
1923	51. 7	. 568	48. 7	. 686				
1925	49. 7	. 591	50. 0	. 688			48. 8	$0. 644
1927	49. 4	. 617	49. 0	. 651	57. 5	$0. 617	48. 0	. 642

[1] Kansas City, Omaha, St. Louis, East St. Louis, and St. Joseph.
[2] Years 1917 and 1921, St. Paul, Milwaukee, and Ottumwa; year 1923, Austin (Minn.), Cedar Rapids, Milwaukee, Ottumwa, and St. Paul; years 1925 and 1927, Austin (Minn.), Cedar Rapids, Des Moines, Mason City, Milwaukee, Ottumwa, Sioux City, Sioux Falls, St. Paul, Topeka, Waterloo, and Wichita.
[3] Years 1917, 1921, and 1923, Oklahoma City and Fort Worth; years 1925 and 1927, Oklahoma City, Dallas, Fort Worth, and Houston.
[4] Not reported.
[5] Years 1917 and 1921, Buffalo, Cleveland, Cincinnati, and Indianapolis; years 1923, 1925, and 1927, Buffalo, Cincinnati, Cleveland, Detroit, Indianapolis, and Pittsburgh.
[6] Years 1917, 1921, and 1923, Boston, New York, and Philadelphia; years 1925 and 1927, Boston, New Haven, New York, Philadelphia, and Springfield (Mass.).
[7] Years 1925 and 1927, Baltimore, Moultrie, and Jacksonville.
[8] Years 1925 and 1927, Denver, Los Angeles, Portland, San Francisco, Seattle, and Tacoma.

TABLE I-31.—*Molders, iron, 1843-1900, by year and State*

Year and State	Sex	Lowest, highest, and average—		Year and State	Sex	Lowest, highest, and average—	
		Hours per week	Rate per day (dollars)			Hours per week	Rate per day (dollars)
1843:				**1860:**			
New York	M.	60-60-60	0.83-1.33-1.15	Connecticut	M.	60-60-60	1.32-2.00-1.57
1844:				Illinois	M.	(1)	3.00-3.00-3.00
New York	M.	60-60-60	1.00-1.38-1.23	Maryland	M.	60-60-60	1.67-2.00-1.87
1845:				Massachusetts	M.	60-60-60	1.34-1.70-1.59
New York	M.	60-60-60	1.00-1.50-1.24	New York	M.	60-60-60	1.13-2.25-1.65
1846:				Pennsylvania	M.	60-60-60	1.50-1.84-1.68
New York	M.	60-60-60	1.00-1.50-1.31	**1861:**			
1847:				Connecticut	M.	60-60-60	1.33-2.00-1.56
New York	M.	60-60-60	1.00-1.75-1.39	Illinois	M.	(1)	3.50-3.50-3.50
1848:				Maryland	M.	60-60-60	1.50-2.00-1.75
New York	M.	60-60-60	1.25-1.75-1.39	Massachusetts	M.	60-60-60	1.42-1.70-1.59
1849:				New York	M.	60-60-60	1.13-2.25 :.74
Massachusetts	M.	60-60-60	1.42-1.83-1.56	Pennsylvania	M.	60-60-60	1.50-2.00-1.82
New York	M.	60-60-60	1.25-1.75-1.44	**1862:**			
1850:				Connecticut	M.	60-60-60	1.50-2.00-1.60
Illinois	M.	(1)	3.00-3.00-3.00	Illinois	M.	(1)	4.50-4.50-4.50
Massachusetts	M.	60-60-60	1.42-1.83-1.56	Maryland	M.	60-60-60	1.67-2.25-1.83
New York	M.	60-60-60	1.00-1.75-1.39	Massachusetts	M.	60-60-60	1.42-1.70-1.58
1851:				New York	M.	60-60-60	1.13-2.25-1.66
Illinois	M.	(1)	3.00-3.00-3.00	Pennsylvania	M.	60-60-60	1.50-2.00-1.80
Massachusetts	M.	60-60-60	1.34-1.75-1.57	**1863:**			
New York	M.	60-60-60	1.00-2.00-1.41	Connecticut	M.	60-60-60	1.50-2.50-1.72
1852:				Illinois	M.	(1)	4.75-4.75-4.75
Illinois	M.	(1)	3.50-3.50-3.50	Maryland	M.	60-60-60	1.83-2.25-1.93
Massachusetts	M.	60-60-60	1.34-1.75-1.56	Massachusetts	M.	60-60-60	1.25-2.00-1.68
New York	M.	60-60-60	1.00-2.00-1.49	New York	M.	60-60-60	1.17-2.40-1.66
1853:				Pennsylvania	M.	60-60-60	1.50-2.20-1.93
Connecticut	M.	60-60-60	1.25-1.75-1.44	**1864:**			
Illinois	M.	(1)	3.50-3.50-3.50	Connecticut	M.	60-60-60	1.50-3.25-1.91
Massachusetts	M.	60-60-60	1.42-1.67-1.56	Illinois	M.	(1)	5.00-5.00-5.00
New York	M.	60-60-60	1.38-2.00-1.67	Maryland	M.	60-60-60	2.00-3.00-2.24
Pennsylvania	M.	60-60-60	1.50-1.50-1.50	Massachusetts	M.	60-60-60	1.30-2.00-1.85
1854:				New York	M.	60-60-60	1.13-3.10-1.88
Connecticut	M.	60-60-60	1.25-1.88-1.49	Pennsylvania	M.	60-60-60	1.84-2.50-2.20
Illinois	M.	(1)	3.50-3.50-3.50	**1865:**			
Massachusetts	M.	60-60-60	1.42-1.75-1.59	Connecticut	M.	60-60-60	1.67-3.25-2.28
New York	M.	60-60-60	1.00-2.13-1.59	Illinois	M.	(1)	5.00-5.00-5.00
Pennsylvania	M.	60-60-60	1.50-1.67-1.54	Maryland	M.	60-60-60	2.33-2.67-2.50
1855:				Massachusetts	M.	60-60-60	1.25-2.75-2.18
Connecticut	M.	60-60-60	1.38-2.00-1.61	Nebraska	M.	54-54-54	2.50-3.75-3.20
Illinois	M.	(1)	3.50-3.50-3.50	New York	M.	60-60-60	1.50-3.75-2.27
Maryland	M.	60-60-60	1.67-2.17-1.84	Pennsylvania	M.	60-60-60	2.17-3.00-2.77
Massachusetts	M.	60-60-60	1.42-1.78-1.61	**1866:**			
New York	M.	60-60-60	1.13-2.00-1.57	Connecticut	M.	60-60-60	1.50-3.25-2.29
Pennsylvania	M.	60-60-60	1.50-1.67-1.55	Illinois	M.	(1)	5.00-5.00-5.00
1856:				Maryland	M.	60-60-60	2.50-3.00-2.64
Connecticut	M.	60-60-60	1.33-1.75-1.55	Massachusetts	M.	60-60-60	1.35-2.75-2.36
Illinois	M.	(1)	3.50-3.50-3.50	New York	M.	60-60-60	1.38-3-95-2.35
Maryland	M.	60-60-60	1.67-2.17-1.89	Pennsylvania	M.	60-60-60	2.50-3.00-2.86
Massachusetts	M.	60-60-60	1.34-1.75-1.57	**1867:**			
New York	M.	60-60-60	1.13-2.25-1.63	Connecticut	M.	60-60-60	1.50-3.50-2.30
Pennsylvania	M.	60-60-60	1.50-1.84-1.56	Illinois	M.	(1)	4.50-4.50-4.50
1857:				Maryland	M.	60-60-60	2.50-3.00-2.03
Connecticut	M.	60-60-60	1.33-1.75-1.60	Massachusetts	M.	60-60-60	2.00-3.00-2.45
Illinois	M.	(1)	3.00-3.00-3.00	New York	M.	60-60-60	1.50-3.50-2.37
Maryland	M.	60-60-60	1.67-2.00-1.81	Pennsylvania	M.	60-60-60	2.50-3.00-2.76
Massachusetts	M.	60-60-60	1.34-1.75-1.59	**1868:**			
New York	M.	60-60-60	1.25-2.25-1.73	Connecticut	M.	60-60-60	1.67-3.50-2.37
Pennsylvania	M.	60-60-60	1.50-1.84-1.56	Illinois	M.	(1)	4.00-4.00-4.00
1858:				Maryland	M.	60-60-60	2.50-3.00-2.44
Connecticut	M.	60-60-60	1.33-1.75-1.60	Massachusetts	M.	60-60-60	2.00-3.00-2.44
Illinois	M.	(1)	3.00-3.00-3.00	New York	M.	60-60-60	1.50-3.60-2.42
Maryland	M.	60-60-60	1.67-2.00-1.85	Pennsylvania	M.	60-60-60	2.50-2.60-2.55
Massachusetts	M.	60-60-60	1.30-1."0-1.45	**1869:**			
New York	M.	60-60-60	1.00-2.25-1.72	Connecticut	M.	60-60-60	1.67-3.50-2.30
Pennsylvania	M.	60-60-60	1.50-1.84-1.58	Illinois	M.	(1)	3.75-3.75-3.75
1859:				Maryland	M.	60-60-60	2.50-3.00-2.67
Connecticut	M.	60-60-60	1.33-2.00-1.60	Massachusetts	M.	60-60-60	1.50-3.00-2.36
Illinois	M.	(1)	3.00-3.00-3.00	New York	M.	60-60-60	1.50-3.60-2.48
Maryland	M.	60-60-60	1.67-2.00-1.85	Pennsylvania	M.	60-60-60	2.50-2.60-2.54
Massachusetts	M.	60-60-60	1.34-2.00-1.59	**1870:**			
New York	M.	60-60-60	1.13-2.25-1.65	California	M.	60-60-60	3.00-4.00-3.72
Pennsylvania	M.	60-60-60	1.50-1.84-1.55	Connecticut	M.	60-60-60	1.75-3.50-2.49

1 Not reported.

TABLE I-31.—*Molders, iron, 1843–1900, by year and State*—Continued

Year and State	Sex	Hours per week	Rate per day (dollars)	Year and State	Sex	Hours per week	Rate per day (dollars)
1870—Continued.				**1876:**			
Illinois	M.	60–60–60	2.50–3.75–3.07	California	M.	60–60–60	3.25–4.25–3.52
Louisiana	M.	60–60–60	3.25–3.50–3.44	Connecticut	M.	60–60–60	1.80–3.00–2.35
Maryland	M.	60–60–60	2.00–3.33–2.33	Illinois	M.	60–60–60	2.50–3.25–2.70
Massachusetts	M.	60–60–60	1.33–4.50–2.63	Louisiana	M.	60–60–60	2.75–3.00–2.88
Minnesota	M.	60–60–60	2.50–3.00–2.72	Maryland	M.	60–60–60	2.00–3.00–2.28
Missouri	M.	60–60–60	3.00–3.00–3.00	Massachusetts	M.	60–60–60	1.50–3.15–2.14
New York	M.	60–60–60	1.50–3.70–2.60	Minnesota	M.	60–60–60	2.50–3.00–2.72
Ohio	M.	60–60–60	3.33–3.33–3.33	Missouri	M.	54–54–54	2.65–2.65–2.65
Pennsylvania	M.	60–60–60	1.67–3.50–2.54	New Hampshire	M.	72–72–72	1.25–3.33–2.03
1871:				New York	M.	60–60–60	1.50–3.30–2.43
California	M.	60–60–60	3.00–3.75–3.36	Ohio	M.	60–60–60	2.00–2.83–2.56
Connecticut	M.	60–60–60	1.75–3.75–2.38	Pennsylvania	M.	60–60–60	1.25–3.08–2.03
Illinois	M.	60–60–60	2.50–3.75–3.40	Virginia	M.	60–60–60	2.00–2.00–2.00
Maryland	M.	60–60–60	2.00–3.33–2.35	**1877:**			
Massachusetts	M.	53–60–58	1.33–4.50–3.06	California	M.	60–60–60	3.25–4.00–3.50
Minnesota	M.	60–60–60	2–50–3.00–2.72	Connecticut	M.	60–60–60	1.40–2.85–2.16
Missouri	M.	60–60–60	3.00–3.00–3.00	Illinois	M.	60–60–60	2.50–3.25–2.63
New York	M.	60–60–60	1.50–3.70–2.58	Louisiana	M.	60–60–60	2.50–3.50–2.88
Ohio	M.	60–60–60	3.33–3.33–3.33	Maryland	M.	60–60–60	2.00–2.50–2.17
Pennsylvania	M.	60–60–60	2.00–3.50–2.52	Massachusetts	M.	60–60–60	1.33–3.15–2.04
1872:				Minnesota	M.	60–60–60	2.50–3.00–2.72
California	M.	60–60–60	3.25–3.75–3.53	Missouri	M.	54–54–54	2.50–2.50–2.50
Connecticut	M.	60–60–60	1.75–3.75–2.52	New Hampshire	M.	72–72–72	1.25–3.33–1.96
Illinois	M.	60–60–60	2.50–3.75–3.32	New Jersey	M.	55–55–55	1.30–2.75–1.58
Louisiana	M.	60–60–60	2.75–3.75–3.30	New York	M.	60–60–60	1.50–3.20–2.30
Maryland	M.	60–60–60	2.00–3.33–2.36	Ohio	M.	48–63–59	1.61–5.00–2.53
Massachusetts	M.	54–60–60	1.50–5.45–2.55	Pennsylvania	M.	48–60–56	1.70–3.45–2.30
Minnesota	M.	60–60–60	2.50–3.00–2.72	Virginia	M.	60–60–60	2.00–2.00–2.00
Missouri	M.	60–60–60	3.00–3.00–3.00	**1878:**			
New Hampshire	M.	72–72–72	1.00–4.00–1.88	California	M.	60–60–60	3.25–4.00–3.50
New York	M.	60–60–60	1.50–3.80–2.65	Connecticut	M.	60–60–60	1.40–2.75–2.04
Ohio	M.	60–60–60	2.00–5.00–3.49	Illinois	M.	60–60–60	2.25–3.50–2.55
Pennsylvania	M.	60–60–60	1.90–3.50–2.63	Louisiana	M.	60–60–60	2.50–3.50–2.88
1873:				Maryland	M.	60–60–60	2.00–2.50–2.18
California	M.	60–60–60	3.25–4.50–3.68	Massachusetts	M.	60–60–60	1.25–3.15–2.23
Connecticut	M.	60–60–60	2.00–3.25–2.53	Minnesota	M.	60–60–60	2.50–3.00–2.72
Illinois	M.	60–60–60	2.50–3.50–3.38	Missouri	M.	54–54–54	2.50–2.50–2.50
Louisiana	M.	60–60–60	2.75–3.75–3.25	New Hampshire	M.	72–72–72	1.00–3.33–1.95
Maryland	M.	60–60–60	2.00–3.33–2.36	New Jersey	M.	(¹)	2.00–2.00–2.00
Massachusetts	M.	60–60–60	1.50–4.00–2.42	New York	M.	60–60–60	1.50–3.20–2.29
Minnesota	M.	60–60–60	2.50–3.00–2.72	Ohio	M.	60–60–60	1.83–2.83–2.44
Missouri	M.	60–60–60	2.75–2.75–2.75	Pennsylvania	M.	48–60–58	.76–2.75–1.95
New Hampshire	M.	72–72–72	1.00–3.50–1.90	Virginia	M.	60–60–60	1.75–1.75–1.75
New Jersey	M.	(¹)	3.33–5.00–3.65	**1879:**			
New York	M.	60–60–60	1.60–3.80–2.64	California	M.	60–60–60	3.00–4.00–3.43
Ohio	M.	60–60–60	3.33–3.33–3.33	Connecticut	M.	60–60–60	1.40–2.50–1.94
Pennsylvania	M.	60–60–60	1.90–3.50–2.52	Illinois	M.	60–60–60	2.25–3.50–2.47
1874:				Do	M.	(¹)	3.50–3.50–3.50
California	M.	60–60–60	3.25–4.00–3.59	Louisiana	M.	60–60–60	2.50–3.00–2.75
Connecticut	M.	60–60–60	2.00–3.25–2.58	Maryland	M.	60–60–60	2.00–2.50–2.18
Illinois	M.	60–60–60	2.50–3.50–3.14	Massachusetts	M.	60–60–60	1.25–3.50–2.08
Louisiana	M.	60–60–60	3.25–3.75–3.42	Minnesota	M.	60–60–60	2.50–3.00–2.72
Maryland	M.	60–60–60	2.00–3.33–2.33	Missouri	M.	54–54–54	2.00–2.50–2.42
Massachusetts	M.	60–60–60	1.50–3.50–2.31	New Hampshire	M.	72–72–72	1.00–3.00–2.08
Minnesota	M.	54–54–54	2.50–3.00–2.72	New Jersey	M.	60–60–60	1.40–2.50–2.13
Missouri	M.	60–60–60	2.75–2.75–2.75	New York	M.	60–60–60	1.40–3.00–2.25
New Hampshire	M.	72–72–72	1.25–4.08–2.01	Ohio	M.	60–60–60	1.67–3.15–2.21
New York	M.	60–60–60	1.50–3.50–2.44	Pennsylvania	M.	54–66–59	1.00–3.33–2.04
Ohio	M.	60–60–60	2.25–3.00–2.79	Virginia	M.	60–60–60	1.50–1.80–1.67
Pennsylvania	M.	60–60–60	1.25–3.25–2.28	**1880:**			
Virginia	M.	60–60–60	2.00–2.25–2.11	California	M.	60–60–60	3.00–3.80–3.51
1875:				Connecticut	M.	60–60–60	1.50–2.50–1.94
California	M.	60–60–60	3.25–4.25–3.59	Illinois	M.	54–60–59	1.50–3.50–2.21
Connecticut	M.	60–60–60	1.80–3.25–2.49	Louisiana	M.	60–60–60	2.50–3.00–2.75
Illinois	M.	60–60–60	3.00–3.25–3.04	Maryland	M.	60–60–60	2.00–2.75–2.22
Louisiana	M.	60–60–60	3.25–3.25–3.25	Massachusetts	M.	60–60–60	1.25–3.00–2.08
Maryland	M.	60–60–60	2.00–3.00–2.26	Minnesota	M.	60–60–60	2.50–3.00–2.72
Massachusetts	M.	60–60–60	1.50–3.30–2.28	Missouri	M.	54–60–58	2.30–2.40–2.33
Minnesota	M.	60–60–60	2.50–3.00–2.72	New Hampshire	M.	72–72–72	1.25–3.00–2.10
Missouri	M.	54–54–54	2.75–2.75–2.75	New Jersey	M.	60–60–60	1.50–3.25–2.16
New Hampshire	M.	72–72–72	1.37–3.50–1.99	New York	M.	60–60–60	1.40–3.00–2.16
New York	M.	60–60–60	1.50–3.40–2.44	Ohio	M.	60–60–60	2.00–3.15–2.21
Ohio	M.	60–60–60	2.00–3.00–2.67	Pennsylvania	M.	48–60–60	1.40–3.00–2.29
Pennsylvania	M.	60–60–60	1.55–3.25–1.90	Virginia	M.	60–60–60	1.75–2.00–1.87
Virginia	M.	60–60–60	2.00–2.25–2.11				

¹ Not reported.

TABLE I–31.—*Molders, iron, 1843–1900, by year and State*—Continued

Year and State	Sex	Hours per week	Rate per day (dollars)	Year and State	Sex	Hours per week	Rate per day (dollars)
1881:				**1885:**			
California	M.	60–60–60	2.75–3.80–3.41	California	M.	60–60–60	2.75–3.80–3.41
Colorado	M.	60–60–60	3.00–8.00–3.00	Connecticut	M.	54–60–60	1.11–2.75–1.52
Connecticut	M.	60–60–60	1.45–2.75–1.74	Delaware	M.	60–60–60	2.25–2.50–2.37
Georgia	M.	60–60–60	3.00–3.00–3.00	Illinois	M.	60–60–60	2.00–4.00–2.98
Illinois	M.	60–60–60	2.00–3.50–2.35	Indiana	M.	60–60–60	1.15–3.00–1.87
Kentucky	M.	60–60–60	2.25–3.00–2.69	Kansas	M.	60–60–60	2.25–2.50–2.39
Louisiana	M.	60–60–60	2.50–3.00–2.75	Kentucky	M.	60–60–60	2.00–2.75–2.24
Maryland	M.	60–60–60	2.00–2.50–2.32	Louisiana	M.	60–60–60	2.50–3.00–2.75
Massachusetts	M.	60–60–60	1.25–3.00–2.05	Maryland	M.	60–60–60	2.00–2.50–2.36
Michigan	M.	59–59–59	2.10–2.10–2.10	Massachusetts	M.	59–60–59	1.50–3.20–2.77
Minnesota	M.	60–66–62	2.50–3.00–2.64	Michigan	M.	60–60–60	.55–5.00–2.26
Missouri	M.	54–60–59	2.35–3.00–2.54	Minnesota	M.	60–60–60	2.50–3.00–2.73
New Hampshire	M.	72–72–72	1.25–3.00–2.12	Missouri	M.	60–60–60	2.25–2.40–2.29
New Jersey	M.	59–60–60	1.95–3.37–2.16	New Hampshire	M.	59–72–64	1.50–3.00–2.05
New York	M.	60–60–60	1.50–3.25–2.57	New Jersey	M.	48–60–59	1.33–3.08–2.45
Ohio	M.	48–60–60	1.25–4.17–2.50	New York	M.	60–72–60	1.30–4.16–3.01
Oregon	M.	60–60–60	3.60–4.00–3.80	North Carolina	M.	60–60–60	2.35–2.35–2.35
Pennsylvania	M.	60–60–60	2.00–3.30–2.67	Ohio	M.	60–60–60	1.00–3.33–2.42
Virginia	M.	60–60–60	1.83–2.17–2.06	Pennsylvania	M.	40–60–59	1.80–3.65–2.61
Wisconsin	M.	59–60–60	2.25–2.40–2.29	Tennessee	M.	60–60–60	2.25–2.25–2.25
1882:				Vermont	M.	60–60–60	2.25–2.25–2.25
California	M.	60–60–60	2.75–3.80–3.49	Virginia	M.	48–60–55	1.80–2.20–2.05
Connecticut	M.	54–60–58	1.67–2.75–2.05	West Virginia	M.	60–60–60	2.50–2.50–2.50
Illinois	M.	59–60–60	2.25–3.50–2.76	Wisconsin	M.	59–60–59	2.00–3.55–2.07
Iowa	M.	60–60–60	2.25–2.25–2.25	**1886:**			
Louisiana	M.	60–60–60	2.50–3.00–2.80	Alabama	M.	59–59–59	1.87–1.87–1.87
Maryland	M.	60–60–60	2.00–3.00–2.34	California	M.	60–60–60	2.75–4.25–3.46
Massachusetts	M.	60–60–60	1.33–3.20–2.07	Do	M.	60–60–60	²2.30–2.30–2.30
Minnesota	M.	54–60–59	2.50–3.50–3.12	Connecticut	M.	54–60–60	1.50–2.75–1.88
Missouri	M.	59–60–60	2.00–4.17–2.45	Illinois	M.	54–60–59	1.00–3.00–2.61
New Hampshire	M.	72–72–72	1.35–3.00–2.11	Indiana	M.	60–60–60	2.50–2.50–2.50
New Jersey	M.	60–72–67	1.50–2.50–2.09	Iowa	M.	48–57–54	.90–3.50–1.64
New York	M.	60–60–60	1.50–3.25–2.72	Kansas	M.	60–60–60	2.75–3.50–3.00
Ohio	M.	60–60–60	2.50–2.75–2.66	Louisiana	M.	60–60–60	2.34–3.00–2.57
Do	(¹)	48–75–60	1.00–4.50–2.51	Maryland	M.	60–60–60	2.00–3.00–2.37
Pennsylvania	M.	60–60–60	1.50–3.00–2.78	Massachusetts	M.	60–60–60	1.50–3.00–2.05
Virginia	M.	60–60–60	1.83–2.17–2.04	Michigan	M.	60–60–60	2.50–2.50–2.50
Wisconsin	M.	60–60–60	2.15–2.25–2.19	Missouri	M.	60–60–60	2.50–3.00–2.72
1883:				New Hampshire	M.	60–72–67	1.60–3.00–2.29
Connecticut	M.	60–60–60	2.00–2.75–2.22	New Jersey	M.	54–66–61	1.67–3.33–2.02
Illinois	M.	60–60–60	2.25–3.50–2.70	New York	M.	60–60–60	1.40–3.75–2.37
Louisiana	M.	60–60–60	2.50–3.00–2.88	Ohio	M.	54–60–60	1.75–3.29–2.61
Maryland	M.	60–60–60	2.00–3.00–2.36	Pennsylvania	M.	60–60–60	2.00–3.48–2.56
Massachusetts	M.	60–60–60	1.50–4.00–2.43	Virginia	M.	59–60–59	2.00–2.50–2.31
Michigan	M.	(¹)	.65–5.30–2.25	**1887:**			
Minnesota	M.	60–66–63	2.50–4.50–3.37	California	M.	60–60–60	2.75–4.00–3.65
Missouri	M.	60–60–60	2.00–3.00–2.43	Connecticut	M.	60–60–60	1.67–3.00–2.24
New Hampshire	M.	72–72–72	1.35–3.00–2.13	Florida	M.	(¹)	2.25–2.60–2.31
New Jersey	M.	48–60–58	.83–3.50–2.32	Illinois	M.	60–60–60	2.25–3.50–2.63
New York	M.	60–60–60	1.50–3.25–2.35	Kansas	M.	54–60–59	1.83–3.50–2.73
Ohio	M.	48–66–60	1.50–4.48–2.65	Louisiana	M.	60–60–60	2.75–3.00–2.88
Pennsylvania	M.	60–60–60	2.00–3.00–2.52	Maryland	M.	60–60–60	1.50–3.00–1.86
Virginia	M.	60–60–60	1.92–2.25–1.99	Masssachusetts	M.	60–60–60	1.50–3.00–2.10
1884:				Minnesota	M.	60–60–60	2.50–3.00–2.73
California	M.	60–60–60	2.75–3.80–3.47	Missouri	M.	60–60–60	2.30–2.35–2.31
Connecticut	M.	54–60–57	1.75–2.75–2.13	Nebraska	M.	54–60–54	2.00–3.75–3.16
Illinois	M.	60–60–56	2.00–3.50–2.73	New Hampshire	M.	60–72–62	1.70–3.00–2.15
Indiana	M.	60–60–60	2.50–2.50–2.50	New York	M.	60–60–60	1.50–4.00–2.38
Iowa	M.	42–48–45	1.80–3.85–3.28	Do	M.	(¹)	² .22– .28– .23½
Kentucky	M.	60–60–60	2.50–2.50–2.50	North Carolina	M.	60–60–60	1.00–1.50–1.25
Louisiana	M.	60–60–60	2.50–3.00–2.80	Ohio	M.	48–60–59	1.00–4.00–2.44
Maryland	M.	60–60–60	2.00–3.00–2.37	Pennsylvania	M.	60–72–60	1.50–3.48–2.51
Massachusetts	M.	60–60–60	1.50–3.20–2.20	Rhode Island	M.	60–60–60	2.50–2.50–2.50
Michigan	M.	(¹)	.50–4.00–2.27	Virginia	M.	60–60–60	1.25–2.50–2.06
Minnesota	M.	60–60–60	2.50–3.00–2.72	Wisconsin	M.	(¹)	2.28–2.28–2.28
Missouri	M.	60–60–60	2.33–3.50–2.42	**1888:**			
New Hampshire	M.	72–72–72	1.40–3.00–2.11	California	M.	60–60–60	2.75–4.00–3.66
New Jersey	M.	54–60–60	1.50–3.50–2.47	Connecticut	M.	60–60–60	1.75–3.00–2.17
New York	M.	60–60–60	1.40–3.25–1.73	Illinois	M.	60–60–60	2.25–3.30–2.67
Ohio	M.	56–60–60	2.75–3.07–2.55	Iowa	M.	54–54–54	2.60–2.60–2.60
Oregon	M.	60–60–60	3.50–4.00–3.75	Kansas	M.	(¹)	2.42–3.50–2.60
Pennsylvania	M.	60–60–60	1.80–3.90–2.68				
Virginia	M.	60–60–60	1.83–2.17–1.95				

¹Not reported. ²And board. ³Per hour.

TABLE I–31.—*Molders, iron, 1843–1900, by year and State*—Continued

Year and State	Sex	Lowest, highest, and average—		Year and State	Sex	Lowest, highest, and average—	
		Hours per week	Rate per day (dollars)			Hours per week	Rate per day (dollars)
1888—Continued.				**1892—Continued.**			
Louisiana	M.	60–60–60	2. 75–3. 00–2. 88	Ohio	M.	60–60–60	2. 75–2. 92–2. 81
Maryland	M.	60–60–60	2. 00–3. 00–2. 38	Pennsylvania	M.	60–60–60	2. 00–3. 50–2. 37
Massachusetts	M.	60–60–60	1. 50–3. 00–2. 10	Virginia	M.	60–60–60	1. 67–2. 25–2. 10
Minnesota	M.	60–60–60	2. 50–3. 00–2. 71	**1893:**			
Missouri	M.	60–60–60	2. 25–2. 35–2. 28	California	M.	60–60–60	3. 25–4. 50–3. 67
New Hampshire	M.	60–72–61	1. 25–2. 92–1. 67	Illinois	M.	40–78–58	1. 00–3. 50–2. 62
New Jersey	M.	42–60–56	1. 60–4. 00–2. 22	Louisiana	M.	60–60–60	2. 50–3. 00–2. 75
New York	M.	51–60–58	1. 50–6. 30–2. 69	Maryland	M.	48–72–60	. 42–3. 00–2 01
Ohio	M.	60–60–60	1. 25–3. 34–2. 38	Massachusetts	M.	60–60–60	1. 50–3. 25–2 25
Pennsylvania	M.	60–60–60	2. 00–3. 48–2. 48	Michigan	M.	54–60–58	1. 23–2. 88–2. 07
Tennessee	M.	(1)	1. 25–2. 50–1. 71	Minnesota	M.	60–60–60	2. 50–3. 00–2. 71
Virginia	M.	60–84–61	1. 25–2. 33–2 09	Missouri	M.	54–60–59	2. 00–2. 40–2. 08
1889:				Montana	M.	54–54–54	3. 50–6. 00–4. 21
Alabama	M.	84–84–84	1. 75–2. 00–1. 83	New York	M.	58–60–59	1. 17–2. 00–1. 59
California	M.	60–60–60	3. 25–4. 00–3. 69	Ohio	M.	30–60–58	. 66–3. 25–2. 24
Connecticut	M.	60–60–60	1. 75–3. 00–2. 22	Pennsylvania	M.	48–66–60	. 58–3. 50–2 40
Georgia	M.	84–84–84	1. 25–1. 25–1. 25	Rhode Island	M.	(1)	1. 50–3. 00–1. 85
Illinois	M.	60–60–60	2. 25–3. 50–2. 67	Virginia	M.	60–60–60	1. 67–2. 25–2. 10
Kansas	M.	60–60–60	2. 50–2. 75–2. 63	**1894:**			
Louisiana	M.	60–60–60	2. 75–3. 00–2. 88	California	M.	60–60–60	3. 50–4. 50–3. 63
Maryland	M.	60–60–60	2. 00–3. 00–2 39	Illinois	M.	60–60–60	2. 25–3. 25–2. 64
Massachusetts	M.	60–60–60	1. 50–3. 25–2 16	Indiana	M.	54–60–58	1. 86–3. 05–2 47
Michigan	M.	60–60–60	3. 00–3. 00–3. 00	Iowa	M.	54–60–60	1. 00–3. 00–2. 20
Minnesota	M.	60–60–60	2. 50–3. 00–2. 71	Louisiana	M.	60–60–60	2. 50–3. 00–2. 67
Missouri	M.	60–72–60	1. 50–2. 35–2. 14	Maryland	M.	60–60–60	2. 00–3. 00–2 32
New Hampshire	M.	60–60–60	1. 25–2. 50–1. 76	Massachusetts	M.	60–60–60	1. 50–2. 93–2. 02
New York	M.	60–60–60	. 95–3. 75–2. 39	Minnesota	M.	60–60–60	2. 50–3. 00–2 94
				Missouri	M.	54–60–59	2. 00–2. 60–2. 12
Ohio	M.	60–84–70	1. 65–2. 67–2. 18	New Hampshire	M.	48–60–58	1. 25–4. 50–2. 13
Pennsylvania	M.	56–84–61	1. 25–3. 33–2. 42	North Carolina	M.	60–60–60	1. 00–3. 00–1. 77
Tennessee	M.	84–84–84	. 60–1. 25–1. 12	Ohio	M.	30–60–58	1. 20–4. 20–2. 20
Virginia	M.	60–60–60	1. 67–2. 17–1. 94	Pennsylvania	M.	60–60–60	2. 00–3. 25–2. 34
1890:				Virginia	M.	60–60–60	1. 67–2. 33–2. 10
Alabama	M.	84–84–84	2. 00–2. 00 2 00	**1895:**			
California	M.	60–60–60	3. 25. 4. 50–3. 66	California	M.	60–60–60	3. 25–4. 50–3. 69
Connecticut	M.	60–60–60	1. 75–3. 00–2. 20	Illinois	M.	60–60–60	2. 25–3. 50–2. 72
Illinois	M.	60–60–60	2. 25–3. 30–2. 75	Kansas	M.	72–72–72	3. 45–3. 45–3. 45
Kansas	M.	(1)	2. 25–3. 00–2. 56	Louisiana	M.	60–60–60	2. 50–3. 00–2. 67
Louisiana	M.	60–60–60	2. 75–3. 00–2. 88	Maryland	M.	60–60–60	2. 00–3. 00–2 32
Maryland	M.	60–60–60	2. 00–3. 00–2 39	Massachusetts	M.	60–60–60	1. 33–3. 00–2 06
Massachusetts	M.	60–60–60	1. 50–3. 00 2 18	Minnesota	M.	60–60–60	2. 50–3. 00–2. 70
Michigan	M.	60–60–60	. 45–5. 00–2. 00	Missouri	M.	54–60–59	2. 00–2. 50–2. 10
Minnesota	M.	60–60–60	1. 50–3. 25–2. 75	New Hampshire	M.	59–59–59	1. 29–1. 99–1. 66
Missouri	M.	60–60–60	2. 00–2. 40–2. 10	New York	M.	00–60–60	2. 00–2. 00–2. 00
Nebraska	(1)	54–54–54	2. 50–3. 75–3. 15	North Carolina	M.	60–60–60	1. 50–3. 50–2. 17
New Hampshire	M.	60–60–60	1. 25–2. 50–1. 74	Ohio	M.	48–60–58	1. 00–3. 09–2. 24
New York	M.	60–60–60	. 63–4. 19–2. 43	Pennsylvania	M.	60–60–60	2. 00 3. 25–2. 30
Ohio	M.	42–72–58	1. 25–4. 00–2. 39	Virginia	M.	60–60–60	1. 50–2. 25–2. 00
Pennsylvania	M.	60–60–60	2. 00–3. 50–2. 51	**1896:**			
Virginia	M.	60–60–60	1. 75–2. 00–1. 86	California	M.	60–60–60	3. 25–4. 50–3. 59
1891:				Colorado	M.	60–60–60	3. 00–3. 00–3. 00
California	M.	60–60–60	3. 25–4. 50–3. 63	Florida	M.	(1)	1. 25–1. 25–1. 25
Connecticut	M.	60–60–60	1. 75–3. 00–2. 22	Georgia	M.	(1)	1. 17–1. 17–1. 17
Illinois	M.	60–60–60	2. 25–3. 50–2. 82	Illinois	M.	60–60–60	1. 50–3. 00–2. 55
Louisiana	M.	60–60–00	2. 75–3. 00–2. 88	Kansas	M.	60–60–60	1. 50–1. 75–1. 58
Maryland	M.	60–60–60	2. 00–3. 00–2 37	Louisiana	M.	60–60–60	2. 50–3. 00–2. 75
Massachusetts	M.	60–60–60	1. 50–3. 00–2 12	Maryland	M.	60–60–60	2. 00–2. 75–2 54
Minnesota	M.	60–60–60	2. 75–3. 25–2. 97	Massachusetts	M.	60–60–60	1. 50–3. 00–2 12
Missouri	M.	60–60–60	1. 74–2. 80–2. 17	Minnesota	M.	60–60–60	2. 50–3. 00–2. 70
New Hampshire	M.	60–72–60	1. 25–2. 50–1. 77	Missouri	M.	48–60–57	1. 60–4. 25–2. 21
New York	M.	60–60–60	. 50–5. 00–2. 42	Nebraska	M.	54–54–54	2. 50–7. 25–4. 88
North Carolina	M.	60–60–60	. 75–2. 50–1. 82	New Jersey	M.	60–60–60	2. 50–2. 50–2. 50
Ohio	M.	42–72–59	1. 00–3. 08–2. 26	New York	M.	55–55–55	. 75–3. 00–1. 73
Pennsylvania	M.	60–60–60	2. 40–3. 50–2. 55	North Carolina	M.	59–60–60	. 50–2. 50–1. 60
Virginia	M.	60–60–60	1. 67–2. 25–2. 09	Ohio	M.	48–60–56	1. 50–3. 00–2. 21
1892:				Pennsylvania	M.	60–60–60	1. 10–3. 25–2. 10
California	M.	56–60–60	1. 17–4. 50–3. 52	Virginia	M.	60–60–60	1. 50–2. 25–1. 94
Connecticut	M.	60–60–60	1. 75–3. 00–2. 36	**1897:**			
Illinois	M.	60–60–60	2. 35–3. 50–2. 83	California	M.	60–60–60	3. 25–4. 50–3. 57
Indiana	M.	48–84–60	1. 74–2. 87–2. 30	Illinois	M.	60–60–60	2. 25–3. 00–2. 74
Louisiana	M.	60–60–60	2. 50–3. 00–2. 67	Kansas	M.	60–60–60	2. 00–2. 40–2. 10
Maryland	M.	60–60–60	2. 00–3. 00–2 39	Do	M.	(1)	[2] 22– . 22– . 22
Massachusetts	M.	60–60–60	1. 50–3. 25–2. 22	Louisiana	M.	60–60–60	2. 50–3. 00–2. 75
Missouri	M.	54–60–59	2. 00–5. 00–2. 45	Maryland	M.	60–60–60	2. 00–2. 50–2. 18
New York	M.	60–60–60	1. 80–3. 60–2. 53	Massachusetts	M.	60–60–60	1. 50–3. 00–2. 33

[1] Not reported.   [2] Per hour.

TABLE I-31.—*Molders, iron, 1843–1900, by year and State*—Continued

Year and State	Sex	Lowest, highest, and average—		Year and State	Sex	Lowest, highest, and average—	
		Hours per week	Rate per day (dollars)			Hours per week	Rate per day (dollars)
1897—Continued.				1898—Continued.			
Michigan	(¹)	(¹)	2.25-3.00-2.50	Ohio	M.	60-60-60	2.50-2.67-2.52
Minnesota	M.	60-60-60	2.50-3.00-2.69	Pennsylvania	M.	60-60-60	1.95-3.25-2.34
Missouri	M.	54-60-59	2.00-2.30-2.05	Virginia	M.	60-60-60	1.50-2.25-1.94
Nebraska	M.	60-60-60	2.00-2.00-2.00	Do	(¹)	54-54-54	2.57-2.57-2.57
New York	M.	54-60-59	1.00-4.00-2.39	1899:			
Ohio	M.	60-60-60	2.50-2.67-2.52	Alabama	M.	60-60-60	2.75-3.00-2.90
Pennsylvania	M.	60-60-60	2.00-3.25-2.37	Georgia	M.	59-60-60	1.50-3.00-1.96
Virginia	M.	48-60-58	1.31-3.00-2.04	Massachusetts	M.	59-59-59	2.25-4.00-2.71
1898:				New York	M.	60-60-60	1.90-2.70-2.23
California	M.	60-60-60	3.25-4.50-3.57	North Carolina	M.	60-60-60	2.50-2.50-2.50
Illinois	M.	60-60-60	2.25-3.00-2.71	Ohio	M.	60-60-60	2.00-3.10-2.56
Louisiana	M.	60-60-60	2.50-3.00-2.75	Pennsylvania	M.	(¹)	1.95-1.95-1.95
Maryland	M.	60-60-60	2.00-2.50-2.18	1900:			
Massachusetts	M.	60-60-60	2.33-2.33-2.33	Alabama	M.	60-60-60	2.75-3.00-2.97
Michigan	(¹)	(¹)	2.33-2.33-2.33	Georgia	M.	59-60-59	1.50-3.00-2.02
Minnesota	M.	60-60-60	2.50-3.00-2.69	Massachusetts	M.	59-59-59	2.75-4.00-2.91
Missouri	M.	60-60-60	2.00-2.40-2.06	New York	M.	60-60-60	2.00-3.50-2.51
Nebraska	(¹)	52-60-52	1.50-3.00-2.17	North Carolina	M.	60-60-60	2.50-2.50-2.50
New Jersey	M.	54-60-58	1.33-3.67-2.28	Ohio	M.	60-60-60	2.20-3.40-2.81
New York	M.	48-60-59	1.25-3.60-2.50				

¹ Not reported.

TABLE I-32.—*Molders, iron, males, 1890–1906, by city and year*

Year	Atlanta, Ga.		Birmingham, Ala.		Boston, Mass.		Chicago, Ill	
	Hours per week	Rate per hour	Hours per week	Rate per hour	Hours per week	Rate per hour	Hours per week	Rate per hour
1890	59.8	$0.253			59.8	$0.263	59.9	$0.268
1891	59.9	.260			59.8	.263	59.8	.275
1892	59.9	.257			58.3	.270	59.2	.273
1893	59.9	.252			58.4	.271	56.4	.272
1894	59.9	.243			58.5	.265	58.6	.256
1895	59.8	.246			58.3	.267	58.9	.250
1896	59.8	.266			58.3	.264	58.9	.255
1897	59.8	.258			58.3	.274	58.2	.255
1898	59.8	.260			58.2	.275	58.9	.257
1899	59.8	.258			58.3	.275	58.9	.267
1900	59.8	.270			58.4	.276	58.6	.284
1901	59.9	.267			56.3	.293	57.4	.286
1902	59.7	.271			55.4	.295	57.8	.292
1903	59.8	.278			55.1	.299	54.0	.326
1904	59.7	.292	59.5	$0.292	55.2	.301	54.0	.334
1905	59.7	.300	59.5	.308	54.0	.307	54.0	.325
1906	59.8	.296	59.4	.316	54.0	.324	52.2	.337

Year	Cincinnati, Ohio		Denver, Colo.		Detroit, Mich.		New Orleans, La.	
	Hours per week	Rate per hour	Hours per week	Rate per hour	Hours per week	Rate per hour	Hours per week	Rate per hour
1890					60.0	$0.252	60.0	$0.284
1891					60.0	.253	60.0	.284
1892					60.0	.254	60.0	.283
1893					60.0	.250	60.0	.284
1894					60.0	.228	60.0	.283
1895					60.0	.227	60.0	.284
1896					60.0	.243	60.0	.289
1897					60.0	.250	60.0	.289
1898					60.0	.252	60.0	.288
1899					60.0	.274	60.0	.282
1900					60.0	.284	60.0	.290
1901					60.0	.279	54.0	.325
1902					60.0	.284	54.0	.321
1903	60.0	$0.321			59.4	.300	54.0	.322
1904	60.0	.329	53.6	$0.392	59.3	.301	54.0	.331
1905	60.0	.315	53.4	.391	59.6	.305	54.0	.333
1906	57.0	.335	54.0	.419	59.5	.296	54.0	.333

TABLE **I-32.**—*Molders, iron, males, 1890-1906, by city and year*—Continued

Year	New York, N. Y.		Philadelphia, Pa.		St. Louis, Mo.		San Francisco, Calif.	
	Hours per week	Rate per hour	Hours per week	Rate per hour	Hours per week	Rate per hour	Hours per week	Rate per hour
1890	59. 2	$0. 274	58. 6	$0. 250	60. 0	$0. 260	55. 1	$0. 355
1891	59. 2	. 272	58. 8	. 253	60. 0	. 256	59. 2	. 352
1892	59. 2	. 271	59. 0	. 252	60. 0	. 263	59. 2	. 357
1893	59. 1	. 267	58. 5	. 247	57. 6	. 269	59. 2	. 352
1894	59. 0	. 275	58. 7	. 235	57. 8	. 282	59. 1	. 328
1895	59. 2	. 273	58. 2	. 236	58. 0	. 279	59. 1	. 315
1896	59. 2	. 275	58. 8	. 243	58. 8	. 273	54. 3	. 316
1897	59. 2	. 274	58. 8	. 257	58. 5	. 275	59. 2	. 318
1898	59. 2	. 273	59. 0	. 244	60. 0	. 271	59. 2	. 319
1899	59. 2	. 280	57. 4	. 250	60. 0	. 274	59. 3	. 294
1900	59. 2	. 293	56. 1	. 258	60. 0	. 281	59. 2	. 307
1901	59. 0	. 296	56. 1	. 261	60. 0	. 305	59. 2	. 329
1902	54. 0	. 332	56. 3	. 283	60. 0	. 316	57. 3	. 333
1903	54. 0	. 333	56. 3	. 340	54. 0	. 346	56. 5	. 349
1904	54. 0	. 336	55. 3	. 316	54. 0	. 322	54. 0	. 387
1905	54. 0	. 335	55. 5	. 334	54. 0	. 342	54. 0	. 384
1906	54. 0	. 347	56. 1	. 345	54. 0	. 341	54. 0	. 444

TABLE **I-33.**—*Molders, iron, males, 1907-1924, by city and year*

Year	Atlanta, Ga.		Birmingham, Ala.		Boston, Mass.[1]		Chicago, Ill.[2]	
	Hours per week	Rate per hour	Hours per week	Rate per hour	Hours per week	Rate per hour	Hours per week	Rate per hour
1907	60. 0	$0. 300	60. 0	$0. 300	54. 0	$0. 333	54. 0	$0. 361
1908	60. 0	. 325	60. 0	. 300	54. 0	. 333	54. 0	. 361
1909	60. 0	. 325	60. 0	. 300	54. 0	. 333	54. 0	. 361
1910	60. 0	. 350	60. 0	. 300	54. 0	. 361	54. 0	. 389
1911	60. 0	. 350	60. 0	. 300	54. 0	. 361	54. 0	. 389
1912	60. 0	. 350	60. 0	. 300	54. 0	. 361	54. 0	. 389
1913	60. 0	. 350	54. 0	. 361	54. 0	. 389	54. 0	. 444
1914	60. 0	. 350	54. 0	. 361	54. 0	. 389	54. 0	. 444
1915	60. 0	. 350	54. 0	. 361	54. 0	. 389	54. 0	. 444
1916	60. 0	. 350	54. 0	. 361	54. 0	. 444	48. 0	. 500
1917	54. 0	. 417	54. 0	. 361	54. 0	. 500	48. 0	. 563
1918	54. 0	. 500	48. 0	. 563	54. 0	. 583	48. 0	. 688
1919	54. 0	. 700	48. 0	. 680	54. 0	. 583	48. 0	. 800
1920	50. 0	. 800	48. 0	. 800	48. 0	. 900	48. 0	1. 050
1921	50. 0	. 800			48. 0	. 900	48. 0	. 900
1922	50. 0	. 600			48. 0	. 750	48. 0	. 750
1923 [3]	50. 0	. 700			48. 0	. 900	48. 0	. 875
1924 [3]	50. 0	. 700			48. 0	. 900	[4] 44. 0	1. 000

Year	Cincinnati, Ohio		Denver, Colo.[1]		Detroit, Mich.[2]		New Orleans, La.	
1907	54. 0	$0. 356	54. 0	$0. 444	54. 0	$0. 347	54. 0	$0. 361
1908	54. 0	. 356	54. 0	. 417	54. 0	. 347	54. 0	. 361
1909	54. 0	. 356	54. 0	. 417	54. 0	. 347	54. 0	. 361
1910	54. 0	. 356	54. 0	. 417	54. 0	. 347	54. 0	. 361
1911	54. 0	. 361	54. 0	. 444	54. 0	. 361	54. 0	. 361
1912	54. 0	. 361	54. 0	. 444	54. 0	. 361	54. 0	. 361
1913	54. 0	. 361	54. 0	. 444	54. 0	. 389	54. 0	. 361
1914	54. 0	. 389	54. 0	. 444	54. 0	. 389	54. 0	. 361
1915	54. 0	. 389	54. 0	. 444	54. 0	. 389	54. 0	. 361
1916	54. 0	. 444	54. 0	. 444	54. 0	. 444	54. 0	. 389
1917	54. 0	. 444	48. 0	. 500	54. 0	. 500	48. 0	. 500
1918	54. 0	. 555	[5] 48. 0	. 594	54. 0	. 611	48. 0	. 625
1919	54. 0	. 583	[5] 48. 0	. 750	48. 0	. 800	48. 0	. 800
1920	48. 0	. 813	[5] 48. 0	. 800	48. 0	1. 000	48. 0	. 800
1921	48. 0	. 750	[5] 48. 0	1. 000	48. 0	. 900	48. 0	. 800
1922	48. 0	. 688	48. 0	. 781	48. 0	. 750	48. 0	. 750
1923 [3]	48. 0	. 750	[5] 48. 0	. 781	48. 0	. 850	48. 0	. 750
1924 [3]	48. 0	. 875	48. 0	. 800	48. 0	. 900	44. 0	. 800

[1] Iron and brass molders, 1913–1917, inclusive.
[2] Iron and brass molders, 1913–1916, inclusive.
[3] Core makers included.
[4] 48, November to April, inclusive.
[5] Full holiday alternate Saturdays, June to August, inclusive.

TABLE **I-33.**—*Molders, iron, males, 1907–1924, by city and year*—Continued

Year	New York, N. Y.		Philadelphia, Pa.		St. Louis, Mo.		San Francisco, Calif.[6]	
	Hours per week	Rate per hour	Hours per week	Rate per hour	Hours per week	Rate per hour	Hours per week	Rate per hour
1907	54.0	$0.361	54.0	$0.322	54.0	$0.350	54.0	$0.444
1908	54.0	.361	54.0	.322	54.0	.350	54.0	.444
1909	54.0	.361	54.0	.322	54.0	.350	52.5	.457
1910	54.0	.389	54.0	.322	54.0	.350	49.5	.485
1911	54.0	.389	54.0	.361	54.0	.372	48.0	.500
1912	54.0	.389	54.0	.361	54.0	.372	48.0	.500
1913	54.0	.389	54.0	.361	54.0	.389	48.0	.500
1914	54.0	.417	54.0	.389	54.0	.389	48.0	.500
1915	54.0	.417	54.0	.389	54.0	.389	48.0	.500
1916	54.0	.417	54.0	.444	54.0	.417	48.0	.500
1917	54.0	.472	54.0	.500	54.0	.500	48.0	.531
1918	54.0	.528	48.0	.688	54.0	.611	[7] 48.0	.725
1919	48.0	.750	48.0	[8] .688	48.0	.750	44.0	.800
1920	48.0	[9] .880	48.0	1.000	48.0	.900	44.0	.880
1921	48.0	[10] .880	48.0	.900	48.0	.850	44.0	1.000
1922	48.0	.781	48.0	.780	48.0	.750	44.0	.800
1923 [3]	48.0	.781	48.0	.850	48.0	.875	44.0	.875
1924 [3]	48.0	1.000	48.0	.969	48.0	.938	44.0	.938

[3] Core makers included.
[6] Iron and brass molders, 1914–1916, inclusive.
[7] 44, June to August, inclusive.
[8] 75 per cent received 50 cents to $1.50 more per day.
[9] More than 50 per cent received more.
[10] More than 75 per cent received more.

TABLE **I-34.**—*Molders, hand, floor, males, 1923, 1925, and 1927, by State and year*

Year	Alabama		California		Illinois		Louisiana	
	Hours per week	Rate per hour	Hours per week	Rate per hour	Hours per week	Rate per hour	Hours per week	Rate per hour
1923	50.9	$0.636	46.2	$0.798	51.1	$0.765	51.8	$0.752
1925	51.5	.688	46.9	.873	50.9	.857	49.4	.711
1927	54.1	.714	45.5	.960	47.3	.831	50.3	.703

Year	Maryland		Massachusetts		Michigan		Missouri	
1923	48.9	$0.710	48.9	$0.776	50.9	$0.685	50.5	$0.734
1925	49.1	.763	47.9	.975	49.2	.781	52.1	.745
1927	50.2	.773	48.4	.971	51.2	.789	50.5	.817

Year	New Hampshire		New York		Ohio		Pennsylvania	
1923	49.5	$0.728	50.2	$0.767	49.7	$0.757	54.9	$0.737
1925	49.4	.771	49.1	.843	51.6	.800	50.3	.808
1927	49.1	.735	49.2	.832	50.7	.848	50.6	.817

TABLE I–35.—*Molders, machine, males, 1923, 1925, and 1927, by State and year*

Year	Alabama		California		Illinois		Louisiana	
	Hours per week	Rate per hour	Hours per week	Rate per hour	Hours per week	Rate per hour	Hours per week	Rate per hour
1923			45. 8	$0. 698	51. 5	$0. 701		
1925			50. 2	. 755	51. 9	. 669	49. 3	$0. 702
1927			49. 7	. 955	50. 5	. 787		$0. 702

	Maryland		Massachusetts		Michigan		Missouri	
1923	48. 8	$0. 712	49. 2	$0. 760	52. 2	$0. 669	56. 2	$0. 579
1925	52. 8	. 622	48. 8	. 810	49. 2	. 773	54. 8	. 703
1927	53. 6	. 639	48. 5	. 836	51. 0	. 730	54. 0	. 657

	New Hampshire		New York		Ohio		Pennsylvania	
1923	52. 0	$0. 483	51. 2	$0. 689	49. 9	$0. 736	53. 5	$0. 612
1925	48. 9	. 918	49. 5	. 785	51. 5	. 709	49. 3	. 727
1927	49. 9	. 793	47. 5	. 787	50. 1	. 765	49. 7	. 700

TABLE I–36.—*Pattern makers, 1844–1900, by year and State*

Year and State	Sex	Lowest, highest, and average—		Year and State	Sex	Lowest, highest, and average—	
		Hours per week	Rate per day (dollars)			Hours per week	Rate per day (dollars)
1844:				**1854:**			
New York	M.	60–60–60	1. 13–2. 00–1. 38	Connecticut	M.	60–60–60	1. 50–2. 25–1. 75
1845:				Massachusetts	M.	66–66–66	1. 50–1. 93–1. 78
Massachusetts	M.	72–72–72	1. 56–1. 56–1. 56	New Hampshire	M.	60–60–60	1. 50–1. 50–1. 50
New Hampshire	M.	66–66–66	1. 00–1. 00–1. 00	New York	M.	60–60–60	1. 25–2. 00–1. 62
New York	M.	60–60–60	1. 00–2. 00–1. 41	**1855:**			
1846:				Connecticut	M.	60–60–60	1. 50–2. 25–1. 82
Massachusetts	M.	72–72–72	1. 56–1. 56–1. 56	Maryland	M.	60–60–60	1. 50–2. 00–1. 56
New Hampshire	M.	66–66–66	1. 08–1. 08–1. 08	Massachusetts	M.	66–66–66	1. 50–1. 93–1. 82
New York	M.	60–60–60	1. 25–1. 75–1. 39	New Hampshire	M.	60–60–60	1. 67–1. 67–1. 67
1847:				New York	M.	60–60–60	1. 00–2. 50–1. 66
Massachusetts	M.	72–72–72	1. 56–1. 56–1. 56	Pennsylvania	M.	60–60–60	1. 50–1. 80–1. 60
New Hampshire	M.	66–66–66	1. 00–1. 25–1. 14	**1856:**			
New York	M.	60–60–60	1. 25–1. 75–1. 41	Connecticut	M.	60–60–60	1. 50–2. 00–1. 80
1848:				Maryland	M.	60–60–60	1. 50–2. 00–1. 58
Massachusetts	M.	72–72–72	1. 56–1. 56–1. 56	Massachusetts	M.	60–60–60	1. 50–1. 75–1. 69
New Hampshire	M.	60–60–60	1. 17–1. 50–1. 34	New Hampshire	M.	60–60–60	1. 67–1. 67–1. 67
New York	M.	60–60–60	1. 00–1. 75–1. 37	New York	M.	60–60–60	1. 25–2. 50–1. 73
1849:				Pennsylvania	M.	60–60–60	1. 50–1. 80–1. 63
Massachusetts	M.	72–72–72	1. 56–1. 56–1. 56	**1857:**			
New Hampshire	M.	60–60–60	1. 17–1. 50–1. 34	Connecticut	M.	60–60–60	1. 50–2. 00–1. 79
New York	M.	60–60–60	1. 00–1. 75–1. 41	Maryland	M.	60–60–60	1. 50–2. 50–1. 68
Pennsylvania	M.	60–60–60	1. 50–1. 50–1. 50	Massachusetts	M.	60–66–62	1. 60–1. 75–1. 71
1850:				New Hampshire	M.	60–60–60	1. 50–1. 67–1. 59
Massachusetts	M.	72–72–72	1. 56–1. 56–1. 56	New York	M.	60–60–60	1. 25–3. 00–1. 71
New Hampshire	M.	60–60–60	1. 25–1. 25–1. 25	Pennsylvania	M.	60–60–60	1. 50–1. 80–1. 65
New York	M.	60–60–60	1. 00–1. 75–1. 42	**1858:**			
Pennsylvania	M.	60–60–60	1. 50–1. 50–1. 50	Connecticut	M.	60–60–60	1. 50–2. 00–1. 68
1851:				Maryland	M.	60–60–60	1. 50–2. 00–1. 69
Massachusetts	M.	66–66–66	1. 54–1. 54–1. 54	Massachusetts	M.	60–66–62	1. 85–1. 88–1. 87
New Hampshire	M.	60–60–60	1. 25–1. 25–1. 25	New Hampshire	M.	60–60–60	1. 67–1. 67–1. 67
New York	M.	60–60–60	1. 25–1. 75–1. 41	New York	M.	60–60–60	1. 50–2. 50–1. 75
Pennsylvania	M.	60–60–60	1. 50–1. 50–1. 50	Pennsylvania	M.	60–60–60	1. 50–1. 67–1. 57
1852:				**1859:**			
Massachusetts	M.	66–66–66	1. 54–1. 54–1. 54	Connecticut	M.	60–60–60	1. 50–2. 00–1. 71
New Hampshire	M.	60–60–60	1. 33–1. 75–1. 54	Maryland	M.	60–60–60	1. 50–2. 50–1. 72
New York	M.	60–60–60	1. 00–1. 75–1. 44	Massachusetts	M.	60–66–62	1. 85–1. 88–1. 87
Pennsylvania	M.	60–60–60	1. 50–1. 50–1. 50	New Hampshire	M.	60–60–60	1. 42–1. 42–1. 42
1853:				New York	M.	60–60–60	1. 25–2. 00–1. 56
Connecticut	M.	60–60–60	1. 25–2. 00–1. 69	Pennsylvania	M.	60–60–60	1. 50–1. 67–1. 56
Massachusetts	M.	66–66–66	1. 40–1. 54–1. 49	**1860:**			
New Hampshire	M.	60–60–60	1. 33–1. 33–1. 33	Connecticut	M.	60–60–60	1. 75–2. 00–1. 81
New York	M.	60–60–60	1. 38–1. 78–1. 54	Maryland	M.	60–60–60	1. 50–2. 50–1. 65

[1] Not reported.

TABLE I-36.—*Pattern makers, 1844–1900, by year and State*—Continued

Year and State	Sex	Hours per week	Rate per day (dollars)	Year and State	Sex	Hours per week	Rate per day (dollars)
1860—Continued.				**1870:**			
Massachusetts	M.	60-66-62	1.75-2.00-1.94	California	M.	60-60-60	3.00-3.00-3.00
New Hampshire	M.	60-60-60	1.67-1.67-1.67	Connecticut	M.	60-60-60	2.50-4.00-3.25
New York	M.	60-60-60	1.25-2.13-1.61	Illinois	M.	60-60-60	2.90-3.25-3.23
Ohio	M.	(1)	1.50-3.00-2.25	Louisiana	M.	60-60-60	4.00-4.50-4.25
Pennsylvania	M.	60-60-60	1.50-1.67-1.56	Maryland	M.	60-60-60	2.50-4.00-2.99
1861:				Massachusetts	M.	59-60-60	2.00-5.00-2.80
Connecticut	M.	60-60-60	1.50-2.00-1.72	Minnesota	M.	60-60-60	3.50-4.00-3.75
Maryland	M.	60-60-60	1.33-1.50-1.44	Missouri	M.	59-60-59	2.50-3.00-2.84
Massachusetts	M.	60-66-62	1.75-2.10-2.01	New Hampshire	M.	60-60-60	3.00-3.00-3.00
New Hampshire	M.	60-60-60	1.58-1.58-1.58	New Jersey	M.	60-60-60	3.00-3.75-3.38
New York	M.	60-60-60	1.38-2.13-1.72	New York	M.	60-60-60	1.50-4.50-2.84
Pennsylvania	M.	60-60-60	1.50-1.84-1.65	Ohio	M.	60-60-60	3.00-3.25-3.08
1862:				Pennsylvania	M.	60-60-60	1.90-3.50-2.54
Connecticut	M.	60-60-60	1.50-2.50-1.81	**1871:**			
Maryland	M.	60-60-60	1.33-2.25-1.60	California	M.	60-60-60	3.33-3.50-3.45
Massachusetts	M.	60-66-62	1.75-2.25-2.13	Connecticut	M.	60-60-60	2.50-4.00-3.28
New Hampshire	M.	60-60-60	1.50-1.50-1.50	Illinois	M.	60-60-60	3.10-3.25-3.24
New York	M.	60-60-60	1.25-2.13-1.62	Louisiana	M.	60-60-60	3.00-4.50-3.83
Pennsylvania	M.	60-60-60	1.50-1.84-1.71	Maryland	M.	60-60-60	2.50-4.00-3.00
1863:				Massachusetts	M.	53-60-59	2.00-5.00-3.03
Connecticut	M.	60-60-60	1.50-2.10-1.82	Minnesota	M.	60-60-60	3.50-4.00-3.75
Maryland	M.	60-60-60	1.67-3.00-1.87	Missouri	M.	59-60-59	2.50-3.00-2.84
Massachusetts	M.	60-66-62	1.75-2.50-2.31	New Hampshire	M.	60-60-60	3.00-3.00-3.00
New Hampshire	M.	60-60-60	1.50-1.50-1.50	New Jersey	M.	60-60-60	3.00-3.75-3.42
New York	M.	60-60-60	1.00-2.13-1.64	New York	M.	60-60-60	1.50-4.50-2.92
Pennsylvania	M.	60-60-60	1.67-2.00-1.87	Ohio	M.	60-60-60	3.00-3.25-3.08
1864:				Pennsylvania	M.	60-60-60	1.95-3.50-2.59
Connecticut	M.	60-60-60	1.75-3.00-2.16	**1872:**			
Maryland	M.	60-60-60	1.63-3.50-2.25	California	M.	60-60-60	3.25-3.75-3.47
Massachusetts	M.	60-66-62	2.00-3.00-2.75	Connecticut	M.	60-60-60	3.00-4.00-3.41
New Hampshire	M.	60-60-60	2.00-2.00-2.00	Illinois	M.	60-60-60	2.90-3.35-3.24
New Jersey	M.	60-60-60	2.75-3.50-3.17	Louisiana	M.	60-60-60	3.50-4.50-3.88
New York	M.	60-60-60	1.25-3.25-2.11	Maryland	M.	60-60-60	2.50-4.00-2.98
Pennsylvania	M.	60-60-60	1.80-2.50-2.18	Minnesota	M.	59-60-60	2.00-4.50-2.81
1865:				New Hampshire	M.	60-60-60	3.50-4.00-3.75
Connecticut	M.	60-60-60	1.67-3.50-2.48	New Jersey	M.	60-60-60	3.00-3.50-3.42
Maryland	M.	60-60-60	2.00-4.00-2.60	New York	M.	60-60-60	1.50-4.50-2.99
Massachusetts	M.	60-66-62	2.40-3.50-3.23	Ohio	M.	60-60-60	2.25-3.25-2.81
New Hampshire	M.	60-60-60	2.00-2.00-2.00	Pennsylvania	M.	60-60-60	1.90-4.00-2.62
New Jersey	M.	60-60-60	2.75-3.50-3.17	**1873:**			
New York	M.	60-60-60	1.75-3.25-2.48	California	M.	60-60-60	3.50-4.00-3.89
Pennsylvania	M.	60-60-60	2.20-2.84-2.57	Connecticut	M.	60-60-60	2.00-4.00-3.27
1866:				Illinois	M.	60-60-60	3.15-3.25-3.25
Connecticut	M.	60-60-60	1.67-3.50-2.66	Louisiana	M.	60-60-60	4.00-4.00-4.00
Maryland	M.	60-60-60	2.67-4.00-2.93	Maryland	M.	60-60-60	2.50-3.50-2.95
Massachusetts	M.	60-60-60	2.50-3.50-3.30	Massachusetts	M.	59-60-60	2.12-5.00-2.90
New Hampshire	M.	60-60-60	2.50-2.50-2.50	Minnesota	M.	60-60-60	3.50-4.00-3.67
New Jersey	M.	60-60-60	2.88-3.38-3.08	Missouri	M.	59-60-60	2.50-3.00-2.79
New York	M.	60-60-60	1.75-3.25-2.48	New Jersey	M.	60-60-60	3.00-3.75-3.38
Pennsylvania	M.	60-60-60	2.60-2.84-2.72	New York	M.	60-60-60	1.34-4.50-2.88
1867:				Ohio	M.	60-60-60	2.50-3.25-2.94
Connecticut	M.	60-60-60	2.50-3.50-3.04	Pennsylvania	M.	60-60-60	2.10-4.00-2.65
Maryland	M.	60-60-60	2.50-4.00-2.83	Virginia	M.	48-48-48	4.00-4.00-4.00
Massachusetts	M.	60-60-60	2.50-3.50-3.33	**1874:**			
New Hampshire	M.	60-60-60	3.00-3.00-3.00	California	M.	60-60-60	3.50-4.00-3.75
New Jersey	M.	60-60-60	2.88-3.25-3.13	Connecticut	M.	60-60-60	3.25-4.25-3.61
New York	M.	60-60-60	1.75-3.25-2.64	Illinois	M.	60-60-60	3.00-3.10-3.01
Pennsylvania	M.	60-60-60	2.67-2.84-2.78	Louisiana	M.	60-60-60	4.00-4.00-4.00
1868:				Maryland	M.	60-60-60	2.50-3.50-2.95
Connecticut	M.	60-60-60	2.25-3.50-3.02	Massachusetts	M.	59-60-60	1.80-5.00-2.83
Maryland	M.	60-60-60	2.50-4.00-2.78	Minnesota	M.	59-60-60	3.50-4.00-3.67
Massachusetts	M.	60-60-60	2.50-3.50-3.33	Missouri	M.	59-60-60	2.50-3.00-2.79
New Hampshire	M.	60-60-60	3.00-3.00-3.00	New Jersey	M.	60-60-60	3.00-3.75-3.50
New Jersey	M.	60-60-60	3.25-3.50-3.38	New York	M.	60-60-60	1.34-4.50-2.75
New York	M.	60-60-60	2.00-3.50-2.85	Ohio	M.	60-60-60	2.50-3.00-2.75
Pennsylvania	M.	60-60-60	2.34-2.84-2.67	Pennsylvania	M.	60-60-60	1.50-3.67-2.62
1869:				Virginia	M.	60-60-60	2.00-2.25-2.15
Connecticut	M.	60-60-60	2.25-3.75-3.13	**1875:**			
Maryland	M.	60-60-60	2.50-4.00-2.83	California	M.	60-60-60	3.50-4.00-3.79
Massachusetts	M.	60-60-60	2.50-3.20-3.08	Connecticut	M.	60-60-60	2.00-4.25-2.86
New Hampshire	M.	60-60-60	3.00-3.00-3.00	Illinois	M.	60-60-60	2.75-3.00-2.99
New Jersey	M.	60-60-60	3.00-3.75-3.38	Louisiana	M.	60-60-60	4.00-4.00-4.00
New York	M.	60-60-60	2.00-3.75-2.97	Maryland	M.	60-60-60	2.50-3.58-2.95
Pennsylvania	M.	60-60-60	2.34-2.84-2.63				

1 Not reported.   2 Per hour.

Table I-36.—*Pattern makers, 1844–1900, by year and State*—Continued

Year and State	Sex	Hours per week	Rate per day (dollars)
1875—Continued.			
Massachusetts....	M.	59–60–60	2.00–4.60–2.73
Minnesota........	M.	60–60–60	3.50–4.00–3.63
Missouri.........	M.	59–60–59	2.50–3.00–2.72
New Jersey.......	M.	60–60–60	3.00–3.75–3.38
New York.........	M.	60–60–60	1.50–4.50–2.88
Ohio.............	M.	60–60–60	2.50–3.00–2.75
Pennsylvania.....	M.	60–60–60	1.80–4.00–2.42
Virginia.........	M.	60–60–60	2.00–2.25–2.20
1876:			
California.......	M.	60–60–60	3.00–3.75–3.37
Connecticut......	M.	60–60–60	2.00–4.25–2.95
Illinois.........	M.	60–60–60	2.75–3.00–2.97
Louisiana........	M.	60–60–60	3.00–3.00–3.00
Maryland.........	M.	60–60–60	2.25–3.50–2.71
Massachusetts....	M.	59–60–60	1.75–4.60–2.54
Minnesota........	M.	60–60–60	3.50–4.00–3.63
Missouri.........	M.	59–60–59	2.50–3.00–2.69
New Jersey.......	M.	60–60–60	3.00–3.75–3.25
New York.........	M.	60–60–60	2.20–4.50–2.76
Ohio.............	M.	60–60–60	2.50–3.00–2.75
Pennsylvania.....	M.	60–60–60	1.50–4.00–2.20
Do...............	M.	(1)	².23–.23–.23
Virginia.........	M.	60–60–60	2.00–2.00–2.00
1877:			
California.......	M.	60–60–60	3.00–3.50–3.30
Connecticut......	M.	60–60–60	2.00–4.25–2.98
Illinois.........	M.	60–60–60	2.25–2.85–2.74
Louisiana........	M.	60–60–60	3.00–3.00–3.00
Maryland.........	M.	60–60–60	2.25–3.50–2.72
Massachusetts....	M.	59–60–60	1.60–4.00–2.44
Minnesota........	M.	60–60–60	3.25–3.75–3.40
Missouri.........	M.	59–60–60	2.50–3.00–2.87
New Jersey.......	M.	60–60–60	3.00–3.40–3.20
New York.........	M.	60–60–60	1.70–4.50–2.63
Ohio.............	M.	60–60–60	1.67–4.00–2.48
Pennsylvania.....	M.	48–60–58	1.90–3.33–2.37
Virginia.........	M.	60–60–60	1.67–2.00–1.84
1878:			
California.......	M.	60–60–60	3.00–3.50–3.18
Connecticut......	M.	60–72–62	2.00–4.25–2.93
Illinois.........	M.	60–60–60	2.50–2.75–2.72
Louisiana........	M.	60–60–60	3.00–3.00–3.00
Maryland.........	M.	60–60–60	2.25–3.50–2.79
Massachusetts....	M.	59–60–60	1.60–4.00–2.39
Minnesota........	M.	60–60–60	3.25–3.75–3.40
Missouri.........	M.	59–60–60	2.50–3.00–2.87
New Jersey.......	M.	60–60–60	2.50–3.40–2.97
New York.........	M.	60–60–60	1.50–4.50–2.46
Ohio.............	M.	60–60–60	1.67–3.33–2.35
Pennsylvania.....	M.	48–60–58	1.67–3.33–2.17
Virginia.........	M.	60–60–60	1.67–2.00–1.84
1879:			
California.......	M.	60–60–60	3.00–3.50–3.14
Connecticut......	M.	60–60–60	2.00–2.70–2.31
Illinois.........	M.	60–60–60	2.25–2.75–2.70
Louisiana........	M.	60–60–60	2.75–3.00–2.92
Maryland.........	M.	60–60–60	2.25–3.50–2.83
Massachusetts....	M.	59–60–60	1.75–4.00–2.32
Minnesota........	M.	60–60–60	3.25–3.75–3.40
Missouri.........	M.	59–60–60	2.25–3.00–2.73
New Jersey.......	M.	60–60–60	2.50–3.40–2.80
New York.........	M.	60–60–60	1.70–4.50–2.38
Ohio.............	M.	60–60–60	1.50–2.75–2.25
Pennsylvania.....	M.	57–60–60	1.00–3.50–1.94
Virginia.........	M.	60–60–60	1.50–2.00–1.58
1880:			
California.......	M.	60–60–60	2.75–3.25–3.08
Connecticut......	M.	60–60–60	2.00–2.70–2.24
Illinois.........	M.	60–60–60	2.25–2.75–2.70
Louisiana........	M.	60–60–60	3.00–3.00–3.00
Maryland.........	M.	60–60–60	2.25–3.50–2.75
Massachusetts....	M.	59–60–60	1.75–4.00–2.36
Minnesota........	M.	60–60–60	3.25–3.75–3.38
Missouri.........	M.	59–60–59	2.50–3.00–2.84
New Jersey.......	M.	60–60–60	2.50–3.40–2.95
1880—Continued.			
New York.........	M.	60–60–60	1.60–4.50–2.39
Ohio.............	M.	60–60–60	2.17–2.75–2.46
Pennsylvania.....	M.	60–60–60	1.50–3.50–2.23
Virginia.........	M.	60–60–60	1.83–2.50–1.97
1881:			
California.......	M.	60–60–60	2.50–3.50–3.15
Connecticut......	M.	60–60–60	2.00–2.75–2.39
Illinois.........	M.	60–60–60	2.00–3.00–2.87
Louisiana........	M.	60–60–60	3.00–3.00–3.00
Maryland.........	M.	60–60–60	2.25–3.25–2.66
Massachusetts....	M.	59–60–60	1.75–4.00–2.36
Minnesota........	M.	60–60–60	3.25–3.50–3.31
Missouri.........	M.	59–60–59	2.50–3.00–2.86
New Jersey.......	M.	60–60–60	2.08–3.67–2.78
New York.........	M.	60–60–60	1.80–4.50–2.50
Ohio.............	M.	60–60–60	1.50–3.25–2.19
Pennsylvania.....	M.	60–60–60	1.80–4.00–2.41
Virginia.........	M.	60–60–60	2.25–2.25–2.25
1882:			
California.......	M.	60–60–60	3.00–3.75–3.31
Connecticut......	M.	60–60–60	2.00–3.00–2.61
Illinois.........	M.	60–60–60	2.50–3.00–2.95
Louisiana........	M.	60–60–60	3.00–3.00–3.00
Maryland.........	M.	60–60–60	2.25–3.00–2.61
Massachusetts....	M.	59–60–60	2.00–4.00–2.48
Minnesota........	M.	60–60–60	3.25–3.50–3.33
Missouri.........	M.	59–60–60	1.75–3.50–2.79
New Jersey.......	M.	60–60–60	1.75–3.40–2.63
New York.........	M.	59–60–60	1.90–5.00–2.76
Ohio.............	M.	60–60–60	2.00–3.00–2.50
Do...............	M.	(1)	1.50–5.00–2.36
Pennsylvania.....	M.	60–60–60	1.84–4.17–2.45
Virginia.........	M.	60–60–60	2.25–2.25–2.25
1883:			
California.......	M.	60–60–60	3.00–3.75–3.36
Connecticut......	M.	60–60–60	2.25–3.00–2.62
Illinois.........	M.	60–60–60	2.50–3.00–2.93
Louisiana........	M.	60–60–60	3.00–3.00–3.00
Maryland.........	M.	60–60–60	2.25–3.00–2.58
Massachusetts....	M.	59–60–60	1.80–4.00–2.60
Michigan.........	M.	(1)	.65–4.00–2.48
Minnesota........	M.	60–60–60	3.25–3.50–3.33
Missouri.........	M.	59–60–60-	2.50–3.00–2.90
New Jersey.......	M.	60–60–60	2.50–3.75–2.64
New York.........	M.	60–60–60	2.00–3.75–2.92
Ohio.............	M.	54–60–60	1.50–3.17–2.49
Pennsylvania.....	M.	60–60–60	2.00–4.17–2.54
Virginia.........	M.	60–60–60	2.25–2.25–2.25
1884:			
California.......	M.	60–60–60	3.00–3.75–3.31
Connecticut......	M.	60–60–60	2.25–3.00–2.53
Illinois.........	M.	60–60–60	2.70–3.00–2.97
Louisiana........	M.	60–60–60	3.00–3.00–3.00
Maryland.........	M.	60–60–60	2.25–2.75–2.53
Massachusetts....	M.	59–60–60	1.80–4.00–2.42
Michigan.........	M.	(1)	1.75–3.50–2.53
Minnesota........	M.	60–60–60	3.25–3.50–3.33
Missouri.........	M.	59–60–60	2.50–3.00–2.81
New Jersey.......	M.	60–60–60	2.15–3.40–2.65
New York.........	M.	60–60–60	2.00–5.00–2.91
Ohio.............	M.	56–60–58	2.33–4.50–2.45
Pennsylvania.....	M.	60–60–60	2.00–4.50–2.50
Virginia.........	M.	60–60–60	2.08–2.25–2.18
1885:			
California.......	M.	60–60–60	2.50–4.00–3.34
Connecticut......	M.	60–60–60	2.00–3.50–2.56
Delaware.........	M.	60–60–60	2.50–2.50–2.50
Illinois.........	M.	60–60–60	2.00–4.00–2.86
Indiana..........	M.	60–60–60	1.50–3.50–2.34
Kentucky.........	M.	60–60–60	2.50–2.50–2.50
Louisiana........	M.	60–60–60	3.00–3.00–3.00
Maine............	M.	60–60–60	2.25–2.25–2.25
Maryland.........	M.	60–60–60	2.25–2.75–2.59
Massachusetts....	M.	59–60–60	1.60–2.75–2.39
Michigan.........	M.	60–60–60	1.00–5.00–2.30

¹ Not reported. ² Per hour.

TABLE I-36.—*Pattern makers, 1844-1900, by year and State*—Continued

Year and State	Sex	Lowest, highest, and average—	
		Hours per week	Rate per day (dollars)
1885—Continued.			
Minnesota.........	M.	60-60-60	3. 25-3. 50-3. 31
Missouri.........	M.	59-60-59	2. 50-3. 00-2. 78
New Hampshire..	M.	60-60-60	2. 50-2. 50-2. 50
New Jersey.......	M.	54-60-59	1. 00-3. 40-2. 50
New York........	M.	60-60-60	1. 80-5. 00-2. 74
Ohio...........	M.	59-60-60	1. 00-4. 50-2. 42
Pennsylvania.....	M.	60-60-60	1. 90-4. 50-2. 43
Tennessee........	M.	60-60-60	2. 50-2. 50-2. 50
Vermont.........	M.	60-60-60	2. 25-2. 25-2. 25
Virginia.........	M.	48-60-55	2. 00-2. 70-2. 30
West Virginia.....	M.	60-60-60	2. 25-2. 25-2. 25
1886:			
California........	M.	60-60-60	3. 00-6. 00-3. 52
Connecticut.....	M.	60-60-60	2. 25-2. 75-2. 52
Illinois.........	M.	60-60-60	2. 50-3. 00-2. 90
Kansas........	M.	54-60-57	2. 00-2. 25-2. 13
Louisiana......	M.	60-60-60	2. 75-3. 00-2. 88
Maryland......	M.	60-60-60	2. 25-2. 75-2. 56
Massachusetts....	M.	59-60-60	1. 60-3. 00-2. 29
Minnesota.....	M.	60-60-60	3. 25-3. 50-3. 31
Missouri......	M.	59-60-59	2. 50-3. 12-2. 83
New Jersey.....	M.	60-60-60	2. 50-3. 40-3. 01
New York.......	M.	54-60-59	1. 80-5. 00-3. 03
Ohio........	M.	60-60-60	1. 24-3. 11-2. 40
Pennsylvania.....	M.	60-60-60	1. 80-4. 50-2. 50
Virginia.........	M.	60-60-60	2. 17-2. 17-2. 17
1887:			
California........	M.	60-60-60	3. 00-3. 75-3. 41
Connecticut.....	M.	60-60-60	1. 82-3. 00-2. 68
Florida.........	M.	(1)	3. 50-3. 50-3. 50
Illinois.........	M.	60-60-60	2. 50-3. 00-2. 95
Louisiana.......	M.	60-60-60	3. 00-3. 00-3. 00
Maryland.......	M.	60-60-60	1. 50-3. 00-2. 21
Massachusetts....	M.	59-60-60	1. 75-3. 25-2 39
Michigan........	M.	(1)	². 35- . 35
Minnesota.....	M.	60-60-60	3. 25-3. 50-3. 31
Missouri.........	M.	59-60-60	2. 50-3. 13-2 74
Nebraska.......	(1)	54-60-55	2. 90-3. 55-3. 16
New Jersey......	M.	60-60-60	2. 75-3. 40-3. 18
New York.......	M.	54-60-53	1. 80-5. 00-2. 79
Do...........	M.	(1)	². 20-. 28½-. 24
Ohio...........	M.	54-63-60	1. 62-5. 00-2. 39
Do...........	F.	60-60-60	1. 17-1. 17-1. 17
Oregon........	M.	(1)	3. 85-3. 85-3. 85
Pennsylvania.....	M.	60-60-60	1. 55-5. 00-2. 60
Rhode Island.....	M.	(1)	2. 00-2. 00-2. 00
Virginia........	M.	60-60-60	2. 00-2. 50-2. 17
Wisconsin........	M.	(1)	1. 67-3. 00-2. 25
1888:			
California........	M.	60-60-60	3. 00-3. 75-3. 42
Connecticut.....	M.	60-60-60	2. 25-3. 00-2. 74
Illinois.........	M.	60-60-60	2. 50-3. 00-2. 94
Kansas........	M.	(1)	2. 62-2. 62-2. 62
Louisiana......	M.	60-60-60	3. 00-3. 00-3. 00
Maryland......	M.	60-60-60	2. 25-3. 00-2 58
Massachusetts....	M.	59-60-60	1. 80-3. 20-2. 47
Michigan........	M.	60-60-60	2. 68-2. 68-2. 68
Minnesota.....	M.	60-60-60	3. 25-3. 50-3. 33
Missouri......	M.	59-60-59	2. 50-3. 13-2 76
New Jersey......	M.	60-60-60	2. 25-3. 40-2 51
New York.......	M.	48-60-58	1. 50-5. 00-2 81
Do...........	M.	(1)	². 25-. 51-. 33
North Carolina...	M.	60-60-60	1. 50-1. 50-1. 50
Ohio........	M.	60-60-60	1. 65-3. 00-2. 43
Pennsylvania.....	M.	60-60-60	1. 80-5. 00-2. 59
Virginia.........	M.	60-60-60	2. 00-2. 17-2. 10
1889:			
California........	M.	60-60-60	3. 00-3. 75-3. 55
Connecticut.....	M.	60-60-60	2. 25-3. 00-2. 60
Illinois.........	M.	60-60-60	2. 50-3. 00-2. 96
Kansas........	M.	60-60-60	2. 20-3. 00-2. 53
Louisiana......	M.	60-60-60	3. 00-3. 00-3. 00
Maryland.........	M.	60-60-60	2. 50-3. 00-2. 64

Year and State	Sex	Lowest, highest, and average—	
		Hours per week	Rate per day (dollars)
1889—Continued.			
Massachusetts....	M.	59-60-60	1. 80-3. 50-2. 59
Michigan.........	M.	60-60-60	2. 25-2. 50-2. 38
Minnesota........	M.	60-60-60	3. 25-3. 50-3. 33
Missouri.........	M.	59-60-59	1. 67-3. 13-2 57
New Jersey.......	M.	60-60-60	2. 75-3. 40-3. 08
New York........	M.	54-60-58	1. 25-4. 50-2. 75
Ohio...........	M.	60-60-60	2. 00-3. 00-2. 38
Pennsylvania.....	M.	60-60-60	2. 00-5. 00-2. 69
Virginia.........	M.	60-60-60	2. 00-2. 25-2. 15
1890:			
California........	M.	60-60-60	3. 25-3. 75-3. 57
Connecticut.....	M.	60-60-60	2. 25-3. 50-2. 82
Illinois.........	M.	60-60-60	2. 70-3. 00-2. 96
Louisiana......	M.	60-60-60	2. 75-3. 00-2. 88
Maryland......	M.	60-60-60	2. 25-3. 00-2. 59
Massachusetts....	M.	59-60-60	1. 80-3. 50-2. 67
Michigan........	M.	60-60-60	. 40-4. 17-2. 27
Minnesota.....	M.	60-60-60	1. 25-3. 50-2. 81
Missouri......	M.	59-60-59	1. 67-3. 13-2. 69
New Jersey.....	M.	60-60-60	2. 75-3. 40-3. 18
New York.......	M.	54-60-58	1. 00-5. 00-2. 69
Ohio........	M.	60-60-60	2. 33-3. 00-2. 50
Do...........	(1)	54-60-60	1. 97-3. 50-2. 51
Pennsylvania.....	M.	60-60-60	2. 00-5. 00-2. 71
Virginia.........	M.	60-60-60	2. 00-2. 42-2. 21
1891:			
California........	M.	60-60-60	3. 50-3. 75-3. 58
Connecticut.....	M.	60-60-60	2.25-3. 50-2. 83
Illinois.........	M.	60-60-60	2. 50-3. 30-3. 22
Louisiana......	M.	60-60-60	2. 75-3. 00-2 88
Maine..........	M.	60-60-60	3. 00-3. 00-3. 00
Maryland......	M.	60-60-60	2. 25-3. 00-2. 59
Massachusetts....	M.	50-60-60	1. 80-4. 00-2 66
Minnesota.....	M.	60-60-60	3. 50-3. 50-3. 50
Missouri......	M.	59-60-59	1. 66-3. 30-2. 59
New Jersey.....	M.	60-60-60	2. 75-3. 40-3. 18
New York.......	M.	54-60-58	. 90-5. 00-2. 59
Ohio........	M.	48-60-59	1. 50-3. 50-2. 45
Pennsylvania.....	M.	54-60-59	2. 00-5. 00-2. 73
Virginia...........	M.	60-60-60	2. 00-2. 33-2. 20
1892:			
California........	M.	56-60-58	3. 00-4. 00-3. 42
Connecticut.....	M.	60-60-60	1. 50-3. 00-2. 60
Illinois.........	M.	60-60-60	2. 50-3. 30-3. 23
Indiana........	M.	54-60-59	1. 81-3. 00-2. 40
Louisiana......	M.	60-60-60	2. 75-3. 00-2. 88
Maryland......	M.	60-60-60	2. 25-3. 00-2. 65
Massachusetts....	M.	59-60-60	1. 75-4. 00-2. 59
Michigan........	M.	(1)	2. 07-2. 07-2. 07
Minnesota.....	M.	60-60-60	3. 50-3. 50-3. 50
Missouri......	M.	59-60-60	1. 66-3. 13-2. 68
New Jersey.....	M.	60-60-60	3. 25-3. 50-3. 38
New York.......	M.	54-60-58	1. 80-5. 00-2. 85
Ohio........	M.	60-60-60	2. 33-3. 00-2. 62
Pennsylvania.....	M.	54-60-60	1. 60-5. 00-2. 75
Virginia.........	M.	60-60-60	2. 00-2. 42-2. 13
1893:			
California........	M.	60-60-60	2. 50-3. 75-3. 15
Illinois.........	M.	60-60-60	2. 70-3. 50-3. 47
Indiana........	M.	60-60-60	2. 25-2. 25-2. 25
Louisiana......	M.	60-60-60	2. 75-3. 00-2. 83
Maryland......	M.	60-60-60	1. 50-3. 00-2. 59
Massachusetts....	M.	60-60-60	1. 80-4. 00-2. 68
Michigan........	M.	57-60-60	2. 00-2. 75-2. 25
Minnesota.....	M.	60-60-60	3. 25-3. 50-3. 34
Missouri......	M.	59-60-59	3. 50-3. 50-3. 34
Montana........	M.	54-56-55	3. 50-5. 75-4. 44
New Hampshire..	M.	53-53-53	3. 00-3. 00-3. 00
New York.......	M.	60-60-60	2. 75-5. 00-3. 36
Ohio........	M.	48-60-59	1. 50-4. 00-2. 51
Do...........	F.	60-60-60	1. 00-1. 00-1. 00
Pennsylvania.....	M.	54-60-60	1. 60-5. 00-2. 66
Virginia.........	M.	60-60-60	2. 25-2. 42-2. 34

¹ Not reported.   ² Per hour.

TABLE **I–36.**—*Pattern makers, 1844–1900, by year and State*—Continued

Year and State	Sex	Lowest, highest, and average—		Year and State	Sex	Lowest, highest, and average—	
		Hours per week	Rate per day (dollars)			Hours per week	Rate per day (dollars)
1894:				**1897:**			
California	M.	60–60–60	3. 50–3. 75–3. 58	California	M.	60–60–60	3. 00–3. 50–3. 35
Illinois	M.	60–60–60	2. 70–2. 90–2. 88	Illinois	M.	60–60–60	2. 50–3. 00–2. 94
Indiana	M.	48–60–54	2. 00–3. 25–2. 53	Kansas	M.	60–60–60	2. 00–2. 00–2. 00
Iowa	M.	48–60–59	1. 80–3. 75–2. 41	Louisiana	M.	60–60–60	2. 75–3. 00–2. 88
Louisiana	M.	60–60–60	2. 75–2. 75–2. 75	Maryland	M.	60–60–60	2. 50–2. 75–2. 61
Maryland	M.	60–60–60	2. 50–3. 00–2. 66	Massachusetts	M.	59–60–60	1. 97–4. 00–2. 77
Massachusetts	M.	59–60–60	1. 80–4. 00–2. 61	Michigan	M.	(1)	2. 22–2. 22–2. 22
Minnesota	M.	60–60–60	3. 25–3. 50–3. 32	Minnesota	M.	60–60–60	3. 25–3. 50–3. 32
Missouri	M.	59–60–59	2. 00–3. 33–2. 79	Missouri	M.	59–60–59	2. 25–3. 08–2. 68
New Hampshire	M.	36–59–50	2. 00–3. 00–2. 38	Nebraska	M.	48–48–48	2. 50–2. 50–2. 50
New York	M.	60–60–60	1. 50–5. 00–3. 24	New York	M.	60–60–60	1. 60–4. 50–2. 80
Ohio	M.	45–60–59	1. 00–4. 00–2. 27	Ohio	M.	60–60–60	2. 17–2. 27–2. 22
Do	F.	(1)	. 50–. 50–. 50	Pennsylvania	M.	54–60–59	1. 80–5. 00–2. 63
Pennsylvania	M.	54–60–59	1. 60–5. 00–2. 42	Virginia	M.	54–60–60	1. 25–3. 00–2. 21
Virginia	M.	60–60–60	2. 25–2. 42–2. 34	**1898:**			
West Virginia	M.	60–60–60	1. 66–1. 66–1. 66	California	M.	60–60–60	3. 00–3. 50–3. 35
1895:				Illinois	M.	60–60–60	2. 50–3. 00–2. 95
California	M.	60–60–60	2. 75–3. 50–3. 39	Louisiana	M.	60–60–60	2. 75–3. 00–2. 83
Illinois	M.	60–60–60	2. 70–3. 00–2. 96	Maryland	M.	60–60–60	2. 50–2. 75–2. 61
Louisiana	M.	60–60–60	2. 75–3. 00–2. 88	Massachusetts	M.	59–60–60	2. 00–4. 00–2. 79
Maryland	M.	60–60–60	2. 50–3. 00–2. 66	Michigan	M.	(1)	1. 82–2. 75–2. 34
Massachusetts	M.	55–60–59	2. 00–4. 00–2. 75	Minnesota	M.	60–60–60	3. 25–3. 50–3. 31
Minnesota	M.	60–60–60	3. 25–3. 50–3. 35	Missouri	M.	59–60–59	2. 25–3. 08–2. 68
Missouri	M.	59–60–59	1. 77–3. 33–2. 68	Nebraska	M.	(1)	2. 25–3. 50–3. 40
New Jersey	M.	60–60–60	2. 42–2. 42–2. 42	New Jersey	M.	60–60–60	2. 42–2. 75–2. 55
New York	M.	60–60–60	2. 50–4. 50–3. 23	New York	M.	60–60–60	2. 50–4. 50–2. 83
Ohio	M.	48–72–59	1. 55–4. 00–2. 38	Ohio	M.	60–60–60	2. 17–2. 50–2. 31
Do	F.	48–48–48	1. 62–1. 62–1. 62	Pennsylvania	M.	54–60–59	2. 00–3. 33–2. 74
Pennsylvania	M.	54–60–59	1. 93–5. 00–2. 57	Virginia	M.	60–60–60	1. 67–2. 25–1. 98
Virginia	M.	60–60–60	1. 83–2. 25–2. 01	**1899:**			
1896:				Alabama	M.	60–60–60	2. 25–3. 00–2. 82
California	M.	60–60–60	3. 00–3. 50–3. 32	Georgia	M.	59–60–59	2. 00–3. 00–2. 40
Colorado	M.	54–60–57	2. 25–3. 00–2. 63	Illinois	M.	60–60–60	2. 48–3. 30–2. 08
Illinois	M.	60–60–60	2. 50–3. 00–2. 93	Massachusetts	M.	54–54–54	2. 25–3. 00–2. 70
Louisiana	M.	60–60–60	2. 75–2. 75–2. 75	New York	M.	60–60–60	3. 00–3. 25–3. 13
Maryland	M.	60–60–60	2. 50–3. 00–2. 79	Ohio	M.	60–60–60	2. 50–3. 00–2. 75
Massachusetts	M.	56–60–59	1. 97–4. 00–2. 88	**1900:**			
Minnesota	M.	60–60–60	3. 25–3. 50–3. 32	Alabama	M.	60–60–60	2. 25–3. 00–2. 91
Missouri	M.	48–60–55	1. 35–3. 33–2. 36	Georgia	M.	59–60–59	2. 00–3. 00–2. 45
Nebraska	M.	(1)	1. 75–2. 50–2. 10	Illinois	M.	60–60–60	2. 48–3. 30–3. 10
New York	M.	60–60–60	1. 75–4. 50–2. 73	Massachusetts	M.	54–54–54	2. 25–3. 00–2. 70
Ohio	M.	54–60–59	1. 35–3. 00–2. 31	New York	M.	60–60–60	3. 25–3. 25–3. 25
Pennsylvania	M.	54–60–60	1. 66–5. 00–2. 78	Ohio	M.	60–60–60	2. 50–3. 50–2. 76
Vermont	M.	60–60–60	1. 75–1. 75–1. 75				
Virginia	M.	60–60–60	2. 00–2. 25–2. 08				

¹ Not reported.

TABLE **I–37.**—*Pattern makers; males, 1890–1906, by city and year*

Year	Atlanta, Ga.		Birmingham, Ala.		Boston, Mass.		Chicago, Ill.	
	Hours per week	Rate per hour	Hours per week	Rate per hour	Hours per week	Rate per hour	Hours per week	Rate per hour
1890	59. 6	$0. 277			59. 1	$0. 298	59. 5	$0. 320
1891	59. 6	. 277			59. 1	. 298	59. 5	. 316
1892	59. 6	. 277			59. 1	. 298	58. 9	. 316
1893	59. 6	. 277			58. 7	. 303	55. 0	. 335
1894	59. 6	. 270			58. 6	. 292	58. 0	. 275
1895	59. 6	. 270			58. 6	. 297	58. 6	. 274
1896	59. 6	. 268			58. 7	. 276	58. 5	. 276
1897	59. 6	. 270			58. 7	. 283	57. 9	. 276
1898	59. 6	. 271			58. 7	. 285	58. 6	. 275
1899	59. 6	. 264			57. 3	. 287	58. 6	. 279
1900	59. 6	. 264			56. 9	. 284	58. 6	. 291
1901	59. 7	. 279			56. 5	. 295	56. 3	. 307
1902	59. 7	. 285			55. 8	. 310	55. 8	. 320
1903	59. 7	. 285			55. 3	. 323	54. 1	. 370
1904	59. 7	. 288	59. 6	$0. 314	55. 7	. 321	54. 0	. 371
1905	59. 6	. 302	59. 7	. 308	54. 0	. 340	54. 0	. 378
1906	59. 7	. 307	59. 7	. 322	54. 0	. 346	52. 6	. 403

Year	Cincinnati, Ohio		Denver, Colo.		Detroit, Mich.		New Orleans, La.	
1890	60. 0	$0. 245			60. 0	$0. 239	60. 0	$0. 292
1891	60. 0	. 256			60. 0	. 244	60. 0	. 292
1892	60. 0	. 256			60. 0	. 254	60. 0	. 292
1893	60. 0	. 240			60. 0	. 259	60. 0	. 290
1894	60. 0	. 224			60. 0	. 247	60. 0	. 290
1895	60. 0	. 231			60. 0	. 246	60. 0	. 292
1896	60. 0	. 234			60. 0	. 243	60. 0	. 290
1897	60. 0	. 254			60. 0	. 253	60. 0	. 291
1898	60. 0	. 258			60. 0	. 250	60. 0	. 292
1899	60. 0	. 260			60. 0	. 264	58. 8	. 307
1900	60. 0	. 262			60. 0	. 266	59. 1	. 309
1901	60. 0	. 264			60. 0	. 267	54. 0	. 345
1902	58. 7	. 287			60. 0	. 281	54. 0	. 331
1903	56. 6	. 290			59. 6	. 281	53. 2	. 340
1904	55. 0	. 318	53. 7	$0. 330	59. 5	. 248	54. 0	. 337
1905	55. 0	. 325	57. 2	. 348	59. 3	. 282	54. 0	. 340
1906	55. 0	. 319	56. 3	. 365	59. 4	. 298	54. 0	. 333

Year	New York, N. Y.		Philadelphia, Pa.		St. Louis, Mo.		San Francisco, Calif.	
1890	56. 4	$0. 335	60. 0	$0. 262	59. 6	$0. 298	59. 1	$0. 355
1891	56. 4	. 321	60. 0	. 266	59. 6	. 298	59. 2	. 358
1892	56. 4	. 360	60. 0	. 269	59. 6	. 298	59. 2	. 354
1893	56. 0	. 313	60. 0	. 273	59. 4	. 298	59. 2	. 347
1894	55. 9	. 343	60. 0	. 240	59. 5	. 302	59. 2	. 327
1895	55. 2	. 331	60. 0	. 247	59. 5	. 302	59. 1	. 318
1896	54. 8	. 387	60. 0	. 262	59. 6	. 314	59. 1	. 320
1897	54. 9	. 328	60. 0	. 262	59. 5	. 302	59. 2	. 325
1898	54. 8	. 365	60. 0	. 267	57. 3	. 317	59. 3	. 328
1899	54. 7	. 327	58. 2	. 276	57. 3	. 319	59. 1	. 331
1900	54. 8	. 352	57. 3	. 281	57. 5	. 320	59. 1	. 333
1901	55. 0	. 355	57. 5	. 284	57. 1	. 327	59. 2	. 341
1902	53. 9	. 380	57. 1	. 300	55. 1	. 341	57. 7	. 347
1903	54. 0	. 389	56. 8	. 301	54. 0	. 351	57. 6	. 365
1904	54. 1	. 401	56. 3	. 315	54. 0	. 353	54. 0	. 411
1905	54. 0	. 405	56. 3	. 312	54. 0	. 357	54. 0	. 422
1906	54. 0	. 410	56. 5	. 323	54. 0	. 400	54. 0	. 535

324 PART 2.—FROM 1840 TO 1928

TABLE I-38.—*Pattern makers, wood, males, jobbing shops, 1907–1924, by city and year*

Year	Birmingham, Ala.		Boston, Mass.		Chicago, Ill.	
	Hours per week	Rate per week	Hours per week	Rate per week	Hours per week	Rate per week
1907					49.5	$0.500
1908					49.5	.500
1909					49.5	.500
1910					49.5	.530
1911					44.0	.563
1912					44.0	.563
1913					44.0	.600
1914			50.0	$0.450	44.0	.600
1915			50.0	.450	44.0	.600
1916	44.0	$0.500	50.0	.470	44.0	.700
1917	44.0	.600	48.0	.600	44.0	.750
1918	44.0	.700	48.0	.800	44.0	.900
1919	44.0	.900	48.0	.900	44.0	1.100
1920	44.0	1.000	44.0	1.150	44.0	1.350
1921	48.0	.750	44.0	1.000	44.0	1.200
1922	48.0	.750	44.0	[1].800		
1923	48.0	.850	44.0	.900		
1924	48.0	.850	44.0	.900		

Year	Cincinnati, Ohio		Denver, Colo.[2]		Detroit, Mich.	
	Hours per week	Rate per week	Hours per week	Rate per week	Hours per week	Rate per week
1907	54.0	$0.420	54.0	$0.400		
1908	54.0	.420	54.0	.400		
1909	54.0	.420	54.0	.400		
1910	54.0	.420	54.0	.400		
1911	50.0	.420	54.0	.450		
1912	50.0	.420	54.0	.450	55.0	$0.425
1913	50.0	.420	54.0	.450	55.0	.450
1914	50.0	.420			55.0	.450
1915	50.0	.420			50.0	.450
1916	50.0	.500	54.0	.500	50.0	.450
1917	50.0	.600	54.0	.600	44.0	.650
1918	50.0	.700			44.0	.850
1919	50.0	.800			44.0	1.100
1920	44.0	1.250			44.0	1.400
1921					44.0	1.250
1922					44.0	1.000
1923					44.0	1.250
1924					44.0	1.250

Year	New York, N.Y.		Philadelphia, Pa.[3]		St. Louis, Mo.	
	Hours per week	Rate per week	Hours per week	Rate per week	Hours per week	Rate per week
1907	46.3	$0.485			54.0	$0.450
1908	46.3	.485			54.0	.450
1909	46.3	.485			54.0	.480
1910	46.3	.515			54.0	.550
1911	46.3	.515			54.0	.550
1912	44.0	.531	50.0	$0.400	54.0	.550
1913	44.0	.531	50.0	.420	44.0	.600
1914	44.0	.540	50.0	.420	44.0	.600
1915	44.0	.540	50.0	.420	44.0	.600
1916	44.0	.600			44.0	.600
1917	44.0	.750	44.0	.625	44.0	.600
1918	44.0	.850	44.0	.750	44.0	.750
1919	44.0	1.000	44.0	.860	44.0	.900
1920	44.0	1.350	44.0	1.000	44.0	1.250
1921	44.0	1.150	44.0	[4]1.000	44.0	1.250
1922	44.0	1.150	44.0	1.000	44.0	1.000
1923	44.0	1.150	44.0	1.100	44.0	1.100
1924	44.0	1.150	44.0	1.100	44.0	1.100

[1] More than 25 per cent received more.
[2] Manufacturing and jobbing shops, 1913.
[3] Manufacturing and jobbing shops, 1920 and 1921.
[4] 25 per cent received more, $1.10 to $1.25 per hour.

TABLE I-39.—*Pattern makers, wood, males, manufacturing shops, 1907-1924, by city and year*

Year	Atlanta, Ga.		Birmingham, Ala.		Boston, Mass.		Chicago, Ill.[1]	
	Hours per week	Rate per hour	Hours per week	Rate per hour	Hours per week	Rate per hour	Hours per week	Rate per hour
1907	60.0	$0.325	60.0	$0.375	54.0	$0.390	54.0	$0.400
1908	60.0	.325	60.0	.350	54.0	.390	54.0	.425
1909	60.0	.350	60.0	.350	54.0	.400	54.0	.450
1910	54.0	.350	60.0	.350	54.0	.400	54.0	475
1911	54.0	.375	60.0	.350	54.0	.400	54.0	.475
1912	54.0	.375	60.0	.350	54.0	.400	54.0	.475
1913	60.0	.375	60.0	.375	54.0	.450	54.0	.500
1914	60.0	.375	60.0	.375	54.0	.450	54.0	.500
1915	60.0	.375	60.0	.375	54.0	.450	54.0	.500
1916	54.0	.400	54.0	.500	54.0	.470	54.0	.550
1917	54.0	.450	54.0	.600	48.0	.600	54.0	.550
1918	50.0	².550	54.0	.700	50.0	.750	54.0	.750
1919	50.0	.750	48.0	.800	50.0	.860	54.0	1.050
1920			48.0	.900	48.0	.860	54.0	1.350
1921			48.0	.750	48.0	.860	44.0	1.200
1922			48.0	.750	48.0	.760	44.0	1.200
1923			48.0	.750	48.0	.800	44.0	1.200
1924			48.0	.750	48.0	.800	44.0	1.250

Year	Cincinnati, Ohio		Denver, Colo.[3]		Detroit, Mich.[1]		New Orleans, La.	
1907	60.0	$0.350					54.0	$0.333
1908	60.0	.350					54.0	.361
1909	60.0	.350					54.0	.361
1910	60.0	.350					54.0	.361
1911	55.0	.350					54.0	.361
1912	55.0	.350	54.0	$0.450	60.0	$0.420	54.0	.361
1913	55.0	.350	54.0	.450	60.0	.450	54.0	.361
1914	55.0	.350	54.0	.450	55.0	.450	54.0	.361
1915	55.0	.400	54.0	.450	55.0	.450		
1916	52.5	.440	54.0	.500	55.0	.450		
1917	52.5	.480	54.0	.600	50.0	.550		
1918	52.5	.650	48.0	⁴.650	50.0	.750		
1919	52.5	.700	48.0	⁵.750	50.0	.850		
1920	48.0	1.250	48.0	⁵1.000	50.0	1.250		
1921	48.0	1.250	48.0	1.000	50.0	1.000		
1922	48.0	.900	48.0	.900	50.0	⁵.800		
1923	48.0	.900			50.0	1.000		
1924	48.0	.900			50.0	1.000		

Year	New York, N.Y.		Philadelphia, Pa.		St. Louis, Mo.		San Francisco, Calif.	
1907			50.0	$0.350	50.0	$0.400	54.0	$0.556
1908			50.0	.350	50.0	.400	54.0	.556
1909			50.0	.350	50.0	.435	52.5	.571
1910			50.0	.350	50.0	.450	49.5	.606
1911			50.0	.375	50.0	.480	48.0	.625
1912	53.0	$0.453	50.0	.375	50.0	.480	48.0	.625
1913	53.0	.453	50.0	.375	50.0	.480	48.0	.625
1914	50.0	.472	50.0	.375	50.0	.480	48.0	.625
1915	50.0	.472	50.0	.375	50.0	.480	48.0	.625
1916	50.0	.530	50.0	.450	50.0	.480	48.0	.625
1917	44.0	.563	50.0	.550	50.0	.530	48.0	.625
1918	44.0	.900	49.5	.750	50.0	.700	⁶48.0	.894
1919	44.0	1.000	49.5	.860	44.0	.850	44.0	.940
1920	44.0	1.100	44.0	1.000	44.0	1.250	44.0	1.080
1921	44.0	1.100	44.0	⁷1.000	44.0	1.250	44.0	1.080
1922	44.0	1.000	44.0	1.000	44.0	.950	44.0	1.000
1923	44.0	1.000	44.0	1.000	44.0	1.000	44.0	1.000
1924	44.0	1.100	44.0	1.000	44.0	1.000	44.0	1.000

[1] Wood and metal, 1915, 1916, and 1917.
² 65 cents June 1.
³ Manufacturing and jobbing shops, 1913 and 1915.
⁴ 75 cents June 11.
⁵ More than 50 per cent received more.
⁶ 44, June to August, inclusive.
⁷ 25 per cent received, $1.10 to $1.25.

TABLE I-40.—*Pattern makers, foundries, 1923, 1925, and 1927, by State and year*

Year	Alabama		California		Illinois		Louisiana	
	Hours per week	Rate per hour	Hours per week	Rate per hour	Hours per week	Rate per hour	Hours per week	Rate per hour
1923	54. 0	$0. 683	46. 1	$0. 884	52. 9	$0. 711	50. 1	$0. 825
1925	53. 4	. 738	46. 5	. 935	50. 0	. 843	49. 7	. 807
1927	54. 0	. 785	45. 7	1. 003	48. 8	. 891	49. 3	. 759

	Maryland		Massachusetts		Michigan		Missouri	
1923	49. 7	$0. 739	49. 5	$0. 654	51. 8	$0. 688	48. 9	$0. 809
1925	50. 2	. 738	48. 7	. 726	51. 8	. 812	49. 6	. 857
1927	48. 9	. 741	48. 8	. 752	51. 4	. 846	46. 5	1. 070

	New Hampshire		New York		Ohio		Pennsylvania	
1923	49. 7	$0. 752	48. 5	$0. 841	50. 4	$0. 714	54. 8	$0. 745
1925	50. 7	. 778	49. 6	. 832	52. 1	. 804	50. 8	. 832
1927	50. 0	. 773	50. 0	. 815	50. 8	. 836	51. 0	. 836

TABLE I-41.—*Tool makers, 1870–1897, by year and State*

Year and State	Sex	Lowest, highest, and average—		Year and State	Sex	Lowest, highest, and average—	
		Hours per week	Rate per day (dollars)			Hours per week	Rate per day (dollars)
1870:				1887—Continued.			
Maine	M.	60–60–60	2. 50–2. 50–2. 50	Rhode Island	M.	(1)	2. 75–2. 75–2. 75
1872:				Wisconsin	M.	(1)	1. 40–1. 40–1. 40
Connecticut	M.	60–60–60	3. 50–3. 50–3. 50	1888:			
Ohio	M.	(1)	3. 00–3. 00–3. 00	New Jersey	M.	60–63–61	1. 25–5. 33–2. 37
1874:				Do	F.	(1)	. 67–1. 33– . 95
Connecticut	M.	(1)	4. 00–4. 00–4. 00	New York	M.	50–60–58	2. 00–4. 50–2. 62
1876:				1890:			
Pennsylvania	M.	(1)	3. 00–3. 00–3. 00	Michigan	M.	60–60–60	1. 50–4. 13–2. 56
1877:				New York	M.	(1)	1. 21–4. 17–2. 66
Ohio	M.	60–60–60	2. 00–2. 00–2. 00	1891:			
Pennsylvania	M.	60–60–60	2. 75–2. 75–2. 75	Maine	M.	60–60–60	2. 50–2. 50–2. 50
1878:				New York	M.	(1)	1. 21–4. 31–2. 88
Ohio	M.	60–60–60	2. 38–2. 38–2. 38	Ohio	M.	54–60–59	1. 35–3. 50–2. 22
1880:				1892:			
Connecticut	M.	60–60–60	1. 50–4. 00–2. 50	California	M.	57–57–57	3. 00–3. 00–3. 00
New Jersey	(1)	59–59–59	. 75–2. 00–1. 38	Indiana	M.	60–60–60	3. 00–3. 00–3. 00
1881:				Massachusetts	M.	60–60–60	2. 25–3. 25–2. 69
Ohio	M.	60–60–60	2. 25–2. 75–2. 50	1893:			
1882:				Massachusetts	M.	60–60–60	2. 50–3. 00–2. 74
Missouri	M.	60–60–60	1. 50–3. 50–2. 24	Ohio	M.	42–60–57	1. 50–3. 00–2. 19
New Jersey	M.	60–60–60	1. 67–3. 00–2. 44	1894:			
Pennsylvania	M.	60–60–60	1. 67–2. 67–2. 15	Indiana	M.	48–60–57	2. 25–2. 50–2. 31
1883:				Massachusetts	M.	60–60–60	2. 16–3. 00–2. 70
Massachusetts	M.	(1)	2. 50–2. 50–2. 50	New Hampshire	M.	58–58–58	1. 83–2. 00–1. 92
1884:				North Carolina	(1)	60–60–60	2. 00–2. 00–2. 00
Michigan	M.	(1)	2. 25–2. 50–2. 38	Ohio	M.	36–60–55	1. 43–4. 00–1. 97
New Jersey	M.	60–60–60	2. 00–2. 00–2. 00	1895:			
Ohio	M.	60–60–60	2. 00–2. 00–2. 00	Connecticut	M.	59–60–60	2. 00–3. 50–2. 72
1885:				Maine	M.	60–60–60	2. 50–2. 50–2. 50
Connecticut	M.	(1)	2. 96–3. 00–2. 98	Massachusetts	M.	54–60–56	1. 67–4. 00–2. 65
Illinois	M.	60–60–60	1. 15–3. 25–2. 32	New Jersey	M.	54–60–59	2. 00–4. 00–2. 63
Maine	M.	66–66–66	1. 80–1. 80–1. 80	New York	M.	59–59–59	2. 50–5. 00–4. 00
Massachusetts	M.	58–58–58	2. 00–4. 00–3. 25	Ohio	M.	42–72–57	1. 35–3. 50–2. 28
New Jersey	M.	59–60–60	1. 83–4. 00–2 51	Pennsylvania	M.	54–54–54	2. 07–2. 07–2. 07
New York	M.	59–59–59	2. 17–5. 42–4. 18	Rhode Island	M.	55–55–55	2. 50–2. 50–2. 50
Ohio	M.	60–60–60	1. 75–1. 75–1. 75	1896:			
1886:				Connecticut	M.	60–60–60	3. 00–4. 00–3. 44
New Jersey	M.	60–60–60	2. 00–2. 00–2. 00	Michigan	M.	60–60–60	2. 25–3. 00–2. 59
New York	M.	(1)	2. 67–2. 67–2. 67	New York	M.	60–60–60	2. 75–2. 75–2. 75
Ohio	M.	(1)	1. 92–2. 55–2. 24	Ohio	M.	48–60–58	1. 70–3. 12. 2. 48
1887:				Pennsylvania	M.	60–60–60	2. 00–3. 00–2. 56
Connecticut	M.	(1)	2. 37–2. 68–2. 48	Rhode Island	M.	60–60–60	4. 00–4. 00–4. 00
Maine	M.	72–72–72	2. 00–2. 00–2. 00	1897:			
Ohio	M.	60–60–60	1. 50–3. 00–2. 23	Connecticut	M.	60–60–60	3. 00–4. 00–3. 60
Pennsylvania	M.	60–60–60	2. 00–2. 75–2. 46				

1 Not reported.

TABLE I-42.—*Tool and die makers, males, 1907-1924, by city and year*

Year	Boston, Mass.		Chicago, Ill.		Cincinnati, Ohio		Detroit, Mich.	
	Hours per week	Rate per hour	Hours per week	Rate per hour	Hours per week	Rate per hour	Hours per week	Rate per hour
1907	54. 0	$0. 361			55. 0	$0. 350	55. 0	$0. 375
1908	54. 0	. 361			55. 0	. 350	55. 0	. 425
1909	54. 0	. 389			55. 0	. 350	55. 0	. 425
1910	54. 0	. 444			55. 0	. 350	55. 0	. 425
1911	54. 0	. 444	49. 5	$0. 450	55. 0	. 350	55. 0	. 425
1912	54. 0	. 444	49. 5	. 450	55. 0	. 350	55. 0	. 350
1913	54. 0	. 444	48. 0	. 545	55. 0	. 350	50. 0	. 400
1914	54. 0	. 444	48. 0	. 495	52. 5	. 350	50. 0	. 400
1915	54. 0	. 444	48. 0	. 495	52. 5	. 350	50. 0	. 400
1916	54. 0	. 444	48. 0	. 529	48. 0	. 425	50. 0	. 450
1917	48. 0	. 580	48. 0	. 610	48. 0	. 480	50. 0	. 520
1918	48. 0	. 650	1 48. 0	. 710	48. 0	. 600	48. 0	. 800
1919	48. 0	. 750	44. 0	. 860	48. 0	. 700	48. 0	2. 850
1920	48. 0	. 750	44. 0	2 1. 060	48. 0	. 900	50. 0	2. 950
1921	48. 0	2. 900	44. 0	2. 960	48. 0	. 900		
1922	48. 0	3. 900	44. 0	4. 900	48. 0	. 800		
1923	44. 0	. 800	44. 0	1. 060	48. 0	. 900		
1924	44. 0	. 800	44. 0	1. 080	48. 0	. 900		

Year	New York, N. Y.[5]		Philadelphia, Pa.		St. Louis, Mo.		San Francisco, Calif.[6]	
1907					54. 0	$0. 400		
1908					54. 0	. 400		
1909					54. 0	. 400		
1910					54. 0	. 400		
1911					54. 0	. 400		
1912			54. 0	$0. 375	54. 0	. 400		
1913			54. 0	. 375	54. 0	. 420	48. 0	$0. 438
1914			54. 0	. 375	54. 0	. 450	48. 0	. 438
1915	51. 0	$0. 480	54. 0	. 375	54. 0	. 450	48. 0	. 438
1916	48. 0	. 550	54.	. 580	54. 0	. 450	48. 0	. 500
1917	48. 0	. 650	48. 0	. 600	54. 0	. 550	48. 0	. 500
1918	48. 0	. 820	48. 0	. 780	48. 0	. 650	7 48. 0	. 725
1919	48. 0	. 900	48. 0	. 900	48. 0	. 750		
1920	48. 0	. 900	48. 0	1. 070	48. 0	. 900	44. 0	. 900
1921	44. 0	3. 950	48. 0	. 900				
1922	44. 0	3. 900	48. 0	. 750	48. 0	. 700		
1923	44. 0	. 950	48. 0	. 750	48. 0	. 850		
1924	44. 0	1. 250	48. 0	. 750	48. 0	. 950		

1 44, June to September, inclusive.
2 More than 50 per cent received more.
3 More than 25 per cent received more.
4 More than 75 per cent received more.
5 And printing-press repair men, 1919 and 1920.
6 And all-round men, 1913 to 1918.
7 44, June to August, inclusive.

TABLE I-43.—*Tool makers, 1925 and 1927, by State and year*

Year	California		Connecticut		Illinois		Indiana	
	Hours per week	Rate per hour	Hours per week	Rate per hour	Hours per week	Rate per hour	Hours per week	Rate per hour
1925	46. 3	$0. 873	51. 0	$0. 702	50. 8	$0. 780	52. 6	$0. 677
1927	46. 0	. 867	50. 4	. 735	50. 2	. 818	50. 5	. 703

Year	Massachusetts		Michigan		New Jersey		New York	
1925	49. 3	$0. 705	50. 8	$0. 754	49. 1	$0. 794	48. 1	$0. 781
1927	48. 8	. 723	50. 8	. 809	49. 3	. 789	48. 2	. 818

Year	Ohio		Pennsylvania		Rhode Island		Wisconsin	
1925	50. 1	$0. 691	49. 4	$0. 729	50. 5	$0. 687	51. 9	$0. 683
1927	49. 4	. 726	51. 2	. 722	50. 4	. 708	52. 5	. 702

J.—MINING INDUSTRY

The sources from which these wage data were taken are the Fifteenth Annual Report of the Commissioner of Labor Statistics and bulletins of the Bureau of Labor Statistics Nos. 279, 316, 394 and 454.

Data for iron miners are shown only in the Fifteenth Annual Report of the Commissioner of Labor Statistics and Bulletin No. 394 of the Bureau of Labor Statistics.

A very large per cent of miners and loaders of coal are paid piece rates of a specified amount per ton. This means that no record of time worked is usually kept for these employees. In all such mines arrangements were made with officials of the company for a day-by-day record of the hours actually worked. These hours divided into the earnings of each employee for a representative pay period were the means of ascertaining the earnings per hour for employees in each of these tonnage-work occupations. Machine mining has largely supplanted pick mining. In 1891 there were 545 cutting machines in use in bituminous mines in the United States as compared with 15,261 in 1927. In 1891 only 5.3 per cent of bituminous coal was machine mined, compared with 73.8 per cent in 1927.

TABLE J-1.—*Drivers, coal mining, 1874–1900, year and State*

Year and State	Sex	Lowest, highest, and average—		Year and State	Sex	Lowest, highest, and average—	
		Hours per week	Rate per day (dollars)			Hours per week	Rate per day (dollars)
1874:				**1889—Continued.**			
Pennsylvania	M.	(¹)	1.00-1.00-1.00	Indiana	M.	60-60-60	1.15-2.05-1.91
1875:				Kansas	M.	54-60-56	1.75-2.25-1.87
Pennsylvania	M.	(¹)	.60-3.00-1.45	Maryland	M.	60-60-60	1.50-1.85-1.85
1876:				Missouri	(¹)	(¹)	1.12-2.50-1.90
Pennsylvania	M.	(¹)	.34-6.75-1.42	Ohio	M.	48-60-55	1.25-2.20-1.88
1877:				Pennsylvania	M.	48-60-59	.81-4.00-2.02
Ohio	M.	(¹)	.50-1.75-1.46	Tennessee	M.	60-60-60	1.15-1.15-1.15
Pennsylvania	M.	42-72-58	.39-5.00-1.26	Virginia	M.	72-72-72	1.00-1.00-1.00
1878:				West Virginia	M.	54-60-59	1.25-1.50-1.49
Pennsylvania	M.	36-60-58	.50-2.50-1.14	**1890:**			
1879:				Alabama	M.	60-60-60	1.50-1.50-1.50
Ohio	M.	(¹)	.69-1.66-1.20	Pennsylvania	M.	54-54-54	1.80-2.00-1.89
Pennsylvania	M.	42-60-58	.25-2.50-1.18	**1891:**			
1881:				Ohio	M.	(¹)	.75-2.25-1.78
Ohio	M.	(¹)	.90-3.00-1.80	Pennsylvania	M.	60-60-60	2.00-2.00-2.00
1882:				**1892:**			
Iowa	M.	60-60-60	2.00-2.00-2.00	Ohio	(¹)	(¹)	.75-3.00-1.79
1883:				**1893:**			
Ohio	M.	(¹)	1.67-2.37-1.86	Missouri	M.	(¹)	1.50-2.25-1.87
1885:				Ohio	M.	(¹)	1.20-2.05-1.78
Indiana	M.	60-60-60	1.25-1.50-1.40	**1894:**			
Maryland	M.	66-66-66	1.60-1.60-1.60	Montana	M.	(¹)	3.06-3.06-3.06
Missouri	M.	60-60-60	1.93-2.00-1.99	West Virginia	M.	60-60-60	1.75-1.75-1.75
Ohio	M.	54-60-59	1.25-2.25-1.56	**1895:**			
Pennsylvania	M.	60-60-60	2.50-2.50-2.50	Ohio	M.	(¹)	.60-1.75-1.49
Virginia	M.	60-60-60	.75-.75-.75	Pennsylvania	M.	60-60-60	1.50-2.00-1.61
West Virginia	M.	54-66-60	.75-2.25-1.47	**1897:**			
1886:				Pennsylvania	M.	60-60-60	1.25-2.00-1.92
Iowa	M.	60-60-60	2.00-2.00-2.00	**1898:**			
1887:				Pennsylvania	M.	(¹)	1.45-1.70-1.69
Ohio	M.	48-60-56	1.00-2.25-1.64	Tennessee	M.	(¹)	.80-.80-.80
1888:				**1899:**			
Illinois	M.	60-60-60	1.50-2.00-1.87	Alabama	M.	(¹)	1.27-1.58-1.43
Indiana	M.	(¹)	1.50-2.00-1.88	Michigan	M.	(¹)	1.76-1.76-1.76
Kansas	M.	(¹)	2.25-2.25-2.25	Pennsylvania	M.	(¹)	1.65-1.90-1.88
1889:				Tennessee	M.	(¹)	1.00-1.84-1.38
Alabama	M.	48-60-59	.40-5.00-1.32	**1900:**			
Illinois	M.	60-60-60	.77-2.50-1.77	Alabama	M.	(¹)	1.58-1.58-1.58

¹ Not reported.

TABLE J-2.—*Drivers, males, coal mining, 1919-1926, by State and year*

Year	Alabama Hours per week	Rate per hour	Colorado Hours per week	Rate per hour	Illinois Hours per week	Rate per hour	Indiana Hours per week	Rate per hour
1919	48.0	$0.440	48.0	$0.662	48.0	$0.625	48.0	$0.63C
1922	(1)	.385	(1)	.956	(1)	.930	(1)	.942
1924	(1)	.350	(1)	.939	(1)	.938	(1)	.944
1926	(1)	.356	(1)	.706	(1)	.936	(1)	.912

	Kansas Hours per week	Rate per hour	Kentucky Hours per week	Rate per hour	Ohio Hours per week	Rate per hour	Pennsylvania Hours per week	Rate per hour
1919	48.0	$0.627	48.0	$0.493	48.0	$0.649	48.4	$0.635
1922			(1)	.718	(1)	.938	(1)	.704
1924	(1)	.940	(1)	.637	(1)	.932	(1)	.779
1926	(1)	.943	(1)	.558	(1)	.936	(1)	.760

	Tennessee Hours per week	Rate per hour	Virginia Hours per week	Rate per hour	West Virginia Hours per week	Rate per hour	Wyoming Hours per week	Rate per hour
1919	48.0	$0.419	48.0	$0.383	48.5	$0.559	48.0	$0.677
1922					(1)	.801	(1)	.984
1924	(1)	.414	(1)	.463	(1)	.636		
1926	(1)	.396	(1)	.416	(1)	.573		

1 Not reported.

TABLE J-3.—*Loaders, males, coal and ore mining, 1876-1900, by year and State*

Year and State	Sex	Lowest, highest, and average— Hours per week	Rate per day (dollars)	Year and State	Sex	Lowest, highest, and average— Hours per week	Rate per day (dollars)
1876:				1889—Continued			
Pennsylvania	M.	(1)	1.80-2.00-1.87	Michigan	M.	60-60-60	1.30-2.25-2.10
1877:				Missouri	(1)	(1)	1.09-1.38-1.14
Ohio	M.	(1)	1.42-1.50-1.49	New York	M.	(1)	1.22-1.22-1.22
Pennsylvania	M.	60-60-60	1.66-1.66-1.66	Ohio	M.	54-55-54	1.35-1.50-1.49
1878:				Pennsylvania	M.	60-60-60	.90-3.25-1.95
Pennsylvania	M.	60-60-60	1.38-1.84-1.61	Tennessee	M.	(1)	1.00-1.00-1.00
1881:				Wisconsin	M.	60-60-60	1.72-1.72-1.72
Pennsylvania	M.	66-72-69	1.15-1.30-1.23	1890:			
1884:				Pennsylvania	M.	(1)	.60-1.75- .95
New Jersey	M.	60-60-60	1.65-1.68-1.67	1891:			
1885:				Michigan	M.	60-60-60	2.00-2.00-2.00
Pennsylvania	M.	60-60-60	2.75-2.75-2.75	1892:			
1886:				Indiana	M.	(1)	1.39-2.20-1.77
New Jersey	M.	60-60-60	2.00-2.00-2.00	Iowa	M.	60-60-60	1.50-1.50-1.50
1887:				1893:			
Colorado	M.	(1)	2.50-2.50-2.50	Illinois	M.	(1)	1.65-2.25-1.77
Ohio	M.	54-60-54	1.37-2.60-2.52	Missouri	M.	(1)	1.14-1.34-1.22
1888:				1894:			
Illinois	M.	60-60-60	.96-2.00-1.74	Montana	M.	(1)	2.50-2.50-2.50
Michigan	M.	60-60-60	1.34-1.92-1.75	1895:			
1889:				Illinois	M.	(1)	1.50-2.00-1.75
Alabama	M.	54-60-59	1.25-1.50-1.30	1899:			
Illinois	M.	60-60-60	1.50-2.75-1.65	Alabama	M.	(1)	1.15-1.38-1.26
Indiana	M.	60-60-60	1.72-2.10-1.96	1900:			
Maryland	M.	60-60-60	1.50-1.50-1.50	Alabama	M.	(1)	1.38-1.38-1.38

1 Not reported.

TABLE J–4.—*Loaders, males, coal mining, 1922–1926, by State and year*

Year	Alabama		Colorado		Illinois		Indiana	
	Hours per week	Rate per hour	Hours per week	Rate per hour	Hours per week	Rate per hour	Hours per week	Rate per hour
1922	(¹)	² $0.497	(¹)	² $0.927	(¹)	² $1.197	(¹)	² $1.146
1924	(¹)	². 492	(¹)	². 858	(¹)	² 1.092	(¹)	² 1.083
1926	(²)	². 478	(¹)	². 789	(¹)	² 1.078	(¹)	² 1.116

	Kansas		Kentucky		Ohio		Pennsylvania	
1922			(¹)	$0.752	(¹)	$0.973	(¹)	$0.739
1924			(¹)	.693	(¹)	.860	(¹)	.743
1926			(¹)	.617	(¹)	.817	(¹)	.711

	Tennessee		Virginia		West Virginia		Wyoming	
1922					(¹)	² $0.904	(¹)	² $1.158
1924	(¹)	² $0.508	(¹)	² $0.604	(¹)	². 831		
1926	(¹)	². 436	(¹)	². 597	(¹)	². 776		

¹ Not reported.
²Average earnings per hour based on time at face, including lunch.

TABLE J–5.—*Miners, coal, 1840–1900, by year and State*

Year and State	Sex	Lowest, highest, and average—		Year and State	Sex	Lowest, highest, and average—	
		Hours per week	Rate per day (dollars)			Hours per week	Rate per day (dollars)
1840:				1859:			
Pennsylvania	M.	(¹)	1.20–1.20–1.20	Pennsylvania	M.	(¹)	1.16–1.16–1.16
1841:				1860:			
Pennsylvania	M.	(¹)	1.00–1.00–1.00	Pennsylvania	M.	(¹)	1.16–1.16–1.16
1842:				1861:			
Pennsylvania	M.	(¹)	1.00–1.00–1.00	Pennsylvania	M.	(¹)	1.00–1.00–1.00
1843:				1862:			
Pennsylvania	M.	(¹)	.92–.92–.92	Pennsylvania	M.	(¹)	1.16–1.16–1.16
1844:				1863:			
Pennsylvania	M.	(¹)	1.00–1.00–1.00	Pennsylvania	M.	(¹)	1.66–1.66–1.66
1845:				1864:			
Pennsylvania	M.	(¹)	1.16–1.16–1.16	Pennsylvania	M,	(¹)	2.58–2.58–2.58
1846:				1865:			
Pennsylvania	M.	(¹)	1.16–1.16–1.16	Pennsylvania	M.	(¹)	1.75–1.75–1.75
1847:				1866:			
Pennsylvania	M.	(¹)	1.16–1.16–1.16	Pennsylvania	M.	(¹)	2.00–2.00–2.00
1848:				1867:			
Pennsylvania	M.	(¹)	1.16–1.16–1.16	Pennsylvania	M.	(¹)	1.79–1.79–1.79
1849:				1868:			
Pennsylvania	M.	(¹)	1.16–1.16–1.16	Pennsylvania	M.	(¹)	2.50–2.50–2.50
1850:				1869:			
Pennsylvania	M.	(¹)	1.16–1.16–1.16	Pennsylvania	M.	(¹)	3.44–3.44–3.44
1851:				1870:			
Pennsylvania	M.	(¹)	1.16–1.16–1.16	Pennsylvania	M.	(¹)	2.59–2.59–2.59
1852:				1871:			
Pennsylvania	M.	(¹)	1.16–1.16–1.16	Pennsylvania	M.	(¹)	2.34–2.34–2.34
1853:				1872:			
Pennsylvania	M.	(¹)	1.08–1.08–1.08	Pennsylvania	M.	(¹)	2–25–2.25–2.25
1854:				1873:			
Pennsylvania	M.	(¹)	1.25–1.25–1.25	Pennsylvania	M.	(¹)	2.44–4.00–3.34
1855:				1874:			
Pennsylvania	M	(¹)	1.16–1.16–1.16	Pennsylvania	M.	42–42–42	1.00–2.59–1.71
1856:				1875:			
Pennsylvania	M.	(¹)	1.25–1.25–1.25	Pennsylvania	M.	(¹)	1.00–7.17–2.85
1857:				1876:			
Pennsylvania	M.	(¹)	1.16–1.16–1.16	Pennsylvania	M.	(¹)	². 40–.75–.64
1858:				Do	M.	(¹)	³ .03–.03–.03
Pennsylvania	M.	(¹)	.90–.90–.90	Do	M.	(¹)	.75–4.00–2.43

¹ Not reported.   ² Per ton.   ³ Per bushel.

TABLE J-5.—*Miners, coal, 1840–1900, by year and State*—Continued

Year and State	Sex	Hours per week	Rate per day (dollars)
1877:			
Ohio	M.	([1])	1.00-2.33-1.69
Pennsylvania	M.	42-54-47	[2].37-.75-.55
Do	M.	36-72-57	.75-6.67-2.02
1878:			
Ohio	M.	48-66-58	.75-2.66-1.61
Do	M.	([1])	[2].70-.70-.70
Pennsylvania	M.	([1])	[4].40-.40-.40
Do	M.	42-60-51	[2].30-.75-.53
Do	M.	36-72-59	1.00-3.60-1.90
1879:			
Ohio	M.	([1])	.96-2.50-1.44
Pennsylvania	M.	([1])	[2].34-.56-.40
Do	([2])	([1])	[2].02-.02-.02
Do	M.	42-96-60	.99-4.75-1.87
1880:			
Iowa	M.	60-60-60	2.00-2.00-2.00
Ohio	M.	48-78-60	1.00-3.33-1.90
Pennsylvania	M.	48-84-61	1.03-3.74-2.07
1881:			
Illinois	M.	60-60-60	1.50-2.50-2.02
Indiana	M.	([1])	1.25-1.54-1.40
Iowa	M.	60-60-60	1.75-2.25-2.13
Kentucky	M.	([1])	2.08-2.20-2.14
Michigan	M.	([1])	2.00-2.40-2.20
Missouri	M.	60-60-60	2.25-3.50-3.23
Ohio	M.	44-72-56	.50-4.17-2.17
Pennsylvania	M.	48-84-65	1.40-3.78-2.37
West Virginia	M.	60-66-61	1.55-2.00-1.82
1882:			
Alabama	M.	60-60-60	2.00-2.50-2.35
Colorado	M.	60-60-60	2.50-2.75-2.63
Illinois	M.	60-60-60	1.50-2.25-1.89
Indiana	M.	([1])	1.37-1.54-1.46
Iowa	M.	60-60-60	1.50-2.50-2.00
Missouri	M.	([1])	1.33-2.40-1.98
North Dakota	M.	60-60-60	1.50-1.50-1.50
Ohio	M.	54-60-56	1.35-3.60-1.75
Do	([1])	([1])	1.25-4.00-2.01
Pennsylvania	M.	54-72-59	1.35-3.20-1.95
1883:			
Colorado	M.	60-60-60	2.75-2.75-2.75
Illinois	M.	60-60-60	1.50-2.00-1.83
Indiana	M.	([1])	1.25-1.54-1.42
Iowa	M.	([1])	1.75-2.50-2.09
Kansas	M.	([1])	1.75-2.00-1.88
North Dakota	M.	60-60-60	1.75-1.75-1.75
Ohio	M.	54-72-56	1.00-3.33.1.99
Pennsylvania	M.	54-60-56	1.40-2.30-1.65
1884:			
Alabama	M.	54-60-58	1.85-2.00-1.97
Arkansas	M.	48-48-48	2.00-2.25-2.13
Colorado	M.	60-60-60	2.25-2.75-2.41
Illinois	M.	48-60-60	1.50-2.00-1.88
Indiana	M.	([1])	1.15-1.54-1.36
Iowa	M.	57-72-60	.90-2.50-1.89
Kansas	M.	([1])	2.00-2.00-2.00
Michigan	M.	([1])	2.00-2.00-2.00
Montana	M.	56-70-63	3.25-4.00-3.63
New Mexico	M.	60-60-60	2.25-2.75-2.52
Ohio	M.	48-70-59	1.33-2.85-2.14
Pennsylvania	M.	60-60-60	.70-4.40-1.41
West Virginia	M.	60-60-60	1.75-1,75-1.75
1885:			
Alabama	M.	60-60-60	2.00-2.00-2.00
Arkansas	M.	48-48-48	1.75-2.00-1.88
Colorado	M.	60-60-60	2.00-2.50-2.38
Illinois	M.	59-60-60	1.50-2.50-1.84
Do	M.	([1])	[2].30-1.75-.79
Indiana	M.	60-60-60	.94-2.00-1.40
Iowa	M.	60-60-60	1.50-2.00-1.88
Kansas	M.	([1])	1.75-2.00-1.88
Kentucky	M.	([1])	1.75-2.01-1.89
Maryland	M.	66-66-66	1.56-1.73-1.62
Michigan	M.	50-50-50	1.75-1.75-1.75
1885—Continued.			
Missouri	M.	([1])	[2]0.52-1.00-0.78
Do	M.	36-60-54	1.33-2.46-1.57
Ohio	M.	48-70-59	1.12-4.58-1.53
Pennsylvania	M.	48-60-57	1.25-2.45-1.68
Virginia	M.	60-60-60	1.25-1.75-1.50
West Virginia	M.	54-66-60	1.20-2.00-1.60
Wyoming	M.	60-60-60	3.00-3.50-3.09
1886:			
Arkansas	M.	48-48-48	2.75-2.80-2.78
Colorado	M.	60-60-60	1.73-2.50-2.09
Illinois	M.	42-60-60	.84-2.40-1.79
Indiana	M.	([1])	1.54-1.65-1.62
Iowa	M.	60-60-60	1.50-2.75-1.98
Kansas	M.	60-60-60	.87-3.69-1.75
Kentucky	M.	([1])	1.34-1.95-1.61
Maryland	M.	60-60-60	1.60-1.60-1.60
Missouri	M.	([1])	1.75-2-64-2.16
North Dakota	M.	60-60-60	1.50-1.50-1.50
Ohio	M.	48-60-59	1.35-2.84-1.69
Pennsylvania	M.	54-72-60	1.18-2.40-1.48
Tennessee	M.	48-48-48	1.48-1.90-1.88
West Virginia	M.	60-60-60	1.50-1.60-1.53
1887:			
Illinois	M.	([1])	[2].38-2.00-.76
Kansas	M.	([1])	1.00-4.52-1.96
Ohio	M.	48-66-56	1.00-4.84-1.76
Do	M.	48-60-56	[2].33-.90-.65
Pennsylvania	M.	([1])	[2].55-.55-.55
Do	M.	48-60-60	1.50-3.34-1.80
1888:			
Illinois	M.	60-60-60	1.46-3.94-2.19
Indiana	M.	([1])	1.82-2.32-2.19
Iowa	M.	54-60-59	1.24-1.92-1.53
Kansas	M.	([1])	.80-4.00-2.13
Michigan	M.	42-6-48	1.00-2.00-1.52
Missouri	M.	([1])	[2].52-1.25-.83
Pennsylvania	M.	([1])	1.84-4.32-2.69
1889:			
Alabama	M.	48-60-55	1.00-4.25-2.19
Do	M.	([1])	[2].37-.58-.53
Do	([1])	([1])	2.11-2.37-2.15
Arkansas	([1])	([1])	2.10-2.42-2.20
Colorado	([1])	([1])	2.25-3.10-2.65
Illinois	M.	([4])	[2].70-.70-.70
Do	([1])	([1])	[2].31-1.50-.78
Do	([1])	([1])	1.10-3.15-1.98
Do	M.	60-60-60	.47-4.92-2.08
Indiana	M.	60-60-60	1.75-2.75-2.01
Do	([1])	([1])	1.00-2.25-1.89
Indian Territory	([1])	([1])	3.25-3.25-3.25
Iowa	([1])	([1])	1.74-3.14-2.32
Kansas	([1])	([1])	1.31-2.55-1.89
Do	M.	54-60-57	2.00-3.79-2.38
Kentucky	([1])	([1])	1.51-1.98-1.75
Maryland	M.	60-60-60	2.23-2.36-2.32
Do	([1])	([1])	2.45-2.45-2.45
Michigan	([1])	([1])	1.73-1.75-1.74
Missouri	([1])	([1])	1.40-2.62-2.24
Do	([1])	([1])	1.44-3.12-2.26
Do	M.	([1])	[2].40-1.75-.85½
Montana	([1])	([1])	3.08-3.35-3.19
New Mexico	([1])	([1])	2.97-3.69-3.08
North Dakota	([1])	([1])	2.15-2.15-2.15
Ohio	M.	48-48-48	[2].62½-.80-.66
Do	([1])	([1])	1.39-2.50-1.95
Do	M.	42-60-53	1.05-2.82-1.79
Pennsylvania	M.	50-60-52	[2].40-.79-.59½
Do	([1])	([1])	[2].02½-.03-.03
Do	([1])	([1])	1.57-3.16-2.15
Do	M.	42-60-55	.65-6.33-2.12
Tennessee	M.	60-60-60	2.02-2.02-2.02
Do	([1])	([1])	1.78-2.12-1.98
Texas	([1])	([1])	2.00-2.00-2.00
Utah	([1])	([1])	3.21-3.21-3,21

[1] Not reported.   [2] Per ton.   [3] Per bushel.   [4] Per gross ton.

TABLE J–5.—*Miners, coal, 1840–1900, by year and State*—Continued

| Year and State | Sex | Lowest, highest, and average— | | Year and State | Sex | Lowest, highest, and average— | |
		Hours per week	Rate per day (dollars)			Hours per week	Rate per day (dollars)
1889—Continued.				**1894:**			
Virginia	M.	72–72–72	2. 50–2. 50–2. 50	Iowa	M.	48–60–57	0. 96–2. 00–1. 70
Do	(¹)	(¹)	. 96–1. 95–1. 53	West Virginia	M.	54–90–61	. 75–2. 50–1. 38
Washington	(¹)	(¹)	2. 88–3. 77–3. 26	**1895:**			
West Virginia	M.	48–60–53	. 91–2. 48–2. 21	Illinois	M.	(¹)	1. 75–2. 50–2. 26
Do	(¹)	(¹)	1. 52–2. 11–1. 86	Do	M.	(¹)	². 17–1. 37½–. 59
Wyoming	(¹)	(¹)	2. 57–2. 98–2. 71	Missouri	M.	(¹)	1. 79–3. 17–2. 37
1890:				Ohio	M.	(¹)	². 55–1. 00–. 56
Alabama	M.	60–60–60	1. 75–1. 75–1. 75	**1896:**			
Illinois	M.	(¹)	². 25–1. 38–. 72½	Illinois	M.	60–60–60	1. 05–1. 33–1. 19
Do	M.	60–60–60	1. 82–2. 50–2. 01	**1897:**			
Pennsylvania	M.	(¹)	². 40–. 50–. 44½	Illinois	(¹)	(¹)	⁴. 17–1. 25–. 35½
Do	M.	54–54–54	1. 91–2. 00–2. 00	Do	M.	(¹)	⁵. 25–1. 25–. 67
1891:				Kansas	M.	36–72–55	. 90–2. 00–1. 55
Illinois	M.	(¹)	1. 50–2. 50–2. 17	Do	M.	(¹)	². 41–1. 25–. 91½
Do	M.	(¹)	². 34–1. 50–. 72½	**1898:**			
Pennsylvania	M.	(¹)	1. 91–1. 91–1. 91	Illinois	(¹)	(¹)	2. 00–2. 00–2. 00
1892:				Do	(¹)	(¹)	⁴. 25–1. 37½–. 54
Illinois	M.	(¹)	². 25–1. 50–. 68	Do	(¹)	(¹)	⁵. 45–1. 25–. 73½
Indiana	M.	48–60–54	. 56–3. 55–1. 42	Do	(¹)	(¹)	⁶. 67½–. 72½–. 70½
Iowa	M.	60–60–60	1. 15–2. 50–1. 85	Pennsylvania	M.	(¹)	1. 82–1. 82–1. 82
Ohio	(¹)	(¹)	². 40–1. 00–. 73	Tennessee	M.	(¹)	². 30–. 30–. 30
Pennsylvania	M.	(¹)	1. 91–1. 91–1. 91	**1899:**			
1893:				Illinois	M.	(¹)	1. 50–1. 50–1. 50
Illinois	M.	(¹)	2. 25–2. 50–2. 27	Do	M.	(¹)	². 23–. 50–. 32
Do	(¹)	(¹)	². 24–1. 50–. 74	Do	M.	(¹)	⁴. 25–1. 37½–. 52
Do	(¹)	(¹)	⁴. 30–1. 00–. 55	Do	M.	(¹)	⁵. 33–1. 25–. 53½
Missouri	M.	(¹)	. 90–6. 91–2. 32	Do	M.	(¹)	⁶. 52½–. 72½–. 67½
Montana	M.	47–54–52	3. 00–3. 50–3. 24	Michigan	M.	(¹)	1. 66–1. 66–1. 66
Do	M.	48–57–53	². 85–1. 00–. 97½	Pennsylvania	M.	(¹)	1. 95–1. 95–1. 95
Ohio	M.	48–48–48	. 70–2. 50–1. 52	**1900:**			
				Alabama	M.	(¹)	². 47½–. 55–. 53½

¹ Not reported.   ² Per ton.   ⁴ Per gross ton.   ⁵ Per ton screened.   ⁶ Per ton forked.

TABLE J–6.—*Miners, hand or pick, males, coal mining, 1919–1926, by State and year*

| Year | Alabama | | Colorado | | Illinois | | Indiana | |
	Hours per week	Rate per hour	Hours per week	Rate per hour	Hours per week	Rate per hour	Hours per week	Rate per hour
1922	(¹)	² $0. 548	(¹)	² $0. 993	(¹)	² $0. 865	(¹)	² $0. 827
1924	(¹)	². 577	(¹)	². 929	(¹)	². 912	(¹)	² 1. 087
1926	(¹)	². 540	(¹)	². 787	(¹)	². 923	(¹)	² 1. 047

| | Kansas | | Kentucky | | Ohio | | Pennsylvania | |
	Hours per week	Rate per hour	Hours per week	Rate per hour	Hours per week	Rate per hour	Hours per week	Rate per hour
1922			(¹)	² $0. 825	(¹)	² $0. 916	(¹)	² $0. 767
1924	(¹)	² $0. 901	(¹)	². 776	(¹)	² 1. 041	(¹)	². 777
1926		². 809	(¹)	². 647	(¹)	². 879	(¹)	². 768

| | Tennessee | | West Virginia | | Wyoming | | | |
	Hours per week	Rate per hour	Hours per week	Rate per hour	Hours per week	Rate per hour		
1922			(¹)	² $1. 019	(¹)	² $1. 215		
1924		² $0. 541	(¹)	². 831				
1926	(¹)	². 436	(¹)	². 794				

¹ Not reported.   ² Average earnings per hour based on time at face, including lunch.

TABLE J–7.—*Miners, iron, 1840–1898, by year and State*

Year and State	Sex	Lowest, highest, and average—		Year and State	Sex	Lowest, highest, and average—	
		Hours per week	Rate per day (dollars)			Hours per week	Rate per day (dollars)
1840:				**1863:**			
New Jersey	M.	72–72–72	0. 69–0. 69–0. 69	Michigan	M.	(¹)	2. 25–2. 25–2. 25
New York	M.	(¹)	. 75–. 75–. 75	New Jersey	M.	60–60–60	1. 25–1. 25–1. 25
1841:				New York	M.	60–60–60	1. 40–1. 40–1. 40
New Jersey	M.	72–72–72	. 69–. 69–. 69	**1864:**			
New York	M.	(¹)	. 75–. 75–. 75	Michigan	M.	(¹)	3. 00–3. 00–3. 00
1842:				New Jersey	M.	60–60–60	1. 75–1. 75–1. 75
New Jersey	M.	72–72–72	. 73–. 73–. 73	New York	M.	60–60–60	2. 50–2. 50–2. 50
New York	M.	(¹)	1. 00–1. 00–1. 00	**1865:**			
1843:				Michigan	M.	(¹)	2. 50–2. 50–2. 50
New Jersey	M.	72–72–72	. 73–. 73–. 73	New Jersey	M.	60–60–60	1. 88–1. 88–1. 88
New York	M.	(¹)	1. 00–1. 00–1. 00	New York	M.	60–60–60	1. 50–1. 50–1. 50
1844:				**1866:**			
New Jersey	M.	72–72–72	. 73–. 73–. 73	Michigan	M.	(¹)	2. 50–2. 50–2. 50
New York	M.	(¹)	1. 00–1. 00–1. 00	New Jersey	M.	60–60–60	1. 50–1. 50–1. 50
1845:				New York	M.	60–60–60	1. 65–1. 65–1. 65
New Jersey	M.	72–72–72	. 73–. 73–. 73	**1867:**			
New York	M.	(¹)	1. 00–1. 00–1. 00	Michigan	M.	(¹)	2. 40–2. 40–2. 40
1846:				New Jersey	M.	60–60–60	1. 50–1. 50–1. 50
New Jersey	M.	72–72–72	. 73–. 73–. 73	New York	M.	60–60–60	2. 05–2. 05–2. 05
New York	M.	(¹)	1. 00–1. 00–1. 00	**1868:**			
1847:				Michigan	M.	(¹)	2. 25–2. 25–2. 25
New Jersey	M.	72–72–72	. 73–. 73–. 73	New Jersey	M.	60–60–60	1. 50–1. 50–1. 50
New York	M.	(¹)	. 94–. 94–. 94	New York	M.	60–60–60	2. 05–2. 05–2. 05
1848:				**1869:**			
New Jersey	M.	72–72–72	. 73–. 73–. 73	Michigan	M.	(¹)	2. 25–2. 25–2. 25
New York	M.	(¹)	. 94–. 94–. 94	New Jersey	M.	60–60–60	1. 50–1. 50–1. 50
1849:				New York	M.	60–60–60	2. 05–2. 05–2. 05
New Jersey	M.	72–72–72	. 69–. 69–. 69	**1870:**			
New York	M.	(¹)	. 94–. 94–. 94	Michigan	M.	(¹)	2. 25–2. 25–2. 25
1850:				New Jersey	M.	60–60–60	1. 63–1. 63–1. 63
New Jersey	M.	72–72–72	. 69–. 69–. 69	New York	M.	60–60–60	2. 05–2. 05–2. 05
New York	M.	(¹)	. 94–. 94–. 94	**1871:**			
1851:				Michigan	M.	(¹)	2. 25–2. 25–2. 25
New Jersey	M.	72–72–72	. 69–. 69–. 69	New Jersey	M.	60–60–60	1. 50–1. 50–1. 50
New York	M.	(¹)	1. 00–1. 00–1. 00	New York	M.	60–60–60	2. 05–2. 05–2. 05
1852:				**1872:**			
New Jersey	M.	72–72–72	. 73–. 73–. 73	Michigan	M.	(¹)	2. 25–2. 25–2. 25
New York	M.	(¹)	1. 25–1. 25–1. 25	New Jersey	M.	60–60–60	2. 00–2. 00–2. 00
1853:				New York	M.	60–60–60	2. 05–2. 05–2. 05
New Jersey	M.	72–72–72	. 92–. 92–. 92	**1873:**			
New York	M.	(¹)	1. 25–1. 25–1. 25	Michigan	M.	(¹)	2. 75–2. 75–2. 75
1854:				New Jersey	M.	60–60–60	2. 13–2. 13–2. 13
New Jersey	M.	60–60–60	1. 13–1. 13–1. 13	New York	M.	60–60–60	2. 30–2. 30–2. 30
New York	M.	(¹)	1. 25–1. 25–1. 25	**1874:**			
1855:				Michigan	M.	(¹)	1. 50–1. 50–1. 50
New Jersey	M.	60–60–60	1. 00–1. 00–1. 00	New Jersey	M.	60–60–60	1. 50–1. 50–1. 50
New York	M.	(¹)	1. 25–1. 25–1. 25	New York	M.	60–60–60	2. 60–2. 60–2. 60
1856:				Pennsylvania	M.	(¹)	1. 10–2. 25–1. 63
New Jersey	M.	60–60–60	1. 00–1. 00–1. 00	**1875:**			
New York	M.	(¹)	1. 25–1. 25–1. 25	Michigan	M.	(¹)	1. 50–1. 50–1. 50
1857:				New Jersey	M.	60–60–60	1. 25–1. 25–1. 25
Michigan	M.	(¹)	. 90–. 90–. 90	New York	M.	60–60–60	1. 75–1. 75–1. 75
New Jersey	M.	60–60–60	1. 00–1. 13–1. 07	**1876:**			
New York	M.	(¹)	1. 25–1. 25–1. 25	Michigan	M.	(¹)	1. 50–1. 50–1. 00
1858:				New Jersey	M.	60–60–60	1. 13–1. 13–1. 13
Michigan	M.	(¹)	. 90–. 90–. 90	New York	M.	60–60–60	1. 75–1. 75–1. 75
New Jersey	M.	60–60–60	. 80–. 80–. 80	Pennsylvania	M.	(¹)	. 40–2. 00–1. 13
New York	M.	(¹)	1. 25–1. 25–1. 25	**1877:**			
1859:				Michigan	M.	(¹)	1. 50–1. 50–1. 50
Michigan	M.	(¹)	. 90–. 90–. 90	New Jersey	M.	60–60–60	1. 00–1. 00–1. 00
New Jersey	M.	60–60–60	1. 00–1. 00–1. 00	New York	M.	60–60–60	1. 50–1. 50–1. 50
New York	M.	(¹)	1. 25–1. 25–1. 25	**1878:**			
1860:				Michigan	M.	(¹)	1. 50–1. 50–1. 50
Michigan	M.	(¹)	1. 35–1. 35–1. 35	New Jersey	M.	60–60–60	1. 00–1. 00–1. 00
New Jersey	M.	60–60–60	1. 00–1. 00–1. 00	New York	M.	60–60–60	1. 50–1. 50–1. 50
New York	M.	60–60–60	1. 25–1. 25–1. 25	Ohio	M.	(¹)	. 83–1. 42–1. 02
1861:				Pennsylvania	M.	48–72–63	. 60–1. 50–. 95
Michigan	M.	(¹)	1. 15–1. 15–1. 15	**1879:**			
New Jersey	M.	60–60–60	. 90–. 90–. 90	Michigan	M.	(¹)	1. 50–1. 50–1. 50
New York	M.	60–60–60	1. 25–1. 25–1. 25	New Jersey	M.	60–60–60	1. 00–1. 00–1. 00
1862:				New York	M.	60–60–60	1. 50–1. 50–1. 50
Michigan	M.	(¹)	1. 10–1. 10–1. 10	Ohio	M.	(¹)	1. 00–1. 67–1. 14
New Jersey	M.	60–60–60	1. 00–1. 00–1. 00	Pennsylvania	M.	48–66–60	. 70–2. 00–1. 17
New York	M.	60–60–60	1. 35–1. 35–1. 35	Do	M.	(¹)	².77–. 77–. 77

¹ Not reported.　　　　　　　　　² And rent.

TABLE J-7.—*Miners, iron, 1840–1898, by year and State—Continued*

Year and State	Sex	Hours per week	Rate per day (dollars)
1880:			
Alabama	(1)	(1)	1.92–1.92–1.92
Colorado	(1)	(1)	3.00–3.00–3.00
Michigan	M.	(1)	1.75–1.75–1.75
Do	(1)	(1)	2.23–2.23–2.23
Minnesota	(1)	(1)	2.55–2.55–2.55
Missouri	(1)	(1)	1.58–1.58–1.58
New Jersey	M.	60–60–60	1.25–1.25–1.25
Do	(1)	(1)	1.39–1.39–1.39
New York	M.	60–60–60	1.60–1.60–1.60
Do	(1)	(1)	1.47–1.47–1.47
Ohio	(1)	(1)	1.25–1.25–1.25
Pennsylvania	(1)	(1)	1.39–1.39–1.39
Do	M.	60–60–60	1.00–2.30–1.42
Tennessee	(1)	(1)	1.20–1.20–1.20
Wisconsin	(1)	(1)	2.00–2.00–2.00
1881:			
Michigan	M.	(1)	1.70–1.70–1.70
New Jersey	M.	48–60–56	1.25–1.67–1.43
New York	M.	60–60–60	1.75–1.75–1.75
Ohio	M.	48–60–56	1.17–1.87–1.34
Pennsylvania	M.	60–70–62	.75–.85–.81
1882:			
Michigan	M.	(1)	1.85–1.85–1.85
New Jersey	M.	45–45–45	1.50–1.50–1.50
New York	M.	60–60–60	1.85–1.85–1.85
1883:			
Michigan	M.	50–60–55	1.70–2.10–1.93
New Jersey	M.	45–45–45	1.25–1.25–1.25
Do	(1)	48–48–48	1.25–1.50–1.25
New York	M.	60–60–60	1.75–1.75–1.75
1884:			
Michigan	M.	60–60–60	1.60–1.95–1.60
New Jersey	M.	45–60–60	1.10–1.25–1.25
New York	M.	60–60–60	1.65–1.65–1.65
Ohio	M.	51–60–57	1.00–1.60–1.18
1885:			
Michigan	M.	(1)	1.90–1.90–1.90
Missouri	M.	60–60–60	1.25–1.25–1.25
New Jersey	M.	45–60–49	.88–1.10–1.01
New York	M.	60–60–60	1.50–1.50–1.50
Ohio	M.	(1)	.83–1.30–1.17
Virginia	M.	60–60–60	1.00–1.05–1.04
1886:			
Michigan	M.	(1)	1.90–1.90–1.90
New Jersey	M.	45–45–45	1.10–1.10–1.10
New York	M.	60–60–60	1.65–1.65–1.65
Ohio	M.	(1)	1.65–1.65–1.65
1887:			
Michigan	M.	(1)	2.05–2.05–2.05
New Jersey	M.	45–45–45	1.20–1.20–1.20

Year and State	Sex	Hours per week	Rate per day (dollars)
1887—Continued.			
New York	M.	60–60–60	1.75–1.75–1.75
Ohio	M.	60–60–60	1.00–1.25–1.02
1888:			
Michigan	M.	(1)	2.00–2.00–2.00
Missouri	M.	(1)	1.10–1.10–1.10
New Jersey	M.	45–45–45	1.20–1.20–1.20
New York	M.	60–60–60	1.25–1.75–1.27
Pennsylvania	M.	(1)	1.10–1.35–1.25
Virginia	M.	66–72–68	.50–1.15–1.05
1889:			
Alabama	M.	48–60–52	1.50–3.00–2.05
Do	(1)	(1)	1.92–1.92–1.92
Colorado	(1)	(1)	3.00–3.00–3.00
Georgia	M.	(1)	1.00–1.00–1.00
Michigan	M.	57–60–60	1.75–3.25–2.27
Do	(1)	(1)	2.23–2.23–2.23
Minnesota	M.	60–60–60	2.25–2.40–2.32
Do	(1)	(1)	2.55–2.55–2.55
Missouri	M.	(1)	.90–1.35–1.25
Do	(1)	(1)	1.58–1.58–1.58
Do	(1)	(1)	1.16–1.55–1.35
New Jersey	(1)	(1)	1.39–1.39–1.39
Do	M.	45–45–45	1.20–1.20–1.20
New York	M.	60–60–60	1.20–1.65–1.44
Do	(1)	(1)	1.47–1.47–1.47
Ohio	M.	48–60–54	.84–2.96–1.12
Pennsylvania	(1)	(1)	1.25–1.25–1.25
Do	M.	54–60–58	.60–1.55–1.29
Tennessee	(1)	(1)	1.39–1.39–1.39
Wisconsin	M.	(1)	1.20–1.20–1.20
Do	M.	60–60–60	1.50–2.25–1.97
Do	(1)	(1)	2.00–2.00–2.00
1890:			
Michigan	M.	60–60–60	2.60–2.60–2.60
Do	M.	(1)	1.75–1.75–1.75
New Jersey	M.	45–45–45	1.20–1.20–1.20
New York	M.	60–60–60	1.34–1.75–1.34
Pennsylvania	M.	(1)	.80–1.30–.87
1891:			
Michigan	M.	(1)	1.75–1.75–1.75
New Jersey	M.	45–45–45	1.20–1.20–1.20
New York	M.	60–60–60	1.44–1.65–1.44
1892:			
Michigan	M.	(1)	1.70–1.70–1.70
New York	M.	60–60–60	1.65–1.65–1.65
1893:			
Michigan	M.	(1)	1.50–1.50–1.50
1898:			
Tennessee	M.	(1)	². 07¼–. 07¼–. 07

¹ Not reported.　　　² Per hour.

TABLE J-8.—*Muckers, males, iron mining, 1924, by State and year*

Year	Alabama		Michigan	
	Hours per week	Rate per hour	Hours per week	Rate per hour
1924	60.0	$0.429	47.3	$0.531

TABLE J-9.—*Drilling-machine operators, company, males, iron mining, 1924, by State and Year*

Year	Alabama		Michigan		Minnesota	
	Hours per week	Rate per hour	Hours per week	Rate per hour	Hours per week	Rate per hour
1924	60. 0	$0. 483	47. 2	$0. 625	47. 8	$0. 584

TABLE J-10.—*Timbermen, mining, 1878-1899, by year and State*

Year and State	Sex	Lowest, highest, and average—		Year and State	Sex	Lowest, highest, and average—	
		Hours per week	Rate per day (dollars)			Hours per week	Rate per day (dollars)
1878:				1889—Continued			
Pennsylvania	M.	(¹)	1. 12-1. 12-1. 12	Virginia	M.	72-72-72	2. 25-2. 25-2. 25
1879:				West Virginia	M.	54-60-58	1. 50-2. 00-1. 70
Pennsylvania	M.	60-60-60	1. 00-1. 00-1. 00	Wisconsin	M.	60-60-60	1. 98-2. 25-2. 00
1883:				1890:			
New Jersey	M.	48-48-48	1. 50-1. 50-1. 50	Alabama	M.	60-60-60	1. 50-1. 50-1. 50
1884:				Pennsylvania	M.	(¹)	1. 05-1. 05-1. 05
Michigan	M.	(¹)	1. 75-2. 68-1. 96	1891:			
1885:				Ohio	M.	(¹)	1. 35-2. 25-1. 94
Virginia	M.	60-60-60	1. 25-2. 00-1. 44	1892:			
1888:				Iowa	M.	60-60-60	1. 92-2. 50-2. 38
Illinois	M.	60-60-60	1. 75-2. 30-2. 02	Ohio	(¹)	(¹)	1. 50-2. 50-1. 94
Michigan	M.	48-72-60	1. 23-3. 45-1. 91	1893:			
Virginia	M.	66-66-66	1. 00-1. 56-1. 14	Illinois	M.	(¹)	1. 75-2. 25-2. 01
1889:				Missouri	M.	(¹)	2. 00-2. 25-2. 11
Alabama	M.	48-60-58	1. 25-2. 50-1. 70	Montana	M.	54-54-54	4. 00-4. 00-4. 00
Illinois	M.	60-60-60	1. 50-2. 57-1. 92	Ohio	M.	(¹)	1. 28-2. 13-1. 92
Indiana	M.	60-60-60	1. 75-2. 40-2. 23	1894:			
Maryland	M.	60-60-60	1. 40-2. 00-1. 59	Montana	M.	(¹)	3. 12-3. 12-3. 12
Michigan	M.	57-60-59	1. 65-2. 50-1. 77	1895:			
Minnesota	M.	60-60-60	1. 95-3. 83-2. 10	Illinois	M.	(¹)	1. 50-2. 00-1. 96
Missouri	M.	(¹)	1. 35-1. 35-1. 35	Ohio	M.	(¹)	1. 40-2. 00-1. 66
Do	(¹)	(¹)	1. 35-1. 54-1. 38	1899:			
New York	M.	(¹)	1. 90-2. 00-1. 97	Michigan	M.	(¹)	1. 84-1. 84-1. 84
Ohio	M.	(¹)	1. 40-1. 40-1. 40	Tennessee	M.	(¹)	1. 00-2. 00-1. 50
Pennsylvania	M.	48-48-48	1. 25-2. 00-1. 66				

¹ Not reported.

TABLE J-11.—*Bratticemen and timbermen, coal mining, 1919-1926, by State and year*

Year	Alabama		Colorado		Illinois		Indiana	
	Hours per week	Rate per hour	Hours per week	Rate per hour	Hours per week	Rate per hour	Hours per week	Rate per hour
1919	48. 0	$0. 498	48. 0	$0. 672	48. 0	$0. 626	48. 0	$0. 625
1922	(¹)	. 424	(¹)	. 983	(¹)	. 938	(¹)	. 942
1924	(¹)	. 436	(¹)	. 934	(¹)	. 937	(¹)	. 937
1926	(¹)	. 450	(¹)	. 705	(¹)	. 938	(¹)	. 915
	Kansas		Kentucky		Ohio		Pennsylvania	
1919	48. 0	$0. 627	48. 0	$0. 513	48. 0	$0. 625	48. 8	$0. 625
1922			(¹)	. 693	(¹)	. 937	(¹)	. 701
1924	(¹)	. 940	(¹)	. 619	(¹)	. 932	(¹)	. 799
1926	(¹)	. 941	(¹)	. 600	(¹)	. 983	(¹)	. 746
	Tennessee		Virginia		West Virginia		Wyoming	
1919	48. 0	$0. 448	48. 0	$0. 476	51. 2	$0. 516	48. 0	$0. 677
1922					(¹)	. 759	(¹)	. 990
1924	(¹)	. 457	(¹)	. 488	(¹)	. 613		
1926	(¹)	. 431	(¹)	. 503	(¹)	. 614		

¹ Not reported.

K.—PRINTING AND PUBLISHING

The sources from which these wage data were taken are the fifteenth and the nineteenth annual reports of the Commissioner Labor Statistics and bulletins of the Bureau of Labor Statistics Nos. 59, 65, 71, 77, 131, 143, 171, 194, 214, 245, 259, 274, 286, 302, 325, 354, 388, 404, 431, 457, and 482. These later reports represent union wage scales which are further explained under "Building trades" (p. 153).

The details on wages and hours for the early periods of this report and extending to 1907 were in most instances copied direct from pay rolls of representative establishments in the various cities. Both hours and earnings represent averages computed from these reports.

For the period from 1907 to 1928 the rates represent the minimum union scale of wages which was accepted and agreed to by the union men and the employers or group of employers. The hours represent the maximum which may be worked beyond which extra payment for overtime is usually made.

The remarkable efficiency of the modern newspaper is largely due to the invention of the type-casting and typesetting machines. The Mergenthaler linotype was the first of these machines to be put into practical use. This was done by a large New York City newspaper in 1886. The use of this machine was followed about one year later by the Lanston monotype. These machines were instrumental in bringing about a rapid change from the hand method of typesetting, the change being especially notable in the newspaper field. The modern printing presses are also responsible for a large share in the great strides made in all branches of the printing business.

In some cities compositors and machine operators of the newspaper printing trades have agreements with their employees whereby they are provided with work for a minimum number of hours per day or payment is made in full if a man starts a day's work.

TABLE **K–1.**—*Bookbinders, 1856–1900, by year and State*

Year and State	Sex	Lowest, highest, and average—		Year and State	Sex	Lowest, highest, and average—	
		Hours per week	Rate per day (dollars)			Hours per week	Rate per day (dollars)
1856:				**1863:**			
New York	M.	60–60–60	2. 00–2. 00–2. 00	New York	(¹)	60–60–60	1. 42–1. 42–1. 42
1857:				**1864:**			
New York	(¹)	60–60–60	. 92–1. 42–1. 25	New York	(¹)	60–60–60	1. 67–2. 17–1. 89
1858:				**1865:**			
New York	(¹)	60–60–60	1. 33–1. 42–1. 39	New York	(¹)	60–60–60	2. 00–2. 17–2. 03
1859:				**1866:**			
New York	(¹)	60–60–60	1. 42–1. 42–1. 42	New York	(¹)	60–60–60	2. 00–2. 67–2. 11
1860:				**1867:**			
New York	M.	60–60–60	2. 00–2. 00–2. 00	New York	(¹)	60–60–60	2. 00–2. 67–2. 19
Do	(¹)	60–60–60	1. 42–1. 42–1. 42	**1868:**			
1861:				New York	(¹)	60–60–60	2. 50–3. 00–2. 60
New York	(¹)	60–60–60	1. 42–1. 42–1. 42	**1869:**			
1862:				Massachusetts	(¹)	(¹)	2. 33–2. 33–2. 33
New York	(¹)	60–60–60	1. 42–1. 42–1. 42	New York	(¹)	59–59–59	2. 50–3. 00–2. 60

¹ Not reported.

TABLE K-1.—*Bookbinders, 1856-1900, by year and State*—Continued

Year and State	Sex	Hours per week	Rate per day (dollars)	Year and State	Sex	Hours per week	Rate per day (dollars)
1870:				**1886:**			
New York	(1)	59-59-59	1.50-3.00-2.42	California	M.	60-60-60	2.30-4.00-3.38
1871:				Do	(1)	(1)	[2]2.50-2.50-2.50
Massachusetts	M.	(1)	1.46-1.46-1.46	Florida	M.	60-60-60	1.00-1.00-1.00
New York	(1)	59-59-59	1.50-3.00-2.40	Kansas	M.	54-57-56	2.66-3.00-2.83
1872:				New York	(1)	59-59-59	2.00-2.00-2.00
Massachusetts	M.	60-60-60	3.33-3.33-3.33	Pennsylvania	M.	59-59-59	1.17-2.58-1.81
Do	F.	(1)	1.13-1.13-1.13	**1887:**			
New York	(1)	59-59-59	1.75-3.00-2.38	Connecticut	M.	(1)	.66-2.48-2.03
1873:				Do	F.	(1)	1.30-3.07-1.60
New York	(1)	59-59-59	2.00-3.00-2.50	Kansas	M.	55-60-56	2.50-3.00-2.79
Pennsylvania	M.	(1)	2.00-2.00-2.00	New York	(1)	59-59-59	2.00-2.00-2.00
1874:				Ohio	M.	(1)	.70-2.50-1.76
New York	(1)	59-59-59	2.50-3.00-2.58	Do	F.	60-60-60	.60-1.00-.63
1875:				Wisconsin	(1)	(1)	1.90-2.00-1.90
New York	(1)	59-59-59	2.50-3.00-2.60	**1888:**			
Virginia	M.	(1)	2.00-2.00-2.00	California	F.	48-54-53	1.00-1.67-1.31
1876:				Colorado	F.	54-60-58	1.00-1.50-1.22
New York	(1)	59-59-59	2.50-3.00-2.63	Kansas	M.	(1)	2.66-2.66-2.66
1877:				New York	(1)	59-59-59	2.00-2.00-2.00
New York	(1)	59-59-59	2.33-3.00-2.58	Do	M.	48-68-59	.75-3.00-1.53
1878:				Do	(1)	60-60-60	.54-.54-.54
New York	(1)	59-59-59	2.33-3.00-2.56	**1889:**			
Ohio	M.	(1)	2.76-2.76-2.76	New York	(1)	59-59-59	2.00-2.00-2.00
1879:				Rhode Island	F.	60-60-60	.50-.50-.50
New York	(1)	59-59-59	1.83-1.83-1.83	**1890:**			
1880:				Illinois	M.	(1)	2.00-2.00-2.00
Georgia	M.	60-60-60	2.50-2.50-2.50	Minnesota	M.	(1)	1.00-3.20-2.14
Kentucky	M.	60-60-60	2.08-2.52-2.31	New York	(1)	59-59-59	2.00-2.00-2.00
New Jersey	(1)	59-59-59	2.25-2.25-2.25	Do	M.	(1)	.54-3.33-1.02
New York	M.	60-60-60	2.25-2.67-2.42	Do	F.	(1)	1.00-1.67-1.34
1881:				**1891:**			
Ohio	M.	59-59-59	2.00-2.00-2.00	Illinois	M.	(1)	2.00-2.00-2.00
1882:				Michigan	F.	(1)	.42-1.33-.70
Massachusetts	M.	59-59-59	1.83-1.83-1.83	New York	M.	(1)	.54-3.33-.90
Missouri	M.	60-60-60	1.67-2.85-2.13	Do	F.	(1)	1.00-1.67-1.34
Ohio	(1)	60-60-60	1.75-1.75-1.75	North Carolina	M.	60-60-60	2.00-2.50-2.25
1883:				Ohio	M.	54-60-60	.75-3.00-1.99
Massachusetts	M.	(1)	1.00-3.00-2.08	Do	F.	54-60-59	.40-1.25-.89
Michigan	M.	(1)	1.35-2.50-1.87	**1892:**			
Missouri	M.	53-53-53	2.50-3.00-2.79	California	M.	48-60-50	.50-4.00-1.98
New York	M.	59-59-59	2.33-2.33-2.33	Do	F.	48-54-50	.33-3.67-.90
Do	(1)	59-59-59	1.83-1.83-1.83	Connecticut	M.	60-60-60	1.75-3.25-2.46
Ohio	M.	59-59-59	3.33-3.33-3.33	Illinois	M.	51-59-56	.50-1.50-.98
1884:				Maine	F.	60-60-60	.50-1.33-.82
California	M.	60-60-60	4.00-4.00-4.00	Missouri	M.	(1)	2.83-3.00-2.89
Kentucky	M.	59-59-59	2.00-3.00-2.50	**1893:**			
Michigan	M.	(1)	.65-3.00-1.87	Connecticut	M.	60-60-60	2.00-3.25-2.47
Do	F.	(1)	.58-1.33-.83	Illinois	M.	54-66-59	.83-3.00-1.97
Missouri	M.	(1)	1.67-2.50-2.09	Do	F.	46-64-59	.50-1.83-.97
Do	(1)	(1)	1.75-1.75-1.75	Maryland	M.	60-60-60	1.50-2.92-2.02
New Jersey	M.	60-60-60	2.67-2.67-2.67	Montana	M.	48-48-48	4.50-4.89-4.79
Do	F.	60-60-60	1.08-1.08-1.08	New York	M.	53-66-59	.58-3.50-1.96
New York	(1)	59-59-59	2.00-2.00-2.00	Do	F.	49-60-56	.50-2.00-1.07
North Carolina	M.	60-60-60	2.00-3.00-2.50	Ohio	M.	45-60-58	.75-3.34-2.01
Ohio	M.	51-51-51	2.00-3.00-2.50	Do	F.	45-60-58	.49-1.26-.93
Tennessee	M.	59-59-59	1.50-2.33-1.94	Pennsylvania	M.	45-60-60	.58-2.50-1.61
Virginia	M.	59-59-59	2.00-2.00-2.00	Do	F.	58-58-58	1.00-1.00-1.00
West Virginia	M.	59-59-59	1.67-1.67-1.67	**1894:**			
1885:				Connecticut	M.	60-60-60	2.00-3.25-2.51
Connecticut	M.	59-59-59	2.17-2.17-2.17	Iowa	M.	54-60-60	.75-3.33-2.10
Florida	M.	60-60-60	2.50-2.50-2.50	Do	F.	60-60-60	.50-1.33-.91
Georgia	M.	60-60 60	1.67-1.67-1.67	Kansas	F.	55-55-55	1.14-1.14-1.14
Illinois	M.	60-60-60	2.10-2.10-2.10	Montana	M.	(1)	4.58-4.58-4.58
Louisiana	M.	60-60-60	2.00-2.00-2.00	New Hampshire	M.	57-57-57	2.00-2.00-2.00
Massachusetts	M.	60-60-60	.95-2.00-1.53	Ohio	M.	48-60-58	.75-3.00-2.39
Missouri	F.	(1)	.58-.58-.58	Do	F.	48-60-58	.50-1.50-.97
Do	M.	59-59-59	2.00-2.50-2.25	**1895:**			
New Jersey	M.	59-59-59	2.00-3.00-2.67	Connecticut	M.	59-60-60	2.00-3.25-2.48
New York	M.	60-60-60	1.58-2.50-1.92	Kentucky	M.	60-60-60	1.82-3.04-2.47
Do	(1)	59-59-59	2.00-2.00-2.00	Louisiana	M.	59-59-59	1.43-2.93-1.98
Virginia	M.	58-58-58	2.50-2.50-2.50	Massachusetts	M.	58-58-58	1.35-1.90-1.68

[1] Not reported.   [2] And board.

TABLE **K–1.**—*Bookbinders, 1856–1900, by year and State*—Continued

Year and State	Sex	Lowest, highest, and average—		Year and State	Sex	Lowest, highest, and average—	
		Hours per week	Rate per day (dollars)			Hours per week	Rate per day (dollars)
1895—Continued.				1897:			
Missouri	M.	53–60–56	2. 00–3. 67–2. 60	Kansas	M.	48–62–54	1. 07–2. 83–2. 28
Montana	M.	53–53–53	4. 00–4. 00–4. 00	Do	F.	48–48–48	. 50–1. 60–1. 05
New Jersey	M.	59–60–59	2. 00–3. 00–2. 33	Michigan	M.	(¹)	1. 65–1. 65–1. 65
New York	M.	59–60–60	1. 43–3. 00–1. 95	New York	M.	60–60–60	1. 25–3. 50–2. 54
North Carolina	M.	54–54–54	2. 00–2. 33–2. 08	Do	F.	57–60–58	1. 17–1. 07–1. 21
Ohio	M.	45–60–59	1. 03–3. 33–2. 06	Virginia	M.	54–60–59	1. 25–2. 50–2. 06
Do	F.	45–60–59	. 70–1. 50– . 95	Do	F.	54–60–58	. 60–1. 00– . 75
South Carolina	M.	54–54–54	3. 00–3. 00–3. 00	1898:			
Tennessee	M.	59–59–59	1. 33–2. 00–1. 75	Nebraska	(¹)	54–60–54	1. 00–2. 10–1. 55
Virginia	M.	57–59–58	2. 00–2. 50–2. 29	New York	M.	60–60–60	2. 50–3. 50–2. 67
Wisconsin	(¹)	60–60–60	1. 50–3. 33–2. 54	1899:			
1896:				Alabama	M.	60–60–60	2. 75–3. 33–2. 94
Florida	M.	60–60–60	1. 00–1. 00–1. 00	California	M.	59–59–59	3. 00–4. 00–3. 23
Georgia	M.	54–60–55	1. 33–3. 17–2. 38	Georgia	M.	60–60–60	2. 00–3. 00–2. 43
Illinois	F.	45–45–45	. 50– . 50– . 50	Illinois	M.	54–54–54	3. 00–3. 00–3. 00
Kansas	M.	54–60–57	1. 50–3. 00–2. 25	North Carolina	M.	54–59–55	1. 67–2. 50–2. 13
Kentucky	M.	59–59–59	1. 00–1. 83–1. 42	1900:			
Missouri	M.	48–60–59	1. 00–2. 66–1. 89	Alabama	M.	60–60–60	2. 75–3. 33–2. 94
Do	F.	48–60–57	. 75–1. 69– . 87	California	M.	59–59–59	2. 75–4. 00–3. 13
Nebraska	(¹)	60–60–60	1. 67–2. 50–2. 09	Georgia	M.	60–60–60	2. 00–3. 00–2. 43
New York	M.	57–60–59	1. 33–3. 00–1. 91	Illinois	M.	54–54–54	3. 00–3. 00–3. 00
Ohio	M.	54–60–59	. 98–3. 25–1. 97	New York	M.	54–54–54	2. 50–3. 33–2. 83
Do	F.	54–60–59	. 72–1. 23– . 91	North Carolina	M.	54–59–55	1. 67–2. 50–2. 06
West Virginia	M.	59–59–59	1. 50–2. 50–2. 00				

¹ Not reported.

TABLE **K–2.**—*Bookbinders, males, 1890–1907, by geographic division and year*

Year	North Atlantic		South Atlantic		North Central		Western	
	Hours per week	Rate per hour	Hours per week	Rate per hour	Hours per week	Rate per hour	Hours per week	Rate per hour
1890	59. 3	$0. 270	59. 7	$0. 197	57. 5	$0. 279	59. 0	$0. 305
1891	59. 3	. 270	59. 7	. 197	57. 4	. 279	59. 0	. 305
1892	59. 3	. 272	59. 7	. 200	57. 2	. 285	59. 0	. 305
1893	59. 3	. 275	59. 7	. 201	56. 9	. 292	59. 0	. 305
1894	59. 3	. 274	59. 0	. 208	57. 0	. 286	59. 0	. 305
1895	59. 3	. 277	59. 2	. 203	57. 3	. 285	59. 0	. 305
1896	59. 2	. 279	59. 3	. 209	57. 1	. 289	59. 0	. 305
1897	59. 2	. 278	59. 0	. 205	56. 4	. 298	59. 0	. 305
1898	57. 4	. 287	59. 1	. 207	56. 2	. 301	59. 0	. 305
1899	56. 8	. 295	58. 1	. 207	55. 0	. 304	59. 0	. 305
1900	55. 9	. 302	58. 6	. 206	54. 5	. 302	59. 0	. 305
1901	55. 3	. 326	58. 3	. 210	54. 2	. 309	57. 0	. 316
1902	54. 2	. 339	56. 0	. 227	54. 3	. 310	57. 0	. 316
1903	54. 3	. 328	54. 8	. 241	54. 0	. 303	55. 1	. 346
1904	53. 8	. 339	54. 8	. 287	53. 9	. 309	52. 4	. 362
1905	53. 6	. 340	54. 4	. 292	53. 9	. 309	51. 6	. 368
1906	53. 3	. 344	54. 0	. 308	53. 8	. 315	49. 6	. 395
1907	52. 8	. 351	53. 1	. 327	53. 6	. 320	49. 6	. 417

TABLE K-3.—*Bookbinders, journeymen, males, book and job, 1907–1928, by city and year*

Year	Atlanta, Ga.		Birmingham, Ala.		Boston, Mass.		Chicago, Ill.	
	Hours per week	Rate per hour	Hours per week	Rate per hour	Hours per week	Rate per hour	Hours per week	Rate per hour
1907	52.0	$0.317					54.0	$0.361
1908	52.0	.317					48.0	.427
1909	52.0	.346					48.0	.427
1910	52.0	.346					48.0	.427
1911	52.0	.346			48.0	$0.438	48.0	.427
1912	48.0	.375	48.0	$0.375	48.0	.438	48.0	.427
1913	48.0	.375	48.0	.375	48.0	.438	48.0	.427
1914	48.0	.406	48.0	.375	48.0	.500	48.0	.438
1915	48.0	.406	48.0	.375	48.0	.500	48.0	.438
1916	48.0	.406	48.0	.375	48.0	.500	48.0	.438
1917	48.0	.406	48.0	.448	48.0	.375	48.0	.458
1918	48.0	.469	48.0	.448	48.0	.500	48.0	.510
1919	48.0	.583	48.0	.521	48.0	.563	48.0	.672
1920	48.0	.750	48.0	.688	48.0	.740	48.0	.880
1921	48.0	.750	44.0	.750			44.0	.975
1922	48.0	.750	44.0	.800			44.0	.892
1923	48.0	.750	44.0	.800			44.0	.965
1924	48.0	.750	44.0	.800			44.0	1.025
1925	44.0	.909	48.0	.800			44.0	1.025
1926	44.0	.909	44.0	.966			44.0	1.070
1927	44.0	.909	44.0	.966	48.0	.865	44.0	1.070
1928	44.0	.909	44.0	.800	48.0	.865	44.0	1.070

Year	Cincinnati, Ohio		Denver, Colo.		Detroit, Mich.		New Orleans, La.	
1907	54.0	$0.333	48.0	$0.375	54.0	$0.296	48.0	$0.375
1908	48.0	.375	48.0	.375	48.0	.333	48.0	.375
1909	48.0	.375	48.0	.417	48.0	.333	48.0	.375
1910	48.0	.375	48.0	.417	48.0	.333	48.0	.375
1911	48.0	.375	48.0	.458	48.0	.333	48.0	.375
1912	48.0	.375	48.0	.479	48.0	.333	48.0	.375
1913	48.0	.375	48.0	.500	48.0	.375	48.0	.375
1914	48.0	.375	48.0	.500	48.0	.375	48.0	.375
1915	48.0	.375	48.0	.500	48.0	.375	48.0	.375
1916			48.0	.500	48.0	.375	48.0	.375
1917	48.0	.375	48.0	.500	48.0	.438	48.0	.375
1918	48.0	.375	48.0	.552	48.0	.438	48.0	.375
1919	48.0	.417	48.0	.615	48.0	.625	48.0	.469
1920	48.0	.583	48.0	.813	48.0	.833	48.0	.625
1921					48.0	.833	48.0	.833
1922	44.0	.773			48.0	.833	48.0	.781
1923	44.0	.773			48.0	.833	48.0	.781
1924	44.0	.818			48.0	.938	48.0	.781
1925	44.0	.841			48.0	.938	48.0	.761
1926	44.0	.864			48.0	.938	48.0	.781
1927	44.0	.864			44.0	1.023	48.0	.781
1928	44.0	.864			48.0	.938	48.0	.781

Year	New York, N. Y.		Philadelphia, Pa.		St. Louis, Mo.		San Francisco, Calif.	
1907	54.0	$0.389	54.0	$0.259	54.0	$0.352	48.0	$0.438
1908	48.0	.438	48.0	.292	48.0	.396	48.0	.438
1909	48.0	.438	48.0	.292	48.0	.396	48.0	.438
1910	48.0	.438	48.0	.292	48.0	.396	48.0	.438
1911	48.0	.438	48.0	.333	48.0	.396	48.0	.469
1912	48.0	.438	48.0	.333	48.0	.396	48.0	.500
1913	48.0	.500	48.0	.333	48.0	.396	48.0	.500
1914	48.0	.500	48.0	.333	48.0	.396	48.0	.500
1915	48.0	.500	48.0	.333	48.0	.396	48.0	.500
1916	48.0	.500	48.0	.333	48.0	.417	48.0	.500
1917	48.0	.500	48.0	.354	48.0	.438	48.0	.500
1918	48.0	.563	48.0	.458	48.0	.481	48.0	.542
1919			48.0	.563	48.0	.546	48.0	.625
1920			48.0	.729	48.0	.771	48.0	.813
1921			48.0	.833	48.0	.906	44.0	1.045
1922			48.0	.833	48.0	.906	44.0	1.045
1923	44.0	1.068	48.0	.833	48.0	.904	44.0	1.045
1924	44.0	1.068	48.0	.833	48.0	.960	44.0	1.045
1925	44.0	1.068	48.0	.833	48.0	.960	44.0	1.136
1926	44.0	1.068	48.0	.833	48.0	.960	44.0	1.136
1927	44.0	1.068	48.0	.833	44.0	1.002	44.0	1.136
1928	44.0	1.068	48.0	.833	44.0	1.002	44.0	1.136

TABLE **K-4.**—*Press feeders, book and job, 1842–1900, by year and State*

Year and State	Sex	Lowest, highest, and average—		Year and State	Sex	Lowest, highest, and average—	
		Hours per week	Rate per day (dollars)			Hours per week	Rate per day (dollars)
1842:				**1868:**			
Connecticut	F.	60–60–60	0.50–0.50–0.50	Connecticut	F.	60–60–60	1.00–1.50–1.05
1843:				New York	(1)	(1)	.58–.97–.77
Connecticut	F.	60–60–60	.50–.50–.50	Pennsylvania	F.	54–54–54	.84–.92–.89
1844:				**1869:**			
Connecticut	F.	60–60–60	.50–.50–.50	Connecticut	F.	60–60–60	1.00–1.50–1.07
1845:				New York	(1)	(1)	.78–.97–.83
Connecticut	F.	60–60–60	.50–.50–.50	Pennsylvania	F.	54–54–54	.84–.92–.89
1846:				**1870:**			
Connecticut	F.	60–60–60	.50–.50–.50	New York	(1)	(1)	.18–1.17–.77
1847:				Pennsylvania	F.	54–54–54	.84–.92–.88
Connecticut	F.	60–60–60	.50–.50–.50	**1871:**			
1848:				New York	(1)	(1)	.21–1.08–.82
Connecticut	F.	60–60–60	.50–.50–.50	Pennsylvania	F.	54–54–54	.84–1.00–.89
1849:				**1872:**			
Connecticut	F.	60–60–60	.50–.50–.50	Connecticut	M.	60–60–60	1.00–1.25–1.08
1850:				Do	F.	60–60–60	.92–1.17–1.00
Connecticut	F.	60–60–60	.50–.50–.50	New York	(1)	(1)	.78–1.56–1.14
1851:				Pennsylvania	F.	54–54–54	.92–1.00–.98
Connecticut	F.	60–60–60	.50–.50–.50	**1873:**			
1852:				Connecticut	M.	60–60–60	1.00–1.00–1.00
Connecticut	F.	60–60–60	.42–.50–.48	Do	F.	60–60–60	1.00–1.17–1.01
Pennsylvania	F.	54–54–54	.84–.84–.84	New York	(1)	(1)	.22–1.39–1.00
1853:				Pennsylvania	F.	54–54–54	1.00–1.00–1.00
Connecticut	F.	60–60–60	.42–.58–.50	Do	M.	(1)	1.00–1.00–1.00
Pennsylvania	F.	54–54–54	.84–.84–.84	**1874:**			
1854:				Connecticut	M.	60–60–60	1.00–1.50–1.25
Connecticut	F.	60–60–60	.58–.58–.58	Do	F.	60–60–60	1.00–1.17–1.01
Pennsylvania	F.	54–54–54	.84–.84–.84	New York	(1)	(1)	.58–.99–.81
1855:				Pennsylvania	F.	54–54–54	1.00–1.00–1.00
Connecticut	F.	60–60–60	.58–.58–.58	**1875:**			
Pennsylvania	F.	54–54–54	.84–.84–.84	Connecticut	F.	59–60–60	.83–1.33–1.00
1856:				Do	M.	60–60–60	.67–1.17–1.01
Connecticut	F.	60–60–60	.58–.58–.58	New York	(1)	(1)	.58–.97–.83
Pennsylvania	F.	54–54–54	.84–.84–.84	Pennsylvania	F.	54–54–54	1.00–1.00–1.00
1857:				**1876:**			
Connecticut	F.	60–60–60	.58–.58–.58	Connecticut	M.	60–60–60	.50–1.34–1.01
Pennsylvania	F.	54–54–54	.84–.84–.84	Do	F.	60–60–60	1.00–1.00–1.00
1858:				New York	(1)	(1)	.58–.97–.88
Connecticut	F.	60–60–60	.58–.58–.58	Pennsylvania	F.	54–54–54	1.00–1.00–1.00
Pennsylvania	F.	54–54–54	.84–.84–.84	**1877:**			
1859:				Connecticut	M.	60–60–60	.50–1.67–1.16
Pennsylvania	F.	54–54–54	.84–.84–.84	Do	F.	60–60–60	.75–1.00–.98
1860:				New York	(1)	(1)	.97–.97–.97
New York	M.	60–60–60	.75–.75–.75	Pennsylvania	F.	54–54–54	1.00–1.00–1.00
Pennsylvania	F.	54–54–54	.84–.84–.84	**1878:**			
1861:				Connecticut	M.	60–60–60	.67–1.50–1.15
New York	(1)	(1)	.39–.39–.39	Do	F.	60–60–60	.84–.84–.84
Pennsylvania	F.	54–54–54	.84–.84–.84	New York	(1)	(1)	.97–.97–.97
1862:				Ohio	M.	(1)	.83–1.44–1.04
New York	(1)	(1)	.58–.58–.58	Do	F.	(1)	.67–1.06–.97
Pennsylvania	F.	54–54–54	.84–.84–.84	Pennsylvania	F.	54–54–54	1.00–1.00–1.00
1863:				**1879:**			
New York	(1)	(1)	.58–.58–.58	Connecticut	M.	60–60–60	.50–1.84–1.15
Pennsylvania	F.	54–54–54	.84–.84–.84	Do	F.	60–60–60	.75–.84–.83
1864:				New York	(1)	(1)	.97–.99–.98
Connecticut	F.	60–60–60	.38–.84–.79	Pennsylvania	F.	54–54–54	1.00–1.00–1.00
New York	(1)	(1)	.58–.60–.59	**1880:**			
Pennsylvania	F.	54–54–54	.84–.92–.85	Connecticut	M.	60–60–60	.42–2.00–1.24
1865:				Do	F.	60–60–60	.75–1.00–.84
Connecticut	F.	60–60–60	.67–.83–.81	Kentucky	M.	60–60–60	.75–.75–.75
New York	(1)	(1)	.58–.61–.60	Missouri	M.	(1)	.83–.83–.83
Pennsylvania	F.	54–54–54	.82–.92–.85	New York	(1)	(1)	.97–1.01–.98
1866:				Pennsylvania	F.	54–60–57	.83–1.17–1.01
Connecticut	M.	60–60–60	1.00–1.00–1.00	Rhode Island	M.	58–58–58	.42–.83–.63
Do	F.	60–60–60	.92–1.00–.98	West Virginia	F.	(1)	.67–.67–.67
New York	(1)	(1)	.78–.78–.78	**1881:**			
Pennsylvania	F.	54–54–54	.84–.92–.88	Connecticut	M.	60–60–60	.42–1.50–.97
1867:				Do	F.	60–60–60	.50–1.00–.96
Connecticut	M.	60–60–60	1.00–1.00–1.00	Illinois	M.	60–60–60	1.25–1.25–1.25
Do	F.	60–60–60	1.00–1.00–1.00	New York	(1)	(1)	.58–.97–.87
New York	(1)	(1)	.58–.97–.74	Pennsylvania	F.	54–54–54	1.00–1.00–1.00
Pennsylvania	F.	54–54–54	.84–.92–.89				

1 Not reported.

TABLE **K-4.**—*Press feeders, book and job, 1842–1900, by year and State*—Contd.

Year and State	Sex	Lowest, highest, and average—		Year and State	Sex	Lowest, highest, and average—	
		Hours per week	Rate per day (dollars)			Hours per week	Rate per day (dollars)
1882:				1887—Continued.			
Connecticut	M.	60–60–60	0.50–1.34–.95	New York	(¹)	(¹)	0.60–1.83–1.02
Do	F.	60–60–60	.84–1.00–.99	Ohio	(¹)	59–61–60	.50–1.15–.88
Missouri	M.	59–59–59	.67–.92–.78	Do	F.	54–60–60	.50–3.00–1.59
New York	(¹)	(¹)	.58–.97–.87	Pennsylvania	F.	54–60–55	.50–1.00–.94
Ohio	M.	(¹)	1.50–1.50–1.50	Wisconsin	(¹)	(¹)	.92–.92–.92
Do	(¹)	(¹)	.56–.56– 56	1888:			
Pennsylvania	M.	60–60–60	.75–1.00–.88	Connecticut	M.	60–60–60	.67–1.67–1.17
Do	F.	54–60–55	.75–1.00–.95	Do	F.	60–60–60	.84–1.50–1.13
1883:				Georgia	F.	59–60–60	.36–.83–.58
Connecticut	M.	60–60–60	.50–1.50–.90	Indiana	F.	57–60–59	.45–.83–.67
Do	F.	60–60–60	.92–1.00–.98	New York	(¹)	(¹)	.58–1.83–.99
Massachusetts	M.	(¹)	.83–1.67–1.33	Do	M.	53–60–59	.42–2.00–1.11
Do	F.	(¹)	1.00–1.17–1.09	Do	F.	59–60–59	.58–1.50–1.08
Do	(¹)	(¹)	.83–1.67–1.39	Pennsylvania	F.	54–54–54	1.00–1.00–1.00
Missouri	F.	(¹)	.58–.58–.58	South Carolina	F.	60–60–60	.42–.83–.64
New York	F.	56–56–56	.33–1.00–.64	1889:			
Do	(¹)	(¹)	.97–.97–.97	Connecticut	M.	60–60–60	.42–1.67–1.08
Pennsylvania	F.	54–54–54	1.00–1.00–1.00	Do	F.	60–60–60	1.00–1.34–1.13
1884:				New York	(¹)	(¹)	.58–1.83–1.00
Connecticut	M.	60–60–60	.50–1.84–.91	Pennsylvania	F.	54–54–54	1.00–1.17–1.02
Do	F.	60–60–60	.92–1.00–.99	1890:			
Georgia	M.	54–54–54	1.17–1.25–1.20	Connecticut	M.	60–60–60	.50–1.67–.98
Do	F.	54–54–54	1.00–1.00–1.00	Do	F.	60–60–60	1.00–1.34–1.15
Kentucky	M.	59–59–59	.75–.75–.75	Illinois	M.	(¹)	.75–2.00–1.50
Missouri	M.	(¹)	.83–.83–.83	Minnesota	M.	59–59–59	.75–.75–.75
Do	(¹)	(¹)	.87–.87–.87	New York	(¹)	(¹)	.40–1.83–.98
New York	(¹)	(¹)	.97–1.50–1.08	Do	M.		.33–2.00–1.08
Ohio	M.	51–59–57	1.00–1.25–1.19	Do	F.		.50–1.17–.98
Pennsylvania	F.	54–59–56	.83–1.00–.97	Pennsylvania	F.	54–54–54	1.17–1.17–1.17
Virginia	M.	59–59–59	.75–.75–.75	Do	F.	54–54–54	1.00–1.00–1.00
West Virginia	F.	60–60–60	.75–.75–.75	1891:			
1885:				Connecticut	M.	60–60–60	.67–2.00–1.15
Connecticut	M.	59–60–60	.33–1.25–.79	Do	F.	60–60–60	1.17–1.50–1.20
Do	F.	59–60–60	.67–1.00–.96	Illinois	M.	60–60–60	.67–2.33–1.50
Georgia	M.	59–60–59	1.17–2.00–1.46	Michigan	(¹)	(¹)	.60–.83–.72
Do	F.	59–59–59	.25–.67–.58	New York	(¹)	(¹)	.78–1.83–1.06
Illinois	M.	59–59–59	1.33–1.33–1.33	Do	F.	(¹)	.33–2.17–1.13
Louisiana	M.	60–60–60	.83–.83–.83	Do	M.	(¹)	.50–1.17–.99
Massachusetts	M.	59–59–59	1.67–1.67–1.67	Ohio	M.	54–60–60	.50–2.00–.99
Do	F.	59–59–59	.67–1.33–1.17	Do	F.	54–60–60	.42–1.00–.74
Missouri	M.	59–59–59	1.00–1.50–1.33	Pennsylvania	F.	54–54–54	1.00–1.17–1.03
New Jersey	M.	59–59–59	1.17–1.17–1.17	1892:			
New York	M.	59–60–59	.42–2.17–1.13	California	M.	57–63–60	.83–1.17–.94
Do	F.	59–59–59	.58–1.17–.85	Do	F.	60–60–60	1.33–1.50–1.42
Do	(¹)	(¹)	.60–1.83–1.02	Connecticut	M.	60–60–60	.58–1.67–1.02
Ohio	M.	59–59–59	.67–.67–.67	Do	F.	60–60–60	1.17–1.17–1.17
Pennsylvania	F.	54–54–54	1.00–1.00–1.00	Illinois	M.	59–60–59	.83–2.00–1.60
South Carolina	F.	59–59–59	.42–.75–.57	Iowa	(¹)	48–60–58	.30–1.00–.62
1886:				Maine	F.	60–60–60	.50–1.17–.75
Connecticut	M.	60–60–60	.50–1.34–.93	New York	M.	60–60–60	.84–.84–.84
Do	F.	60–60–60	1.00–1.17–1.08	1893:			
Florida	M.	60–60–60	1.17–1.17–1.17	Connecticut	M.	60–60–60	.67–1.00–.85
Illinois	M.	60–60–60	.67–.67–.67	Do	F.	60–60–60	1.17–1.17–1.17
Do	F.	60–60–60	.83–1.00–.92	Illinois	M.	48–60–60	.50–2.00–1.64
Iowa	M.	60–60–60	.50–1.17–.73	Do	F.	59–59–59	.83–1.00–.92
Maryland	F.	50–60–56	.54–1.02–.73	Maryland	M.	60–60–60	.83–.83–.83
Michigan	M.	59–59–59	.58–.83–.71	Do	F.	60–60–60	83–.83–.83
Do	F.	59–59–59	.67–.83–.75	Montana	(¹)	(¹)	1.24–1.24–1.24
Missouri	F.	59–60–59	.42–1.42–.88	New York	M.	59–60–60	.67–2.00–1.37
New Jersey	M.	60–60–60	.83–.83–.83	Do	F.	54–60–59	.50–1.17–.80
New York	(¹)	59–59–59	1.16–1.16–1.16	Ohio	M.	54–60–60	.50–1.75–1.31
Do	(¹)	(¹)	.60–1.83–.96	Do	F.	57–60–59	.58–1.25–.96
Do	M.	(¹)	.50–1.00–.67	Pennsylvania	M.	60–60–60	.67–1.33–.94
Do	F.	54–61–55	.67–1.17–.86	Do	F.	30–60–46	.50–1.33–1.03
Pennsylvania	F.	52–62–56	.75–1.08–.97	1894:			
1887:				Connecticut	M.	60–60–60	.75–1.50–1.06
Connecticut	M.	60–60–60	.50–1.67–1.11	Do	F.	60–60–60	1.17–1.17–1.17
Do	F.	60–60–60	1.00–1.29–1.09	Indiana	F.	59–59–59	.42–1.00–.60
Illinois	F.	48–60–58	.50–1.50–.98	Iowa	M.	54–63–59	.42–1.67–1.14
Kentucky	F.	59–59–59	1.00–1.00–1.00	Montana	M.		1.47–1.47–1.47
Massachusetts	F.	45–59–52	.58–1.17–.89	New Hampshire	M.	54–59–57	1.00–1.25–1.13
New York	F.	54–60–58	.58–1.22–.82	Ohio	M.	54–60–59	.50–3.75–1.25
Do	M.	(¹)	.50–1.00–.71	Do	F.	48–60–59	.46–1.25–.84

¹ Not reported.

TABLE K-4.—*Press feeders, book and job, 1842-1900, by year and State*—Contd.

Year and State	Sex	Lowest, highest, and average—		Year and State	Sex	Lowest, highest, and average—	
		Hours per week	Rate per day (dollars)			Hours per week	Rate per day (dollars)
1895:				**1896—Continued.**			
Connecticut	M.	59-60-60	0. 67-1. 50-1. 13	Illinois	M.	54-59-57	0. 67-1. 75-1. 27
Do	F.	59-60-60	. 50-1. 17-1. 09	Do	F.	54-54-54	. 83-1 00- . 91
Georgia	M.	59-59-59	1. 67-1. 67-1. 67	Iowa	M.	60-60-60	1. 00-1. 67-1. 45
Do	F.	59-59-59	. 65- . 75- . 72	Kentucky	M.	59-59-59	. 60- . 67- . 64
Kentucky	M.	60-60-60	. 75- . 75- . 75	Michigan	M.	59-59-59	. 42-1. 50- . 96
Louisiana	M.	59-59-59	1. 00-1. 08-1. 04	Do	F.	59-59-59	1. 00-1. 00-1. 00
Massachusetts	M.	55-60-59	. 67-1. 67-1. 39	New York	M.	59-60-60	. 50-2. 50-1. 27
Do	F.	55-58-57	. 46-1. 67-1. 07	Do	F.	54-60-58	. 67-1. 06- . 92
Missouri	M.	59-60-59	. 58-1. 50- . 93	Ohio	M.	54 60-59	. 60-2. 00-1. 18
Do	F.	60-60-60	. 67- . 67- . 67	Do	F.	50-60-57	. 73- . 97- . 83
New Jersey	M.	59-59-59	. 83-1. 17-1. 00	Pennsylvania	M.	60-60-60	. 83-1. 33-1. 16
New York	M.	58-60-59	. 67-1. 67-1. 17	Do	F.	59-60-60	. 67-1. 50- . 99
Do	F.	56-60-58	. 58-1. 17- . 96	West Virginia	F.	60-60-60	. 42- . 83- . 77
Ohio	M.	45-60-57	. 50-1. 35-1. 10	**1897:**			
Do	F.	45-60-59	. 46-1. 25- . 92	New York	M.	54-54-54	1. 50-1. 50-1. 50
Pennsylvania	M.	60-60-60	. 75-1. 67-1. 31	Pennsylvania	M.	60-60-60	1. 50-1. 50-1. 50
Do	F.	54-54-54	1. 00-1. 00-1. 00	**1899:**			
Rhode Island	M.	56-56-56	1. 00-1. 42-1. 21	California	M.	59-59-59	1. 25-2. 00-1. 37
South Carolina	F.	54-59-58	. 42- . 67- . 58	Illinois	M.	54-54-54	1. 92-1. 92-1. 92
Virginia	M.	59-59-59	. 83- . 83- . 83	Massachusetts	M.	54-54-54	1. 50-2. 00-1. 67
1896:				New York	M.	54-54-54	1. 67-2. 33-2. 32
Connecticut	M.	60-60-60	1. 00-1. 00-1. 00	**1900:**			
Florida	M.	60-60-60	1-17-1. 17-1. 17	California	M.	59-59-59	1. 25-4. 17-2. 09
Do	F.	60-60-60	. 42-1. 33- . 88	Illinois	M.	54-54-54	1. 92-1. 92-1. 92
Georgia	M.	54-60-55	. 50-2. 00- . 92	Massachusetts	M.	54-54-54	2. 00-2. 00-2. 00
Do	F.	54-54-54	1. 00-1. 00-1. 00	New York	M.	54-54-54	1. 67-2. 33-2. 32

TABLE K-5.—*Press feeders, males, book and job, 1890-1907, by geographic division and year*

Year	North Atlantic		South Atlantic		North Central		South Central	
	Hours per week	Rate per hour	Hours per week	Rate per hour	Hours per week	Rate per hour	Hours per week	Rate per hour
1890	59. 7	$0. 155	59. 3	$0 112	56. 9	$0. 143	60. 0	$0. 083
1891	59. 7	. 156	59. 3	. 113	56. 6	. 148	60. 0	. 083
1892	59. 7	. 154	59. 3	. 112	56. 6	. 146	60. 0	. 083
1893	59. 8	. 153	59. 2	. 113	56. 6	. 144	60. 0	. 092
1894	59. 7	. 155	59. 3	. 112	56. 4	. 149	60. 0	. 092
1895	59. 8	. 160	59. 3	. 112	56. 8	. 147	60. 0	. 092
1896	59. 7	. 157	59. 2	. 118	57. 1	. 142	60. 0	. 092
1897	59. 7	. 154	59. 1	. 116	57. 1	. 144	60. 0	. 092
1898	57. 5	. 159	58. 9	. 117	56. 9	. 148	60. 0	. 100
1899	57. 3	. 164	59. 0	. 122	56. 6	. 149	60. 0	. 100
1900	55. 1	. 186	58. 2	. 124	54. 6	. 178	60. 0	. 092
1901	55. 2	. 188	58. 1	. 130	54. 6	. 178	60. 0	. 092
1902	54. 0	. 190	56. 2	. 140	54. 6	. 173	60. 0	. 075
1903	53. 7	. 202	54. 6	. 131	54. 1	. 195	54. 0	. 162
1904	53. 4	. 201	54. 9	. 145	53. 9	. 187	53. 6	. 154
1905	53. 2	. 206	54. 5	. 151	53. 9	. 187	53. 6	. 154
1906	52. 4	. 209	53. 8	. 161	53. 9	. 190	53. 2	. 165
1907	52. 5	. 226	52. 8	. 162	53. 5	. 195	52. 9	. 171

TABLE **K-6.**—*Press feeders, cylinder, both sexes, book and job, 1907–1928, by city and year*

Year	Atlanta, Ga.		Birmingham, Ala.		Boston, Mass.[1]		Chicago, Ill.[2]	
	Hours per week	Rate per hour	Hours per week	Rate per hour	Hours per week	Rate per hour	Hours per week	Rate per hour
1907	54.0	$0.157			54.0	$0.259	54.0	$0.278
1908	48.0	.177			48.0	.292	48.0	.313
1909	48.0	.177			48.0	.292	48.0	.313
1910	48.0	.177			48.0	.313	48.0	.313
1911	48.0	.177			48.0	.313	48.0	.344
1912	48.0	.177			48.0	.313	48.0	.344
1913	48.0	.177			48.0	.313	48.0	.344
1914	48.0	.177			48.0	.333	48.0	.365
1915	48.0	.177			48.0	.333	48.0	.365
1916	48.0	.177			48.0	.333	48.0	.365
1917	48.0	.177			48.0	.333	48.0	.385
1918	48.0	.250			48.0	.396	48.0	.438
1919	48.0	.375			48.0	.458	48.0	.594
1920	48.0	.431			48.0	.656	48.0	.813
1921	44.0	.568	44.0	$0.532	48.0	.781	44.0	.901
1922	44.0	.568	44.0	.532	48.0	.781	44.0	.833
1923	44.0	.568	44.0	.532	48.0	.781	44.0	.943
1924	44.0	.568	44.0	.532	48.0	.781	44.0	.943
1925	44.0	.568	44.0	.602	44.0	.852	44.0	.943
1926	44.0	.568	44.0	.602	44.0	.852	44.0	.983
1927	44.0	.568	44.0	.602	44.0	.852	44.0	.983
1928	44.0	.568	44.0	.602	44.0	.852	44.0	.983

Year	Cincinnati, Ohio		Denver, Colo.		Detroit, Mich.[3]		New Orleans, La.[4]	
1907	54.0	$0.222	48.0	$0.292	54.0	$0.185	48.0	$0.250
1908	48.0	.229	48.0	.292	48.0	.208	48.0	.250
1909	48.0	.250	48.0	.292	48.0	.250	48.0	.250
1910	48.0	.250	48.0	.313	48.0	.250	48.0	.281
1911	48.0	.281	48.0	.313	48.0	.250	48.0	.281
1912	48.0	.281	48.0	.333	48.0	.271	48.0	.313
1913	48.0	.302	48.0	.344	48.0	.292	48.0	.313
1914	48.0	.302	48.0	.354	48.0	.313	48.0	.313
1915	48.0	.302	48.0	.354	48.0	.313	48.0	.313
1916	48.0	.302	48.0	.354	48.0	.313	48.0	.313
1917	48.0	.333	48.0	.354	48.0	.354	48.0	.313
1918	48.0	.375	48.0	.396	48.0	.375	48.0	.344
1919	48.0	.448	48.0	.479	48.0	.479	48.0	.396
1920	48.0	.573	48.0	.625	48.0	.729	48.0	.521
1921	44.0	.761	48.0	.760	48.0	.729	44.0	.568
1922	44.0	.761	44.0	.723	48.0	.729	44.0	.568
1923			44.0	.723	48.0	.729	44.0	.568
1924			44.0	.723	48.0	.800	44.0	.625
1925			44.0	.723	48.0	.800	44.0	.625
1926	44.0	.761	44.0	.795	48.0	.800	44.0	.625
1927	44.0	.801	44.0	.795	48.0	.800	44.0	.625
1928	44.0	.801	44.0	.795	48.0	.800	44.0	.625

Year	New York, N. Y.[5]		Philadelphia, Pa.[6]		St. Louis, Mo.[7]		San Francisco, Calif.	
1907	54.0	$0.296			54.0	$0.278	48.0	$0.313
1908	48.0	.333			54.0	.278	48.0	.313
1909	48.0	.333			48.0	.313	48.0	.313
1910	48.0	.333			48.0	.313	48.0	.344
1911	48.0	.333	48.0	$0.250	48.0	.313	48.0	.344
1912	48.0	.344	48.0	.250	48.0	.313	48.0	.344
1913	48.0	.354	48.0	.281	48.0	.313	48.0	.344
1914	48.0	.354	48.0	.281	48.0	.313	48.0	.344
1915	48.0	.354	48.0	.281	48.0	.333	48.0	.344
1916	48.0	.354	48.0	.281	48.0	.333	48.0	.344
1917	48.0	.365	48.0	.313	48.0	.354	48.0	.344
1918	48.0	.458	[8] 48.0	[8] .417	48.0	.390	48.0	.406
1919	48.0	.625	48.0	.458	48.0	.431	48.0	.438
1920	48.0	.813	48.0	.729	48.0	.625	48.0	.531
1921	44.0	.852	45.0	.778	48.0	.740	44.0	.682
1922	44.0	.830	44.0	.729	44.0	.739	44.0	.682
1923	44.0	.920	44.0	.729	44.0	.739	44.0	.682
1924	44.0	.966	44.0	.729	44.0	.780	44.0	.682
1925	44.0	.966	44.0	.729	44.0	.784	44.0	.818
1926	44.0	.989	44.0	.729	44.0	.780	44.0	.818
1927	44.0	1.011	44.0	.795	44.0	.825	44.0	.818
1928	44.0	1.034	44.0	.795	44.0	.825	44.0	.818

[1] Not classified, 1907–1912.
[2] Cylinder press 25 by 38 and over, 1917–1928, inclusive.
[3] Cylinder press 25 by 38 and over, 1913–1918, inclusive.
[4] Not classified, 1922–1928, inclusive.
[5] Hand press, 1907–1912.
[6] Presses 25 by 38 inches and over, 1911–1920; competitive offices only, 1914–1927; union offices only, 1922–1928.
[7] Presses 24 by 36 and over, 1912–1928, inclusive.
[8] Flat-bed perfecting presses.

TABLE **K-7.**—*Press feeders, platen, both sexes, book and job, 1907–1928, by city and year*

Year	Atlanta, Ga.		Birmingham, Ala.		Chicago, Ill.		Denver, Colo.	
	Hours per week	Rate per hour	Hours per week	Rate per hour	Hours per week	Rate per hour	Hours per week	Rate per hour
1907	54.0	$0.130			54.0	$0.176		
1908	48.0	.146			48.0	.198		
1909	48.0	.146			48.0	.198		
1910	48.0	.146			48.0	.198		
1911	48.0	.146			48.0	.219	48.0	$0.188
1912	48.0	.146			48.0	.219	48.0	.188
1913	48.0	.146			48.0	.219	48.0	.198
1914	48.0	.146			48.0	.240	48.0	.198
1915	48.0	.156			48.0	.240		
1916	48.0	.156			48.0	.240		
1917					48.0	.260		
1918					48.0	.292		
1919					48.0	.385		
1920					48.0	.510		
1921	44.0	.534	44.0	$0.395	44.0	.566		
1922	44.0	.534	44.0	.395	44.0	.525		
1923	44.0	.534	44.0	.395	44.0	.591		
1924	44.0	.534	44.0	.395	44.0	.591		
1925	44.0	.534	44.0	.443	44.0	.591		
1926	44.0	.534	44.0	.443	44.0	.615		
1927	44.0	.534	44.0	.443	44.0	.615		
1928	44.0	.534	44.0	.443	44.0	.615		

Year	Detroit, Mich.		New York, N. Y.		St. Louis, Mo.[1]		San Francisco, Calif.	
	Hours per week	Rate per hour	Hours per week	Rate per hour	Hours per week	Rate per hour	Hours per week	Rate per hour
1907					54.0	$0.222	48.0	$0.250
1908					54.0	.222	48.0	.250
1909					48.0	.250	48.0	.250
1910					48.0	.250	48.0	.281
1911	48.0	$0.208			48.0	.250	48.0	.281
1912	48.0	.229	[2] 48.0	[3] $0.250	48.0	.250	48.0	.281
1913	48.0	.250	48.0	.250	48.0	.250	48.0	.281
1914	48.0	.250	48.0	.250	48.0	.250	48.0	.281
1915	48.0	.250	48.0	.250	48.0	.250	48.0	.281
1916	48.0	.250	48.0	.250	48.0	.271	48.0	.281
1917	48.0	.292	48.0	.260	48.0	.292	48.0	.281
1918	48.0	.313	48.0	.354			48.0	.344
1919	48.0	.396	48.0	.417			48.0	.375
1920	48.0	.521	48.0	.604	48.0	.365	48.0	.469
1921	48.0	.521	[2] 44.0	[2] .636	48.0	.427	44.0	.568
1922	48.0	.521	44.0	.591	44.0	.427	44.0	.568
1923	48.0	.521	44.0	.636	44.0	.427	44.0	.568
1924	48.0	.552	44.0	.659	44.0	.449	44.0	.568
1925	48.0	.552	44.0	.659	44.0	.449	44.0	.614
1926	48.0	.552	44.0	.682	44.0	.450	44.0	.614
1927	48.0	.552	44.0	.705	44.0	.472	44.0	.614
1928	48.0	.552	44.0	.705	44.0	.472	44.0	.614

[1] Lithographic No. 2 or less, 1907–1917, inclusive.   [3] Job presses.

TABLE **K-8.**—*Press feeders, females, book and job, 1890–1907, by geographic division and year*

Year	North Atlantic		North Central		South Atlantic		South Central	
	Hours per week	Rate per hour	Hours per week	Rate per hour	Hours per week	Rate per hour	Hours per week	Rate per hour
1890	59.0	$0.091	59.8	$0.091				
1891	59.0	.091	59.8	.091				
1892	59.0	.092	59.8	.092				
1893	59.0	.090	59.8	.092				
1894	59.0	.090	59.8	.091				
1895	59.0	.091	59.7	.084				
1896	59.0	.092	59.8	.092				
1897	59.0	.091	59.8	.093				
1898	57.3	.094	59.9	.095				
1899	56.2	.097	59.3	.095				
1900	54.0	.098	54.9	.105				
1901	54.0	.102	54.8	.104				
1902	54.0	.105	54.6	.106				
1903	53.9	.117	53.8	.125	54.0	$0.090	54.0	$0.111
1904	53.7	.118	53.8	.148	54.8	.106	54.2	.113
1905	54.5	.124	54.0	.142	54.0	.107	54.1	.104
1906	54.0	.127	53.9	.145	54.0	.114	53.8	.099
1907	54.0	.124	53.4	.141	53.7	.121	53.7	.117

TABLE **K-9.**—*Proof readers, 1872–1900, by year and State*

Year and State	Sex	Lowest, highest, and average—		Year and State	Sex	Lowest, highest, and average—	
		Hours per week	Rate per day (dollars)			Hours per week	Rate per day (dollars)
1872:				1886:			
Connecticut	F.	60–60–60	1.67–1.67–1.67	Iowa	F.	60–60–60	1.00–1.00–1.00
Massachusetts	F.	60–60–60	1.17–1.67–1.29	New York	M.	59–59–59	2.50–3.33–2.92
1873:				Pennsylvania	F.	(¹)	1.33–1.33–1.33
Connecticut	F.	60–60–60	2.00–2.00–2.00	1887:			
1874:				Connecticut	M.	60–60–60	1.50–2.40–2.18
Connecticut	F.	60–60–60	2.00–2.00–2.00	Do.	F.	60–60–60	1.00–1.00–1.00
1875:				New York	M.	(¹)	3.00–3.00–3.00
Connecticut	M.	59–59–59	3.33–3.33–3.33	Ohio	M.	60–60–60	1.50–3.33–2.83
Do.	F.	60–60–60	2.00–2.00–2.00	Do.	F.	60–60–60	1.25–1.25–1.25
1876:				Wisconsin	(¹)	(¹)	2.75–2.75–2.75
Pennsylvania	M.	60–60–60	2.50–2.50–2.50	1888:			
1877:				Connecticut	M.	60–60–60	2.25–2.25–2.25
Connecticut	M.	60–60–60	3.00–3.00–3.00	Do.	F.	60–60–60	1.42–1.42–1.42
1878:				South Carolina	F.	60–60–60	1.33–1.33–1.33
Connecticut	M.	60–60–60	2.50–2.50–2.50	1889:			
Ohio	M.	(¹)	1.83–4.00–2.51	Connecticut	M.	60–60–60	2.42–2.42–2.42
Do.	F.	(¹)	1.00–1.00–1.00	Do.	F.	60–60–60	1.75–1.75–1.75
1879:				1890:			
Connecticut	M.	60–60–60	2.00–2.00–2.00	Connecticut	M.	60–60–60	2.50–2.50–2.50
1880:				Do.	F.	60–60–60	1.67–1.67–1.67
South Carolina	M.	(¹)	3.33–3.33–3.33	Illinois	M.	(¹)	2.50–3.33–3.02
1881:				Do.	F.	(¹)	2.17–3.00–2.56
Connecticut	M.	60–60–60	2.34–2.34–2.34	New York	M.	(¹)	.83–3.67–3.18
1882:				Ohio	(¹)	48–72–59	1.00–3.50–2.25
Connecticut	M.	60–60–60	2.50–2.50–2.60	1891:			
Illinois	F.	51–51–51	1.33–1.33–1.33	Connecticut	M.	60–60–60	2.75–2.75–2.75
Ohio	(¹)	51–51–51	3.08–3.08–3.08	Do.	F.	60–60–60	1.75–1.75–1.75
1883:				Illinois	M.	(¹)	3.33–5.03–3.44
Massachusetts	F.	(¹)	1.33–2.00–1.57	Do.	F.	(¹)	2.17–3.00–2.56
Do.	M.	(¹)	3.17–3.17–3.17	Michigan	M.	(¹)	.83–1.81–1.58
Michigan	(¹)	(¹)	1.00–1.00–1.00	New York	M.	(¹)	.83–3.67–3.18
1884:				1892:			
Michigan	M.	(¹)	2.15–2.15–2.15	California	M.	60–60–60	3.00–3.33–3.17
Missouri	(¹)	(¹)	2.50–2.50–2.50	Do.	F.	54–54–54	2.17–2.17–2.17
1885:				Connecticut	M.	60–60–60	1.67–4.17–2.92
Massachusetts	M.	44–59–56	1.67–5.75–2.95	Do.	F.	60–60–60	1.50–1.50–1.50
Do.	F.	59–59–59	1.00–2.00–1.25	Illinois	M.	59–60–59	3.00–3.50–3.26
New York	M.	59–59–59	3.33–3.67–3.53	Do.	F.	54–60–56	1.17–2.50–2.07
Do.	F.	60–60–60	1.00–3.00–2.00	Maine	F.	60–60–60	1.00–1.67–1.34
South Carolina	F.	59–59–59	1.33–1.33–1.33	Missouri	(¹)	(¹)	3.33–3.33–3.33

¹ Not reported.

TABLE K-9.—*Proof readers, 1872-1900, by year and State*—Continued

Year and State	Sex	Lowest, highest, and average—		Year and State	Sex	Lowest, highest, and average—	
		Hours per week	Rate per day (dollars)			Hours per week	Rate per day (dollars)
1893:				**1895—Continued**			
Connecticut	M.	60-60-60	1. 67-4. 17-2. 61	Pennsylvania	M.	60-60-60	2. 50-2. 50-2. 50
Do	F.	60-60-60	1. 50-1. 50-1. 50	South Carolina	M.	54-54-54	3. 33-3. 67-3. 50
Illinois	F.	59-60-59	1. 00-2. 50-1. 94	Do	F.	59-59-59	1. 33-1. 33-1. 33
Do	M.	59-60-59	3. 00-3. 50-3. 21	**1896:**			
Ohio	F.	60-60-60	1. 50-1. 50-1. 50	Illinois	F.	51-51-51	1. 33-1. 33-1. 33
Pennsylvania	F.	60-60-60	1. 67-1. 67-1. 67	Iowa	M.	60-60-60	1. 00-1. 00-1. 00
1894:				New York	M.	59-59-59	2. 33-3. 00-2. 57
Connecticut	M.	60-60-60	1. 75-4. 17-2. 97	Do	F.	59-59-59	1. 33-1. 33-1. 33
Do	F.	60-60-60	1. 67-2. 25-1. 96	Ohio	M.	48-60-58	2. 50-3. 50-2. 90
Indiana	F.	59-59-59	1. 33-1. 33-1. 33	Do	F.	48-60-56	1. 35-2. 25-2. 05
1895:				Pennsylvania	F.	60-60-60	1. 33-1. 33-1. 33
Connecticut	M.	59-60-60	1. 75-4. 17-2. 95	**1897:**			
Do	F.	59-60-60	1. 67-2. 50-1. 98	Kansas	M.	54-54-54	3. 33-3. 33-3. 33
Massachusetts	M.	48-60-56	2. 17-3. 00-2. 85	**1898:**			
Do	F.	48-60-57	1. 00-3. 67-1. 78	Michigan	F.	(1)	1. 60-1. 60-1. 60
Montana	M.	53-53-53	5. 00-5. 00-5. 00	**1899:**			
New York	M.	48-60-57	2. 70-4. 05-3. 39	Massachusetts	F.	53-53-53	1. 67-4. 17-2. 51
Do	F.	48-60-55	. 83-2. 50-1. 71	**1900:**			
Ohio	M.	48-48-48	2. 33-2. 33-2. 33	Massachusetts	F.	53-53-53	1. 67-4. 17-2. 43
Do	F.	60-60-60	1. 20-2. 00-1. 57				

¹ Not reported.

TABLE K-10.—*Proof readers, males,¹ book and job, 1890-1907, by geographic division and year*

Year	North Atlantic		South Atlantic		North Central		South Central	
	Hours per week	Rate per hour	Hours per week	Rate per hour	Hours per week	Rate per hour	Hours per week	Rate per hour
1890	59. 9	$0. 329	60. 0	$0. 333	60. 0	$0. 318		
1891	59. 9	. 332	60. 0	. 333	60. 0	. 318		
1892	59. 9	. 327	60. 0	. 300	60. 0	. 318		
1893	59. 9	. 327	60. 0	. 300	60. 0	. 326		
1894	59. 8	. 323	60. 0	. 300	60. 0	. 326		
1895	59. 9	. 333	60. 0	. 300	60. 0	. 329		
1896	59. 9	. 325	60. 0	. 300	60. 0	. 329		
1897	59. 9	. 331	60. 0	. 300	60. 0	. 323		
1898	59. 2	. 338	60. 0	. 300	60. 0	. 323		
1899	56. 4	. 306	60. 0	. 267	55. 6	. 348		
1900	55. 1	. 355	60. 0	. 267	52. 8	. 364		
1901	54. 9	. 357	60. 0	. 267	52. 9	. 389		
1902	51. 8	. 403	56. 0	. 313	52. 9	. 386		
1903	52. 4	. 392	55. 4	. 318	53. 9	. 372	54. 0	$0. 361
1904	52. 6	. 370	54. 7	. 320	53. 8	. 370	54. 0	. 386
1905	52. 5	. 381	54. 7	. 324	54. 0	. 368	53. 0	. 394
1906	50. 2	. 410	53. 7	. 326	52. 9	. 382	53. 5	. 360
1907	49. 8	. 420	51. 9	. 340	51. 3	. 402	53. 5	. 348

¹ For rates after 1907 use those of "Compositors, daywork; newspaper." See Table K-13, p. 353.

TABLE **K-11.**—*Proof readers, females,[1] book and job, 1890–1907, by geographic division and year*

Year	North Atlantic		North Central		South Central		Western	
	Hours per week	Rate per hour	Hours per week	Rate per hour	Hours per week	Rate per hour	Hours per week	Rate per hour
1890	59.8	$0.271	60.0	$0.222			48.0	$0.438
1891	59.8	.301	60.0	.252			48.0	.438
1892	57.3	.289	60.0	.230			48.0	.438
1893	57.8	.296	60.0	.200			48.0	.438
1894	57.3	.303	60.0	.160			48.0	.438
1895	57.1	.280	60.0	.174			48.0	.438
1896	56.7	.265	60.0	.210			48.0	.438
1897	57.2	.261	60.0	.187			48.0	.438
1898	56.6	.265	60.0	.197			48.0	.438
1899	56.6	.269	57.0	.256			48.0	.438
1900	55.0	.286	54.9	.303			48.0	.438
1901	54.0	.292	54.0	.254			48.0	.438
1902	54.0	.320	54.0	.281			48.0	.438
1903	51.0	.351	54.0	.325	54.0	$0.207	50.0	.343
1904	51.4	.302	53.4	.326	55.4	.162	50.4	.313
1905	51.6	.298	53.6	.291			50.4	.337
1906	52.4	.293	52.4	.274	53.2	.239	50.4	.310
1907	51.7	.320	52.0	.280	51.1	.279	49.5	.393

[1] For rates after 1907 use those of "Compositors, daywork; newspaper." See Table K-13, p. 353.

TABLE **K-12.**—*Compositors, 1842–1900, by year and State*

Year and State	Sex	Lowest, highest, and average—		Year and State	Sex	Lowest, highest, and average—	
		Hours per week	Rate per day (dollars)			Hours per week	Rate per day (dollars)
1842:				1856:			
Connecticut	M.	60–60–60	1.50–1.50–1.50	Connecticut	M.	60–60–60	[1] 0.25–0.25–0.25
Do	M.	60–60–60	[1] .24– .25– .24	New York	(²)	(²)	1.67–2.17–1.79
1843:				1857:			
Connecticut	M.	60–60–60	1.50–1.50–1.50	Connecticutt	M.	60–60–60	2.00–2.00–2.00
Do	M.	60–60–60	[1] .25– .25– .25	Do	M.	60–60–60	[1] .25– .25– .25
1844:				New York	(²)	60–60–60	1.34–2.50–1.79
Connecticut	M.	60–60–60	[1] .25– .25– .25	Pennsylvania	M.	60–60–60	1.67–1.67–1.67
1845:				1858:			
Connecticut	M.	60–60–60	1.45–1.45–1.45	Connecticut	M.	60–60–60	[1] .25– .25– .25
Do	M.	60–60–60	[1] .25– .25– .25	New York	(²)	60–60–60	1.67–2.50–1.75
1846::				Pennsylvania	M.	60–60–60	1.67–1.67–1.67
Connecticut	M.	60–60–60	1.67–1.67–1.67	Do	M.	60–60–60	[1] .40– .40– .40
Do	M.	60–60–60	[1] .25– .25– .25	1859:			
1847:				New York	(²)	60–60–60	1.34–2.50–1.76
Connecticut	M.	60–60–60	1.67–1.67–1.67	Pennsylvania	M.	60–60–60	1.67–1.67–1.67
Do	M.	60–60–60	[1] .25– .25– .25	Do	M.	60–60–60	[1] .40– .40– .40
1848:				1860:			
Connecticut	M.	60–60–60	1.67–1.67–1.67	New York	M.	60–60–60	2.00–2.00–2.00
Do	M.	60–60–60	[1] .25– .25– .25	Do	(²)	60–60–60	1.67–2.83–1.80
1849:				Ohio	M.	(²)	3.00–3.00–3.00
Connecticut	M.	60–60–60	[1] .30– .30– .30	Pennsylvania	M.	60–60–60	1.67–1.88–1.72
1850:				Do	M.	60–60–60	[1] .40– .40– .40
Connecticut	M.	60–60–60	[1] .30– .30– .30	1861:			
1851:				Maryland	M.	59–59–59	1.67–1.67–1.67
Connecticut	M.	60–60–60	[1] .30– .30– .30	New York	(²)	59–60–59	1.34–2.83–1.80
New York	M.	(²)	1.50–1.50–1.50	Pennsylvania	M.	60–60–60	1.67–1.67–1.67
1852:				Do	M.	6C–60–60	[1] .40– .40– .40
Connecticut	M.	60–60–60	[1] .30– .30– .30	1862:			
New York	M.	(²)	1.50–1.50–1.50	Maryland	M.	59–59–59	1.67–1.67–1.67
1853:				New York	(²)	60–60–60	1.34–2.83–1.83
Connecticut	M.	60–60–60	[1] .30– .30– .30	Pennsylvania	M.	60–60–60	1.67–1.67–1.67
New York	(²)	(²)	1.50–1.67–1.54	Do	M.	60–60–60	[1] .40– .40– .40
1854:				1863:			
Connecticut	M.	60–60–60	[1] .30– .30– .30	Maryland	M.	59–59–59	1.67–1.67–1.67
New York	(²)	(²)	1.67–2.00–1.71	New York	(²)	59–60–59	1.34–2.83–1.82
1855:				Pennsylvania	M.	60–60–60	1.67–1.67–1.67
Connecticut	M.	60–60–60	[1] .30– .30– .30	Do	M.	6J–60–60	[1] .40– .40– .40
New York	(²)	(²)	1.67–2.00–1.70				

[1] Per 1,000 ems. ² Not reported.

TABLE **K-12.**—*Compositors, 1842-1900, by year and State*—Continued

Year and State	Sex	Hours per week	Rate per day (dollars)	Year and State	Sex	Hours per week	Rate per day (dollars)
1864:				**1872:**			
Connecticut	M.	60-60-60	2.00-2.50-2.17	California	M.	60-60-60	3.00-5.00-3.36
Do	M.	60-60-60	[1] .37-.40-.37½	Connecticut	M.	60-60-60	1.67-3.67-2.92
Maryland	M.	59-59-59	2.50-2.50-2.50	Do	M.	60-60-60	[1] .38-.38-.38
New York	(²)	59-59-59	1.67-2.50-2.32	Do	F.	60-60-60	[1] .36-.36-.36
Pennsylvania	M.	60-60-60	1.50-1.84-1.67	Illinois	M.	60-60-60	3.50-3.50-3.50
Do	M.	60-60-60	[1] .40-.40-.40	Louisiana	M.	59-60-59	3.00-3.00-3.00
1865:				Maryland	M.	59-60-60	3.00-3.00-3.00
Connecticut	M.	60-60-60	2.50-3.00-2.75	Massachusetts	M.	59-72-59	2.50-5.00-2.82
Do	M.	60-60-60	[1] .40-.40-.40	Do	F.	60-60-60	1.00-1.67-1.40
Maryland	M.	59-59-59	3.00-3.00-3.00	Minnesota	M.	60-60-60	1.50-1.50-1.50
New York	(²)	59-59-59	2.17-3.00-2.56	Do	M.	52-52-52	[1] .38-.38-.38
Pennsylvania	M.	60-60-60	1.67-1.84-1.76	Missouri	M.	54-60-59	2.17-3.00-2.86
1866:				Do	M.	(²)	[1] .45-.45-.45
Connecticut	M.	60-60-60	2.50-2.50-2.50	New York	M.	60-60-60	3.00-3.33-3.06
Do	M.	60-60-60	[1] .40-.40-.40	Do	(²)	59-59-59	2.83-3.67-3.04
Maryland	M.	59-59-59	3.00-3.00-3.00	Ohio	M.	59-59-59	2.33-4.17-3.28
New York	(²)	59-59-59	2.00-2.83-2.53	Pennsylvania	M.	59-59-59	2.50-3.34-3.00
Pennsylvania	M.	60-60-60	1.50-2.67-1.87	Do	M.	60-60-60	[1] .40-.40-.40
Do	M.	60-60-60	[1] .40-.40-.40	Virginia	M.	58-58-58	3.33-3.33-3.33
1867:				**1873:**			
Connecticut	M.	60-60-60	[1] .43-.43-.43	California	M.	60-60-60	3.00-5.00-3.45
Maryland	M.	59-59-59	3.00-3.00-3.00	Connecticut	M.	60-60-60	1.67-3.67-2.86
New York	(²)	59-59-59	2.50-3.33-2.62	Do	M.	60-60-60	[1] .38-.38-.38
Pennsylvania	M.	60-60-60	2.75-2.75-2.75	Do	F.	60-60-60	[1] .36-.36-.36
Do	M.	60-60-60	[1] .40-.40-.40	Illinois	M.	60-60-60	3.50-3.50-3.50
1868:				Louisiana	M.	59-60-59	3.00-3.00-3.00
Connecticut	M.	60-60-60	2.67-3.17-2.87	Maryland	M.	59-60-60	3.00-3.00-3.00
Do	M.	60-60-60	[1] .43-.48-.43½	Massachusetts	M.	59-59-59	2.50-4.00-2.75
Maryland	M.	59-59-59	3.00-3.00-3.00	Minnesota	M.	60-60-60	1.67-1.67-1.67
New York	(²)	59-59-59	3.00-3.33-3.05	Do	M.	52-52-52	[1] .38-.38-.38
Pennsylvania	M.	60-60-60	3.00-3.00-3.00	Missouri	M.	54-60-59	2.17-3.00-2.86
Do	M.	60-60-60	[1] .40-.40-.40	Do	M.	(²)	[1] .45-.45-.45
1869:				New York	M.	60-60-60	3.00-3.33-3.07
Connecticut	M.	60-60-60	3.00-3.67-3.25	Do	(²)	59-59-59	2.44-3.67-3.03
Do	M.	60-60-60	[1] .43-.43-.43	Ohio	M.	59-59-59	3.50-4.17-3.65
Maryland	M.	59-59-59	3.00-3.00-3.00	Pennsylvania	M.	59-60-59	1.42-3.34-2.36
New York	(²)	59-59-59	3.00-3.33-3.07	Do	F.	(²)	1.00-1.00-1.00
Pennsylvania	M.	60-60-60	3.00-3.00-3.00	Virginia	M.	58-58-58	3.33-3.33-3.33
Do	M.	60-60-60	[1] .40-.40-.40	**1874:**			
1870:				California	M.	60-60-60	3.00-5.00-?.48
California	M.	60-60-60	3.00-5.00-3.41	Connecticut	M.	60-60-60	2.00-3.67-2.92
Illinois	M.	60-60-60	3.50-3.50-3.50	Do	M.	60-60-60	[1] .38-.38-.38
Louisiana	M.	59-60-59	3.00-3.00-3.00	Do	F.	60-60-60	[1] .36-.36-.36
Maryland	M.	59-60-60	2.50-3.00-2.86	Illinois	M.	60-60-60	3.50-3.50-3.50
Massachusetts	M.	59-59-59	2.50-5.00-2.75	Do	(²)	59-59-59	3.50-3.50-3.50
Minnesota	M.	60-60-60	1.50-1.50-1.50	Louisiana	M.	59-60-59	3.00-3.00-3.00
Do	M.	52-52-52	[1] .38-.38-.38	Massachusetts	M.	59-59-59	2.50-3.50-2.85
Missouri	M.	54-60-59	2.17-3.00-2.87	Minnesota	M.	60-60-60	1.67-1.67-1.67
Do	M.	(²)	[1] .45-.45-.45	Do	M.	52-52-52	[1] .38-.38-.38
New York	M.	60-60-60	3.00-3.33-3.07	Missouri	M.	54-60-59	2.17-3.00-2.87
Do	(²)	59-59-59	3.00-3.33-3.08	Do	M.	(²)	[1] .45-.45-.45
Ohio	M.	59-59-59	3.00-3.67-3.38	New York	M.	60-60-60	2.83-3.33-2.89
Pennsylvania	M.	59-60-59	2.00-3.33-3.04	Do	(²)	59-59-59	2.44-3.67-2.90
Do	M.	60-60-60	[1] .40-.40-.40	Ohio	M.	59-59-59	3.50-4.17-3.57
Virginia	M.	58-58-58	3.33-3.33-3.33	Oregon	M.	60-60-60	4.58-4.58-4.58
1871:				Pennsylvania	M.	59-60-59	1.83-3.34-2.98
California	M.	60-60-60	3.00-5.00-3.45	Do	M.	60-60-60	[1] .40-.40-40
Illinois	M.	60-60-60	3.50-3.50-3.50	Virginia	M.	58-58-58	3.33-3.33-3.33
Louisiana	M.	59-60-59	3.00-3.00-3.00	**1875:**			
Maryland	M.	59-60-60	3.00-3.00-3.00	California	M.	60-60-60	3.00-5.00-3.54
Massachusetts	M.	59-59-59	2.50-5.00-2.79	Connecticut	M.	59-60-60	1.50-3.34-2.56
Do	(²)	(²)	3.00-3.00-3.00	Do	M.	60-60-60	[1] .35-.35-.35
Minnesota	M.	60-60-60	1.50-1.50-1.50	Do	F.	60-60-60	[1] .33-.33-.33
Do	M.	52-52-52	[1] .38-.38-.38	Illinois	M.	60-60-60	3.50-3.50-3.50
Missouri	M.	54-60-59	2.17-3.00-2.85	Louisiana	M.	59-60-59	3.00-3.00-3.00
Do	M.	(²)	[1] .45-.45-.45	Maryland	M.	59-60-60	3.00-3.00-3.00
New York	M.	60-60-60	3.00-3.33-3.06	Massachusetts	M.	59-59-59	2.50-3.83-2.81
Do	(²)	59-59-59	2.83-3.67-3.05	Minnesota	M.	60-60-60	1.67-1.67-1.67
Ohio	M.	59-59-59	3.50-4.17-3.62	Do	M.	52-52-52	[1] .38-.38-.38
Pennsylvania	M.	59-60-59	2.50-3.33-3.01	Missouri	M.	54-60-59	2.17-3.00-2.85
Do	M.	60-60-60	[1] .40-.40-.40				
Virginia	M.	58-58-58	3.33-3.33-3.33				

[1] Per 1,000 ems.   [2] Not reported.

TABLE **K-12**.—*Compositors, 1842-1900, by year and State*—Continued

Year and State	Sex	Hours per week	Rate per day (dollars)
1875—Continued.			
Missouri..........	M.	(²)	¹0.40-0.40-0.40
New York........	M.	60-60-60	2.83-3.83-2.90
Do...........	(²)	59-59-59	2.83-3.83-3.05
Ohio.............	M.	59-59-59	3.50-4.17-3.71
Pennsylvania.....	M.	59-60-59	1.33-3.34-2.84
Do...........	M.	60-60-60	¹.40-.40-.40
Virginia..........	M.	58-58-58	3.33-3.33-3.33
1876:			
California........	M.	60-60-60	2.67-5.00-3.41
Connecticut......	M.	60-60-60	2.00-3.00-2.74
Do...........	M.	60-60-00	¹.35-.35-.35
Do...........	F.	60-60-60	¹.40-.40-.40
Illinois...........	M.	60-60-60	3.50-3.50-3.50
Louisiana........	M.	59-60-60	3.00-3.00-3.00
Maryland........	M.	59-60-60	3.00-3.00-3.00
Massachusetts....	M.	59-59-59	2.33-3.83-2.71
Minnesota........	M.	60-60-60	1.67-1.67-1.67
Do...........	M.	52-52-52	¹.38-.38-.38
Missouri.........	M.	54-60-59	2.17-3.00-2.88
Do...........	M.	(²)	¹.40-.40-.40
New York........	M.	60-60-60	3.00-3.33-3.22
Do...........	(²)	59-59-59	2.67-3.83-3.06
Ohio.............	M.	59-59-59	3.00-4.17-3.67
Pennsylvania.....	M.	59-60-59	1.00-3.34-2.65
Do...........	M.	60-60-60	¹.40-.40-.40
Virginia..........	M.	58-58-58	2.67-2.67-2.67
1877:			
California........	M.	60-60-60	2.67-5.00-3.36
Connecticut......	M.	60-60-60	1.67-3.34-2.60
Do...........	M.	60-60-60	¹.37-.37-.37
Do...........	F.	60-60-60	¹.35-.35-.35
Illinois...........	M.	60-60-60	3.50-3.50-3.50
Louisiana........	M.	59-60-59	3.00-3.00-3.00
Maryland........	M.	59-60-60	2.70-2.70-2.70
Massachusetts....	M.	59-59-59	2.33-2.83-2.75
Minnesota........	M.	60-60-60	1.75-1.75-1.75
Do...........	M.	52-52-52	¹.38-.38-.38
Missouri.........	M.	54-60-59	2.17-3.00-2.86
Do...........	M.	(²)	¹.40-.40-.40
New Jersey.......	M.	59-59-59	1.00-2.17-1.42
New York........	M.	60-60-60	2.83-3.33-3.01
Do...........	(²)	59-59-59	2.50-3.83-2.81
Ohio.............	M.	59-60-59	1.97-4.17-2.53
Pennsylvania.....	M.	59-59-59	.83-3.34-2.62
Do...........	M.	60-60-60	¹.40-.40-.40
Virginia..........	M.	58-58-58	2.67-2.67-2.67
1878:			
California........	M.	60-60-60	3.00-5.00-3.40
Connecticut......	M.	60-60-60	1.67-3.00-2.51
Do...........	M.	60-60-60	¹.35-.37-.37
Do...........	F.	60-60-60	¹.35-.35-.35
Illinois...........	M.	60-60-60	3.00-3.00-3.00
Louisiana........	M.	59-60-59	3.00-3.00-3.00
Maryland........	M.	59-60-60	2.70-2.70-2.70
Massachusetts....	M.	59-59-59	2.33-3.33-2.66
Minnesota........	M.	60-60-60	1.75-1.75-1.75
Do...........	M.	52-52-52	¹.38-.38-.38
Missouri.........	M.	54-60-59	2.17-3.00-2.86
Do...........	M.	(²)	¹.40-.40-.40
New York........	M.	60-60-60	2.83-3.33-2.96
Do...........	(²)	59-59-59	2.50-4.17-2.65
Ohio.............	M.	59-78-62	1.36-3.50-2.01
Do...........	F.	(²)	1.05-1.33-1.09
Pennsylvania.....	M.	59-60-59	1.67-3.34-2.43
Do...........	M.	60-60-60	¹.40-.40-.40
Virginia..........	M.	58-58-58	2.67-2.67-2.67
1879:			
California........	M.	60-60-60	3.00-5.00-3.38
Connecticut......	M.	60-60-60	1.50-2.84-2.19
Do...........	M.	60-60-60	¹.37-.37-.37
Do...........	F.	60-60-60	¹.35-.35-.35
Illinois...........	M.	60-60-60	3.00-3.00-3.00
Louisiana........	M.	59-60-59	3.00-3.00-3.00
Maryland.........	M.	59-60-60	2.70-2.70-2.70
1879—Continued.			
Massachusetts....	M.	59-59-59	2.33-3.17-2.53
Minnesota........	M.	60-60-60	1.75-1.75-1.75
Do...........	M.	52-52-52	¹.38-.38-.38
Missouri.........	M.	54-60-58	1.00-4.58-2.01
Do...........	M.	(²)	¹.40-.40-.40
New Jersey.......	(²)	59-65-62	2.50-3.00-2.75
New York........	M.	60-60-60	2.83-3.17-2.89
Do...........	(²)	59-59-59	2.33-4.17-2.66
Ohio.............	M.	59-59-59	1.50-3.50-2.67
Pennsylvania.....	M.	54-60-59	1.00-3.34-2.05
Do...........	M.	60-60-60	¹.40-.40-.40
Virginia..........	M.	58-58-58	2.67-2.67-2.67
1880:			
California........	M.	60-60-60	3.00-4.17-3.28
Connecticut......	M.	60-60-60	1.17-2.50-2.01
Do...........	M.	60-60-60	¹.35-.35-.35
Do...........	F.	60-60-60	¹.33-.33-.33
Georgia..........	M.	60-60-60	2.00-2.00-2.00
Illinois...........	M.	60-60-60	3.00-3.00-3.00
Kentucky........	M.	60-60-60	1.00-3.00-2.43
Louisiana........	M.	59-60-59	3.00-3.00-3.00
Maryland........	M.	59-60-60	2.70-2.70-2.70
Massachusetts....	M.	59-59-59	2.17-3.33-2.57
Michigan........	M.	55-55-55	2.50-2.50-2.50
Minnesota........	M.	60-60-60	1.75-1.75-1.75
Do...........	M.	52-52-52	¹.38-.38-.38
Missouri.........	M.	54-60-59	2.67-3.00-2.93
Do...........	M.	(²)	¹.40-.40-.40
New Jersey.......	(²)	45-75-66	1.00-3.00-2.13
New York........	M.	60-60-60	1.67-3.17-2.79
Do...........	(²)	59-59-59	2.33-4.17-2.67
Ohio.............	M.	59-59-59	2.00-3.67-2.84
Pennsylvania.....	M.	54-60-59	1.17-3.34-2.29
Do...........	M.	60-60-60	¹.40-.40-.40
Rhode Island.....	M.	58-58-58	1.25-3.33-2.22
South Carolina....	M.	(²)	2.00-3.67-2.91
Virginia..........	M.	58-58-58	2.67-2.67-2.67
West Virginia.....	M.	(²)	2.00-3.00-2.42
1881:			
California........	M.	60-60-60	2.50-4.17-3.28
Connecticut......	M.	60-60-60	1.25-2.84-2.19
Do...........	M.	60-60-60	¹.35-.35-.35
Do...........	F.	60-60-60	¹.31-.31-.31
Illinois...........	M.	60-60-60	2.50-3.00-2.83
Indiana..........	M.	(²)	1.80-1.80-1.80
Iowa............	M.	60-60-60	2.00-2.00-2.00
Louisiana........	M.	59-60-60	3.00-3.50-3.33
Maryland........	M.	59-60-60	2.70-2.70-2.70
Massachusetts....	M.	59-59-59	2.17-4.17-2.61
Minnesota........	M.	54-60-57	1.75-2.88-2.25
Do...........	M.	52-52-52	¹.38-.38-.38
Missouri.........	M.	42-60-57	2.67-3.00-2.94
Do...........	M.	(²)	¹.40-.40-.40
New Jersey.......	M.	54-60-55	1.17-2.50-2.21
New York........	M.	60-60-60	1.75-3.17-2.56
Do...........	(²)	59-59-59	2.00-4.00-2.63
Ohio.............	M.	59-72-67	1.33-6.67-2.75
Pennsylvania.....	M.	60-60-60	1.33-3.58-2.60
Do...........	M.	60-60-60	¹.40-.40-.40
Virginia..........	M.	58-58-58	2.67-2.67-2.67
1882:			
California........	M.	60-60-60	2.50-4.17-3.33
Connecticut......	M.	60-60-60	1.25-3.00-2.38
Do...........	M.	60-60-60	¹.35-.35-.35
Do...........	F.	60-60-60	¹.31-.31-.31
Georgia..........	M.	70-70-70	2.50-2.50-2.50
Illinois...........	F.	51-51-51	1.17-1.17-1.17
Do...........	M.	60-60-61	2.50-3.00-2.81
Iowa............	M.	54-70-63	2.00-2.50-2.21
Kansas..........	M.	60-60-60	2.50-2.50-2.50
Kentucky........	(²)	60-60-60	3.00-3.00-3.00
Louisiana........	M.	59-60-59	3.00-3.00-3.00
Maryland........	M.	59-60-60	2.70-2.70-2.70
Massachusetts....	M.	59-59-59	2.00-3.17-2.75

¹ Per 1,000 ems.   ² Not reported.

TABLE **K-12.**—*Compositors, 1842–1900, by year and State*—Continued

Year and State	Sex	Hours per week	Rate per day (dollars)	Year and State	Sex	Hours per week	Rate per day (dollars)
1882—Continued.				**1884—Continued.**			
Michigan	M.	72-72-72	2.60-2.60-2.60	New York	M.	48-70-58	2.00-3.33-2.69
Minnesota	M.	59-72-65	1.75-3.00-2.61	Do	([2])	50-59-55	2.00-4.17-2.84
Do	M.	52-52-52	[1].40-.40-.40	North Carolina	M	60-60-60	2.00-2.33-2.22
Missouri	M.	54-60-59	2.00-3.50-2.88	North Dakota	M.	59-60-59	3.50-3.50-3.50
Do	M.	([2])	[1].40-.40-.40	Ohio	M.	51-60-58	2.36-3.67-2.85
New York	([2])	59-59-59	2.00-4.00-2.56	Pennsylvania	M.	59-60-59	1.50-4.00-2.66
Do	M.	54-63-59	2.00-3.20-2.67	Do	M.	60-60-60	[1].40-.40-.40
North Dakota	M.	60-60-60	3.50-3.50-3.50	Tennessee	M.	59-59-59	2.00-2.92-2.47
Ohio	M.	59-59-59	3.00-3.67-3.22	Texas	M.	60-60-60	3.00-3.00-3.00
Do	([2])	55-84-56	1.33-3.00-2.20	Virginia	M.	58-58-58	2.67-2.67-2.67
Pennsylvania	M.	59-60-59	1.50-4.00-2.66	West Virginia	M.	59-59-59	1.17-1.67-1.44
Do	M.	60-60-60	[1].40-.40-.40	Do	F.	59-59-59	.83-.83-.83
Rhode Island	M.	60-60-60	2.67-2.67-2.67	Wyoming	M.	59-59-59	3.50-3.50-3.50
Tennessee	M.	45-72-51	1.79-2.00-1.90	**1885:**			
Texas	M.	60-60-60	2.50-2.50-2.50	Alabama	([2])	([2])	2.50-3.33-2.97
Virginia	M.	58-66-64	1.64-2.67-1.95	Arkansas	([2])	([2])	2.67-2.67-2.67
1883:				California	M.	60-60-60	2.50-4.00-3.49
California	M.	60-60-60	2.50-4.50-4.17	Do	([2])	([2])	3.00-3.50-3.08
Connecticut	M.	60-60-60	1.25-3.00-2.36	Colorado	([2])	([2])	3.50-4.33-3.62
Do	M.	60-60-60	[1].35-.35-.35	Connecticut	M.	60-60-60	1.50-3.09-2.46
Do	F.	60-60-60	[1].31-.31-.31	Do	M.	60-60-60	[1].35-.35-.35
Georgia	M.	59-59-59	2.00-2.00-2.00	Do	F.	60-60-60	[1].31-.31-.31
Illinois	F.	60-60-60	2.00-2.00-2.00	Do	([2])	([2])	2.50-2.50-2.50
Do	M.	60-60-60	1.50-3.00-2.81	Dist. of Columbia	M.	54-54-54	2.00-2.70-2.34
Iowa	M.	66-66-66	3.00-3.00-3.00	Do	([2])	([2])	3.20-3.20-3.20
Louisiana	M.	59-60-59	3.00-3.00-3.00	Florida	M.	60-60-60	2.00-3.00-2.47
Maryland	M.	59-60-60	2.70-2.70-2.70	Do	([2])	([2])	2.50-2.50-2.50
Massachusetts	([2])	59-59-59	1.82-1.82-1.82	Georgia	M.	60-60-60	2.00-3.00-2.63
Do	M.	59-70-61	2.00-4.33-2.82	Illinois	M.	60-60-60	3.00-3.00-3.00
Do	F	([2])	.82-3.00-1.52	Do	([2])	([2])	2.00-3.00-2.97
Michigan	M.	([2])	.75-5.00-2.24	Indiana	M.	([2])	1.67-1.67-1.67
Minnesota	M.	59-72-64	1.75-2.75-2.37	Do	M.	([2])	[1].30-.30-.30
Do	M.	52-52-52	[1].40-.40-.40	Do	([2])	([2])	2.00-2.50-2.32
Missouri	M.	54-60-60	2.25-3.00-2.53	Iowa	M.	60-72-67	2.00-3.00-2.60
Do	M.	([2])	[1].40-.40-.40	Do	([2])	([2])	2.00-2.33-2.21
Nebraska	M.	66-66-66	2.85-2.95-2.90	Kansas	M.	48-60-60	1.66-2.50-2.08
New Jersey	M.	54-60-57	2.13-2.80-2.40	Kentucky	([2])	([2])	3.00-3.00-3.00
Do	F.	54-54-54	1.67-2.00-1.81	Louisiana	([2])	60-60-60	2.75-3.00-2.98
New Mexico	M.	54-54-54	3.00-3.00-3.00	Do	M.	59-60-59	1.82-3.00-2.78
New York	([2])	59-59-59	2.00-4.00-2.76	Maine	M.	60-60-60	1.00-1.50-1.35
Do	M.	42-60-49	1.50-3.50-2.88	Do	F.	60-60-60	1.25-1.25-1.25
Ohio	M.	54-72-63	1.33-4.00-2.84	Do	([2])	([2])	2.33-2.33-2.33
Pennsylvania	M.	59-60-60	2.33-4.50-3.19	Maryland	M.	59-60-60	2.70-2.70-2.70
Do	M.	60-60-60	[1].40-.40-.40	Do	([2])	([2])	2.70-2.70-2.70
Tennessee	M.	60-60-60	2.00-2.00-2.00	Massachusetts	M.	54-70-60	1.17-4.17-2.45
Texas	M.	70-70-70	2.50-2.75-2.63	Do	F.	54-59-57	.71-3.13-1.62
Virginia	M.	58-58-58	2.67-2.67-2.67	Do	([2])	([2])	2.00-2.50-2.49
Wyoming	M.	59-59-59	3.50-3.50-3.50	Michigan	([2])	([2])	1.75-1.75-1.75
1884:				Minnesota	M.	60-60-60	1.75-1.75-1.75
California	M.	60-60-60	2.00-4.17-2.72	Do	M.	52-52-52	[1].40-.40-.40
Do	F.	48-48-48	2.50-2.50-2.50	Do	([2])	([2])	2.50-2.67-2.56
Connecticut	M.	60-60-60	1.25-3.17-2.42	Missouri	M.	54-60-59	2.50-3.00-2.90
Do	M.	60-60-60	[1].35-.35-.35	Do	([2])	60-60-60	1.67-3.00-2.81
Do	F.	60-60-60	[1].31-.31-.31	Do	([2])	([2])	[1].40-.40-.40
Delaware	M.	40-40-40	3.00-3.00-3.00	Montana	M.	60-60-60	4.00-4.50-4.25
Georgia	M.	54-54-54	2.33-3.00-2.69	Nebraska	([2])	([2])	2.50-2.50-2.50
Illinois	M.	60-60-60	1.60-4.00-2.78	New Jersey	M.	48-60-60	1.25-3.67-1.98
Do	F.	([2])	3.25-3.25-3.25	Do	([2])	([2])	2.33-2.33-2.33
Indiana	M.	60-60-60	1.00-2.25-1.45	New York	([2])	54-70-59	1.60-4.17-2.76
Iowa	M.	48-72-64	1.25-4.16-2.61	Do	M.	47-60-59	.83-3.51-2.65
Kansas	M.	60-60-60	2.00-2.00-2.00	Do	F.	47-60-56	.37-3.00-1.51
Kentucky	M.	59-59-59	2.67-2.67-2.67	Ohio	M.	59-81-63	2.00-3.67-2.74
Louisiana	M.	59-60-59	3.00-3.00-3.00	Do	([2])	([2])	2.33-2.50-2.41
Maryland	M.	59-60-60	2.70-2.70-2.70	Oregon	([2])	([2])	3.50-3.50-3.50
Massachusetts	M.	59-59-59	2.00-4.17-2.70	Pennsylvania	M.	59-60-59	1.17-3.40-2.70
Michigan	M.	54-54-54	.50-3.00-1.72	Do	M.	60-60-60	[1].40-.40-.40
Do	F.	([2])	.75-.75-.75	Do	([2])	([2])	2.25-3.00-2.47
Minnesota	M.	60-60-60	1.75-2.50-2.38	South Carolina	M.	59-59-59	1.50-2.83-2.40
Do	M.	52-52-52	[1].40-.40-.40	Do	([2])	([2])	1.50-1.50-1.50
Missouri	M.	54-60-59	2.00-3.00-2.85	Tennessee	M.	45-45-45	1.75-1.75-1.75
Do	F.	([2])	.88-1.33-1.11	Do	([2])	([2])	2.00-3.00-2.67
Do	M.	([2])	[1].40-.40-.40	Texas	M.	60-60-60	3.20-3.20-3.20
Do	([2])	([2])	1.43-1.43-1.43	Utah	([2])	([2])	3.00-3.00-3.00
Nebraska	M.	66-66-66	3.00-3.00-3.00	Virginia	M.	58-58-58	2.67-2.67-2.67
New Jersey	M.	48-60-56	1.00-4.00-2.17	Do	([2])	([2])	2.67-2.67-2.67
New Mexico	M.	54-54-54	3.00-3.00-3.00	Washington	([2])	([2])	3.00-3.50-3.28

[1] Per 1,000 ems.   [2] Not reported.

TABLE **K-12.**—*Compositors, 1842-1900, by year and State*—Continued

Year and State	Sex	Hours per week	Rate per day (dollars)	Year and State	Sex	Hours per week	Rate per day (dollars)
1885—Continued.				1888:			
West Virginia	(²)	(²)	2.50-2.50-2.50	California	M.	60-60-60	3.00-4.17-3.43
Wisconsin	M.	60-72-66	3.00-3.33-3.17	Do	F.	47-60-53	.17-1.67-.84
1886:				Do	F.	(²)	¹.25-.25-.25
California	(²)	48-72-60	1.00-4.17-2.46	Colorado	M.	72-90-81	4.17-6.00-5.09
Do	F.	60-60-60	1.00-2.30-1.08	Connecticut	M.	60-60-60	1.25-3.00-2.38
Do	F.	(²)	³1.53-1.53-1.53	Do	M.	60-60-60	¹.35-.35-.35
Connecticut	M.	60-60-60	1.42-3.09-2.42	Do	F.	60-60-60	¹.31-.31-.31
Do	M.	60-60-60	¹.35-.35-.35	Georgia	F.	56-60-57	.96-1.50-1.15
Do	F.	60-60-60	¹.31-.31-.31	Illinois	M.	60-60-60	3.00-3.00-3.00
Florida	M.	60-60-60	2.24-2.24-2.24	Indiana	F.	56-59-58	.19-1.17-.72
Illinois	M.	60-72-61	1.25-3.00-2.70	Iowa	M.	54-60-56	1.50-2.25-1.99
Indiana	M.	(²)	¹.30-.30-.30	Do	F.	60-60-60	.90-2.25-1.54
Iowa	M.	54-63-58	.70-5.00-1.61	Kansas	M.	(²)	2.00-2.58-2.29
Kansas	F.	54-54-54	1.11-1.11-1.11	Louisiana	M.	59-60-59	3.00-3.00-3.00
Kansas	M.	48-108-56	1.50-4.30-2.43	Maine	M.	60-60-60	2.33-2.33-2.33
Louisiana	(²)	51-51-51	3.25-3.25-3.25	Do	F.	54-60-59	1.00-1.50-1.30
Do	M.	59-60-59	3.00-3.00-3.00	Maryland	M.	59-60-60	2.70-2.70-2.70
Maryland	M.	59-60-60	2.70-2.70-2.70	Massachusetts	M.	59-59-59	2.50-4.17-2.67
Massachusetts	M.	59-59-59	2.50-4.17-2.72	Minnesota	M.	60-60-60	1.75-1.75-1.75
Michigan	(²)	55-60-55	1.89-2.16-1.97	Do	M.	52-52-52	¹.40-.40-.40
Do	M.	59-59-59	1.50-2.50-2.05	Missouri	M.	54-60-59	2.50-3.00-2.88
Do	F.	59-59-59	1.29-2.23-1.71	Do	M.	(²)	¹.42-.43-.42½
Minnesota	(²)	59-59-59	1.97-2.50-2.24	New Jersey	F.	60-60-60	.66-.66-.66
Do	M.	60-60-60	1.75-1.75-1.75	Do	(²)	48-60-57	2.00-3.50-2.47
Do	M.	52-52-52	¹.40-.40-.40	New York	M.	42-66-57	.67-4.17-2.23
Missouri	M.	54-60-59	2.00-3.00-2.42	Do	(²)	59-59-59	2.50-4.17-2.87
Do	(²)	58-59-59	2.50-2.83-2.67	Do	M.	59-60-60	³.50-.75-.56
Do	F.	52-59-56	.67-2.00-1.28	Do	M.	48-78-60	¹.16-.35-.29
Do	M.	(²)	¹.40-.40-.40	Do	F.	59-60-59	1.25-2.33-1.69
New Jersey	(²)	59-59-59	1.90-1.90-1.90	North Carolina	M.	36-72-60	.62-2.83-1.37
Do	M.	54-60-60	2.50-3.00-2.98	Ohio	M.	59-59-59	1.00-3.50-2.30
New York	M.	54-63-60	1.01-3.33-2.68	Pennsylvania	M.	59-60-59	2.00-3.34-2.68
Do	F.	54-60-59	1.00-2.00-1.32	Do	M.	60-60-60	¹.40-.40-.40
Do	(²)	59-59-59	2.00-4.17-2.78	Rhode Island	M.	(²)	2.95-3.00-2.98
Ohio	M.	59-60-60	.99-4.00-3.54	Virginia	M.	58-58-58	2.67-2.67-2.67
Pennsylvania	M.	59-60-59	1.33-3.34-2.51	1889:			
Do	M.	60-60-60	¹.40-.40-.40	California	M.	60-60-60	3.00-4.00-3.42
Rhode Island	F.	49-59-54	.50-1.83-1.17	Connecticut	M.	60-60-60	1.25-3.17-2.41
Texas	(²)	60-60-60	2.33-2.33-2.33	Do	M.	60-60-60	¹.35-.35-.35
Virginia	M.	58-60-59	1.31-2.67-2.21	Do	F.	60-60-60	¹.31-.31-.31
West Virginia	M.	60-77-71	2.50-2.80-2.55	Illinois	M.	60-60-60	3.00-3.00-3.00
Wisconsin	F.	(²)	1.33-1.33-1.33	Kansas	M.	(²)	.50-4.00-1.89
1887:				Do	F.	(²)	.29-2.50-1.05
California	F.	47-60-53	.17-1.67-.88	Louisiana	M.	59-60-59	3.00-3.00-3.00
Do	M.	60-60-60	3.00-4.17-3.44	Maryland	M.	59-60-59	2.70-2.70-2.70
Connecticut	M.	60-60-60	.88-3.00-2.29	Massachusetts	M.	59-59-59	2.50-4.17-2.68
Do	M.	60-60-60	¹.35-.35-.35	Minnesota	M.	60-60-60	1.15-1.75-1.48
Do	F.	60-60-60	¹.31-.31-.31	Do	M.	52-52-52	¹.40-.40-.40
Illinois	F.	49-50-50	.75-1.00-.88	Missouri	M.	54-60-59	2.50-3.00-2.88
Do	M.	60-60-60	3.00-3.00-3.00	Do	M.	(²)	¹.42-.43-.42½
Kansas	M.	54-78-62	2.00-3.00-2.66	New York	M.	60-60-60	3.00-3.38-3.01
Kentucky	F.	59-59-59	1.33-1.33-1.33	Do	(²)	60-60-60	2.50-4.17-2.93
Louisiana	M.	60-60-60	3.00-3.00-3.00	North Carolina	M.	60-60-60	1.67-1.67-1.67
Maine	M.	60-60-60	1.00-2.00-1.50	Ohio	M.	59-59-59	3.00-3.50-3.11
Maryland	M.	59-60-60	2.70-2.70-2.70	Pennsylvania	M.	59-60-59	1.67-3.34-2.62
Massachusetts	F.	50-59-53	.58-1.67-1.21	Do	M.	60-60-60	¹.40-.40-.40
Do	M.	59-59-59	2.50-4.17-2.69	Virginia	M.	58-58-58	2.67-2.67-2.67
Minnesota	F.	54-59-57	.42-2.66-1.11	1890:			
Do	M.	60-60-60	1.75-1.75-1.75	California	M.	60-60-60	2.67-4.00-3.38
Do	M.	52-52-52	¹.40-.40-.40	Connecticut	M.	60-60-60	1.50-3.00-2.45
Missouri	M.	54-60-59	2.50-3.00-2.89	Do	M.	60-60-60	¹.35-.35-.35
Do	M.	(²)	¹.42-.43-.42½	Do	F.	60-60-60	¹.31-.31-.31
New York	F.	54-54-54	.50-2.50-1.27	Illinois	M.	60-60-60	1.67-3.50-2.85
Do	M.	60-60-60	1.46-3.33-2.81	Kansas	M.	(²)	1.20-4.00-2.68
Do	(²)	59-59-59	2.50-4.17-2.79	Do	F.	(²)	.85-3.50-2.18
North Carolina	M.	60-60-60	1.00-2.33-1.47	Louisiana	M.	59-60-59	3.00-3.00-3.00
Ohio	M.	48-60-59	.25-6.66-1.01	Maryland	M.	59-60-60	2.70-2.70-2.70
Do	F.	60-60-60	¹.20-.20-.20	Massachusetts	M.	59-59-59	2.50-4.17-2.66
Do	M.	48-72-58	.34-6.66-2.25	Minnesota	M.	60-60-60	1.00-3.75-2.81
Do	M.	54-60-60	¹.25-.30-.30	Do	M.	52-52-52	¹.40-.40-.40
Pennsylvania	M.	59-60-59	1.67-3.50-2.70	Missouri	M.	54-60-59	2.50-3.00-2.88
Virginia	M.	58-58-58	2.67-2.67-2.67	Do	M.	(²)	¹.42-.43-.42½
Wisconsin	F.	59-59-59	1.83-1.83-1.83	Nebraska	M.	(²)	2.50-2.50-2.50
Do	M.	(²)	1.65-2.50-2.19	New York	(²)	59-59-59	2.50-4.17-2.88
				Do	F.	(²)	.75-1.33-.94

¹ Per 1,000 ems.   ² Not reported.   ³ And board.

TABLE **K-12.**—*Compositors, 1842-1900, by year and State*—Continued

Year and State	Sex	Hours per week	Rate per day (dollars)
1890—Continued.			
New York	M.	60-60-60	0.42-5.00-2.47
Ohio	M.	59-59-59	3.00-3.50-3.15
Do	(²)	42-72-58	.50-7.69-2.08
Pennsylvania	M.	59-60-59	2.17-3.34-2.58
Do	M.	60-60-60	¹.40-.40-.40
Virginia	M.	58-58-58	2.67-2.67-2.67
1891:			
California	M.	60-60-60	2.50-4.00-3.24
Connecticut	M.	60-60-60	2.00-3.00-2.52
Do	M.	60-60-60	¹.35-.35-.35
Do	F.	60-60-60	¹.31-.31-.31
Illinois	M.	60-60-60	2.00-3.50-2.95
Do	F.		2.50-2.50-2.50
Louisiana	M.	59-60-59	3.00-3.00-3.00
Maryland	M.	60-60-60	2.70-2.70-2.70
Massachusetts	M.	59-59-59	2.50-4.17-2.73
Michigan	F.	(²)	.58-1.75-1.13
Minnesota	M.	60-60-60	1.75-2.00-1.79
Do	M.	52-52-52	¹.40-.40-.40
Missouri	M.	54-60-59	2.50-3.00-2.88
Do	M.	(²)	¹.42-.43-.42½
New York	(¹)	59-59-59	2.50-4.17-2.91
Do	F.	(²)	.83-1.33-1.00
Do	M.	60-60-60	.42-5.00-2.45
North Carolina	M.	48-60-59	.83-3.00-1.79
Ohio	M.	42-60-57	.50-4.00-2.21
Do	F.	42-60-58	.50-1.50-.95
Pennsylvania	M.	59-60-59	1.17-3.34-2.39
Do	M.	60-60-60	¹.40-.40-.40
Virginia	M.	58-58-58	2.67-2.67-2.67
1892:			
California	M.	50-60-60	1.50-5.50-3.28
Do	F.	47-60-56	1.00-3.50-2.14
Connecticut	M.	60-60-60	1.50-3.00-2.58
Illinois	M.	59-60-59	1.67-3.50-2.92
Do	F.	48-57-54	.75-2.67-1.66
Iowa	(²)	48-60-55	.70-3.25-2.22
Louisiana	M.	59-60-59	3.00-3.00-3.00
Maine	F.	60-60-60	.42-1.83-1.03
Maryland	M.	60-60-60	2.70-2.75-2.71
Massachusetts	M.	54-59-57	2.50-4.17-2.67
Minnesota	M.	52-60-54	1.75-3.90-3.30
Missouri	M.	54-60-59	1.00-5.83-3.18
Do	M.	(²)	¹.42-.43-.42½
Do	F.	(²)	1.25-1.25-1.25
New York	M.	60-60-60	2.50-3.33-2.83
Ohio	M.	59-59-59	3.00-3.50-3.09
Pennsylvania	M.	59-59-59	1.67-2.67-2.36
Virginia	M.	58-58-58	2.67-2.67-2.67
1893:			
California	M.	60-60-60	2.50-4.17-3.23
Connecticut	M.	60-60-60	2.17-3.00-2.66
Illinois	M.	48-72-58	.58-3.00-2.10
Do	M.	48-72-59	.58-3.50-2.87
Iowa	F.	45-60-57	.50-1.75-.95
Louisiana	M.	59-60-59	3.00-3.00-3.00
Maryland	F.	60-60-60	.67-.67-.67
Do	M.	48-72-60	.50-5.00-2.63
Massachusetts	M.	54-59-56	2.50-3.67-2.67
Minnesota	M.	52-60-54	1.75-3.90-3.30
Missouri	M.	54-60-58	2.50-3.00-2.87
Do	M.	(²)	¹.42-.43-.42½
Montana	M.	42-57-52	1.67-6.67-3.96
Do	M.	35-57-47	¹.35-.55-.48
Do	M.	48-48-48	⁴.96-1.15-1.06
Do	F.	54-51-54	1.00-1.00-1.00
Do	F.	54-54-54	¹.45-.45-.45
New Jersey	F.	55-55-55	.50-1.33-.84
New York	M.	30-78-59	.50-5.83-2.63
Do	F.	47-50-49	.83-1.00-.88
Ohio	M.	45-60-52	1.00-3.50-2.22
Do	F.	45-60-59	.35-2.16-1.22
Pennsylvania	M.	42-75-59	.83-3.00-2.16
Rhode Island	M.	(²)	1.50-4.00-2.61
Virginia	M.	58-58-58	2.67-2.67-2.67
1894:			
California	M.	60-60-60	2.50-4.17-3.31
Connecticut	M.	60-60-60	2.33-3.17-2.77
Illinois	M.	60-60-60	3.00-3.00-3.00
Indiana	F.	59-59-59	1.00-2.75-1.58
Iowa	M.	36-90-58	.83-4.17-2.38
Do	F.	48-60-57	.92-2.67-1.87
Kansas	M.	59-59-59	1.60-1.60-1.60
Do	F.	54-54-54	1.08-1.08-1.08
Louisiana	M.	59-60-59	3.00-3.00-3.00
Maryland	M.	60-60-60	2.70-2.70-2.70
Massachusetts	M.	54-59-56	2.50-3.83-2.65
Minnesota	M.	52-60-55	2.00-3.90-3.32
Missouri	M.	54-60-59	2.50-4.00-3.69
Do	M.	(²)	¹.42-.43-.42½
Montana	M.	(²)	3.53-3.53-3.53
New Hampshire	M.	55-60-59	1.50-2.67-1.99
New York	M.	60-60-60	3.00-3.33-3.03
North Carolina	(²)	54-108-65	.50-2.35-1.37
Ohio	M.	48-60-59	.83-3.50-2.18
Do	F.	48-60-58	.75-2.00-1.42
Pennsylvania	M.	59-59-59	1.87-3.00-2.38
Virginia	M.	58-58-58	2.67-2.67-2.67
1895:			
California	M.	59-60-59	2.50-4.17-3.26
Connecticut	M.	59-60-60	1.47-3.20-2.64
Do	F.	59-59-59	2.38-2.42-2.40
Georgia	M.	60-60-60	1.33-2.00-1.71
Illinois	M.	60-60-60	3.00-3.00-3.00
Kansas	(²)	45-90-56	.67-3.75-2.19
Kentucky	M.	60-60-60	1.00-3.00-2.60
Louisiana	M.	59-60-59	1.91-3.00-2.76
Maine	M.	60-60-60	1.50-2.50-1.68
Maryland	M.	60-60-60	2.70-2.70-2.70
Massachusetts	M.	48-60-57	1.30-3.67-2.48
Do	F.	48-60-57	.84-2.65-1.67
Minnesota	M.	52-60-54	2.25-3.90-3.42
Missouri	M.	54-60-59	1.50-4.00-3.51
Do	F.	60-60-60	.92-1.67-1.25
Do	M.	(²)	¹.42-.42-.42
Montana	M.	53-53-53	3.10-4.39-4.05
New Jersey	M.	54-59-56	.83-3.33-2.11
Do	F.	54-54-54	2.07-2.50-2.24
New York	M.	60-60-60	1.00-3.67-2.78
Do	F.	47-59-50	1.00-3.17-1.68
North Carolina	M.	45-60-58	1.50-3.00-2.34
Ohio	M.	45-60-58	1.00-3.50-2.21
Do	F.	54-60-58	.60-2.66-1.37
Pennsylvania	M.	59-59-59	2.00-3.00-2.47
Rhode Island	M.	56-60-56	1.67-3.00-2.23
Do	F.	56-56-56	1.67-1.83-1.72
South Carolina	M.	54-59-55	1.50-3.67-2.69
Do	F.	59-59-59	1.50-1.50-1.50
Tennessee	M.	59-59-59	2.00-3.50-2.60
Virginia	M.	58-59-58	1.00-2.67-2.43
Wisconsin	(²)	48-60-55	2.00-3.83-2.73
1896:			
California	M.	59-60-59	2.50-5.00-3.35
Colorado	(²)	48-54-52	3.25-4.25-3.59
Florida	M.	60-60-60	1.33-3.33-2.40
Do	F.	60-60-60	2.00-2.00-2.00
Georgia	M.	54-60-55	2.00-2.83-2.31
Illinois	M.	57-57-57	1.88-3.80-2.86
Do	M.	57-72-59	.79-3.80-2.90
Do	F.	51-51-51	1.17-1.17-1.17
Iowa	M.	59-60-60	1.17-3.00-2.34
Kansas	M.	42-66-57	.46-8.33-1.63
Kentucky	M.	59-59-59	2.33-2.33-2.33
Louisiana	M.	48-59-55	2.40-3.00-2.25
Maryland	M.	58-60-60	2.50-2.70-2.70
Massachusetts	M.	54-59-56	2.50-4.00-2.63
Michigan	M.	59-59-59	1.17-3.33-2.13
Minnesota	M.	52-60-54	2.50-3.90-3.49
Missouri	M.	48-60-59	1.10-4.00-2.68

¹ Per 1,000 ems.　　　² Not reported.　　　⁴ And board and lodging

TABLE **K-12.**—*Compositors, 1842–1900, by year and State*—Continued

| Year and State | Sex | Lowest, highest, and average— | | Year and State | Sex | Lowest, highest, and average— | |
		Hours per week	Rate per day (dollars)			Hours per week	Rate per day (dollars)
1896—Continued.				1898—Continued.			
Missouri	M.	([2])	[1]0.42-0.42-0.42	Maryland	M.	60-60-60	2.70-2.70-2.70
Do	F.	54-60-59	.66-2.70-1.40	Massachusetts	M.	54-54-54	2.50-4.00-2.63
Nebraska	([2])	60-60-60	1.33-3.00-1.99	Michigan	M.	([2])	1.25-2.38-2.00
New York	M.	54-60-58	.67-4.00-2.71	Minnesota	M.	52-60-54	2.50-3.90-3.49
Do	F.	60-60-60	1.35-1.78-1.55	Missouri	M.	54-60-59	2.50-4.00-3.77
North Carolina	M.	54-60-58	1.00-3.00-2.00	Do	M.	([2])	[1].42-.42-.42
Ohio	M.	45-60-56	.67-3.50-2.21	Nebraska	([2])	48-72-59	.50-3.45-1.55
Do	F.	48-60-57	.50-1.67-1.40	New York	M.	54-60-59	1.25-4.50-2.45
Pennsylvania	M.	59-60-60	1.17-3.33-2.47	Ohio	M.	59-59-59	3.00-3.50-3.13
Do	F.	60-60-60	2.00-2.67-2.34	Pennsylvania	M.	59-59-59	2.00-3.00-2.46
Virginia	M.	58-58-58	2.67-2.67-2.67	Virginia	M.	58-58-58	2.67-2.67-2.67
West Virginia	M.	59-60-60	1.17-3.00-2.16	1899:			
Do	F.	59-60-59	.50-2.50-1.08	Alabama	M.	54-54-54	2.67-3.75-3.01
1897:				California	M.	59-59-59	2.67-4.33-3.02
California	M.	59-60-59	2.50-4.58-3.25	Georgia	M.	60-60-60	1.50-3.00-2.11
Illinois	M.	60-60-60	3.00-3.00 3.00	Illinois	M.	54-54-54	3.00-3.00-3.00
Kansas	M.	36-102-55	.50-3.00-1.57	Massachusetts	M.	54-54-54	2.50-3.17-2.66
Do	F.	48-60-56	.33-2.00-1.04	Do	F.	53-53-53	.86-2.65-1.75
Louisiana	M.	48-59-54	2.40-3.00-2.73	Montana	M.	53-53-53	4.00-4.00-4.00
Maryland	M.	60-60-60	2.70-2.70-2.70	New York	M.	54-54-54	3.00-3.00-3.00
Massachusetts	M.	54-59-55	2.50-4.00-2.64	North Carolina	M.	48-72-55	.70-3.00-1.77
Minnesota	M.	52-60-54	2.50-3.90-3.49	Ohio	M.	53-53-53	2.21-2.50-2.23
Missouri	M.	54-60-59	2.50-4.00-3.73	Pennsylvania	M.	60-60-60	.79-2.67-1.58
Do	M.	([2])	[1].42-.42-.42	1900:			
New York	M.	48-60-54	1.33-11.31-3.53	Alabama	M.	54-54-54	2.67-3.75-3.01
Do	F.	60-60-60	1.83-5.00-3.25	California	M.	59-59-59	2.50-4.50-3.03
Ohio	M.	59-59-59	3.00-3.50-3.08	Georgia	M.	60-60-60	1.50-3.00-2.11
Pennsylvania	M.	59-59-59	1.00-3.00-2.33	Illinois	M.	54-54-54	3.00-3.00-3.00
Virginia	M.	48-60-59	1.00-2.67-2.21	Massachusetts	M.	54-54-54	2.50-3.17-2.63
Do	F.	54-60-57	.70-1.25-1.01	Do	F.	53-53-53	1.15-2.60-1.60
1898:				Montana	M.	53-53-53	4.00-4.00-4.00
California	M.	59-60-59	2.50-4.58-3.28	New York	M.	54-54-54	3.00-3.00-3.00
Illinois	M.	60-60-60	3.00-3.00-3.00	North Carolina	M.	54-59-56	1.50-2.50-2.09
Kansas	M.	54-63-59	1.80-3.15-2.48	Ohio	M.	50-50-50	2.50-2.83-2.54
Louisiana	M.	48-59-54	2.40-3.00-2.73	Pennsylvania	M.	60-60-60	1.23-2.69-1.82

[1] Per 1,000 ems.   [2] Not reported.

TABLE **K-13.**—*Compositors, males, daywork, newspaper, 1890–1928, by city and year*

| Year | Atlanta, Ga. | | Birmingham, Ala. | | Boston, Mass. | | Chicago, Ill. | |
	Hours per week	Rate per hour	Hours per week	Rate per hour	Hours per week	Rate per hour	Hours per week	Rate per hour
1890	48.0	$0.372					60.0	$0.300
1891	48.0	.372					60.0	.300
1892	48.0	.374					60.0	.300
1893	48.0	.374					60.0	.300
1894	48.0	.370					60.0	.300
1895	48.0	.370					60.0	.300
1896	48.0	.370					60.0	.300
1897	48.0	.370					59.6	.301
1898	48.0	.372					59.6	.301
1899	48.0	.371					54.0	.358
1900	48.0	.386					54.0	.358
1901	51.6	.370					54.0	.371
1902	51.9	.371					54.4	.371
1903	49.0	.368			36.3	$0.550	49.1	.589
1904	49.6	.404	54.0	$0.419	42.0	.575	49.3	.607
1905	48.0	.430	51.9	.431	42.0	.573	47.7	.635
1906	48.0	.418	48.0	.463	42.0	.586	46.1	.659
1907	48.0	.375	[1]42.0	.520	42.0	.610	45.0	.550
1908	48.0	.375	[1]42.0	.520	42.0	.610	45.0	.550
1909	48.0	.438	[1]42.0	.520	42.0	.610	45.0	.550
1910	48.0	.438	[1]42.0	.520	42.0	.610	45.0	.550
1911	48.0	.438	[1]42.0	.525	42.0	.610	45.0	.620
1912	48.0	.438	[1]42.0	.525	42.0	.630	45.0	.620
1913	48.0	.438	[1]42.0	.525	42.0	.630	45.0	.620
1914	48.0	.438	[1]42.0	.530	42.0	.630	45.0	.620
1915	48.0	.438	[1]42.0	.545	42.0	.630	45.0	.620
1916	48.0	.438	[1]42.0	.555	42.0	.630	45.0	.620
1917	48.0	.438	[1]42.0	.565	42.0	.680	45.0	.620
1918	48.0	.500	[1]42.0	.575	42.0	.680	45.0	.660

[1] Minimum; maximum, 48.

TABLE **K-13.**—*Compositors, males, daywork, newspaper, 1890–1928, by city and year*—Continued

Year	Atlanta, Ga.		Birmingham, Ala.		Boston, Mass.		Chicago, Ill.	
	Hours per week	Rate per hour	Hours per week	Rate per hour	Hours per week	Rate per hour	Hours per week	Rate per hour
1919	48.0	$0.606	1 42.0	$0.675	42.0	$0.830	45.0	$0.790
1920	48.0	.638	1 42.0	.675	42.0	.950	45.0	.890
1921	48.0	.910	1 42.0	.675	42.0	.950	48.0	1.150
1922	48.0	.865	1 42.0	.825	48.0	1.070	48.0	1.150
1923	48.0	.865	1 42.0	.825	48.0	1.070	48.0	1.150
1924	48.0	.938	1 42.0	.825	44.0	1.120	45.0	1.290
1925	48.0	.938	1 42.0	.825	44.0	1.170	45.0	1.290
1926	48.0	1.000	1 42.0	.925	44.0	1.170	45.0	1.290
1927	48.0	1.000	1 42.0	.950	44.0	1.250	45.0	1.356
1928	48.0	1.000	1 42.0	.975	44.0	1.250	45.0	1.380

Year	Cincinnati, Ohio		Denver, Colo.		Detroit, Mich.		New Orleans, La.	
1903	48.0	$0.514					48.3	$0.573
1904	48.0	.525	47.2	$0.566			48.5	.580
1905	48.2	.525	47.2	.565			48.4	.580
1906	48.0	.523	46.0	.575			48.4	.580
1907	48.0	.500	46.0	.500	48.0	$0.500	42.5	.550
1908	48.0	.500	46.0	.500	48.0	.500	42.5	.550
1909	48.0	.521	46.0	.550	48.0	.500	42.5	.550
1910	47.7	.524	46.0	.550	48.0	.500	42.5	.550
1911	47.7	.524	45.0	.633	48.0	.500	42.5	.550
1912	47.7	.524	45.0	.633	48.0	.500	42.5	.550
1913	47.7	.524	45.0	.633	48.0	.550	42.5	.550
1914	48.0	.542	45.0	.633	48.0	.550	42.5	.560
1915	48.0	.563	45.0	.633	48.0	.550	42.5	.570
1916	48.0	.563	45.0	.633	48.0	.550	42.5	.570
1917	48.0	.563	45.0	.633	48.0	.605	42.5	.570
1918	48.0	.563	45.0	.727	48.0	.605	42.5	.570
1919	48.0	.875	45.0	.867	48.0	.745		
1920	45.0	1.073	45.0	.978	48.0	.870		
1921	45.0	1.073	45.0	.978	48.0	.969		
1922	45.0	1.073	45.0	.933	48.0	.970		
1923	45.0	1.133	45.0	.933	48.0	.970		
1924	45.0	1.133	45.0	1.033	48.0	1.130		
1925	45.0	1.138	45.0	1.033	48.0	1.130		
1926	45.0	1.138	45.0	1.033	48.0	1.200		
1927	45.0	1.138	45.0	1.033	45.0	1.250		
1928	45.0	1.183	45.0	1.106	45.0	1.250		

Year	New York, N. Y.[2]		Philadelphia, Pa.		St. Louis, Mo.		San Francisco, Calif.	
1890	53.6	$0.491	52.3	$0.349	45.0	$0.583	56.8	$0.476
1891	50.7	.509	51.9	.343	45.0	.606	56.8	.469
1892	50.7	.504	50.6	.361	45.0	.611	56.8	.474
1893	50.6	.515	55.7	.335	45.0	.544	56.8	.491
1894	48.0	.548	55.7	.335	45.0	.548	56.8	.481
1895	48.0	.577	55.6	.337	45.0	.562	56.2	.486
1896	48.0	.581	50.0	.394	45.0	.579	56.0	.482
1897	48.0	.579	51.4	.358	45.0	.593	56.0	.478
1898	48.0	.576	51.4	.358	45.0	.581	52.5	.546
1899	48.0	.579	51.6	.356	45.0	.572	51.9	.556
1900	48.0	.585	50.0	.372	45.0	.561	53.7	.566
1901	48.0	.590	50.5	.373	45.0	.563	45.0	.635
1902	48.0	.584	50.4	.373	45.0	.579	45.0	.629
1903	48.7	.568	48.7	.422	45.0	.592	45.0	.654
1904	48.6	.577	48.9	.422	45.0	.544	45.0	.667
1905	49.0	.581	49.2	.420	45.3	.592	45.0	.667
1906	47.8	.581	49.5	.429	45.3	.582	45.0	.670
1907	45.0	.622	48.0	.417	46.0	.505	45.0	.600
1908	45.0	.622	48.0	.417	46.0	.505	45.0	.600
1909	45.0	.622	48.0	.417	46.0	.505	45.0	.644
1910	45.0	.644	48.0	.417	46.0	.505	45.0	.644
1911	45.0	.644	48.0	.417	46.0	.505	45.0	.644
1912	45.0	.644	48.0	.417	46.0	.587	45.0	.644
1913	45.0	.667	48.0	.417	46.0	.587	45.0	.644
1914	45.0	.667	48.0	.417	46.0	.587	45.0	.644
1915	45.0	.667	48.0	.417	46.0	.587	42.0	.690
1916	45.0	.667	48.0	.417	46.0	.587	42.0	.690
1917	45.0	.667	48.0	.417	46.0	.634	42.0	.690
1918	45.0	.711	48.0	.500	46.0	.634	45.0	.689
1919	45.0	.967	48.0	.667	46.0	.634	45.0	.756
1920	45.0	1.222	48.0	.813	46.0	.913	45.0	.933
1921	45.0	1.222	48.0	.792	46.0	.913	45.0	1.078
1922	45.0	1.222	48.0	.792	46.0	.913	45.0	1.078
1923	45.0	1.222	48.0	.792	46.0	.913	45.0	1.078
1924	45.0	1.289	48.0	.875	46.0	1.022	45.0	1.078
1925	45.0	1.333	48.0	.875	46.0	1.065	45.0	1.156
1926	45.0	1.333	48.0	.875	46.0	1.109	45.0	1.156
1927	45.0	1.400	46.0	.913	46.0	1.109	45.0	1.156
1928	45.0	1.422	46.0	.913	46.0	1.141	45.0	1.200

[1] Minimum; maximum, 48.   [2] Greater New York, 1903–1907, inclusive.

Table **K-14.**—*Pressmen, 1840-1900, by year and State*

Year and State	Sex	Lowest, highest, and average—Hours per week	Lowest, highest, and average—Rate per day (dollars)
1840:			
Pennsylvania	M.	60-60-60	2.00-2.00-2.00
1845:			
Pennsylvania	M.	72-72-72	1.75-1.75-1.75
1847:			
Connecticut	M.	60-60-60	1.50-1.67-1.59
1848:			
Connecticut	M.	60-60-60	1.25-2.00-1.60
1849:			
Connecticut	M.	60-60-60	1.50-2.00-1.67
1850:			
Connecticut	M.	60-60-60	1.34-2.00-1.58
1851:			
Connecticut	M.	60-60-60	1.34-2.00-1.57
New York	M.	(1)	1.67-1.67-1.67
1852:			
Connecticut	M.	60-60-60	1.50-1.67-1.59
New York	M.	72-72-72	1.50-2.00-1.84
1853:			
Connecticut	M.	60-60-60	1.67-2.00-1.71
New York	M.	(1)	1.50-1.67-1.59
1854:			
Connecticut	M.	60-60-60	1.25-2.24-1.77
New York	M.	(1)	1.67-2.00-1.84
1855:			
Connecticut	M.	60-60-60	1.25-2.24-1.75
New York	M.	(1)	1.67-2.00-1.84
1856:			
Connecticut	M.	60-60-60	1.50-2.24-1.89
New York	M.	1 60-60-60	1.67-2.00-1.94
1857:			
Connecticut	M.	60-60-60	1.00-2.24-1.77
New York	M.	60-60-60	1.50-2.50-1.56
1858:			
Connecticut	M.	60-60-60	1.34-2.17-1.72
New York	M.	(1)	2.17-2.17-2.17
1859:			
New York	M.	(1)	2.17-2.17-2.17
1860:			
New York	M.	60-60-60	1.67-2.33-1.84
1861:			
New York	M.	60-60-60	1.67-2.17-1.84
1862:			
New York	M.	60-60-60	1.67-2.17-1.84
1863:			
New York	M.	60-60-60	1.67-2.17-1.84
1864:			
Connecticut	M.	60-60-60	1.25-3.00-2.16
New York	M.	60-60-60	2.17-2.50-2.39
1865:			
Connecticut	M.	60-60-60	1.34-3.00-2.40
New York	M.	60-60-60	1.50-2.50-2.17
1866:			
Connecticut	M.	60-60-60	1.25-3.50-2.36
New York	M.	60-60-60	1.50-2.50-2.25
1867:			
Connecticut	M.	60-60-60	1.34-3.00-2.48
New York	M.	60-60-60	1.50-2.50-2.17
1868:			
Connecticut	M.	60-60-60	1.50-3.34-2.58
New York	M.	60-60-60	1.67-3.00-2.67
1869:			
Connecticut	M.	60-60-60	1.50-3.34-2.59
New York	M.	59-59-59	1.67-3.33-2.70
1870:			
New York	M.	59-59-59	.83-3.33-2.27
1871:			
New York	M.	59-59-59	.83-3.33-2.43
1872:			
Connecticut	M.	60-60-60	2.00-3.34-2.99
New York	M.	59-59-59	1.33-3.33-2.42
1873:			
Connecticut	M.	60-60-60	2.00-3.34-3.03
New York	M.	59-59-59	1.83-3.33-2.67
Pennsylvania	M.	(1)	3.00-3.17-3.10
1874:			
Connecticut	M.	60-60-60	2.34-3.34-3.05
Illinois	M.	59-59-59	2.50-2.50-2.50
New York	M.	59-59-59	2.00-3.33-2.66
Oregon	M.	60-60-60	5.00-5.00-5.00
1875:			
Connecticut	M.	59-59-59	1.17-3.34-2.86
Maryland	M.	60-60-60	1.67-1.67-1.67
New York	M.	59-59-59	2.00-3.33-2.69
1876:			
Connecticut	M.	60-60-60	1.17-3.34-2.63
New York	M.	59-59-59	2.00-3.33-2.77
Pennsylvania	M.	60-60-60	1.67-1.67-1.67
1877:			
Connecticut	M.	60-60-60	1.17-3.67-2.70
New York	M.	59-59-59	1.83-3.33-2.78
Pennsylvania	M.	60-60-60	1.17-1.17-1.17
1878:			
Connecticut	M.	60-60-60	1.17-3.00-2.55
Maryland	M.	60-60-60	2.70-2.70-2.70
New York	M.	59-59-59	2.08-3.00-2.75
Ohio	M.	(1)	1.27-3.08-1.79
Pennsylvania	M.	60-60-60	1.17-1.17-1.17
1879:			
Connecticut	M.	60-60-60	1.17-2.67-2.15
Missouri	M.	60-60-60	1.25-3.00-1.89
New York	M.	59-59-59	1.67-3.00-2.49
Pennsylvania	M.	60-60-60	1.17-1.17-1.17
1880:			
Connecticut	M.	60-60-60	1.50-2.67-2.22
Georgia	M.	60-60-60	2.33-2.33-2.33
Kentucky	M.	60-60-60	2.67-2.67-2.67
New York	M.	59-59-59	1.00-3.00-2.17
Pennsylvania	M.	60-60-60	1.25-2.67-2.10
Rhode Island	M.	58-58-58	1.67-2.92-2.09
South Carolina	M.	(1)	1.67-3.00-2.11
West Virginia	M.	(1)	2.50-2.50-2.50
1881:			
Connecticut	M.	60-60-60	1.50-3.00-2.33
New York	M.	59-59-59	1.50-3.00-2.38
Ohio	M.	59-59-59	1.67-1.67-1.67
Pennsylvania	M.	60-60-60	1.34-1.42-1.38
1882:			
Connecticut	M.	60-60-60	1.50-2.84-2.46
Missouri	M.	60-60-60	2.50-2.50-2.50
New York	M.	59-59-59	1.50-3.00-2.38
Ohio	(1)	53-60-56	1.83-3.14-2.58
Pennsylvania	M.	60-60-60	1.34-2.17-1.78
Rhode Island	M.	60-60-60	1.00-2.67-1.74
1883:			
Connecticut	M.	60-60-60	1.42-2.84-2.30
Massachusetts	M.	(1)	2.00-5.83-2.62
New Jersey	M.	59-59-59	2.00-2.50-2.08
New York	M.	59-59-59	1.67-3.00-2.35
Ohio	M.	58-60-59	2.50-3.33-2.94
Pennsylvania	M.	60-60-60	1.42-1.50-1.46
1884:			
Connecticut	M.	60-60-60	1.75-2.75-2.31
Georgia	M.	54-54-54	2.67-2.67-2.67
Kentucky	M.	59-59-59	2.50-2.50-2.50
Michigan	M.	(1)	1.00-2.15-1.71
Missouri	M.	(1)	1.69-1.69-1.69
New Jersey	M.	60-60-60	2.17-3.00-2.30
New York	M.	59-59-59	1.67-3.00-2.34
North Carolina	M.	60-60-60	2.00-2.00-2.00
Ohio	M.	59-59-59	2.50-2.50-2.50
Pennsylvania	M.	59-59-59	1.34-2.67-1.96
Virginia	M.	59-59-59	1.50-1.50-1.50
West Virginia	M.	59-59-59	2.00-2.00-2.00
1885:			
Connecticut	M.	59-59-59	1.17-2.75-2.17
Florida	M.	60-60-60	2.00-2.67-2.33
Georgia	M.	(1)	2.08-2.08-2.08
Illinois	M.	59-59-59	2.00-3.50-2.75
Do	(1)	(1)	3.50-3.50-3.50

1 Not reported.

TABLE K–14.—*Pressmen, 1840–1900, by year and State*—Continued

Year and State	Sex	Lowest, highest, and average— Hours per week	Rate per day (dollars)
1885—Continued.			
Louisiana	M.	60–60–60	2.50–2.50–2.50
Maine	M.	60–60–60	1.75–1.75–1.75
Maryland	M.	60–60–60	1.00–1.08–1.04
Massachusetts	M.	44–60–58	1.00–3.67–2.30
Michigan	(1)	(1)	2.50–2.50–2.50
Missouri	M.	59–59–59	3.33–3.33–3.33
New Jersey	M.	54–60–57	1.25–3.00–1.90
New York	M.	59–60–59	1.33–3.67–2.27
Ohio	M.	59–60–59	2.50–4.38–3.14
Pennsylvania	M.	60–60–60	1.34–1.50–1.45
Do	(1)	(1)	2.50–2.50–2.50
South Carolina	M.	59–59–59	1.67–2.67–2.28
Wisconsin	(1)	(1)	3.00–3.00–3.00
1886:			
Connecticut	M.	60–60–60	1.84–2.84–2.48
Florida	M.	60–60–60	2.00–2.00–2.00
Illinois	M.	60–60–60	1.33–1.33–1.33
Iowa	M.	59–60–60	1.67–2.67–2.23
Michigan	M.	59–59–59	1.67–2.00–1.89
New Jersey	M.	60–60–60	2.33–3.33–2.68
New York	M.	54–59–56	1.67–3.17–2.31
Pennsylvania	M.	59–60–60	1.00–3.00–2.30
1887:			
Connecticut	M.	60–60–60	1.50–3.00–2.39
New York	M.	59–59–59	1.00–3.00–2.13
Ohio	M.	48–60–58	1.00–3.50–1.92
Pennsylvania	M.	60–60–60	1.67–1.84–1.76
Wisconsin	M.	(1)	2.16–2.16–2.16
1888:			
Connecticut	M.	60–60–60	1.75–3.00–2.45
New York	M.	47–60–59	.73–3.50–2.75
Pennsylvania	M.	54–60–57	1.67–2.00–1.88
1889:			
Connecticut	M.	60–60–60	1.25–3.00–2.40
Kansas	M.	(1)	2.94–2.94–2.94
New York	M.	59–59–59	1.83–3.00–2.52
Pennsylvania	M.	60–60–60	1.67–1.84–1.76
1890:			
Connecticut	M.	60–60–60	2.00–3.00–2.56
Illinois	M.	(1)	2.00–4.00–3.24
New York	M.	59–59–59	.83–5.83–2.59
Ohio	(1)	36–60–59	1.00–3.50–2.15
Pennsylvania	M.	60–60–60	1.84–1.84–1.84
1891:			
Connecticut	M.	60–60–60	2.00–3.00–2.40
Illinois	M.	(1)	2.16–4.00–3.28
New York	M.	59–59–59	.85–5.83–2.63
North Carolina	M.	84–84–84	.80–1.92–1.36
Ohio	M.	30–60–59	1.00–5.00–1.93
Pennsylvania	M.	60–60–60	1.84–1.84–1.84
1892:			
California	M.	48–60–59	1.50–4.00–2.71
Connecticut	M.	60–60–60	1.00–3.00–2.07
Illinois	M.	59–60–59	2.00–4.00–3.09
Iowa	M.	30–60–50	1.50–3.00–2.30
New York	M.	60–60–60	2.17–3.34–2.81
1893:			
Connecticut	M.	60–60–60	1.25–3.00–2.33
Illinois	M.	48–60–59	1.25–4.00–3.08
Maryland	M.	60–60–60	1.00–2.50–1.75
Montana	M.	51–51–51	2.92–5.00–3.33
New York	M.	42–63–54	.58–2.50–1.64
Ohio	M.	45–60–59	1.02–3.50–2.04
Pennsylvania	M.	30–60–48	2.50–3.00–2.72
1894:			
Connecticut	M.	60–60–60	1.50–3.50–2.42
Iowa	M.	24–90–58	1.67–3.83–2.52

Year and State	Sex	Lowest, highest, and average— Hours per week	Rate per day (dollars)
1894—Continued.			
Montana	M.	(1)	4.53–4.53–4.53
New Hampshire	M.	36–60–54	1.33–2.33–1.98
Ohio	M.	54–60–59	1.00–4.00–2.18
1895:			
Connecticut	M.	59–60–60	1.50–4.00–2.53
Georgia	M.	60–60–60	2.00–2.00–2.00
Kentucky	M.	60–60–60	2.92–2.92–2.92
Louisiana	M.	59–59–59	3.00–3.00–3.00
Maine	M.	60–60–60	1.25–2.00–1.50
Maryland	M.	60–60–60	1.08–1.08–1.08
Massachusetts	M.	41–60–58	1.00–5.00–2.72
Missouri	M.	59–59–59	1.33–3.33–1.78
Montana	M.	53–53–53	4.54–4.54–4.54
New Jersey	M.	54–59–58	1.22–3.33–2.15
New York	M.	49–60–60	.83–3.67–2.53
North Carolina	M.	54–54–54	2.08–2.08–2.08
Ohio	M.	45–72–60	.44–3.16–1.70
Pennsylvania	M.	42–60–54	1.00–4.50–3.10
Rhode Island	M.	56–60–58	1.00–3.00–2.16
South Carolina	M.	54–59–56	1.67–3.00–2.33
Virginia	M.	59–59–59	1.33–1.67–1.52
1896:			
Colorado	(1)	60–60–60	2.00–2.00–2.00
Connecticut	M.	60–60–60	2.50–3.50–3.00
Florida	M.	60–60–60	1.67–2.50–2.21
Georgia	M.	54–54–54	1.50–2.75–2.34
Illinois	M.	54–57–56	1.33–3.50–2.30
Iowa	M.	59–60–60	1.79–3.00–2.26
Kansas	M.	36–36–36	.42–.42–.42
Kentucky	M.	59–59–59	2.33–2.33–2.33
Michigan	M.	59–59–59	2.00–2.67–2.38
Missouri	M.	48–60–58	1.08–4.00–2.21
Do	F.	60–60–60	1.00–1.25–1.05
Nebraska	(1)	60–60–60	.67–2.50–1.73
New York	M.	36–60–57	1.50–5.00–2.80
North Carolina	M.	54–54–54	1.75–1.75–1.75
Ohio	M.	54–60–59	1.50–4.17–1.97
Do	F.	55–60–60	1.00–1.05–1.05
Pennsylvania	M.	59–60–60	1.00–3.33–2.37
West Virginia	M.	59–60–59	2.00–2.50–2.33
1897:			
Kansas	M.	54–55–55	1.33–1.67–1.50
Pennsylvania	M.	60–60–60	3.00–3.00–3.00
Virginia	M.	48–60–56	1.00–2.66–1.46
Do	F.	48–60–58	.75–.75–.75
1898:			
Kansas	M.	54–54–54	2.67–3.33–3.00
Nebraska	(1)	54–60–56	.96–3.50–1.66
New York	M.	60–60–60	1.00–6.67–2.79
Alabama	M.	60–60–60	2.17–3.00–2.59
California	M'	59–59–59	2.50–4.17–2.85
Georgia	M.	60–60–60	2.50–3.33–2.94
Illinois	M.	54–54–54	3.50–3.50–3.50
Massachusetts	M.	54–54–54	2.50–4.17–3.18
New York	M.	54–54–54	3.33–6.67–3.83
North Carolina	M.	54–59–55	1.25–2.00–1.40
Pennsylvania	M.	60–60–60	2.67–3.33–2.93
1900:			
Alabama	M.	60 60–60	2.17–3.00–2.59
Georgia	M.	60–60–60	2.50–3.33–2.94
Illinois	M.	54–54–54	3.50–3.50–3.50
Massachusetts	M.	54–54–54	2.50–4.17–3.15
New York	M.	54–54–54	3.33–6.67–3.83
North Carolina	M.	54–59–55	1.25–2.00–1.40
Pennsylvania	M.	60–60–60	3.00–3.42–3.16

1 Not reported.

TABLE **K–15.**—*Pressmen, web, males, newspaper, 1890–1904, by city and year*

Year	Atlanta, Ga.		Boston, Mass.		Chicago, Ill.		Cincinnati, Ohio		Detroit, Mich.	
	Hours per week	Rate per hour	Hours per week	Rate per hour	Hours per week	Rate per hour	Hours per week	Rate per hour	Hours per week	Rate per hour
1890	60. 7	$0. 297	46. 4	$0. 435	63. 8	$0. 294			49. 3	$0. 254
1891	60. 7	. 297	46. 5	. 452	63. 8	. 294			49. 1	. 272
1892	60. 7	. 297	46. 3	. 450	63. 8	. 294			49. 0	. 257
1893	60. 7	. 297	46. 8	. 446	63. 8	. 294			48. 9	. 259
1894	60. 7	. 297	46. 9	. 442	63. 8	. 294			48. 8	. 235
1895	60. 7	. 297	46. 5	. 446	63. 8	. 294			48. 8	. 235
1896	60. 7	. 297	46. 7	. 441	63. 8	. 294			48. 8	. 254
1897	60. 7	. 278	46. 5	. 443	63. 4	. 294			48. 8	. 254
1898	60. 7	. 278	46. 5	. 470	57. 4	. 294			48. 8	. 306
1899	60. 7	. 278	46. 7	. 466	57. 4	. 351			48. 8	. 321
1900	60. 7	. 278	46. 3	. 475	57. 4	. 351			48. 9	. 314
1901	67. 0	. 262	46. 4	. 473	57. 4	. 351			48. 7	. 321
1902	67. 0	. 262	46. 8	. 491	57. 8	. 351			48. 7	. 322
1903	54. 0	. 268	47. 0	. 491	50. 6	. 368	51. 0	$0. 306	48. 7	. 348
1904	54. 0	. 245	45. 9	. 491	50. 4	. 366	50. 9	. 309	48. 8	. 375

Year	New Orleans, La.		New York, N. Y.		Philadelphia, Pa.		St. Louis, Mo.		San Francisco, Calif.	
1890			45. 3	$0. 591	54. 8	$0. 340	48. 0	$0. 309	60. 7	$0. 269
1891			45. 6	. 588	54. 9	. 339	48. 0	. 302	60. 7	. 266
1892			45. 4	. 594	55. 1	. 349	48. 0	. 291	60. 7	. 265
1893			46. 1	. 591	55. 1	. 349	48. 0	. 322	60. 7	. 265
1894			46. 2	. 593	55. 2	. 346	48. 0	. 322	60. 3	. 262
1895			46. 0	. 611	55. 2	. 346	48. 0	. 326	60. 3	. 261
1896			46. 0	. 600	55. 1	. 364	48. 0	. 322	60. 3	. 262
1897			45. 9	. 608	55. 1	. 364	48. 0	. 322	51. 4	. 311
1898			45. 7	. 600	55. 3	. 364	48. 0	. 289	51. 2	. 311
1899			45. 5	. 610	55. 6	. 370	48. 0	. 293	50. 8	. 312
1900			45. 7	. 608	53. 7	. 386	48. 0	. 295	50. 8	. 318
1901			45. 4	. 598	53. 8	. 388	48. 0	. 300	48. 0	. 415
1902			45. 0	. 609	53. 6	. 396	48. 0	. 303	48. 0	. 433
1903	64. 4	$0. 315	44. 1	. 475	52. 8	. 398	48. 0	. 379	46. 9	. 463
1904	64. 4	. 315	43. 8	. 479	53. 7	. 375	48. 0	. 390	46. 6	. 476

TABLE **K-16.**—*Pressmen, web, head, males, night work, newspaper, 1907–1928, by city and year*

Year	Atlanta, Ga. Hours per week	Rate per hour	Birmingham, Ala. Hours per week	Rate per hour	Boston, Mass. Hours per week	Rate per hour	Chicago, Ill. Hours per week	Rate per hour
1907					36.0	$0.667	42.0	$0.571
1908					36.0	.667	42.0	.571
1909					36.0	.667	42.0	.571
1910					36.0	.667	42.0	.571
1911					36.0	.667	42.0	.571
1912	48.0	$0.500	48.0	$0.625	36.0	.692	42.0	.571
1913	48.0	.500	48.0	.625	36.0	.692	42.0	.571
1914	48.0	.500	42.0	.714	36.0	.692	42.0	.571
1915	48.0	.500	42.0	.714	36.0	.692	42.0	.571
1916	48.0	.500	42.0	.833	36.0	.692	48.0	.688
1917	48.0	.500	42.0	.833	36.0	.740	48.0	.688
1918	48.0	.719	42.0	.833	36.0	.740	48.0	.688
1919	48.0	.625	42.0	.833	36.0	.888	48.0	.688
1920	48.0	.813	42.0	.833	36.0	1.083	42.0	1.071
1921	48.0	.813	42.0	1.131	36.0	1.250	42.0	1.071
1922	48.0	.813	42.0	1.131	36.0	1.250	42.0	1.071
1923	48.0	.813	42.0	.893	36.0	1.250	42.0	1.071
1924	48.0	.875	42.0	1.036	36.0	1.308	42.0	1.190
1925	48.0	.938	42.0	1.036	36.0	1.308	44.0	1.227
1926	48.0	1.094	42.0	1.036	36.0	1.308	44.0	1.227
1927	48.0	1.094	42.0	1.107	36.0	1.408	44.0	1.341
1928	48.0	.969	42.0	1.143	36.0	1.408	44.0	1.341

Year	New York, N. Y. Hours per week	Rate per hour	Philadelphia, Pa. Hours per week	Rate per hour	St. Louis, Mo. Hours per week	Rate per hour	San Francisco, Calif. Hours per week	Rate per hour
1907	38.0	$0.816	48.0	$0.521	48.0	$0.500	45.0	$0.567
1908	38.0	.816	48.0	.521	48.0	.500	45.0	.689
1909	38.0	.816	48.0	.521	48.0	.500	45.0	.689
1910	38.0	.816	48.0	.521	45.0	.580	45.0	.689
1911	38.0	.816	48.0	.521	45.0	.580	45.0	.689
1912	38.0	.816	48.0	.521	45.0	.580	45.0	.689
1913	38.0	.842	38.0	.658	45.0	.613	45.0	.689
1914	38.0	.842	38.0	.658	45.0	.613	45.0	.689
1915	38.0	.842	38.0	.658	45.0	.613	45.0	.689
1916	38.0	.842	38.0	.658	45.5	.613	45.0	.689
1917	37.5	.853	38.0	.658	45.5	.607	45.0	.689
1918	37.5	.907	38.0	.789	45.5	.659	45.0	.733
1919	37.5	1.227	38.0	.947	45.5	.712	45.0	.756
1920	37.5	1.387	36.0	1.167	45.5	.778	45.0	.889
1921	38.0	1.334	36.0	1.167	45.5	.910	45.0	1.053
1922	48.0	1.125	38.0	1.105	45.5	.910	48.0	.990
1923	48.0	1.125	38.0	1.105	42.0	1.084	48.0	.990
1924	41.0	1.415	38.0	1.105	42.0	1.167	48.0	.990
1925	41.0	1.439	38.0	1.105	42.0	1.214	48.0	1.052
1926	41.0	1.464	38.0	1.105	42.0	1.214	48.0	1.052
1927	41.0	1.598			42.0	1.250	48.0	1.052
1928	41.0	1.646			42.0	1.262	45.0	1.167

Year	Cincinnati, Ohio Hours per week	Rate per hour	Denver, Colo. Hours per week	Rate per hour	Detroit, Mich. Hours per week	Rate per hour	New Orleans, La. Hours per week	Rate per hour
1907					48.0	$0.396		
1908					48.0	.396		
1909					48.0	.396		
1910	43.0	$0.523			48.0	.438		
1911	43.0	.523			48.0	.438		
1912	48.0	.500	48.0	$0.625	48.0	.479		
1913	48.0	.500	48.0	.625	45.0	.511		
1914	48.0	.500	48.0	.625	45.0	.511		
1915	48.0	.500	48.0	.625	45.0	.511	48.0	$0.646
1916	48.0	.531	48.0	.625	45.0	.511	48.0	.667
1917	48.0	.531	48.0	.625	44.0	.625	48.0	.667
1918	48.0	.531	48.0	.656	44.0	.625	48.0	.729
1919	48.0	.656	48.0	.677	44.0	.818	48.0	.438
1920	48.0	.750	48.0	.719	44.0	.909	48.0	.719
1921	48.0	.917	48.0	.813	44.0	1.159		
1922	48.0	.917	43.0	.988	44.0	1.023		
1923	48.0	.917	43.0	.988	44.0	1.136		
1924	48.0	1.000	43.0	1.093	44.0	1.136		
1925	48.0	1.000	43.0	1.093	44.0	1.205		
1926	48.0	1.035	43.0	1.128	44.0	1.227		
1927	48.0	1.052	43.0	1.128	44.0	1.295		
1928	48.0	1.083	43.0	1.163	44.0	1.295		

TABLE K-17.—*Pressmen, web, first assistants, males, night work, newspaper, 1907-1928, by city and year*

Year	Atlanta, Ga.		Birmingham, Ala.		Boston, Mass.		Chicago, Ill.	
	Hours per week	Rate per hour	Hours per week	Rate per hour	Hours per hour	Rate per hour	Hours per hour	Rate per hour
1907	54.0	$0.306	--------	--------	36.0	$0.625	42.0	$0.500
1908	54.0	.306	--------	--------	36.0	.625	42.0	.500
1909	48.0	.344	--------	--------	36.0	.625	42.0	.500
1910	48.0	.344	--------	--------	36.0	.625	42.0	.500
1911	48.0	.438	--------	--------	36.0	.625	42.0	.500
1912	48.0	.438	48.0	$0.500	36.0	.575	42.0	.500
1913	48.0	.438	48.0	.500	36.0	.575	42.0	.500
1914	48.0	.438	42.0	.500	36.0	.575	42.0	.500
1915	48.0	.438	42.0	.548	36.0	.575	42.0	.500
1916	48.0	.438	42.0	.571	36.0	.575	48.0	.550
1917	48.0	.438	42.0	.571	36.0	.615	48.0	.550
1918	48.0	.594	42.0	.571	36.0	.615	48.0	.550
1919	48.0	.531	42.0	.714	36.0	.740	48.0	.550
1920	48.0	.750	42.0	.786	36.0	.917	42.0	.929
1921	48.0	.750	42.0	.893	36.0	1.083	42.0	.929
1922	48.0	.750	42.0	.803	36.0	1.083	42.0	.929
1923	48.0	.750	42.0	.786	36.0	1.083	42.0	.929
1924	48.0	.854	42.0	.929	36.0	1.142	42.0	1.048
1925	48.0	.813	42.0	.929	36.0	1.142	44.0	1.091
1926	48.0	.906	42.0	.929	36.0	1.142	44.0	1.091
1927	48.0	.906	42.0	1.000	36.0	1.242	44.0	1.170
1928	48.0	.906	42.0	1.036	36.0	1.242	44.0	1.170

Year	Cincinnati, Ohio		Denver, Colo.		Detroit, Mich.		New Orleans, La.	
1907	--------	--------	--------	--------	48.0	$0.354	--------	--------
1908	--------	--------	--------	--------	48.0	.354	--------	--------
1909	--------	--------	--------	--------	48.0	.354	--------	--------
1910	43.0	$0.454	--------	--------	48.0	.385	--------	--------
1911	43.0	.454	--------	--------	48.0	.385	--------	--------
1912	48.0	.438	48.0	$0.500	48.0	.406	--------	--------
1913	48.0	.438	48.0	.500	45.0	.433	--------	--------
1914	48.0	.438	48.0	.500	45.0	.433	--------	--------
1915	48.0	.438	48.0	.500	45.0	.433	48.0	$0.438
1916	48.0	.463	48.0	.500	45.0	.433	48.0	.458
1917	48.0	.463	48.0	.500	44.0	.545	48.0	.458
1918	48.0	.463	48.0	.531	44.0	.545	48.0	.438
1919	48.0	.563	48.0	.552	44.0	.750	48.0	.438
1920	48.0	.656	48.0	.594	44.0	.841	48.0	.688
1921	48.0	.854	48.0	.719	44.0	1.023	--------	--------
1922	48.0	.854	43.0	.884	44.0	.909	--------	--------
1923	48.0	.854	43.0	.884	44.0	1.000	--------	--------
1924	48.0	.938	43.0	.988	44.0	1.000	--------	--------
1925	48.0	.938	43.0	.988	44.0	1.068	--------	--------
1926	48.0	.971	43.0	1.023	44.0	1.091	--------	--------
1927	48.0	.979	43.0	1.023	44.0	1.159	--------	--------
1928	48.0	1.010	43.0	1.058	44.0	1.159	--------	--------

Year	New York, N. Y.		Philadelphia, Pa.		St. Louis, Mo.		San Francisco, Calif.	
1907	38.0	$0.658	48.0	$0.375	48.0	$0.406	45.0	$0.500
1908	38.0	.658	48.0	.375	48.0	.406	45.0	.600
1909	38.0	.658	48.0	.375	48.0	.406	45.0	.600
1910	38.0	.658	48.0	.375	45.0	.487	45.0	.600
1911	38.0	.658	48.0	.375	45.0	.487	45.0	.600
1912	38.0	.658	48.0	.375	45.0	.487	45.0	.607
1913	38.0	.684	38.0	.474	45.0	.520	45.0	.607
1914	38.0	.684	38.0	.474	45.0	.520	45.0	.607
1915	38.0	.684	38.0	.474	45.0	.520	45.0	.607
1916	38.0	.684	38.0	.474	45.5	.520	45.0	.607
1917	37.5	.693	38.0	.474	45.5	.514	45.0	.607
1918	37.5	.747	38.0	.632	45.5	.571	45.0	.653
1919	37.5	1.067	38.0	.632	45.5	.612	45.0	.689
1920	37.5	1.227	36.0	1.000	45.5	.673	45.0	.844
1921	38.0	1.184	36.0	1.000	45.5	.804	45.0	.987
1922	48.0	1.000	38.0	.947	45.5	.804	48.0	.927
1923	48.0	1.000	38.0	.947	42.0	.959	48.0	.927
1924	41.0	1.268	38.0	.947	42.0	1.048	48.0	.927
1925	41.0	1.293	38.0	1.105	42.0	1.095	48.0	.990
1926	41.0	1.317	38.0	1.105	42.0	1.095	48.0	.990
1927	41.0	1.378	--------	--------	42.0	1.131	48.0	.990
1928	41.0	1.427	--------	--------	42.0	1.143	45.0	1.100

TABLE K-18.—*Stereotypers, 1857-1900, by year and State*

Year and State	Sex	Lowest, highest, and average—		Year and State	Sex	Lowest, highest, and average—	
		Hours per week	Rate per day (dollars)			Hours per week	Rate per day (dollars)
1857:				1886:			
New York	M.	60-60-60	1. 67-2. 00-1. 84	New York	M.	59-59-59	2. 33-3. 67-3. 00
1858:				Do	(¹)	(¹)	2. 50-2. 50-2. 50
New York	M.	60-60-60	1. 00-1. 67-1. 33	1887:			
1859:				New York	(¹)	(¹)	2. 50-3. 00-2. 63
New York	M.	60-60-60	1. 00-1. 67-1. 33	Ohio	M.	60-60-60	1. 59-4. 00-2. 11
1860:				Wisconsin	(¹)	(¹)	2. 48-2. 48-2. 48
New York	M.	60-60-60	1. 33-1. 67-1. 50	1888:			
1861:				New York	(¹)	(¹)	2. 67-2. 67-2. 67
New York	M.	60-60-60	1. 67-1. 67-1. 67	1889:			
1862:				Kansas	M.	(¹)	3. 38-3. 38-3. 38
New York	M.	60-60-60	1. 67-1. 83-1. 75	New York	(¹)	(¹)	2. 67-3. 00-2. 75
1863:				1890:			
New York	M.	60-60-60	1. 67-1. 83-1. 75	New York	(¹)	(¹)	2. 67-3. 00-2. 75
1865:				Do	M.	(¹)	. 67-3. 33-2. 00
New York	M.	60-60-60	1. 67-2. 33-2. 00	1891:			
1866:				New York	(¹)	(¹)	2. 67-3. 00-2. 78
New York	M.	60-60-60	2. 00-2. 00-2. 00	Do	M.	(¹)	. 67-3. 33-1. 88
1871:				1892:			
New York	(¹)	(¹)	3. 00-3. 00-3. 00	New York	M.	60-60-60	2. 67-2. 67-2. 67
1872:				1893:			
New York	M.	59-59-59	3. 00-3. 00-3. 00	Montana	M.	(¹)	5. 83-6. 00-5. 92
1873:				Ohio	M.	60-60-60	2. 33-2. 33-2. 33
New York	(¹)	(¹)	3. 00-3. 00-3. 00	Pennsylvania	M.	36-60-46	. 83-3. 33-2. 39
1874:				1894:			
New York	(¹)	(¹)	2. 44-2. 44-2. 44	Iowa	M.	30-60-51	1. 50-3. 33-2. 11
1875:				Montana	M.	(¹)	4. 93-4. 93-4. 93
New York	(¹)	(¹)	3. 00-3. 00-3. 00	Ohio	M.	(¹)	2. 25-2. 25-2. 25
1876:				1895:			
New York	(¹)	(¹)	3. 00-3. 00-3. 00	Kansas	(¹)	54-60-57	1. 67-2. 50-2. 09
1877:				Massachusetts	M.	48-48-48	2. 38-3. 13-2. 76
New York	(¹)	(¹)	2. 83-2. 83-2. 83	Missouri	M.	59-59-59	4. 00-4. 00-4. 00
1878:				Montana	M.	53-53-53	4. 50-4. 50-4. 50
New York	(¹)	(¹)	2. 67-2. 67-2. 67	Ohio	M.	51-60-58	2. 25-3. 66-2. 47
Ohio	M	(¹)	1. 83-2. 24-2. 09	1896:			
1879:				Colorado	M.	48-48-48	4. 00-4. 00-4. 00
New Jersey	(¹)	60-60-60	1. 00-1. 00-1. 00	Kansas	M.	60-60-60	1. 33-1. 33-1. 33
1882:				New York	M.	59-59-59	1. 96-3. 33-2. 70
Ohio	(¹)	52-52-52	2. 55-2. 55-2. 55	Ohio	M.	51-59-52	2. 33-3. 25-2. 64
1883:				1897:			
Massachusetts	M.	(¹)	1. 83-3. 00-2. 42	New York	M.	48-48-48	3. 00-4. 11-3. 42
1884:				1898:			
Missouri	(¹)	(¹)	2. 58-2. 58-2. 58	New York	M.	48-60-59	2. 00-4. 50-3. 14
New Jersey	M.	48-48-48	2. 33-2. 33-2. 33	1899:			
New York	(¹)	(¹)	2. 00-2. 00-2. 00	New York	M.	54-54-54	4. 00-4. 50-4. 30
1885:				1900:			
Missouri	M.	59-59-59	3. 50-3. 50-3. 50	New York	M.	54-54-54	4. 00-4. 50-4. 31
New York	(¹)	(¹)	2. 00-2. 00-2. 00				
Ohio	M.	59-59-59	2. 50-2. 50-2. 50				

¹ Not reported.

TABLE K-19.—*Stereotypers, males, daywork, newspaper, 1890-1928, by city and year*

Year	Atlanta, Ga.		Birmingham, Ala.		Boston, Mass.		Chicago, Ill.	
	Hours per week	Rate per hour	Hours per week	Rate per hour	Hours per week	Rate per hour	Hours per week	Rate per hour
1890					47. 7	$0. 539	52. 4	$0. 375
1891					47. 5	. 541	52. 4	. 375
1892					47. 7	. 539	52. 4	. 375
1893					47. 7	. 539	52. 4	. 375
1894					47. 6	. 540	52. 4	. 392
1895					47. 5	. 541	52. 4	. 392
1896					47. 7	. 539	52. 4	. 392
1897					47. 7	. 539	52. 4	. 392
1898					47. 8	. 538	52. 4	. 392
1899					47. 8	. 538	52. 4	. 406
1900					47. 7	. 538	52. 4	. 406

TABLE K-19.—*Stereotypers, males, daywork, newspaper, 1890-1928, by city and year*—Continued

Year	Atlanta, Ga.		Birmingham, Ala.		Boston, Mass.[1]		Chicago, Ill.	
	Hours per week	Rate per hour	Hours per week	Rate per hour	Hours per week	Rate per hour	Hours per week	Rate per hour
1901					47.5	0.544	52.4	0.406
1902					47.4	.544	52.4	.406
1903	42.7	$0.502			47.4	.544	48.0	.445
1904	48.0	.438	51.0	$0.370	42.0	.610	48.0	.463
1905	48.0	.363	51.0	.397	42.0	.609	48.0	.513
1906	48.0	.363	55.5	.373	42.0	.613	49.3	.495
1907					42.0	.571	46.5	.484
1908					42.0	.571	46.5	.549
1909					42.0	.571	46.5	.549
1910	48.0	.406			42.0	.571	46.5	.549
1911	48.0	.438			42.0	.571	46.5	.581
1912	48.0	.438	48.0	.417	42.0	.571	46.5	.581
1913	48.0	.438	48.0	.438	42.0	.595	48.0	.563
1914	48.0	.469	48.0	.438	42.0	.595	48.0	.563
1915	48.0	.469	48.0	.469	42.0	.595	48.0	.563
1916	48.0	.469	48.0	.469	42.0	.595	48.0	.563
1917	48.0	.469	48.0	.500	42.0	.643	48.0	.563
1918	48.0	.510	48.0	.544	42.0	.643	48.0	.563
1919	48.0	.510	48.0	.544	42.0	.750	48.0	.604
1920	48.0	.781	48.0	.734	42.0	.929	48.0	.813
1921	48.0	.844	48.0	.813	42.0	1.097	48.0	.813
1922	48.0	.813	48.0	.750	42.0	1.097	48.0	.813
1923	48.0	.813	48.0	.813	42.0	1.097	48.0	.875
1924	48.0	.881	48.0	.813	42.0	1.147	48.0	.875
1925	48.0	.886	48.0	.813	42.0	1.147	48.0	.958
1926	48.0	.943	48.0	.875	42.0	1.147	48.0	.979
1927	48.0	.943	48.0	.875	42.0	1.147	48.0	1.000
1928	48.0	.943	48.0	.906	42.0	1.193	48.0	1.020

Year	Cincinnati, Ohio		Denver, Colo.		Detroit, Mich.		New Orleans, La.	
1890					49.1	$0.230		
1891					49.1	.230		
1892					49.1	.264		
1893					48.9	.261		
1894					48.9	.261		
1895					48.9	.261		
1896					48.9	.296		
1897					48.9	.300		
1898					48.9	.327		
1899					48.8	.363		
1900					48.8	.363		
1901					48.8	.363		
1902					48.8	.363		
1903	50.0	$0.328			48.8	.401	53.0	$0.358
1904	50.1	.348	47.4	$0.408	49.0	.391	53.0	.397
1905	49.0	.398	47.4	.408	48.9	.398	53.2	.384
1906	48.6	.402	47.7	.440	48.9	.398	53.2	.384
1907	[1]57.0	.379	48.0	.469	42.0	.500	48.0	.313
1908	[1]57.0	[2].379	48.0	.469	42.0	.500	48.0	.321
1909	57.0	[2].379	48.0	.469	42.0	.500	48.0	.321
1910	[3]51.0	[4].435	48.0	.500	42.0	.514	48.0	.321
1911	[3]51.0	[4].435	48.0	.531	42.0	.529	48.0	.321
1912	[3]51.0	[5].441	48.0	.531	42.0	.571	48.0	.321
1913	[3]51.0	[6].471	48.0	.531	48.0	.500	48.0	.321
1914	48.0	.500	48.0	.563	48.0	.500	42.0	.439
1915	48.0	.500	48.0	.563	48.0	.500	42.0	.460
1916	48.0	.500	48.0	.563	48.0	.500	42.0	.500
1917	48.0	.510	48.0	.563	48.0	.578	42.0	.500
1918	48.0	.521	48.0	.589	48.0	.578	42.0	.500
1919	48.0	.646	48.0	.661	48.0	.578	48.0	.525
1920	48.0	.719	48.0	.746	48.0	.833	48.0	.688
1921	48.0	.854	48.0	.865	48.0	.833	47.5	.688
1922	48.0	.854	48.0	.844	48.0	.875	47.5	.688
1923	44.0	.854	48.0	.844	48.0	.875	47.5	.688
1924	48.0	.938	48.0	.875	48.0	.938	47.5	.750
1925	48.0	.938	48.0	.917	48.0	1.000	47.5	.750
1926	48.0	.979	48.0	.917	48.0	1.000	47.5	.750
1927	48.0	.979	48.0	.958	48.0	1.075	47.5	.758
1928	48.0	1.021	47.5	.968	48.0	1.075	47.5	.821

[1] 54 hours, October to March.
[2] 40 cents, October to March.
[3] 48 hours, October to March.
[4] 46½ cents, October to March.
[5] 46⅔ cents, October to March.
50 cents, October to March.

TABLE **K-19.**—*Stereotypers, males, daywork, newspaper, 1890–1928, by city and year*—Continued

Year	New York, N. Y.[7]		Philadelphia, Pa.		St. Louis, Mo.		San Francisco, Calif.	
	Hours per week	Rate per hour	Hours per week	Rate per hour	Hours per week	Rate per hour	Hours per week	Rate per hour
1890	43.3	$0.675	40.2	$0.383	48.0	$0.301	56.0	$0.295
1891	43.8	.675	40.2	.386	48.0	.333	56.0	.287
1892	43.9	.672	41.1	.370	48.0	.412	56.0	.287
1893	44.9	.655	41.1	.370	48.0	.385	56.0	.294
1894	45.1	.652	41.1	.374	48.0	.412	56.0	.277
1895	45.2	.650	41.4	.374	48.0	.425	56.0	.276
1896	45.3	.650	41.4	.384	48.0	.422	56.0	.279
1897	45.9	.642	41.4	.384	48.0	.394	46.8	.366
1898	45.4	.652	41.7	.394	48.0	.430	47.6	.369
1899	45.4	.648	42.0	.395	48.0	.434	47.3	.441
1900	45.7	.648	42.3	.394	48.0	.409	47.3	.441
1901	45.7	.653	42.3	.394	48.0	.421	47.3	.455
1902	45.5	.653	42.8	.416	48.0	.435	46.9	.459
1903	44.0	.646	46.4	.409	48.0	.446	45.0	.544
1904	43.7	.647	46.4	.416	48.0	.445	45.0	.544
1905	43.2	.658	46.4	.420	45.0	.493	45.0	.544
1906	42.5	.654	47.3	.411	45.4	.500	45.0	.600
1907	48.0	.563	54.0	.375	48.0	.469	45.0	.533
1908	48.0	.563	54.0	.375	48.0	.469	45.0	.533
1909	48.0	.563	54.0	.375	48.0	.500	45.0	.600
1910	48.0	.563	48.0	.406	48.0	.500	45.0	.600
1911	48.0	.563	48.0	.406	48.0	.500	45.0	.600
1912	48.0	.563	48.0	.406	48.0	.500	45.0	.600
1913	48.0	.625	48.0	.438	48.0	.538	45.0	.600
1914	48.0	.625	48.0	.438	48.0	.538	45.0	.667
1915	48.0	.625	48.0	.438	48.0	.538	45.0	.667
1916	48.0	.625	48.0	.438	48.0	.575	45.0	.667
1917	48.0	.625	48.0	.438	48.0	.575	45.0	.667
1918	48.0	.667	48.0	.521	48.0	.625	45.0	.667
1919	48.0	.729	48.0	.563	48.0	.669	45.0	.733
1920	48.0	.833	48.0	.667	48.0	.798	45.0	.889
1921	48.0	1.042	48.0	.729	48.0	.861	45.0	1.033
1922	48.0	1.042	48.0	.729	48.0	.861	45.0	1.033
1923	48.0	1.042	48.0	.729	48.0	.875	45.0	1.000
1924	48.0	1.042	48.0	.792	48.0	.969	45.0	1.000
1925	48.0	1.042	48.0	.792	48.0	1.031	45.0	1.033
1926	48.0	1.042	48.0	.833	48.0	1.031	45.0	1.033
1927	48.0	1.042	48.0	.875	48.0	1.031	45.0	1.044
1928	48.0	1.042	48.0	.875	48.0	1.073	45.0	1.044

[7] Greater New York—1903–1907.

L.—TEXTILES

COTTON

The sources from which this information was taken are the fifteenth and the nineteenth annual reports of the Commissioner of Labor Statistics and bulletins of the Bureau of Labor Statistics Nos. 59, 65, 71, 77, 128, 150, 190, 239, 262, 288, 345, 371, 446, and 492. The data shown here has been taken from the above-noted reports in the identical form as presented during each period of years. A large per cent of this material is shown by States, in other periods it is by geographic divisions, and during certain other periods no reports were available.

These reports on wages and hours in the cotton-goods manufacturing industry also include data for employees engaged in cotton finishing and cotton dyeing.

TABLE L–1.—*Doffers, cotton goods, 1849–1900, by year and State*

Year and State	Sex	Hours per week	Rate per day (dollars)	Year and State	Sex	Hours per week	Rate per day (dollars)
1849:				**1861:**			
Massachusetts____	(1)	75–75–75	0. 40–0. 40–0. 40	Massachusetts____	M.	66–66–66	0. 20–0. 45–0. 31
1850:				Do_____	F.	66–66–66	. 30– . 38– . 34
Massachusetts____	(1)	75–75–75	. 40– . 40– . 40	New York_____	F.	72–72–72	. 46– . 46– . 46
1851:				**1862:**			
Massachusetts____	M.	72–75–73	. 20– . 45– . 31	Massachusetts____	M.	66–66–66	. 20– . 50– . 32
Do_____	F.	72–72–72	. 18– . 18– . 18	Do_____	F.	66–66–66	. 33– . 33– . 33
1852:				New York_____	F.	72–72–72	. 54– . 54– . 54
Massachusetts____	M.	72–75–72	. 25– . 45– . 31	**1863:**			
Do_____	F.	72–72–72	. 17– . 17– . 17	Massachusetts____	M.	66–66–66	. 20– . 60– . 38
1853:				Do_____	F.	66–66–66	. 25– . 33– . 28
Massachusetts____	M.	72–75–72	. 20– . 45– . 28	**1864:**			
Do_____	F.	72–72–72	. 17– . 22– . 19	Massachusetts____	M.	66–66–66	. 22– . 71– . 44
New York_____	F.	72–72–72	. 36– . 36– . 36	Do_____	F.	66–66–66	. 25– . 25– . 25
1854:				**1865:**			
Massachusetts____	M.	66–72–71	. 20– . 45– . 28	Massachusetts____	M.	66–66–66	. 40– . 88– . 55
Do_____	F.	72–72–72	. 17– . 22– . 19	Do_____	F.	66–66–66	. 40– . 60– . 49
New York_____	F.	72–72–72	. 50– . 50– . 50	New York_____	F.	72–72–72	. 67– . 67– . 67
1855:				**1866:**			
Massachusetts____	M.	66–72–71	. 21– . 50– . 31	Massachusetts____	M.	66–66–66	. 40– . 88– . 58
Do_____	F.	72–72–72	. 17– . 17– . 17	Do_____	F.	66–66–66	. 50– . 50– . 50
New York_____	F.	72–72–72	. 47– . 47– . 47	Missouri_____	F.	61–61–61	. 42– . 42– . 42
1856:				New York_____	F.	72–72–72	. 67– . 67– . 67
Massachusetts____	M.	66–72–72	. 21– . 50– . 33	**1867:**			
Do_____	F.	72–72–72	. 17– . 17– . 17	Georgia_____	M.	66–66–66	. 30– . 30– . 30
New York_____	F.	72–72–72	. 54– . 54– . 54	Massachusetts____	M.	66–66–66	. 50– . 88– . 69
1857:				Do_____	F.	66–66–66	. 40– . 67– . 53
Massachusetts____	M.	66–72–71	. 21– . 50– . 33	New York_____	F.	72–72–72	. 77– . 77– . 77
Do_____	F.	72–72–72	. 17– . 33– . 20	**1868:**			
New York_____	F.	72–72–72	. 63– . 63– . 63	Massachusetts____	M.	66–66–66	. 58– . 83– . 72
1858:				Do_____	F.	66–66–66	. 50– . 63– . 61
Massachusetts____	M.	66–72–71	. 21– . 50– . 30	New York_____	F.	66–66–66	. 77– . 77– . 77
Do_____	F.	72–72–72	. 33– . 33– . 33	**1869:**			
New York_____	F.	72–72–72	. 39– . 39– . 39	Massachusetts____	M.	66–66–66	. 58– . 83– . 70
1859:				Do_____	F.	66–66–66	. 54– . 68– . 59
Massachusetts____	M.	66–72–71	. 25– . 50– . 31	New York_____	F.	66–66–66	. 77– . 77– . 77
Do_____	F.	72–72–72	. 25– . 33– . 30	**1870:**			
New York_____	F.	72–72–72	. 50– . 50– . 50	Massachusetts____	M.	66–66–66	. 50– . 75– . 65
1860:				Do_____	F.	66–66–66	. 33– . 60– . 50
Massachusetts____	M.	66–72–72	. 25– . 46– . 32	New York_____	F.	66–66–66	. 77– . 77– . 77
Do_____	F.	72–72–72	. 30– . 33– . 32	**1871:**			
New York_____	F.	72–72–72	. 46– . 46– . 46	Massachusetts____	M.	66–66–66	. 50– . 88– . 64
Rhode Island____	F.	60–60–60	. 83– . 83– . 83	Do_____	F.	66–66–66	. 50– . 63– . 56
				New York_____	F.	66–66–66	. 84– . 84– . 84

1 Not reported.

TABLE L–1.—*Doffers, cotton goods, 1849–1900, by year and State*—Continued

Year and State	Sex	Hours per week	Rate per day (dollars)	Year and State	Sex	Hours per week	Rate per day (dollars)
1872:				**1883—Continued.**			
Massachusetts	M.	66-66-66	0.50-1.00-0.76	Georgia	M.	66-66-66	0.25-0.50-0.43
Do	F.	66-66-66	.50-.83-.61	Kentucky	F.	(¹)	.33-.33-.33
New York	F.	66-66-66	.84-.84-.84	Massachusetts	M.	60-66-61	.30-.78-.57
South Carolina	M.	72-72-72	.30-.40-.35	Do	F.	60-60-60	.35-.41-.38
1873:				Do	(¹)	(¹)	.40-1.00-.64
Massachusetts	M.	66-66-66	.40-1.00-.76	Mississippi	M.	(¹)	.42-.42-.42
Do	F.	66-66-66	.50-.83-.61	New Jersey	M.	50-65-64	.50-2.50-.00
New York	F.	66-66-66	.84-.84-.84	Do	F.	60-60-60	.33-.42-.42
1874:				New York	F.	66-66-66	.50-.71-.66
Massachusetts	M.	60-66-64	.40-.85-.68	North Carolina	M.	(¹)	.35-.40-.27
Do	F.	66-66-66	.50-.83-.72	South Carolina	M.	70-72-71	.30-.35-.34
New York	F.	66-66-66	.58-.88-.81	Tennessee	M.	66-66-66	.30-.55-.42
1875:				Do	F.	66-66-66	.40-.50-.46
Massachusetts	M.	60-60-60	.30-.97-.55	**1884:**			
Do	F.	60-60-60	.54-.54-.54	Georgia	M.	66-70-68	.25-.40-.35
New York	F.	66-66-66	.42-.84-.69	Louisiana	M.	63-66-64	.33-.50-.47
1876:				Massachusetts	F.	60-60-60	.25-.90-.47
Massachusetts	M.	60-60-60	.40-.85-.54	Do	M.	60-60-60	.30-.80-.55
Do	F.	60-60-60	.53-.53-.53	Missouri	F.	(¹)	.30-.30-.30
New York	F.	66-66-66	.42-.69-.62	New Jersey	M.	60-60-60	.50-1.67-.73
Pennsylvania	M.	(¹)	.40-.82-.42	New York	F.	66-66-66	.67-.67-.67
Do	F.	(¹)	.50-.50-.50	North Carolina	M.	69-72-71	.39-.33-.33
South Carolina	M.	66-66-66	.35-.35-.35	Pennsylvania	F.	(¹)	.25-.25-.25
1877:				Rhode Island	F.	(¹)	.50-.50-.50
Georgia	M.	66-66-66	.40-.40-.40	South Carolina	M.	69-69-69	.30-.45-.36
Maine	M.	66-66-66	.45-.73-.54	Tennessee	F.	66-66-66	.35-.70-.38
Do	F.	66-66-66	.35-.90-.53	Virginia	F.	69-69-69	.29-.29-.29
Massachusetts	M.	60-60-60	.30-.80-.52	**1885:**			
Do	F.	60-60-60	.41-.41-.41	Alabama	M.	63-63-63	.30-.46-.40
New York	F.	66-66-66	.67-.67-.67	Connecticut	M.	60-66-65	.50-.75-.58
1878:				Do	F.	66-66-66	.60-.60-60
Massachusetts	M.	60-60-60	.30-.75-.51	Delaware	M.	60-60-60	.70-1.00-.85
Do	F.	60-60-60	.39-.52-.49	Georgia	M.	69-69-69	.30-.42-.35
New York	F.	66-66-66	.67-.67-.67	Maine	M.	66-66-66	.39-.80-.46
North Carolina	M.	72-72-72	.30-.40-.37	Do	F.	66-66-66	.36-.55-.46
Do	F.	72-72-72-	.30-.30-.30	Maryland	M.	66-66-66	.30-.50-.40
1879:				Do	F.	66-66-66	.30-.40-.37
Massachusetts	M.	60-60-60	.30-.80-.50	Massachusetts	M.	60-60-60	.25-.89-.58
Do	F.	60-60-60	.35-.41-.38	Do	F.	60-60-60	.35-.73-.57
Missouri	F.	(¹)	.25-.25-.25	Missouri	F.	(¹)	.30-.33-.32
New York	F.	66-66-66	.69-.69-.69	New Hampshire	M.	60-65-64	.50-.80-.69
1880:				Do	F.	60-65-64	.50-1.06-.61
Georgia	M.	66-69-68	.22-.45-.40	New Jersey	F.	60-60-60	.45-.45-.45
Massachusetts	M.	60-60-60	.30-.80-.52	Do	M.	60-60-60	1.67-1.67-1.67
Do	F.	60-60-60	.30-.45-.41	New York	M.	60-69-65	.33-.75-.42
New York	F.	66-66-66	.75-.75-.75	Do	F.	66-66-66	.33-.77-.51
Pennsylvania	M.	60-60-60	.21-.67-.31	North Carolina	F.	69-69-69	.30-.42-.33
Virginia	M.	68-68-68	.33-.33-.33	Do	M.	69-69-69	.30-.42-.36
1881:				Pennsylvania	F.	60-60-60	.50-.50-.50
Georgia	M.	66-66-66	.35-.50-.43	Vermont	M.	66-66-66	.42-.60-.46
Massachusetts	M.	60-60-60	.30-.75-.53	Do	F.	66-66-66	.42-.42-.42
Do	F.	60-60-60	.30-.45-.40	Virginia	M.	66-66-66	.33-.50-.39
New Hampshire	F.	65-65-65	.45-.88-.61	**1886:**			
New York	F.	66-66-66	.73-.73-.73	Maryland	F.	60-61-60	.29-.67-.45
North Carolina	M.	(¹)	.40-.40-.40	Massachusetts	M.	60-60-60	.45-.81-.63
Rhode Island	M.	66-66-66	.64-.90-.78	Do	F.	60-60-60	.40-.50-.46
Do	F.	66-66-66	.58-.80-.73	Missouri	F.	61-66-64	.27-.42-.32
Tennessee	M.	66-66-66	.30-.30-.30	New Hampshire	M.	60-60-60	.42-.85-.47
1882:				Do	F.	60-60-60	.42-.60-.43
Georgia	M.	70-72-72	.30-.50-.42	New Jersey	M.	58-60-60	.38-.58-.39
Kentucky	M.	66-66-66	.60-.60-.60	Do	M.	60-60-60	.58-.67-.64
Massachusetts	M.	60-66-61	.30-.78-.54	New York	(¹)	60-60-60	.58-.58-.58
Do	F.	60-60-60	.30-.45-.40	Do	F.	59-66-62	.50-.61-.56
Missouri	F.	(¹)	.29-.29-.29	Pennsylvania	F.	57-61-60	.30-.75-.51
New Hampshire	M.	66-66-66	.45-1.60-.63	Do	M.	58-64-60	.33-.83-.64
Do	F.	66-66-66	.45-.90-.64	Rhode Island	F.	59-60-60	.40-.67-.51
New York	F.	66-66-66	.75-.75-.75	**1887:**			
North Carolina	M.	65-72-68	.30-.40-.36	California	F.	63-63-63	.40-.40-.40
Do	F.	(¹)	.25-.25-.25	Connecticut	M.	(¹)	.80-.87-.84
South Carolina	M.	69-76-70	.30-.40-.38	Do	F.	(¹)	.74-.74-.74
Do	F.	76-76-76	.30-.30-.30	Georgia	F.	66-66-66	.75-.75-.75
1883:				Louisiana	F.	60-60-60	.17-.25-.21
Alabama	M.	(¹)	.40-.67-.50	Massachusetts	F.	60-60-60	.40-1.08-.62
Connecticut	F.	(¹)	.75-.75-.75	Do	M.	60-60-60	.44-.95-.65

¹ Not reported.

TABLE L-1.—*Doffers, cotton goods, 1849-1900, by year and State*—Continued

Year and State	Sex	Hours per week	Rate per day (dollars)	Year and State	Sex	Hours per week	Rate per day (dollars)
1887—Continued.				**1891:**			
New York	F.	57-60-59	0.42-0.83-0.58	Massachusetts	M.	60-60-60	0.44-1.02-0.70
Ohio	F.	60-60-60	.32-.33-.32	Do	F.	60-60-60	.50-1.00-.69
Pennsylvania	F.	60-60-60	.50-.67-.58	New York	M.	(1)	.50-1.00-.59
Rhode Island	M.	60-60-60	1.15-1.35-1.28	Do	F.	60-60-60	.60-.90-.76
Wisconsin	(1)	(1)	.56-.67-.59	**1892:**			
1888:				Maine	M.	60-60-60	.45-1.10-.63
California	F.	63-63-63	.40-.40-.40	Do	F.	60-60-60	.50-1.17-.62
Delaware	M.	(1)	.67-1.00-.83	Massachusetts	M.	58-60-59	.50-1.30-.75
Georgia	M.	66-66-66	.25-.60-.40	Do	F.	58-60-58	.25-1.00-.56
Indiana	F.	60-60-60	.33-.33-.33	New York	F.	60-60-60	.87-.87-.87
Maine	F.	60-60-60	.42-.42-.42	**1893:**			
Massachusetts	M.	60-60-60	.32-1.25-.70	Massachusetts	M.	58-58-58	.55-1.09-.76
Do	F.	60-60-60	.50-1.00-.62	New Jersey	F.	60-60-60	.33-1.00-.67
New Hampshire	M.	60-60-60	.50-.70-.57	**1894:**			
Do	F.	60-60-60	.60-.75-.70	Massachusetts	(1)	(1)	.92-1.17-1.08
New Jersey	F.	60-60-60	.41-.41-.41	Do	M.	58-58-58	.17-1.35-.71
New York	M.	60-60-60	.33-1.25-.54	New York	M.	60-60-60	.60-.65-.63
Do	F.	60-60-60	.25-.75-.48	Do	F.	60-60-60	.39-.70-.56
North Carolina	M.	(1)	.20-.50-.30	North Carolina	M.	69-69-69	.40-.40-.40
Do	F.	(1)	.20-.20-.20	Do	F.	60-60-60	.30-.30-.30
Rhode Island	M.	60-60-60	.50-1.58-.63	Rhode Island	(1)	(1)	.71-2.23-1.29
Do	F.	60-60-60	.35-.46-.38	South Carolina	M.	66-66-66	.30-.30-.30
South Carolina	M.	66-71-68	.20-.50-.33	**1895:**			
Do	(1)	66-66-66	.28-.42-.32	Alabama	M.	60-66-63	.30-.60-.41
Virginia	M.	60-60-60	.35-.75-.48	Georgia	M.	66-66-66	.25-.50-.42
1889:				Kentucky	M.	60-60-60	.40-.60-.49
Connecticut	M.	60-60-60	.58-.80-.63	Louisiana	M.	60-63-62	.25-.80-.43
Georgia	M.	66-66-66	.25-.75-.43	Maine	M.	60-60-60	.35-1.00-.66
Do	F.	66-66-66	.35-.50-.37	Do	F.	60-60-60	.50-1.05-.93
Maine	M.	60-60-60	.25-.80-.55	Massachusetts	M.	58-58-58	.42-1.35-.72
Do	F.	60-60-60	.42-1.00-.69	Do	F.	58-58-58	1.00-1.00-1.00
Do	(1)	60-60-60	.42-.75-.53	Mississippi	M.	60-60-60	.40-.40-.40
Maryland	M.	(1)	.20-.45-.30	New Hampshire	M.	60-60-60	.40-1.16-.82
Do	F.	(1)	.19-.60-.26	Do	F.	60-60-60	.40-1.45-.83
Massachusetts	M.	60-60-60	.30-1.08-.74	New Jersey	M.	58-60-59	.46-.58-.51
Do	F.	60-60-60	.20-1.05-.66	New York	M.	60-60-60	.45-1.50-.80
Mississippi	M.	(1)	.15-.50-.32	Do	F.	60-60-60	.42-.82-.46
New Hampshire	M.	60-60-60	.30-1.05-.73	North Carolina	M.	65-72-69	.25-.40-.34
Do	F.	60-60-60	.25-1.05-.64	Do	F.	66-72-69	.25-.35-.30
Do	(1)	60-60-60	.46-1.17-.66	South Carolina	M.	66-66-66	.25-.50-.37
New Jersey	M.	60-60-60	.42-.50-.43	Do	F.	66-66-66	.25-.25-.25
Do	F.	60-60-60	.50-.50-.50	Tennessee	M.	66-66-66	.25-.55-.34
New York	M.	60-60-60	.50-1.00-.67	Do	F.	66-66-66	.25-.55-.30
Do	F.	60-60-60	.45-.84-.54	Virginia	M.	60-60-60	.50-.50-.50
North Carolina	M.	69-69-69	.40-.40-.40	Do	F.	60-60-60	.29-.33-.30
Pennsylvania	M.	(1)	.75-.84-.79	**1896:**			
Do	F.	(1)	.75-.75-.75	Georgia	M.	63-66-65	.20-.75-.42
Rhode Island	M.	(1)	.46-.83-.66	Do	F.	63-63-63	.35-.35-.35
Do	F.	60-60-60	.35-.80-.55	Indiana	M.	60-60-60	1.35-1.35-1.35
South Carolina	M.	66-69-68	.25-.50-.37	Kentucky	F.	63-63-63	.30-.30-.30
Tennessee	M.	66-66-66	.25-.60-.31	New Hampshire	M.	60-60-60	.45-1.25-.58
Do	F.	66-66-66	.25-.60-.32	Do	F.	60-60-60	.40-.55-.47
Do	(1)	66-66-66	.30-.38-.36	New York	F.	60-60-60	.88-.88-.88
Virginia	M.	(1)	.15-.75-.33	North Carolina	M.	68-69-69	.35-.90-.42
Do	F.	(1)	.25-.60-.48	Do	F.	69-69-69	.40-.40-.40
1890:				Pennsylvania	M.	57-60-59	.30-.79-.48
Alabama	M.	63-69-66	.30-.54-.36	Do	F.	57-60-59	.26-.83-.46
Connecticut	M.	(1)	.64-.74-.68	Rhode Island	M.	60-60-60	.70-1.05-.93
Kentucky	(1)	(1)	.40-.75-.49	Do	F.	60-60-60	.70-.70-.70
Louisiana	M.	(1)	.25-.65-.39	South Carolina	M.	66-66-66	.21-.45-.44
Do	F.	(1)	.40-.40-.40	Tennessee	M.	69-69-69	.30-.30-.30
Massachusetts	M.	60-60-60	.50-1.02-.73	**1897:**			
Do	F.	60-60-60	.50-1.00-.68	Georgia	M.	66-66-66	.40-.40-.40
Mississippi	M.	66-66-66	.33-.45-.39	**1899:**			
New Jersey	M.	60-60-60	.63-.63-.63	Alabama	M.	70-70-70	.35-.35-.35
Do	F.	60-60-60	.50-.50-.50	Georgia	M.	66-66-66	.30-.50-.39
New York	F.	60-60-60	.84-.84-.84	North Carolina	M.	69-69-69	.25-.40-.31
Do	M.		.50-1.00-.57	**1900:**			
North Carolina	M.	66-69-68	.15-.80-.40	Alabama	M.	70-70-70	.35-.35-.35
Do	F.	(1)	.40-.40-.40	Georgia	M.	66-66-66	.35-.50-.44
Tennessee	M.	(1)	.30-.50-.36	North Carolina	M.	69-69-69	.25-.40-.31
Do	F.	(1)	.30-.52-.37				

1 Not reported.

TABLE L–2.—*Doffers, males, cotton goods, 1916–1928, by State and year*

Year	Alabama		Connecticut		Georgia		Maine	
	Hours per week	Rate per hour	Hours per week	Rate per hour	Hours per week	Rate per hour	Hours per week	Rate per hour
1916	60.2	$0.131	55.0	$0.168	60.0	$0.124	58.0	$0.158
1918	58.8	.189	51.4	.248	59.7	.213	53.8	.278
1920	58.6	.356	49.1	.444	55.9	.437	53.2	.429
1922	55.7	.228	51.6	.318	56.0	.259	53.5	.382
1924	55.6	.255	52.5	.369	56.1	.283	54.0	.358
1926	54.5	.263	52.3	.323	56.9	.282	54.0	.316
1928	55.0	.264	51.6	.340	56.3	.282	54.0	.352

Year	Massachusetts		New Hampshire		New York		North Carolina	
	Hours per week	Rate per hour	Hours per week	Rate per hour	Hours per week	Rate per hour	Hours per week	Rate per hour
1916	53.3	$0.183	55.0	$0.184	54.8	$0.194	60.0	$0.104
1918	52.7	.278	53.4	.301	54.4	.288	56.6	.191
1920	47.9	.519	47.8	.506	49.5	.511	53.7	.468
1922	48.3	.403	53.2	.422	50.4	.380	54.5	.279
1924	48.9	.472	54.0	.459	49.9	.466	55.4	.310
1926	48.5	.414	52.9	.446	49.4	.426	55.9	.282
1928	49.6	.395	53.9	.406	48.7	.439	56.0	.289

Year	Pennsylvania		Rhode Island		South Carolina		Virginia	
	Hours per week	Rate per hour	Hours per week	Rate per hour	Hours per week	Rate per hour	Hours per week	Rate per hour
1916			54.0	$0.197	60.0	$0.100		
1918			53.7	.337	58.1	.188		
1920			49.8	.569	54.2	.445	54.3	$0.382
1922	53.1	$0.266	49.3	.419	54.9	.245	54.3	.311
1924	52.9	.389	50.9	.470	55.0	.262	55.3	.362
1926	52.7	.436	49.7	.381	55.0	.260	55.3	.287
1928			52.6	.409	55.0	.270	54.7	.300

TABLE L–3.—*Doffers, females, cotton goods, 1916–1928, by State and year*

Year	Connecticut		Maine		Massachusetts	
	Hours per week	Rate per hour	Hours per week	Rate per hour	Hours per week	Rate per hour
1916			58.0	$0.150	52.2	$0.168
1918			53.2	.254	51.9	.258
1920			53.7	.372	47.1	.423
1922	52.4	$0.285	54.0	.295	47.7	.344
1924	50.8	.379	53.9	.338	47.9	.428
1926			53.8	.304	48.0	.382
1928			54.0	.272	48.0	.377

Year	New Hampshire		New York		North Carolina	
	Hours per week	Rate per hour	Hours per week	Rate per hour	Hours per week	Rate per hour
1916	55.0	$0.179				
1918	54.0	.273				
1920	48.0	.418				
1922	53.1	.357				
1924	54.0	.394			55.0	$0.235
1926	54.0	.334	48.0	$0.385	55.0	.314
1928	53.4	.342			55.0	.271

Year	Pennsylvania		Rhode Island		South Carolina	
	Hours per week	Rate per hour	Hours per week	Rate per hour	Hours per week	Rate per hour
1916	53.7	$0.126				
1918	53.7	.168				
1920	50.8	.269				
1922	51.6	.259				
1924	51.5	.345	48.0	$0.453	55.0	$0.264
1926	53.2	.409			55.0	.236
1928					55.0	.247

Table L-4.—*Drawers-in, cotton goods, 1842-1897, by year and State*

Year and State	Sex	Hours per week	Rate per day (dollars)	Year and State	Sex	Hours per week	Rate per day (dollars)
1842:				**1865:**			
Massachusetts____	F.	78–78–78	0.40–0.45–0.43	Connecticut_____	F.	66–66–66	1.25–1.25–1.25
1843:				Massachusetts____	F.	66–72–70	.50–.86–.68
Massachusetts____	F.	78–78–78	.45–.45–.42	New York_____	F.	72–72–72	1.00–1.00–1.00
1844:				Rhode Island_____	F.	78–78–78	1.04–1.04–1.04
Massachusetts____	F.	78–78–78	.42–.44–.42	**1866:**			
1845:				Connecticut_____	F.	66–66–66	1.38–1.38–1.38
Massachusetts____	F.	78–78–78	.42–.46–.43	Massachusetts____	F.	66–72–70	.67–1.12–.88
1846:				New York_____	F.	72–72–72	1.10–1.10–1.10
Massachusetts____	F.	78–78–78	.42–.50–.44	**1867:**			
1847:				Connecticut_____	F.	66–66–66	.50–1.50–1.50
Massachusetts____	F.	78–78–78	.42–.45–.43	Georgia_____	F.	66–66–66	.65–.65–.65
1848:				Massachusetts____	F.	66–72–70	.67–1.30–1.03
Massachusetts____	F.	75–78–77	.40–.82–.51	New Hampshire__	F.	66–66–66	.79–.79–.79
1849:				New York_____	F.	72–72–72	1.20–1.20–1.20
Massachusetts____	F.	75–78–77	.34–.83–.53	**1868:**			
1850:				Connecticut_____	F.	66–66–66	1.25–1.25–1.25
Massachusetts____	F.	75–78–77	.34–.85–.60	Massachusetts____	F.	66–66–66	.67–1.28–.98
Rhode Island_____	F.	84–84–84	1.00–1.00–1.00	New York_____	F.	66–66–66	1.25–1.25–1.25
1851:				**1869:**			
Massachusetts____	F.	75–78–76	.38–.80–.61	Connecticut_____	F.	66–66–66	1.25–1.25–1.25
Rhode Island_____	F.	84–84–84	1.00–1.00–1.00	Massachusetts____	F.	66–66–66	.67–1.23–.98
1852:				New York_____	F.	66–66–66	1.30–1.30–1.30
Massachusetts____	F.	75–78–77	.30–.85–.57	**1870:**			
Rhode Island_____	M.	84–84–84	1.50–1.50–1.50	Connecticut_____	F.	66–66–66	1.25–1.25–1.25
1853:				Massachusetts____	F.	66–66–66	.62–1.23–.95
Massachusetts____	F.	75–78–77	.38–.84–.54	New York_____	F.	66–66–66	1.20–1.20–1.20
New York_____	F.	72–72–72	.50–.50–.50	**1871:**			
Rhode Island_____	F.	84–84–84	1.04–1.04–1.04	Connecticut_____	F.	66–66–66	1.25–1.25–1.25
1854:				Massachusetts____	F.	66–66–66	.62–1.15–.88
Massachusetts____	F.	66–78–75	.38–.72–.52	New York_____	F.	66–66–66	1.10–1.10–1.10
New York_____	F.	72–72–72	.80–.80–.80	**1872:**			
Rhode Island_____	F.	84–84–84	1.04–1.04–1.04	Connecticut_____	F.	66–66–66	1.25–1.25–1.25
1855:				Massachusetts____	F.	66–66–66	.62–1.31–1.01
Massachusetts____	F.	66–78–75	.30–.85–.57	New York_____	F.	66–66–66	1.20–1.20–1.20
New York_____	F.	72–72–72	.70–.70–.70	**1873:**			
Rhode Island_____	F.	84–84–84	1.04–1.04–1.04	Connecticut_____	F.	66–66–66	1.25–1.30–1.28
1856:				Massachusetts____	F.	66–66–66	.58–1.24–.95
Massachusetts____	F.	66–66–66	.84–.84–.84	New York_____	F.	66–66–66	1.30–1.30–1.30
New York_____	F.	72–72–72	.65–.65–.65	**1874:**			
Rhode Island_____	F.	84–84–84	1.04–1.04–1.04	Connecticut_____	F.	66–66–66	1.00–1.38–1.26
1857:				Massachusetts____	F.	66–66–66	.58–1.29–.94
Massachusetts____	F.	66–66–66	.84–.84–.84	New York_____	F.	66–66–66	1.08–1.08–1.08
New York_____	F.	72–72–72	.65–.65–.65	**1875:**			
Rhode Island_____	F.	84–84–84	1.04–1.04–1.04	Connecticut_____	F.	66–66–66	1.00–1.25–1.11
1858:				Massachusetts____	F.	60–60–60	.58–1.56–1.00
Massachusetts____	F.	66–78–73	.42–.86–.64	Do_____	M.	(¹)	1.26–1.26–1.26
New York_____	F.	72–72–72	.60–.60–.60	New York_____	F.	66–66–66	1.20–1.20–1.20
Rhode Island_____	F.	84–84–84	1.04–1.04–1.04	**1876:**			
1859:				Connecticut_____	F.	66–66–66	1.00–1.20–1.10
Connecticut_____	F.	72–72–72	.58–.58–.58	Massachusetts____	F.	60–60–60	.58–1.43–.94
Maine_____	F.	(¹)	.50–.50–.50	New Hampshire__	F.	66–66–66	1.00–1.00–1.00
Massachusetts____	F.	66–78–74	.38–.84–.58	New York_____	F.	66–66–66	1.05–1.05–1.05
New York_____	F.	72–72–72	.65–.65–.65	Pennsylvania_____	M.	(¹)	1.83–1.83–1.83
Rhode Island_____	F.	84–84–84	1.00–1.00–1.00	Do_____	F.	(¹)	.66–.89–.82
1860:				South Carolina____	F.	66–66–66	.50–.60–.55
Massachusetts____	F.	66–78–74	.40–.80–.57	**1877:**			
New York_____	F.	72–72–72	.62–.62–.62	Connecticut_____	F.	66–66–66	1.12–1.25–1.19
Pennsylvania_____	M.	60–60–60	.50–1.20–.90	Georgia_____	F.	66–66–66	.40–1.00–.77
Rhode Island_____	F.	78–78–78	1.00–1.00–1.00	Maine_____	F.	66–66–66	.58–1.12–.83
1861:				Massachusetts____	F.	60–60–60	.50–1.37–.85
Connecticut_____	F.	72–72–72	.62–.62–.62	New York_____	F.	66–66–66	.80–.80–.80
Massachusetts____	F.	66–78–74	.30–.80–.57	**1878:**			
New York_____	F.	72–72–72	.60–.60–.60	Connecticut_____	F.	66–66–66	1.10–1.52–1.38
Rhode Island_____	F.	78–78–78	1.00–1.00–1.00	Massachusetts____	F.	60–60–60	.50–1.36–.86
1862:				New Hampshire__	M.	60–60–60	.75–.90–.83
Connecticut_____	F.	72–72–72	.74–.74–.74	Do_____	F.	60–60–60	.50–.90–.70
Massachusetts____	F.	66–72–70	.40–.94–.63	New York_____	F.	66–66–66	.85–.85–.85
New York_____	F.	72–72–72	.50–.50–.50	**1879:**			
Rhode Island_____	F.	78–78–78	1.04–1.04–1.04	Connecticut_____	F.	66–66–66	1.48–1.48–1.48
1863:				Massachusetts____	F.	60–60–60	.45–1.42–.88
Connecticut_____	F.	72–72–72	.74–.74–.74	New York_____	F.	66–66–66	.86–.86–.86
Massachusetts____	F.	66–72–69	.40–.86–.69	Pennsylvania_____	F.	(¹)	.75–.75–.75
Rhode Island_____	F.	78–78–78	1.04–1.04–1.04	Do_____	F.	60–60–60	1.75–1.75–1.75
1864:				**1880:**			
Connecticut_____	F.	72–72–72	.83–.83–.83	Connecticut_____	F.	66–66–66	1.53–1.53–1.53
Massachusetts____	F.	66–72–70	.44–.82–.66	Georgia_____	F.	66–69–67	.45–.90–.62
Rhode Island_____	F.	78–78–78	1.04–1.04–1.04	Maine_____	F.	(¹)	1.00–1.00–1.00

¹ Not reported.

TABLE L-4.—*Drawers-in, cotton goods, 1842-1897, by year and State—Con.*

Year and State	Sex	Lowest, highest, and average— Hours per week	Lowest, highest, and average— Rate per day (dollars)
1880—Continued.			
Massachusetts....	F.	60-60-60	0.45-1.50-0.95
Do.	(¹)	80-63-61	.75-1.00-.90
New Hampshire..	(¹)	66-66-66	1.00-1.00-1.00
New York	F.	66-66-66	.90-.90-.90
Rhode Island	(¹)	66-66-66	1.17-1.17-1.17
Virginia	F.	68-68-68	.55-.55-.55
1881:			
Connecticut	F.	66-66-66	1.83-1.83-1.83
Georgia	F.	66-66-66	.75-1.00-.88
Massachusetts	F.	60-60-60	.45-1.35-.95
New Hampshire	M.	65-65-65	1.55-1.56-1.55
Do.	F.	65-65-65	.60-1.44-1.00
New York	F.	66-66-66	1.05-1.05-1.05
South Carolina	F.	72-72-72	.50-.50-.50
1882:			
Connecticut	F.	66-66-66	1.63-1.63-1.63
Georgia	F.	72-72-72	.75-.90-.84
Massachusetts	F.	60-60-60	.45-1.22-.88
New Hampshire	F.	66-66-66	.51-1.56-.97
New York	F.	66-66-66	1.17-1.17-1.17
North Carolina	M.	65-65-65	.58-.58-.50
Do.	F.	72-72-72	.60-.60-.60
South Carolina	F.	69-69-69	.75-.80-.79
1883:			
Alabama	F.	(¹)	.72-.94-.82
Connecticut	F.	66-66-66	2.32-2.32-2.32
Georgia	F.	66-69-68	.83-1.10-.99
Massachusetts	M.	(¹)	1.05-1.05-1.05
Do.	F.	60-60-60	.40-1.46-.97
Mississippi	F.	(¹)	.78-.84-.81
New York	F.	66-66-66	.90-.90-.90
Tennessee	F.	66-66-66	.40-.55-.50
1884:			
Connecticut	F.	66-66-66	2.02-2.02-2.02
Georgia	M.	70-70-70	.75-.75-.75
Do.	F.	66-70-69	.67-1.00-.80
Kentucky	F.	66-66-66	.40-.55-.47
Louisiana	F.	63-66-64	.75-1.06-.92
Massachusetts	F.	60-60-60	.45-1.33-.94
New Hampshire	F.	60-60-60	.61-1.09-.89
New York	F.	66-66-66	.94-.94-.94
North Carolina	M.	72-72-72	.55-.55-.55
Do.	F.	69-69-69	.40-.40-.40
Rhode Island	F.	(¹)	1.17-1.17-1.17
South Carolina	M.	69-69-69	.67-.67-.67
Do.	F.	(¹)	.85-.85-.85
1885:			
Alabama	M.	63-63-63	.90-.90-.90
Do.	F.	(¹)	.49-.71-.60
Connecticut	F.	66-69-67	1.15-1.70-1.49
Delaware	M.	60-60-60	.50-1.25-.88
Georgia	F.	69-69-69	.55-.55-.55
Indiana	M.	66-66-66	.92-.92-.92
Maine	F.	66-66-66	.50-.84-.66
Maryland	F.	66-66-66	.50-1.32-1.00
Massachusetts...	F.	60-60-60	.75-.75-.75
Do.	F.	60-60-60	.45-1.37-.87
New Hampshire..	M.	60-60-60	.75-.75-.75
Do.	F.	66-66-66	.81-1.16-.93
New York	M.	60-66-65	.50-1.50-.92
Do.	F.	60-66-62	.42-1.40-.76
North Carolina...	M.	66-69-69	.40-.75-.67
Do.	F.	(¹)	.70-.70-.70
Rhode Island	F.	60-60-60	1.00-1.00-1.00
Tennessee	F.	66-66-66	1.00-1.00-1.00
Vermont	F.	66-66-66	.90-.90-.90
Virginia	F.	66-66-66	.75-1.10-.93
1886:			
Connecticut	F.	66-66-66	1.44-1.44-1.44
Indiana	F.	60-60-60	.25-.25-.25
Iowa	F.	60-60-60	.75-.75-.75
Massachusetts...	F.	60-60-60	.65-1.24-.98
New Hampshire..	F.	60-60-60	.43-1.19-.82
1886—Continued.			
New York	F.	66-66-66	0.84-0.84-0.84
Pennsylvania	M.	60-60-60	1.83-2.00-1.96
Do.	F.	60-60-60	1.17-1.17-1.17
Rhode Island	F.	60-60-60	1.00-1.33-1.17
1887:			
Connecticut	M.		.83-.83-.83
Do.	F.	60-60-60	.91-1.40-.96
Georgia	F.	66-72-67	.46-.83-.65
Louisiana	F.	60-60-60	.67-.75-.71
Massachusetts...	F.	60-60-60	.50-1.22-.93
New York	F.	57-60-60	.70-1.00-.81
Wisconsin	(¹)	(¹)	.75-.95-.93
1888:			
California	M.	(¹)	1.00-1.00-1.00
Connecticut	M.	(¹)	.75-.75-.75
Do.	F.	60-60-60	1.12-1.78-1.46
Delaware	M.	(¹)	.58-.83-.71
Georgia	F.	66-71-66	.22-1.20-.66
Do.	M.	66-66-66	.15-.80-.48
Do.	(¹)	(¹)	.32-.32-.32
Maine	F.	60-60-60	.86-.90-.88
Massachusetts...	F.	60-60-60	.50-1.12-.89
New Hampshire	M.	(¹)	.78-.78-.78
New Jersey	F.	(¹)	1.67-1.67-1.67
New York	F.	60-60-60	.46-1.00-.85
Do.	M.	(¹)	.90-1.19-1.10
North Carolina	M.	(¹)	1.75-1.75-1.75
Pennsylvania	F.	(¹)	.42-.42-.42
Rhode Island	M.	60-60-60	.70-.70-.70
Do.	F.	60-60-60	1.00-1.93-1.41
Virginia	F.	60-60-60	.75-1.54-1.07
1889:			
California	M.	(¹)	.90-1.25-1.13
Connecticut	M.	60-60-60	1.95-1.95-1.95
Do.	F.	60-60-60	.50-1.70-1.23
Georgia	F.	66-66-66	.55-.55-.55
Maine	M.	(¹)	.50-.53-.51
Do.	F.	60-60-60	.45-1.50-.95
Do.	(¹)	56-60-56	.84-.94-.85
Maryland	M.	(¹)	.37-.84-.59
Do.	F.	(¹)	.24-.60-.35
Massachusetts...	F.	60-60-60	.50-1.15-.89
Missouri	F.	(¹)	.84-.84-.84
New Hampshire	M.	60-60-60	.97-1.30-1.15
Do.	F.	60-60-60	.39-1.19-.76
New York	F.	60-60-60	.65-1.90-1.02
North Carolina	M.	69-69-69	.75-.75-.75
Rhode Island	M.	(¹)	.70-1.30-1.12
Do.	F.	60-60-60	.50-1.76-1.11
South Carolina	F.	66-66-66	.78-.78-.78
Tennessee	M.	66-66-66	.80-.80-.80
Do.	F.	66-66-66	.90-.90-.90
Do.	(¹)	66-66-66	.85-.85-.85
Virginia	M.	(¹)	.60-.60-.60
Do.	F.	(¹)	.55-.65-.59
1890:			
Alabama	F.	63-69-66	.90-1.67-1.15
Connecticut	M.	(¹)	1.25-1.25-1.25
Do.	F.	60-60-60	1.25-1.92-1.41
Kentucky	(¹)	66-66-66	.80-.80-.80
Louisiana	M.	(¹)	1.25-1.25-1.25
Maine	F.	60-60-60	1.00-1.42-1.17
Massachusetts	F.	60-60-60	.50-1.25-.93
Mississippi	F.	66-66-66	.90-.90-.90
Missouri	F.	(¹)	.50-1.25-.82
New Hampshire..	F.	60-60-60	1.50-1.60-1.53
New Jersey	F.	60-60-60	.50-.60-.54
New York	F.	60-60-60	.60-.97-.88
Do.	M.	(¹)	.95-1.00-.99
North Carolina...	F.	69-69-69	.40-.80-.62
Do.	(¹)	(¹)	.60-.60-.60
Rhode Island	F.	(¹)	1.38-1.74-1.54
Tennessee	F.	69-69-69	1.18-1.18-1.18

¹ Not reported.

TABLE L-4.—*Drawers-in, cotton goods, 1842-1897, by year and State—*Con.

Year and State	Sex	Lowest, highest, and average—		Year and State	Sex	Lowest, highest, and average—	
		Hours per week	Rate per day (dollars)			Hours per week	Rate per day (dollars)
1891:				**1895—Continued.**			
Connecticut	F.	60-60-60	1.75-1.94-1.91	Maine	M.	60-60-60	0.58-1.96-0.89
Maine	F.	60-60-60	1.00-1.00-1.00	Do	F.	60-60-60	.67-1.28-1.01
Massachusetts	F.	60-60-60	.50-1.25-.89	Massachusetts	M.	58-58-58	.70-.70-.70
New Jersey	F.	60-60-60	.90-1.00-.93	Do	F.	58-58-58	.87-1.69-1.19
New York	F.	60-60-60	.67-1.00-.84	Mississippi	F.	60-60-60	.68-.98-.83
Do	M.	(¹)	.42-1.00-.67	New Hampshire	M.	60-60-60	.90-1.45-1.20
1892:				Do	F.	60-60-60	.45-1.71-.97
Connecticut	F.	60-60-60	1.15-2.12-1.67	New York	M.	60-60-60	1.00-1.00-1.00
Maine	M.	60-60-60	.85-.91-.90	Do	F.	60-60-60	.44-1.00-.66
Do	F.	60-60-60	.67-1.25-.95	North Carolina	M.	65-72-68	.40-.85-.68
Massachusetts	M.	58-60-58	.85-1.23-1.20	Do	F.	66-72-69	.25-.83-.62
Do	F.	58-60-68	1.00-1.22-1.12	Pennsylvania	M.	60-60-60	1.95-2.75-2.30
New York	F.	60-60-60	.90-.92-.91	Rhode Island	F.	60-60-60	.67-1.08-1.04
1893:				South Carolina	M.	66-66-66	.40-1.25-.67
Massachusetts	M.	58-58-58	.73-.73-.73	Do	F.	66-76-66	.40-.85-.77
New Jersey	F.	60-60-60	.67-1.00-.82	Tennessee	M.	66-66-66	.50-.50-.50
New York	F.	60-60-60	.72-.78-.75	Do	F.	66-66-66	.40-1.05-.52
Ohio	F.	60-60-60	.83-.83-.83	Virginia	F.	60-80-60	.55-.55-.55
1894:				**1896:**			
Indiana	(¹)	60-60-60	.91-.91-.91	Georgia	M.	66-66-66	.75-1.50-1.05
Massachusetts	M.	58-58-58	.70-.70-.70	Do	F.	66-66-66	.45-1.25-.74
New York	M.	60-66-62	.75-2.25-1.40	Indiana	M.	60-60-60	1.00-1.25-1.13
Do	F.	60-60-60	.50-.66-.58	Do	F.	60-65-64	.58-.97-.78
North Carolina	M.	60-66-63	.80-.80-.80	Iowa	F.	60-60-60	.70-.70-.70
Ohio	F.	60-66-60	.83-.83-.83	Kentucky	F.	60-60-60	.40-.50-.44
Rhode Island	(¹)	(¹)	.90-1.20-1.06	Minnesota	F.	60-60-60	1.10-1.10-1.10
South Carolina	M.	66-66-66	.55-.55-.88	New Hampshire	F.	60-60-60	.50-1.37-.89
Do	F.	66-66-66	1.00-1.00-1.00	New York	F.	60-60-60	.69-.84-.77
1895:				North Carolina	M.	69-69-69	.45-.48-.46
Alabama	M.	63-63-63	1.00-1.00-1.00	Do	F.	68-69-69	.40-.75-.60
Do	F.	60-66-62	.20-1.00-.55	Pennsylvania	M.	60-60-60	1.83-2.00-1.92
Connecticut	F.	60-60-60	.42-.83-.58	Do	F.	60-60-60	.42-1.00-.78
Georgia	F.	66-66-66	.35-1.20-.88	South Carolina	F.	66-66-66	.65-.83-.73
Louisiana	F.	60-63-62	;74-1.23-.97	**1897:**			
				Georgia	F.	66-66-66	.40-.80-.67

¹ Not reported.

TABLE L-5.—*Drawers-in, females, cotton goods, 1916-1928, by State and year*

Year	Alabama		Connecticut		Georgia		Maine	
	Hours per week	Rate per hour	Hours per week	Rate per hour	Hours per week	Rate per hour	Hours per week	Rate per hour
1916	60.3	$0.123	55.0	$0.232	60.0	$0.131	58.0	$0.180
1918	60.2	.162	54.'5	.326	60.0	.169	54.0	.308
1920	57.3	.294	48.7	.612	56.8	.402	54.0	.483
1922	55.4	.184	52.5	.451	56.7	.268	54.0	.396
1924	55.8	.199	52.3	.389	55.3	.270	54.0	.388
1926	55.0	.208	51.7	.427	55.3	.269	54.0	.364
1928	55.0	.216	52.7	.407	55.2	.284	54.0	.339

Year	Massachusetts		New Hampshire		New York		North Carolina	
1916	53.9	$0.215	55.0	$0.214	---------	---------	60.0	$0.128
1918	53.7	.303	54.0	.312	---------	---------	60.0	.200
1920	47.9	.525	48.0	.585	48.2	$0.558	55.4	.465
1922	48.0	.419	53.3	.419	49.1	.420	55.4	.297
1924	47.9	.453	54.0	.482	48.1	.495	55.2	.322
1926	48.0	.448	54.0	.364	48.0	.439	55.3	.323
1928	48.0	.417	53.9	.369	48.6	.375	55.3	.328

Year	Pennsylvania		Rhode Island		South Carolina		Virginia	
1916	54.0	$0.172	54.0	$0.213	60.0	$0.135	---------	---------
1918	54.0	.209	54.0	.280	59.6	.179	---------	---------
1920	51.1	.325	49.6	.457	54.6	.403	55.7	$0.368
1922	51.3	.256	48.0	.342	54.8	.219	55.3	.328
1924	52.8	.296	48.9	.457	55.0	.252	55.3	.427
1926	52.5	.320	48.4	.435	55.0	.232	55.3	.302
1928	---------	---------	51.9	.479	55.0	.266	55.2	.312

TABLE L-6.—*Drawing-frame tenders, cotton goods, 1849–1897, by year and State*

Year and State	Sex	Hours per week	Rate per day (dollars)	Year and State	Sex	Hours per week	Rate per day (dollars)
1849:				**1875:**			
Massachusetts....	F.	75-75-75	0.47-0.47-0.47	Massachusetts....	F.	60-60-60	0.75-0.75-0.75
1850:				New York........	F.	66-66-66	.67-.67-.67
Massachusetts....	F.	75-75-75	.47-.47-.47	**1876:**			
1851:				Massachusetts....	F.	60-60-60	.75-.75-.75
Massachusetts....	F.	75-75-75	.47-.47-.47	New York........	F.	66-66-66	.59-.59-.59
1852:				Pennsylvania....	M.	(1)	.40-.83-.54
Massachusetts....	F.	72-75-73	.46-.47-.46	Do........	F.	(1)	.50-1.75-.82
1853:				South Carolina....	F.	66-66-66	.50-.50-.50
Massachusetts....	F.	72-75-73	.45-.50-.48	**1877:**			
New York........	F.	72-72-72	.42-.42-.42	Georgia........	M.	66-66-66	.65-.65-.65
1854:				Massachusetts....	F.	60-60-60	.67-.67-.67
Massachusetts....	M.	66-66-66	.45-.45-.45	New York........	F.	66-66-66	.54-.54-.54
Do........	F.	72-72-72	.54-.54-.54	**1878:**			
New York........	F.	72-72-72	.42-.42-.42	Massachusetts....	F.	60-60-60	.67-.67-.67
1855:				New Hampshire..	M.	60-60-60	.83-.83-.83
Massachusetts....	F.	66-72-70	.45-.58-.53	Do........	F.	60-60-60	.48-.92-.73
New York........	F.	72-72-72	.42-.42-.42	New York........	F.	66-66-66	.54-.54-.54
1856:				North Carolina..	F.	72-72-72	.50-.50-.50
Massachusetts....	F.	66-66-66	.49-.49-.49	Pennsylvania....	F.	60-66-62	.70-1.08-.84
New York........	F.	72-72-72	.42-.42-.42	**1879:**			
1857:				Massachusetts....	F.	60-60-60	.67-.67-.67
Massachusetts....	F.	66-66-66	.49-.49-.49	New York........	F.	66-66-66	.54-.54-.54
New York........	F.	72-72-72	.46-.46-.46	Pennsylvania....	M.	60-60-60	.60-.75-.61
1858:				Do........	F.	66-66-66	.60-.60-.60
Massachusetts....	F.	66-66-66	.49-.49-.49	**1880:**			
New York........	F.	72-72-72	.38-.38-.38	Georgia........	M.	(1)	.75-.75-.75
1859:				Massachusetts....	F.	60-60-60	.67-.67-.67
Massachusetts....	F.	66-66-66	.49-.49-.49	New York........	F.	66-66-66	.67-.67-.67
New York........	F.	72-72-72	.44-.44-.44	**1881:**			
1860:				Massachusetts....	F.	60-60-60	.80-.80-.80
Massachusetts....	F.	66-66-66	.49-.49-.49	New Hampshire..	M.	65-65-65	1.05-2.00-1.27
New York........	F.	72-72-72	.42-.42-.42	Do........	F.	65-65-65	.61-1.15-.87
1861:				New York........	F.	66-66-66	.73-.73-.73
Massachusetts....	F.	66-66-66	.50-.50-.50	North Carolina..	F.	(1)	.40-.40-.40
New York........	F.	72-72-72	.42-.42-.42	Rhode Island....	F.	66-66-66	.80-.80-.80
1862:				**1882:**			
Massachusetts....	F.	66-66-66	.50-.50-.50	Georgia........	M.	70-70-70	.75-.75-.75
New York........	F.	72-72-72	.42-.42-.42	Massachusetts....	F.	60-60-60	.85-.85-.85
1863:				New Hampshire..	M.	66-66-66	1.26-1.26-1.26
Massachusetts....	F.	66-66-66	.50-.50-.50	Do........	F.	66-66-66	1.01-1.31-1.22
1864:				New Jersey........	M.	66-66-66	2.00-2.00-2.00
Massachusetts....	F.	66-66-66	.55-.55-.55	Do........	(1)	60-60-60	.60-.60-.60
1865:				New York........	F.	66-66-66	.73-.73-.73
Massachusetts....	F.	66-66-66	.65-.65-.65	North Carolina..	M.	(1)	.25-.25-.25
New York........	F.	72-72-72	.59-.59-.59	Do........	F.	(1)	.45-.45-.45
1866:				South Carolina..	M.	69-69-69	.40-.50-.47
Massachusetts....	F.	66-66-66	.80-.80-.80	Do........	F.	69-69-69	.40-.70-.62
New York........	F.	72-72-72	.59-.59-.59	**1883:**			
1867:				Alabama........	M.	(1)	.58-.58-.58
Massachusetts....	F.	66-66-66	.85-.85-.85	Georgia........	M.	(1)	.65-.75-.69
New York........	F.	72-72-72	.67-.67-.67	Do........	F.	66-66-66	.60-.75-.65
1868:				Massachusetts....	F.	60-60-60	.85-1.42-.99
Massachusetts....	F.	66-66-66	.82-.82-.82	New Jersey........	M.	60-60-60	.83-.83-.83
New York........	F.	66-66-66	.67-.67-.67	Do........	F.	60-60-60	.33-.67-.42
1869:				New York........	F.	66-66-66	.67-.67-.67
Massachusetts....	F.	66-66-66	.82-.82-.82	North Carolina..	M.	(1)	.45-.45-.45
New York........	F.	66-66-66	.67-.67-.67	South Carolina..	M.	70-70-70	.75-.75-.75
1870:				Do........	F.	70-70-70	.75-.75-.75
Massachusetts....	F.	66-66-66	.82-.92-.83	**1884:**			
New York........	F.	66-66-66	.75-.75-.75	Georgia........	F.	66-70-69	.50-.70-.65
1871:				Louisiana........	M.	66-66-66	.50-.60-.53
Massachusetts....	F.	66-66-66	.82-.82-.82	Do........	F.	63-63-63	.42-.50-.46
New York........	F.	66-66-66	.75-.75-.75	Massachusetts....	M.	60-60-60	.65-.80-.74
1872:				Do........	F.	60-60-60	.75-.80-.76
Massachusetts....	F.	66-66-66	.82-.82-.82	New York........	F.	66-66-66	.67-.67-.67
New York........	F.	66-66-66	.71-.71-.71	North Carolina..	F.	69-69-69	.40-.40-.40
1873:				South Carolina..	M.	69-69-69	.75-.75-.75
Massachusetts....	F.	66-66-66	.82-.82-.82	**1885:**			
New York........	F.	66-66-66	.75-.75-.75	Georgia........	F.	69-69-69	.58-.72-.66
1874:				Maine........	F.	66-66-66	1.00-1.00-1.00
Massachusetts....	F.	66-66-66	.82-.82-.82	Do........	M.	66-66-66	.80-.80-.80
New York........	F.	66-66-66	.67-.67-.67	Massachusetts....	M.	60-60-60	1.00-1.00-1.00
Pennsylvania....	F.	(1)	1.13-1.13-1.13	Do........	F.	60-60-60	.42-1.00-.89

1 Not reported.

TABLE **L-6.**—*Drawing-frame tenders, cotton goods, 1849–1897, by year and State*— Continued

Year and State	Sex	Hours per week	Rate per day (dollars)
1885—Continued.			
New Hampshire..	F.	65-65-65	1.00-1.16-1.15
New York........	F.	66-66-66	.61-1.25-1.10
1886:			
Massachusetts....	F.	60-60-60	.76-ʳ.76-.76
New Hampshire....	F.	60-60-60	.51-1.29-.82
New Jersey.......	F.	58-60-60	.67-1.00-.85
New York........	F.	66-66-66	.61-.61-.61
Pennsylvania.....	F.	60-64-60	.71-1.25-.93
1887:			
Massachusetts....	M.	(1)	.68-.68-.68
Do........	F.	60-60-60	.68-1.21-.92
New York........	F.	60-60-60	.50-.61-.59
Wisconsin.......	(1)	(1)	.67-.67-.67
1888:			
California........	F.	66-66-66	1.00-1.00-1.00
Georgia...........	M.	(1)	.60-.75-.67
Do...........	F.	(1)	.65-.75-.66
Do...........	(1)	(1)	.45-.90-.72
Massachusetts....	M.	60-60-60	.72-.75-.74
Do...........	F.	60-60-60	.55-1.17-.77
New York........	F.	60-60-60	.61-1.00-.78
Do...........	M.	(1)	.83-.83-.83
North Carolina...	F.	(1)	.50-.50-.50
Rhode Island.....	M.	(1)	.83-1.04-.89
Do...........	F.	60-60-60	.90-.90-.90
South Carolina...	M.	66-71-67	.25-.65-.41
Do...........	F.	66-71-67	.40-.65-.55
Do...........	(1)	66-66-66	.45-.60-.53
Virginia.........	F.	(1)	.35-.85-.58
1889:			
Connecticut......	M.	60-60-60	.63-.84-.70
Georgia..........	M.	66-66-66	.60-.75-.62
Do...........	F.	66-66-66	.60-.65-.61
Maine...........	M.	60-60-60	.50-1.00-.64
Do...........	F.	(1)	.63-1.00-.74
Maryland........	M.	(1)	.25-.64-.50
Massachusetts....	M.	60-60-60	.50-2.00-.79
Do...........	F.	60-60-60	.50-1.20-.73
Mississippi......	M.	(1)	.75-.75-.75
New Hampshire..	M.	(1)	.70-.75-.70
Do...........	F.	60-60-60	.60-.97-.81
Do...........	(1)	60-60-60	.67-.67-.67
New Jersey.......	F.	60-60-60	.92-.92-.92
New York........	M.	(1)	1.00-1.00-1.00
Do...........	F.	60-60-60	.60-.80-.73
North Carolina...	F.	69-69-69	.50-.60-.53
Pennsylvania.....	M.	(1)	.75-.75-.75
Do...........	F.	(1)	.75-.97-.91
Rhode Island.....	M.	(1)	.67-.79-.74
Do...........	F.	60-60-60	.79-1.17-1.00
South Carolina...	M.	69-69-69	.20-.60-.41
Do...........	F.	66-66-66	.60-.60-.60
Tennessee........	M.	(1)	.40-.40-.40
Do...........	F.	66-66-66	.50-.91-.59
Virginia.........	M.	(1)	.52-.52-.52
Do...........	F.	(1)	.46-.60-.55
1890:			
Alabama.........	M.	63-69-66	.40-.90-.64
Do...........	F.	66-67-66	.50-.90-.57
Connecticut......	M.	(1)	.67-.67-.67
Do...........	F.	(1)	.67-1.14-1.12
Kentucky........	(1)	66-66-66	.50-.50-.50
Louisiana........	F.	(1)	.45-.55-.51
Massachusetts....	F.	60-60-60	.80-.80-.80
Mississippi........	M.	(1)	.40-.50-.46
1890—Continued.			
Mississippi........	F.	(1)	0.40-0.40-0.40
Do...........	(1)	66-66-66	.40-.50-.47
New York........	F.	60-60-60	.67-.67-.67
Do...........	M.	(1)	.54-1.00-.69
North Carolina...	M.	66-69-68	.35-1.00-.62
Do...........	F.	69-69-69	.70-.75-.73
Pennsylvania.....	M.	60-60-60	.75-.75-.75
Do...........	F.	60-60-60	.75-1.08-.89
Tennessee........	M.	(1)	.50-.65-.58
Do...........	F.	69-69-69	.50-.60-.57
1891:			
Massachusetts....	F.	60-60-60	.80-.80-.80
New York........	F.	60-60-60	.71-.71-.71
Do...........	M.	(1)	.54-1.12-.89
North Carolina...	(1)	71-71-71	.40-.40-.40
1892:			
Maine...........	M.	60-60-60	.58-.75-.67
Do...........	F.	60-60-60	.75-1.44-1.19
Massachusetts....	M.	58-60-59	.65-1.00-.80
Do...........	F.	58-60-60	.60-.80-.63
New York........	F.	60-60-60	.75-.75-.75
1893:			
Massachusetts....	M.	58-58-58	.80-.80-.80
Do...........	F.	58-58-58	.60-.65-.63
New Jersey.......	F.	55-60-58	.50-1.08-.91
1894:			
Indiana..........	F.	60-60-60	.50-.58-.53
Massachuseits....	M.	58-58-58	.79-.79-.79
Do...........	F.	58-58-58	.60-.60-.60
New York........	F.	60-60-60	.67-.67-.67
North Carolina...	M.	60-69-66	.45-.75-.55
South Carolina...	M.	66-66-66	.75-.75-.75
1895:			
Alabama.........	M.	66-66-66	.50-.55-.54
Georgia..........	M.	66-66-66	.40-1.10-.69
Do...........	F.	66-66-66	.60-1.10-.76
Louisiana........	M.	60-60-60	.50-.60-.52
Do...........	F.	63-63-63	.42-.50-.43
Maine...........	M.	60-60-60	.80-.80-.80
Do...........	F.	60-60-60	1.28-1.74-1.41
Massachusetts....	M.	58-58-58	.68-.97-.73
Do...........	F.	58-58-58	.65-1.15-.78
Do...........	F.	58-58-58	.60-1.02-.69
New Hampshire..	M.	60-60-60	.73-1.05-.94
Do...........	F.	60-60-60	.50-1.51-1.03
New York........	F.	60-60-60	1.00-1.25-1.20
North Carolina...	M.	66-70-68	.40-.75-.56
Do...........	F.	66-66-66	.50-.50-.50
South Carolina...	M.	66-66-66	.75-.75-.75
Do...........	F.	66-66-66	.65-.80-.73
Do...........	M.	66-66-66	.50-.50-.50
1896:			
Georgia..........	M.	63-66-65	.30-1.00-.64
Do...........	F.	63-66-66	.35-1.12-.83
New Hampshire..	F.	60-60-60	.62-1.40-1.04
New York.......	F.	60-60-60	.75-.75-.75
North Carolina...	M.	66-69-68	.30-.75-.52
Do...........	F.	69-69-69	.40-.65-.55
Pennsylvania.....	F.	60-60-60	.67-1.08-.83
Rhode Island.....	M.	60-60-60	.83-.83-.83
Do...........	F.	60-60-60	.83-.87-.86
Do...........	M.	66-66-66	.40-.70-.59
Do...........	F.	66-66-66	.70-.70-.70
1897:			
Georgia..........	F.	66-66-66	.40-.40-.40

¹ Not reported.

TABLE L-7.—*Drawing frame-tenders, males, cotton goods, 1907–1928, by State and year*

Year	Alabama		Connecticut		Georgia		Maine	
	Hours per week	Rate per hour	Hours per week	Rate per hour	Hours per week	Rate per hour	Hours per week	Rate per hour
1907	66.0	$0.069			65.6	$0.080	60.0	$0.108
1908	62.1	.066			64.1	.089	60.0	.098
1909	61.8	.070			65.5	.088	60.0	.099
1910	62.2	.070			63.8	.090	58.0	.090
1911	62.0	.080			63.6	.086	58.0	.105
1912	62.3	.087			60.0	.098	58.0	.111
1913	61.0	.087			60.0	.100	58.0	.109
1914	60.2	.094			60.0	.107	58.0	.112
1916	60.2	.101			60.0	.107	58.0	.130
1918	90.3	.163			60.0	.164	53.3	.251
1920	57.2	.279	49.8	$0.458	56.3	.339	54.0	.431
1922	54.4	.179	51.7	.278	56.1	.200	52.3	.291
1924	55.1	.211	53.6	.350	56.6	.214	55.7	.350
1926	54.1	.233	50.2	.326	57.9	.231	51.7	.297
1928	55.0	.235	50.0	.367	56.4	.245	54.0	.268

Year	Massachusetts		New Hampshire		New York		North Carolina	
1907	58.0	$0.115					66.0	$0.086
1908	58.0	.116					63.8	.086
1909	58.0	.114					63.9	.082
1910	56.0	.113	58.0	$0.100			62.6	.094
1911	56.0	.110	58.0	.106			62.4	.095
1912	54.0	.125	58.0	.124			60.0	.098
1913	54.0	.135	58.0	.138			60.0	.100
1914	54.0	.133	55.0	.148			60.0	.119
1916	54.3	.164	55.0	.180			60.0	.126
1918	54.4	.249	54.0	.261			60.0	.206
1920	51.7	.523			54.2	$0.470	55.1	.468
1922	49.6	.361			53.3	.330	55.1	.295
1924	51.3	.415	54.4	.400	54.2	.378	55.4	.304
1926	51.6	.368	54.3	.315			55.7	.280
1928	51.5	.347	54.3	.417			56.0	.272

Year	Pennsylvania		Rhode Island		South Carolina		Virginia	
1907			58.0	$0.118	62.0	$0.080		
1908			58.0	.113	60.0	.078		
1909			58.0	.111	60.0	.086		
1910			56.0	.112	60.0	.083		
1911			56.0	.116	60.0	.086		
1912			56.0	.126	60.0	.090		
1913			56.0	.125	60.0	.095		
1914			54.0	.131	60.0	.102		
1916			54.8	.157	60.0	.103		
1918			49.5	.276	57.6	.162		
1920	50.6	$0.271	50.3	.444	54.9	.407	55.4	$0.419
1922	50.7	.256	48.0	.348	54.5	.221	55.2	.314
1924	50.7	.325	54.2	.418	55.0	.260	55.1	.350
1926			54.1	.379	55.0	.242	55.2	.296
1928			51.9	.339	55.0	.256	55.2	.300

TABLE L-8.—*Drawing frame-tenders, females, cotton goods, 1907–1928, by State and year*

Year	Alabama		Georgia		Maine		Massachusetts	
	Hours per week	Rate per hour	Hours per week	Rate per hour	Hours per week	Rate per hour	Hours per week	Rate per hour
1907	66.0	$0.067	63.8	$0.073	60.0	$0.089	58.0	$0.109
1908	61.9	.058	62.2	.084	60.0	.084	58.0	.114
1909	61.7	.058	61.8	.085	60.0	.086	58.0	.108
1910	61.7	.061	62.3	.081	58.0	.087	56.0	.099
1911	61.4	.065	61.7	.089	58.0	.087	56.0	.102
1912	62.0	.080	60.0	.103	58.0	.100	54.0	.117
1913	60.0	.081	60.0	.107	58.0	.104	54.0	.117
1914	60.0	.069	60.0	.104	58.0	.108	53.8	.118
1916	60.0	.086	60.0	.097	58.0	.106	53.9	1.49
1918	59.8	.144	60.0	.143	52.1	.210	53.8	.223
1920	59.0	.253	56.1	.311	54.0	.336	47.9	.409
1922	56.3	.162	56.2	.189	54.0	.271	48.0	.314
1924	55.6	.183	55.5	.206	54.0	.306	48.0	.366
1926	55.0	.184	55.9	.202	53.6	.263	48.0	.331
1928	55.0	.195	55.9	.208	54.5	.234	48.0	.324

Year	New Hampshire		New York		North Carolina		Pennsylvania	
1910	58.0	$0.091						
1911	58.0	.098						
1912	58.0	.113						
1913	58.0	.121						
1914	55.0	.131						
1916	55.0	.156						
1918	53.9	.235						
1920	48.0	.395			55.0	$0.383	50.1	$0.354
1922	53.8	.301	48.3	$0.295			53.3	.247
1924	54.0	.336	48.0	.342			52.3	.316
1926	54.0	.328	48.0	.315	55.0	.299	52.3	.377
1928	53.6	.318	48.0	.320	58.3	.262		

TABLE L-9.—*Dyers, cotton goods, 1848–1900, by year and State*

Year and State	Sex	Lowest, highest, and average—		Year and State	Sex	Lowest, highest, and average—	
		Hours per week	Rate per day (dollars)			Hours per week	Rate per day (dollars)
1848:				1858:			
Massachusetts	M.	75–75–75	1.00–1.00–1.00	Connecticut	M.	72–72–72	1.50–1.50–1.50
1849:				Massachusetts	M.	66–66–66	1.00–1.00–1.00
Massachusetts	M.	75–75–75	1.00–1.00–1.00	Rhode Island	M.	84–84–84	1.08–1.08–1.08
1850:				1859:			
Massachusetts	M.	75–75–75	1.00–1.00–1.00	Connecticut	M.	72–72–72	1.50–1.50–1.50
Rhode Island	M.	84–84–84	1.00–1.00–1.00	Massachusetts	M.	66–66–66	1.00–1.00–1.00
1851:				Rhode Island	M.	84–84–84	1.08–1.08–1.08
Massachusetts	M.	75–75–75	1.00–1.00–1.00	1860:			
Rhode Island	M.	84–84–84	1.00–1.00–1.00	Massachusetts	M.	66–66–66	1.00–1.00–1.00
1852:				Pennsylvania	M.	60–60–60	.75–.75–.75
Massachusetts	M.	75–75–75	1.00–1.00–1.00	Rhode Island	M.	78–78–78	1.10–1.10–1.10
Rhode Island	M.	84–84–84	1.00–1.00–1.00	1861:			
1853:				Massachusetts	M.	66–66–66	1.00–1.00–1.00
Massachusetts	M.	75–75–75	1.00–1.00–1.00	Rhode Island	M.	78–78–78	1.20–1.20–1.20
Rhode Island	M.	84–84–84	1.00–1.00–1.00	1862:			
1854:				Connecticut	M.	72–72–72	1.00–1.00–1.00
Massachusetts	M.	66–66–66	1.00–1.00–1.00	Massachusetts	M.	66–66–66	1.00–1.00–1.00
Rhode Island	M.	84–84–84	1.00–1.00–1.00	Rhode Island	M.	78–78–78	1.25–1.25–1.25
1855:				1863:			
Massachusetts	M.	66–66–66	1.00–1.00–1.00	Connecticut	M.	72–72–72	.85–1.00–.94
Rhode Island	M.	84–84–84	1.00–1.00–1.00	Massachusetts	M.	66–66–66	1.00–1.00–1.00
1856:				Rhode Island	M.	78–78–78	1.20–1.20–1.20
Massachusetts	M.	66–66–66	1.00–1.00–1.00	1864:			
Rhode Island	M.	84–84–84	1.05–1.05–1.05	Connecticut	M.	72–72–72	1.00–1.65–1.19
1857:				Massachusetts	M.	66–66–66	1.25–1.25–1.25
Massachusetts	M.	66–66–66	1.00–1.00–1.00	Rhode Island	M.	78–78–78	1.25–1.25–1.25
Rhode Island	M.	84–84–84	1.08–1.08–1.08				

TABLE L-9.—*Dyers, cotton goods, 1848–1900, by year and State*—Continued

Year and State	Sex	Lowest, highest, and average—		Year and State	Sex	Lowest, highest, and average—	
		Hours per week	Rate per day (dollars)			Hours per week	Rate per day (dollars)
1865:				**1880—Continued.**			
Connecticut	M.	66-66-66	1.35-1.50-1.39	New Hampshire	M.	69-69-69	1.50-1.50-1.50
Massachusetts	M.	66-66-66	1.50-1.50-1.50	Do	(¹)	66-66-66	1.33-1.67-1.42
Rhode Island	M.	78-78-78	1.25-1.25-1.25	New York	M.	66-66-66	1.13-1.13-1.13
1866:				Rhode Island	M.	72-72-72	1.28-1.28-1.28
Connecticut	M.	66-66-66	1.35-1.50-1.40	**1881:**			
Massachusetts	M.	66-66-66	1.75-1.75-1.75	Connecticut	M.	66-66-66	1.25-1.35-1.26
Rhode Island	M.	78-78-78	1.25-1.25-1.25	Massachusetts	M.	60-60-60	1.25-1.45-1.43
1867:				New Hampshire	M.	65-65-65	.58-2.50-1.30
Connecticut	M.	66-66-66	1.50-1.50-1.50	New Jersey	M.	(¹)	1.33-1.33-1.33
Georgia	M.	66-66-66	1.00-1.50-1.24	North Carolina	M.	(¹)	.60-.75-.65
Massachusetts	M.	66-66-66	1.75-1.75-1.75	Ohio	M.	60-66-62	1.00-2.25-1.44
New Hampshire	M.	66-66-66	1.33-1.33-1.33	Rhode Island	M.	72-72-72	1.28-1.28-1.28
Rhode Island	M.	78-78-78	1.35-1.35-1.35	Tennessee	M.	66-66-66	.80-.80-.80
1868:				**1882:**			
Connecticut	M.	66-66-66	1.35-1.35-1.35	Connecticut	M.	66-66-66	1.28-1.50-1.33
Massachusetts	M.	66-66-66	1.75-1.75-1.75	Kentucky	M.	66-66-66	.90-1.50-1.20
Rhode Island	M.	72-72-72	1.45-1.45-1.45	Maine	M.	66-66-66	1.25-1.25-1.25
1869:				Massachusetts	M.	60-60-60	1.45-1.45-1.45
Connecticut	M.	66-66-66	1.25-1.50-1.36	New Jersey	M.	60-60-60	1.00-2.50-1.35
Massachusetts	M.	66-66-66	1.63-1.63-1.63	Ohio	(¹)	60-66-62	1.50-3.50-2.10
Rhode Island	M.	72-72-72	1.45-1.45-1.45	**1883:**			
1870:				Connecticut	(¹)	66-66-66	1.28-2.50-1.40
Connecticut	M.	66-66-66	1.35-1.50-1.40	Georgia	M.	69-69-69	.67-1.75-1.03
Massachusetts	M.	66-66-66	1.50-1.70-1.68	Massachusetts	M.	60-60-60	1.05-3.00-1.25
Rhode Island	M.	72-72-72	1.33-1.33-1.33	Do	F.	(¹)	1.00-1.00-1.00
1871:				New Jersey	M.	60-60-60	.83-3.00-1.53
Connecticut	M.	66-66-66	1.35-1.50-1.40	Ohio	M.	60-60-60	.98-1.20-1.10
Maine	M.	66-66-66	1.25-1.25-1.25	Rhode Island	M.	72-72-72	1.28-1.28-1.28
Massachusetts	M.	66-66-66	1.70-1.70-1.70	Tennessee	M.	65-65-65	.75-1.00-.83
Rhode Island	M.	72-72-72	1.50-1.50-1.50	West Virginia	M.	60-60-60	1.50-1.50-1.50
1872:				**1884:**			
Connecticut	M.	66-66-66	1.35-1.50-1.40	Connecticut	M.	66-66-66	1.25-1.28-1.26
Massachusetts	M.	66-66-66	1.70-1.70-1.70	Georgia	M.	66-66-66	1.00-1.17-1.03
Rhode Island	M.	72-72-72	1.50-1.50-1.50	Kentucky	M.	66-66-66	1.08-2.00-1.39
1873:				Massachusetts	M.	40-60-44	1.35-1.40-1.36
Connecticut	M.	66-66-66	1.50-1.50-1.50	New Jersey	M.	60-60-60	.33-2.67-1.53
Massachusetts	M.	66-66-66	1.70-1.70-1.70	Ohio	M.	60-60-60	1.33-1.33-1.33
Pennsylvania	M.	(¹)	2.00-2.00-2.00	Rhode Island	M.	72-72-72	1.28-1.28-1.28
Rhode Island	M.	72-72-72	1.50-1.50-1.50	**1885:**			
Tennessee	M.	57-57-57	1.00-1.00-1.00	Alabama	M.	(¹)	1.00-1.33-1.11
1874:				California	M.	60-69-64	1.87-1.87-1.87
Connecticut	M.	66-66-66	1.50-1.75-1.56	Connecticut	M.	60-69-64	1.00-3.00-1.53
Massachusetts	M.	66-66-66	1.70-1.70-1.70	Delaware	M.	60-60-60	1.50-3.00-1.71
Pennsylvania	M.	62-62-62	.68-2.28-1.44	Illinois	M.	63-63-63	1.35-1.35-1.35
Rhode Island	M.	72-72-72	1.27-1.27-1.27	Indiana	M.	60-60-60	1.00-2.50-1.38
1875:				Iowa	M.	60-60-60	1.50-1.50-1.50
Connecticut	M.	66-66-66	1.35-1.50-1.39	Kentucky	M.	66-66-66	1.10-1.54-1.39
Massachusetts	M.	60-60-60	1.60-3.50-1.85	Maine	M.	60-60-64	.60-2.00-1.35
Rhode Island	M.	72-72-72	1.50-1.50-1.50	Do	F.	64-64-64	1.00-1.00-1.00
1876:				Maryland	M.	66-66-66	1.25-1.25-1.25
Connecticut	M.	66-66-66	1.25-1.38-1.31	Massachusetts	M.	60-60-60	.52-2.50-1.09
Massachusetts	M.	60-60-60	1.70-1.70-1.70	Minnesota	M.	(¹)	1.35-1.50-1.40
New Hampshire	M.	66-66-66	1.00-1.50-1.25	Missouri	M.	60-60-60	1.25-1.25-1.25
Pennsylvania	M.	(¹)	1.13-3.66-1.65	New Hampshire	M.	60-60-61	1.00-1.75-1.29
Rhode Island	M.	72-72-72	1.50-1.50-1.50	New Jersey	M.	60-63-60	1.00-2.67-1.62
1877:				New York	M.	60-66-63	1.12-2.00-1.46
Connecticut	M.	66-66-66	1.25-1.38-1.27	North Carolina	M.	66-69-69	.75-.75-.75
Massachusetts	M.	60-60-60	1.50-1.50-1.50	Pennsylvania	M.	60-60-60	1.25-2.33-1.39
Rhode Island	M.	72-72-72	1.12-1.12-1.12	Rhode Island	M.	72-72-72	1.50-1.50-1.50
1878:				Tennessee	M.	66-67-67	.80-1.75-1.03
Connecticut	M.	66-66-66	1.25-2.00-1.38	Vermont	M.	60-66-64	.53-1.25-.94
Georgia	M.	66-66-66	.75-.75-.75	Virginia	M.	66-66-66	1.00-1.00-1.00
Massachusetts	M.	60-60-60	1.40-1.40-1.40	**1886:**			
Pennsylvania	M.	60-60-60	1.00-3.33-1.57	Connecticut	M.	60-66-60	1.20-1.30-1.25
Rhode Island	M.	72-72-72	1.33-1.33-1.33	Indiana	M.	60-60-60	1.00-1.67-1.25
1879:				Iowa	M.	60-60-60	2.25-3.00-2.50
Connecticut	M.	66-66-66	1.13-1.38-1.25	Massachusetts	(¹)	60-60-60	1.40-1.40-1.40
Massachusetts	M.	60-60-60	1.40-1.40-1.40	Do	M.	40-60-42	1.33-1.60-1.52
New Jersey	(¹)	60-60-60	1.40-1.60-1.50	New Jersey	M.	60-60-60	.83-3.00-1.84
Pennsylvania	M.	60-72-61	1.00-2.50-1.60	Pennsylvania	M.	60-60-60	1.00-4.33-1.55
Rhode Island	M.	72-72-72	1.33-1.33-1.33	Rhode Island	M.	60-60-60	1.50-1.67-1.52
1880:				**1887:**			
Connecticut	M.	66-66-66	1.25-1.81-1.75	Connecticut	M.	60-60-60	.75-1.65-1.42
Massachusetts	M.	60-60-60	1.35-1.35-1.35	Massachusetts	M	60-60-60	1.50-1.50-1.50

¹ Not reported.

TABLE L-9.—*Dyers, cotton goods, 1848-1900, by year and State*—Continued

| Year and State | Sex | Lowest, highest, and average— | | Year and State | Sex | Lowest, highest, and average— | |
		Hours'per week	Rate per day (dollars)			Hours per week	Rate per day (dollars)
1887—Continued.				**1894—Continued**			
Ohio	M.	60–60–60	1. 35–3. 00–1. 62	Massachusetts	M.	58–58–58	1. 26–1. 26–1. 26
Rhode Island	M.	60–60–60	1. 50–1. 50–1. 50	New York	M.	60–66–61	1. 35–6. 39–2. 41
Wisconsin	(¹)	(¹)	1. 52–2. 88–1. 97	Ohio	M.	60–66–60	. 66–2. 50–1. 38
1888:				Do	F.	60–60–60	. 75– . 75– . 75
Connecticut	M.	60–60–60	1. 10–1. 40–1. 26	Rhode Island	(¹)	(¹)	. 92–4. 50–1. 67
Massachusetts	M.	60–60–60	1. 50–1. 50–1. 50	South Carolina	M.	66–66–66	. 50–1. 00– . 90
New Hampshire	M.	(¹)	1. 72–1. 72–1. 72	**1895:**			
New Jersey	M.	60–63–62	1. 25–3. 33–2. 20	Alabama	M.	60–60–60	1. 00–1. 50–1. 19
New York	M.	55–60–57	. 50–6. 00–1. 61	Georgia	M.	66–66–66	. 83–1. 75–1. 04
North Carolina	M.	(¹)	3. 33–3. 33–3. 33	Kentucky	M.	60–60–60	1. 00–1. 00–1. 00
Rhode Island	(¹)	(¹)	1. 16–4. 00–2. 22	Louisiana	M.	60–60–60	1. 50–1. 50–1. 50
Do	M.	60–60–60	1. 00–1. 50–1. 09	Maine	M.	60–60–60	. 70–2. 50–1. 19
Virginia	M.	(¹)	. 50–1. 20–1. 01	Massachusetts	M.	58–60–59	1. 25–2. 50–1. 31
1889:				New Hampshire	M.	60–60–60	. 70–2. 00–1. 20
California	M.	(¹)	1. 35–2. 00–1. 55	New Jersey	M.	55–60–56	1. 26–2. 70–1. 57
Connecticut	M.	60–60–60	1. 13–1. 40–1. 24	New York	M.	60–60–60	1. 17–3. 00–1. 72
Maine	M.	60–60–60	1. 25–2. 06–1. 42	North Carolina	M.	66–72–71	. 75– . 90– . 82
Massachusetts	M.	60–60–60	1. 50–3. 00–1. 53	Ohio	M.	60–60–60	. 75–2. 50–1. 00
Missouri	M.	(¹)	1. 25–1. 25–1. 25	Pennsylvania	M.	60–60–60	1. 33–2. 21–1. 67
New Hampshire	M.	60–60–60	1. 25–1. 73–1. 49	Tennessee	M.	60–67–66	. 50–1. 75– . 93
New York	M.	60–60–60	1. 00–1. 50–1. 15	Vermont	M.	60–60–60	. 90–1. 20– . 93
Pennsylvania	M.	(¹)	1. 17–2. 75–1. 47	**1896:**			
Rhode Island	M.	60–60–60	1. 50–1. 50–1. 50	Connecticut	M.	60–60–60	1. 00–3. 00–1. 32
1890:				Georgia	M.	63–66–65	. 60–1. 67–1. 09
Connecticut	M.	60–60–60	. 90–1. 50–1. 25	Indiana	M.	60–60–60	. 75–1. 75–1. 29
Maine	M.	60–60–60	1. 25–2. 00–1. 63	Iowa	M.	60–60–60	1. 83–2. 50–2. 17
Massachusetts	M.	60–60–60	1. 20–1. 50–1. 47	Kentucky	M.	60–60–60	. 90–1. 80–1. 18
Missouri	M.	(¹)	1. 40–1. 40–1. 40	Minnesota	M.	60–60–60	1. 15–1. 40–1. 28
New Hampshire	M.	60–60–60	1. 25–1. 25–1. 25	Missouri	M.	60–60–60	1. 00–1. 06–1. 03
New Jersey	M.	60–60–60	1. 00–1. 00–1. 00	New Hampshire	M.	60–60–60	1. 25–1. 50–1. 28
New York	M.	60–60–60	. 60–7. 00–1. 58	North Carolina	M.	69–69–69	. 70– . 70– . 70
North Carolina	M.	72–72–72	. 75–1. 25– . 89	Ohio	M.	60–60–60	1. 07–1. 58–1. 43
Rhode Island	M.	60–60–60	1. 50–1. 50–1. 50	Pennsylvania	M.	51–60–60	. 75–6. 66–1. 59
1891:				Rhode Island	M.	60–60–60	1. 50–1. 50–1. 50
Connecticut	M.	60–60–60	1. 13–1. 50–1. 28	Tennessee	M.	69–69–69	. 85– . 85– . 85
Maine	M.	60–60–00	1. 25–1. 33–1. 27	West Virginia	M.	60–60–60	1. 67–1. 67–1. 67
Massachusetts	M.	60–60–60	1. 50–1. 50–1. 50	**1897:**			
New Jersey	M.	60–60–60	1. 25–1. 25–1. 25	Virginia	M.	60–66–62	. 65–1. 75–1. 16
New York	M.	60–60–60	. 60–7. 00–1. 53	Do	F.	60–60–60	. 75– . 75– . 75
Rhode Island	M.	60–60–60	1. 50–1. 50–1. 50	**1898:**			
1892:				New Jersey	M.	60–60–60	2. 50–2. 50–2. 50
Connecticut	M.	60–60–60	1. 25–2. 00–1. 31	**1899:**			
Indiana	M.	48–66–59	1. 25–1. 84–1. 52	New Jersey	M.	60–60–60	1. 08–1. 45–1. 12
Maine	M.	60–60–60	1. 35–1. 83–1. 40	New York	M.	59–59–59	2. 00–2. 00–2. 00
Massachusetts	M.	60–60–60	1. 50–1. 50–1. 50	North Carolina	M.	66–66–66	. 75– . 75– . 75
Rhode Island	M.	60–60–60	1. 25–1. 50–1. 29	Pennsylvania	M.	60–60–60	. 49–2. 32–1. 75
1893:				**1900:**			
Maryland	M.	60–60–60	1. 42–1. 42–1. 42	New Jersey	M.	60–60–60	1. 25–1. 67–1. 30
Massachusetts	M.	58–58–58	1. 45–1. 45–1. 45	New York	M.	59–59–59	2. 00–2. 00–2. 00
Ohio	M.	60–60–60	1. 10–2. 50–1. 35	North Carolina	M.	66–66–66	. 75– . 75– . 75
Do	F.	60–60–60	. 75– . 75– . 75	Pennsylvania	M.	60–60–60	. 53–2. 26–1. 69
1894:							
Indiana	M.	60–60–60	1. 80–2. 16–2. 07				
Maine	M.	48–48–48	1. 44–1. 44–1. 44				

¹ Not reported.

TABLE L-10.—*Dyers, males, cotton goods, 1890-1907, by State and year*

Year	Massachusetts		Pennsylvania		Rhode Island		New Jersey	
	Hours per week	Rate per hour	Hours per week	Rate per hour	Hours per week	Rate per hour	Hours per week	Rate per hour
1890	60.0	$0.122	60.0	$0.174	60.0	$0.130		
1891	60.0	.120	60.0	.174	60.0	.130		
1892	59.4	.122	60.0	.174	60.0	.130		
1893	58.0	.128	60.0	.174	60.0	.131		
1894	55.6	.122	60.0	.170	60.0	.131		
1895	58.0	.121	60.0	.170	60.0	.130		
1896	58.0	.127	60.0	.171	60.0	.131		
1897	55.6	.126	60.0	.170	60.0	.131		
1898	58.0	.125	60.0	.170	60.0	.131		
1899	58.0	.124	60.0	.170	60.0	.131		
1900	58.0	.131	60.0	.174	60.0	.132		
1901	58.0	.130	60.0	.174	60.0	.133		
1902	58.0	.131	60.0	.180	60.0	.133		
1903	58.0	.132	60.0	.180	59.0	.135		
1904	58.0	.129	60.0	.178	59.6	.135		
1905	58.0	.129	60.0	.176	59.5	.136	58.8	$0.144
1906	58.0	.132	60.0	.182	58.5	.138	58.7	.144
1907	58.0	.139	60.0	.181	58.3	.146	58.8	.151

TABLE L-11.—*Laborers, dyehouse, males, cotton goods, 1911-1918, by State and year*

Year	Connecticut		Massachusetts		New Hampshire		New Jersey	
	Hours per week	Rate per hour	Hours per week	Rate per hour	Hours per week	Rate per hour	Hours per week	Rate per hour
1911	59.7	$0.148	56.8	$0.142	58.0	$0.148	58.0	$0.155
1912	59.6	.158	56.0	.150	58.0	.162	60.0	.163
1913	59.8	.148	55.2	.150	58.0	.163	60.0	.162
1914	57.5	.150	55.1	.152	55.0	.172	60.0	.162
1916	59.4	.180	55.3	.178	55.7	.196	58.3	.195
1918	57.3	.263	55.4	.272	54.8	.317	55.8	.255

Year	North Carolina		Pennsylvania		Rhode Island	
1911	63.0	$0.097			56.7	$0.150
1912	60.0	.106			56.7	.153
1913	60.0	.110			57.8	.140
1914	60.0	.113	55.3	$0.162	54.0	.153
1916	60.0	.118	55.7	.169	54.0	.183
1918	60.0	.188			54.0	.290

TABLE L-12.—*Loom fixers, cotton goods, 1848-1900, by year and State*

Year and State	Sex	Hours per week	Rate per day (dollars)
1848:			
Massachusetts	M.	75-75-75	1.25-1.25-1.25
1849:			
Massachusetts	M.	75-75-75	1.40-1.40-1.40
1850:			
Massachusetts	M.	75-75-75	1.40-1.40-1.40
1851:			
Massachusetts	M.	75-75-75	1.25-1.37-1.35
1852:			
Massachusetts	M.	75-75-75	1.00-1.50-1.27
1853:			
Massachusetts	M.	75-78-75	1.00-1.50-1.26
1854:			
Massachusetts	M.	66-66-66	1.00-1.50-1.25
1855:			
Massachusetts	M.	66-66-66	1.00-1.50-1.25
1856:			
Massachusetts	M.	66-66-66	1.26-1.94-1.66
1857:			
Massachusetts	M.	66-66-66	1.33-1.98-1.69
1858:			
Massachusetts	M.	66-66-66	1.21-1.87-1.56
1859:			
Massachusetts	M.	66-78-67	1.22-1.97-1.58
1860:			
Massachusetts	M.	66-78-67	1.23-1.91-1.56
1861:			
Connecticut	M.	72-72-72	1.25-1.25-1.25
Massachusetts	M.	66-78-67	1.20-1.80-1.52
1862:			
Connecticut	M.	72-72-72	1.00-1.25-1.13
Massachusetts	M.	66-78-67	1.00-1.85-1.50
1863:			
Connecticut	M.	72-72-72	1.25-1.50-1.38
Massachusetts	M.	66-78-68	1.00-2.40-1.65
1864:			
Connecticut	M.	72-72-72	1.50-2.20-1.88
Massachusetts	M.	66-78-71	1.25-2.00-1.59
1865:			
Connecticut	M.	66-66-66	2.00-2.40-2.27
Massachusetts	M.	66-66-66	1.50-2.50-2.07
1866:			
Connecticut	M.	66-66-66	1.75-2.00-1.88
Massachusetts	M.	66-66-66	1.75-2.63-2.33
1867:			
Connecticut	M.	66-66-66	1.75-2.00-1.92
Georgia	M.	66-66-66	1.00-1.35-1.19
Massachusetts	M.	66-66-66	1.50-2.63-2.24
1868:			
Connecticut	M.	66-66-66	1.50-2.00-1.86
Massachusetts	M.	66-66-66	1.50-2.63-2.18
1869:			
Connecticut	M.	66-66-66	1.50-2.00-1.83
Massachusetts	M.	66-66-66	1.38-2.63-2.14
1870:			
Connecticut	M.	66-66-66	1.50-2.13-1.81
Massachusetts	M.	66-06-66	1.38-2.63-2.20
1871:			
Connecticut	M.	66-66-66	1.50-2.13-1.77
Massachusetts	M.	66-66-66	1.75-2.63-2.25
1872:			
Connecticut	M.	66-66-66	1.50-2.00-1.78
Massachusetts	M.	66-66-66	1.50-2.75-2.24
South Carolina	M.	72-72-72	1.25-1.50-1.40
1873:			
Connecticut	M.	66-66-66	1.60-2.00-1.80
Massachusetts	M.	66-66-66	1.38-3.00-2.20
1874:			
Connecticut	M.	66-66-66	1.38-2.25-1.93
Massachusetts	M.	66-66-66	1.50-3.00-2.21
1875:			
Connecticut	M.	66-66-66	2.00-2.00-2.00
Massachusetts	M.	60-66-62	1.49-3.00-1.91

Year and State	Sex	Hours per week	Rate per day (dollars)
1876:			
Connecticut	M.	66-66-66	2.00-2.00-2.00
Massachusetts	M.	60-60-60	1.50-2.39-2.08
Pennsylvania	M.	(1)	1.52-2.08-1.71
South Carolina	M.	66-66-66	1.25-1.50-1.33
1877:			
Connecticut	M.	66-66-66	1.75-2.50-2.05
Georgia	M.	66-66-66	1.50-1.50-1.50
Massachusetts	M.	60-60-60	1.50-2.27-1.97
1878:			
Connecticut	M.	66-66-66	1.75-2.50-2.05
Massachusetts	M.	60-60-60	1.73-2.27-1.97
North Carolina	M.	72-72-72	1.25-1.25-1.25
Pennsylvania	M.	66-66-66	1.88-1.88-1.88
1879:			
Connecticut	M.	60-66-65	1.38-2.50-1.97
Massachusetts	M.	60-60-60	1.73-2.27-1.97
1880:			
Connecticut	M.	66-66-66	1.95-2.00-1.98
Do	(1)	66-66-66	1.25-1.25-1.25
Georgia	M.	69-69-69	1.25-1.75-1.50
Maine	(1)	66-66-66	1.58-1.58-1.58
Massachusetts	M.	60-60-60	1.35-2.15-1.86
Do	(1)	60-62-60	1.50-1.67-1.63
New Hampshire	(1)	65-66-65	1.60-1.90-1.78
New Jersey	(1)	67-67-67	1.70-1.70-1.70
Pennsylvania	M.	60-60-60	1.33-1.58-1.50
Rhode Island	(1)	66-66-66	1.50-1.50-1.50
Virginia	M.	63-68-68	1.25-1.25-1.25
1881:			
Connecticut	M.	66-66-66	1.95-2.00-1.98
Georgia	M.	66-66-66	1.17-1.17-1.17
Massachusetts	M.	60-60-60	1.35-2.27-2.00
North Carolina	M.	(1)	1.00-1.25-1.08
1882:			
Connecticut	M.	66-66-66	2.00-2.17-2.09
Georgia	M.	72-72-72	1.25-1.25-1.25
Kentucky	M.	66-66-66	1.20-1.20-1.20
Massachusetts	M.	60-60-60	1.35-2.27-1.99
New Hampshire	M.	66-66-66	1.15-1.50-1.24
South Carolina	M.	69-69-69	1.25-1.75-1.50
1883:			
Alabama	M.	(1)	1.39-1.39-1.39
Connecticut	M.	66-66-66	2.17-2.17-2.17
Georgia	M.	69-69-69	1.25-1.90-1.73
Massachusetts	M.	60-60-60	1.50-2.20-1.93
Mississippi	M.	(1)	1.50-1.67-1.61
New Jersey	M.	60-60-60	2.33-2.58-2.47
Do	(1)	60-60-60	1.50-2.50-1.81
South Carolina	M.	70-70-71	1.00-1.25-1.13
1884:			
Connecticut	M.	66-66-66	2.20-2.20-2.20
Georgia	M.	66-70-68	1.25-1.50-1.33
Indiana	M.	(1)	.88-1.30-1.09
Kentucky	M.	66-66-66	2.00-2.25-2.14
Louisiana	M.	63-66-64	1.50-1.67-1.57
Massachusetts	M.	60-60-60	1.50-2.20-1.92
New Jersey	M.	60-60-60	1.67-2.67-1.87
New York	M.	60-60-60	2.50-2.50-2.50
North Carolina	M.	69-69-69	1.50-1.50-1.17
South Carolina	M.	69-69-69	1.50-1.50-1.50
1885:			
Alabama	M.	63-63-63	1.50-1.67-1.62
California	M.	60-60-60	1.75-1.75-1.75
Connecticut	M.	66-66-66	1.35-2.20-1.88
Delaware	M.	60-60-60	1.40-2.25-1.94
Indiana	M.	66-66-66	1.50-2.00-1.74
Kentucky	M.	66-66-66	1.75-1.75-1.75
Maine	M.	66-66-66	1.50-1.75-1.65
Maryland	M.	66-66-66	1.25-1.75-1.56
Massachusetts	M.	60-60-60	1.08-2.70-1.82
Minnesota	M.	(1)	2.00-2.50-2.25
New Hampshire	M.	66-66-66	1.75-1.90-1.88

1 Not reported.

TABLE L–12.—*Loom fixers, cotton goods, 1848–1900, by year and State*—Continued

Year and State	Sex	Hours per week	Rate per day (dollars)	Year and State	Sex	Hours per week	Rate per day (dollars)
1885—Continued.				**1891—Continued.**			
New Jersey	M.	60–60–60	1.50–3.00–1.85	Massachusetts	M.	60–60–60	1.35–2.75–1.94
New York	M.	60–69–63	1.25–2.63–2.17	New Jersey	M.	60–60–60	2.00–2.17–2.09
North Carolina	M.	69–69–69	.75–1.50–1.15	New York	M.	60–60–60	1.25–3.75–2.07
Pennsylvania	(1)	60–60–60	2.50–2.50–2.50	**1892:**			
Do	M.	60–60–60	1.17–3.00–2.42	Connecticut	M.	60–60–60	2.20–2.20–2.20
Tennessee	M.	66–67–67	1.25–2.00–1.53	Indiana	M.	60–60–60	1.25–3.00–1.75
Vermont	M.	60–66–63	.80–1.86–1.45	Maine	M.	60–60–60	2.00–2.00–2.00
Do	F.	60–60–60	.45–1.53–.79	Massachusetts	M.	58–60–59	1.16–2.45–1.90
Virginia	M.	66–66–66	1.20–1.50–1.32	New York	M.	60–60–60	1.75–1.75–1.75
1886:				Rhode Island	M.	60–60–60	2.25–2.25–2.25
Connecticut	M.	66–66–66	1.50–2.20–1.91	**1893:**			
Indiana	M.	60–60–60	1.67–3.00–2.56	Massachusetts	M.	58–58–58	1.55–2.53–1.99
Iowa	M.	60–60–60	1.65–1.75–1.70	New York	M.	60–60–60	1.75–1.75–1.75
Maine	M.	66–66–66	1.80–1.80–1.80	Ohio	M.	60–60–60	2.00–2.00–2.00
Massachusetts	M.	60–60–60	1.50–2.09–1.84	Rhode Island	M.	60–60–60	2.25–2.25–2.25
New Jersey	M.	55–60–60	1.67–3.00–2.13	**1894:**			
Pennsylvania	M.	58–60–60	1.58–3.33–2.33	Iowa	M.	60–60–60	2.00–2.00–2.00
1887:				Maine	M.	60–60–60	1.50–1.90–1.70
Connecticut	M.	60–60–60	.75–2.20–1.86	Massachusetts	M.	58–58–58	1.70–2.28–1.87
Do	F.	(1)	1.00–1.00–1.00	New York	M.	60–60–60	1.25–2.25–1.80
Maine	M.	60–60–60	1.75–1.90–1.83	North Carolina	M.	60–72–66	.75–1.50–1.18
Massachusetts	M.	60–60–60	1.38–2.25–1.89	Ohio	M.	60–60–60	1.40–1.50–1.41
New York	M.	60–60–60	1.67–1.67–1.67	Do	F.	60–60–60	.80–.80–.80
Rhode Island	M.	60–60–60	2.00–2.00–2.00	Rhode Island	M.	60–60–60	2.05–2.05–2.05
Wisconsin	M.	(1)	1.78–1.78–1.78	Do	(1)	(1)	1.00–2.50–1.72
1888:				South Carolina	M.	66–66–66	1.75–1.75–1.75
California	M.	(1)	3.00–3.00–3.00	**1895:**			
Connecticut	M.	60–60–60	1.38–2.50–2.00	Alabama	M.	60–66–62	1.35–1.67–1.57
Delaware	M.	(1)	2.00–2.00–2.00	Connecticut	M.	60–60–60	2.00–2.50–2.21
Georgia	M.	66–66–66	1.50–1.90–1.63	Georgia	M.	66–66–66	.80–1.75–1.32
Maine	M.	60–60–60	1.67–2.00–1.85	Kentucky	M.	60–60–60	1.50–1.50–1.50
Massachusetts	M.	60–60–60	1.38–2.25–1.82	Louisiana	M.	60–63–62	1.58–1.83–1.65
New Hampshire	M.	(1)	1.88–1.88–1.88	Maine	M.	60–60–60	1.50–1.79–1.67
New Jersey	M.	63–63–63	1.33–3.75–2.35	Massachusetts	M.	58–58–58	1.16–2.28–1.85
New York	M.	60–60–60	1.19–2.75–1.84	Mississippi	M.	60–60–60	1.50–1.50–1.50
North Carolina	M.	(1)	1.25–1.50–1.37	New Hampshire	M.	60–60–60	1.10–1.95–1.65
Pennsylvania	M.	(1)	2.50–2.50–2.50	New Jersey	M.	55–60–56	1.83–3.33–2.46
Rhode Island	M.	60–60–60	1.75–2.50–2.10	New York	M.	60–60–60	1.75–3.00–2.26
Do	(1)	(1)	1.60–2.50–2.03	North Carolina	M.	66–72–69	.80–1.50–1.22
South Carolina	M.	66–66–66	.85–1.70–1.25	Ohio	M.	60–60–60	1.50–2.00–1.82
Virginia	M.	60–60–60	1.20–2.25–1.43	Do	F.	60–60–60	1.01–1.01–1.01
1889:				Pennsylvania	M.	60–60–60	1.67–2.83–2.54
California	M.	(1)	2.50–3.00–2.75	Rhode Island	M.	60–60–60	1.33–2.33–1.95
Connecticut	M.	60–60–60	1.08–2.50–1.78	South Carolina	M.	66–66–66	.90–1.75–1.28
Georgia	M.	66–66–66	1.75–1.75–1.75	Tennessee	M.	66–67–67	1.15–2.00–1.65
Maine	M.	60–60–60	1.50–2.00–1.72	Vermont	M.	60–60–60	.42–2.25–1.36
Maryland	M.	(1)	1.00–1.63–1.28	Do	F.	60–60–60	.42–1.25–.87
Massachusetts	M.	60–60–60	1.50–3.50–1.91	Virginia	M.	60–60–60	1.25–1.25–1.25
Mississippi	M.	(1)	1.40–1.50–1.46	**1896:**			
New Hampshire	M.	60–60–60	1.25–2.00–1.75	Connecticut	M.	60–60–60	2.00–2.00–2.00
New York	M.	60–60–60	1.50–2.92–2.01	Georgia	M.	66–66–66	.60–1.85–1.53
North Carolina	M.	69–69–69	1.60–1.60–1.60	Indiana	M.	60–65–61	1.35–2.25–1.84
Pennsylvania	M.	(1)	2.17–2.75–2.23	Iowa	M.	60–60–60	1.50–2.00–1.83
Rhode Island	M.	(1)	1.33–1.92–1.77	Kentucky	M.	60–60–60	1.80–2.17–1.97
South Carolina	M.	66–66–66	1.43–1.43–1.43	Minnesota	M.	60–60–60	1.50–2.00–1.75
Tennessee	M.	66–66–66	1.20–1.75–1.54	New York	M.	60–60–60	1.67–1.75–1.71
Do	F.	66–66–66	1.25–1.25–1.25	North Carolina	M.	69–69–69	.50–1.25–.87
Virginia	M.	(1)	1.25–1.25–1.25	Ohio	M.	60–60–60	1.25–1.99–1.85
1890:				Do	F.	60–60–60	1.10–1.10–1.10
Alabama	M.	63–69–66	1.13–1.67–1.36	Pennsylvania	M.	51–60–60	1.17–3.17–2.22
Connecticut	M.	60–60–60	1.82–2.20–1.85	South Carolina	M.	66–66–66	1.17–1.50–1.37
Kentucky	M.	66–66–66	1.45–1.45–1.45	**1897:**			
Louisiana	M.	(1)	1.00–1.75–1.51	Georgia	M.	66–66–66	1.60–1.60–1.60
Maine	M.	60–60–60	1.40–2.00–1.63	New York	M.	60–60–60	1.83–1.83–1.83
Massachusetts	M.	60–60–60	1.35–2.25–1.91	**1898:**			
Mississippi	M.	66–66–66	1.35–1.50–1.46	New York	M.	60–60–60	1.83–1.83–1.83
Missouri	M.	(1)	1.60–2.00–1.87	**1899:**			
New Hampshire	M.	60–60–60	1.90–1.90–1.90	Alabama	M.	70–70–70	1.50–1.50–1.50
New Jersey	M.	60–60–60	2.00–2.25–2.11	Georgia	M.	66–66–66	.90–1.50–1.50
New York	M.	60–60–60	1.25–3.67–2.20	New York	M.	60–60–60	1.75–2.85–2.54
North Carolina	M.	66–69–68	.90–1.50–1.31	North Carolina	M.	66–72–68	.95–1.50–1.37
Do	M.	69–69–69	1.50–1.50–1.50	South Carolina	M.	66–66–66	1.75–1.75–1.75
Do	M.	66–69–68	.90–1.50–1.32	**1900:**			
Rhode Island	M.	(1)	1.75–2.00–1.95	Alabama	M.	70–70–70	1.50–1.50–1.50
Tennessee	M.	69–69–69	1.00–1.82–1.50	Georgia	M.	66–66–66	1.50–1.55–1.52
1891:				New York	M.	60–60–60	1.83–3.00–2.67
Connecticut	M.	60–60–60	1.75–2.20–2.03	North Carolina	M.	66–69–68	.95–1.50–1.38
Maine	M.	60–60–60	1.65–2.00–1.79	South Carolina	M.	66–66–66	1.75–1.75–1.75

¹ Not reported.

TABLE L-13.—*Loom fixers, males, cotton goods, 1890–1906, by State and year*

Year	Maine		Massachusetts		Rhode Island		South Carolina	
	Hours per week	Rate per hour	Hours per week	Rate per hour	Hours per week	Rate per hour	Hours per week	Rate per hour
1890	60.0	$0.188	60.0	$0.184	60.0	$0.177	66.0	$0.133
1891	60.0	.188	60.0	.180	60.0	.178	69.0	.122
1892	60.0	.191	60.0	.180	60.0	.179	68.4	.127
1893	60.0	.189	58.0	.191	60.0	.183	66.0	.127
1894	60.0	.180	54.2	.181	60.0	.169	66.0	.123
1895	60.0	.179	58.0	.172	60.0	.171	66.0	.123
1896	60.0	.185	58.0	.187	60.0	.174	66.0	.113
1897	60.0	.191	56.4	.187	60.0	.171	66.0	.126
1898	60.0	.178	58.0	.184	60.0	.166	66.0	.127
1899	60.0	.184	58.0	.178	60.0	.178	66.0	.127
1900	60.0	.204	58.0	.203	60.0	.198	66.0	.132
1901	60.0	.204	58.0	.203	60.0	.195	66.0	.131
1902	60.0	.205	58.0	.205	58.0	.218	66.0	.131
1903	60.0	.202	58.0	.212	58.0	.217	---------	--------
1904	60.0	.198	58.0	.219	58.0	.204	66.0	.130
1905	60.0	.194	58.0	.217	58.0	.206	66.0	.132
1906	60.0	.208	58.0	.230	58.0	.217	---------	--------

TABLE L-14.—*Loom fixers, males, cotton goods, 1907–1928, by State and year*

Year	Alabama		Georgia		Maine		Massachusetts	
	Hours per week	Rate per hour	Hours per week	Rate per hour	Hours per week	Rate per hour	Hours per week	Rate per hour
1907	66.0	$0.160	64.4	$0.152	60.0	$0.230	58.0	$0.247
1908	61.6	.166	63.5	.157	60.0	.211	58.0	.242
1909	62.2	.165	63.4	.160	60.0	.208	58.0	.225
1910	62.7	.165	63.1	.160	58.0	.213	56.0	.228
1911	62.0	.170	63.1	.161	58.0	.216	56.0	.231
1912	62.3	.174	60.0	.175	58.0	.240	54.0	.259
1913	61.7	.177	60.0	.183	58.0	.241	54.0	.261
1914	60.1	.188	60.0	.183	58.0	.258	54.0	.264
1916	60.1	.198	60.0	.193	58.0	.278	54.0	.315
1918	60.2	.284	60.0	.270	54.0	.444	54.0	.455
1920	57.4	.529	56.7	.527	54.0	.742	48.0	.791
1922	55.7	.363	57.2	.353	54.0	.577	48.2	.620
1924	55.7	.396	56.2	.363	54.1	.650	48.6	.696
1926	54.9	.394	57.6	.372	54.1	.600	48.3	.620
1928	55.0	.395	56.2	.379	54.0	.548	49.4	.592

Year	North Carolina		Rhode Island		South Carolina		New Hampshire	
	Hours per week	Rate per hour	Hours per week	Rate per hour	Hours per week	Rate per hour	Hours per week	Rate per hour
1907	66.0	$0.144	58.0	$0.254	62.0	$0.168	---------	--------
1908	64.2	.151	58.0	.235	60.0	.172	---------	--------
1909	63.9	.153	58.0	.236	60.0	.171	---------	--------
1910	62.8	.152	56.0	.238	60.0	.167	58.0	$0.215
1911	62.8	.152	56.0	.243	60.0	.163	58.0	.220
1912	60.0	.169	56.0	.265	60.0	.173	58.0	.249
1913	60.0	.170	56.0	.266	60.0	.176	58.0	.249
1914	60.0	.170	54.0	.276	60.8	.177	55.0	.264
1916	60.0	.189	54.0	.332	60.3	.193	55.0	.325
1918	60.0	.286	54.0	.503	61.1	.275	54.0	.463
1920	55.2	.658	49.6	.767	55.9	.596	48.0	.814
1922	55.2	.420	49.0	.617	55.8	.360	53.2	.628
1924	55.3	.457	51.0	.695	55.0	.391	54.1	.705
1926	55.7	.411	50.0	.623	55.3	.377	54.2	.667
1928	56.1	.418	51.9	.615	55.0	.377	53.7	.647

TABLE L-15.—*Slasher tenders, cotton goods, 1855-1896, by year and State*

Year and State	Sex	Hours per week	Rate per day (dollars)	Year and State	Sex	Hours per week	Rate per day (dollars)
1855:				**1884:**			
Massachusetts	M.	78-78-78	0.80-0.80-0.80	Georgia	M.	66-70-68	1.25-1.25-1.25
1858:				Indiana	M.	(1)	1.30-1.75-1.53
Massachusetts	M.	78-78-78	.83-.83-.83	Louisiana	M.	63-66-65	1.50-1.67-1.58
1859:				Massachusetts	M.	60-60-60	1.40-1.60-1.48
Massachusetts	M.	78-78-78	.90-1.08-1.04	North Carolina	M.	69-69-69	.58-.58-.58
1860:				South Carolina	M.	69-69-69	1.17-1.17-1.17
Massachusetts	M.	78-78-78	.90-1.08-1.01	Virginia	M.	69-69-69	1.00-1.00-1.00
1861:				**1885:**			
Massachusetts	M.	78-78-78	.90-.90-.90	Alabama	M.	63-63-63	1.25-1.25-1.25
1862:				Connecticut	M.	66-66-66	1.67-1.67-1.67
Massachusetts	M.	72-72-72	.91-.91-.91	Georgia	M.	69-69-69	1.15-1.25-1.22
1863:				Maine	M.	66-66-66	1.40-1.58-1.45
Massachusetts	M.	72-72-72	1.05-1.05-1.05	Massachusetts	M.	60-60-60	1.06-1.66-1.43
1864:				New Hampshire	M.	65-66-65	1.54-1.60-1.59
Massachusetts	M.	72-72-72	1.00-1.25-1.20	New York	M.	60-69-69	.87-1.87-1.12
1865:				North Carolina	M.	69-69-69	.90-1.40-1.08
Massachusetts	M.	72-72-72	1.25-1.50-1.38	Vermont	M.	66-66-66	.90-1.50-1.20
1866:				Virginia	M.	66-66-66	1.70-1.70-1.70
Massachusetts	M.	72-72-72	1.16-1.75-1.60	**1886:**			
1867:				Connecticut	M.	(1)	1.65-1.65-1.65
Massachusetts	M.	72-72-72	2.00-2.16-2.11	Massachusetts	M.	60-60-60	1.55-1.60-1.58
1868:				New Hampshire	M.	60-60-60	1.25-1.50-1.47
Massachusetts	M.	66-66-66	1.72-1.90-1.83	New Jersey	M.	60-60-60	1.00-1.08-1.04
1869:				**1887:**			
Massachusetts	M.	66-66-66	1.72-2.00-1.85	Massachusetts	M.	60-60-60	1.55-1.75-1.64
1870:				Rhode Island	M.	60-60-60	2.75-2.75-2.75
Massachusetts	M.	66-66-66	1.87-2.08-1.99	Wisconsin	(1)	(1)	2.50-2.50-2.50
1871:				**1888:**			
Massachusetts	M.	66-66-66	1.16-2.25-1.96	Georgia	M.	66-66-66	1.15-1.50-1.31
1872:				Massachusetts	M.	60-60-60	1.60-1.75-1.69
Massachusetts	M.	66-66-66	1.25-2.25-1.98	New York	M.	60-60-60	1.00-1.75-1.62
South Carolina	M.	72-72-72	1.10-1.10-1.10	Rhode Island	M.	(1)	1.54-1.63-1.59
1873:				South Carolina	M.	66-66-66	.75-1.25-.91
Massachusetts	M.	66-66-66	1.25-2.25-1.92	Virginia	M.	60-60-60	1.00-1.75-1.38
1874:				**1889:**			
Massachusetts	M.	66-66-66	1.25-2.08-1.67	Connecticut	M.	60-60-60	.84-2.17-1.32
1875:				Georgia	M.	66-70-67	1.00-2.00-1.29
Massachusetts	M.	60-60-60	1.67-1.82-1.79	Maine	M.	56-60-59	1.00-2.50-1.55
1876:				Maryland	M.	(1)	.70-2.25-1.47
Massachusetts	M.	60-60-60	1.60-1.73-1.64	Massachusetts	M.	60-60-60	1.50-2.30-2.09
South Carolina	M.	66-66-66	.95-1.00-.96	Mississippi	M.	(1)	1.50-1.50-1.50
1877:				New Hampshire	M.	60-60-60	1.45-2.00-1.65
Georgia	M.	66-66-66	.85-1.75-1.30	New York	M.	60-60-60	1.75-1.75-1.75
Massachusetts	M.	60-60-60	1.60-1.62-1.61	Pennsylvania	M.	(1)	1.67-1.67-1.67
1878:				Rhode Island	M.	(1)	1.68-1.84-1.73
Massachusetts	M.	60-60-60	1.52-1.60-1.55	South Carolina	M.	66-66-66	1.20-1.20-1.20
1879:				Tennessee	M.	66-66-66	.65-1.50-1.01
Massachusetts	M.	60-60-60	1.40-1.62-1.53	Virginia	M.	(1)	1.75-1.79-1.77
1880:				**1890:**			
Georgia	M.	66-69-67	1.25-1.50-1.31	Alabama	M.	63-69-66	1.00-1.80-1.55
Massachusetts	M.	60-60-60	1.40-1.78-1.52	Connecticut	M.	(1)	2.00-2.00-2.00
New Hampshire	(1)	66-66-66	1.80-1.80-1.80	Kentucky	(1)	66-66-66	1.40-1.60-1.50
Pennsylvania	M.	60-60-60	1.35-1.35-1.35	Louisiana	M.	(1)	1.25-1.25-1.25
Rhode Island	(1)	66-66-66	1.57-1.57-1.57	Massachusetts	M.	60-60-60	1.60-1.75-1.64
Virginia	M.	68-68-68	1.75-1.75-1.75	Mississippi	M.	66-66-66	1.00-1.50-1.25
1881:				New York	M.	(1)	.58-1.75-1.37
Georgia	M.	66-66-66	1.33-1.33-1.33	North Carolina	M.	69-69-69	1.25-1.50-1.38
Massachusetts	M.	60-60-60	1.00-1.78-1.38	Tennessee	M.	69-69-69	1.40-1.50-1.43
New Hampshire	M.	65-65-65	1.20-1.75-1.58	**1891:**			
1882:				Maine	M.	60-60-60	1.67-2.00-1.77
Georgia	M.	70-72-71	1.00-1.75-1.38	Massachusetts	M.	60-60-60	1.60-1.90-1.70
Massachusetts	M.	60-60-60	1.05-1.78-1.57	New York	M.	(1)	.58-1.75-1.41
New Hampshire	M.	66-66-66	.90-1.85-1.51	North Carolina	(1)	69-72-71	1.00-1.13-1.07
North Carolina	M.	65-65-65	.40-1.00-.80	**1892:**			
South Carolina	M.	69-69-69	.90-.90-.90	Massachusetts	M.	58-60-59	1.55-2.10-1.64
1883:				Maine	M.	60-60-60	1.60-1.85-1.66
Alabama	M.	(1)	1.17-1.17-1.17	New York	M.	60-60-60	2.25-2.25-2.25
Georgia	M.	(1)	1.50-1.75-1.63	**1893:**			
Massachusetts	M.	60-60-60	1.05-1.60-1.42	Massachusetts	M.	58-58-58	1.60-2.25-1.68
Do	(1)	(1)	.70-2.40-1.63	New York	M.	60-60-60	2.25-2.25-2.25
Mississippi	M.	(1)	1.67-1.67-1.67	**1894:**			
South Carolina	M.	70-72-71	.85-1.25-1.01	Maine	M.	60-60-60	2.00-2.00-2.00
Tennessee	M.	66-66-66	1.00-1.50 1.25	Massachusetts	M.	58-58-58	1.50-1.94-1.55

1 Not reported.

Table L-15.—*Slasher tenders, cotton goods, 1855-1896, by year and State*—Con.

Year and State	Sex	Hours per week	Rate per day (dollars)	Year and State	Sex	Hours per week	Rate per day (dollars)
1894—Continued.				1895—Continued.			
New York	M.	60-60-60	2.25-2.25-2.25	North Carolina	M.	66-72-70	1.00-1.50-1.19
North Carolina	M.	60-72-67	.45-1.00-.78	South Carolina	M.	66-66-66	.65-1.25-.99
Rhode Island	M.	(¹)	.70-2.50-1.77	Tennessee	M.	66-66-66	.80-1.75-1.24
1895:				Virginia	M.	60-60-60	1.00-1.75-1.38
Alabama	M.	63-66-65	1.25-1.50-1.38	1896:			
Georgia	M.	66-66-66	.85-1.75-1.37	Georgia	M.	66-66-66	.75-1.75-1.30
Louisiana	M.	60-63-62	1.25-2.08-1.53	Indiana	M.	65-65-65	1.25-1.75-1.44
Maine	M.	60-60-60	.65-2.00-1.19	New Hampshrie	M.	60-60-60	1.65-1.75-1.67
Massachusetts	M.	58-58-58	1.50-1.94-1.66	North Carolina	M.	69-69-69	.60-1.25-.84
Mississippi	M.	60-60-60	1.50-1.50-1.50	Pennsylvania	M.	60-60-60	1.67-1.67-1.67
New Hampshire	M.	60-60-60	1.05-2.00-1.42	South Carolina	M.	66-66-66	.90-1.15-1.03
New York	M.	60-60-60	1.50-2.25-1.85				

¹ Not reported.

Table L-16.—*Slasher tenders, males, cotton goods, 1907-1928, by State and year*

Year	Alabama Hours per week	Alabama Rate per hour	Connecticut Hours per week	Connecticut Rate per hour	Georgia Hours per week	Georgia Rate per hour	Maine Hours per week	Maine Rate per hour
1907	66.0	$0.117			64.3	$0.126	60.0	$0.195
1908	60.8	.129			63.2	.129	60.0	.185
1909	61.1	.129			62.5	.132	60.0	.185
1910	61.2	.131			62.2	.140	58.0	.185
1911	61.0	.139	58.0	$0.233	62.7	.138	58.0	.186
1912	61.8	.145	58.0	.243	60.0	.154	58.0	.206
1913	61.2	.144			60.0	.146	58.0	.205
1914	60.2	.144			60.0	.147	58.0	.205
1916	60.1	.145			60.0	.154	58.0	.237
1918	60.0	.216			60.0	.236	54.0	.374
1920	57.3	.391	49.3	.686	56.4	.442	54.0	.671
1922	55.5	.271	51.9	.519	56.8	.299	54.0	.499
1924	55.7	.286	52.1	.575	55.9	.303	54.8	.562
1926	55.0	.279	51.7	.501	56.3	.306	54.0	.507
1928	55.0	.286	52.1	.493	56.3	.304	54.0	.429

Year	Massachusetts Hours per week	Massachusetts Rate per hour	New Hampshire Hours per week	New Hampshire Rate per hour	New York Hours per week	New York Rate per hour	North Carolina Hours per week	North Carolina Rate per hour
1907	58.0	$0.221					66.0	$0.137
1908	58.0	.231					65.3	.141
1909	58.0	.219					65.3	.127
1910	56.0	.211	58.0	$0.191			62.8	.135
1911	56.0	.211	58.0	.251			62.5	.134
1912	54.0	.230	58.0	.283			60.0	.142
1913	54.0	.234	58.0	.286			60.0	.151
1914	53.9	.240	55.0	.292			60.0	.153
1916	54.0	.286	55.0	.332			60.0	.179
1918	54.0	.415	54.0	.456			60.2	.245
1920	48.0	.706	48.0	.736	49.0	$0.652	55.2	.561
1922	48.0	.564	53.6	.575	49.1	.485	55.2	.360
1924	48.0	.636	54.0	.619	48.9	.581	55.3	.382
1926	48.4	.549	54.0	.544	48.9	.513	55.5	.355
1928	48.6	.512	53.7	.532	48.5	.520	55.4	.365

Year	Pennsylvania Hours per week	Pennsylvania Rate per hour	Rhode Island Hours per week	Rhode Island Rate per hour	South Carolina Hours per week	South Carolina Rate per hour	Virginia Hours per week	Virginia Rate per hour
1907			58.0	$0.223	62.0	$0.126		
1908			58.0	.216	60.0	.136		
1909			58.0	.215	60.0	.132		
1910			56.0	.216	60.0	.136		
1911			56.0	.217	60.0	.141		
1912			56.0	.238	60.0	.153		
1913					60.0	.138		
1914					60.0	.133		
1916					60.0	.137		
1918					60.0	.206		
1920	51.1	$0.460	49.2	.695	55.0	.449	55.4	$0.455
1922	51.8	.419	48.7	.526	55.0	.260	55.7	.373
1924	51.4	.509	51.6	.593	55.0	.288	55.3	.405
1926	51.5	.507	50.4	.540	55.0	.280	56.1	.361
1928			52.3	.551	55.0	.286	55.3	.369

382   PART 2.—FROM 1840 TO 1928

TABLE L-17.—*Speeder tenders, cotton goods, 1840–1900, by year and State*

Year and State	Sex	Hours per week	Rate per day (dollars)
1840:			
Massachusetts	M.	84-84-84	0.42-0.48-0.45
Do	F.	84-84-84	.43-.55-.49
1841:			
Massachusetts	M.	84-84-84	.40-.50-.45
Do	F.	84-84-84	.42-.56-.49
1842:			
Massachusetts	M.	84-84-84	.48-.52-.51
Do	F.	78-84-81	.42-.56-.49
1843:			
Massachusetts	M.	84-84-84	.46-.48-.47
Do	F.	78-84-80	.42-.50-.45
1844:			
Massachusetts	M.	84-84-84	.46-.56-.50
Do	F.	78-84-81	.38-.48-.44
1845:			
Massachusetts	M.	84-84-84	.48-.56-.51
Do	F.	84-84-84	.38-.50-.43
1846:			
Massachusetts	M.	84-84-84	.46-.48-.47
Do	F.	78-84-84	.42-.52-.46
1847:			
Massachusetts	M.	84-84-84	.54-.56-.55
Do	F.	78-84-83	.42-.54-.48
1848:			
Massachusetts	M.	84-84-84	.50-.70-.55
Do	F.	78-84-83	.46-.58-.50
1849:			
Massachusetts	M.	84-84-84	.48-.60-.53
Do	F.	75-84-82	.44-.58-.51
1850:			
Massachusetts	M.	84-84-84	.46-.58-.53
Do	F.	75-84-80	.46-.60-.54
1851:			
Massachusetts	M.	72-84-74	.42-.50-.43
Do	F.	72-84-77	.38-.55-.47
1852:			
Massachusetts	M.	72-72-72	.50-.50-.50
Do	F.	72-78-73	.38-.55-.45
1853:			
Massachusetts	M.	72-72-72	.50-.50-.50
Do	F.	72-78-74	.40-.58-.47
New York	F.	72-72-72	.70-.70-.70
1854:			
Massachusetts	M.	72-72-72	.50-.50-.50
Do	F.	66-78-72	.40-.60-.48
New York	F.	72-72-72	.70-.70-.70
1855:			
Massachusetts	M.	72-72-72	.46-.55-.53
Do	F.	66-78-71	.46-.56-.51
New York	F.	72-72-72	.70-.70-.70
1856:			
Massachusetts	M.	72-72-72	.46-.54-.51
Do	F.	66-72-72	.46-.54-.52
New York	F.	72-72-72	.70-.70-.70
1857:			
Massachusetts	M.	72-72-72	.50-.60-.53
Do	F.	66-72-70-	.42-.56-.52
New York	F.	72-72-72	.76-.76-.76
1858:			
Massachusetts	M.	72-72-72	.46-.50-.49
Do	F.	66-78-71	.46-.57-.52
New York	F.	72-72-72	.60-.60-.60
1859:			
Massachusetts	M.	72-72-72	.46-.52-.50
Do	F.	66-78-72	.48-.57-.52
New York	F.	72-72-72	.65-.65-.65
1860:			
Massachusetts	M.	72-72-72	.46-.54-.50
Do	F.	66-78-71	.42-.60-.55
New York	F.	72-72-72	.70-.70-.70
1861:			
Massachusetts	M.	66-66-66	.46-.54-.49
Do	F.	66-78-69	.50-.60-.56
New York	F.	72-72-72	.73-.73-.73
1862:			
Massachusetts	M.	66-66-66	0.46-0.54-0.49
Do	F.	66-72-68	.50-.60-.57
New York	F.	72-72-72	.66-.66-.66
1863:			
Massachusetts	M.	66-66-66	.44-.44-.44
Do	F.	66-72-67	.48-.60-.57
1864:			
Massachusetts	F.	66-72-67	.50-.85-.67
1865:			
Massachusetts	F.	66-72-67	.57-.85-.75
New York	F.	72-72-72	.90-.90-.90
1866:			
Massachusetts	F.	66-72-67	.74-.95-.89
New York	F.	72-72-72	.81-.81-.81
1867:			
Massachusetts	F.	66-72-67	.48-1.00-.92
New York	F.	72-72-72	1.04-1.04-1.04
1868:			
Massachusetts	F.	66-66-66	.75-1.00-.94
New York	F.	66-66-66	1.14-1.14-1.14
1869:			
Massachusetts	F.	66-66-66	.75-1.00-.94
New York	F.	66-66-66	1.20-1.20-1.20
1870:			
Massachusetts	F.	66-66-66	.75-1.16-.96
New York	F.	66-66-66	1.02-1.02-1.02
1871:			
Massachusetts	F.	66-66-66	.80-1.16-1.02
New York	F.	66-66-66	1.08-1.08-1.08
1872:			
Massachusetts	F.	66-66-66	.85-1.16-1.02
New York	F.	66-66-66	1.05-1.05-1.05
South Carolina	M.	72-72-72	1.00-1.08-1.02
1873:			
Massachusetts	F.	66-66-66	.75-1.22-1.12
New York	F.	66-66-66	1.14-1.14-1.14
1874:			
Massachusetts	F.	66-66-66	.65-1.15-1.04
New York	F.	66-66-66	.84-.84-.84
Pennsylvania	M.	(¹)	.85-.85-.85
Do	F.	(¹)	1.00-1.00-1.00
1875:			
Massachusetts	M.	(¹)	1.51-1.51-1.51
Do	F.	60-66-61	.50-1.13-1.01
New York	F.	66-66-66	.72-.72-.72
1876:			
Massachusetts	F.	60-60-60	.60-1.05-.97
New York	F.	66-66-66	.85-.85-.85
Pennsylvania	F.	(¹)	.53-1.23-.85
Rhode Island	F.	(¹)	1.00-1.00-1.00
1877:			
Georgia	M.	66-66-66	1.10-1.10-1.10
Maine	F.	66-66-66	.83-1.31-1.12
Massachusetts	F.	60-60-60	.60-1.00-.86
New York	F.	66-66-66	.77-.77-.77
1878:			
Massachusetts	F.	60-66-64	.60-1.00-.89
New Hampshire	F.	60-60-60	.65-1.06-.81
New York	F.	66-66-66	.74-.74-.74
North Carolina	F.	72-72-72	.48-.50-.49
Pennsylvania	F.	60-66-64	.62-1.25-.90
Rhode Island	F.	(¹)	.75-.75-.75
1879:			
Massachusetts	M.	60-60-60	.60-.75-.66
Do	F.	60-66-64	.60-1.00-.91
New York	F.	66-66-66	.73-.73-.73
Pennsylvania	M.	60-66-63	.50-1.00-.65
Do	F.	(¹)	.60-.60-.60
1880:			
Georgia	M.	(¹)	.90-1.00-.95
Do	F.	66-69-67	.75-1.00-.90
Massachusetts	M.	60-60-60	.60-.70-.65
Do	F.	60-60-60	.60-1.05-.87
New York	F.	60-66-63	.72-.74-.73

¹ Not reported.

TABLE L-17.—*Speeder tenders, cotton goods, 1840-1900, by year and State*—Con.

Year and State	Sex	Hours per week	Rate per day (dollars)	Year and State	Sex	Hours per week	Rate per day (dollars)
1880—Continued.				**1886:**			
Pennsylvania-----	F.	60-60-60	0.44-0.66-0.58	Connecticut------	M.	(1)	0.25-0.25-0.25
South Carolina----	F.	(1)	.83-.83-.83	Do----------	F.	(1)	.34-.34-.34
Virginia----------	F.	68-68-68	.75-.75-.75	Maine-----------	F.	66-66-66	.85-.95-.90
1881:				Maryland--------	F.	60-61-60	.90-1.17-1.01
Georgia----------	F.	66-66-66	.75-.75-.75	Massachusetts----	F.	60-60-60	.65-1.05-.83
Indiana----------	F.	(1)	.92-.92-.92	Missouri---------	F.	66-66-66	.67-.67-.67
Massachusetts----	M.	60-60-60	.50-.65-.59	New Hampshire--	F.	60-60-60	.69-1.33-1.07
Do----------	F.	60-60-60	.60-1.05-.85	New Jersey-------	F.	60-60-60	.58-.92-.77
New Hamshire--	F.	65-65-65	.50-1.65-.93	New York--------	F.	66-66-66	.66-.66-.66
New York--------	F.	66-66-66	.80-.80-.80	Pennsylvania-----	F.	60-64-60	1.00-1.45-1.19
North Carolina---	F.	(1)	.40-.40-.40	Rhode Island-----	F.	59-60-60	.75-1.17-.98
Rhode Island-----	F.	66-66-66	.80-.94-.90	**1887:**			
South Carolina----	F.	72-72-72	.70-.70-.70	Alabama---------	F.	66-66-66	.88-.92-.89
1882:				Connecticut------	M.	(1)	1.00-1.25-1.11
Georgia----------	F.	70-72-72	.65-.90-.75	Do----------	F.	(1)	1.06-1.09-1.08
Massachusetts----	M.	60-60-60	.60-.65-.61	Georgia----------	F.	65-72-67	.40-1.00-.73
Do----------	F.	60-60-60	.55-1.10-.90	Louisiana--------	F.	60-60-60	.75-.75-.75
New Hampshire--	M.	66-66-66	.50-1.26-.83	Massachusetts----	F.	60-60-60	.55-1.15-.86
Do----------	F.	66-66-66	.80-1.27-1.01	New York--------	F.	60-60-60	.68-.83-.73
New Jersey-------	M.	60-60-60	2.00-2.00-2.00	Ohio------------	F.	60-60-60	.45-.83-.69
New York--------	F.	66-66-66	.79-.79-.79	Wisconsin--------	(1)	(1)	.93-.93-.93
North Carolina---	M.	(1)	.67-.67-.67	**1888:**			
Do----------	F.	65-72-68	.45-.75-.60	Georgia----------	F.	58-71-66	.50-1.33-.91
South Carolina----	M.	69-69-69	.75-1.00-.88	Do----------	M.	66-66-66	.75-1.11-.90
Do----------	F.	69-76-71	.40-1.00-.71	Indiana----------	M.	60-60-60	.96-.96-.96
1883:				Massachusetts----	F.	60-60-60	.60-1.52-1.06
Alabama----------	M.	(1)	.64-1.01-.80	New Hampshire--	F.	(1)	.95-.95-.95
Georgia----------	F.	66-66-66	.60-1.12-.76	New York--------	M.	(1)	.46-1.25-.87
Massachusetts----	M.	60-60-60	.55-1.25-1.13	Do----------	F.	60-60-60	.60-1.10-.83
Do----------	F.	60-60-60	.55-1.40-.93	North Carolina---	M.	(1)	.30-.80-.53
Mississippi-------	F.	(1)	.50-1.02-.71	Do----------	F.	(1)	.30-1.00-.62
New Jersey-------	M.	66-66-66	.58-2.00-1.70	Rhode Island-----	M.	(1)	.80-1.17-.92
Do----------	F.	60-66-61	.67-1.00-.88	Do----------	(1)	(1)	.66-2.25-1.32
New York--------	F.	66-66-66	.72-.72-.72	South Carolina----	F.	65-65-65	.78-.82-.80
North Carolina---	F.	(1)	.60-.60-.60	Do----------	M.	(1)	.20-.70-.49
South Carolina----	F.	70-70-70	.83-.90-.87	Virginia----------	F.	60-61-60	.50-.83-.65
Tennessee--------	M.	66-66-66	.87-1.07-.97	Do----------	M.	(1)	.75-1.00-.83
Do----------	F.	66-66-66	.50-.86-.70	**1889:**			
1884:				Connecticut------	M.	(1)	1.00-1.00-1.00
Georgia----------	F.	60-70-68	.70-1.00-.84	Georgia----------	M.	66-70-69	.50-1.15-1.01
Louisiana--------	F.	63-66-64	.62-.87-.76	Do----------	M.	66-66-66	.50-.90-.68
Massachusetts----	F.	60-60-60	.65-1.05-.94	Maine-----------	F.	(1)	.60-1.55-1.04
New Jersey-------	M.	60-60-60	1.00-1.00-1.00	Do----------	M.	(1)	.66-1.20-.93
Do----------	F.	60-60-60	.67-.83-.80	Maryland--------	F.	(1)	.39-.90-.69
New York--------	F.	66-66-66	.79-.79-.79	Massachusetts----	F.	60-60-60	.90-1.20-1.05
North Carolina---	F.	69-72-71	.40-.60-.53	Do----------	F.	60-60-60	.70-1.77-1.14
South Carolina----	M.	69-69-69	1.00-1.00-1.00	Mississippi-------	M.	(1)	.60-.92-.78
Do----------	F.	69-69-69	.67-.90-.81	Do----------	F.	(1)	.73-.97-.80
Virginia----------	F.	69-69-69	.67-.67-.67	Do----------	(1)	(1)	.60-.89-.71
1885:				New Hampshire--	M.	60-60-60	1.10-1.50-1.26
Alabama----------	M.	63-63-63	.61-.96-.74	Do----------	F.	60-60-60	.69-1.43-.99
Do----------	F.	66-66-66	.49-.62-.57	New York--------	F.	60-60-60	.70-.70-.70
Connecticut-------	M.	66-66-66	.95-.95-.95	Pennsylvania-----	M.	(1)	1.16-1.25-1.20
Do----------	F.	66-66-66	1.12-1.12-1.12	Do----------	F.	(1)	.57-1.48-1.05
Georgia----------	F.	(1)	.75-.75-.75	Rhode Island-----	M.	(1)	.84-1.04-.94
Maine-----------	M.	66-66-66	.98-.98-.98	Do----------	F.	60-60-60	.67-1.57-1.17
Maryland--------	M.	66-66-66	.60-.60-.60	South Carolina----	M.	69-69-69	.50-.65-.55
Do----------	F.	66-66-66	.75-.84-.82	Do----------	F.	69-69-69	.40-.60-.52
Massachusetts----	M.	60-60-60	.75-.95-.88	Tennessee--------	M.	(1)	.30-.75-.51
Do----------	F.	60-60-60	.50-1.05-.82	Do----------	M.	66-66-66	.60-.80-.66
New Hampshire--	M.	65-65-65	1.00-1.00-1.00	Virginia----------	F.	(1)	.50-.63-.60
Do----------	F.	60-65-64	.70-1.00-.83	Do----------	F.	(1)	.38-.63-.59
New Jersey-------	F.	60-60-60	.79-.90-.88	**1890:**			
Do----------	F.	60-60-60	.83-.83-.83	Alabama---------	M.	(1)	.68-1.08-.20
New York--------	M.	69-69-69	.35-.35-.35	Do----------	F.	63-66-65	.50-1.08-.84
Do----------	F.	69-69-69	.50-1.05-.62	Connecticut------	M.	(1)	1.14-1.14-1.19
North Carolina---	F.	69-69-69	.60-.60-.60	Louisiana--------	F.	(1)	.52-1.01-.73
Do----------	M.	69-69-68	.60-.60-.60	Massachusetts----	F.	60-60-60	.60-1.25-1.00
Pennsylvania----	F.	60-60-60	1.12-1.12-1.12	New York--------	M.	(1)	.75-1.13-.86
Vermont---------	M.	66-66-66	.82-.82-.82	North Carolina---	M.	66-69-69	.48-1.20-.76
Do----------	F.	66-66-66	.90-.90-.90	Do----------	F.	60-60-60	.50-.89-.66
Virginia----------	M.	66-66-66	.42-.42-.42	Pennsylvania----	M.	60-60-60	.83-1.08-.96
Do----------	F.	66-66-66	.55-.75-.61	Tennessee--------	M.	(1)	.70-.70-.70
				Do----------	F.	(1)	.55-.75-.67

1 Not reported.

TABLE **L-17.**—*Speeder tenders, cotton goods, 1840-1900, by year and State*—Con.

Year and State	Sex	Hours per week	Rate per day (dollars)	Year and State	Sex	Hours per week	Rate per day (dollars)
1891:				**1895—Continued.**			
Massachusetts	F.	60-60-60	0.80-1.25-1.07	Massachusetts	F.	58-60-58	0.73-1.21-0.97
New York	F.	60-60-60	.80-.80-.80	Mississippi	F.	60-60-60	.39-1.04-.58
Do	M.	(1)	.75-1.13-.85	New Hampshire	M.	60-60-60	.73-1.70-1.18
North Carolina	(1)	72-72-72	.65-.65-.65	Do	F.	60-60-60	.25-1.77-1.09
1892:				North Carolina	M.	65-72-70	.50-1.00-.68
Maine	M.	60-60-60	1.20-1.33-1.27	Do	F.	65-72-69	.50-1.00-.60
Do	F.	60-60-60	1.00-1.33-1.17	South Carolina	M.	66-66-66	.50-.85-.80
Massachusetts	M.	58-60-60	.63-1.07-.97	Do	F.	66-66-66	.50-.90-.82
Do	F.	60-60-60	.45-1.29-.98	Tennessee	M.	66-66-66	.53-1.21-.95
New York	F.	60-60-60	.83-.83-.83	Do	F.	66-66-66	.51-1.22-.73
1893:				Virginia	F.	60-60-60	.67-.83-.72
Massachusetts	M.	58-58-58	1.06-1.08-1.07	**1896:**			
New Jersey	F.	60-60-60	.50-1.56-1.01	Georgia	M.	63-66-65	.90-1.12-1.05
1894:				Do	F.	63-66-65	.50-1.30-.82
Indiana	F.	60-60-60	.75-.88-.79	Indiana	F.	65-65-65	.70-1.00-.87
Massachusetts	(1)	(1)	1.57-1.57-1.57	New Hampshire	M.	60-60-60	.95-1.06-1.01
Do	M.	58-58-58	1.01-1.01-1.01	Do	F.	60-60-60	.85-1.38-1.16
New York	F.	60-60-60	.88-.88-.88	New York	F.	60-60-60	.83-.88-.85
North Carolina	M.	60-69-65	.40-.70-.58	North Carolina	M.	66-69-68	.40-.60-.51
Do	F.	60-60-63	.60-.65-.62	Pennsylvania	F.	60-60-60	.51-1.61-1.06
Rhode Island	(1)	(1)	.80-1.50-1.05	Rhode Island	F.	60-60-60	.83-1.40-1.11
South Carolina	F.	66-66-66	.60-.70-.67	South Carolina	M.	66-66-66	.85-1.15-1.01
1895:				Do	F.	66-66-66	.85-1 15-1.03
Alabama	M.	60-66-62	.56-1.19-.83	**1897:**			
Do	F.	66-66-66	.38-.70-.54	Georgia	F.	66-66-66	.80-.80-.80
Georgia	M.	66-66-66	.60-1.40-.98	**1899:**			
Do	F.	66-66-66	.45-1.10-.86	Gerogia	F.	66-66-66	.70-.70-.70
Louisiana	F.	60-63-62	.32-1.00-.69	North Carolina	F.	66-69-66	.65-.96-.85
Maine	M.	60-60-60	1.00-1.10-1.07	**1900:**			
Do	F.	60-60-60	.55-1.37-1.12	Georgia	F.	66-66-66	.70-.70-.70
Massachusetts	M.	58-58-58	.80-1.01-.99	North Carolina	F.	60-69-66	.65-.96-.85

[1] Not reported.

TABLE **L-18.**—*Fine speeders, males, cotton goods, 1907-1928, by State and year*

Year	Alabama Hours per week	Alabama Rate per hour	Connecticut Hours per week	Connecticut Rate per hour	Georgia Hours per week	Georgia Rate per hour	Maine Hours per week	Maine Rate per hour
1907	66.0	$0.092			64.8	$0.105		
1908	60.9	.107			63.0	.112		
1909	61.0	.114			63.1	.129		
1910	61.6	.110			61.9	.121		
1911	61.4	.115			62.8	.128		
1912	62.4	.109	58.0	$0.143	60.0	.128	58.0	$0.151
1913	61.4	.132			60.0	.142		
1914	60.0	.137			60.0	.152		
1916	60.0	.147			60.0	.155		
1918	60.0	.204			60.0	.229		
1920	58.8	.400	50.0	.613	56.8	.460	54.0	.507
1922	55.6	.253	52.1	.450	56.2	.293	54.0	.420
1924	55.2	.284	52.5	.515	56.4	.306	55.7	.477
1926	54.9	.293	51.2	.451	57.4	.291	53.6	.467
1928	55.0	.276	50.7	.453	55.9	.307	55.0	.390

Year	Massachusetts Hours per week	Massachusetts Rate per hour	New Hampshire Hours per week	New Hampshire Rate per hour	New York Hours per week	New York Rate per hour	North Carolina Hours per week	North Carolina Rate per hour
1907							66.0	$0.115
1908							63.8	.109
1909							63.9	.114
1910							63.1	.131
1911							62.9	.140
1912	54.0	$0.156	58.0	$0.159			60.0	.117
1913	54.0	.148					60.0	.145
1914	54.0	.156					60.0	.157
1916	54.0	.229					60.0	.159
1918	54.0	.349					60.0	.249
1920	49.5	.674	48.0	.619	51.7	$0.626	55.2	.559
1922	49.4	.501	53.6	.463	53.1	.431	55.2	.353
1924	49.9	.565	54.1	.515	50.2	.562	55.3	.371
1926	51.1	.460	54.1	.467	49.0	.495	56.0	.333
1928	52.7	.461	53.8	.481	48.5	.476	56.2	.333

TABLE L-18.—*Fine speeders, males, cotton goods, 1907–1928, by State and year—*
Continued

Year	Rhode Island		South Carolina		Virginia	
	Hours per week	Rate per hour	Hours per week	Rate per hour	Hours per week	Rate per hour
1907			62.0	$0.129		
1908			60.0	.133		
1909			60.0	.138		
1910			60.0	.141		
1911			60.0	.136		
1912	56.0	$0.162	60.0	.129		
1913			60.0	.145		
1914			60.0	.151		
1916			60.0	.148		
1918			60.1	.220		
1920	50.3	.574	54.9	.500	55.4	$0.494
1922	50.8	.450	55.0	.414	55.2	.391
1924	52.9	.495	55.0	.302	55.3	.470
1926	51.3	.462	55.0	.294	55.3	.378
1928	52.7	.488	55.0	.296	55.2	.385

TABLE L-19.—*Fine speeders, females, cotton goods, 1907–1928, by State and year*

Year	Alabama		Connecticut		Georgia		Maine	
	Hours per week	Rate per hour	Hours per week	Rate per hour	Hours per week	Rate per hour	Hours per week	Rate per hour
1907	66.0	$0.103			63.8	$0.105	60.0	$0.145
1908	62.9	.098			62.2	.116	60.0	.136
1909	62.7	.104			62.4	.122	60.0	.139
1910	62.5	.101			63.0	.116	58.0	.137
1911	62.7	.100	58.0	$0.130	62.8	.116	58.0	.138
1912	62.4	.109	58.0	.143	60.0	.128	58.0	.151
1913	61.7	.122	58.0	.134	60.0	.133	58.0	.155
1914	60.2	.123	55.0	.147	60.0	.135	58.0	.154
1916	60.1	.139	55.0	.203	60.0	.152	58.0	.189
1918	60.1	.177	55.0	.274	60.0	.197	54.0	.296
1920	58.7	.331	48.7	.537	56.6	.441	54.0	.475
1922	55.6	.230	50.7	.384	56.5	.263	54.0	.382
1924	55.9	.262	50.9	.440	56.0	.289	54.0	.330
1926	55.0	.251	50.0	.381	56.1	.278	53.6	.393
1928	55.0	.276	50.7	.453	55.9	.307	55.0	.390

Year	Massachusetts		New Hampshire		New York		North Carolina	
1907	58.0	$0.148					66.0	$0.113
1908	58.0	.152					63.5	.112
1909	58.0	.142					65.0	.115
1910	56.0	.143	58.0	$0.130			62.5	.109
1911	56.0	.144	58.0	.143			62.2	.112
1912	54.0	.156	58.0	.159			60.0	.117
1913	54.0	.158	58.0	.159	54.0	$0.176	60.0	.124
1914	54.0	.160	55.0	.167	54.0	.173	60.0	.119
1916	54.0	.197	55.0	.202	54.0	.204	60.0	.143
1918	54.0	.291	54.0	.302	54.0	.267	60.0	.208
1920	48.0	.514	48.0	.523	48.8	.462	55.0	.482
1922	48.0	.402	53.6	.419	49.0	.357	55.1	.322
1924	48.0	.462	54.0	.467	48.4	.449	55.4	.349
1926	48.0	.390	53.3	.446	48.5	.392	55.9	.300
1928	52.7	.461	53.8	.481	48.5	.476	56.2	.333

Year	Pennsylvania		Rhode Island		South Carolina		Virginia	
1907			58.0	$0.145	62.0	$0.132		
1908			58.0	.153	60.0	.118		
1909			58.0	.148	60.0	.132		
1910			56.0	.141	60.0	.126		
1911			56.0	.147	60.0	.125		
1912			56.0	.162	60.0	.129		
1913			56.0	.165	60.0	.128		
1914			54.0	.167	60.0	.130		
1916			54.0	.197	60.0	.134		
1918			54.0	.305	59.8	.198		
1920	50.8	$0.408	49.6	.496	54.8	.438	55.7	$0.441
1922	52.6	.296	49.4	.393	54.9	.250	55.3	.328
1924	52.3	.326	51.8	.440	55.0	.286	55.3	.424
1926	53.1	.365	50.5	.386	55.0	.267	55.2	.327
1928			52.7	.488	55.0	.297	55.2	.385

TABLE L–20.—*Spinners, cotton goods, 1842–1900, by year and State*

Year and State	Sex	Hours per week	Rate per day (dollars)	Year and State	Sex	Hours per week	Rate per day (dollars)
1842:				**1866:**			
Massachusetts	F.	78-78-78	0.43-0.48-0.46	Massachusetts	M.	66-66-66	0.55-1.00-0.78
1843:				Do	F.	66-78-69	.55-1.00-.86
Massachusetts	F.	78-78-78	.40-.48-.45	New York	M.	72-72-72	1.38-1.38-1.38
1844:				Do	F.	72-72-72	.50-.50-.50
Massachusetts	F.	78-78-78	.35-.50-.43	**1867:**			
1845:				Massachusetts	M.	66-66-66	.55-.55-.55
Massachusetts	F.	78-78-78	.40-.50-.44	Do	F.	66-72-69	.50-1.00-.84
1846:				New York	M.	72-72-72	1.50-1.50-1.50
Massachusetts	F.	78-78-78	.37-.48-.43	Do	F.	72-72-72	.52-.52-.52
1847:				**1868:**			
Massachusetts	F.	78-78-78	.40-.48-.44	Massachusetts	M.	66-66-66	.58-1.00-.80
1848:				Do	F.	66-66-66	.50-1.04-.83
Massachusetts	F.	75-78-77	.35-.63-.51	New York	M.	66-66-66	1.50-1.50-1.50
1849:				Do	F.	66-66-66	.52-.52-.52
Massachusetts	F.	75-78-77	.40-.50-.47	**1869:**			
1850:				Massachusetts	M.	66-66-66	.58-1.00-.86
Massachusetts	F.	75-78-77	.30-.72-.52	Do	F.	66-66-66	.54-1.25-.83
1851:				New York	M.	66-66-66	1.75-1.75-1.75
Massachusetts	F.	75-78-77	.30-.50-.45	Do	F.	66-66-66	.52-.52-.52
1852:				**1870:**			
Massachusetts	F.	75-78-77	.30-.53-.46	Massachusetts	F.	66-72-66	.50-1.67-.93
1853:				Do	M.	60-66-64	.83-1.80-1.21
Massachusetts	F.	75-78-77	.30-.64-.46	New York	M.	66-66-66	1.75-1.75-1.75
New York	M.	72-72-72	.67-.67-.67	Do	F.	66-66-66	.54-.54-.54
Do	F.	72-72-72	.29-.29-.29	**1871:**			
1854:				Massachusetts	M.	58-66-64	1.09-2.25-1.91
Georgia	F.	(1)	.23-.23-.23	Do	F.	66-66-66	.50-1.67-1.03
Massachusetts	F.	66-78-74	.30-.64-.48	New York	M.	66-66-66	1.75-1.75-1.75
New York	M.	72-72-72	.67-.67-.67	Do	F.	66-66-66	.67-.67-.67
Do	F.	72-72-72	.42-.42-.42	**1872:**			
1855:				Massachusetts	M.	66-66-66	1.33-2.33-2.13
Massachusetts	F.	66-78-74	.30-.64-.47	Do	F.	66-66-66	.40-2.00-1.03
New York	M.	72-72-72	.75-.75-.75	New York	M.	66-66-66	1.75-1.75-1.75
Do	F.	72-72-72	.42-.42-.42	Do	F.	66-66-66	.67-.67-.67
1856:				South Carolina	F.	72-72-72	.50-.65-.59
Massachusetts	F.	66-66-66	.56-.56-.56	**1873:**			
New York	M.	72-72-72	.75-.75-.75	Massachusetts	M.	66-66-66	1.67-2.25-2.13
Do	F.	72-72-72	.42-.42-.42	Do	F.	66-66-66	.67-2.10-1.03
1857:				New York	M.	66-66-66	1.75-1.75-1.75
Massachusetts	F.	66-66-66	.56-.56-.56	Do	F.	66-66-66	.67-.67-.67
New York	M.	72-72-72	.75-.75-.75	Pennsylvania	(1)	(1)	.50-1.05-.54
Do	F.	72-72-72	.42-.42-.42	**1874:**			
1858:				Maine	M.	66-66-66	.50-1.50-1.00
Massachusetts	F.	66-78-74	.30-.64-.50	Do	F.	66-66-66	.60-1.00-.89
New York	M.	72-72-72	.63-.63-.63	Massachusetts	M.	66-66-66	.80-2.25-1.85
Do	F.	72-72-72	.34-.34-.34	Do	F.	66-66-66	.50-1.75-1.00
1859:				New York	M.	66-66-66	1.50-1.50-1.50
Maine	M.	(1)	.40-.40-.40	Do	F.	66-66-66	.71-.71-.71
Do	F.	(1)	.33-.50-.39	Pennsylvania	M.	(1)	.68-1.75-.91
Massachusetts	M.	72-72-72	.96-.96-.96	Do	F.	(1)	1.00-1.00-1.00
Do	F.	66-78-74	.36-.64-.50	**1875:**			
New York	M.	72-72-72	.38-.67-.46	Georgia	F.	(1)	.60-.60-.60
1860:				Massachusetts	M.	60-60-60	.80-2.05-1.83
Massachusetts	F.	66-78-73	.30-.64-.50	Do	F.	60-60-60	.50-1.60-.91
New York	M.	72-72-72	.73-.73-.73	New York	M.	66-66-66	1.69-1.69-1.69
Do	F.	72-72-72	.37-.37-.37	Do	F.	66-66-66	.75-.75-.75
1861:				**1876:**			
Massachusetts	F.	66-78-75	.30-.67-.47	Massachusetts	M.	60-60-60	.65-2.05-1.84
New York	M.	72-72-72	.75-.75-.75	Do	F.	60-60-60	.50-1.35-.85
Do	F.	72-72-72	.37-.37-.37	New York	M.	66-66-66	1.48-1.48-1.48
1862:				Do	F.	66-66-66	.65-.65-.65
Massachusetts	F.	60-78-70	.30-.59-.50	Pennsylvania	M.	(1)	.28-2.00-.60
New York	M.	72-72-72	.75-.75-.75	Do	F.	(1)	.50-1.07-.67
Do	F.	72-72-72	.49-.49-.49	South Carolina	M.	66-66-66	.40-.50-.47
1863:				Do	F.	66-66-66	.40-.50-.45
Massachusetts	F.	66-72-71	.40-.59-.49	**1877:**			
1864:				Georgia	F.	66-66-66	.55-.55-.55
Massachusetts	M.	66-66-66	.40-.40-.40	Maine	M.	66-66-66	1.02-2.00-1.56
Do	F.	66-72-70	.50-.75-.61	Do	F.	66-66-66	.35-.75-.63
1865:				Massachusetts	M.	60-60-60	.60-2.00-1.76
Massachusetts	F.	66-72-69	.45-.83-.68	Do	F.	60-60-60	.50-1.30-.99
New York	M.	72-72-72	1.25-1.25-1.25	New York	M.	66-66-66	1.34-1.34-1.34
Do	F.	72-72-72	.50-.50-.50	Do	F.	66-66-66	.61-.61-.61

1 Not reported.

TABLE L-20.—*Spinners, cotton goods, 1842–1900, by year and State*—Continued

Year and State	Sex	Hours per week	Rate per day (dollars)
1878:			
Alabama	F.	(1)	0.40-0.40-0.40
Georgia	F.	(1)	.60-.60-.60
Massachusetts	M.	60-60-60	.65-2.00-1.81
Do	F.	60-66-60	.60-1.50-.84
New Hampshire	M.	60-60-60	.40-1.75-1.03
Do	F.	60-60-60	.40-.80-.70
New York	M.	66-66-66	1.34-1.34-1.34
Do	F.	66-66-66	.61-.61-.61
North Carolina	F.	72-72-72	.40-.45-.43
Pennsylvania	M.	60-66-63	.30-2.33-.48
Do	F.	60-60-60	.50-1.00-.78
1879:			
Georgia	F.	(1)	.17-.42-.29
Massachusetts	M.	60-60-60	.70-1.90-1.72
Do	F.	60-60-60	.70-1.50-.90
New Jersey	(1)	65-65-65	1.25-1.25-1.25
New York	M.	66-66-66	1.34-1.34-1.34
Do	F.	66-66-66	.67-.67-.67
Pennsylvania	M.	60-60-60	.50-2.00-1.02
Do	F.	66-66-66	.70-.70-.70
Do	(1)	60-60-62	.33-.65-.55
1880:			
Connecticut	(1)	65-69-67	1.25-1.92-1.53
Georgia	F.	66-69-68	.30-.75-.59
Do	M.	69-69-69	1.30-1.40-1.35
Maine	(1)	66-72-66	.83-1.75-1.48
Massachusetts	M.	60-60-60	.70-1.75-1.66
Do	F.	60-60-60	.70-1.50-.93
Do	(1)	60-63-61	.92-1.67-1.38
New Hampshire	(1)	66-66-66	1.00-2.00-1.61
New York	M.	66-66-66	1.38-1.38-1.38
Do	F.	66-66-66	.67-.67-.67
Do	(1)	66-66-66	1.00-1.58-1.29
Pennsylvania	M.	60-60-60	.79-.90-.85
Rhode Island	(1)	66-66-66	1.00-1.67-1.40
Virginia	F.	68-68-68	.50-.50-.50
1881:			
Georgia	F.	(1)	.25-.79-.47
Massachusetts	M.	60-60-60	1.50-1.75-1.62
Do	F.	60-60-60	.70-1.50-.98
New Hampshire	M.	65-65-65	.45-2.00-.93
Do	F.	65-65-65	.25-1.30-.74
New Jersey	M.	68-68-68	1.50-1.50-1.50
New York	M.	66-66-66	1.50-1.50-1.50
Do	F.	66-66-66	.67-.67-.67
North Carolina	F.	(1)	.40-.40-.40
Rhode Island	M.	66-66-66	.60-1.60-1.36
Do	F.	66-66-66	.83-.83-.83
South Carolina	M.	72-72-72	.40-.40-.40
Do	F.	72-72-72	.40-.40-.40
1882:			
Georgia	F.	70-70-70	.35-.80-.49
Massachusetts	(1)	60-60-60	1.30-1.55-1.47
Do	M.	60-60-60	1.50-1.75-1.72
Do	F.	60-60-60	.70-1.55-.94
New Hampshire	M.	66-66-66	.33-1.75-1.04
Do	F.	66-66-66	.25-1.00-.80
New Jersey	M.	66-66-66	2.00-2.00-2.00
New York	M.	66-66-66	1.75-1.75-1.75
Do	F.	66-66-66	.67-.67-.67
North Carolina	M.	72-72-72	.40-.45-.43
Do	F.	65-72-68	.30-.60-.48
Ohio	(1)	60-60-60	1.50-1.50-1.50
Rhode Island	F.	(1)	.83-.83-.83
South Carolina	M.	69-69-69	.30-.90-.57
Do	F.	69-76-70	.29-.70-.51
1883:			
Alabama	F.	(1)	.27-.67-.42
Georgia	F.	66-66-66	.35-.80-.61
Do	M.	66-66-66	.60-1.00-.79
Massachusetts	(1)	60-60-60	1.72-1.72-1.72
Do	M.	60-60-60	1.00-2.11-1.60
Do	F.	60-60-60	.68-1.55-.83
Do	(1)	(1)	.45-1.00-.80
Mississippi	F.	(1)	.33-.88-.63
1883—Continued.			
New Jersey	M,	60-60-60	2.00-2.00-2.00
Do	F.	60-60-60	.33-1.17-.58
New York	M.	66-66-66	1.75-1.75-1.75
Do	F.	66-66-66	.67-.67-.67
North Carolina	F.	(1)	.60-.60-.60
Rhode Island	F.	(1)	.58-.58-.58
South Carolina	F.	70-72-71	.30-.75-.56
Do	M.	70-72-71	.30-.65-.52
Tennessee	M.	66-66-66	.46-1.18-.70
Do	F.	66-66-66	.49-.73-.60
1884:			
Georgia	F.	66-70-69	.38-.93-.52
Indiana	M.	(1)	.35-1.26-.92
Do	F.	(1)	.30-.70-.48
Louisiana	M.	66-66-66	.45-.50-.48
Do	F.	63-66-64	.33-.85-.60
Massachusetts	M.	59-60-60	1.50-1.80-1.57
Do	F.	60-60-60	.60-1.45-.92
Do	(1)	60-60-60	1.36-1.70-1.46
New Hampshire	M.	60-60-60	.35-1.70-.90
New Jersey	M.	60-60-60	.50-2.75-1.10
Do	F.	60-60-60	.38-1.50-.55
New York	M.	66-66-66	1.65-1.65-1.65
Do	F.	66-66-66	.71-.71-.71
North Carolina	F.	69-72-70	.35-.50-.43
South Carolina	F.	69-69-69	.40-.65-.48
Do	M.	69-69-69	.40-.65-.48
Tennessee	F.	66-66-66	.33-.83-.56
Virginia	F.	69-69-69	.50-.50-.50
1885:			
Alabama	M.	63-66-64	.24-.50-.34
Do	F.	63-66-64	.29-.68-.43
Connecticut	M.	66-66-66	.26-1.80-1.10
Do	M.	66-66-66	.26-.58-.42
Delaware	M.	66-66-66	2.50-2.50-2.50
Georgia	M.	60-60-60	.37-.85-.53
Do	F.	69-69-69	.35-.80-.43
Maine	M.	64-66-66	.30-1.75-1.30
Do	F.	64-66-66	.30-.85-.58
Maryland	M.	66-66-66	.45-.45-.45
Do	F.	66-66-66	.45-.79-.68
Massachusetts	M.	60-60-60	.43-1.80-1.06
Do	F.	60-60-60	.25-1.45-.91
New Hampshire	M.	60-66-65	.25-1.62-.85
Do	F.	60-66-65	.25-1.02-.73
New Jersey	M.	54-60-60	.67-2.33-1.02
Do	F.	55-60-59	.33-1.67-.70
New York	M.	66-69-69	.62-1.75-.99
Do	F.	66-69-69	.35-1.25-.40
North Carolina	M.	69-69-69	.45-.50-.46
Do	F.	66-69-68	.45-.55-.49
Pennsylvania	F.	66-66-66	.88-.88-.88
South Carolina	F.	66-66-66	.25-.65-.65
Vermont	M.	66-66-66	1.20-1.20-1.20
Do	F.	66-66-66	.65-.65-.65
Virginia	M.	66-66-66	.44-.50-.45
Do	F.	66-66-66	.38-.55-.49
1886:			
Connecticut	M.	66-66-65	.43-.140-.88
Do	F.	60-60-60	.30-1.12-.89
Georgia	F.	(1)	.25-.40-.33
Maine	(1)	66-66-66	1.88-1.96-1.92
Maryland	F.	60-61-60	.32-.88-.68
Massachusetts	M.	60-60-60	1.40-1.80-1.55
Do	F.	60-60-60	.60-1.65-.96
Missouri	F.	66-66-66	.33-.67-.50
New Hampshire	M.	60-65-61	1.34-1.73-1.47
Do	F.	60-60-60	.36-1.41-.76
New Jersey	M.	60-60-60	1.33-2.00-1.65
Do	F.	60-60-60	.83-1.33-1.08
New York	(1)	66-66-66	1.40-1.40-1.40
Do	M.	66-66-66	1.65-1.65-1.65
Do	F.	66-66-66	.67-.67-.67
Pennsylvania	F.	60-64-61	.45-1.25-.79

1 Not reported.

TABLE L-20.—*Spinners, cotton goods, 1842-1900, by year and State*—Continued

Year and State	Sex	Hours per week	Rate per day (dollars)	Year and State	Sex	Hours per week	Rate per day (dollars)
1886—Continued.				1890:			
Pennsylvania	M.	60–60–60	0.54–2.17–1.24	Alabama	M.	63–67–65	0.37–0.54–0.40
Rhode Island	(1)	60–60–60	1.24–1.49–1.42	Do	F.	63–69–65	.20–.68–.40
Do	F.	59–60–60	.60–.83–.73	Connecticut	M.	(1)	.67–1.75–1.47
1887:				Do	F.	(1)	.67–.67–.67
Alabama	F.	66–68–67	.31–.55–.43	Kentucky	M.	66–66–66	1.67–1.67–1.67
California	F.	60–60–60	.60–1.50–.96	Do	F.	66–66–66	.54–.54–.54
Connecticut	M.	(1)	.73–1.17–1.06	Louisiana	F.	(1)	.25–.80–.47
Do	F.	(1)	.61–.90–.75	Massachusetts	M.	60–60–60	.75–1.90–1.61
Georgia	F.	65–72–67	.08–1.00–.46	Do	F.	60–60–60	.60–1.70–.96
Louisiana	F.	60–60–60	.40–.44–.42	Mississippi	F.	66–66–66	.40–.40–.40
Maine	(1)	66–66–66	1.33–1.50–1.42	New York	M.	90–60–60	.38–3.00–.87
Do	M.	60–60–60	1.33–1.75–1.46	Do	F.	60–60–60	.90–.90–.90
Massachusetts	M.	60–60–60	.32–1.80–1.42	North Carolina	M.	(1)	.25–.95–.39
Do	F.	60–60–60	.16–1.65–.96	Do	F.	66–69–68	.15–.90–.45
New York	M.	60–60–60	1.40–1.50–1.47	Pennsylvania	M.	60–60–60	.67–.67–.67
Do	F.	60–60–60	.50–.90–.70	Do	F.	60–60–60	.37–.83–.70
Ohio	F.	60–60–60	.35–.83–.62	Tennessee	M.	(1)	.44–1.36–1.12
Pennsylvania	M.	60–60–60	2.00–2.00–2.00	Do	F.	(1)	.38–1.04–.65
Rhode Island	M.	60–60–60	1.40–1.50–1.47	Do	(1)	69–69–69	.39–.39–.39
South Carolina	F.	65–65–65	.60–.60–.60	1891:			
Wisconsin	(1)	(1)	.65–1.33–.76	Maine	M.	60–60–60	1.50–2.25–1.75
1888:				Do	F.	60–60–60	.65–.90–.80
California	F.	62–62–62	.60–1.50–.96	Massachusetts	M.	60–60–60	.83–1.90–1.63
Georgia	F.	66–71–66	.20–1.11–.61	Do	F.	60–60–60	.70–1.65–1.01
Do	M.	66–66–66	.27–1.20–.61	New York	M.	60–60–60	.38–3.00–.90
Indiana	F.	60–60–60	.67–.83–.75	Do	F.	60–60–60	1.00–1.00–1.00
Maine	F.	60–60–60	.75–.92–.84	North Carolina	(1)	66–66–66	1.75–1.75–1.75
Massachusetts	M.	60–60–60	.29–2.00–1.46	Tennessee	F.	(1)	.68–.68–.68
Do	F.	60–60–60	.37–1.65–.90	1892:			
New Hampshire	F.	60–60–60	.30–1.00–.94	Maine	M.	60–60–60	1.42–1.92–1.74
Do	(1)	60–60–60	.45–.90–.69	Do	F.	60–60–60	.63–1.08–.79
New Jersey	(1)	57–60–58	.58–1.00–.75	Massachusetts	M.	58–60–58	.99–2.09–1.15
New York	M.	60–60–60	.67–2.50–1.24	Do	F.	58–60–59	.25–1.02–.88
Do	F.	60–60–60	.50–.84–.66	New York	M.	60–60–60	.50–1.94–1.19
North Carolina	M.	(1)	.40–.40–.40	Do	F.	60–60–60	.50–1.00–.86
Do	F.	(1)	.20–.80–.41	1893:			
Rhode Island	M.	(1)	1.54–1.54–1.54	Massachusetts	M.	58–58–58	1.70–1.70–1.70
Do	F.	(1)	.47–.52–.51	Do	F.	58–58–58	.94–.94–.94
Do	(1)	(1)	.93–.93–.93	New Jersey	F.	60–60–60	.33–.92–.67
Do	(1)	(1)	1.25–1.84–1.48	New York	M.	60–60–60	.42–1.98–1.03
South Carolina	F.	65–71–67	.10–.75–.33	Do	F.	60–60–60	.50–1.00–.87
Do	M.	66–66–66	.20–.85–.37	1894:			
Virginia	F.	60–61–60	.23–.75–.45	Indiana	M.	60–60–60	2.00–2.00–2.00
Do	M.	(1)	.30–.50–.44	Do	F.	60–60–60	.58–.88–.72
1889:				Maine	M.	60–60–60	1.50–1.92–1.80
Connecticut	M.	60–60–60	.22–1.50–.55	Massachusetts	(1)	(1)	1.06–3.27–1.77
Do	F.	60–60–60	.63–.83–.67	Do	M.	58–58–58	1.50–1.50–1.50
Georgia	M.	66–66–66	.20–.50–.34	Do	F.	58–58–58	.74–.74–.74
Do	F.	66–70–67	.20–.68–.59	New York	M.	60–60–60	.42–1.00–.83
Maine	M.	60–60–60	.17–1.85–1.13	Do	M.	60–60–60	.50–1.94–1.12
Do	F.	60–60–60	.25–1.01–.69	North Carolina	F.	60–69–64	.40–.50–.45
Maryland	M.	(1)	.15–.82–.56	Rhode Island	(1)	(1)	.75–3.50–1.63
Do	F.	(1)	.25–.66–.57	South Carolina	F.	66–66–66	.45–.45–.45
Massachusetts	M.	60–60–60	.45–2.08–1.61	1895:			
Do	F.	60–60–60	.30–1.65–.84	Alabama	M.	60–66–63	.19–.53–.34
Mississippi	M.	(1)	.12–.69–.38	Do	F.	60–66–64	.18–.67–.39
Do	F.	(1)	.10–.51–.31	Georgia	M.	66–66–66	.40–1.25–.82
Do	(1)	(1)	.13–.70–.39	Do	F.	66–66–66	.25–.75–.54
New Hampshire	M.	60–60–60	.50–2.39–1.57	Louisiana	F.	60–60–60	.40–.86–.61
Do	F.	60–60–60	.40–1.08–.79	Maine	F.	60–60–60	.30–2.07–1.06
Do	F.	60–60–60	.45–1.88–.96	Do	F.	60–60–60	.20–1.00–.72
Do	(1)	60–60–60	.50–1.50–1.11	Massachusetts	M.	58–58–58	1.00–1.50–1.27
New York	M.	60–60–60	.33–.90–.56	Do	F.	58–58–58	.80–1.25–.81
Do	F.	60–60–60	.40–.40–.40	Mississippi	F.	60–60–60	.28–.97–.51
North Carolina	F.	69–69–69	.40–.40–.40	New Hampshire	F.	60–60–60	.30–2.31–1.15
Pennsylvania	M.	(1)	.25–2.21–.64	Do	F.	60–60–60	.30–1.35–.80
Do	F.	(1)	.25–.98–.64	New Jersey	F.	53–53–53	.97–.97–.97
Rhode Island	F.	(1)	.31–2.04–1.56	New York	M.	60–60–60	.75–1.93–1.23
Do	F.	60–60–60	.18–1.00–.61	Do	F.	60–60–60	.50–1.00–.83
South Carolina	M.	66–69–67	.25–1.00–.54	North Carolina	M.	69–72–70	.30–.40–.38
Do	F.	66–69–68	.10–.55–.40	Do	F.	65–72–69	.20–.80–.52
Tennessee	M.	66–66–66	.91–1.60–1.49	Do	(1)	66–66–66	.40–.40–.40
Do	F.	66–66–66	.41–.82–.69	Ohio	F.	60–60–60	.55–.62–.60
Virginia	M.	(1)	.17–.55–.41				
Do	F.	(1)	.15–.60–.41				

1 Not reported.

TABLE **L–20.**—*Spinners, cotton goods, 1842–1900, by year and State*—Continued

Year and State	Sex	Hours per week	Rate per day (dollars)	Year and State	Sex	Hours per week	Rate per day (dollars)
1895—Continued.				1898:			
South Carolina____	M.	66–66–66	0. 30–0. 60–0. 43	Louisiana_____	F.	63–63–63	0. 22–0. 85–0. 52
Do_____	F.	66–66–66	. 30– . 60– . 44	New York_____	M.	60–60–60	1. 33–1. 85–1. 68
Tennessee_____	M.	66–66–66	. 36–1. 31– . 70	1899:			
Do_____	F.	66–66–66	. 31–1. 00– . 51	Alabama_____	M.	70–70–70	. 30– . 47– . 41
Virginia_____	F.	60–60–60	. 47– . 54– . 50	Do_____	F.	70–70–70	. 20– . 80– . 42
1896:				Georgia_____	F.	66–66–66	. 21– . 80– . 48
Georgia_____	M.	63–66–64	. 60–1. 25– . 82	Massachusetts____	M.	58–58–58	1. 67–1. 82–1. 79
Do_____	F.	63–66–65	. 25– . 80– . 58	Do_____	(¹)	58–58–58	. 64–1. 06– . 84
Indiana_____	M.	65–65–65	. 50–1. 66–1. 32	North Carolina___	F.	66–69–69	. 25–1. 00– . 52
Do_____	F.	65–65–65	. 35– . 80– . 53	Do_____	(¹)	66–66–66	. 30– . 50– . 37
New Hampshire__	M.	60–60–60	. 93–2. 28–1. 88	South Carolina____	F.	66–66–66	. 36– . 54– . 45
Do_____	F.	60–60–60	. 46–1. 08– . 81	Do_____	(¹)	66–66–66	. 20– . 66– . 56
New York_____	M.	60–60–60	1. 52–1. 94–1. 73	1900:			
Do_____	F.	60–60–60	. 67–1. 00– . 85	Alabama_____	M.	70–70–70	. 30– . 47– . 41
North Carolina___	M.	68–69–69	. 30–1. 00– . 58	Do_____	F.	70–70–70	. 20– . 80– . 42
Do_____	F.	66–69–68	. 30– . 90– . 48	Georgia_____	F.	66–66–66	. 21– . 88– . 51
Ohio_____	F.	42–42–42	. 83– . 83– . 83	Massachusetts____	M.	58–58–58	1. 81–1. 93–1. 87
Pennsylvania_____	M.	60–60–60	. 46–1. 92–1. 13	Do_____	(¹)	58–58–58	. 70–1. 17– . 96
Do_____	F.	60–60–60	. 29–1. 17– . 73	North Carolina___	F.	66–69–69	. 25–1. 00– . 52
Rhode Island_____	M.	60–60–60	1. 67–1. 67–1. 67	Do_____	(¹)	66–66–66	. 30– . 50– . 37
Do_____	F.	60–60–60	. 90– . 90– . 90	South Carolina____	F.	66–66–66	. 36– . 54– . 45
South Carolina____	M.	66–66–66	. 30– . 90– . 59	Do_____	(¹)	66–66–66	. 20– . 66– . 56
Do_____	F.	66–66–66	. 40– . 70– . 58				
1897:							
Georgia_____	F.	66–66–66	. 40– . 40– . 40				
New York_____	M.	60–63–61	1. 50–2. 00–1. 81				

¹ Not reported.

TABLE **L–21.**—*Spinners, frame, females, cotton goods, 1890–1906, by State and year*

Year	Massachusetts		New Hampshire		Rhode Island		South Carolina	
	Hours per week	Rate per hour	Hours per week	Rate per hour	Hours per week	Rate per hour	Hours per week	Rate per hour
1890_____	60. 0	$0. 091	60. 0	$0. 080	60. 0	$0. 053	66. 0	$0. 030
1891_____	60. 0	. 089	60. 0	. 081	60. 0	. 053	68. 3	. 031
1892_____	60. 0	. 091	60. 0	. 091	60. 0	. 055	68. 1	. 025
1893_____	58. 0	. 099	60. 0	. 094	60. 0	. 061	66. 0	. 025
1894_____	55. 0	. 089	60. 0	. 089	60. 0	. 058	66. 0	. 030
1895_____	58. 0	. 091	60. 0	. 092	60. 0	. 059	66. 0	. 028
1896_____	58. 0	. 097	60. 0	. 088	60. 0	. 068	66. 0	. 034
1897_____	56. 2	. 096	60. 0	. 083	60. 0	. 063	66. 0	. 035
1898_____	58. 0	. 092	60. 0	. 078	60. 0	. 059	66. 0	. 033
1899_____	58. 0	. 089	60. 0	. 080	60. 0	. 063	66. 0	. 034
1900_____	58. 0	. 104	60. 0	. 092	60. 0	. 076	66. 0	. 036
1901_____	58. 0	. 103	60. 0	. 081	60. 0	. 073	66. 0	. 041
1902_____	58. 0	. 103	60. 0	. 088	58. 0	. 094	66. 0	. 041
1903_____	58. 0	. 106	60. 0	. 091	58. 0	. 098	_____	_____
1904_____	58. 0	. 101	60. 0	. 095	58. 0	. 085	66. 0	. 060
1905_____	58. 0	. 106	60. 0	. 097	58. 0	. 098	66. 0	. 075
1906_____	58. 0	. 122	60. 0	. 104	58. 0	. 110	65. 7	. 079

390 PART 2.—FROM 1840 TO 1928

TABLE L–22.—*Spinners, frame, females, cotton goods, 1907–1928, by State and year*

Year	Alabama		Georgia		Maine		Massachusetts	
	Hours per week	Rate per hour	Hours per week	Rate per hour	Hours per week	Rate per hour	Hours per week	Rate per hour
1907	66.0	$0.073	64.3	$0.087	60.0	$0.121	58.0	$0.138
1908	61.9	.078	62.6	.088	60.0	.105	58.0	.132
1909	62.3	.080	62.8	.089	60.0	.109	58.0	.124
1910	61.5	.083	62.9	.090	58.0	.121	56.0	.131
1911	62.1	.084	62.9	.096	58.0	.117	56.0	.130
1912	62.6	.099	60.0	.107	58.0	.133	54.0	.146
1913	61.8	.097	60.0	.104	58.0	.141	54.0	.149
1914	60.1	.098	60.0	.108	58.0	.142	53.9	.150
1916	60.1	.105	60.0	.114	58.0	.174	53.9	.185
1918	59.0	.169	59.8	.170	53.8	.290	53.7	.277
1920	57.5	.293	54.6	.356	54.0	.449	47.9	.506
1922	55.7	.179	55.8	.225	54.0	.331	48.0	.386
1924	55.5	.202	56.1	.223	54.0	.333	48.0	.437
1926	54.5	.209	57.0	.220	53.9	.295	48.0	.378
1928	55.0	.215	56.1	.222	54.0	.311	48.0	.350

Year	North Carolina		Rhode Island		South Carolina		New Hampshire	
	Hours per week	Rate per hour	Hours per week	Rate per hour	Hours per week	Rate per hour	Hours per week	Rate per hour
1907	66.0	$0.084	58.0	$0.135	62.0	$0.095	--------	--------
1908	64.2	.076	58.0	.125	60.1	.094	--------	--------
1909	64.1	.084	58.0	.120	60.0	.095	--------	--------
1910	63.1	.079	56.0	.140	60.0	.090	58.0	$0.121
1911	63.0	.085	56.0	.132	60.0	.096	58.0	.125
1912	60.0	.095	56.0	.121	60.0	.102	58.0	.144
1913	60.0	.101	56.0	.144	60.0	.102	58.0	.148
1914	60.0	.110	54.0	.151	60.0	.106	55.0	.154
1916	60.0	.111	54.0	.190	60.0	.104	55.0	.188
1918	58.5	.186	53.8	.303	56.5	.168	53.9	.279
1920	54.2	.420	49.4	.500	54.0	.391	47.9	.513
1922	54.5	.251	49.6	.374	54.2	.206	53.7	.393
1924	55.3	.256	51.2	.425	55.0	.219	54.0	.456
1926	56.0	.230	50.0	.362	55.0	.213	53.5	.409
1928	55.9	.242	52.5	.367	55.0	.215	53.6	.407

TABLE L–23.—*Weavers, cotton goods, 1841–1900, by year and State*

Year and State	Sex	Hours per week	Rate per day (dollars)	Year and State	Sex	Hours per week	Rate per day (dollars)
1841:				1852:			
Massachusetts	M.	84-84-84-	0.33-0.33-0.33	Massachusetts	M.	72-72-72	0.58-0.84-0.81
1842:				Do.	F.	78-78-78	.30- .67- .62
Massachusetts	F.	78-78-78	.33-1.25- .61	1853:			
1843:				Massachusetts	M.	(¹)	.83- .83- .83
Massachusetts	F.	78-78-78	.30-1.25- .60	Do.	F.	72-78-77	.23- .79- .61
1844:				New York	F.	72-72-72	.30- .70- .50
Massachusetts	F.	78-84-80	.30- .46- .40	1854:			
1845:				Massachusetts	M.	(¹)	.81- .81- .81
Massachusetts	F.	78-78-78	.38- .50- .43	Do.	F.	72-78-78	.23- .75- .58
1846:				New York	F.	72-72-72	.30- .84- .63
Massachusetts	F.	78-84-79	.38- .63- .45	1855:			
Rhode Island	(¹)	(¹)	1.33-1.33-1.33	Massachusetts	M.	72-72-72	.54-1.00- .88
1847:				Do.	F.	72-78-77	.23- .75- .64
Massachusetts	F.	78-84-79	.38- .71- .46	New York	M.	72-72-72	.84- .84- .84
1848:				Do.	F.	72-72-72	.50- .80- .58
Massachusetts	F.	78-84-79	.35- .71- .45	1856:			
1849:				Massachusetts	M.	72-72-72	.67-1.00- .94
Massachusetts	M.	(¹)	.88- .88- .88	Do.	F.	72-72-72	.54- .83- .70
Do.	F.	78-84-79	.38- .90- .76	New York	M.	72-72-72	.86- .86- .86
1850:				Do.	F.	72-72-72	.50- .85- .61
Massachusetts	M.	(¹)	1.05-1.05-1.05	1857:			
Do.	F.	78-84-79	.38- .88- .82	Massachusetts	M.	72-72-72	.58- .96- .95
1851:				Do.	F.	72-72-72	.23- .73- .71
Massachusetts	M.	(¹)	.93- .93- .93	New York	M.	72-72-72	1.05-1.05-1.05
Do.	F.	78-78-78	.30- .60- .64	Do.	F.	72-72-72	.50- .70- .65

¹ Not reported.

TABLE **L–23.**—*Weavers, cotton goods, 1841–1900, by year and State*—Con.

Year and State	Sex	Hours per week	Rate per day (dollars)
1858:			
Massachusetts	M.	(1)	1.01-1.01-1.01
Do	F.	72-78-78	.23-.78-.72
New York	M.	72-72-72	.80-.80-.80
Do	F.	72-72-72	.40-.75-.58
1859:			
Maine	F.	(1)	.38-.54-.46
Massachusetts	M.	72-72-72	.33-.93-.90
Do	F.	72-78-76	.17-.71-.66
New York	M.	72-72-72	.90-.90-.90
Do	F.	72-72-72	.40-.78-.62
1860:			
Massachusetts	M.	72-72-72	.33-.93-.91
Do	F.	72-78-76	.24-.75-.66
New York	M.	72-72-72	1.00-1.00-1.00
Do	F.	72-72-72	.40-.82-.73
1861:			
Massachusetts	M.	66-66-66	.33-.93-.91
Do	F.	66-78-75	.24-.75-.65
New York	M.	72-72-72	1.05-1.05-1.05
Do	F.	72-72-72	.40-.90-.74
1862:			
Massachusetts	M.	66-66-66	.33-.90-.88
Do	F.	66-72-70	.24-.75-.67
New York	M.	72-72-72	.77-.77-.77
Do	F.	72-72-72	.60-.80-.76
1863:			
Massachusetts	M.	(1)	.90-.90-.90
Do	F.	72-72-72	.45-.77-.73
1864:			
Massachusetts	M.	(1)	.92-.92-.92
Do	F.	72-72-72	.45-.75-.71
1865:			
Massachusetts	M.	(1)	1.20-1.20-1.20
Do	F.	66-72-71	.40-.97-.89
New York	M.	72-72-72	1.00-1.00-1.00
Do	F.	72-72-72	.50-1.05-.78
1866:			
Massachusetts	M.	(1)	1.55-1.55-1.55
Do	F.	72-72-72	.70-1.19-1.15
New York	M.	72-72-72	1.00-1.00-1.00
Do	F.	72-72-72	.50-1.00-.77
1867:			
Massachusetts	M.	66-66-66	.92-1.65-1.63
Do	F.	66-72-71	.50-1.35-1.27
New York	M.	72-72-72	1.29-1.29-1.29
Do	F.	72-72-72	.53-1.18-.90
1868:			
Massachusetts	M.	(1)	1.53-1.53-1.53
Do	F.	66-66-66	.50-1.27-1.22
New York	M.	66-66-66	1.34-1.34-1.34
Do	F.	66-66-66	.56-1.28-.99
1869:			
Massachusetts	M.	(1)	1.62-1.62-1.62
Do	F.	66-66-66	.63-1.50-1.21
New York	M.	66-66-66	1.25-1.25-1.25
Do	F.	66-66-66	.60-1.25-1.05
1870:			
Massachusetts	M.	(1)	1.58-1.58-1.58
Do	F.	66-66-66	.42-1.33-1.19
New York	M.	66-66-66	1.26-1.26-1.26
Do	F.	66-66-66	.63-1.17-.93
1871:			
Massachusetts	M.	(1)	1.78-1.78-1.78
Do	F.	66-66-66	.50-1.67-1.27
New York	M.	66-66-66	1.26-1.26-1.26
Do	F.	66-66-66	.62-1.16-.97
1872:			
Massachusetts	M.	(1)	1.91-1.91-1.91
Do	F.	66-66-66	.50-1.67-1.45
New York	M.	66-66-66	1.38-1.38-1.38
Do	F.	66-66-66	.64-1.20-1.00
South Carolina	M.	72-72-72	.83-1.08-.97
Do	F.	72-72-72	.67-1.08-.88

Year and State	Sex	Hours per week	Rate per day (dollars)
1873:			
Massachusetts	M.	(1)	1.84-1.84-1.84
Do	F.	66-66-66	.63-2.00-1.41
New York	M.	66-66-66	1.03-1.03-1.03
Do	F.	66-66-66	.63-1.15-.99
Pennsylvania	M.	(1)	2.00-2.00-2.00
Do	F.	(1)	.92-1.42-1.16
Do	(1)	(1)	.50-.50-.50
1874:			
Georgia	F.	(1)	.83-.83-.83
Maine	M.	66-66-66	.75-1.33-1.04
Do	F.	66-66-66	.90-1.00-.96
Massachusetts	M.	(1)	1.70-1.70-1.70
Do	F.	66-66-66	.55-1.80-1.33
New York	M.	66-66-66	1.17-1.17-1.17
Do	F.	66-66-66	.50-1.10-.90
Pennsylvania	M.	(1)	1.25-1.66-1.51
Do	F.	(1)	1.50-1.50-1.50
1875:			
Massachusetts	M.	(1)	1.18-1.72-1.58
Do	F.	60-60-60	.50-1.40-1.16
New York	M.	66-66-66	1.19-1.19-1.19
Do	F.	66-66-66	.63-1.15-.95
1876:			
Georgia	F.	(1)	.58-1.25-.94
Massachusetts	M.	(1)	1.65-1.65-1.65
Do	F.	60-60-60	.33-1.40-1.22
New York	M.	66-66-66	1.18-1.18-1.18
Do	F.	66-66-66	.60-1.04-.85
Pennsylvania	M.	(1)	1.17-2.00-1.44
Do	F.	(1)	.79-1.50-1.04
South Carolina	M.	66-66-66	.75-.98-.88
Do	F.	66-66-66	.67-.98-.82
1877:			
Georgia	F.	66-66-66	1.25-1.25-1.25
Maine	M.	66-66-66	.63-2.00-1.14
Do	F.	66-66-66	.41-1.30-.94
Massachusetts	M.	(1)	1.36-1.36-1.36
Do	F.	60-60-60	.33-1.30-1.07
New York	M.	66-66-66	1.00-1.00-1.00
Do	F.	66-66-66	.57-1.02-.79
1878:			
Georgia	F.	(1)	.46-.46-.46
Massachusetts	M.	(1)	1.42-1.42-1.42
Do	F.	60-60-60	.50-1.50-1.18
New Hampshire	M.	60-60-60	.67-1.75-1.10
Do	F.	60-60-60	.58-1.33-.96
New York	M.	66-66-66	.63-1.04-.76
North Carolina	F.	72-72-72	.46-.58-.49
Pennsylvania	M.	60-60-60	1.15-1.50-1.23
Do	F.	60-60-63	.80-1.20-.99
1879:			
Georgia	F.	(1)	1.00-1.00-1.00
Massachusetts	M.	(1)	1.34-1.34-1.34
New York	F.	60-60-60	.50-1.50-1.15
Pennsylvania	M.	66-66-66	.60-1.17-.84
Do	F.	60-60-61	.75-1.75-1.02
1880:			
Connecticut	(1)	65-72-68	.83-2.00-1.27
Georgia	M.	66-66-66	.75-1.00-.89
Do	F.	66-69-67	.67-1.25-.85
Maine	M.	66-66-66	1.00-1.42-1.15
Massachusetts	M.	(1)	1.31-1.31-1.31
Do	F.	60-60-60	.50-1.50-1.16
Do	M.	60-63-60	.83-1.67-1.30
New Hampshire	(1)	65-69-67	.83-1.50-1.18
New Jersey	M.	(1)	1.88-2.08-1.98
New York	F.	66-66-66	.60-1.06-.80
Pennsylvania	F.	60-60-60	.22-.90-.56
Rhode Island	(1)	66-66-66	.83-1.50-1.25
Virginia	F.	68-68-68	.67-.92 .80
1881:			
Georgia	F.	(1)	.75-.77-.76
Massachusetts	M.	(1)	.96-1.00-.98
Do	M.	(1)	1.23-1.23-1.23

1 Not reported.

Table L-23.—*Weavers, cotton goods, 1841-1900, by year and State*—Con.

Year and State	Sex	Lowest, highest, and average— Hours per week	Lowest, highest, and average— Rate per day (dollars)	Year and State	Sex	Lowest, highest, and average— Hours per week	Lowest, highest, and average— Rate per day (dollars)
1881—Continued.				**1885—Continued.**			
Massachusetts	F.	60–60–60	0.50–1.50–1.13	Delaware	F.	60–60–60	0.76–0.84–0.82
New Hampshire	(¹)	66–66–66	1.35–1.50–1.43	Georgia	M.	69–69–69	.85–.87–.86
Do	M.	65–65–65	.33–2.25–1.25	Do	F.	69–69–69	.75–1.17–.77
Do	F.	65–65–65	.27–2.12–1.05	Indiana	F.	65–65–65	.76–.85–.81
New York	F.	66–66–66	.62–1.17–.97	Maine	M.	64–66–66	.45–2.50–1.14
North Carolina	M.	(¹)	.67–.83–.74	Do	F.	64–66–65	.58–1.90–1.15
Do	F₁	(¹)	.50–.83–.65	Maryland	M.	66–66–66	.84–.84–.84
Ohio	F.	65–65–65	.90–.90–.90	Do	F.	66–66–66	.80–.92–.85
Rhode Island	(¹)	66–66–66	.80–.85–.83	Massachusetts	M.	60–60–60	.40–1.69–1.14
South Carolina	F.	72–72–72	.50–.90–.65	Do	F.	60–60–60	.35–1.50–.94
Do	M.	72–72–72	.50–1.00–.81	Do	(¹)	60–60–60	1.11–1.11–1.11
1882:				New Hampshire	M.	60–66–65	.36–2.50–1.08
Georgia	F.	72–72–72	.65–.90–.80	Do	F.	60–66–65	.38–2.20–1.00
Do	M.	72–72–72	.75–1.08–.91	New Jersey	F.	60–60–60	.42–1.19–.74
Massachusetts	M.	(¹)	1.26–1.26–1.26	Do	M.	60–60–60	.50–1.28–.84
Do	F.	60–60–60	.45–1.50–1.10	New York	M.	66–69–68	.44–1.29–.89
New Hampshire	M.	66–66–66	.43–1.76–1.18	Do	F.	66–69–68	.35–1.12–.90
Do	F.	66–66–66	.38–2.05–1.10	North Carolina	M.	66–69–69	.67–1.17–.80
New York	F.	66–66–66	.60–1.08–1.00	Do	F.	66–69–69	.67–1.17–.78
North Carolina	M.	72–72–72	.65–.75–.70	Pennsylvania	M.	60–60–60	1.12–1.12–1.12
Do	F.	72–72–72	.50–.83–.67	Do	F.	60–60–60	1.12–1.12–1.12
Ohio	(¹)	60–60–60	1.50–1.50–1.50	Do	(¹)	60–60–60	.92–1.66–1.23
South Carolina	M.	69–69–69	.65–1.17–.81	Rhode Island	M.	60–66–66	.67–1.65–1.65
Do	F.	69–69–69	.65–1.00–.77	Do	F.	60–60–60	1.17–1.67–1.40
1883:				Do	(¹)	66–66–66	1.24–1.24–1.24
Alabama	M.	(¹)	.36–1.02–.68	South Carolina	M.	66–66–66	.92–.92–.92
Do	F.	(¹)	.42–1.08 .71	Vermont	M.	66–66–66	1.00–1.00–1.00
Georgia	F.	66–69–69	.65–1.33–.84	Do	F.	66–66–66	.82–.82–.82
Do	M.	66–69–68	.67–1.40–.95	Virginia	M.	66–66–66	1.10–1.10–1.10
Maine	(¹)	65–65–65	1.20–1.20–1.20	Do	F.	66–66–66	.75–1.10–.79
Massachusetts	M.	(¹)	.85–1.50–1.37	**1886:**			
Do	F.	60–60–60	.40–1.60–1.06	Connecticut	M.	65–66–65	.65–1.80–1.24
Do	(¹)	(¹)	1.10–1.10 -1.10	Do	F.	65–66–65	.50–1.30–1.14
Mississippi	F.	(¹)	.60–1.17–.88	Do	(¹)	60–60–60	.89–.93–.91
New Jersey	M.	60–60–60	.67–1.50–1.17	Georgia	F.	(¹)	.50–.80–.68
Do	F.	60–60–60	.67–1.43–.88	Maryland	F.	60–61–60	.74–1.33–1.09
Do	(¹)	60–60–60	1.00–1.21–1.11	Massachusetts	(¹)	60–60–60	.96–1.51–1.30
New York	F.	66–66–66	.50–1.00–.84	Do	M.	(¹)	1.17–1.17–1.17
Rhode Island	(¹)	66–66–66	.90–1.50–1.13	Do	F.	60–60–60	.45–1.50–.98
Do	F.		.83–.83–.83	Missouri	F.	66–66–66	.88–1.08–.96
South Carolina	M.	70–72–71	.65–1.00–.83	New Hampshire	(¹)	65–65–65	1.00–1.25–1.13
Do	F.	70–72–71	.50–1.00–.77	Do	M.	60–60–60	.50–1.45–.94
Tennessee	M.	66–66–66	.49–1.32–.92	Do	F.	60–60–60	.50–1.48–.93
Do	F.	66–66–66	.46–1.08–.76	New Jersey	M.	60–60–60	.33–2.00–1.28
Wisconsin	(¹)	66–66–66	.75–.86–.81	Do	F.	60–60–60	.33–2.00–1.30
1884:				New York	(¹)	60–60–60	.90–.90–.90
Connecticut	(¹)	66–66–64	1.00–1.35–1.12	Do	F.	66–66–66	.60–1.05–.87
Georgia	F.	66–72–68	.65–1.17–.82	Pennsylvania	(²)	60–60–60	.92–1.33–1.13
Do	M.	66–70–69	.65–1.17–.84	Do	F.	53–61–60	.63–2.21–1.29
Indiana	M.	(¹)	.75–1.60–1.21	Do	M.	60–60–60	.70–2.11–1.43
Do	F.	(¹)	.30–1.13–.78	Rhode Island	(¹)	60–60–60	.90–1.63–1.11
Louisiana	F.	63–66–64	.43–1.08–.78	Do	F.	59–60–60	.54–2.13–1.19
Massachusetts	(¹)	60–60–60	1.40–1.40–1.40	Vermont	(¹)	66–66–66	1.00–1.00–1.00
Do	M.	60–60–60	.82–1.50–1.26	**1887:**			
Do	F.	60–60–60	.56–1.50–.96	California	F.	60–60–60	1.00–1.67–1.32
Do	F.	60–60–60	.45–1.50–1.08	Connecticut	M.	(¹)	1.36–1.36–1.36
New Hampshire	M.	60–60–60	.73–1.71–1.11	Do	F.	(¹)	.96–.99–.97
Do	F.	60–60–60	.68–1.42–1.02	Georgia	F.	65–72–67	.25–1.33–.80
New Jersey	M.	60–60–60	.83–1.17–.98	Louisiana	F.	60–60–60	.29–1.25–.71
Do	F.	60–60–60	.49–.88–.70	Maine	M.	60–66–62	1.30–1.65–1.48
New York	(¹)	66–66–66	1.25–1.65–1.45	Massachusetts	M.	(¹)	.82–1.45–1.32
Do	F.	60–66–63	.61–1.50–1.10	Do	F.	60–60–60	.45–1.50–1.08
North Carolina	M.	69–69–69	.50–.80–.68	New York	F.	59–72–61	.36–1.26–.79
Do	F.	69–69–69	.50–.80–.67	Ohio	F.	60–60–60	.67–1.33–.94
Pennsylvania	(¹)	60–60–60	1.50–1.66–1.58	Pennsylvania	F.	60–60–60	1.00–1.33–1.13
Rhode Island	(¹)	66–66–66	1.87–1.87–1.87	Rhode Island	M.	60–60–60	1.20–2.25–1.60
South Carolina	F.	69–69–69	.65–1.00–.83	**1888:**			
Do	M.	69–69–69	.65–1.00–.86	California	F.	62–62–62	1.00–1.67–1.32
Tennessee	M.	66–66–66	.47–.86–.67	Georgia	F.	66–71–66	.25–1.66–.86
Do	F.	66–66–66	.42–.65–.54	Do	M.	66–66–66	.38–1.66–.93
Virginia	(¹)	69–69–69	1.00–1.25–1.13	Maine	F.	60–60–60	.75–1.50–1.09
Do	F.	69–69–69	.75–1.08–.82	Massachusetts	M.	60–60–60	.36–1.80–1.21
1885:				Do	F.	60–60–60	.23–1.77–.99
Alabama	F.	63–63–63	.43–1.29–.80	Do	(¹)	60–60–60	1.00–1.90–1.45
Do	M.	63–63–63	.50–1.14–.76	New Hampshire	M.	60–60–60	.99–.99–.99
Connecticut	F.	66–66–66	.80–1.17–1.09	Do	F.	60–60–60	.48–1.34–.79
Do	F.	66–66–66	.80–.95–.94	Do	(¹)	(¹)	.40–1.31–.81

¹ Not reported.

TABLE L–23.—*Weavers, cotton goods, 1841–1900, by year and State—Con.*

Year and State	Sex	Hours per week	Rate per day (dollars)	Year and State	Sex	Hours per week	Rate per day (dollars)
1888—Continued.				**1893:**			
New Jersey	F.	60–60–60	0.80–1.16–0.93	Massachusetts	M.	58–58–58	1.34–1.55–1.52
Do	[1]	60–63–61	1.50–2.40–1.81	Do	F.	58–58–58	1.35–1.35–1.35
New York	M.	60–60–60	1.00–2.24–1.23	New Jersey	F.	60–60–60	.33–1.83–.97
Do	F.	60–60–60	.43–1.49–.92	New York	F.	60–60–60	.50–1.85–1.08
Do	[1]	60–60–60	1.10–1.10–1.10	**1894:**			
North Carolina	M.	[1]	.30–1.30–.76	Indiana	F.	60–60–60	.83–1.00–.92
Do	F.	[1]	.25–1.01–.67	Do	[1]	60–60–60	.85–.85–.85
Rhode Island	M.	[1]	1.25–1.25–1.25	Maine	M.	60–60–60	1.00–1.50–1.25
Do	F.	[1]	1.25–1.25–1.25	Massachusetts	M.	58–58–58	1.20–1.50–1.49
Do	[1]	[1]	.83–1.75–1.31	Do	F.	58–58–58	1.07–1.07–1.07
South Carolina	F.	65–66–66	.25–1.00–.69	New York	F.	60–60–60	.45–1.51–.97
Do	M.	66–66–66	.30–.75–.60	North Carolina	F.	60–60–60	.65–.92–.74
Virginia	F.	60–61–60	.38–.96–.66	Do	[1]	72–72–72	.88–.88–.88
Do	M.	[1]	.75–.75–.75	Rhode Island	[1]	[1]	.58–3.25–1.25
Do	[1]	60–60–60	.83–.83–.83	South Carolina	M.	66–66–66	.90–.90–.90
1889:				**1895:**			
Alabama	[1]	67–67–67	.60–1.00–.95	Alabama	M.	60–66–64	.37–1.13–.77
Connecticut	F.	60–60–60	1.12–1.12–1.12	Do	F.	60–66–63	.30–1.35–.74
Georgia	M.	66–66–66	.30–.96–.82	Georgia	M.	66–66–66	.50–1.33–.93
Do	F.	66–66–66	.25–1.13–.86	Do	F.	66–66–66	.60–1.67–.88
Do	[1]	70–70–70	.85–.85–.85	Louisiana	F.	60–63–62	.42–1.36–.86
Maine	M.	60–60–60	.34–1.69–1.06	Maine	M.	60–60–60	.60–2.10–1.28
Do	F.	60–60–60	.34–1.45–1.05	Do	F.	60–60–60	.56–1.89–1.20
Maryland	M.	[1]	.29–1.25–.67	Massachusetts	M.	58–58–58	.58–1.75–1.21
Do	F.	[1]	.19–1.33–.74	Do	F.	58–58–58	.88–1.68–1.12
Massachusetts	M.	60–60–60	.64–2.00–1.38	Mississippi	F.	60–60–60	.54–1.15–.92
Do	F.	60–60–60	.40–2.13–1.29	New Hampshire	M.	60–60–60	.35–2.50–1.33
New Hampshire	M.	60–60–60	.70–1.75–.99	Do	F.	60–60–60	.33–2.50–1.22
Do	F.	60–60–60	.27–1.44–.97	New Jersey	M.	55–55–55	1.17–2.25–1.96
Do	[1]	60–60–60	.44–1.91–1.07	New York	F.	60–60–60	.50–1.87–1.20
New York	M.	60–60–60	.45–1.49–.91	North Carolina	M.	66–72–70	.50–1.25–.85
Do	F.	60–60–60	.45–1.34–.82	Do	F.	66–72–69	.60–1.17–.78
North Carolina	M.	69–69–69	.75–1.00–.85	Do	[1]	72–72–72	.70–.70–.70
Do	F.	69–69–69	.75–1.00–.82	Ohio	M.	60–60–60	2.16–2.16–2.16
Pennsylvania	M.	[1]	.58–2.42–1.35	Do	F.	60–60–60	.58–.58–.58
Do	F.	[1]	.69–1.73–1.20	Pennsylvania	M.	60–60–60	.67–1.00–.77
Rhode Island	F.	60–60–60	.35–1.77–1.17	Rhode Island	M.	60–60–60	.85–1.77–1.37
South Carolina	M.	66–66–66	.88–.88–.88	Do	F.	60–60–60	.50–1.50–1.13
Do	F.	66–66–66	.88–.88–.88	South Carolina	M.	66–66–66	.50–1.25–.86
Tennessee	M.	[1]	.50–.63–.57	Do	F.	66–66–66	.46–1.25–.84
Do	F.	66–66–66	.45–.97–.96	Tennessee	M.	66–66–66	.39–1.31–.82
Do	[1]	66–66–66	.95–1.29–1.19	Do	F.	66–66–66	.32–1.33–.80
Virginia	F.	[1]	.55–1.00–.73	Virginia	F.	60–60–60	.60–1.00–.72
1890:				**1896:**			
Alabama	M.	63–69–66	.29–1.34–.92	Georgia	M.	66–66–66	.65–1.25–.87
Do	F.	63–69–65	.25–1.16–.78	Do	F.	66–66–66	.55–1.42–.82
Do	[1]	67–67–67	.75–.85–.84	Indiana	M.	65–65–65	.75–1.57–1.38
Connecticut	M.	[1]	1.25–1.25–1.25	Do	F.	65–65–65	.35–1.38–.93
Do	F.	[1]	1.25–1.25–1.25	New Hampshire	M.	60–60–60	.50–1.94–1.12
Kentucky	M.	66–66–66	1.30–1.30–1.30	Do	F.	60–60–60	.50–1.83–1.08
Do	[1]	66–66–66	.66–1.00–.91	New York	F.	60–60–60	.54–1.52–1.01
Louisiana	M.	[1]	.90–.90–.90	North Carolina	M.	68–69–69	.50–1.15–.81
Do	F.	[1]	.21–.90–.55	Do	F.	68–69–69	.48–1.43–.73
Maryland	M.	[1]	1.25–1.25–1.25	Pennsylvania	M.	60–60–60	.67–2.00–1.31
Massachusetts	M.	[1]	1.39–1.39–1.39	Do	F.	60–60–60	.37–2.02–1.12
Do	F.	60–60–60	.35–1.50–1.16	Rhode Island	[1]	[1]	1.00–1.00–1.00
Mississippi	F.	66–66–66	.70–1.10–.82	South Carolina	M.	66–66–66	.65–1.00–.82
New York	F.	60–60–60	.64–1.20–1.02	Do	F.	66–66–66	.67–1.00–.84
Do	M.	[1]	.63–3.00–.97	**1897:**			
North Carolina	M.	66–66–66	.56–1.26–.93	Georgia	F.	66–66–66	.85–.85–.85
Do	F.	66–69–68	.45–1.80–.84	**1899:**			
Do	[1]	69–69–69	.50–1.13–.82	Alabama	M.	70–70–70	.73–1.50–1.03
Tennessee	[1]	69–69–69	.83–1.25–1.19	Do	F.	70–70–70	.75–1.20–.96
1891:				Georgia	M.	66–66–66	.50–1.30–.90
Maine	M.	60–60–60	1.08–1.50–1.31	Do	F.	66–66–66	.50–1.25–.83
Do	F.	60–60–60	1.00–1.30–1.13	Massachusetts	F.	58–58–58	.87–.90–.89
Massachusetts	[1]	[1]	.29–1.60–1.09	Do	[1]	58–58–58	.48–1.68–1.23
Do	M.	[1]	1.42–1.42–1.42	North Carolina	M.	66–69–68	.55–1.45–.93
Do	F.	60–60–60	.35–1.50–1.19	Do	F.	66–69–68	.38–1.15–.70
New York	F.	60–60–60	.70–1.17–1.02	Do	[1]	66–66–66	.75–1.25–.97
Do	M.	[1]	.63–3.00–.97	South Carolina	M.	66–66–66	.80–1.75–1.07
North Carolina	[1]	69–69–69	1.00–1.00–1.00	Do	F.	66–66–66	.80–1.00–.86
1892:				Do	[1]	66–66–66	.40–1.20–.87
Maine	M.	60–60–60	1.00–1.60–1.27	**1900:**			
Do	F.	60–60–60	1.00–1.67–1.21	Alabama	M.	70–70–70	.73–1.50–1.07
Massachusetts	M.	58–60–59	.87–1.48–1.43	Do	F.	70–70–70	.77–1.20–.99
Do	F.	58–60–59	.86–1.34–1.03	Georgia	M.	66–66–66	.50–1.30–.92
New York	F.	60–60–60	.50–1.51–1.20	Do	F.	66–66–66	.50–1.35–.85

[1] Not reported.

TABLE **L-23.**—*Weavers, cotton goods, 1841-1900, by year and State*—Con.

Year and State	Sex	Lowest, highest, and average—		Year and State	Sex	Lowest, highest, and average—	
		Hours per week	Rate per day (dollars)			Hours per week	Rate per day (dollars)
1900—Continued.				1900—Continued.			
Massachusetts	(¹)	58-58-58	0. 59-1. 82-1. 37	South Carolina	M.	66-66-66	0. 80-2. 00-1. 07
North Carolina	M.	66-69-68	. 55-1. 45- . 93	Do	F.	66-66-66	. 80-1. 00- . 86
Do	F.	66-69-68	. 38-1. 15- . 70	Do	(¹)	66-66-66	. 40-1. 20- . 87
Do	(¹)	66-66-66	. 75-1. 25- . 96				

¹ Not reported.

TABLE **L-24.**—*Weavers, males, cotton goods, 1890-1906, by State and year*

Year	Massachusetts		New Hampshire		Rhode Island		South Carolina	
	Hours per week	Rate per hour	Hours per week	Rate per hour	Hours per week	Rate per hour	Hours per week	Rate per hour
1890	60. 0	$0. 135	60. 0	$0. 136	60. 0	$0. 160	66. 0	$0. 069
1891	60. 0	. 134	60. 0	. 140	60. 0	. 138	68. 6	. 060
1892	60. 0	. 137	60. 0	. 142	60. 0	. 141	68. 3	. 056
1893	58. 0	. 146	60. 0	. 151	60. 0	. 153	66. 0	. 059
1894	56. 8	. 132	60. 0	. 147	60. 0	. 136	66. 0	. 060
1895	58. 0	. 127	60. 0	. 142	60. 0	. 142	66. 0	. 054
1896	58. 0	. 138	60. 0	. 142	60. 0	. 139	66. 0	. 060
1897	57. 2	. 137	60. 0	. 145	60. 0	. 134	66. 0	. 065
1898	58. 0	. 135	60. 0	. 126	60. 0	. 119	66. 0	. 066
1899	58. 0	. 127	60. 0	. 131	60. 0	. 131	66. 0	. 067
1900	58. 0	. 149	60. 0	. 155	60. 0	. 151	66. 0	. 070
1901	58. 0	. 150	60. 0	. 151	60. 0	. 141	66. 0	. 073
1902	58. 0	. 153	60. 0	. 152	58. 0	. 159	66. 0	. 078
1903	58. 0	. 160	60. 0	. 153	58. 0	. 167		
1904	58. 0	. 165	60. 0	. 158	58. 0	. 143	66. 0	. 102
1905	58. 0	. 165			58. 0	. 148	66. 0	. 103
1906	58. 0	. 174			58. 0	. 165	65. 5	. 111

TABLE **L-25.**—*Weavers, males, cotton goods, 1907-1928, by State and year*

Year	Alabama		Georgia		Maine		Massachusetts	
	Hours per week	Rate per hour	Hours per week	Rate per hour	Hours per week	Rate per hour	Hours per week	Rate per hour
1907	66. 0	$0. 124	64. 9	$0. 116	60. 0	$0. 192	58. 0	$0. 179
1908	61. 0	. 124	64. 1	. 128	60. 0	. 174	58. 0	. 184
1909	61. 7	. 128	64. 1	. 127	60. 0	. 171	58. 0	. 161
1910	62. 1	. 131	62. 9	. 130	58. 0	. 169	56. 0	. 163
1911	61. 5	. 135	62. 8	. 128	58. 0	. 178	56. 0	. 164
1912	62. 1	. 141	60. 0	. 143	58. 0	. 197	54. 0	. 180
1913	61. 4	. 144	60. 0	. 145	58. 0	. 199	54. 0	. 182
1914	60. 0	. 140	60. 0	. 159	58. 0	. 197	54. 0	. 186
1916	60. 0	. 163	60. 0	. 161	58. 0	. 235	53. 9	. 225
1918	60. 0	. 235	60. 0	. 218	53. 9	. 382	53. 9	. 327
1920	57. 4	. 439	56. 2	. 476	54. 0	. 658	48. 0	. 598
1922	55. 8	. 255	56. 8	. 282	54. 0	. 471	48. 4	. 460
1924	55. 5	. 298	56. 1	. 314	54. 1	. 539	48. 0	. 543
1926	54. 9	. 298	57. 3	. 297	54. 1	. 485	49. 0	. 459
1928	55. 0	. 311	56. 1	. 309	54. 0	. 424	50. 0	. 431

Year	North Carolina		Rhode Island		South Carolina		New Hampshire	
1907	66. 0	$0. 124	58. 0	$0. 192	61. 5	$0. 132		
1908	64. 0	. 129	58. 0	. 190	60. 5	. 133		
1909	63. 8	. 128	58. 0	. 187	60. 0	. 134		
1910	62. 7	. 132	56. 0	. 179	60. 0	. 136	58. 0	$0. 155
1911	62. 7	. 139	56. 0	. 182	60. 0	. 138	58. 0	. 167
1912	60. 0	. 144	56. 0	. 192	60. 0	. 140	58. 0	. 190
1913	60. 0	. 146	56. 0	. 195	60. 0	. 143	58. 0	. 191
1914	60. 0	. 156	54. 0	. 201	60. 0	. 148	55. 0	. 196
1916	60. 0	. 167	54. 0	. 245	59. 9	. 153	55. 0	. 235
1918	59. 8	. 251	53. 9	. 359	59. 9	. 232	54. 0	. 344
1920	55. 1	. 582	49. 4	. 607	55. 0	. 532	48. 0	. 626
1922	55. 1	. 350	49. 1	. 454	55. 0	. 286	52. 9	. 466
1924	55. 3	. 401	52. 6	. 542	55. 0	. 328	54. 2	. 532
1926	55. 6	. 353	50. 1	. 494	55. 0	. 314	54. 4	. 514
1928	55. 9	. 370	52. 2	. 498	55. 0	. 313	54. 3	. 501

TABLE **L-26.**—*Weavers, females, cotton goods, 1890–1906, by State and year*

Year	Massachusetts		New Hampshire		Rhode Island		South Carolina	
	Hours per week	Rate per hour	Hours per week	Rate per hour	Hours per week	Rate per hour	Hours per week	Rate per hour
1890	60. 0	$0. 119	60. 0	$0. 104	60. 0	$0. 128	66. 0	$0. 062
1891	60. 0	. 119	60. 0	. 105	60. 0	. 129	67. 9	. 057
1892	60. 0	. 122	60. 0	. 111	60. 0	. 127	68. 3	. 054
1893	58. 0	. 132	60. 0	. 117	60. 0	. 140	66. 0	. 055
1894	54. 0	. 121	60. 0	. 113	60. 0	. 125	66. 0	. 057
1895	58. 0	. 119	60. 0	. 115	60. 0	. 124	66. 0	. 050
1896	58. 0	. 125	60. 0	. 121	60. 0	. 127	66. 0	. 055
1897	55. 6	. 123	60. 0	. 119	60. 0	. 122	66. 0	. 060
1898	58. 0	. 125	60. 0	. 107	60. 0	. 115	66. 0	. 060
1899	58. 0	. 120	60. 0	. 107	60. 0	. 119	66. 0	. 059
1900	58. 0	. 136	60. 0	. 131	60. 0	. 131	66. 0	. 060
1901	58. 0	. 137	60. 0	. 124	60. 0	. 130	66. 0	. 063
1902	58. 0	. 137	60. 0	. 126	58. 0	. 144	66. 0	. 068
1903	58. 0	. 141	60. 0	. 124	58. 0	. 146		
1904	58. 0	. 149	60. 0	. 152	58. 0	. 137	66. 0	. 077
1905	58. 0	. 148			58. 0	. 136	66. 0	. 092
1906	58. 0	. 156			58. 0	. 151	65. 5	. 099

TABLE **L-27.**—*Weavers, females, cotton goods, 1907–1928, by State and year*

Year	Alabama		Georgia		Maine		Massachusetts	
	Hours per week	Rate per hour	Hours per week	Rate per hour	Hours per week	Rate per hour	Hours per week	Rate per hour
1907	66. 0	$0. 112	63. 8	$0. 109	60. 0	$0. 162	58. 0	$0. 162
1908	61. 9	. 119	62. 0	. 141	60. 0	. 149	58. 0	. 163
1909	62. 3	. 123	61. 9	. 113	60. 0	. 151	58. 0	. 151
1910	62. 1	. 122	62. 2	. 120	58. 0	. 149	56. 0	. 150
1911	61. 6	. 126	62. 2	. 120	58. 0	. 152	56. 0	. 148
1912	62. 1	. 125	60. 0	. 131	58. 0	. 163	54. 0	. 167
1913	61. 5	. 128	60. 0	. 133	58. 0	. 167	54. 0	. 166
1914	60. 3	. 132	60. 0	. 140	58. 0	. 166	54. 0	. 168
1916	60. 2	. 147	60. 0	. 144	58. 0	. 204	53. 9	. 206
1918	60. 2	. 190	59. 9	. 187	53. 9	. 341	53. 9	. 303
1920	57. 4	. 378	56. 7	. 430	54. 0	. 560	48. 0	. 548
1922	55. 8	. 231	56. 7	. 274	54. 0	. 419	48. 0	. 415
1924	55. 5	. 262	55. 8	. 286	54. 0	. 458	48. 1	. 487
1926	54. 7	. 278	57. 0	. 284	54. 0	. 449	48. 0	. 420
1928	55. 0	. 299	56. 0	. 292	54. 0	. 397	48. 0	. 405

Year	North Carolina		Rhode Island		South Carolina		New Hampshire	
1907	66. 0	$0. 114	58. 0	$0. 170	62. 0	$0. 122		
1908	64. 2	. 121	58. 0	. 169	60. 4	. 122		
1909	64. 5	. 118	58. 0	. 166	60. 0	. 121		
1910	62. 8	. 121	56. 0	. 195	60. 0	. 122	58. 0	$0. 145
1911	62. 6	. 125	56. 0	. 161	60. 0	. 127	58. 0	. 160
1912	60. 0	. 131	56. 0	. 171	60. 0	. 127	58. 0	. 180
1913	60. 0	. 134	56. 0	. 173	60. 0	. 129	58. 0	. 180
1914	60. 0	. 139	54. 0	. 181	60. 0	. 130	55. 0	. 188
1916	60. 0	. 151	54. 0	. 224	60. 0	. 140	55. 0	. 226
1918	59. 6	. 221	53. 9	. 333	59. 4	. 200	54. 0	. 319
1920	54. 8	. 519	50. 5	. 538	54. 3	. 468	48. 0	. 575
1922	55. 1	. 313	49. 5	. 405	54. 9	. 260	53. 7	. 428
1924	55. 2	. 351	50. 6	. 515	55. 0	. 299	54. 0	. 495
1926	55. 5	. 316	50. 3	. 455	55. 0	. 276	53. 3	. 488
1928	55. 9	. 333	52. 0	. 469	55. 0	. 277	52. 5	. 493

HOSIERY AND UNDERWEAR

The sources from which this information was taken are the fifteenth and the nineteenth annual reports of the Commissioner of Labor Statistics and bulletins of the Bureau of Labor Statistics Nos. 59, 65, 71, 77, 134, 154, 177, 265, 328, 376, 452, and 504. In the early reports wages and hours of labor were shown for employees reported as knitters; in later reports employees who were performing similar work were reported as footers, toppers, or transfer knitters.

In nearly all reports the information is presented by States, when not available it is shown by geographic divisions or for the United States.

TABLE L-28.—*Knitters, hosiery and underwear, 1842–1900, by year and State*

Year and State	Sex	Lowest, highest, and average—		Year and State	Sex	Lowest, highest, and average—	
		Hours per week	Rate per day (dollars)			Hours per week	Rate per day (dollars)
1842:				1876:			
Massachusetts____	F.	78–78–78	0. 60–0. 60–0. 60	Massachusetts____	M.	60–60–60	0. 75–0. 75–0. 75
1843:				1877:			
Massachusetts____	M.	78–78–78	1. 13–1. 13–1. 13	Massachusetts____	M.	60–60–60	. 75– . 75– . 75
Do_____	F.	78–78–78	. 60– . 60– . 60	1878:			
1846:				Massachusetts____	M.	60–60–60	. 71– . 71– . 71
Massachusetts____	F.	78–78–78	. 58– . 58– . 58	1879:			
1847:				Massachusetts____	M.	60–60–60	. 71– . 71– . 71
Massachusetts____	F.	78–78–78	. 58– . 58– . 58	1880:			
1848:				Ohio_____	F.	(¹)	. 43– . 63– . 53
Massachusetts____	F.	78–78–78	. 58– . 58– . 58	1882:			
1849:				Connecticut_____	M.	66–66–66	. 58– . 83– . 73
Massachusetts____	F.	78–78–78	. 56– . 56– . 56	Do_____	F.	66–66–66	. 42– . 90– . 74
1850:				Kentucky_____	F.	60–60–60	. 54– . 88– . 72
Massachusetts____	F.	78–78–78	. 56– . 56– . 56	Missouri_____	M.	60–60–60	1. 10–1. 10–1. 10
1851:				1883:			
Massachusetts____	F.	78–78–78	. 54– . 56– . 55	Massachusetts____	M.	(¹)	1. 49–3. 00–1. 55
1852:				Do_____	F.	(¹)	. 89–1. 50– . 94
Massachusetts____	F.	78–78–78	. 54– . 54– . 54	Michigan_____	F.	(¹)	. 40–1. 50– . 67
1853:				Ohio_____	F.	60–60–60	. 50– . 67– . 58
Massachusetts____	F.	78–78–78	. 50– . 54– . 52	1884:			
1854:				Georgia_____	F.	(¹)	. 75– . 75– . 75
Massachusetts____	F.	78–78–78	. 50– . 50– . 50	Michigan_____	M.	(¹)	. 35– . 70– . 52
1858:				Do_____	F.	(¹)	1. 00–1. 00–1. 00
Massachusetts____	F.	78–78–78	. 54– . 73– . 58	New Hampshire__	F.	66–66–66	. 76–1. 48–1. 01
1859:				New Jersey_____	F.	60–60–60	. 67–1. 17–1. 08
Massachusetts____	F.	78–78–78	. 50– . 73– . 62	Pennsylvania_____	M.	(¹)	1. 59–1. 59–1. 59
1860:				1885:			
Massachusetts____	F.	78–78–78	. 50– . 73– . 59	Alabama_____	M.	(¹)	. 67–1. 00– . 88
1861:				Do_____	F.	(¹)	. 25–1. 00– . 66
Massachusetts____	F.	78–78–78	. 50– . 73– . 57	Massachusetts____	M.	60–60–60	1. 00–1. 13–1. 07
1862:				Do_____	F.	60–60–60	. 50–1. 25– . 73
Massachusetts____	F.	72–72–72	. 54–1. 00– . 69	Minnesota_____	F.	60–60–60	. 33–1. 75– . 73
1863:				Missouri_____	F.	55–60–58	. 67–1. 25– . 88
Massachusetts____	F.	72–72–72	. 67–1. 00– . 84	New Hampshire__	M.	66–66–66	. 77–2. 00–1. 21
1865:				Do_____	F.	66–66–66	. 57–1. 61–1. 09
Massachusetts____	F.	72–72–72	. 83– . 83– . 83	New York_____	M.	66–66–63	. 67–2. 00–1. 41
1866:				Do_____	F.	60–66–65	. 50–1. 89–1. 17
Massachusetts____	F.	72–72–72	. 67– . 75– . 71	Pennsylvania_____	F.	60–60–60	. 50– . 50– . 50
1869:				Rhode Island_____	F.	(¹)	1. 08–1. 08–1. 08
Massachusetts____	(¹)	60–60–60	2. 00–2. 00–2. 00	Vermont_____	M.	64–64–64	. 75–1. 25–1. 00
1872:				Do_____	F.	64–64–64	. 63–1. 89–1. 06
Massachusetts____	M.	66–66–66	1. 17–1. 17–1. 17	Virginia_____	M.	60–60–60	. 60–1. 75– . 98
Do___ _____	F.	(¹)	. 83– . 83– . 83	Do_____	F.	60–60–60	. 50– . 50– . 50
1873:				1886:			
Massachusetts__	M.	66–66–66	1. 17–1. 17–1. 17	Connecticut_____	F.	60–60–60	1. 10–1. 20–1. 15
1874:				Illinois_____	F.	(¹)	. 50–1. 21–. 84
Massachusetts____	M.	66–66–66	1. 00–1. 00–1. 00	Michigan_____	F.	(¹)	. 67–1. 06– . 87
1875:				Missouri_____	F.	54–60–57	. 24– . 83– . 59
Massachusetts____	M.	60–60–60	. 80– . 80– . 80	New Jersey_____	F.	60–60–60	1. 00–1. 00–1. 00

¹ Not reported.

TABLE L–28.—*Knitters, hosiery and underwear, 1842–1900, by year and State—Con.*

Year and State	Sex	Lowest, highest, and average—		Year and State	Sex	Lowest, highest, and average—	
		Hours per week	Rate per day (dollars)			Hours per week	Rate per day (dollars)
1886—Continued.				**1894—Continued.**			
New York	F.	53–58–58	0. 83–1. 50–1. 16	Ohio	F.	48–60–58	0. 50–2. 50–0. 74
Pennsylvania	(¹)	60–60–60	1. 66–2. 00–1. 92	Rhode Island	(¹)	(¹)	. 92–2. 83–1. 57
Do	M.	60–60–60	. 50–2. 94–1. 64	**1895:**			
Do	F.	47–60–57	. 34–2. 27–1. 01	Connecticut	F.	60–60–60	. 39–1. 00– . 80
Rhode Island	F.	60–61–60	. 92–1. 50–1. 33	Massachusetts	F.	58–60–58	. 76–1. 50–1. 07
Vermont	M.	66–66–66	1. 00–1. 00–1. 00	Do	M.	58–60–60	. 86–2. 50–1. 54
Do	F.	66–66–66	. 67–2. 04–1. 13	New Hampshire	F.	66–66–66	. 70–2. 00–1. 19
Wisconsin	M.	60–60–60	. 40– . 40– . 40	Do	F.	60–60–60	. 52–2. 01–1. 05
1887:				New York	M.	60–60–60	. 94–2. 00–1. 66
Connecticut	M.	(¹)	. 48– . 48– . 48	Do	F.	60–60–60	1. 00–2. 16–1. 78
Do	F.	(¹)	. 66– . 76– . 67	North Carolina	M.	60–66–63	. 25– . 50– . 38
Georgia	F.	65–65–65	. 42– . 98– . 66	Do	F.	60–60–60	. 30– . 30– . 30
Illinois	F.	48–60–56	. 25–1. 33– . 82	Ohio	M.	48–48–48	1. 50–1. 50–1. 50
Kentucky	F.	60–62–62	. 33– . 75– . 57	Do	F.	48–60–56	. 50– . 87– . 71
Massachusetts	F.	54–59–56	. 92–1. 50–1. 37	Pennsylvania	M.	60–60–60	1. 66–2. 00–1. 70
New York	F.	50–60–58	. 21–1. 33– . 70	Do	F.	60–60–60	1. 00–1. 15–1. 06
Ohio	M.	60–60–60	. 85–1. 10– . 97	Rhode Island	F.	60–60–60	1. 00–1. 17–1. 06
Do	F.	48–72–61	. 25–1. 15– . 65	**1896:**			
Wisconsin	(¹)	(¹)	. 62– . 62– . 62	Alabama	M.	63–63–63	. 25– . 90– . 38
1888:				Do	F.	63–63–63	. 25– . 90– . 59
Indiana	F.	48–57–54	. 50–1. 08– . 67	Georgia	M.	63–63–63	1. 00–1. 15–1. 09
Maine	F.	60–60–60	. 45–1. 40–1. 00	Do	F.	63–63–63	. 67–1. 00– . 89
New Jersey	M.	(¹)	3. 33–3. 33–3. 33	Illinois	M.	54–54–54	1. 17–2. 00–1. 56
Do	F.	(¹)	1. 00–1. 25–1. 02	Do	F.	54–57–57	. 43–1. 25– . 76
New York	M.	45–60–55	. 67–3. 50–1. 12	Kentucky	F.	60–60–60	. 49– . 88– . 66
Do	F.	59–60–60	. 33–1. 38– . 86	Michigan	M.	60–60–60	. 50–1. 21– . 87
Do	(¹)	(¹)	1. 00–1. 00–1. 00	Minnesota	F.	54–54–54	. 55–1. 20– . 81
Rhode Island	(¹)	(¹)	1. 50–1. 70–1, 60	New York	M.	58–58–58	. 26–1. 32– . 84
1889:				Ohio	M.	48–55–52	1. 75–1. 84–1. 81
Rhode Island	F.	60–72–66	1. 17–1. 50–1. 34	Do	F.	42–60–49	. 36–1. 00– . 73
1890:				Pennsylvania	F.	60–60–60	. 42–2. 17–1. 25
New York	M.	(¹)	. 50–4. 00–1. 33	Do	F.	60–60–60	. 28–1. 74–1. 02
Do	F.	(¹)	1. 41–1. 50–1. 42	Rhode Island	F.	60–60–60	. 67–1. 33–1. 02
1891:				Vermont	M.	60–64–62	1. 00–1. 50–1. 18
Michigan	F.	(¹)	. 60–1. 04– . 72	Do	F.	64–66–65	. 75–1. 78–1. 18
New York	M.	(¹)	. 65–4. 00–1. 35	**1897:**			
Do	F.	(¹)	1. 41–1. 50–1. 42	Massachusetts	M.	63–63–63	2. 50–2. 50–2. 50
1892:				New Hampshire	M.	60–60–60	1. 10–1. 10–1. 10
Indiana	F.	54–60–56	. 41– . 55– . 46	New York	M.	60–60–60	2. 00–2. 00–2. 00
New York	F.	54–54–54	1. 33–1. 33–1. 33	North Carolina	M.	75–75–75	. 30– . 30– . 30
1893:				Pennsylvania	F.	(¹)	. 68–4. 57–1. 52
Illinois	F.	40–60–52	. 67–1. 00– . 86	Do	F.	(¹)	. 67– . 67– . 67
Maryland	F.	60–60–60	. 25– . 50– . 38	**1898:**			
New Jersey	F.	55–60–55	. 42–1. 45– . 99	New Jersey	F.	60–60–60	. 96–1. 33–1. 06
New York	F.	54–58–56	1. 33–2. 00–1. 67	**1899:**			
Ohio	F.	48–60–53	. 52–1. 25– . 88	North Carolina	M.	66–66–66	. 49–1. 00– . 72
Pennsylvania	F.	55–55–55	. 83– . 83– . 83	Do	F.	66–66–66	. 26– . 55– . 37
1894:				**1900:**			
Indiana	(¹)	60–60–60	1. 31–1. 31–1. 31	North Carolina	M.	66–66–66	. 49–1. 00– . 80
New Hampshire	M.	59–59–59	1. 50–1. 50–150.	Do	F.	66–66–66	. 26– . 55– . 37

¹ Not reported.

TABLE L–29.—*Knitters, males, hosiery and underwear, 1890–1907, by geographic division and year*

Year	North Atlantic		South Atlantic		North Central	
	Hours per week	Rate per hour	Hours per week	Rate per hour	Hours per week	Rate per hour
1890	60. 0	$0. 175				
1891	60. 0	. 193				
1892	60. 0	. 163				
1893	58. 7	. 185				
1894	53. 3	. 179				
1895	58. 6	. 183				
1896	58. 5	. 147				
1897	58. 3	. 133				
1898	58. 3	. 139				
1899	58. 3	. 131				
1900	57. 6	. 148				
1901	57. 7	. 150				
1902	57. 7	. 156				
1903	56. 9	. 202				
1904	58. 9	. 185	65. 5	$0. 104	58. 2	$0. 295
1905	61. 5	. 184	65. 4	. 111	58. 2	. 293
1906	63. 3	. 203	64. 3	. 110	57. 5	. 274
1907	60. 4	. 203	64. 4	. 124	57. 2	. 302

TABLE L–30.—*Knitters, females, hosiery and underwear, 1890–1907, by geographic division and year*

Year	North Atlantic		North Central		South Atlantic	
	Hours per week	Rate per hour	Hours per week	Rate per hour	Hours per week	Rate per hour
1890	60. 0	$0. 113	59. 5	$0. 058		
1891	60. 0	. 118	59. 6	. 064		
1892	60. 0	. 115	59. 7	. 064		
1893	59. 8	. 109	59. 8	. 064		
1894	54. 6	. 114	59. 7	. 063		
1895	59. 8	. 120	59. 7	. 066		
1896	60. 0	. 118	59. 6	. 065		
1897	60. 0	. 123	59. 6	. 062		
1898	60. 0	. 116	59. 6	. 065		
1899	60. 0	. 122	59. 7	. 064		
1900	58. 0	. 126	59. 6	. 063		
1901	58. 4	. 130	59. 6	. 076		
1902	58. 2	. 131	59. 7	. 082		
1903	57. 6	. 121	59. 5	. 084		
1904	58. 5	. 120	58. 6	. 093		
1905	58. 8	. 128	58. 8	. 097	57. 5	$0. 096
1906	58. 4	. 135	56. 3	. 107	59. 4	. 100
1907	58. 1	. 138	56. 1	. 116	59. 3	. 106

TABLE L–31.—*Knitters, footers or toppers, males, hosiery, 1910–1919, United States, by year*

Year	United States		Year	United States	
	Hours per week	Rate per hour		Hours per week	Rate per hour
1910	58. 2	$0. 136	1913	58. 0	$0. 150
1911	57. 8	. 147	1914	56. 3	. 151
1912	57. 7	. 156	1919	54. 3	. 298

TABLE **L–32.**—*Knitters, footers or toppers, females, hosiery, 1907–1910, United States, by year*

| Year | United States | | Year | United States | |
	Hours per week	Rate per hour		Hours per week	Rate per hour
1907	58. 1	$0. 123	1909	58. 1	$0. 133
1908	58. 1	. 134	1910	57. 5	. 121

TABLE **L–33.**—*Knitters, footers or toppers, males, hosiery, 1913–1926, by State and Year*

| Year | Alabama | | North Carolina | | Pennsylvania | | Indiana | |
	Hours per week	Rate per hour	Hours per week	Rate per hour	Hours per week	Rate per hour	Hours per week	Rate per hour
1919 [1]			59. 7	$0. 357	53. 8	$0. 564	49. 5	$0. 624
1922	53. 3	$0. 159			56. 7	1. 071		
1924			55. 0	. 299	49. 8	. 539	49. 6	. 534
1926 [2]	[3] 55. 1	[3] . 192	55. 2	. 375	53. 4	. 509		

| | New Hampshire | | Georgia | | Tennessee | | Virginia | |
	Hours per week	Rate per hour	Hours per week	Rate per hour	Hours per week	Rate per hour	Hours per week	Rate per hour
1913	58. 0	$0. 179	58. 3	$0. 127	58. 8	$0. 132	56. 7	$0. 156
1914	55. 0	. 195	58. 9	. 121	58. 0	. 119	57. 8	. 143
1919 [1]	50. 9	. 368	56. 8	. 297	55. 4	. 263	54. 6	. 330
1922	51. 1	. 483			53. 5	. 243	52. 4	. 277
1924					52. 5	. 293	51. 5	. 334
1926 [2]			54. 7	. 252	54. 3	. 274	51. 4	. 378

[1] All knitters.   [2] Knitters, transfer.   [3] Includes Louisiana.

TABLE **L–34.**—*Knitters, footers or toppers, females, hosiery, 1910–1926, by State and Year*

| Year | New Hampshire | | Georgia | | Illinois | | Massachusetts | |
	Hours per week	Rate per hour	Hours per week	Rate per hour	Hours per week	Rate per hour	Hours per week	Rate per hour
1910	58. 0	$0. 143	57. 8	$0. 093	59. 4	$0. 110	56. 0	$0. 132
1911	58. 0	. 140	57. 5	. 105	59. 5	. 103	56. 0	. 121
1912	58. 0	. 137	57. 1	. 116	59. 0	. 103	54. 0	. 135
1913	58. 0	. 153	57. 3	. 109	54. 6	. 128	54. 0	. 147
1914	55. 0	. 141	57. 4	. 114	53. 8	. 112	54. 0	. 153
1919 [1]	49. 0	. 343	58. 3	. 270			48. 0	. 336
1922			53. 5	. 225	48. 4	. 223	48. 0	. 369
1924	48. 2	. 527	55. 0	. 212	49. 3	. 238	48. 0	. 364
1926 [2]	[3] 48. 0	[3] . 368	55. 0	. 212	51. 6	. 267	48. 0	. 297

| | Michigan | | North Carolina | | Pennsylvania | | Wisconsin | |
	Hours per week	Rate per hour	Hours per week	Rate per hour	Hours per week	Rate per hour	Hours per week	Rate per hour
1910	53. 7	$0. 132	60. 0	$0. 072	57. 7	$0. 127	55. 0	$0. 141
1911	53. 7	. 141	59. 2	. 083	57. 3	. 150	55. 0	. 140
1912	53. 7	. 149	59. 1	. 103	55. 5	. 147	55. 0	. 147
1913	53. 7	. 143	59. 2	. 089	55. 6	. 166	55. 0	. 163
1914			59. 1	. 099	53. 9	. 167	55. 0	. 163
1919 [1]	53. 9	. 262	60. 0	. 199	53. 6	. 312	53. 0	. 276
1922	50. 3	. 297	55. 0	. 200	48. 9	. 387		
1924	50. 3	. 307	56. 0	. 194	49. 4	. 439	49. 7	. 545
1926 [2]	50. 6	. 394	55. 8	. 263	50. 8	. 425	49. 6	. 417

[1] All knitters.   [2] Knitters, transfer.   [3] Includes Vermont.

SILK

The sources from which this information was taken are the fifteenth and the nineteenth annual reports of the Commissioner of Labor Statistics and bulletins of the Bureau of Labor Statistics Nos. 65, 71, 77, 128, 150, 190, and 265.

These reports include the wages of employees engaged principally in the manufacture of broad silks and ribbons and those employed in silk throwing.

In this report details showing wages and hours of labor are presented by States in all years where data in this form are available.

On account of the incomplete State figures, details are shown for the United States from 1890 to 1910, inclusive. A part of this table overlaps that shown by States.

In the wage data shown for winders, the details are presented for employees working on both hard and soft silk for the specified years in the period from 1907 to 1919.

No data in this industry have been published by the Bureau of Labor Statistics since 1919.

TABLE **L–35.**—*Weavers, silk goods, 1877–1900, by year and State*

Year and State	Sex	Lowest, highest, and average—		Year and State	Sex	Lowest, highest, and average—	
		Hours per week	Rate per day (dollars)			Hours per week	Rate per day (dollars)
1877:				**1887:**			
New Jersey	(¹)	62–62–62	0.83–2.50–1.58	Connecticut	M.	(¹)	0.72–1.67–1.57
1879:				Do	F.	(¹)	1.07–1.07–1.07
Connecticut	F.	60–60–60	.22–1.69–.97	New York	F.	59–61–60	.46–1.75–1.04
New Jersey	(¹)	51–62–59	1.00–2.25–1.42	Pennsylvania	F.	60–60–60	.83–.92–.88
1880:				**1888:**			
New Jersey	(¹)	50–75–60	1.00–3.25–1.56	Maine	F.	60–60–60	1.25–1.50–1.38
1881:				New Jersey	M.	(¹)	1.50–3.67–2.45
New Jersey	M.	60–60–60	1.25–2.00–1.99	Do	F.	60–60–60	1.00–2.00–1.76
1882:				Do	(¹)	56–62–60	1.66–4.75–2.43
New Jersey	M.		1.89–2.50–2.20	New York	M.	55–59–56	2.33–3.67–3.02
New York	M.	60–60–60	2.25–2.25–2.25	Do	(¹)	59–59–59	2.08–2.08–2.08
1883:				**1889:**			
Connecticut	M.	60–60–60	1.60–1.60–1.60	Connecticut	F.	60–60–60	1.15–1.15–1.15
Do	F.	60–60–60	1.60–1.60–1.60	**1890:**			
New Jersey	M.	60–60–60	1.25–4.00–2.07	New York	M.	(¹)	2.00–2.67–2.37
Do	(¹)	60–60–60	1.43–1.43–1.43	**1891:**			
Do	(¹)	60–63–61	1.25–4.00–2.10	Michigan	F.	(¹)	.75–.75–.75
Do	F.	60–63–60	1.00–2.17–1.56	New York	M.	(¹)	1.92–2.67–2.29
1884:				**1893:**			
New Jersey	M.	60–60–60	.92–3.75–2.00	New Jersey	F.	55–55–55	.50–1.83–1.21
Do	F.	60–60–60	1.17–1.71–1.22	Pennsylvania	F.	60–60–60	.75–.75–.75
Do	(¹)	54–60–57	.97–.98–.98	**1895:**			
New York	M.	59–59–59	1.75–2.50–2.13	Connecticut	M.	60–60–60	.50–1.00–.68
1885:				Do	F.	60–60–60	.30–2.75–1.21
Connecticut	M.	60–60–60	1.65–1.65–1.65	New Jersey	M.	55–60–55	1.33–3.33–2.40
Do	F.	60–60–60	.26–1.65–1.30	Do	F.	55–55–55	1.42–2.50–1.86
New Jersey	M.	58–60–60	.83–5.00–2.39	New York	M.	60–60–60	.83–3.03–1.89
Do	F.	60–60–60	.83–2.00–1.69	Do	F.	60–60–60	.50–1.50–.99
New York	M.	60–60–60	.85–2.68–2.12	**1896:**			
Do	F.	60–68–60	.50–1.38–1.13	Pennsylvania	M.	60–60–60	.34–3.73–1.52
1886:				Do	F.	60–60–60	.33–1.91–1.03
Connecticut	M.	60–60–60	2.17–2.17–2.17	**1897:**			
Massachusetts	(¹)	60–60–60	2.00–2.00–2.00	New York	M.	60–60–60	1.86–1.86–1.86
New Jersey	M.	55–60–59	1.00–3.25–2.11	**1899:**			
Do	(¹)	60–60–60	1.40–1.80–1.54	New York	M.	59–59–59	1.67–3.00–2.33
Do	F.	55–60–60	.83–2.00–1.71	**1900:**			
New York	M.	58–58–58	1.40–1.40–1.40	New York	M.	59–59–59	1.67–3.00–2.33
Pennsylvania	M.	58–60–60	1.00–2.00–1.03				
Do	F.	58–60–58	.29–1.95–.80				

¹ Not reported.

TABLE L–36.—*Weavers, males, silk goods, 1890–1910, United States, by year*

Year	United States		Year	United States	
	Hours per week	Rate per hour		Hours per week	Rate per hour
1890	58. 0	$0. 163	1901	56. 7	$0. 154
1891	58. 5	. 167	1902	56. 9	. 165
1892	57. 0	. 174	1903	56. 6	. 160
1893	55. 4	. 180	1904	57. 9	. 195
1894	55. 4	. 172	1905	57. 7	. 196
1895	55. 5	. 165	1906	57. 7	. 209
1896	55. 3	. 189	1907	57. 7	. 206
1897	56. 0	. 166	1908	57. 4	. 185
1898	56. 5	. 162	1909	57. 5	. 200
1899	56. 5	. 161	1910	56. 9	. 213
1900	56. 5	. 168			

TABLE L–37.—*Weavers, females, silk goods, 1890–1910, United States, by year*

Year	United States		Year	United States	
	Hours per week	Rate per hour		Hours per week	Rate per hour
1890	58. 6	$0. 148	1901	57. 7	$0. 146
1891	59. 3	. 139	1902	57. 8	. 156
1892	58. 5	. 156	1903	58. 0	. 151
1893	57. 4	. 163	1904	57. 9	. 147
1894	57. 6	. 172	1905	58. 0	. 149
1895	57. 4	. 157	1906	58. 3	. 154
1896	58. 3	. 176	1907	57. 1	. 143
1897	58. 2	. 149	1908	56. 9	. 127
1898	58. 1	. 147	1909	56. 7	. 128
1899	58. 2	. 144	1910	56. 7	. 141
1900	58. 2	. 149			

TABLE L–38.—*Weavers, males, broad silk goods, 1904–1919, by State and year*

Year	Connecticut		Pennsylvania		New Jersey		New York	
	Hours per week	Rate per hour	Hours per week	Rate per hour	Hours per week	Rate per hour	Hours per week	Rate per hour
1904	60. 0	$0. 193			55. 0	$0. 212	57. 2	$0. 167
1905	60. 0	. 195	59. 1	$0. 135	55. 0	. 202	55. 7	. 205
1906	60. 0	. 205	59. 4	. 167	55. 0	. 215	55. 7	. 200
1907	59. 7	. 212	58. 7	. 145	55. 0	. 210	56. 2	. 205
1910	57. 9	. 217	55. 3	. 117				
1911	57. 9	. 204	58. 0	. 170				
1912	57. 9	. 220	57. 4	. 186	55. 0	. 244	54. 6	. 260
1913	57. 9	. 232	57. 3	. 214	54. 8	. 285	54. 1	. 248
1914	55. 0	. 254	54. 1	. 186	54. 8	. 270	54. 2	. 229
1919	(¹)	. 481	(¹)	. 467	(¹)	. 492	(¹)	. 460

¹ Not reported.

TABLE L–39.—*Weavers, females, broad silk goods, 1904–1919, by State and year*

Year	Connecticut		Pennsylvania		New Jersey		New York	
	Hours per week	Rate per hour	Hours per week	Rate per hour	Hours per week	Rate per hour	Hours per week	Rate per hour
1904	60. 0	$0. 151	58. 1	$0. 114	55. 0	$0. 196	58. 7	$0. 170
1905	60. 0	. 155	58. 2	. 122	55. 0	. 180	59. 7	. 169
1906	60. 0	. 164	58. 4	. 125	55. 0	. 200	59. 6	. 166
1907	59. 5	. 167	57. 9	. 140	55. 0	. 213	59. 8	. 168
1910	57. 9	. 166	56. 6	. 130				
1911	57. 9	. 160	58. 2	. 142				
1912	57. 9	. 164	55. 9	. 161	55. 0	. 230		
1913	57. 9	. 182	56. 2	. 181	55. 0	. 258	54. 0	. 215
1914	55. 0	. 192	54. 0	. 153	55. 0	. 236	54. 0	. 184
1919	(¹)	. 396	(¹)	. 278	(¹)	. 454	(¹)	. 374

¹ Not reported.

Table **L–40.**—*Winders, silk goods, 1845–1900, by year and State*

Year and State	Sex	Hours per week	Rate per day (dollars)
1845:			
New York	F.	78–78–78	0. 38–0. 38–0. 38
1848:			
Massachusetts	F.	(1)	. 90– . 90– . 90
1849:			
Massachusetts	F.	(1)	. 65– . 65– . 65
1850:			
Massachusetts	F.	(1)	. 62– . 62– . 62
1851:			
Massachusetts	F.	(1)	. 55– . 55– . 55
1852:			
Massachusetts	F.	(1)	. 53– . 53– . 53
1853:			
Massachusetts	F.	(1)	. 45– . 45– . 45
1854:			
Massachusetts	F.	(1)	. 48– . 48– . 48
1855:			
Massachusetts	F.	(1)	. 48– . 48– . 48
1856:			
Massachusetts	F.	(1)	. 52– . 52– . 52
1857:			
Massachusetts	F.	(1)	. 55– . 55– . 55
1858:			
Massachusetts	F.	(1)	. 55– . 55– . 55
1859:			
Massachusetts	F.	(1)	. 60– . 60– . 60
1860:			
Massachusetts	F.	(1)	. 56– . 56– . 56
Pennsylvania	M.	60–60–60	25– . 25– . 25
Do	F.	60–60–60	. 42– . 75– . 59
1861:			
Massachusetts	F.	(1)	. 60– . 60– . 60
1862:			
Massachusetts	F.	(1)	. 68– . 68– . 68
1863:			
Massachusetts	F.	(1)	. 68– . 68– . 68
1864:			
Massachusetts	F.	(1)	. 68– . 68– . 68
1865:			
Massachusetts	F.	(1)	. 80– . 80– . 80
1866:			
Massachusetts	F.	(1)	. 98– . 98– . 98
1867:			
Massachusetts	F.	(1)	1. 02–1. 02–1. 02
1868:			
Massachusetts	F.	(1)	1. 07–1. 07–1. 07
1869:			
Massachusetts	F.	(1)	1. 08–1. 08–1. 08
1870:			
Connecticut	F.	66–66–66	1. 00–1. 00–1. 00
Massachusetts	F.	(1)	1. 07–1. 07–1. 07
1871:			
Connecticut	F.	66–66–66	1. 00–1. 00–1. 00
Massachusetts	F.	(1)	1. 27–1. 27–1. 27
1872:			
Connecticut	F.	66–66–66	1. 00–1. 00–1. 00
Massachusetts	F.	(1)	1. 24–1. 24–1. 24
1873:			
Connecticut	F.	66–66–66	1. 00–1. 13–1. 02
Massachusetts	F.	(1)	1. 35–1. 35–1. 35
1874:			
Connecticut	F.	66–66–66	1. 06–1. 06–1. 06
Massachusetts	F.	(1)	1. 24–1. 24–1. 24
Pennsylvania	F.	(1)	. 90– . 90– . 90
1875:			
Massachusetts	F.	(1)	1. 12–1. 12–1. 12
1876:			
Massachusetts	F.	(1)	1. 00–1. 00–1. 00
1877:			
Connecticut	F.	66–66–66	. 89– . 89– . 89
Massachusetts	F.	(1)	. 96– . 96– . 96
1878:			
Connecticut	F.	66–66–66	. 93– . 93– . 93
Massachusetts	F.	(1)	. 96– . 96– . 96
Pennsylvania	F.	(1)	. 62– . 62– . 62

Year and State	Sex	Hours per week	Rate per day (dollars)
1879:			
Connecticut	F.	66–66–66	0. 96–0. 96–0. 96
Massachusetts	F.	(1)	. 96– . 96– . 96
1880:			
Connecticut	F.	66–66–66	. 95– . 95– . 95
Massachusetts	F.	(1)	. 98– . 98– . 98
Ohio	F.	(1)	. 60– . 75– . 65
Rhode Island	(1)	66–66–66	1. 17–1. 17–1. 17
1881:			
Connecticut	F.	66–66–66	. 87– . 87– . 87
Massachusetts	F.	(1)	. 96– . 96– . 96
New Hampshire	M.	65–65–65	. 60–1. 10– . 78
Do	F.	65–65–65	. 52–2. 05–1. 03
Rhode Island	F.	66–66–66	. 88– . 88– . 88
1882:			
Connecticut	F.	66–66–66	. 88–1. 46 1. 07
Kentucky	F.	60–60–60	. 40– . 40– . 40
Massachusetts	F.	(1)	1. 04–1. 04–1. 04
New Hampshire	M.	66–66–66	. 30– . 75– . 65
Do	F.	66–66–66	. 58–1. 02– . 79
South Carolina	F.	61–61–61	. 60– . 83– . 77
1883:			
Connecticut	F.	66–66–66	1. 07–1. 07–1. 07
Massachusetts	M.	(1)	. 50–2. 50–1. 01
Do	F.	(1)	. 60–1. 25– . 95
Do	(1)	(1)	. 50– . 95– . 73
New York	F.	60–60–60	. 67–1. 27–1. 03
1884:			
Connecticut	F.	66–66–66	. 80–1. 02– . 98
Georgia	F.	66–66–66	. 67– . 90– . 75
Louisiana	F.	66–66–66	. 40– . 40– . 40
Massachusetts	M.	60–60–60	. 65– . 85– . 67
Do	F.	60–60–60	. 90–1. 00–1. 00
New Hampshire	F.	66–66–66	. 54–1. 22–1. 01
New Jersey	F.	60–60–60	. 83– . 83– . 83
New York	F.	60–60–60	. 50– . 75– . 65
1885:			
Connecticut	F.	60–66–63	. 65–1. 07– . 87
Georgia	M.	69–69–69	. 75– . 75– . 75
Maine	M.	66–66–66	. 58–1. 15–1. 10
Massachusetts	M.	60–60–60	. 50–1. 70–1. 11
Do	F.	60–60–60	. 48–1. 50– . 91
Minnesota	M.	(1)	. 75–1. 35– . 90
New Hampshire	F.	60–60–60	. 45–1. 00– . 76
New Jersey	F.	55–55–55	. 92–1. 17–1. 04
New York	M.	60–66–66	. 62–1. 67–1. 27
Do	F.	66–66–66	. 55–1. 60– . 96
North Carolina	M.	69–69–69	. 75– . 75– . 75
Do	F.	69–69–69	. 75– . 75– . 75
Pennsylvania	M.	60–60–60	. 66– . 66– . 66
Do	F.	60–60–60	. 42–1. 83– . 77
Rhode Island	M.	60–60–60	. 42– . 42– . 42
Do	F.	60–60–60	. 58– . 58– . 58
Vermont	F.	64–66–65	. 43– . 75– . 54
1886:			
Connecticut	F.	66–66–66	. 58–1. 06–1. 05
Massachusetts	F.	(1)	. 94– . 94– . 94
Missouri	F.	61–61–61	. 71– . 83– . 76
New Jersey	F.	51–60–59	. 29–1. 29– . 73
New York	F.	54–60–58	. 58–1. 50– . 97
Do	M.	(1)	1. 08–1. 08–1. 08
Ohio	F.	(1)	. 33– . 33– . 33
Pennsylvania	F.	57–72–61	. 46–1. 51– . 91
Rhode Island	F.	60–60–60	. 83– . 96– . 90
Vermont	M.	66–66–66	. 67– . 75– . 70
Do	F.	66–66–66	. 74–1. 63– . 91
1887:			
California	F.	60–60–60	1. 00–1. 00–1. 00
Connecticut	F.	60–60–60	. 52–1. 32–1. 15
Do	M.	(1)	. 49–1. 33–1. 07
Illinois	F.	56–60–58	. 25– . 67– . 42
Kentucky	F.	62–62–62	. 21– . 33– . 27
Massachusetts	F.	56–60–59	. 50–1. 25– . 93
New York	F.	53–60–58	. 42–1. 33– . 86
Ohio	F.	51–57–55	. 25– . 50– . 36
Pennsylvania	F.	60–61–60	. 50–1. 42– . 94

1 Not reported.

TABLE L–40.—*Winders, silk goods, 1845–1900, by year and State—Continued*

Year and State	Sex	Hours per week	Rate per day (dollars)	Year and State	Sex	Hours per week	Rate per day (dollars)
1888:				**1892—Continued.**			
Connecticut	F.	60–60–60	1.16–1.16–1.16	Illinois	F.	54–54–54	0.83–0.83–0.83
Do	F.	60–60–60	.75–1.16–1.08	Indiana	F.	54–54–54	.25–.25–.25
Massachusetts	M.	60–60–60	.60–1.00–.82	Maine	F.	60–60–60	.75–1.00–.93
Do	F.	60–60–60	.60–.98–.95	Massachusetts	F.	58–60–59	.99–1.06–1.02
New Jersey	F.	57–60–59	.71–1.17–.97	Do	M.	58–58–58	1.31–1.31–1.31
Do	(¹)	(¹)	.58–.58–.58	**1893:**			
New York	M.	53–60–60	.42–1.00–.83	Massachusetts	F.	58–58–58	1.00–1.10–1.05
Do	F.	60–60–60	.50–1.00–.82	New Jersey	F.	55–60–58	.75–1.67–1.02
Do	(¹)	(¹)	.75–.75–.75	**1894:**			
Pennsylvania	F.	(¹)	.50–.50–.50	Massachusetts	F.	54–60–58	.67–1.25–.92
Rhode Island	M.	60–60–60	.70–1.00–.85	New York	M.	60–60–60	.70–1.50–1.23
Do	F.	60–60–60	.71–1.00–.87	Do	F.	60–60–60	.75–.75–.75
South Carolina	F.	60–60–60	.58–1.00–.79	North Carolina	F.	60–66–66	.35–.35–.35
1889:				Ohio	F.	60–60–60	.75–.75–.75
Connecticut	M.	(¹)	.90–.90–.90	Rhode Island	(¹)	(¹)	.80–.83–.82
Do	F.	60–60–60	1.07–1.07–1.07	**1895:**			
Georgia	F.	66–66–66	.75–.75–.75	Connecticut	F.	60–60–60	.85–1.37–1.15
Maine	M.	(¹)	1.30–1.30–1.30	Louisiana	F.	60–60–60	.40–.40–.40
Do	F.	60–60–60	.75–1.00–.86	Massachusetts	F.	54–60–58	.39–1.51–.94
Maryland	M.	(¹)	.40–.69–.46	New Hampshire	M.	60–60–60	.50–1.40–.98
Do	F.	(¹)	.27–.27–.27	Do	F.	60–60–60	.60–1.67–.99
Massachusetts	M.	60–60–60	.33–.85–.68	New Jersey	F.	53–55–53	.83–1.17–1.00
Do	F.	60–60–60	.34–1.15–1.07	New York	M.	60–60–60	.67–.67–.67
New Hampshire	F.	60–60–60	.70–1.20–.91	Do	F.	55–60–59	.33–1.38–1.06
New Jersey	M.	60–60–60	.75–.75–.75	North Carolina	M.	66–66–66	.75–.75–.75
New York	M.	(¹)	.70–.70–.70	Do	F.	66–66–66	.55–.55–.55
Do	F.	60–60–60	.30–1.08–.72	Pennsylvania	M.	60–60–60	1.67–1.67–1.67
Pennsylvania	M.	(¹)	1.01–1.05–1.03	Do	F.	60–60–60	.75–1.00–.89
Do	F.	(¹)	.82–1.63–1.04	South Carolina	F.	61–61–61	.67–.83–.74
Rhode Island	F.	60–60–60	.67–2.50–1.34	**1896:**			
Tennessee	F.	(¹)	.30–.40–.35	Connecticut	F.	60–60–60	1.00–1.00–1.00
1890:				Georgia	F.	63–66–65	.50–.90–.72
Connecticut	F.	60–60–60	1.24–1.24–1.24	Do	M.	66–66–66	.40–.40–.40
Massachusetts	F.	(¹)	1.03–1.03–1.03	Kentucky	F.	60–60–60	.33–.33–.33
Missouri	M.	(¹)	1.25–1.25–1.25	Minnesota	F.	54–60–58	.60–1.18–.94
Do	F.	(¹)	.40–.50–.43	New York	F.	60–60–56	.56–1.17–.76
New Hampshire	F.	60–60–60	.90–.90–.90	Ohio	F.	42–60–55	.50–1.00–.77
New York	M.	(¹)	.38–2.50–1.00	Pennsylvania	M.	60–60–60	1.00–2.00–1.50
Do	F.	(¹)	.60–1.00–.91	Do	F.	51–60–59	.23–2.01–.84
Pennsylvania	F.	60–60–60	.75–.75–.75	Rhode Island	F.	60–60–60	.88–1.24–.97
Rhode Island	M.	(¹)	.60–1.00–.88	Vermont	M.	66–66–66	.64–1.50–1.05
Tennessee	M.	(¹)	.35–.35–.35	Do	F.	64–66–65	.50–1.44–.97
1891:				**1897:**			
Connecticut	F.	60–60–60	1.28–1.28–1.28	Massachusetts	F.	63–63–63	1.00–1.00–1.00
Maine	F.	60–60–60	1.00–1.00–.72	**1898:**			
Massachusetts	F.	(¹)	1.05–1.05–1.05	New Jersey	F.	60–60–60	.83–.83–.83
Michigan	F.	(¹)	.67–.67–.67	**1899:**			
New Jersey	F.	60–60–60	.60–.60–.60	New York	F.	60–60–60	.78–1.39–1.12
New York	F.	60–60–60	.58–1–13–.89	Pennsylvania	F.	60–60–60	.84–1.67–1.27
Do	M.	(¹)	.50–2.50–.97	**1900:**			
1892:				New York	F.	60–60–60	.82–1.47–1.18
Connecticut	F.	60–60–60	1.13–1.13–1.13	Pennsylvania	F.	60–60–60	.74–1.91–1.35

¹ Not reported.

TABLE L-41.—*Winders, females, silk goods, 1890–1910, United States, by year*

[In 1890 to 1903 the grade of silk on which employees worked was not reported]

| Year | United States | | Year | United States | |
	Hours per week	Rate per hour		Hours per week	Rate per hour
1890	59. 8	$0. 093	HARD SILK		
1891	59. 9	. 082			
1892	59. 3	. 090	1907	57. 6	$0. 099
1893	57. 1	. 096	1908	57. 1	. 087
1894	57. 3	. 104	1909	56. 5	. 089
1895	57. 3	. 103	1910	56. 4	. 093
1896	57. 5	. 100			
1897	57. 5	. 099	SOFT SILK		
1898	57. 4	. 104	1907	58. 0	. 103
1899	57. 5	. 100	1908	57. 6	. 099
1900	57. 6	. 102	1909	57. 6	. 104
1901	57. 6	. 106	1910	57. 2	. 108
1902	57. 6	. 108			
1903	57. 7	. 112			

TABLE L-42.—*Winders, females, silk goods, 1904–1919, by State and year*

[In 1904 to 1907 and in 1919 the grade of silk on which employees worked was not reported]

| Year | Connecticut | | New Jersey | | New York | | Pennsylvania | |
	Hours per week	Rate per hour	Hours per week	Rate per hour	Hours per week	Rate per hour	Hours per week	Rate per hour
1904			55. 0	$0. 134	58. 2	$0. 137	58. 8	$0. 087
1905	60. 0	$0. 108	55. 0	. 127	57. 4	. 133	58. 9	. 092
1906	60. 0	. 106	55. 0	. 124	57. 2	. 139	59. 1	. 091
1907	59. 8	. 110	55. 0	. 134	57. 3	. 145	58. 6	. 102
1919	(¹)	. 295	(¹)	. 310	(¹)	. 243	(¹)	. 228
HARD SILK								
1910			55. 0	. 121			57. 7	. 086
1911	57. 9	. 126	55. 0	. 121			56. 9	. 090
1912	57. 9	. 128	55. 0	. 120			57. 0	: 094
1913	57. 9	. 133	55. 0	. 127	52. 1	. 104	56. 6	. 103
1914	55. 0	. 142	55. 0	. 130	52. 1	. 106	54. 0	. 110
SOFT SILK								
1910	57. 9	. 125	55. 0	. 124			57. 7	: 099
1911	57. 9	. 128	55. 0	. 141			58. 0	. 105
1912	57. 9	. 126	55. 0	. 156			55. 4	. 117
1913	57. 9	. 129	54. 9	. 164	52. 3	. 146	56. 2	. 122
1914	55. 0	. 146	55. 0	. 169	52. 1	. 159	54. 0	. 131

¹ Not reported.

WOOLEN AND WORSTED GOODS

The sources from which this information was taken are the fifteenth and the nineteenth annual reports of the Commissioner of Labor Statistics and bulletins of the Bureau of Labor Statistics Nos. 59, 65, 71, 77, 128, 150, 190, 238, 261, 289, 327, 377, 443, and 487.

The fabrics known as woolen and worsted cloths are both made from wool. Many of the processes of manufacture are identical and for this reason the two groups of employees are shown together. There are some differences, however. The wool which is to be used for woolen yarn is prepared with the object in view of retaining the natural curly, springy quality of the fiber while in preparing it for worsted yarn the object is to take out as much of the curl as possible and make the fibers parallel so that they will spin into a smoother and harder yarn than the woolen.

In addition to employees engaged in the manufacturing processes these reports show the wages and hours of work of those engaged in wool dyeing. The data are presented by States whenever possible; certain sections are shown by geographic divisions only; in other instances there are overlapping periods, and for other years no reports were available. The details are shown here in the same manner as published in the above-noted reports.

TABLE L–43.—*Doffers, males, woolen and worsted goods, 1916–1928,[1] by State and year*

Year	Massachusetts		Pennsylvania		Rhode Island	
	Hours per week	Rate per hour	Hours per week	Rate per hour	Hours per week	Rate per hour
1916	49.4	$0.164			54.0	$0.125
1918	51.0	.297			49.1	.179
1920	46.4	.525				
1922	46.9	.307				
1924	45.8	.328	53.1	$0.272		
1926	48.0	.290			48.7	.286
1928			52.7	.307		

[1] For earlier years see doffers, cotton goods.

TABLE L–44.—*Doffers, females, woolen and worsted goods, 1916–1928,[1] by State and year*

Year	Massachusetts		New Jersey		Pennsylvania		Rhode Island	
	Hours per week	Rate per hour	Hours per week	Rate per hour	Hours per week	Rate per hour	Hours per week	Rate per hour
1916	49.5	$0.147			50.6	$0.109	53.9	$0.124
1918	48.6	.233			53.7	.188	50.5	.186
1920	46.1	.398	48.0	$0.348	45.9	.339	46.7	.312
1922	46.7	.291			52.5	.286	47.6	.239
1924	46.7	.337			52.3	.306	47.8	.275
1926	48.0	.295			52.3	.273	48.3	.269
1928	48.0	.322	48.0	.345	53.6	.260	48.3	.272

[1] For earlier years see doffers, cotton goods.

TABLE L–45.—*Dressers, woolen and worsted goods, 1842–1896, by year and State*

Year and State	Sex	Lowest, highest, and average—		Year and State	Sex	Lowest, highest, and average—	
		Hours per week	Rate per day (dollars)			Hours per week	Rate per day (dollars)
1842:				1849:			
Massachusetts	F.	78–78–78	0.55–0.98–0.64	Massachusetts	M.	75–75–75	1.35–1.35–1.35
1843:				Do	F.	78–78–78	.58–.65–.62
Massachusetts	F.	84–84–84	.58–.58–.58	1850:			
1844:				Massachusetts	M.	75–75–75	1.50–1.50–1.50
Massachusetts	F.	84–84–84	.38–.71–.57	Do	F.	78–78–78	.60–.75–.65
1845:				Rhode Island	M.	84–84–84	1.08–1.08–1.08
Massachusetts	F.	78–84–83	.38–.70–.44	1851:			
1846:				Massachusetts	M.	72–75–73	.58–1.63–1.15
Massachusetts	F.	78–78–78	.66–.70–.68	Do	F.	78–78–78	.82–.82–.82
1847:				Rhode Island	M.	84–84–84	1.08–1.08–1.08
Massachusetts	F.	78–84–83	.21–.60–.42	1852:			
1848:				Massachusetts	M.	72–75–73	.58–1.63–1.10
Massachusetts	M.	75–75–75	1.25–1.25–1.25	Do	F.	72–78–77	.45–.62–.56
Do	F.	78–84–80	.58–.65–.60	Rhode Island	M.	84–84–84	1.08–1.08–1.08

TABLE L-45.—*Dressers, woolen and worsted goods, 1842-1896. by year and State—*
Continued

Year and State	Sex	Lowest, highest, and average—		Year and State	Sex	Lowest, highest, and average—	
		Hours per week	Rate per day (dollars)			Hours per week	Rate per day (dollars)
1853:				**1871:**			
Massachusetts____	M.	75-75-75	1. 52-1. 52-1. 52	Massachusetts____	M.	66-66-66	1. 25-2. 76-2. 47
Do_____	F.	78-78-78	. 50- . 72- . 65	Rhode Island_____	M.	72-72-72	1. 75-1. 75-1. 75
Rhode Island_____	M.	84-84-84	1. 08-1. 08-1. 08	**1872:**			
1854:				Massachusetts____	M.	60-60-60	1. 75-2. 81-2. 54
Massachusetts____	M.	66-66-66	1. 60-1. 60-1. 60	Do_____	F.	66-66-66	1. 75-1. 75-1. 75
Do_____	F.	78-78-78	. 50- . 72- . 60	Rhode Island_____	M.	72-72-72	1. 75-1. 75-1. 75
Rhode Island_____	M.	84-84-84	1. 08-1. 08-1. 08	**1873:**			
1855:				Massachusetts____	M.	60-66-66	1. 40-2. 76-2. 44
Massachusetts____	M.	66-72-70	. 63-1. 67-1. 05	Do_____	F.	66-66-66	. 83-1. 75-1. 29
Do_____	F.	78-78-78	. 50- . 65- . 54	Pennsylvania_____	M.	(1)	2. 45-2. 45-2. 45
Rhode Island_____	M.	84-84-84	1. 00-1. 00-1. 00	Do_____	F.	(1)	1. 16-1. 16-1. 16
1856:				Do_____	(1)	(1)	. 50- . 50- . 50
Massachusetts____	M.	66-66-66	1. 74-1. 74-1. 74	Rhode Island_____	M.	72-72-72	1. 75-1. 75-1. 75
Rhode Island_____	M.	84-84-84	1. 00-1. 00-1. 00	**1874:**			
1857:				Connecticut_____	M.	66-66-66	1. 50-1. 80-1. 68
Massachusetts____	M.	66-72-68	. 60-1. 68-1. 45	Massachusetts____	M.	66-66-66	1. 40-2. 58-2. 34
Do_____	F.	72-72-72	. 40-1. 25- . 90	Do_____	F.	66-66-66	. 60- . 60- . 60
Rhode Island_____	M.	84-84-84	1. 00-1. 00-1. 00	Rhode Island_____	M.	72-72-72	1. 50-1. 50-1. 50
1858:				**1875:**			
Massachusetts____	M.	66-72-68	. 60-1. 74-1. 49	Connecticut_____	M.	66-66-66	1. 75-1. 80-1. 78
Do_____	F.	72-78-73	. 48-1. 08- . 84	Maine_____	M.	64-64-64	1. 75-1. 75-1. 75
Rhode Island_____	M.	84-84-84	1. 00-1. 00-1. 00	Massachusetts____	M.	60-60-60	. 70-4. 00-2. 03
1859:				Do_____	F.	60-60-60	. 60-1. 89-1. 17
Massachusetts____	M.	66-72-67	1. 00-1. 79-1. 69	Rhode Island_____	M.	72-72-72	1. 67-1. 67-1. 67
Do_____	F.	72-78-73	. 50-1. 10- . 86	**1876:**			
Rhode Island_____	M.	84-84-84	1. 00-1. 00-1. 00	Connecticut_____	M.	66-66-66	1. 80-1. 80-1. 80
1860:				Massachusetts____	M.	60-60-60	. 70-2. 83-2. 18
Massachusetts____	M.	66-72-67	. 74-1. 64-1. 56	Do_____	F.	60-60-60	. 60- . 60- . 60
Do_____	F.	72-78-73	. 50-1. 38- . 98	New Hampshire__	M.	66-66-66	1. 40-1. 40-1. 40
Rhode Island_____	M.	78-78-78	1. 00-1. 00-1. 00	Pennsylvania_____	M.	(1)	. 67-2. 50-1. 54
1861:				Do_____	F.	(1)	1. 00-1. 00-1. 00
Massachusetts____	M.	66-66-66	. 86-1. 80-1. 66	Rhode Island_____	M.	72-72-72	1. 67-1. 67-1. 67
Do_____	F.	66-78-69	. 65-1. 30-1. 03	**1877:**			
Rhode Island_____	M.	78-78-78	. 92- . 92- . 92	Connecticut_____	M.	66-66-66	1. 50-1. 80-1. 73
1862:				Maine_____	M.	66-66-66	. 88-1. 17-1. 03
Massachusetts____	M.	66-66-66	. 68-1. 87-1. 70	Massachusetts____	M.	60-60-60	. 70-2. 59-2. 04
Do_____	F.	66-72-68	. 40- . 90- . 74	Do_____	F.	60-60-60	. 60- . 60- . 60
Rhode Island_____	M.	78-78-78	. 92- . 92- . 92	Rhode Island_____	M.	72-72-72	1. 75-1. 75-1. 75
1863:				**1878:**			
Massachusetts____	M.	66-66-66	. 86- . 86- . 86	Connecticut_____	M.	66-66-66	1. 50-1. 80-1. 70
Do_____	F.	66-66-66	. 45-1. 92-1. 61	Massachusetts____	M.	60-60-60	. 70-2. 36-1. 97
Rhode Island_____	M.	78-78-78	. 92- . 92- . 92	Do_____	F.	60-60-60	. 60- . 80- . 70
1864:				New Hampshire__	M.	60-60-60	1. 00-1. 50-1. 25
Massachusetts____	M.	66-66-66	. 85-1. 80-1. 67	Pennsylvania_____	M.	(1)	1. 20-1. 20-1. 20
Do_____	F.	66-66-66	. 67-1. 50-1. 11	Rhode Island_____	M.	72-72-72	1. 75-1. 75-1. 75
Rhode Island_____	M.	78-78-78	. 92- . 92- . 92	**1879:**			
1865:				Connecticut_____	M.	66-66-66	1. 25-1. 38-1. 32
Massachusetts____	M.	66-66-66	. 58-1. 94-1. 59	Massachusetts____	M.	60-60-60	. 50-2. 48-1. 94
Do_____	F.	66-66-66	. 58-1. 50- . 94	Do_____	F.	60-60-60	. 50- . 50- . 50
Rhode Island_____	M.	78-78-78	1. 00-1. 00-1. 00	Pennsylvania_____	M.	66-66-66	1. 60-1. 60-1. 60
1866:				Do_____	(1)	(1)	. 75- . 75- . 75
Connecticut_____	M.	66-66-66	1. 50-1. 50-1. 50	Rhode Island_____	M.	72-72-72	1. 75-1. 75-1. 75
Massachusetts____	M.	66-66-66	. 92-2. 25-1. 78	**1880:**			
Do_____	F.	66-66-66	. 72-2. 00-1. 23	Connecticut_____	M.	66-66-66	1. 53-1. 53-1. 53
Rhode Island_____	M.	78-78-78	1. 25-1. 25-1. 25	Do_____	(1)	66-66-66	1. 25-1. 50-1. 38
1867:				Massachusetts____	M.	60-60-60	. 40-2. 21-1. 79
Connecticut_____	M.	66-66-66	1. 38-1. 50-1. 44	Do_____	F.	60-60-60	. 55- . 55- . 55
Massachusetts____	M.	66-66-66	1. 33-2. 27-2. 15	New York_____	(1)	66-66-66	2. 50-2. 50-2. 50
Do_____	F.	66-66-66	. 75-2. 10-1. 59	Rhode Island_____	M.	72-72-72	1. 50-1. 50-1. 50
New Hampshire__	F.	74-74-74	. 67-1. 00- . 86	**1881:**			
Rhode Island_____	M.	78-78-78	1. 50-1. 50-1. 50	Connecticut_____	M.	66-66-66	1. 58-1. 58-1. 58
1868:				Massachusetts____	M.	60-60-60	1. 00-2. 14-1. 85
Massachusetts____	M.	66-66-66	1. 98-2. 25-2. 19	Do_____	F.	60-60-60	. 60- . 70- . 67
Do_____	F.	66-66-66	1. 00-2. 10-1. 51	New Hampshire__	M.	65-65-65	. 80-2. 16-1. 61
Rhode Island_____	M.	72-72-72	1. 50-1. 50-1. 50	Do_____	F.	65-65-65	. 80-1. 85-1. 28
1869:				Rhode Island_____	M.	72-72-72	1. 50-1. 50-1. 50
Massachusetts____	M.	66-66-66	2. 00-2. 18-2. 15	**1882:**			
Do_____	F.	66-66-66	. 96-1. 86-1. 51	Connecticut_____	M.	66-66-66	1. 55-1. 58-1. 56
Rhode Island_____	M.	72-72-72	1. 50-1. 50-1. 50	Massachusetts____	M.	60-60-60	1. 10-2. 00-1. 84
1870:				Do_____	F.	60-60-60	. 60- . 80- . 73
Massachusetts____	M.	66-66-66	1. 75-2. 26-2. 20	New Hampshire__	M.	66-66-66	1. 15-1. 72-1. 34
Do_____	F.	66-66-66	. 92-2. 00-1. 46	Do_____	F.	66-66-66	1. 10-1. 15-1. 12
Rhode Island_____	M.	72-72-72	1. 75-1. 75-1. 75	Rhode Island_____	M.	72-72-72	1. 50-1. 50-1. 50
				South Carolina____	M.	69-69-69	1. 00-1. 25-1. 10

[1] Not reported.

TABLE **L-45.**—*Dressers, woolen and worsted goods, 1842–1896, by year and State—*
Continued

Year and State	Sex	Lowest, highest, and average—	
		Hours per week	Rate per day (dollars)
1883:			
Connecticut_____	M.	66–66–66	1.60–1.60–1.60
Georgia_____	M.	66–66–66	1.75–1.75–1.75
Massachusetts____	M.	60–60–60	.85–2.34–1.82
Do_____	F.	60–60–60	.70–1.42–1.03
Do_____	(¹)	(¹)	.45–.75–.51
New Hampshire__	M.	66–66–66	1.90–1.90–1.90
Rhode Island_____	M.	72–72–72	1.50–1.50–1.50
1884:			
Connecticut_____	M.	66–66–66	1.45–1.45–1.45
Massachusetts____	M.	60–60–60	.90–2.14–1.94
Do_____	F.	60–60–60	1.00–1.20–1.10
New Hampshire__	M.	60–60–60	1.00–1.40–1.20
Rhode Island_____	M.	72–72–72	1.50–1.50–1.50
1885:			
California_____	M.	60–60–60	2.75–2.75–2.75
Connecticut_____	M.	66–69–66	1.30–1.60–1.51
Delaware_____	M.	60–60–60	.91–2.33–1.11
Illinois_____	F.	63–63–63	.44–.44–.44
Indiana_____	M.	66–66–66	1.33–1.75–1.53
Maine_____	M.	64–66–64	.38–2.50–1.24
Do_____	F.	64–64–64	.42–1.57–.86
Maryland_____	M.	66–66–66	.80–.80–.80
Do_____	F.	66–66–66	.80–.80–.80
Massachusetts____	M.	60–60–60	1.00–2.11–1.73
Do_____	F.	60–60–60	.60–1.50–.88
New Hampshire__	M	60–66–65	.96–1.85–1.16
Do_____	F.	60–65–65	.65–.97–.92
New Jersey_____	M.	60–60–60	1.54–1.54–1.54
New York_____	M.	60–69–67	1.00–2.25–1.52
Pennsylvania_____	M.	60–60–60	.67–2.00–1.26
Rhode Island_____	M.	72–72–72	1.67–1.67–1.67
Tennessee_____	M.	67–67–67	.90–.90–.90
Vermont_____	M.	60–60–60	1.00–1.35–1.26
Virginia_____	M.	66–66–66	.50–.75–.63
1886:			
Connecticut_____	M.	66–66–66	1.60–1.60–1.60
Iowa_____	M.	60–60–60	1.67–1.67–1.67
Massachusetts____	M.	60–60–60	1.10–2.07–1.93
Do_____	F.	60–60–60	1.20–1.20–1.20
New Hampshire__	M.	60–60–60	1.05–1.72–1.32
Pennsylvania_____	M.	(¹)	1.67–2.50–1.93
Rhode Island_____	M.	60–60–60	1.67–1.67–1.67
1887:			
Connecticut_____	M.	60–60–60	.79–1.80–1.51
Do_____	F.	(¹)	.80–1.00–.83
Maine_____	M.	60–60–60	2.25–2.25–2.25
Massachusetts____	M.	60–60–60	1.00–2.08–1.87
Do_____	F.	60–60–60	1.20–1.20–1.20
New York_____	M.	60–60–60	.50–2.50–1.67
Ohio_____	M.	60–60–60	1.75–1.75–1.75
Rhode Island_____	M.	60–60–60	1.65–1.67–1.67
Wisconsin_____	(¹)		1.75–2.25–2.13
1888:			
California_____	M.	(¹)	2.50–2.50–2.50
Connecticut_____	M.	60–66–62	1.38–1.80–1.65
Maine_____	F.	60–60–60	1.00–1.00–1.00
Massachusetts____	M.	60–60–60	1.00–2.24–1.98
New Hampshire__	M.	(¹)	1.75–2.00–1.88
New Jersey_____	M.	(¹)	1.50–2.75–2.13
New York_____	M.	(¹)	1.00–2.50–2.25

Year and State	Sex	Lowest, highest, and average—	
		Hours per week	Rate per day (dollars)
1888—Continued.			
Pennsylvania_____	M.	(¹)	0.50–2.50–2.05
Do_____	F.	(¹)	0.50–.50–.50
Rhode Island_____	M.	60–60–60	1.67–2.00–1.94
Do_____	(¹)	(¹)	1.65–1.75–1.72
1889:			
California_____	M.	(¹)	1.40–2.50–1.95
Connecticut_____	M.	60–60–60	1.25–1.75–1.59
Maine_____	M.	60–60–60	1.50–1.84–1.69
Massachusetts____	M.	60–60–60	1.10–2.74–1.94
New Hampshire__	F.	60–60–60	1.00–1.00–1.00
New York_____	M.	60–60–60	.96–1.75–1.60
Rhode Island_____	M.	60–60–60	1.67–1.67–1.67
1890:			
Connecticut_____	M.	60–60–60	1.25–1.75–1.58
Maine_____	M.	(¹)	1.75–1.75–1.75
Massachusetts____	M.	60–60–60	1.10–3.12–2.50
Missouri_____	M.	(¹)	2.25–2.25–2.25
New York_____	M.	(¹)	.50–3.00–1.50
Rhode Island_____	M.	60–60–60	1.67–1.75–1.72
1891:			
Connecticut_____	M.	60–60–60	1.25–1.75–1.61
Massachusetts____	M.	60–60–60	1.20–3.10–2.41
New York_____	M.	60–60–60	.50–3.00–1.51
Do_____	(¹)	(¹)	.80–.90–.85
Rhode Island_____	M.	60–60–60	1.67–1.67–1.67
1892:			
Connecticut_____	M.	60–60–60	1.75–2.75–2.03
Maine_____	M.	60–60–60	1.86–1.86–1.86
Massachusetts____	M.	58–58–58	1.26–2.06–1.75
Rhode Island_____	M.	60–60–60	1.75–1.75–1.75
1893:			
Rhode Island_____	M.	60–60–60	1.75–1.75–1.75
1894:			
Maine_____	M.	60–60–60	1.65–1.65–1.65
New York_____	M.	60–60–60	2.25–2.25–2.25
Ohio_____	M.	60–60–60	1.45–1.45–1.45
Do_____	F.	60–60–60	.60–.60–.60
Rhode Island_____	M.	60–60–60	1.60–1.60–1.60
Do_____	(¹)	(¹)	1.17–3.25–1.84
1895:			
Georgia_____	M.	66–66–66	.65–1.80–1.23
Maine_____	M.	60–60–60	.27–2.50–1.24
Do_____	M.	60–60–60	.26–1.68–.90
Massachusetts____	M.	58–58–58	1.38–2.99–2.09
New Hampshire__	M.	60–60–60	.90–3.00–1.62
Do_____	F.	60–60–60	.73–1.60–1.18
Rhode Island_____	M.	60–60–60	1.75–1.75–1.75
Tennessee_____	M.	67–67–67	.70–1.00–.95
Vermont_____	M.	60–60–60	.55–1.35–.78
Do_____	F.	60–60–60	.56–1.00–.88
1896:			
Georgia_____	F.	66–66–66	1.00–1.25–1.11
Iowa_____	M.	60–60–60	1.75–1.75–1.75
New Hampshire__	M.	60–60–60	1.00–2.00–1.43
New York_____	M.	60–60–60	.58–1.67–1.13
Ohio_____	M.	60–60–60	1.00–1.74–1.56
Do_____	F.	60–60–60	.61–.61–.61
Pennsylvania_____	M.	60–60–60	1.67–2.00–1.93
South Carolina____	M.	66–66–66	.90–1.50–1.08

¹ Not reported.

TABLE L-46.—*Dresser tenders,*[1] *males, woolen and worsted goods, 1911-1926, by State and year*

Year	Connecticut		Maine		Massachusetts		New Hampshire	
	Hours per week	Rate per week	Hours per week	Rate per week	Hours per week	Rate per week	Hours per week	Rate per week
1911					56. 1	$0. 256		
1912					54. 6	. 278		
1913			58. 2	$0. 229	54. 6	. 277	57. 8	$0. 249
1914	56. 1	$0. 261	58. 2	. 228	54. 0	. 280	54. 7	. 269
1916	55. 4	. 295	58. 0	. 278	54. 0	. 332	54. 6	. 300
1918	54. 8	. 428	54. 0	. 410	54. 0	. 498	54. 3	. 427
1920	47. 9	. 739	48. 8	. 822	48. 0	. 662	48. 0	. 784
1922	48. 3	. 591	48. 7	. 668	48. 0	. 677	49. 0	. 624
1924	48. 7	. 673	49. 7	. 743	48. 0	. 758	50. 9	. 735
1926	48. 8	. 641	49. 4	. 680	48. 0	. 719	48. 8	. 683

Year	New York		Pennsylvania		Rhode Island		Vermont	
1911					56. 0	$0. 265		
1912					56. 0	. 280		
1913					56. 0	. 280		
1914	60. 0	$0. 278			54. 0	. 294		
1916	58. 9	. 275	54. 6	$0. 344	54. 0	. 338	57. 8	$0. 302
1918	59. 0	. 400	54. 5	. 453	54. 0	. 470	56. 0	. 440
1920	48. 0	. 736	50. 2	. 838	48. 2	. 845	48. 0	. 783
1922	48. 0	. 575	51. 4	. 720	48. 3	. 641	50. 6	. 616
1924	48. 0	. 663	51. 2	. 874	48. 3	. 716	52. 2	. 697
1926	49. 2	. 582	50. 4	. 821	48. 4	. 674	52. 1	. 645

[1] Classified as "dressers" prior to 1914.

TABLE L-47.—*Dyers, males, woolen and worsted goods, 1890-1906, by State and year*

Year	California		Maine		Massachusetts		Pennsylvania	
	Hours per week	Rate per hour	Hours per week	Rate per hour	Hours per week	Rate per hour	Hours per week	Rate per hour
1890 [1]	62. 5	$0. 143	60. 0	$0. 125	59. 8	$0. 111	60. 1	$0. 150
1891	62. 5	. 154	60. 0	. 128	59. 8	. 113	60. 2	. 151
1892	63. 4	. 155	60. 0	. 129	59. 6	. 109	60. 1	. 155
1893	62. 5	. 163	60. 0	. 130	54. 6	. 113	60. 1	. 152
1894	62. 3	. 147	60. 0	. 129	58. 0	. 106	60. 0	. 136
1895	62. 3	. 147	60. 0	. 134	58. 0	. 106	60. 1	. 139
1896	62. 6	. 143	60. 0	. 132	58. 0	. 107	60. 1	. 139
1897	63. 1	. 148	60. 0	. 132	44. 2	. 107	60. 1	. 142
1898	63. 7	. 139	60. 0	. 132	58. 0	. 107	60. 1	. 149
1899	63. 7	. 139	60. 0	. 130	58. 0	. 107	60. 1	. 150
1900	57. 3	. 172	60. 0	. 130	58. 0	. 124	60. 1	. 157
1901	58. 8	. 160	60. 0	. 130	58. 0	. 118	60. 1	. 156
1902	58. 8	. 169	60. 0	. 131	58. 0	. 121	60. 1	. 156
1903	60. 5	. 158	60. 0	. 130	58. 0	. 127	60. 0	. 153
1904			60. 0	. 138	56. 6	. 129	60. 0	. 154
1905			60. 0	. 140	58. 0	. 129	60. 0	. 155
1906			60. 0	. 142	58. 0	. 139	59. 0	. 159

[1] For data for previous years, see dyers, cotton goods, Tables L-9 ond L-10, pp. 373-376.

TABLE L-48.—*Dyers, laborers, dyehouse, males, woolen and worsted goods, 1907-1926, by State and year*

Year	Connecticut Hours per week	Rate per hour	Maine Hours per week	Rate per hour	Massachusetts Hours per week	Rate per hour	New Hampshire Hours per week	Rate per hour
1907 ¹					58. 0	$0. 152		
1908					58. 0	. 139		
1909					58. 0	. 140		
1910					56. 0	. 144		
1911					56. 0	. 144	57. 9	$0. 150
1912					54. 2	. 157	57. 8	. 164
1913	58. 5	$0. 157	58. 1	$0. 158	54. 2	. 155	57. 8	. 166
1914	56. 5	. 161	58. 2	. 160	54. 0	. 158	54. 8	. 178
1916	55. 5	. 198	58. 0	. 194	54. 1	. 194	54. 9	. 200
1918	55. 2	. 313	54. 2	. 315	53. 8	. 305	54. 2	. 307
1920	48. 0	. 524	50. 1	. 510	48. 0	. 571	48. 0	. 546
1922	49. 1	. 409	49. 1	. 418	48. 1	. 446	48. 0	. 419
1924	48. 9	. 462	49. 7	. 457	48. 1	. 496	52. 0	. 471
1926	49. 7	. 443	50. 0	. 426	48. 4	. 446	50. 4	. 429

Year	New Jersey Hours per week	Rate per hour	New York Hours per week	Rate per hour	Pennsylvania Hours per week	Rate per hour	Rhode Island Hours per week	Rate per hour
1907							58. 0	$0. 136
1908							58. 0	. 135
1909							58. 0	. 129
1910	55. 3	$0. 152					56. 0	. 140
1911	55. 6	. 155					56. 0	. 146
1912	55. 1	. 163					56. 0	. 157
1913	55. 2	. 173					56. 0	. 155
1914	55. 3	. 173	60. 0	$0. 141			54. 0	. 155
1916	55. 7	. 213	59. 4	. 174	54. 4	$0. 207	55. 8	. 188
1918	55. 5	. 313	58. 5	. 289	54. 8	. 301	54. 0	. 288
1920	49. 1	. 631	48. 0	. 567	50. 6	. 538	48. 2	. 540
1922	48. 9	. 489	48. 0	. 421	54. 1	. 397	48. 6	. 414
1924	48. 7	. 568	48. 0	. 485	50. 6	. 511	48. 5	. 464
1926			49. 6	. 429	52. 0	. 535	49. 0	. 434

¹ For data for previous years, see dyers, cotton goods, Tables L-9 and L-10, pp. 373-376.

TABLE L-49.—*Loom fixers, males, woolen and worsted goods, 1890-1906, by State and year*

Year	California Hours per week	Rate per hour	Maine Hours per week	Rate per hour	Massachusetts Hours per week	Rate per hour	Pennsylvania Hours per week	Rate per hour
1890	63. 5	$0. 210	60. 0	$0. 194	58. 3	$0. 199	60. 6	$0. 249
1891	63. 5	. 210	60. 0	. 188	58. 4	. 199	60. 6	. 245
1892	63. 5	. 235	60. 0	. 197	58. 3	. 198	60. 6	. 248
1893	63. 5	. 235	60. 0	. 197	58. 0	. 210	60. 3	. 238
1894	63. 5	. 210	60. 0	. 198	53. 5	. 202	60. 4	. 217
1895	63. 5	. 212	60. 0	. 196	58. 0	. 203	60. 5	. 222
1896	63. 5	. 212	60. 0	. 193	58. 0	. 214	60. 4	. 223
1897	63. 5	. 201	60. 0	. 199	58. 0	. 215	60. 4	. 234
1898	63. 5	. 225	60. 0	. 194	58. 0	. 210	60. 4	. 240
1899	63. 5	. 225	60. 0	. 198	58. 0	. 213	60. 4	. 240
1900	63. 5	. 225	60. 0	. 200	58. 0	. 236	60. 3	. 254
1901	63. 5	. 225	60. 0	. 200	58. 0	. 236	60. 3	. 254
1902	63. 5	. 225	60. 0	. 200	58. 0	. 241	60. 3	. 254
1903	60. 5	. 236	60. 0	. 197	58. 0	. 238	60. 0	. 265
1904			60. 0	. 216	57. 0	. 236	60. 0	. 273
1905			60. 0	. 221	58. 0	. 238	60. 0	. 276
1906			60. 0	. 245	58. 0	. 252	58. 5	. 306

TABLE L–50.—*Loom fixers, male, woolen and worsted goods, 1907–1928, by State and year*

Year	Connecticut		Maine		New York		Vermont	
	Hours per week	Rate per hour	Hours per week	Rate per hour	Hours per week	Rate per hour	Hours per week	Rate per hour
1914	56.7	$0.298	58.2	$0.258	60.0	$0.278	57.8	$0.288
1916	55.7	.354	58.0	.312	59.2	.309	57.9	.383
1918	54.8	.505	54.0	.472	59.2	.447	59.1	.467
1920	47.8	.851	49.2	.864	48.0	.960	48.0	.956
1922	48.5	.702	49.1	.686	48.0	.756	48.0	.743
1926	48.9	.762	50.2	.783	49.7	.750	50.8	.716
1928	49.1	.755	50.5	.769	50.4	.707	48.0	.819

	Massachusetts		New Hampshire		Rhode Island		New Jersey	
	Hours per week	Rate per hour	Hours per week	Rate per hour	Hours per week	Rate per hour	Hours per week	Rate per hour
1907	58.0	$0.274			58.0	$0.266		
1908	58.0	.257			58.0	.271		
1909	58.0	.257			58.0	.271		
1910	56.0	.276			56.0	.296		
1911	56.0	.283	57.9	$0.232	56.0	.300		
1912	54.2	.326	57.9	.256	56.0	.320		
1913	54.2	.302	57.9	.257	56.0	.322		
1914	54.0	.326	54.9	.272	54.0	.329	55.0	$0.327
1916	54.0	.410	54.8	.315	54.0	.387	55.8	.334
1918	54.0	.646	54.2	.463	54.0	.541	54.8	.387
1920	48.0	1.091	48.0	.835	48.2	.931	54.7	.557
1922	48.0	.806	48.2	.646	48.2	.730	49.0	.828
1926	48.0	.839	51.0	.723	48.3	.789	47.8	.761
1928	48.2	.840	50.5	.692	48.5	.814	48.9	.937

TABLE L–51.—*Spinners, woolen and worsted goods, 1850–1900, by year and State*

Year and State	Sex	Lowest, highest, and average—		Year and State	Sex	Lowest, highest, and average—	
		Hours per week	Rate per day (dollars)			Hours per week	Rate per day (dollars)
1850:				1861—Continued.			
Rhode Island	M.	84–84–84	0.92–0.92–0.92	Massachusetts	M.	78–78–78	0.46–1.25–0.74
1851:				Do	F.	78–78–78	.29–.75–.51
Rhode Island	M.	84–84–84	.92–.92–.92	Rhode Island	M.	78–78–78	.95–.95–.95
1852:				1862:			
Rhode Island	M.	84–84–84	.92–.92–.92	Connecticut	M.	72–72–72	1.00–1.00–1.00
1853:				Massachusetts	M.	78–78–78	.31–1.50–.87
Massachusetts	M.	78–78–78	.61–.61–.61	Do	F.	78–78–78	.31–.50–.45
Do	F.	78–78–78	.67–.67–.67	Rhode Island	M.	78–78–78	.95–.95–.95
Rhode Island	M.	84–84–84	.95–.95–.95	1863:			
1854:				Connecticut	M.	72–72–72	1.30–1.30–1.30
Rhode Island	M.	84–84–84	.95–.95–.95	Massachusetts	M.	78–78–78	.61–1.50–1.10
1855:				Do	F.	78–78–78	.58–.58–.58
Rhode Island	M.	84–84–84	.95–.95–.95	Rhode Island	M.	78–78–78	1.00–1.00–1.00
1856:				1864:			
Rhode Island	M.	84–84–84	.95–.95–.95	Connecticut	M.	72–72–72	1.35–1.35–1.35
1857:				Massachusetts	M.	78–78–78	.61–1.75–1.17
Rhode Island	M.	84–84–84	.95–.95–.95	Do	F.	78–78–78	.42–.67–.53
1858:				Rhode Island	M.	78–78–78	1.19–1.19–1.19
Connecticut	M.	72–72–72	.87–.87–.87	1865:			
Rhode Island	M.	84–84–84	.95–.95–.95	Connecticut	M.	66–66–66	1.68–1.68–1.68
1859:				Massachusetts	M.	66–66–66	1.00–1.75–1.33
Connecticut	M.	66–72–71	.84–1.13–.89	Rhode Island	M.	78–78–78	1.17–1.17–1.17
Maine	M.	(1)	.65–1.06–.92	1866:			
Massachusetts	M.	78–78–78	.54–1.50–.93	Connecticut	M.	66–66–66	.95–1.80–1.18
Do	F.	78–78–78	.38–.42–.41	Massachusetts	M.	66–66–66	1.25–1.75–1.65
Rhode Island	M.	84–84–84	.95–.95–.95	Rhode Island	M.	78–78–78	1.20–1.20–1.20
1860:				1867:			
Connecticut	M.	72–72–72	1.05–1.05–1.05	Connecticut	M.	66–66–66	1.93–1.93–1.93
Massachusetts	M.	78–78–78	.31–1.25–.63	Massachusetts	M.	66–66–66	.62–1.50–1.18
Do	F.	78–78–78	.42–.42–.42	Do	F.	66–66–66	.75–1.75–1.05
Rhode Island	M.	78–78–78	.95–.95–.95	New Hampshire	M.	66–74–71	1.33–1.87–1.55
1861:				Rhode Island	M.	78–78–78	1.31–1.31–1.31
Connecticut	M.	72–72–72	1.05–1.05–1.05				

1 Not reported.

TABLE L–51.—*Spinners, woolen and worsted goods, 1850–1900, by year and State—*
Continued

Year and State	Sex	Hours per week	Rate per day (dollars)	Year and State	Sex	Hours per week	Rate per day (dollars)
1868:				**1880—Continued.**			
Connecticut	M.	60–60–60	1.33–1.75–1.40	New York	(¹)	63–66–65	1.38–1.83–1.61
Massachusetts	M.	66–66–66	1.00–1.50–1.35	Rhode Island	M.	72–72–72	1.24–1.25–1.24
Do	F.	66–66–66	.75–.85–.82	Do	(¹)	66–66–66	1.00–1.67–1.21
Pennsylvania	M.	62–62–62	1.00–1.75–1.38	**1881:**			
Rhode Island	M.	72–72–72	1.27–1.27–1.27	Connecticut	M.	66–66–66	1.50–1.50–1.50
1869:				Do	F.	66–66–66	.89–.89–.89
Connecticut	M.	66–66–66	1.75–1.85–1.84	Kentucky	M.	(¹)	.58–.77–.66
Massachusetts	M.	66–66–66	.60–1.50–1.30	Do	F.	(¹)	.53–.85–.65
Do	F.	66–66–66	.65–1.00–.84	Massachusetts	M.	60–60–60	1.00–1.50–1.25
Rhode Island	M.	72–72–72	1.30–1.30–1.30	New Jersey	M.	(¹)	1.50–1.67–1.59
1870:				Ohio	M.	60–72–63	1.00–2.00–1.66
Connecticut	M.	66 66 66	1.70–1.75–1.70	Rhode Island	M.	72–72–72	1.26–1.26–1.26
Massachusetts	M.	66–66–66	1.00–1.50–1.35	**1882:**			
Do	F.	66–66–66	.75–.75–.75	Connecticut	M.	66–66–66	1.50–1.50–1.50
Rhode Island	M.	72–72–72	1.34–1.34–1.34	Maine	M.	66–66–66	1.25–1.25–1.25
1871:				Massachusetts	M.	60–60–60	.75–1.50–1.08
Connecticut	M.	66–66–66	1.86–1.86–1.86	New Jersey	M.	60–66–61	.33–.83–.45
Maine	M.	66–66–66	1.72–2.08–1.95	Ohio	(¹)	60–72–61	.50–2.75–1.42
Massachusetts	M.	66–66–66	.50–1.50–1.18	Rhode Island	M.	72–72–72	1.23–1.23–1.23
Do	F.	66–66–66	.65–1.00–.79	**1883:**			
Do	(¹)	(¹)	.75–.75–.75	Connecticut	M.	66–66–66	1.13–1.13–1.13
Rhode Island	M.	72–72–72	1.33–1.33–1.33	Massachusetts	M.	60–60–60	.75–1.50–1.08
1872:				Do	M.	60–60–60	.69–2.00–1.15
Connecticut	M.	66–66–66	1.50–1.85–1.79	Do	F.	(¹)	.45–1.04–.79
Massachusetts	M.	66–66–66	.60–1.75–.91	Do	(¹)	(¹)	.50–.95–.72
Do	F.	66–66–66	.50–1.00–.76	New Hampshire	M.	66–66–66	.75–1.72–1.41
Rhode Island	M.	72–72–72	1.32–1.32–1.32	New Jersey	M.	60–60–60	.33–3.00–1.05
1873:				Rhode Island	M.	72–72–72	1.23–1.23–1.23
Connecticut	M.	66–66–66	1.50–1.65–1.58	West Virginia	M.	60–60–60	1.25–1.25–1.25
Massachusetts	M.	66–66–66	.70–2.25–1.33	**1884:**			
Rhode Island	M.	72–72–72	1.29–1.29–1.29	Connecticut	M.	66–66–66	1.13–1.25–1.22
1874:				Massachusetts	M.	60–60–60	.75–1.50–.92
Connecticut	M.	66–66–66	1.37–1.65–1.44	New Hampshire	M.	(¹)	.84–1.35–1.06
Massachusetts	M.	66–66–66	.50–2.25–1.33	Do	F.	(¹)	.50–1.11–.84
Do	F.	66–66–66	.50–1.75–1.13	New Jersey	F.	60–60–60	.50–.96–.80
Pennsylvania	M.	62–62–62	.75–2.32–2.00	Do	M.	60–60–60	.42–2.00–1.29
Rhode Island	M.	72–72–72	1.32–1.32–1.32	Rhode Island	F.	(¹)	.50–.50–.50
1875:				Do	M.	72–72–72	1.28–1.28–1.28
Connecticut	M.	66–66–66	1.50–1.68–1.64	**1885:**			
Maine	M.	64–64–64	.67–1.00–.89	California	M.	60–60–60	1.00–1.00–1.00
Massachusetts	M.	66–66–66	.81–2.00–1.53	Connecticut	M.	66–69–67	1.15–1.50–1.29
Do	F.	(¹)	.63–1.00–.83	Do	(¹)	66–66–66	1.25–1.25–1.25
Rhode Island	M.	72–72–72	1.33–1.33–1.33	Delaware	M.	60–60–60	1.66–2.70–2.31
1876:				Illinois	M.	63–63–63	1.02–1.02–1.02
Connecticut	M.	66–66–66	1.59–1.59–1.59	Do	F.	63–63–63	1.02–1.02–1.02
Massachusetts	M.	60–60–60	1.25–2.00–1.58	Indiana	M.	60–66–66	.29–1.25–.66
New Hampshire	M.	66–66–66	.75–1.67–1.44	Do	F.	66–66–66	.42–.75–.62
Pennsylvania	M.	(¹)	.48–3.25–1.52	Iowa	M.	60–60–60	1.25–1.25–1.25
Rhode Island	F.	(¹)	.67–.67–.67	Do	F.	60–60–60	.75–.75–.75
Do	M.	72–72–72	1.28–1.28–1.28	Kentucky	M.	66–66–66	.88–.88–.88
1877:				Do	F.	66–66–66	.60–.75–.67
Connecticut	M.	66–66–66	1.44–1.44–1.44	Maine	M.	66–66–65	.80–2.04–1.50
Ohio	M.	(¹)	1.50–1.50–1.50	Maryland	M.	60–60–60	1.35–1.35–1.35
Rhode Island	M.	72–72–72	1.30–1.30–1.30	Massachusetts	M.	60–60–60	.56–1.65–1.20
1878:				Do	F.	60–60–60	.60–.98–.66
Connecticut	M.	66–66–66	1.50–1.52–1.51	Minnesota	M.	(¹)	.95–1.50–1.10
Pennsylvania	M.	60–60–60	1.50–2.50–1.80	Do	F.	(¹)	.85–.90–.89
Rhode Island	M.	72–72–72	1.29–1.29–1.29	Missouri	M.	60–60–60	1.25–1.25–1.25
1879:				New Hampshire	M.	66–66–66	1.00–2.20–1.66
Connecticut	M.	66–66–66	1.25–1.50–1.38	New Jersey	M.	60–60–60	.37–2.00–.96
Massachusetts	M.	60–60–60	.65–.75–.70	Do	F.	60–60–60	.42–.42–.42
Do	F.	60–60–60	.75–.75–.75	New York	M.	60–66–64	.75–2.50–1.17
Pennsylvania	M.	57–72–61	1.00–3.00–1.87	Do	M.	60–66–61	.45–1.33–.98
Do	(¹)	57–60–59	1.00–2.25–1.89	North Carolina	M.	69–69–69	1.25–1.25–1.25
Rhode Island	M.	72–72–72	1.24–1.24–1.24	Pennsylvania	M.	60–60–60	1.50–1.83–1.74
1880:				Do	F.	60–60–60	.42–.83–.68
Connecticut	M.	66–66–66	1.50–1.50–1.50	Rhode Island	M.	63–63–63	.92–.92–.92
Do	(¹)	66–71–67	1.33–1.96–1.56	Do	M.	72–72–72	1.25–1.25–1.25
Maine	(¹)	66–66–66	1.42–1.67–1.55	Vermont	M.	60–66–63	.45–1.60–1.22
Massachusetts	M.	60–60–60	.75–1.00–.88	**1886:**			
Do	(¹)	60–60–60	1.08–1.42–1.26	Connecticut	M.	66–66–66	.75–1.35–.92
New Hampshire	M.	69–69–69	1.29–1.84–1.62	Do	F.	(¹)	.75–.75–.75
Do	(¹)	66–66–66	1.17–1.83–1.36	Indiana	F.	60–60–60	.50–.67–.61

¹ Not reported.

TABLE L–51.—*Spinners, woolen and worsted goods, 1850–1900, by year and State—*
Continued

| Year and State | Sex | Lowest, highest, and average— | | Year and State | Sex | Lowest, highest, and average— | |
		Hours per week	Rate per day (dollars)			Hours per week	Rate per day (dollars)
1886—Continued.				**1891:**			
Iowa	M.	60–60–60	0. 60–1. 67–1. 23	Connecticut	M.	60–60–60	1. 31–1. 31–1. 31
Do	F.	60–60–60	. 67– . 70– . 67	Maine	M.	60–60–60	1. 70–1. 70–1. 70
Maine	(¹)	66–66–66	1. 50–1. 50–1. 50	Massachusetts	M.	60–60–60	. 75–1. 50–1. 15
Massachusetts	M.	60–60–60	. 68–1. 50– . 97	New Jersey	M.	60–60–60	1. 41–1. 41–1. 41
Missouri	F.	36–36–36	. 21– . 21– . 21	New York	M.	60–60–60	. 37–3. 00–1. 19
New Jersey	M.	60–60–60	1. 25–2. 50–1. 44	Do	F.	(¹)	. 65– . 75– . 70
Do	F.	60–60–60	. 67–1. 17–1. 00	Do	(¹)	(¹)	. 60– . 90– . 82
Pennsylvania	M.	60–60–60	. 67–2. 66–1. 40	Rhode Island	M.	60–60–60	1. 26–1. 31–1. 29
Do	F.	58–60–60	. 42–1. 00– . 73	**1892:**			
Rhode Island	F.	57–61–60	. 66–1. 00– . 84	Connecticut	M.	60–60–60	1. 35–1. 35–1. 35
Do	M.	60–60–60	1. 25–1. 28–1. 26	Indiana	(¹)	54–60–58	1. 00–1. 87–1. 35
1887:				Iowa	F.	60–60–60	. 67– . 67– . 67
Connecticut	M.	60–60–60	. 41–1. 37–1. 22	Maine	M.	60–60–60	1. 47–1. 47–1. 47
Do	F.	(¹)	. 84– . 99– . 97	Do	F.	60–60–60	. 75– . 75– . 75
Kentucky	F.	60–60–60	. 42– . 72– . 54	Rhode Island	M.	60–60–60	1. 37–1. 45–1. 41
Maine	M.	60–60–60	1. 25–1. 25–1. 25	**1893:**			
Massachusetts	M.	60–60–60	1. 00–1. 50–1. 23	New Jersey	F.	60–60–60	. 58– . 83– . 73
Do	F.	60–60–60	. 75– . 75– . 75	Ohio	M.	60–60–60	1. 50–2. 00–1. 67
New York	F.	60–60–60	1. 25–1. 46–1. 36	Do	F.	60–60–60	. 60– . 62– . 60
Pennsylvania	F.	60–60–60	. 50– . 83– . 64	**1894:**			
Rhode Island	M.	60–60–60	1. 25–1. 37–1. 26	Iowa	M.	60–60–60	1. 18–1. 18–1. 18
Wisconsin	(¹)	(¹)	. 50–1. 19– . 65	Do	F.	60–60–60	. 67– . 67– . 67
1888:				Maine	M.	60–60–60	1. 45–1. 50–1. 48
California	M.	(¹)	1. 00–1. 00–1. 00	New York	M.	60–66–61	1. 00–2. 00–1. 36
Connecticut	M.	60–60–60	. 95–1. 45–1. 21	Do	F.	60–60–60	. 65– . 75– . 71
Delaware	M.	(¹)	1. 67–2. 50–2. 09	North Carolina	M.	66–66–66	1. 67–1. 67–1. 67
Indiana	F.	60–60–60	. 42– . 50– . 46	Ohio	M.	60–60–60	. 75–2. 00–1. 06
Maine	M.	60–60–60	1. 50–1. 50–1. 50	Do	F.	60–60–60	. 45– . 70– . 51
Massachusetts	M.	60–60–60	. 75–1. 50–1. 15	Rhode Island	(¹)	(¹)	. 75–2. 35–1. 27
New Jersey	M.	(¹)	. 75–1. 50–1. 00	**1895:**			
Do	M.	(¹)	1. 50–1. 50–1. 50	Maine	M.	60–60–60	. 73–2. 12–1. 50
Do	M.	(¹)	. 75–1. 50–1. 25	Massachusetts	M.	58–58–58	1. 44–2. 61–1. 86
Do	F.	(¹)	. 67– . 67– . 67	Missouri	M.	(¹)	. 60–1. 00– . 82
Do	(¹)	(¹)	. 50– . 58– . 58	Do	F.	(¹)	. 63–1. 25– . 86
New York	M.	60–60–60	. 75–1. 75–1. 55	New Hampshire	M.	60–60–60	. 50–2. 05–1. 47
Do	F.	(¹)	. 60–1. 20– . 64	Do	F.	60–60–60	. 50–1. 49– . 83
Rhode Island	M.	60–60–60	1. 08–2. 00–1. 26	New Jersey	F.	55–60–56	. 50–1. 67– . 73
Do	F.	60–60–60	. 75– . 75– . 75	Do	M.	55–60–60	. 58– . 83– . 70
Do	(¹)	(¹)	1. 25–2. 00–1. 48	New York	F.	60–60–60	. 75– . 75– . 75
1889:				Ohio	M.	60–60–60	. 90–2. 00–1. 09
California	M.	(¹)	. 50–1. 00– . 82	Do	F.	60–60–60	. 47– . 70– . 54
Connecticut	M.	60–60–60	1. 12–1. 12–1. 12	Pennsylvania	M.	60–60–60	. 42– . 80– . 65
Maine	M.	60–60–60	1. 12–2. 52–1. 61	Vermont	M.	60–60–60	. 88–1. 68–1. 20
Massachusetts	M.	60–60–60	1. 20–1. 60–1. 42	**1896:**			
Missouri	M.	(¹)	. 50– . 84– . 67	Indiana	F.	60–60–60	. 50– . 67– . 64
New Hampshire	M.	60–60–60	1. 30–1. 74–1. 66	Iowa	M.	60–60–60	. 70–1. 50–1. 13
Do	F.	60–60–60	. 85– . 85– . 85	Do	F.	60–60–60	. 50– . 67– . 62
New Jersey	F.	60–60–60	. 58– . 58– . 58	Kentucky	M.	60–60–60	. 49– . 49– . 49
New York	M.	60–60–60	. 50–1. 98– . 80	Do	M.	60–60–60	. 61– . 73– . 68
Rhode Island	M.	60–60–60	. 45–1. 13– . 67	Minnesota	M.	60–60–60	. 65–1. 27– . 97
Rhode Island	M.	60–60–60	1. 26–1. 26–1. 26	Missouri	M.	54–60–55	1. 00–1. 07–1. 06
Do	F.	60–60–60	. 40– . 92– . 74	Do	F.	54–60–58	. 73– . 75– . 74
1890:				Ohio	M.	59–60–60	. 82–1. 07–1. 00
Connecticut	M.	60–60–60	1. 25–1. 89–1. 74	Do	F.	60–60–60	. 50– . 67– . 55
Maine	M.	60–60–60	1. 21–2. 01–1. 47	Pennsylvania	M.	60–60–60	. 75–2. 50–1. 32
Massachusetts	M.	60–60–60	. 75–1. 53–1. 30	Do	F.	60–60–60	. 42– . 88– . 68
Missouri	M.	(¹)	. 30– . 80– . 56	West Virginia	M.	60–60–60	1. 25–1. 25–1. 25
Do	F.	(¹)	. 40– . 80– . 66	**1897:**			
New Hampshire	M.	60–60–60	1. 90–1. 90–1. 90	Virginia	M.	60–60–60	. 50–1. 25– . 97
New Jersey	M.	60–60–60	. 58–2. 10– . 95	Do	F.	60–66–62	. 50– . 60– . 58
Do	F.	(¹)	. 50– . 50– . 50	**1899:**			
New York	M.	60–60–60	. 37–3. 00–1. 18	New Jersey	M.	60–60–60	1. 06–1. 85–1. 38
Do	F.	60–60–60	. 65–1. 00– . 72	**1900:**			
North Carolina	M.	60–60–60	. 50– . 50– . 50	New Jersey	M.	60–60–60	1. 17–2. 07–1. 51
Pennsylvania	F.	60–60–60	. 67– . 75– . 73				
Rhode Island	M.	60–60–60	1. 00–1. 55–1. 25				

¹ Not reported.

TABLE L-52.—*Spinners, mule, males, woolen and worsted goods, 1890-1907, by geographic division and year*

Year	North Atlantic		Western		Year	North Atlantic		Western	
	Hours per week	Rate per hour	Hours per week	Rate per hour		Hours per week	Rate per hour	Hours per week	Rate per hour
1890	60.0	$0.129	66.0	$0.080	1899	60.0	$0.134	66.0	$0.086
1891	60.0	.128	66.0	.085	1900	59.3	.157	66.0	.088
1892	60.0	.125	66.0	.086	1901	59.5	.153	66.0	.085
1893	57.8	.136	66.0	.084	1902	59.1	.151	66.0	.098
1894	52.1	.132	66.0	.082	1903	59.3	.180	60.2	.114
1895	59.5	.128	66.0	.083	1904	58.6	.183	60.1	.121
1896	59.5	.138	66.0	.086	1905	58.5	.189		
1897	54.9	.140	66.0	.081	1906	58.6	.203		
1898	59.4	.150	66.0	.079	1907	58.5	.207		

TABLE L-53.—*Spinners, mule, males, woolen and worsted goods, 1907-1928, by State and year*

Year	Connecticut		New Jersey		New York		Vermont	
	Hours per week	Rate per hour	Hours per week	Rate per hour	Hours per week	Rate per hour	Hours per week	Rate per hour
1913	59.0	$0.206	55.4	$0.272				
1914	58.1	.194	55.3	.292	60.0	$0.236	58.8	$0.221
1916	56.2	.280	54.1	.372	56.4	.301	57.8	.264
1918	54.7	.418	54.4	.444	59.4	.458	57.8	.472
1920	48.0	.705	49.5	.734	48.0	.987	48.0	.789
1922	48.5	.569	49.8	.561	48.0	.724	51.0	.695
1926	49.3	.641			50.4	.689	51.0	.619
1928	49.3	.627	48.0	.793	50.9	.654	48.0	.658

Year	Maine		Massachusetts		New Hampshire		Rhode Island	
	Hours per week	Rate per hour	Hours per week	Rate per hour	Hours per week	Rate per hour	Hours per week	Rate per hour
1907			58.0	$0.242	58.6	$0.199	58.0	$0.228
1908			58.0	.218	58.0	.185	58.0	.235
1909			58.0	.232	58.0	.201	58.0	.215
1910			56.0	.233	58.0	.218	56.0	.238
1911	58.0	$0.211	56.0	.235	58.0	.211	56.0	.222
1912	58.0	.225	54.2	.253	58.0	.231	56.0	.248
1913	58.2	.218	54.2	.253	58.0	.224	56.0	.243
1914	58.3	.224	54.1	.268	54.9	.239	54.0	.254
1916	58.1	.290	54.5	.336	54.8	.306	54.0	.323
1918	54.6	.600	54.2	.551	54.3	.527	54.0	.427
1920	49.2	.793	48.0	1.000	48.0	.819	48.3	.740
1922	49.3	.680	48.2	.753	48.9	.699	48.0	.645
1926	50.0	.666	48.0	.763	49.5	.770	48.0	.755
1928	49.1	.668	48.6	.767	50.3	.684	48.0	.758

TABLE L–54.—*Spinners, mule, females, woolen and worsted goods, 1890–1903, by geographic division and year*

Year	North Atlantic		North Central		Year	North Atlantic		North Central	
	Hours per week	Rate per hour	Hours per week	Rate per hour		Hours per week	Rate per hour	Hours per week	Rate per hour
1890	60. 0	$0. 056	60. 0	$0. 050	1897	60. 0	$0. 056	60. 0	$0. 050
1891	60. 0	. 056	60. 0	. 050	1898	60. 0	. 056	60. 0	. 050
1892	60. 0	. 056	60. 0	. 050	1899	60. 0	. 056	60. 0	. 050
1893	60. 0	. 064	60. 0	. 050	1900	60. 0	. 058	60. 0	. 050
1894	60. 0	. 055	60. 0	. 050	1901	60. 0	. 061	60. 0	. 050
1895	60. 0	. 055	60. 0	. 050	1902	60. 0	. 072	60. 0	. 050
1896	60. 0	. 055	60. 0	. 050	1903	60. 0	. 070	60. 0	. 050

TABLE L–55.—*Spinners, frame, females, woolen and worsted goods, 1890–1907, by geographic division and year*

Year	North Atlantic		Year	North Atlantic	
	Hours per week	Rate per hour		Hours per week	Rate per hour
1890	60. 0	$0. 090	1899	59. 1	$0. 099
1891	60. 0	. 091	1900	59. 0	. 110
1892	60. 0	. 092	1901	59. 1	. 107
1893	59. 2	. 096	1902	58. 1	. 114
1894	59. 4	. 088	1903	58. 3	. 115
1895	59. 4	. 088	1904	58. 3	. 102
1896	59. 3	. 094	1905	58. 3	. 104
1897	59. 2	. 095	1906	58. 7	. 107
1898	59. 2	. 097	1907	58. 0	. 119

TABLE L–56.—*Spinners, frame, females, woolen and worsted goods, 1907–1928, by State and year*

Year	Massachusetts		New Jersey		Rhode Island		Pennsylvania	
	Hours per week	Rate per hour	Hours per week	Rate per hour	Hours per week	Rate per hour	Hours per week	Rate per hour
1907					58. 0	$0. 119		
1908					58. 0	. 126		
1909					58. 0	. 124		
1910	56. 0	$0. 124			56. 0	. 129		
1911	56. 0	. 131	55. 3	$0. 116	56. 0	. 130		
1912	54. 0	. 157	55. 2	. 122	56. 0	. 136		
1913	54. 0	. 146	55. 2	. 128	56. 0	. 138		
1914	53. 8	. 145	55. 4	. 142	54. 0	. 145		
1916	53. 9	. 188	52. 9	. 194	54. 0	. 172	53. 0	$0. 149
1918	53. 6	. 299	53. 0	. 287	54. 0	. 252	54. 0	. 231
1920	48. 0	. 515	48. 0	. 510	47. 9	. 441	49. 8	. 428
1922	47. 9	. 350	48. 0	. 287	48. 0	. 340	52. 2	. 343
1926	48. 0	. 384			48. 3	. 365	52. 9	. 317
1928	48. 0	. 401	48. 0	. 420	48. 2	. 367	53. 5	. 335

TABLE **L-57.**—*Weavers, woolen goods, 1850–1900, by year and State*

Year and State	Sex	Hours per week	Rate per day (dollars)
1850:			
Rhode Island	M.	84–84–84	0.77–0.77–0.77
Do	F.	84–84–84	.50–.50–.50
1851:			
Rhode Island	M.	84–84–84	.74–.74–.74
Do	F.	84–84–84	.49–.49–.49
1852:			
Rhode Island	M.	84–84–84	.79–.79–.79
Do	F.	84–84–84	.50–.50–.50
1853:			
Massachusetts	M.	78–78–78	.77–.77–.77
Rhode Island	M.	84–84–84	.82–.82–.82
Do	F.	84–84–84	.55–.55–.55
1854:			
Rhode Island	M.	84–84–84	.85–.85–.85
Do	F.	84–84–84	.54–.54–.54
1855:			
Rhode Island	M.	84–84–84	.84–.84–.84
Do	F.	84–84–84	.55–.55–.55
1856:			
Rhode Island	M.	84–84–84	.87–.87–.87
Do	F.	84–84–84	.58–.58–.58
1857:			
Rhode Island	M.	84–84–84	.86–.86–.86
Do	F.	84–84–84	.60–.60–.60
1858:			
Connecticut	M.	72–72–72	.48–.48–.48
Do	F.	72–72–72	.46–.46–.46
Rhode Island	M.	84–84–84	.89–.89–.89
Do	F.	84–84–84	.62–.62–.62
1859:			
Connecticut	M.	72–72–72	.49–.49–.49
Do	F.	72–72–72	.46–.46–.46
Maine	M.	(1)	.51–1.02–.84
Do	F.	(1)	.50–.66–.56
Massachusetts	M.	78–78–78	.46–1.00–.67
Rhode Island	M.	84–84–84	.93–.93–.93
Do	F.	84–84–84	.66–.66–.66
1860:			
Connecticut	M.	72–72–72	.93–.93–.93
Do	F.	72–72–72	.81–.81–.81
Massachusetts	M.	78–78–78	.46–1.00–.79
Rhode Island	M.	78–78–78	.94–.94–.94
Do	F.	78–78–78	.70–.70–.70
1861:			
Connecticut	M.	72–72–72	1.16–1.16–1.16
Do	F.	72–72–72	1.10–1.10–1.10
Massachusetts	M.	78–78–78	.46–1.00–.84
Do	F.	78–78–78	.27–.85–.61
Rhode Island	M.	78–78–78	.95–.95–.95
Do	F.	78–78–78	.73–.73–.73
1862:			
Connecticut	M.	72–72–72	1.12–1.12–1.12
Do	F.	72–72–72	1.07–1.07–1.07
Massachusetts	M.	78–78–78	.58–1.25–.94
Do	F.	78–78–78	.27–.67–.51
Rhode Island	M.	78–78–78	.98–.98–.98
Do	F.	78–78–78	.82–.82–.82
1863:			
Connecticut	M.	72–72–72	1.35–1.35–1.35
Do	F.	72–72–72	1.30–1.30–1.30
Massachusetts	M.	78–78–78	.69–1.25–.97
Do	F.	78–78–78	.27–.27–.27
Rhode Island	M.	78–78–78	1.03–1.03–1.03
Do	F.	78–78–78	.81–.81–.81
1864:			
Connecticut	M.	72–72–72	1.23–1.23–1.23
Do	F.	72–72–72	1.14–1.14–1.14
Massachusetts	M.	78–78–78	.50–1.25–.85
Rhode Island	M.	78–78–78	1.00–1.00–1.00
Do	F.	78–78–78	.91–.91–.91
1865:			
Connecticut	M.	66–66–66	1.60–1.60–1.60
Do	F.	66–66–66	1.46–1.46–1.46
Massachusetts	M.	66–66–66	.58–1.25–.96
Do	F.	66–66–66	.46–.67–.59
Rhode Island	M.	78–78–78	1.10–1.10–1.10
Do	F.	78–78–78	.98–.98–.98
1866:			
Connecticut	M.	66–66–66	1.47–1.47–1.47
Do	F.	66–66–66	1.22–1.22–1.22
Massachusetts	M.	66–66–66	.69–1.25–.93
Do	F.	66–66–66	.50–1.00–.71
Rhode Island	M.	78–78–78	1.18–1.18–1.18
Do	F.	78–78–78	1.06–1.06–1.06
1867:			
Connecticut	M.	66–66–66	1.36–1.36–1.36
Do	F.	66–66–66	1.23–1.23–1.23
Massachusetts	M.	66–66–66	.77–1.13–.95
Do	F.	66–66–66	.50–1.00–.76
New Hampshire	F.	66–74–69	.53–1.40–1.01
Rhode Island	M.	78–78–78	1.26–1.26–1.26
Do	F.	78–78–78	1.07–1.07–1.07
1868:			
Connecticut	M.	66–66–66	1.19–1.19–1.19
Do	F.	66–66–66	1.15–1.15–1.15
Massachusetts	M.	66–66–66	.85–1.13–.99
Do	F.	66–66–66	.50–1.00–.77
Pennsylvania	F.	62–62–62	.83–.92–.86
Rhode Island	M.	72–72–72	1.27–1.27–1.27
Do	F.	72–72–72	1.09–1.09–1.09
1869:			
Connecticut	M.	66–66–66	1.50–1.50–1.50
Do	F.	66–66–66	1.35–1.35–1.35
Massachusetts	M.	66–66–66	.60–1.13–.86
Do	F.	66–66–66	.50–1.00–.84
Rhode Island	M.	72–72–72	1.21–1.21–1.21
Do	F.	72–72–72	1.12–1.12–1.12
1870:			
Connecticut	M.	66–66–66	1.33–1.33–1.33
Do	F.	66–66–66	1.04–1.04–1.04
Massachusetts	M.	66–66–66	.60–1.00–.86
Do	F.	66–66–66	.50–1.00–.85
Rhode Island	M.	72–72–72	1.27–1.27–1.27
Do	F.	72–72–72	1.15–1.15–1.15
1871:			
Connecticut	M.	66–66–66	1.26–1.26–1.26
Do	F.	66–66–66	1.08–1.08–1.08
Maine	M.	66–66–66	.42–2.00–1.43
Do	F.	66–66–66	1.32–2.16–1.56
Massachusetts	M.	66–66–66	.70–1.25–.92
Do	F.	66–66–66	.50–1.00–.75
Rhode Island	M.	72–72–72	1.32–1.32–1.32
Do	F.	72–72–72	1.18–1.18–1.18
1872:			
Connecticut	M.	66–66–66	1.25–1.25–1.25
Do	F.	66–66–66	1.02–1.02–1.02
Massachusetts	M.	66–66–66	.60–1.25–.99
Do	F.	66–66–66	.45–1.00–.73
Rhode Island	M.	72–72–72	1.34–1.34–1.34
Do	F.	72–72–72	1.22–1.22–1.22
1873:			
Connecticut	M.	66–66–66	1.25–1.25–1.25
Do	F.	66–66–66	1.05–1.05–1.05
Massachusetts	M.	66–66–66	.75–1.10–.89
Do	F.	66–66–66	.45–1.00–.58
Rhode Island	M.	72–72–72	1.30–1.30–1.30
Do	F.	72–72–72	1.18–1.18–1.18
1874:			
Connecticut	M.	66–66–66	1.33–1.33–1.33
Do	F.	66–66–66	1.40–1.40–1.40
Massachusetts	M.	66–66–66	.45–1.10–.81
Do	F.	66–66–66	.45–1.50–.77
Pennsylvania	M.	62–62–62	.69–1.50–1.24
Do	F.	62–62–62	.34–1.40–1.25
Rhode Island	M.	72–72–72	1.34–1.34–1.34
Do	F.	72–72–72	1.22–1.22–1.22
1875:			
Connecticut	M.	66–66–66	1.38–1.38–1.38
Do	F.	66–66–66	1.23–1.23–1.23
Maine	M.	64–64–64	1.00–1.00–1.00
Do	F.	64–64–64	.80–1.25–1.01
Massachusetts	M.	66–66–66	.50–1.62–1.42
Do	F.	66–66–66	.45–1.50–1.26
Rhode Island	M.	72–72–72	1.33–1.33–1.33
Do	F.	72–72–72	1.24–1.24–1.24

¹ Not reported.

TABLE L-57.—*Weavers, woolen goods, 1850–1900, by year and State*—Continued

Year and State	Sex	Lowest, highest, and average—		Year and State	Sex	Lowest, highest, and average—	
		Hours per week	Rate per day (dollars)			Hours per week	Rate per day (dollars)
1876:				**1883:**			
Connecticut	M.	66–66–66	1. 31–1. 31–1. 31	Connecticut	M.	66–66–66	1. 61–1. 61–1. 61
Do	F.	66–66–66	1. 20–1. 20–1. 20	Do	F.	66–66–66	1. 55–1. 55–1. 55
Massachusetts	M.	60–60–60	. 50–1. 13– . 86	Massachusetts	M.	60–60–60	1. 00–1. 67–1. 23
Do	F.	60–60–60	. 45–1. 25– . 83	Do	F.	60–60–60	. 54–1. 41–1. 15
New Hampshire	F.	66–66–66	. 70–1. 20– . 91	Do	(¹)	(¹)	. 70– . 85– . 78
Pennsylvania	M.	(¹)	. 45–1. 83–1. 33	New Hampshire	M.	66–66–66	1. 25–1. 27–1. 26
Do	F.	(¹)	. 41–1. 38–1. 17	Do	F.	66–66–66	. 68–1. 35–1. 00
Rhode Island	M.	72–72–72	1. 32–1. 32–1. 32	New Jersey	M.	60–60–60	. 83–1. 67–1. 32
Do	F.	72–72–72	1. 25–1. 25–1. 25	Do	(¹)	60–60–60	1. 26–1. 69–1. 50
1877:				Do	F.	60–60–60	. 83–1. 50–1. 06
Connecticut	M.	66–66–66	1. 20–1. 20–1. 20	Rhode Island	M.	72–72–72	1. 31–1. 31–1. 31
Do	F.	66–66–66	1. 14–1. 14–1. 14	Do	F.	72–72–72	1. 23–1. 23–1. 23
Massachusetts	M.	60–60–60	1. 00–1. 25–1. 13	West Virginia	F.	60–60–60	. 83–1. 08—. 95
Do	F.	60–60–60	. 50–1. 25– . 79	**1884:**			
New Jersey	(¹)	60–60–60	1. 33–2. 50–2. 11	Connecticut	M.	66–66–66	1. 50¹–1. 50–1. 50
Ohio	M.	(¹)	. 67–1. 50–1. 06	Do	F.	66–66–66	1. 36–1. 36–1. 36
Rhode Island	M.	72–72–72	1. 36–1. 36–1. 36	Kentucky	F.	66–66–66	. 70–1. 21– . 99
Do	F.	72–72–72	1. 23–1. 23–1. 23	Massachusetts	M.	60–60–60	. 60–1. 20– . 85
1878:				Do	F.	60–60–60	. 60–1. 25– . 91
Connecticut	M.	66–66–66	1. 30–1. 30–1. 30	New Jersey	M.	60–60–60	. 83–1. 50–1. 12
Do	F.	66–66–66	1. 31–1. 31–1. 31	Do	F.	60–60–60	. 67–1. 33– . 93
Massachusetts	M.	60–60–60	. 35–1. 25– . 83	Pennsylvania	M.	60–60–60	1. 00–1. 60–1. 60
Do	F.	60–60–60	. 40–1. 25– . 80	Rhode Island	M.	72–72–72	1. 34–1. 34–1. 34
Pennsylvania	M.	60–60–60	1. 00–1. 00–1. 00	Do	F.	72–72–72	1. 25–1. 25–1. 25
Do	F.	60–60–60	1. 00–1. 25–1. 08	**1885:**			
Rhode Island	M.	72–72–72	1. 37–1. 37–1. 37	California	M.	60–60–60	1. 00–1. 50–1. 42
Do	F.	72–72–72	1. 28–1. 28–1. 28	Connecticut	F.	66–69–67	. 70–1. 60–1. 15
1879:				Do	(¹)	84–84–84	. 95– . 95– . 95
Connecticut	M.	66–66–66	1. 18–1. 18–1. 18	Do	M.	66–66–66	1. 40–1. 40–1. 40
Do	F.	66–66–66	1. 35–1. 35–1. 35	Delaware	M.	60–60–60	1. 25–2. 00–1. 71
Massachusetts	M.	60–60–60	1. 00–1. 25–1. 13	Do	F.	60–60–60	1. 25–2. 00–1. 36
Do	F.	60–60–60	. 35–1. 25– . 66	Illinois	M.	63–66–64	1. 25–2. 12–1. 43
Pennsylvania	M.	60–60–62	1. 00–2. 00–1. 43	Do	F.	66–66–66	1. 25–1. 25–1. 25
Rhode Island	M.	72–72–72	1. 33–1. 33–1. 33	Indiana	M.	66–66–66	. 83–1. 08– . 91
Do	F.	72–72–72	1. 29–1. 29–1. 29	Do	F.	66–66–66	1. 00–1. 07–1. 05
1880:				Iowa	M.	66–66–66	1. 25–1. 25–1. 25
Connecticut	M.	66–66–66	1. 20–1. 20–1. 20	Do	F.	60–60–60	1. 20–1. 20–1. 20
Do	F.	66–66–66	1. 39–1. 39–1. 39	Kentucky	F.	66–66–66	. 60–1. 10– . 79
Do	(¹)	65–71–67	. 75–2. 00–1. 36	Maine	M.	60–60–60	. 53–2. 49–1. 30
Maine	(¹)	66–66–66	1. 00–1. 83–1. 38	Do	F.	66–66–65	. 50–2. 11–1. 16
Massachusetts	M.	60–60–60	. 40–1. 25– . 82	Maryland	M.	66–66–66	. 90–1. 10–1. 05
Do	F.	60–60–60	. 45–1. 25– . 78	Do	F.	66–66–66	. 90–1. 10– . 99
Do	(¹)	60–60–60	. 83–1. 33–1. 13	Massachusetts	M.	60–60–60	. 39–2. 00–1. 29
New Hampshire	M.	69–69–69	. 90–1. 37–1. 17	Do	F.	60–60–60	. 37–1. 64–1. 13
Do	F.	69–69–69	. 89–1. 37–1. 11	Do	(¹)	60–60–60	1. 30–1. 30–1. 30
Do	(¹)	66–66–66	1. 17–1. 67–1. 39	Minnesota	M.	(¹)	. 75–1. 55–1. 28
New Jersey	(¹)	60–60–60	1. 50–2. 50–2. 00	Do	F.	(¹)	. 65–1. 61–1. 13
New York	(¹)	63–66–65	1. 00–1. 67–1. 41	Missouri	M.	60–60–60	1. 50–1. 50–1. 50
Rhode Island	M.	72–72–72	1. 32–1. 32–1. 32	Do	F.	60–60–60	1. 50–1. 50–1. 50
Do	F.	72–72–72	1. 24–1. 24–1. 24	New Hampshire	M.	66–66–66	1. 05–1. 82–1. 47
Do	(¹)	66–66–66	1. 00–1. 42–1. 23	Do	F.	66–66–66	. 56–1. 88–1. 38
1881:				New Jersey	M.	60–60–60	. 50–1. 75–1. 04
Connecticut	M.	66–84–72	. 90–1. 30–1. 16	Do	F.	60–60–60	. 50–1. 75– . 78
Do	F.	66–84–80	. 90–1. 21– . 97	Do	(¹)	60–60–60	1. 00–1. 00–1. 00
Massachusetts	M.	60–60–60	. 75–1. 25– . 98	New York	M.	66–66–66	. 81–1. 37–1. 08
Do	F.	60–60–60	. 40–1. 25– . 68	Do	F.	66–66–66	1. 02–1. 20–1. 11
Ohio	M.	60–72–66	1. 00–1. 66–1. 02	North Carolina	F.	69–69–69	. 75– . 75– . 75
Do	F.	60–60–60	. 60–1. 10– . 92	Pennsylvania	M.	60–60–60	1. 33–1. 92–1. 77
Rhode Island	(¹)	66–66–66	1. 65–1. 83–1. 74	Do	F.	60–60–60	1. 33–1. 33–1. 33
Do	M.	72–72–72	1. 33–1. 33–1. 33	Do	(¹)	60–60–60	1. 25–1. 50–1. 33
Do	F.	72–72–72	. 71–1. 26–1. 24	Rhode Island	(¹)	66–66–66	2. 00–2. 00–2. 00
1882:				Do	M.	72–72–72	1. 32–1. 50–1. 33
Connecticut	M.	66–66–66	1. 10–1. 31–1. 29	Do	F.	72–72–72	1. 27–1. 27–1. 27
Do	(¹)	60–72–68	. 86–1. 75–1. 11	Vermont	M.	60–66–64	. 58–1. 31–1. 07
Do	F.	66–66–66	1. 10–1. 31–1. 21	Do	F.	60–66–63	. 54–1. 34–1. 02
Illinois	F.	60–60–60	1. 00–1. 00–1. 00	**1886:**			
Maine	M.	66–66–66	1. 16–1. 63–1. 47	Connecticut	M.	60–66–65	. 86–1. 50–1. 39
Do	F.	66–66–66	. 75–1. 66–1. 22	Do	F.	60–66–64	. 70–1. 50–1. 30
Massachusetts	M.	60–60–60	. 75–1. 20–1. 02	Do	(¹)	66–66–66	1. 37–1. 37–1. 37
Do	F.	60–60–60	. 45–1. 25– . 91	Indiana	F.	66–66–66	. 50–1. 25– . 93
Ohio	M.	60–72–63	1. 00–2. 00–1. 38	Iowa	M.	60–60–60	1. 46–1. 61–1. 53
Do	F.	60–66–63	. 50–1. 25– . 92	Do	F.	60–60–60	. 41–1. 54– . 99
Pennsylvania	(¹)	60–60–60	1. 16–1. 25–1. 21	Maine	M.	65–65–65	1. 60–1. 60–1. 60
Rhode Island	M.	72–72–72	1. 32–1. 32–1. 32	Do	(¹)	65–66–66	1. 40–1. 50–1. 42
Do	F.	72–72–72	1. 24–1. 24–1. 24	Massachusetts	M.	60–60–60	. 60–1. 71–1. 64

¹ Not reported.

TABLE L-57.—*Weavers, woolen goods, 1850-1900, by year and State*—Continued

| Year and State | Sex | Lowest, highest, and average— | | Year and State | Sex | Lowest, highest, and average— | |
		Hours per week	Rate per day (dollars)			Hours per week	Rate per day (dollars)
1886—Continued.				**1890—Continued.**			
Massachusetts....	F.	60-60-60	0. 60-1. 50-1. 36	Rhode Island.....	M.	60-60-60	0. 96-1. 91-1. 43
Do...........	(¹)	60-60-60	1. 50-1. 50-1. 50	Do...........	F.	60-60-60	. 80-1. 79-1. 36
New Hampshire..	(¹)	60-66-65	1. 05-1. 50-1. 33	**1891:**			
New Jersey.......	M.	60-60-60	1. 00-1. 83-1. 35	Connecticut......	M.	60-60-60	1. 58-1. 58-1. 58
Do...........	F.	60-60-60	. 83-1. 42-1. 05	Do...........	F.	60-60-60	1. 63-1. 63-1. 63
New York........	F.	60-60-60	1. 05-1. 05-1. 05	Maine...........	M.	60-60-60	1. 31-1. 77-1. 61
Pennsylvania.....	(¹)	60-60-60	1. 20-1. 25-1. 23	Massachusetts....	M.	60-60-60	1. 20-1. 25-1. 23
Do...........	F.	60-61-60	. 71-2. 44-1. 40	Do...........	F.	60-60-60	. 60-1. 50-1. 08
Do...........	M.	60-60-60	. 98-2. 72-1. 58	New Jersey.......	M.	60-60-60	1. 67-1. 67-1. 67
Rhode Island.....	(¹)	60-60-60	1. 25-1. 60-1. 43	Do...........	F.	60-60-60	. 80-1. 44-1. 35
Do...........	M.	60-60-60	1. 35-1. 35-1. 35	New York........	M.	60-60-60	. 50-5. 00-1. 46
Do...........	F.	60-60-60	. 83-1. 58-1. 27	Do...........	F.	60-60-60	. 42-1. 36-1. 11
1887:				Rhode Island.....	M.	60-60-60	1. 35-1. 35-1. 35
California........	F.	64-64-64	1. 67-1. 67-1. 67	Do...........	F.	60-60-60	1. 31-1. 31-1. 31
Connecticut......	M.	60-60-60	. 63-1. 74-1. 51	**1892:**			
Do...........	F.	60-60-60	. 50-1. 69-1. 38	Connecticut......	M.	60-60-60	1. 67-1. 83-1. 76
Kentucky.........	F.	60-61-60	. 38-1. 13- . 84	Do...........	F.	60-60-60	1. 67-1. 83-1. 75
Maine...........	M.	60-60-60	1. 25-1. 25-1. 25	Indiana..........	(¹)	54-66-61	1. 44-2. 87-1. 56
Massachusetts....	M.	60-60-60	1. 00-1. 20-1. 10	Maine...........	M.	60-60-60	1. 34-1. 34-1. 34
Do...........	F.	60-60-60	. 60-1. 50- . 95	Do...........	F.	60-60-60	. 75-1. 50-1. 32
Ohio............	F.	60-60-60	. 60- . 90- . 77	Rhode Island.....	M.	60-60-60	1. 50-1. 50-1. 50
Pennsylvania.....	F.	60-61-60	1. 25-1. 75-1. 46	Do...........	F.	60-60-60	1. 50-1. 50-1. 50
Rhode Island.....	M.	60-60-60	1. 10-1. 60-1. 33	**1893:**			
Do...........	F.	60-60-60	1. 26-1. 26-1. 26	Ohio............	M.	60-60-60	1. 00-2. 00-1. 28
Wisconsin........	(¹)	(¹)	1. 06-1. 06-1. 06	Do...........	F.	60-60-60	. 70-1. 25-1. 07
1888:				**1894:**			
California........	M.	(¹)	1. 00-1. 00-1. 00	Indiana..........	F.	60-60-60	1. 00-1. 50-1. 36
Do...........	F.	66-66-66	1. 50-1. 67-1. 53	Iowa............	M.	60-60-60	1. 40-1. 40-1. 40
Connecticut......	M.	60-60-60	1. 50-1. 54-1. 53	Do...........	F.	60-60-60	1. 00-1. 33-1. 14
Do...........	F.	60-60-60	1. 42-1. 50-1. 47	Maine...........	M.	60-60-60	1. 00-1. 55-1. 44
Delaware........	M.	(¹)	1. 62-2. 12-1. 98	New York........	M.	60-66-62	1. 25-2. 50-1. 67
Do...........	F.	(¹)	1. 50-2. 05-1. 86	Do...........	F.	60-66-64	. 66-1. 25-1. 05
Indiana..........	M.	60-60-60	. 79-1. 50-1. 21	Ohio............	M.	60-60-60	1. 00-2. 25-1. 41
Maine...........	M.	60-60-60	1. 31-1. 31-1. 31	Do...........	F.	48-66-60	. 64-1. 25- . 96
Do...........	F.	60-60-60	1. 00-2. 00-1. 71	Rhode Island.....	(¹)	(¹)	. 67-2. 75-1. 29
Massachusetts....	M.	60-60-60	1. 00-1. 25-1. 18	**1895:**			
Do...........	F.	60-60-60	. 60-1. 50- . 95	Maine...........	M.	60-60-60	. 50-2. 43-1. 43
New Hampshire..	F.	60-60-60	. 97-1. 21-1. 07	Do...........	F.	60-60-60	. 45-2. 23-1. 28
New Jersey.......	M.	(¹)	1. 25-2. 38-1. 47	Massachusetts....	M.	58-58-58	. 80-2. 42-1. 74
Do...........	F.	(¹)	. 92-2. 16-1. 31	Do...........	F.	58-58-58	. 98-2. 06-1. 58
New York........	M.	60-60-60	1. 00-2. 25-1. 17	Missouri.........	M.	(¹)	. 54-2. 00-1. 29
Do...........	F.	(¹)	1. 25-1. 40-1. 31	Do...........	F.	(¹)	. 60-1. 53-1. 15
Pennsylvania.....	M.	(¹)	. 75-1. 30-1. 05	New Hampshire..	M.	60-60-60	. 58-2. 00-1. 26
Do...........	F.	(¹)	. 79-1. 24-1. 02	Do...........	F.	60-60-60	. 42-1. 83-1. 14
Rhode Island.....	M.	60-60-60	1. 30-1. 50-1. 47	New Jersey.......	M.	55-55-55	1. 33-1. 80-1. 57
Do...........	F.	60-60-60	1. 30-1. 50-1. 46	Do...........	F.	55-55-55	. 83-1. 28-1. 09
Do...........	(¹)	(¹)	. 83-2. 25-1. 44	Ohio............	M.	60-60-60	. 50-2. 00-1. 12
1889:				Do...........	F.	60-60-60	. 50-1. 90- . 99
Connecticut......	M.	60-60-60	1. 51-1. 60-1. 52	Vermont.........	M.	60-60-60	. 68-1. 87-1. 16
Do...........	F.	60-60-60	1. 60-1. 69-1. 62	Do...........	F.	60-60-60	. 76-1. 61-1. 17
Maine...........	M.	60-60-60	. 84-2. 51-1. 42	**1896:**			
Do...........	F.	60-60-60	. 61-2. 22-1. 37	Indiana..........	F.	60-60-60	. 46-1. 30- . 85
Massachusetts....	M.	60-60-60	1. 20-1. 50-1. 47	Iowa............	M.	60-60-60	. 91-1. 42-1. 14
Do...........	F.	60-60-60	. 60-1. 50-1. 38	Do...........	F.	60-60-60	. 50-1. 58-1. 02
New Hampshire..	M.	60-60-60	1. 50-1. 50-1. 50	Kentucky.........	F.	60-60-60	. 73-1. 23-1. 00
Do...........	F.	60-60-60	1. 21-1. 47-1. 22	Minnesota.......	M.	60-60-60	. 70- . 89- . 83
New York........	M.	60-60-60	. 99-2. 51-1. 63	Do...........	F.	60-60-60	. 60-1. 44- . 94
Do...........	F.	60-60-60	. 94-2. 33-1. 51	Missouri.........	M.	54-60-58	1. 00-1. 40-1. 16
Rhode Island.....	M.	60-60-60	1. 33-1. 33-1. 33	Do...........	F.	54-54-54	. 75- . 75- . 75
Do...........	F.	60-60-60	. 67-2. 00-1. 39	Ohio............	M.	60-60-60	. 59-1. 25-1. 17
1890:				Do...........	F.	58-60-59	. 83-1. 08- . 91
Connecticut......	M.	60-60-60	1. 71-1. 71-1. 71	Pennsylvania.....	M.	60-60-60	. 77-2. 17-1. 40
Do...........	F.	60-60-60	1. 56-1. 56-1. 56	Do...........	F.	60-60-60	. 44-2. 28-1. 25
Maine...........	M.	60-60-60	. 98-2. 38-1. 53	Rhode Island.....	(¹)	(¹)	1. 05-1. 05-1. 05
Do...........	F.	60-60-60	. 57-1. 85-1. 28	West Virginia.....	F.	60-60-60	. 92-1. 67-1. 21
Massachusetts....	M.	60-60-60	. 90-1. 91-1. 52	**1897:**			
Do...........	F.	60-60-60	. 60-1. 74-1. 39	Virginia..........	M.	60-60-60	. 60-1. 00- . 92
New Hampshire..	(¹)	60-60-60	1. 62-1. 62-1. 62	Do...........	F.	60-66-61	. 50- . 76- . 66
New Jersey.......	M.	60-60-60	1. 23-2. 55-1. 41	**1899:**			
Do...........	F.	60-60-60	. 92-1. 73-1. 30	New Jersey.......	(¹)	60-60-60	1. 09-1. 74-1. 39
New York........	M.	60-60-60	. 50-5. 00-1. 45	**1900:**			
Do...........	F.	60-60-60	. 42-1. 40-1. 13	New Jersey.......	(¹)	60-60-60	1. 25-2. 00-1. 60
North Carolina...	F.	66-66-66	. 60- . 60- . 60				

¹ Not reported.

TABLE L-58.—*Weavers, males, woolens and worsted goods, 1890–1906, by State and year*

Year	Maine		Massachusetts		New Jersey		Pennsylvania	
	Hours per week	Rate per hour	Hours per week	Rate per hour	Hours per week	Rate per hour	Hours per week	Rate per hour
1890	60.0	$0.151	60.0	$0.134			60.0	$0.157
1891	60.0	.156	60.0	.132			60.0	.160
1892	60.0	.150	60.0	.139			60.0	.165
1893	60.0	.166	58.0	.151			60.0	.168
1894	60.0	.131	58.0	.136			60.0	.148
1895	60.0	.129	58.0	.138			60.0	.147
1896	60.0	.130	58.0	.144			60.0	.136
1897	60.0	.129	58.0	.149			60.0	.150
1898	60.0	.138	58.0	.142			60.0	.156
1899	60.0	.132	58.0	.143			60.0	.165
1900	60.0	.153	58.0	.158			60.0	.177
1901	60.0	.146	58.0	.161			60.0	.188
1902	60.0	.147	58.0	.181			60.0	.193
1903	60.0	.153	58.0	.184	57.7	$.0146	60.0	.198
1904	60.0	.155	57.5	.158	57.6	.174	60.0	.200
1905	60.0	.146	58.0	.173	56.8	.181	60.0	.211
1906	60.0	.163	58.0	.196	56.6	.199	59.3	.227

TABLE L-59.—*Weavers, males, woolen and worsted goods, 1907–1928, by State and year*

Year	Connecticut		Maine		Massachusetts		New Hampshire	
	Hours per week	Rate per hour	Hours per week	Rate per hour	Hours per week	Rate per hour	Hours per week	Rate per hour
1907	58.8	$0.239	60.0	$0.198	58.0	$0.195	59.1	$0.205
1908	58.0	.221	60.0	.214	58.0	.176	58.0	.178
1909	58.0	.248	60.0	.210	58.0	.175	58.0	.201
1910	58.0	.229	58.0	.187	56.0	.213	58.0	.198
1911	58.4	.227	58.0	.206	56.0	.215	57.8	.185
1912	58.3	.249	58.0	.215	54.4	.252	57.8	.214
1913	58.6	.248	58.2	.230	54.4	.239	57.8	.212
1914	56.5	.241	58.3	.221	54.0	.248	54.6	.215
1916	55.5	.311	58.0	.297	54.0	.318	54.6	.294
1918	54.8	.466	54.0	.553	54.0	.485	53.8	.463
1920	47.8	.774	48.7	.827	48.0	.846	48.0	.795
1922	48.4	.603	48.6	.567	48.0	.644	48.5	.566
1926	49.0	.635	49.8	.611	48.0	.678	49.6	.627
1928	48.9	.681	49.9	.659	48.2	.676	49.3	.599

Year	New Jersey		New York		Rhode Island		Vermont	
1907			60.0	$0.196	58.0	$0.219		
1908			60.0	.182	58.0	.210		
1909			60.0	.187	58.0	.197		
1910	55.7	$0.187	60.0	.205	56.0	.215		
1911	56.4	.210	60.0	.204	56.0	.223		
1912	55.0	.223	60.0	.208	56.0	.250		
1913	55.0	.218	56.6	.225	56.0	.244	57.9	$0.218
1914	55.6	.214	60.0	.225	54.0	.249	57.8	.235
1916	54.1	.270	58.7	.258	54.0	.320	57.9	.308
1918	54.0	.406	58.4	.366	54.0	.480	56.2	.493
1920	49.2	.756	48.0	.765	48.7	.760	48.0	.889
1922	47.1	.603	48.0	.612	48.5	.598	48.0	.680
1926			49.3	.665	48.2	.676	50.0	.680
1928	49.4	.688	49.8	.636	48.3	.664	48.0	.584

TABLE L–60.—*Weavers, females, woolen and worsted goods, 1890–1906, by State and year*

Year	Maine		Massachusetts		New Jersey		Pennsylvania	
	Hours per week	Rate per hour	Hours per week	Rate per hour	Hours per week	Rate per hour	Hours per week	Rate per hour
1890	60.0	$0.127	60.0	$0.130				
1891	60.0	.129	60.0	.132				
1892	60.0	.123	60.0	.124				
1893	60.0	.150	58.0	.134				
1894	60.0	.121	58.0	.138				
1895	60.0	.128	58.0	.128				
1896	60.0	.133	58.0	.131				
1897	60.0	.119	58.0	.139				
1898	60.0	.128	58.0	.135				
1899	60.0	.128	58.0	.129				
1900	60.0	.144	58.0	.137				
1901	60.0	.135	58.0	.145				
1902	60.0	.130	58.0	.148				
1903	60.0	.138	58.0	.146	55.2	$0.138	60.0	$0.189
1904	60.0	.159	56.9	.145	55.3	.147	60.0	.179
1905	60.0	.148	58.0	.148	55.4	.160	60.0	.193
1906	60.0	.145	58.0	.169	55.4	.165	59.1	.216

TABLE L–61.—*Weavers, females, woolen and worsted goods, 1907–1928, by State and year*

Year	Connecticut		Maine		Massachusetts		New Hampshire	
	Hours per week	Rate per hour	Hours per week	Rate per hour	Hours per week	Rate per hour	Hours per week	Rate per hour
1907					58.0	$0.191	58.8	$0.200
1908					58.0	.167	58.0	.177
1909					58.0	.170	58.0	.188
1910					56.0	.195	58.0	.204
1911			58.0	$0.191	56.0	.199	57.9	.187
1912			58.0	.199	54.0	.231	57.9	.191
1913	58.0	$0.226	58.0	.210	54.0	.216	57.9	.184
1914	54.8	.212	58.0	.193	54.0	.228	54.9	.193
1916	54.7	.336	58.0	.271	54.0	.298	54.9	.267
1918	54.7	.478	54.0	.498	54.0	.449	54.0	.387
1920	48.0	.724	49.4	.714	48.0	.800	48.0	.692
1922	48.7	.592	49.1	.540	48.0	.616	48.5	.491
1926	49.2	.607	50.2	.608	48.0	.647	50.8	.575
1928	49.3	.637	50.1	.622	48.0	.634	50.9	.496

Year	New Jersey		New York		Rhode Island		Vermont	
	Hours per week	Rate per hour	Hours per week	Rate per hour	Hours per week	Rate per hour	Hours per week	Rate per hour
1907			60.0	$0.190	58.0	$0.190		
1908			60.0	.174	58.0	.173		
1909			60.0	.181	58.0	.169		
1910	55.1	$0.146	60.0	.195	56.0	.179		
1911	55.4	.147	60.0	.183	56.0	.181		
1912	55.0	.172	60.0	.213	56.0	.195		
1913	55.0	.169	58.2	.203	56.0	.199	57.9	$0.217
1914	55.2	.168	54.0	.215	54.0	.195	57.9	.234
1916	54.2	.252	54.0	.235	54.0	.249	57.9	.310
1918	54.1	.357	54.0	.316	53.8	.388	56.0	.458
1920	49.6	.710	48.0	.729	48.1	.694	48.0	.843
1922	48.5	.572	48.0	.688	48.1	.561	48.0	.701
1926			50.5	.633	48.0	.615	51.9	.535
1928	48.2	.655	49.3	.596	48.0	.610	48.0	.562

TABLE L-62.—*Wool sorters, woolen and worsted goods, 1859-1896, by year and State*

| Year and State | Sex | Lowest, highest, and average— | | Year and State | Sex | Lowest, highest, and average— | |
		Hours per week	Rate per day (dollars)			Hours per week	Rate per day (dollars)
1859:				**1885—Continued.**			
Massachusetts	M.	78-78-78	1.25-1.25-1.25	New Jersey	M.	60-60-60	0.80-3.00-2.27
1860:				Do	F.	60-60-60	.67-.67-.67
Massachusetts	M.	78-78-78	1.50-1.50-1.50	**1885:**			
1861:				New York	M.	60-66-62	1.20-1.84-1.86
Massachusetts	M.	78-78-78	1.50-1.50-1.50	North Carolina	M.	69-69-69	1.00-1.00-1.00
1862:				Pennsylvania	M.	60-60-60	1.50-2.47-1.65
Massachusetts	M.	78-78-78	.61-.69-.68	Do	F.	60-60-60	.75-.75-.75
1863:				Vermont	M.	60-66-63	.54-4.00-1.67
Massachusetts	M.	78-78-78	.61-1.50-.76	Do	F.	60-60-60	.45-.54-.51
1864:				**1886:**			
Massachusetts	M.	78-78-78	.61-1.50-.84	Connecticut	M.	(1)	1.65-1.65-1.65
1866:				Iowa	M.	60-60-60	1.50-1.50-1.50
Massachusetts	M.	66-66-66	.61-2.00-1.23	Massachusetts	M.	60-60-60	1.50-1.50-1.38
1867:				New Jersey	M.	60-60-60	2.25-3.33-2.73
Massachusetts	M.	66-66-66	.61-1.50-1.12	Pennsylvania	M.	58-60-60	1.21-4.72-2.38
New Hampshire	M.	66-66-66	.79-1.18-.99	Do	F.	(1)	1.88-1.88-1.88
1868:				**1887:**			
Massachusetts	M.	66-66-66	.69-1.50-1.27	Maine	M.	60-60-60	1.25-1.25-1.25
Pennsylvania	M.	62-62-62	1.67-1.67-1.67	Massachusetts	M.	60-60-60	1.25-1.50-1.38
1869:				Ohio	M.	60-60-60	1.50-1.67-1.61
Massachusetts	M.	66-66-66	.50-1.50-1.14	Pennsylvania	F.	49-57-52	.58-.92-.72
1870:				**1888:**			
Massachusetts	M.	66-66-66	.75-2.00-1.44	California	M.	(1)	1.20-2.50-1.98
1871:				Connecticut	M.	(1)	1.00-1.80-1.69
Massachusetts	M.	66-66-66	1.25-2.00-1.56	Massachusetts	M.	60-60-60	1.25-1.50-1.38
1872:				New Jersey	M.	(1)	1.67-3.00-2.44
Massachusetts	M.	66-66-66	.75-3.00-1.75	New York	M.	60-60 60	1.82-2.25-2.00
1873:				Rhode Island	M.	60-60-60	1.25-2.00-1.85
Massachusetts	M.	66-66-66	1.50-3.00-1.88	**1889:**			
1875:				Maine	M.	60-60-60	1.50-2.00-1.65
Maine	M.	64-64-64	1.83-1.83-1.83	Massachusetts	M.	60-60-60	.90-1.75-1.43
1876:				New Hampshire	M.	60-60-60	1.40-2.50-1.97
New Hampshire	M.	66-66-66	1.00-1.00-1.00	New Jersey	M.	60-60-60	2.50-2.50-2.50
Pennsylvania	M.	(1)	.54-2.50-1.35	New York	M.	60-60-60	1.75-1.75-1.75
Do	F.	(1)	.95-.95-.95	**1890:**			
1877:				Maine	M.	60-60-60	1.84-1.84-1.84
Maine	M.	66-66-66	.35-1.17-.84	Massachusetts	M.	60-60-60	.75-1.50-.98
Ohio	M.	(1)	1.25-1.25-1.25	New Hampshire	M.	60-60-60	1.50-1.80-1.64
1878:				New Jersey	M.	60-60-60	2.25-2.25-2.25
Pennsylvania	M.	60-60-60	1.15-1.15-1.15	New York	M.	60-60-60	.75-3.00-1.52
1879:				Pennsylvania	M.	60-60-60	2.50-2.50-2.50
Pennsylvania	M.	57-66-61	.80-2.50-2.10	**1891:**			
Do	(1)	57-60-60	1.34-2.50-2.40	Massachusetts	M.	60-60-60	1.25-1.50-1.29
1880:				New Jersey	M.	60-60-60	1.25-1.25-1.25
New Hampshire	M.	69-69-69	1.25-1.25-1.25	New York	M.	60-60-60	.75-3.00-1.54
1881:				**1892:**			
Connecticut	M.	60-60-60	1.65-1.65-1.65	Indiana	M.	60-60-60	1.50-1.50-1.50
Kentucky	M.	(1)	1.50-2.50-1.83	Maine	M.	60-60-60	1.57-1.57-1.57
New Hampshire	M.	65-65-65	1.17-2.53-1.95	Rhode Island	M.	60-60-60	1.85-1.85-1.85
1883:				**1893:**			
Massachusetts	M.	(1)	1.10-2.20-1.51	Illinois	M.	60-60-60	2.00-2.00-2.00
Do	F.	(1)	.62-.62-.62	Ohio	M.	(1)	1.58-1.58-1.58
New Hampshire	M.	66-66-66	1.40-1.75-1.63	Rhode Island	M.	60-60-60	1.85-1.85-1.85
New Jersey	M.	60-65-60	1.33-2.50-2.17	**1894:**			
Do	(1)	(1)	2.00-2.00-2.00	Indiana	M.	54-54-54	1.27-1.27-1.27
Pennsylvania	F.	56-56-56	.48-.48-.48	Iowa	M.	60-60-60	1.75-1.75-1.75
1884:				New Hampshire	M.	60-60-60	2.00-2.00-2.00
Connecticut	M.	60-60-60	1.75-1.85-1.80	New York	M.	66-66-66	1.50-1.50-1.50
Kentucky	M.	66-66-66	1.67-1.75-1.69	Ohio	M.	60-60-60	1.10-1.35-1.32
New Hampshire	M.	66-66-66	1.00 1.80 1.31	Rhode Island	M.	60-60-60	1.00-3.00-1.75
Do	F.	(1)	1.00-1.00-1.00	**1895:**			
New Jersey	M.	60-60-60	2.50-2.50-2.50	Maine	M.	60-60-60	.58-2.00-1.36
Do	M.	60-60-60	2.00-2.50-2.31	Massachusetts	M.	58-60-60	1.44-1.83-1.81
1885:				New Hampshire	M.	60-60-60	.72-3.00-1.86
California	M.	60-60-60	1.25-1.25-1.25	Do	F.	60-60-60	1.15-1.15-1.15
Delaware	M.	60-60-60	1.25-1.66-1.46	New Jersey	M.	55-60-57	1.67-2.50-2.09
Illinois	M.	63-63-63	1.92-1.92-1.92	Ohio	M.	60-60-60	1.08-2.00-1.37
Indiana	M.	60-66-66	.75-2.00-1.19	Pennsylvania	M.	60-60-60	2.00-2.19-2.12
Iowa	M.	60-60-60	2.00-2.00-2.00	Rhode Island	M.	60-60-60	1.85-1.85-1.85
Kentucky	M.	66-66-66	.44-1.65-.96	Vermont	M.	60-60-60	1.01-2.00-1.48
Maine	M.	60-66-66	1.17-1.87-1.57	Do	F.	60-60-60	.55-.60-.57
Maryland	M.	66-66-66	.80-2.20-1.27	**1896:**			
Massachusetts	M.	60-60-60	1.50-2.00-1.79	Iowa	M.	60-60-60	1.50-1.50-1.50
Do	F.	60-60-60	1.68-1.68-1.68	Kentucky	M.	60-60-60	1.50-2.50-1.76
Minnesota	M.	(1)	1.60-2.25-2.01	Minnesota	M.	60-60-60	1.33-2.00-1.65
Missouri	M.	60-60-60	1.50-1.50-1.50	Ohio	M.	58-60-60	1.31-1.36-1.32
New Hampshire	M.	66-66-66	.50-3.05-1.71	Pennsylvania	M.	60-60-60	1.17-4.34-2.06

1 Not reported.

TABLE **L-63.**—*Wool sorters, males, woolen and worsted goods, 1907–1926, by State and year*

Year	Connecticut		Maine		Massachusetts		New Hampshire	
	Hours per week	Rate per hour	Hours per week	Rate per hour	Hours per week	Rate per hour	Hours per week	Rate per hour
1907					58.0	$0.251		
1908					58.0	.242		
1909					58.0	.244		
1910					56.0	.250		
1911					56.0	.240		
1912					54.0	.267		
1913					54.0	.278	58.0	$0.292
1914					54.0	.268	54.9	.296
1916					54.0	.322	54.9	.338
1918					54.0	.476	54.0	.436
1920	48.0	$0.866	51.0	$0.498	48.0	.913	48.0	.900
1922	50.4	.558			48.0	.703	48.0	.695
1924			52.0	.426	48.0	.770	53.6	.779
1926	52.0	.693	54.0	.715	48.0	.713	53.8	.853

Year	New Jersey		Pennsylvania		Rhode Island	
	Hours per week	Rate per hour	Hours per week	Rate per hour	Hours per week	Rate per hour
1907					58.0	$0.217
1908					58.0	.218
1909					58.0	.245
1910					56.0	.261
1911					56.0	.261
1912					56.0	.274
1913					56.0	.296
1914	55.5	$0.238			54.0	.316
1916	54.2	.283			54.0	.361
1918	55.0	.416			54.0	.488
1920	48.0	.822	48.6	$0.713	48.0	.953
1922	48.0	.736	54.0	.705	48.0	.736
1924	48.0	.879	53.2	.720	48.0	.802
1926			53.5	.697	48.2	.736

M.—TOBACCO INDUSTRY

The sources from which these wage data were taken are the fifteenth and the nineteenth annual reports of the Commissioner of Labor Statistics and bulletins Nos. 59, 65, 71, 77, 135, 161, and 265 of the Bureau of Labor Statistics. No wage data are available for any occupation in the tobacco industry after the year 1919.

TABLE M–1.—*Cigar makers, 1860–1900, by year and State*

Year and State	Sex	Hours per week	Rate per day (dollars)	Year and State	Sex	Hours per week	Rate per day (dollars)
1860:				**1882—Continued.**			
Ohio	M.	(1)	1.17-2.67-1.65	Ohio	M	54-60-56	1.09-2.25-1.77
1870:				Do	(1)	56-56-56	1.41-2.25-2.05
West Virginia	M.	72-72-72	1.67-2.67-2.17	Pennsylvania	(1)	56-60-59	1.40-1.76-1.69
1871:				Do	M.	54-60-58	1.00-2.00-1.47
Massachusetts	M.	(1)	(2)	Virginia	M.	54-60-58	1.75-2.00-1.92
Do	F.	(1)	³9.00-9.00-9.00	Wisconsin	(1)	59-59-59	1.43-1.43-1.43
Do	(1)	(1)	3.00-3.00-3.00	Do	M.	48-48-48	1.82-3.39-2.69
1872:				Do	F.	48-48-48	1.03-1.64-1.26
Ohio	M.	(1)	2.00-4.67-2.45	**1883:**			
1877:				Connecticut	M.	60-60-60	2.00-2.38-2.12
New Jersey	(1)	60-60-60	1.25-1.25-1.25	Dist. of Columbia	M.	58-58-58	1.50-2.00-1.75
Ohio	M.	54-60-58	1.17-3.33-1.35	Illinois	M.	48-60-59	1.50-2.25-1.56
Do	(1)	55-60-58	.83-1.00-.96	Indiana	M.	54-60-59	1.33-2.00-1.76
1878:				Iowa	M.	58-60-59	1.18-2.25-1.65
Ohio	M.	(1)	1.08-2.03-1.47	Do	F.	60-60-60	.75-1.18-1.04
Do	F.	(1)	.92-1.78-1.21	Kansas	M.	60-60-60	3.00-3.00-3.00
1879:				Kentucky	M.	60-60-60	1.00-1.25-1.13
New Jersey	(1)	50-60-56	.85-2.00-1.47	Louisiana	M.	63-63-63	.64-1.67-.99
Ohio	M.	(1)	1.00-2.50-1.41	Do	F.	63-63-63	.30-1.68-.81
1880:				Maryland	M.	56-60-58	1.45-1.83-1.59
Maryland	M.	55-55-55	1.67-2.25-1.98	Massachusetts	M.	48-60-58	1.75-2.20-1.84
Do	F.	55-55-55	1.04-1.67-1.37	Do	F.	58-58-58	1.75-1.88-1.81
New Jersey	(1)	54-60-59	1.00-2.50-1.47	Do	(1)	50-60-55	1.51-2.50-1.88
Ohio	F.	(1)	.50-.50-.50	Michigan	M.	54-60-56	.83-3.50-1.71
Pennsylvania	M.	60-72-64	1.20-2.45-1.63	Do	(1)	(1)	.58-.58-.58
1881:				Minnesota	M.	60-60-60	1.50-2.50-2.09
Connecticut	M.	60-60-60	1.33-2.00-1.63	Missouri	M.	48-60-51	1.50-2.00-1.68
Illinois	M.	48-48-48	1.60-1.65-1.63	Nebraska	M.	60-60-60	2.50-2.50-2.50
Indiana	M.	60-60-60	1.50-1.50-1.50	New Hampshire	(1)	60-60-60	2.30-2.50-2.40
Iowa	M.	58-66-58	1.75-2.00-1.85	New Jersey	M.	48-60-58	1.00-3.00-1.51
Kentucky	M.	56-60-58	1.00-1.90-1.43	Do	F.	60-60-60	.33-1.67-.75
Massachusetts	(1)	58-58-58	1.36-1.39-1.38	New York	M.	54-60-58	1.35-3.37-2.54
Michigan	(1)	48-60-55	1.45-2.25-1.79	Do	F.	58-58-58	1.25-1.25-1.25
Missouri	M.	59-59-59	2.00-2.00-2.00	Do	(1)	54-72-55	1.25-2.25-1.73
Do	(1)	60-60-60	.67-1.42-1.23	Ohio	M.	42-60-58	1.10-2.60-1.73
New Jersey	M.	59-59-59	1.25-1.75-1.50	Do	(1)	54-60-56	1.25-2.15-1.76
New York	(1)	57-60-60	1.45-2.13-1.65	Pennsylvania	M.	48-60-54	1.25-2.15-1.76
Ohio	M.	36-66-59	1.00-2.25-1.75	Do	(1)	50-60-52	1.79-2.60-1.83
Pennsylvania	(1)	48-60-52	.92-2.00-1.75	Rhode Island	M.	48-60-54	2.20-2.25-2.24
Do	M.	60-60-60	1.00-1.00-1.00	Tennessee	M.	60-60-60	2.00-2.16-2.08
West Virginia	M.	(1)	1.50-1.65-1.58	Virginia	M.	48-60-57	1.96-3.27-2.41
Wisconsin	(1)	56-60-59	1.25-1.65-1.47	Wisconsin	M.	54-59-56	1.40-1.55-1.49
1882:				**1884:**			
Connecticut	M.	60-60-60	1.98-2.17-2.07	Alabama	M.	60-60-60	2.00-2.00-2.00
Georgia	M.	48-48-48	1.67-2.08-1.86	California	M.	50-60-56	1.03-2.30-1.26
Illinois	(1)	51-51-51	2.00-2.00-2.00	Do	(1)	50-57-52	1.08-1.31-1.17
Indiana	M.	60-60-60	2.00-2.10-2.03	Florida	M.	48-48-48	2.00-3.67-2.94
Iowa	M.	53-60-58	1.52-2.25-1.71	Illinois	M.	48-60-51	1.50-3.00-1.84
Do	F.	60-60-60	1.52-1.52-1.52	Indiana	M.	60-60-60	1.50-2.00-1.61
Massachusetts	(1)	58-58-58	1.48-1.48-1.48	Iowa	M.	51-60-58	.58-3.15-1.83
Michigan	M.	56-56-56	1.58-1.85-1.74	Kansas	M.	60-60-60	1.50-1.50-1.50
Minnesota	M.	66-66-66	2.00-2.00-2.00	Do	(1)	60-60-60	2.00-2.00-2.00
Missouri	M.	60-60-60	2.10-2.80-2.22	Maryland	M.	56-56-56	1.50-1.66-1.58
Do	(1)	60-60-60	1.00-2.00-1.44	Do	(1)	56-56-56	1.50-1.60-1.55
New Jersey	M.	60-60-60	1.25-2.00-1.57	Massachusetts	(1)	58-58-58	2.50-2.50-2.50
New York	(1)	57-60-60	1.52-2.35-1.73	Do	(1)	54-58-57	1.75-2.40-1.88

1 Not reported. 2 $12-$12-$12 per 1,000 cigars. 3 Per 1,000 cigars.

TABLE M-1.—*Cigar makers, 1860–1900, by year and State*—Continued

Year and State	Sex	Hours per week	Rate per day (dollars)
1884—Continued.			
Michigan	M.	50-58-55	0.38-3.50-1.99
Minnesota	(1)	48-48-48	2.25-2.25-2.25
Missouri	M.	60-60-60	1.75-2.10-1.94
Do	(1)	60-60-60	1.00-3.00-1.57
New Jersey	M.	48-60-58	1.35-2.85-1.99
New York	M.	54-54-54	1.75-2.20-1.93
Do	F.	60-60-60	1.50-1.50-1.50
Do	(1)	54-60-57	1.25-2.00-1.68
Ohio	M.	54-59-57	1.30-1.92-1.53
Do	(1)	54-60-57	1.06-2.25-1.31
Pennsylvania	M.	60-60-60	1.67-2.34-2.01
Rhode Island	M.	60-60-60	2.00-2.00-2.00
Virginia	M.	60-60-60	2.00-2.58-2.30
West Virginia	M.	57-60-57	1.33-2.83-2.09
Wisconsin	M.	60-60-60	1.75-1.75-1.75
1885:			
Connecticut	M.	60-60-60	2.25-2.25-2.25
Florida	M.	60-60-60	1.66-2.09-2.01
Do	F.	60-60-60	1.94-2.09-2.02
Illinois	M.	48-60-54	1.22-2.88-1.67
Do	F.	44-60-51	.50-2.00-1.16
Indiana	M.	54-60-59	1.75-2.10-2.01
Kansas	M.	48-60-58	1.00-2.50-1.66
Kentucky	M.	55-60-60	1.25-2.10-1.71
Louisiana	F.	55-55-55	.65-1.20-.88
Maryland	M.	60-60-60	1.08-2.63-1.68
Do	F.	60-60-60	1.00-2.04-1.38
Massachusetts	M.	54-60-57	1.67-3.85-2.52
Michigan	M.	48-52-51	1.50-2.00-1.82
Do	(1)	52-60-54	1.17-2.40-1.59
Minnesota	M.	54-54-54	2.00-2.20-2.05
Do	F	(1)	2.00-2.07-2.05
Missouri	M.	60-60-60	1.75-2.50-1.96
New Hampshire	M.	60-60-60	2.50-2.65-2.58
New Jersey	M.	50-60-56	.92-4.00-2.08
Do	F.	54-58-56	.67-1.33-.98
New York	M.	46-60-59	1.04-8.00-1.74
Do	F.	46-108-72	.50-2.32-1.31
Do	(1)	40-70-56	1.38-2.18-1.69
Do	(1)	57-57-57	[6]6.70-6.70-6.70
Ohio	M.	45-60-57	.63-2.00-1.65
Do	F.	45-60-54	.58-1.58-1.19
Do	(1)	56-66-60	1.27-2.00-1.45
Pennsylvania	M.	56-56-56	1.50-1.67-1.50
Do	(1)	56-56-56	1.48-1.67-1.58
Rhode Island	M.	60-60-60	1.83-2.33-2.11
Virginia	F.	(1)	.67-1.08-.87
West Virginia	M.	60-60-60	1.33-1.67-1.51
1886:			
California	M.	60-60-60	1.50-2.50-1.87
Do	M.	(1)	[2]2.50-2.50-2.50
Colorado	M.	54-54-54	2.50-2.75-2.63
Connecticut	M.	48-60-55	1.66-2.67-2.16
Florida	M.	60-60-60	3.40-3.40-3.40
Illinois	M.	48-60-50	1.50-2.60-1.73
Iowa	M.	48-60-52	.64-3.00-1.84
Kansas	M.	48-60-60	1.80-1.80-1.80
Maine	(1)	45-45-45	2.33-2.53-2.43
Maryland	M.	40-60-53	1.00-3.00-2.06
Do	F.	47-57-54	.75-1.67-1.03
Massachusetts	M.	48-60-53	1.40-2.68-2.10
Do	(1)	48-54-53	1.58-2.24-1.81
Michigan	(1)	48-50-49	1.00-1.63-1.54
Do	M.	45-60-54	1.63-2.70-2.18
Minnesota	M.	48-48-48	2.00-2.50-2.05
Missouri	M.	48-60-54	1.16-1.75-1.43
Do	F.	52-52-52	.58-1.08-.78
Nebraska	M.	60-60-60	1.75-1.92-1.84
New Jersey	M.	47-60-59	1.33-3.33-2.15
Do	F.	45-56-54	.83-1.50-1.18
New York	M.	45-60-52	1.17-2.63-1.83
Do	F.	48-52-48	.67-1.17-.89
Do	(1)	48-60-54	1.09-2.50-1.51
1886—Continued.			
New York	M.	47-59-58	[5]6.00-7.00-6.04
Do	F.	58-58-58	[7]7.00-7.00-7.00
Ohio	M.	48-56-49	1.04-2.10-1.87
Do	(1)	54-56-56	1.22-1.92-1.77
Pennsylvania	M.	55-60-57	.63-2.25-1.61
Do	F.	44-58-54	.50-1.83-1.04
Do	(1)	50-72-61	1.17-2.16-1.42
Rhode Island	F.	40-60-52	.67-1.67-1.15
South Dakota	M.	48-48-48	2.75-2.75-2.75
Virginia	M.	48-60-54	2.00-2.25-2.08
West Virginia	M.	58-58-58	1.50-1.67-1.60
Wisconsin	M.	58-58-58	1.75-1.75-1.75
1887:			
Illinois	F.	51-58-55	1.00-1.75-1.36
Kansas	M.	48-48-48	1.66-3.50-2.19
Kentucky	F.	46-57-55	.79-2.00-1.15
Louisiana	F.	46-57-52	.58-1.92-.96
Massachusetts	F.	48-48-48	1.42-2.50-1.85
Minnesota	F.	51-51-51	1.67-1.67-1.67
New York	F.	34-75-51	.58-2.67-1.44
Do	M.	44-48-45	1.67-3.00-2.40
Ohio	F.	41-60-58	.50-2.00-1.23
Do	M.	48-60-58	.34-3.34-1.46
Do	M.	60-60-60	[5]6.00-9.00-6.75
Pennsylvania	F.	48-52-50	1.00-1.50-1.21
Rhode Island	M.	(1)	1.08-2.00-1.37
Wisconsin	(1)	(1)	1.00-1.77-1.77
1888:			
California	F.	55-56-55	1.00-1.33-1.13
Colorado	F.	48-60-54	.75-1.33-1.00
Iowa	M.	48-48-48	1.70-2.35-1.86
Kansas	M.	(1)	2.00-2.34-2.15
New Jersey	(1)	48-60-51	1.50-3.00-2.12
New York	M.	44-60-47	.83-2.50-1.98
Do	M.	44-60-50	(5)
Do	F.	47-47-47	1.33-1.67-1.54
Ohio	M.	(1)	1.29-2.05-1.48
Virginia	F.	40-60-52	.42-1.50-.76
1889:			
California	F.	(1)	2.70-2.70-2.70
Kansas	M.	(1)	2.15-2.25-2.19
Rhode Island	F.	60-60-60	.87-1.33-1.00
1890:			
Kansas	M.	(1)	2.00-4.00-2.53
Minnesota	M.	(1)	1.00-2.65-1.89
New York	M.	(1)	.33-4.50-1.77
Do	F.	(1)	1.17-2.50-1.58
Ohio	(1)	42-60-52	1.00-2.60-1.69
1891:			
Michigan	F.	(1)	.50-1.72-1.34
New York	F.	(1)	.33-4.50-1.78
Do	F.	(1)	1.17-2.50-1.50
North Carolina	M.	60-60-60	3.00-3.00-3.00
Ohio	M.	36-66-52	.80-3.00-1.75
Do	F.	45-60-56	.50-1.75-1.06
1892:			
California	M.	48-48-48	.67-3.83-2.01
Do	F.	48-48-48	.83-2.00-1.40
Illinois	F.	45-54-52	.56-2.00-1.25
Iowa	(1)	48-60-49	1.25-2.94-2.04
Missouri	M.	48-48-48	1.67-2.17-2.01
1893:			
Illinois	M.	35-72-53	.67-4.17-1.76
Do	F.	46-63-56	.33-1.67-1.05
Maryland	M.	45-72-61	.42-3.33-1.54
Do	F.	60-72-63	.50-1.50-.91
Missouri	M.	48-48-48	1.75-2.25-1.86
Montana	M.	42-42-42	3.00-3.00-3.00
Do	M.	42-48-45	(6)
Do	F.	48-48-48	(7)
New Hampshire	M.	47-47-47	3.50-3.50-3.50
New Jersey	F.	58-58-58	.50-1.83-1.17
New York	M.	48-84-58	.67-3.67-1.61

[1] Not reported.
[2] Per 1,000 cigars.
[4] And board.
[5] $2.50–$17.00–$7.93½ per 1,000 cigars.
[6] $14–$19–$15.60 per 1,000 cigars.
[7] $14–$14–$14 per 1,000 cigars.

TABLE **M-1.**—*Cigar makers, 1860–1900, by year and State*—Continued

Year and State	Sex	Hours per week	Rate per day (dollars)	Year and State	Sex	Hours per week	Rate per day (dollars)
1893—Continued.				**1896—Continued.**			
New York	F.	60–60–60	0.50–1.33–0.75	Michigan	M.	40–48–46	1.30–2.80–2.07
Ohio	M.	42–60–52	.90–3.00–1.72	Minnesota	M.	48–48–48	1.87–1.87–1.87
Do	F.	42–60–54	.40–2.00–1.23	Do	F.	48–48–48	1.90–1.90–1.90
Pennsylvania	M.	45–66–57	.42–4.17–1.70	Missouri	M.	48–60–49	1.30–3.50–2.24
Do	F.	49–60–57	.83–2.00–1.23	Do	F.	48–60–51	.50–3.50–1.33
Rhode Island	M.	(¹)	1.50–2.60–2.05	Nebraska	M.	42–48–46	.70–3.50–2.53
1894:				Do	F.	48–48–48	1.25–2.25–1.50
Iowa	M.	42–60–51	1.00–3.25–1.88	Do	(¹)	42–48–44	.35–3.00–.80
Do	F.	54–60–58	.50–1.50–.99	New York	M.	46–48–48	.58–3.00–1.73
Kansas	M.	54–54–54	1.55–1.55–1.55	Do	F.	48–48–48	.53–1.17–.87
Do	F.	60–60–60	1.03–1.03–1.03	Ohio	M.	44–60–46	1.05–2.07–1.52
New Hampshire	M.	47–48–48	1.50–5.33–2.69	Do	F.	44–60–54	.75–2.02–1.02
North Carolina	M.	60–60–60	.60–2.40–1.80	Pennsylvania	M.	52–54–52	.58–2.67–1.40
Ohio	M.	42–72–52	.67–3.33–1.66	Do	F.	52–60–54	.43–2.10–.96
Do	F.	42–60–54	.40–1.83–1.22	West Virginia	M.	54–60–57	1.03–3.33–1.86
Pennsylvania	F.	51–63–57ᵉ	.33–1.58–.60	Do	F.	54–58–57	.32–1.00–.80
1895:				Wisconsin	M.	48–48–48	1.33–4.20–2.37
Kansas	(¹)	30–54–48	1.00–3.33–1.93	Do	F.	48–48 48	1.00–2.01–1.24
Louisiana	M.	63–63–63	.41–1.95–1.02	**1897:**			
Do	F.	55–63–62	.23–1.70–.65	Connecticut	M.	45–45–45	2.57–2.57–2.57
Maryland	M.	55–55–55	1.17–3.33–1.88	Kansas	M.	22–72–46	.67–2.50–1.69
Do	F.	55–55–55	.67–2.25–1.19	Do	F	36–61–55	.75–1.67–.93
Massachusetts	M.	54–54–54	1.75–5.00–3.01	Michigan	M.	45–45–45	1.66–2.00–1.72
New Jersey	F.	56–56–56	.69–1.68–1.07	Do	F.	(¹)	1.17–2.50–1.49
New York	M.	46–48–47	1.23–3.33–2.11	Nebraska	M.	48–48–48	2.00–2.00–2.00
Do	F.	46–48–47	1.55–2.35–1.95	Do	F.	48–48–48	.50–.50–.50
Ohio	M.	42–72–52	.55–5.00–1.68	Do	(¹)	48–48–48	2.50–2.50–2.50
Do	F.	42–60–54	.50–1.80–1.16	New York	M.	38–48–48	.50–4.50–1.88
Virginia	F.	54–54–54	.67–1.08–.88	Do	F.	48–48–48	1.33–2.00–1.54
Wisconsin	(¹)	30–54–47	.83–3.00–1.55	Virginia	M.	48–48–48	.55–5.00–1.55
1896:				Do	M.	(¹)	7.00–7.00–7.00
Colorado	(¹)	36–45–43	1.67–2.00–1.75	**1898:**			
Florida	M.	48–48–48	1.50–4.17–2.89	Kansas	M.	42–60–49	1.67–2.50–1.94
Georgia	M.	48–48–48	1.50–1.67–1.59	Do	M.	48–60–53	(⁸)
Do	F.	48–48–48	1.08–1.17–1.13	Michigan	M.	(¹)	1.25–2.67–1.96
Illinois	M.	36–48–44	1.00–3.75–2.05	New Jersey	M.	48–48–48	1.50–2.83–2.06
Do	F.	44–48–45	1.00–2.04–1.43	New York	M.	48–48–48	.68–6.13–1.88
Iowa	M.	48–58–53	.63–2.61–1.42	Virginia	(¹)	48–48–48	1.73–1.73–1.73
Do	F.	48–58–54	1.00–1.93–1.31	**1899:**			
Kansas	M.	36–60–48	1.17–3.45–2.08	Massachusetts	M.	(¹)	1.25–5.75–3.09
Maryland	M.	48–48–48	.33–1.83–1.00	**1900:**			
Do	F.	48–48–48	.38–1.04–.74	Massachusetts	M.	(¹)	1.38–5.25–3.20

¹ Not reported.   ⁸ $7–$10–$8 per 1,000 cigars.

TABLE **M-2.**—*Cigar makers, males, 1890–1907, by geographic division and year*

Year	North Atlantic Hours per week	Rate per hour	South Atlantic Hours per week	Rate per hour	North Central Hours per week	Rate per hour	South Central Hours per week	Rate per hour
1890	48.8	$0.286	60.0	$0.267	46.3	$0.271		
1891	49.0	.274	60.0	.264	46.1	.302		
1892	48.9	.294	60.0	.266	46.7	.291		
1893	49.0	.295	60.0	.263	46.8	.268		
1894	49.3	.276	60.0	.253	46.8	.277		
1895	49.4	.264	60.0	.253	46.7	.269		
1896	50.3	.257	60.0	.232	47.2	.277		
1897	51.0	.246	60.0	.238	47.1	.272		
1898	50.6	.247	60.0	.276	47.4	.269		
1899	51.5	.233	60.0	.256	47.6	.285		
1900	50.0	.252	60.0	.257	47.3	.281		
1901	50.8	.259	60.0	.275	47.4	.287		
1902	51.1	.257	60.0	.276	47.5	.291		
1903	48.6	.366	60.0	.275	47.1	.307		
1904	49.2	.325	59.8	.292	47.5	.298		
1905	49.5	.314	59.9	.289	47.1	.318		
1906	49.0	.348	59.9	.302	47.2	.320	49.0	$0.274
1907	48.9	.360	59.9	.296	47.1	.333	48.9	.305

TABLE M-3.—*Cigar makers, males, 1911-1913 and 1919, by city and year*

Year	Baltimore, Md.		Boston, Mass.		Chicago, Ill.		Cincinnati, Ohio	
	Hours per week	Rate per hour	Hours per week	Rate per hour	Hours per week	Rate per hour	Hours per week	Rate per hour
1911	(1)	$0.251			(1)	$0.417	(1)	$0.289
1912	(1)	.245			(1)	.404	(1)	.303
1913	(1)	.270			(1)	.418	(1)	.352
1919	(1)	.437	(1)	$0.685	(1)	.584	(1)	.389

Year	Detroit, Mich.		Key West, Fla.		Lancaster, Pa.		New York, N. Y.	
1911	(1)	$0.340					(1)	$0.300
1912	(1)	.332					(1)	.336
1913	(1)	.331					(1)	.340
1919	(1)	.474	(1)	$0.348	(1)	$0.369	(1)	.435

Year	Philadelphia, Pa.		Reading, Pa.		Tampa, Fla.			
1911	(1)	$0.289			(1)	$0.298		
1912	(1)	.281			(1)	.293		
1913	(1)	.294			(1)	.293		
1919	(1)	.398	(1)	$0.383	(1)	.340		

1 Not reported.

TABLE M-4.—*Cigar makers, females, 1911-1913 and 1919, by city and year*

Year	Boston, Mass.		Chicago, Ill.		Cleveland, Ohio		Lancaster, Pa.	
	Hours per week	Rate per hour	Hours per week	Rate per hour	Hours per week	Rate per hour	Hours per week	Rate per hour
1911			(1)	$0.357				
1912			(1)	.437				
1913			(1)	.401				
1919	(1)	$0.561	(1)	(1)	(1)	$0.427	(1)	$0.346

Year	New York, N. Y.		Philadelphia, Pa.		Reading, Pa.		Tampa, Fla.	
1911	(1)	$0.312	(1)	$0.236			(1)	$0.241
1912	(1)	.287	(1)	.248			(1)	.258
1913	(1)	.278	(1)	.233			(1)	.257
1919			(1)	.376	(1)	$0.337	(1)	.360

1 Not reported.

TABLE M-5.—*Strippers, tobacco, 1870-1900, by year and State*

Year and State	Sex	Lowest, highest, and average—		Year and State	Sex	Lowest, highest, and average—	
		Hours per week	Rate per day (dollars)			Hours per week	Rate per day (dollars)
1870:				1880:			
West Virginia	F.	72-72-72	0.75-0.75-0.75	Maryland	M.	55-55-55	1.00-1.00-1.00
1871:				Pennsylvania	M.	47-50-48	.67-1.33-.89
Massachusetts	F.	(1)	.75-1.20-.98	1881:			
1877:				Ohio	M.	54-60-59	.40-1.00-.51
Ohio	(1)	(1)	.40-.50-.48	1882:			
1878:				Georgia	M.	48-48-48	.42-.58-.50
Ohio	M.	(1)	.29-.78-.57	Do	F.	48-48-48	.50-.50-.50
Do	F.	(1)	.32-.63-.43	Missouri	(1)	60-60-60	1.00-1.00-1.00

1 Not reported.

TABLE **M-5.**—*Strippers, tobacco, 1870-1900, by year and State*—Continued

| Year and State | Sex | Lowest, highest, and average— | | Year and State | Sex | Lowest, highest, and average— | |
		Hours per week	Rate per day (dollars)			Hours per week	Rate per day (dollars)
1882—Continued.				**1888—Continued.**			
Ohio	M.	60-60-60	0. 50-0. 50-0. 50	New York	F.	60-60-60	0. 67-0. 67-0. 67
Do	F.	60-60-60	.64- .64- .64	Virginia	F.	59-59-59	.50- .50- .50
Virginia	M.	(1)	.29- .60- .52	**1889:**			
Do	F.	(1)	.25- .50- .39	California	F.	(1)	.83- .83- .83
Wisconsin	F.	48-48-48	.33- .58- .43	**1890:**			
1883:				New York	M.	(1)	.17-2. 67- .84
Louisiana	F.	63-63-63	.29- .68- .46	**1891:**			
New Jersey	(1)	60-60-60	.42- .42- .42	Michigan	F.	(1)	.21- .83- .49
Ohio	F.	(1)	.17- .17- .17	New York	M.	(1)	.19-2. 67- .85
1884:				Ohio	M.	48-60-55	.20-1. 35- .52
Florida	F.	48-48-48	.83-1. 17- .95	Do	F.	42-60-58	.30-1. 00- .63
Iowa	F.	58-58-58	.30- .70- .45	**1892:**			
Michigan	M.	(1)	.33- .85- .62	California	M.	48-68-56	.50- .67- .58
New Jersey	M.	60-60-60	.30-2. 17-1. 24	Do	F.	48-48-48	.83-1. 17- .96
Ohio	F.	(1)	.33- .33- .33	Illinois	F.	52-60-53	.44- .92- .70
1885:				Maine	F.	60-60-60	.33-1. 50- .77
Connecticut	F.	60-60-60	.58-1. 17- .79	**1893:**			
Illinois	M.	48-60-59	.33- .83- .49	Illinois	M.	48-60-54	.50- .67- .58
Do	F.	60-60-58	.33-1. 00- .54	Do	F.	60-60-60	.58- .58- .58
Kentucky	M.	60-60-60	.80- .80- .80	Maryland	M.	45-60-57	.25-1. 00- .60
Do	F.	60-60-60	.80-1. 00- .83	New Jersey	F.	58-58-58	.25-1. 00- .65
Louisiana	M.	55-55-55	.32- .57- .44	New York	M.	53-72-59	.33-2. 00-1. 04
Do	F.	55-55-55	.37- .69- .56	Do	F.	47-60-58	.42-1. 33- .81
Maryland	M.	60-60-60	.50-1. 25- .80	Ohio	M.	48-60-52	.38-2. 00- .88
Massachusetts	F.	(1)	.67-1. 50- .92	Do	F.	36-60-54	.40-1. 25- .68
Michigan	M.	60-60-60	.80- .80- .80	Pennsylvania	M.	50-60-58	.50- .83- .65
Do	F.	60-60-60	.80- .80- .80	Do	F.	40-60-52	.33- .83- .60
Minnesota	M.	(1)	.50- .50- .50	**1894:**			
Do	F.	(1)	.50- .83- .67	Iowa	M.	54-57-56	.42- .50- .46
Missouri	M.	60-60-60	1. 00-1. 00-1. 00	Do	F.	48-60-55	.33- .83- .53
New Jersey	F.	54-58-56	.46- .66- .58	New York	M.	48-48-48	.40- .40- .40
Do	M.	57-60-58	.33-3. 33-1. 67	Do	F.	48-60-58	1. 00-1. 00-1. 00
New York	M.	58-58-58	.25- .58- .46	Ohio	M.	39-60-53	.38-1. 00- .62
Do	(1)	46-62-54	.25-1. 18- .89	Do	F.	36-60-53	.45-1. 00- .63
North Carolina	M.	69-69-69	.45- .45- .45	**1895:**			
Ohio	M.	60-60-60	.40- .51- .44	Louisiana	M.	55-55-55	.24- .47- .37
Do	F.	45-60-56	.21- .69- .50	Do	F.	55-63-62	.27-1. 01- .57
Rhode Island	F.	60-60-60	1. 00-1. 00-1. 00	Maryland	M.	55-55-55	.50-1. 33- .88
Virginia	M.	60-60-60	.30- .50- .45	Massachusetts	F.	50-50-50	.58-1. 33- .99
Do	F.	60-60-60	.50- .60- .55	New Jersey	F.	56-56-56	.50-1. 00- .67
West Virginia	F.	60-60-60	.50- .58- .51	New York	F.	46-60-54	.25-1. 17- .80
Wisconsin	M.	60-60-60	.63- .96- .81	Do	M.	48-54-49	.50- .50- .50
1886:				Ohio	M.	24-60-53	.25-1. 33- .63
Iowa	F.	48-60-58	.25- .83- .53	Do	F.	42-60-53	.35-1. 00- .61
Maryland	F.	48-55-51	.33-1. 13- .65	Virginia	M.	54-54-54	.42- .58- .49
Michigan	F.	45-60-57	.50-1. 01- .80	Do	F.	54-54-54	.21- .50- .41
Missouri	F.	45-47-46	1. 08-1. 33-1. 21	**1896:**			
New Jersey	F.	48-56-53	.50-1. 00- .70	Florida	F.	48-48-48	.83-1. 17- .97
Do	M.	48-60-60	.33-3. 33-1. 59	Georgia	F.	48-48-48	.33- .42- .39
New York	F.	49-57-51	.33- .83- .60	Illinois	F.	44-60-46	.50-1. 33- .71
Ohio	F.	(1)	.25- .25- .25	Iowa	F.	48-58-52	.25-1. 17- .51
Pennsylvania	F.	48-60-57	.26-1. 00- .56	Michigan	F.	40-55-52	.33-1. 18- .70
Do	M.	(1)	.32- .87- .53	Maryland	F.	48-48-48	.33-1. 13- .77
Rhode Island	F.	50-61-54	.50-1. 00- .74	Minnesota	M.	48-48-48	.42- .83- .63
West Virginia	M.	58-58-58	.50- .58- .58	Do	F.	48-48-48	.67- .67- .67
Do	F.	58-58-58	.58- .58- .58	North Carolina	F.	54-54-54	.50- .50- .50
1887:				Ohio	F.	45-60-53	.28- .94- .58
California	F.	50-55-53	.50-1. 17- .82	Do	M.	48-60-53	.42-1. 00- .54
Illinois	F.	40-61-53	.25-1. 17- .69	Pennsylvania	M.	52-52-52	.27-1. 17- .58
Kentucky	F.	55-57-56	.33- .38- .35	Do	F.	52-60-55	.27-1. 17- .64
Louisiana	F.	45-60-54	.21-1. 00- .52	West Virginia	M.	58-58-58	.58- .67- .64
Massachusetts	F.	47-54-51	.58-1. 33- .89	Do	F.	54-60-58	.28- .83- .65
Minnesota	F.	53-59-56	.33- .92- .63	Wisconsin	M.	48-48-48	.50-1. 03- .80
New York	F.	42-69-55	.31-2. 50- .84	Do	F.	48-48-48	.33- .58- .41
Ohio	F.	46-60-58	.18-1. 08- .63	**1897:**			
Do	M.	54-60-60	.40- .85- .75	Virginia	M.	48-52-52	.62- .75- .62
Pennsylvania	F.	45-53-49	.23- .75- .51	Do	F.	52-52-52	.62- .62- .62
Wisconsin	(1)	(1)	.43- .67- .46	**1898:**			
1888:				Michigan	F.	(1)	.65- .65- .65
California	F.	54-56-55	.50-1. 17- .82	**1899:**			
Indiana	F.	53-59-54	.42- .75- .49	Massachusetts	F.	53-54-53	.58-1. 50- .99
Maine	F.	60-60-60	.67- .75- .71	**1900:**			
New Jersey	(1)	60-60-60	1. 50-1. 50-1. 50	Massachusetts	F.	47-54-49	.55-1. 50- .99
New York	M.	44-60-53	.25-1. 25- .76				

1 Not reported.

TABLE **M–6.**—*Stemmers or strippers, males, 1890–1904, by geographic division and year*

Year	North Atlantic		South Atlantic		North Central		South Central	
	Hours per week	Rate per hour	Hours per week	Rate per hour	Hours per week	Rate per hour	Hours per week	Rate per hour
1890	59.8	$0.085	60.0	$0.102				
1891	59.9	.095	60.0	.093				
1892	59.8	.091	60.0	.086				
1893	59.7	.084	60.0	.081				
1894	59.8	.095	60.0	.085				
1895	59.7	.092	60.0	.082				
1896	59.7	.098	60.0	.083				
1897	59.8	.104	60.0	.096				
1898	60.0	.121	60.0	.092				
1899	60.0	.114	60.0	.092				
1900	60.0	.111	60.0	.107				
1901	60.0	.116	60.0	.100				
1902	60.0	.118	60.0	.095				
1903	50.0	.091	60.0	.073	48.0	$0.125	46.0	$0.135
1904	50.0	.057	58.9	.070	48.0	.125	46.0	.108

TABLE **M–7.**—*Stemmers or strippers, females, 1890–1904, by geographic division and year*

Year	North Atlantic		South Atlantic		North Central		South Central	
	Hours per week	Rate per hour	Hours per week	Rate per hour	Hours per week	Rate per hour	Hours per week	Rate per hour
1890	59.6	$0.064			50.7	$0.065		
1891	59.6	.063			50.4	.064		
1892	59.6	.072			50.4	.065		
1893	59.5	.070			50.0	.064		
1894	59.7	.075			49.8	.066		
1895	59.6	.074			49.8	.062		
1896	58.3	.075			50.6	.069		
1897	58.8	.087			50.1	.068		
1898	58.9	.083			50.3	.068		
1899	59.1	.078			50.2	.068		
1900	58.8	.077			50.3	.071		
1901	58.8	.092			50.1	.074		
1902	58.8	.086			50.2	.077		
1903	52.8	.105	60.0	$0.118	51.1	.097	46.0	$0.091
1904	53.0	.114	59.8	.114	51.4	.097	46.0	.073

TABLE **M–8.**—*Strippers, males, 1911–1913 and 1919, by city and year*

Year	Baltimore, Md.		Evansville, Ind.		New York, N.Y.		Philadelphia, Pa.	
	Hours per week	Rate per hour	Hours per week	Rate per hour	Hours per week	Rate per hour	Hours per week	Rate per hour
1911	(1)	$0.150			(1)	$0.124	(1)	$0.125
1912	(1)	.136			(1)	.170	(1)	.131
1913	(1)	.156			(1)	.168	(1)	.145
1919	(1)	.245	(1)	$0.141	(1)	.285	(1)	.204

[1] Not reported.

Table **M-9.**—*Stemmers, or strippers, females, 1904–1919, by city and year*

Year	Baltimore, Md. Hours per week	Baltimore, Md. Rate per hour	Binghamton, N.Y. Hours per week	Binghamton, N.Y. Rate per hour	Boston, Mass. Hours per week	Boston, Mass. Rate per hour	Chicago, Ill. Hours per week	Chicago, Ill. Rate per hour	Cincinnati, Ohio Hours per week	Cincinnati, Ohio Rate per hour	Cleveland, Ohio Hours per week	Cleveland, Ohio Rate per hour
1904	50.6	$0.078			46.0	$0.144	48.0	$0.127	53.0	$0.110	44.0	$0.124
1905	57.9	.072			45.9	.143	48.0	.133	53.1	.114	44.0	.127
1906	53.2	.088			45.0	.142	48.0	.142	51.9	.107	44.0	.131
1907	53.8	.080			45.0	.156	48.0	.146	51.8	.099	44.0	.130
1911	(1)	.081					(1)	.167	(1)	.123		
1912	(1)	.085					(1)	.137	(1)	.130		
1913	(1)	.093					(1)	.144	(1)	.159		
1919	(1)	.192	(1)	$0.216			(1)	.257	(1)	.169		

Year	Dayton, Ohio Hours per week	Dayton, Ohio Rate per hour	Detroit, Mich. Hours per week	Detroit, Mich. Rate per hour	Evansville, Ind. Hours per week	Evansville, Ind. Rate per hour	Key West, Fla. Hours per week	Key West, Fla. Rate per hour	Lancaster, Pa. Hours per week	Lancaster, Pa. Rate per hour	Louisville, Ky. Hours per week	Louisville, Ky. Rate per hour
1904			55.0	$0.065								
1905			53.0	.071								
1906			52.0	.082							51.4	$0.081
1907			52.6	.089							52.2	.094
1911			(1)	.104								
1912	(1)	$0.116	(1)	.117					(1)	$0.105		
1913	(1)	.146	(1)	.115					(1)	.119		
1919	(1)	.194	(1)	.256	(1)	$0.151	(1)	$0.183	(1)	.199		

Year	Milwaukee, Wis. Hours per week	Milwaukee, Wis. Rate per hour	New York, N.Y. Hours per week	New York, N.Y. Rate per hour	Philadelphia, Pa. Hours per week	Philadelphia, Pa. Rate per hour	Pittsburgh and Allegheny, Pa. Hours per week	Pittsburgh and Allegheny, Pa. Rate per hour	Rochester, N.Y. Hours per week	Rochester, N.Y. Rate per hour	Tampa, Fla. Hours per week	Tampa, Fla. Rate per hour
1904	49.8	$0.082	56.5	$0.101	48.6	$0.092	48.9	$0.124	52.7	$0.098	60.0	$0.133
1905	49.8	.082	56.4	.100	46.4	.099	49.0	.119	51.0	.105	60.0	.134
1906	49.8	.067	55.8	.105	46.3	.096	46.5	.120	51.0	.105	60.0	.142
1907	49.8	.094	55.3	.111	49.4	.102	46.7	.131	50.7	.104	60.0	.136
1911			(1)	.108	(1)	.104					(1)	.111
1912			(1)	.134	(1)	.111					(1)	.121
1913			(1)	.134	(1)	.117					(1)	.123
1919			(1)	.233	(1)	.188					(1)	.196

1 Not reported.

N.—TRANSPORTATION

Railroad trainmen.—The wage data for this group of railroad employees, which includes brakemen, conductors, engineers, and firemen, were taken from the Fifteenth Annual Report of the Commissioner of Labor Statistics. Similar, but not strictly comparable, data for later years may be found in reports of the United States Railroad Labor Board and the Interstate Commerce Commission, reproduced in the Monthly Labor Review of November, 1920; April, 1922; June, 1924; and February and November, 1927.

Street-railway men.—Wage data for street-railway conductors and motormen are taken from the Fifteenth Annual Report of the Commissioner of Labor Statistics and from bulletins of the Bureau of Labor Statistics Nos. 204, 302, 325, 354, 388, 404, 431, 457, and 482. No report of similar character is available for the periods from 1900 to 1914 nor from 1915 to 1920.

Longshoremen and teamsters.—The sources from which wage data for these employees were taken are the Fifteenth Annual Report of the Commissioner of Labor Statistics and the bulletins of the Bureau of Labor Statistics Nos. 143, 171, 194, 214, 245, 259, 274, 286, 302, 325, 354, 388, 404, 431, 457, and 482.

A great variation of terms is used in the classification of teamsters, drivers, etc. In some localities they are designated as 1-horse, 2-horse, etc.; in others as 1-ton, 2-ton, etc., and in still others as ice, milk, laundry, furniture, etc. This method of reporting makes comparison for the various cities difficult. Wherever possible, the selection of a uniform designation for the various years was made in each city.

The wage data reported here for street-railway conductors and motormen for the period from 1920 to 1928 and for longshoremen and teamsters for the period from 1913 to 1928, inclusive, represent minimum rates of wages paid to union workers through agreements with their employers or group of employers. The hours represent the maximum which may be worked, beyond which extra for overtime is usually paid. The reports for other periods were copied by agents of the Bureau of Labor Statistics direct from pay rolls or other records of representative establishments in the various localities. Both hours and earnings as shown here represent averages computed from these reports. For further explanation of the source and method of computing these details, see "Building trades," page 153.

429

TABLE **N–1.**—*Brakemen, railroad, 1840–1900, by year and State*

Year and State	Sex	Lowest, highest, and average—		Year and State	Sex	Lowest, highest, and average—	
		Hours per week	Rate per day (dollars)			Hours per week	Rate per day (dollars)
1840:				**1875:**			
Massachusetts____	M.	70–70–70	1.00–1.15–1.07	Massachusetts____	M.	70–70–70	2.00–2.25–2.07
1841:				Pennsylvania_____	M.	(¹)	1.25–2.03–1.79
Massachusetts____	M.	70–70–70	1.00–1.15–1.06	**1876:**			
1842:				Massachusetts____	M.	70–70–70	1.75–2.25–1.91
Massachusetts____	M.	70–70–70	1.00–1.15–1.09	Pennsylvania_____	M.	56–98–67	.85–2.25–1.72
1843:				**1877:**			
Massachusetts____	M.	70–70–70	1.00–1.15–1.12	Massachusetts____	M.	70–70–70	1.65–1.80–1.74
1844:				New Jersey_____	M.	70–70–70	1.15–1.80–1.76
Massachusetts____	M.	70–70–70	1.00–1.15–1.04	Pennsylvania_____	M.	56–91–71	1.00–2.75–1.75
1845:				**1878:**			
Massachusetts____	M.	70–70–70	1.00–1.15–1.09	Massachusetts____	M.	70–70–70	1.65–1.80–1.73
1846:				Pennsylvania_____	M.	56–84–72	.82–1.84–1.60
Massachusetts____	M.	70–70–70	1.00–1.15–1.07	**1879:**			
1847:				Massachusetts____	M.	70–70–70	1.65–1.80–1.75
Massachusetts____	M.	70–70–70	1.00–1.15–1.08	Missouri_____	M.	63–63–63	1.83–1.83–1.83
1848:				New Jersey_____	(¹)	24–72–59	1.20–1.80–1.57
Massachusetts____	M.	70–70–70	1.00–1.15–1.13	Pennsylvania_____	(¹)	70–77–74	.66–2.57–1.65
1849:				**1880:**			
Massachusetts____	M.	70–70–70	1.00–1.15–1.11	Illinois_____	M.	(¹)	1.46–1.85–1.73
1850:				Massachusetts____	M.	70–70–70	1.75–2.00–1.90
Massachusetts____	M.	70–70–70	1.00–1.15–1.11	New Jersey_____	(¹)	55–72–67	1.47–1.90–1.79
1851:				**1881:**			
Massachusetts____	M.	70–70–70	1.00–1.15–1.10	Arkansas_____	M.	60–60–60	1.70–1.85–1.77
1852:				Indiana_____	M.	(¹)	.96–2.00–1.65
Massachusetts____	M.	70–70–70	1.00–1.15–1.06	Massachusetts____	M.	70–70–70	1.75–2.00–1.91
1853:				New Jersey_____	M.	(¹)	1.48–1.48–1.48
Massachusetts____	M.	70–70–70	1.00–1.15–1.06	**1882:**			
1854:				Illinois_____	M.	(¹)	.99–1.97–1.37
Massachusetts____	M.	70–70–70	1.00–1.34–1.11	Indiana_____	M.	(¹)	1.43–2.05–1.61
1855:				Massachusetts____	M.	70–70–70	1.75–2.00–1.90
Massachusetts____	M.	70–70–70	1.60–1.34–1.13	Michigan_____	M.	72–72–72	1.90–1.90–1.90
1856:				New York_____	M.	54–54–54	1.75–2.00–1.83
Massachusetts____	M.	70–70–70	1.00–1.34–1.21	**1883:**			
1857:				Indiana_____	M.	(¹)	1.15–2.00–1.80
Massachusetts____	M.	70–70–70	1.00–1.25–1.15	Massachusetts____	M.	70–70–70	1.75–2.50–1.78
1858:				Michigan_____	M.	(¹)	1.32–1.81–1.53
Massachusetts____	M.	70–70–70	1.17–1.25–1.21	Ohio_____	M.	60–60–60	1.61–1.61–1.61
1859:				**1884:**			
Massachusetts____	M.	70–70–70	1.17–1.25–1.21	Indiana_____	M.	(¹)	1.20–2.50–1.61
1860:				Iowa_____	M.	49–84–65	1.40–2.00–1.71
Massachusetts____	M.	70–70–70	1.17–1.25–1.22	Massachusetts____	M.	70–70–70	1.75–2.00–1.82
1861:				Michigan_____	M.	(¹)	1.15–2.00–1.56
Massachusetts____	M.	70–70–70	1.17–1.25–1.22	New Jersey_____	M.	70–84–81	1.15–1.75–1.19
1862:				Pennsylvania_____	M.	(¹)	1.36–1.40–1.40
Massachsetts_____	M.	70–70–70	1.17–1.25–1.22	Wisconsin_____	M.	(¹)	1.46–1.52–1.47
1863:				**1885:**			
Massachusetts____	M.	70–70–70	1.25–1.40–1.34	Illinois_____	M.	60–60–60	1.60–1.83–1.72
1864:				Indiana_____	M.	(¹)	1.50–3.00–1.81
Massachusetts____	M.	70–70–70	1.25–1.40–1.34	Iowa_____	M.	49–84–59	1.33–1.94–1.69
1865:				Kansas_____	M.	63–91–74	1.50–2.25–1.81
Massachusetts____	M.	70–70–70	1.40–1.92–1.73	Massachusetts____	M.	70–70–70	1.75–2.00–1.84
1866:				Michigan_____	M.	(¹)	1.10–2.65–1.62
Massachusetts____	M.	70–70–70	1.40–1.92–1.73	Missouri_____	M.	(¹)	1.48–1.64–1.59
1867:				New Jersey_____	M.	(¹)	.99–1.32–1.18
Massachusetts____	M.	70–70–70	1.65–2.30–2.09	Ohio_____	M.	60–60–60	1.75–1.75–1.75
1868:				Pennsylvania_____	M.	(¹)	1.41–1.41–1.41
Massachusetts____	M.	70–70–70	2.00–2.30–2.19	**1886:**			
1869:				Illinois_____	M.	60–70–61	1.60–2.50–2.10
Massachusetts____	M.	70–70–70	2.00–2.11–2.02	Indiana_____	M.	60–60–60	1.00–2.00–1.63
1870:				Iowa_____	M.	49–98–65	.75–3.50–1.73
Massachusetts____	M.	70–70–70	2.00–2.00–2.00	Kansas_____	M.	42–112–72	1.55–2.53–1.87
1871:				Kentucky_____	M.	55–66–57	1.50–2.00–1.84
Massachusetts____	M.	70–70–70	2.00–2.25–2.13	Louisiana_____	M.	60–60–60	2.08–2.30–2.19
1872:				Massachusetts____	M.	70–70–70	1.75–2.00–1.86
Massachusetts____	M.	70–70–70	2.00–2.25–2.11	Mississippi_____	M.	60–60–60	1.83–1.92–1.88
1873:				New Jersey_____	M.	(¹)	1.15–1.48–1.26
Massachusetts____	M.	70–70–70	2.00–2.25–2.10	New York_____	M.	72–72–72	1.38–1.38–1.38
Pennsylvania_____	M.	(¹)	2.33–2.33–2.33	Ohio_____	M.	75–75–75	1.75–1.75–1.75
1874:				Tennessee_____	M.	72–72–72	1.75–1.75–1.75
Illinois_____	M.	(¹)	1.03–1.71–1.44	Wyoming_____	M.	60–60–60	2.31–2.31–2.31
Indiana_____	M.	(¹)	.80–1.48–1.41	**1887:**			
Iowa_____	M.	(¹)	1.58–1.58–1.58	Connecticut_____	M.	(¹)	1.15–2.75–1.43
Massachusetts____	M.	70–70–70	1.75–2.25–1.85	Delaware_____	M.	(¹)	.49–1.90–1.59
Ohio_____	M.	(¹)	1.48–1.48–1.48	Do_____	M.	(¹)	².15–.15–.15
Pennsylvania_____	M.	(¹)	1.98–1.98–1.98				

¹ Not reported. ² Per hour.

TABLE N-1.—*Brakemen, railroad, 1840–1900, by year and State*—Continued

Year and State	Sex	Lowest, highest, and average—		Year and State	Sex	Lowest, highest, and average—	
		Hours per week	Rate per day (dollars)			Hours per week	Rate per day (dollars)
1887—Continued.				1893—Continued.			
Florida	M.	(¹)	0. 75–1. 50–1. 25	Kansas	M.	(¹)	1. 50–2. 47–1. 92
Illinois	(¹)	(¹)	1. 61–1. 61–1. 61	Maryland	M.	60–84–72	1. 71–2. 14–1. 97
Kansas	M.	68–84–71	1. 53–2. 31–1. 86	Michigan	M.	35–1. 40–81	. 74–3. 00–1. 73
Maine	M.	(¹)	. 85–1. 71–1. 39	Minnesota	M.	(¹)	³ 1. 15–1. 64–1. 27
Maryland	M.	70–70–70	. 82–3. 25–1. 69	Montana	M.	56–63–62	1. 91–3. 29–2. 40
Massachusetts	M.	70–70–70	1. 15–2. 75–1. 88	Do	M.	(¹)	(⁴)
Michigan	M.	70–70–70	. 82–2. 30–1. 71	New York	M.	70–70–70	1. 70–1. 71–1. 70
Missouri	M.	(¹)	1. 32–2. 79–1. 96	Pennsylvania	M.	60–84–72	1. 97–2. 86–2. 42
Do	(¹)	(¹)	1. 33–1. 98–1. 97	1894:			
Nebraska	(¹)	49–70–66	1. 33–2. 60–1. 86	Indiana	M.	70–84–78	1. 33–3. 31–2. 15
New Hampshire	M.	(¹)	1. 00–1. 50–1. 29	Iowa	M.	70–77–74	2. 00–2. 14–2. 07
New Jersey	M.	(¹)	. 99–2. 50–1. 79	Minnesota	M.	(¹)	³ 1. 15–1. 32–1. 19
New York	M.	(¹)	1. 00–2. 30–1. 72	Montana	M.	(¹)	1. 82–2. 92–2. 12
North Carolina	M.	56–84–72	. 54–1. 19– . 89	New Hampshire	M.	45–74–58	1. 21–2. 00–1. 53
Ohio	M.	70–70–70	1. 80–2. 50–1. 92	West Virginia	M.	(¹)	. 77–1. 79–1. 31
Oregon	M.	(¹)	. 99–2. 30–1. 97	1895:			
Pennsylvania	M.	(¹)	. 82–2. 75–1. 79	Indiana	M.	(¹)	1. 50–3. 13–2. 19
Do	M.	(¹)	², 16– . 16– . 16	Minnesota	M.	(¹)	³ 1. 15–1. 32–1. 18
Rhode Island	M.	(¹)	. 38–1. 81–1. 56	Montana	M.	(¹)	1. 99–2. 92–2. 11
Virginia	M.	(¹)	1. 25–1. 90–1. 60	Wisconsin	(¹)	70–70–70	2. 50–2. 50–2. 50
West Virginia	M.	(¹)	1. 50–1. 60–1. 51	1896:			
Wisconsin	M.	(¹)	1. 48–2. 80–1. 77	Alabama	M.	(¹)	1. 75–1. 75–1. 75
1888:				Colorado	M.	70–84–78	2. 50–3. 25–2 95
Colorado	M.	(¹)	1. 84–2. 63–2. 29	Indiana	M.	(¹)	1. 43–3. 75–2. 18
Indiana	M.	70–84–78	1. 22–2. 47–1. 79	Kansas	M.	56–91–76	1. 64–2. 50–2. 05
Iowa	M.	42–89–67	1. 33–2. 17–1. 84	Minnesota	M.	60–60–60	³ 1. 15–1. 35–1. 21
Kansas	M.	56–77–64	1. 33–2. 35–1. 79	Montana	M.	(¹)	1, 57–2. 47–2. 04
Massachusetts	M.	70–70–70	1. 75–2. 00–1. 87	New Jersey	M.	60–60–60	2. 00–2. 00–2. 00
Missouri	(¹)	(¹)	1. 25–1. 97–1. 80	South Carolina	M.	(¹)	. 71– . 71– . 71
New Jersey	(¹)	70–70–70	1. 57–1. 57–1. 57	Tennessee	M.	(¹)	1. 79–1. 79–1. 79
Rhode Island	M.	(¹)	2. 00–2. 00–2. 00	1897:			
1889:				Kansas	(¹)	70–84–77	1. 96–1. 97–1. 97
Indiana	M.	56–84–79	1. 25–2. 50–1. 87	Do	(¹)	70–91–77	⁴, 02– . 02– . 02
Iowa	M.	42–84–59	1. 00–2. 32–1. 84	Maryland	(¹)	42–70–67	1. 16–2. 20–1. 90
Kansas	M.	42–84–70	1. 17–2. 88–1. 80	Michigan	(¹)	56–91–81	1. 48–2. 12–1. 70
Massachusetts	M.	70–70–70	1. 75–2. 00–1. 86	Do	(¹)	77–84–79	(⁶)
1890:				Montana	(¹)	(¹)	1. 78–2. 50–2. 04
Indiana	M.	63–84–79	1. 13–2. 80–1. 98	1898:			
Kansas	M.	(¹)	1. 80–1. 80–1. 80	Indiana	(¹)	42–84–71	1. 25–3. 05–2. 16
Massachusetts	M.	70–70–70	1. 75–2. 00–1. 83	Kansas	M.	56–77–70	1. 97–2. 12–2. 11
Ohio	(¹)	42–91–67	1. 00–2. 43–1. 86	Do	M.	49–112–74	(⁷)
1891:				Missouri	(¹)	56–84–69	1. 35–2. 18–1. 96
Indiana	M.	63–84–77	1. 12–2. 70–2. 05	Nebraska	(¹)	56–112–70	1. 00–3. 46–1. 92
Maine	M.	70–91–74	1 55–1. 73–1. 66	Do	(¹)		⁵, 02– . 02– . 02
Massachusetts	M.	70–70–70	1. 75–2. 00–1. 93	New Jersey	M.	(¹)	1. 71–1. 80–1. 79
Minnesota	M.	(¹)	1. 15–1. 64–1. 27	Washington	(¹)	(¹)	1. 96–2. 50–2. 23
1892:				1899:			
Indiana	M.	63–84–76	1. 25–2. 83–2. 14	Massachusetts	M.	(¹)	1. 50–2. 20–1. 87
Maryland	M.	63–70–69	1. 20–2. 20–1. 94	Pennsylvania	M.	(¹)	1. 50–2. 30–1. 79
Massachusetts	M.	70–70–70	1. 75–2. 00–1. 93	Do	(¹)	(¹)	(⁶)
Minnesota	M.	(¹)	³ 1. 15–1. 64–1. 27	1900:			
1893:				Massachusetts	M.	(¹)	1. 50–2. 20–1. 87
Illinois	M.	65–65–65	1. 71–2. 00–1. 81	Pennsylvania	M.	(¹)	1. 50–2. 30–1. 84
Indiana	M.	70–84–79	1. 31–3. 06–2. 16	Do	(¹)	(¹)	(⁸)

¹ Not reported.
² Per hour.
³ And board.
⁴ $0.02–$0.025–$0.0221 per mile.

⁵ Per mile.
⁶ $0.019–$0.02–$0.02 per mile.
⁷ $0.02–$0.0225–$0.0201 per mile.
⁸ $0.15–$0.16–$0.155 per hour.

Table **N-2.**—*Conductors, passenger, railroad, 1840–1900, by year and State*

Year and State	Sex	Hours per week	Rate per day (dollars)	Year and State	Sex	Hours per week	Rate per day (dollars)
		Lowest, highest, and average—				Lowest, highest, and average—	
1840:				**1872—Continued.**			
Massachusetts....	M.	70–70–70	2.11–2.11–2.11	Massachusetts....	M.	70–70–70	3.29–3.84–3.50
1841:				Minnesota........	M.	(1)	3.29–3.29.29
Massachusetts....	M.	70–70–70	2.11–2.11–2.11	Ohio.............	M.	60–60–60	4.11–4.11–4.11
1842:				Virginia.........	M.	(1)	2.63–2.63–2.63
Massachusetts....	M.	70–70–70	2.11–2.11–2.11	**1873:**			
1843:				California........	M.	(1)	3.62–3.78–3.70
Massachusetts....	M.	70–70–70	2.11–2.11–2.11	Illinois..........	M.	(1)	2.74–3.29–2.82
1844:				Louisiana........	M.	(1)	3.29–3.29–3.29
Massachusetts....	M.	70–70–70	2.11–2.11–2.11	Massachusetts....	M.	70–70–70	3.29–3.84–3.45
1845:				Minnesota........	M.	(1)	3.29–3.29–3.29
Massachusetts....	M.	70–70–70	2.11–2.11–2.11	Ohio.............	M.	60–60–60	4.11–4.11–4.11
1846:				Virginia.........	M.	(1)	2.63–2.63–2.63
Massachusetts....	M.	70–70–70	2.30–2.30–2.30	**1874:**			
1847:				California........	M.	(1)	3.62–3.78–3.72
Massachusetts....	M.	70–70–70	2.30–2.30–2.30	Illinois..........	M.	(1)	2.74–3.29–2.88
1848:				Louisiana........	M.	(1)	3.29–3.29–3.29
Massachusetts....	M.	70–70–70	2.30–2.30–2.30	Massachusetts....	M.	70–70–70	2.96–3.84–3.32
1850:				Minnesota........	M.	(1)	3.29–3.29–3.29
Massachusetts....	M.	70–70–70	2.30–2.30–2.30	Ohio.............	M.	60–60–60	4.11–4.11–4.11
1851:				Pennsylvania.....	M.	(1)	2.90–2.90–2.90
Massachusetts....	M.	70–70–70	2.30–2.30–2.30	Virginia.........	M.	(1)	2.63–2.63–2.63
1852:				**1875:**			
Massachusetts....	M.	70–70–70	2.30–2.30–2.30	California........	M.	(1)	3.62–3.78–3.72
1853:				Illinois..........	M.	(1)	2.74–3.29–2.90
Massachusetts....	M.	70–70–70	2.49–2.49–2.49	Louisiana........	M.	(1)	3.29–3.29–3.29
1854:				Massachusetts....	M.	70–70–70	2.96–3.84–3.15
Massachusetts....	M.	70–70–70	2.49–2.49–2.49	Minnesota........	M.	(1)	3.29–3.29–3.29
1855:				Ohio.............	M.	60–60–60	3.62–3.62–3.62
Massachusetts....	M.	70–70–70	2.49–2.49–2.49	Pennsylvania.....	M.	(1)	1.54–3.42–2.88
1856:				Virginia.........	M.	(1)	2.63–2.63–2.63
Massachusetts....	M.	70–70–70	2.49–2.49–2.49	**1876:**			
1857:				California........	M.	(1)	3.62–3.78–3.72
Massachusetts....	M.	70–70–70	2.49–2.49–2.49	Illinois..........	M.	(1)	2.47–3.29–2.79
1858:				Louisiana........	M.	(1)	3.29–3.29–3.29
Massachusetts....	M.	70–70–70	2.83–2.83–2.83	Massachusetts....	M.	70–70–70	2.96–3.45–3.17
1859:				Minnesota........	M.	(1)	3.29–3.29–3.29
Massachusetts....	M.	70–70–70	3.20–3.20–3.20	Ohio.............	M.	60–60–60	3.29–3.29–3.29
1860:				Pennsylvania.....	M.	56–98–67	1.16–4.23–2.84
Massachusetts....	M.	70–70–70	3.20–3.20–3.20	Virginia.........	M.	(1)	2.63–2.63–2.63
1861:				**1877:**			
Massachusetts....	M.	70–70–70	3.20–3.20–3.20	California........	M.	(1)	3.62–3.78–3.72
1862:				Illinois..........	M.	(1)	2.47–3.29–2.87
Massachusetts....	M.	70–70–70	3.20–3.20–3.20	Louisiana........	M.	(1)	3.29–3.29–3.29
1863:				Massachusetts....	M.	70–70–70	3.29–3.45–3.34
Massachusetts....	M.	70–70–70	3.20–3.20–3.20	Minnesota........	M.	(1)	3.29–3.29–3.29
1864:				Ohio.............	M.	60–60–60	3.29–3.29–3.29
Massachusetts....	M.	70–70–70	3.20–3.20–3.20	Pennsylvania.....	M.	(1)	1.33–3.66–2.78
1865:				Virginia.........	M.	(1)	2.63–2.63–2.63
Massachusetts....	M.	70–70–70	3.84–3.84–3.84	**1878:**			
1866:				California........	M.	(1)	3.62–3.78–3.69
Massachusetts....	M.	70–70–70	3.84–3.84–3.84	Illinois..........	M.	(1)	2.47–2.96–2.75
1867:				Louisiana........	M.	(1)	3.29–3.29–3.29
Massachusetts....	M.	70–70–70	3.84–3.84–3.84	Massachusetts....	M.	70–70–70	3.29–3.45–3.37
1868:				Minnesota........	M.	(1)	3.29–3.29–3.29
Massachusetts....	M.	70–70–70	3.84–3.84–3.84	Ohio.............	M.	60–60–60	3.29–3.29–3.29
1869:				Pennsylvania.....	M.	56–84–65	1.48–3.58–2.60
Massachusetts....	M.	70–70–70	3.84–3.84–3.84	Virginia.........	M.	(1)	2.63–2.63–2.63
1870:				**1879:**			
California........	M.	(1)	4.11–4.11–4.11	California........	M.	(1)	3.62–3.78–3.68
Illinois..........	M.	(1)	2.74–3.29–2.81	Illinois..........	M.	(1)	2.47–2.96–2.75
Louisiana........	M.	(1)	3.29–3.29–3.29	Louisiana........	M.	(1)	3.29–3.29–3.29
Massachusetts....	M.	70–70–70	3.29–3.84–3.50	Massachusetts....	M.	70–70–70	3.29–3.45–3.36
Ohio.............	M.	60–60–60	4.11–4.11 4.11	Minnesota........	M.	(1)	3.29–3.29–3.29
Virginia.........	M.	(1)	2.63–2.63–2.63	Ohio.............	M.	60–60–60	3.29–3.29–3.29
1871:				Pennsylvania.....	(1)	(1)	1.25–3.46–2.60
California........	M.	(1)	3.62–3.78–3.72	Virginia.........	M.	(1)	2.63–2.63–2.63
Illinois..........	M.	(1)	2.74–3.29–2.81	**1880:**			
Louisiana........	M.	(1)	3.29–3.29–3.29	California........	(1)	(1)	3.62–3.78–3.69
Massachusetts....	M.	70–70–70	3.29–3.84–3.42	Illinois..........	M.	(1)	2.30–3.26–2.99
Ohio.............	M.	60–60–60	4.11–4.11–4.11	Louisiana........	M.	(1)	3.29–3.29–3.29
Virginia.........	M.	(1)	2.63–2.63–2.63	Massachusetts....	M.	70–70–70	3.29–3.84–3.52
1872:				Minnesota........	M.	(1)	3.29–3.29–3.29
California........	M.	(1)	3.62–3.78–3.70	Ohio.............	M.	60–60–60	2.96–3.29–3.25
Illinois..........	M.	(1)	2.74–3.29–2.81	Pennsylvania.....	M.	70–70–70	2.86–2.86–2.86
Louisiana........	M.	(1)	3.29–3.29–3.29	Virginia.........	M.	(1)	2.63–2.63–2.63

1 Not reported.

TABLE N-2.—*Conductors, passenger, railroad, 1840-1900, by year and State—* Continued

Year and State	Sex	Hours per week	Rate per day (dollars)	Year and State	Sex	Hours per week	Rate per day (dollars)
1881:				**1887—Continued.**			
California	M.	(1)	3.62-3.78-3.68	Minnesota	M.	(1)	3.62-3.62-3.62
Illinois	M.	(1)	2.74-2.96-2.77	Missouri	M.	(1)	1.97-3.75-3.06
Indiana	M.	(1)	1.73-4.00-3.13	Do	(1)	(1)	2.47-3.33-3.29
Louisana	M.	(1)	3.29-3.29-3.29	Nebraska	(1)	49-70-49	2.50-3.32-2.96
Massachusetts	M.	70-70-70	3.29-3.84-3.44	New Jersey	M.	(1)	2.50-2.79-2.68
Minnesota	M.	(1)	3.29-3.29-3.29	New York	M.	(1)	2.14-3.29-2.83
Ohio	M.	60-60-60	2.96-3.29-3.25	North Carolina	M.	70-84-72	1.17-3.00-2.68
Virginia	M.	(1)	2.63-2.63-2.63	Ohio	M.	60-60-60	3.60-3.60-3.60
1882:				Oregon	M.	(1)	3.29-3.29-3.29
California	M.	(1)	3.62-3.78-3.66	Pennsylvania	M.	70-70-70	2.00-3.40-2.75
Illinois	M.	(1)	1.64-3.26-2.66	Rhode Island	M.	(1)	2.79-2.96-2.80
Indiana	M.	(1)	2.35-4.00-3.32	Virginia	M.	(1)	2.63-3.06-2.83
Louisiana	M.	(1)	3.29-3.29-3.29	West Virginia	M.	(1)	2.00-2.30-2.15
Massachusetts	M.	70-70-70	3.29-3.84-3.48	Wisconsin	M.	(1)	1.48-3.29-3.03
Minnesota	M.	(1)	3.29-3.29-3.29	**1888:**			
Ohio	M.	60-60-60	2.96-3.29-3.25	California	M.	(1)	3.62-3.78-3.69
Virginia	M.	(1)	2.63-2.63-2.63	Colorado	M.	(1)	3.29-3.68-3.51
1883:				Illinois	M.	(1)	2.74-3.29-2.87
California	M.	(1)	3.62-3.78-3.68	Indiana	M.	(1)	2.14-3.98-3.19
Illinois	M.	(1)	2.74-2.96-2.76	Iowa	M.	35-84-61	1.60-4.71-3.41
Indiana	M.	(1)	2.20-4.37-3.33	Kansas	M.	56-74-63	2.30-4.65-3.01
Louisiana	M.	(1)	3.29-3.29-3.29	Louisiana	M.	(1)	3.29-3.29-3.29
Massachusetts	M.	70-70-70	3.29-3.84-3.47	Massachusetts	M.	70-70-70	3.29-3.84-3.45
Minnesota	M.	(1)	3.62-3.62-3.62	Minnesota	M.	(1)	3.62-3.62-3.62
Ohio	M.	60-60-60	3.35-3.35-3.35	Missouri	(1)	(1)	1.53-3.33-3.13
Virginia	M.	(1)	2.63-2.63-2.63	Ohio	M.	60-60-60	3.60-3.60-3.60
1884:				Virginia	M.	(1)	3.06-3.06-3.06
California	M.	(1)	3.62-3.78-3.69	**1889:**			
Illinois	M.	(1)	2.74-3.29-3.00	California	M.	(1)	3.62-3.78-3.70
Indiana	M.	(1)	2.25-4.30-3.22	Illinois	M.	(1)	2.74-3.29-2.90
Iowa	M.	35-84-53	2.50-3.58-3.18	Indiana	M.	(1)	2.37-4.50-3.23
Louisiana	M.	(1)	3.29-3.29-3.29	Iowa	M.	35-98-55	1.67-3.64-3.26
Massachusetts	M.	70-70-70	3.29-3.84-3.50	Kansas	M.	56-77-69	2.78-4.00-3.27
Minnesota	M.	(1)	3.62-3.62-3.62	Louisiana	M.	(1)	3.29-3.29-3.29
Ohio	M.	60-60-60	3.35-3.35-3.35	Massachusetts	M.	70-70-70	3.29-3.84-3.44
Pennsylvania	M.	(1)	2.24-2.24-2.24	Minnesota	M.	(1)	3.62-3.62-3.62
Virginia	M.	(1)	2.63-2.63-2.63	Ohio	M.	60-60-60	3.60-3.60-3.60
Wisconsin	M.	(1)	2.92-2.92-2.92	Virginia	M.	(1)	3.00-3.00-3.00
1885:				**1890:**			
California	M.	(1)	3.62-3.78-3.69	California	M.	(1)	3.62-3.78-3.70
Illinois	M.	(1)	2.74-3.29-2.91	Illinois	M.	(1)	2.74-3.29-2.86
Indiana	M.	(1)	2.50-4.00-3.00	Indiana	M.	(1)	2.50-5.00-3.32
Iowa	M.	49-77-68	2.00-3.56-2.96	Louisiana	M.	(1)	3.44-3.44-3.44
Kansas	M.	56-70-69	2.47-3.41-3.25	Massachusetts	M.	70-70-70	3.29-3.84-3.43
Louisiana	M.	(1)	3.29-3.29-3.29	Minnesota	M.	(1)	3.62-3.62-3.62
Massachusetts	M.	70-70-70	3.29-3.84-3.50	Ohio	M.	60-60-60	3.60-3.68-3.61
Minnesota	M.	(1)	3.62-3.62-3.62	Virginia	M.	(1)	3.00-3.00-3.00
Missouri	M.	(1)	2.96-3.29-3.24	**1891:**			
Ohio	M.	60-60-60	3.52-3.52-3.52	California	M.	(1)	3.62-4.11-3.87
Pennsylvania	M.	(1)	2.50-2.50-2.50	Illinois	M.	(1)	2.29-3.95-3.47
Virginia	M.	(1)	2.63-2.63-2.63	Indiana	M.	(1)	2.50-4.10-3.70
1886:				Louisiana	M.	(1)	4.11-4.11-4.11
California	M.	(1)	3.62-3.78-3.69	Massachusetts	M.	70-70-70	3.29-3.84-3.42
Illinois	M.	(1)	2.74-3.29-2.91	Minnesota	M.	(1)	4.11-4.11-4.11
Indiana	M.	(1)	2.23-4.40-2.58	Ohio	M.	60-60-60	3.69-3.76-3.70
Iowa	M.	25-84-58	1.60-4.00-3.21	Virginia	M.	(1)	3.16-3.16-3.16
Kansas	M.	42-84-64	2.90-3.88-3.31	**1892:**			
Louisiana	M.	(1)	3.29-3.29-3.29	California	M.	(1)	3.62-4.11-3.87
Massachusetts	M.	70-70-70	3.29-3.84-3.53	Illinois	M.	(1)	2.29-3.95-3.48
Minnesota	M.	(1)	3.62-3.62-3.62	Indiana	M.	(1)	3.00-4.82-3.74
Ohio	M.	60-60-60	3.52-3.52-3.52	Louisiana	M.	(1)	4.27-4.27-4.27
Virginia	M.	(1)	2.63-2.63-2.63	Maryland	M.	63-70-68	2.45-4.00-3.48
1887:				Massachusetts	M.	70-70-70	3.29-3.84-3.42
California	M.	(1)	3.62-3.78-3.69	Minnesota	M.	(1)	4.11-4.11-4.11
Connecticut	M.	(1)	1.81-1.97-1.89	Ohio	M.	60-60-60	3.52-3.59-3.53
Florida	M.	(1)	1.64-3.00-2.81	Virginia	M.	(1)	3.02-3.02-3.02
Illinois	M.	(1)	2.74-3.29-2.85	**1893:**			
Do	(1)	(1)	3.19-3.19-3.19	California	M.	(1)	3.62-4.11-3.86
Kansas	M.	49-84-67	2.66-3.84-3.23	Illinois	M.	(1)	3.29-3.95-3.46
Louisiana	M.	(1)	3.29-3.29-3.29	Indiana	M.	(1)	2.63-6.12-3.51
Maryland	M.	(1)	1.64-3.98-2.82	Kansas	M.	(1)	3.29-4.11-3.48
Massachusetts	M.	70-70-70	1.60-3.84-3.28	Louisiana	M.	(1)	4.97-4.97-4.97
Michigan	M.	(1)	1.48-3.00-2.54	Massachusetts	M.	(1)	3.29-3.29-3.29

1 Not reported.

TABLE **N-2.**—*Conductors, passenger, railroad, 1840–1900, by year and State*—
Continued

Year and State	Sex	Lowest, highest, and average—		Year and State	Sex	Lowest, highest, and average—	
		Hours per week	Rate per day (dollars)			Hours per week	Rate per day (dollars)
1893—Continued.				1896—Continued.			
Minnesota	M.	(¹)	4. 11–4. 11–4. 11	Ohio	M.	60–60–60	3. 56–3. 56–3. 56
Ohio	M.	60–60–60	3. 52–3. 59–3. 53	Virginia	M.	(¹)	3. 05–3. 05–3. 05
Virginia	M.	(¹)	3. 14–3. 14–3. 14	1897:			
1894:				California	M.	(¹)	3. 62–4. 11–3. 81
California	M.	(¹)	3. 62–4. 11–3. 85	Illinois	M.	(¹)	3. 29–3. 95–3. 58
Illinois	M.	(¹)	3. 29–3. 95–3. 56	Louisiana	M.	(¹)	5. 04–5. 04–5. 04
Indiana	M.	(¹)	2. 63–6. 12–3. 50	Massachusetts	M.	(¹)	3. 29–3. 29–3. 29
Louisiana	M.	(¹)	3. 97–3. 97–3. 97	Michigan	M.	(¹)	2. 47–3. 95–3. 21
Massachusetts	M.	(¹)	3. 29–3. 29–3. 29	Minnesota	M.	(¹)	3. 70–3. 70–3. 70
Minnesota	M.	(¹)	3. 70–3. 70–3. 70	Ohio	M.	60–60–60	3. 52–3. 52–3. 52
Ohio	M.	60–60–60	3. 45–3. 45–3. 45	Virginia	M.	(¹)	3. 05–3. 05–3. 05
Virginia	M.	(¹)	3. 25–3. 25–3. 25	1898:			
1895:				California	M.	(¹)	3. 62–4. 11–3. 81
California	M.	(¹)	3. 62–4. 11–3. 84	Illinois	M.	(¹)	3. 29–3. 95–3. 53
Illinois	M.	(¹)	3. 29–3. 95–3. 56	Indiana	(¹)	42–84–68	1. 50–6. 11–3. 85
Indiana	M.	(¹)	3. 00–5. 78–3. 93	Louisiana	M.	(¹)	4. 65–4. 65–4. 65
Louisiana	M.	(¹)	4. 58–4. 58–4. 58	Massachusetts	M.	(¹)	3. 29–3. 29–3. 29
Massachusetts	M.	(¹)	3. 29–3. 29–3. 29	Minnesota	M.	(¹)	3. 70–3. 70–3. 70
Minnesota	M.	(¹)	3. 70–3. 70–3. 70	Missouri	M.	56–84–69	1. 80–3. 98–3. 30
Ohio	M.	60–60–60	3. 66–3. 66–3. 66	Nebraska	M.	70–70–70	2. 47–3. 62–3. 42
Virginia	M.	(¹)	3. 12–3. 12–3. 12	Ohio	M.	60–60–60	3. 59–3. 59–3. 59
1896:				Virginia	M.	(¹)	3. 05–3. 05–3. 05
California	M.	(¹)	3. 62–4. 11–3. 82	1899:			
Illinois	M.	(¹)	3. 29–3. 95–3. 55	Massachusetts	(¹)	(¹)	2. 88–3. 84–3. 81
Indiana	M.	(¹)	2. 70–5. 39–3. 62	Pennsylvania	(¹)	(¹)	2. 15–3. 69–3. 22
Louisiana	M.	(¹)	4. 92–4. 92–4. 92	1900:			
Massachusetts	M.	(¹)	3. 29–3. 29–3. 29	Massachusetts	(¹)	(¹)	3. 20–3. 84–3. 83
Minnesota	M.	(¹)	3. 70–3. 70–3. 70	Pennsylvania	(¹)	(¹)	2. 15–3. 69–3. 27

¹ Not reported.

TABLE **N-3.**—*Conductors, freight, railroad, 1840–1900, by year and State*

Year and State	Sex	Lowest, highest, and average—		Year and State	Sex	Lowest, highest, and average—	
		Hours per week	Rate per day (dollars)			Hours per week	Rate per day (dollars)
1840:				1855:			
Massachusetts	M.	70–70–70	1. 54–1. 92–1. 80	Massachusetts	M.	70–70–70	1. 54–1. 92–1. 57
1841:				1856:			
Massachusetts	M.	70–70–70	1. 54–1. 92–1. 75	Massachusetts	M.	70–70–70	1. 54–1. 92–1. 61
1842:				1857:			
Massachusetts	M.	70–70–70	1. 54–1. 92–1. 66	Massachusetts	M.	70–70–70	1. 54–1. 92–1. 60
1843:				1858:			
Massachusetts	M.	70–70–70	1. 54–1. 92–1. 72	Massachusetts	M.	70–70–70	1. 54–1. 92–1. 58
1844:				1859:			
Massachusetts	M.	70–70–70	1. 54–1. 92–1. 64	Massachusetts	M.	70–70–70	1. 54–1. 92–1. 58
1845:				1860:			
Massachusetts	M.	70–70–70	1. 54–1. 92–1. 76	Massachusetts	M.	70–70–70	1. 54–1. 92–1. 64
1846:				1861:			
Massachusetts	M.	70 70–70	1. 54–1. 92–1. 73	Massachusetts	M.	70–70–70	1. 73–1. 92–1. 74
1847:				1862:			
Massachusetts	M.	70–70–70	1. 54–1. 92–1. 70	Massachusetts	M.	70–70–70	1. 73–1. 92–1. 77
1848:				1863:			
Massachusetts	M.	70–70–70	1. 54–1. 92–1. 70	Massachusetts	M.	70–70–70	1. 73–1. 92–1. 83
1849:				1864:			
Massachusetts	M.	70–70–70	1. 54–2. 30–1. 96	Massachusetts	M.	70–70–70	1. 73–1. 92–1. 78
1850:				1865:			
Massachusetts	M.	70–70–70	1. 54–1. 92–1. 68	Massachusetts	M.	70–70–70	2. 49–3. 07–2. 66
1851:				1866:			
Massachusetts	M.	70–70–70	1. 54–1. 92–1. 63	Massachusetts	M.	70–70–70	2. 49–3. 07–2. 57
1852:				1867:			
Massachusetts	M.	70–70–70	1. 54–1. 92–1. 73	Massachusetts	M.	70–70–70	2. 49–3. 07–2. 68
1853:				1868:			
Massachusetts	M.	70–70–70	1. 54–1. 92–1. 58	Massachusetts	M.	70–70–70	2. 49–3. 07–2. 58
1854:				1869:			
Massachusetts	M.	70–70–70	1. 54–1. 92–1. 59	Massachusetts	M.	70–70–70	2. 49–3. 07–2. 57

TABLE **N-3.**—*Conductors, freight, railroad, 1840-1900, by year and State*—Con.

Year and State	Sex	Lowest, highest, and average—		Year and State	Sex	Lowest, highest, and average—	
		Hours per week	Rate per day (dollars)			Hours per week	Rate per day (dollars)
1870:				**1887—Continued.**			
Massachusetts____	M.	70-70-70	2.30-3.45-2.61	Massachusetts____	M.	70-70-70	1.48-2.88-2.51
1871:				Michigan____	M.	(1)	2.30-2.30-2.30
Massachusetts____	M.	70-70-70	2.30-2.49-2.36	Missouri____	M.	(1)	1.97-3.75-2.81
1872:				Do____	(1)	(1)	1.97-3.01-2.89
Massachusetts____	M.	70-70-70	2.30-3.07-2.39	Nebraska____	M.	70-70-70	1.50-3.75-2.49
1873:				New Jersey____	M.	(1)	2.14-2.96-2.55
Massachusetts____	M.	70-70-70	2.30-3.07-2.44	New York____	M.	(1)	1.85-2.87-2.73
1874:				North Carolina____	M.	70-84-71	1.97-2.35-2.22
Massachusetts____	M.	70-70-70	2.30-3.07-2.58	Oregon____	M.	(1)	2.96-3.29-2.97
Pennsylvania____	M.	(1)	2.30-2.30-2.30	Pennsylvania____	M.	70-70-70	1.00-3.50-2.62
1875:				Rhode Island____	M.	(1)	1.97-2.52-2.29
Massachusetts____	M.	70-70-70	2.49-3.07-2.63	Virginia____	M.	(1)	2.30-3.06-2.66
Pennsylvania____	M.	(1)	1.78-2.75-2.25	West Virginia____	M.	(1)	2.00-2.00-2.00
1876:				Wisconsin____	M.	(1)	1.48-3.29-2.71
Massachusetts____	M.	70-70-70	2.30-3.07-2.46	**1888:**			
Pennsylvania____	M.	56-84-67	1.32-2.88-2.39	Colorado____	M.	(1)	2.70-3.68-2.93
1877:				Indiana____	M.	(1)	1.91-3.39-2.60
Massachusetts____	M.	70-70-70	2.30-2.50-2.37	Iowa____	M.	70-89-73	1.60-3.00-2.83
Pennsylvania____	M.	56-84-71	1.30-3.00-2.47	Kansas____	M.	56-77-63	2.00-3.80-2.75
1878:				Massachusetts____	M.	70-70-70	2.88-2.88-2.88
Massachusetts____	M.	70-70-70	2.30-2.50-2.32	Missouri____	(1)	(1)	2.47-3.29-2.98
Pennsylvania____	M.	56-84-84	1.32-2.70-2.32	**1889:**			
1879:				Indiana____	M.	(1)	2.12-3.50-2.79
Massachusetts____	M.	70-70-70	2.25-2.50-2.26	Iowa____	M.	49-84-56	1.75-3.48-2.67
Pennsylvania____	(1)	(1)	.82-2.70-2.11	Kansas____	M.	42-84-70	1.92-3.84-2.72
1880:				Massachusetts____	M.	70-70-70	2.50-2.88-2.54
Illinois____	M.	(1)	2.34-2.79-2.70	**1890:**			
Massachusetts____	M.	70-70-70	2.49-2.88-2.58	Indiana____	M.	(1)	2.50-3.53-2.99
Pennsylvania____	M.	(1)	2.51-2.51-2.51	Massachusetts____	M.	70-70-70	2.50-2.88-2.60
1881:				**1891:**			
Massachusetts____	M.	70-70-70	2.50-2.88-2.60	Indiana____	M.	(1)	1.91-3.77-3.05
1882:				Massachusetts____	M.	70-70-70	2.50-2.88-2.57
Illinois____	M.	(1)	1.32-2.71-2.24	**1892:**			
Massachusetts____	M.	70-70-70	2.50-2.88-2.57	Indiana____	M.	(1)	2.15-3.52-3.02
1883:				Massachusetts____	M.	70-70-70	2.50-2.88-2.57
Massachusetts____	M.	70-70-70	2.50-2.88-2.60	**1993:**			
1884:				Indiana____	M.	(1)	2.50-3.89-3.21
Iowa____	M.	49-84-67	2.00-5.50-2.80	Kansas____	M.	(1)	2.47-2.96-2.85
Massachusetts____	M.	70-70-70	2.50-2.88-2.61	Maryland____	M.	84-84-84	2.57-2.57-2.57
Pennsylvania____	M.	(1)	2.07-2.07-2.07	**1894:**			
Wisconsin____	M.	(1)	2.21-2.21-2.21	Indiana____	M.	(1)	2.49-3.89-3.15
1885:				New Hampshire__	M.	60-60-60	1.79-1.79-1.79
Iowa____	M.	49-84-70	2.00-3.00-2.62	**1895:**			
Do____	M.	(1)	[2]2.70-2.70-2.70	Indiana____	M.	(1)	2.50-3.90-3.11
Kansas____	M.	63-84-73	2.34-3.22-2.69	**1896:**			
Massachusetts____	M.	70-70-70	2.50-2.88-2.64	Indiana____	M.	(1)	2.50-4.85-3.15
Missouri____	M.	(1)	1.97-2.47-2.37	**1897:**			
Ohio____	M.	70-70-70	4.07-4.07-4.07	Michigan____	(1)	77-91-82	2.30-3.00-2.54
Pennsylvania____	M.	(1)	2.10-2.10-2.10	Do____	(1)	84-84-84	[3].02½-.02½-.02½
1886:				**1898:**			
Iowa____	M.	23-84-64	.87-3.00-2.64	Indiana____	(1)	42-84-70	2.00-4.16-3.13
Kansas____	M.	63-84-71	2.09-3.42-2.74	Missouri____	(1)	56-84-69	1.80-3.66-3.21
Massachusetts____	M.	70-70-70	2.50-2.88-2.58'	**1899:**			
1887:				Pennsylvania____	(1)	(1)	2.03-3.00-2.47
Connecticut____	M.	(1)	1.81-2.30-2.18	Do____	(1)	(1)	[4].17- .19-.17½
Florida____	M.	(1)	2.47-3.00-2.52	**1900:**			
Illinois____	(1)	(1)	2.34-2.34-2.34	Pennsylvania____	(1)	(1)	2.00-3.00-2.59
Kansas____	M.	62-84-70	2.09-3.84-2.85	Do____	(1)	(1)	[4].17- .19- 17½
Maryland____	M.	(1)	1.32-3.43-2.46				

[1] Not reported.   [2] Per 100 miles.   [3] Per mile.   [4] Per hour.

TABLE N-4.—*Conductors (not specified), railroad, 1870–1900, by year and State*

Year and State	Sex	Lowest, highest, and average—	
		Hours per week	Rate per day (dollars)
1870:			
Pennsylvania	M.	([1])	2.63-3.45-2.95
1871:			
Pennsylvania	M.	([1])	2.87-3.25-2.97
1872:			
Pennsylvania	M.	([1])	2.96-3.50-3.06
1873:			
Pennsylvania	M.	([1])	2.35-5.20-3.75
1874:			
Illinois	M.	([1])	1.64-3.29-2.49
Indiana	M.	([1])	1.68-2.47-2.35
Iowa	M.	([1])	2.61-2.61-2.61
Ohio	M.	([1])	2.51-2.51-2.51
Pennsylvania	M.	([1])	2.47-4.68-3.50
1875:			
Pennsylvania	M.	([1])	2.47-4.68-3.53
1876:			
Pennsylvania	M.	84-84-84	2.24-4.68-2.87
1877:			
New Jersey	M.	72-72-72	1.81-2.63-2.56
Pennsylvania	M.	70-84-77	1.60-4.68-3.09
1878:			
Pennsylvania	M.	70-84-74	1.32-4.25-2.96
1879:			
Missouri	M.	63-63-63	2.92-2.92-2.92
Pennsylvania	M.	70-70-70	2.17-4.21-3.13
1880::			
Illinois	M.	([1])	2.03-2.03-2.03
New Jersey	([1])	72-72-72	2.75-2.75-2.75
Pennsylvania	M.	([1])	2.66-4.68-3.62
1881:			
Pennsylvania	M.	([1])	2.30-4.68-3.76
1882:			
Pennsylvania	M.	([1])	2.66-2.96-2.81
1883:			
Michigan	M.	([1])	1.64-3.62-2.49
Pennsylvania	M.	([1])	2.63-4.68-3.81
1884:			
California	M.	35-98-73	1.25-2.50-1.79
Michigan	M.	([1])	.82-4.11-2.37
New Jersey	M.	70-70-70	2.14-2.30-2.15
Pennsylvania	M.	([1])	2.15-4.68-2.68
1885:			
Kansas	M.	70-70-70	2.90-2.90-2.90
Michigan	M.	([1])	1.15-3.85-2.48
New Jersey	M.	84-84-84	1.78-2.37-2.09
Pennsylvania	M.	([1])	2.96-4.68-3.69
Do	M.	([1])	2.10-2.10-2.10
1886:			
California	M.	84-84-84	3.29-3.29-3.29
Illinois	M.	70-70-70	3.00-3.00-3.00
Indiana	M.	([1])	2.60-3.00-2.80
Kansas	M.	70-70-70	2.91-2.91-2.91
New Jersey	M.	([1])	1.78-2.37-2.03
Pennsylvania	M.	([1])	2.63-4.68-3.50
1887:			
Connecticut	M.	([1])	1.48-3.29-2.48
Delaware	M.	([1])	.66-2.65-2.41
Florida	M.	([1])	1.97-3.00-2.45
Kansas	M.	70-70-70	2.97-2.97-2.97
Maine	M.	([1])	1.58-1.83-1.66
Maryland	M.	([1])	1.48-3.94-2.39
Massachusetts	M.	([1])	1.32-3.84-2.57
Missouri	M.	([1])	2.63-3.29-2.73
Do	([1])	([1])	1.51-1.51-1.51
Nebraska	([1])	70-70-70	1.93-3.42-2.55
New Hampshire	M.	([1])	2.00-2.00-2.00
New Jersey	M.	([1])	1.15-3.50-2.57
New York	M.	([1])	1.48-3.46-2.52
North Carolina	M.	84-84-84	1.48-1.48-1.48
Oregon	M.	([1])	2.47-3.29-2.97
Pennsylvania	M.	([1])	1.32-4.68-2.51
Rhode Island	M.	([1])	1.97-2.47-2.21
Virginia	M.	([1])	2.30-2.90-2.57
Wisconsin	M.	([1])	1.97-2.96-2.55

Year and State	Sex	Lowest, highest, and average—	
		Hours per week	Rate per day (dollars)
1888:			
Kansas	M.	56-56-56	2.69-2.94-2.71
Missouri	([1])	([1])	1.64-2.89-2.55
New York	M.	([1])	[2] .02-.02-.02
Pennsylvania	M.	([1])	2.35-4.68-2.44
1889:			
Iowa	M.	70-84-75	2.14-3.16-2.91
Kansas	M.	56-70-69	2.00-3.67-2.67
New York	M.	([1])	2.35-2.98-2.58
Do	M.	([1])	[2] .02-.02-.02
Pennsylvania	M.	([1])	2.35-4.68-2.43
1890:			
Iowa	M.	([1])	1.21-3.50-2.97
New York	M.	([1])	2.70-3.50-2.89
Do	M.	([1])	[2] .02-.02-.02
Ohio	M.	35-105-68	1.70-4.68-3.06
Pennsylvania	M.	([1])	2.67-4.68-2.73
1891:			
Indiana	M.	([1])	2.43-3.09-2.83
Kansas	M.	47-98-79	3.41-6.24-4.59
Maine	M.	70-77-74	1.50-3.13-2.70
New York	M.	([1])	2.56-3.53-2.85
Do	([1])	([1])	[2] .02-.02-.02
North Carolina	([1])	([1])	1.64-3.00-2.33
Pennsylvania	M.	([1])	2.38-4.68-2.45
Wisconsin	M.	([1])	2.00-2.00-2.00
1892:			
Indiana	M.	([1])	2.62-3.00-2.76
Maryland	M.	70-70-70	1.90-4.00-3.22
New York	M.	([1])	2.48-3.51-2.72
Do	M.	([1])	[2] .02-.02-.02
North Carolina	([1])	([1])	1.00-3.39-2.47
Pennsylvania	M.	([1])	2.45-4.68-2.49
1893:			
Illinois	M.	72-119-96	2.43-3.57-3.00
Maryland	M.	36-84-66	1.43-2.86-2.08
Michigan	M.	32-112-81	1.32-5.25-2.69
Montana	M.	47-81-66	3.00-5.92-3.94
Do	M.	84-84-84	[2] .03-.03½-.0312
New York	M.	([1])	2.48-3.52-2.76
Do	M.	([1])	[2] .02-.02-.02
North Carolina	M.	([1])	1.29-3.09-2.46
Pennsylvania	M.	72-72-72	2.14-4.30-2.42
1894:			
Iowa	M.	63-70-67	2.97-3.00-2.99
Montana	M.	([1])	2.88-4.56-3.39
New Hampshire	M.	47-72-60	1.50-2.71-2.02
New York	M.	([1])	2.63-5.55-2.84
Do	M.	([1])	[2] .02-.02-.02
North Carolina	M.	([1])	1.15-3.06-2.39
Pennsylvania	M.	([1])	2.52-4.68-2.59
West Virginia	M.	([1])	.82-3.01-2.06
1895:			
Iowa	([1])	([1])	1.39-4.15-3.11
Montana	M.	([1])	3.12-5.75-3.35
New York	M.	([1])	2.50-3.54-2.78
Do	M.	([1])	[2] .02-.02-.02
North Carolina	M.	([1])	.97-3.05-2.44
Pennsylvania	M.	([1])	2.47-4.68-2.54
1896:			
Colorado	M.	49-84-68	3.50-4.25-4.05
Indiana	M.	([1])	2.55-4.85-4.09
Iowa	M.	([1])	1.24-3.80-3.00
Missouri	([1])	([1])	2.08-3.78-3.16
Montana	M.	([1])	2.52-5.02-3.23
New York	M.	70-70-70	1.75-3.49-2.19
Do	M.	([1])	[2] .02-.02-.02
North Carolina	M.	([1])	1.42-2.91-2.40
Pennsylvania	M.	([1])	2.49-4.68-2.55
1897:			
Iowa	([1])	([1])	1.01-3.80-3.18
Kansas	([1])	70-72-71	3.29-3.45-3.37
Do	([1])	56-84-72	[2] .03-.03-.03
Maryland	M.	42-70-67	1.87-3.59-3.09
Montana	([1])	([1])	2.66-3.72-3.10
New York	M.	([1])	[2] .02-.02-.02

[1] Not reported.   [2] Per mile.

TABLE N-4.—*Conductors (not specified), railroad, 1870–1900, by year and State—Continued*

Year and State	Sex	Hours per week	Rate per day (dollars)	Year and State	Sex	Hours per week	Rate per day (dollars)
1897—Continued.				**1898—Continued.**			
New York	M.	63–84–77	1. 80–4. 00–2. 76	Pennsylvania	M.	(1)	2. 46–4. 68–2. 53
North Carolina	(1)	(1)	. 40–2. 84–2. 39	Washington	(1)	(1)	2. 47–3. 33–2. 87
Pennsylvania	M.	(1)	2. 45–4. 68–2. 52	**1899:**			
1898:				Massachusetts	(1)	(1)	2. 00–4. 00–2. 79
Iowa	(1)	(1)	1. 01–4. 15–3. 47	New Jersey	(1)	(1)	2. 89–2. 89–2. 89
Kansas	M.	56–105–75	2. 14–4. 11–3. 29	New York	M.	(1)	2. 96–3. 26–3. 13
Do	M.	70–112–80	[2]. 02⅜–. 03–. 0298	North Carolina	M.	(1)	. 96–3. 32–2. 61
Nebraska	(1)	42–84–71	1. 20–5. 00–3. 15	Pennsylvania	(1)	(1)	2. 15–2. 50–2. 34
Do	(1)	(1)	[2]. 03–. 03–. 03	Virginia	(1)	(1)	1. 53–3. 83–2. 92
New Jersey	M.	(1)	2. 47–2. 91–2. 76	**1900:**			
New York	M.	(1)	[2]. 02–. 02–. 02	Massachusetts	(1)	(1)	2. 00–4. 00–2. 76
Do	M.	70–84–77	1. 50–4. 50–2. 85	New Jersey	(1)	(1)	2. 86–2. 86–2. 86
North Carolina	(1)	(1)	. 96–3. 73–2. 61	Pennsylvania	(1)	(1)	2. 15–2. 50–2. 35

[1] Not reported. [2] Per mile.

TABLE N-5.—*Engineers, locomotive, railroad, 1840–1900, by year and State*

Year and State	Sex	Hours per week	Rate per day (dollars)	Year and State	Sex	Hours per week	Rate per day (dollars)
1840:				**1861:**			
Massachusetts	M.	70–70–70	1. 97–1. 97–1. 97	Massachusetts	M.	70–70–70	1. 97–2. 30–2. 10
1841:				**1862:**			
Massachusetts	M.	70–70–70	1. 97–1. 97–1. 97	Massachusetts	M.	70–70–70	1. 97–2. 30–2. 05
1842:				**1863:**			
Massachusetts	M.	70–70–70	1. 97–1. 97–1. 97	Massachusetts	M.	70–70–70	2. 14–2. 30–2. 19
1843:				**1864:**			
Massachusetts	M.	70–70–70	1. 97–1. 97–1. 97	Massachusetts	M.	70–70–70	2. 14–2. 30–2. 18
1844:				**1865:**			
Massachusetts	M.	70–70–70	1. 97–1. 97–1. 97	Massachusetts	M.	70–70–70	2. 63–2. 88–2. 73
1845:				**1866:**			
Massachusetts	M.	70–70–70	1. 97–1. 97–1. 97	Massachusetts	M.	70–70–70	2. 63–2. 88–2. 69
1846:				**1867:**			
Massachusetts	M.	70–70–70	1. 97–1. 97–1. 97	Massachusetts	M.	70–70–70	2. 96–3. 07–2. 98
1847:				**1868:**			
Massachusetts	M.	70–70–70	1. 97–1. 97–1. 97	Massachusetts	M.	70–70–70	2. 96–3. 07–3. 00
1848:				**1869:**			
Massachusetts	M.	70–70–70	1. 97–1. 97–1. 97	Massachusetts	M.	70–70–70	3. 29–3. 45–3. 31
1849:				**1870:**			
Massachusetts	M.	70–70–70	1. 97–2. 00–1. 98	California	M.	(1)	4. 11–4. 11–4. 11
1850:				Illinois	M.	(1)	[2]. 35–. 37–. 36½
Massachusetts	M.	70–70–70	1. 97–2. 00–1. 98	Louisiana	M.	(1)	3. 78–3. 78–3. 78
1851:				Massachusetts	M.	70–70–70	3. 29–4. 22–3. 35
Massachusetts	M.	70–70–70	1. 97–2. 00–1. 98	Ohio	M.	60–60–60	2. 30–2. 79–2. 62
1852:				Pennsylvania	M.	(1)	3. 00–4. 88–3. 47
Massachusetts	M.	70–70–70	1. 97–2. 00–1. 98	Virginia	M.	(1)	2. 96–3. 12–3. 03
1853:				**1871:**			
Massachusetts	M.	70–70–70	2. 00–2. 00–2. 00	California	M.	(1)	3. 85–4. 01–3. 95
1854:				Illinois	M.	(1)	[2]. 35–. 37–. 36½
Massachusetts	M.	70–70–70	2. 14–2. 49–2. 26	Louisiana	M.	(1)	3. 78–3. 78–3. 78
1855:				Massachusetts	M.	70–70–70	2. 47–2. 79–2. 74
Massachusetts	M.	70–70–70	2. 14–2. 49–2. 23	Ohio	M.	60–60–60	3. 00–5. 04–3. 66
1856:				Pennsylvania	M.	(1)	2. 96–3. 12–3. 03
Massachusetts	M.	70–70–70	2. 14–2. 49–2. 23	Virginia	M.	(1)	2. 96–3. 12–3. 03
1857:				**1872:**			
Massachusetts	M.	70–70–70	2. 14–2. 30–2. 18	California	M.	(1)	3. 85–4. 01–3. 93
1858:				Illinois	M.	(1)	[2]. 35–. 37–. 36½
Massachusetts	M.	70–70–70	2. 14–2. 30–2. 18	Louisiana	M.	(1)	3. 78–3. 78–3. 78
1859:				Massachusetts	M.	70–70–70	3. 29–4. 22–3. 40
Massachusetts	M.	70–70–70	1. 97–2. 30–2. 10	Ohio	M.	60–60–60	3. 22–3. 23–3. 22
1860:				Pennsylvania	M.	(1)	3. 00–5. 50–3. 89
Massachusetts	M.	70–70–70	1. 97–2. 30–2. 03	Virginia	M.	(1)	2. 96–3. 12–3. 03

[1] Not reported. [2] Per hour.

TABLE N-5.—*Engineers, locomotives, railroad, 1840–1900, by year and State*—Con.

Year and State	Sex	Lowest, highest, and average—		Year and State	Sex	Lowest, highest, and average—	
		Hours per week	Rate per day (dollars)			Hours per week	Rate per day (dollars)
1873:				**1880:**			
California	M.	[1]	3.85–4.01–3.94	California	M.	[1]	3.85–4.01–3.92
Illinois	M.	[1]	[2].37–.37–.37	Illinois	M.	[1]	[2].37–.37–.37
Louisiana	M.	[1]	3.78–3.78–3.78	Do	M.	70–70–70	2.75–3.59–3.22
Massachusetts	M.	70–70–70	3.29–3.45–3.31	Louisiana	M.	[1]	3.78–3.78–3.78
Minnesota	M.	[1]	[3].03½–.03½–.03½	Massachusetts	M.	70–70–70	3.29–3.45–3.30
Ohio	M.	60–60–60	3.58–3.58–3.58	Minnesota	M.	[1]	[3].03½–.03½–.03½
Pennsylvania	M.	[1]	3.09–5.50–4.10	New Jersey	[1]	78–84–81	2.00–2.50–2.25
Virginia	M.	[1]	2.96–3.12–3.03	Ohio	M.	60–60–60	3.45–3.45–3.45
1874:				Pennsylvania	M.	[1]	3.15–4.90–3.73
California	M.	[1]	3.85–4.01–3.95	Virginia	M.	[1]	2.96–3.12–3.03
Illinois	M.	[1]	[2].35–.37–.36	**1881:**			
Do	M.	[1]	1.64–3.78–2.88	California	M.	[1]	3.85–4.01–3.91
Indiana	M.	[1]	2.96–3.33–2.98	Illinois	M.	[1]	[2].37–.37–.37
Iowa	M.	[1]	2.86–2.86–2.86	Indiana	M.	[1]	2.04–5.00–3.76
Louisiana	M.	[1]	3.78–3.78–3.78	Louisiana	M.	[1]	3.78–3.78–3.78
Massachusetts	M.	70–70–70	2.96–3.45–3.16	Massachusetts	M.	70–70–70	3.29–3.45–3.31
Minnesota	M.	[1]	[3].03½–.03½–.03½	Minnesota	M.	[1]	[3].03½–.03½–.03½
Ohio	M.	60–60–60	3.58–3.58–3.58	Ohio	M.	60–66–60	1.93–3.45–3.32
Do	[1]	[1]	2.80–2.80–2.80	Pennsylvania	M.	[1]	3.15–4.90–3.88
Pennsylvania	M.	[1]	2.57–4.95–2.97	Virginia	M.	[1]	2.96–3.12–3.03
Virginia	M.	[1]	2.96–3.12–3.03	**1882:**			
1875:				California	M.	[1]	3.85–4.01–3.89
California	M.	[1]	3.85–4.01–3.95	Illinois	M.	[1]	[2].37–.37–.37
Illinois	M.	[1]	[2].32½–.37–.35½	Do	M.	[1]	1.97–4.27–2.46
Louisiana	M.	[1]	3.78–3.78–3.78	Indiana	M.	[1]	2.04–4.20–3.57
Massachusetts	M.	70–70–70	2.96–3.45–3.17	Louisiana	M.	[1]	3.78–3.78–3.78
Minnesota	M.	[1]	[3].03½–.03½–.03½	Massachusetts	M.	70–70–70	3.29–3.45–3.30
Ohio	M.	60–60–60	3.34–3.34–3.34	Minnesota	M.	[1]	[3].03½–.03½–.03½
Pennsylvania	M.	[1]	1.00–6.85–3.04	Ohio	M.	60–60–60	3.57–3.57–3.57
Virginia	M.	[1]	2.96–3.12–3.03	Pennsylvania	M.	70–84–79	2.00–4.00–3.42
1876:				Virginia	M.	[1]	2.96–3.12–3.03
California	M.	[1]	3.85–4.01–3.95	**1883:**			
Illinois	M.	[1]	[2].37–.37–.37	California	M.	[1]	3.85–4.01–3.91
Louisiana	M.	[1]	3.78–3.78–3.78	Illinois	M.	[1]	[2].37–.37–.37
Massachusetts	M.	70–70–70	2.96–3.45–3.16	Indiana	M.	[1]	2.63–4.25–3–32
Minnesota	M.	[1]	[3].03½–.03½–.03½	Louisiana	M.	[1]	3.78–3.78–3.78
Ohio	M.	60–60–60	3.45–3.45–3.45	Massachusetts	M.	70–70–70	3.29–3.45–3.32
Pennsylvania	M.	56–91–67	1.50–5.45–3.17	Michigan	M.	[1]	1.48–4.93–2.72
Virginia	M.	[1]	2.96–3.12–3.03	Minnesota	M.	[1]	[3].03½–.03½–.03½
1877:				Ohio	M.	60–72–61	2.14–3.45–3.31
California	M.	[1]	3.85–4.01–3.95	Pennsylvania	M.	[1]	3.15–4.00–3.59
Illinois	M.	[1]	[2].32½–.37–.35½	Virginia	M.	[1]	2.96–3.12–3.03
Louisiana	M.	[1]	3.78–3.78–3.78	**1884:**			
Massachusetts	M.	70–70–70	2.96–3.36–3.14	California	M.	[1]	3.85–4.01–3.92
Minnesota	M.	[1]	[3].03½–.03½–.03½	Illinois	M.	[1]	[2].37–.37–.37
New Jersey	M.	75–75–75	2.63–2.96–2.95	Indiana	M.	[1]	2.17–4.00–3.14
Ohio	M.	60–60–60	3.45–3.45–3.45	Iowa	M.	49–77–70	3.00–3.88–3.39
Pennsylvania	M.	56–84–68	1.81–5.45–3.43	Louisiana	M.	[1]	3.78–3.78–3.78
Virginia	M.	[1]	2.96–3.12–3.03	Massachusetts	M.	70–70–70	2.96–3.45–3.26
1878:				Michigan	M.	[1]	.99–3.29–2.59
California	M.	[1]	3.85–4.01–3.93	Minnesota	M.	[1]	[3].037–.037–.037
Illinois	M.	[1]	[2].32½–.37–.35½	New Jersey	M.	70–84–77	2.37–3.29–2.51
Louisiana	M.	[1]	3.78–3.78–3.78	New York	M.	[1]	2.50–3.50–3.32
Massachusetts	M.	70–70–70	2.96–3.36–3.14	Ohio	M.	60–60–60	3.45–3.45–3.45
Minnesota	M.	[1]	[3].03½–.03½–.03½	Pennsylvania	M.	[1]	1.56–4.00–2.30
Ohio	M.	55–60–60	3.00–3.45–3.42	Virginia	M.	[1]	2.96–3.12–3.03
Pennsylvania	M.	56–84–69	1.32–4.45–3.12	Wisconsin	M.	[1]	3.81–3.81–3.81
Virginia	M.	[1]	2.96–3.12–3.03	**1885:**			
1879:				California	M.	[1]	3.85–4.01–3.92
California	M.	[1]	3.85–4.01–3.92	Illinois	M.	[1]	[2].37–.37–.37
Illinois	M.	[1]	[2].37–.37–.37	Indiana	M.	[1]	2.50–4.00–3.14
Louisiana	M.	[1]	3.78–3.78–3.78	Iowa	M.	39–77–68	2.50–4.00–3.56
Massachusetts	M.	70–70–70	2.96–3.36–3.11	Do	M.	[1]	[4]
Minnesota	M.	[1]	[3].03½–.03½–.03½	Kansas	M.	56–84–76	2.58–3.92–3.52
Missouri	M.	56–100–65	2.43–4.29–3.21	Louisiana	M.	[1]	3.78–3.78–3.78
New Jersey	[1]	72–72–72	3.25–3.25–3.25	Massachusetts	M.	70–70–70	2.96–3.45–3.23
Ohio	M.	60–60–60	3.45–3.45–3.45	Michigan	M.	[1]	2.00–5.60–3.17
Pennsylvania	M.	77–91–84	.82–4.60–2.89	Minnesota	M.	[1]	[3].037–.037–.037
Virginia	M.	[1]	2.96–3.12–3.03	Missouri	M.	[1]	3.56–5.04–4.41

[1] Not reported.   [2] Per hour.   [3] Per mile.   [4] $0.0312–$0.0312–$0.0312 per mile.

TABLE N-5.—*Engineers, locomotive, railroad, 1840–1900, by year and State*—Con.

Year and State	Sex	Lowest, highest, and average— Hours per week	Lowest, highest, and average— Rate per day (dollars)
1885—Continued.			
New Jersey	M.	(1)	1.97-2.63-2.30
New York	M.	(1)	3.00-3.50-3.41
Ohio	M.	60-60-60	3.68-3.68-3.68
Pennsylvania	M.	(1)	2.40-4.00-2.60
Virginia	M.	(1)	2.96-3.12-3.03
1886:			
California	M.	(1)	3.85-4.01-3.92
Illinois	M.	(1)	[2] .37-.37-.37
Indiana	M.	(1)	2.37-4.50-2.91
Iowa	M.	35-112-60	.75-5.50-3.48
Kansas	M.	42-98-73	3.00-4.80-3.62
Louisiana	M.	(1)	3.78-3.78-3.78
Massachusetts	M.	70-70-70	3.29-3.45-3.32
Minnesota	M.	(1)	[3] .04-.04-.04
New Jersey	M.	(1)	1.97-2.63-2.34
New York	M.	(1)	2.50-3.50-3.40
Ohio	M.	60-60-60	2.16-3.68-3.50
Pennsylvania	M.	(1)	3.15-4.00-3.60
Virginia	M.	(1)	2.96-3.12-3.03
1887:			
California	M.	(1)	3.85-4.01-3.92
Connecticut	M.	(1)	1.64-4.00-2.86
Delaware	M.	(1)	2.25-3.78-2.87
Florida	M.	(1)	1.32-3.70-2.79
Illinois	M.	(1)	[2] .37-.37-.37
Do	(1)	(1)	4.68-4.68-4.68
Kansas	M.	53-84-67	3.00-4.81-3.71
Louisiana	M.	(1)	3.78-3.78-3.78
Maine	M.	(1)	1.97-1.97-1.97
Maryland	M.	(1)	1.32-5.50-3.07
Massachusetts	M.	70-70-70	3.29-3.84-3.47
Michigan	M.	70-70-70	2.10-3.50-2.54
Minnesota	M.	(1)	[3] .04-.04-.04
Missouri	M.	(1)	1.75-4.93-3.52
Do	(1)	(1)	2.08-3.56-3.44
Nebraska	(1)	60-60-60	2.25-5.50-3.67
Do	(1)	(1)	[3] .03½-.04-.0367
New Hampshire	M.	(1)	2.25-2.50-2.38
New Jersey	M.	(1)	1.97-3.50-3.39
New York	M.	(1)	1.50-5.75-3.30
North Carolina	M.	70-84-71	1.25-3.84-3.07
Ohio	M.	60-60-60	3.68-3.68-3.68
Pennsylvania	M.	(1)	1.30-5.75-2.86
Rhode Island	M.	(1)	1.64-6.58-2.84
Virginia	M.	(1)	1.25-3.50-2.61
West Virginia	M.	(1)	2.50-3.00-2.93
Wisconsin	M.	(1)	2.25-3.00-2.78
1888:			
California	M.	(1)	3.85-4.01-3.92
Colorado	M.	(1)	3.85-4.51-4.26
Illinois	M.	(1)	[2] .37-.37-.37
Do	M.	(1)	2.43-2.43-2.43
Indiana	M.	56-84-81	2.24-4.93-3.29
Iowa	M.	42-95-66	2.16-5.21-3.64
Kansas	M.	63-98-71	2.54-4.95-3.75
Louisiana	M.	(1)	3.78-3.78-3.78
Massachusetts	M.	70-70-70	3.29-3.84-3.67
Minnesota	M.	(1)	[3] .04-.04-.04
Missouri	(1)	(1)	2.50-4.38-3.79
New Jersey	(1)	84-84-84	2.79-3.80-3.30
New York	M.	(1)	2.50-3.50-3.39
Do	M.	(1)	[3] .03½-.03½-.03½
Ohio	M.	60-60-60	3.68-3.68-3.68
Pennsylvania	M.	(1)	3.15-4.20-3.27
Virginia	M.	(1)	3.78-3.78-3.78
1889:			
California	M.	(1)	3.85-4.01-3.93
Illinois	M.	(1)	[2] .37-.37-.37
Indiana	M.	56-84-81	2.00-5.07-3.41
Iowa	M.	42-98-60	2.25-5.25-3.61
Kansas	M.	42-84-70	2.33-8.86-3.87
Louisiana	M.	(1)	3.78-3.78-3.78
Massachusetts	M.	70-70-70	3.29-3.84-3.67
Minnesota	M.	(1)	[3] .04-.04-.04
1889—Continued.			
New York	M.	(1)	2.50-3.53-3.46
Do	M.	(1)	[3] .03½-.03½-.03½
Ohio	M.	60-60-60	3.80-3.80-3.80
Pennsylvania	M.	(1)	3.00-4.20-3.06
Virginia	M.	(1)	3.78-3.78-3.78
1890:			
California	M.	(1)	3.85-4.01-3.93
Illinois	M.	(1)	[2] .37-.38½-.37½
Indiana	M.	63-84-77	1.75-5.50-3.66
Iowa	M.	(1)	1.64-4.79-3.62
Louisiana	M.	(1)	3.78-3.78-3.78
Massachusetts	M.	70-70-70	3.29-4.00-3.67
Minnesota	M.	(1)	[3] .04-.04-.04
New York	M.	(1)	2.50-3.79-3.52
Do	M.	(1)	[3] .03½-.03½-.03½
Ohio	M.	60-60-60	3.80-3.80-3.80
Do	(1)	42-84-69	2.24-4.20-3.50
Pennsylvania	M.	(1)	3.00-5.00-3.08
Virginia	----	(1)	3.78-3.78-3.78
1891:			
California	M.	(1)	3.85-4.01-3.94
Illinois	M.	(1)	[2] .37-.43-.39
Indiana	M.	56-84-75	1.75-5.50-3.73
Kansas	M.	35-103-70	3.50-9.00-5.36
Louisiana	M.	(1)	4.29-4.29-4.29
Maine	M.	70-70-70	1.69-3.50-3.05
Massachusetts	M.	70-70-70	3.29-4.00-3.65
Minnesota	M.	(1)	[3] .04-.04-.04
New York	M.	(1)	2.50-3.78-3.45
Do	M.	(1)	[3] .03½-.03½-.03½
North Carolina	M.	70-70-70	3.00-3.00-3.00
Do	(1)	(1)	1.53-4.17-3.38
Ohio	M.	60-60-60	3.80-3.80-3.80
Pennsylvania	M.	(1)	3.00-5.00-3.07
Virginia	M.	(1)	3.88-3.88-3.88
Wisconsin	M.	(1)	2.75-2.75-2.75
1892:			
California	M.	(1)	3.85-4.01-3.94
Illinois	M.	(1)	[2] .37-.43-.39
Indiana	M.	56-84-72	2.30-5.50-3.74
Louisiana	M.	(1)	5.24-5.24-5.24
Maryland	M.	70-70-70	2.50-4.50-3.90
Massachusetts	M.	70-70-70	3.29-4.00-3.65
Minnesota	M.	(1)	[3] .04-.04-.04
New York	M.	(1)	2.50-3.79-3.39
Do	M.	(1)	[3] .03½-.03½-.03½
North Carolina	(1)	(1)	1.64-4.61-3.43
Ohio	M.	60-60-60	4.03-4.03-4.03
Pennsylvania	M.	(1)	3.00-6.60-3.13
Virginia	M.	(1)	4.00-4.00-4.00
1893:			
California	M.	(1)	3.85-4.01-3.93
Illinois	M.	59-84-70	2.29-3.57-3.04
Do	M.	(1)	[2] .37-.43-.39½
Indiana	M.	56-84-74	2.31-5.00-3.79
Kansas	M.	(1)	2.30-5.69-3.72
Louisiana	M.	(1)	5.16-5.16-5.16
Maryland	M.	56-77-68	1.86-4.29-3.10
Massachusetts	M.	(1)	3.29-3.29-3.29
Michigan	M.	32-126-81	1.32-5.26-3.18
Minnesota	M.	(1)	[3] .04-.04-.04
Montana	M.	63-77-68	2.96-5.00-4.00
Do	M.	(1)	[2] .40-.40-.40
Do	M.	(1)	[3] .03¾-.04½-.04
New York	M.	60-60-60	2.14-3.80-3.42
Do	M.	(1)	[3] .03½-.03½-.03½
North Carolina	M.	(1)	1.66-4.63-3.52
Ohio	M.	60-60-60	4.26-4.26-4.26
Pennsylvania	M.	60-60-60	1.71-6.60-3.18
Rhode Island	M.	(1)	2.93-3.50-3.25
Virginia	M.	(1)	4.14-4.14-4.14
1894:			
California	M.	(1)	3.85-4.01-3.93
Illinois	M.	(1)	[2] .37½-.43½-.39½

[1] Not reported. [2] Per hour. [3] Per mile.

Table N-5.—*Engineers, locomotive, railroad, 1840–1900, by year and State*—Con.

Year and State	Sex	Lowest, highest, and average—		Year and State	Sex	Lowest, highest, and average—	
		Hours per week	Rate per day (dollars)			Hours per week	Rate per day (dollars)
1894—Continued.				1897—Continued.			
Indiana	M.	56–84–76	1. 68–4. 95–3. 72	Kansas	(1)	49–91–70	2. 22–3. 45–2. 86
Iowa	M.	28–98–72	1. 71–4. 29–3. 21	Do	(1)	42–84–67	³. 03½–. 04–. 0386
Louisiana	M.	(1)	4. 24–4. 24–4. 24	Louisiana	M.	(1)	5. 43–5. 43–5. 43
Massachusetts	M.	(1)	3. 29–3. 29–3. 29	Maryland	(1)	42–70–67	1. 97–4. 21–3. 66
Minnesota	M.	(1)	³. 03½–. 03½–. 03¾	Massachusetts	M.	(1)	3. 29–3. 29–3. 29
Montana	M.	(1)	3. 30–4. 75–3. 92	Michigan	(1)	68–84–77	1. 75–4. 00–2. 88
New Hampshire	M.	54–84–64	1. 50–3. 00–2. 45	Do	(1)	(1)	³. 25–. 25–. 25
New York	M.	(1)	2. 50–3. 77–3. 50	Do	(1)	42–95–73	³. 03–. 04–. 0352
Do	M.	(1)	³. 03½–. 03½–. 03½	Minnesota	M.	(1)	³. 03½–. 03½–. 03½
North Carolina	M.	(1)	1. 50–4. 30–3. 24	Montana	(1)	(1)	3. 63–4. 13–3. 95
Ohio	M.	60–60–60	3. 62–3. 62–3. 62	New York	M.	(1)	³. 03½–03½–. 03½
Pennsylvania	M.	(1)	2. 50–6. 60–3. 17	Do	M.	70–84–83	1. 15–7. 00–3. 57
Virginia	M.	(1)	4. 04–4. 04–4. 04	North Carolina	(1)	(1)	1. 50–4. 35–3. 35
West Virginia	M.	(1)	2. 24–3. 75–2. 70	Ohio	M.	60–60–60	3. 62–3. 62–3. 62
1895:				Pennsylvania	M.	(1)	2. 50–6. 60–3. 44
California	M.	(1)	3. 46–3. 61–3. 53	Virginia	M.	(1)	4. 13–4. 13–4. 13
Illinois	M.	(1)	³. 37–. 43–. 39½	1898:			
Indiana	M.	(1)	2. 31–5. 01–3. 79	California	M.	(1)	3. 46–3. 61–3. 52
Iowa	(1)	(1)	1. 64–4. 82–3. 65	Illinois	M.	(1)	³. 37–. 43–. 40½
Louisiana	M.	(1)	5. 51–5. 51–5. 51	Indiana	(1)	42–91–74	2. 00–5. 97–3. 75
Massachusetts	M.	(1)	3. 29–3. 29–3. 29	Iowa	(1)	(1)	1. 32–4. 65–3. 74
Minnesota	M.	(1)	³. 03½–. 03½–. 03½	Kansas	M.	42–91–71	2. 47–4. 77–3. 86
Montana	M.	(1)	3. 91–4. 35–4. 01	Do	M.	35–98–63	(8)
New York	M.	(1)	2. 50–3. 79–3. 53	Louisiana	M.	(1)	4. 95–4. 95–4. 95
Do	M.	(1)	³. 03½–. 03½–. 03½	Massachusetts	M.	(1)	3. 29–3. 29–3. 29
North Carolina	(1)	(1)	1. 50–4. 04–3. 29	Minnesota	M.	(1)	³. 03½–. 03½–. 03½
Ohio	M.	60–60–60	3. 42–3. 42–3. 42	Missouri	(1)	56–84–69	1. 92–4. 63–3. 83
Pennsylvania	M.	(1)	2. 50–6. 60–3. 22	Nebraska	(1)	49–84–70	1. 00–6. 00–3. 43
Virginia	M.	(1)	4. 09–4. 09–4. 09	Do	(1)	(1)	³. 03–. 03½–. 03½
Wisconsin	(1)	70–70–70	3. 70–3. 70–3. 70	New Jersey	M.	(1)	2. 70–3. 55–3. 31
1896:				New York	M.	(1)	³. 03½–. 03½–. 03½
California	M.	(1)	3. 46–3. 61–3. 53	Do	M.	63–84–79	2. 00–5. 50–3. 40
Colorado	M.	56–70–60	4. 00–4. 00–4. 00	North Carolina	(1)	(1)	1. 50–4. 04–3. 37
Illinois	M.	(1)	³. 37–. 43–. 39½	Ohio	M.	60–60–60	3. 62–3. 62–3. 62
Indiana	M.	(1)	2. 31–7. 08–3. 85	Pennsylvania	M.	(1)	2. 50–6. 60–3. 44
Iowa	(1)	(1)	1. 71–5. 00–3. 65	Virginia	M.	(1)	4. 13–4. 13–4. 13
Kansas	M.	42–84–67	1. 15–6. 58–3. 37	Do	(1)	84–84–84	4. 35–4. 35–4. 35
Louisiana	M.	(1)	5. 98–5. 98–5. 98	Washington	(1)	(1)	2. 50–4. 48–3. 82
Massachusetts	M.	(1)	3. 29–3. 29–3. 29	1899:			
Minnesota	M.	(1)	³. 03½–. 03½–. 03½	Massachusetts	(1)	(1)	2. 20–4. 50–3. 33
Missouri	(1)	(1)	2. 49–4. 66–3. 80	Do	(1)	(1)	³. 03½–. 04–. 0358
Montana	M.	(1)	3. 65–4. 37–3. 90	New Jersey	(1)	(1)	3. 34–3. 34–3. 34
New York	M.	(1)	³. 03½–. 03½–. 03½	New York	(1)	(1)	3. 49–3. 82–3. 65
Do	M.	60–70–64	3. 00–3. 83–3. 49	North Carolina	(1)	(1)	1. 35–4. 49–3. 72
North Carolina	M.	(1)	1. 50–4. 16–3. 21	Pennsylvania	(1)	(1)	2. 47–4. 07–3. 17
Ohio	M.	60–60–60	3. 62–3. 62–3. 62	Do	(1)	(1)	³. 20–. 28–. 26
Pennsylvania	M.	(1)	2. 50–6. 60–3. 20	Virginia	(1)	(1)	1. 57–4. 82–4. 07
Virginia	M.	(1)	4. 13–4. 13–4. 13	1900:			
1897:				Massachusetts	(1)	(1)	2. 25–4. 50–3. 36
California	M.	(1)	3. 46–3. 61–3. 52	Do	(1)	(1)	³. 03½–. 04–. 0358
Illinois	M.	(1)	³. 37–. 43–. 39½	New Jersey	(1)	(1)	3. 37–3. 37–3. 37
Iowa	(1)	(1)	2. 05–4. 55–3. 66	Pennsylvania	(1)	(1)	2. 47–5. 50–3. 29
				Do	(1)	(1)	³. 21–. 28–. 26

¹ Not reported.
² Per hour.
³ Per mile.
⁵ $0.035–$0.045–$0–.0384 per mile.

TABLE **N-6.**—*Firemen, locomotive, 1840-1900, by year and State*

Year and State	Sex	Lowest, highest, and average— Hours per week	Rate per day (dollars)	Year and State	Sex	Lowest, highest, and average— Hours per week	Rate per day (dollars)
1840:				**1872:**			
Massachusetts	M.	70-70-70	0.96-1.15-1.06	California	M.	(¹)	2.14-2.30-2.22
1841:				Illinois	M.	(¹)	1.64-1.81-1.74
Massachusetts	M.	70-70-70	.96-1.15-1.10	Louisiana	M.	(¹)	2.14-2.14-2.14
1842:				Massachusetts	M.	70-70-70	2.00-2.25-2.02
Massachusetts	M.	70-70-70	.96-1.15-1.11	Minnesota	M.	(¹)	²2.00-2.00-2.00
1843:				Ohio	M.	60-60-60	1.71-2.53-1.86
Massachusetts	M.	70-70-70	.96-1.15-1.06	Pennsylvania	M.	(¹)	1.75-2.85-2.08
1844:				Virginia	M.	(¹)	.99-.99-.99
Massachusetts	M.	70-70-70	.96-1.15-1.07	**1873:**			
1845:				California	M.	(¹)	2.14-2.30-2.23
Massachusetts	M.	70-70-70	.96-1.15-1.06	Illinois	M.	(¹)	1.81-1.81-1.81
1846:				Louisiana	M.	(¹)	2.14-2.14-2.14
Massachusetts	M.	70-70-70	.96-1.15-1.08	Massachusetts	M.	70-70-70	2.00-2.00-2.00
1847:				Minnesota	M.	(¹)	²2.00-2.00-2.00
Massachusetts	M.	70-70-70	.96-1.15-1.05	Ohio	M.	60-60-60	1.67-1.67-1.67
1848:				Pennsylvania	M.	((¹))	1.75-2.85-2.10
Massachusetts	M.	70-70-70	1.15-1.15-1.15	Virginia	M.	(¹)	.99-.99-.99
1849:				**1874:**			
Massachusetts	M.	70-70-70	1.15-1.15-1.15	California	M.	(¹)	2.14-2.30-2.24
1850:				Illinois	M.	(¹)	1.64-1.81-1.74
Massachusetts	M.	70-70-70	1.15-1.15-1.15	Louisiana	M.	(¹)	2.14-2.14-2.14
1851:				Massachusetts	M.	70-70-70	1.80-2.00-1.85
Massachusetts	M.	70-70-70	1.15-1.15-1.15	Minnesota	M.	(¹)	²2.00-2.00-2.00
1852:				Ohio	M.	60-60-60	1.81-1.81-1.81
Massachusetts	M.	70-70-70	1.15-1.15-1.15	Pennsylvania	M.	(¹)	1.43-2.57-1.99
1853:				Virginia	M.	(¹)	.99-.99-.99
Massachusetts	M.	70-70-70	1.15-1.15-1.15	**1875:**			
1854:				California	M.	(¹)	2.14-2.30-2.24
Massachusetts	M.	70-70-70	1.34-1.34-1.34	Illinois	M.	(¹)	1.81-1.81-1.81
1855:				Louisiana	M.	(¹)	2.14-2.14-2.14
Massachusetts	M.	70-70-70	1.34-1.34-1.34	Massachusetts	M.	70-70-70	1.80-2.00-1.88
1856:				Minnesota	M.	(¹)	2.00-2.00-2.00
Massachusetts	M.	70-70-70	1.34-1.34-1.34	Ohio	M.	60-60-60	1.69-1.69-1.69
1857:				Pennsylvania	M.	(¹)	1.00-2.57-1.81
Massachusetts	M.	70-70-70	1.34-1.34-1.34	Virginia	M.	(¹)	.99-.99-.99
1858:				**1876:**			
Massachusetts	M.	70-70-70	1.34-1.34-1.34	California	M.	(¹)	2.14-2.30-2.24
1859:				Illinois	M.	(¹)	1.64-1.81-1.74
Massachusetts	M.	70-70-70	.90-1.25-1.20	Louisiana	M.	(¹)	2.14-2.14-2.14
1860:				Massachusetts	M.	70-70-70	1.80-1.80-1.80
Massachusetts	M.	70-70-70	1.00-1.30-1.16	Minnesota	M.	(¹)	²2.00-2.00-2.00
1861:				Ohio	M.	60-60-60	1.75-1.75-1.75
Massachusetts	M.	70-70-70	1.30-1.30-1.30	Pennsylvania	M.	63-98-70	.89-2.57-1.76
1862:				Virginia	M.	(¹)	.99-.99-.99
Massachusetts	M.	70-70-70	1.30-1.30-1.30	**1877:**			
1863:				California	M.	(¹)	2.14-2.30-2.24
Massachusetts	M.	70-70-70	1.34-1.34-1.34	Illinois	M.	(¹)	1.64-1.81-1.75
1864:				Louisiana	M.	(¹)	2.14-2.14-2.14
Massachusetts	M.	70-70-70	1.34-1.34-1.34	Massachusetts	M.	70-70-70	1.80-2.00-1.91
1865:				Minnesota	M.	(¹)	²2.00-2.00-2.00
Massachusetts	M.	70-70-70	1.75-1.75-1.75	New Jersey	M.	70-75-71	1.23-2.00-1.92
1866:				Ohio	M.	60-60-60	1.75-1.75-1.75
Massachusetts	M.	70-70-70	1.75-1.75-1.75	Pennsylvania	M.	56-84-68	.89-2.57-1.82
1867:				Virginia	M.	(¹)	.99-.99-.99
Massachusetts	M.	70-70-70	1.75-2.00-1.83	**1878:**			
1868:				California	M.	(¹)	2.14-2.30-2.22
Massachusetts	M.	70-70-70	1.75-1.75-1.75	Illinois	M.	(¹)	1.81-1.81-1.81
1869:				Louisiana	M.	(¹)	2.14-2.14-2.14
Massachusetts	M.	70-70-70	2.00-2.00-2.00	Massachusetts	M.	70-70-70	1.30-2.00-1.77
1870:				Minnesota	M.	(¹)	²2.00-2.00-2.00
California	M.	(¹)	2.63-2.63-2.63	Ohio	M.	60-60-60	1.75-1.75-1.75
Illinois	M.	(¹)	1.64-1.97-1.76	Pennsylvania	M.	63-98-69	.82-2.60-1.74
Louisiana	M.	(¹)	2.14-2.14-2.14	Virginia	M.	(¹)	.99-.99-.99
Massachusetts	M.	70-70-70	2.00-2.00-2.00	**1879:**			
Ohio	----	60-60-60	1.56-1.56-1.56	California	M.	(¹)	2.14-2.30-2.22
Pennsylvania	M.	(¹)	1.65-2.50-1.90	Illinois	M.	(¹)	1.81-1.81-1.81
Virginia	----	(¹)	.99-.99-.99	Louisiana	M.	(¹)	2.14-2.14-2.14
1871:				Massachusetts	M.	70-70-70	²2.00-2.00-2.00
California	M.	(¹)	2.14-2.30-2.24	Minnesota	M.	(¹)	²2.00-2.00-2.00
Illinois	M.	(¹)	1.64-1.97-1.78	Missouri	M.	63-63-63	1.89-1.89-1.89
Louisiana	M.	(¹)	2.14-2.14-2.14	Ohio	M.	60-60-60	1.71-1.83-1.75
Massachusetts	M.	70-70-70	2.00-2.25-2.02	Pennsylvania	M.	70-98-71	.49-2.60-1.77
Ohio	M.	60-60-60	1.56-1.56-1.56	Virginia	M.	(¹)	.99-.99-.99
Pennsylvania	M.	(¹)	1.75-2.85-2.11				
Virginia	M.	(¹)	.99-.99-.99				

¹ Not reported.　　² Per 100 miles.

TABLE **N-6.**—*Firemen, locomotive, 1840-1900, by year and State*—Continued

Year and State	Sex	Hours per week	Rate per day (dollars)	Year and State	Sex	Hours per week	Rate per day (dollars)
1880:				**1886—Continued.**			
California	M.	(1)	2.14-2.30-2.21	Louisiana	M.	(1)	2.14-2.14-2.14
Illinois	M.	(1)	1.48-1.90-1.68	Massachusetts	M.	70-70-70	1.75-2.00-1.96
Louisiana	M.	(1)	2.14-2.14-2.14	Minnesota	M.	(1)	²2.10-2.10-2.10
Massachusetts	M.	70-70-70	2.00-2.00-2.00	Do	M.	68-68-68	2.00-2.00-2.00
Minnesota	M.	(1)	²2.00-2.00-2.00	New Jersey	M.	(1)	1.32-1.64-1.47
Ohio	M.	60-60-60	1.75-1.75-1.75	New York	M.	(1)	1.65-1.75-1.74
Pennsylvania	M.	(1)	1.65-2.60-1.81	North Carolina	M.	60-72-66	.90-.95-.93
Virginia	M.	(1)	.99-.99-.99	Ohio	M.	60-60-60	1.79-2.47-1.83
1881:				Pennsylvania	M.	(1)	1.75-1.85-1.80
California	M.	(1)	2.14-2.30-2.20	Virginia	M.	(1)	.99-.99-.99
Illinois	M.	(1)	1.81-1.81-1.81	**1887:**			
Louisiana	M.	(1)	2.14-2.14-2.14	California	M.	(1)	2.14-2.30-2.22
Massachusetts	M.	70-70-70	2.00-2.00-2.00	Connecticut	M.	(1)	1.32-2.50-1.71
Minnesota	M.	(1)	²2.00-2.00-2.00	Delaware	M.	(1)	1.00-2.40-1.77
New Jersey	M.	(1)	1.64-1.64-1.64	Florida	M.	(1)	.90-1.50-1.28
Ohio	M.	60-60-60	1.75-1.75-1.75	Illinois	M.	(1)	³.22-.22-.22
Pennsylvania	M.	(1)	1.65-2.00-1.79	Do	(1)	(1)	2.77-2.77-2.77
Virginia	M.	(1)	.99-.99-.99	Kansas	M.	53-84-68	1.85-2.57-2.14
1882:				Louisiana	M.	(1)	2.14-2.14-2.14
California	M.	(1)	2.14-2.30-2.18	Maine	M.	(1)	1.25-1.92-1.51
Illinois	M.	(1)	³.25-.25-.25	Maryland	M.	70-70-70	1.10-2.75-1.67
Do	M.	(1)	1.32-1.97-1.69	Massachuetts	M.	70-70-70	1.35-3.45-1.92
Louisiana	M.	(1)	2.14-2.14-2.14	Michigan	M.	70-70-70	.83-2.00-1.33
Massachusetts	M.	70-70-70	1.75-2.00-1.97	Do	M.	(1)	³.12-.30-.16
Minnesota	M.	(1)	²2.00-2.00-2.00	Minnesota	M.	(1)	²2.10-2.10-2.10
Ohio	M.	60-60-60	1.80-1.80-1.80	Missouri	M.	(1)	1.25-3.50-2.10
Pennsylvania	M.	(1)	1.75-2.70-1.86	Do	(1)	(1)	1.10-2.12-2.07
Virginia	M.	(1)	.99-.99-.99	Nebraska	(1)	70-70-70	1.50-3.40-2.22
1883:				Do	(1)	(1)	²2.00-2.25-2.08
California	M.	(1)	2.14-2.30-2.20	New Hampshire	M.	(1)	.50-1.50-1.13
Illinois	M.	(1)	1.81-1.81-1.81	New Jersey	M.	(1)	1.00-2.25-2.15
Do	M.	(1)	³.25-.25-.25	New York	M.	(1)	1.07-2.47-1.71
Louisiana	M.	(1)	2.14-2.14-2.14	North Carolina	M.	(1)	.50-1.55-1.19
Massachusetts	M.	70-70-70	2.00-2.00-2.00	Ohio	M.	56-84-70	1.74-1.84-1.75
Minnesota	M.	(1)	²2.00-2.00-2.00	Pennsylvania	M.	60-60-60	.99-3.15-1.65
Ohio	M.	60-72-61	1.50-1.80-1.68	Do	M.	(1)	³.12½-.27-.16
Pennsylvania	M.	(1)	1.80-2.00-1.84	Rhode Island	M.	(1)	1.15-1.97-1.61
Virginia	M.	(1)	.99-.99-.99	Virginia	M.	(1)	.99-2.30-1.58
1884::				West Virginia	M.	(1)	1.50-1.75-1.53
California	M.	(1)	2.14-2.30-2.21	Wisconsin	M.	(1)	1.35-1.75-1.55
Illinois	M.	(1)	1.81-1.81-1.81	**1888:**			
Do	M.	(1)	³.26-.26-.26	California	M.	(1)	2.14-2.30-2.21
Iowa	M.	60-84-70	1.50-2.15-1.98	Colorado	M.	(1)	2.24-2.63-2.49
Louisiana	M.	(1)	2.14-2.14-2.14	Illinois	M.	(1)	³.22-.22-.22
Massachusetts	M.	70-70-70	1.75-2.00-1.99	Indiana	M.	70-84-81	1.32-2.73-1.82
Minnesota	M.	(1)	²2.00-2.00-2.00	Iowa	M.	42-95-66	1.33-2.87-2.08
New Jersey	M.	70-70-70	1.48-1.97-1.52	Kansas	M.	70-77-70	1.55 2.97-2.11
New York	M.	(1)	1.65-1.75-1.73	Louisiana	M.	(1)	2.14-2.14-2.14
Ohio	M.	60-60-60	1.68-1.68-1.68	Massachusetts	M.	70-70-70	1.75-2.00-1.94
Pennsylvania	M.	(1)	1.40-1.85-1.50	Minnesota	Sex.	(1)	²2.10-2.10-2.10
Virginia	M.	(1)	.99-.99-.99	Missouri	(1)	(1)	1.25-2.47-2.06
Wisconsin	M.	(1)	1.77-1.89-1.86	New York	M.	(1)	1.65-1.75-1.73
1885:				Do	M.	(1)	²1.90-1.90-1.90
California	M.	(1)	2.14-2.30-2.21	Ohio	M.	60-60-60	1.74-1.84-1.75
Illinois	M.	(1)	1.81-1.81-1.81	Pennsylvania	M.	(1)	1.75-2.10-1.98
Do	M.	(1)	³.26-.26-.26	Virginia	M.	(1)	1.16-1.16-1.16
Iowa	M.	49-84-68	1.33-2.16-2.02	**1889:**			
Do	M.	(1)	²1.92-1.92-1.92	California	M.	(1)	2.14-2.30-2.22
Kansas	M.	56-84-75	1.65-2.09-1.94	Illinois	M.	(1)	³.22-.22-.22
Louisiana	M.	(1)	2.14-2.14-2.14	Indiana	M.	56-84-79	1.25-3.25-1.87
Massachusetts	M.	70-70-70	1.75-2.00-1.99	Iowa	M.	42-98-61	1.40-2.80-2.07
Michigan	M.	(1)	1.10-2.80-1.70	Kansas	M.	42-84-70	1.50-5.06-2.27
Minnesota	M.	(1)	²2.10-2.10-2.10	Louisiana	M.	(1)	2.14-2.14-2.14
Missouri	M.	(1)	1.81-2.72-2.41	Massachusetts	M.	70-70-70	1.75-2.00-1.99
New Jersey	Sex.	(1)	1.32-2.14-1.50	Minnesota	Sex.	(1)	²2.10-2.10-2.10
New York	M.	(1)	1.65-1.75-1.73	New York	M.	(1)	1.72-1.85-1.76
Ohio	M.	60-72-63	1.50-1.79-1.72	Do	M.	(1)	²1.90-1.90-1.90
Pennsylvania	M.	(1)	1.45-1.85-1.54	Ohio	M.	60-60-60	2.01-2.01-2.01
Virginia	M.	(1)	.99-.99-.99	Pennsylvania	M.	84-84-84	1.15-2.00-1.98
1886:				Virginia	M.	(1)	1.16-1.16-1.16
California	M.	(1)	2.14-2.30-2.21	**1890:**			
Illinois	M.	(1)	³.22-.22-.22	California	M.	(1)	2.14-2.30-2.22
Iowa	M.	44-70-60	1.33-2.30-1.96	Illinois	M.	(1)	³.22-.23½-.23
Kansas	M.	42-98-73	1.64-2.40-2.10	Indiana	M.	63-84-78	1.20-2.97-2.04

¹ Not reported.   ² Per 100 miles.   ³ Per hour.

TABLE N-6.—*Firemen, locomotive, 1840–1900, by year and State*—Continued

Year and State	Sex	Hours per week	Rate per day (dollars)	Year and State	Sex	Hours per week	Rate per day (dollars)
1890—Continued.				1894—Continued.			
Iowa	M.	([1])	0.67-2.74-2.12	Ohio	M.	60-60-60	1.99-1.99-1.99
Louisiana	M.	([1])	2.14-2.14-2.14	Pennsylvania	M.	([1])	1.40-3.85-1.89
Massachusetts	M.	70-70-70	1.75-2.25-1.99	Virginia	M.	([1])	1.52-1.52-1.52
Minnesota	M.	([1])	[2]2.25-2.25-2.25	West Virginia	M.	([1])	.95-1.98-1.38
Nebraska	M.	([1])	1.75-1.75-1.75	1895:			
New York	M.	(·)	1.75-2.23-1.97	California	M.	([1])	1.92-2.07-1.99
Do	M.	([1])	[2]1.90-1.90-1.90	Illinois	M.	([1])	[3].22-.28-.25
Ohio	M.	60-60-60	2.01-2.01-2.01	Indiana	M.	([1])	1.35-2.75-2.13
Do	([1])	42-84-68	1.25-2.42-1.84	Iowa	M.	([1])	1.34-3.18-2.16
Pennsylvania	M.	([1])	1.75-2.03-2.03	Louisiana	M.	([1])	2.99-2.99-2.99
Virginia	M.	([1])	1.33-1.33-1.33	Massachusetts	M.	([1])	2.00-2.00-2.00
1891:				Minnesota	M.	([1])	[2]2.15-2.15-2.15
California	M.	([1])	2.14-2.30-2.23	Do	M.·	([1])	[4]1.32-1.32-1.32
Illinois	M.	([1])	[3].22-.28-.24	Montana	M.	([1])	2.14-2.63-2.27
Indiana	M.	56-84-75	1.20-3.00-2.07	New York	M.	([1])	,1.75-2.23-2.03
Louisiana	M.	([1])	2.34-2.34-2.34	Do	M.	([1])	[2]1.90-1.90-1.90
Maine	M.	70-70-70	1.15-2.10-1.85	North Carolina	([1])	([1])	.56-1.66-1.23
Massachusetts	M.	70-70-70	1.75-2.25-1.98	Ohio	M.	60-60-60	1.88-1.88-1.88
Minnesota	M.	([1])	[2]2.25-2.25-2.25	Pennsylvania	M.	([1])	1.40-3.85-2.03
Do	M.	([1])	[4]1.64-1.64-1.64	Virginia	M.	([1])	1.51-1.51-1.51
New York	M.	([1])	1.75-2.23-1.98	1896:			
Do	M.	([1])	[2]1.90-1.90-1.90	Alabama	M.	([1])	.82-2.00-1.41
North Carolina	([1])	([1])	.66-1.85-1.17	California	M.	([1])	1.92-2.07-1.99
Ohio	M.	60-60-60	2.09-2.09-2.09	Colorado	M.	70-84-75	1.75-2.65-2.10
Pennsylvania	M.	([1])	1.75-2.25-1.98	Georgia	M.	([1])	.99-.99-.99
Virginia	M.	([1])	1.47-1.47-1.47	Illinois	M.	([1])	[3].22-.28-.25
Wisconsin	M.	([1])	1.50-1.50-1.50	Indiana	M.	([1])	1.35-3.89-2.20
1892:				Iowa	M.	([1])	1.30-2.86-2.19
California	M.	([1])	2.14-2.30-2.23	Kansas	M.	46-84-73	1.32-2.89-1.96
Illinois	M.	([1])	[3].22-.28-.24	Louisiana	M.	([1])	3.25-2.35-3.25
Indiana	M.	56-84-73	1.20-3.00-2.12	Massachusetts	M.	([1])	2.00-2.00-2.00
Louisiana	M.	([1])	3.12-3.12-3.12	Minnesota	M.	([1])	[2]2.15-2.15-2.15
Maryland	M.	63-70-69	1.00-2.80-2.01	Do	M.	([1])	[4]1.32-1.32-1.32
Massachusetts	M.	70-70-70	1.75-2.25-2.13	Missouri	([1])	([1])	1.38-2.67-2.24
Minnesota	M.	([1])	[2]2.25-2.25-2.25	Montana	M.	([1])	1.74-2.72-2.23
Do	M.	([1])	[4]1.64-1.64-1.64	New York	M.	([1])	1.75-2.25-2.02
New York	M.	([1])	1.75-2.23-1.96	Do	M.	([1])	[2]1.90-1.90-1.90
Do	M.	([1])	[2]1.90-1.90-1.90	North Carolina	M.	([1])	.68-1.73-1.21
North Carolina	([1])	([1])	.66-1.85-1.17	Ohio	M.	60-60-60	1.99-1.99-1.99
Ohio	M.	60-60-60	2.22-2.22-2.22	Pennsylvania	M.	([1])	1.40-3.85-1.99
Pennsylvania	M.	([1])	1.75-3.65-2.11	Tennessee	M.	([1])	1.04-1.04-1.04
Virginia	M.	([1])	1.42-1.42-1.42	Virginia	M.	([1])	1.48-1.48-1.48
1893:				1897:			
California	M.	([1])	2.14-2.30-2.22	California	M.	([1])	1.92-2.07-1.98
Illinois	M.	42-72-58	2.14-2.14-2.14	Illinois	M.	([1])	[3].22-.28-.24
Do	M.	([1])	.22-.28-.24	Iowa	M.	([1])	1.19-3.16-2.20
Indiana	M.	56-84-75	1.40-3.00-2.15	Kansas	([1])	84-84-84	1.81-2.07-1.92
Louisiana	M.	([1])	2.81-2.81-2.81	Do	([1])	49-91-74	[5].01½-.02½-.02½
Maryland	M.	60-84-66	1.29-2.14-1.63	Louisiana	M.	([1])	2.98-2.98-2.98
Massachusetts	M.	([1])	2.00-2.00-2.00	Maryland	([1])	42-70-68	1.16-2.24-1.83
Michigan	M.	35-126-79	.62-2.96-1.89	Massachusetts	M.	([1])	2.00-2.00-2.00
Minnesota	M.	([1])	[2]2.25-2.25-2.25	Michigan	M.	70-84-78	1.25-1.81-1.62
Do	M.	([1])	[4]1.64-1.64-1.64	Do	M.	70-91-79	[5].01½-.02½-.02
Montana	M.	58-79-65	1.75-3.00-2.36	Minnesota	M.	([1])	[2]2.15-2.15-2.15
Do	M.	([1])	2.25-2.50-2.42	Montana	([1])	([1])	1.78-2.74-2.27
New York	M.	([1])	1.75-2.24-1.98	New York	M.	([1])	1.75-2.30-2.02
Do	M.	([1])	[2]1.90-1.90-1.90	Do	M.	([1])	[2]1.90-1.90-1.90
North Carolina	M.	([1])	.49-1.95-1.24	Do	M.	70-88-82	1.50-4.00-2.25
Ohio	M.	60-60-60	2.34-2.34-2.34	North Carolina	([1])	([1])	.66-1.74-1.25
Pennsylvania	M.	60-70-63	1.65-3.85-2.13	Ohio	M.	60-60-60	1.99-1.99-1.99
Virginia	M.	([1])	1.50-1.50-1.50	Pennsylvania	M.	([1])	1.40-3.85-1.99
1894:				Virginia	M.	([1])	1.48-1.48-1.48
California	M.	([1])	2.14-2.30-2.22	1898:			
Illinois	M.	([1])	.22-.28-.24	California	M.	([1])	1.92-2.07-1.98
Indiana	M.	56-84-75	1.35-2.75-2.14	Illinois	M.	([1])	[3].22-.28-.26
Iowa	M.	28-84-70	1.65-2.71-2.13	Indiana	M.	([1])	1.25-3.28-2.18
Louisiana	M.	([1])	2.36-2.36-2.36	Iowa	M.	42-91-74	1.12-2.89-2.24
Massachusetts	M.	([1])	2.00-2.00-2.00	Kansas	M.	([1])	2.15-2.83-2.31
Minnesota	M.	([1])	[2]2.15-2.15-2.15	Do	M.	([1])	[5].02½-.02½-.02½
Do	M.	([1])	[4]1.32-1.32-1.32	Louisiana	M.	([1])	2.62-2.62-2.62
Montana	M.	([1])	2.01-3.00-2.24	Massachusetts	M.	([1])	2.00-2.00-2.00
New Hampshire	M.	36-78-57	1.07-1.71-1.60	Minnesota	M.	([1])	[2]2.15-2.15-2.15
New York	M.	([1])	1.75-2.22-2.04	Missouri	M.	([1])	1.00-2.66-2.18
Do	M.	([1])	[2]1.90-1.90-1.90	Nebraska	M.	56-48-69	1.00-3.60-2.21
North Carolina	M.	([1])	.60-2.17-1.24	Do	M.	56-84-69	[5].01½-.02½-.02

[1] Not reported.　[2] Per 100 miles.　[3] Per hour.　[4] And board.　[5] Per mile.

TABLE **N–6**.—*Firemen, locomotive, 1840–1900, by year and State*—Continued

| Year and State | Sex | Lowest, highest, and average— | | Year and State | Sex | Lowest, highest, and average— | |
		Hours per week	Rate per day (dollars)			Hours per week	Rate per day (dollars)
1898—Continued.				**1899—Continued.**			
New Jersey	M.	(1)	1.72-2.15-2.08	New Jersey	(1)	(1)	2.12-2.12-2.12
New York	M.	(1)	²1.90-1.90-1.90	New York	(1)	(1)	2.08-2.11-2.08
Do	M.	84-90-84	1.50-2.90-2.18	North Carolina	(1)	(1)	.58-2.22-1.36
North Carolina	(1)	(1)	.66-1.81-1.29	Pennsylvania	(1)	(1)	1.60-2.62-2.02
Ohio	M.	60-60-60	1.99-1.99-1.99	Do	(1)	(1)	³.15-.18-.17
Pennsylvania	M.	(1)	1.80-3.85-1.99	Virginia	(1)	(1)	.82-2.36-1.98
Virginia	M.	(1)	1.48-1.48-1.48	**1900:**			
Do	(1)	77-77-77	1.91-1.91-1.91	Massachusetts	(1)	(1)	1.50-2.50-1.92
Washington	(1)	(1)	1.50-2.67-2.44	Do	(1)	(1)	⁵.02-.02¼-.0203
1899:				New Jersey	(1)	(1)	2.14-2.14-2.14
Massachusetts	(1)	(1)	1.50-2.50-1.90	Pennsylvania	(1)	(1)	1.40-3.15-2.07
Do	(1)	(1)	⁵.02-.02¼-.0204	Do	(1)	(1)	³.15-.18-.17

¹ Not reported. ² Per 100 miles. ³ Per hour. ⁵ Per mile.

TABLE **N–7**.—*Conductors, street railways, 1871–1900, by year and State*

| Year and State | Sex | Lowest, highest, and average— | | Year and State | Sex | Lowest, highest, and average— | |
		Hours per week	Rate per day (dollars)			Hours per week	Rate per day (dollars)
1871:				**1892:**			
Massachusetts	M.	(1)	1.67-1.75-1.75	California	M.	51-75-70	1.50-2.75-2.30
1877:				Iowa	M.	72-72-72	1.00-2.00-1.79
New Jersey	M.	90-90-90	1.60-1.60-1.60	Ohio	M.	60-105-70	1.00-2.00-1.79
1880:				**1893:**			
Pennsylvania	M.	96-96-96	2.00-2.00-2.00	Illinois	M.	60-84-72	1.20-1.44-1.32
1882:				Maryland	M.	60-105-83	1.50-2.33-1.91
Missouri	M.	78-108-93	2.00-2.00-2.00	Missouri	M.	27-90-62	.83-2.40-1.90
Ohio	M.	72-90-81	.83-2.00-1.81	Do	M.	(1)	³.15-.19-.18
1883:				Montana	M.	60-64-62	2.50-3.50-2.79
New Jersey	M.	66-78-69	1.67-2.08-1.74	New York	M.	54-84-76	1.33-2.33-1.89
1884:				**1894:**			
California	M.	78-78-78	1.00-2.50-2.22	Ohio	M.	(1)	3.33-3.33-3.33
Illinois	M.	78-96-88	2.00-2.60-2.20	**1895:**			
Missouri	M.	62-90-75	.50-2.50-2.01	Kansas	M.	69-78-73	1.33-2.15-1.86
New Jersey	M.	72-96-84	.96-2.33-1.97	Michigan	M.	(1)	.46-2.47-1.68
Pennsylvania	M.	60-102-91	1.00-2.09-2.03	Wisconsin	(1)	60-60-60	2.00-2.00-2.00
1885:				**1896:**			
Iowa	M.	72-78-74	1.50-1.50-1.50	Colorado	M.	72-72-72	2.10-2.40-2.32
Do	M.	60-60-60	³.83-.83-.83	Illinois	M.	63-63-63	2.67-2.67-2.67
Kansas	M.	102-102-102	1.50-1.50-1.50	Kansas	M.	57-72-70	1.00-2.08-1.58
Missouri	M.	69-75-73	1.85-2.03-1.96	Maryland	M.	72-72-72	1.75-2.00-1.76
Pennsylvania	M.	72-102-91	1.00-2.50-2.00	**1897:**			
1886:				Michigan	(1)	54-78-58	³.10-.27½-.19
California	M.	72-72-72	2.11-2.11-2.11	**1898:**			
Kansas	M.	98-98-98	1.50-1.64-1.52	Missouri	(1)	54-66-63	1.25-2.00-1.74
1887:				Washington	(1)	(1)	1.25-2.25-1.95
Kansas	M.	63-91-73	1.50-2.00-1.83	**1899:**			
Missouri	M.	72-84-73	1.53-2.50-2.00	Alabama	M.	(1)	1.50-1.75-1.58
Wisconsin	M.	(1)	1.80-1.80-1.80	Georgia	M.	(1)	1.20-1.80-1.67
1888:				Michigan	(1)	(1)	1.76-1.76-1.76
Kansas	M.	84-84-84	1.50-2.50-2.04	North Carolina	M.	(1)	1.15-1.20-1.17
Ohio	M.	54-96-72	1.34-2.30-1.87	New York	M.	(1)	1.46-1.75-1.68
Rhode Island	M.	(1)	1.66-2.75-2.38	Ohio	(1)	(1)	2.00-2.00-2.00
1889:				Virginia	(1)	(1)	1.00-2.10-1.50
Kansas	M.	54-84-75	1.45-2.40-1.85	**1900:**			
1890:				Alabama	M.	(1)	1.50-1.75-1.58
Connecticut	M.	65-100-84	1.50-2.00-1.80	Georgia	M.	(1)	1.20-1.80-1.67
Kansas	M.	(1)	1.50-2.40-2.18	New York	M.	(1)	1.46-1.75-1.68
1891:				North Carolina	M.	(1)	1.15-1.30-1.20
Maine	M.	(1)	1.43-1.43-1.43	Ohio	M.	(1)	2.00-2.00-2.00

¹ Not reported. ³ And board. ⁴ Per hour.

TABLE N-8.—*Conductors and motormen, street railways, 1914, 1920-1928*

Year	Atlanta, Ga.		Birmingham, Ala.		Boston, Mass.		Chicago, Ill.	
	Hours per week	Rate per hour	Hours per week	Rate per hour	Hours per week	Rate per hour	Hours per week	Rate per hour
1914 [1]	([2])	$0.233	([2])	$0.221	([2])	$0.308	([2])	$0.315
1914 [3]	([2])	.230	([2])	.215	([2])	.300	([2])	.310
1920	([2])	[4].460	([2])	[5].500	([2])	[4].700	([2])	[4].650
1921	([2])	[5].480	([2])	[5].500	([2])	[4].700	([2])	[4].800
1922	([2])	[5].480	([2])	[5].500	([2])	[4].650	([2])	[4].800
1923	([2])	[5].480	([2])	[5].500	([2])	[4].610	([2])	[4].700
1924	([2])	[6].510	([2])	[5].500	([2])	[4].700	([2])	[4].730
1925	([2])	[6].540	([2])	[5].500	([2])	[4].725	([2])	[4].750
1926	([2])	[6].540	([2])	[5].500	([2])	[4].725	([2])	[4].750
1927	([2])	[6].540	([2])	[5].540	([2])	[4].725	([2])	[4].750
1928	([2])	[6].580	([2])	[5].540	([2])	[4].750	([2])	[4].750

Year	Cincinnati, Ohio		Denver, Colo.		Detroit, Mich.		New Orleans, La.	
1914 [1]	([2])	$0.258	([2])	$0.296	([2])	$0.317	([2])	$0.240
1914 [3]	([2])	.248	([2])	.293	([2])	.314	([2])	.240
1920	([2])	[4].500	--------	--------	([2])	[4].750	([2])	[4].420
1921	([2])	[4].590	--------	--------	([2])	[4].600	([2])	[4].550
1922	([2])	[4].500	--------	--------	([2])	[4].600	([2])	[4].510
1923	([2])	[4].480	--------	--------	([2])	[4].625	([2])	[4].510
1924	([2])	[4].530	--------	--------	([2])	[4].700	([2])	[4].510
1925	([2])	[4].530	--------	--------	([2])	[4].700	([2])	[4].510
1926	([2])	[4].530	--------	--------	([2])	[4].730	([2])	[4].510
1927	([2])	[4].560	--------	--------	([2])	[4].750	([2])	[4].510
1928	([2])	[4].580	--------	--------	([2])	[4].750	([2])	[4].510

Year	New York, N. Y.		Philadelphia, Pa.		St. Louis, Mo.		San Francisco, Calif.	
1914 [1]	([2])	[7]$0.368	([2])	$0.298	([2])	$0.263	([2])	$0.375
1914 [3]	([2])	[7].256	([2])	.295	([2])	.254	([2])	.375
1920	([2])	[8].860	--------	--------	([2])	[5].600	--------	--------
1921	([2])	[8].860	--------	--------	([2])	[5].650	([2])	[10].625
1922	([2])	[8].780	--------	--------	([2])	[9].650	([2])	[10].625
1923	([2])	[8].780	--------	--------	([2])	[9].650	([2])	[10].625
1924	([2])	[8].820	--------	--------	([2])	[9].670	([2])	[10].675
1925	([2])	[9].820	--------	--------	([2])	[9].670	([2])	[10].675
1926	([2])	[9].820	--------	--------	([2])	[9].670	([2])	[10].725
1927	([2])	[9].861	--------	--------	([2])	[9].670	([2])	[10].750
1928	([2])	[8].861	--------	--------	([2])	[9].670	([2])	[10].750

[1] Motormen. [3] Conductors. [5] After 2 years. [7] One large elevated line. [9] After 3 years.
[2] Not reported. [4] After 1 year [6] After 18 months. [8] After 4 years. [10] Municipal lines.

TABLE N-9.—*Motormen, street railways, 1889–1900, by year and State*

Year and State	Sex	Hours per week	Rate per day (dollars)	Year and State	Sex	Hours per week	Rate per day (dollars)
1889:				**1897:**			
Kansas	M.	72-84-81	1.50-1.50-1.50	Connecticut	M.	63-70-67	1.71-1.75-1.73
1890:				**1897:**			
Connecticut	M.	65-91-82	1.50-2.15-1.96	Michigan	(¹)	54-78-59	1.25-2.48-1.80
Kansas	M.	(¹)	1.33-1.33-1.33	**1898:**			
1891:				Missouri	(¹)	54-66-61	1.50-2.00-1.74
Maine	M.	(¹)	1.43-1.43-1.43	Washington	(¹)	(¹)	1.25-2.25-1.98
1892:				**1899:**			
Iowa	M.	72-84-73	1.50-2.40-1.89	Alabama	M.	(¹)	1.30-1.40-1.35
Ohio	M.	60-96-72	1.42-2.10-1.75	Georgia	M.	(¹)	1.20-1.80-1.68
1893:				Michigan	(¹)		1.71-1.71-1.71
Maryland	M.	72-72-72	2.00-2.00-2.00	New York	M.	(¹)	1.46-1.75-1.68
Missouri	M.	27-78-62	1.00-2.10-1.86	North Carolina	M.	(¹)	1.15-1.20-1.17
Do.	M.	(¹)	²12½-.20-.19	Ohio	(¹)	(¹)	2.00-2.00-2.00
Montana	M.	54-66-60	2.50-3.00-2.78	Virginia	(¹)	(¹)	1.00-2.20-1.57
1894:				**1900:** ³			
Ohio	M.	(¹)	1.67-3.50-3.59	Alabama	M.	(¹)	1.30-1.40-1.35
1895:				Georgia	M.	72-72-72	1.20-1.80-1.68
Kansas	M.	66-77-74	1.17-2.09-1.65	New York	M.	(¹)	1.46-1.75-1.68
Michigan	M.	(¹)	.50-2.25-1.69	North Carolina	M.	(¹)	1.15-1.30-1.20
1896:				Ohio	(¹)	(¹)	2.00-2.00-2.00
Colorado	M.	72-72-72	2.10-2.40-2.32				
Kansas	M.	60-72-69	1.25-1.80-1.52				
Maryland	M.	72-72-72	1.75-2.25-1.81				

¹ Not reported.   ² Per hour.   ³ For data of following years see Table N-8, p. 445.

TABLE N-10.—*Longshoremen, 1859–1898, by year and State*

Year and State	Sex	Hours per week	Rate per day (dollars)	Year and State	Sex	Hours per week	Rate per day (dollars)
1859:				**1886—Continued.**			
New York	M.	60-60-60	3.00-3.00-3.00	Louisiana	M.	60-60-60	4.00-5.00-4.51
1880:				New Jersey	M.	60-60-60	2.00-2.00-2.00
Illinois	M.	60-60-60	2.00-2.00-2.00	New York	M.	42-42-42	2.10-2.10-2.10
Minnesota	M.	(¹)	2.00-2.00-2.00	Washington	M.	60-60-60	3.00-4.00-3.50
New Jersey	(¹)	30-59-47	1.00-2.75-2.06	**1887:**			
1881:				Maine	M.	60-60-60	2.50-8.65-5.58
Illinois	M.	60-60-60	2.00-3.00-2.20	New York	M.	60-60-60	3.00-3.00-3.00
New York	M.	(¹)	1.50-1.75-1.63	Wisconsin	M.	(¹)	4.00-4.00-4.00
1882:				**1888:**			
Illinois	M.	60-60-60	2.00-3.00-2.27	New Jersey	(¹)	60-60-60	3.00-3.00-3.00
Massachusetts	M.	60-60-60	1.80-2.00-1.93	Do.	(¹)		³.30-.30-.30
Oregon	M.	60-60-60	3.00-4.00-3.50	New York	M.	48-60-55	2.00-4.00-3.03
1883:				Do.	M.	(¹)	³.30-.40-.36½
California	M.	(¹)	1.50-1.50-1.50	**1891:**			
Illinois	M.	60-60-60	2.00-3.00-2.27	Maine	M.	60-60-60	1.60-2.25-1.81
Michigan	M.	60-60-60	1.35-4.00-3.23	Do.	M.	(¹)	³.17½-.17½-.17½
Minnesota	M.	60-60-60	2.50-3.00-2.75	**1892:**			
New York	M.	38-45-41	1.20-3.00-1.66	California	M.	54-60-56	5.50-5.50-5.50
Pennsylvania	M.	55-55-55	1.75-1.75-1.75	**1893:**			
Texas	M.	73-73-73	5.00-5.00-5.00	Illinois	M.	42-70-55	1.17-3.00-1.76
1884:				Maryland	M.	60-72-65	.83-2.00-1.37
Illinois	M.	60-60-60	2.90-3.00-2.19	New York	M.	46-84-60	.58-3.50-1.78
Michigan	M.	(¹)	2.00-2.25-2.09	Ohio	M.	60-60-60	3.10-3.10-3.10
New York	M.	60-60-60	2.50-2.50-2.50	Pennsylvania	M.	48-72-59	1.25-3.00-1.89
Oregon	M.	54-60-57	4.00-4.95-4.48	**1894:**			
Pennsylvania	M.	50-50-50	1.73-1.73-1.73	Massachusetts	M.	(¹)	1.75-1.75-1.75
South Carolina	M.	54-54-54	4.50-4.50-4.50	**1896:**			
1885:				Florida	M.	(¹)	1.67-1.67-1.67
Illinois	M.	60-60-60	2.00-3.00-2.22	New York	M.	60-60-60	2.50-3.50-2.89
New York	M.	36-39-37	1.05-1.25-1.15	**1897:**			
Texas	M.	60-72-71	4.00-5.00-4.92	Michigan	(¹)	(¹)	1.25-3.00-2.27
1886:				Do.	(¹)	(¹)	³.30-.50-.39
California	M.	60-60-60	2.68-2.68-2.68	New York	M.	60-60-60	3.00-3.00-3.00
Do.	M.	72-72-72	²1.92-1.92-1.92	**1898:**			
Florida	M.	60-60-60	2.00-2.50-2.25	New York	M.	48-48-48	2.00-2.50-2.15
Illinois	M.	60-60-60	2.00-3.00-2.19				

¹ Not reported.   ² And board.   ³ Per hour.

TABLE **N-11.**—*Longshoremen, 1913–1928, by city and year*

Year	Baltimore, Md.		Boston, Mass.		New Orleans, La.		New York, N. Y.	
	Hours per week	Rate per hour	Hours per week	Rate per hour	Hours per week	Rate per hour	Hours per week	Rate per hour
1913	60.0	$0.250	59.0	$0.330	59.0	$0.400	60.0	$0.330
1914	[1] 60.0	[1].250	59.0	.330	[2] 59.0	[2].400	60.0	.330
1915	[1] 60.0	[1].250	59.0	.230	[2] 59.0	[2].400	60.0	.330
1916			59.0	.250	[2] 59.0	[2].400	60.0	.350
1917			59.0	.250	[2] 59.0	[2].400	60.0	[2].400
1918			59.0	.305	[2] 58.0	[2].500	[3] 54.0	[3].500
1919			44.0	.650	[4] 48.0	[4].650	[3] 44.0	[3].650
1920	44.0	.850	44.0	.800	[4] 44.0	[4].800	[3] 44.0	[3].800
1921	44.0	.850	44.0	.800	[4] 44.0	[4].800	44.0	.800
1922	48.0	.700	48.0	.650	[4] 48.0	[4].650	48.0	.650
1923	[5] 48.0	[5].750	48.0	.700	[4] 48.0	[4].650	48.0	.700
1924	48.0	[6].800	48.0	.800	[4] 48.0	[4].800	48.0	.800
1925	[6] 44.0	[6].800	44.0	.800	[4] 48.0	[4].800	44.0	.800
1926	44.0	.800	44.0	.800	48.0	.800	44.0	.800
1927	44.0	.800	44.0	.800	48.0	.800	44.0	.800
1928	44.0	.800	44.0	.850	48.0	.800	44.0	.850

Year	Philadelphia, Pa.		Portland, Me.		San Francisco, Calif.	
1913	60.0	$0.200			54.0	$0.500
1914	60.0	.300			54.0	.500
1915	60.0	.300			54.0	.500
1916	60.0	.350			54.0	.500
1917	60.0	.400	[7] 60.0	[7] $0.350	54.0	.550
1918	60.0	.500	54.0	.500	54.0	.650
1919	44.0	.650	44.0	.650	48.0	.800
1920	44.0	.800	44.0	.800	48.0 / 48.0	[8] .990 / [9] 1.000
1921	44.0	.800	44.0	.800	48.0	.900
1922	50.0	.650	48.0	.650	48.0	.800
1923	50.0	.700	48.0	.700	48.0	.800
1924	50.0	.800	48.0	.800	48.0	.900
1925	50.0	.800	48.0	.800	48.0	.900
1926	50.0	.800	44.0	.800	48.0	.900
1927	44.0	.800	44.0	.800	48.0	.900
1928	44.0	.850	44.0	.850	48.0	.900

[1] Freight and coal handlers.
[2] Longshoremen and stevedores.
[3] Freight handlers, general cargo, foreign-bound vessels.
[4] Docks and vessels.
[5] Deckmen.
[6] Hold men and truckers.
[7] Freight handlers.
[8] Including a bonus of 9 cents per hour.
[9] Including a bonus of 10 cents per hour.

TABLE N-12.—*Teamsters, 1840-1900, by year and State*

Year and State	Sex	Lowest, highest, and average—		Year and State	Sex	Lowest, highest, and average—	
		Hours per week	Rate per day (dollars)			Hours per week	Rate per day (dollars)
1840:				**1859:**			
Massachusetts	M.	78-84-82	1.00-1.50-1.33	Maryland	M.	60-60-60	1.00-1.13-1.07
Pennsylvania	M.	(1)	1.00-1.00-1.00	Massachusetts	M.	60-72-63	.90-1.50-1.13
1841:				New York	M.	60-66-64	.50-2.00-1.01
Massachusetts	M.	84-84-84	1.50-1.50-1.50	**1860:**			
1842:				Maryland	M.	60-60-60	.92-1.13-1.04
Massachusetts	M.	78-84-82	1.00-1.50-1.33	Massachusetts	M.	60-72-62	.85-1.50-1.07
New York	M.	66-66-66	1.50-1.50-1.50	New Jersey	M.	72-72-72	.50-.50-.50
Pennsylvania	M.	(1)	1.00-1.00-1.00	New York	M.	60-66-65	1.00-2.00-1.10
1843:				Pennsylvania	M.	60-60-60	1.50-1.50-1.50
Massachusetts	M.	78-84-81	1.00-1.50-1.25	**1861:**			
New York	M.	66-66-66	1.50-1.50-1.50	Maryland	M.	60-60-60	.75-1.12-.84
Pennsylvania	M.	(1)	1.00-1.00-1.00	Massachusetts	M.	60-66-61	.85-1.50-1.08
1844:				New York	M.	60-66-64	.75-2.00-1.07
Massachusetts	M.	78-84-81	1.00-1.50-1.25	**1862:**			
New York	M.	66-66-66	1.50-1.50-1.50	Maryland	M.	60-60-60	.83-1.00-.94
Pennsylvania	M.	(1)	1.00-1.00-1.00	Massachusetts	M.	60-66-61	.85-1.50-1.14
1845:				New York	M.	60-66-64	.75-2.00-1.06
Massachusetts	M.	78-84-83	1.00-1.75-1.40	**1863:**			
New York	M.	66-66-66	1.50-1.50-1.50	Maryland	M.	60-60-60	1.13-1.25-1.17
Pennsylvania	M.	(1)	1.00-1.00-1.00	Massachusetts	M.	60-66-62	.80-1.50-1.17
1846:				New York	M.	60-66-64	.75-2.00-1.21
Massachusetts	M.	78-84-83	1.00-1.75-1.22	Pennsylvania	M.	(1)	1.00-1.00-1.00
New York	M.	66-66-66	1.50-1.50-1.50	**1864:**			
Pennsylvania	M.	(1)	1.00-1.00-1.00	Maryland	M.	60-60-60	1.33-1.67-1.50
1947:				Massachusetts	M.	60-66-62	.75-1.50-1.22
Massachusetts	M.	78-84-83	1.00-1.75-1.40	New York	M.	60-66-64	1.00-2.00-1.39
New York	M.	60-66-64	.60-1.50-1.20	Pennsylvania	M.	60-60-60	1.50-1.75-1.63
Pennsylvania	M.	(1)	1.00-1.00-1.00	**1865:**			
1848:				Maryland	M.	60-60-60	1.60-1.75-1.64
Massachusetts	M.	78-84-83	1.00-1.75-1.32	Massachusetts	M.	60-66-62	1.25-1.50-1.39
New York	M.	60-66-64	.60-1.50-1.20	New York	M.	60-66-64	1.00-2.00-1.51
Pennsylvania	M.	(1)	1.00-1.00-1.00	Pennsylvania	M.	60-60-60	1.75-1.83-1.79
1849:				**1866:**			
Massachusetts	M.	60-84-76	.85-1.83-1.19	Connecticut	M.	66-66-66	2.00-2.00-2.00
New York	M.	60-66-64	.60-1.50-1.20	Maine	M.	66-66-66	1.67-2.00-1.84
Pennsylvania	M.	(1)	1.00-1.00-1.00	Maryland	M.	60-60-60	1.60-2.00-1.70
1850:				Massachusetts	M.	60-66-62	1.25-2.00-1.56
Massachusetts	M.	60-84-78	.85-1.83-1.27	New Jersey	M.	(1)	1.38-1.38-1.38
New York	M.	60-66-64	.80-2.00-1.23	New York	M.	60-66-64	1.25-2.00-1.53
1851:				Pennsylvania	M.	60-60-60	1.67-1.83-1.75
Massachusetts	M.	60-84-74	.85-1.83-1.23	**1867:**			
New York	M.	60-66-64	.80-2.00-1.23	Connecticut	M.	66-66-66	1.50-1.50-1.50
1852:				Georgia	M.	66-66-66	.83-.83-.83
Massachusetts	M.	60-72-70	.90-2.50-1.55	Maryland	M.	60-60-60	1.60-2.00-1.70
New York	M.	60-66-62	.75-2.00-1.06	Massachusetts	M.	60-66-62	1.50-2.00-1.58
Pennsylvania	M.	(1)	1.00-1.00-1.00	New York	M.	60-66-64	1.25-1.50-1.47
1853:				Pennsylvania	M.	60-60-60	2.00-2.00-2.00
Massachusetts	M.	60-72-67	.90-1.75-1.21	**1868:**			
New York	M.	60-66-63	.80-2.00-1.44	Connecticut	M.	66-66-66	1.50-1.50-1.50
Pennsylvania	M.	(1)	1.00 1.00 1.00	Maryland	M.	60-60-60	1.60-1.75-1.65
1854:				Massachusetts	M.	60-66-62	1.50-2.00-1.58
Maryland	M.	60-60-60	1.00-1.00-1.00	New York	M.	60-66-63	1.50-1.67-1.51
Massachusetts	M.	60-72-69	1.00-1.83-1.33	Pennsylvania	M.	60-62-61	1.17-2.17-1.75
New York	M.	60-66-65	.62-2.00-.90	**1869:**			
1855:				Connecticut	M.	60-66-61	1.50-1.83-1.77
Maryland	M.	60-60-60	1.00-1.12-1.02	Maryland	M.	60-60-60	1.50-1.75-1.62
Massachusetts	M.	60-72-67	1.00-1.83-1.26	Massachusetts	M.	60-72-63	1.50-2.00-1.70
New York	M.	60-66-65	.83-2.00-.97	New Hampshire	M.	(1)	2.00-2.00-2.00
1856:				New York	M.	60-66-64	1.50-2.00-1.54
Maryland	M.	60-60-60	1.00-1.13-1.07	Pennsylvania	M.	60-60-60	1.17-2.17-1.71
Massachusetts	M.	60-72-67	1.00-1.50-1.20	**1870:**			
New York	M.	60-66-64	.75-2.00-1.03	California	M.	72-72-72	2.00-3.00-2.63
Pennsylvania	M.	72-72-72	.77-.77-.77	Connecticut	M.	60-66-61	1.50-1.83-1.70
1857:				Illinois	M.	63-63-63	1.92-2.30-2.12
Maryland	M.	60-60-60	1.00-1.13-1.07	Louisiana	M.	72-72-72	1.65-2.50-2.24
Massachusetts	M.	60-72-66	1.00-1.50-1.20	Maryland	M.	60-60-60	1.60-2.00-1.75
New York	M.	60-66-64	.88-2.00-1.05	Massachusetts	M.	60-66-62	1.50-2.50-1.86
Pennsylvania	M.	(1)	1.00-1.00-1.00	Minnesota	M.	60-60-60	1.50-1.50-1.50
1858:				Missouri	M.	60-60-60	1.34-2.11-1.67
Maryland	M.	60-60-60	1.00-1.13-1.07	New York	M.	60-72-65	1.50-2.17-1.64
Massachusetts	M.	60-72-65	1.00-1.50-1.17	Ohio	M.	60-60-60	1.75-2.00-1.81
New York	M.	60-66-64	.75-2.00-1.04	Pennsylvania	M.	60-72-62	1.33-2.08-1.74
				Virginia	M.	60-60-60	1.00-1.00-1.00

1 Not reported.

TABLE N-12.—*Teamsters, 1840–1900, by year and State*—Continued

Year and State	Sex	Hours per week	Rate per day (dollars)	Year and State	Sex	Hours per week	Rate per day (dollars)
1871:				1876—Continued.			
California	M.	72-72-72	2.00-3.00-2.64	Maryland	M.	60-60-60	1.33-2.00-1.72
Connecticut	M.	66-66-66	2.00-2.00-2.00	Massachusetts	M.	60-60-62	1.50-2.67-1.93
Illinois	M.	63-63-63	1.90-2.30-2.11	Minnesota	M.	60-60-60	1.50-1.50-1.50
Louisiana	M.	72-72-72	1.65-2.50-2.29	Missouri	M.	60-60-60	1.34-2.11-1.69
Maryland	M.	60-60-60	1.60-2.00-1.75	New Hampshire	M.	66-72-68	1.25-1.50-1.40
Massachusetts	M.	53-70-62	1.25-2.50-1.91	New York	M.	60-72-65	1.25-2.17-1.62
Minnesota	M.	60-60-60	1.50-1.50-1.50	Ohio	M.	60-60-60	1.83-2.17-1.96
Missouri	M.	60-60-60	1.34-2.11-1.68	Pennsylvania	M.	60-72-62	.65-3.00-1.31
New York	M.	60-72-65	1.50-2.17-1.64	South Carolina	M.	66-66-66	.67-.75-.72
Ohio	M.	60-60-60	1.75-2.00-1.87	Vermont	M.	72-72-72	1.80-1.80-1.80
Pennsylvania	M.	60-72-62	1.25-2.08-1.71	Virginia	M.	60-60-60	1.00-1.25-1.20
Virginia	M.	60-60-60	1.25-1.25-1.25	1877:			
1872:				California	M.	72-72-72	2.00-3.00-2.64
California	M.	72-72-72	2.00-3.00-2.64	Connecticut	M.	60-60-60	1.50-1.67-1.56
Connecticut	M.	66-66-66	2.00-2.00-2.00	Illinois	M.	63-63-63	1.92-2.11-2.03
Illinois	M.	63-63-63	1.92-2.30-2.09	Louisiana	M.	72-72-72	1.65-2.50-2.33
Louisiana	M.	72-72-72	1.65-2.50-2.33	Maine	M.	66-66-66	1.00-1.00-1.00
Maryland	M.	60-60-60	1.60-2.00-1.75	Maryland	M.	60-60-60	1.33-2.00-1.70
Massachusetts	M.	54-66-57	1.17-3.33-2.08	Massachusetts	M.	60-66-60	1.50-2.17-1.87
Michigan	M.	60-60-60	²1.00-1.30-1.15	Minnesota	M.	60-60-60	1.50-1.50-1.50
Minnesota	M.	60-60-60	1.50-1.50-1.50	Missouri	M.	60-60-60	1.34-2.11-1.68
Missouri	M.	60-60-60	1.34-2.11-1.68	New Hampshire	M.	72-72-72	1.50-1.50-1.50
New Hampshire	M.	72-72-72	1.50-1.50-1.50	New York	M.	60-72-65	1.00-2.17-1.58
New York	M.	60-72-64	1.25-2.17-1.64	Ohio	M.	60-60-60	.75-2.50-1.71
Ohio	M.	60-60-60	1.75-2.17-1.98	Pennsylvania	M.	60-72-62	1.12-2.00-1.62
Pennsylvania	M.	54-72-62	1.25-2.67-1.77	Virginia	M.	60-60-60	1.00-1.25-1.22
Virginia	M.	60-60-60	1.25-1.25-1.25	1878:			
1873:				California	M.	72-72-72	2.00-3.00-2.64
California	M.	72-72-72	2.00-3.00-2.64	Connecticut	M.	66-66-66	2.00-2.00-2.00
Connecticut	M.	66-66-66	2.00-2.00-2.00	Georgia	M.	66-66-66	.83-1.00-.93
Illinois	M.	63-63-63	1.92-2.11-2.01	Illinois	M.	63-63-63	1.92-2.11-2.04
Louisiana	M.	72-72-72	1.65-2.50-2.33	Louisiana	M.	72-72-72	1.65-2.50-2.26
Maryland	M.	60-60-60	1.67-2.00-1.78	Maryland	M.	60-60-60	1.33-2.00-1.70
Massachusetts	M.	60-66-62	1.17-2.50-1.83	Massachusetts	M.	60-66-60	1.25-2.50-1.85
Minnesota	M.	60-60-60	1.50-1.50-1.50	Missouri	M.	60-60-60	1.34-2.11-1.68
Missouri	M.	60-60-60	1.34-2.11-1.69	New Hampshire	M.	72-72-72	1.50-1.50-1.50
New Hampshire	M.	72-72-72	1.50-1.50-1.50	New York	M.	60-72-65	1.25-2.17-1.64
New York	M.	60-72-64	1.50-2.17-1.68	Ohio	M.	59-60-60	1.50-2.00-1.70
Ohio	M.	60-60-60	1.75-2.67-2.11	Pennsylvania	M.	54-72-62	.70-2.00-1.30
Pennsylvania	M.	60-72-62	1.50-2.50-1.85	Virginia	M.	60-60-60	1.00-1.25-1.19
Virginia	M.	60-60-60	1.25-1.25-1.25	1879:			
1874:				California	M.	72-72-72	2.00-3.00-2.65
California	M.	72-72-72	2.00-3.00-2.63	Connecticut	M.	66-66-66	1.25-1.25-1.25
Connecticut	M.	60-66-63	1.00-2.00-1.75	Illinois	M.	63-63-63	1.92-2.11-2.05
Illinois	M.	63-63-63	1.92-2.50-2.06	Louisiana	M.	72-72-72	1.65-2.50-2.22
Louisiana	M.	72-72-72	1.65-2.50-2.29	Maryland	M.	60-60-60	1.25-2.00-1.65
Maryland	M.	60-60-60	1.67-2.00-1.78	Massachusetts	M.	60-60-60	1.25-2.50-1.80
Massachusetts	M.	60-66-61	1.25-3.00-2.04	Minnesota	M.	60-60-60	1.75-1.75-1.75
Minnesota	M.	60-60-60	1.50-1.50-1.50	Missouri	M.	54-108-60	1.34-2.25-1.68
Missouri	M.	60-60-60	1.34-2.11-1.69	New Hampshire	M.	72-72-72	1.45-1.45-1.45
New Hampshire	M.	72-72-72	1.50-1.50-1.50	New Jersey	M.	(¹)	2.00-2.00-2.00
New York	M.	60-72-64	1.50-2.17-1.68	Do.	(¹)	60-72-66	1.25-1.50-1.38
Ohio	M.	60-60-60	1.67-2.17-1.80	New York	M.	60-72-66	1.00-2.17-1.61
Pennsylvania	M.	42-72-55	.80-2.17-1.33	Ohio	M.	60-60-60	1.50-1.83-1.71
Virginia	M.	60-60-60	1.00-1.25-1.22	Pennsylvania	M.	60-72-62	.75-4.00-1.62
1875:				Do.	(¹)		².58-.58-.58
California	M.	72-72-72	2.00-2.83-2.56	Virginia	M.	60-60-60	1.00-1.25-1.21
Connecticut	M.	60-66-61	1.50-2.00-1.55	1880:			
Illinois	M.	63-63-63	1.92-2.11-2.03	California	M.	72-72-72	2.00-3.00-2.68
Louisiana	M.	72-72-72	1.65-2.50-2.36	Connecticut	M.	66-66-63	1.50-1.75-1.63
Maryland	M.	60-60-60	1.33-2.00-1.68	Illinois	M.	60-63-63	1.53-2.59-2.09
Massachusetts	M.	60-66-60	1.50-2.67-1.95	Louisiana	M.	72-72-72	1.65-2.50-2.22
Minnesota	M.	60-60-60	1.50-1.50-1.50	Maryland	M.	60-60-60	1.25-2.00-1.66
Missouri	M.	60-60-60	1.34-2.11-1.69	Massachusetts	M.	60-60-60	1.00-2.50-1.70
New Hampshire	M.	72-72-72	1.50-1.50-1.50	Minnesota	M.	60-60-60	1.50-1.75-1.62
New York	M.	57-72-65	1.50-2.50-1.75	Missouri	M.	60-60-60	1.34-2.11-1.69
Ohio	M.	60-60-00	1.67-2.17-1.83	New Hampshire	M.	72-72-72	1.45-1.45-1.45
Pennsylvania	M.	60-72-63	1.25-2.00-1.67	New Jersey	(¹)	60-72-63	1.00-1.40-1.13
Virginia	M.	60-60-60	1.00-1.25-1.20	New York	M.	52-72-60	1.25-2.75-1.76
1876:				Ohio	M.	60-60-60	1.67-2.17-1.78
California	M.	72-72-72	2.00-3.00-2.63	Pennsylvania	M.	53-72-62	1.17-2.25-1.69
Connecticut	M.	60-66-63	1.67-2.00-1.84	Rhode Island	M.	72-72-72	1.25-1.50-1.38
Illinois	M.	63-63-63	1.92-2.11-2.02	Virginia	M.	60-60-60	1.00-1.25-1.18
Louisiana	M.	72-72-72	1.65-2.50-2.32				

¹ Not reported. ² And board.

TABLE **N-12.**—*Teamsters, 1840–1900, by year and State*—Continued

Year and State	Sex	Hours per week	Rate per day (dollars)	Year and State	Sex	Hours per week	Rate per day (dollars)
1881:				**1884—Continued.**			
California	M.	72–72–72	2.00–3.00–2.64	New Hampshire	M.	72–72–72	1.45–1.67–1.56
Connecticut	M.	66–66–66	1.50–1.50–1.50	New Jersey	M.	56–60–60	1.20–2.17–1.52
Illinois	M.	.63–63–63	1.92–2.11–2.05	New York	M.	60–72–65	1.25–2.17–1.77
Louisiana	M.	72–72–72	1.65–2.50–2.22	Ohio	M.	51–60–59	1.00–2.75–1.91
Maryland	M.	60–60–60	1.33–2.00–1.66	Pennsylvania	M.	54–78–61	1.00–2.03–1.67
Massachusetts	M.	60–66–60	1.15–2.50–1.69	Rhode Island	M.	72–72–72	1.25–1.50–1.38
Michigan	M.	60–60–60	1.25–1.25–1.25	South Carolina	M.	69–69–69	.75–.83–.77
Minnesota	M.	60–60–60	1.50–1.75–1.62	Tennessee	M.	66–66–66	1.00–1.00–1.00
Missouri	M.	60–60–60	1.34–2.11–1.68	Virginia	M.	55–60–59	1.00–1.75–1.27
New Hampshire	M.	65–72–66	1.40–1.50–1.49	West Virginia	M.	60–60–60	.83–.83–.83
New Jersey	M.	[1]	1.15–1.15–1.15	Wisconsin	M.	60–60–60	2.00–2.00–2.00
New York	M.	60–72–65	1.25–2.17–1.63	**1885:**			
Ohio	M.	48–72–60	1.00–3.50–1.49	Alabama	M.	72–72–72	1.25–1.25–1.25
Pennsylvania	M.	54–72–60	1.33–2.25–1.41	California	M.	60–72–71	2.00–3.33–2.65
Rhode Island	M.	72–72–69	1.25–2.25–1.67	Connecticut	M.	60–66–62	1.13–1.80–1.43
South Carolina	M.	72–72–72	.50–.60–.57	Delaware	M.	60–60–60	1.17–1.50–1.43
Virginia	M.	60–60–60	1.00–1.25–1.19	Georgia	M.	66–69–68	1.00–1.05–1.03
1882:				Illinois	M.	60–72–65	1.50–2.50–1.85
California	M.	72–72–72	2.00–3.00–2.62	Indiana	M.	60–72–63	1.25–2.00–1.52
Connecticut	M.	66–66–66	1.50–1.67–1.56	Kansas	M.	60–60–60	1.33–3.00–1.93
Georgia	M.	72–72–72	1.00–1.00–1.00	Kentucky	M.	54–60–56	1.00–2.50–1.47
Illinois	M.	63–66–64	1.80–2.11–1.95	Louisiana	M.	72–72–72	1.65–2.50–2.30
Iowa	M.	60–60–60	1.35–1.50–1.43	Maine	M.	60–72–66	1.00–1.73–1.37
Louisiana	M.	72–72–72	1.65–2.50–2.18	Maryland	M.	60–72–68	1.00–2.00–1.40
Maine	M.	66–66–66	1.25–1.25–1.25	Massachusetts	M.	54–66–60	1.05–2.50–1.59
Maryland	M.	60–60–60	1.33–2.00–1.70	Michigan	M.	60–66–66	.75–2.67–1.36
Massachusetts	M.	60–60–60	1.15–2.50–1.77	Minnesota	M.	60–60–60	1.75–1.75–1.75
Minnesota	M.	60–60–60	1.50–1.75–1.62	Missouri	M.	60–60–60	1.34–2.33–1.70
Missouri	M.	59–60–60	1.00–2.11–1.69	New Hampshire	M.	60–72–66	1.17–1.50–1.42
New Hampshire	M.	72–72–72	1.35–1.35–1.35	New Jersey	M.	45–72–55	1.00–2.33–1.48
New Jersey	M.	[1]	1.25–1.25–1.25	New York	M.	52–72–63	.75–2.37–1.74
New York	M.	60–72–60	1.25–4.00–3.66	North Carolina	M.	69–69–69	.75–1.00–.81
North Carolina	M.	60–60–60	.67–.75–.70	Ohio	M.	51–72–66	1.00–2.88–1.57
Ohio	M.	60–60–60	1.67–2.17–1.85	Pennsylvania	M.	48–84–59	1.00–2.25–1.53
Do	[1]	54–72–61	.75–3.00–1.54	Rhode Island	M.	48–72–58	1.25–2.25–1.69
Pennsylvania	M.	54–72–56	1.33–2.25–1.73	Vermont	M.	66–66–66	1.22–1.25–1.23
Rhode Island	M.	72–72–72	1.25–1.50–1.38	Virginia	M.	60–72–64	.50–1.25–1.18
South Carolina	M.	69–76–71	.50–.75–.67	West Virginia	M.	60–60–60	1.66–1.66–1.66
Virginia	M.	60–60–60	1.00–1.25–1.18	Wisconsin	M.	59–66–60	1.14–2.00–1.83
West Virginia	M.	59–59–59	1.40–1.40–1.40	**1886:**			
1883:				California	M.	60–72–66	1.50–3.00–1.98
Alabama	M.	[1]	1.00–1.00–1.00	Do	M.	60–72–70	[2]1.00–2.30–1.56
California	M.	72–72–72	2.00–3.00–2.63	Connecticut	M.	54–60–57	1.10–1.80–1.47
Connecticut	M.	66–66–66	1.50–1.50–1.50	Illinois	M.	60–84–80	1.00–2.50–1.61
Georgia	M.	[1]	.80–1.10–1.00	Kansas	M.	60–72–64	1.10–2.00–1.93
Illinois	M.	63–63–63	1.92–2.11–2.05	Louisiana	M.	72–72–72	1.65–2.50–2.22
Louisiana	M.	72–72–72	1.65–2.50–2.26	Maryland	M.	60–60–60	1.50–1.67–1.55
Maryland	M.	60–66–65	1.33–2.00–1.66	Massachusetts	M.	60–60–60	1.05–2.50–1.74
Massachusetts	M.	60–66 60	1.00 3.21–1.92	Michigan	M.	58–60–60	1.17–2.00–1.44
Michigan	M.	[1]	.75–2.25–1.54	Minnesota	M.	60–60–60	1.75–1.83–1.76
Minnestoa	M.	60–60–60	1.75–1.75–1.75	Missouri	M.	60–60–60	1.34–2.11–1.68
Missouri	M.	59–60–60	1.34–2.11–1.68	New Hampshire	M.	60–72–61	1.17–1.50–1.22
New Hampshire	M.	72–72–72	1.40–1.40–1.40	New Jersey	M.	60–60–60	1.14–1.67–1.34
New Jersey	M.	[1]	1.50–2.67–2.00	New York	M.	58–72–62	1.25–2.17–1.87
New York	M.	60–72–65	1.25–2.17–1.75	Ohio	M.	60–72–65	1.50–2.17–1.76
North Carolina	M.	[1]	.75–.75–.75	Pennsylvania	M.	48–72–60	1.25–2.50–1.82
Ohio	M.	60–60–60	1.17–2.00–1.75	Rhode Island	M.	60–60–60	1.25–1.83–1.61
Pennsylvania	M.	60–72–62	1.34–2.25–1.65	Virginia	M.	60–60–60	1.00–1.50–1.40
Rhode Island	M.	72–72–72	1.25–1.50–1.38	**1887:**			
Tennessee	M.	66–66–66	1.00–1.00–1.00	California	M.	72–72–72	2.00–3.00–2.60
Virginia	M.	60–60–60	1.00–1.25–1.20	Connecticut	M.	60–72–72	1.18–3.65–1.77
1884:				Florida	M.	[1]	1.15–1.15–1.15
California	M.	60–84–64	1.92–3.00–2.12	Illinois	M.	63–63–63	1.92–2.11–2.05
Connecticut	M.	66–66–66	1.50–1.50–1.50	Kansas	M.	60–72–65	1.25–3.00–2.38
Georgia	M.	66–70–68	.75–.85–.80	Louisiana	M.	72–72–72	1.65–2.50–2.34
Illinois	M.	63–78–63	1.50–4.00–2.09	Maryland	M.	60–60–60	1.10–1.92–1.53
Iowa	M.	63–63–63	1.29–3.00–1.89	Massachusetts	M.	60–60–60	1.40–2.50–1.85
Kentucky	M.	66–66–66	1.50–1.50–1.50	Minnesota	M.	60–60–60	1.75–1.75–1.75
Louisiana	M.	66–72–72	1.50–2.50–2.27	Missouri	M.	60–72–60	1.35–2.30–1.89
Maryland	M.	60–60–60	1.33–1.67–1.53	New Hampshire	M.	60–60–60	1.50–1.50 1.50
Massachusetts	M.	60–60–60	1.15–2.50–1.80	New York	M.	60–72–66	1.35–2.17–1.75
Michigan	M.	[1]	.40–3.50–1.54	Ohio	M.	48–72–60	.40–4.00–1.74
Minnesota	M.	60–60–60	1.75–1.75–1.75	Pennsylvania	M.	60–72–62	1.00–2.17–1.72
Missouri	M.	60–60–60	1.34–2.11–1.73	Do	M.	[1]	[3].13½–.13½–.13½

[1] Not reported.　　　[2] And board.　　　[3] Per hour.

TABLE N-12.—*Teamsters, 1840-1900, by year and State*—Continued

Year and State	Sex	Hours per week	Rate per day (dollars)
1887—Continued.			
Rhode Island	M.	60–60–60	1.25–1.50–1.38
Virginia	M.	60–60–60	1.00–1.50–1.40
Wisconsin	M.	(1)	1.50–2.00–1.55
1888:			
California	M.	72–72–72	2.00–3.00–2.60
Colorado	M.	60–60–60	1.20–2.00–1.60
Connecticut	M.	60–60–60	1.62–1.62–1.62
Delaware	M.	(1)	1.50–1.50–1.50
Georgia	M.	(1)	1.00–1.00–1.00
Illinois	M.	63–63–63	1.92–2.11–2.04
Indiana	M.	(1)	1.25–1.25–1.25
Kansas	M.	54–72–64	.96–3.00–1.46
Louisiana	M.	72–72–72	1.65–2.50–2.36
Maine	M.	66–66–66	1.33–1.33–1.33
Maryland	M.	60–60–60	1.50–1.67–1.54
Massachusetts	M.	60–60–60	1.30–2.50–1.87
Michigan	M.	60–60–60	.61–1.99–1.38
Minnesota	M.	60–60–60	1.75–1.75–1.75
Missouri	M.	60–60–60	1.73–2.30–1.91
New Hampshire	M.	60–60–60	1.50–1.50–1.50
New Jersey	M.	60–78–67	1.25–2.50–1.69
New York	M.	48–74–60	.80–4.00–1.73
Do	M.	(1)	[3].20–.20–.20
Do	M.	62–62–62	[4]2.00–2.00–2.00
Do	M.	58–60–59	[2].77–1.67–1.07
North Carolina	M.	(1)	1.00–1.00–1.00
Ohio	M.	60–60–60	1.50–2.17–1.66
Pennsylvania	M.	60–72–62	.84–2.17–1.69
Rhode Island	M.	60–60–60	1.25–1.50–1.42
South Carolina	M.	66–66–66	.75–1.05–.83
Tennessee	M.	60–60–60	1.15–1.25–1.18
Virginia	M.	60–60–60	.83–1.50–1.32
1889:			
Alabama	M.	60–60–60	1.00–1.50–1.08
California	M.	72–72–72	2.00–3.00–2.61
Connecticut	M.	60–60–60	1.34–1.75–1.50
Delaware	M.	60–60–60	1.42–1.42–1.42
Illinois	M.	60–72–63	1.13–2.75–1.86
Indiana	M.	60–60–60	1.25–2.00–1.40
Kansas	M.	54–72–65	.58–2.50–1.38
Louisiana	M.	72–72–72	1.65–2.25–2.10
Maine	M.	60–60–60	1.25–1.80–1.48
Maryland	M.	60–60–60	1.25–1.67–1.53
Massachusetts	M.	60–66–60	1.25–2.67–1.75
Michigan	M.	60–60–60	.75–2.25–1.39
Minnesota	M.	60–60–60	1.75–1.75–1.75
Mississippi	M.	(1)	1.00–1.00–1.00
Missouri	M.	60–60–60	1.73–2.30–1.90
New Hampshire	M.	60–60–60	1.00–2.30–1.54
New Jersey	M.	60–60–60	1.34–1.67–1.41
New York	M.	60–72–66	1.25–3.00–1.83
North Carolina	M.	(1)	1.00–1.00–1.00
Ohio	M.	54–66–59	.75–2.17–1.56
Pennsylvania	M.	60–84–62	.60–2.17–1.56
Do	(1)	M.	1.50–1.92–1.86
Rhode Island	M.	60–60–60	1.25–1.50–1.38
South Carolina	M.	69–69–69	.65–.65–.65
Tennessee		72–72–72	1.00–1.25–1.06
Virginia	M.	60–72–63	1.00–1.50–1.35
West Virginia	M.	(1)	1.55–2.15–1.84
1890:			
Alabama	M.	60–72–71	.54–1.15–.94
California	M.	72–72–72	2.00–3.00–2.62
Connecticut	M.	54–60–57	1.62–1.80–1.71
Illinois	M.	60–63–62	1.50–2.50–1.96
Indiana	M.	54–54–54	1.25–1.25–1.25
Louisiana	M.	72–72–72	1.65–2.25–2.10
Maine	M.	60–60–60	1.25–1.50–1.38
Maryland	M.	48–60–59	1.50–1.67–1.55
Massachusetts	M.	60–66–60	1.30–2.33–1.77
Michigan	M.	60–60–60	1.00–2.00–1.45
Minnesota	M.	60–60–60	1.40–2.75–2.53
Mississippi	M.	(1)	.75–1.00–.90
Missouri	M.	60–60–60	1.54–2.30–1.90
1890—Continued.			
Nebraska	M.	(1)	.77–1.50–1.24
New Hampshire	M.	60–60–60	1.25–1.75–1.42
New Jersey	M.	60–60–60	1.20–1.67–1.38
New York	M.	54–72–66	.44–5.33–1.66
North Carolina	M.	(1)	.68–1.00–.78
Ohio	M.	54–60–58	1.50–2.17–1.76
Do	(1)	54–66–60	1.60–2.15–1.81
Pennsylvania	M.	60–72–61	1.50–2.17–1.82
Rhode Island	M.	60–60–60	1.25–1.50–1.38
Virginia	M.	60–60–60	1.00–1.50–1.44
1891:			
California	M.	72–72–72	2.00–3.00–2.60
Connecticut	M.	54–60–57	1.62–1.80–1.71
Florida	M.	55–60–60	1.00–1.25–1.18
Illinois	M.	(2)	3.85–3.85–3.85
Do	M.	58–63–63	1.92–2.11–2.03
Louisiana	M.	72–72–72	1.65–2.25–2.10
Maine	M.	60–72–62	1.25–1.80–1.54
Maryland	M.	60–60–60	1.50–1.67–1.55
Massachusetts	M.	60–60–60	1.30–2.50–1.82
Michigan	M.	60–60–60	1.38–1.50–1.45
Minnesota	M.	60–60–60	1.50–1.75–1.70
Do	M.	(1)	1.00–1.34–1.09
Missouri	M.	60–60–60	1.24–2.30–1.91
New Hampshire	M.	60–60–60	1.75–1.75–1.75
New Jersey	M.	60–60–60	1.50–1.67–1.59
New York	M.	54–72–66	.50–6.67–1.66
Ohio	M.	30–72–59	.75–2.50–1.56
Pennsylvania	M.	54–72–62	1.50–2.17–1.78
Rhode Island	M.	60–60–60	1.25–1.50–1.38
Virginia	M.	60–60–60	1.00–1.50–1.44
Wisconsin	M.	60–60–60	1.00–2.25–1.66
1892:			
California	M.	60–72–70	1.25–3.00–2.49
Do	M.	60–60–60	[2]1.25–1.25–1.25
Connecticut	M.	54–60–59	1.60–2.00–1.77
Florida	M.	54–66–60	.88–1.25–1.03
Illinois	M.	63–63–63	1.92–2.11–2.02
Indiana	M.	60–60–60	2.25–2.25–2.25
Louisiana	M.	72–72–72	1.65–2.25–2.16
Maine	M.	60–60–60	1.50–1.75–1.62
Maryland	M.	60–60–60	1.13–2.00–1.55
Massachusetts	M.	58–66–59	1.07–2.50–1.70
Michigan	M.	60–60–60	1.38–1.50–1.45
Minnesota	M.	60–60–60	1.50–1.75–1.69
Do	M.	(1)	[2]1.00–1.34–1.10
Missouri	M.	60–60–60	1.73–2.30–1.91
New Hampshire	M.	66–72–70	1.50–2.00–1.83
New York	M.	54–72–67	1.50–2.33–2.00
Ohio	M.	48–60–57	.75–3.50–1.77
Pennsylvania	M.	60–60–62	1.50–2.36–1.78
Rhode Island	M.	54–60–58	1.25–2.00–1.54
Virginia	M.	60–60–60	1.00–1.50–1.44
Wisconsin	M.	60–60–60	1.60–1.60–1.60
1893:			
California	M.	72–72–72	2.00–2.83–2.36
Connecticut	M.	54–60–59	1.60–2.00–1.96
Illinois	M.	48–84–61	.50–4.17–1.93
Kansas	M.	(1)	2.50–2.50–2.50
Louisiana	M.	72–72–72	1.65–2.00–1.91
Maryland	M.	48–96–64	.33–3.00–1.59
Massachusetts	M.	58–66–60	1.16–2.33–1.82
Michigan	M.	60–60–60	1.15–1.50–1.40
Minnesota	M.	60–60–60	1.50–1.75–1.65
Do	M.	(1)	[2].77–1.00–.91
Missouri	M.	60–60–60	1.73–2.30–1.90
Montana	M.	(1)	(1) [5]1.69–1.69–1.69
New York	M.	35–103–65	.33–4.17–1.89
Ohio	M.	42–72–59	.66–3.50–1.57
Pennsylvania	M.	35–94–63	.42–3.33–1.69
Rhode Island	M.	60–60–60	1.25–1.83–1.48
Virginia	M.	60–60–60	1.00–1.50–1.44
Wisconsin	M.	60–60–60	1.42–2.70–2.59
Do	M.	(1)	[2]1.00–1.00–1.00

1 Not reported.
2 And board.
3 Per hour.
4 And a commission.
5 And board and lodging.

TABLE N-12.—*Teamsters, 1840–1900, by year and State*—Continued

Year and State	Sex	Lowest, highest, and average—		Year and State	Sex	Lowest, highest, and average—	
		Hours per week	Rate per day (dollars)			Hours per week	Rate per day (dollars)
1894:				**1896—Continued.**			
California	M.	72–72–72	2. 00–2. 83–2. 37	Indiana	M.	65–65–65	1. 50–1. 50–1. 50
Connecticut	M.	54–60–59	1. 60–2. 00–1. 95	Kentucky	M.	60–63–61	1. 00–2. 50–1. 49
Georgia	M.	72–72–72	. 70–1. 00– . 85	Louisiana	M.	72–72–72	1. 50–1. 83–1. 77
Illinois	M.	63–63–63	1. 92–2. 11–2. 04	Maryland	M.	48–84–63	. 70–1. 67–1. 14
Iowa	M.	48–96–61	. 83–3. 00–1. 74	Massachusetts	M.	48–84–60	1. 50–2. 33–1. 79
Kansas	M.	(¹)	2. 50–2. 50–2. 50	Michigan	M.	54–72–60	. 85–2. 50–1. 38
Louisiana	M.	72–72–72	1. 65–2. 00–1. 93	Minnesota	M.	60–60–60	1. 25–1. 75–1. 54
Maine	M.	60–66–61	1. 12–2. 00–1. 58	Do	M.	60–60–60	. 61–1. 00– . 68
Maryland	M.	(¹)	1. 50–1. 67–1. 56	Missouri	M.	48–72–60	. 75–2. 45–1. 84
Massachusetts	M.	54–66–60	1. 16–2. 33–1. 78	Nebraska	M.	60–90–64	. 65–1. 75–1. 26
Michigan	M.	60–60–60	1. 25–1. 38–1. 27	New York	M.	52–72–65	1. 00–3. 00–1. 82
Minnesota	M.	60–60–60	1. 25–1. 75–1. 56	North Carolina	M.	69–69–69	. 70–1. 50– . 81
Do	M.	(¹)	² . 77–1. 00– . 86	Ohio	----	45–72–60	1. 00–2. 75–1. 79
Missouri	M.	60–60–60	1. 73–2. 30–1. 90	Pennsylvania	M.	48–72–60	1. 00–2. 75–1. 59
Montana	M.	(¹)	⁴ 1. 58–1. 58–1. 58	Rhode Island	M.	60–60–60	1. 67–2. 50–1. 76
New Hampshire	M.	53–60–58	1. 00–1. 67–1. 29	South Carolina	M.	66–66–66	. 50– . 85– . 70
New York	M.	54–72–70	1. 00–2. 33–2. 07	Tennessee	M.	69–69–69	. 50–1. 67–1. 06
North Carolina	M.	60–69–61	. 50–1. 50– . 77	Vermont	M.	64–64–64	1. 67–1. 67–1. 67
Do	(¹)	60–60–60	. 75– . 75– . 75	Virginia	M.	60–60–60	1. 00–1. 50–1. 44
Ohio	M.	45–72–60	. 50–5. 00–1. 77	West Virginia	M.	60–60–60	1. 50–1. 50–1. 50
Pennsylvania	M.	54–72–62	1. 40–2. 17–1. 74	Wisconsin	M.	48–60–58	1. 10–2. 00–1. 70
Rhode Island	M.	60–60–60	1. 25–1. 50–1. 33	**1897:**			
Virginia	M.	60–60–60	1. 00–1. 50–1. 44	California	M.	72–72–72	2. 00–2. 83–2. 38
West Virginia	M.	60–60–60	1. 25–1. 50–1. 38	Connecticut	M.	55–60–58	1. 50–1. 75–1. 63
Wisconsin	M.	60–60–60	1. 25–1. 25–1. 25	Illinois	M.	63–63–63	1. 92–2. 11–2. 02
1895:				Kansas	M.	48–105–63	. 50–2. 50–1. 46
Alabama	M.	66–66–66	. 75–1. 00– . 89	Louisiana	M.	72–72–72	1. 50–1. 83–1. 77
California	M.	72–72–72	2. 00–2. 83–2. 37	Maryland	M.	(¹)	1. 50–1. 67–1. 56
Connecticut	M.	45–72–60	1. 17–2. 25–1. 88	Massachusetts	M.	60–66–61	1. 00–2. 33–1. 90
Georgia	M.	54–66–65	. 75–1. 25– . 94	Michigan	M.	(¹)	1. 63–1. 63–1. 63
Illinois	M.	63–63–63	1. 92–2. 11–2. 04	Minnesota	M.	60–60–60	1. 75–1. 75–1. 75
Kansas	M.	60–60–60	1. 00–1. 00–1. 00	Missouri	M.	60–60–60	1. 73–2. 30–1. 90
Louisiana	M.	60–72–71	1. 65–2. 00–1. 91	Nebraska	M.	54–72–62	1. 00–2. 00–1. 64
Maine	M.	60–60–60	1. 17–2. 00–1. 49	New York	M.	60–72–67	1. 67–3. 50–2. 71
Maryland	M.	57–60–59	1. 08–1. 67–1. 52	Ohio	M.	48–60–53	1. 50–2. 00–1. 76
Massachusetts	M.	55–72–60	1. 16–2. 33–1. 75	Pennsylvania	M.	54–72–62	1. 25–2. 17–1. 76
Michigan	M.	60–60–60	1. 00–2. 00–1. 31	Virginia	M.	54–72–63	. 43–1. 75–1. 05
Minnesota	M.	60–60–60	1. 25–1. 75–1. 56	**1898:**			
Do	M.	(¹)	² . 69–1. 00– . 75	California	M.	72–72–72	2. 00–2. 83–2. 38
Missouri	M.	59–60–60	1. 25–2. 33–1. 86	Illinois	M.	63–63–63	1. 92–2. 11–2. 00
New Hampshire	M.	59–66–60	1. 10–1. 85–1. 41	Kansas	M.	30–66–52	1. 50–2. 00–1. 83
New Jersey	M.	48–60–56	. 50–2. 50–1. 55	Louisiana	M.	72–72–72	1. 50–1. 50–1. 50
New York	M.	52–72–67	. 85–2. 50–1. 99	Maryland	M.	(¹)	1. 50–1. 67–1. 56
North Carolina	M.	60–72–62	. 50–1. 00– . 67	Massachusetts	M.	60–66–61	1. 50–2. 33–2. 02
Ohio	M.	36–72–60	. 50–3. 00–1. 65	Michigan	M.	(¹)	1. 00–2. 36–1. 38
Pennsylvania	M.	54–72–61	1. 50–2. 17–1. 78	Minnesota	M.	60–60–60	1. 75–1. 75–1. 75
Rhode Island	M.	55–60–58	1. 25–2. 67–1. 70	Missouri	M.	60–60–60	1. 73–2. 30–1. 90
South Carolina	M.	66–66–66	. 50– . 95– . 83	Nebraska	(¹)	54–66–60	. 50–4. 50–1. 77
Tennessee	M.	66–67–66	1. 00–1. 25–1. 08	New York	M.	60–72–63	1. 67–3. 50–2. 74
Virginia	M.	48–60–58	1. 00–1. 75–1. 46	Ohio	M.	54–60–55	1. 25–2. 00–1. 60
West Virginia	M.	59–59–59	1. 50–1. 50–1. 50	Pennsylvania	M.	54–72–62	1. 26–2. 17–1. 70
Wisconsin	M.	59–60–60	1. 25–2. 00–1. 44	Virginia	M.	60–60–60	1. 00–1. 50–1. 40
Do	(¹)	60–72–62	1. 15–1. 90–1. 42	Washington	(¹)	(¹)	. 96–2. 49–1. 78
1896:				**1899:**			
Alabama	M.	(¹)	1. 17–1. 17–1. 17	Michigan	M.	61–61–61	1. 33–1. 33–1. 33
California	M.	72–72–72	2. 00–2. 83–2. 37	New York	M.	59–60–59	1. 50–1. 83–1. 64
Colorado	M.	60–60–60	2. 00–3. 25–2. 42	Ohio	M.	(¹)	1. 50–1. 50–1. 50
Connecticut	M.	60–60–60	1. 25–1. 67–1. 47	Pennsylvania	M.	(¹)	1. 15–2. 20–1. 63
Dist. of Columbia	M.	(¹)	. 67–1. 17– . 89	**1900:**			
Florida	M.	60–60–60	. 75–2. 50–1. 21	Massachusetts	M.	60–60–60	1. 50–1. 50–1. 50
Georgia	M.	63–66–66	. 50–3. 33– . 96	New York	M.	59–59–59	1. 67–1. 83–1. 75
Illinois	M.	48–72–60	1. 17–3. 00–1. 91				

¹ Not reported.   ² And board.   ⁴ And a commission.

TABLE **N-13.**—*Teamsters, general, 1-horse, 1913–1928, by city and year*

Year	Boston, Mass.		Chicago, Ill.		Cincinnati, Ohio		New York, N. Y.	
	Hours per week	Rate per hour	Hours per week	Rate per hour	Hours per week	Rate per hour	Hours per week	Rate per hour
1913	60.0	$0.233	66.0	[1]$0.205	60.0	$0.233	[2]60.0	[2]$0.233
1914	66.0	.212	66.0	[1].205	60.0	.217	[2]60.0	[2].250
1915	66.0	.212	66.0	[1].205	60.0	.217	[2]60.0	[2].250
1916	66.0	.212	66.0	[1].227	[3]60.0	[3].217	60.0	.250
1917	66.0	.242	66.0	.227	[3]60.0	[3].233	60.0	.283
1918	66.0	.303	64.0	.281	[3]60.0	[3].275	54.0	.352
1919	66.0	.348	60.0	.383	[3]60.0	[3].317	54.0	.444
1920	60.0	.467	60.0	.483	[3]57.0	[3].404	54.0	.537
1921	58.0	.483	60.0	.483	[3]57.0	[3].404	54.0	.537
1922	58.0	.483	60.0	.433	[3]57.0	[3].456	54.0	.537
1923	58.0	.483	60.0	.483	[3]57.0	[3].456	54.0	.537
1924	58.0	.517	60.0	.483	[3]57.0	[3].491	54.0	.630
1925	58.0	.517	60.0	[4].517	[3]57.0	[5].491	[5]54.0	[5].630
1926	58.0	.517	60.0	[4].517	[3]54.5	[3].550	[5]54.0	[5].630
1927	52.5	.571	60.0	[4].517	[3]54.5	[3].550	[5]54.0	[5].630
1928	52.5	.571	60.0	.517	[3]54.5	[3].550	[5]54.8	[5].722

Year	Philadelphia, Pa.		St. Louis, Mo.		San Francisco, Calif.	
1913	[6]70.0	[6]$0.129	66.0	$0.174	[7]60.0	[7]$0.250
1914	[8]56.0	[8].214	66.0	.189	[7]60.0	[7].250
1915	[8]56.0	[8].214	66.0	.189	[7]60.0	[7].250
1916	[9]65.0	[9].162	63.0	.206	[7]60.0	[7].250
1917	[9]63.0	[9].190	63.0	.206	[7]60.0	[7].300
1918	63.0	.222	63.0	.230	[10]60.0	[10].300
1919	63.0	.286	63.0	.325	[10]60.0	[10].350
1920	61.0	.377	63.0	.341	[10]48.0	[10].500
1921			57.0	.456	[10]48.0	[10].563
1922			57.0	.412	[10]48.0	[10].563
1923			57.0	.412		
1924			57.0	.412		
1925			57.0	.456		
1926			[11]57.0	[11].456		
1927			[11]57.0	[11].474		
1928	55.5	.450	[11]57.0	[11].491		

[1] Union N.
[2] Drivers, Union F.
[3] Heavy wagons.
[4] Union A.
[5] Single trucks.
[6] Drivers, coal.
[7] Large wagon.
[8] Drivers, Union A.
[9] Teaming.
[10] Grocery.
[11] General transfer.

TABLE **N-14.**—*Teamsters, general, 2-horse, 1913–1928, by city and year*

Year	Boston, Mass.		Chicago, Ill.		Cincinnati, Ohio		New York, N. Y.	
	Hours per week	Rate per hour	Hours per week	Rate per hour	Hours per week	Rate per hour	Hours per week	Rate per hour
1913	60.0	$0.267	66.0	[1]$0.250	60.0	$0.250	[2]60.0	[2]$0.267
1914	66.0	.242	66.0	[1].250	[3]60.0	[3].250	[2]60.0	[2].283
1915	66.0	.242	66.0	[1].250	[3]60.0	[3].250	[2]60.0	[2].283
1916	66.0	.242	66.0	[1].273	[3]60.0	[3].250	60.0	.283
1917	66.0	.273	69.0	.290	60.0	.267	60.0	.317
1918	66.0	.333	64.0	.328	60.0	.308	54.0	.389
1919	66.0	.377	60.0	.433	60.0	.350	54.0	.481
1920	60.0	.500	60.0	.533	[3]57.0	[3].439	54.0	.574
1921	58.0	.517	60.0	.533	[3]57.0	[3].439	54.0	.574
1922	58.0	.517	[4]60.0	[4].483	[3]57.0	[3].491	54.0	.574
1923	58.0	.517	[4]60.0	[4].533	[3]57.0	[3].491	54.0	.574
1924	58.0	.552	[4]60.0	[4].533	[3]57.0	[3].526	54.0	.667
1925	58.0	.552	[4]60.0	[4].567	[3]57.0	[3].526	[5]54.0	[5].667
1926	58.0	.552	[4]60.0	[4].567	[3]54.5	[3].587	[5]54.0	[5].667
1927	52.5	.610	[4]60.0	[4].567	[3]54.5	[3].587	[5]54.0	[5].667
1928	52.5	.610	[4]60.0	[4].567	[3]54.5	[3].587	[5]54.0	[5].759

[1] Union N.
[2] Drivers, Union F.
[3] Heavy wagons.
[4] Union A.
[5] Single trucks.

TABLE **N-14.**—*Teamsters, general, 2-horse, 1913-1928, by city and year*—Contd.

Year	Philadelphia, Pa.		St. Louis, Mo.		San Francisco, Calif.	
	Hours per week	Rate per hour	Hours per week	Rate' per hour	Hours per week	Rate per hour
1913	6 70.0	6 $0.143	7 66.0	7 $0.200	8 60.0	8 $0.350
1914	9 65.0	9 .286	7 66.0	7 .215	8 60.0	8 .350
1915	9 56.0	9 .286	7 66.0	7 .215	8 60.0	8 .350
1916	10 56.0	10 .286	7 63.0	7 .233	8 60.0	8 .350
1917	10 57.0	10 .263	7 63.0	7 .233	8 60.0	8 .400
1918	57.0	.333	7 63.0	7 .257	8 57.0	8 .474
1919	63.0	.381	7 63.0	7 .357	8 53.5	8 .556
1920	61.0	.459	7 63.0	7 .373	8 52.5	8 .667
1921	11 61.0	11 .393	7 57.0	7 .526	8 52.5	8 .722
1922	11 61.0	11 .393	7 57.0	7 .474	8 52.5	8 .667
1923	11 55.0	11 .491	7 57.0	7 .474	8 52.5	8 .722
1924	11 55.0	11 .491	7 57.0	7 .474	9 52.5	9 .722
1925	11 55.0	11 .491	7 57.0	7 .526	8 52.5	8 .722
1926	11 55.0	11 .491	7 57.0	7 .526	8 50.0	8 .780
1927	11 55.0	11 .491	7 57.0	7 .544	8 50.0	8 .780
1928	11 55.0	11 .491	7 57.0	7 .561	8 50.0	8 .780

6 Drivers, coal.   9 Drivers, Union A.
7 Hauling less than 5,000 pounds tonnage.   10 Teaming.
8 2-horse truck.   11 Lumber drivers

O.—WOODWORKING TRADES (INCLUDING LUMBER)

The sources from which data for cabinetmakers were taken are the fifteenth and the nineteenth annual reports of the Commissioner of Labor Statistics and bulletins of the Bureau of Labor Statistics Nos. 59, 65, 71, 77, 129, 153, 225, and 265. Reports showing data for coopers are found in the fifteenth and the nineteenth annual reports of the Commissioner of Labor Statistics and bulletins of the Bureau of Labor Statistics Nos. 294, 373, 421, and 472. No details are available for the years 1904 to 1917. The data for occupations in the lumber industry were taken from the fifteenth and the nineteenth annual reports of the Commissioner of Labor Statistics and bulletins of the Bureau of Labor Statistics Nos. 59, 65, 71, 77, 129, 153, 225, 265, 317, 363, 413, and 497. Wage data for laborers in the lumber industry are included here, other laborers are shown under the titles of Laborers (kind of work not designated), Table G-1, and Farm Laborers, Tables D-1, D-2, and D-3, and are also reported in the group of building trades, Table B-12, and of metal trades, Tables I-16, I-17, and I-18. The wage data for machine woodworkers in planing mills was taken from the fifteenth and the nineteenth annual reports of the Commissioner of Labor Statistics and from bulletins of the Bureau of Labor Statistics Nos. 59, 65, 71, 77, 129, 153, 225, and 265. No reports are available for any period after the year 1919.

TABLE O-1.—*Cabinetmakers, 1845–1900, by year and State*

Year and State	Sex	Lowest, highest, and average—		Year and State	Sex	Lowest, highest, and average—	
		Hours per week	Rate per day (dollars)			Hours per week	Rate per day (dollars)
1845:				**1867:**			
New Jersey	M.	72–72–72	1.50–1.50–1.50	Delaware	M.	60–60–60	2.50–2.50–2.50
1850:				New York	M.	72–72–72	2.00–2.00–2.00
Massachusetts	M.	60–66–62	1.50–1.75–1.58	**1869:**			
1852:				Massachusetts	M.	60–60–60	1.50–1.50–1.50
Massachusetts	M.	60–60–60	1.75–1.75–1.75	**1870:**			
1854:				Illinois	M.	60–60–60	3.20–3.50–3.44
Massachusetts	M.	60–60–60	2.50–2.50–2.50	Louisiana	M.	60–60–60	3.25–3.75–3.50
1855:				Maryland	M.	60–60–60	2.00–3.00–2.28
Massachusetts	M.	66–66–66	1.75–1.75–1.75	Massachusetts	M.	59–59–59	2.00–3.50–3.00
New Jersey	M.	60–60–60	1.50–1.75–1.58	Minnesota	M.	60–60–60	2.00–2.25–2.10
New York	M.	60–60–60	1.50–2.00–1.67	Missouri	M.	54–60–57	2.00–4.00–2.33
1856:				New York	M.	60–60–60	2.00–3.00–2.04
Massachusetts	M.	60–60–60	1.25–1.50–1.38	Ohio	M.	60–60–60	2.00–2.50–2.17
1858:				Pennsylvania	M.	60–60–60	2.00–3.00–2.47
New York	M.	60–60–60	1.50–1.50–1.50	Virginia	M.	60–60–60	2.25–2.50–2.38
1860:				**1871:**			
New Jersey	M.	60–60–60	1.50–2.00–1.63	Delaware	M.	60–60–60	2.00–3.33–2.50
New York	M.	60–60–60	1.50–1.50–1.50	Illinois	M.	60–60–60	2.80–3.50–3.30
Ohio	M.	(¹)	1.33–1.33–1.33	Louisiana	M.	60–60–60	2.75–3.25–3.00
Pennsylvania	M.	60–60–60	2.00–2.00–2.00	Maryland	M.	60–60–60	2.00–2.50–2.13
1861:				Massachusetts	M.	59–60–59	2.08–4.17–2.88
New Jersey	M.	60–60–60	2.00–2.50–2.45	Minnesota	M.	60–60–60	2.00–2.25–2.08
1866:				Missouri	M.	54–60–57	2.00–4.00–2.35
Delaware	M.	60–60–60	2.25–2.50–2.25	New York	M.	60–60–60	2.00–3.00–2.03
New York	M.	72–72–72	3.00–3.00–3.00	Ohio	M.	60–60–60	1.67–2.00–1.83
Pennsylvania	M.	60–60–60	2.50–2.50–2.50	Pennsylvania	M.	60–60–60	2.00–3.00–2.39
				Virginia	M.	60–60–60	2.25–2.50–2.38

¹ Not reported.

TABLE **O–1.**—*Cabinetmakers, 1845–1900, by year and State*—Continued

Year and State	Sex	Hours per week	Rate per day (dollars)
1872:			
Delaware	M.	60–60–60	2.33–3.00–2.64
Illinois	M.	60–60–60	2.80–3.50–3.18
Louisiana	M.	60–60–60	3.00–3.75–3.33
Maryland	M.	60–60–60	2.00–3.00–2.39
Massachusetts	M.	59–59–59	2.00–3.50–2.88
Minnesota	M.	60–60–60	2.00–2.25–2.22
Missouri	M.	54–60–57	2.00–4.00–2.36
New York	M.	60–60–60	2.00–3.00–2.04
Ohio	M.	60–60–60	1.67–2.83–2.24
Pennsylvania	M.	60–60–60	2.00–3.00–2.43
Virginia	M.	60–60–60	2.25–2.50–2.38
1873:			
Delaware	M.	60–60–60	2.00–3.00–2.56
Illinois	M.	60–60–60	3.00–3.15–3.10
Louisiana	M.	60–60–60	2.75–3.25–3.00
Maryland	M.	60–60–60	2.00–3.00–2.52
Massachusetts	M.	59–59–59	2.00–3.50–2.94
Minnesota	M.	60–60–60	2.00–2.25–2.22
Missouri	M.	54–60–56	2.00–4.00–2.37
New York	M.	60–60–60	1.75–2.50–1.79
Ohio	M.	60–60–60	1.67–2.00–1.83
Pennsylvania	M.	60–60–60	2.00–3.00–2.47
Virginia	M.	60–60–60	2.25–2.50–2.38
1874:			
Delaware	M.	60–60–60	2.00–2.67–2.30
Illinois	M.	60–60–60	3.00–3.15–3.05
Louisiana	M.	60–60–60	3.00–3.50–3.25
Maryland	M.	60–60–60	2.00–3.00–2.33
Massachusetts	M.	59–59–59	2.17–4.17–2.81
Minnesota	M.	60–60–60	2.25–2.25–2.25
Missouri	M.	54–60–56	2.00–4.00–2.37
New York	M.	60–60–60	1.75–2.50–1.79
Ohio	M.	60–60–60	1.67–2.00–1.83
Pennsylvania	M.	60–60–60	2.00–3.00–2.46
Virginia	M.	60–60–60	1.50–2.00–1.75
1875:			
Delaware	M.	?0–60–60	1.92–2.50–2.16
Illinois	M.	?0–60–60	2.35–3.00–2.63
Louisiana	M.	60–60–60	3.25–3.50–3.38
Maryland	M.	60–60–60	2.00–3.00–2.35
Massachusetts	M.	59–59–59	1.87–3.25–2.47
Minnesota	M.	60–60–60	2.25–2.25–2.25
Missouri	M.	54–60–56	2.17–4.00–2.45
New York	M.	60–60–60	1.75–2.50–1.80
Ohio	M.	60–60–60	1.67–2.00–1.83
Pennsylvania	M.	60–60–60	2.00–2.70–2.30
Virginia	M.	60–60–60	1.50–2.00–1.75
1876:			
Delaware	M.	60–60–60	1.67–2.50–1.95
Illinois	M.	60–60–60	2.40–3.00–2.50
Louisiana	M.	60–60–60	3.25–3.50–3.38
Maryland	M.	60–60–60	2.00–3.00–2.46
Massachusetts	M.	59–59–59	1.75–3.33–2.47
Minnesota	M.	60–60–60	2.25–2.25–2.25
Missouri	M.	54–60–56	2.17–4.00–2.45
New York	M.	60–60–60	1.75–2.50–1.84
Ohio	M.	60–60–60	1.83–2.17–1.97
Pennsylvania	M.	60–60–60	2.00–2.50–2.25
Virginia	M.	60–60–60	1.50–2.00–1.75
1877:			
Delaware	M.	60–60–60	1.67–2.33–1.79
Illinois	M.	60–60–60	2.30–3.00–2.45
Louisiana	M.	60–60–60	3.25–3.50–3.33
Maryland	M.	60–60–60	2.00–3.00–2.43
Massachusetts	M.	59–59–59	1.67–3.33–2.26
Minnesota	M.	60–60–60	2.25–2.25–2.25
Missouri	M.	54–60–56	2.17–4.00–2.44
New Jersey	M.	59–59–59	1.75–2.27–1.94
New York	M.	60–60–60	1.75–2.50–1.88
Ohio	M.	60–60–60	1.50–2.25–1.69
Pennsylvania	M.	60–60–60	1.50–2.50–1.89
Virginia	M.	60–60–60	1.50–2.00–1.75
1878:			
Delaware	M.	60–60–60	1.17–2.33–1.42
Illinois	M.	60–60–60	2.30–3.00–2.43
Louisiana	M.	60–60–60	3.00–3.25–3.08
Maryland	M.	60–60–60	2.00–2.50–2.28
Massachusetts	M.	59–59–59	1.67–3.67–1.99
Minnesota	M.	60–60–60	2.25–2.25–2.25
Missouri	M.	54–60–56	2.17–4.00–2.44
New York	M.	60–60–60	1.75–2.50–1.88
Ohio	M.	60–60–60	1.67–2.17–1.94
Pennsylvania	M.	60–60–60	2.00–3.00–2.42
Virginia	M.	60–60–60	1.50–2.00–1.75
1879:			
Delaware	M.	60–60–60	1.17–2.33–1.67
Illinois	M.	60–60–60	2.20–3.00–2.35
Louisiana	M.	60–60–60	3.00–3.25–3.08
Maryland	M.	60–60–60	2.00–2.50–2.29
Massachusetts	M.	59–59–59	1.83–3.67–2.18
Minnesota	M.	60–60–60	2.25–2.25–2.25
Missouri	M.	54–60–56	2.17–4.00–2.45
New Jersey	(1)	59–60–59	1.25–2.83–1.77
New York	M.	60–60–60	1.75–2.50–1.94
Ohio	M.	60–60–60	1.00–2.00–1.53
Pennsylvania	M.	54–60–59	1.25–3.00–1.81
Virginia	M.	60–60–60	1.50–2.00–1.75
1880:			
Illinois	M.	60–60–60	2.30–3.00–2.65
Louisiana	M.	60–60–60	2.50–3.25–2.88
Maryland	M.	60–60–60	2.00–2.50–2.17
Massachusetts	M.	59–59–59	1.67–3.50–2.19
Minnesota	M.	60–60–60	2.25–2.25–2.25
Missouri	M.	54–60–56	2.25–4.00–2.47
New Jersey	M.	59–60–59	1.50–3.00–2.18
New York	M.	60–60–60	1.75–2.50–1.94
Ohio	M.	60–60–60	1.67–2.00–1.88
Pennsylvania	M.	60–60–60	1.62–3.00–2.38
Virginia	M.	60–60–60	1.25–2.00–1.63
1881:			
Delaware	M.	60–60–60	1.50–3.00–1.94
Illinois	M.	60–60–60	2.20–3.00–2.43
Louisiana	M.	60–60–60	2.50–3.25–2.88
Maryland	M.	60–60–60	2.00–2.50–2.28
Massachusetts	M.	59–59–59	2.00–3.33–2.53
Minnesota	M.	60–60–60	2.25–2.25–2.25
Missouri	M.	54–60–56	2.25–4.00–2.47
New Jersey	M.	57–57–57	2.83–2.83–2.83
New York	M.	60–60–60	2.00–3.00–2.22
Ohio	M.	60–60–60	1.33–2.75–1.79
Pennsylvania	M.	60–60–60	1.25–3.00–2.36
Virginia	M.	60–60–60	1.25–2.00–1.63
1882:			
Delaware	M.	60–60–60	1.75–3.00–2.12
Illinois	M.	60–60–60	2.30–3.00–2.53
Louisiana	M.	60–60–60	2.50–3.25–2.88
Maryland	M.	60–60–60	2.00–2.50–2.20
Massachusetts	M.	59–59–59	2.17–3.33–2.55
Minnesota	M.	60–60–60	2.25–2.25–2.25
Missouri	M.	54–60–57	1.25–4.00–2.38
New York	M.	60–60–60	2.00–3.00–2.23
Ohio	M.	60–60–60	1.50–2.00–1.77
Do	(1)	54–60–59	1.50–2.50–2.07
Pennsylvania	M.	60–60–60	1.75–3.00–2.58
Virginia	M.	60–60–60	1.25–2.00–1.63
1883:			
Delaware	M.	60–60–60	1.75–3.33–2.07
Illinois	M.	60–60–60	2.30–2.40–2.38
Louisiana	M.	60–60–60	2.25–3.25–2.58
Maryland	M.	60–60–60	2.00–2.50–2.23
Massachusetts	M.	59–59–59	1.17–4.17–2.30
Michigan	M.	(1)	.65–6.00–1.94
Minnesota	M.	60–60–60	2.25–2.25–2.25
Missouri	M.	54–60–56	2.25–4.00–2.47
New Jersey	M.	60–60–60	3.00–3.00–3.00

[1] Not reported.

TABLE **O-1.**—*Cabinetmakers, 1845-1900, by year and State*—Continued

Year and State	Sex	Hours per week	Rate per day (dollars)	Year and State	Sex	Hours per week	Rate per day (dollars)
1883—Continued.				**1888:**			
New York	M.	60-60-60	2.00-3.00-2.23	Delaware	M.	60-60-60	1.83-2.75-2.12
Ohio	M.	54-60-60	1.42-2.50-1.90	Illinois	M.	60-60-60	2.30-2.50-2.40
Pennsylvania	M.	60-60-60	2.00-3.00-2.44	Indiana	F.	60-60-60	2.00-2.00-2.00
Virginia	M.	60-60-60	1.25-2.00-1.63	Iowa	M.	60-60-60	1.43-2.25-2.04
1884:				Kansas	M.	(1)	2.05-2.50-2.29
California	M.	60-60-60	2.00-3.00-2.40	Louisiana	M.	60-60-60	2.25-3.25-2.67
Delaware	M.	60-60-60	1.75-3.33-2.11	Maryland	M.	54-54-54	2.00-2.50-2.25
Florida	M.	60-60-60	2.33-2.33-2.33	Massachusetts	M.	59-59-59	1.83-3.80-2.61
Illinois	M.	60-60-60	2.20-2.50-2.28	Minnesota	M.	60-60-60	2.25-2.25-2.25
Iowa	M.	60-60-60	1.75-2.50-1.95	Missouri	M.	54-60-56	2.25-4.00-2.61
Louisiana	M.	60-60-60	2.50-3.25-2.88	New Jersey	M.	54-58-57	1.50-3.25-1.51
Maryland	M.	60-60-60	2.00-2.50-2.26	New York	M.	45-60-58	1.28-3.26-2.31
Massachusetts	M.	59-59-59	1.67-3.50-2.65	North Carolina	M.	60-72-64	.58-2.50-1.54
Michigan	M.	(1)	.40-3.00-1.91	Ohio	M.	60-60-60	1.40-2.50-2.00
Minnesota	M.	60-60-60	2.25-2.25-2.25	Pennsylvania	M.	54-60-60	1.67-3.33-2.44
Missouri	M.	54-60-56	2.00-4.00-2.46	Rhode Island	M.	(1)	1.70-2.25-2.07
New Jersey	M.	60-60-60	2.00-2.75-2.35	Virginia	M.	60-60-60	2.25-2.50-2.38
New York	M.	60-60-60	2.00-3.20-2.28	**1889:**			
Ohio	M.	57-60-58	1.42-2.00-1.84	Delaware	M.	60-60-60	1.83-3.00-2.18
Pennsylvania	M.	60-60-60	2.00-3.00-2.45	Illinois	M.	60-60-60	2.30-2.50-2.38
Virginia	M.	60-60-60	1.25-2.00-1.63	Louisiana	M.	60-60-60	2.25-3.00-2.63
1885:				Maryland	M.	54-54-54	2.00-2.50-2.29
Delaware	M.	60-60-60	1.50-2.17-1.65	Massachusetts	M.	54-59-59	1.83-3.50-2.53
Illinois	M.	60-60-60	2.20-2.50-2.35	Michigan	M.	60-60-60	.38-3.50-1.60
Indiana	M.	60-60-50	1.50-2.00-1.59	Minnesota	M.	60-60-60	2.25-2.50-2.32
Kansas	M.	54-60-59	1.50-2.00-1.73	Missouri	M.	54-60-56	2.25-4.00-2.61
Kentucky	M.	54-54-54	1.80-1.80-1.80	New York	M.	60-60-60	2.00-3.20-2.28
Louisiana	M.	60-60-60	2.50-3.50-3.06	Ohio	M.	60-60-60	1.33-2.50-1.71
Maryland	M.	.60 60 60	2.00-2.50-2.28	Pennsylvania	M.	54-60-60	1.67-3.33-2.41
Massachusetts	M.	'59-59-59	1.83-3.50-2.56	Virginia	M.	60-60-60	1.50-1.75-1.63
Michigan	M.	60-72-61	.50-3.00-1.83	**1890:**			
Minnesota	M.	60-60-60	2.25-2.25-2.25	Delaware	M.	60-60-60	1.83-3.33-2.24
Missouri	M.	54-60-56	2.25-4.00-2.47	Illinois	M.	60-60-60	2.30-2.50-2.35
New Jersey	M.	60-60-60	2.50-2.75-2.63	Kansas	M.	(1)	1.75-2.28-2.11
New York	M.	60-60-60	2.00-3.20-2.40	Louisiana	M.	60-60-60	2.50-3.50-2.83
Ohio	M.	60-60-60	1.42-2.00-1.60	Maryland	M.	54-54-54	2.00-2.50-2.26
Pennsylvania	M.	60-60-60	1.50-3.00-2.34	Massachusetts	M.	54-66-59	1.83-3.50-2.52
Rhode Island	M.	48-48-48	2.54-2.54-2.54	Michigan	M.	60-60-60	1.50-2.25-1.93
Virginia	M.	60-60-60	1.25-2.00-1.63	Minnesota	M.	60-60-60	1.25-2.50-2.17
1886:				Missouri	M.	54-60-56	2.25-4.00-2.61
California	M.	60-60-60	2.00-4.00-2.89	New York	M.	60-60-60	1.25-4.17-2.14
Do.	M.	60-72-68	[2] 2.50-2.88-2.64	Ohio	M.	60-60-60	1.17-2.50-1.74
Connecticut	M.	60-60-60	2.30-2.30-2.30	Do.	M.	48-60-60	1.10-2.50-1.84
Delaware	M.	60-60-60	1.50-2.17-1.67	Do.	M.	48-60-60	1.10-2.50-1.83
Illinois	M.	60-60-60	1.33-3.20-2.11	Pennsylvania	M.	54-60-60	1.67-3.33-2.41
Iowa	M.	51-72-60	.96-5.00-2.24	Virginia	M.	60-60-60	1.50-1.75-1.63
Kansas	M.	60-60-60	2.00-2.00-2.00	**1891:**			
Louisiana	M.	60-60-60	2.50-3.25-2.75	Delaware	M.	60-60-60	1.83-3.33-2.17
Maryland	M.	60-60-60	2.00-2.50-2.28	Illinois	M.	60-60-60	2.30-2.50-2.38
Massachusetts	M.	59-60-59	1.83-3.50-2.63	Louisiana	M.	60-60-60	2.25-3.50-2.75
Michigan	M.	60-60-60	2.25-2.25-2.25	Maryland	M.	54-54-54	2.00-2.50-2.27
Minnesota	M.	60-60-60	2.25-2.25-2.25	Massachusetts	M.	54-54-54	1.71-4.00-2.43
Missouri	M.	54-60-59	1.75-4.00-2.03	Minnesota	M.	60-60-60	2.50-2.50-2.50
New York	M.	60-60-60	2.00-3.20-2.29	Missouri	M.	54-60-56	2.25-4.00-2.61
Ohio	M.	54-60-58	.68-2.50-1.92	New York	M.	60-60-60	1.00-4.17-2.19
Pennsylvania	M.	48-60-59	1.50-3.00-2.00	North Carolina	M.	60-60-60	1.50-1.50-1.50
Virginia	M.	60-60-60	2.25-2.50-2.38	Ohio	M.	48-60-59	1.00-2.50-1.94
1887:				Pennsylvania	M.	54-60-60	1.67-3.50-2.46
Connecticut	M.	(1)	2.39-2.39-2.39	Virginia	M.	60-60-60	1.50-1.75-1.63
Delaware	M.	60-60-60	1.83-2.75-2.10	**1892:**			
Illinois	M.	60-60-60	2.30-3.20-2.43	California	M.	54-60-55	1.17-3.50-2.52
Kansas	M.	72-72-72	2.17-2.75-2.53	Delaware	M.	60-60-60	1.50-3.00-2.08
Louisiana	M.	60-60-60	2.25-3.25-2.53	Illinois	M.	60-60-60	2.30-2.50-2.35
Maryland	M.	54-54-54	1.60-2.50-2.18	Indiana	M.	54-60-60	1.47-2.64-1.71
Massachusetts	M.	59-59-59	2.00-3.50-2.55	Louisiana	M.	54-54-54	2.50-3.50-2.92
Michigan	M.	60-60-60	2.10-2.50-2.30	Maryland	M.	54-54-54	2.00-2.50-2.28
Minnesota	M.	60-60-60	2.25-2.25-2.25	Massachusetts	M.	54-54 54	1.65-4.00-2.52
Missouri	M.	54-60-56	2.25-4.00-2.60	Minnesota	M.	54-60-60	2.50-2.50-2.50
New Jersey	M.	(1)	2.50-2.50-2.50	Missouri	M.	48-60-60	1.83-4.00-2.53
New York	M.	60-60-60	2.00-3.20-2.27	New York	M.	60-60-60	2.00-2.75-2.17
North Carolina	M.	60-60-60	1.00-1.75-1.44	Ohio	M.	60-60-60	1.33-2.50-1.79
Ohio	M.	48-60-59	.75-2.75-1.58	Pennsylvania	M.	54-60-59	1.58-3.50-2.45
Pennsylvania	M.	54-60-60	1.67-3.00-2.37	Virginia	M.	60-60-60	1.50-1.75-1.63
Virginia	M.	60-60-60	2.25-2.50-2.38				
Wisconsin	M.	(1)	1.25-1.97-1.97				

[1] Not reported.   [2] And board.

458 PART 2.—FROM 1840 TO 1928

TABLE O–1.—*Cabinetmakers, 1845–1900, by year and State*—Continued

| Year and State | Sex | Lowest, highest, and average— | | Year and State | Sex | Lowest, highest, and average— | |
		Hours per week	Rate per day (dollars)			Hours per week	Rate per day (dollars)
1893:				**1896:**			
Delaware	M.	60–60–60	1.50–3.00–2.02	Florida	M.	60–60–60	2.08–2.08–2.08
Illinois	M.	48–72–58	1.00–3.33–2.15	Georgia	M.	(¹)	1.17–1.25–1.21
Louisiana	M.	60–60–60	2.50–3.25–2.55	Illinois	M.	60–60–60	2.20–3.00–2.36
Maryland	M.	48–72–57	.67–4.17–2.05	Kansas	M.	60–60–60	1.25–1.25–1.25
Massachusetts	M.	54–54–54	1.65–4.00–2.49	Louisiana	M.	54–54–54	2.25–2.50–2.38
Michigan	M.	57–57–57	2.30–2.30–2.30	Maryland	M.	54–54–54	2.00–2.50–2.27
Minnesota	M.	60–60–60	2.25–2.25–2.25	Massachusetts	M.	54–54–54	1.65–3.50–2.51
Missouri	M.	54–60–56	2.25–4.00–2.60	Minnesota	M.	60–60–60	1.52–2.25–2.06
Montana	M.	54–60–57	3.33–4.50–3.77	Missouri	M.	48–60–59	.95–4.00–2.01
New York	M.	45–60–60	1.00–2.50–2.10	New York	M.	54–60–60	.83–3.33–2.45
Ohio	M.	48–60–58	1.00–2.50–1.92	North Carolina	M.	60–60–60	1.00–1.25–1.19
Pennsylvania	M.	54–66–60	1.00–3.50–2.37	Ohio	M.	48–60–57	1.25–2.50–1.59
Virginia	M.	60–60–60	1.50–1.75–1.63	Pennsylvania	M.	54–60–59	2.00–3.50–2.49
1894:				Virginia	M.	60–60–60	1.50–1.75–1.63
Delaware	M.	60–60–60	1.67–3.00–1.97	**1897:**			
Georgia	M.	60–60–60	1.50–1.70–1.68	Illinois	M.	60–60–60	2.20–2.40–2.33
Illinois	M.	60–60–60	2.30–2.40–2.33	Louisiana	M.	60–60–60	2.25–2.25–2.25
Indiana	M.	43–60–52	1.34–2.50–1.68	Maryland	M.	54–54–54	2.00–2.50–2.22
Iowa	M.	54–54–54	2.00–2.00–2.00	Massachusetts	M.	54–60–58	1.50–3.50–2.47
Louisiana	M.	54–54–54	2.25–3.25–2.34	Michigan	M.	(¹)	1.40–1.40–1.40
Maine	M.	60–60–60	1.50–2.00–1.89	Minnesota	M.	60–60–60	2.25–2.25–2.25
Maryland	M.	54–54–54	2.00–2.50–2.27	Missouri	M.	54–60–56	2.00–4.00–2.44
Massachusetts	M.	54–54–54	1.65–3.50–2.51	New York	M.	60–60–60	1.50–3.00–2.36
Minnesota	M.	60–60–60	2.25–2.25–2.25	Ohio	M.	60–60–60	1.00–2.00–1.53
Missouri	M.	54–60–55	2.00–4.00–2.57	Pennsylvania	M.	54–60–59	1.80–3.33–2.46
New Hampshire	M.	57–60–59	1.42–1.75–1.56	Virginia	M.	57–60–60	.85–2.00–1.53
New York	M.	60–60–60	1.20–2.50–2.05	**1898:**			
North Carolina	M.	60–60–60	1.25–2.00–1.63	Illinois	M.	60–60–60	2.30–2.40–2.33
Ohio	M.	48–72–58	.98–2.50–1.80	Louisiana	M.	60–60–60	2.00–2.25–2.13
Pennsylvania	M.	54–60–58	2.00–3.50–2.45	Maryland	M.	54–54–54	2.00–2.50–2.22
Virginia	M.	60–60–60	1.50–1.75–1.63	Massachusetts	M.	54–54–54	1.65–3.60–2.63
1895:				Michigan	M.	(¹)	1.25–1.81–1.58
Delaware	M.	60–60–60	1.09–3.00–1.78	Minnesota	M.	60–60–60	2.25–2.25–2.25
Illinois	M.	60–60–60	2.30–2.40–2.33	Missouri	M.	54–60–57	2.25–4.00–2.51
Louisiana	M.	54–54–54	2.25–2.50–2.41	Nebraska	M. (¹)	52–60–56	1.00–2.00–1.58
Maryland	M.	54–54–54	2.00–2.50–2.27	New York	M.	60–60–60	1.66–3.50–2.57
Massachusetts	M.	54–60–54	1.65–4.00–2.49	Ohio	M.	60–60–60	1.00–2.00–1.53
Minnesota	M.	60–60–60	2.25–2.25–2.25	Pennsylvania	M.	54–60–59	1.98–3.67–2.41
Missouri	M.	54–60–55	2.00–4.00–2.57	Virginia	M.	60–60–60	1.50–1.75–1.63
New York	M.	48–60–58	2.00–3.17–2.31	**1899:**			
North Carolina	M.	60–60–60	.75–2.00–1.42	Georgia	M.	60–60–60	1.25–2.25–1.57
Ohio	M.	45–60–56	1.00–3.00–1.83	New York	M.	48–48–48	2.25–2.50–2.38
Pennsylvania	M.	54–60–59	2.00–3.50–2.47	North Carolina	M.	60–72–61	.90–2.00–1.23
Rhode Island	M.	55–55–55	1.38–1.65–1.52	**1900:**			
Virginia	M.	60–60–60	1.50–1.75–1.63	Georgia	M.	60–60–60	1.25–2.25–1.57
Wisconsin	(¹)	48–60–59	1.00–2.50–1.58	New York	M.	48–48–48	2.50–2.75–2.63
				North Carolina	M.	60–60–60	1.00–1.25–1.10

¹Not reported.

TABLE **O-2.**—*Cabinetmakers, male, furniture, 1890–1907, by city and year*

Year	Boston, Mass.		Chicago, Ill.		Cincinnati, Ohio		Detroit, Mich.	
	Hours per week	Rate per hour	Hours per week	Rate per hour	Hours per week	Rate per hour	Hours per week	Rate per hour
1890	57.4	$0.258			60.0	$0.174	60.0	$0.206
1891	56.5	.256			60.0	.174	57.2	.220
1892	56.3	.260			60.0	.178	55.6	.229
1893	55.2	.269			60.0	.171	55.2	.229
1894	55.2	.260			60.0	.169	56.8	.227
1895	55.6	.266			60.0	.165	57.2	.209
1896	54.6	.259			60.0	.165	57.7	.211
1897	55.5	.268			60.0	.164	56.2	.216
1898	55.6	.268			60.0	.167	57.0	.205
1899	55.5	.267			60.0	.170	56.6	.214
1900	53.6	.278			60.0	.182	57.4	.239
1901	51.1	.307			60.0	.185	56.1	.221
1902	50.4	.318			56.7	.210	51.6	.268
1903	50.8	.330	56.6	$0.249	58.6	.215	53.3	.261
1904	50.4	.338	53.1	.263	59.2	.223	51.9	.275
1905	50.4	.349	54.5	.261	55.6	.234	51.6	.286
1906	49.2	.354	54.1	.274	55.3	.256	50.9	.310
1907	48.9	.354	54.2	.283	56.1	.252	51.8	.294
	New York, N. Y.		Philadelphia, Pa.		St. Louis, Mo.		San Francisco, Calif.	
1890	56.4	$0.258	60.0	$0.237	56.5	$0.261	54.0	$0.264
1891	55.5	.273	60.0	.242	56.5	.261	54.0	.264
1892	55.2	.278	60.0	.242	56.6	.257	54.0	.271
1893	56.6	.255	60.0	.245	56.3	.262	54.0	.268
1894	54.4	.264	60.0	.243	56.4	.262	54.0	.255
1895	54.0	.271	60.0	.242	56.4	.262	54.0	.255
1896	53.8	.278	60.0	.239	56.8	.257	54.0	.264
1897	53.4	.301	60.0	.242	57.3	.247	54.0	.268
1898	53.9	.288	60.0	.239	57.7	.240	54.0	.268
1899	51.4	.310	60.0	.238	57.8	.242	54.0	.268
1900	51.4	.310	60.0	.239	57.9	.240	54.0	.268
1901	51.7	.307	60.0	.248	58.3	.233	48.0	.350
1902	48.2	.392	60.0	.242	58.9	.237	48.0	.375
1903	47.4	.408	60.0	.245	55.8	.266	48.0	.387
1904	57.7	.254	57.2	.252	56.3	.242		
1905	58.0	.251	56.4	.259	56.5	.244		
1906	57.4	.261	53.9	.289	56.7	.241		
1907	56.9	.263	55.2	.282	56.6	.242		

TABLE **O-3.**—*Cabinetmakers, male, furniture, 1907–1919, by State and year*

Year	Illinois		Indiana		Maryland		Massachusetts	
	Hours per week	Rate per hour	Hours per week	Rate per hour	Hours per week	Rate per hour	Hours per week	Rate per hour
1907	54.3	$0.252	59.5	$0.221				
1908	54.4	.263	59.5	.213				
1909	54.4	.260	59.4	.207				
1910	56.6	.274	59.4	.207			49.1	$0.359
1911	57.8	.269	59.4	.227	59.8	$0.180	49.6	.352
1912	58.4	.265	59.0	.218	58.6	.186	49.9	.312
1913	58.1	.272	59.0	.224	56.5	.206	50.7	.312
1915	57.4	.272	58.2	.243	55.5	.204	50.1	.351
1919	(1)	.386	(1)	.376	(1)	.431	(1)	.531
	Michigan		Missouri		New York		North Carolina	
1907	58.1	$0.216						
1908	58.0	.216						
1909	57.4	.217						
1910	58.6	.235			59.2	$0.226	59.8	$0.137
1911	57.6	.262	60.0	$0.223	58.6	.225	59.9	.140
1912	57.8	.242	60.0	.226	57.3	.235	59.6	.148
1913	54.2	.257	60.0	.222	55.9	.240	59.9	.150
1915	54.1	.277	58.1	.240	55.7	.243	60.0	.156
1919	(1)	.419	(1)	.357	(1)	.390	(1)	.336
	Ohio		Pennsylvania		Tennessee		Wisconsin	
1910			57.2	$0.213			59.4	$0.195
1911	59.2	$0.231	58.8	.198	59.7	$0.173	59.5	.189
1912	59.3	.222	58.8	.202	59.7	.191	59.7	.193
1913	58.9	.239	58.5	.220	60.0	.187	59.9	.192
1915	56.5	.244	58.6	.207	60.0	.184	59.8	.197
1919	(1)	.364	(1)	.364	(1)	.399	(1)	.382

1 Not reported.

TABLE **O-4.**—*Coopers, 1844-1900, by year and State*

| Year and State | Sex | Lowest, highest, and average— | | Year and State | Sex | Lowest, highest, and average— | |
		Hours per week	Rate per day (dollars)			Hours per week	Rate per day (dollars)
1844:				**1881:**			
New York	M.	(¹)	0. 83-0. 83-0. 83	Illinois	M.	60-60-60	2. 00-2. 00-2. 00
1855:				Michigan	M.	66-66-66	1. 50-1. 50-1. 50
New York	M.	72-72-72	1. 38-1. 46-1. 42	Minnesota	M.	60-60-60	2. 00-2. 75-2. 20
1856:				Missouri	M.	59-59-59	2. 50-2. 75-2. 63
New York	M.	72-72-72	1. 25-1. 54-1. 43	New York	M.	72-72-72	2. 00-2. 75-2. 67
1857:				Ohio	M.	60-72-62	1. 00-2. 00-1. 62
New York	M.	72-72-72	1. 25-1. 54-1. 47	**1882:**			
1858:				Illinois	M.	60-60-60	2. 00-2. 75-2. 32
New York	M.	72-72-72	1. 38-1. 54-1. 44	Indiana	M.	60-60-60	1. 25-1. 70-1. 51
1859:				Iowa	M.	(¹)	2. 25-2. 25-2. 25
New York	M.	72-72-72	1. 38-1. 54-1. 47	Minnesota	M.	55-60-60	1. 75-2. 50-2. 11
1860:				Missouri	M.	60-60-60	1. 00-3. 00-1. 82
New York	M.	72-72-72	1. 50-1. 63-1. 52	New Jersey	M.	60-60-60	1. 75-2. 50-2. 25
Ohio	M.	(¹)	1. 50-1. 50-1. 50	New York	M.	60-72-60	. 92-2. 75-2. 28
1861:				Ohio	(¹)	54-75-61	1. 00-2. 67-1. 94
New York	M.	72-72-72	1. 38-1. 63-1. 50	Pennsylvania	M.	60-60-60	2. 00-2. 50-2. 25
1862:				**1883:**			
New York	M.	72-72-72	1. 50-1. 63-1. 52	California	M.	60-60-60	2. 75-3. 00-2. 90
1863:				Indiana	M.	60-60-60	1. 00-3. 00-1. 72
New York	M.	72-72-72	1. 50-1. 75-1. 55	Massachusetts	M.	(¹)	1. 17-3. 00-2. 05
1864:				Michigan	M.	(¹)	. 50-3. 00-1. 87
New York	M.	72-72-72	1. 50-2. 25-1. 98	Missouri	M.	59-59-59	2. 00-2. 13-2. 07
1865:				New York	M.	72-72-72	2. 00-2. 75-2. 56
New York	M.	72-72-72	1. 50-2. 25-2. 08	Ohio	M.	48-65-58	1. 50-2. 50-2. 01
1866:				Tennessee	M.	60-60-60	1. 05-1. 20-1. 13
New York	M.	72-72-72	2. 00-2. 25-2. 17	**1884:**			
1867:				California	M.	60-60-60	3. 00-3. 00-3. 00
New York	M.	72-72-72	2. 00-2. 75-2. 29	Do	M.	60-60-60	² 2. 30-2. 30-2. 30
1868:				Iowa	M.	60-60-60	1. 71-1. 75-1. 73
New York	M.	72-72-72	2. 25-3. 00-2. 46	Michigan	M.	(¹)	. 85-3. 00-1. 83
1869:				Minnesota	M.	55-60-59	2. 00-2. 25-2. 04
New York	M.	72-72-72	2. 00-3. 00-2. 53	Missouri	M.	59-59-59	1. 33-1. 83-1. 58
1870:				New Jersey	M.	48-60-60	1. 67-2. 50-2. 37
New York	M.	72-72-72	2. 25-3. 00-2. 67	New York	M.	72-72-72	2. 75-2. 75-2. 75
1871:				**1885:**			
Massachusetts	M.	60-70-63	2. 25-3. 00-2. 61	California	M.	60-60-60	2. 25-2. 50-2. 49
New York	M.	72-72-72	2. 25-3. 00-2. 71	Georgia	M.	60-60-60	2. 10-2. 10-2. 10
1872:				Illinois	M.	60-72-60	1. 83-3. 00-2. 74
Massachusetts	M.	60-60-60	2. 00-2. 00-2. 00	Indiana	M.	60-60-60	1. 37-1. 60-1. 49
New York	M.	60-72-71	2. 25-3. 00-2. 82	Iowa	M.	60-60-60	1. 25-1. 50-1. 38
Ohio	M.	(¹)	1. 50-3. 50-2. 46	Kansas	M.	60-60-60	1. 00-1. 50-1. 35
1873:				Maryland	M.	54-60-56	1. 17-1. 67-1. 50
New York	M.	72-72-72	2. 25-3. 00-2. 88	Michigan	M.	66-66-66	. 75-3. 00-1. 95
Pennsylvania	M.	(¹)	2. 50-3. 00-2. 83	New Hampshire	M.	60-60-60	1. 80-1. 90-1. 85
1874:				New Jersey	M.	60-60-60	2. 50-2. 50-2. 50
New York	M.	72-72-72	3. 00-3. 00-3. 00	New York	M.	60-72-67	1. 50-2. 75-2. 25
Pennsylvania	M.	(¹)	1. 45-2. 40-1. 92	Ohio	M.	60-72-66	1. 00-1. 55-1. 28
1875:				Pennsylvania	M.	60-60-60	1. 75-1. 75-1. 75
New York	M.	72-72-72	2. 00-3. 00-2. 80	Virginia	M.	60-60-60	1. 50-1. 50-1. 50
1876:				Wisconsin	M.	60-60-60	1. 93-1. 93-1. 93
New York	M.	72-72-72	3. 00-3. 00-3. 00	**1886:**			
Pennsylvania	M.	(¹)	1. 50-2. 00-1. 86	California	M.	48-72-60	2. 00-3. 00-2. 91
1877:				Do	M.	(¹)	² 2. 30-2. 30-2. 30
New York	M.	72-72-72	3. 00-3. 00-3. 00	Illinois	M.	48-66-56	1. 00-2. 90-2. 01
Ohio	M.	(¹)	1. 00-2. 67-1. 32	Iowa	M.	60-60-60	1. 75-2. 50-2. 33
Pennsylvania	M.	60-60-60	1. 25-1. 25-1. 25	Iowa	M.	48-66-60	1. 00-2. 75-1. 78
1878:				Kansas	M.	60-60-60	1. 25-1. 50-1. 38
New York	M.	72-72-72	2. 75-3. 00-2. 77	Minnesota	M.	55-60-57	1. 60-2. 25-1. 70
Ohio	M.	60-60-60	1. 00-1. 00-1. 00	New York	M.	72-72-72	2. 75-2. 75-2. 75
Pennsylvania	M.	(¹)	1. 44-1. 44-1. 44	Pennsylvania	M.	54-60-59	1. 28-1. 93-1. 45
1879:				Virginia	M.	60-60-60	1. 51-2. 00-1. 72
Missouri	M.	45-70-57	. 58-2. 00-1. 23	Wisconsin	M.	60-60-60	. 90-1. 00- . 95
New York	M.	72-72-72	2. 75-2. 75-2. 75	**1887:**			
Ohio	M.	(¹)	1. 00-1. 50-1. 26	Kansas	M.	(¹)	1. 50-1. 50-1. 50
Pennsylvania	M.	72-72-72	1. 00-1. 25-1. 13	Maine	M.	66-84-75	1. 17-2. 00-1. 59
1880:				Maryland	M.	(¹)	1. 53-2. 30-1. 78
New Jersey	(¹)	60-60-60	2. 00-2. 00-2. 00	Massachusetts	M.	(¹)	1. 67-2. 25-2. 08
New York		72-72-72	2. 75-2. 75-2. 75	Michigan	M.	(¹)	1. 25-1. 50-1. 33
Ohio	M.	60-60-60	3. 00-3. 00-3. 00	Do	M.	(¹)	³ . 15- . 15- . 15
Pennsylvania	M.	(¹)	1. 67-2. 33-2. 00				

¹Not reported.   ² And board.   ³ Per hour.

TABLE O-4.—*Coopers, 1844-1900, by year and State*—Continued

Year and State	Sex	Lowest, highest, and average—		Year and State	Sex	Lowest, highest, and average—	
		Hours per week	Rate per day (dollars)			Hours per week	Rate per day (dollars)
1887—Continued.				**1924—Continued.**			
Missouri	M.	(1)	1.92-1.92-1.92	Maine	M.	60-60-60	1.75-1.75-1.75
New York	M.	72-72-72	1.40-3.00-1.86	New Hampshire	M.	58-84-62	.83-3.00-1.69
North Carolina	M.	66-66-66	.83-.83-.83	New York	M.	54-54-54	2.75-2.75-2.75
Ohio	M.	48-66-57	.50-2.85-1.75	North Carolina	M.	60-60-60	.75ᵃ.75-.75
Oregon	M.	(1)	2.49-2.59-2.54	Ohio	M.	42-72-58	.75-4.83-1.68
Pennsylvania	M.	(1)	1.34-2.30-1.74	West Virginia	M.	60-60-60	1.00-1.46-1.23
Wisconsin	M.	(1)	1.20-2.50-1.96	**1895:**			
1888:				Kansas	M.	36-60-52	.50-2.75-1.13
Iowa	M.	60-60-60	1.40-1.40-1.40	Maryland	M.	54-60-57	.83-2.00-1.42
Kansas	M.	(1)	2.50-2.50-2.50	Missouri	M.	(1)	1.56-3.00-2.50
Maine	M.	48-72-66	1.00-1.75-1.36	New Jersey	M.	60-60-60	2.50-3.20-2.81
Michigan	M.	48-60-58	1.61-2.88-2.14	New York	M.	54-60-60	1.00-3.00-1.84
New Jersey	(1)	60-60-60	2.50-3.00-2.63	North Carolina	M.	60-60-60	1.00-1.25-1.13
New York	M.	44-72-58	1.00-3.50-2.37	Ohio	M.	36-72-56	1.00-2.66-1.71
North Carolina	M.	60-60-60	1.00-1.50-1.25	West Virginia	M.	59-59-59	1.50-1.50-1.50
Ohio	M.	(1)	1.00-2.25-1.86	Wisconsin	(1)	36-66-58	.50-2.50-1.49
1889:				**1896:**			
Maine	M.	72-72-72	1.50-1.50-1.50	Colorado	M.	60-60-60	2.75-2.88-2.82
New York	M.	72-72-72	2.75-3.00-2.79	Georgia	M.	(1)	1.33-1.33-1.33
North Carolina	M.	(1)	.67-.67-.67	Illinois	M.	60-60-60	2.00-2.29-2.19
Ohio	M.	55-60-57	1.50-1.58-1.55	Kansas	M.	36-60-53	.75-2.25-1.11
1890:				Missouri	M.	48-72-59	1.00-2.62-1.87
Kansas	M.	(1)	1.60-2.50-2.06	Nebraska	M.	48-60-59	1.90-3.00-2.61
Michigan	M.	60-60-60	.75-3.00-1.46	New York	M.	60-60-60	1.50-1.83-1.65
Minnesota	M.	(1)	1.50-3.00-2.15	North Carolina	M.	60-60-60	1.50-1.50-1.50
Nebraska	M.	(1)	2.00-2.75-2.42	Ohio	M.	48-72-56	1.00-2.50-1.63
New York	M.	72-72-72	.50-3.50-2.03	Pennsylvania	M.	60-60-60	1.00-2.50-1.78
Ohio	(1)	48-69-58	1.00-3.00-2.02	Tennessee	M.	(1)	1.50-1.50-1.50
1891:				**1897:**			
Missouri	M.	(1)	2.07-2.94-2.41	Kansas	M.	30-70-49	.86-2.57-1.69
New York	M.	72-72-72	.50-3.00-2.05	Michigan	M.	(1)	1.10-1.86-1.50
Ohio	M.	48-72-59	1.25-2.75-1.84	Nebraska	M.	(1)	2.45-2.45-2.45
1892:				New York	M.	54-60-59	1.00-3.00-2.42
California	M.	54-60-57	1.50-4.17-2.70	Ohio	M.	(1)	2.00-2.00-2.00
Indiana	M.	54-60-56	1.16-1.73-1.37	Virginia	M.	48-72-60	1.00-2.75-1.60
Missouri	M.	60-60-60	1.25-3.00-1.79	**1898:**			
New York	M.	54-60-58	2.75-2.75-2.75	Kansas	M.	42-60-56	³.15-.29-.19
Ohio	(1)	57-58-57	2.00-2.50-2.25	Michigan	M.	(1)	1.03-2.06-1.88
1893:				New York	M.	59-60-59	1.50-3.50-2.61
Illinois	M.	48-65-58	1.17-3.00-2.07	**1899:**			
Maryland	M.	60-72-61	.67-2.50-1.57	Massachusetts	M.	59-59-59	2.50-5.83-3.67
Michigan	M.	72-72-72	1.50-1.50-1.50	New York	M.	48-48-48	1.00-1.83-1.38
Montana	M.	54-59-57	⁴2.00-3.00-2.50	North Carolina	M.	60-60-60	1.50-1.50-1.50
New York	M.	52-66-60	.83-3.00-2.02	**1900:**			
Ohio	M.	36-69-55	.75-3.00-1.64	Massachusetts	M.	59-59-59	2.50-5.83-3.67
Pennsylvania	M.	54-60-59	1.25-3.00-2.05	New York	M.	48-48-48	1.04-1.92-1.42
1894:							
Indiana	M.	55-60-57	1.16-1.82-1.35				
Iowa	M.	54-72-61	.67-2.50-1.41				

¹ Not reported.   ² And board.   ³ Per hour.   ⁴ And board and lodging.

TABLE O-5.—*Coopers, males, tight barrels, 1890-1903, by geographic division and year*

Year	North Atlantic		North Central		South Central	
	Hours per week	Rate per hour	Hours per week	Rate per hour	Hours per week	Rate per hour
1890	58.6	$0.254	59.9	$0.207	60.0	$0.185
1891	58.3	.256	59.9	.206	60.0	.185
1892	58.6	.246	59.9	.202	60.0	.185
1893	58.4	.250	59.9	.192	60.0	.185
1894	59.0	.242	59.9	.189	60.0	.185
1895	58.8	.247	59.9	.187	60.0	.185
1896	58.8	.243	59.9	.197	60.0	.200
1897	58.6	.243	59.9	.195	60.0	.200
1898	58.5	.245	59.6	.196	60.0	.201
1899	58.5	.252	59.7	.198	60.0	.201
1900	57.3	.259	59.7	.198	60.0	.218
1901	55.6	.269	59.7	.206	60.0	.218
1902	55.8	.288	59.5	.205	60.0	.224
1903	55.9	.287	57.9	.216	60.0	.230

TABLE O–6.—*Coopers, males, slack barrels, 1890–1903, by geographic division and year*

Year	North Atlantic		North Central		Year	North Atlantic		North Central	
	Hours per week	Rate per hour	Hours per week	Rate per hour		Hours per week	Rate per hour	Hours per week	Rate per hour
1890	59.7	$0.217	59.1	$0.238	1897	59.8	$0.230	59.0	$0.224
1891	59.7	.216	59.2	.239	1898	59.7	.236	57.1	.216
1892	59.6	.221	59.0	.218	1899	59.7	.236	57.1	.223
1893	59.7	.226	59.0	.222	1900	59.7	.234	57.8	.247
1894	59.8	.232	59.0	.249	1901	59.8	.244	57.8	.233
1895	59.9	.230	59.0	.249	1902	59.8	.251	58.1	.250
1896	59.8	.230	59.0	.238	1903	59.8	.271	57.4	.249

TABLE O–7.—*Coopers (repairers), males, 1917–1927, by district and year*

Year	District No. 1, Chicago		District No. 2 [1]		District No. 3 [2]		District No. 4 [3]	
	Hours per week	Rate per hour	Hours per week	Rate per hour	Hours per week	Rate per hour	Hours per week	Rate per hour
1917	([4])	$0.292	([4])	$0.345	([4])	$0.347	([4])	$0.385
1921	47.8	.560	48.0	.570	48.0	[5].574	48.0	.614
1923	53.6	.569	49.5	.596	49.0	.634	48.0	.624
1925	50.4	.575	48.5	.603	48.8	.596	49.0	.557
1927	48.3	.588	47.8	.603	50.0	.617	48.4	.603

Year	District No. 5 [6]		District No. 6 [7]		District No. 7 [8]		District No. 8 [9]	
1917	([4])	$0.311	([4])	$0.401				
1921	52.4	.549	48.0	.625				
1923	50.4	.589	53.8	.620				
1925	51.4	.581	53.7	.594	52.5	$0.530	50.0	$0.622
1927	51.1	.566	52.7	.577	55.0	.542	49.6	.646

[1] Kansas City, Omaha, St. Louis, East St. Louis, and St. Joseph.
[2] 1917 and 1921, St. Paul, Milwaukee, and Ottumwa; 1923, Austin (Minn.), Cedar Rapids, Milwaukee, Ottumwa, and St. Paul; 1925 and 1927, Austin (Minn.), Cedar Rapids, Des Moines, Mason City, Milwaukee, Ottumwa, Sioux City, Sioux Falls, St. Paul, Topeka, Waterloo, and Wichita.
[3] 1917, 1921, and 1923, Oklahoma City and Fort Worth; 1925 and 1927, Oklahoma City, Dallas, Fort Worth, and Houston.
[4] Not reported.
[5] Not including data for 1 establishment in which employees are paid biweekly.
[6] 1917 and 1921, Buffalo, Cleveland, Cincinnati, and Indianapolis; 1923, 1925, and 1927, Buffalo, Cleveland, Cincinnati, Detroit, Indianapolis, and Pittsburgh.
[7] 1917, 1921, and 1923, Boston, New York, and Philadelphia; 1925 and 1927, Boston, New Haven, New York, Philadelphia, and Springfield (Mass.).
[8] 1925 and 1927, Baltimore, Moultrie, and Jacksonville.
[9] 1925 and 1927, Denver, Los Angeles, Portland, San Francisco, Seattle, and Tacoma.

TABLE O–8.—*Choppers and sawyers (felling trees), males, logging, 1891–1896, by year and State*

Year and State	Sex	Lowest, highest, and average—		Year and State	Sex	Lowest, highest, and average—	
		Hours per week	Rate per day (dollars)			Hours per week	Rate per day (dollars)
1891: Minnesota	M.	([1])	[2] 0.84–1.15–0.96	1894: Minnesota	M.	([1])	[2] 0.61–0.77–0.74
1892: Minnesota	M.	([1])	[2].84–1.15–.96	1895: Minnesota	M.	([1])	[2].61–.69–.63
1893: Minnesota	M.	([1])	[2].61–.77–.74	1896: Minnesota	M.	([1])	[2].54–.69–.56

[1] Not reported.   [2] And board.

TABLE **O–9.**—*Choppers and sawyers, males, logging, 1890–1907, by geographic division and year*

Year	North Atlantic		North Central		South Central		Western	
	Hours per week	Rate per hour	Hours per week	Rate per hour	Hours per week	Rate per hour	Hours per week	Rate per hour
1890	54. 0	$0. 189	60. 2	$0. 150	65. 0	$0. 135	66. 1	$0. 219
1891	54. 0	. 192	60. 3	. 149	65. 0	. 135	66. 1	. 218
1892	54. 0	. 191	60. 3	. 150	65. 0	. 135	66. 1	. 219
1893	54. 0	. 190	60. 2	. 151	64. 3	. 133	66. 1	. 197
1894	54. 0	. 190	60. 3	. 151	64. 5	. 134	66. 2	. 194
1895	54. 0	. 190	60. 2	. 162	64. 5	. 134	66. 2	. 193
1896	54. 0	. 190	60. 3	. 161	64. 2	. 133	66. 2	. 194
1897	54. 0	. 190	60. 3	. 165	64. 0	. 141	66. 2	. 203
1898	54. 0	. 190	60. 2	. 170	64. 0	. 141	66. 2	. 227
1899	54. 0	. 195	60. 2	. 171	64. 0	. 141	66. 3	. 233
1900	54. 0	. 195	60. 3	. 170	53. 7	. 166	66. 3	. 235
1901	54. 0	. 200	60. 3	. 171	63. 7	. 175	66. 1	. 257
1902	54. 0	. 200	60. 2	. 173	63. 0	. 180	66. 1	. 259
1903			60. 2	. 177	61. 4	. 143	64. 0	. 284
1904			60. 2	. 170	62. 0	. 144	64. 3	. 270
1905			60. 3	. 182	63. 3	. 158	64. 2	. 266
1906			60. 3	. 183	60. 4	. 179	61. 6	. 294
1907			60. 5	. 191	60. 4	. 184	61. 5	. 314

TABLE **O–10.**—*Choppers and sawyers, males, logging, 1915–1928, by State and year*

Year	Alabama		California		Florida		Georgia	
	Hours per week	Rate per hour	Hours per week	Rate per hour	Hours per week	Rate per hour	Hours per week	Rate per hour
1915	{ 66. 0	[1] $0. 085	60. 0	$0. 269	66. 0	[1] $0. 107	66. 0	$0. 108
	{ 66. 0	. 032–. 045	60. 0	[1]. 191			65. 0	[2]
1919			(³)	. 484	(³)	. 201		
1921			57. 0	. 574				
1921			4 54. 0	4. 479				
1925			54. 0	. 654				
1928			53. 8	. 666				

Year	Louisiana		Michigan		Mississippi		North Carolina	
1915	{ 60. 0	(²)			60. 0	$0. 142	63. 3	$0. 145
	{				60. 0	(²)		
1919			(³)	$0. 299			64. 0	(²)
1921	60. 0	$0. 275					(³)	. 358
1925	{ 49. 2	. 465			59. 8	. 345	60. 0	. 231
	{				60. 0	1. 311	60. 0	. 259
1928	{ 60. 0	. 457			60. 0	. 326	59. 7	. 303
	{ 4 60. 0	4. 310						

Year	Pennsylvania		Washington		Wisconsin	
1915			4 60. 0	4 $0. 315		
1919	(³)	$0. 475	(³)	. 652	(³)	$0. 321
1921	{		4 48. 0	4. 615		
	{		48. 0	1. 361		
1925			4 48. 0	4. 652		
1928	{		48. 0	. 618		
	{		4 48. 0	4. 744		

And board. [1] Piecework. [2] Not reported. [4] Listed as fallers.

TABLE O-11.—*Laborers, males, lumber, 1890–1907, by geographic division and year*

Year	North Atlantic		South Atlantic		North Central		South Central	
	Hours per week	Rate per hour	Hours per week	Rate per hour	Hours per week	Rate per hour	Hours per week	Rate per hour
1890	62.7	$0.154	63.6	$0.087	64.4	$0.151	60.0	$0.124
1891	63.8	.147	63.6	.087	64.3	.151	60.0	.119
1892	63.8	.145	63.7	.087	64.6	.150	60.0	.119
1893	63.1	.141	63.7	.088	64.4	.150	60.0	.118
1894	63.4	.140	63.8	.088	64.4	.140	60.0	.118
1895	63.2	.140	63.8	.088	64.3	.135	60.0	.116
1896	62.8	.143	63.8	.088	64.4	.138	60.0	.116
1897	63.2	.142	63.8	.088	64.7	.137	60.0	.111
1898	63.8	.140	63.9	.088	64.0	.145	60.0	.110
1899	63.9	.145	63.9	.088	64.4	.152	60.0	.116
1900	63.9	.146	63.9	.089	64.4	.158	60.0	.114
1901	63.9	.146	63.5	.091	64.1	.163	60.0	.115
1902	63.8	.147	63.5	.090	62.6	.173	60.0	.127
1903	59.2	.162	62.3	.106	60.8	.163	60.9	.135
1904	59.4	.166	62.2	.111	60.2	.162	63.3	.135
1905	59.5	.171	61.3	.116	60.2	.166	63.2	.137
1906	60.0	.169	60.7	.133	60.3	.174	61.0	.151
1907	60.0	.180	60.0	.137	60.2	.180	60.7	.160

TABLE O-12.—*Laborers, males, lumber, 1907–1928, by State and year*

Year	Alabama		California		Florida		Georgia	
	Hours per week	Rate per hour	Hours per week	Rate per hour	Hours per week	Rate per hour	Hours per week	Rate per hour
1907	62.2	$0.131	60.0	$0.219	60.0	$0.150		
1908	62.3	.125	60.0	.207	60.0	.141		
1909	62.3	.126	60.0	.201	60.0	.145		
1910	64.2	.118	60.1	.203	62.1	.132	63.7	$0.120
1911	64.5	.120	60.1	.201	63.2	.129	64.3	.120
1912	65.4	.120	60.1	.202	63.5	.133	64.0	.127
1913	64.8	.126	60.0	.207	63.7	.134	63.6	.131
1915	65.2	.106	60.1	.198	63.0	.115	64.9	.106
1919	(1)	.242	(1)	.394	(1)	.249	(1)	.197
1921	61.0	.155	55.9	.406	60.4	.159	60.8	.129
1923	60.6	.199	56.5	.456	60.6	.204	60.7	.160
1925	60.4	.201	56.4	.448	60.0	.242	60.2	.188
1928	60.5	.198	56.4	.423	61.4	.207	59.5	.185

Year	Louisiana		Maine		Michigan		Mississippi	
1907			60.0	$0.178	60.0	$0.176		
1908			60.0	.181	60.0	.175		
1909			60.0	.182	60.0	.176		
1910	61.4	$0.153	61.5	.183	60.0	.175	64.6	$0.126
1911	61.4	.153	61.7	.183	60.0	.175	64.5	.128
1912	61.0	.162	61.9	.185	60.0	.176	64.6	.131
1913	60.9	.163	62.1	.185	60.0	.179	60.1	.136
1915	60.6	.155	61.9	.189	60.0	.171	60.6	.126
1919	(1)	.295	(1)	.346	(1)	.315	(1)	.295
1921	60.3	.194	58.2	.311	60.1	.312	60.1	.182
1923	60.4	.228	58.1	.300	58.9	.377	59.9	.231
1925	60.7	.243	57.4	.315	59.7	.351	59.7	.240
1928	59.5	.231	59.5	.301	59.0	.345	59.7	.237

Year	North Carolina		Pennsylvania		Washington		Wisconsin	
1907	62.9	$0.123	63.3	$0.181	60.0	$0.219	60.0	$0.176
1908	63.9	.116	63.0	.182	60.0	.177	60.0	.167
1909	63.9	.114	62.7	.182	60.0	.193	60.0	.168
1910	62.1	.117	63.1	.196	60.0	.211	60.0	.182
1911	63.0	.118	63.4	.193	60.0	.208	60.0	.184
1912	61.7	.123	61.8	.189	60.0	.212	60.0	.185
1913	61.7	.127	61.8	.195	60.0	.230	60.0	.186
1915	62.6	.114	62.0	.200	60.1	.199	60.0	.174
1919	(1)	.260	(1)	.381	(1)	.513	(1)	.325
1921	60.4	.208	60.0	.312	48.0	.407	59.0	.288
1923	60.3	.210	60.0	.400	48.1	.499	59.8	.351
1925	60.2	.213	59.2	.372	48.1	.478	59.4	.349
1928	60.2	.213			48.0	.488	59.6	.322

1 Not reported.

TABLE **O-13.**—*Sawyers, lumber, 1843-1900, by year and State*

Year and State	Sex	Lowest, highest, and average—		Year and State	Sex	Lowest, highest, and average—	
		Hours per week	Rate per day (dollars)			Hours per week	Rate per day (dollars)
1843:				**1884:**			
Florida	M.	66-66-66	1.00-1.00-1.00	Illinois	M.	(1)	2.00-2.00-2.00
1845:				Michigan	M.	(1)	.50-6.00-2.57
Massachusetts	M.	72-72-72	1.50-1.50-1.50	New Jersey	M.	48-60-57	1.00-2.50-1.69
1850:				Ohio	M.	59-59-59	1.77-1.77-1.77
Massachusetts	M.	60-60-60	1.50-1.75-1.58	West Virginia	M.	60-60-60	1.50-1.50-1.50
New York	M.	72-72-72	1.00-1.17-1.09	**1885:**			
1852:				Arkansas	M.	60-60-60	2.25-2.25-2.25
Massachusetts	M.	60-60-60	1.75-1.75-1.75	Connecticut	M.	60-60-60	2.25-2.25-2.25
1854:				Delaware	M.	60-60-60	1.83-1.83-1.83
Wisconsin	M.	72-72-72	2.00-2.00-2.00	Illinois	M.	66-66-66	3.00-3.60-3.33
1855:				Kentucky	M.	(1)	1.25-1.25-1.25
Florida	M.	60-60-60	1.50-2.00-1.67	Maine	M.	63-63-63	2.00-3.00-2.29
1856:				Michigan	M.	60-66-66	.35-5.00-2.25
Massachusetts	M.	60-60-60	1.25-1.25-1.25	New Jersey	M.	48-60-59	.83-3.33-1.76
1857:				New York	M.	58-60-60	1.00-3.00-2.04
Virginia	M.	72-72-72	1.00-1.00-1.00	North Carolina	M.	60-60-60	1.25-2.25-1.45
1860:				Ohio	M.	(1)	2.00-2.00-2.00
New Jersey	M.	72-72-72	1.00-1.00-1.00	Rhode Island	M.	48-48-48	1.50-2.25-1.92
1864:				Virginia	M.	60-60-60	1.00-2.00-1.21
Massachusetts	M.	54-54-54	2.25-2.25-2.25	West Virginia	M.	80-60-60	2.00-2.75-2.38
1867:				Wisconsin	M.	60-66-64	1.10-3.20-1.76
New York	M.	60-60-60	2.00-2.00-2.00	**1886:**			
1868:				Illinois	M.	60-60-60	1.67-2.00-1.92
New York	M.	60-60-60	2.00-2.00-2.00	Kansas	M.	60-60-60	2.50-2.50-2.50
1869:				Michigan	M.	48-60-55	.75-2.00-1.40
New York	M.	60-60-60	2.00-2.00-2.00	Missouri	F.	60-60-60	.75-.75-.75
1870:				Ohio	M.	(1)	.44-.44-.44
New York	M.	60-60-60	2.00-2.00-2.00	**1887:**			
1871:				Kansas	M.	60-60-60	2.50-2.50-2.50
Massachusetts	M.	(1)	1.53-2.25-1.96	North Carolina	M.	60-72-64	.75-2.50-1.21
New York	M.	60-60-60	2.25-2.25-2.25	Ohio	M.	57-72-61	1.00-4.00-1.82
1872:				Wisconsin	M.	(1)	1.17-4.00-2.05
Michigan	M.	60-60-60	²1.15-1.15-1.15	Do	F.	(1)	1.25-1.25-1.25
New York	M.	60-60-60	2.25-2.25-2.25	**1888:**			
Ohio	M.	(1)	2.00-2.00-2.00	New Jersey	M.	(1)	1.67-2.50-2.14
1873:				New York	M.	53-66-59	1.00-3.83-2.03
New York	M.	60-60-60	2.25-2.25-2.25	North Carolina	M.	60-72-67	.60-2.50-1.30
Pennsylvania	M.	(1)	2.15-2.15-2.15	Michigan	M.	60-60-60	.42-2.50-1.35
1874:				New York	(1)	53-60-55	1.67-3.00-2.45
Massachusetts	M.	60-60-60	2.50-2.50-2.50	**1890:**			
New York	M.	60-60-60	2.25-2.25-2.25	Michigan	M.	60-60-60	.54-2.00-1.11
1875:				Minnesota	M.	(1)	1.45-1.45-1.45
Massachusetts	M.	(1)	2.27-3.37-2.63	New York	M.	(1)	.58-3.50-1.82
1876:				**1891:**			
New York	M.	60-60-60	1.67-2.33-2.13	Maine	M.	60-69-64	1.50-3.25-2.15
North Carolina	M.	66-66-66	1.00-1.00-1.00	Michigan	M.	60-60 60	1.38-3.50-2.16
Pennsylvania	M.	(1)	.40-4.00-1.94	Minnesota	M.	60-60-60	1.60-5.50-3.26
1877:				New York	M.	(1)	.58-3.50-1.85
Ohio	M.	(1)	1.67-2.00-1.81	North Carolina	M.	60-60-60	1.50-1.50-1.50
Pennsylvania	M.	60-60-60	1.66-2.00-1.77	Ohio	M.	60-60-60	1.00-3.75-1.71
1878:				Wisconsin	M.	60-60 60	.92-4.00-1.16
Pennsylvania	M.	60-60-60	1.38-1.77-1.54	**1892:**			
1879:				California	M.	54-60-58	1.50-3.33-2.34
Missouri	M.	60-60-60	1.58-1.58-1.58	Indiana	M.	48-60-58	1.15-2.25-1.59
Ohio	M.	(1)	1.33-1.83-1.58	Michigan	M.	60-60-60	1.38-3.50-2.16
Pennsylvania	M	60-72-66	.75-5.83-1.67	Minnesota	M.	60-60-60	1.60-5.00-3.38
Do	(1)	(1)	³.77-1.50-1.14	Missouri	M.	60-60-60	2.00-2.00-2.00
1880:				Wisconsin	M.	60-60-60	1.75-4.00-2.88
Missouri	M.	(1)	1.33-1.67-1.50	**1893:**			
New York	M.	(1)	2.25-2.25-2.25	Illinois	M.	60-60-60	1.75-3.00-2.42
Pennsylvania	M.	60-60-60	1.60-2.75-2.00	Maryland	M.	60-60-60	1.50-2.00-1.83
1881:				Michigan	M.	60-60-60	1.38-3.50-2.16
Ohio	M.	60-60-60	1.25-3.00-1.91	Minnesota	M.	60-60-60	1.60-5.00-3.45
Pennsylvania	M.	72-72-72	2.00-2.00-2.00	Missouri	M.	60-60-60	2.00-2.00-2.00
1882:				Montana	M.	54-60-57	2.70-7.00-4.57
Missouri	M.	60-60-60	2.50-2.50-2.50	Do	M.	(1)	¹1.53-3.71-2.98
New Jersey	M.	60-60-60	2.00-2.00-2.00	New York	M.	59-59-59	2.17-2.17-2.17
Ohio	M.	60-60-60	2.00-2.00-2.00	Ohio	M.	48-72-59	.90-4.50-1.68
Do	(1)	60-60-60	1.25-3.00-1.88	Wisconsin	M.	60-60-60	2.00-5.00-3.50
Pennsylvania	M.	(1)	1.50-2.00-1.75	Do	M.	(1)	1.42-3.50-2.26
1883:				Do	M.	(1)	².92-.92-.92
Massachusetts	M.	(1)	1.17-3.00-2.05	**1894:**			
Do	(1)	(1)	.75-1.25-1.00	Georgia	M.	60-60-60	1.00-2.50-1.53
Michigan	M.	(1)	.80-5.50-2.35	Indiana	M.	48-60-55	1.25-2.09-1.67
Ohio	M.	60-60-60	1.40-2.17-1.81	Iowa	M.	48-66-59	1.28-3.50-2.40

¹ Not reported.　　² And board.　　³ And board and lodging.

TABLE O-13.—*Sawyers, lumber, 1843–1900, by year and State*—Continued

Year and State	Sex	Lowest, highest, and average—		Year and State	Sex	Lowest, highest, and average—	
		Hours per week	Rate per day (dollars)			Hours per week	Rate per day (dollars)
1894—Continued.				**1896—Continued.**			
Maine	M.	60–60–60	1.25–1.25–1.25	Massachusetts	M.	54–60–58	1.50–3.00–2.02
Michigan	M.	60–60–C0	1.25–3.60–2.07	Michigan	M.	48–60–58	.75–3.00–1.71
Minnesota	M.	60–60–60	1.30–4.50–2.91	Minnesota	M.	60–60–60	².69–.69–.69
Montana	M.	(¹)	2.75–2.75–2.75	Do	M.	60–60–60	1.30–5.00–2.82
Do	M.	(¹)	³3.60–3.60–3.00	Missouri	M.	55–60–59	.90–4.00–2.30
New Hampshire	M.	60–90–68	1.00–2.00–1.52	Nebraska	M.	60–60–60	1.00–1.00–1.00
New York	M.	60 60 60	1.00–3.25–1.70	New Hampshire	M.	60–60–60	1.25–1.25–1.25
North Carolina	M.		.55–2.25–1.24	New Jersey	M.	60–60–60	2.00–2.00–2.00
Ohio	M.	48–69–59	.80–4.00–1.64	New York	M.	54–60–59	1.50–3.00–2.13
West Virginia	M.	60–60–C0	1.40–1:40–1.40	Ohio	M.	44–60–57	.50–3.59–1.65
Wisconsin	M.	60–60–60	1.50–4.00–2.75	Pennsylvania	M.	60–60–60	1.00–2.50–1.75
1895:				South Carolina	M.	(¹)	.50–.50–.50
Massachusetts	M.	54–60–59	1.50 .3.00–2.31	West Virginia	M.	60–60–60	1.58–1.58–1.58
Michigan	M.	60–60–60	1.38–3.60–2.09	Wisconsin	M.	48–60–56	.70–4.00–1.73
Minnesota	M.	60–60–60	1.30–5.50–3.02	**1897:**			
Missouri	M.	60–60–60	.98–2.98–1.78	Maine	M.	60–60–60	1.75–1.75–1.75
New Jersey	M.	60–60–58	1.33–4.00–2.22	Massachusetts	M.	54–60–59	1.00–3.00–1.89
New York	M.	48–60–59	1.00–3.00–2.06	Michigan	M.	60–60–C0	1.00–1.50–1.45
North Carolina	M.	60–72–61	.60–2.00–.90	New York	M.	60–60–60	1.35–2.00–1.65
Ohio	M.	45–63–59	.68–3.50–1.66	North Carolina	M.	66–66–66	.60–1.00–.74
Pennsylvania	M.	54–60–58	.72–3.00–1.56	Vermont	M.	60–60–60	1.25–2.00–1.34
Rhode Island	M.	55–55–55	.92–2.29–1.53	Virginia	M.	48–72–52	.75–4.00–1.75
Tennessee	M.	60–60–60	1.25–1.25–1.25	**1898:**			
Vermont	M.	60–60–60	1.15–1.35–1.25	Washington	(¹)	(¹)	1.50–3.41–2.52
Wisconsin	M.	60–60–60	1.75–4.00–2.88	**1899:**			
Do	(¹)	60–60–60	2.00–4.00–3.28	Massachusetts	M.	58–58–58	1.83–3.00–2.21
1896:				New York	M.	59–60–59	2.00–2.50–2.19
Connecticut	M.	60–60–60	2.00–2.50–2.13	North Carolina	M.	60–60–C0	1.00–1.00–1.00
Florida	M.	60–60–60	2.00–2.00–2.00	**1900:**			
Georgia	M.	60–66–63	.33–3.50–1.02	Massachusetts	M.	58–58–58	1.83–3.00–2.21
Illinois	M.	48 48–48	1.67–2.00–1.83	New York	M.	59–60–59	2.00–2.67–2.22
Kentucky	M.	60–60–60	1.50–1.50–1.50				

¹ Not reported.　² And board.　³ And board and lodging.

TABLE O-14.—*Sawyers, band, males, lumber, 1890–1907, by geographic division and year*

Year	North Atlantic		North Central		South Central		Western	
	Hours per week	Rate per hour	Hours per week	Rate per hour	Hours per week	Rate per hour	Hours per week	Rate per hour
1890	64.5	$0.291	62.3	$0.438	62.0	$0.394	60.4	$0.370
1891	64.5	.291	62.2	.443	62.0	.394	60.0	.376
1892	64.8	.287	62.2	.443	62.0	.394	60.0	.379
1893	64.5	.291	62.3	.441	62.0	.394	60.0	.382
1894	64.5	.291	62.2	.410	62.0	.394	60.0	.374
1895	64.5	.291	62.2	.433	62.0	.394	60.0	.364
1896	64.5	.291	62.2	.425	62.0	.394	60.0	.365
1897	64.5	.291	62.1	.429	62.0	.398	60.0	.365
1898	63.6	.283	62.2	.427	61.7	.388	60.0	.372
1899	64.0	.293	62.2	.447	61.5	.386	60.0	.375
1900	63.6	.301	62.0	.475	61.3	.379	60.0	.375
1901	63.6	.307	62.0	.491	61.3	.389	60.0	.379
1902	63.6	.307	61.3	.543	60.7	.423	60.0	.374
1903	60.0	.454	61.6	.564	60.6	.446	60.0	.395
1904	60.0	.458	60.3	.483	63.2	.495	60.0	.412
1905	60.0	.503	60.3	.495	63.2	.516	60.0	.425
1906	60.0	.514	60.3	.506	61.1	.570	60.0	.498
1907	60.0	.487	60.3	.523	60.6	.597	60.0	.507

TABLE **O-15.**—*Sawyers, head, band, males, lumber, 1910–1928, by State and year*

Year	Alabama		California		Florida		Georgia	
	Hours per week	Rate per hour	Hours per week	Rate per hour	Hours per week	Rate per hour	Hours per week	Rate per hour
1910	64. 2	$0. 546	60. 4	$0. 500	62. 7	$0. 598	62. 4	$0. 562
1911	64. 3	. 540	60. 0	. 533	63 0	. 598	63. 3	. 566
1912	65. 1	. 542	60. 0	. 531	63. 0	. 611	62. 9	. 572
1913	64. 0	. 575	60. 0	. 537	63. 0	. 618	62. 7	. 581
1915	65. 1	. 514	60. 0	. 540	63. 0	. 549	64. 1	. 533
1919	(1)	. 781	(1)	. 777	(1)	. 790		
1921	61. 0	. 749	55. 5	. 864	60. 7	. 825	59. 8	. 735
1923	60. 5	. 838	55. 3	. 990	60. 4	1. 018	58. 8	. 882
1925	60. 3	. 881	55. 8	1. 041	60. 0	1. 059	59. 8	. 828
1928	60. 8	. 820	54. 6	1. 029	60. 5	. 893	59. 2	. 828

Year	Louisiana		Maine		Michigan		Mississippi	
1910	60. 9	$0. 650	62. 4	$0. 536	60. 0	$0. 513	64. 9	$0. 554
1911	60. 8	. 655	62. 3	. 532	60. 0	. 512	64. 6	. 554
1912	60. 8	. 664	61. 5	. 513	60. 0	. 505	64. 0	. 572
1913	60. 6	. 688	61. 4	. 512	60. 0	. 505	60. 0	. 597
1915	60. 3	. 657	61. 5	. 513	60. 0	. 490	60. 0	. 553
1919	(1)	. 950	(1)	. 632	(1)	. 608	(1)	. 830
1921	60. 0	. 824	57. 3	. 686	60. 0	. 730	60. 0	. 798
1923	60. 1	. 910	57. 8	. 697	58. 6	. 832	59. 6	. 867
1925	60. 1	. 911	57. 6	. 718	59. 3	. 744	59. 2	. 883
1928	59. 1	. 872	58. 7	. 684	59. 0	. 768	58. 4	. 884

Year	North Carolina		Pennsylvania		Washington		Wisconsin	
1910	62. 1	$0. 489	63. 7	$0. 405	60. 0	$0. 549	60. 0	$0. 543
1911	63. 3	. 467	63. 4	. 378	60. 0	. 569	60. 0	. 556
1912	62. 9	. 485	62. 1	. 384	60. 0	. 564	60. 0	. 551
1913	62. 5	. 488	62. 4	. 404	60. 0	. 591	60. 0	. 550
1915	63. 0	. 475	61. 8	. 402	60. 1	. 580	60. 0	. 541
1919	(1)	. 613	(1)	. 618	(1)	1. 030	(1)	. 639
1921	60. 4	. 647	60. 0	. 621	48. 0	1. 045	59. 1	. 729
1923	60. 8	. 715	60. 0	. 703	48. 0	1. 153	59. 4	. 754
1925	60. 7	. 711	59. 3	. 669	48. 0	1. 140	59. 5	. 759
1928	60. 0	. 697			48. 1	1. 176		

1 Not reported.

TABLE **O-16.**—*Sawyers, circular, males, lumber, 1890–1907, by geographic division and year*

Year	South Atlantic		North Central		South Central		Western	
	Hours per week	Rate per hour	Hours per week	Rate per hour	Hours per week	Rate per hour	Hours per week	Rate per hour
1890	64. 7	$0. 217	60. 0	$0. 600	64. 4	$0. 361	63. 6	$0. 460
1891	64. 7	. 217	60. 0	. 600	64. 4	. 361	62. 4	. 468
1892	64. 7	. 217	60. 0	. 575	64. 4	. 361	63. 0	. 461
1893	64. 7	. 217	60. 0	. 600	64. 4	. 361	55. 5	. 451
1894	64. 7	. 217	60. 0	. 550	64. 4	. 361	55. 5	. 430
1895	64. 7	. 217	60. 0	. 575	64. 4	. 361	62. 4	. 386
1896	64. 7	. 217	60. 0	. 500	64. 1	. 352	62. 4	. 415
1897	64. 7	. 217	60. 0	. 500	63. 2	. 317	63. 0	. 423
1898	64. 7	. 217	60. 0	. 500	62. 9	. 309	62. 4	. 423
1899	64. 7	. 217	60. 0	. 525	62. 6	. 298	62. 4	. 428
1900	64. 7	. 217	60. 0	. 563	62. 3	. 303	60. 0	. 458
1901	63. 4	. 252	60. 0	. 563	62. 3	. 308	60. 0	. 468
1902	63. 4	. 252	60. 0	. 563	60. 9	. 334	60. 0	. 468
1903	62. 8	. 305	60. 0	. 588	60. 7	. 328	60. 0	. 490
1904	63. 0	. 308	59. 9	. 327	61. 7	. 332	60. 0	. 486
1905	62. 1	. 338	59. 9	. 343	62. 1	. 387	60. 0	. 478
1906	61. 7	. 367	60. 0	. 367	60. 0	. 512	60. 0	. 546
1907	60. 8	. 370	60. 0	. 341	60. 0	. 538	60. 0	. 570

TABLE **O-17.**—*Sawyers, head, circular, males, lumber, 1910–1928, by State and year*

Year	Alabama		California		Florida		Georgia	
	Hours per week	Rate per hour	Hours per week	Rate per hour	Hours per week	Rate per hour	Hours per week	Rate per hour
1910	65.0	$0.504			62.6	$0.453	65.2	$0.454
1911	65.1	.511	62.0	$0.517	63.8	.445	65.8	.461
1912	65.1	.501	62.0	.538	64.0	.538	66.0	.407
1913	65.9	.480	62.0	.521	66.0	.524	66.3	.450
1915	65.9	.384			66.0	.408	67.1	.366
1919	(1)	.557			(1)	.673	(1)	.663
1921	61.4	.459			61.5	.639	64.5	.436
1923	60.0	.950			61.2	1.036	63.8	.532
1925	60.0	.762			60.0	1.000	63.6	.416
1928	59.6	.778			64.8	.661	59.3	.514

Year	Louisiana		Maine		Michigan		Mississippi	
	Hours per week	Rate per hour	Hours per week	Rate per hour	Hours per week	Rate per hour	Hours per week	Rate per hour
1910	60.0	$0.638			60.0	$0.502	63.0	$0.476
1911	61.0	.629	65.0	$0.450	60.0	.511	64.9	.479
1912	61.2	.594	64.3	.429	60.0	.521	64.8	.517
1913	60.6	.592	64.3	.441	60.0	.535	60.0	.507
1915	60.8	.573	63.3	.414	60.0	.507	53.0	.581
1919	(1)	.848	(1)	.600			(1)	.694
1921	60.0	.864	60.0	.625	60.0	.721	60.0	.625
1923	60.0	1.011	57.5	.602				
1925	60.4	.904	56.3	.655	60.0	.735		
1928	60.0	.938	56.3	.541	60.0	.763		

Year	North Carolina		Pennsylvania		Washington		Wisconsin	
	Hours per week	Rate per hour	Hours per week	Rate per hour	Hours per week	Rate per hour	Hours per week	Rate per hour
1910	60.0	$0.333	(1)	(1)	60.0	$0.550	60.0	$0.538
1911	60.0	.333	62.5	$0.301	60.0	.588	60.0	.538
1912	60.0	.325	60.6	.343	60.0	.575	60.0	.538
1913	61.0	.278	60.6	.348	60.0	.567	60.0	.538
1915	60.5	.272			60.0	.503		
1919					(1)	.887		
1921	59.7	.461			48.0	1.009	57.5	.680
1923					48.0	1.092	59.9	.810
1925	60.0	.556			48.0	1.071	58.8	.791
1928					48.0	1.098	60.0	.763

¹ Not reported.

TABLE **O-18.**—*Sawyers, gang, males, lumber, 1890–1907, by geographic division and year*

Year	North Atlantic		South Atlantic		North Central		South Central	
	Hours per week	Rate per hour	Hours per week	Rate per hour	Hours per week	Rate per hour	Hours per week	Rate per hour
1890	60.8	$0.134	63.0	$0.132	62.0	$0.287	66.0	$0.273
1891	60.8	.134	63.0	.132	62.0	.287	66.0	.273
1892	60.8	.134	63.0	.132	62.0	.292	66.0	.273
1893	60.8	.134	63.0	.132	62.3	.283	66.0	.284
1894	60.8	.130	63.0	.132	62.3	.263	66.0	.284
1895	60.8	.130	63.0	.132	62.0	.263	66.0	.284
1896	60.8	.130	63.0	.132	62.0	.263	66.0	.296
1897	60.9	.208	63.0	.132	61.7	.271	66.0	.296
1898	60.9	.205	63.0	.121	61.7	.274	66.0	.296
1899	60.9	.213	63.0	.121	61.7	.284	66.0	.296
1900	60.9	.213	63.0	.132	61.3	.296	66.0	.296
1901	60.9	.213	63.0	.132	61.3	.304	66.0	.296
1902	60.9	.213	63.0	.132	60.9	.318	63.0	.309
1903	60.0	.223	63.0	.132	61.5	.319	63.0	.298
1904	60.0	.229	63.0	.132	60.4	.298	66.0	.255
1905	60.0	.229	59.0	.150	60.4	.296	66.0	.255
1906	60.0	.231	59.3	.167	60.4	.307	60.0	.232
1907	60.0	.238	56.0	.183	60.4	.321	60.0	.288

TABLE O-19.—*Woodworkers, 1840-1900, by year and State*

Year and State	Sex	Hours per week	Rate per day (dollars)	Year and State	Sex	Hours per week	Rate per day (dollars)
1840:				**1866:**			
Massachusetts	M.	78-78-78	1.50-1.50-1.50	Massachusetts	M.	60-66-62	2.00-3.00-2.50
1841:				**1867:**			
Massachusetts	M.	78-78-78	1.50-1.50-1.50	Massachusetts	M.	60-66-62	1.84-3.00-2.49
1842:				New Hampshire	M.	60-60-60	2.17-2.17-2.17
Massachusetts	M.	78-78-78	1.50-1.50-1.50	**1868:**			
1843:				Massachusetts	M.	60-66-62	1.50-3.00-2.43
Massachusetts	M.	60-60-60	1.50-1.50-1.50	New Hampshire	M.	60-60-60	2.50-2.50-2.50
1844:				**1869:**			
Massachusetts	M.	78-78-78	1.50-1.50-1.50	Massachusetts	M.	60-66-62	1.50-3.00-2.35
1845:				**1870:**			
Massachusetts	M.	78-78-78	1.50-1.50-1.50	Massachusetts	M.	60-60-60	1.50-3.00-2.30
1846:				New York	M.	60-60-60	2.50-2.50-2.50
Massachusetts	M.	78-78-78	1.50-1.50-1.50	**1871:**			
New Hampshire	M.	66-66-66	.83-.83-.83	Massachusetts	M.	59-60-60	1.50-3.00-2.46
1847:				**1872:**			
Massachusetts	M.	78-78-78	1.50-1.50-1.50	Massachusetts	M.	60-66-60	1.65-3.00-2.40
New Hampshire	M.	66-66-66	1.00-1.00-1.00	Ohio	M.	(¹)	2.00-4.17-2.67
1848:				**1873:**			
Massachusetts	M.	78-78-78	1.50-1.50-1.50	Massachusetts	M.	60-60-60	1.50-3.00-2.36
New Hampshire	M.	60-60-60	.83-.83-.83	Pennsylvania	M.	(¹)	2.25-3.30-2.96
New York	M.	60-60-60	1.50-1.50-1.50	**1874:**			
1849:				Massachusetts	M.	60-60-60	1.75-3.00-2.42
Massachusetts	M.	78-78-78	1.50-1.50-1.50	**1875:**			
New Hampshire	M.	60-60-60	.92-.92-.92	Massachusetts	M.	60-60-60	1.75-3.00-2.45
1850:				**1876:**			
Massachusetts	M.	72-72-72	1.33-1.50-1.42	Massachusetts	M.	60-60-60	1.50-3.00-2.21
New Hampshire	M.	60-60-60	.92-.92-.92	Pennsylvania	M.	(¹)	2.00-2.50-2.16
1851:				**1877:**			
Massachusetts	M.	72-72-72	1.33-1.75-1.54	Massachusetts	M.	60-60-60	1.35-2.75-1.95
New Hampshire	M.	60-60-60	.92-1.42-1.17	Ohio	M.	60-60-60	1.67-2.25-1.94
1852:				Pennsylvania	M.	60-60-60	1.00-2.50-1.95
Massachusetts	M.	72-72-72	1.33-1.75-1.54	**1878:**			
New Hampshire	M.	60-60-60	1.00-1.00-1.00	Massachusetts	M.	60-60-60	1.35-2.75-2.01
1853:				Ohio	M.	60-60-60	1.98-3.33-1.99
Massachusetts	M.	72-72-72	1.50-1.75-1.63	Pennsylvania	M.	60-66-61	1.83-2.25-2.06
New Hampshire	M.	60-60-60	1.17-1.50-1.34	**1879:**			
1854:				Massachusetts	M.	60-60-60	1.35-2.50-1.98
Massachusetts	M.	72-72-72	1.50-1.75-1.63	Missouri	M.	60-60-60	1.90-1.90-1.90
New Hampshire	M.	60-60-60	1.25-1.50-1.42	Ohio	M.	(¹)	1.50-3.50-2.15
1855:				Pennsylvania	(¹)	60-60-60	1.25-1.25-1.25
Massachusetts	M.	66-66-66	1.50-1.75-1.64	**1880:**			
New Hampshire	M.	60-60-60	1.33-1.33-1.33	Massachusetts	M.	60-60-60	1.30-2.50-1.85
1856:				New Jersey	M.	60-60-60	1.50-1.50-1.50
Massachusetts	M.	60-66-63	1.33-1.75-1.50	New York	M.	60-60-60	2.50-2.50-2.50
New Hampshire	M.	60-60-60	1.33-1.33-1.33	**1881:**			
1857:				Massachusetts	M.	60-60-60	1.30-2.75-1.90
Massachusetts	M.	60-66-63	1.25-1.67-1.46	Ohio	M.	54-60-59	1.35-2.75-1.91
New Hampshire	M.	60-60-60	1.33-1.33-1.33	**1882:**			
1858:				Massachusetts	M.	60-60-60	1.50-2.75-2.01
Massachusetts	M.	60-66-65	1.50-1.67-1.53	Missouri	M.	60-60-60	1.67-3.33-2.30
New Hampshire	M.	60-60-60	1.33-1.33-1.33	New Jersey	M.	(¹)	1.75-1.75-1.75
1859:				Ohio	M.	54-60-60	1.20-2.75-1.95
Massachusetts	M.	60-66-64	1.31-1.75-1.57	**1883:**			
New Hampshire	M.	60-60-60	1.17-1.17-1.17	Massachusetts	M.	60-60-60	1.15-4.00-1.94
1860:				New Jersey	M.	60-60-60	2.00-2.50-2.15
Massachusetts	M.	60-66-63	1.25-1.75-1.54	**1884:**			
New Hampshire	M.	60-60-60	1.25-1.50-1.38	Massachusetts	M.	60-60-60	1.50-2.75-2.02
Ohio	M.	(¹)	1.67-1.67-1.67	Michigan	M.	(¹)	.50-3.00-1.74
1861:				Missouri	M.	60-60-60	1.67-2.50-2.09
Massachusetts	M.	60-66-64	1.25-2.00-1.71	New Jersey	M.	60-60-60	1.50-2.67-1.91
1862:				Ohio	M.	(¹)	1.25-2.75-1.86
Massachusetts	M.	60-66-65	1.50-2.00-1.83	**1885:**			
New Hampshire	M.	60-60-60	1.25-1.25-1.25	Illinois	M.	60-60-60	1.00-3.25-1.85
1863:				Indiana	M.	60-60-60	1.25-1.75-1.45
Massachusetts	M.	60-66-64	1.50-2.25-1.83	Kentucky	M.	60-60-60	2.50-2.50-2.50
New Hampshire	M.	60-60-60	1.67-1.67-1.67	Maine	M.	60-60-60	2.25-2.25-2.25
1864:				Massachusetts	M.	60-60-60	1.40-2.75-2.07
Massachusetts	M.	60-66-63	1.50-2.50-1.92	New Jersey	M.	60-60-60	1.67-1.67-1.67
New Hampshire	M.	60-60-60	1.50-1.50-1.50	Ohio	M.	60-60-60	1.25-2.60-1.70
1865:				Pennsylvania	M.	60-60-60	1.91-1.91-1.91
Massachusetts	M.	66-66-62	2.00-2.60-2.31	Vermont	M.	60-60-60	1.50-1.90-1.75
New Hampshire	M.	60-60-60	2.25-2.25-2.25				
New York	M.	60-60-60	2.00-3.00-2.33				

¹ Not reported.

TABLE O-19.—*Woodworkers, 1840-1900, by year and State*—Continued

| Year and State | Sex | Lowest, highest, and average— | | Year and State | Sex | Lowest, highest, and average— | |
		Hours per week	Rate per day (dollars)			Hours per week	Rate per day (dollars)
1886:				**1893:**			
Illinois	M.	60-60-60	1. 75-2. 25-1. 79	Maryland	M.	54-60-57	. 50-2. 67-1. 59
Maryland	M.	60-60-60	1. 50-3. 00-2. 20	Massachusetts	M.	58-58-58	1. 79-2. 18-1. 96
Massachusetts	M.	60-60-60	1. 50-2. 75-2. 07	Michigan	M.	54-60-56	1. 25-2. 10-1. 63
Michigan	M.	60-60-60	1. 50-1. 50-1. 50	Missouri	M.	54-60-60	1. 67-2. 75-2. 30
Minnesota	M.	60-60-60	1. 00-3. 00-1. 99	Montana	M.	54-55-55	4. 00-4. 00-4. 00
Ohio	M.	(¹)	1. 19-1. 46-1. 33	New York	M.	53-53-53	3. 00-3. 00-3. 00
1887:				Ohio	M.	30-60-56	1. 00-3. 00-1. 79
Connecticut	M.	(¹)	. 70-2. 75-1. 69	Pennsylvania	M.	60-60-60	2. 67-2. 67-2. 67
Massachusetts	M.	60-60-60	1. 50-3. 00-1. 95	**1894:**			
Michigan	M.	60-60-60	1. 25-2. 20-1. 59	Indiana	M.	54-60-56	1. 17-2. 50-1. 64
Ohio	M.	48-60-59	. 75-3. 00-1. 96	Iowa	M.	48-66-57	. 50-3. 25-1. 52
Pennsylvania	M.	(¹)	1. 00-1. 00-1. 00	Maine	M.	60-60-60	2. 50-2. 50-2. 50
Wisconsin	M.	(¹)	1. 25-2. 50-1. 70	Massachusetts	M.	54-58-57	1. 79-3. 42-2. 25
1888:				New Hampshire	M.	48-64-58	1. 25-2. 50-1. 95
Massachusetts	M.	60-60-60	1. 50-2. 75-2. 10	New York	M.	60-60-60	. 75-2. 50-1. 75
New Jersey	M.	(¹)	2. 50-2. 50-2. 50	North Carolina	M.	60-60-60	. 96-2. 00-1. 43
New York	M.	35-60-59	. 35-3. 75-2. 08	Ohio	M.	42-60-56	. 40-3. 00-1. 70
North Carolina	M.	60-60-60	1. 50-2. 00-1. 65	**1895:**			
1889:				Kansas	M.	60-60-60	1. 38-1. 38-1. 38
Massachusetts	M.	60-60-60	1. 50-2. 75-2. 04	Massachusetts	M.	54-58-57	1. 79-3. 00-2. 31
Michigan	M.	60-60-60	1. 08-2. 00-1. 56	New York	M.	60-60-60	1. 25-2. 00-1. 63
Tennessee	M.	66-66-66	1. 50-1. 75-1. 63	North Carolina	M.	60-60-60	1. 00-1. 50-1. 25
1890:				Ohio	M.	42-72-57	1. 00 4. 00-1. 65
Massachusetts	M.	60-60-60	1. 50-2. 75-2. 01	Do	(¹)	60-60-60	1. 50-1. 50-1. 50
Michigan	M.	60-60-60	. 42-4. 00-1. 65	Wisconsin	(¹)	48-72-59	. 75-2. 42-1. 39
New York	M.	(¹)	. 40-4. 00-1. 79	**1896:**			
Ohio	M.	48-60-58	1. 25-2. 75-1. 68	Colorado	M.	54-54-54	1. 50-1. 50-1. 50
1891:				Maryland	M.	60-60-60	1. 50-3. 00-2. 04
Maine	M.	60-60-60	1. 40-1. 50-1. 43	Michigan	M.	54-60-60	. 50-3. 00-1. 69
Massachusetts	M.	60-60-60	1. 25-2. 75-1. 95	Minnesota	M.	60-60-60	. 90-2. 50-1. 57
New York	M.	(¹)	. 40-4. 00-1. 83	Missouri	M.	50-60-56	1. 17-3. 00-1. 85
Do	F.	(¹)	. 50-2. 17-. 84	New York	M.	60-60-60	2. 25-2. 25-2. 25
Do	(¹)	(¹)	. 50-. 50-. 50	Ohio	M.	42-60-56	. 97-2. 41-1. 62
Ohio	M.	48-72-58	1. 10-3. 00-1. 80	**1897:**			
1892:				Nebraska	M.	60-60-60	2. 50-2. 50-2. 50
California	M.	60-60-60	2. 00-2. 50-2. 25	New York	M.	54-60-55	1. 50-3. 00-2. 41
Indiana	M.	48-60-58	1. 35-2. 25-1. 67	Virginia	M.	54-60-60	1. 00-2. 25-1. 38
Iowa	M.	60-60-60	. 55-3. 50-1. 52	**1898:**			
Massachusetts	M.	58-60-57	1. 50-3. 50-2. 04	Michigan	M.	(¹)	1. 21-1. 80-1. 42
Michigan	M.	(¹)	1. 29-1. 29-1. 29	New York	M.	54-59-57	1. 75-3. 50-2. 71
Missouri	M.	(¹)	2. 00-2. 00-2. 00	**1899:**			
Ohio	M.	60-72-61	1. 50-2. 50-2. 03	Massachusetts	M.	53-53-53	3. 00-3. 00-3. 00
				Virginia	(¹)	(¹)	1. 00-2. 25-1. 90
				1900:			
				Massachusetts	M.	53-53-53	3. 00-3. 00-3. 00

¹ Not reported.

TABLE **O-20.**—*Machine woodworkers, males, planing mill, 1890–1907, by city and year*

Year	Atlanta, Ga.		Boston, Mass.		Chicago, Ill.		Cincinnati, Ohio		Detroit, Mich.	
	Hours per week	Rate per hour	Hours per week	Rate per hour	Hours per week	Rate per hour	Hours per week	Rate per hour	Hours per week	Rate per hour
1890			53.9	$0.302	57.1	$0.237			54.0	$0.238
1891			53.9	.304	57.1	.249			54.0	.239
1892			53.9	.300	57.1	.249			54.0	.235
1893			53.9	.295	57.5	.237			54.0	.238
1894			53.9	.298	57.3	.219			51.5	.224
1895			53.8	.299	57.7	.219			51.6	.222
1896			53.9	.302	57.8	.217			51.1	.215
1897			53.9	.302	57.1	.216			51.0	.227
1898			52.2	.314	57.4	.217			51.1	.219
1899			52.2	.314	54.6	.232			51.5	.230
1900			51.8	.317	52.2	.250			50.7	.234
1901			51.7	.314	54.5	.246			50.9	.236
1902			51.8	.315	54.4	.252			50.8	.263
1903	59.2	$0.224	53.5	.318	54.0	.271	54.3	$0.262	50.8	.275
1904	59.3	.212	53.4	.313	54.0	.277	54.3	.282	51.1	.304
1905	59.3	.223	50.7	.338	57.0	.289	54.3	.284	51.0	.283
1906	60.0	.235	48.0	.345	57.1	.304	54.4	.296	51.1	.297
1907	60.0	.241	48.0	.371	56.9	.325	54.4	.308	50.3	.318

Year	New Orleans, La.		New York, N. Y.		Philadelphia, Pa.		St. Louis, Mo.		San Francisco, Calif.	
1890	60.0	$0.245	55.0	$0.284	60.0	$0.243	60.0	$0.258	60.0	$0.336
1891	54.6	.279	55.1	.282	60.0	.243	60.0	.259	60.0	.338
1892	54.7	.287	55.0	.284	60.0	.243	60.0	.258	60.0	.330
1893	54.7	.286	55.1	.285	60.0	.243	60.0	.253	60.0	.310
1894	54.8	.292	53.8	.291	60.0	.243	60.0	.244	60.0	.280
1895	54.8	.292	53.8	.295	60.0	.243	60.0	.242	60.0	.281
1896	54.8	.291	53.8	.296	60.0	.241	60.0	.240	60.0	.292
1897	60.0	.253	53.9	.300	60.0	.241	60.0	.241	60.0	.306
1898	60.0	.244	54.0	.300	60.0	.241	60.0	.250	60.0	.305
1899	60.0	.248	53.5	.318	60.0	.241	60.0	.252	60.0	.315
1900	60.0	.248	53.4	.323	60.0	.241	60.0	.265	55.7	.358
1901	60.0	.239	53.3	.319	60.0	.255	60.0	.266	48.0	.420
1902	54.6	.257	50.0	.342	54.0	.286	60.0	.267	48.0	.438
1903	54.0	.244	50.2	.333	54.0	.295	60.0	.265	48.0	.469
1904	54.0	.230	52.2	.308	54.0	.290	60.0	.264	48.0	.463
1905	55.0	.251	52.8	.317	54.0	.297	60.0	.268	48.0	.462
1906	54.0	.252	50.3	.379	52.6	.320	60.0	.273	48.0	.656
1907	54.0	.269	49.0	.414	52.3	.325	60.0	.272	48.0	.651

TABLE **O-21.**—*Machine hands,[1] males, planing mill, 1907–1919, by State and year*

Year	California		Georgia		Illinois		Iowa	
	Hours per week	Rate per hour	Hours per week	Rate per hour	Hours per week	Rate per hour	Hours per week	Rate per hour
1907	48. 0	$0. 385	60. 0	$0. 234	57. 3	$0. 294	59. 1	$0. 208
1908	48. 0	. 407	60. 0	. 228	56. 7	. 294	59. 1	. 211
1909	48. 0	. 410	60. 0	. 230	56. 8	. 309	59. 1	. 214
1910	52. 2	. 377	58. 8	. 220	55. 2	. 328	58. 9	. 223
1911	51. 2	. 390	58. 8	. 222	55. 7	. 333	58. 8	. 228
1912	51. 6	. 399	57. 7	. 215	55. 0	. 340	58. 7	. 236
1913	51. 5	. 404	57. 3	. 227	54. 0	. 352	58. 6	. 238
1915	53. 4	. 375	55. 9	. 210	52. 7	. 354	59. 0	. 240
1919	(²)	. 622	(²)	. 408	(²)	. 485	(²)	. 378

	Massachusetts		Michigan		Minnesota		New York	
1907	49. 6	$0. 351	57. 8	$0. 210	59. 6	$0. 221	52. 6	$0. 322
1908	49. 9	. 347	58. 0	. 200	59. 7	. 218	53. 0	. 315
1909	49. 7	. 353	57. 8	. 212	59. 6	. 222	53. 1	. 318
1910	52. 4	. 300	57. 8	. 236	59. 8	. 226	54. 9	. 291
1911	52. 1	. 321	57. 7	. 245	60. 0	. 228	54. 6	. 294
1912	51. 2	. 322	56. 9	. 260	59. 6	. 241	53. 7	. 296
1913	50. 6	. 327	56. 6	. 275	59. 8	. 246	53. 1	. 304
1915	49. 8	. 332	56. 4	. 271	59. 8	. 248	53. 9	. 301
1919	(²)	. 504	(²)	. 389	(²)	. 346	(²)	. 467

Year	Ohio		Pennsylvania		Wisconsin	
1907	56. 6	$0. 283	56. 7	$0. 279	59. 9	$0. 184
1908	56. 6	. 279	57. 3	. 261	59. 9	. 183
1909	56. 8	. 277	57. 6	. 261	59. 9	. 187
1910	55. 8	. 273	55. 9	. 267	60. 0	. 185
1911	55. 6	. 282	55. 0	. 271	60. 0	. 191
1912	55. 1	. 284	54. 6	. 275	60. 0	. 181
1913	54. 9	. 305	54. 6	. 282	59. 9	. 203
1915	55. 9	. 298	54. 1	. 280	59. 6	. 204
1919	(²)	. 421	(²)	. 465	(²)	. 314

[1] Employees reported as machine woodworkers and sawyers for 1890–1907 are reported as machine hands for subsequent years.
[2] Not reported.

APPENDIXES

APPENDIX A.—EARLY WAGE LEGISLATION

While the following bill,[1] introduced into the court of Essex County, Mass., in 1670 and again in 1672, did not become law, it illustrates forcibly the kind of wage legislation in which the New England colonies persisted, in spite of admitted inability to enforce it.

This Court considering the great difficultie and discouragement, that at present lyes pressing vpon many inhabitants of this jurisdiction, especially vpon such, as whose callings are in husbandry, not onely by reason of the afflicting hand of God vpon them seuerall yeares in blasting their principall grayne, and abating their increase in other corne, and slowenes of market, and exceeding low price for what the husbandman can raise, vnto whose afflicting hand all ought to submitt and humble themselves, and yet with the prophet confesse, "Thou, Lord, hast afflicted vs lesse than we deserue;"—but also difficultie and discouragement are yet heaped and increasing vpon them and others by reason of the excessive deerenes of labour by artificers, labourers, and servants, contrary to reason and equitie, to the great prejudice of many householders and their familyes, and tending to their vtter ruein and vndoeing, and the produce thereof is by many spent to mayntayne such brauery in apparell which is altogether vnbecomeing their place and ranck, and in idleness of life and a great part spent viciously in taverns and alehouses and other sinful practices, much to the dishonour of God, scandall of Religion, and great offence and griefe to sober and godly people amongst vs. All which timely to prevent, this Court account it their duty carefully by all good meanes to provide, and therefore doe order as followeth.

It is therefore ordered by this Court and the authoritie thereof that no person within this jurisdiction, directly or indirectly, shall hereafter either paye or receaue for worke, labour or comoditie, more or aboue, then is in this present order appointed, and that vpon the penalties therein heere after expressed.

Imprimis. Labourers by the daye, from the end of September to the end of March dyeting themselues _____ 1/3 per day (21¢)
   From end of March to the end of June _____ 1/8 " " (28¢)
   From the end of June to the end of Septr. they workeing
     10 houres in the daye, besides repast _____ 2/ " " (33.3¢)
2. Taske worke. One acre of salt marsh and one acre of
   English grasse well mowen _____ 2/ per acre (33.3¢)
   One acre of fresh meadowe well mowen _____ 1/6 " " (25¢)
   " " Wheat " reapeing _____ 4/ " " (66.7¢)
   " " Rye " reapeing _____ 3/ " " (50¢)
   " " Barly and one of oats, each well mowen_ 1/ " " (16.7¢)
   " " Peas, cutting _____ 3/ " " (33.3¢)
   " coarde of woode, cutting and well coarding ____ 1/3. (21¢)

These wages are allowed as aboue to workemen dyeting themselues.

3. Carpenters and Masons, and Stone-layers, from 1 March to 10 of October, 2/ [33.3 cents] per day; and all worke taken by the great or piece by carpenters, masons, joyners, or shinglers, is to be apportioned according to the equitie of the value of daye's worke as above, they dyeting themselues.

4. Master Taylors, and such as are fully workemen of that trade, for one daye's worke of 12 hours, 1/8 [28 cents]. Apprentices to that trade the first four yeares, the like daye, 1/ [16.7 cents]. And all weauers for their worke at 12 hours per day, are to haue the like wages as taylors.

5. All men and women seruants shall in their respective wages be moderated according to the proportion of labour aboue limitted.

<hr>

[1] Taken from Felt's Massachusetts Currency, pp. 243–245.

6. No person shall pay, neither shall any shoemaker receaue, more than 5/ [83.3 cents] for men's shoes of eleuens or twelues, nor for women's shoes of seauens or eights more than 3/8 [61 cents]; and all bootes and shoes of other sizes proporiona ble to the rates abouesaide.

7. Cowpers shall not receaue nor any person paye for a thight barrel of 32 gallons aboue 2/8 [44.5 cents], and other cowper's worke proportionable in price to barrels.

8. Smythes shall not take nor any person paye for great worke, as for ships, mills, plough irones, all irones for cart wheeles well layd vpon the wheeles, and other the like great worke, above 5d [7 cents] per lb. For smaller worke as chaynes and other the like solde by weight, not aboue 6d [8.4 cents] per lb. For the largest horse shoe well set with seven nayles, not above 6d per lb. For remoueing a horse shoe, 2d [2.8 cents]. For an ordinary felling axe, 3/6 [58 cents]. For one broadaxe, 5/6 [91.7 cents]. One broad hough, 3/ [50 cents]. All being good and well steeled; and all other smithe's worke not named to be proportioned according to the prices abouesaid.

9. And whereas it apears that Glouers, Sadlers, Hatters, and seuerall other artificers doe at present greatly exceed the rules of equitie in their prizes, they are all required to moderate the same according to the rules prescribed to others, or know that in neglect thereof they are lyeable to presentment and proceeded against according to the Lawe,—Title Oppression.

Innkeepers and ordinary keepers are required to attend the dutie of them expected according to Lawe—Title Innkeepers, sec. 11, which order ought more carefully and strictly to be executed for the prevention of oppression in selling of wine, and as for selling beere they are to attend the Lawe, that orders what quantitie of malte is to be putt into each hogshead of beere, and that when malt is vnder 4/ [66.7 cents] per bushell then to sell no less than one quarte for 1½d [2 cents], and for entertaynment of horses in Sumer not to take more than 4d [5.6 cents] for one daye and night, and in winter not to exceed 6d [8.4 cents] for the like time.

All these payments are to be made in merchantable Corne at the price from yeare to yeare, set by the Generall Courte, prouided that when the materials are brought from the market by the artificer, as shoemakers, smythes, and the like, allowance may be made for that charge by the buyer according to what the transportation may be.

If any person shall paye or receaue more then according to the rates aboue expressed, he or they, both buyer and seller, shall forfeit the full treble value of what shall be payed or receaued, one-halfe to the enformer and the other halfe to the Treasurer of the seuerall Countie Courts.

The President of euery Countie Courte shall at euery such Court giue in charge to the Grand Jury to enquire carefully into the breach of this order in euery particular thereof. And all Grand Jurymen are required vpon their oath to present all offences against this Lawe, and if it shall apeere to the Court of the Countie at any time within one yeare after the offence is committed, that any Grand Juryman has knoweingly neglected his dutie heerein, he shall vpon conuiction before the Courte be fined Tenn times so much as the offenders should have payed whome he ought to have been presented.

The Deputyes having considered of this Bill about regulating workmen's wages, doe think it meete to refer the same to consideration vntill the next Court of election, our honoured Magistrates consenting hereto.

WM. TORREY, *Cleric.*

May 17, 1670. The Magistrates haue passed this Bill for an order of this Court, desiring ye consent of our brethren ye deputyes.

JOHN PYNCHON, *per order.*

The Deputyes consent not hereto.

WILLIAM TORREY, *Cleric.*

Tried again Oct. 11, 1672—Magistrates consented.
Deputies non-concurred.

APPENDIX B.—BUILDING TRADES

BUILDING CONTRACT FOR POHICK CHURCH

Fairfax County, Va., 1769

ARTICLES OF AGREEMENT made the 7th day of April in the year 1769 between the vestry of Truro Parish in the County of Fairfax, of the one part, and Daniel French of the County of Fairfax (Gent.) of the other part, as follows, viz.:

The said Daniel French doth agree and undertake to build and finish in a workmanlike manner a church near the forks of the road above Robert Boggess, to be placed as the vestry shall hereafter direct, of the following dimensions and materials, viz.:

Sixty-six feet in length and forty-five and a half feet in breadth from out to out. The walls twenty-eight feet high from the foundation. To be built of good bricks well burnt and of the ordinary size, that is, 9 inches long, four and one-half inches broad and three inches thick. To be three bricks thick to the water-table and two and one half afterward. The outside bricks to be laid with mortar two-thirds lime and one-third sand and the inside with mortar half and half. The corners of the House, the Pedestals, and doors with Pediment heads to be of good white free-stone. And the returns and arches of the windows to be of rubbed bricks. The doors to be made of pine plank two inches thick with moulded and raised panels on both sides and the frames thereof to be of pine clear of knots and sap with locust sills. The sashes to be made of pine plank one and one-half inch thick clear of sap. The lights to be of the best brown glass, eighteen in each window eleven inches by nine. The window and the door cases to be made with proper archatraves and the lower windows to have weights and pullies. The frames of the Roof to be of pine except the Kingposts which are to be of oak and the scantling to be of a size in proportion to the building. The roof to be covered with inch pine plank well seasoned and cyphered and laid one inch and one-half and then with cypress shingles 20 inches long and to show six inches. A Medallion cornice on the outside and a cove cornice on the inside. The roof to be framed agreeable to the plan thereto annexed. The floors to be framed with good oak clear of sap and laid with pine planks one inch and one-half thick and well seasoned. The ends of the Sleepers next to the walls of the House to have a least six inches hold thereof and their other end next the aisles to be supported by flush and entire brick walls in underpinning 9 inches thick and of a proper height. The aisles to be laid with Flagg-stone well squared and pointed. The pews to be wainscoted with pine plank an inch and one-half well seasoned and be quarter-rounded on both sides with raised panels on one side. The seats to be of one inch and onehalf pine plank fourteen inches wide and well supported. The Alter-Peice to be twenty feet high and fifteen feet wide and done with wainscot after the Ionic order. The Floor of the Communion place to be raised 12 inches higher than the floor of the House with hand rails and bannisters of pine and the Communion table of black walnut of the proper size. The Apostles' Creed, the Lord's Prayer and the Ten Commandments to be neatly painted on the Alter-Peice in black letters. The Pulpit Canopy and Reading Desk to be on pine wainscoted with proper cornice and exceuted in the Ionic order. The Inside to be ceiled, plaistered and whitewashed, no lome or clay to be used in the plaistering. The outside cornice and all the wooden-work on the inside of the House (except the floors) to be neatly painted of the proper colors. Stone steps to be put at the doors and locks and hinges to the Pews, Pulpit and Communion place.

The whole building to be completed and finished by the first of September in the Year of Our Lord 1772 in a sufficient and workmanlike manner.

And the said Daniel French doth further agree to build two horse-blocks with each two flight of steps and to fix six benches for the people to sit on under the trees and to clear and remove all the rubbish and litter from the church yard and to fix it for the reception of the congregation and to have these additional works done by the time appointed for the finishing of the church.

On condition of the above promises, said vestry do agree to pay to the said Daniel French the sum of £877 sterling in the manner following, to wit:

Two hundred pounds on the first of September next; two hundred and twenty-five pounds thirteen shillings and four pence on the first day of September, 1770; two hundred and twenty-five pounds thirteen shillings and four pence on the first day of September 1771 and the remaining two hundred and twenty-five pounds thirteen and four pence on the first day of September 1772 at which time the church is to be completed.

In witness whereof the said parties (to wit) members of the vestry here present and the said Daniel French have hereunto interchangeable set their hands on the day and year above written.

Signed and delivered in the presence of

JOHN BARRY
WILLIAM TRIPLETT } *Witnesses*

DANIEL FRENCH

ALEXANDER HENDERSON
DANIEL MCCARTY
EDWARD PAYNE
GEORGE WASHINGTON
GEORGE WILLIAM FAIRFAX
WILLIAM GARDNER
TOMEZIN ELLEZEY } *Vestrymen*

(From a transcript.)

CONSTRUCTION COSTS OF MONTICELLO, THOMAS JEFFERSON'S HOME, AT CHARLOTTESVILLE, VA., 1770–1772

(*From Jefferson's Account Books, in possession of the Massachusetts Historical Society*)

Moran & Maddox, masonry	$1, 557. 25
Hope do	28. 50
Chisholm, brickwork	142. 50
Blagden, marble	3. 50
Lime	124. 25
Plaistering	247. 15
Negro Hire	200. 00
Hauling	319. 60
Planks, sawing, etc	189. 11
I. Pery, carpentry	516. 00
R. Perry, do	24. 23
Oldham, joinery	122. 30
Andrews, composition	113. 53
	3, 587. 92

The whole of the nails used for Monticello and smith's work are omitted, because no account was kept of them.

RULES OF WORK OF CARPENTERS IN THE TOWN OF BOSTON

(Formed, and most accurately corrected, by a large number of the first Workmen of the Town, 1800.)

INTRODUCTION

That certain rules for Carpenters, specifying the various kinds of work they perform, the manner of finishing, and the value, are extremely necessary and highly useful, must be obvious to everyone. They assist the workman in stating his price, upon fair and equitable terms, in uniformity with his brethren and other mechanics; they enable the employer to ascertain the true amount of work performed; they serve as a test to prove the accuracy of accounts; and tend to prevent or remove all uneasiness between those who employ and those who perform.

Upon these principles "the Carpenters' rules of work in the town of Boston" were formed and published in the year 1774; and several have held them up as a direction to this day, not considering that they were calculated upon a scale which bears no proportion to the price of other labor *now*, and which is by no means an equivalent compensation for the service, in reference to the raised price of the necessaries of life; and that not only the low rate at which they are cast render them a very incompetent guide at present, but that they are besides greatly deceptive in not specifying one-quarter part of the work now in demand. Wherefore, the Carpenters of the Town have met at sundry times to consider the propriety of forming new arrangements and new Rules, more accurate and more complete, and calculated on a scale better adjusted to the means of an honest livelihood in an equitable award to faithful industry. They chose, accordingly, a large and respectable Committee, out of their number, to form such Rules; which, being reported and unanimously approved by the whole body, they now publish for the service of the Craft—expecting that all work will be measured by them, and executed in the best possible manner.

At a Meeting of the CARPENTERS of the Town of Boston at Marean's Hall
August 21, 1800

Voted, that the names of the Committee of twenty-one who drew up the Rules of Work be published with the book, and attested by the Secretary.

The Committee, accordingly, gave their signatures as follows:

WILLIAM ELLISON	WILLIAM ANDREW	JAMES BOLTER
NATHANIEL BRADLEE	BRADDOCK LORING	JONATHAN LORING
AMOS LINCOLN	JAMES ROBBINS	THOMAS BARRY
WILLIAM TODD	JOHN MILLER	THOMAS W SUMNER
MOSES AYRES	JEDEDIAH LINCOLN	JOSEPH STODDER
SAMUEL TODD	THOMAS HEARSEY	CHARLES CLEMENT
JOSIAH WHEELER	WARD JACKSON	MOSES GARDNER

Attest:

(Signed in ink)   THOS. STUTSON,
Secretary.

RULES OF WORK

Framing floors of all kinds

	D	O
Framing brick or wooden house floors with summers or planks, from 10 to 12 inches deep, at per square	1	33
And where the summers or planks are deeper, for every inch in depth add per square		33

Framing sides and ends

	D	O
Framing sides and ends where the girts are from 10 to 12 inches deep, and the posts not less than 7 nor more than 10 inches square, at per square	1	33

Small framing

	D	O
Framing small frames, such as woodhouse, &c., of small timber or large joist, including the roof, at per square	1	25
Framing hips and gutters, at per foot		12½

Framing roofs

	D	O
Framing a plain pitched roof, with rafters of 8 inches deep, at per square	1	50
Framing a plain gambol roof, with timber of the above size, including collar beams, at per square	1	91
Framing a hipped roof, with rafters of 8 inches deep, at per square	1	75
And where the rafters are more than 8 inches deep, add for every inch in depth, per square		13
And all beams under hips whole framing and all others half framing; and if any joists are let into dit. at per square for dit		50
Rafters framed with one king post, half framing; rafters framed with one king post and two braces, whole framing. Rafters framed with king post, two struts, and two braces, add one-fourth. If more work in any of the above add in the same proportion:		
Framing gutters and hips at per foot		25
Framing flat roofs with beams on a curve, at per square	1	54
Framing flat trussed roof, with regular pitch, including beam and hip rafters, at per square	2	

Framing middles

			D	C
Laying out middles for stores with one summer			1	50
dit.	dit.	with two summers	2	
dit.	dit.	with three summers	3	

Putting on floors, hewing and plaining timber, scaffolding, shoring, sawing and shooting plank, for framing, collecting materials, stocking boards, hewing and laying sleepers, to be paid for by the day.

Raising wooden house frames, and putting on all roofs, to be paid for by the day.

Rough boarding

	D	C
Rough boarding per square		50
If shot dit		75
If feather-edged dit		83
If Rabbeted dit	1	12
If on a roof more than two stories high	1	
If grooved with match planes	1	83
Boarding hips and gutters at per foot		6
Laying rough floors at per square		58
If shot and well laid dit		83
Laying rough plank floors with hewed joints, at per square	1	50
If planed, suitable for store floors, at per square	2	50

Window frames of all kinds

	D	C
Making a window frame to contain 24 panes or less, of 6 by 8 glass	1	25
If for 7 by 9, or 10 by 14	1	50
If 8 by 10, or 11 by 15	1	71
If 12 by 18	1	83
If 13 by 21	1	96
If larger, add in the same proportion		
If any of the above are sunk from 3 to 4 inches, add		25
If plain OGG, add		33
If double moulding, add		40
If cased to receive shutters outside, add		50
If double architrave, add	1	
If solid flat cap, worked with lip and OGG, add		40
For setting any of the above, add		25
If any of the above frames have a compass head, add for dit	1	50
For setting dit. add		37
If OGG on dit. add for the sweep per foot		9
If double architrave, add for the sweep per foot		30
If the stool is rabbeted, add		25
A plain Venetian window frame, the center part of which is to contain not more than 12 panes of 12 by 18 glass	6	25
If larger, add in proportion. If to receive pilasters 8 inches wide or less, and an entablature from 7 to 15 inches wide, add	2	
For setting dit		50
For a plain bow window to contain not more than 30 panes of 18 by 12 glass, or less, at per frame	6	
If larger, add in the same proportion.		
Setting dit. to be paid for by the day.		
Boxing any of the above frames		25
For letting in iron or brass box pullies, each		6
Making a cellar window frame (with bars put in) from 2 to 3 feet from out to out	1	
If larger, add in proportion.		
Setting dit		25
Making plank lintels, each		17
Making centers, to be paid for by the day.		

Window caps outside

	D	C
Equal to the Tuscan order	2	
Equal to the Doric or Corinthian	4	
Equal to the Ionic	2	50
Equal to the Composite	5	

Sashes of all kinds, and hanging dit.

	D	C
Making sashes 7 by 9, or 8 by 10 with ovolo, per light		8
If larger each way, per inch		1
Nosing sashes add one fourth to the prices of ovolo sashes per light.		
Plain sashes 6 by 8, 7 by 9, or 8 by 10 glass, per light		6
Hanging sashes single, with line or hinges, per window		17
Hanging dit. double with 4 laths and 4 weights		50
Sashes in bow windows, add 100 per Ct. per light. If in two sashes, add 150 per Ct. per light.		
A true sweep sash, from a segment to a semicircle per light		38
If Elipsis		50

Clapboarding, butting, and scribing

	D	C
For shooting Clapboards per hundred		25
Plaining dit. per dit	1	25
Laying dit. per dit	1	50
Scribing on shingles at per foot		8
Plain scribing, and butting per foot		2

Shingling crippels, gutters boards and weather boards

	D	C
Laying shingles, per square	1	50
Shingling hips per foot		10
Shingling gutters per foot		18
Building cripples behind chimnies at per foot, measuring on the ridge		33
Ripping up old shingles and clearing the nailes, at per square		33
Half gutter boards per foot		2
Whole gutter boards per foot		4
Plain weather boards, 6 inches wide or under, at per foot		6
If wider, add for every inch in width more		½
If OGG on dit		8
If plancere		12
Hip ridge and eave pieces for slating at per foot		6

Facia under eaves

	D	C
If 6 inches wide or under, per foot		6
If wider, for every inch in width add per foot		½
OGG on dit, per foot		2
If single cornice on dit		6
If dentil cornice on dit		18

Water tables, corner boards, and saddle boards

	D	C
Water tables of plank 6 inches wide or under, at per foot		6
If wider, add for every inch in width		½
Water tables of timber, worked with a moulding, at per foot		18
Corner boards, double, 6 inches wide or under, per foot		10
If wider, add for every inch in width more, per foot		½
Corner boards single, half price of double		
Saddle boards at per foot, run		8
If made of plank		10

Rustic corners, fronts, plain sheathing and belts

	D	C
Rustic corners, including the ground work, at per foot, superficial		21
Rusticated fronts at per foot dit		18
Butting and scribing dit. at per foot, run		6
Plain sheathing with 1¼ inch stuff, at per foot superficial		13
If 1 inch stuff dit. dit		10
Butting, scribing, and mitring 1¼ inch stuff, at per foot, run		6
Butting, scribing, and mitring 1 inch stuff, at per foot, run		5
Belts from 7 to 12 inches wide, per foot, run		10
If moulding underneath, add for dit. per foot, run		6

Trunks and gutters

	D	C
Making a square trunk, at per foot		8
Making round trunk per foot		12
Single cornice head to square trunk		50
Dentil cornice and necking to dit	1	
Solid cornice gutters per foot, run		18
If rabbeted to lodge on bricks, add per foot		1
Plain cant gutters per foot		9
Cant gutters worked with cornice		12
Putting up trunks and gutters to be paid for by the day		

Casing coveing and cornices of all kinds

Casing coveing with plancere and facia only, at per foot, run	16
Single cornice at per dit	6
Tuscan dit. at per inch in height, for every foot, run	3
Doric and Corinthian cornices from 5 to 7 inches, per foot	73
For every inch in height more, add per inch	4
If a double fret dentril	75
For every inch in height more, add	4½
Ionic cornice from 5 to 7 inches, per foot	60
For every inch in height more, add per foot	2
Composite cornice from 5 to 7 inches, at per foot	75

And for every inch in height, add 4½ cents for every foot.

Single cornice with fluted frize and astragal neck, from 5 to 7 inches, per foot	35
For every inch in height more, add	4
Block cornice form, 5 to 7 inches, per foot	37
For every inch in height more, add per inch	4
Gothic cornice with modillion and chain dentril from 5 to 7 inches, per foot	75
For every inch in height more, add per inch	4½
Gothic dit. without modillion from 5 to 7 inches, per foot	55
For every inch in height more, add per inch	2
Gothic dit. without fret and with modillion from 5 to 7 inches, per foot	60
For every inch in height more, add per inch	3
Composite cornice with modillion, and the frize to be ornamented, from 5 to 7 inches, at per foot	67
For every inch in height more, add	3

(If any of the above cornices have a regular frize and architrave, add per foot one third the price of the cornice; except the Doric, which add one half the price per foot of the cornice. All mitres and scribes equal to a foot of Cornice.)

Outside pedastals and pilasters

Plain pilasters, including base and necking, at per inch in width	50
Fluting columns and pilasters, add per inch	20
Tuscan pedastal at per inch in width	20
Doric dit. dit. dit	25
Corinthian dit. dit. dit	28
Ionic dit. dit. dit	25
Composite dit. dit. dit	30

If for pilaster or ¾ column measure one face; if for a whole column measure 2 faces.

Luthern windows

Hip'd luthern window boarded, with single cornice broke round dit	3
Pitched pediment with cornice and bed mould broke round, dit	6
Dit. dit. with dentil cornice	8
Dit. dit. with compass head	10

Turrets

	D	O
Plain posts and rails with plancere, per foot		17
Dit. posts morticed, rails made with boards, and moulding under plancere, per foot		25
If plank rails		33
Diamond work turrets at per foot, run		40
Chinese dit. at per foot, run		50
Ballustrade straight work at per foot, run		75
Dit. broke over posts at per dit	1	

Frontispieces and porticos of all kinds

	D	O
Plain casing doors with plancere, cap, truss, architrave and straight light over the door	7	
With dentil cornice, fluted trusses, open pilasters and cased for fan light	20	
With fret, or eye dentil, fluted frize and trusses, and cased for fan light	25	
Plain Tuscan frontispiece, straight cap and plain pilasters	20	
Tuscan dit. with pediment, brake and pilasters	26	
If with columns, add	4	
Doric frontispiece, straight cap, plain ground and fluted pilasters	33	
If a pediment, add	10	
If rustic ground, add	6	
If brake and columns, add	6	
Ionic frontispiece, straight cap	30	
If with pediment, add	9	
Corinthian frontispiece the same as Doric		
Open pediment with plain columns, equal to the Ionic order	40	
Open dit. equal to the Doric or Corinthian order	40	
If with columns	45	
If any of the above have fluted columns, add	5	
If any of the above frontispieces have rusticated grounds, add	6	
Tuscan portico, plain ground, pilasters and columns	50	50
Doric dit. plain ground, pilasters and fluted columns	80	
Corinthian dit. the same as Doric		
Ionic dit. plain ground, pilasters and fluted columns	65	
Swelled portico with two columns equal to the Ionic order	85	
Dit. dit. with four columns dit. dit.	113	
Dit. dit. with six columns equal to the Doric or Corinthian order	150	

Outside door cases for brick walls

	D	O
Plank door cases for brick or stone walls, per foot superficial		8
Door cases made with pine timber, 9 inches wide and 4 inches thick or under, at per foot, run		15
Dit. from 9 to 12 inches wide, and from 4 to 6 inches thick, per foot, run		20
If larger, add per inch in width		2
If oak thresholds, add per foot for dit		20
Door cases made of hard wood, add 100 per cent for dit		
Compass heads or door cases, per foot		50

Outside cellar doors

	D	O
Cellar doors with head, sills and strings, slanted to the house	3	
If plank top and bottom, add		50
Cellar doors with solid cheeks, plank top and bottom	7	
If with pediment, add	2	

Rough partitions, rough ceilings, and rough furrings

	D	C
Rough partitions, solid, of plank, per square_____	1	25
Dit. dit. open, of dit. per square, including sawing_____	1	
If the planks are sawed from 3 to 4 inches in width, and set edgewise, at per square_____	1	50
Rough furring, and rough ceiling, per square_____	1	
All circular ceilings to be paid for by the day_____		

Inside door cases

Inside door cases with framed heads_____		95
Rough dit. with stops, and hardwood threshold_____		75
Dit. dit. with stops and pine threshold_____		67

Casing outside doors

Edge casing, outside doors on studs, including threshold_____	1	
Casing on outside with plank_____		60
Dit. on three sides, with board casings_____	1	75

Double doors and shutters, with boards planed to a thickness

Doors and shutters with boards planed to a thickness, at per foot, superficial_____	15
All kinds of fastenings for dit. each_____	25

Casing windows

Casings five inches wide, or less, at per foot_____	3
For every inch more in width, add_____	$\frac{1}{2}$
Box casings, per foot_____	$2\frac{1}{2}$

Casing timber

Casing timber, at per foot, measuring on the corners_____	6
Strips for stopping plastering, per foot_____	2

Planed partitions, battened doors, and shutters

Planed partitions of boards on one side, battened, or matched, at per foot, superficial_____	3
If planed on both sides_____	$4\frac{1}{2}$
Plank partitions, planed on one side, battened or match, at per foot, superficial_____	$4\frac{1}{2}$
Dit. planed on both sides_____	6
All battened doors planed on one side, at per foot, superficial_____	6
. Dit. on both sides, dit._____	7

The above prices for doors include the stops.
All battened shutters the same price as doors.

Architraves and mouldings

Single face architrave, per foot, running_____	6
Double face dit, per foot, dit._____	10
Dit. with extra moulding_____	12
Fluted architrave per foot_____	17
Compass double face architrave_____	30
Dit. single face_____	18
OGG, ovolo or cove, straight work, at per foot, run_____	3
Dit. dit. dit. compass per foot_____	9

Inside door caps

	D	C
Door cap equal to the Tuscan order	1	75
Dit. equal to the Doric	3	50
Dit. equal to the Ionic	2	25
Dit. equal to the Corinthian	3	50
Dit. equal to the Composite	4	38

(If any of the above doors are more or less than 3 feet wide and 7 feet high, add or deduct in proportion.)

Inside window shutters

Shutters made with planed boards, and ends cleated, per foot, run	8
Two paneled shutters, square joints, at per foot	12
Dit. with quarter round work, at per foot	15
Three paneled shutters, with quarter round, at per foot	18
Two paneled shutters, with ovolo, or OGG, at per foot	17
Three paneled dit. with ovolo or OGG, at per foot	23
Two paneled dit. with ovolo or quirk OGG sunk panel, and astragal neck, at per foot	23
Three paneled dit. dit. dit.	26
Two paneled dit. with ovolo, or quirk OGG on one side, and bead, and flush on the other, at per foot	30
Three paneled dit. dit. dit. at per foot	36

If any of the above shutters are bead and but, deduct from the two paneled 3 cents, and the three paneled 4 cents.

Hanging stiles, each	25
Fitting shutters into box, per window	33

(Shutters, bead and flush on both sides, at per foot the same price as quirk OGG and neck on one side, and bead and flush on the other. And if any of the preceding shutters are more than 12 inches wide, to be measured superficial, at per foot the same as running).

The foregoing prices include hanging.

Fastenings

Plain fastenings to windows, each	12½
Dit. spring fastenings to dit. each	25

Stairs of all kinds

	D	C
Common rough plank stairs, straight run, per step		33
Dit. if winders		50
Planed plank stairs, straight run, at per step		42
If winders		60
If planed both sides, straight run, per step		50
Dit. if winders		67
If posts and hand rails to either of the above stairs, per foot, run, for the rail		16
Rough stairs of boards, straight run, per step		25
Dit. if winders		30
Planed stairs of boards, straight run, per step		30
Dit. if winders		35
Back stairs, straight run, with moulding underneath the step, per step		33
Dit. if winders		40

(The above plank stairs is considered to be not more than four feet long, and the board steps not more than three feet long; if longer add in the same proportion.)

	D	C
Framed stairs, straight run, with banisters and risers mitred in the stringboard, per step	1	
Dit. if winders, per step	1	25
If short platform	2	
If long platform	3	
If gallery, per foot		50
Bracket stairs made with boards, per step	1	25
Dit. with plank steps and nails hid, per step	1	55

	D	C
If with double bracket	1	75
If cased underneath, add per step		75
If short platform	2	75
If long dit	4	50
Straight gallery, per foot, run		77
Working a common quarter twist rail and capping the first post	4	
Working a scroll (including the curtailed step)	10	
Working knees, each	1	50
Working mahogany rail, per foot, run		25
Cylinder stairs, per step	3	50
Casing dit. underneath, per step	1	34
Gallery, per foot	1	75
Circular rails on galleries, per foot	1	
Working twists in a continued rail, at per foot	2	50
Fitting banisters of pine, per dozen		25
Dit. dit. of hard wood		50

Wainscoting, dadoing rooms and stairs

Wainscoting rooms from floor to ceiling, with quarter round work, per foot, superficial	8
Dit. with small ovolo	9
Dit. with quirk OGG and sunk panel, and astragal neck	12
Low wainscoting in rooms up to the windows, quarter round work, at per foot, superficial	10
Dit. dit. ovolo	11
Dit. with quirk OGG, sunk panel and astragal neck	15
If upstairs, add one third to their respective prices.	
If any of the above wainscoting have frize panels, add to their respective prices one-fifth part.	
Bolexion work in rooms, per foot, superficial	16
Dados in rooms, &c., per foot, superficial	6
Each but in dado	8
Each mitre in dit	16
Dado on stairs, per foot, superficial	7
Capping on Dado equal to the Tuscan order, per foot, run	9
Dit. on dit. equal to Doric, per foot, run	11
Base suitable to Tuscan or Doric cappings, per foot, run	11
Capping on dado equal to the Ionic order, per foot, run	13
Base suitable for such order, per foot, run	12
Capping on dado equal to the Corinthian order, per foot, run	25
Base suitable for such order, per foot, run	20

N. B.—Mop boards and plinths are included in the bases of dado. Mitres in capping, and bases, each the same as their respective price per foot, run.

The above prices of capping and bases are estimated for dados two feet eight inches high, or under. If the dados are higher, add for such height one tenth part of their respective prices for every three inches.

Finishing windows inside

Plain risers and returns for seats, per foot, superficial	11
Dit. dit. with panels and quarter round work, per foot, superficial	15
Dit. dit. with ovolo dit	16
Dit. dit. with quirk OGG, sunk panel and astragal neck, per foot, superficial	18
Plain back boards and elbows, per foot, superficial	18
Back boards and elbows with quarter round work, and panels raised, per foot, superficial	30
Dit. dit. ovolo dit. dit	32
Dit. quirk OGG, sunk panel, astragal neck, per foot, super	35
Plain soffita, per foot, superficial	8
Quarter round dit. panels raised, per foot, superficial	22
Ovolo dit. per foot, superficial	24
Quirk OGG, sunk panels and astragal neck, per foot, superficial	25

	D	C
Circular soffita, if plain, per foot superficial.........................		22
Dit. dit., quarter round work, panels raised, per foot, super.....		60
Dit. dit. ovolo, dit. dit...................................		62
Dit. dit. quirk OGG and astragal neck, per foot, superficial......		75

N. B.—The above prices of circular soffitas are estimated for openings about three feet, and soffita one foot wide. Smaller openings and narrower soffitas are worth more. Larger openings and wider soffitas are worth less, per foot.

	D	C
Back linings to windows, plain, per foot, superficial..................		4½
Dit. dit. bead and but, per foot, superficial.....................		14
Dit. dit. with quarter round work, ovolo or quirk OGG, the same prices respectively as risers and returns.		
Window seats of pine, per foot, superficial........................		8
Dit. of mahogany dit..		20

Doors of all kinds

	D	C
Eight panel door, quarter round work, one side, raised one side, per foot, superficial...		15
Dit. dit. two sides, raised one side, per foot, superficial.........		17
Eight panel door, two sides, raised two sides, per foot, super........		20
Eight panel door, ovolo moulding one side, raised one side, per foot superficial..		16
Dit. dit. two sides, raised one side, per foot, superficial.........		18
Dit. dit. raised two sides, per foot superficial..................		21
Eight panel door, quirk OGG, astragal neck one side, quarter round, and panel raised on other side, per foot, superficial..............		22
Dit. dit. with quirk OGG and astragal neck on both sides, per foot, superficial..		24
Six panel door, quarter round one side, raised one side, per foot superficial..		13
Dit. dit. two sides, raised one side, dit......................		16
Dit. dit. two sides, raised two sides, dit....................		19
Dit. dit. ovolo moulding one side, raised one side, per foot superficial..		14
Dit. dit. two sides, raised one side, per foot superficial.........		17
Dit. dit. two sides, raised two sides, per foot superficial........		20
Six panel door quirk OGG and astragal neck on one side, ovolo and raised panel on the other, per foot, superficial..................		21
Dit. dit. with quirk OGG, and astragal neck on both sides, per foot, superficial..		22
Four panel door, quarter round on one side, raised one side, per foot superficial..		10
Dit. dit. two sides, raised one side, per foot superficial.........		12
Four panel door, two sides, raised two sides, per foot superficial....		14
Four panel door, ovolo moulding one side, raised one side, per foot superficial..		11
Dit. dit. two sides, raised one side, dit......................		13
Dit. dit. two sides, raised two sides, dit....................		15
Four panel door, quirk OGG and astragal neck on one side, raised one side, per foot, superficial...............................		14
Dit. dit. quirk OGG and astragal neck both sides, per foot superficial..		16
Two panel door, quarter round one side, six feet high and two feet wide or under..	1	25
Two panel door, ovolo moulding on one side, raised on one side, six feet high and two feet wide or under.........................	1	33
Two panel door, quirk OGG, and astragal neck on one side, six feet high and two feet wide or under, at per door...................	1	50
Two panel door, quarter round one side, raised one side, from six feet high, two feet wide, and upwards, per foot, superficial..........		8
Dit. dit. two sides, raised two sides, dit. dit, per foot, superficial.		10
Dit. quirk OGG and astragal neck one side, from six feet high two feet wide and upwards, at per foot, superficial..........		9

D C

Dit. dit. quirk OGG and astragal neck on two sides, from six
feet high two feet wide and upwards, at per foot, superficial__   12
N. B.—If any of the above doors are worked with wide muntin,
with bead in the center, add 2 cents to their respective prices.
The above prices include the hanging of doors, with H or HL
ninges. If hung with but hinges, add, per door, 25 cents.
Putting on mortise locks, each_____   75
Putting on iron stock locks, wood stock locks, and closet locks_   25
Putting on knob latches, thumb latches, plate bolts and plain bolts,
each_____   12½

Chimney pieces, casings, &c.

	D	C
Casing kitchen chimney with shelf and single cornice, per shelf_____	1	50
Stiles to stop plastering, per foot, run_____		2
Plain chimney casings, each_____		75
If one moulding around dit. add_____		25
Panel breast work to chimneys, per foot superficial_____		8
Large ovolo round dit. per foot, run_____		5
Ovolo and OGG round dit. per foot, run_____		7
Each mitre in the above moulding_____		4
A plain chimney piece, or equal to the Tuscan order_____	5	50
Dit. equal to the Ionic order_____	7	50
Dit. equal to the Corinthian or Doric order_____	13	
Dit. equal to the Composite order_____	18	
If any of the above chimney pieces have double pilasters or columns, add to their respective prices_____	2	

Putting on composition ornaments to be paid for by the day.

Linings in rooms, and closets, with their mouldings

	D	C
Plain linings, boards grooved, per foot, superficial_____		5
Nozing, capping, per foot, run_____		2½
Astragal dit, per foot, run_____		2

Floors of all kinds

	D	C
Floors laid with merchantable boards not planed to a thickness, at per square_____	2	
If rabbeted_____	2	25
Dit. dit, planed to a thickness_____	2	75
Floors laid with narrow boards of the best sort, per square_____	3	50
Keyed or grooved floors, with nails hid, at per square_____	6	

When floors are laid in places measuring less than 100 feet superficial add to their respective prices one fourth.

Mop boards

	D	C
Under mop boards for plastering, at per foot, run_____		2
Planed mop boards, per foot, run_____		4
Dit. with a moulding, per foot, run_____		6
Mop boards from 5 to 8 inches wide, per foot, run_____		7

If wider, add in proportion_____
For mitres, in mop boards, one half the price per foot, run, each.

Fences, posts, gates, &c

	D	C
Gate post framed with sill, yoke or braces, post planed and capped with bed mould, or cornice, the opening from four feet to six feet, per pair_____	7	25
Single post, planed and capped with single cornice, per post_____	2	37
Gate post framed as above, the opening from six feet to twelve feet, capped as above_____	10	
Single post, cased plain, with a cornice equal to the Tuscan order___	4	62
Dit. dit. dit. cornice equal to the Doric or Corinthian order_____	6	
Dit. dit. dit. equal to the Ionic order_____	5	25
If a sunk panel in front and architraves round, add to their respective prices_____	1	82

	D	C
If a sunk panel on more than one side, add for each side		75
If plain pilaster, mouldings broke over it, add	2	50
If fluted pilaster and mouldings broke over it, add	3	
If either of the above posts have rusticated grounds, add to their respective prices	2	

Hewing and trimming posts, digging holes, and setting posts, to be paid for by the day.

	D	C
Panel gates, per foot, superficial		16
Panel gates, with pales in upper part, per foot superficial		18
Dit. dit. with wings, at per foot, superficial		25
Single pale fence, moulding on rail and cant, per foot, run		70
Single pale fence, plain cant and rail, per foot, run		55
Single pale gates and piers to dit. per foot, run	1	40
Double pale fence with moulding on rail and cant, per foot, run		80
Double pale fence palin cant and rails, per foot, run		60
Double pale gates with piers, per foot, run	1	60
Any ornaments in frizes of gate paid for by the day		
Plain plinths to fence under cants, per foot, superficial		5
Rusticated plinths to fence under cants, per foot superficial		7
Planed board fence, boards grooved, per foot, superficial		2
If planed both sides, add		1
Single cornice facia and plancere, per foot, run		9
Planed battens on fence, per foot, run		2
Double or Tuscan cornice on fence, per foot, run		16
Rough fence, not shot or feathcredged, at per square		75
Rough fence, shot or featheredged, per square	1	
Dit. dit. shot and grooved, per square	1	25
Dit. dit. boards an end, shot and pickets sawed, at per square	1	25
Dit. dit. boards an end, shot and grooved, and pickets sawed, at per square	1	50
If plank at bottom and rabbeted, add per foot, run		5
Planed board fence, boards an end, shot and pickets sawed, per square	2	
Planed board fence, boards an end, grooved and pickets sawed, per square	2	25
Plain picket open fence, per foot, run		25
Dit. dit. if the pickets are worked, per foot, run		33
Plain posts, capped plain for such fence, each	1	

Gates for picket fence measure double.

	D	C
Rough batten gates, at per foot, superficial		4
Planed batten gates, at per foot superficial		8
Planed gates, with battens laid on in front to form panels, per foot, superficial		11

Blinds

	D	C
Blinds for windows for 24 squares or less, of 7 by 9 or 8 by 10 glass in two parts, per window	4	25
If larger, per foot, superficial		20
If circular heads to blinds, at per foot, superficial for the circle		60

Cants on walls

	D	C
Plank cant on battlement, at per foot, run		12½
Timber cant on dit. at per foot, run		25

APPENDIX C.—GLASS

List of Prices for Blowing Vials and Bottles, for the Blast Commencing September 1, 1846, and Ending June 1, 1847

(Adopted by the Western Glass Blowers, assembled in mass convention in Pittsburg, June 22, 1846)

VIALS

	N. L. Cts.	W.L. Cts.	P. Cts.	N.P.W. Cts.
1 and ½ oz	50	53	55	58
1½ and 2 oz	55	58	60	63
3 oz	58	61	63	66
4 oz	63	67	68	72
6 oz	70	74	75	79
8 oz	80	84	85	89
1½, and 2 drachm	55	—	60	63
Harlem Oils				48
British Oils				55
Batemans				55
Durable Inks				50
1 oz. Inks, plain				52
Do. Iron Mold				50
2 oz. Inks, Plain				58
Do. Iron Mold				55
3 oz. Inks, Plain				64
Do. Iron Mold				58
4 oz. Inks, Plain				67
Do. Iron Mold				60
6 oz. Inks, Plain				76
Do. Iron Mold				72
8 oz. Inks, Plain				86
Do. Iron Mold				80
Turlington's Balsam				50
Peppermints				50
Bear's Oil				54
Maccassar Oil				55
Godfrey's Cordial				55
Opodeldoc (S)				55
Do. (L)				58
Liquid Opodeldoc				58
Lemon Acid				50
Fahnestock's Vermifuge				48
London Mustard				69
Calcined Magnesia				66
Varnish Bottles				76
Gothic Cologne				80
Plain do				80
Salter's Ginseng				70
Square Inks				50
Red Inks				50
Squat do				63
Inks, 40 to gal				63
Do. 50 to gal				60
Nerve and Bone Linament				55
Lindsay's Linament				63
Dalbt's Carminative				55
Cayenne Peppers				63
Seller's Inks				63
Sargent's Inks				63
Fahnestock's Cough Balsam				55
Do. Rubefacient				55
Thompson's Carminative (S)				70
Do. Do. (L)				80
Bates & Co				70
Winan's ¼ pint R Waters				80

BOTTLES

	Cts.
Castor Oils, 6 to gal. per doz	13½
" " 8 " " " "	12
" " 10 " " " "	11
" " 12 " " " "	11
" " 16 " " " "	9
" " 20 " " " "	8½
" " 24 " " " "	8½
" " 30 " " " "	8¼
" " 30 Iron Mold, gross	80
Octagon Pints " " doz	12
" " 20 " " "	8½
Quarter Pints " " gross	80
Concave Pints " " doz	12
" ½ " " " "	8½
" ¼ " " " gross	80
Rose Waters, pints " " doz	12
" " ½ " " " "	8½
" " ¼ " " " gross	80
Fancy Flasks, pints " " doz	8¾
Eagle Flasks, " " " "	8½
Fancy Flasks, ½ " " " "	7½
Eagle " ½ " " " "	7
Quart Bottles, Round " " "	13½
½ Gal " " " " "	21
One Gal " " " " "	32
Seltzers, ½ pints NM 8½, WM	9
" 1 " " 12, "	12½
" 1 quart " 14, "	15
" ½ gal " 23, "	25
" 3 quarts " 28, "	30
" 1 gal " 38, "	40
" 6 quarts " 50, "	52
Cap and Tye-over Jars, same as wide-mouth Seltzers.	
Wines, Claret	14
Muscat Wines	15
Lemon Syrup	13½
Mineral Waters, 12 oz	14
Ague Bottles	8½
" Mixture	9¼
Quart Pickle Jars, Square	14
Warner's Pint Bottles	12
" Quart "	14
Baltimore Pint Inks	12
" Quart "	14
Robinson's ½ Pint Bottles	8½
Smith's " " "	8½
Wilder's " " "	7
American Oils	11
Wheeler's Quart Syrup	14
" Pint "	12
Pittsburgh Pint Tonic	9
House's Syrup	12
Fahnestock's Quart Syrup	14
Emanuel's Bottles	8½
Liverwort & Hoarhound	8
Houses Indian Tonic	7¼
Thorn's Mixture	7¼
Concave's ½ Pint, Iron Mould	7½
Porter Bottles (L)	16
" " (S)	14

APPENDIX D.—TIME TABLE OF LOWELL TEXTILE MILLS

Arranged to make the working time throughout the year average 11 hours per day

To Take Effect September 21, 1853

From March 20 to Sept. 19 incl

Commence work at 6.30 A M
Leave off work at 6.30 P M except Saturday
Breakfast 6 a m.   Dinner at 12 M
Commence work after dinner at 12.45 P M

Sept 20 to March 19 incl

Commence work at 7 A M
Leave off work at 7 P M except Saturday
Breakfast 6.30 A M.   Dinner 12.30 P M
Commence work after dinner at 1.15 P M
(Saturday hours vary from 4 p m to 6 p m with daylight)

APPENDIX E.—PRINTING

SCALE OF PRICES ADOPTED OCTOBER 7, 1815, BY THE NEW YORK TYPOGRAPHICAL
SOCIETY

COMPOSITION

1. All works in the English language, common matter, from English to minion inclusive, 27 cents per 1,000; in nonpareil, 29 cents; in pearl, 37½ cents; in diamond, 50 cents: In all cases headlines and directions, or signatures and blank lines to be included. An odd en in width or length, to be reckoned an em; if less than an en, not to be counted.

2. All works done in foreign languages, common matter, to be paid 4 cents extra per 1,000 ems.

3. Works printed in great primer, or larger type, to be computed as English.—script, 30 cents per 1,000.

4. All workmen employed by the week, shall receive not less than $9 in book offices and on evening papers, and on morning papers not less than $10.

5. Works done in the English language, in which words of Greek, Hebrew, Saxon, etc., or any of the dead characters occur, should they average one word per page, it shall be considered sufficient to become a charge, which shall be settled between the employer and employed.

6. Works done in Hebrew and Greek, without points, shall be paid 15 cents per 1,000 ems higher than common matter; with points, to be counted half body and half points, and paid double.

7. That making-up a set of furniture for a work of five sheets or under, if an octavo, be paid 25 cents. All other impositions to be 3 cents extra, progressively, in proportion to the size—a single form shall constitute a set.

8. Works done partly in figures and partly plain, such as arithmetical works, etc., to be paid 30 cents per 1,000 ems. Rule and figure work to be paid double.

9. Broadsides, such as leases, deeds, etc., done on English or smaller type, to be paid 27 cents per thousand ems. Play bills, posting bills, etc., to be paid for at the rate of 15 cents per hour.

10. Algebraical works, or those where characters of music are the principal part, and works composed principally of medical, astronomical, or other signs, to be paid double.

11. Time lost by alteration from copy, or by casing or distributing letter, to be paid for at the rate of 15 cents per hour.

12. All works composed from manuscript copy, 2 cents extra.

13. Side, bottom, or cut-in notes, to be agreed on between the employer and the employed.

PRESSWORK

1. Bookwork, done on brevier or larger type, on medium or smaller paper, 33 cents per token; on smaller type, 35 cents. Royal paper, on brevier or larger type, 35 cents per token; on smaller type, 37½ cents per token. Super royal paper, on brevier or larger type, 36 cents per token; on smaller type, 39 cents per token.

2. A token of paper, if on bookwork, to consist of no more than 10½ quires; and if on a daily paper, no more than 10. For covering tympans, 37½ cents each; tympan and drawer to be considered as two.

3. Jobs, folio, quarto, etc., to be paid 33 cents per token.

4. Cards, if 100 or under, 30 cents; for each additional pack, if not more than 5, 12½ cents; if over 5, 10 cents.

5. Broadsides, on bourgeois or larger type, 45 cents; on smaller type, 50 cents per token.

6. Three cents extra to be paid on forms containing wood engravings.

7. No journeyman working at press on a morning daily paper, shall receive a less sum than $10 for his weekly services; nor those on an evening paper a less sum than $9. If the quantity of work should exceed 8 tokens per day, the whole to be charged, if on a morning paper, at the rate of 45 cents per token; if an evening paper, 40 cents per token. Daily papers not exceeding 6 tokens per day, if a morning paper, $9 per week, if an evening paper, $8 per week.

8. All works done on parchment to be settled between the employer and employed.

9. Working down a new press to be settled between the employer and employed.

10. If at any time a pressman should be obliged to lift his form before it is worked off, he shall be allowed 33 cents for the same.

11. A pressman shall receive, for teaching an apprentice presswork, for the first three months, 5 cents per token, and for the three months following, 3 cents per token.

PETER FORCE, *President.*

THOS. SNOWDEN, *Secretary.*

LIST OF PRICES OF THE COLUMBIA TYPOGRAPHICAL SOCIETY, WASHINGTON, D. C., ADOPTED NOVEMBER 4, 1815

COMPOSITORS

During the recess of Congress, in book or newspaper offices, to receive not less than $9 per week. During the session, in offices engaged on congressional work, or in newspaper offices, to receive not less than $10 per week, and $2 for each and every Sunday.

By the piece: For every 1,000 ems, from brevier to pica, 28 cents; for smaller letter than brevier, 33⅓ cents; on newspapers, not less than 30 cents per 1,000 ems; above pica, to be charged as pica.

Rule or figure work: All common rule or figure work, from brevier and upward, not less than 45 cents per 1,000 ems; below brevier, 50 cents per 1,000 ems.

Rule and figure work: All common rule and figure work, from brevier and upward, not less than 56¼ cents per 1,000 ems; below brevier, not less than 65 cents per 1,000 ems; above pica, to be charged as pica.

For all foreign languages, printed in the Roman character, an addition of 5 cents per 1,000 ems.

All words printed in Greek, or other foreign characters, to be paid for at the rate of 60 cents per 1,000 ems.

Side notes to be calculated separate from the text.

An addition of 3 cents on each 1,000 ems for pronouncing dictionaries.

Alterations: Compositors to receive, for alterations from copy, at the rate of 25 cents per hour.

PRESSMEN

During the recess of Congress, shall receive not less than $9 per week; by the piece, in newspaper offices, not less than 27½ cents per token, for royal or super-royal; nor less than 45 cents per token for imperial.

During the session, in offices engaged on congressional work, or in newspaper offices, not to receive less than $10 per week, and $2 for each and every Sunday.

Paper: Medium, and below medium, when the form consists of brevier, or larger letter, 33⅓ cents per token; below brevier, not less than 35 cents per token; royal and upward, on brevier or larger letter, not less than 37½ cents per token; all under brevier, not less than 50 cents per token.

Quarto, on medium paper, above 44 pica ems in width, to be paid as royal; octavo, above 24 pica ems, to be paid as royal; 12mo. above 21 pica ems, to be paid as royal; 18mo. above 17 pica ems, to be paid as royal.

Jobs not less than 35 cents per token.

Cards, for one pack, and not exceeding two packs, 35 cents; when exceeding two packs, to be paid at the rate of 15 cents per pack.

Broadsides shall be paid for double, according to the size of the paper.

All work on parchment, if one pull, 6¼ cents; if two pulls, 12½ cents.

For taking down or putting up a press, $3.

For working down a new press, $6.

For lifting a form before completed, 33⅓ cents.

For covering a tympan and drawer, $1, or 50 cents for either.

When an alteration in a form takes place, each pressman shall be paid 16½ cents per hour.

No pressman shall teach an apprentice presswork, without the benefit of his work for 13 weeks, or half his wages for 6 months; nor shall he teach an apprentice who is more than 18 years old, and who is bound for less than three years.

LIST OF PRICES OF THE BALTIMORE TYPOGRAPHICAL SOICETY, ADOPTED JUNE 2, 1832

COMPOSITION

I. Works done in the English language, common matter, from pica to minion, inclusive, 25 cents per 1,000 ems; nonpareil, 30 cents; agate, 31¼ cents; pearl, 33⅓ cents; diamond, 50 cents. The headline, with the blank after, and the foot line, in all cases to be counted not less than three lines; and odd en in width or length, to be counted an em; if less than an en, not to be reckoned.

II. Works printed in pica, or larger type, to be counted as if done in pica.

III. Works printed in Latin or Spanish, 3 cents extra per 1,000 ems; in French, 5 cents extra. Dictionaries in the above languages to be advanced as in Art. VI.

IV. Works in which Greek, Hebrew, Saxon or other foreign characters may occur, when they amount to one line per 1,000 ems, 2 cents extra, and in proportion for a greater or less quantity.

V. All works done in Greek and Latin, or Greek and English, to be charged a price and a half.

VI. English dictionaries, printed with figured vowels and accents, 5 cents advance; without figured vowels, but with accents, 2 cents advance. Geographical, biographical, and medical dictionaries, gazetteers, dictionaries of the arts and sciences, and works of a similar character, are not included in this article, unless they be attended with extra trouble, beyond the usual descriptive matter.

VII. Arithmetical works, 5 cents advance per 1,000 ems; rule work to be charged a price and a half; rule and figure work, double; algebraical works, and works composed principally of medical, astronomical, or other signs, to be charged double price.

VIII. Works done in Hebrew, without points, 15 cents advance per 1,000 ems; with points (to be counted half body and half points), double price.

IX. Works done in Greek, without accents, 40 cents per 1,000 ems; with accents, 50 cents; the asper and lenis not to be considered as accents.

X. Spelling books, and works of that description, 5 cents in advance per 1,000 ems.

XI. Side and center notes in Bibles and Testaments, to be counted the full length of the page (including the lead or one rule), according to the type in which they are set, and charged 5 cents extra per 1,000 ems. Cut-in notes in the above works to be cast up according to the type in which they are set, and charged a price and a half.

XII. Side notes, in law and historical works, to be counted the full length of the page, and charged according to the type in which they are set; and when cut into the text to be charged 4 cents extra per 1,000 ems.

XIII. Quotations, mottoes, contents of chapters, and bottom notes, in smaller type than the body, to be paid for according to the size of type in which they are set.

XIV. Works where the measure does not exceed 14 ems in width, to be paid 2 cents in advance per 1,000 ems.

XV. Time occupied by alterations from copy, or by casing or distributing letter not used by the compositor, to be paid for at the rate of 15 cents per hour.

XVI. When compositors, in book and job offices, shall be required to work after regular hours, they shall be allowed 20 cents per hour, or 5 cents advance per 1,000 ems.

XVII. All letter cast on a body larger than the face, to be counted according to the face of the type; and all letter cast on a smaller body than the face to be counted according to the body.

XVIII. For all matter made up and imposed by the employer, no more than 2 cents per 1,000 ems shall be allowed. The compositor in all cases to furnish the head, blank, and foot line, and count the same.

XIX. Making up a set of furniture, to be charged for by the time occupied, at the rate of 15 cents per hour.

XX. Compositors shall, in all cases, charge for every blank page at the end of a work imposed—each form to be graduated by the following rule: In octavo forms, if less than 2 pages, to be charged as 2; for 3 pages, 4 to be charged; for 5, 6 or 7, a full form, etc.

XXI. Compositors employed by the week shall not receive less than $8 per week. Ten hours shall be considered a day's work in book and job offices.

PRESSWORK

With balls or rollers before the press

	Per token
Medium and royal	$0. 30
Superroyal	. 37½
Imperial	. 45
Job work	. 33⅓
Broadsides	. 60

Cards, two packs and under to be considered a token, all over, 12½ cents per pack.

With rollers behind the press

	Per token
Medium and royal	$0. 23
Superroyal	. 25
Imperial	. 27

All fine works to receive an extra price, to be determined by the employer and pressman, according to its quality. All book work under four tokens to be charged 2 cents extra per token.

All broadsides to be 45 cents per token.

Job work, 25 cents per token.

Cards, two packs and under, 25 cents; all over two packs, 10 cents per pack.

All colors to be charged double.

In all cases, where the employer finds the roller boy, 4 cents to be deducted on book or job work; on cards, 2 cents per pack.

Machine rollers: Medium, four tokens or less, 30 cents per token; over four tokens, 27 cents. Other works in proportion. Fine work, extra price.

Lifting forms: When there are not more than eight tokens, the pressman shall receive the price of one token extra for every form he shall be necessitated to lift.

Standing: After a form shall have been put to press, the pressman shall receive 15 cents for the first half hour, and 20 cents for every subsequent hour that he is delayed by corrections or alterations.

Pressmen working by the piece, required to count the paper from the press, to be paid 2 cents extra per token.

Pressmen employed by the week to receive not less than $8 per week. Ten hours shall be considered a day in book and job offices.

When pressmen, in book and job offices, shall be required to work after regular hours, they shall be allowed 20 cents per hour, or 4 cents extra per token.

Pressmen employed on morning papers, to be paid not less than $9; on evening papers, not less than $8 per week.

For covering tympan or drawer, 50 cents.

COMPOSITION

1. Works done in the English language, common matter, from English to nonpareil, 25 cents per 1,000 ems; agate, 27 cents; pearl, 30 cents; diamond, 37½ cents. The headline, with blank after, and the foot line, in all cases to be counted not less than three lines. When a measure exceeds even ems in width, and is less than an en, an en only to be counted; but if an en, or over, to be counted an em. Where guard lines are required to pages, they shall be furnished by the employer in a solid shape, or shall be charged by the compositor.

2. Works printed in great primer, or larger type, to be counted as if done in English.

3. All jobs done in plain script, to be counted as English, and charged at 30 cents per 1,000 ems; those in analytical or combination script, on inclined bodies, to be counted as above, and charged 37½ cents.

4. Works printed in Latin or Spanish, 3 cents extra per 1,000 ems; in French, 5 cents extra. Dictionaries in the above languages to be advanced in proportion, as in article 7.

5. Greek, Hebrew, Saxon, etc., or any of the other characters not in common use, if amounting to one word, and not exceeding three words per 1,000 ems, to be charged 2 cents extra. Where the characters are of a different size from the body of the matter, and are to be justified in they shall be charged 4 cents extra. All exceeding three words to be charged in proportion.

6. All works done in Greek and Latin, or Greek and English, to be charged a price and a half

7. English dictionaries, printed with figured vowels and accents, 5 cents advance; without figured vowels, but with accents, 2 cents advance. Concordances, and works of a similar description, where figures and points predominate, or any work where capitals, small capitals, or italic, are profusely used, 3 cents advance. Where superior letters or references are used, as in Bibles, or works of that character, 1 cent extra per 1,000 ems shall be charged. Geographical, biographical, and medical dictionaries, gazetteers, dictionaries of the arts and sciences, and works of a similar character are not included in this article, except they are attended with extra trouble, beyond the usual descriptive matter.

8. Arithmetical works, 5 cents extra per 1,000 ems. Rule work, part plain and part figures, and figure work where no rules are used and figures are required to be placed in columns, to be charged a price and a half; rule and figure work, double. Algebraical works, and works composed principally of medical, astronomical, or other signs, to be charged double.

9. Works done in Hebrew, without points, 15 cents advance per 1,000 ems; when with points, the body and the points to be cast up each according to its size, and to be charged double.

10. Works done in Greek, without accents, printed copy, page for page, 37½ cents; other reprints, 40 cents per 1,000 ems; with accents 50 cents; the asper and lenis n^t to be considered as accen*s.

11. Church music, whether analytical or solid, to be charged a single price, according to the size of the type in which it is set. Piano music to be charged a price and a half, according to the size, except where it is condensed, when it shall be charged double.

12. Works done from manuscript copy, to be charged 2 cents extra per 1,000 ems, except foreign languages, which shall be 5 cents; printed copy, with frequent interlineations, to be considered as manuscript.

13. Spelling books, and works of that description, 5 cents advance per 1,000 ems.

14. Side and center notes in Bibles and Testaments to be counted the full length of the page (including the lead, or one rule, which shall count at least one em), according to the type in which they are set, and charged 5 cents extra per 1,000 ems. Cut-in notes, in the above works, to be charged 4 cents extra each note, and the whole page to be counted as text.

15. Side notes in law and historical works, to be counted the full length of the page, according to the type in which they are set; and when cut into the text, to be charged 4 cents extra each note.

16. Quotations, mottoes, contents of chapters, and bottom notes, in smaller type than the body, to be paid for according to the size of the type in which they are set.

17. Works where the measure does not exceed 16 ems in width, to be paid 2 cents advance per 1,000 ems.

18. Time occupied by alterations from copy, by casing or distributing letter, not used by the compositor, or other work appointed by the employer, to be paid for at the rate of 15 cents per hour.

19. When compositors are required to work more than regular hours, they shall be allowed 20 cents an hour, or 5 cents advance per 1,000 ems.

20. All letter cast on a body larger than the face (as bourgeois on long primer) to be counted according to the face; and all letter cast on a body smaller than the face (as minion on nonpareil) to be counted according to the body.

21. In all cases where a companionship may deem it necessary that matter should be made up by one person, the compositors may either appoint, from among themselves, or authorize the employer to appoint, a person to perform that duty, on terms to be agreed upon between themselves and the person employed to make up: *Provided, however,* That no more than 2 cents per 1,000 ems shall be allowed to the employer for making up, imposing, taking the necessary proofs, and keeping the schedule.

22. When a compositor is required to take out bad letters, and replace them, in consequence of faults in the founder, miscasts, or worn-out fonts, he shall be paid at the rate of 15 cents an hour.

23. For imposing forms, no more shall be allowed than 3 cents per page for quarto, 2 for octavo, 1½ for duodecimo, 1¼ for sexadecimo, and the like sum for all forms of a larger number of pages—the compositor, in all cases, to lay the pages in regular order, or to be responsible for their being so done.

24. It shall be the duty of the compositor imposing, to take two proofs of each form. All proofs taken afterwards shall be paid for at the rate of 8 cents each, for letterpress forms and for stereotype forms and small jobs, 2 cents each. When an extra proof, or proofs, are required by the carelessness of the compositor, they shall be at his expense.

25. Making up furniture for a quarto form, 18 cents; an octavo, 25 cents; and 3 cents extra for all other impositions progressively.

26. Compositors employed on morning newspapers shall receive not less than $12 per week; on evening papers and in book and job offices, not less than $9 per week. Ten hours shall be considered a day in book and job offices.

PRESSWORK

With balls: Medium, 30 cents per token; royal, 33⅓ cents; superroyal, 37½ cents; medium, and a half, 39 cents; imperial, 40 cents; and everything above imperial, 45 cents. Cards, the first hundred, 30 cents; for all over one hundred, 10 cents a pack. The charge with hand rollers to be the same as with balls.

With rollers: Medium, when there shall be but 4 tokens or less on a form, 25 cents per token; if over 4 tokens, 23 cents. Royal, 4 tokens or less, 27 cents; over 4 tokens, 26 cents. Superroyal, 4 tokens or less, 30 cents; over 4 tokens, 28 cents. Medium and a half, 4 tokens or less, 32 cents; over 4 tokens, 30 cents. Imperial, 4 tokens or less, 35 cents; over 4 tokens, 33 cents. For any size above imperial, the charge shall be, when there are 4 tokens or less, 40 cents; over 4 tokens, 35 cents. All broadsides, 40 cents per token. Cards, the first hundred, 25 cents; all over one hundred, 15 cents per hundred. All fine work to receive an extra price, to be arranged between the employer and journeyman. Work done after regular hours, to receive an advance of 5 cents per token.

Roller boys: When the employer shall furnish a roller boy, there shall be 18 per cent deducted from the wages of the pressman until it amounts to $2 per week, when the deduction shall cease.

Machine rollers: Medium, 4 tokens or less, 21 cents per token; over 4 tokens, 20 cents. Other sizes in proportion. Fine work, extra price.

Lifting forms: When there are not more than 8 tokens, the pressman shall receive the price of 1 token extra for every form he shall be required to lift.

Covering tympans: The sum of 37½ cents shall be allowed for covering a tympan; and the like sum for covering a drawer, or inner tympan.

For putting up or removing presses: Twenty cents per hour shall be allowed.

Standing: After a form shall have been put to press, the pressman shall receive 15 cents for the first half hour, and 20 cents for every subsequent hour, that he is delayed by corrections or alterations.

When a pressman is employed by the week, he shall receive not less than $9 per week; ten hours, in all cases, to be the limit of a day's work. Overwork, 20 cents an hour.

Scale of variation for the sizes of forms

Size of form	Octavo pages or smaller	Quarto or larger pages
	Pica ems	*Pica ems*
Medium, to contain	9, 000	11, 000
Royal, to contain	11, 000	13, 500
Superroyal, to contain	13, 500	16, 000
Medium and a half, to contain	16, 000	18, 000
Imperial, to contain	18, 000	22, 000

Any form exceeding either of these, by 250 ems, to be charged as the next highest.

BILL OF PRICES OF THE NASHVILLE, TENN., TYPOGRAPHICAL SOCIETY, ADOPTED 1837

COMPOSITION

Compositors to receive per week _____ $11. 00
Bookwork, MS. copy, per 1,000 ems _____ . 35
Bookwork, reprint _____ . 33⅓
Newspaper, manuscript and reprint _____ . 32
Pamphlets (100 pages, or less,) _____ . 37½
Rule or figure work, to be counted price and a half.
Rule and figure work, double price.
For all works in foreign languages, an advance of _____ . 12½
Dictionaries, arithmetics, and algebraical works, an advance of _____ . 12½
Side notes to be calculated separate from the text, an advance of ____ . 02
All measures under 12 ems pica, an advance of _____ . 02
Letters cast on a different body from the face, to be counted by the
  body one way and the face the other.
Alterations from copy, per hour _____ . 25
All sizes larger than pica, and not exceeding double pica, to be counted
  pica.
Larger than double pica to be charged by the time.
All type smaller than nonpareil, an advance of _____ . 02
Dressing furniture for book or pamphlet form _____ . 50
Ten hours shall be considered a day's work.
All extra work to be charged per hour.

PRESSWORK

Pressmen to receive per week _____ $12. 00
Mammoth or elephant (book or news), per token _____ . 40
Imperial and superroyal _____ . 33⅓
Royal and medium _____ . 25
Jobs _____ . 37½
Cards, first pack _____ . 37½
Cards, each additional pack on same form _____ . 18¾
Hat tips, same as cards.
Jobs on silk or bank-note paper _____ . 50
Broadsides, on medium paper, or smaller _____ . 37½
Broadsides, larger than medium _____ . 50
Lifting forms before finished, to be charged a token.
All jobs with colored ink, per hour _____ . 25
Parchment, each pull _____ . 06¼
Covering tympan and drawer, each _____ . 75
All works containing woodcuts, an advance of _____ . 10
Corrections made in a form, after being put to press, to be charged per
  hour _____ . 25
Ten hours considered a day's work.
Ten quires to be considered a token on a newspaper form—10½ quires
  on a book form.

LIST OF PRICES OF THE COLUMBIA TYPOGRAPHICAL SOCIETY, WASHINGTON, D. C., AMENDED AND ADOPTED JANUARY, 1837

COMPOSITION

1. Compositors, during the recess of Congress, in book, or newspaper offices, to receive not less than $10 per week. Ten hours to constitute a day's work.

2. During the session of Congress, in offices employed on the current Congress work, and in all offices engaged on other work done for, or by the authority of that body, or in newspaper offices, to receive not less than $11 per week.

3. In all offices, and at all seasons to receive not less than $2 for each and every Sunday (to consist of eight hours), and for extra hours on Sunday, 25 cents; and at all other times, 20 cents per hour.

PIECEWORK

1. All works done in the English language, common matter, from pica to minion, 31 cents per 1,000 ems; minion and nonpareil, 37 cents; agate, 39 cents; pearl, 41 cents; diamond, 50 cents. The headline, with the blank after it, and the foot line, in all cases to be counted as three lines. An en, in length or width, to be counted an em; if less than an en, not to be reckoned. Above pica to be charged as pica.

2. Newspapers: Brevier and upward, 33½ cents per 1,000 ems; minion and nonpareil, 37 cents; agate, 39 cents; pearl, 41 cents; diamond, 50 cents.

3. Rule or figure work: All rule or figure work a price and a half, according to the type in which it is set. All matter in which two or more rules are inserted, to constitute rule work; and two or more columns of figures, without rules, to constitute figure work.

4. Rule and figure work: All rule and figure work to be paid double the price of common matter. One column of figures and one rule in a page of other matter shall constitute rule and figure work: *Provided, however,* That on works, the pages of which are uniformly made up of two or more columns (as on periodical publications), no charge beyond that of common matter shall be made for, or on account of the rules separating the columns.

5. All heads and foot lines attached to rule or figure work, or rule and figure work, to be reckoned the same as the body of the matter.

6. For all foreign languages, printed in the Roman characters, an addition of 6 cents per 1,000 ems.

7. All works printed in Greek or other foreign characters, to be paid for at the rate of 66 cents per 1,000 ems.

8. Arithmetical works to be paid an advance of 6 cents per 1,000 ems on the price of common matter.

9. Algebraical works to be charged double price.

10. Spelling books, or other work containing more than two columns in a page, to be paid an advance of one-half on the price of common matter.

11. Music, double price.

12. Side notes to be counted the full length of the page, and charged according to the type in which they are set.

13. Cut-in notes to be cast up according to the type in which they are set, and charged 10 cents extra per 1,000 ems; and the whole page to be counted as text.

14. All bottom notes, contents of chapters, etc., in smaller type than the text, to be paid for according to the type in which they are set.

15. All letter cast upon a larger body than the face, as bourgeois on long primer, to be counted according to the face; and all letter cast upon a smaller body than the face, as minion on nonpareil, to be counted according to the body.

16. All works where the measure does not exceed 14 ems in width, to be 3 cents per 1,000 ems advance.

17. For making up a set of furniture, not exceeding 16 pages, 31 cents; when exceeding, 55 cents.

Alterations: Compositors to receive for alterations from copy, at the rate of 25 cents per hour.

PRESSWORK

1. Pressmen, during the recess of Congress, shall receive not less than $10 per week—ten hours to constitute a day's work.

2. During the session of Congress, in offices employed on the current Congress work, and in all offices engaged on other work done for, or by the authority of that body, or in newspaper offices, to receive not less than $11 per week.

3. In all offices, and at all seasons, to receive not less than $2 for each and every Sunday (to consist of eight hours), and for extra hours on Sundays, 25 cents; and at all other times, 20 ents per hour.

1. Piecework

Kind of work—per token	With balls or hand rollers	With rollers and roller boys [1] or machine rollers
Medium and below medium, when the form consists of brevier or larger letter	$0.37	$0.27
Below brevier, not less than	.39	.29
Royal, on brevier or larger letter	.41	.31
Royal, below brevier	.43	.33
Superroyal, on brevier or larger letter	.45	.35
Superroyal, below brevier	.47	.37
Medium and a half, on brevier or larger letter	.46	.36
Medium and a half, below brevier	.48	.38
Imperial, on brevier or larger letter	.50	.40
Imperial, below brevier	.52	.42
Newspapers, when printed on imperial	.50	.40
Newspapers, when printed on royal or superroyal	.41	.31
For any size above imperial, the charge shall be	.60	.50

[1] Pressman to find his own roller boy.

2. Scale of variation for the size of forms

Size of form	Octavo or smaller	Quarto or larger
	Pica ems	*Pica ems*
Medium, to contain	9,000	11,000
Royal, to contain	11,000	13,500
Superroyal, to contain	13,500	16,000
Medium and half, to contain	16,000	18,000
Imperial, to contain	18,000	22,000

Any form exceeding either of these by 250 ems to be charged as the next highest.

Scale for jobs

	Inches
Medium to measure	18 by 22
Royal to measure	19 by 24
Superroyal to measure	20 by 27
Imperial to measure	21 by 31

3. All bookwork less than 4 tokens to be charged 2 cents extra per token.

4. Jobs, 39 cents per token, when worked on medium, or paper below medium; when on royal or upward, on brevier or larger letter, not less than 43 cents; below brevier 45 cents; when on imperial, 50 cents per token.

5. Work done in colors, double price.

6. Cards, for 1 pack, and not exceeding 2 packs, 39 cents; when **exceeding 2** packs, to be paid at the rate of 16 cents per pack.

7. Broadsides shall be paid for double, according to the size of the paper. To constitute a broadside, the matter to extend across the sheet without a break. A foolscap sheet, and all above, to be considered a broadside.

8. All work on parchments, when not done by the piece, to be paid $2.20 per day, and no charge to be made for less than half a day; when done by the piece, if 1 pull, 7 cents; if 2 pulls, 14 cents.

9. All matter that is required to be made up and imposed in pages, to be considered bookwork.

10. Tokens: On newspaper work, not over 10 quires, or 240 sheets; and on other work, not more than 250 sheets; or 10½ quires to constitute a token.

11. For taking down or putting up a press, 20 cents per hour.

12. For working down a new Ramage press, $6.

13. For lifting a form before completed, 37 cents.

14. For covering a tympan and drawer $1.10, or 55 cents for either.

15. When an alteration in a form takes place, each pressman shall be paid at the rate of 18 cents per hour for the time occupied, or 25 cents per hour if but one pressman, with roller boy.

16. No pressman shall teach an apprentice presswork without the benefit of his work for 15 weeks, or half his wages for six months; nor shall he teach an apprentice who is more than 18 years old, and who is bound for less than four years.

No alteration or amendment shall be made to the foregoing list of prices unless two-thirds of the members present concur therein; nor then, without one month's previous notice having been given.

REGULATIONS RESPECTING APPRENTICES

1. Every apprentice shall serve until he be 21 years of age; and, at the time of entering as an apprentice, shall not be more than 16 years of age; and every boy taken as an apprentice shall be bound to his employer in due form of law.

2. No runaway apprentice to be received into any office in the District of Columbia, either as an apprentice or journeyman.

3. That on the death of his master, or if, from any cause, the office wherein he was indented shall be discontinued, he may be taken into another office, and be regularly indented to finish the term of his apprenticeship.

4. After the 1st day of January, 1844, the Columbia Typographical Society will not consider any application for membership unaccompanied by sufficient proof that the applicant has served the period of five years as a regularly indented apprentice at the printing business.

5. That after the 1st day of January, 1839, the Columbia Typographical Society will not permit members of said society to work in any office where boys may be taken as apprentices to the printing business to serve for a less period than five years.

6. The Columbia Typographical Society recognizes but two classes of printers— employers and journeymen; that is, persons who carry on business solely as employers, and those who work as journeymen in the manner prescribed, and at the prices demanded by this society.

SCALE OF PRICES OF THE NEW ORLEANS TYPOGRAPHICAL SOCIETY, ADOPTED SEPTEMBER 14, 1839

COMPOSITION

Compositors employed on morning newspapers to work by the piece only, at the following rates: Plain matter, in the English, French, or Spanish language, 62½ cents per 1,000 ems, for manuscript or printed copy; pearl, 75 cents per 1,000 ems; ruby, 81¼ cents per 1,000 ems; diamond, $1 per 1,000 ems; rule and figure work, $1.25 per 1,000 ems; rule or figure work separately, 93¾ cents per 1,000 ems. A foreman not to receive less than $25 per week.

On evening papers, and in book and job offices, compositors not to receive less than $19 per week, ten hours constituting a day's work; and all extra hours to be charged at the rate of 40 cents per hour. Work done by the piece to be charged the same as morning papers. Foremen on evening papers not to receive less than $22.50 per week. Where two foremen are employed on one paper in two languages, the foreman on the English side not to receive less than $20 per week.

On bookwork, the running title, white line under it, and the foot line of the page, to be considered as regular matter.

An odd en in width or depth to be counted an em; but if less than an en, it is not to be reckoned.

Bookwork and jobs done by the piece, with pica or larger letter, to be charged as pica.

Bookwork and jobs done by the piece, in which Hebrew, Greek, or other foreign characters occur, to be charged when they amount to one line, 16 cents extra per 1,000 ems.

Bookwork done by the piece in the dead languages to be charged at the rate of $1.25 per 1,000 ems; but work done in the dead and modern languages (an equal proportion of each) to be charged at the rate of 93⅗ cents per 1,000 ems.

Bookwork with side notes, to be charged as follows: The text and side notes to be charged separately, and the notes to be charged according to the letter in which they are set, and calculated the full length of the page; when they are cut in the text, 16 cents extra to be charged.

Music, $1.25 per 1,000 ems.

Letter cast on a body smaller than the face to be charged according to the body; and letter cast on a body larger than the face to be charged according to the face.

Compositors making up a set of furniture, to charge at the rate of 40 cents per hour.

Compositors, in all cases, to charge the blank pages which may occur in a work. For alterations from copy, if a single one, 25 cents; per hour, 40 cents.

PRESSWORK

(With balls or rollers)

Bookwork done on medium, royal, or superroyal paper to be charged per token	$1.00
Imperial	1.25
Broadside, posting bills, superroyal or imperial	1.50
Broadside, posting bills, under superroyal	1.00
Cards:	
Plain, two packs or under	.75
Glazed	1.25
For each succeeding pack, if plain	.25
For each succeeding pack, if glazed	.37½
Work done on parchment, each impression	.12½
Standing after a form shall have been put to press, per hour	.40
Covering tympan and drawer, each	1.00
Putting up a press	5.00
Taking down a press	2.50
Pressmen working on morning and evening papers, or other periodicals, by the piece, to charge for medium, or superroyal, per token	.75
Imperial or larger	1.00

For all extra fine work an additional price to be charged, to be agreed on between the employer and employed.

All work done in colors to be charged according to the time employed thereon.

Lifting a form before the whole impression is worked off, to be charged as one token.

When a roller boy is furnished by the employer, no more than 25 per cent shall be deducted.

When a pressman may be employed by the week in a book or job office, or on an evening paper, he shall not charge less than $19 per week, ten hours constituting a day; and all work done after the regular hours, 40 cents per hour.

On morning papers, pressmen working by the week, not to receive less than $22.

SCALE OF PRICES OF THE PITTSBURG TYPOGRAPHICAL ASSOCIATION, ADOPTED NOVEMBER 21, 1849

Pittsburg Typographical Association, organized in 1849, issued a bill of prices together with apprenticeship recommendations, November 21, 1849, as follows:

REPORT ON BILL OF PRICES

To the Officers and Members of the Pittsburg Typographical Association.

Your committee appointed to fix a bill of prices respectfully offer the following for the consideration of the association:

Composition

1. Composition, manuscript, and reprint, per 1,000 ems	$0.25
2. Any size smaller than nonpareil	.28

(The headline, with the blank after, and the foot line, in all cases to be counted three lines; over an en in length or width, to be counted an em; if less, not to be reckoned.)

3. Work done in foreign languages, in Roman characters, extra per 1,000 ems_____ $0. 10
4. Work done in foreign languages, and not in Roman characters, except the German, which shall be the same as English per 1,000 ems_____ . 50
5. Algebraical work, and works having a great number of astronomical, medical, and other signs_____ . 50
6. Spelling books and similar works, advance per 1,000_____ . 05
7. Arithmetical work, advance_____ . 05
8. English dictionaries with figured vowels and accents, advance_____ . 10
9. English dictionaries without figured vowels, advance_____ . 05
10. Side and center notes in Bibles, Testaments, and other works, to be counted the full length of the page (including the lead or rule), according to the type in which they are set, and an advance per 1,000 of_____ . 03
11. Cut-in notes to be cast up according to the type in which they are set, and charged an advance of_____ . 05
12. Quotations, notes, mottoes, etc., in smaller type, to be counted according to the type in which they are set.
13. Works where the measure does not exceed 14 ems, advance per 1,000 of_____ . 03
14. All letter cast on a body larger than the face to be counted according to the face; and all letter cast on a smaller body than the face, to be counted according to the body.
15. Composition on music to be done as agreed upon by the employer and journeyman.
16. Rule and figure work, per 1,000_____ . 50
17. Rule or figure work, per 1,000_____ . 37½
18. Letter list, or names set two or three in newspaper column, per 1,000_____ . 37½
19. Time lost in alterations from copy, extra casing of letter, or anything not coming legitimately under the preceding articles, to be charged by the hour_____ . 20
20. Journeymen working by the week (ten hours a day's work) to receive not less than_____ 8. 00
21. Journeymen working on morning papers, per week not less than____ 9. 00
22. Foremen shall not receive less per week than_____ 10. 00

Job work

(Forms to be distributed by the journeyman)

Common medium sheet bills_____ $1. 00
Common medium sheet bills (with border)_____ 1. 25
Common medium half-sheet bills_____ . 50
Common medium half-sheet bills (with borders)_____ . 75
Common medium quarto bills_____ . 37½
Programs (eight to a sheet)_____ . 50
Posters for theater, circus, etc_____ . 50
Bills of lading_____ . 50
Circulars for balls, etc. (script)_____ . 25
Business cards or exhibition tickets_____ . 25
   Plain composition in script to be counted as pica.
   All job work not above enumerated, or any of the before mentioned with an extra quantity of matter, to be agreed upon by the parties.

Presswork

(Office to find the roller boy)

Medium, or under, per token_____ $0. 20
Imperial, per token_____ . 25
Double medium, per token_____ . 28
Music, per token_____ . 23
Steamboat bills, per token (black)_____ . 25
Steamboat bills, per token (colored)_____ . 35

Alterations on steamboat bills	$0. 10
Bills of lading, circulars, invitations, billheads, checks, drafts, etc., per token	. 25
Colored work, per token	. 30
Cap or quarto post, per token	. 25
Cards, first pack	. 12½
Cards, every additional pack	. 06¼
Posters, 100 or less	. 25
Posters, each additional 100 or less	. 12½
Books of not more than one token, an advance of	. 05
All work done on parchment, each pull	. 04
Covering tympan	. 50
Covering drawer	. 50
Making roller	. 25

Lifting forms before their completion, an extra token to be charged; provided the full complement does not exceed 8 tokens.

Extra charges on engravings.

Pressmen employed by the week, ten hours to constitute a day's work, $9 per week; power pressmen, $10.

Your committee, without wishing to be considered as dictating to employers, would earnestly recommend that hereafter no apprentice shall be taken for a less period than three years, and that regular and formal indentures be made between the parties, that justice may be done both.

SCALE OF PRICES OF THE JOURNEYMEN PRINTERS' UNION OF PHILADELPHIA, UNANIMOUSLY ADOPTED AUGUST 10, 1850

MORNING NEWSPAPERS

1. Composition in agate, and in all larger type, of regular body and face, 30 cents per 1,000 ems.

2. Composition in type smaller than agate, of regular body and face, 35 cents per 1,000 ems.

3. Letter cast on a body larger than the face, to be charged according to the face; and letter cast on a body smaller than the face to be counted according to the body.

4. Rule and figure work, double price.

5. Composition requiring three justifications, such as three columns of figures, lists of letters, as at present published, etc., a price and a half.

6. Work by the hour, and all waiting after 8 o'clock, p. m., for mails, or for any other purpose, 25 cents per hour.

7. On each occasion where a hand shall be called to go to work, after being through the regular work, $1 shall be charged extra.

8. Every hand employed upon a morning newspaper shall be entitled to 24 consecutive hours' intermission from labor in each week, and if called upon to work during such intermission, he shall be paid $1 extra, whether the said intermission occurs on Saturday, or any other day of the week.

9. Work by the week, $12 per week, 10 hours constituting a day's work.

WEEKLY AND AFTERNOON NEWSPAPERS

1. Composition, 28 cents per 1,000 ems.

2. Hour work, 20 cents per hour.

3. Ten dollars per week, 10 hours constituting a day's work.

BOOK AND JOB WORK

1. Work in the English language, printed copy, from pica to nonpareil inclusive, 27 cents per 1,000 ems; from agate to diamond, 30 cents per 1,000 ems. Manuscript copy, 2 cents per 1,000 ems extra. Printed copy, with 10 interlineations or alterations per 1,000 ems, to be charged as manuscript.

2. Work in foreign languages, Roman characters, printed copy, 5 cents per 1,000 ems extra; manuscript, 7 cents per 1,000 ems extra.

3. Work in the Hebrew language, 35 cents per 1,000 ems. Where points are used, they shall be counted according to their body, and charged 40 cents per 1,000 ems.

4. Work in the Greek language, 45 cents per 1,000 ems.
5. Work in which Hebrew and Greek words, and words in other than Roman characters occur, 1 cent extra for every three words.
6. Spelling books, dictionaries, primers, and all works in which figured vowels and accents are used, printed copy, 33 cents per 1,000 ems; manuscript, 35 cents extra per 1,000 ems.
7. Arithmetical work, 10 cents extra per 1,000 ems.
8. Algebraical work, 50 cents per 1,000 ems.
9. Work in which cuts, excepting initial letters, are run into the matter, 2 cents per 1,000 ems extra on the pages in which such cuts occur.
10. Quotations, mottoes, contents of chapters, footnotes, descriptions, undercuts, to be charged according to the type in which they are set.
11. Jobs in script to be counted as pica, 33 cents per 1,000 ems.
12. Work in which the lines or paragraphs are in different sized type alternately, 2 cents per 1,000 ems extra.
13. All matter in which there are a number of braces, requiring more than two justifications, a price and a half. (In this section reference is made to tables of classification, as a botanical work, etc.)
14. Side and center notes, or references to Bibles, Testaments, law and historical works, and work of a similar description, to be counted according to the type in which they are set, and measured the whole length of the page, including the leads and rules, 3 cents per 1,000 ems extra.
15. Cut-in notes, 2 cents per note, and the matter to be counted as text.
16. In letterpress offices, cuts and blank pages to be charged by the compositor; and all cuts to be charged according to the type of the page in which they respectively occur.
17. Letter cast on a body larger than the face, to be charged according to the face; and letter cast on a body smaller than the face, to be counted according to the body.
18. The headline, the blank after it, and the foot line, to be counted three lines. An en in width to be counted an en; if more than an en, to be counted an em; if less than an en, not to be counted.
19. When the measure does not exceed 14 ems in width, 3 cents per 1,000 ems extra.
20. When the measure does not exceed 18 ems in width, 2 cents per 1,000 ems extra.
21. When the measure does not exceed 21 ems in width, 1 cent per 1,000 ems extra.
22. The compositor shall not be required to correct alterations (including alterations of punctuations) from printed copy.
23. In tabular work, three or more columns of rules and figures to constitute rule and figure work. Three or more columns of rules to constitute rule work. Three or more columns of figures to constitute figure work. Rule and figure work, double price. Rule work, a price and a half. Figure work, a price and a half.
24. No work shall be measured by any type larger than pica.
25. Making up a set of furniture to be charged for according to the time occupied.
26. In stereotype offices, the forms to be revised, or prepared for molding, at the employer's expense, and reimposed matter to be in the care of the office.
27. The lowest charge for any piece of work, 27 cents.
28. All work on time (except week work), 20 cents per hour.
29. Compositors employed by the week, $10 per week; ten hours to constitute a day's work.

MUSIC

1. Plain choral music, 18 cents per 1,000 ems; plain choral music, containing two parts on a staff, or with organ accompaniment, 22 cents per 1,000 ems; where a single staff on the page contains two parts, 20 cents per 1,000 ems.
2. Piano and other instrumental music, 20 cents per 1,000 ems.
3. Rudiments to be counted as music.
4. Music jobs, containing less than 15,000 ems, 3 cents per 1,000 ems extra.

List of Prices of the Columbia (Washington, D. C.) Typographical Society, Adopted November 2, 1850

COMPOSITION

1. Compositors to receive not less than $12 per week; ten hours to constitute a day's work; and for extra hours, 25 cents per hour.

2. In all offices, and at all seasons, to receive not less than $2.50 for each and every Sunday (to consist of eight hours); and for extra hours on said day, 30 cents per hour.

PIECEWORK

1. All works done in the English language, common matter, from pica to nonpareil, 40 cents per 1,000 ems; nonpareil, 44 cents; agate, 47 cents; pearl, 49 cents; diamond, 60 cents. The headline, with the blank after it, and the foot line, in all cases, to be counted as three lines. An en, in length or width, to be counted an em; if less than an en, not to be reckoned. Above pica, to be charged as pica.

2. Rule or figure work: All rule or figure work a price and a half, according to the type in which it is set. All matter in which two or more rules are inserted to constitute rule work; and two or more columns of figures without rules to constitute figure work.

3. Rule and figure work: All rule and figure work to be paid double the price of common matter. One column of figures and one rule, in a page or other matter, shall constitute rule and figure work: *Provided, however,* That on works the pages of which are uniformly made up of two or more columns (as on periodical publications), no charge beyond that of common matter shall be made for, or on account of, the rules separating the columns.

4. All heads and foot lines attached to rule or figure work, or rule and figure work, to be reckoned the same as the body of the matter.

5. All foreign languages, printed in Roman characters, an addition of 6 cents per 1,000 ems.

6. All work printed in Greek or other foreign characters to be paid for at the rate of 79 cents per 1,000 ems.

7. Arithmetical works to be paid an advance of 6 cents per 1,000 ems on the price of common matter.

8. Algebraical or mathematical works to be charged double price.

9. Spelling books, or other work containing more than two columns in a page, to be paid an advance of one-half on the price of common matter.

10. Music, double price.

11. Side notes to be counted the full length of the page, and charged according to the type in which they are set.

12. Cut-in notes to be cast up according to the type in which they are set, and charged 10 cents extra per 1,000 ems; and the whole page to be counted as text.

13. All bottom notes, contents of chapters, etc., in smaller type than the text, to be paid for according to the type in which they are set.

14. All letter cast upon a larger body than the face, as bourgeois on long primer, to be counted according to its face; all letter cast upon a smaller body than the face, as minion on nonpareil, to be counted according to the body; and all letters shall measure 12½ ems to the alphabet.

15. All works, where the measure does not exceed 14 ems in width, to be 3 cents per 1,000 ems advance.

16. For making up a set of furniture, not exceeding 16 pages, 37 cents; exceeding, 66 cents.

Alterations: Compositors to receive for alternations from copy at the rate of 30 cents per hour.

PRESSWORK

1. Pressmen shall receive not less than $12 per week; ten hours to constitute a day's work; and for extra hours 25 cents per hour.

2. At all times to receive not less than $2.50 for each and every Sunday (to consist of eight hours); and for extra hours on said day 30 cents per hour.

1. Piecework

Kind of work	With balls or hand rollers	With rollers and roller boys [1] or machine rollers
	Cents	Cents
Medium and below medium, when the form consists of brevier or larger letter	43	33
Below brevier, not less than	46	36
Royal, on brevier or larger letter	48	38
Royal, below brevier	51	41
Superroyal, on brevier or larger letter	53	43
Superroyal, below brevier	55	45
Medium and a half, on brevier or larger letter	54	44
Medium and a half, below brevier	57	47
Imperial, on brevier or larger letter	59	49
Imperial, below brevier	61	51
Newspapers, when printed on imperial	59	49
Newspapers, when printed on royal or superroyal	48	38
For any size above imperial the charge shall be	71	61

[1] Pressman to pay his roller boy.

2. Scale of variation for the size of forms, showing the number of pica ems [1] to be contained in each

Numerical denomination	Medium	Royal	Superroyal	Medium and a half	Imperial
Twos	11,966	13,780	16,318	17,948	19,672
Fours	9,960	11,468	13,580	14,720	16,372
Sixes	9,306	10,716	12,690	13,960	15,298
Eights	8,816	10,152	12,044	13,224	14,494
Twelves	8,712	10,032	11,880	13,068	14,322
Sixteens	8,254	9,504	11,276	12,380	13,524
Eighteens	8,206	9,450	11,190	12,312	13,492
Twenty-fours	8,024	9,240	10,942	12,036	13,192
Thirty-twos	7,948	9,152	10,838	11,922	13,066

[1] This table is based upon 6 pica ems to the statute inch. The English standard (see Penny Magazine Vol. II, p. 422) is 71½ pica ems to the foot; but most fonts in this country are a slight degree smaller.

3. Legitimate sizes of paper

	Inches
Medium	16 by 22
Royal	19 by 24
Superroyal	20 by 27
Medium and a half	22 by 27
Imperial	21 by 31

Any form exceeding either of these by 300 ems, to be charged as the next size.

4. All bookwork less than 4 tokens to be charged 2 cents extra per token.

5. Jobs 48 cents per token, when worked on medium or paper below medium; when on royal or upward, on brevier or larger letter, not less than 52 cents; below brevier, 54 cents; when on imperial, 60 cents per token.

6. Work done in colors, double price.

7. Cards, for one pack, and not exceeding two packs, 47 cents; when exceeding two packs, to be paid for at the rate of 19 cents per pack.

8. Broadsides shall be a price and a half, according to the size of the paper. To constitute a broadside, the matter to extend across the sheet without a break. A foolscap sheet, and all above, to be considered a broadside.

9. Parchments to be 50 cents per token.

10. All matter that is required to be made up and imposed in pages, to be considered bookwork, except newspapers of 4, 8, or 16 pages.

11. A token shall consist of 240 sheets.

12. For taking down or putting up a press, 25 cents per hour.

13. For lifting a form before completed, 44 cents.

14. For covering a tympan and drawer, $1.50, or 75 cents for either.

15. When an alteration in a form takes place, each pressman shall be paid at the rate of 25 cents per hour for the time occupied; or 30 cents per hour, if but one pressman, with a roller boy.

16. No pressman shall teach an apprentice presswork without the benefit of his work for fifteen weeks, or half his wages for six months; and he shall be a regular apprentice of the office.

SCALE OF PRICES OF THE PRINTERS' UNION OF THE CITY OF NEW YORK, PROCLAIMED FEBRUARY 1, 1851 (ADOPTED OCTOBER 26, 1850)

(Somewhat abridged and condensed)

The scale for bookwork occupies 15 pages of the pamphlet containing the scale.[1] The most essential points of this book scale are:

ARTICLE 1. Works done in the English language, common matter, (reprint) from pica to agate, inclusive, 27 cents per 1,000 ems; pearl, 32 cents; diamond, 40 cents.

ART. 2. Works done in the English language, common matter (manuscript), from pica to agate, inclusive, 29 cents per 1,000 ems; pearl, 34 cents; diamond, 42 cents.

ART. 3. Works done in pica, or any larger type, to be counted as pica.

Then follow several articles specifying extras: Works in Latin or Spanish, 3 cents extra per 1,000 ems; French, 5 cents extra; grammars, 5 cents. Works printed in both Greek and Latin or in Greek and English are charged price and a half; so too of work in Greek alone.

ART. 15. Side and center notes in Bibles and Testaments to be counted the full length of the page (including the lead, or one rule, which shall count at least 1 em), according to the type in which they are set, and charged a price and a half. Cut-in notes, in the above works, to be charged 4 cents extra each note, and the whole page to be counted as text.

ART. 19. The headline, with the blank after it. and foot line, to be charged by the maker-up, and counted not less than 3 lines.

ART. 21. Time occupied by alterations from copy, by casing or distributing letter not used by the compositor, etc., to be paid for at the rate of 18 cents per hour. When compositors are required to work beyond regular hours, they shall be paid at the rate of 21 cents per hour, or 5 cents advance per 1,000 ems.

ART. 22. All letter cast on a body larger than the face (as bourgeois on long primer) to be counted according to the face; all letter cast on a body smaller than the face (as minion on nonpareil) to be counted according to the body. All fonts, the alphabets of which measure less than 12½ ems, to be counted in width according to the next smaller size.

ART. 23. In all cases where a companionship may deem it necessary that matter should be made up by one person, the compositors may appoint from among themselves, or authorize the employer to appoint a person to perform that duty, on terms to be agreed upon between themselves and the person employed to make-up: *Provided, however,* That no more than 2 cents per 1,000 ems shall be allowed for making-up, imposing, taking the necessary proofs, and keeping the schedule.

---

[1] The following preface to the scale is issued "To the trade," and is of historical value:

To the Trade

The following "scale of prices" has been adopted, after mature deliberation, by the "New York Printers' Union," and, so far as their members are concerned, will be fully supported from the 1st day of February, 1851.

We submit these prices to the trade at large, and ask for them the support of journeymen and employers; because we believe them to be in every respect just and reasonable,—because a number of the largest and best establishments in the city now pay them,—because the recent great increase in the necessaries of life, and the general advance of wages by other trades, render these enhanced prices in our business imperatively necessary,—because they will tend to the physical and consequently the moral improvement of printers,—because they will protect good workmen against quacks, and thus become of pecuniary interest both to the employer and the workman,—and because they will form what has been long needed in this city, a uniform and well-known tariff of wages.

With these brief, but we think cogent reasons, we submit the "New York Union scale" to the trade; and by our signatures hereunto appended, do certify the following to be a correct transcript of the original copy.

F. J. OTTARSON,
President of the New York Printers' Union.

C. WALKER COLBURN,
Recording Secretary.
JANUARY 25, 1851.

ART. 24. When a compositor is required to take out bad letters, and replace them, in consequence of faults in the founder, miscasts, or worn-out fonts, he shall be paid at the rate of 18 cents per hour.

ART. 25. For imposing forms, no more shall be allowed than 3 cents per page for quarto, 2 cents for octavo, 1½ cents for duodecimo, 1¼ cents for sexadecimo, and the like sum for all forms of a larger number of pages—the compositor, in all cases, to lay the pages in regular order, or be responsible for their being so done.

ART. 27. Making-up furniture for a quarto form, 18 cents; an octavo, 25 cents; and 3 cents extra for all other impositions progressively.

ART. 28. Compositors employed by the week shall receive not less than $10, ten hours to be considered a day's work.

ART. 29. The compositors on a work are entitled to correct the author's proofs, for which they shall be paid at the rate of 18 cents per hour.

ART. 32. When woodcuts are inserted in the matter, or worked in pages along with the body of the work, such cuts belong to the compositors; but where the cuts are worked entirely separate, the same as copperplate engravings or lithographic plates, they shall not be claimed by the compositors.

ART. 34. In large book rooms, the establishment has the privilege of claiming full titles and dedications, but in no case shall piece-paying establishments claim half titles, or any other prefixed matter, nor cull the fat portions of any work.

ART. 37. When a compositor (working by the piece) receives copy of contents, indexes, or any other copy where more than the usual quantity of capitals, figures, periods, and italics are used, the establishment shall furnish the compositor with the necessary sorts.

ART. 39. The compositor shall in all cases be exempt from clearing away, tying up, or in any manner taking charge of matter which he has set: *Provided, always,* That this article shall not interfere with the custom existing as to headlines, titles, taking out leads, etc.

ART. 40. When works, or portions of works, are required to be leaded, and the leads are not furnished by the office at the time of composition, such matter to be afterwards leaded, but at the expense of the employer, and the compositor to charge such matter the same as if he himself had originally put in the leads.

ART. 43. When compositors are required to remain in the office unemployed, awaiting orders from the employers, etc., they shall be paid at the rate of 18 cents per hour.

The newspapers scales, job work and presswork scales are in full, as follows:

MORNING NEWSPAPER WORK

ARTICLE 1. Compositors employed by the piece shall receive not less than 32 cents per 1,000 ems, for common matter. When compositors are employed at night, only, by the piece, they shall receive 36 cents per 1,000 ems.

ART. 2. Compositors employed by the week (six days) shall receive not less than $14 per week; twelve hours to constitute a day's work. When employed on night situations, two hours shall be devoted in the afternoon to distribution, and seven hours at night (from 7 to 2 o'clock) to composition; and they shall be paid $11 per week. For all times beyond 2 o'clock at night, in either of the above situations, 25 cents per hour shall be charged, or the time deducted from the following day, at the option of the employer.

ART. 3. Compositors may be employed during the day, on morning papers, at 28 cents per 1,000 ems, or $10 per week.

ART. 4. When required to remain in the office unemployed during the stipulated hours for composition, the compositor shall receive not less than 25 cents per hour for such standing time; it being understood, of course, that he shall perform any other reasonable work that the employer may appoint during such standing time. Time occupied in casing or distributing letter not to be used by the person distributing or casing, alterations from copy, lifting forms, etc., to be paid for at not less than 25 cents per hour.

ART. 5. When compositors are called upon before the regular hour for commencing composition, in case of the arrival of a steamer, etc., they shall be paid not less than $1 each for such call, and be entitled to the matter they set. This is understood to apply to both week and piece work.

ART. 6. Tabular work, etc., containing three or four columns, either of figures or words, or figures and words, without rules, shall be charged a price and a half. All work, as above, with brass or other rules, or where there are five or more columns of figures, or figures and words, with or without rules, shall be paid double price.

ART. 7. For work done in pearl, or smaller type, an advance of 4 cents per 1,000 ems shall be charged. For work done in French, German, and other foreign languages, an advance of 5 cents per 1,000 ems shall be charged.

ART. 8. When a measure exceeds even ems in width, and is less than a 3-em space, no extra charge is to be made; if a 3-em space, an en to be counted; if an en, an en to be counted; if over an en, an em to be counted.

ART. 9. Bastard letter to be cast up as described in article 22 of book scale.

ART. 10. Where intricate work, etc., occurs, which the newspaper scale can not reach, the price to be agreed upon between employer and journeyman.

ART. 11. In offices where both week and piece hands are employed, the fat and lean copy to be distributed equally among them.

EVENING NEWSPAPER WORK

ARTICLE 1. Compositors employed by the piece shall receive 28 cents per 1,000 ems for common matter.

ART. 2. Compositors employed by the week (six days) shall receive not less than $10—ten hours to constitute a day's work.

ART. 3. For time (as laid down in art. 4 of morning paper scale), a charge of 18 cents per hour shall be made.

Articles 6, 7, 8, 9, 10, and 11, of morning paper scale shall apply to evening papers.

WEEKLY, SEMIWEEKLY, AND TRIWEEKLY PAPERS

ARTICLE 1. Compositors employed by the piece shall receive not less than 28 cents per 1,000 ems for common matter.

ART. 2. Compositors employed by the week (six days) shall receive not less than $10—ten hours to constitute a day's work.

ART. 3. Compositors employed by the piece on Sunday papers shall receive not less than 28 cents per 1,000 ems for common matter. When employed by the week (six days), they shall receive not less than $11—ten hours to constitute a day's work, with the exception of Saturday, when it is expected that a week hand will work during the evening.

ART. 4. For time (as laid down in art. 4 of morning paper scale), a charge of 18 cents per hour shall be made.

Articles 6, 7, 8, 9, 10, and 11 of morning paper scale shall apply to weekly, semiweekly, triweekly, and Sunday papers.

JOB WORK

ARTICLE 1. All job work of a fancy or display character shall be either paid for on time or by special agreement, according to its relative value—that is to say, all that class of jobs styled posters, show cards, handbills, circulars, billheads, cards, labels, and others of a similar description. All pamphlets, catalogues, sermons, tracts, by-laws, and other works of a like nature, when making not more than one sheet, to be considered jobs; and, if done on the piece, to be paid for at the rate of 28 cents per 1,000 ems, for either manuscript or reprint, without the usual extras belonging to bookwork; but when making over one sheet, to be charged in accordance with the book scale with the extras belonging thereto.

ART. 2. All men employed by the week shall be paid at the rate of $10; when paid by the hour, the price shall correspond to the amount per week—ten hours to constitute a day's work. When required to work beyond regular hours, such extra time shall be paid for at the rate of 21 cents per hour; and if by the piece, the compositor shall receive 5 cents advance per 1,000 ems.

PRESSWORK

ARTICLE 1. Power pressmen: No power pressman shall work for a less sum than $10 per week, for day work, or $12 per week, for night work. The day's work in all cases to consist of ten hours. Overwork shall be paid for at the rate of 21 cents per hour.

ART. 2. The pressman shall not be held responsible for any accident that may happen at a press at which he is not actually working, provided such press was all right when it was started.

Art. 3. No pressman shall take charge of more than two presses, unless temporarily, as in the case of the sickness of a fellow-workman, or other emergency.

Art. 4. Hand pressmen: No hand pressman, employed by the week, shall work for a less sum than $10 per week, for day work, or less than $12 per week, for night work. The day's work in all cases to consist of ten hours. Overwork shall be paid for at the rate of 21 cents per hour.

Art. 5. Bookwork on the piece: Ordinary bookwork to be paid at the following rates: Medium, 18 by 22 inches, 25 cents per token; royal, 20 by 25 inches, 27 cents per token; superroyal, 22 by 29 inches, 29 cents per token; medium and a half, 24 by 29 inches, 31 cents per token; imperial, 23 by 33 inches, 33 cents per token. Double medium, or larger, to be subject to special agreement. For all jobs of bookwork of 4 tokens, or less, 2 cents extra per token shall be charged.

Job work on the piece: No job, the number of which does not exceed 1,000, shall be done for less than 25 cents per token of 250 sheets; nor shall any description of work, of what number soever, be done for less than 23 cents per token.

Art. 6. Any number of sheets exceeding 12 over the regular surplus, shall be reckoned as a token, and charged.

Art. 7. Pulling clean proofs shall be charged on time.

Art. 8. Extra bookwork to be paid as may be agreed upon. By extra bookwork is meant such bookwork forms as have cuts in them, where the pages are surrounded with rules, where there are more than 24 pages in the form, or any other thing which causes extra trouble to the pressman.

Art. 9. Show bills to be paid 50 cents per token. If two or more colors are required, or any extra care be required in the making ready or working, they shall be charged on time, or by special agreement.

Art. 10. Cards: Small or ordinary business cards shall be paid 25 cents for the first pack and 10 cents for each subsequent pack. Extra size cards, as show cards, etc., 50 cents for the first pack and 25 cents for every succeeding pack.

Art. 11. Extra work: All kinds of extra work, as headings, show cards with cuts in them, wood engravings, colored work, or printing in gold, silver, bronze, etc., to be paid for either on time or by special agreement.

Art. 12. Standing to be paid for at the rate of 18 cents per hour.

Art. 13. When the press is not furnished with a self-inking apparatus the employer shall furnish a roller boy at his own expense.

Art. 14. When the inking apparatus is not worked by steam, the pressman shall be entitled to charge 2 cents per token extra.

Art. 15. Lifting forms: When a pressman is required to lift his form he shall be entitled to charge 1 token therefor.

Art. 16. Putting on tympans: The pressman shall be entitled to 50 cents for putting on a new tympan, either outer or inner.

Art. 17. Pressmen employed in cleaning, putting up, or removing presses, shall be paid 21 cents per hour.

Art. 18. Pressmen required to cast rollers, cut paper, or do any other work not fairly to be considered presswork, in their own time, shall be paid 18 cents per hour for the same.

This scale of prices shall at no time be altered or amended, unless notice of such alteration or amendment shall have been given at least one month previously to being acted upon; nor then, except by a two-third vote of the members present.

Scale of Prices of the Cincinnati Typographical Union, To Take Effect On Thursday, November 24, 1853

COMPOSITION

Article I

Section 1. No office shall be entitled to more than three apprentices. The number in small offices to be regulated by the standing committee.

Article II

Section 1. Composition on morning papers, common matter, shall be charged at the rate of 35 cents per 1,000 ems, and all standing time shall be charged as follows, namely: For half an hour or less, 15 cents; over half an hour, and not exceeding an hour, 30 cents. All matter composed in a morning newsroom to be regarded as belonging to a morning paper and to be charged as such.

Sec. 2. Composition on other than morning papers, common matter, 30 cents per 1,000 ems; and all matter composed on Sundays, and after 9 o'clock p. m., on Mondays, Tuesdays, Wednesdays, Thursdays, and Fridays, and after 5 p. m. on Saturdays shall be charged a price and a half.

Article III

Section 1. Composition on bookwork, common matter, from pica to agate, inclusive, 32 cents per 1,000 ems; pearl, 33½ cents; diamond, 35 cents. All work done in larger type than pica to be counted as pica.

Sec. 2. All foreign languages, in the Roman characters (reprint), an advance per 1,000 ems of 5 cents; in manuscript, 10 cents.

Sec. 3. Spelling books and works of that description, an advance, on the entire work, of 5 cents per 1,000 ems.

Sec. 4. English dictionaries, printed with figured vowels or accents, an advance per 1,000 ems of 5 cents; without figured vowels or accents, an advance of 2 cents.

Sec. 5. All work where figures, points, capitals, small capitals, or italics are profusely used, an advance of 3 cents per 1,000 ems.

Sec. 6. Grammars and arithmetics to be charged an advance of 5 cents per 1,000 ems.

Sec. 7. Works in algebra, where matter is generally plain, 3 cents advance per 1,000 ems; all other algebraical works, 18 cents advance per 1,000 ems.

Sec. 8. Works done in the Hebrew, without points, 15 cents per 1,000 ems advance; when with points, the body and the points to be cast up, each according to its size, and to be charged double.

Sec. 9. Works in Greek, with accents attached, 8 cents advance per 1,000 ems; with kerns, 18 cents advance per 1,000 ems; in Greek and Latin combined, 8 cents advance per 1,000 ems.

Sec. 10. When Greek, Hebrew, Saxon, or any other character not in common use, occasionally occurs, to be charged 1 cent per word.

Sec. 11. Plain choral music, 20 cents per 1,000 ems; plain choral music containing two parts on a staff, or with organ accompaniment, 24 cents per 1,000 ems; when a single staff on a page contains two parts, 22 cents per 1,000 ems; piano and other instrumental music, 22 cents per 1,000 ems; rudiments to be charged the same as the music accompanying. All music jobs containing less than 15,000 ems, an advance of 3 cents per 1,000 ems.

Sec. 12. Side and center notes to be counted the full length of the page, including the lead or one rule, according to the type in which they are set, and charged 5 cents advance per 1,000 ems. Cut-in notes, when in type foreign to the text, to be charged at the rate of 50 cents per 1,000 ems, and no deduction to be made from the regular page.

Sec. 13. Works on natural philosophy, chemistry, astronomy, botany, etc., where woodcuts are inserted in the matter which cause overrunning in making up, and especially when questions are appended at the bottom of the page, 25 cents per hour shall be charged for the time so lost.

Sec. 14. Medical, astronomical, and philosophical works, where signs frequently occur, a price and a half.

Sec. 15. Small, isolated tables, occurring in works of a narrow measure, as in double-column octavo, to be paid for according to the time consumed in composing them, at the rate of 25 cents per hour.

Sec. 16. All cuts shall be charged by the compositor, and estimated according to the body of the work.

Sec. 17. Works in which the lines or paragraphs occur frequently in different sized type, to be cast up separately, and charged an advance of 3 cents per 1,000 ems.

Sec. 18. All matter in which there are a number of braces requiring two or more justifications, as in botanical works, a price and a half to be charged.

Sec. 19. All matter made up and proved by the employer, except on newspapers, to be charged 2 cents less per 1,000 ems. No matter, however, to be made up by the employer or other persons, without the consent of the journeyman composing the same; nor is this to be construed as giving to the employer the headings, the blank pages, head or foot lines, or any portion of matter, which, according to usage, belongs to the journeyman when he makes up himself; and all guard lines to be charged with body of the page.

Sec. 20. Headlines, when set in type smaller than the body of the work, or spaced, the folios justified, or altered for each alternate page, 1 cent extra per page shall be charged.

Sec. 21. The compositor shall, in all cases, be exempt from clearing away, tying up, unleading, or in any manner taking charge of matter which he has set, except to distribute, and clear away bearer, head, and foot lines, titles, and blanks, and, also, to leave his tabular or column work free of rules: *Provided*, That such matter shall be ready to clear away while the compositor holds his situation.

Sec. 22. Compositors shall, in all cases, charge for every blank page at the end of the work imposed—each form to be graduated by the following rule: In octavo forms, if less than 2 pages, to be charged as 2; for 3 pages, 4 to be charged; for 5, 6, or 7 pages, a full form to be charged.

Sec. 23. It shall be the duty of the compositor to take two proofs of each form he imposes. All proofs taken afterwards shall be charged at the rate of 1 cent per page and for small jobs, 5 cents each. Where extra proofs are required from the carelessness of the compositor. no additional charge shall be made.

Article IV

Section 1. Tabular or column work, etc., containing three or four columns of figures, or words, or figures and words, shall be charged a price and a half. All work, as above, with brass or other rules, or where there are five or more columns of figures, or words, or figures and words, with or without rules, shall be charged double price.

Sec. 2. Where a measure exceeds even ems in width, and is less than an en, an en only to be counted; but if over an en, to be counted an em.

Sec. 3. Where a measure does not exceed 8 ems in width, 4 cents extra per 1,000 ems; 8 and less than 14, 3 cents extra per 1,000 ems; 14 and under 18, 2 cents extra per 1,000 ems; 18 and under 21, 1 cent extra per 1,000 ems.

Sec. 4. All letter cast on a body larger than the face, as bourgeois on long primer, to be counted according to the face; and all letter cast on a smaller body than the face, to be counted according to the body. The standard for all regular fonts of letter, from pica to diamond inclusive, shall be as follows: For pica, 11 ems; small pica, 12 ems; long primer, 12 ems; bourgeois, 12 ems; brevier, 13 ems; minion, 13 ems; nonpareil, 14 ems; agate, 15 ems; pearl, 16 ems; and diamond, 17 ems; all fonts of letter, the alphabets of which fall below the number of ems above established, shall in all cases be charged, for every 3-em space of such deficiency, 1 cent extra per 1,000 ems.

Sec. 5. Making up furniture, casing new letter pulling out or putting in leads (after the matter shall have been set), alterations in proof from copy, in phraseology, punctuation, capitalization, italicization, small capitalization, or in any other particular, shall be charged according to the time consumed, at the rate of 25 cents per hour.

Sec. 6. All fat matter shall be equally distributed, in such manner as the journeymen in each office, respectively, may agree upon.

Sec. 7. All work not coming legitimately under the above scale shall be charged at the rate of 25 cents per hour.

Article V

Section 1. Foremen and assistant foremen on morning papers shall receive not less than $15 per week.

Sec. 2. Foremen and assistant foremen on other than morning papers shall receive not less than $13 per week.

Sec. 3. Compositors in book or job offices shall receive not less than $12 per week.

Sec. 4. Ten hours shall be considered a day's work, except on Saturday, when it shall be nine, and end at 5 o'clock, p. m.

PRESSWORK

1. Medium size or under, per token _____ $0. 25
2. Imperial or medium and a half or under _____ . 30
3. Double medium, or mammoth _____ . 38
4. On forms of but one token, advance_____ . 10
5. Lifting form before completed, to be charged same as token.
6. Poetical works of 24s and under 72s, superroyal and under (where the number does not exceed 1,000 copies, 2 cents advance) per token___ . 38
7. Steamboat bills, on post or cap paper, per ream_____ 1. 00
8. Steamboat bills, on post or cap paper, one-half ream_____ . 50
9. Broadsides, cap or letter, per token _____ . 35

10. Broadsides, medium or larger, per token _____ $0. 50
11. Posters, medium or under, first hundred _____ . 40
12. Posters, medium or under, each additional hundred _____ . 30
13. Posters, imperial to double medium, first hundred _____ . 45
14. Posters, imperial to double medium, each additional hundred _____ . 35
15. Handbills, half-sheet medium or under, per first token _____ . 40
16. Handbills, half-sheet medium or under, each additional token _____ . 30
17. Cap or letter jobs, including circulars, bill heads, bills of lading, dray tickets, magistrates' and constables' blanks, wood receipts, etc., per single token _____ . 35
18. Each additional token _____ . 30
19. Steamboat registers, headings, etc., on demy, per single token, or under _____ . 50
20. Each additional token _____ . 35
21. Blank checks, on post or demy, single token _____ . 50
22. Each additional token _____ . 35
23. Blank checks, on cap or letter paper, per token _____ . 35
24. All jobs done in colors, to be charged by the hour _____ . 25
25. All jobs on bank-note, silk or linen paper _____ . 50
26. Policies of insurance, on folio post or proposition paper, per token ___ . 50
27. Steamboat bills, medium or royal paper, per ream _____ 1. 25
28. Steamboat bills, medium or royal paper, one-half ream _____ . 75
29. Cards, No. 7 or under, per hundred _____ . 20
30. Cards, larger size _____ . 50
31. Hat tips, same as cards.
32. All parchments on letter-sheet size or over, per pull _____ . 05
33. All parchments under letter-sheet size, per hour _____ . 25
34. Covering tympan and drawer, each _____ . 50
35. All work done with machine rollers, advance, per token _____ . 05
36. Working a new hand press, first month, advance, per token _____ . 05
37. For each roller that a pressman casts he shall receive _____ . 50
38. After a form is put to press, the pressman shall receive 25 cents per hour for detentions caused by alterations or corrections.

For all work done by the hour, pressmen shall receive not less than 25 cents per hour; and at not less than this rate, fine work, requiring extra trouble, and all work not coming legitimately under the above scale, shall be arranged between the employer and the employed.

1. Pressmen on daily morning papers, working by the week, to receive not less than $15; all other pressmen, not less than $12 per week.

2. Ten hours to be considered a day's work, except on Saturday, which shall be nine hours, and end at 5 o'clock, p. m. Presswork done after 9 o'clock at night or after 5 o'clock on Saturday evening, and all work done on Sunday, to be charged a price and a half.

This scale of prices shall not prevent superior workmen from getting a higher rate of pay. But no workmen shall work for less than the prices herein specified.

PRICE LIST OF COLUMBIA TYPOGRAPHICAL SOCIETY, WASHINGTON, D. C., ADOPTED NOVEMBER 1, 1854

COMPOSITION

1. Compositors to receive not less than $14 per week; ten hours to constitute a day's work; and for extra hours 30 cents per hour.

2. In all offices, and at all seasons, to receive not less than $3 for each and every Sunday (to consist of eight hours); and for extra hours on said day, 37½ cents per hour.

PIECEWORK

1. All work done in the English language, common matter, from pica to nonpareil, 42 cents per 1,000 ems; nonpareil, 46 cents; agate, 49 cents; pearl, 51 cents; diamond, 62 cents. The headline, with the blank after it, and the foot line, in all cases, to be counted as three lines. An en, in length or width, to be counted an en; if less than an en, not to be reckoned. Above pica, to be charged as pica.

2. Rule or figure work: All rule or figure work a price and a half, according to the type in which it is set. All matter in which two or more rules are inserted to constitute rule work; and two or more columns of figures, without rules, to constitute figure work.

3. Rule and figure work: All rule and figure work to be paid double the price of common matter. One column of figures and one rule, in a page or other matter, shall constitute rule and figure work: *Provided, however,* That on works the pages of which are uniformly made up of two or more columns (as on periodical publications), no charge beyond that of common matter shall be made for, or on account of, the rules separating the columns.

4. All heads and foot lines attached to rule or figure work, or rule and figure work, to be reckoned the same as the body of the matter.

5. All foreign languages, printed in Roman characters, an addition of 8 cents per 1,000 ems.

6. All work printed in Greek or other foreign characters, to be paid for at the rate of 81 cents per 1,000 ems.

7. Arithmetical works to be paid an advance of 8 cents per 1,000 ems on the price of common matter.

8. Algebraical or mathematical works to be charged double price.

9. Spelling books, or other work containing more than two columns in a page, to be paid an advance of one-half on the price of common matter.

10. Music to be charged for according to the size of the type in which it is set. The head and foot lines to be charged the same as the body of the matter.

11. Side notes to be counted the full length of the page, and charged according to the type in which they are set.

12. Cut-in notes to be cast up according to the type in which they are set, and charged 17 cents extra per 1,000 ems; and the whole page to be counted as text.

13. All bottom notes, contents of chapters, etc., in smaller type than the text, to be paid for according to the type in which they are set.

14. All letter cast upon a larger body than the face, as bourgeois on long primer, to be counted according to its face; all letter cast upon a smaller body than the face, as minion on nonpareil, to be counted according to the body; and all letter shall measure 12½ ems to the alphabet.

15. All works, where the measure does not exceed 14 ems in width, to be 5 cents per 1,000 ems advance.

16. For making up a set of furniture, not exceeding 16 pages, 40 cents; exceeding, 66 cents.

Alterations: Compositors to receive for alterations from copy at the rate of 35 cents per hour.

PRESSWORK

1. Pressmen shall receive not less than $14 per week; ten hours to constitute a day's work; and for extra hours, 30 cents per hour.

2. At all times to receive not less than $3 for each and every Sunday (to consist of eight hours); and for extra hours on said day 37½ cents per hour.

1. Piecework

Kind of work	With balls or hand rollers	With rollers and roller boys,[1] or machine rollers
	Cents	*Cents*
Medium and below medium, when the form consists of brevier or larger letter	43	33
Below brevier, not less than	46	36
Royal, on brevier or larger letter	48	38
Royal, below brevier	51	41
Superroyal, on brevier or larger letter	53	43
Superroyal, below brevier	55	45
Medium and a half, on brevier or larger letter	54	44
Medium and a half, below brevier	57	47
Imperial, on brevier or larger letter	59	49
Imperial, below brevier	61	51
Newspapers, when printed on imperial	59	49
Newspapers, when printed on royal or superroyal	48	38
For any size above imperial, the charge shall be	71	61

[1] Pressman to pay his roller boy.

2. Scale of variation for the size of forms, showing the number of pica ems [1] to be contained in each

Numerical denomination	Medium	Royal	Super-royal	Medium and a half	Imperial
Twos	11,966	13,770	16,318	17,948	19,672
Fours	9,960	11,468	13,580	14,720	16,372
Sixes	9,306	10,716	12,690	13,960	15,298
Eights	8,816	10,152	12,044	13,224	14,494
Twelves	8,712	10,032	11,880	13,068	14,322
Sixteens	8,254	9,504	11,276	12,380	13,524
Eighteens	8,206	9,450	11,190	12,312	13,492
Twenty-fours	8,024	9,240	10,942	12,036	13,192
Thirty-twos	7,948	9,152	10,838	11,922	13,066

[1] This table is based upon 6 pica ems to the statute inch. The English standard (see Penny Magazine, Vol. II, p. 422) is 71½ pica ems to the foot; but most fonts in this country are a slight degree smaller.

3. Legitimate sizes of paper

	Inches
Medium	18 by 22
Royal	19 by 24
Superroyal	20 by 27
Medium and a half	22 by 27
Imperial	21 by 31

Any form exceeding either of these by 300 ems, to be charged as the next size.

4. All bookwork less than four tokens to be charged 2 cents extra per token.

5. Jobs 48 cents per token, when worked on medium or paper below medium; when on royal or upward, on brevier or larger letter, not less than 52 cents; below brevier, 54 cents; when on imperial, 60 cents per token.

6. Work done in colors, double price.

7. Cards, for one pack, and not exceeding two packs, 47 cents; when exceeding two packs, to be paid for at the rate of 19 cents per pack.

8. Broadsides shall be a price and a half, according to the size of the paper To constitute a broadside, the matter to extend across the sheet without a break. A foolscap sheet, and all above, to be considered a broadside.

9. Parchments to be 50 cents per token.

10. All matter that is required to be made up and imposed in pages, to be considered bookwork, except newspapers of 4, 8, or 16 pages.

11. A token shall consist of 240 sheets.

12. For taking down or putting up a press, 25 cents per hour.

13. For lifting a form before completed, 44 cents.

14. For covering a tympan and drawer, $1.50, or 75 cents for either.

15. When an alteration in a form takes place, each pressman shall be paid at the rate of 25 cents per hour for the time occupied; or 30 cents per hour, if but one pressman, with a roller boy.

16. No pressman shall teach an apprentice presswork without the benefit of his work for fifteen weeks, or half his wages for six months; and he shall be a regular apprentice of the office.

SCALE OF PRICES OF THE COLUMBIA TYPOGRAPHICAL SOCIETY, WASHINGTON CITY, D. C., REVISED AND ADOPTED MARCH, 1856

COMPOSITION

1. Compositors to receive not less than $14 per week, ten hours to constitute a day's work, and for extra hours 32 cents per hour; Sunday work to be paid for at the rate of $3 per day of eight hours.

PRESSWORK

Pressmen are to be paid not less than the same rates that compositors working by the week receive.

PIECEWORK

1. All works done in the English language, common matter, from pica to nonpareil, 40 cents; agate, 44 cents; pearl, 49 cents; diamond, 60 cents; the headline with the blank after it and the foot line in all cases to be counted as three lines.

An en in length or width to be counted an em; if less than an en, not to be reckoned. Above pica, to be charged as pica.

2. Rule or figure work: All rule or figure work, "or where three or more justifications occur in a page or column," a price and a half, according to the type in which it is set. All matter in which two or more rules are inserted to constitute rule work, and two or more columns of figures without rules, to constitute figure work.

3. Rule and figure work; All rule and figure work to be paid double the price of common matter. One column of figures and one rule, in a page or other matter shall constitute rule and figure work: *Provided, however,* That on works the pages of which are uniformly made up of two or more columns (as on periodical publications), no charge beyond that of common matter shall be made for or on account of the rules separating the columns.

4. All heads or foot lines attached to rule or figure work or rule and figure work, to be reckoned the same as the body of the matter.

5. All foreign languages, printed in Roman characters, an addition of 10 cents per 1,000 ems.

6. All works printed in Greek, or other foreign characters, to be paid for at the rate of 80 cents per 1,000 ems.

7. Arithmetical works to be paid an advance of 10 cents per 1,000 ems on the price of common matter.

8. Music double price.

9. Side notes to be counted the full length of the page and charged according to the type in which they are set.

10. Cut-in notes to be cast up according to the type in which they are set, and charged 10 cents extra per 1,000 ems; and the whole page to be counted as text.

11. Algebraical or mathematical works to be charged double price.

12. All bottom notes, contents or chapters, etc., in smaller type than the text, to be paid for according to the type in which they are set.

13. All letter cast upon a larger body than the face, as bourgeois on long primer, to be counted according to its face; all letter cast upon a smaller body than the face, as minion on nonpareil, to be counted according to the body; and all letter shall measure 12½ ems to the alphabet.

14. All works where the measure does not exceed 14 ems in width, to be 3 cents per 1,000 ems advance.

15. For making up a set of furniture, not exceeding 16 pages, 37 cents; exceeding, 66 cents.

Alterations: Compositors to receive for alterations from copy, or other time work at the rate of 32 cents per hour.

SCALE OF PRICES OF THE COLUMBIA TYPOGRAPHICAL SOCIETY, WASHINGTON, D. C., ADOPTED FEBRUARY 21, 1863

WEEKLY RATES

1. Compositors in book and job offices, and on evening and weekly newspapers, to receive not less than $16 per week, ten hours to constitute a day's work; and for extra hours 40 cents per hour.

2. The regular hours of work shall be as follows: From the 10th of October, inclusive, to the 10th of March, 8 a. m. to 7 p. m.; from the 10th of March, inclusive, to the 10th of October, 7 a. m. to 6 p. m.

The regular holidays shall be as follows: Fourth of July, Thanksgiving Day, and Christmas Day; and all work required to be done on those days shall be paid the same as Sunday work.

On the eve of regular holidays and days generally observed as such, and on every Saturday evening throughout the year, work shall cease at 5 p. m.

4. In all offices and at all seasons compositors to receive not less than $4 for Sunday work, the day to consist of eight hours, and 60 cents per hour for all extra work.

5. No work shall be done at the weekly rates for less than three days—all jobs that last for a less time to be done by the piece.

Book, job, and evening paper offices

1. All works done in the English language, common matter, from pica to agate, inclusive, 45 cents per 1,000 ems; pearl, 50 cents; diamond, 60 cents. An en in length or width to be counted an em; if less than an en, not to be counted. Works set in type larger than pica to be counted as pica.

2. All works in foreign languages (Roman characters) shall be paid 5 cents extra per 1,000.

3. Works in foreign characters shall be paid for as follows: Greek, without accents, 60 cents per 1,000; accented, 65 cents; German, 45 cents; Hebrew without points, 60 cents; with points (to be cast up half body and half points), 80 cents.

4. Where words of Greek or Hebrew occur in common matter the charge shall be for the first three words or less 5 cents, and 1 cent a word thereafter; unless the foreign character shall amount to 1,000 ems in a mass, then to be paid as per scale for such character.

5. Arithmetical works 10 cents per 1,000 ems extra.

6. Algebraical or mathematical works, double price.

7. Side notes to be counted the full length of the page, and charged according to the type in which they are set.

8. Cut-in notes to be charged 3 cents a note, the whole page to be counted as text.

9. All bottom notes, contents of chapters, etc., in smaller type than the text, to be paid for according to the type in which they are set.

10. All works under fourteen ems in width, 3 cents per 1,000 ems extra.

11. All letter cast on a body larger than its face, as bourgeois on long primer, to be paid by the face; and all cast on a smaller body than the face to be paid by the body.

12. All letter must measure 12½ ems to the alphabet.

13. Compositors shall correct proof and one revise. All alterations made by the author to be paid for at the rate of 40 cents per hour.

14. For making up a set of furniture, 16 pages, 37 cents; exceeding 16 pages, 66 cents.

Rule and figure work

15. Rule or figure work: All rule or figure work, or where three or more justifications occur in a page or column, a price and a half, according to the type in which it is set. All matter in which two or more rules are inserted, to constitute rule work; and two or more columns of figures, without rules, to constitute figure work.

16. Rule and figure work: All rule and figure work to be paid double the price of common matter. One column of figures and one rule, in a page or other matter, shall constitute rule and figure work: *Provided, however,* That on works the pages of which are uniformly made up of two or more columns (as on periodical publications), no charge beyond that of common matter shall be made for, or on account of, the rules separating the columns.

17. All heads and foot lines attached to rule or figure work, or rule and figure work, to be reckoned the same as the body of the matter.

1. Compositors employed on morning papers shall receive 45 cents per 1,000 ems (all letters included), and shall in all cases work by the piece.

2. Rule work, figure work, and rule and figure work shall be charged at the rates laid down in articles 15, 16, and 17 of book rates.

3. If the hook, stone, table, desk, or place where copy is taken from be cleared after 7 o'clock at night, compositors to receive pay while on the wait, at 40 cents per hour; for fractions of hours the charge shall be as follows: 15 minutes and under, one-fourth hour; over 20 and not exceeding 35, one-half hour; over 35 and not exceeding 50, three-fourths hour; over 50 minutes, one hour.

4. At least two hours' composition shall be supplied between the hours of 3 and 6 o'clock p. m.

5. Compositors to correct one proof.

6. In consideration that the office in which the official debates of Congress are printed can not obtain the copy until the Houses of Congress adjourn and the reporters' notes are written out, the proprietor thereof shall have the privilege to commute all time for waiting and afternoon copy by paying 5 cents per 1,000 ems over and above the foregoing scale of prices: *Provided*, That such system shall continue throughout each session of Congress.

PRESSWORK

1. Pressmen shall receive not less than $16 per week, ten hours to constitute a day's work; and for extra hours 40 cents per hour.
2. At all times to receive not less than $4 for each and every Sunday (to consist of eight hours), and for extra hours on said day, 60 cents per hour.
3. In any office where there are more than four presses, no pressman shall have charge of more than two power presses, except in the case of an unavoidable exigency.

SCALE OF PRICES OF THE COLUMBIA TYPOGRAPHICAL SOCIETY, WASHINGTON, D. C., ADOPTED JULY 2, 1864

WEEKLY RATES

1. Compositors in book and job offices and on weekly newspapers to receive not less than $21 per week, ten hours to constitute a day's work; and for extra hours 50 cents per hour.
2. The regular hours of work shall be as follows:
From the 10th of October, inclusive, to the 10th of March, 8 a. m. to 7 p. m.; from the 10th of March, inclusive, to the 10th of October, 7 a. m. to 6 p. m.
3. The regular holidays shall be as follows: Fourth of July, Thanksgiving Day, and Christmas Day; and all work required to be done on those days shall be paid the same as Sunday work.
On the eve of regular holidays and days generally observed as such, and on every Saturday evening throughout the year, work shall cease at 5 p. m.
4. In all offices and at all seasons compositors to receive not less than $5 for Sunday work, the day to consist of eight hours, and 70 cents per hour for all extra work.
5. No work shall be done at the weekly rates for less than three days, all jobs that last for a less time to be done by the piece.

PIECEWORK

Book, job, and evening paper offices

1. All works done in the English language, common matter, from pica to agate, inclusive, 60 cents per 1,000 ems; pearl, 65 cents; diamond, 75 cents. An en in length or width to be counted an em; if less than an en, not to be counted. Works set in type larger than pica to be counted as pica.
2. All works in foreign languages (Roman characters) shall be paid 10 cents extra per 1,000.
3. Works in foreign characters shall be paid for as follows: Greek, without accents, 75 cents per 1,000; accented, 80 cents; German, 60 cents; Hebrew, without point, 75 cents; with points (to be cast up half body and half points), $1.
4. Where words of Greek or Hebrew occur in common matter the charge shall be for the first three words or less 5 cents, and 1 cent a word thereafter; unless the foreign character shall amount to 1,000 ems in a mass, then to be paid as per scale for such character.
5. Arithmetical works 10 cents per 1,000 ems extra.
6. Algebraical or mathematical works, double price.
7. Side notes to be counted the full length of the page, and charged according to the type in which they are set.
8. Cut-in notes to be charged 3 cents a note, the whole page to be counted as text.
9. All bottom notes, contents of chapters, etc., in smaller type than the text, to be paid for according to the type in which they are set.
10. All works under 14 ems in width, 3 cents per 1,000 ems extra.
11. All letter cast on a body larger than its face, as bourgeois on long primer, to be paid by the face; and all cast on a smaller body than the face to be paid by the body.

12. All letter must measure 12½ ems to the alphabet.

13. Compositors shall correct one proof and one revise. All alterations made by the author to be paid for at the rate of 45 cents per hour.

14. For making up a set of furniture, 16 pages, 50 cents; exceeding 16 pages, 75 cents.

Rule and figure work

15. Rule or figure work: All rule or figure work, or where three or more justifications occur in a page or column, a price and a half, according to the type in which it is set. All matter in which two or more rules are inserted to constitute rule work, and two or more columns of figures, without rules, or one column of figures and one rule, to constitute figure work.

16. Rule and figure work: All rule and figure work to be paid double the price of common matter. Two columns of figures and two rules in a page or other matter, shall constitute rule and figure work: *Provided, however,* That on works the pages of which are uniformly made up of two or more columns (as on periodical publications), no charge beyond that of common matter shall be made for, or on account of, the rules separating the columns.

17. All heads and foot lines attached to rule or figure work, or rule and figure work, to be reckoned the same as the body of the matter.

Evening papers

1. Compositors on evening papers shall, in all cases, work by the piece, and have at least six hours' composition each day; and if, during said six hours, they may be compelled to wait, they shall be paid while on the wait 45 cents per hour. For fractions of an hour the charge shall be: For 15 minutes and under 20 minutes, one-fourth hour; over 20 and not exceeding 35 minutes, one-half hour; over 35 and not exceeding 50 minutes, three-fourths hour; over 50 minutes, one hour.

2. On all evening or weekly newspapers where the foreman or maker-up sets type, he shall take his regular turn for copy. All copy shall be placed on the hook, and fat advertisements or any other description of fat matter shall not be culled.

Morning papers

1. Compositors employed on morning papers shall receive 60 cents per 1,000 ems (all letters included) and shall, in all cases, work by the piece.

2. Rule work, figure work, and rule and figure work shall be charged at the rates laid down in articles 15, 16, and 17 of book rates.

3. If the hook, stone, table, desk, or place where copy is taken from be cleared after 7 o'clock at night, compositors to receive pay while on the wait, at 50 cents per hour; for fractions of hours the charge shall be as follows: For 15 minutes and under 20, one-fourth hour; over 20 and not exceeding 35, one-half hour; over 35 and not exceeding 50, three-fourths hour; over 50 minutes, one hour.

4. At least two hours' composition shall be supplied between the hours of 3 and 6 o'clock.

5. Compositors to correct one proof.

6. In consideration that the office in which the official debates of Congress are printed can not obtain the copy until the Houses of Congress adjourn and the reporters' notes are written out, the proprietor thereof shall have privilege to commute all time for waiting and afternoon copy by paying 10 cents per 1,000 ems over and above the aforegoing scale of prices: *Provided,* That such system shall continue throughout each session of Congress.

PRESSWORK

1. Pressmen shall receive not less than $21 per week, ten hours to constitute a day's work; and for extra hours, 50 cents per hour.

2. At all times to receive not less than $5 for each and every Sunday (to consist of eight hours); and for extra hours on said day, 70 cents per hour.

3. In any office where there are more than four presses, no pressman shall have charge of more than two power presses, except in the case of a fellow pressman being absent by sickness or other temporary cause, in which case the man attending the presses shall be paid the full amount of the absentee's wages: *Provided,* That no pressman shall have claim for any such extra service for more than three days in any one month.

Scale of Prices of Columbia Typographical Society, Washington, D. C.,
Adopted October 13, 1866

BOOK AND JOB WORK

1. All works in the English language, common matter, from pica to agate, inclusive, 60 cents per 1,000 ems; pearl, 65 cents; diamond, 75 cents. An en in length or width to be counted as an em; less than an en not to be counted. Type larger than pica to be cast up as pica.

2. Works in foreign languages (Roman characters) shall be paid price and a half per 1,000 ems.

3. Where words of Greek or Hebrew occur in common matter the charge shall be 5 cents extra for the first three words or less and 1 cent per word thereafter, unless the foreign characters shall amount to 1,000 ems in a mass, in which case they shall be charged a price and a half.

4. Arithmetical works 20 cents per 1,000 ems extra.

5. Algebraical or mathematical works, double price. Should lines or small portions of algebra occur in an ordinary work, 50 cents per hour shall be charged for the time consumed in composing them.

6. Works printed with the old English spelling, contractions, superiors, etc., shall be charged 10 cents per 1,000 ems extra.

7. Prefaces, contents, or any prefixed matter are cast up to the type in which they are composed, and take the extras of the work to which they belong.

8. Blank pages in a form shall be charged by the compositor only when the matter is made up or imposed by him, but chapter heads and concluding pages shall be charged by the compositor, whether made up by him or not, at the same rate as the body of the work to which they belong.

9. The office has the privilege of claiming full titles and dedications, but in no case shall piece-paying establishments claim half titles, or any other prefixed matter, nor cull the fat portions of any work.

10. Headlines, etc., giving a synopsis of the contents of each page, when filled up by the proof reader after the matter has been made up, to be charged 50 cents per hour for the time consumed in inserting.

11. The establishment shall furnish the necessary sorts for all works requiring an unusual quantity of capitals, figures, italics, points, etc. Sorts furnished subsequent to matter being set up shall be inserted at the expense of the office.

12. When matter is set without leads, and is afterwards required to be leaded, such matter shall be leaded at the expense of the employer, and the compositor shall charge for it the same as if he had originally put in the leads.

13. Compositors may be required to clear away or distribute all fat or objectionable matter charged by them, when the sorts in it have been supplied by the office, and take out leads from dead matter when the leads have been supplied by the office; except in cases where the matter has been kept standing for a second edition, in which case the office shall take charge of it.

14. Side notes shall be counted the full length of the page, and charged according to the type in which they are set.

15. Cut-in notes shall be paid 25 cents each, and the whole page charged as text.

16. Bottom notes, contents of chapters, etc., in smaller type than the text, shall be cast up to the type in which they are set.

(Casting up side notes, etc.: When a compositor is required to cast up his pages to ascertain their value, he is entitled to reckon in his calculation all that constitutes part and parcel of his page. It is upon this rule that he acts when he casts up a page of two columns, for he includes in the width of his page the reglet or rule which separates his columns. In table work he reckons the rules or blank columns which may occur in his page. So, also, in casting of bottom notes, he reckons the reglet, rule or white which separates the text and the note; and upon the same principle he is entitled to reckon the reglet in the square of his page.)

17. All matter set in a measure less than 16 ems in width, of whatever type may be composed, shall be charged 5 cents per 1,000 ems extra.

(Note.—When more than two columns appear on the face of a page, this article shall not apply, but the case shall be governed by article 20.)

18. When cuts are inserted in the matter or worked in pages along with the body of the work, such cuts belong to the compositors; but when the cuts are worked entirely separate, the same as copperplate engravings or lithographic plates, they are not claimed by the compositors.

19. When cuts inserted in matter cause overrunning in making up—as works on natural philosophy, chemistry, etc.—and also when questions are appended to the page, 50 cents per hour shall be paid for the time occupied in overrunning or appending the questions.

20. All work where three justifications or columns (words or figures), without rules, occur in a page or column shall be charged a price and a half, according to the type in which it is set; when more than three columns occur, to be charged double price.

21. All rule and figure work to be charged double the price of common matter. Three or more columns (figures or words), with rules, in a page or other matter, shall constitute rule and figure work: *Provided, however,* That on works the pages of which are uniformly made up of two or more columns (such as periodical publications) no charge beyond that of common matter shall be made for (or) on account of the rules separating the columns.

22. Title headings and foot lines to column and tabular work shall be considered as part of such matter and paid for accordingly.

23. Short pages in a series of tables are charged as full pages.

24. Matter consisting of four or five blank columns (forms, etc.) to be charged a price and a half; but when the columns are six or more, to be charged double, cast up to the type used in the work in which they occur.

25. It shall be the duty of the compositor imposing to take two proofs of each form. All proofs taken afterwards shall be paid for at the rate of 15 cents each for letterpress forms, and for stereotype forms and small jobs 5 cents each. When extra proofs are required through the carelessness of a compositor, they shall be taken at his expense.

26. Compositors shall correct one proof and one revise. All alterations made by the author to be paid for at the rate of 50 cents per hour.

27. In all cases where bad letters are marked by the proof reader in consequence of worn-out defective fonts, the same shall be corrected at the expense of the establishment.

28. All letter cast on a larger body than the face (as bourgeois on long primer) shall be cast up according to the face, and all letter cast on a smaller body than the face (as minion on nonpareil) shall be counted according to the body.

29. All fonts of type, the alphabet of which measures less than 12½ ems, shall be cast up in depth to the body of the type used, and in width to that of the next smaller type.

30. When necessary to facilitate work, the employer may appoint a maker-up: *Provided,* That not more than 4 cents per 1,000 ems shall be deducted for making-up, imposing, taking the necessary proofs, etc.; the compositor to charge the entire page, including head and foot lines.

31. For bad manuscript, works of an intricate nature, etc., not governed by these articles, 50 cents per hour shall be charged.

TIME WORK

32. Compositors and pressmen employed by the week shall receive not less than $24 per week, eight hours to constitute a day from the 1st of October to the 31st of March, and ten hours to constitute a day from the 1st of April to the 30th of September inclusive. For extra work 50 cents per hour. After 12 o'clock midnight, 75 cents per hour.

33. The regular hours of work shall be as follows: From the 1st of October to the 31st of March, inclusive, 8 a. m. to 5 p. m., and from the 1st of April to the 30th of September, inclusive, 7 a. m. to 6 p. m.

34. The regular holidays shall be as follows: Fourth of July, Thanksgiving Day, and Christmas Day; and all work required to be done on those days shall be paid the same as Sunday work. On the eve of regular holidays, and days generally observed as such, and every Saturday evening, throughout the year, work shall cease at 5 p. m.

35. In all offices and at all seasons compositors to receive not less than $5 for Sunday work, the day to consist of eight hours, and 75 cents per hour for all extra work.

36. No composition shall be done at the weekly rates for less than three days; all jobs that last for a less time to be done by the piece or at the rate of 50 cents per hour.

37. In any case where a compositor or pressman employed by the week shall be recalled, without previous notice, after working hours to do extra work, $1 extra shall be charged.

38. In any office where there are more than three presses, no pressman shall have charge of more than two power presses, except in case of a pressman being absent by reason of sickness or other unavoidable circumstance, in which event his fellow-pressmen, with the approbation of the employer, may take charge of his presses: *Provided*, That the absentee be paid the full amount of his wages: *Provided, further*, That he shall not be absent more than one week in any one month.

MORNING PAPERS

1. Compositors employed upon morning papers shall receive not less than 60 cents per 1,000 ems (all letter included) and shall in all cases work by the piece.

2. Column and tabular work: See articles 20, 21, and 22 of book scale.

3. Bastard type: See articles 28 and 29 of book scale.

4. Work done by the hour shall be charged at the rate of 50 cents per hour; and all time consumed in waiting for copy after 7 p. m. shall be similarly charged. For fractions of hours the charge shall be as follows: For 10 minutes and not exceeding 20, one-fourth hour; over 20 and not exceeding 35 minutes, one-half hour; over 35 and not exceeding 50 minutes, three-fourths hour; over 50 minutes, one hour.

5. At least two consecutive hours' composition shall be supplied between the hours of 2 and 6 p. m.

(NOTE.—In consideration that the office in which the official debates of Congress are printed can not obtain the copy until the House of Congress adjourns and the reporters' notes are written out, the proprietor thereof shall have the privilege of commuting all time for waiting and afternoon copy by paying 10 cents per 1,000 ems over and above the foregoing scale: *Provided*, That such system shall continue throughout each session of Congress.)

6. A cut or stereotype plate, whether complete in itself or not, belongs to the compositor.

7. On each and every occasion when a man after having left the office for the night, shall be recalled to work before 10 a. m. $1 extra shall be charged.

8. All matter set for newspapers during the week, whether published or not, shall be placed upon the compositors' bills and paid for at the end of the week, or at whatever time may be specified for the closing of the weekly bills.

9. A majority of the hands in each newspaper office shall regulate all matters in relation to departments or other fat matter, subject to the approval of the employer, but no copy shall be culled except under such regulation.

10. Compositors to correct one proof.

EVENING PAPERS

1. Compositors on evening papers shall in all cases work by the piece, and have at least six consecutive hours' composition each day; and if at any time they may be compelled to wait for copy they shall be paid at the rate of 50 cents per hour— fractions of hours to be charged as prescribed in article 4 of morning newspaper scale.

2. Articles 1, 2, 3, 6, 8, 9, and 10 of the scale for morning papers shall apply to evening papers.

APPENDIX F.—INDEX NUMBERS OF WAGES

GENERAL INDEX OF HOURLY RATES

Table 1 gives index numbers of wage rates per hour from 1840 to 1926 for all industries, other than agriculture, for which data are available. The table was compiled by the Bureau of Labor Statistics from all accessible sources.

TABLE 1.—*Index numbers of wage rates per hour, 1840 to 1926 (exclusive of agriculture)*

[Currency basis during Civil War period. 1913=100]

Year	Index number	Year	Index number	Year	Index number	Year	Index number
1840	33	1862	41	1884	64	1906	85
1841	34	1863	44	1885	64	1907	89
1842	33	1864	50	1886	64	1908	89
1843	33	1865	58	1887	67	1909	90
1844	32	1866	61	1888	67	1910	93
1845	33	1867	63	1889	68	1911	95
1846	34	1868	65	1890	69	1912	97
1847	34	1869	66	1891	69	1913	100
1848	35	1870	67	1892	69	1914	102
1849	36	1871	68	1893	69	1915	103
1850	35	1872	69	1894	67	1916	111
1851	34	1873	69	1895	68	1917	128
1852	35	1874	67	1896	69	1918	162
1853	35	1875	67	1897	69	1919	184
1854	37	1876	64	1898	69	1920	234
1855	38	1877	61	1899	70	1921	218
1856	39	1878	60	1900	73	1922	208
1857	40	1879	59	1901	74	1923	217
1858	39	1880	60	1902	77	1924	223
1859	39	1881	62	1903	80	1925	226
1860	39	1882	63	1904	80	1926	229
1861	40	1883	64	1905	82		

INDEX NUMBERS OF UNION WAGE RATES, 1907 TO 1928

Table 2 shows by index numbers the change in union wage rates and hours of labor from 1907 to 1928, the base (100) being 1913. These index numbers include all trades and all cities covered in preceding years except street-railway motormen and conductors and bus drivers. While rates of wages per hour were obtained for these occupations, no attempt was made to report them because the hours of labor are so variable. Since of necessity they could not be included in the second and third columns, these occupations are omitted from the three columns of index numbers. Piece rates are also omitted, because hourly rates can not be computed therefrom.

The number of trades and cities included in the data has varied from year to year.

TABLE 2.—*Index numbers of union wage rates and hours of labor in the United States as of May each year, 1907 to 1928*

[1913=100]

Year	Index numbers of—			Year	Index numbers of—		
	Rate of wages per hour	Hours per full-time week	Rate of wages per full-time week		Rate of wages per hour	Hours per full-time week	Rate of wages per full-time week
1907	89.7	102.6	91.5	1918	132.7	97.0	129.6
1908	91.0	102.1	92.5	1919	154.5	94.7	147.8
1909	91.9	101.9	93.3	1920	199.0	93.8	188.5
1910	94.4	101.1	95.2	1921	205.3	93.9	193.3
1911	96.0	100.7	96.5	1922	193.1	94.4	183.0
1912	97.6	100.3	97.7	1923	210.6	94.3	198.6
1913	100.0	100.0	100.0	1924	228.1	93.9	214.3
1914	101.9	99.6	101.6	1925	237.9	93.0	222.3
1915	102.8	99.4	102.3	1926	250.3	92.8	233.4
1916	107.2	98.8	106.2	1927	259.5	92.4	240.8
1917	114.2	98.4	112.4	1928	260.6	91.9	240.6

SUPPLEMENT, 1929–1933

SUPPLEMENT, 1929-1933

The first edition of this bulletin was published in 1929 and the series of wage tables therein were brought down to 1928. In the preparation of this revised edition it was impracticable, for reasons of printing cost, to recast the original tables so as to include the data for later years. The method adopted—that of presenting the additional material in the form of a supplement—is by no means as satisfactory as a completely revised bulletin would be, but by the use of identical table headings and page references to the original tables, it is believed that the use of the material is made reasonably convenient.

525

A.—BAKERY TRADES

BAKERS

TABLE **A–5** (continued from p. 150).—*Bakers, first hands, hand, day work, males, 1929–1933, by city and year*

Year	Cincinnati, Ohio [1]		Dallas, Tex. [2]		Denver, Colo.		Fall River, Mass.	
	Hours per week	Rate per hour	Hours per week	Rate per hour	Hours per week	Rate per hour	Hours per week	Rate per hour
1929	48.0	$0.771	51.0	$0.765	48.0	$0.792		
1930	48.0	.771	51.0	.765	48.0	.792		
1931	48.0	.771	48.0	.813	48.0	.792		
1932	48.0	.694	48.0	.731	48.0	.792		
1933	48.0	.694	48.0	.658	48.0	.675		

Year	Indianapolis, Ind. [3]		Kansas City, Mo. [4]		Louisville, Ky. [1]		New York, N.Y.	
1929	54.0	$0.694	48.0	$0.896	48.0	$0.625	48.0	$0.979
1930	54.0	.694	48.0	.896	48.0	.625	48.0	.979
1931			48.0	.896	48.0	.625	48.0	.979
1932			48.0	.896	48.0	.500	48.0	.979
1933			40.0	.833			48.0	.979

Year	Omaha, Nebr.		San Francisco, Calif. [4]		Seattle, Wash. [4]		Washington, D.C. [5]	
1929			48.0	$0.958	48.0	$1.000	48.0	$1.000
1930			48.0	.958	48.0	1.000	48.0	1.000
1931			48.0	.958	48.0	1.000	48.0	1.000
1932			48.0	.958	48.0	1.000	48.0	.900
1933			48.0	.863	48.0	.900	48.0	.900

[1] Ovenmen.
[2] Foremen, 1929–1933, inclusive.
[3] Foremen, 1929 and 1930.
[4] Ovenmen, 1929–1933, inclusive.
[5] Journeymen, 1929–1933, inclusive.

TABLE **A–6** (continued from p. 151).—*Bakers, first hands, machine, day work, males, 1929–1933, by city and year*

Year	Kansas City, Mo.		Washington, D.C.		Cincinnati, Ohio		New York, N.Y.		San Francisco, Calif.		Denver, Colo. [1]	
	Hours per week	Rate per hour	Hours per week	Rate per hour	Hours per week	Rate per hour	Hours per week	Rate per hour	Hours per week	Rate per hour	Hours per week	Rate per hour
1929	[2] 48.0	[2] $0.833									48.0	$0.708
1930	[2] 48.0	[2] .833									48.0	.708
1931	[2] 48.0	[2] .833									48.0	.667
1932	[2] 48.0	[2] .833									48.0	.667
1933	[2] 40.0	[2] .771									48.0	.563

[1] Ovenmen, 1929–1933.
[2] Benchmen and machine hands.

BAKERS—Continued

TABLE A-8 (continued from p. 152).—*Bakers, second hands, hand, day work, males, 1929-1933, by city and year*

Year	Cincinnati, Ohio [1]		Dallas, Tex. [1]		Denver, Colo. [1]		Fall River, Mass.	
	Hours per week	Rate per hour	Hours per week	Rate per hour	Hours per week	Rate per hour	Hours per week	Rate per hour
1929	48.0	$0.708	51.0	$0.676	48.0	$0.667	---------	---------
1930	48.0	.708	51.0	.676	48.0	.667	---------	---------
1931	48.0	.708	48.0	.719	48.0	.667	---------	---------
1932	48.0	.638	48.0	.647	48.0	.667	---------	---------
1933	48.0	.638	48.0	.608	48.0	.563	---------	---------

Year	Indianapolis, Ind. [1]		Kansas City, Mo. [1]		Louisville, Ky. [1]		New York, N.Y.	
1929	54.0	$0.556	48.0	$0.833	48.0	$0.583	48.0	$0.917
1930	54.0	.556	48.0	.833	48.0	.583	48.0	.917
1931	---------	---------	48.0	.833	48.0	.583	48.0	.917
1932	---------	---------	48.0	.833	48.0	.417	48.0	.917
1933	---------	---------	40.0	.771	---------	---------	48.0	.917

Year	Omaha, Nebr.		San Francisco, Calif. [1]		Seattle, Wash. [1]	
1929	---------	---------	48.0	$0.896	48.0	$0.938
1930	---------	---------	48.0	.896	48.0	.938
1931	---------	---------	48.0	.896	48.0	.938
1932	---------	---------	48.0	.896	48.0	.938
1933	---------	---------	48.0	.806	48.0	.844

[1] Benchmen.

B.—BUILDING TRADES

TABLE **B-2** (continued from p. 159).—*Bricklayers, males, 1929–1933, by city and year*

Year	Atlanta, Ga.		Birmingham, Ala.		Boston, Mass.		Chicago, Ill.	
	Hours per week	Rate per hour	Hours per week	Rate per hour	Hours per week	Rate per hour	Hours per week	Rate per hour
1929	44.0	$1.250	44.0	$1.500	44.0	$1.500	44.0	$1.625
1930	44.0	1.250	44.0	1.500	44.0	1.500	44.0	1.700
1931	44.0	1.250	44.0	1.500	40.0	1.500	44.0	1.700
1932	44.0	1.125	44.0	1.000	40.0	1.300	40.0	1.375
1933	44.0	1.125	44.0	1.000	40.0	1.300	40.0	1.375

Year	Cincinnati, Ohio		Denver, Colo.		Detroit, Mich.		New Orleans, La.	
1929	44.0	$1.625	44.0	$1.500	44.0	$1.575	44.0	$1.500
1930	40.0	1.625	44.0	1.500	40.0	1.575	44.0	1.500
1931	40.0	1.625	40.0	1.500	40.0	1.500	44.0	1.000
1932	40.0	1.375	40.0	1.313	40.0	1.250	44.0	1.000
1933	40.0	1.375	40.0	1.313	40.0	1.250	44.0	1.000

Year	New York, N.Y.		Philadelphia, Pa.		St. Louis, Mo.		San Francisco, Calif.	
1929	40.0	$1.875	40.0	$1.625	44.0	$1.750	44.0	$1.375
1930	40.0	1.925	40.0	1.750	44.0	1.750	40.0	1.375
1931	40.0	1.925	40.0	1.750	40.0	1.750	40.0	1.375
1932	40.0	1.650	¹ 24.0	1.500	40.0	1.500	40.0	1.375
1933	40.0	1.650	40.0	1.500	40.0	1.500	40.0	1.375

¹ Worked but 3 days per week.

TABLE **B-4** (continued from p. 167).—*Carpenters, males, 1929–1933, by city and year*

Year	Atlanta, Ga.		Birmingham, Ala.		Boston, Mass.		Chicago, Ill.	
	Hours per week	Rate per hour	Hours per week	Rate per hour	Hours per week	Rate per hour	Hours per week	Rate per hour
1929	44.0	$0.800	44.0	$1.000	44.0	$1.375	44.0	$1.500
1930	44.0	.800	40.0	1.000	44.0	1.375	44.0	1.625
1931	44.0	.900	40.0	1.000	40.0	1.375	44.0	1.625
1932	44.0	.900	44.0	1.000	40.0	1.175	40.0	1.313
1933	44.0	.900	44.0	.750	40.0	1.175	40.0	1.313

Year	Cincinnati, Ohio		Denver, Colo.		Detroit, Mich.		New Orleans, La.	
1929	44.5	$1.375	40.0	$1.250	44.0	$1.150	44.0	$0.900
1930	44.5	1.400	40.0	1.250	44.0	1.150	44.0	.900
1931	40.0	1.400	40.0	1.250	44.0	1.000	44.0	.900
1932	40.0	1.200	40.0	1.094	44.0	1.000	44.0	.900
1933	40.0	1.200	40.0	1.094	44.0	1.000	44.0	.750

Year	New York, N.Y.		Philadelphia, Pa.		St. Louis, Mo.		San Francisco, Calif.	
1929	44.0	$1.500	44.0	$1.250	40.0	$1.500	44.0	$1.125
1930	40.0	1.650	¹ 44.0	1.250	40.0	1.500	40.0	1.125
1931	40.0	1.650	¹ 44.0	1.250	40.0	1.500	40.0	1.125
1932	40.0	1.250	¹ 44.0	1.050	40.0	1.250	40.0	.900
1933	40.0	1.400	40.0	1.000	40.0	1.250	40.0	.900

¹ 40 hours per week, June to August, inclusive.

TABLE **B**-7 (continued from p. 169).—*Inside wiremen, males, 1929-1933, by city and year*

Year	Atlanta, Ga. Hours per week	Atlanta, Ga. Rate per hour	Birmingham, Ala. Hours per week	Birmingham, Ala. Rate per hour	Boston, Mass. Hours per week	Boston, Mass. Rate per hour	Chicago, Ill. Hours per week	Chicago, Ill. Rate per hour
1929	44.0	$1.125	40.0	$1.250	44.0	$1.375	44.0	$1.625
1930	44.0	1.125	40.0	1.250	40.0	1.500	44.0	1.625
1931	44.0	1.125	40.0	1.250	40.0	1.500	44.0	1.625
1932	44.0	1.125	40.0	1.250	40.0	1.500	40.0	1.500
1933	44.0	1.125	40.0	{ 1.250 / 1.000 }	40.0	1.250	40.0	1.500

Year	Cincinnati, Ohio Hours per week	Cincinnati, Ohio Rate per hour	Denver, Colo. Hours per week	Denver, Colo. Rate per hour	Detroit, Mich. Hours per week	Detroit, Mich. Rate per hour	New Orleans, La. Hours per week	New Orleans, La. Rate per hour
1929	44.5	$1.375	44.0	$1.375	44.0	$1.500	44.0	$1.250
1930	44.5	1.400	40.0	1.375	40.0	1.550	44.0	1.250
1931	40.0	1.400	40.0	1.375	40.0	1.550	44.0	1.250
1932	40.0	1.250	40.0	1.375	40.0	1.400	44.0	1.250
1933	40.0	1.250	30.0	.900	40.0	1.400	40.0	{ 1.250 / 1.000 }

Year	New York, N.Y. Hours per week	New York, N.Y. Rate per hour	Philadelphia, Pa. Hours per week	Philadelphia, Pa. Rate per hour	St. Louis, Mo. Hours per week	St. Louis, Mo. Rate per hour	San Francisco, Calif. Hours per week	San Francisco, Calif. Rate per hour
1929	40.0	$1.650	¹ 44.0	$1.250	40.0	$1.500	44.0	$1.125
1930	40.0	1.650	40.0	1.250	40.0	1.650	40.0	1.125
1931	40.0	1.650	40.0	1.500	40.0	1.650	40.0	1.125
1932	40.0	1.650	40.0	1.500	40.0	1.675	40.0	1.000
1933	40.0	1.400	40.0	1.250	40.0	1.675	40.0	1.000

¹ 40 hours per week, June to August, inclusive.

TABLE **B**-11 (continued from p. 184).—*Hod carriers, males, 1929-1933, by city and year*

Year	Atlanta, Ga. Hours per week	Atlanta, Ga. Rate per hour	Birmingham, Ala. Hours per week	Birmingham, Ala. Rate per hour	Boston, Mass. Hours per week	Boston, Mass. Rate per hour	Chicago, Ill. Hours per week	Chicago, Ill. Rate per hour
1929					44.0	$0.850	44.0	$0.900
1930					44.0	.850	44.0	.975
1931					44.0	.850	44.0	.975
1932					40.0	.700	44.0	.825
1933					40.0	.700	40.0	.825

Year	Cincinnati, Ohio Hours per week	Cincinnati, Ohio Rate per hour	Denver, Colo. Hours per week	Denver, Colo. Rate per hour	Detroit, Mich. Hours per week	Detroit, Mich. Rate per hour	New Orleans, La. Hours per week	New Orleans, La. Rate per hour
1929	45.0	$0.975	44.0	{ $0.813 / .844 }	44.0	$0.700		
1930	45.0	1.000	44.0	{ .813 / .844 }	44.0	.750		
1931	40.0	1.000	40.0	{ .813 / .844 }	44.0	.650		
1932	40.0	.700	40.0	.750	44.0	.600		
1933	40.0	.700	40.0	{ .750 / .781 }				

Year	New York, N.Y. Hours per week	New York, N.Y. Rate per hour	Philadelphia, Pa. Hours per week	Philadelphia, Pa. Rate per hour	St. Louis, Mo. Hours per week	St. Louis, Mo. Rate per hour	San Francisco, Calif. Hours per week	San Francisco, Calif. Rate per hour
1929	40.0	{ $1.188 / 1.125 }	44.0	{ $0.850 / 1.000 }	44.0	$1.150	44.0	$0.875
1930	40.0	1.238	44.0	.850	44.0	1.150	40.0	.875
1931	40.0	{ 1.238 / 1.125 }	44.0	.850	40.0	1.150	40.0	.875
1932	40.0	{ 1.125 / 1.000 }	44.0	1.000	40.0	1.000	40.0	.875
1933	40.0	{ 1.000 / .750 }			40.0	1.000	40.0	.875

TABLE **B**-12 (continued from p. 186).—*Laborers, males, 1929–1933, by city and year*

Year	Atlanta, Ga.		Birmingham, Ala.		Boston, Mass.		Chicago, Ill.	
	Hours per week	Rate per hour	Hours per week	Rate per hour	Hours per week	Rate per hour	Hours per week	Rate per hour
1929					48.0	$0.800	44.0	$0.900
1930					48.0	.800	44.0	.975
1931					48.0	.800	44.0	.975
1932					40.0	.700	44.0	.825
1933					40.0	.700	44.0	.825

	Cincinnati, Ohio		Denver, Colo.		Detroit, Mich.		New Orleans, La.	
1929	50.0	$0.600			44.0	$0.600		
1930	50.0	.600			44.0	.600		
1931	45.0	.600	44.0	$0.625	44.0	.650		
1932	40.0	.450	44.0	.500	44.0	.500	54.0	$0.350
1933	40.0	.450	44.0	.500	40.0	.500		

	New York, N.Y.		Philadelphia, Pa.		St. Louis, Mo.		San Francisco, Calif.	
1929	44.0	$1.200 / 1.300	44.0	$0.600	44.0	$0.750	44.0	$0.688
1930	44.0	1.250 / 1.350	44.0	.500	44.0	.875	44.0	.688
1931	44.0	1.000 / 1.100	44.0	.500	44.0	.875	40.0	.688
1932	40.0	.650 / .750	44.0	.500	40.0	.788	40.0	.688
1933	40.0	.600 / .500	44.0	.500	40.0	.788	40.0	.688

TABLE **B**-17 (continued from p. 194).—*Stone masons, males, 1929–1933, by city and year*

Year	Atlanta, Ga.		Birmingham, Ala.		Boston, Mass.		Chicago, Ill.	
	Hours per week	Rate per hour	Hours per week	Rate per hour	Hours per week	Rate per hour	Hours per week	Rate per hour
1929	44.0	$1.250	44.0	$1.500	44.0	$1.500	44.0	$1.625
1930	44.0	1.250	44.0	1.500	44.0	1.500	44.0	1.700
1931	44.0	1.250	44.0	1.500	40.0	1.500	44.0	1.700
1932	44.0	1.125	44.0	1.000	40.0	1.300	40.0	1.375
1933	44.0	1.125	44.0	1.000	40.0	1.300	40.0	1.375

	Cincinnati, Ohio		Denver, Colo.		Detroit, Mich.		New Orleans, La.	
1929	45.0	$1.500	44.0	$1.500	44.0	$1.575	44.0	$1.500
1930	40.0	1.500	44.0	1.500	40.0	1.575	44.0	1.500
1931	40.0	1.500	40.0	1.500	40.0	1.500	44.0	1.000
1932	40.0	1.375	40.0	1.313	40.0	1.250	44.0	1.000
1933	40.0	1.250	40.0	1.313	40.0	1.250	44.0	1.000

	New York, N.Y.		Philadelphia, Pa.		St. Louis, Mo.		San Francisco, Calif.	
1929	40.0	$1.875 / 1.925	[1] 44.0	$1.500	44.0	$1.500	44.0	$1.375
1930	40.0	1.925	40.0	1.500	44.0	1.500	40.0	1.375
1931	40.0	1.925	40.0	1.500	40.0	1.500	40.0	1.375
1932	40.0	1.650	40.0	1.250 / 1.500	40.0	1.250	40.0	1.375
1933	40.0	1.650	40.0	1.375	40.0	1.250	40.0	1.375

[1] 40 hours per week, July and August.

TABLE **B-19** (continued from p. 201).—*Painters, males, 1929-1933, by city and year*

Year	Atlanta, Ga.		Birmingham, Ala.		Boston, Mass.		Chicago, Ill.	
	Hours per week	Rate per hour	Hours per week	Rate per hour	Hours per week	Rate per hour	Hours per week	Rate per hour
1929	44.0	$0.850	44.0	$1.000	40.0	$1.375	40.0	$1.625
1930	44.0	.850	40.0	1.000	40.0	1.375	40.0	1.750
1931	44.0	.850	40.0	1.000	40.0	1.375	40.0	1.750
1932	44.0	.850	40.0	.750	40.0	1.125	40.0	1.410
1933	44.0	.850	40.0	.750	40.0	1.125	40.0	1.410

Year	Cincinnati, Ohio		Denver, Colo.		Detroit, Mich.		New Orleans, La.	
1929	40.0	$1.313	40.0	$1.250	44.0	$1.250	44.0	$0.900
1930	40.0	1.338	40.0	1.250	44.0	1.250	44.0	.900
1931	40.0	1.338	40.0	1.250	44.0	1.250	44.0	.900
1932	40.0	1.100	40.0	1.094	44.0	1.000	44.0	.900
1933	40.0	1.150	40.0	.750	44.0	1.000	44.0	.750

Year	New York, N. Y.		Philadelphia, Pa.		St. Louis, Mo.		San Francisco, Calif.	
1929	40.0	$1.500	44.0	$1.050	40.0	$1.438	44.0	$1.125
1930	40.0	[1] 1.500 / [1] 1.650	44.0	1.050	40.0	1.500	40.0	1.125
1931	40.0	[1] 1.500 / [1] 1.650 / [3] 1.400	[3] 44.0	1.125	40.0	1.500	40.0	1.125
1932	40.0	[3] 1.250 / [3] 1.000	[1] 44.0	1.000	40.0	1.250	40.0	1.125
1933	40.0	[1] 1.250 / [1] 1.400	44.0	1.000	40.0	1.250	40.0	.875

[1] 2 organizations.   [3] 2 organizations; $1 is for repair work only.
[2] 40 hours per week, June to August, inclusive.

TABLE **B-21** (continued from p. 205).—*Plasterers, males, 1929-1933, by city and year*

Year	Atlanta, Ga.		Birmingham, Ala.		Boston, Mass.		Chicago, Ill.	
	Hours per week	Rate per hour	Hours per week	Rate per hour	Hours per week	Rate per hour	Hours per week	Rate per hour
1929	44.0	$1.250	44.0	$1.250	40.0	$1.500	44.0	$1.625
1930	44.0	1.250	40.0	1.250	40.0	1.625	40.0	1.700
1931	44.0	1.000	----	----	40.0	1.625	40.0	1.700
1932	44.0	1.000	40.0	1.000	40.0	1.375	40.0	1.375
1933	44.0	1.000	40.0	1.000	40.0	1.375	40.0	1.375

Year	Cincinnati, Ohio		Denver, Colo.		Detroit, Mich.		New Orleans, La.	
1929	44.5	$1.500	44.0	$1.500	44.0	$1.625	45.0	$1.250
1930	44.5	1.500	44.0	1.500	44.0	1.625	45.0	1.250
1931	40.0	1.625	40.0	1.500	44.0	1.375	45.0	1.250
1932	40.0	1.375	40.0	1.313	44.0	1.375	45.0	1.000
1933	40.0	1.375	40.0	1.000	40.0	1.250	45.0	1.000

Year	New York, N. Y.		Philadelphia, Pa.		St. Louis, Mo.		San Francisco, Calif.	
1929	40.0	$1.750	40.0	[1] $1.250 / [1] 1.500	40.0	$1.750	44.0	$1.375
1930	40.0	1.925	40.0	[1] 1.250 / [1] 1.625	40.0	1.750	40.0	1.875
1931	40.0	1.925	40.0	1.625	40.0	1.750	40.0	1.875
1932	40.0	1.500	[2] 24.0	1.625	40.0	1.500	40.0	1.100
1933	40.0	1.500	40.0	1.375	40.0	1.500	40.0	1.250

[1] 2 organizations.   [3] Worked but 3 days per week.

TABLE **B-23** (continued from p. 210).—*Plumbers and gas fitters, males, 1929–1933, by city and year*

Year	Atlanta, Ga.		Birmingham, Ala.		Boston, Mass.		Chicago, Ill.	
	Hours per week	Rate per hour	Hours per week	Rate per hour	Hours per week	Rate per hour	Hours per week	Rate per hour
1929	44.0	$1.250	40.0	$1.500	44.0	$1.375	44.0	$1.625
1930	44.0	1.250	40.0	1.500	40.0	1.500	44.0	1.625
1931	40.0	1.250	40.0	1.500	40.0	1.500	44.0	1.700
1932	40.0	1.250	40.0	1.000	40.0	1.250	44.0	1.375
1933	40.0	1.000	40.0	1.000	40.0	1.250	44.0	1.375

Year	Cincinnati, Ohio		Denver, Colo.		Detroit, Mich.		New Orleans, La.	
1929	44.0	$1.375	44.0	$1.375	44.0	$1.500	44.0	$1.050
1930	44.0	1.400	40.0	1.375	44.0	1.500	44.0	1.050
1931	40.0	1.400	40.0	1.375	40.0	1.500	44.0	1.050
1932	40.0	1.250	40.0	1.188	40.0	1.250	44.0	1.050
1933	40.0	1.250	40.0	1.000	40.0	1.250	44.0	1.050

Year	New York, N.Y.		Philadelphia, Pa.		St. Louis, Mo.		San Francisco, Calif.	
1929	44.0	$1.500	44.0	$1.150	40.0	$1.625	44.0	$1.250
1930	40.0	1.650	40.0	1.250	40.0	1.625	40.0	1.250
1931	40.0	1.650	40.0	1.250	40.0	1.625	40.0	1.250
1932	40.0	1.400	40.0	1.040	40.0	1.625	40.0	1.250
1933	40.0	1.500	40.0	1.040	40.0	1.438	40.0	1.250

TABLE **B-26** (continued from p. 215).—*Stonecutters, soft stone, males, 1929–1933, by city and year*

Year	Atlanta, Ga.		Birmingham, Ala.		Boston, Mass.		Chicago, Ill.	
	Hours per week	Rate per hour	Hours per week	Rate per hour	Hours per week	Rate per hour	Hours per week	Rate per hour
1929					44.0	$1.375	44.0	$1.500
1930					44.0	1.375	44.0	1.500
1931					40.0	1.375	44.0	1.500
1932					40.0	1.175	44.0	1.200
1933					40.0	1.175	44.0	1.000

Year	Cincinnati, Ohio		Denver, Colo.		Detroit, Mich.[1]		New Orleans, La.	
1929	44.0	$1.500	44.0	$1.250	44.0	$1.375	44.0	$1.250
1930	40.0	1.500	44.0	1.250	44.0	1.375	44.0	1.250
1931	40.0	1.500	44.0	1.250	44.0	1.375	44.0	1.000
1932	40.0	1.375	40.0	1.250	44.0	1.125	44.0	1.125
1933	40.0	1.250	44.0	1.125	44.0	1.000		

Year	New York, N.Y.		Philadelphia, Pa.		St. Louis, Mo.		San Francisco, Calif.	
1929	44.0	$1.688	44.0	$1.313	44.0	$1.250	44.0	$1.125
1930	40.0	1.688	44.0	1.313	44.0	1.250	44.0	1.125
1931	40.0	1.688	44.0	1.313	44.0	1.250	44.0	1.125
1932	40.0	1.688	40.0	1.313	40.0	1.000	40.0	1.125
1933	40.0	1.500	40.0	1.000	40.0	1.000	40.0	.850

[1] Outside men.

TABLE **B-28** (continued from p. 217).—*Granite cutters, inside, males, 1929-1933, by city and year*

Year	Atlanta, Ga.		Boston, Mass.		Chicago, Ill.[1]		Cincinnati, Ohio	
	Hours per week	Rate per hour	Hours per week	Rate per hour	Hours per week	Rate per hour	Hours per week	Rate per hour
1929			44. 0	$1. 180	[2] 44. 0	$1. 625	[2] 44. 0	$1. 125
1930			[3] 44. 0	1. 240	[2] 44. 0	1. 500	[2] 44. 0	1. 125
1931			[3] 44. 0	1. 240	40. 0	1. 500	[2] 44. 0	1. 125
1932			[3] 44. 0	1. 150	40. 0	1. 325		
1933			[3] 44. 0	1. 000			[2] 44. 0	1. 063

Year	Denver, Colo.		Detroit, Mich.		New Orleans, La.		New York, N. Y.	
1929	44. 0	$1. 125	44. 0	$1. 125	44. 0	$1. 125	44. 0	$1. 375
1930	44. 0	1. 125	44. 0	1. 125	44. 0	1. 125	40. 0	1. 500
1931	40. 0	1. 125	44. 0	1. 125	44. 0	1. 125	40. 0	1. 500
1932	44. 0	1. 125			44. 0	1. 000	40. 0	1. 250
1933	44. 0	1. 125					40. 0	1. 250

Year	Philadelphia, Pa.		St. Louis, Mo.		San Francisco, Calif.	
1929	[4] 44. 0	$1. 250	44. 0	$1. 125	44. 0	$1. 125
1930	[3] 44. 0	1. 250	44. 0	1. 125	44. 0	1. 125
1931	[3] 44. 0	1. 250	[5] 40. 0	1. 125	40. 0	1. 125
1932	[3] 44. 0	1. 250	[6] 44. 0	1. 000	40. 0	1. 063
1933	40. 0	1. 000	[6] 44. 0	1. 000	40. 0	1. 063

[1] Outside building work.
[2] 40 hours per week, November to March, inclusive.
[3] 40 hours per week, June to August, inclusive.
[4] 40 hours per week, July and August.
[5] 44 hours per week, June to August, inclusive.
[6] 40 hours per week, July to March, inclusive.

TABLE **B-30** (continued from p. 218).—*Tile layers, males, 1929-1933, by city and year*

Year	Atlanta, Ga.		Birmingham, Ala.		Boston, Mass.		Chicago, Ill.	
	Hours per week	Rate per hour	Hours per week	Rate per hour	Hours per week	Rate per hour	Hours per week	Rate per hour
1929	44. 0	$1. 250	44. 0	$1. 500	44. 0	$1. 500	44. 0	$1. 625
1930	44. 0	1. 250	44. 0	1. 500	44. 0	1. 500	44. 0	1. 625
1931	44. 0	1. 250	44. 0	1. 500	40. 0	1. 500	44. 0	1. 625
1932	44. 0	1. 250	44. 0	1. 000	40. 0	1. 500	44. 0	1. 375
1933	44. 0	1. 000	44. 0	1. 000	40. 0	1. 300	44. 0	1. 375

Year	Cincinnati, Ohio		Denver, Colo.		Detroit, Mich.		New Orleans, La.	
1929	44. 0	$1. 500	44. 0	$1. 375	44. 0	$1. 500	44. 0	$1. 250
1930	40. 0	1. 500	40. 0	1. 500	44. 0	1. 500	44. 0	1. 250
1931	40. 0	1. 500	40. 0	1. 500	40. 0	1. 500	44. 0	1. 250
1932	40. 0	1. 250	40. 0	1. 250	40. 0	1. 250	44. 0	1. 250
1933	40. 0	1. 000	40. 0	1. 000	40. 0	1. 250		

Year	New York, N. Y.		Philadelphia, Pa.		St. Louis, Mo.		San Francisco, Calif.	
1929	44. 0	$1. 500	44. 0	$1. 500	44. 0	$1. 500	44. 0	$1. 250
1930	40. 0	1. 650	40. 0	1. 500	44. 0	1. 500	40. 0	1. 250
1931	40. 0	1. 688	40. 0	1. 500	40. 0	1. 500	40. 0	1. 250
1932	40. 0	1. 438	40. 0	1. 250	40. 0	1. 250	40. 0	1. 125
1933	40. 0	1. 438	40. 0	1. 250	40. 0	1. 250	40. 0	1. 000

C.—CLOTHING INDUSTRY

TABLE **C-5** (continued from p. 223).—*Operators, coat, men's clothing, males, 1930 and 1932, by city and year*

Year	Baltimore, Md.		Boston, Mass.		Chicago, Ill.		Cincinnati, Ohio	
	Hours per week	Rate per hour	Hours per week	Rate per hour	Hours per week	Rate per hour	Hours per week	Rate per hour
1930	44.0	$0.725	44.0	$0.870	44.0	$1.132	42.6	$0.997
1932	44.0	.494	44.0	.600	44.0	.757	44.0	.651
	Cleveland, Ohio		New York, N. Y.		Philadelphia, Pa.		Rochester, N. Y.	
1930	44.0	$0.846	44.2	$0.960	44.0	$0.934	44.0	$0.969
1932	44.2	.391	44.1	.707	44.0	.666	44.0	.746

TABLE **C-6** (continued from p. 224).—*Operators, coat, females, men's clothing, 1930 and 1932, by city and year*

Year	Baltimore, Md.		Boston, Mass.		Chicago, Ill.		Cincinnati, Ohio	
	Hours per week	Rate per hour	Hours per week	Rate per hour	Hours per week	Rate per hour	Hours per week	Rate per hour
1930	44.0	$0.426	44.0	$0.496	44.0	$0.987	37.6	$0.702
1932	44.0	.262	44.0	.312	44.0	.680	44.0	.457
	Cleveland, Ohio		New York, N. Y.		Philadelphia, Pa.		Rochester, N. Y.	
1930	44.0	$0.559	44.7	$0.588	44.0	$0.513	44.0	$0.656
1932	44.1	.407	44.4	.434	44.0	.410	44.0	.502

535

D.—FARMING

FARM LABORERS

TABLE **D**-2 (continued from p. 227).—*Farm laborers, males, 1928–1933, by year and index number*

Year	Average farm wage				Index numbers of farm wages— 1910–1914 = 100
	Per month—		Per day—		
	With board	Without board	With board	Without board	
1928	$34. 66	$48. 65	$1. 88	$2. 43	169
1929	34. 74	49. 08	1. 88	2. 42	170
1930	31. 14	44. 59	1. 65	2. 16	152
1931	23. 60	35. 03	1. 22	1. 65	116
1932	17. 53	26. 67	. 88	1. 21	86
1933	15. 86	24. 51	. 86	1. 18	80

536

FARM LABORERS—Continued

TABLE **D-3** (continued from p. 228).—*Farm laborers, males, 1929–1933, by geographic division, State, and year*

Per month with board

Geographic division and State	1929	1930	1931	1932	1933
NORTH ATLANTIC					
Maine	$49.00	$45.00	$38.50	$24.25	$26.50
New Hampshire	49.00	45.00	35.25	27.25	25.50
Vermont	49.00	44.00	32.25	24.25	23.25
Massachusetts	51.00	48.75	41.75	31.75	29.00
Rhode Island	56.00	52.50	45.00	33.25	36.75
Connecticut	54.00	47.00	38.00	28.75	29.00
New York	50.50	45.00	35.25	25.50	22.50
New Jersey	51.00	45.25	36.50	29.25	25.50
Pennsylvania	40.25	36.00	29.50	21.25	21.25
Average	47.72	42.89	34.50	25.23	(¹)
NORTH CENTRAL					
Ohio	38.75	32.75	26.00	19.00	17.50
Indiana	37.25	32.25	26.00	19.50	18.00
Illinois	43.00	38.00	30.25	21.25	18.75
Michigan	44.25	32.50	23.50	16.75	15.75
Wisconsin	49.25	40.25	28.00	19.25	17.25
Minnesota	46.25	40.25	27.90	20.00	18.00
Iowa	48.75	47.25	31.75	21.25	18.00
Missouri	34.50	31.25	25.75	18.25	16.50
North Dakota	47.75	37.50	25.25	20.50	18.50
South Dakota	46.50	43.00	24.50	20.25	15.75
Nebraska	44.00	41.00	28.50	20.00	18.25
Kansas	39.00	34.50	25.50	19.00	17.75
Average	42.79	(¹)	27.33	19.59	(¹)
SOUTH ATLANTIC					
Delaware	35.50	33.25	21.50	20.50	19.75
Maryland	35.25	34.25	27.25	21.25	20.25
Virginia	31.00	26.75	22.00	17.00	17.00
West Virginia	33.50	28.50	23.25	18.00	18.50
North Carolina	28.75	22.25	16.00	11.50	13.75
South Carolina	19.50	16.50	11.00	9.00	9.50
Georgia	19.50	17.00	11.00	8.25	9.00
Florida	23.75	20.50	17.25	11.25	14.00
Average	25.52	21.75	16.07	12.19	13.06
SOUTH CENTRAL					
Kentucky	27.50	24.25	21.25	14.50	14.50
Tennessee	25.00	21.50	17.00	13.00	14.00
Alabama	21.00	17.00	11.00	8.50	9.25
Mississippi	22.50	17.75	12.00	9.75	10.50
Arkansas	24.50	21.00	15.00	12.50	13.00
Louisiana	24.50	20.50	15.75	11.75	12.50
Oklahoma	30.50	25.00	18.50	15.25	17.00
Texas	29.00	25.50	18.75	15.00	17.75
Average	25.86	21.96	16.40	12.75	(¹)
WESTERN					
Montana	57.25	45.00	31.00	26.00	25.00
Idaho	58.00	52.50	36.75	27.50	27.00
Wyoming	53.00	47.75	35.50	25.25	25.50
Colorado	45.50	40.50	29.50	21.00	21.50
New Mexico	36.00	37.75	26.75	20.25	22.00
Arizona	50.00	48.50	40.00	30.00	33.75
Utah	64.75	56.25	40.80	29.50	30.50
Nevada	65.00	54.00	43.25	33.50	32.50
Washington	54.50	43.75	29.50	21.50	23.75
Oregon	54.00	48.00	31.75	24.75	25.50
California	64.00	60.00	44.00	32.00	33.00
Average	56.54	51.23	36.95	27.35	(¹)
United States	35.90	31.31	23.31	17.29	17.19

¹ Not reported.

FARM LABORERS—Continued

TABLE **D-3** (continued from p. 229).—*Farm laborers, males, 1929–1933, by geographic division, State, and year*

Per month without board

Geographic division and State	1929	1930	1931	1932	1933
NORTH ATLANTIC					
Maine	$71.00	$66.00	$56.50	$41.00	$40.00
New Hampshire	72.00	73.00	59.75	46.00	44.50
Vermont	72.00	67.75	50.75	38.50	38.75
Massachusetts	80.00	78.50	72.50	57.50	52.00
Rhode Island	85.00	81.00	78.00	55.75	58.75
Connecticut	86.00	77.25	62.50	48.75	49.25
New York	70.75	64.75	53.50	41.25	36.00
New Jersey	76.00	71.25	60.75	50.00	43.00
Pennsylvania	60.00	54.25	46.00	35.00	34.25
Average	69.90	64.65	54.34	41.94	(¹)
NORTH CENTRAL					
Ohio	54.50	48.25	37.75	29.00	27.50
Indiana	50.00	43.25	36.50	28.25	26.50
Illinois	55.25	49.25	40.25	29.50	26.25
Michigan	61.75	47.75	36.50	26.75	26.25
Wisconsin	67.50	56.25	42.25	30.00	27.50
Minnesota	63.00	54.75	39.60	30.75	27.00
Iowa	60.25	58.00	41.50	29.25	25.25
Missouri	45.75	41.50	34.90	26.00	25.50
North Dakota	63.75	53.50	34.75	30.50	28.25
South Dakota	66.75	57.00	36.00	30.75	24.75
Nebraska	57.75	54.25	40.40	29.75	27.25
Kansas	54.75	49.00	37.75	29.50	27.50
Average	57.41	(¹)	38.51	28.98	(¹)
SOUTH ATLANTIC					
Delaware	53.50	45.00	40.00	32.00	30.50
Maryland	50.75	49.00	40.50	32.75	31.00
Virginia	43.00	38.50	32.00	25.00	24.75
West Virginia	48.50	43.25	34.50	27.50	28.00
North Carolina	39.25	31.25	23.10	17.25	20.00
South Carolina	27.50	24.25	16.25	13.25	13.75
Georgia	27.75	24.50	16.50	12.25	14.00
Florida	36.25	35.00	28.00	20.50	21.25
Average	36.02	31.65	23.88	18.45	19.46
SOUTH CENTRAL					
Kentucky	38.75	34.25	29.50	20.75	21.00
Tennessee	34.75	30.25	23.25	18.25	19.25
Alabama	27.00	25.00	16.00	13.25	13.25
Mississippi	32.25	25.75	18.75	14.50	15.25
Arkansas	35.25	26.25	21.00	18.00	18.75
Louisiana	37.75	30.25	24.00	17.75	18.00
Oklahoma	42.50	36.25	26.90	22.25	24.25
Texas	42.00	36.75	27.75	22.75	25.00
Average	36.70	31.23	23.78	18.85	(¹)
WESTERN					
Montana	77.00	60.00	45.00	38.50	36.00
Idaho	80.75	73.00	54.25	40.00	38.75
Wyoming	75.75	67.50	50.50	37.50	37.75
Colorado	66.50	57.00	46.75	34.75	33.50
New Mexico	52.00	52.00	40.25	31.25	31.25
Arizona	66.50	70.00	52.00	40.00	38.00
Utah	82.50	75.00	57.75	40.50	43.75
Nevada	91.00	84.50	63.75	57.00	45.75
Washington	78.00	69.75	49.00	38.75	41.25
Oregon	74.00	69.50	49.25	40.00	40.00
California	90.00	88.00	67.00	52.00	53.00
Average	78.93	73.97	55.83	43.26	(¹)
United States	50.00	44.36	34.22	26.36	25.89

¹ Not reported.

FARM LABORERS—Continued

TABLE **D-3** (continued from p. 230).—*Farm laborers, males, 1929–1933, by geographic division, State, and year*

Per day with board

Geographic division and State	1929	1930	1931	1932	1933
NORTH ATLANTIC					
Maine	$2.80	$2.60	$2.10	$1.40	$1.55
New Hampshire	2.60	2.35	2.00	1.35	1.40
Vermont	2.60	2.30	1.70	1.30	1.30
Massachusetts	2.80	2.35	2.25	1.60	1.60
Rhode Island	2.80	2.70	2.40	1.75	1.90
Connecticut	3.10	2.45	2.20	1.40	1.70
New York	3.05	2.70	2.10	1.45	1.35
New Jersey	2.75	2.70	2.00	1.60	1.35
Pennsylvania	2.60	2.25	1.80	1.25	1.25
Average	2.83	2.50	2.00	1.40	(¹)
NORTH CENTRAL					
Ohio	2.50	2.05	1.45	1.05	1.05
Indiana	2.30	1.85	1.40	1.00	1.00
Illinois	2.40	1.90	1.50	1.05	1.00
Michigan	2.75	1.95	1.30	1.00	1.00
Wisconsin	2.55	2.00	1.40	1.00	.95
Minnesota	2.60	2.15	1.55	1.10	1.05
Iowa	2.55	2.35	1.50	1.00	1.00
Missouri	1.75	1.55	1.15	.85	.85
North Dakota	2.45	1.85	1.10	1.00	1.05
South Dakota	2.80	2.20	1.20	1.00	.85
Nebraska	2.50	2.25	1.45	1.00	1.05
Kansas	2.50	2.00	1.30	1.00	1.05
Average	2.43	(¹)	1.39	1.00	(¹)
SOUTH ATLANTIC					
Delaware	2.40	2.05	1.70	1.05	1.35
Maryland	2.20	1.85	1.30	1.10	1.15
Virginia	1.60	1.40	1.00	.80	.85
West Virginia	1.65	1.35	1.10	.85	.95
North Carolina	1.40	1.10	.85	.60	.70
South Carolina	.95	.80	.55	.45	.50
Georgia	1.05	.85	.60	.45	.55
Florida	1.15	1.00	.80	.65	.65
Average	1.32	1.10	.82	.62	.70
SOUTH CENTRAL					
Kentucky	1.40	1.20	1.05	.70	.75
Tennessee	1.20	1.05	.85	.60	.70
Alabama	1.10	.85	.50	.45	.50
Mississippi	1.15	.85	.55	.45	.55
Arkansas	1.30	1.00	.75	.55	.60
Louisiana	1.25	1.00	.80	.60	.65
Oklahoma	1.70	1.30	.95	.80	.90
Texas	1.45	1.20	.90	.70	.90
Average	1.32	1.07	.80	.61	(¹)
WESTERN					
Montana	3.05	2.20	1.50	1.25	1.30
Idaho	2.90	2.50	1.65	1.25	1.45
Wyoming	2.65	2.35	1.65	1.15	1.20
Colorado	2.45	2.15	1.40	1.00	1.10
New Mexico	1.90	1.70	1.10	.85	1.00
Arizona	1.90	2.10	1.70	1.20	1.25
Utah	2.55	2.40	2.00	1.45	1.45
Nevada	2.75	2.35	1.75	1.45	1.35
Washington	2.80	2.25	1.70	1.20	1.30
Oregon	2.70	2.40	1.60	1.25	1.25
California	2.60	2.60	1.90	1.35	1.40
Average	2.57	2.36	1.69	1.24	(¹)
United States	1.92	1.61	1.18	.87	.91

¹ Not reported.

FARM LABORERS—Continued

TABLE **D-3** (continued from p. 231).—*Farm laborers, males, 1929–1933, by geographic division, State, and year*

Per day without board

Geographic division and State	1929	1930	1931	1932	1933
NORTH ATLANTIC					
Maine	$3.45	$3.20	$2.80	$1.95	$2.05
New Hampshire	3.50	3.20	2.90	2.10	2.15
Vermont	3.45	3.10	2.50	1.90	1.85
Massachusetts	3.80	3.45	3.20	2.50	2.35
Rhode Island	3.85	3.60	3.00	2.35	2.35
Connecticut	4.00	3.55	3.10	2.40	2.35
New York	3.85	3.50	2.75	2.00	1.90
New Jersey	3.65	3.40	2.70	2.15	1.90
Pennsylvania	3.30	2.90	2.40	1.75	1.70
Average	3.63	3.27	2.70	2.00	(¹)
NORTH CENTRAL					
Ohio	3.15	2.70	1.95	1.40	1.45
Indiana	2.85	2.40	1.75	1.30	1.30
Illinois	2.90	2.45	1.90	1.30	1.35
Michigan	3.35	2.60	1.80	1.35	1.40
Wisconsin	3.15	2.65	2.00	1.45	1.40
Minnesota	3.40	2.85	2.15	1.55	1.50
Iowa	3.20	2.95	2.05	1.35	1.35
Missouri	2.15	2.00	1.55	1.15	1.10
North Dakota	3.75	2.70	1.60	1.35	1.60
South Dakota	3.55	2.90	1.85	1.45	1.30
Nebraska	3.30	2.90	2.00	1.40	1.45
Kansas	3.20	2.70	1.80	1.40	1.40
Average	3.07	(¹)	1.88	1.36	(¹)
SOUTH ATLANTIC					
Delaware	3.05	2.55	2.05	1.40	1.60
Maryland	2.85	2.40	2.00	1.50	1.55
Virginia	2.00	1.85	1.35	1.10	1.10
West Virginia	2.30	1.90	1.55	1.20	1.25
North Carolina	1.80	1.45	1.05	.80	.90
South Carolina	1.20	1.05	.75	.60	.70
Georgia	1.35	1.10	.75	.60	.70
Florida	1.60	1.50	1.20	.90	.90
Average	1.71	1.46	1.08	.84	.91
SOUTH CENTRAL					
Kentucky	1.80	1.55	1.40	.95	1.00
Tennessee	1.50	1.30	1.05	.80	.90
Alabama	1.40	1.10	.80	.60	.70
Mississippi	1.60	1.15	.75	.60	.75
Arkansas	1.70	1.40	1.00	.75	.85
Louisiana	1.55	1.30	1.10	.80	.85
Oklahoma	2.20	1.70	1.20	1.00	1.25
Texas	1.90	1.60	1.20	.95	1.10
Average	1.72	1.40	1.07	.82	(¹)
WESTERN					
Montana	3.80	3.05	2.20	1.85	1.85
Idaho	3.80	3.15	2.20	1.65	1.80
Wyoming	3.45	3.25	2.00	1.55	1.75
Colorado	3.00	2.90	2.00	1.45	1.55
New Mexico	2.30	2.10	1.50	1.20	1.30
Arizona	2.60	2.50	2.00	1.35	1.40
Utah	3.25	3.00	2.50	1.80	1.80
Nevada	3.75	3.00	2.55	2.25	1.85
Washington	3.65	3.40	2.60	1.80	2.00
Oregon	3.40	3.40	2.25	1.70	1.75
California	3.60	3.40	2.60	2.00	2.15
Average	3.39	3.14	2.32	1.75	(¹)
United States	2.46	2.12	1.59	1.19	1.25

¹ Not reported.

E.—GLASS AND CLAY PRODUCTS

TABLE E-4 (continued from p. 234).—*Blowers, hand, males, 1932, by State*

Year	Indiana		New Jersey		New York		Ohio	
	Hours per week	Rate per hour	Hours per week	Rate per hour	Hours per week	Rate per hour	Hours per week	Rate per hour
1932	44.4	$0.874	46.3	$0.958	46.9	$1.024	47.7	$0.997

Year	Pennsylvania		Virginia		West Virginia			
1932	47.1	$1.122			45.9	$0.806		

TABLE E-7 (continued from p. 235).—*Jiggers, males, 1932, by group and kind of ware*

[For semivitreous potteries the geographical groups are: Group 1, East Liverpool, Ohio, and nearby potteries in West Virginia directly across the Ohio River from East Liverpool; Group 2, Ohio, outside East Liverpool and Pennsylvania, Illinois, and Indiana; Group 3, Maryland, Tennessee, and Virginia; Group 4, West Virginia, other than those near East Liverpool and those in New Jersey. The geographical groups of vitreous potteries are: Group 1, New York; group 2, Pennsylvania; group 3, Ohio and West Virginia]

Year	Semivitreous ware							
	Group 1		Group 2		Group 3		Group 4	
	Hours per week	Earnings per hour	Hours per week	Earnings per hour	Hours per week	Earnings per hour	Hours per week	Earnings per hour
1932	(¹)	$0.694	(¹)	$0.635	(¹)	$0.701	(¹)	$0.702

Year	Vitreous ware							
1932	(¹)	$0.691	(¹)	$0.847	(¹)	$0.704		

¹ Not reported.

TABLE **E-9** (continued from p. 236).—*Kiln placers, bisque, and glost, males, 1932, by group and kind of ware*

Year	Bisque—semivitreous ware							
	Group 1		Group 2		Group 3		Group 4	
	Hours per week	Rate per hour	Hours per week	Rate per hour	Hours per week	Rate per hour	Hours per week	Rate per hour
1932	(¹)	$0. 729	(¹)	$0. 749	(¹)	$0. 848	(¹)	$0. 900
	Bisque—vitreous ware							
1932	(¹)	$0. 711	(¹)	$0. 816	(¹)	$0. 870		
	Glost—semivitreous ware							
1932	(¹)	$0. 744	(¹)	$0. 747	(¹)	$0. 853	(¹)	$0. 742

¹ Not reported.

TABLE **E-12** (continued from p. 237).—*Turners, males, 1932, by group and kind of ware*

Year	Semivitreous ware							
	Group 1		Group 2		Group 3		Group 4	
	Hours per week	Rate per hour	Hours per week	Rate per hour	Hours per week	Rate per hour	Hours per week	Rate per hour
1932	(¹)	$0. 870	(¹)	$0. 631	(¹)	$1. 035	(¹)	$0. 662
	Vitreous ware							
1932	(¹)	$0. 619	(¹)	$0. 768	(¹)	$0. 735		

¹ Not reported.

F.—IRON AND STEEL INDUSTRY

TABLE **F-3** (continued from p. 241).—*Catchers, males, bar mills, 1929, 1931, and 1933, by geographic division and year*

Year	Eastern		Pittsburgh		Great Lakes and Middle West		Southern	
	Hours per week	Rate per hour	Hours per week	Rate per hour	Hours per week	Rate per hour	Hours per week	Rate per hour
1929	55.1	$0.742	53.9	$0.991	54.2	$0.953	62.8	$0.647
1931	58.6	.658	56.2	.886	51.3	.884	57.2	.631
1933	55.3	.493	56.5	.611	52.9	.618	56.9	.430

TABLE **F-6** (continued from p. 243).—*Rollers, males, bar mills, 1929, 1931, and 1933, by geographic division*

Year	Eastern		Pittsburgh		Great Lakes and Middle West		Southern	
	Hours per week	Rate per hour	Hours per week	Rate per hour	Hours per week	Rate per hour	Hours per week	Rate per hour
1929	55.7	$1.430	54.6	$1.996	52.1	$1.905	61.1	$1.635
1931	58.9	1.291	54.8	1.711	52.8	1.445	57.0	1.513
1933	55.5	.901	54.4	1.118	52.5	.829	57.1	1.047

TABLE **F-9** (continued from p. 245).—*Roughers, males, bar mills, 1929, 1931, and 1933, by geographic division*

Year	Eastern		Pittsburgh		Great Lakes and Middle West		Southern	
	Hours per week	Rate per hour	Hours per week	Rate per hour	Hours per week	Rate per hour	Hours per week	Rate per hour
1929	54.5	$0.785	55.4	$0.967	53.5	$1.015	61.8	$0.641
1931	58.7	.660	56.5	.895	53.7	.900	57.8	.657
1933	56.2	.487	55.3	.671	53.8	.633	57.9	.438

TABLE **F-12** (continued from p. 247).—*Puddlers, males, puddling mills, 1929, 1931, and 1933, by year*

Year	United States	
	Hours per week	Rate per hour
1929	52.1	$0.784
1931	54.3	.793
1933	52.6	.634

543

TABLE **F-15** (continued from p. 249).—*Keepers, males, blast furnaces, 1929, 1931, and 1933, by geographic division and year*

Year	Eastern		Pittsburgh		Great Lakes and Middle West		Southern	
	Hours per week	Rate per hour	Hours per week	Rate per hour	Hours per week	Rate per hour	Hours per week	Rate per hour
1929	61.9	$0.543	55.1	$0.632	55.5	$0.624	69.3	$0.368
1931	57.4	.525	52.7	.630	55.4	.611	57.3	.421
1933	53.6	.399	54.5	.468	53.7	.465	55.1	.361

TABLE **F-20** (continued from p. 252).—*Skip operators, males, blast furnaces, 1929, 1931, and 1933, by geographic division and year*

Year	Eastern		Pittsburgh		Great Lakes and Middle West		Southern	
	Hours per week	Rate per hour	Hours per week	Rate per hour	Hours per week	Rate per hour	Hours per week	Rate per hour
1929	65.0	$0.494	55.3	$0.601	55.5	$0.612	69.3	$0.351
1931	68.6	.491	53.3	.572	55.5	.611	58.2	.408
1933	56.0	.420	56.7	.439	53.6	.439	56.5	.359

H.—LEATHER AND ITS PRODUCTS

BOOTS AND SHOES

TABLE **H-5** (continued from p. 264).—*Cutters, vamp and whole shoe, hand, males, 1930 and 1932, by State and year*

Year	Massachusetts		New Hampshire		New York		Ohio	
	Hours per week	Rate per hour	Hours per week	Rate per hour	Hours per week	Rate per hour	Hours per week	Rate per hour
1930	48.3	$0.859	49.4	$0.649	47.6	$0.894	49.6	$0.780
1932	48.5	.695	48.5	.508	47.8	.713	49.7	.549

TABLE **H-10** (continued from p. 266).—*Vampers, males, 1930 and 1932, by State and year*

Year	Massachusetts		New Hampshire		New York	
	Hours per week	Rate per hour	Hours per week	Rate per hour	Hours per week	Rate per hour
1930	48.2	$0.666	48.0	$0.340	46.4	$0.791
1932	48.2	.601	48.0	.392	46.3	.649

TABLE **H-13** (continued from p. 267).—*Vampers, females, 1930 and 1932, by State and year*

Year	Massachusetts		New Hampshire		New York		Ohio	
	Hours per week	Rate per hour	Hours per week	Rate per hour	Hours per week	Rate per hour	Hours per week	Rate per hour
1930	47.9	$0.581	48.7	$0.423	48.6	$0.503	47.3	$0.409
1932	47.9	.447	48.5	.345	48.7	.376	47.3	.328

TABLE **H-17** (continued from p. 269).—*Bed-machine operators, males, 1930 and 1932, by State and year*

Year	Massachusetts		New Hampshire		New York		Ohio	
	Hours per week	Rate per hour	Hours per week	Rate per hour	Hours per week	Rate per hour	Hours per week	Rate per hour
1930	48.2	$0.723	49.1	$0.540	48.4	$0.649	47.7	$0.672
1932	48.2	.596	48.4	.439	48.6	.567	47.5	.523

BOOTS AND SHOES—Continued

Table **H–19** (continued from p. 270).—*Hand-method lasting machine operators, males, 1930 and 1932, by State and year*

Year	Massachusetts		New Hampshire		New York		Ohio	
	Hours per week	Rate per hour	Hours per week	Rate per hour	Hours per week	Rate per hour	Hours per week	Rate per hour
1930	48.5	$0.732	51.5	$0.508	(1)	(1)	(1)	(1)
1932	49.8	.600	(1)	(1)	(1)	(1)	50.0	$0.531

1 Establishments or wage earners too few for which to show data.

Table **H–23** (continued from p. 271).—*McKay sewers, males, 1930 and·1932, by State and year*

Year	Massachusetts		New Hampshire		New York		Ohio	
	Hours per week	Rate per hour	Hours per week	Rate per hour	Hours per week	Rate per hour	Hours per week	Rate per hour
1930	48.4	$0.862	51.6	$0.554	48.1	$0.784	46.0	$0.588
1932	49.1	.621	49.0	.545	48.7	.588	47.5	.590

I.—METAL TRADES (OTHER THAN IRON AND STEEL)

TABLE I-4 (continued from p. 283).—*Blacksmiths, males, machine shops, 1929, 1931, and 1933, by State and year*

Year	California		Connecticut		Illinois		Indiana	
	Hours per week	Rate per hour	Hours per week	Rate per hour	Hours per week	Rate per hour	Hours per week	Rate per hour
1929	46.5	$0.929	50.8	$0.712	50.0	$0.777	51.1	$0.705
1931	46.0	.873	50.1	.708	50.3	.742	51.3	.727
1933	44.4	.673	49.4	.623	49.0	.630	51.3	.580

	Massachusetts		Michigan		Minnesota		New Jersey	
1929	48.6	$0.730	51.2	$0.765	50.1	$0.667	49.8	$0.715
1931	48.1	.737	50.2	.686	49.1	.638	49.6	.729
1933	46.9	.567	50.1	.515	48.6	.515	48.6	.573

	New York		Ohio		Pennsylvania		Wisconsin	
1929	49.0	$0.804	49.8	$0.701	51.4	$0.733	50.9	$0.759
1931	49.4	.743	50.2	.705	56.7	.766	50.8	.754
1933	48.5	.640	49.2	.636	49.2	.608	51.3	.559

TABLE I-11 (continued from p. 292).—*Coremakers, males, 1929, 1931, and 1933, by State and year*

Year	California		Connecticut		Illinois		Indiana	
	Hours per week	Rate per hour	Hours per week	Rate per hour	Hours per week	Rate per hour	Hours per week	Rate per hour
1929	45.0	$0.923	48.6	$0.778	49.4	$0.741	50.9	$0.723
1931	45.3	.916	49.4	.693	49.3	.683	51.3	.602
1933	43.5	.728	50.0	.566	47.8	.523	52.6	.435

	Iowa		Massachusetts		Michigan		New Jersey	
1929	52.1	$0.756	48.6	$0.842	50.9	$0.711	51.5	$0.835
1931	52.5	.677	47.1	.835	51.4	.619	50.0	.770
1933	50.4	.607	46.6	.687	50.9	.433	49.6	.586

	New York		Ohio		Pennsylvania		Wisconsin	
1929	50.1	$0.711	50.1	$0.784	50.2	$0.749	49.0	$0.740
1931	49.1	.707	50.0	.759	50.1	.745	51.1	.695
1933	48.3	.603	50.6	.540	48.0	.617	49.4	.505

547

TABLE **I-17** (continued from p. 296).—*Laborers, males, foundries, 1929, 1931, and 1933, by State and year*

Year	Alabama		California		Illinois		Louisiana	
	Hours per week	Rate per hour	Hours per week	Rate per hour	Hours per week	Rate per hour	Hours per week	Rate per hour
1929	53. 4	$0. 297	46. 4	$0. 585	50. 6	$0. 541	56. 6	$0. 293
1931	53. 6	. 297	46. 3	. 553	49. 9	. 495	52. 3	. 284
1933	50. 0	. 216	44. 4	. 495	48. 3	. 402	47. 3	. 273
	Maryland		Massachusetts		Michigan		Missouri	
1929	53. 3	$0. 391	48. 7	$0. 518	52. 7	$0. 533	53. 7	$0. 431
1931	51. 4	. 391	47. 9	. 487	52. 9	. 470	53. 8	. 407
1933	50. 8	. 305	46. 9	. 480	51. 6	. 355	52. 0	. 336
	New Hampshire		New York		Ohio		Pennsylvania	
1929	50. 5	$0. 456	51. 5	$0. 534	53. 4	$0. 467	52. 7	$0. 468
1931	50. 4	. 409	49. 3	. 485	51. 8	. 460	50. 3	˙. 483
1933	49. 1	. 461	49. 2	. 415	51. 4	. 353	49. 9	. 366

TABLE **I-18** (continued from p. 296).—*Laborers, males, machine shops, 1929, 1931, and 1933, by State and year*

Year	Alabama		California		Illinois		Louisiana	
	Hours per week	Rate per hour	Hours per week	Rate per hour	Hours per week	Rate per hour	Hours per week	Rate per hour
1929	50. 7	$0. 299	46. 1	$0. 573	49. 8	$0. 509	58. 0	$0. 280
1931	53. 3	. 320	44. 9	. 513	50. 0	. 474	56. 5	. 240
1933	53. 5	. 218	44. 5	. 425	49. 0	. 396	53. 0	. 194
	Maryland		Massachusetts		Michigan		Missouri	
1929	51. 0	$0. 429	49. 6	$0. 484	51. 9	$0. 479	52. 0	$0. 408
1931	49. 5	. 422	49. 4	. 471	53. 8	. 475	53. 4	. 407
1933	48. 6	. 359	46. 8	. 414	47. 4	. 410	50. 8	. 313
	New Hampshire		New York		Ohio		Pennsylvania	
1929	48. 5	$0. 462	48. 7	$0. 511	49. 8	$0. 463	52. 0	$0. 443
1931	48. 6	. 487	49. 4	. 501	49. 9	. 449	51. 4	. 446
1933	49. 0	. 443	48. 0	. 426	49. 1	. 357	49. 3	. 385

TABLE I-20 (continued from p. 297).—*Lathe hands and operators, turret, males, 1929, 1931, and 1933, by State and year*

Year	California		Connecticut		Illinois		Indiana	
	Hours per week	Rate per hour	Hours per week	Rate per hour	Hours per week	Rate per hour	Hours per week	Rate per hour
1929	47.1	$0.770	52.1	$0.689	50.5	$0.798	50.7	$0.655
1931	45.2	.803	49.8	.637	48.8	.732	50.7	.644
1933	43.9	.735	46.4	.631	47.7	.615	50.2	.501
	Massachusetts		Michigan		Minnesota		New Jersey	
1929	48.9	$0.695	51.7	$0.670	49.8	$0.673	50.2	$0.789
1931	48.8	.674	52.0	.588	49.5	.644	49.3	.809
1933	46.6	.559	49.6	.549	50.3	.559	49.3	.623
	New York		Ohio		Pennsylvania		Wisconsin	
1929	49.2	$0.705	50.6	$0.703	52.2	$0.673	53.3	$0.706
1931	50.1	.682	49.9	.650	50.5	.653	51.2	.680
1933	49.4	.579	49.4	.522	49.1	.526	50.6	.517

TABLE I-21 (continued from p. 298).—*Lathe hands and operators, engine, males, 1929, 1931, and 1933, by State and year*

Year	California		Connecticut		Illinois		Indiana	
	Hours per week	Rate per hour	Hours per week	Rate per hour	Hours per week	Rate per hour	Hours per week	Rate per hour
1929	45.5	$0.859	51.2	$0.674	50.7	$0.770	51.4	$0.671
1931	44.7	.880	50.2	.668	50.0	.724	51.7	.597
1933	44.7	.665	49.5	.619	48.5	.605	51.0	.512
	Massachusetts		Michigan		New Jersey		New York	
1929	49.9	$0.654	51.2	$0.679	49.7	$0.769	48.6	$0.777
1931	49.2	.708	51.6	.670	49.4	.742	49.3	.748
1933	46.1	.541	50.4	.541	48.4	.623	48.2	.648
	Ohio		Pennsylvania		Rhode Island		Wisconsin	
1929	50.5	$0.702	52.1	$0.732	51.6	$0.614	51.3	$0.722
1931	50.2	.698	50.7	.708	50.1	.599	51.4	.703
1933	50.4	.597	50.3	.570	50.4	.521	50.9	.546

TABLE I-27 (continued from p. 308).—*Machinists, males, machine shops, 1929, 1931, and 1933, by State and year*

Year	Alabama		California		Illinois		Louisiana	
	Hours per week	Rate per hour	Hours per week	Rate per hour	Hours per week	Rate per hour	Hours per week	Rate per hour
1929	51.1	$0.723	44.9	$0.891	46.5	$0.826	49.9	$0.798
1931	52.6	.718	44.9	.915	48.0	.801	49.2	.892
1933	49.9	.524	43.5	.724	48.5	.628	47.2	.633

	Maryland		Massachusetts		Michigan		Missouri	
1929	48.3	$0.690	49.5	$0.661	51.1	$0.774	51.4	$0.708
1931	46.1	.734	47.0	.701	50.1	.773	47.7	.751
1933	45.8	.671	45.9	.656	46.4	.649	49.3	.648

	New Hampshire		New York		Ohio		Pennsylvania	
1929	51.2	$0.674	48.8	$0.766	50.3	$0.756	52.2	$0.690
1931	49.5	.634	48.6	.779	49.7	.705	51.1	.701
1933	49.0	.589	47.7	.688	49.0	.581	48.9	.593

TABLE I-30 (continued from p. 310).—*Millwrights, males, slaughtering and meat packing, 1929 and 1931, by districts*

Year	District 1, Chicago		District 2 [1]		District 3 [2]		District 4 [3]	
	Hours per week	Rate per hour	Hours per week	Rate per hour	Hours per week	Rate per hour	Hours per week	Rate per hour
1929	48.0	$0.735	48.0	$0.621	51.1	$0.633	48.3	$0.627
1931	48.2	.655	48.0	.573	49.2	.587	47.1	.561

	District 5 [4]		District 6 [5]		District 7 [6]		District 8 [7]	
1929	49.7	$0.627	49.0	$0.745	56.5	$0.510	48.8	$0.688
1931	48.9	.583	51.0	.640	57.5	.395	48.0	.652

[1] Kansas City, Omaha, St. Joseph, St. Louis, and East St. Louis.
[2] Austin (Minn.), Cedar Rapids, Des Moines, Mason City, Milwaukee, Ottumwa, Sioux City, Sioux Falls, South St. Paul, Topeka, Waterloo, and Wichita.
[3] Dallas, Fort Worth, Houston, and Oklahoma City.
[4] Buffalo, Cincinnati, Cleveland, Detroit, Indianapolis, Pittsburgh, and Wheeling.
[5] 1929, Boston, New Haven, New York, Philadelphia, and Springfield (Mass.). 1931 included Jersey City.
[6] Baltimore, Jacksonville (Fla.), and Moultrie (Ga.).
[7] Denver, Los Angeles, Portland (Oreg.), San Francisco, Seattle, and Tacoma.

TABLE I–34 (continued from p. 317).—*Molders, hand, floor, males, 1929, 1931, and 1933, by State and year*

Year	Alabama		California		Illinois		Louisiana	
	Hours per week	Rate per hour	Hours per week	Rate per hour	Hours per week	Rate per hour	Hours per week	Rate per hour
1929	53.5	$0.727	44.9	$0.996	49.5	$0.864	56.5	$0.731
1931	53.5	.703	44.9	.978	49.1	.803	53.6	.651
1933	49.3	.538	43.0	.756	48.3	.598	47.1	.565
	Maryland		Massachusetts		Michigan		Missouri	
1929	49.0	$0.790	48.4	$0.918	51.5	$0.804	51.8	$0.785
1931	47.7	.764	47.3	.958	51.8	.694	52.2	.720
1933	47.1	.641	47.0	.723	48.9	.598	52.4	.590
	New Hampshire		New York		Ohio		Pennsylvania	
1929	51.1	$0.714	48.9	$0.847	50.4	$0.878	50.7	$0.805
1931	51.1	.674	50.2	.772	50.5	.825	50.3	.790
1933	46.0	.621	48.5	.680	50.1	.599	48.4	.622

TABLE I–35 (continued from p. 318).—*Molders, machine, males, 1929, 1931, and 1933, by State and year*

Year	Alabama		California		Illinois		Louisiana	
	Hours per week	Rate per hour	Hours per week	Rate per hour	Hours per week	Rate per hour	Hours per week	Rate per hour
1929	(1)	(1)	46.7	$0.685	50.1	$0.780	58.0	$0.397
1931	(1)	(1)	45.0	.733	50.2	.680	52.5	.385
1933	(1)	(1)	46.5	.485	47.9	.505	(1)	(1)
	Maryland		Massachusetts		Michigan		Missouri	
1929	51.2	$0.609	48.4	$0.794	51.5	$0.679	50.6	$0.710
1931	49.7	.600	43.8	.704	50.8	.543	52.8	.652
1933	47.1	.562	46.3	.640	51.4	.401	52.8	.372
	New Hampshire		New York		Ohio		Pennsylvania	
1929	52.8	$0.585	49.5	$0.723	49.4	$0.814	49.8	$0.724
1931	52.0	.565	47.9	.655	50.0	.733	51.7	.683
1933	46.7	.571	48.6	.559	49.7	.494	48.3	.557

1 Establishments or wage earners too few for which to show data.

TABLE **I–40** (continued from p. 326).—*Pattern makers, foundries, 1929, 1931, and 1933, by State and year*

Year	Alabama		California		Illinois		Louisiana	
	Hours per week	Rate per hour	Hours per week	Rate per hour	Hours per week	Rate per hour	Hours per week	Rate per hour
1929	52.7	$0.767	44.8	$1.094	50.2	$0.797	(1)	(1)
1931	55.0	.802	44.3	1.101	48.8	.862	(1)	(1)
1933	50.6	.603	43.2	.804	46.1	.707	53.4	$0.557
	Maryland		Massachusetts		Michigan		Missouri	
1929	48.8	$0.796	48.4	$0.731	50.6	$0.901	49.2	$0.991
1931	47.5	.702	47.9	.813	49.1	.843	50.2	.866
1933	47.8	.619	48.1	.718	51.4	.600	52.1	.602
	New Hampshire		New York		Ohio		Pennsylvania	
1929	53.0	$0.717	49.9	$0.820	50.3	$0.820	51.0	$0.766
1931	50.0	.518	48.1	.825	50.5	.833	51.2	.755
1933	50.0	.505	49.8	.702	50.7	.620	48.2	.651

1 Establishments or wage earners too few for which to show data.

TABLE **I–43** (continued from p. 327).—*Tool makers, 1929, 1931, and 1933, by State and year*

Year	California		Connecticut		Illinois		Indiana	
	Hours per week	Rate per hour	Hours per week	Rate per hour	Hours per week	Rate per hour	Hours per week	Rate per hour
1929	45.9	$0.983	51.4	$0.809	49.9	$0.783	50.4	$0.758
1931	45.4	.909	49.7	.768	49.8	.797	50.9	.673
1933	44.7	.787	49.7	.621	49.2	.659	50.4	.609
	Massachusetts		Michigan		New Jersey		New York	
1929	50.3	$0.737	51.8	$0.827	49.5	$0.797	48.4	$0.826
1931	47.8	.640	52.2	.821	49.4	.785	48.6	.802
1933	47.0	.611	49.7	.591	48.9	.621	48.0	.732
	Ohio		Pennsylvania		Rhode Island		Wisconsin	
1929	49.9	$0.784	51.1	$0.753	51.0	$0.686	50.7	$0.759
1931	49.5	.759	50.6	.750	50.5	.768	51.0	.761
1933	48.3	.570	48.9	.660	50.5	.686	50.8	.605

J.—MINING INDUSTRY

TABLE **J-2** (continued from p. 329).—*Drivers, males, coal mining, 1929, 1931, 1933, by State and year*

Year	Alabama		Colorado		Illinois		Indiana	
	Hours per week	Rate per hour	Hours per week	Rate per hour	Hours per week	Rate per hour	Hours per week	Rate per hour
1929	(¹)	$0.343	(¹)	$0.820	(¹)	$0.763	(¹)	$0.768
1931	(¹)	.366	(¹)	.836	(¹)	.766	(¹)	.740
1933	(¹)	.237	(¹)	.601	(¹)	.621	(¹)	.577
	Kansas		Kentucky		Ohio		Pennsylvania	
1929	(¹)	$0.634	(¹)	$0.522	(¹)	$0.621	(¹)	$0.683
1931	(¹)	.629	(¹)	.470	(¹)	.538	(¹)	.634
1933	(¹)	.439	(¹)	.335	(¹)	.394	(¹)	.410
	Tennessee		Virginia		West Virginia		Wyoming	
1929	(¹)	$0.433	(¹)	$0.408	(¹)	$0.550	--------	--------
1931	(¹)	.399	(²)		(¹)	.509	--------	--------
1933	(¹)	.298	(¹)	.300	(¹)	.367	--------	--------

¹ Not reported.　　　² No data.

TABLE **J-4** (continued from p. 330).—*Loaders, males, coal mining, 1929, 1931, and 1933, by State and year*

Year	Alabama		Colorado		Illinois		Indiana	
	Hours per week	Rate per hour	Hours per week	Rate per hour	Hours per week	Rate per hour	Hours per week	Rate per hour
1929	(¹)	² $0.388	(¹)	² $0.736	(¹)	² $0.857	(¹)	² $0.922
1931	(¹)	² .376	(¹)	² .731	(¹)	² .871	(¹)	² .939
1933	(¹)	² .245	(¹)	² .567	(¹)	² .611	(¹)	² .631
	Kansas		Kentucky		Ohio		Pennsylvania	
1929	(¹)	² $0.719	(¹)	² $0.595	(¹)	² $0.592	(¹)	² $0.601
1931	(¹)	(³)	(¹)	² .538	(¹)	² .482	(¹)	² .534
1933	(¹)	² .327	(¹)	² .348	(¹)	² .331	(¹)	² .329
	Tennessee		Virginia		West Virginia		Wyoming	
1929	(¹)	² $0.464	(¹)	² $0.549	(¹)	² $0.653	--------	--------
1931	(¹)	² .362	(¹)	² .494	(¹)	² .533	--------	--------
1933	(¹)	² .300	(¹)	² .292	(¹)	² .362	--------	--------

¹ Not reported.
² Average earnings per hour based on time at face, including lunch.
³ Not reported separately.

553

TABLE **J-6** (continued from p. 332).—*Miners, hand or pick, males, coal mining, 1929, 1931, and 1933, by State and year*

Year	Alabama		Colorado		Illinois		Indiana	
	Hours per week	Rate per hour	Hours per week	Rate per hour	Hours per week	Rate per hour	Hours per week	Rate per hour
1929	(¹)	² $0. 531	(¹)	² $0. 853	(¹)	² $0. 716	(¹)	² $0. 796
1931	(¹)	² . 463	(¹)	² . 664	(¹)	² . 705	(¹)	² . 856
1933	(¹)	² . 239	(¹)	² . 537	(¹)	² . 509	(¹)	² . 668
	Kansas		Kentucky		Ohio		Pennsylvania	
1929	(¹)	² $0. 711	(¹)	² $0. 623	(¹)	(³)	(¹)	² $0. 657
1931	(¹)	² . 615	(¹)	² . 541	(⁴)	(⁴)	(¹)	² . 560
1933	(¹)	² . 397	(¹)	² . 319	(⁴)	(⁴)	(¹)	² . 340
	Tennessee		Virginia		West Virginia		Wyoming	
1929	(¹)	³ $0. 500			(¹)	² $0. 669		
1931	(¹)	² . 368			(¹)	² . 606		
1933	(¹)	² . 278	(¹)	² $0. 210	(¹)	² . 364		

¹ Not reported.
² Average earnings per hour based on time at face, including lunch.
³ Not reported separately.
⁴ No data.

TABLE **J-8** (continued from p. 334).—*Muckers, males, iron mining, 1931, by State*

Year	Alabama		Michigan	
	Hours per week	Rate per hour	Hours per week	Rate per hour
1931	57. 1	$0. 365	48. 0	$0. 530

TABLE **J-9** (continued from p. 335).—*Drilling-machine operators, company, males, iron mining, 1931, by State*

Year	Alabama		Michigan		Minnesota	
	Hours per week	Rate per hour	Hours per week	Rate per hour	Hours per week	Rate per hour
1931	59. 7	$0. 486	41. 9	$0. 806	49. 5	$0. 646

TABLE **J–11** (continued from p. 335).——*Bratticemen and timbermen, coal mining, 1929, 1931, and 1933, by State and year*

Year	Alabama		Colorado		Illinois		Indiana	
	Hours per week	Rates per hour	Hours per week	Rate per hour	Hours per week	Rate per hour	Hours per week	Rate per hour
1929	([1])	$0. 424	([1])	$0. 827	([1])	$0. 765	([1])	$0. 769
1931	([1])	. 421	([1])	. 833	([1])	. 766	([1])	. 771
1933	([1])	. 285	([1])	. 599	([1])	. 623	([1])	. 594

Year	Kansas		Kentucky		Ohio		Pennsylvania	
1929	([1])	$0. 632	([1])	$0. 569	([1])	$0. 625	([1])	$0. 696
1931	([1])	. 637	([1])	. 538	([1])	. 537	([1])	. 651
1933	([1])	. 406	([1])	. 372	([1])	. 389	([1])	. 448

Year	Tennessee		Virginia		West Virginia		Wyoming	
1929	([1])	$0. 434	([1])	$0. 500	([1])	$0. 579		
1931	([1])	. 428	([1])	. 484	([1])	. 528		
1933	([1])	. 316	([1])	. 354	([1])	. 377		

[1] Not reported.

K.—PRINTING AND PUBLISHING

Table **K–3** (continued from p. 339).—*Bookbinders, journeymen, males, book and job, 1929–1933, by city and year*

Year	Atlanta, Ga. Hours per week	Atlanta, Ga. Rate per hour	Birmingham, Ala. Hours per week	Birmingham, Ala. Rate per hour	Boston, Mass. Hours per week	Boston, Mass. Rate per hour	Chicago, Ill. Hours per week	Chicago, Ill. Rate per hour
1929	44.0	$0.909	44.0	$0.800	48.0	$0.865	44.0	$1.070
1930	44.0	.909	44.0	.800	48.0	.865	44.0	1.070
1931	44.0	.909	44.0	.800	48.0	.865	44.0	1.070
1932	44.0	.909	44.0	.800	44.0	.977	44.0	.968
1933	44.0	.909	44.0	.800	44.0	.880	44.0	.968

Year	Cincinnati, Ohio Hours per week	Cincinnati, Ohio Rate per hour	Denver, Colo. Hours per week	Denver, Colo. Rate per hour	Detroit, Mich. Hours per week	Detroit, Mich. Rate per hour	New Orleans, La. Hours per week	New Orleans, La. Rate per hour
1929	44.0	$0.864	44.0	$1.023	48.0	$0.938	48.0	$0.781
1930	44.0	.898	44.0	1.023	44.0	1.023	48.0	.781
1931	44.0	.932	44.0	1.023	44.0	1.023	44.0	.852
1932	44.0	.932	44.0	1.023	44.0	1.023	48.0	.781
1933	44.0	.841	44.0	.920	44.0	1.023	44.0	.852

Year	New York, N. Y. Hours per week	New York, N. Y. Rate per hour	Philadelphia, Pa. Hours per week	Philadelphia, Pa. Rate per hour	St. Louis, Mo. Hours per week	St. Louis, Mo. Rate per hour	San Francisco, Calif. Hours per week	San Francisco, Calif. Rate per hour
1929	44.0	$1.136	48.0	$0.833	44.0	$1.002	44.0	$1.136
1930	44.0	1.159	48.0	.833	44.0	1.002	44.0	1.136
1931	44.0	1.159	48.0	.833	44.0	1.002	44.0	1.159
1932	44.0	1.091	48.0	.833	44.0	1.002	44.0	1.159
1933	44.0	1.068	48.0	.750	44.0	932	44.0	1.091

Table **K–6** (continued from p. 343).—*Press feeders, cylinder, males, book and job, 1929–1933, by city and year*

Year	Atlanta, Ga. Hours per week	Atlanta, Ga. Rate per hour	Birmingham, Ala. Hours per week	Birmingham, Ala. Rate per hour	Boston, Mass. Hours per week	Boston, Mass. Rate per hour	Chicago, Ill.[1] Hours per week	Chicago, Ill.[1] Rate per hour
1929	44.0	$0.568	44.0	$0.602	44.0	$0.852	44.0	$0.983
1930	44.0	.568	44.0	.602	44.0	.852	44.0	.983
1931	44.0	.568	44.0	.602	44.0	.852	44.0	.983
1932	44.0	.568	44.0	.602			36.0	.914
1933	44.0	.511	44.0	.568	44.0	.740	36.0	.835

Year	Cincinnati, Ohio Hours per week	Cincinnati, Ohio Rate per hour	Denver, Colo. Hours per week	Denver, Colo. Rate per hour	Detroit, Mich. Hours per week	Detroit, Mich. Rate per hour	New Orleans, La. Hours per week	New Orleans, La. Rate per hour
1929	44.0	$0.801	44.0	$0.795	48.0	$0.800	44.0	$0.625
1930	44.0	.835	44.0	.864	48.0	.800	44.0	.625
1931	44.0	.869	44.0	.795	48.0	.800	44.0	.625
1932	44.0	.801	44.0	.795	48.0	.800	44.0	.625
1933	44.0	.761	44.0	.795	48.0	.729	44.0	.625

Year	New York, N. Y. Hours per week	New York, N. Y. Rate per hour	Philadelphia, Pa. Hours per week	Philadelphia, Pa. Rate per hour	St. Louis, Mo.[2] Hours per week	St. Louis, Mo.[2] Rate per hour	San Francisco, Calif. Hours per week	San Francisco, Calif. Rate per hour
1929	44.0	$1.034	44.0	$0.795	44.0	$0.825	44.0	$0.818
1930	44.0	1.057	44.0	.841	44.0	.825	44.0	.818
1931	44.0	1.080	44.0	.841	44.0	.825	44.0	.841
1932	32.0	1.025	44.0	.841	44.0	.825	44.0	.841
1933	40.0	.977	44.0	.C94	44.0	.768	44.0	.841

[1] Cylinder presses 25 by 38 and over.   [2] Presses 24 by 39 and over.

TABLE **K-7** (continued from p. 344).—*Press feeders, platen, males, book and job, 1929–1933, by city and year*

Year	Atlanta, Ga.		Birmingham, Ala.		Chicago, Ill.		Denver, Colo.	
	Hours per week	Rate per hour	Hours per week	Rate per hour	Hours per week	Rate per hour	Hours per week	Rate per hour
1929	44.0	$0.534	44.0	$0.443	44.0	$0.615	44.0	$0.409
1930	44.0	.534	44.0	.443	44.0	.615	44.0	.409
1931	44.0	.534	44.0	.443	44.0	.615	44.0	.409
1932	44.0	.534	44.0	.443	36.0	.572	44.0	.409
1933	44.0	.481	44.0	.375	36.0	.523	---------	---------

Year	Detroit, Mich.		New York, N. Y.		St. Louis, Mo.		San Francisco, Calif.	
1929	48.0	$0.552	44.0	$0.727	44.0	$0.472	44.0	$0.614
1930	48.0	.552	---------	---------	44.0	.472	44.0	.614
1931	48.0	.552	---------	---------	44.0	.472	44.0	.625
1932	48.0	.552	---------	---------	44.0	.472	44.0	.625
1933	48.0	.521	---------	---------	44.0	.439	44.0	.625

TABLE **K-13** (continued from p. 354).—*Compositors, males, day work, newspaper, 1929–1933, by city and year*

Year	Atlanta, Ga.		Birmingham, Ala.		Boston, Mass.		Chicago, Ill.	
	Hours per week	Rate per hour	Hours per week	Rate per hour	Hours per week	Rate per hour	Hours per week	Rate per hour
1929	48.0	$1.031	[1] 42.0	$1.000	[2] 44.0	$1.250	45.0	$1.400
1930	48.0	1.031	[1] 42.0	1.025	[2] 44.0	1.250	45.0	1.400
1931	48.0	1.031	[1] 42.0	1.025	[2] 44.0	1.250	45.0	1.400
1932	48.0	1.031	[1] 42.0	.950	[2] 44.0	1.250	45.0	1.400
1933	40.0	.928	[1] 42.0	.950	[2] 44.0	1.250	37.5	1.280

Year	Cincinnati, Ohio		Denver, Colo.		Detroit, Mich.		New Orleans, La.	
1929	45.0	$1.222	44.0	$1.148	45.0	$1.300	---------	---------
1930	45.0	1.228	44.0	1.199	45.0	1.310	---------	---------
1931	45.0	1.228	44.0	1.199	45.0	1.310	---------	---------
1932	37.5	1.228	44.0	1.199	45.0	1.260	---------	---------
1933	48.0	1.151	44.0	1.096	45.0	1.260	---------	---------

Year	New York, N. Y.		Philadelphia, Pa.		St. Louis, Mo.		San Francisco, Calif.	
1929	45.0	$1.444	46.0	$0.913	46.0	$1.141	45.0	$1.200
1930	45.0	1.444	46.0	.913	46.0	1.207	45.0	1.200
1931	45.0	1.444	46.0	.913	46.0	1.207	45.0	1.200
1932	37.5	1.444	46.0	.913	46.0	1.207	45.0	1.200
1933	45.0	1.300	45.0	.933	46.0	1.085	45.0	1.080

[1] Minimum; maximum, 48 hours per week.
[2] Actual hours worked; minimum, 36; maximum, 48.

TABLE **K-16** (continued from p. 358).—*Pressmen, web, in charge, males, night work, newspaper, 1929–1933, by city and year*

Year	Atlanta, Ga.		Birmingham, Ala.		Boston, Mass.		Chicago, Ill.	
	Hours per week	Rate per hour	Hours per week	Rate per hour	Hours per week	Rate per hour	Hours per week	Rate per hour
1929	48.0	$1.000	42.0	$1.107	36.0	$1.408	44.0	$1.341
1930	48.0	1.000	42.0	1.179	36.0	1.408	44.0	1.341
1931	48.0	1.036	42.0	1.179	36.0	1.408	44.0	1.341
1932	48.0	1.036	42.0	1.107	36.0	1.408	42.0	1.405
1933	48.0	.990	42.0	1.107	36.0	1.306	42.0	1.405

Year	Cincinnati, Ohio		Denver, Colo.		Detroit, Mich.		New Orleans, La.	
1929	48.0	$1.094	43.0	$1.174	44.0	$1.295	48.0	$0.875
1930	48.0	1.125	43.0	1.174	44.0	1.364	48.0	.875
1931	48.0	1.125	43.0	1.174	44.0	1.364	48.0	.875
1932	48.0	1.125	43.0	1.174	44.0	1.364	48.0	.875
1933	48.0	1.013	43.0	1.174	44.0	1.268	48.0	.750

Year	New York, N.Y.		Philadelphia, Pa.		St. Louis, Mo.		San Francisco, Calif.	
1929	41.0	$1.671			42.0	$1.262	45.0	$1.167
1930	41.0	1.695			42.0	1.262	45.0	1.167
1931	41.0	1.720			42.0	1.262	45.0	1.167
1932	41.0	1.744	38.0	$1.263	[1] 35.0	1.262	45.0	1.167
1933	41.0	1.634	37.5	1.280	42.0	1.136	45.0	1.050

[1] 5 days per week.

TABLE **K-17** (continued from p. 359).—*Pressmen, web, first assistants, males, night work, newspaper, 1929–1933, by city and year*

Year	Atlanta, Ga.		Birmingham, Ala.		Boston, Mass.		Chicago, Ill.	
	Hours per week	Rate per hour	Hours per week	Rate per hour	Hours per week	Rate per hour	Hours per week	Rate per hour
1929	48.0	$0.938	42.0	$1.000	36.0	$1.242	44.0	$1.170
1930	48.0	.938	42.0	1.071	36.0	1.242	44.0	1.170
1931	48.0	.974	42.0	1.071	36.0	1.242	44.0	1.170
1932	48.0	.974	42.0	1.000	36.0	1.242	42.0	1.226
1933	48.0	.876	42.0	1.000	36.0	1.142	42.0	1.226

Year	Cincinnati, Ohio		Denver, Colo.		Detroit, Mich.		New Orleans, La.	
1929	48.0	$1.021	43.0	$1.070	44.0	$1.159	48.0	$0.813
1930	48.0	1.052	43.0	1.070	44.0	1.227	48.0	.813
1931	48.0	1.052	43.0	1.070	44.0	1.227	48.0	.813
1932	48.0	1.052	43.0	1.070	44.0	1.227	48.0	.813
1933	48.0	.947	43.0	1.070	44.0	1.141	48.0	.600

Year	New York, N.Y.		Philadelphia, Pa.		St. Louis, Mo.		San Francisco, Calif.	
1929	41.0	$1.451			42.0	$1.143	45.0	$1.100
1930	41.0	1.476			42.0	1.143	45.0	1.100
1931	41.0	1.500			42.0	1.143	45.0	1.100
1932	41.0	1.524	38.0	$1.105	[1] 35.0	1.143	45.0	1.100
1933	41.0	1.415	37.5	1.120	42.0	1.029	45.0	.990

[1] 5 days per week.

TABLE **K-19** (continued from p. 362).—*Stereotypers, males, day work, newspaper, 1929–1933, by city and year*

Year	Atlanta, Ga.		Birmingham, Ala.		Boston, Mass.		Chicago, Ill.	
	Hours per week	Rate per hour	Hours per week	Rate per hour	Hours per week	Rate per hour	Hours per week	Rate per hour
1929	48.0	$0.974	48.0	$0.917	42.0	$1.193	48.0	$1.020
1930	48.0	.974	48.0	.948	42.0	1.193	48.0	1.020
1931	48.0	.974	48.0	.948	42.0	1.193	48.0	1.080
1932	48.0	.974	48.0	.881	42.0	1.193	48.0	1.080
1933	48.0	.877	48.0	.881	42.0	1.097	48.0	.979

Year	Cincinnati, Ohio		Denver, Colo.		Detroit, Mich.		New Orleans, La.	
1929	48.0	$1.052	47.5	$0.968	48.0	$1.175	47.5	$0.821
1930	48.0	1.052	47.5	.968	48.0	1.175	47.5	.821
1931	48.0	1.052	47.5	.968	48.0	1.175	48.0	.844
1932	48.0	1.052	47.5	.968	48.0	1.175	48.0	.844
1933	48.0	.947	47.5	.920	48.0	1.088	48.0	.750

Year	New York, N.Y.		Philadelphia, Pa.		St. Louis, Mo.		San Francisco, Calif.	
1929	45.0	$1.233	48.0	$0.875	48.0	$1.073	45.0	$1.089
1930	45.0	1.233	48.0	.875	48.0	1.073	45.0	1.089
1931	45.0	1.233	48.0	.875	48.0	1.073	45.0	1.089
1932	45.0	1.233	48.0	.788	48.0	1.073	45.0	1.089
1933	45.0	1.233	46.0	.781	40.0	.966	45.0	.900

L.—TEXTILES

COTTON

TABLE **L–2** (continued from p. 366).—*Doffers, males, cotton goods, 1930 and 1932, by State and year*

Year	Alabama		Connecticut		Georgia		Maine	
	Hours per week	Rate per hour	Hours per week	Rate per hour	Hours per week	Rate per hour	Hours per week	Rate per hour
1930	55. 2	$0. 280	51. 8	$0. 311	56. 8	$0. 288	53. 1	$0. 330
1932	55. 3	. 224	54. 2	. 268	56. 0	. 235	55. 3	. 280

Year	Massachusetts		New Hampshire		New York		North Carolina	
1930	49. 3	$0. 394	53. 9	$0. 411	48. 0	$0. 443	55. 0	$0. 303
1932	49. 5	. 347	52. 9	. 329	48. 1	. 391	54. 2	. 245

Year	Pennsylvania		Rhode Island		South Carolina		Virginia	
1930			51. 2	$0. 405	54. 7	$0. 271	54. 7	$0. 261
1932			52. 7	. 286	54. 4	. 220	52. 9	. 249

TABLE **L–3** (continued from p. 366).—*Doffers, females, cotton goods, 1930 and 1932, by State and year*

Year	Connecticut		Maine		Massachusetts		New Hampshire	
	Hours per week	Rate per hour	Hours per week	Rate per hour	Hours per week	Rate per hour	Hours per week	Rate per hour
1930	49. 7	$0. 232	53. 5	$0. 293	48. 0	$0. 366	54. 0	$0. 361
1932	53. 8	. 237	54. 0	. 268	48. 0	. 297	53. 0	. 300

Year	New York		North Carolina		Rhode Island		South Carolina	
1930	(1)	(1)	55. 0	$0. 310	51. 3	$0. 231		
1932	48. 0	$0. 322	55. 0	. 196			55. 0	$0. 176

[1] Establishment or wage earners too few for which to show data.

560

COTTON—Continued

TABLE **L–5** (continued from p. 369).—*Drawers-in, females, cotton goods, 1930 and 1932, by State and year*

Year	Alabama		Connecticut		Georgia		Maine	
	Hours per week	Rate per hour	Hours per week	Rate per hour	Hours per week	Rate per hour	Hours per week	Rate per hour
1930	55.2	$0.220	52.4	$0.440	56.8	$0.301	54.0	$0.336
1932	55.2	.189	55.0	.351	55.4	.234	54.0	.257
	Massachusetts		New Hampshire		New York		North Carolina	
1930	48.0	$0.419	53.9	$0.357	48.0	$0.445	55.1	$0.315
1932	48.0	.368	54.0	.287	48.0	.329	54.9	.257
	Pennsylvania		Rhode Island		South Carolina		Virginia	
1930			51.2	$0.421	55.0	$0.292	55.0	$0.314
1932			53.3	.234	55.0	.220	52.4	.278

TABLE **L–7** (continued from p. 372).—*Drawing-frame tenders, males, cotton goods, 1930–1932, by State and year*

Year	Alabama		Connecticut		Georgia		Maine	
	Hours per week	Rate per hour	Hours per week	Rate per hour	Hours per week	Rate per hour	Hours per week	Rate per hour
1930	55.1	$0.230	49.9	$0.333	56.6	$0.247	51.3	$0.284
1932	55.0	.199	54.0	.302	56.6	.191	56.4	.223
	Massachusetts		New Hampshire		New York		North Carolina	
1930	49.5	$0.373	54.3	$0.332			54.9	$0.279
1932	50.7	.323	56.4	.274	(1)	(1)	53.9	.231
	Pennsylvania		Rhode Island		South Carolina		Virginia	
1930			52.1	$0.346	54.8	$0.248	54.7	$0.288
1932			54.0	.233	54.6	.197	54.5	.257

[1] Establishments or wage earners too few for which to show data.

TABLE **L–8** (continued from p. 373).—*Drawing-frame tenders, females, cotton goods, 1930 and 1932, by State and year*

Year	Alabama		Georgia		Maine		Massachusetts	
	Hours per week	Rate per hour	Hours per week	Rate per hour	Hours per week	Rate per hour	Hours per week	Rate per hour
1930	55.6	$0.219	56.2	$0.210	53.5	$0.241	48.0	$0.367
1932	55.4	.168	55.0	.177	54.0	.194	48.0	.310
	New Hampshire		New York		North Carolina		Pennsylvania	
1930	53.7	$0.316	48.0	$0.341	(1)	(1)		
1932	54.0	.251	48.0	.271				

[1] Establishments or wage earners too few for which to show data.

COTTON—Continued

TABLE **L–14** (continued from p. 379).—*Loom fixers, males, cotton goods, 1930 and 1932, by State and year*

Year	Alabama		Georgia		Maine		Massachusetts	
	Hours per week	Rate per hour	Hours per week	Rate per hour	Hours per week	Rate per hour	Hours per week	Rate per hour
1930	55.6	$0.396	56.7	$0.379	53.9	$0.537	48.8	$0.586
1932	55.3	.336	56.2	.338	53.9	.463	49.2	.530

Year	New Hampshire		North Carolina		Rhode Island		South Carolina	
1930	53.8	$0.613	55.0	$0.457	51.3	$0.590	54.8	$0.403
1932	54.2	.468	54.1	.377	52.6	.423	54.7	.327

TABLE **L–16** (continued from p. 381).—*Slasher tenders, males, cotton goods, 1930 and 1932, by State and year*

Year	Alabama		Connecticut		Georgia		Maine	
	Hours per week	Rate per hour	Hours per week	Rate per hour	Hours per week	Rate per hour	Hours per week	Rate per hour
1930	55.4	$0.274	51.0	$0.483	56.2	$0.309	54.0	$0.451
1932	55.5	.233	53.4	.437	56.7	.270	54.0	.387

Year	Massachusetts		New Hampshire		New York		North Carolina	
1930	48.7	$0.505	53.8	$0.513	48.0	$0.577	55.0	$0.367
1932	48.4	.459	54.0	.427	48.0	.478	54.1	.317

Year	Pennsylvania		Rhode Island		South Carolina		Virginia	
1930			51.8	$0.484	54.9	$0.293	55.0	$0.331
1932			53.2	.366	54.6	.238	52.9	.305

TABLE **L–18** (continued from p. 385).—*Fine speeders, males, cotton goods, 1930 and 1932, by State and year*

Year	Alabama		Connecticut		Georgia		Maine	
	Hours per week	Rate per hour	Hours per week	Rate per hour	Hours per week	Rate per hour	Hours per week	Rate per hour
1930	55.3	$0.292	50.7	$0.423	56.4	$0.300	52.8	$0.344
1932	55.3	.231	52.4	.387	55.5	.257	55.1	.296

Year	Massachusetts		New Hampshire		New York		North Carolina	
1930	54.0	$0.483	53.8	$0.458	48.0	$0.456	55.0	$0.340
1932	52.2	.381	54.0	.344	48.1	.335	54.1	.273

Year	Rhode Island		South Carolina		Virginia			
1930	52.6	$0.441	54.7	$0.312	54.6	$0.319		
1932	53.6	.274	54.4	.245	54.1	.287		

COTTON—Continued

TABLE **L–19** (continued from p. 385).—*Fine speeders, females, cotton goods, 1930 and 1932, by State and year*

Year	Alabama		Connecticut		Georgia		Maine	
	Hours per week	Rate per hour	Hours per week	Rate per hour	Hours per week	Rate per hour	Hours per week	Rate per hour
1930	55.2	$0.257	50.0	$0.377	56.5	$0.297	53.9	$0.319
1932	55.0	.215	52.5	.329	55.3	.254	54.0	.286
	Massachusetts		New Hampshire		New York		North Carolina	
1930	47.9	$0.372	53.2	$0.413	48.0	$0.399	55.1	$0.295
1932	48.0	.335	54.0	.332	48.0	.323	• 54.3	.263
	Pennsylvania		Rhode Island		South Carolina		Virginia	
1930			51.6	$0.385	54.7	$0.284	55.0	$0.288
1932			52.7	.286	55.0	.230	53.3	.263

TABLE **L–22** (continued from p. 390).—*Spinners, frame, females, cotton goods, 1930 and 1932, by State and year*

Year	Alabama		Georgia		Maine		Massachusetts	
	Hours per week	Rate per hour	Hours per week	Rate per hour	Hours per week	Rate per hour	Hours per week	Rate per hour
1930	55.2	$0.215	56.6	$0.222	53.9	$0.311	48.0	$0.342
1932	55.3	.181	56.1	.195	54.0	.261	48.0	.289
	New Hampshire		North Carolina		Rhode Island		South Carolina	
1930	52.2	$0.400	55.0	$0.231	51.0	$0.355	54.8	$0.222
1932	53.0	.290	54.4	.194	52.7	.238	55.0	.166

TABLE **L–25** (continued from p. 394).—*Weavers, males, cotton goods, 1930 and 1932, by State and year*

Year	Alabama		Georgia		Maine		Massachusetts	
	Hours per week	Rate per hour	Hours per week	Rate per hour	Hours per week	Rate per hour	Hours per week	Rate per hour
1930	55.3	$0.327	56.2	$0.308	53.7	$0.449	48.0	$0.460
1932	55.2	.275	56.3	.280	53.8	.353	49.1	.366
	New Hampshire		North Carolina		Rhode Island		South Carolina	
1930	54.1	$0.460	55.1	$0.372	51.3	$0.489	54.8	$0.347
1932	54.6	.371	53.9	.298	52.8	.313	54.5	.272

COTTON—Continued

TABLE **L–27** (continued from p. 395).—*Weavers, females, cotton goods, 1930 and 1932, by State and year*

Year	Alabama		Georgia		Maine		Massachusetts	
	Hours per week	Rate per hour	Hours per week	Rate per hour	Hours per week	Rate per hour	Hours per week	Rate per hour
1930	55. 4	$0. 300	56. 0	$0. 303	53. 9	$0. 408	48. 0	$0. 415
1932	55. 2	. 263	56. 0	. 277	54. 0	. 321	48. 0	. 336

Year	New Hampshire		North Carolina		Rhode Island		South Carolina	
1930	53. 6	$0. 493	55. 1	$0. 337	50. 9	$0. 463	54. 8	$0. 312
1932	54. 0	. 354	53. 9	. 276	52. 6	. 310	54. 8	. 262

HOSIERY AND UNDERWEAR

TABLE **L–33** (continued from p. 399).—*Knitters, footers or toppers, males, hosiery, 1928, 1930, and 1932, by State and year*

Year	Alabama		Georgia		Indiana		New Hampshire	
	Hours per week	Rate per hour	Hours per week	Rate per hour	Hours per week	Rate per hour	Hours per week	Rate per hour
1928 [1]	[3] 56. 4	$0. 213	[2]	[2]				
1930 [1]			52. 5	$0. 327				
1932 [1]	[3] 55. 5	. 131	57. 3	. 154				

Year	North Carolina		Pennsylvania		Tennessee		Virginia	
1928 [1]	55. 0	$0. 322			53. 9	$0. 306	[2]	[2]
1930 [1]	55. 5	. 204			55. 4	. 320	50. 0	$0. 380
1932 [1]	55. 0	. 133	[4] 55. 0	$0. 280	52. 5	. 206		

[1] Knitters, transfer.   [3] Includes Louisiana.
[2] Establishments or wage earners too few for which to show data.   [4] Eastern Pennsylvania only.

TABLE **L–34** (continued from p. 399).—*Knitters, footers or toppers, females, hosiery, 1928, 1930, and 1932, by State and year*

Year	Georgia		Illinois		Massachusetts		Michigan	
	Hours per week	Rate per hour	Hours per week	Rate per hour	Hours per week	Rate per hour	Hours per week	Rate per hour
1928 [1]	55. 3	$0. 199	51. 7	$0. 266			[2]	[2]
1930 [1]	56. 2	. 143	52. 2	. 269			49. 8	$0. 359
1932 [1]	56. 2	. 141	53. 0	. 209			50. 8	. 277

Year	New Hampshire		North Carolina		Pennsylvania		Wisconsin	
1928 [1]	[3] 49. 6	$0. 343	55. 2	$0. 240	51. 6	$0. 390	[4] 49. 7	$0. 395
1930 [1]	49. 9	. 377	56. 8	. 187	52. 6	. 339	[4] 49. 6	. 362
1932 [1]	48. 3	. 266	55. 0	. 172	[5] 54. 1	. 225	[4] 49. 6	. 302

[1] Knitters, transfer.
[2] Establishments or wage earners too few for which to show data.
[3] Includes Vermont.
[4] Includes Minnesota.
[5] Eastern Pennsylvania, excluding Philadelphia.

SILK

TABLE **L–38** (continued from p. 401).—*Weavers, males, broad silk goods, 1931 and 1933, by State and year*

Year	Connecticut		New Jersey		New York		Pennsylvania	
	Hours per week	Rate per hour	Hours per week	Rate per hour	Hours per week	Rate per hour	Hours per week	Rate per hour
1931	52. 2	$0. 517	47. 9	$0. 544	51. 0	$0. 496	51. 7	$0. 504
1933	50. 2	. 321	49. 0	. 298	49. 9	. 302	50. 7	. 279

TABLE **L–39** (continued from p. 401).—*Weavers, females, broad silk goods, 1931 and 1933, by State and year*

Year	Connecticut		New Jersey		New York		Pennsylvania	
	Hours per week	Rate per hour	Hours per week	Rate per hour	Hours per week	Rate per hour	Hours per week	Rate per hour
1931	49. 0	$0. 422	47. 5	$0. 493	47. 3	$0. 428	50. 1	$0. 411
1933	51. 3	. 301	48. 7	. 277	48. 0	. 288	48. 7	. 242

TABLE **L–42** (continued from p. 404).—*Winders, females, silk goods, 1931 and 1933, by State and year*

Year	Connecticut		New Jersey		New York		Pennsylvania	
	Hours per week	Rate per hour	Hours per week	Rate per hour	Hours per week	Rate per hour	Hours per week	Rate per hour
HARD SILK								
1931	49. 0	$0. 375	48. 2	$0. 344	49. 1	$0. 337	50. 3	$0. 284
1933	51. 1	. 199	47. 4	. 216	48. 7	. 214	50. 3	. 211
SOFT SILK								
1931	49. 0	. 364	46. 4	. 409	47. 2	. 390	50. 5	. 304
1933	48. 3	. 293	44. 8	. 288	49. 9	. 242	52. 1	. 210

WOOLEN AND WORSTED GOODS

TABLE **L–43** (continued from p. 405).—*Doffers, males, woolen and worsted goods, 1930 and 1932, by State and year*

Year	Massachusetts		Pennsylvania		Rhode Island	
	Hours per week	Rate per hour	Hours per week	Rate per hour	Hours per week	Rate per hour
1930					(1)	(1)
1932	48. 0	$0. 315			(1)	(1)

[1] Establishments or wage earners too few for which to show data.

WOOLEN AND WORSTED GOODS—Continued

TABLE **L-44** (continued from p. 405).—*Doffers, females, woolen and worsted goods, 1930 and 1932, by State and year*

Year	Massachusetts		New Jersey		Pennsylvania		Rhode Island	
	Hours per week	Rate per hour	Hours per week	Rate per hour	Hours per week	Rate per hour	Hours per week	Rate per hour
1930	48.0	$0.305	(1)	(1)	53.5	$0.264	48.2	$0.265
1932	48.0	.319	(1)	(1)	54.0	.195	48.0	.254

[1] Establishments or wage earners too few for which to show data.

TABLE **L-46** (continued from p. 408).—*Dresser tenders, males, woolen and worsted goods, 1930 and 1932, by State and year*

Year	Connecticut		Maine		Massachusetts		New Hampshire	
	Hours per week	Rate per hour	Hours per week	Rate per hour	Hours per week	Rate per hour	Hours per week	Rate per hour
1930	48.6	$0.625	50.3	$0.606	48.0	$0.665	50.1	$0.675
1932	49.1	.469	53.9	.485	48.5	.611	51.9	.544

Year	New York		Pennsylvania		Rhode Island		Vermont	
1930	49.6	$0.611	53.0	$0.800	48.3	$0.667	48.6	$0.619
1932	50.4	.543	51.6	.739	48.0	.554	53.9	.502

TABLE **L-48** (continued from p. 409).—*Dye-house laborers, males, woolen and worsted goods, 1928, 1930, and 1932, by State and year*

Year	Connecticut		Maine		Massachusetts		New Hampshire	
	Hours per week	Rate per hour	Hours per week	Rate per hour	Hours per week	Rate per hour	Hours per week	Rate per hour
1928	49.3	$0.457	50.2	$0.449	48.0	$0.459	50.9	$0.418
1930	49.1	.443	50.7	.423	49.0	.454	51.2	.411
1932	49.1	.405	53.9	.349	48.4	.382	53.4	.330

Year	New Jersey		New York		Pennsylvania		Rhode Island	
1928	49.3	$0.547	50.2	$0.437	53.0	$0.498	48.2	$0.449
1930	48.7	.572	50.6	.438	54.3	.451	48.1	.440
1932	48.7	.457	51.3	.382	54.0	.433	48.5	.396

WOOLEN AND WORSTED GOODS—Continued

TABLE **L-50** (continued from p. 410).—*Loom fixers, males, woolen and worsted goods, 1930 and 1932, by State and year*

Year	Connecticut		Maine		Massachusetts		New Hampshire	
	Hours per week	Rate per hour	Hours per week	Rate per hour	Hours per week	Rate per hour	Hours per week	Rate per hour
1930	49.1	$0.718	52.1	$0.734	48.2	$0.829	51.5	$0.700
1932	49.4	.641	54.0	.634	49.9	.714	53.2	.560

Year	New Jersey		New York		Rhode Island		Vermont	
1930	48.4	$0.939	49.9	$0.690	49.1	$0.819	48.7	$0.802
1932	58.7	.827	50.9	.586	48.5	.709	55.2	.575

TABLE **L-53** (continued from p. 413).—*Spinners, mule, males, woolen and worsted goods, 1930 and 1932, by State and year*

Year	Connecticut		Maine		Massachusetts		New Hampshire	
	Hours per week	Rate per hour	Hours per week	Rate per hour	Hours per week	Rate per hour	Hours per week	Rate per hour
1930	48.9	$0.669	50.0	$0.672	48.1	$0.666	49.4	$0.742
1932	48.8	.498	54.1	.502	49.0	.557	52.7	.584

Year	New Jersey		New York		Rhode Island		Vermont	
1930	48.0	$0.758	52.5	$0.577	48.0	$0.688	49.7	$0.646
1932	47.1	.676	52.1	.506	48.0	.548	54.2	.463

TABLE **L-56** (continued from p. 414).—*Spinners, frame, females, woolen and worsted goods, 1930 and 1932, by State and year*

Year	Massachusetts		New Jersey		Pennsylvania		Rhode Island	
	Hours per week	Rate per hour	Hours per week	Rate per hour	Hours per week	Rate per hour	Hours per week	Rate per hour
1930	48.0	$0.418	48.0	$0.464	53.5	$0.337	48.3	$0.370
1932	48.0	.388	46.1	.389	54.0	.248	48.0	.330

WOOLEN AND WORSTED GOODS—Continued

TABLE **L–59** (continued from p. 418).—*Weavers, males, woolen and worsted goods, 1930 and 1932, by State and year*

Year	Connecticut		Maine		Massachusetts		New Hampshire	
	Hours per week	Rate per hour	Hours per week	Rate per hour	Hours per week	Rate per hour	Hours per week	Rate per hour
1930	48.8	$0.668	50.6	$0.607	47.8	$0.615	50.8	$0.601
1932	49.3	.522	54.1	.474	50.9	.472	50.9	.510

Year	New Jersey		New York		Rhode Island		Vermont	
1930	48.9	$0.686	50.8	$0.651	49.0	$0.656	48.2	$0.656
1932	53.1	.536	50.6	.457	48.2	.586	53.8	.418

TABLE **L–61** (continued from p. 419).—*Weavers, females, woolen and worsted goods, 1930 and 1932, by State and year*

Year	Connecticut		Maine		Massachusetts		New Hampshire	
	Hours per week	Rate per hour	Hours per week	Rate per hour	Hours per week	Rate per hour	Hours per week	Rate per hour
1930	49.1	$0.591	50.9	$0.528	48.0	$0.567	50.8	$0.504
1932	50.2	.413	54.0	.417	48.0	.419	52.2	.395

Year	New Jersey		New York		Rhode Island		Vermont	
1930	48.3	$0.693	49.6	$0.576	48.2	$0.570	51.0	$0.575
1932	58.3	.535	49.8	.431	48.1	.532	54.6	.368

TABLE **L–63** (continued from p. 421).—*Wool sorters, males, woolen and worsted goods, 1928, 1930, and 1932, by State and year*

Year	Connecticut		Maine		Massachusetts		New Hampshire	
	Hours per week	Rate per hour	Hours per week	Rate per hour	Hours per week	Rate per hour	Hours per week	Rate per hour
1928	52.5	$0.801	54.0	$0.666	48.0	$0.721	(¹)	(¹)
1930	50.0	.643	54.0	.737	48.0	.732	42.5	$0.633
1932	(¹)	(¹)	54.0	.545	48.0	.675	53.8	.595

Year	New Jersey		Pennsylvania		Rhode Island	
	Hours per week	Rate per hour	Hours per week	Rate per hour	Hours per week	Rate per hour
1928	48.0	$0.845	54.0	$0.686	48.0	$0.748
1930	48.0	.767	50.6	.686	48.0	.909
1932	48.0	.648	54.0	.589	48.0	.678

¹ Establishments or wage earners too few for which to show data.

M.—TOBACCO INDUSTRY

Continued from page 428

[No later data for cigar industry, but data collected for cigarette manufacturing in 1930 and here given]

TABLE **M–10.**—*Stemming-machine feeders, females, cigarette manufacturing, 1930, by State*

Year	North Carolina		Virginia		Kentucky	
	Hours per week	Rate per hour	Hours per week	Rate per hour	Hours per week	Rate per hour
1930_____	49. 7	$0. 200	49. 9	$0. 209	(¹)	(¹)

¹ Establishments or wage earners too few for which to show data.

TABLE **M–11.**—*Stemmers, hand, males, cigarette manufacturing, 1930, by State*

Year	North Carolina		Virginia		Kentucky	
	Hours per week	Rate per hour	Hours per week	Rate per hour	Hours per week	Rate per hour
1930_____	49. 9	$0. 212	49. 4	$0. 201	(¹)	(¹)

¹ Establishments or wage earners too few for which to show data.

TABLE **M–12.**—*Stemmers, hand, females, cigarette manufacturing, 1930, by State*

Year	North Carolina		Virginia	
	Hours per week	Rate per hour	Hours per week	Rate per hour
1930_____	49. 9	$0. 193	49. 3	$0. 184

TABLE **M–13.**—*Strip searchers, females, cigarette manufacturing, 1930, by State*

Year	North Carolina		Virginia		Kentucky	
	Hours per week	Rate per hour	Hours per week	Rate per hour	Hours per week	Rate per hour
1930_____	49. 7	$0. 199	49. 9	$0. 184	(¹)	(¹)

¹ Establishments or wage earners too few for which to show data.

N.—TRANSPORTATION

TABLE N-8 (continued from p. 445).—*Conductors and motormen, street railways, 1929–1933, by city and year*

Year	Atlanta, Ga.		Birmingham, Ala.		Boston, Mass.		Chicago, Ill.	
	Hours per week	Rate per hour	Hours per week	Rate per hour	Hours per week	Rate per hour	Hours per week	Rate per hour
1929	(¹)	² $0. 580	(¹)	³ $0. 540	(¹)	⁴ $0. 750	(¹)	⁴ $0. 760
1930	(¹)	². 580	(¹)	³. 540	(¹)	⁴. 750	(¹)	⁴. 770
1931	(¹)	². 580	(¹)	³. 540	(¹)	⁴. 750	(¹)	⁴. 770
1932	(¹)	². 530	(¹)	³. 540	(¹)	⁴. 750	(¹)	⁴. 770
1933	(¹)	². 530	(¹)	³. 450	(¹)	⁴. 685	(¹)	⁴. 700

Year	Cincinnati, Ohio		Denver, Colo.		Detroit, Mich.		New Orleans, La.	
1929	(¹)	⁴ $0. 580	--------	--------	(¹)	⁵ $0. 750	(¹)	⁴ $0. 510
1930	(¹)	⁴. 600	--------	--------	(¹)	⁵. 750	--------	--------
1931	(¹)	⁴. 610	--------	--------	(¹)	⁵. 750	--------	--------
1932	(¹)	⁴. 610	--------	--------	(¹)	⁵. 750	--------	--------
1933	(¹)	⁴. 550	--------	--------	(¹)	⁵. 675	--------	--------

Year	New York, N. Y.		Philadelphia, Pa.		St. Louis, Mo.		San Francisco, Calif.	
1929	(¹)	⁶ $0. 861	--------	--------	(¹)	⁷ $0. 670	(¹)	⁸ $0. 750
1930	(¹)	⁶. 861	--------	--------	(¹)	⁷. 750	(¹)	⁸. 750
1931	(¹)	⁶. 861	--------	--------	(¹)	⁷. 690	(¹)	⁸. 750
1932	(¹)	⁶. 861	--------	--------	(¹)	⁷. 622	(¹)	⁸. 750
1933	(¹)	⁶. 800	--------	--------	(¹)	⁷. 600	(¹)	⁸. 750

¹ Not reported.
² After 18 months.
³ After 2 years.
⁴ After 1 year.
⁵ Municipal lines; after 1 year.
⁶ Motormen; after 2 years.
⁷ After 3 years.
⁸ Municipal lines.

TABLE N-11 (continued from p. 447).—*Longshoremen, 1929–1933, by city and year*

Year	Baltimore, Md.		Boston, Mass.		New Orleans, La.		New York, N. Y.	
	Hours per week	Rate per hour	Hours per week	Rate per hour	Hours per week	Rate per hour	Hours per week	Rate per hour
1929	44. 0	$0. 850	44. 0	$0. 850	48. 0	$0. 800	44. 0	$0. 850
1930	44. 0	. 900	44. 0	. 850	48. 0	. 800	44. 0	. 850
1931	44. 0	. 900	44. 0	. 850	48. 0	. 800	44. 0	. 850
1932	44. 0	. 850	44. 0	. 850	--------	--------	44. 0	. 850
1933	44. 0	. 800	44. 0	. 750	--------	--------	44. 0	. 750

Year	Philadelphia, Pa.		Portland, Maine		San Francisco, Calif.	
	Hours per week	Rate per hour	Hours per week	Rate per hour	Hours per week	Rate per hour
1929	44. 0	$0. 850	44. 0	$0. 850	48. 0	$0. 900
1930	44. 0	. 850	44. 0	. 850	48. 0	. 900
1931	44. 0	. 850	44. 0	. 850	48. 0	. 900
1932	44. 0	. 850	44. 0	. 850	48. 0	. 850
1933	44. 0	. 750	44. 0	. 750	48. 0	. 750

TABLE N-13 (continued from p. 453).—*Teamsters, general, 1-horse, 1929–1933, by city and year*

Year	Boston, Mass.		Chicago, Ill.		Cincinnati, Ohio		New York, N. Y.	
	Hours per week	Rate per hour	Hours per week	Rate per hour	Hours per week	Rate per hour	Hours per week	Rate per hour
1929	[1] 52.5	$0.571	60.0	$0.517	[2] 54.5	[2] $0.550	54.0	$0.722
1930	[1] 52.5	.571	60.0	.517	[2] 54.5	[2] .587	48.0	.813
1931	[1] 52.5	.571	60.0 / 66.0	{ .517 / .523 }	[2] 54.5	[2] .587	48.0	.813
1932	[1] 52.5	.571	60.0	.475	[2] 54.5	[2] .587	48.0	.813
1933	[3] 54.0	.500	60.0	.433	----------	----------	48.0	.708

Year	Philadelphia, Pa.		St. Louis, Mo.		San Francisco, Calif.	
	Hours per week	Rate per hour	Hours per week	Rate per hour	Hours per week	Rate per hour
1929	55.5	$0.450	[4] 57.0	[4] $0.491	48.8	$0.677
1930	55.5	.450	[4] 57.0	[4] .491	48.8	.677
1931	55.5	.450	57.0	.491	----------	----------
1932	----------	----------	57.0	.491	----------	----------
1933	----------	----------	57.0	.439	----------	----------

[1] 50½ hours and same pay per week, June to August, inclusive.
[2] Heavy wagons.
[3] 52 hours and same pay per week, June to August, inclusive.
[4] General transfer.

TABLE N-14 (continued from p. 454).—*Teamsters, general, 2-horse, 1929–1933, by city and year*

Year	Boston, Mass.		Chicago, Ill.		Cincinnati, Ohio		New York, N. Y.	
	Hours per week	Rate per hour	Hours per week	Rate per hour	Hours per week	Rate per hour	Hours per week	Rate per hour
1929	[1] 52.5	$0.610	60.0	$0.567	[2] 54.5	[2] $0.587	54.0	$0.759
1930	[1] 52.5	.610	60.0	.567	[2] 54.5	[2] .624	48.0	.854
1931	[1] 52.5	.610	60.0 / 66.0	{ .567 / .568 }	[2] 54.5	[2] .624	48.0	.854
1932	[1] 52.5	.610	60.0	.525	[2] 54.5	[2] .624	48.0	.854
1933	[3] 54.0	.537	60.0	.483	[2] 54.5	[2] .624	48.0	.750

Year	Philadelphia, Pa.		St. Louis, Mo.		San Francisco, Calif.	
	Hours per week	Rate per hour	Hours per week	Rate per hour	Hours per week	Rate per hour
1929	[3] 55.0	[3] $0.491	[4] 57.0	[4] $0.561	48.8	$0.800
1930	[3] 55.0	[3] .491	[4] 57.0	[4] .561	48.8	.800
1931	[3] 55.0	[3] .491	[4] 57.0	[4] .561	48.8	.800
1932	----------	----------	[4] 57.0	[4] .561	49.3	.731
1933	----------	----------	[4] 57.0	[4] .544	49.3	.731

[1] 50½ hours and same pay per week, June to August, inclusive.
[2] Heavy wagons.
[3] Lumber drivers.
[4] Hauling less than 5,000 pounds tonnage.

O.—WOODWORKING TRADES (INCLUDING LUMBER)

TABLE **O-3** (continued from p. 459).—*Assemblers and cabinetmakers, male, furniture, 1929 and 1931, by State and year*

Year	Illinois		Indiana		Maryland		Massachusetts	
	Hours per week	Rate per hour	Hours per week	Rate per hour	Hours per week	Rate per hour	Hours per week	Rate per hour
1929	50.3	$0.692	52.6	$0.535	51.5	$0.533	48.1	$0.707
1931	50.0	.528	51.7	.429	49.8	.500	48.4	.660
	Michigan		Missouri		New York		North Carolina	
1929	51.2	$0.608	51.9	$0.510	51.8	$0.609	55.0	$0.387
1931	51.1	.455	51.2	.465	52.0	.492	54.0	.334
	Ohio		Pennsylvania		Tennessee		Wisconsin	
1929	53.7	$0.546	53.2	$0.528	54.3	$0.431	53.8	$0.494
1931	53.9	.435	53.4	.422	52.5	.278	53.6	.425

TABLE **O-7** (continued from p. 462).—*Coopers (repairers), males, 1929 and 1931, by district and year*

Year	District no. 1, Chicago		District no. 2 [1]		District no. 3 [2]		District no. 4 [3]	
	Hours per week	Rate per hour	Hours per week	Rate per hour	Hours per week	Rate per hour	Hours per week	Rate per hour
1929	48.2	$0.649	48.1	$0.645	50.5	$0.590	48.2	$0.588
1931	48.2	.562	48.1	.528	49.0	.560	45.9	.533
	District no. 5 [4]		District no. 6 [5]		District no. 7 [6]		District no. 8 [7]	
1929	52.5	$0.591	50.9	$0.640	56.4	$0.524	50.9	$0.652
1931	49.5	.519	53.4	.593	54.5	.456	49.5	.562

[1] Kansas City, Omaha, St. Louis, East St. Louis, and St. Joseph.
[2] Iowa, Kansas, Minnesota, South Dakota, and Wisconsin.
[3] Oklahoma and Texas.
[4] Indiana, Michigan, western New York, Ohio, western Pennsylvania, and West Virginia.
[5] Connecticut, Massachusetts, New Jersey, eastern New York, and eastern Pennsylvania.
[6] Florida, Georgia, and Maryland.
[7] California, Colorado, Oregon, and Washington.

TABLE **O-10** (continued from p. 463).—*Choppers and sawyers, males, logging, 1930 and 1932, by State and year*

Year	California		Louisiana		Mississippi		North Carolina		Washington	
	Hours per week	Rate per hour	Hours per week	Rate per hour	Hours per week	Rate per hour	Hours per week	Rate per hour	Hours per week	Rate per hour
1930	[1] 53.9 [2] 53.8	$0.696 .772	[3] 60.0	$0.310	[3] 60.0 [4] 60.0	$0.272 .355	[3] 60.0 [4] 59.6	$0.246 .211	[2] 48.0	$0.756
1932	[2] 53.5	.602	[3] 60.0	.195	[4] 60.0	.172	[3] 60.0 [2] 60.0 [4] 60.0	.189 .120 .124	[2] 48.0	.508

[1] Choppers and sawyers.   [2] Fallers.   [3] Cutters.   [4] Sawyers.

TABLE **O-12** (continued from p. 464).—*Laborers, males, lumber, 1930 and 1932, by State and year*

Year	Alabama		California		Florida		Georgia	
	Hours per week	Rate per hour	Hours per week	Rate per hour	Hours per week	Rate per hour	Hours per week	Rate per hour
1930	60.6	$0.179	53.5	$0.436	61.7	$0.178	57.9	$0.154
1932	60.6	.106	52.1	.356	59.9	.131	58.6	.094

	Louisiana		Maine		Michigan		Mississippi	
1930	60.0	$0.229	59.1	$0.312	58.2	$0.324	59.6	$0.224
1932	59.3	.148	59.3	.207	58.4	.247	59.3	.114

	North Carolina		Pennsylvania		Washington		Wisconsin	
1930	59.1	$0.179			48.1	$0.473	58.9	$0.310
1932	58.7	.117			48.0	.317	58.3	.257

TABLE **O-15** (continued from p. 467).—*Sawyers, head, band, males, lumber, 1930 and 1932, by State and year*

Year	Alabama		California		Florida		Georgia	
	Hours per week	Rate per hour	Hours per week	Rate per hour	Hours per week	Rate per hour	Hours per week	Rate per hour
1930	57.0	$0.803	53.3	$1.044	54.0	$0.966	57.6	$0.743
1932	57.7	.574	52.5	.749	59.7	.664	57.6	.557

	Louisiana		Maine		Michigan		Mississippi	
1930	60.4	$0.879	58.9	$0.666	58.5	$0.757	57.9	$0.860
1932	58.4	.668	58.9	.550	57.3	.613	58.0	.585

	North Carolina		Pennsylvania		Washington		Wisconsin	
1930	59.6	$0.665			48.0	$1.188	59.2	$0.748
1932	59.0	.466			48.0	.842	58.2	.608

TABLE O-17 (continued from p. 468).—*Sawyers, head, circular, males, lumber, 1930 and 1932, by State and year*

Year	Alabama		California		Florida		Georgia	
	Hours per week	Rate per hour	Hours per week	Rate per hour	Hours per week	Rate per hour	Hours per week	Rate per hour
1930	60.8	$0.605			60.0	$0.615	59.1	$0.448
1932	59.4	.515			59.5	.291	62.0	.240

	Louisiana		Maine		Michigan		Mississippi	
1930	58.0	$0.898	58.5	$0.679	(1)	(1)	60.0	$0.843
1932	60.0	.650	56.0	.353			(1)	(1)

	North Carolina		Pennsylvania		Washington		Wisconsin	
1930	56.9	$0.493			48.0	$1.047	(1)	(1)
1932	56.6	.414					60.0	$0.558

1 Establishments and employees too few for which to show data.

Appendix F.—Index numbers of wages

TABLE 1 (continued from p. 521).—*Index numbers of wage rates per hour, 1927-1932*

[1913=100]

Year	Index number	Year	Index number
1927	231	1930	229
1928	232	1931	217
1929	233	1932	1 186

1 Subject to revision.

TABLE 2 (continued from p. 521).—*Index numbers of union wage rates and hours of labor in the United States as of May each year, 1929-1933*

[1913=100]

Year	Index numbers of—			Year	Index numbers of—		
	Rate of wages per hour	Hours per full-time week	Rate of wages per full-time week		Rate of wages per hour	Hours per full-time week	Rate of wages per full-time week
1929	262.1	91.5	240.7	1932	241.8	87.7	212.2
1930	272.1	89.8	243.8	1933	231.2	88.0	203.0
1931	273.0	89.2	242.9				

LIST OF BULLETINS OF THE BUREAU OF LABOR STATISTICS

The following is a list of all bulletins of the Bureau of Labor Statistics published since July 1912, except that in the case of bulletins giving the results of periodic surveys of the Bureau only the latest bulletin on any one subject is here listed.

A complete list of the reports and bulletins issued prior to July 1912, as well as the bulletins published since that date, will be furnished on application. Bulletins marked thus (*) are out of print.

Collective agreements

 *No. 191. Collective bargaining in the anthracite coal industry. [1916.]
 *No. 198. Collective agreements in the men's clothing industry. [1916.]
 No. 341. Trade agreement in the silk-ribbon industry of New York City. [1923.]
 *No. 402. Collective bargaining by actors. [1926.]
 No. 468. Trade agreements, 1927.

Conciliation and arbitration (including strikes and lockouts)

 *No. 124. Conciliation and arbitration in the building trades of Greater New York. [1913.]
 *No. 133. Report of the industrial council of the British Board of Trade on its inquiry into industrial agreements. [1913.]
 *No. 139. Michigan copper district strike. [1914.]
 *No. 144. Industrial court of the cloak, suit, and skirt industry of New York City. [1914.]
 *No. 145. Conciliation, arbitration, and sanitation in the dress and waist industry of New York City. [1914.]
 No. 233. Operation of the Industrial Disputes Investigation Act of Canada. [1918.]
 No. 255. Joint industrial councils in Great Britain. [1919.]
 No. 283. History of the Shipbuilding Labor Adjustment Board, 1917 to 1919.
 No. 287. National War Labor Board: History of its formation and activities, etc. [1921.]
 *No. 303. Use of Federal power in settlement of railway labor disputes. [1922.]
 No. 481. Joint industrial control in the book and job printing industry. [1928.]

Cooperation

 No. 313. Consumers' cooperative societies in the United States in 1920.
 *No. 314. Cooperative credit societies (credit unions) in America and in foreign countries. [1922.]
 No. 437. Cooperative movement in the United States in 1925 (other than agricultural).
 No. 531. Consumers', credit, and productive cooperative societies, 1929.
 No. 598. Organization and management of consumers' cooperative associations and clubs (with model by-laws). [1934.]

Employment and unemployment

 *No. 109. Statistics of unemployment and the work of employment offices [in the United States]. [1913.]
 *No. 172. Unemployment in New York City, N.Y. [1915.]
 *No. 183. Regularity of employment in the women's ready-to-wear garment industries. [1915.]
 *No. 195. Unemployment in the United States. [1916.]
 *No. 196. Proceedings of Employment Managers' Conference, held at Minneapolis, Minn., January 19 and 20, 1916.
 *No. 202. Proceedings of the conference of Employment Managers' Association of Boston, Mass., held May 10, 1916.
 *No. 206. The British system of labor exchanges. [1916.]
 *No. 227. Proceedings of Employment Managers' Conference, Philadelphia, Pa., April 2 and 3, 1917.
 *No. 235. Employment system of the Lake Carriers' Association. [1918.]
 *No. 241. Public employment offices in the United States. [1918.]
 *No. 247. Proceedings of Employment Managers' Conference, Rochester, N.Y., May 9–11, 1918.
 *No. 310. Industrial unemployment: A statistical study of its extent and causes. [1922.]
 *No. 409. Unemployment in Columbus, Ohio, 1921 to 1925.
 No. 542. Report of the Advisory Committee on Employment Statistics. [1931.]
 No. 544. Unemployment-benefit plans in the United States and unemployment insurance in foreign countries. [1931.]
 *No. 553. Fluctuation in employment in Ohio, 1914 to 1929.
 No. 555. Social and economic character of unemployment in Philadelphia, April 1930.

Housing

 *No. 158. Government aid to home owning and housing of working people in foreign countries. [1914.]
 No. 263. Housing by employers in the United States. [1920.]
 No. 295. Building operations in representative cities, 1920.
 No. 545. Building permits in the principal cities of the United States, [1921 to] 1930.

Industrial accidents and hygiene (including occupational diseases and poisons)

 *No. 104. Lead poisoning in potteries, tile works, and porcelain-enameled sanitary ware factories. [1912.]
 No. 120. Hygiene of the painters' trade. [1913.]
 *No. 127. Dangers to workers from dusts and fumes, and methods of protection. [1913.]
 *No. 141. Lead poisoning in the smelting and refining of lead. [1914.]
 *No. 157. Industrial accident statistics. [1915.]
 *No. 165. Lead poisoning in the manufacture of storage batteries. [1914.]
 *No. 179. Industrial poisons used in the rubber industry. [1915.]
 *No. 188. Report of British departmental committee on the danger in the use of lead in the painting of buildings. [1916.]
 *No. 201. Report of the committee on statistics and compensation insurance costs of the international Association of Industrial Accident Boards and Commissions. [1916.]

Industrial accidents and hygiene (including occupational diseases and poisons)—Continued.

*No. 209. Hygiene of the printing trade. [1917.]
*No. 219. Industrial poisons used or produced in the manufacture of explosives. [1917.]
*No. 221. Hours, fatigue, and health in British munition factories. [1917.]
*No. 230. Industrial efficiency and fatigue in British munition factories. [1917.]
*No. 231. Mortality from respiratory diseases in dusty trades (inorganic dusts). [1918.]
*No. 234. The safety movement in the iron and steel industry, 1907 to 1917.
 No. 236. Effects of the air hammer on the hands of stonecutters. [1918.]
*No. 249. Industrial health and efficiency. Final report of British Health of Munition Workers' Committee. [1919.]
*No. 251. Preventable death in the cotton-manufacturing industry. [1919.]
 No. 256. Accidents and accident prevention in machine building. [1919.]
 No. 267. Anthrax as an occupational disease. [1920.]
 No. 276. Standardization of industrial accident statistics. [1920.]
*No. 280. Industrial poisoning in making coal-tar dyes and dye intermediates. [1921.]
*No. 291. Carbon monoxide poisoning. [1921.]
 No. 293. The problem of dust phthisis in the granite stone industry. [1922.]
 No. 298. Causes and prevention of accidents in the iron and steel industry, 1910–1919.
 No. 392. Survey of hygienic conditions in the printing trades. [1925.]
 No. 405. Phosphorus necrosis in the manufacture of fireworks and in the preparation of phosphorus. [1926.]
 No. 427. Health survey of the printing trades, 1922 to 1925.
 No. 428. Proceedings of the Industrial Accident Prevention Conference, held at Washington, D.C., July 14–16, 1926.
 No. 460. A new test for industrial lead poisoning. [1928.]
 No. 466. Settlement for accidents to American seamen. [1928.]
 No. 488. Deaths from lead poisoning, 1925–1927.
 No. 490. Statistics of industrial accidents in the United States to the end of 1927.
 No. 507. Causes of death, by occupation. [1930.]
 No. 582. Occupation hazards and diagnostic signs: A guide to impairments to be looked for in hazardous occupations. (Revision of Bul. No. 306.) [1933.]

Industrial relations and labor conditions

*No. 237. Industrial unrest in Great Britain. [1917.]
*No. 340. Chinese migrations, with special reference to labor conditions. [1923.]
*No. 349. Industrial relations in the West Coast lumber industry. [1923.]
*No. 361. Labor relations in the Fairmount (W.Va.) bituminous coal field. [1924.]
 No. 380. Post-war labor conditions in Germany. [1925.]
 No. 383. Works council movement in Germany. [1925.]
 No. 384. Labor conditions in the shoe industry in Massachusetts, 1920–1924.
 No. 399. Labor relations in the lace and lace-curtain industries in the United States. [1925.]
 No. 483. Conditons in the shoe industry in Haverhill, Mass., 1928.
 No. 534. Labor conditions in the Territory of Hawaii, 1929–1930.

Labor laws of the United States (including decisions of courts relating to labor)

*No. 211. Labor laws and their administration in the Pacific States. [1917.]
*No. 229. Wage-payment legislation in the United States. [1917.]
 No. 285. Minimum-wage laws of the United States: Construction and operation. [1921.]
 No. 321. Labor laws that have been declared unconstitutional. [1922.]
 No. 322. Kansas Court of Industrial Relations. [1923.]
 No. 343. Laws providing for bureaus of labor statistics, etc. [1923.]
 No. 370. Labor laws of the United States, with decisions of courts relating thereto. [1925.]
 No. 408. Laws relating to payment of wages. [1926.]
 No. 581. Laws relating to employment agencies in the United States, as of January 1, 1933.
 No. 583. Proceedings of the National Conference on Labor Legislation, held at Washington, D.C., February 14 and 15, 1934.
 No. 590. Labor legislation, 1931 and 1932.
 No. 592. Decisions of courts and opinions affecting labor, 1931 and 1932.
 No. 596. Laws relating to prison labor in the United States, as of July 1, 1933.
 No. 603. Comparative digest of labor legislation for the States of Alabama, Florida, Georgia, South Carolina, Tennessee. [1933.]

Labor laws of foreign countries

*No. 142. Administration of labor laws and factory inspection in certain European countries. [1914.]
 No. 494. Labor legislation of Uruguay. [1929.]
 No. 510. Labor legislation of Argentina. [1930.]
 No. 529. Workmen's compensation legislation of the Latin American countries. [1930.]
 No. 549. Labor legislation of Venezuela. [1931.]
 No. 554. Labor legislation of Paraguay. [1931.]
 No. 559. Labor legislation of Ecuador. [1931.]
 No. 569. Labor legislation of Mexico. [1932.]

Labor organizations

 No. 342. International Seamen's Union of America: A study of its history and problems. [1923.]
 No. 461. Labor organizations in Chile. [1928.]
*No. 465. Beneficial activities of American trade unions. [1928.]
 No. 506. Handbook of American trade unions: 1929 edition.

Minimum wage

*No. 167. Minimum-wage legislation in the United States and foreign countries. [1915.]
*No. 176. Effect of minimum-wage determinations in Oregon. [1915.]
 No. 285. Minimum-wage laws of the United States: Construction and operation. [1921.]
 No. 467. Minimum-wage legislation in various countries. [1928.]

Old-age care, pensions and insurance

 No. 386. Cost of American almshouses. [1925.]
*No. 465. Beneficial activities of American trade unions. [1928.]
 No. 477. Public-service retirement systems, United States and Europe. [1929.]
*No. 489. Care of aged persons in United States. [1929.]
 No. 505. Directory of homes for the aged in the United States. [1929.]
 No. 561. Public old-age pensions and insurance in the United States and in foreign countries. [1932.]

Prison labor

No. 372. Convict labor in 1923.
No. 595. Prison labor in the United States, 1932.
No. 596. Laws relating to prison labor in the United States, as of July 1, 1933.

Proceedings of annual conventions of the Association of Governmental Officials in Industry of the United States and Canada. (Name changed in 1928 from Association of Governmental Labor Officials of the United States and Canada)

*No. 266. Seventh, Seattle, Wash., July 12-15, 1920.
No. 307. Eighth, New Orleans, La., May 2-6, 1921.
*No. 323. Ninth, Harrisburg, Pa., May 22-26, 1922.
*No. 352. Tenth, Richmond, Va., May 1-4, 1923.
*No. 389. Eleventh, Chicago, Ill., May 19-23, 1924.
*No. 411. Twelfth, Salt Lake City, Utah, August 13-15, 1925.
*No. 429. Thirteenth, Columbus, Ohio, June 7-10, 1926.
*No. 455. Fourteenth, Paterson, N.J., May 31 to June 3, 1927.
*No. 480. Fifteenth, New Orleans, La., May 21-24, 1928.
No. 508. Sixteenth, Toronto, Canada, June 4-7, 1929.
No. 530. Seventeenth, Louisville, Ky., May 20-23, 1930.
*No. 563. Eighteenth, Boston, Mass., May 18-22, 1931.

Proceedings of annual meetings of the International Association of Industrial Accident Boards and Commissions

No. 210. Third, Columbus, Ohio, April 25-28, 1916.
*No. 248. Fourth, Boston, Mass., August 21-25, 1917.
No. 264. Fifth, Madison, Wis., September 24-27, 1918.
*No. 273. Sixth, Toronto, Canada, September 23-26, 1919.
No. 281. Seventh, San Francisco, Calif., September 20-24, 1920.
No. 304. Eighth, Chicago, Ill., September 19-23, 1921.
No. 333. Ninth, Baltimore, Md., October 9-13, 1922.
*No. 359. Tenth, St. Paul, Minn., September 24-26, 1923.
No. 385. Eleventh, Halifax, Nova Scotia, August 26-28, 1924.
No. 395. Index to proceedings, 1914-1924.
No. 406. Twelfth, Salt Lake City, Utah, August 17-20, 1925.
No. 432. Thirteenth, Hartford, Conn., September 14-17, 1926.
*No. 456. Fourteenth, Atlanta, Ga., September 27-29, 1927.
No. 485. Fifteenth, Paterson, N.J., September 11-14, 1928.
No. 511. Sixteenth, Buffalo, N.Y., October 8-11, 1929.
No. 536. Seventeenth, Wilmington, Del., September 22-26, 1930.
No. 564. Eighteenth, Richmond, Va., October 5-8, 1931.
No. 577. Nineteenth, Columbus, Ohio, September 26-29, 1932.
No. 602. Twentieth, Chicago, Ill., September 11-14, 1933.

Proceedings of annual meetings of the International Association of Public Employment Services

*No. 192. First, Chicago, December 19 and 20, 1913; second, Indianapolis, September 24 and 25, 1914; third, Detroit, July 1 and 2, 1915.
*No. 220. Fourth, Buffalo, N.Y., July 20 and 21, 1916.
No. 311. Ninth, Buffalo, N.Y., September 7-9, 1921.
No. 337. Tenth, Washington, D.C., September 11-13, 1922.
No. 355. Eleventh, Toronto, Canada, September 4-7, 1923.
No. 400. Twelfth, Chicago, Ill., May 19-23, 1924.
No. 414. Thirteenth, Rochester, N.Y., September 15-17, 1925.
No. 478. Fifteenth, Detroit, Mich., October 25-28, 1927.
*No. 501. Sixteenth, Cleveland, Ohio, September 18-21, 1928.
No. 538. Seventeenth, Philadelphia, September 24-27, 1929; eighteenth, Toronto, Canada, September 9-12, 1930.

Productivity of labor and technological unemployment

No. 356. Productivity costs in the common-brick industry. [1924.]
No. 360. Time and labor costs in manufacturing 100 pairs of shoes, 1923.
No. 407. Labor cost of production and wages and hours of labor in the paper box-board industry. [1926.]
*No. 412. Wages, hours, and productivity in the pottery industry, 1925.
No. 441. Productivity of labor in the glass industry. [1927.]
No. 474. Productivity of labor in merchant blast furnaces. [1928.]
No. 475. Productivity of labor in newspaper printing. [1929.]
No. 550. Cargo handling and longshore labor conditions. [1932.]
No. 574. Technological changes and employment in the United States Postal Service. [1932.]
No. 585. Labor productivity in the automobile-tire industry. [1933.]
No. 593. Technological changes and employment in the electric-lamp industry. [1933.]

Retail prices and cost of living

*No. 121. Sugar prices, from refiner to consumer. [1913.]
*No. 130. Wheat and flour prices, from farmer to consumer. [1913.]
*No. 164. Butter prices, from producer to consumer. [1914.]
*No. 170. Foriegn food prices as affected by the war. [1915.]
No. 357. Cost of living in the United States. [1924.]
No. 369. The use of cost-of-living figures in wage adjustments. [1925.]
No. 495. Retail prices, 1890 to 1928.

Safety codes

*No. 336. Safety code for the protection of industrial workers in foundries.
No. 350. Rules governing the approval of headlighting devices for motor vehicles.
*No. 351. Safety code for the construction, care, and use of ladders.
*No. 375. Safety code for laundry machinery and operations.
*No. 382. Code of lighting school buildings.
No. 410. Safety code for paper and pulp mills.
*No. 430. Safety code for power presses and foot and hand presses.
No. 447. Safety code for rubber mills and calenders.
No. 451. Safety code for forging and hot-metal stamping.

[IV]

Women and children in industry—Continued.

Work of Federal and State departments of labor

Workmen's insurance and compensation (including laws relating thereto)

Miscellaneous series

O